Concurrency Verification

Cambridge Tracts in Theoretical Computer Science 54

Titles in the series

Concurrency Verification

Introduction to Compositional and
Noncompositional Methods

Willem-Paul de Roever

Frank de Boer

Ulrich Hannemann

Jozef Hooman

Yassine Lakhnech

Mannes Poel

Job Zwiers

CAMBRIDGE
UNIVERSITY PRESS

PUBLISHED BY THE PRESS SYNDICATE OF THE UNIVERSITY OF CAMBRIDGE
The Pitt Building, Trumpington Street, Cambridge, United Kingdom

CAMBRIDGE UNIVERSITY PRESS
The Edinburgh Building, Cambridge CB2 2RU, UK
40 West 20th Street, New York, NY 10011–4211, USA
10 Stamford Road, Oakleigh, VIC 3166, Australia
Ruiz de Alarcón 13, 28014 Madrid, Spain
Dock House, The Waterfront, Cape Town 8001, South Africa

http://www.cambridge.org

First published 2001

Printed in the United Kingdom at the University Press, Cambridge

Typeset by the author in Times 10/13pt [UPH]

A catalogue record for this book is available from the British Library

Library of Congress Cataloguing in Publication data

ISBN 0 521 80608 9 hardback

Contents

Preface

The subject of this work is the state-based verification of concurrent programs. It is published in two volumes. The leading theme of these volumes is the development of so-called *compositional* techniques for the verification of concurrent programs from noncompositional techniques. There are three reasons for this.

First of all, compositional verification techniques reduce the verification of large programs to the *independent* verification of their parts. Consequently, compositional verification represents one of the hopeful directions for the verification of really large programs.

Secondly, compositional techniques for the verification of concurrent programs originate from noncompositional techniques, and can, therefore, be better understood once a firm grasp of the latter has been obtained.

Thirdly, compositional techniques for program verification are well suited to top-down program development. However, there are many classes of programs for which noncompositional techniques lead to shorter and clearer proofs. Therefore, when faced with the difficult task of proving concurrent programs correct, one needs to master both kinds of techniques.

This explains why in the two volumes both noncompositional and compositional techniques are developed.

This volume offers a self-contained presentation from first principles of the main techniques for the state-based verification of concurrent programs, focussing on proofs of partial correctness, invariance properties and termination. It presents a mathematical semantically-oriented theory for the verification of concurrent programs, which is based on Floyd's inductive assertion method. It covers noncompositional as well as compositional methods, relating Floyd's method to the classical noncompositional Hoare logics for shared-variable concurrency and synchronous message passing, and presents an in-depth analysis of the two main compositional proof methods which are currently used:

Misra & Chandy's assumption-commitment paradigm for synchronous message passing, and Jones' rely-guarantee paradigm for shared-variable concurrency. Also a family of so-called *communication-closed-layer* transformation principles is developed. Whenever applicable, these transformation principles clarify the structure of correctness proofs considerably. This especially holds for certain classes of network protocols, e.g., those described in [Ray88].

The companion volume, *Compositional Theory of Concurrency,* presents a self-contained description of the main compositional Hoare logics for reactive systems as well as for real-time distributed message passing, for both synchronous and asynchronous communication. It illustrates these compositional techniques by correctness proofs for a number of industrially-inspired medium-size applications, and shows how to obtain machine support for the application of these techniques using the Prototype Verification System PVS.

The material contained in the two volumes offers an integrated account of the subject matter of around 15 dissertations and approximately 100 papers, and leads up to state-of-the-art research in the area of compositional methods for concurrent program verification.

Since many themes in the two volumes have not been discussed before in any textbook, we first list the new ones below.

The leading new themes of this volume are:

1. A clear separation between the *mathematical* theory of program verification, which is semantic in nature, and *syntactically*-formulated axiomatic approaches to program verification.
2. A detailed account of the development from *noncompositional* to *compositional* proof methods for concurrent program verification; this development is part of the above-mentioned mathematical theory, and includes comprehensive accounts of the *assumption-commitment* and *rely-guarantee* paradigms.
3. Partial-order based *transformation principles* for concurrency, constituting the *communication-closed-layers paradigm.*

The leading themes of the companion volume are:

4. Compositional Hoare logics for reactive and distributed real-time systems.
5. Applications of these compositional techniques to the verification of *hybrid* systems, *arbitration* and *atomic broadcast* protocols, *control systems for chemical batch processing*, and a *stable storage* medium.
6. Electronic tool support for the correct construction of distributed real-time systems using the *Prototype Verification System* PVS.

Next, each of these themes is briefly discussed.

1. The mathematical theory of concurrency developed in this volume is based on *Floyd's inductive assertion method*. The main advantages we see in such a mathematical theory are:

    (i) it highlights essential concepts without syntactic overhead,

    (ii) most semantic steps can be directly verified by dedicated tool support, and

    (iii) it allows simple soundness and semantic completeness proofs.

    We often mix Floyd's method and Hoare logic, for instance when developing a compositional theory of concurrency in a context of inductive assertions. Then inductive-assertion-based methods for the sequential parts of a program are combined with compositional proof rules for deducing properties of the parallel composition of these parts. For all these methods and logics rigorous proofs of their soundness and (semantic) completeness are given,[1] together with many examples of their application.

2. That the hierarchical decomposition of programs into smaller ones is imperative to master the complexity of large programs is now generally recognised. In 1965 Edsger W. Dijkstra formulated this principle [Dij65b], which consists of *reducing* the development and verification problem of a program to *that of its constituent (i.e., top-level) subprograms* by starting from its top-level specification and *verifying that specification on the basis of the specifications of those subprograms*. The development and verification of the latter then proceed in essentially the same way, until no further decomposition is necessary.

    Essential for this strategy is that the specification of a large program is verified *on the basis of the specifications of its constituent subprograms, only,* i.e., *without any knowledge of the interior construction of those subprograms* [Zwi89]. And this is the principle of *compositional program verification*.

    To make this verification strategy possible, systems and their parts are specified using predicates over only their observable behaviour. Such specifications are called *assertional*. Consequently, assertional specifications of the constituent components of a program never depend on any additional knowledge about the underlying execution mechanism of these components.

    To be precise, compositional verification that a program P satisfies an assertional specification φ involves two kinds of proof techniques:

---

[1] In the experience of the senior author literally *every* alleged proof method for concurrency, which reached his desk and had not been proven complete, turned out to be incomplete, and every such proof method, which had not been proven sound, turned out to be unsound.

(i) *Basic techniques* for proving that a program P, which is not decomposed any further, satisfies φ.

(ii) *Compositional proof techniques* to handle the case that P is composed of parts $P_1, \ldots, P_n$, i.e., $P = op^{lang}(P_1, \ldots, P_n)$, $n \geq 1$, with op^{lang} some operator of the programming language.

For the latter kind of program operators we define *compositional proof rules*, i.e., logical inference rules of the form:

"From P_1 *satisfies* φ_1 and ... P_n *satisfies* φ_n infer P *satisfies* φ." [Zwi89]

The characteristic feature of a compositional proof rule is its so-called *compositional proof (reduction) step*. This step consists essentially of a proof that φ follows from some combination of $\varphi_1, \ldots, \varphi_n$. This proof amounts to checking the validity of a finite number of implications involving the predicates occurring in $\varphi_1, \ldots, \varphi_n$ and φ, and *therefore does not involve any representation of P_i at all*!

Observe that the latter is imposed by the condition *"without any knowledge of the interior construction of those subprograms"* in the formulation of compositional program verification.

Consequently, a *compositional proof rule for a program operator* op^{lang} $(P_1, \ldots, P_n)$ has, essentially, the following form:

$$\frac{for\ i = 1, \ldots, n,\ P_i\ satisfies\ \varphi_i,\quad op^{spec}(\varphi_1, \ldots, \varphi_n, \varphi)}{op^{lang}(P_1, \ldots, P_n)\ satisfies\ \varphi,}$$

where $\varphi_1, \ldots, \varphi_n, \varphi$ express assertional specifications, and $op^{spec}(\varphi_1, \ldots, \varphi_n)$ expresses a *compositional proof (reduction) step*.

Apart from rules such as the above, one needs additional proof rules to *adapt* one specification to another. Since these rules do not depend on the structure of the actual programs involved, they reduce to the case $n = 1$ in the formulation of compositional proof rules above, and can, therefore, also be regarded as compositional proof rules.

Now a *compositional proof method* for establishing program correctness consists of basic rules, dealing with constructs which are not decomposed any further, and compositional proof rules, which deal with constructs which are decomposed, and with adaptation of specifications.

In the present volume this compositional theory is formulated as an extension of Floyd's inductive assertion method, and includes the first textbook treatments of the assumption-commitment (A-C) and rely-guarantee (R-G) paradigms. In general, compositional proof techniques have the advantage that they allow a systematic top-down development of programs from their specification, which is correct by construction, as illustrated by many examples in this and in the companion volumes. Moreover, the A-C and R-G paradigms allow for the development of *open* systems, i.e., systems whose environment is not yet known, but possibly specified; this is also illustrated.

Another advantage of compositional techniques is that as soon as traditional techniques suffice to establish the correctness of a component of a process P, these techniques can be "plugged into" the compositional proof strategy described above. For instance, in case the components of P can be successfully checked using *automatic verification tools* (e.g., for model checking), the top-level compositional verification of P only requires, additionally, a number of compositional proof steps (in the above sense) to be carried out [KL93, DJS95]. If applicable, this is a very practical way of formally verifying really complex systems.

3. Partial-order-based transformation principles for concurrency unify such different theories as, e.g.,

   (i) Lipton's theory of left and right movers for reasoning about synchronisation primitives [Lip75],
   (ii) Elrad & Francez' principle of "Communication-Closed Layers" for transforming distributed programs [EF82], and
   (iii) Mazurkiewicz' trace theory [Maz89], one of the first satisfactory partial-order theories for reasoning about truly concurrent systems.

These transformation principles embody the point of view that, in order to explain and clarify how a network of processes functions, as opposed to its mere verification, *the structure of its correctness proof should reflect the structure of its original design process* rather than that of the resulting final program. These principles for explaining and clarifying complex network protocols have been demonstrated on the basis of many correctness proofs, notably for Gallager, Humblet & Spira's distributed spanning-tree algorithm [GHS83].

4. The compositional Hoare logics for reactive systems discussed in the companion volume include, amongst others, Hoare logics for Misra & Chandy's *assumption-commitment* formalism [MC81] for distributed communication, Jones' *rely-guarantee* formalism [Jon83] for shared-variable concurrency, and Pandya & Joseph's *presupposition-affirmation* formalism [PJ91], which are all proved to be sound (completeness proofs are only discussed in this volume).

Moreover, a logic is presented for reasoning compositionally about distributed real-time reactive systems, which is subsequently applied and provided with PVS-based machine support, as described in the second half of the companion volume.

5. In the last three chapters of that volume the emphasis is on illustrating the systematic top-down derivation of distributed programs from their specifications. The resulting programs are correct by construction. This process of program derivation is therefore called the *verify-while-develop paradigm*. This paradigm can be regarded as the "inversion" of a compositional proof method, in which a development step coincides with the application of a compositional rule in which its conclusion and hypotheses are interchanged. For, as a consequence of using compositional techniques, each compositional proof (reduction) step (as defined above) can be viewed as *the verification of a design step*, which only involves reasoning about (the assertional specification of) that particular step and does not involve any future design steps. This explains why in the above definition of compositional proof techniques we stipulated that in a compositional proof step "no additional knowledge about the underlying execution mechanism of the relevant parts is allowed". For, without that clause, reasoning about a particular design step might have involved reasoning about future design steps, and we want these two stages to be independent. This also explains why compositional techniques can be viewed as the proof-theoretical analogue of hierarchically-structured program development.

6. A compositional formalism is developed for specifying distributed real-time systems, in which program constructs and assertional specifications are combined within a single "mixed" framework. This formalism is formally defined within PVS. The resulting machine-checked theory supports systematic top-down derivation of distributed algorithms, as explained above, and is illustrated by the correct construction of a distributed real-time control system for chemical batch processing.

This does not imply that machine-checked proofs are free from error. E.g., an error might be introduced by the use of inconsistent axioms, a bug in the proof-checker or a bug in the underlying hardware. Yet the probability of such errors leading to the machine outputting that a faulty system is correct, is small when compared with hand-checked proofs, and decreases as proof-checkers become more experienced.

Occasionally we refer to properties which in general cannot be proved in a compositional set-up, such as termination properties of semaphores [Pnu77, Pnu85]. These do not constitute the main focus of our work, and are, amongst others, discussed in [Fra86] and Manna & Pnueli's manuscript for the *Progress* book [MP99]. These properties depend on assumptions of so-called weak and strong fairness, which in essence imply termination of the constructs involved, provided corresponding fairness properties of the underlying scheduling mechanisms are satisfied. As such, weak and strong fairnesses are *abstractions* of *real-time* properties of these mechanisms, since they do not state *when* a construct is executed. Since for practical applications the execution speed of such constructs obviously matters, the principal focus of our companion volume is on applications of compositional theories for real-time concurrency.

The structure of this volume

This volume consists of five parts.

Part I consists of Chapter 1. In this chapter such central questions are answered as:

- How important is verification for the development of correct software?
- Why does one need to give correctness proofs for concurrent programs? Must these be formal? Or even machine checked?
- Which style of proof is more appropriate, a compositional or a noncompositional one?

In order to answer these questions, three concurrent algorithms are discussed, in increasing order of difficulty: Peterson's mutual exclusion algorithm, a concurrent garbage collector due to Dijkstra, Lamport and others, and a distributed mutual-exclusion algorithm due to Szymanski. This discussion leads up to the conclusion of Dijkstra that *"To believe that correct solutions of such problems can be found without a very careful justification is optimism on the verge of foolishness."*

Next the approach taken in this volume is explained. It is a state-based, property-oriented, dual-language, and semantically-oriented approach. The concept of compositionality is explained in relation to the verify-while-develop paradigm, machine verification, and the problem how to specify program modules; also the complexity of compositional reasoning as well as its advantages and disadvantages are discussed. Chapter 1 ends with a short account of the history of the development from noncompositional to compositional methods for program verification.

Part II consists of Chapters 2–5.

In Chapters 2, 3 and 4 semantical formulations are given of Floyd's inductive assertion method for, respectively, a simple model of sequential programming, that of *sequential transition systems*, for shared-variable concurrency in the style of Owicki & Gries, and for synchronous message passing in the styles of

Apt, Francez & de Roever and of Levin & Gries. This set-up of interpreting the inductive assertion method semantically allows for a simple and intuitive formulation of program verification methods, which is based on the systematic generation of so-called *verification conditions*. These are the basic mathematical properties of the underlying state spaces of a program that should be satisfied for that program to be correct. Therefore, this approach leads to the formulation of a *mathematical basis* for state-based program verification. The focus here is on proving partial correctness, absence of deadlock, absence of runtime errors, and termination properties. All proposed program verification methods are proved to be sound and complete. The examples discussed include the correctness proofs for various mutual-exclusion algorithms, amongst others, that of Szymanski (discussed in Chapter 1) and Lamport's ticket algorithm, and a correctness proof for Francez & Rodeh's distributed greatest-common-divisor algorithm.

In Chapters 2–4 the kind of completeness investigated is that of *semantic* completeness. In semantic completeness proofs one disregards the expressibility of predicates in any formal language, and only focusses on their mathematical content, i.e., one regards them as boolean functions. Chapter 5 investigates the expressibility of these boolean functions in the language of first-order predicate logic over the standard model of the natural numbers, establishing that all boolean functions which have been used within the verification methods discussed in Chapters 2–4 can be expressed in this logic. This leads to so-called relatively-complete syntactical formulations of the main verification methods discussed, in which all valid properties of the natural numbers are assumed to be axioms. These formulations are needed for establishing relative completeness of the Hoare logics discussed in later chapters.

Part III consists of Chapters 6–8. It discusses various compositional proof methods for the verification of concurrent programs, and culminates in comprehensive accounts of Misra & Chandy's assumption-commitment paradigm (in order to reason compositionally about synchronous message passing) and Jones' rely-guarantee paradigm (for reasoning compositionally about shared-variable concurrency) [MC81, Jon81, Jon83] in, respectively, Chapters 7 and 8. Chapter 6 contains a general introduction to the subject of compositionality and concurrency, and in particular, to the A-C and R-G paradigms. For all these methods soundness and (semantic) completeness proofs are given. The examples discussed include a top-down derivation of a distributed priority queue, and correctness of mutual-exclusion as well as array-search algorithms.

Part IV consists of Chapters 9–11, and discusses Hoare logics for the programming models discussed in Part II. Soundness and relative completeness of these logics is deduced from the corresponding soundness and semantic completeness results from Part II, in combination with the expressibility results from Chapter 5.

In Chapter 9 Hoare logic is presented as a *structured* syntactic formulation of the various inductive assertion methods formulated in Part II, reflecting the algebraic structure of the programs whose proof is given. In particular, the semantics of a program is defined as the semantics of its corresponding transition system; therefore, programs can be regarded as a structured notation for transition systems. Moreover, for every program operator we introduce within the inductive assertion method an operator upon proofs such that the proof of a program displays the same structure as the program itself. As a consequence, a correctness proof of a program in Hoare logic corresponds to a proof using the inductive assertion method for its associated transition system, and vice versa, with the added difference that a proof in Hoare logic now reflects the algebraic structure of the program in question. This leads to an identification of concepts which, until now, were regarded as being different.

In Chapter 10 a so-called *proof-outline logic* is presented for nested shared-variable concurrency. A proof outline is a *systematic annotation* of the control points of a program *with assertions*, which satisfy the verification conditions generated by the inductive assertion method. Because proof outlines annotate program text, they utilise additional information about the underlying execution mechanism, and therefore any logic based on them is noncompositional. They satisfy the following property: whenever the assertions associated with the initial control points of a (concurrent) program are satisfied, and that program is executed, the states arising during its computation satisfy the assertions annotating the control points encountered. Proof-outline logics therefore capture properties of intermediate states arising during program execution. Consequently, they are appropriate for proving correctness of concurrent programs, because the interaction between the processes of such programs depends on the values of their intermediate states. As illustration of these concepts, correctness is proved of the concurrent garbage collector from Chapter 1.

In Chapter 11 we present the noncompositional Hoare logics of Apt, Francez & de Roever and of Levin & Gries for synchronous message passing. The logic of the latter is applied in order to derive a compositional parallel composition rule for synchronous message passing. The examples include a correctness proof of a set-partitioning algorithm.

The last part of this volume is Part V. It consists of Chapter 12, and introduces various communication-closed-layer transformation principles for concurrency (both for shared-variable concurrency and for a simple form of asynchronous message passing). As already stated, these transformation principles express the point of view that, in order to clarify how a network of distributed processes functions, the structure of its correctness proof should reflect the structure of its original design process rather than that of the resulting final program. Whenever applicable, these principles lead to a much clearer proof structure which has the additional advantage of clarifying the resulting network algorithm. This is illustrated on the basis of correctness proofs for a running example in this volume, that of a simple set-partitioning algorithm, and for the two-phase-commit protocol.

The structure of the companion volume

Next we give a brief description of the structure of our companion volume. The latter can be studied independently from this volume.

The companion volume consists of three parts: Part I presents a concise self-contained introduction to Hoare logics for sequential programming, shared-variable concurrency and synchronous message passing. In Part II various compositional Hoare logics for concurrency are presented, and in Part III a number of industrially-inspired medium-size applications are described together with techniques for machine support for checking compositional verification principles for concurrency using PVS.

Its principal focus is the illustration through many examples of compositional techniques in correctness proofs for concurrent programs. As a result, no attention is paid to completeness proofs (the latter being a focus of the present volume). However, we still give soundness proofs to explain why these techniques work.

Part I consists of Chapters 1–3, and discusses Hoare logics for a simple programming language for guarded commands, and its classical noncompositional extensions to shared-variable concurrency and synchronous message passing.

Part II consists of Chapters 4–7.

Chapter 4 presents a compositional Hoare logic for proving partial correctness of programs which communicate through synchronous message passing and feature nested parallelism. The soundness proof for this logic illustrates the problems which must be solved to obtain such compositional Hoare logics in general, and serves as a contrast with its considerably simpler semantical characterisation within an inductive-assertion-style framework which is presented in Chapter 7 of this volume.

Chapter 5 presents various compositional Hoare logics for reactive programs which communicate through synchronous message passing. The purpose of reactive programs is primarily to maintain an ongoing relationship with the environment, rather than to produce a final value upon termination [HP85]. These Hoare logics are variants of:

(i) Misra & Chandy's assumption-commitment and Pandya & Joseph's presupposition-affirmation formalisms, and
(ii) so-called trace-invariant logics.

In these logics the communication interface of a process is specified using invariants over the communication histories of that process. The focus here is on proving both invariance properties, such as *deadlock freedom*, and certain *progress* properties, such as chatter freedom and divergence freedom, which can be proved compositionally. *Chatter freedom* ensures that the number of consecutive communications in a computation is finite, whereas *divergence freedom* ensures finiteness of the number of consecutive internal actions. In case the relation between an action and its resulting reaction within a reactive program is expressed by execution of a loop body, it is important that this loop body terminates. To prove this, establishing chatter and divergence freedom of that loop body are important, because together these properties imply that no infinite computations are generated – this is called *weak* total correctness. Once the latter has been proved, establishing total correctness requires additional deadlock (and runtime-error) freedom proofs.

As usual, soundness proofs are provided.

Chapter 6 presents a sound rely-guarantee formalism for reasoning compositionally about shared-variable concurrency.

Semantic versions of these proof systems for establishing partial correctness are proved semantically complete in this volume.

In Chapter 7 an assumption-commitment-style Hoare logic is developed for reasoning compositionally about real-time synchronous and asynchronous message passing.

Part III consists of Chapters 8–10, and has been discussed under points 5 and 6 on page xiv.

Chapter 8 applies the compositional proof system for distributed real-time of Chapter 7 to hybrid systems and bus protocols. In particular, a system for chemical batch processing is derived, as well as a distributed real-time arbitration protocol inspired by the IEEE 896 Futurebus specification.

In Chapter 9:

• a mixed formalism is defined in which programs and specifications are combined to a unified framework,

- subsequently, this mixed formalism is formulated inside PVS (for Prototype Verification System) [ORS92], and
- applied to the machine-supported verification of the chemical batch processing system from Chapter 8, and a membership protocol.

Chapter 10 extends the formalism of Chapter 7 for reasoning compositionally about distributed real-time to fault tolerance. In particular, a correctness proof is given for the reliable storage of data, called stable storage, which uses multiple disks.

Instructions for classroom use

The material in these textbooks has been developed and tried out during classroom use for over 10 years in the Netherlands and Germany: at the Eindhoven University of Technology, at the University of Utrecht, and at the Christian-Albrechts University at Kiel. The courses given on their basis vary from quarter courses of 18 hours duration to semester courses of up to 52 hours duration, and include numerous shorter compact courses given at various schools. Outlines of possible courses are discussed below, using the chapter dependencies given in Figures 0.1 and 0.2.

I.1
I.2
I.3
I.4
I.6
I.8
II.6
I.5
I.9
I.10
I.12
I.11
II.4
II.5
II.7
II.8
II.9
II.10
I.6
I.7

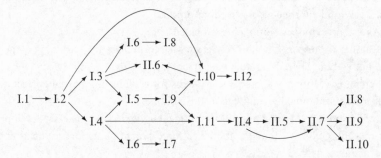

Fig. 0.1. Chapter dependencies: I.j refers to Chapter j of this volume, whereas II.k refers to Chapter k of the companion volume.

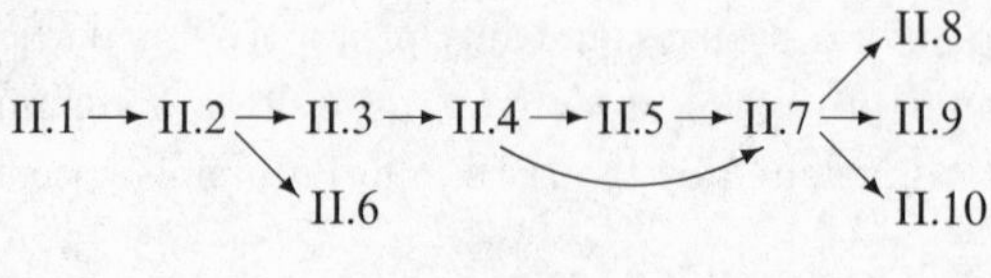

II.1
II.2
II.3
II.4
II.5
II.7
II.8
II.9
II.10
II.6

Fig. 0.2. Chapter dependencies for a course exclusively based on the companion volume.

1. An 18-hours introductory course on the mathematical foundations of program verification, covering Chapters I.2, I.3, I.4 and I.9 (possibly dropping the sections on deadlock-freedom, runtime-error freedom and termination proofs).
2. A one-semester course on the mathematical foundations of compositional program verification, covering Parts I, II and III of this volume.
3. A one-semester course on the verification of programs communicating via shared variables, covering Sections 2–6 of Chapter I.1, and Chapters I.2, I.3, (I.5), I.9, I.10, I.12 and/or II.6, discussing Chapter I.5 only in the exercise sessions.
4. A one-semester course on the verification of distributed message passing programs, covering Sections 2–5 of Chapter I.1, and Chapters I.2, I.4, (I.5), I.9, I.11, II.4 and II.5, discussing Chapter I.5 only in the exercise sessions.
5. A course on compositional logics for program verification, exclusively based on the companion volume (which can be studied independently).
6. A 52-hours course on verification of concurrency, covering this volume and Chapters II.4, II.5 and II.6, with or without Chapters I.5 or I.12.

Corrections

It is inevitable that these books contain errors. Please be so kind as to e-mail any errors or remarks to bkmail2@informatik.uni-kiel.de. A list with corrections can be found under: http://www.informatik.uni-kiel.de/inf/deRoever/ .

Technical Notes

Some sections are called *technical notes;* these can be skipped upon first reading, and are aimed at the already technically-skilled reader.

Acknowledgements

This book contains pictures of many researchers whose work is discussed. We thank them for their permission to publish these, and also those people who provided these pictures. In particular, we are grateful to Manfred Broy for putting his picture archive at our disposal; Michael van Emde Boas for his photograph of Peter van Emde Boas and Theo Janssen; Peter van Emde Boas for his shots of Edsger W. Dijkstra and David Park; Sean Floyd for helping us to obtain pictures of his father Robert W. Floyd; Gerhard Pfeifer for his pictures of flying cranes; Henk Thomas, the photographer of Folia, the weekly of the University of Amsterdam, for his picture of Peter van Emde Boas; the editorial staff of this newspaper for the permission to publish it; and the University of Jena for its picture of Gottlob Frege.

David Tranah and the helpful staff at Cambridge University Press deserve our gratitude for helping us improve and, finally, publish this book. In particular, we owe special thanks to Keith Westmoreland for his careful copy editing and Zoe Naylor for managing to accommodate our request concerning the cover design.

We would like to thank our students and colleagues, especially, Erika Ábrahám-Mumm, Henning Arndt, Roy Bartsch, Kai Baukus, Steve Brooks, Pierre Colette, Antonio Cau, Jaco de Bakker, Edsger W. Dijkstra, Michael Felsberg, Christian Gebken, Oliver Granert, Denise Hodgeson-Möckel, Ralf Huuck, Lasse Kliemann, Lars Kühne, Marcel Kyas, Ben Lukoschus, Jan Lukoschus, Helge Marquardt, Oliver Matz, Jan Meyer, Paritosh Pandya, Jan Paul, Amir Pnueli, Lasse Rempe, Sven Riesenberg, Fred Schneider, Markus Schneider, Carsten Scholz, Dirk Scholz, Natarajan Shankar, Michael Siegel, Karsten Stahl, Änne Straßner, Jan Vianen, Marcus Wieschalla, and Andreas Wortmann for their help and interest, without which writing this book would have been impossible.

We especially thank Ben Lukoschus, without whose TₑXpertise the different parts of this book would never have been integrated into a polished monograph with a uniform typography.

Willem-Paul's special thanks go towards his wife Corinne for her professional advice and for creating such a convivial and stimulating atmosphere when receiving his colleagues at home.

Writing this book would have been impossible without the love, support, and understanding of our partners and children during the many years we have been working on it, and without the engagement and support of our teachers. We dedicate this book to all of them.

Christian-Albrechts-Universität zu Kiel	Willem-Paul de Roever
Rijksuniversiteit Utrecht	Frank de Boer
Katholieke Universiteit Nijmegen	Ulrich Hannemann
Katholieke Universiteit Nijmegen	Jozef Hooman
Université Joseph Fourier, Grenoble	Yassine Lakhnech
Universiteit Twente	Mannes Poel
Universiteit Twente	Job Zwiers

Part I

Introduction and Overview

1

Introduction

1.1 Central Questions

The subject of this work is how to prove correctness of concurrent programs. To argue the relevance of this theme a number of questions should be answered:

- How important is verification for the development of correct software?
- Why does one need to give correctness proofs for concurrent programs? Must these be formal? Or even machine checked?
- Which style of proof method is more appropriate, a compositional or non-compositional one?

These questions will be answered in the present chapter.

Note that here, as elsewhere in this volume, concurrency is used as a generic term covering the execution mechanisms for programs which communicate through distributed message passing as well as through shared variables. Such programs will also be called parallel programs. If we want to focus on programs communicating through distributed message passing we use the term *distributed* programs . Such programs are implemented on distributed locations and communicate by some form of message exchange. When no such physical separation is intended, communication is usually by means of shared variables, and we speak of *shared-variable concurrency*.

1.2 Structure of this Chapter

In Section 1.3 we define some basic concepts in the theory of concurrency which we shall need later. We argue in Section 1.4 that concurrent programs should be proved correct because of their unimaginable and bewildering complexity, thereby answering the first two questions posed above. We do so by starting out with a small refinement problem in the context of a simple mutual exclusion algorithm due to Peterson [Pet83], then discuss several attempted solutions in the area of concurrent garbage collection, consider a distributed mutual exclusion algorithm due to Szymanski [Szy88], and finish Section 1.4 by concluding that operational reasoning gives no guarantee that a program satisfies its specifications. Instead one should always use state-based reasoning for concurrent programs – that is, proofs based on invariance properties. Especially when these proofs are large and complicated, one should use (semi-)automated proof checkers to eliminate errors in hand-checked verification proofs. This answers the first two questions raised above.

Section 1.5 discusses the approach followed in this book, which is a semantically-based dual-language state-based property-oriented approach, gives a brief introduction to Floyd's inductive assertion method and Hoare logic, then discusses their extensions to concurrency – first noncompositional proof methods, and then compositional ones based on the assume-guarantee paradigm and finishes by briefly describing a noncompositional proof method called the communication-closed-layers paradigm suitable for verifying network algorithms and protocols.

Section 1.6 discusses compositionality, one of the leading themes in this work. This central concept is approached from the viewpoint of the verify-while-develop paradigm, thus enabling a detailed analysis of its definition. Then its relationship to machine-supported verification and modularity is explained, followed by a discussion of the complexity of compositional reasoning. We finish the section by answering the third question posed above.

This chapter ends with Section 1.7, which puts the development of noncompositional to compositional state-based proof methods for concurrency into a historical perspective.

1.3 Basic Concepts of Concurrency

Why should one prove concurrent programs correct? As a preparation for answering this question in the next section, we first introduce some basic concepts for reasoning about such programs. Next we sketch a way to understand them by defining their meaning. Then we discuss communication and synchronisation, which are the two main forms of interaction between processes executing in parallel.

1.3.1 Differences between Sequential Programming and Concurrency

But first: *What are the differences between sequential programs on the one hand and concurrent programs on the other?*

First and foremost, a sequential program is intended to run on a single processor, whereas a concurrent program can be executed in principle on as many processors as there are parallel components in the program. The second difference concerns our way of characterising such programs.

For the characterisation of sequential programs it is sufficient to observe their pairs of initial and corresponding final states. For a given program, the set of such pairs is called its *observable behaviour.* (Note that even for sequential programs, there are different notions of such behaviour, varying according to whether or not, e.g., nontermination and/or runtime errors are also observed.) Given such a pair of initial and corresponding final states, it is not necessary to record *how* that final state has been computed from the given initial state. This is so, because two different sequential programs having the same observational behaviour are regarded as equivalent, since, whenever they are plugged as modules inside a third program, this causes no difference in observational behaviour of the latter. That is, from this point of view, sequential programs can be regarded as *atomic* units.

In case of concurrent programs, the same characterisation would not suffice, because the possibility of synchronisation and communication between such programs makes intermediate states as important as final ones. Hence the observational behaviour of these programs should also include some observable form of intermediate states, e.g., the values of those variables which are shared between processes or the messages communicated between them.

In general, a *concurrent program* consists of a collection of processes and shared objects, such as shared channels and/or shared variables. Each process can be considered as a sequential program which can run concurrently with other processes within the same program. The shared objects allow these processes to cooperate in accomplishing some task. They can be implemented in shared memory or might simply be a computer-communication network.

Let us illustrate these concepts.

- *Shared memory* (cf. Figure 1.1): External processes P_1 and P_2 both have access to a pool of shared memory cells. What should be prevented is that P_1 is able to access information in this shared memory while the information is being changed by P_2, and vice versa, because this would cause that information to become temporarily undefined. We want to do this independently of the specific nature of P_1 and P_2, i.e., we need a solution which is canonical w.r.t. programs accessing shared memory. To obtain such a solution, processes P_1 and P_2 have to be synchronised w.r.t. reading and writing memory cells; this is further illustrated in Section 1.4.

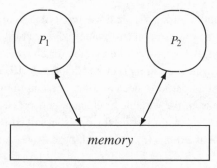

Fig. 1.1. Shared memory concept.

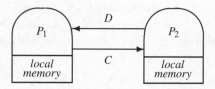

Fig. 1.2. Computer-communication network concept.

- *Computer-communication network* (cf. Figure 1.2): Every process has its own local memory. However, processes share channels. Hence, in order to implement message passing one needs to guarantee that when, e.g., P_1 sends a message along a channel C to P_2, and this message reaches P_2, P_2 eventually reacts to that message. And this again requires some form of synchronisation between, at the very least, P_2 and its environment.

When formulating proof rules and discussing compositionality we need to characterise the observable behaviour of a program component or process more precisely by its so-called *observables*. In a purely sequential context, one sometimes needs to know the precise set of variables occurring, or involved (this term is explained below), in that component, i.e., those variables whose values are read and/or changed during execution of that component. These variables are called the observables of that component. In case of shared-variable concurrency, the observables of a component consist of two sets, the set of variables occurring, or involved, in that component, and the set of variables through which that component communicates with its environment. In a case of message passing, the observables of a component also consist of two sets, the set of variables occurring, or involved, in that component, and the set of channels through which it communicates with its environment. In this book no mixtures of these two communication mechanisms are considered.

In a purely semantic setting we shall use the term "involved in" to express the dependency of a process upon (the values of) variables and/or (the values communicated along) channels, e.g., a variable or channel involved in a process, whereas in a syntactic setting (i.e., in Chapters 5, 10, 11 and 12) we use "occurring in" for this purpose, because then one can point to the particular syntactic occurrences of the variable or channel concerned. These terms will also be defined in a semantic setting for boolean-valued functions, and in a syntactic setting for assertions from first-order predicate logic.

1.3.2 Semantics of Concurrency

Next we give a model for understanding such programs [SA86]. A program *state* σ associates a value with each variable. Execution of a sequential program results in a sequence of *atomic transitions,* each of which transforms the state indivisibly. Execution of a concurrent program results in an interleaving of these sequences of atomic transitions for each component process and can be essentially viewed as a *history* or *computation sequence*

$$\sigma_0 \overset{\alpha_1}{\to} \sigma_1 \overset{\alpha_2}{\to} \cdots \overset{\alpha_i}{\to} \sigma_i \overset{\alpha_{i+1}}{\to} \cdots$$

where the σ_i's denote the states, the α_i's denote atomic transitions, and the sequence $\alpha_1 \alpha_2 \ldots$ is an interleaving of these sequences of atomic transitions resulting from execution of the processes.

The behaviour of a concurrent program is defined by its set of histories, each history corresponding to one possible interleaving of those sequences of atomic actions that result from execution of its processes. For all but trivial programs, this set is apt to be quite large – so large that it might be impossible to enumerate, much less inspect, each of its elements in order to ascertain aspects of the behaviour of the program. This will be illustrated by the examples in Section 1.4. Therefore, we take in Section 1.5 an approach for developing and analysing such programs which is based on the use of abstraction; it is called *assertional reasoning.* Instead of enumerating sets of sequences of states, we characterise the computation sequences in these sets by describing their properties of interest. Instead of enumerating program states, we use *predicates* (boolean functions) which are expressible by *assertions* – formulae of predicate logic – to characterise sets of states. As a result, use of assertional reasoning allows a program to be understood as a *relation between assertions, rather than as an object that is executed.* As will be clear from Section 1.4 onwards, this change of viewpoint is crucial to our understanding of concurrent programs, for it allows us to master their complexity by assertional, or even compositional, reasoning.

1.3.3 Communication and Synchronisation

Thirdly we discuss the important subjects of communication and synchronisation between processes, which have already been introduced above.

In order to interact, processes must communicate and synchronise. *Communication* allows one process to influence execution of another one and can be accomplished using *shared variables* or *message passing*. When shared variables are used, a process writes to a variable that is read by another process; when message passing is used, a process sends a message to another process.

To communicate, one process sets the state of a shared object and the other reads it. This works only if the shared object is read after it has been written – reading the object before it is written can return a meaningful, but erroneous, value. Thus, meaningful communication between processes cannot occur without preventing the latter; this is called synchronisation.

Three notions of synchronisation appear in this book. The first, *mutual exclusion,* groups actions into *critical sections* that are never interleaved during execution. Within these critical sections no program variables are changed which influence the control flow of the synchronisation mechanism implemented (i.e., mutual exclusion). The second form, *conditional synchronisation*, delays a process until the state satisfies some specified condition. This synchronisation mechanism is, e.g., used in order to prevent the value of a shared variable being read in one process before that variable has been written in another process, as discussed above. The third form arises when communication between processes itself is synchronised. Then the acts of sending and receiving messages along given channels are synchronised, and, hence, one speaks of *synchronous communication.* The remaining forms of communication between processes are then called *asynchronous.* For example, communication by shared variables is asynchronous. All these forms of synchronisation restrict interleavings of processes. Mutual exclusion restricts interleavings by preventing interleaving from occurring at certain internal control points in a process; conditional synchronisation and synchronous communication restrict interleavings by causing a process to be delayed at given control points.

A simple example illustrates these types of synchronisation. Communication between a sender process and a receiver process is often implemented using a shared buffer. The sender writes into the buffer; the reader reads from the buffer. Mutual exclusion is used to ensure that a partially written message is not read – access to the buffer by the sender and receiver is made *mutually exclusive.* Conditional synchronisation is used to ensure that the message is not overwritten or read twice – the reader is prevented from reading the buffer until a new message has been written. In a case of synchronous communication, special protocols, which are implemented using such buffers at a lower level of abstraction, convey the impression at a higher level of abstraction that communication between processes along the same channel is simultaneous.

Having introduced these concepts, in the next section we answer the first two questions raised in Section 1.1.[1]

1.4 Why Concurrent Programs Should be Proved Correct

1.4.1 Introduction

In this section we answer the first two questions raised in Section 1.1. In particular, we argue that it is in general impossible to convince oneself of the correctness of concurrent programs without recourse to formal methods. This we do by giving a number of problems which are characteristic for the area, and for which we propose a number of increasingly complicated incorrect approximations until we finally arrive at an alleged correct solution. The separate steps in the derivations of these solutions are certainly in themselves trivial, and yet several errors, sometimes subtle ones, will be shown to creep in. The design of the final solutions proceeds through a disquieting series of trials and errors. It should be clear that an informal justification of programs constructed in such a manner is not sufficient. The difficulties illustrated explain why we are interested in proving the correctness of such programs.[2]

The first example concerns Peterson's mutual exclusion algorithm [Pet83] in a presentation due to Amir Pnueli. The second example deals with the difficult task of concurrent garbage collection; specifically, we discuss a deep logical bug in one of the first concurrent garbage collectors ever written, by E.W. Dijkstra, L. Lamport and others, and how to correct it [DLM+78]. Manna & Pnueli's paper [MP91c] drew our attention to the third example concerning a sophisticated distributed mutual exclusion algorithm due to Szymanski [Szy88].

As pointed out by Leslie Lamport, the history of concurrent algorithms seems to abound with published incorrect algorithms. He writes to de Roever [Lam99]:

To my knowledge, the first published concurrent algorithm was Dijkstra's '65 mutual exclusion paper [Dij65b]. The second one was by H. Hyman in a letter to the *CACM* proposing a simple mutex algorithm for two processors [Hym66]. The third algorithm was by Knuth, also in a letter to the *CACM,* in which he improved Dijkstra's algorithm and pointed out that Hyman's was completely wrong [Knu66].

---

[1] Parts of Section 1.3 originate from [SA86].
[2] This paragraph has been inspired by a similar paragraph in [AO91].

And also, are you aware of the error in Ben-Ari's garbage collection paper [BA82, BA84]? He visited me at SRI soon after that paper was published, and I was discussing proofs with him. ... Going over the proof of one of the algorithms in that paper, and trying to turn it into a real invariance proof, we discovered that the algorithm was wrong.[3]

But sequential algorithms and their correctness proofs also share this fate, as pointed out by Donald Knuth, in an interview with Lád'a Lhotka about structured programming [Knu99, pp. 613–614]:

I was talking with Tony Hoare, who was editor of a series of books ... He told me I ought to *publish* my program for TEX.

As I was writing TEX I was using for the second time in my life a set of ideas called "structured programming", which were revolutionizing the way computer programming was done in the middle 70s (sic). ... Well, this was frightening – a very scary thing, for a professor of computer science to show someone a large program. At best, a professor might publish very small routines as examples of how to write programs. And we could polish those until ... well, every example in the literature about such programs had bugs in it. Tony Hoare was a great pioneer for proving the correctness of programs. But if you looked at the details ... I discovered from reading some of the articles, you know, I could find three bugs in a program that was proved correct. [*laughter*] These were *small* programs. Now, he says, take my *large* program and reveal it to the world, with all its compromises. ... But then I also realized how much need there was for examples of fairly large programs that could be considered as reasonable models of good practice, not just small programs.

1.4.2 First Example: Peterson's Mutual Exclusion Algorithm

Consider the following solution to the mutual exclusion problem:

Example 1.1 Let

$P_1 \equiv \ell_0 :$ **loop forever do**
$\qquad\qquad \ell_1 :$ **noncritical section**;
$\qquad\qquad \ell_2 : (y_1, s) := (1, 1);$
$\qquad\qquad \ell_3 :$ **wait** $(y_2 = 0) \vee (s \neq 1);$
$\qquad\qquad \ell_4 :$ **critical section**;
$\qquad\qquad \ell_5 : y_1 := 0$
$\qquad$ **od**

and

---

[3] The history of concurrent garbage collection and errors in its algorithms is extensively documented in Section 8.10 of [JL96]; e.g., the errors in Ben-Ari's algorithm were published independently by J. van de Snepscheut, C. Pixley, and D. Doligez & X. Leroy.

$P_2 \equiv m_0$: **loop forever do**

        m_1 : **noncritical section**;

        m_2 : $(y_2, s) := (1, 2)$;

        m_3 : **wait** $(y_1 = 0) \vee (s \neq 2)$;

        m_4 : **critical section**;

        m_5 : $y_2 := 0$

    od

and let

$$Pet1 \equiv s := 1; y_1 := 0; y_2 := 0; [P_1 \| P_2].$$ □

The statements **noncritical section** and **critical section** in mutual exclusion algorithms do not change the values of the variables which are used to implement the mutual exclusion mechanism, i.e., in this particular case, do not change the values of y_1, y_2 and s. Here **wait** b is a statement expressing conditional synchronisation. It acts like a traffic light that can only be passed when b evaluates to *true*. Now consider an occurrence of **wait** $(y_j = 0) \vee (s \neq i)$, for $j \neq i$, within a process P_i; then making $(y_j = 0) \vee (s \neq i)$ true is typically done inside another process P_j which operates in parallel with P_i, hence $j \neq i$. This explains the name conditional synchronisation.

Integer variables y_1 and y_2 are used by each process to signal the other process of active interest in entering the critical section. Thus, on leaving the noncritical section, process P_i sets its own variable y_i, $i = 1, 2$, to 1 indicating interest in entering the critical section. In a similar way, on exiting the critical section, P_i resets y_i to 0. Variable s is used to resolve a tie situation between the two processes, which may arise when both processes are actively interested in entering their critical sections at the same time.

Variable s serves as a logbook in which each process that sets its y variable to 1 signs as it does so. The test at ℓ_3 says that P_1 may enter its critical section if either $y_2 = 0$, implying that P_2 is not interested in entering a critical section, or if $s \neq 1$, implying that P_2 performed its assignment to y_2 *after* P_1 assigned 1 to y_1, and, consequently, can only pass m_3 after P_1 has executed its critical section. Since P_1 and P_2 are symmetric, the same kind of reasoning applies when the rôles of P_1 and P_2 are interchanged. Consequently, *Pet1* implements mutual exclusion of the critical sections of P_1 and P_2 (using conditional synchronisation).

Formal methods can help to prove this intuition formally, i.e., proving that no computation of program *Pet1* contains a state in which P_1 is executing at ℓ_4 while P_2 is executing at m_4 (cf. Exercise 3.4). (This can even be verified automatically.)

Program *Pet1* is too demanding in the sense that it forces the processor(s) executing this program to perform the assignments to y_i and to s within the same step. Programs which use these sorts of *multiple assignments* as atomic actions are said to be *of coarse granularity*. Most existing hardware systems cannot perform multiple assignments in one step. Consequently, we wish to refine this working program into a *finer-grained* program in which the assignments to y_i and to s will be performed in two separate assignments. There are two candidates to such a refinement. They are given by programs *Pet2* (solution 2) and *Pet3* (solution 3) respectively. Are both of these programs correct? Let us examine them each in turn.

Example 1.2 Let

$P_1 \equiv \ell_0 :$ **loop forever do**
$\qquad\qquad \ell_1 :$ **noncritical section;**
$\qquad\qquad \ell_2 : s := 1;$
$\qquad\qquad \ell_3 : y_1 := 1;$
$\qquad\qquad \ell_4 :$ **wait** $(y_2 = 0) \vee (s \neq 1);$
$\qquad\qquad \ell_5 :$ **critical section;**
$\qquad\qquad \ell_6 : y_1 := 0$
$\qquad$ **od**

and

$P_2 \equiv m_0 :$ **loop forever do**
$\qquad\qquad m_1 :$ **noncritical section;**
$\qquad\qquad m_2 : s := 2;$
$\qquad\qquad m_3 : y_2 := 1;$
$\qquad\qquad m_4 :$ **wait** $(y_1 = 0) \vee (s \neq 2);$
$\qquad\qquad m_5 :$ **critical section;**
$\qquad\qquad m_6 : y_2 := 0$
$\qquad$ **od**

and let

$$Pet2 \equiv s := 1; y_1 := 0; y_2 := 0; [P_1 \| P_2]. \qquad\qquad \square$$

Program *Pet2* is not correct. Consider the following computation, where states are presented as 5-tuples listing the current location of P_1, the current location of P_2, and the current values of s, y_1, and y_2.

$\langle \ell_0, m_0, 1, 0, 0 \rangle, \quad \langle \ell_1, m_0, 1, 0, 0 \rangle, \quad \langle \ell_1, m_1, 1, 0, 0 \rangle, \quad \langle \ell_2, m_1, 1, 0, 0 \rangle,$
$\langle \ell_2, m_2, 1, 0, 0 \rangle, \quad \langle \ell_3, m_2, 1, 0, 0 \rangle, \quad \langle \ell_3, m_3, 2, 0, 0 \rangle, \quad \langle \ell_3, m_4, 2, 0, 1 \rangle,$
$\langle \ell_3, m_5, 2, 0, 1 \rangle, \quad \langle \ell_4, m_5, 2, 1, 1 \rangle, \quad \langle \ell_5, m_5, 2, 1, 1 \rangle, \quad \ldots$

In this computation, P_2 could move from m_4 to m_5 because y_1 was 0 at the time, while P_1 could move from ℓ_4 to ℓ_5 because s was equal to 2 at the time.

Obviously, the last displayed state in this computation violates the requirement of mutual exclusion since both processes are executing in their critical sections at the same time. This shows that program *Pet2* is incorrect.

Next consider program *Pet3*.

Example 1.3 Let

$P_1 \equiv \ell_0 :$ **loop forever do**

$\qquad\qquad \ell_1 :$ **noncritical section**;

$\qquad\qquad \ell_2 : y_1 := 1;$

$\qquad\qquad \ell_3 : s := 1;$

$\qquad\qquad \ell_4 :$ **wait** $(y_2 = 0) \vee (s \neq 1);$

$\qquad\qquad \ell_5 :$ **critical section**;

$\qquad\qquad \ell_6 : y_1 := 0$

$\qquad$ **od**

and

$P_2 \equiv m_0 :$ **loop forever do**

$\qquad\qquad m_1 :$ **noncritical section**;

$\qquad\qquad m_2 : y_2 := 1;$

$\qquad\qquad m_3 : s := 2;$

$\qquad\qquad m_4 :$ **wait** $(y_1 = 0) \vee (s \neq 2);$

$\qquad\qquad m_5 :$ **critical section**;

$\qquad\qquad m_6 : y_2 := 0$

$\qquad$ **od**

and let

$$Pet3 \equiv s := 1; y_1 := 0; y_2 := 0; [P_1 \| P_2].$$ $\square$

For this program we are unable to produce a violating computation. The program can actually be proved correct. It is due to G.L. Peterson [Pet83]. A formal correctness proof of a variant of this algorithm is the subject of Exercise 3.4.[4]

In this discussion we have presented three programs that attempt to establish mutual exclusion. The programs are very similar and are certainly based on the same idea for coordinating the exclusion. Thus the intuition for all three is

---

[4] In his dissertation [Din99a], J. Dingel proves that the correctness of this algorithm does not depend on any atomicity or granularity assumptions; also, he refines the n-process version of the algorithm in a similar fashion as above.

basically sound. However, two of the three are correct while *Pet2* is incorrect. The differences between *Pet2* and *Pet3* are very small. This just shows that in studying even the simplest concurrent programs, intuition is very useful, but without formal methodologies we are lost.

1.4.3 Second Example: Concurrent Garbage Collection

In the previous example we have seen that when refining atomic actions by a sequence of other atomic actions the order in which the new actions are performed is crucial for the correctness of the refined version. In the following example we will observe the same phenomenon in the context of *concurrent garbage collection*. We have chosen this subject because the correctness of algorithms for concurrent garbage collection has been put in doubt ever since M. Woodger and N. Stenning found a deep logical bug in one of the first concurrent garbage collectors ever written, due to E.W. Dijkstra, L. Lamport and others. Since then several other algorithms for concurrent garbage collection have been published. Some of them have been formally proven correct, but others still suffer from bugs. A good indication of the complexity of developing correct concurrent garbage collection algorithms are the following words of Edsger W. Dijkstra:

It had been surprisingly hard to find the published solution and justification [of this algorithm] ([DLM+78]). We have fallen into nearly every logical trap possible. It was only too easy to design what looked – sometimes even for weeks and to many people – like a perfectly valid solution, until the effort to prove it correct revealed a (sometimes deep) bug. One firm conclusion, however, can be drawn: to believe that such solutions can be found without a very careful justification is optimism on the verge of foolishness.

Leslie Lamport's reaction to this bug goes even further [Lam99]:

The lesson I learned from this is that behavioral proofs are unreliable and one should always use state-based [assertional] reasoning for concurrent algorithms – that is, using a proof based on invariance. All of my later work has been based on this belief.

The problem to be solved is the following. In systems using references or pointer variables, manipulation of these variables may cause certain parts of a dynamically changing data structure to become inaccessible from some designated root. For such systems the operating system has to perform the task of *garbage collection*, meaning identifying and recycling inaccessible nodes.

If we view the memory as an array of *n* homogeneous nodes, we can use the following abstract presentation of the garbage collection problem due to [DLM+78]. We consider a directed graph of varying structure with a fixed number of nodes, where each node has a unique number $i \in \{1, \dots, \#nodes\}$

as identifier and at most two outgoing edges. In the graph there exists a fixed set of so-called *roots*. A node is called *reachable* if it is reachable via a directed path from one of these roots. Nonreachable nodes are called *garbage nodes*. The directed subgraph consisting of all reachable nodes and their outgoing edges represents the current *data structure*. Two extra roots are introduced: one root which points to the *list of free nodes*, i.e., nodes which can be used to modify the data structure, and a root called NIL, to which each node with less than two sons points with its free outgoing edges. The original program modifying the data structure is called the *mutator* in the context of garbage collection. The task of the so-called *collector* is to identify the set of garbage nodes, i.e., the set of nodes which are not reachable from any root, and to append them to the list of free nodes. In algorithms for *garbage-collection-on-the-fly*, the collector has to perform this task concurrently to the activity of a mutator. In this section we focus on such concurrent garbage-collection algorithms.

There are basically two main classes of algorithms. *Marking collectors* work in two phases; first they traverse the graph starting from the roots and mark all nodes they visit during the traversal (*marking phase*). In the second phase they append all non-marked nodes to the list of free nodes and remove all markings (*appending phase*).

In *reference counting* algorithms, in each node the number of references to this node is maintained. When the number of references to a node becomes zero the node is appended to the list of free nodes. A problem in reference counting algorithms is the proper handling of reference cycles between garbage nodes, which may cause the number of references to certain garbage nodes to never become zero.

The algorithms we look at belong to the first class. Thus the activities of the mutator and the collector can be described by repeated execution of:

- the **mutator**: redirecting an outgoing edge of a reachable node towards an already reachable one, and
- the **collector**: marking all reachable nodes, appending all non-marked nodes to the free list and removing all markings.

The correctness criteria which have to be satisfied by the combination of mutator and collector can now be formulated as:

- There are no changes made by the collector in the data structure, except for appending garbage nodes to the free list.
- Every garbage node will eventually be appended by the collector to the list of free nodes.

The first version of our garbage collector works as follows. At the beginning of the marking phase all nodes in the graph are white; several marking sweeps through the memory according to a certain visiting policy for the nodes will blacken all reachable nodes. If no further nodes are marked during a certain sweep, the collector assumes it has marked all reachable nodes and thus starts the appending phase. All remaining white nodes (i.e., garbage nodes, because they are not reachable) are appended to the free list, whereas black nodes are marked white again for the next marking cycle. In the presentation below $< a >$ denotes the atomic version of an arbitrary non-atomic statement a and $\{ \dots \}$ a comment.

Example 1.4 (First approximation) Let

$C_1 \equiv$ {marking phase}
     begin {all nodes are white}
        <blacken all roots>;
        $nnb :=$ #roots; $\{nnb =$ "new number of black nodes"$\}$
        repeat {marking loop}
            $onb := nnb$; $\{onb =$ "previous number of black nodes"$\}$
            for i **from** 1 **to** #nodes **do**
                if color of node $i =$ black **then**
                    <blacken the successors of node i>
                fi
            od;
            $< nnb :=$ #black nodes in the graph>
        until $onb = nnb$
     end;
     {collecting and appending phase}
     begin
        for i **from** 1 **to** #nodes **do**
            if color of node $i =$ white **then**
                <append node i to the free list>
            else <whiten node i >
            fi
        od {there are no more nodes that have been blackened
           during the marking phase}
    end.   □

In all examples of possible runs which are illustrated in this section the numbers identifying the nodes increase from top to bottom. This enumeration imposes a certain visiting policy by the algorithm for the nodes. By convention node number 1 denotes the root of the list of free nodes. Roots of the directed graph are represented by squares and are assumed to have the lowest numbers. We have omitted the special root NIL, as well as all references to it.

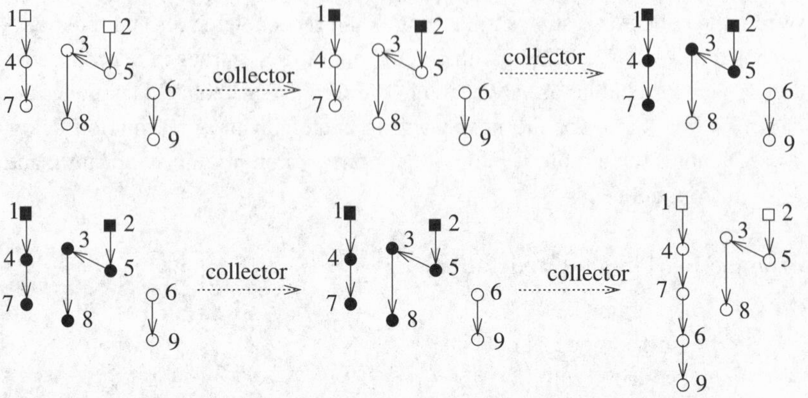

Fig. 1.3. Marking and collecting: The roots are represented by squares; node number 1 denotes the root of the list of free nodes.

Figure 1.3 demonstrates how the algorithm works. At first the collector marks all roots black; one sweep through the marking loop gives the situation shown in the third graph (notice that node number 8 has not been marked in the first sweep, although this node is reachable, because of the visiting policy). The second sweep blackens in this example all reachable nodes. Because the collector does not note a change in the number of black nodes after the third sweep, it starts collecting unmarked nodes, thereby appending node 6 and 9 to the list of free nodes, and removes all markings.

To understand the behaviour of the mutator, we indicate in Figure 1.4 edges to NIL nodes by broken lines. The operations "adding an edge" and "removing an edge" are special cases of "redirecting an edge" where the edge in question is targeted to NIL at the start and at the end of the operation, respectively.

In the example (Figure 1.3) above we only looked at the activities of the collector in isolation. Does this collector work properly if concurrently combined with an arbitrary mutator? Look at the perfectly valid mutator behaviour shown in Figure 1.5.

In Figure 1.5 node 5 has not been marked during the first marking sweep; the collector finds that three nodes are already marked; assume the collector has started the second sweep and is just going to inspect node 3; now the mutator may add edge 2 $\longrightarrow$ 5 and then as its next action remove edge 3 $\longrightarrow$ 5; then node 5 remains unmarked in the second sweep, too; the collector finishes the

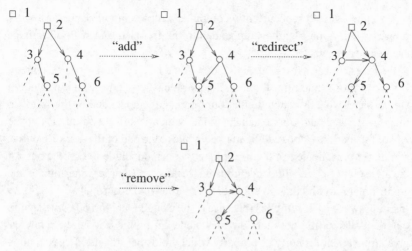

Fig. 1.4. Mutator behaviour: Edges to the NIL node are indicated by broken lines. By repeatedly redirecting an edge, the mutator causes node number 6 to become garbage.

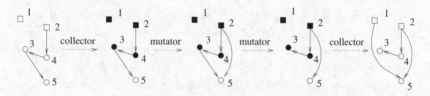

Fig. 1.5. Uncooperative mutator behaviour: By lack of cooperation between collector and mutator, a non-garbage node is appended to the free list.

marking loop and finds the number of black nodes unchanged and thus collects *incorrectly* the unmarked node 5 as garbage.

This incorrectness arises because the mutator made the unmarked node 5 inaccessible to the collector by redirecting edges to this node. It is easy to see that, whatever visiting policy is used by the collector to inspect nodes, there always exists a certain data structure and a certain mutator which makes reachable nodes unreachable for the collector by redirecting edges and thus causes malfunctioning of the garbage collector. This shows *that the mutator itself has to contribute to the garbage collection task*. In order to circumvent problems arising by redirecting edges from and to reachable nodes, we change the action of the mutator (for two arbitrary reachable nodes in the graph) to:

M_1 : < blacken the new target and
              redirect the outgoing edge to the new target >

Does the collector concurrently combined with the modified mutator work properly, i.e., is only garbage appended to the free list, and will all garbage eventually be collected?

We give an informal argument to "show" that the algorithm is indeed correct. If we can prove that, after the marking phase has terminated, all white nodes are garbage, we can conclude that only garbage is appended to the free list. Since it is clear that a nonreachable node, which is still marked black at the end of the marking loop, will be marked white at the end of the marking phase, and hence be collected in the next phase, we can conclude the correctness of the algorithm. So we will concentrate on the former. In order to terminate, the algorithm has to find the same number of marked nodes during two successive marking sweeps. This implies (because no black nodes are turned white again), that the collector did not mark any new node during the last sweep. Now we give an invariant property (a property which holds before and after execution of any action of the algorithm), which implies that all reachable nodes are marked after termination of the marking loop, and thus all unmarked nodes are garbage.

Take as invariant: *whenever the collector arrives at a certain point in the marking loop and has not marked any new node during this sweep, then there is no already inspected black node in the graph which was already black at the moment of inspection and which has an edge to an unmarked white node.*[5]

Readers are encouraged to convince themselves that this property is invariant under all possible steps of the mutator and the collector (Exercise 1.1). After termination of the last sweep, which did not mark any new node, we conclude from the invariant and the fact that the roots are marked, that *all* reachable nodes are marked. This has been shown formally for a similar garbage collector in [BA82].

So we have a first correct version of an algorithm for garbage collection with a very coarse granularity of the atomic actions. We have assumed that actions like "blacken all roots" and "blacken target and redirect edge" are performed *atomically* which requires a high synchronisation effort between collector and mutator and results in low efficiency of the algorithm. In order to find a more efficient solution, where the only form of synchronisation concerns access to shared variables, we refine the coarse atomic actions of M_1 and C_1 by sequences of atomic actions. A possible refinement is the following:

Example 1.5 (Second approximation) Let

---

[5] Node i is considered to have been inspected after "**if** color of node i = black **then** <blacken the successors of node i> **fi**" has been executed.

$M_2 \equiv$ <blacken the new target>;
        <redirect edge to the new target>

and

$C_2 \equiv$ {marking phase}
        begin {all nodes are white}
            for *i* **from** 1 **to** #roots **do**
                <blacken node *i* >;
            od;
            $nnb := \text{\#roots}$; {$nnb = $ "new number of black nodes"}
            repeat {marking loop}
                $onb := nnb$; {$onb = $ "previous number of black nodes"}
                for *i* **from** 1 **to** #nodes **do**
                    if color of node $i = $ black **then**
                        <blacken left successor of node i>;
                        <blacken right successor of node i>
                    fi
                od;
                $nnb := 0$;
                for *i* **from** 1 **to** #nodes **do**
                    if color of node $i = $ black **then**
                        $nnb := nnb + 1$
                    fi
                od
            until $onb = nnb$
        end;
        {collecting and appending phase}
        begin
            for *i* **from** 1 **to** #nodes **do**
                if color of node $i = $ white **then**
                    <append node *i* to the free list>
                else <whiten node *i* >
                fi
            od {there are no more nodes that have been blackened
                during the marking phase}
        end.   □

We have derived a "straightforward" fine-grained solution from the correct coarse-grained solution. But no one will succeed in proving this new version correct. Even such famous researchers as E.W. Dijkstra and L. Lamport were

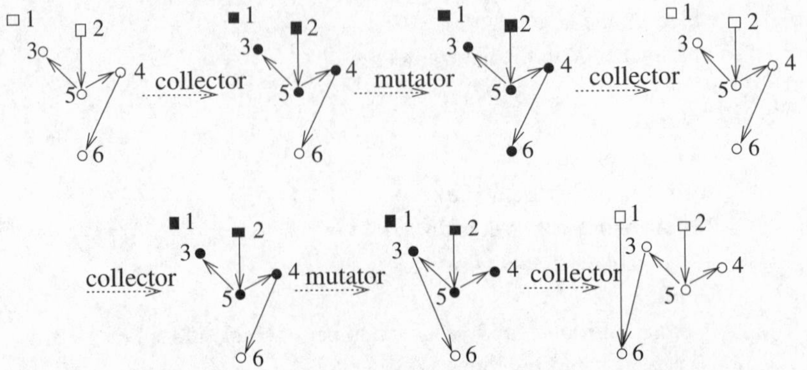

Fig. 1.6. Stenning & Woodger's bug: The mutator marks node number 6 but delays redirecting the edge from node number 3 to its new target, node number 6. Consequently, that node is marked white in the next collector actions, and upon redirecting that edge it remains white and is collected.

convinced of the correctness of the solution, till N. Stenning and M. Woodger found a deep logical bug in this first version of [DLM⁺78].

Figure 1.6 shows the situation where a non-garbage node is erroneously appended to the free list. After the first marking sweep of the collector the mutator wants to establish a reference from node 3 to node 6 and thus blackens node 6; assume that the mutator *delays* establishing this new reference; then the collector will find during the following marking sweep that the number of black nodes did not change and removes all markings; the first sweep of the next marking phase now ends with nodes 1 to 5 marked black and node 6 unmarked (situation 5) and the number of black nodes equal to 5; during the second sweep just before the collector will colour node 6 as a successor of the black node 4, the mutator establishes first the reference from node 3 to 6 and then removes the reference from node 4 to 6; thus node 6 remains unmarked and is thus incorrectly collected as garbage, because the collector finds the number of black nodes unchanged!

In order to fix this bug we could try to swap the actions of the mutator. But what happens, if the colouring of the new target by the mutator is delayed? Do we get other unexpected behaviour? And if not, have we now really considered all possible situations that might occur, when the mutator and the collector act concurrently? A correct version of this algorithm is sketched in Exercise 1.2. It has been formally proved correct in [Gri77]. In Section 10.5 a general strategy is presented for generating correctness proofs for such complex algorithms, using concurrent garbage collection as an example. First an abstract version of a concurrent garbage collector is proved correct, and then a correctness proof is given for a concrete version. The general problem of how to prove correctness of a concurrent algorithm when its atomic actions are refined has been solved by P. Gribomont in [Gri96].

The algorithms that we have investigated above are only partly distributed: the collector and the mutator work in parallel, but the whole data structure resides in one shared memory. The task of garbage collection becomes even more complicated than it is already, if the data structure is *distributed* over a network of nodes, where each node represents a processor. Then we have to deal with several mutators and collectors (possibly spawning new mutator and collector processes), that all work in parallel on a distributed structure. As shown in [Rud90], almost all of the distributed garbage collector algorithms proposed before 1990 contain bugs. In the opinion of M. Rudalics, *it is even doubtful whether some of these incorrect algorithms can be corrected at all!* The relation between garbage collection algorithms and algorithms in other areas of distributed computing, as, e.g., termination detection, global (virtual) time, distributed snapshots, and construction of spanning trees, gives rise to the suspicion, that also in these areas many incorrect published algorithms exist.[6]

We hope that the presented (non-)solutions for the above on-the-fly garbage collection and the incorrect algorithms for distributed garbage collection convince the reader of the truth of the cited words of Dijkstra: *"To believe that [correct] solutions can be found without a very careful justification is optimism on the verge of foolishness."*

To convince the remaining believers in "programming using common sense" that their position is in general untenable, we present in Section 1.4.4 a rather complicated mutual exclusion algorithm due to Szymanski and attempt to justify the correctness of this algorithm using behavioural reasoning. It is our belief that this exercise gives the final deathblow to that position. It is just impossible to survey the informally given arguments for the correctness of that algorithm. Although in this case the final version of the algorithm is correct – a formal proof is given in Section 3.5.2 – we believe that it is not possible to be convinced of this using behavioural reasoning [MP90, MP91c].

The same conclusion is reached by Leslie Lamport on the basis of his experience with [DLM+78], in the following quotation [Lam99]:

I received an early version of this paper [about concurrent garbage collection] from Dijkstra (probably as an EWD[7]) and I made a couple of suggestions. Dijkstra incor-

---

[6] See Section 8.10 of [JL96] for a thorough discussion of the history of concurrent garbage collection and the errors found in these algorithms.

[7] At an early stage Edsger W. Dijkstra started numbering all his professional writings, labelling them by "EWD", followed by their number.

porated them and, rather generously, added me to the list of authors. He submitted the paper to *CACM*. The next I heard about it was when I received a copy of a letter from Dijkstra to the editor withdrawing the paper. The letter said that someone had found an error in the algorithm, but gave no indication of what the error was. Since Dijkstra's proof was so convincing, I figured that it must be a trivial error that could easily be corrected.

I had fairly recently developed my version of what was to become known as the Owicki–Gries method. So, I decided to write a proof using this method, thinking that I would then find and correct the error. In about 15 minutes, the proof method led me to the error. To my surprise, it was a serious error.

I had a hunch that the algorithm could be fixed by changing the order in which two operations were performed. But I had no good reason to believe that would work. Indeed, I could see no simple informal argument to show that it worked. However, I decided to go ahead and try to write a formal correctness proof. It took me about two days of solid work, but I constructed the proof. When I was through, I was convinced that the algorithm was now correct, but I had no intuitive understanding of why it worked.

In the meantime, Dijkstra figured out that the algorithm could be fixed by interchanging two other operations, and wrote the same kind of behavioural proof as before. His fix produced an arguably more efficient algorithm, so that's the version we used. I sketched an assertional (Owicki–Gries style) proof of that algorithm. Given the evidence of the unreliability of his style of proof, I tried to get Dijkstra to agree to a rigorous assertional proof. He was unwilling to do that, though he did agree to make his proof somewhat more assertional and less operational.

Gries later published an Owicki–Gries style proof of the algorithm that was essentially the same as the one I had sketched. He simplified things a bit by combining two atomic operations into one. He mentioned that in a footnote, but the *CACM* failed to print the footnote. (However, they did print the footnote number in the text.)

The lesson I learned from this is that behavioral proofs are unreliable and one should always use state-based [assertional] *reasoning for concurrent algorithms – that is, using a proof based on invariance.* All of my later work, leading up to TLA, has been based on this belief.

We conclude this discussion with another quotation from Dijkstra's work [Dij75b]:

The first moral of this story is *never* to believe the correctness of a solution without a proof for it. The second moral of this story is *never* to forget the first one. The third moral is that for the design of multiprocessor installations we cannot rely on the traditional approach of the optimistic engineer, who, when the design looks reasonable, puts it together to see if it works.

With VLSI-technology existing it seems unavoidable that multiprocessor installations will be built, and, people being as they are, it seems equally unavoidable that many of them will be put together by the aforementioned optimistic engineer. I shudder at the thought of all the new bugs: they will only delight the Devil. Am I too pessimistic? Nobody knows the trouble I have seen . . . .

1.4.4 Third Example: Szymanski's Mutual Exclusion Algorithm

In their paper [MP91c], Zohar Manna and Amir Pnueli prove a rather complicated mutual exclusion algorithm correct, which is due to B.K. Szymanski [Szy88]. This algorithm represented at the beginning of the 1990s the state of the art in mutual exclusion algorithms for distributed processes. In this algorithm each shared variable, although read in all processes, is updated in only one of them; moreover it enjoys the property of so-called linear delay, expressing that the period of waiting associated with entering critical sections and their "waiting rooms" is linearly bounded in the number of processes.

Manna and Pnueli write in [MP91c]:

Although the algorithm appears to be quite simple and innocuous, the only way we could convince ourselves of its correctness was to construct the formal proof outlined in this paper. Szymanski presented an informal proof, which is as convincing as informal proofs can be. In fact, our formal proof derives its main ideas from a formalisation of his informal arguments. However, if the question of correctness is crucial, such as having to decide whether to include this algorithm as a contention-resolving component in a hardware chip, we see no way but to carry out a formal verification.

The interested reader is advised to read their paper, also because it contains a quick and effective introduction to temporal logic "for the practicing verifier".

Below we present the algorithm in a style dubbed "derivation of a correct algorithm through incorrect intermediate approximations". This style can be made formal, as argued in [CKdR92], and is particularly suitable for explaining mutual exclusion algorithms. In fact, Dijkstra was the first one to pioneer this style in his presentation of the first-ever published mutual exclusion algorithm [Dij65b, Dij68a] which was based on the ideas of T.J. Dekker.

But first we present, as a deliberate shock, Szymanski's complete program. Just study it for an hour or so to see whether you can make head or tail of it! Its full text is given below.

Example 1.6 (Final version of Szymanski's algorithm) Let

$P_i \equiv l_0$: **loop forever do**
   l_1 : **noncritical section**;
   l_2 : $flag[i] := 1$;
   l_3 : **wait** $\forall j : 0 \leq j < n.(flag[j] < 3)$;
   l_4 : $flag[i] := 3$;
   l_5 : **if** $\exists j : 0 \leq j < n.(flag[j] = 1)$ **then**
      l_6 : $flag[i] := 2$;
      l_7 : **wait** $\exists j : 0 \leq j < n.(flag[j] = 4)$;
   fi;

$$l_8 \; : flag[i] := 4;$$
$$l_9 \; : \textbf{wait } \forall j : 0 \le j < i.(flag[j] < 2);$$
$$l_{10} : \textbf{critical section};$$
$$l_{11} : \textbf{wait } \forall j : i < j < n.(flag[j] < 2 \lor flag[j] > 3);$$
$$l_{12} : flag[i] := 0$$
   od

and let

$$\textbf{mutex5} \equiv flag := 0; [P_0 \| P_1 \| \dots \| P_{n-1}]. \qquad \qquad \square$$

Before we start explaining this algorithm, we quote Szymanski's original explanation in [Szy90]:

The idea behind the algorithm is simple. The prologue section simulates a waiting room with a door. All processes requesting entry to the critical section at roughly the same time gather first in the waiting room. Then, when there are no more processes requesting entry, processes inside the waiting room shut the door and move to the exit from the waiting room. From there, one by one, they enter their critical sections in the order of their numbering. Any process requesting access to its critical section at that time has to wait in the initial part of the prologue section (at the entry to the waiting room).

The door to the waiting room is initially opened. The door is closed when a process inside the waiting room does not see any new processes requesting entry. The door is opened again when the last process inside the waiting room leaves the exit section of the algorithm.

Our first approximation towards explaining the algorithm starts below.

Example 1.7 (First approximation) Let

$$P_i \equiv l_0 \; : \; \textbf{loop forever do}$$
$$\qquad\qquad l_1 \; : \textbf{noncritical section};$$
$$\qquad\qquad l_2 \; : flag[i] := 1;$$
$$\qquad\qquad l_3 \; : \textbf{wait } \forall j : 0 \le j < n \land j \ne i.(flag[j] = 0);$$
$$\qquad\qquad l_4 \; : \textbf{critical section};$$
$$\qquad\qquad l_5 \; : flag[i] := 0$$
$$\qquad \textbf{od}$$

and let

$$\textbf{mutex1} \equiv flag := 0; [P_0 \| P_1 \| \dots \| P_{n-1}]. \qquad \qquad \square$$

Observe that each process P_i has a variable $flag[i]$, which is read by all other processes, and changed only by P_i. The assignment $flag := 0$ is an abbreviation of $flag[0] := 0; \dots ; flag[n-1] := 0$.

This solution satisfies the mutual exclusion property for the following reason. When a process P_i is in its **critical section** then its *flag*[i] equals 1. Because of the **wait** statement at l_3 a process P_j with $j \neq i$ can only enter its **critical section** when all other processes have their *flag*s set to 0, but we know *flag*[i] equals to 1 so P_j cannot enter its **critical section**.

However, **mutex1** suffers from danger of deadlock: if all processes P_i execute their l_2 instructions simultaneously then all the *flag*[i]s are set equal to 1. Then no process can pass l_3, because there is no process with a *flag* equal to 0, and now and in the future all processes remain suspended at l_3.

A possible solution for this problem might be that the **wait** statement at l_3 can also be passed when $\forall j : 0 \leq j < n.flag[j] = 0 \vee flag[j] = 1$. But then the **wait** statement could always be passed because *flag* has only value 0 or 1. This can be solved as follows: a process which passes the **wait** statement at l_3 sets its *flag* to 4 before it enters the **critical section**. Then all processes trying to pass l_3 afterwards are suspended, until that one process has executed its **critical section** and has set its *flag* to 0. The passing of l_3 and the setting of the *flag* to 4, however, is not atomic so several other processes could pass l_3 before that process sets its *flag* to 4. So the mutual exclusion property is violated because more than one process can enter its **critical section**.

The solution to this problem is that from the processes that have passed l_3, the process with the smallest process number will first enter its **critical section**, followed by the process with the smallest process number of the remaining processes, and so on. The following **wait** statement will do this job: **wait** $\forall j : 0 \leq j < i.(flag[j] = 0 \vee flag[j] = 1)$. This statement is placed in between the assignment of *flag*[i] to 4 and the **critical section**. A process can only pass this statement when all processes with a smaller process number are non-critical. So we obtain the following program **mutex2**:

Example 1.8 (Second approximation) Let

$P_i \equiv l_0$: **loop forever do**

        l_1 : **noncritical section**;

        l_2 : $flag[i] := 1$;

        l_3 : **wait** $\forall j : 0 \leq j < n.(flag[j] = 0 \vee flag[j] = 1)$;

        l_4 : $flag[i] := 4$;

        l_5 : **wait** $\forall j : 0 \leq j < i.(flag[j] = 0 \vee flag[j] = 1)$;

        l_6 : **critical section**;

        l_7 : $flag[i] := 0$

    od

and let

$$\mathbf{mutex2} \equiv flag := 0; [P_0 \| P_1 \| \dots \| P_{n-1}]. \qquad \square$$

Unfortunately **mutex2** does not satisfy the mutual exclusion property. Let $n = 2$, $l_k \to l_{k+1}$ indicate a move of P_0 and $l'_k \to l'_{k+1}$ indicate a move of P_1. Consider the following computation, where states are presented as 4-tuples listing the current location l_k of P_0, the current location l'_k of P_1, and the current values of $flag[0]$ and $flag[1]$:

$$
\begin{aligned}
&\langle l_0, l'_0, 0, 0 \rangle \;\to\; \langle l_1, l'_0, 0, 0 \rangle \;\to\; \langle l_1, l'_1, 0, 0 \rangle \;\to\; \langle l_2, l'_1, 0, 0 \rangle \;\to\; \\
&\langle l_2, l'_2, 0, 0 \rangle \;\to\; \langle l_3, l'_2, 1, 0 \rangle \;\to\; \langle l_3, l'_3, 1, 1 \rangle \;\to\; \langle l_4, l'_3, 1, 1 \rangle \;\to\; \\
&\langle l_4, l'_4, 1, 1 \rangle \;\to\; \langle l_4, l'_5, 1, 4 \rangle \;\to\; \langle l_4, l'_6, 1, 4 \rangle \;\to\; \langle l_5, l'_6, 4, 4 \rangle \;\to\; \\
&\langle l_6, l'_6, 4, 4 \rangle \;\to\; \dots
\end{aligned}
$$

Since l_6 and l'_6 label critical sections, the mutual exclusion property is not satisfied.

How can we avoid this sequence being generated? We must force process P_0 to set its *flag* to 4 *before* process P_1 inspects the **wait** statement at l'_5. Or, in general, all the processes that have passed l_3 must wait with the inspection of the **wait** statement at l_5 until processes, which passed l_3 and have a lower index than the inspecting process, have set their *flag* to 4. We know that the value of the *flag* equals 1 before it is set to 4. By inserting the following test in front of label l_5 below we can check whether there are processes that have not yet set their *flag* to 4 by inserting the test: **if** $\exists j : 0 \le j < n.(flag[j] = 1)$ **then**. But this test does not solve the problem when there is a process suspended at l_3. We can let such processes pass l_3 if we move the test in front of the assignment of $flag[i]$ to 4. We assign the value 2 to the *flag* of the process for which this test is true. And also we change l_3 into **wait** $\forall j : 0 \le j < n.(flag[j] = 0 \lor flag[j] = 1 \lor flag[j] = 2)$. So processes can slip through the **wait** statement at l_3 if there is not yet a process that has assigned its *flag* to 4. But before this is possible the process that has assigned 2 to its *flag* must wait until there is a process that has passed the test between l_3 and l_4, and set its *flag* to 4. This results in **mutex3**, which is as follows:

Example 1.9 (Third approximation) Let

$P_i \equiv l_0$: **loop forever do**
      l_1 : **noncritical section**;
      l_2 : $flag[i] := 1$;
      l_3 : **wait** $\forall j : 0 \le j < n.(flag[j] = 0 \lor flag[j] = 1 \lor flag[j] = 2)$;
      l_4 : **if** $\exists j : 0 \le j < n.(flag[j] = 1)$ **then**
            l_5 : $flag[i] := 2$;

l_6 : **wait** $\exists j : 0 \le j < n.(flag[j] = 4)$
fi;
l_7 : $flag[i] := 4$;
l_8 : **wait** $\forall j : 0 \le j < i.(flag[j] = 0 \lor flag[j] = 1)$;
l_9 : **critical section**;
l_{10} :$flag[i] := 0$
od

and let

$$\mathbf{mutex3} \equiv flag := 0; [P_0 \| P_1 \| \ldots \| P_{n-1}]. \qquad \square$$

This approximation has a terrible fault. All the processes passing l_3 will go to l_5 because for these processes their own *flag* equals to 1. And thus all these processes get suspended at l_6 because there is no process that can set its *flag* to 4. This is a deadlock situation because now no process can enter its **critical section**.

How can we solve this problem? This is easy, just put between l_3 and l_4 the following statement: $flag[i] := 3$. The sequence described above cannot be generated because the process that checks the test at l_4 in the third approximation as the last one will go to l_7 and thus also awake the processes that are suspended at l_6, since such a process will eventually set its *flag* to 4. It can be proved that the resulting program **mutex4** satisfies the mutual exclusion property and does not deadlock.

Example 1.10 (Fourth approximation) Let

$P_i \equiv l_0$: **loop forever do**
$\quad\quad\quad l_1$: **noncritical section**;
$\quad\quad\quad l_2$: $flag[i] := 1$;
$\quad\quad\quad l_3$: **wait** $\forall j : 0 \le j < n.(flag[j] = 0 \lor flag[j] = 1 \lor flag[j] = 2)$;
$\quad\quad\quad l_4$: $flag[i] := 3$;
$\quad\quad\quad l_5$: **if** $\exists j : 0 \le j < n.(flag[j] = 1)$ **then**
$\quad\quad\quad\quad\quad l_6$: $flag[i] := 2$;
$\quad\quad\quad\quad\quad l_7$: **wait** $\exists j : 0 \le j < n.(flag[j] = 4)$
$\quad\quad\quad$**fi**;
$\quad\quad\quad l_8$: $flag[i] := 4$;
$\quad\quad\quad l_9$: **wait** $\forall j : 0 \le j < i.(flag[j] = 0 \lor flag[j] = 1)$;
$\quad\quad\quad l_{10}$: **critical section**;
$\quad\quad\quad l_{11}$:$flag[i] := 0$
$\quad$**od**

and let

$$\textbf{mutex4} \equiv flag := 0; [P_0 \| P_1 \| \dots \| P_{n-1}].\qquad \square$$

Program **mutex4**, however, does not satisfy the linear delay property. This property expresses that the time that a process waits in program segment labelled by l_4 to l_9 is linear in the number of processes. Look for instance at the following sequence:

$$
\begin{array}{llll}
\langle l_0, l_0', 0, 0 \rangle & \to \ \langle l_1, l_0', 0, 0 \rangle & \to \ \langle l_1, l_1', 0, 0 \rangle & \to \ \langle l_2, l_1', 0, 0 \rangle \ \to \\
\langle l_2, l_2', 0, 0 \rangle & \to \ \langle l_3, l_2', 1, 0 \rangle & \to \ \langle l_3, l_3', 1, 1 \rangle & \to \ \langle l_4, l_3', 1, 1 \rangle \ \to \\
\langle l_4, l_4', 1, 1 \rangle & \to \ \langle l_4, l_5', 1, 3 \rangle & \to \ \langle l_4, l_6', 1, 3 \rangle & \to \ \boxed{\langle l_4, l_7', 1, 2 \rangle} \ \to \\
\langle l_5, l_7', 3, 2 \rangle & \to \ \langle l_8, l_7', 3, 2 \rangle & \to \ \langle l_9, l_7', 4, 2 \rangle & \to \ \langle l_{10}, l_7', 4, 2 \rangle \ \to \\
\langle l_{11}, l_7', 4, 2 \rangle & \to \ \langle l_1, l_7', 0, 2 \rangle & \to \ \langle l_2, l_7', 0, 2 \rangle & \to \ \langle l_3, l_7', 1, 2 \rangle \ \to \\
\boxed{\langle l_4, l_7', 1, 2 \rangle} & \to \qquad \dots
\end{array}
$$

Since state $\langle l_4, l_7', 1, 2 \rangle$ occurred earlier in this sequence, P_1 can be infinitely often bypassed by P_0, i.e., P_1 can possibly be starved, i.e., wait forever! Hence, the waiting time of P_1 is not linear.

What can we do about this situation? We must suspend process P_0 after l_{10} and before l_{11}, because then P_1 is forced to pass l_7, since the *flag* of P_0 is then still 4 and P_0 has already executed its **critical section**. How long should we suspend P_0? Until P_1 has passed l_7 and set its *flag* to 4, because then process P_0 can set its *flag* to 0 without suspending process P_1 at l_9 (P_0 has to be resumed, otherwise P_1 gets suspended at l_9 since the *flag* of P_0 is still 4). Process P_1 has to set its *flag* to 4 because then P_0 can also not reenter its **critical section** since it gets suspended at l_3.

In general this means that a process has to wait at l_{11} until all processes that are suspended at l_7 have passed l_7 and have set their *flag* to 4. This can be done by inserting the statement: **wait** $\forall j : i < j < n.(flag[j] < 2 \lor flag[j] > 3)$. We must have $i < j < n$ because the processes that are between l_4 and l_9 will enter their **critical section** in increasing order of their process numbers. So process P_i has to be suspended until all processes that are between l_4 and l_9 (these are processes with a process number higher than i) have set their *flag* to 1 or 4. Notice that we have to take processes P_i with $flag[i] = 1$ into account, because such processes may pass l_3. This culminates in the final program **mutex5**:

Example 1.11 (Fifth and final approximation) Let

$P_i \equiv l_0 \ : \ \textbf{loop forever do}$
$\qquad\qquad\ l_1 \ : \ \textbf{noncritical section};$
$\qquad\qquad\ l_2 \ : flag[i] := 1;$

l_3 : **wait** $\forall j : 0 \leq j < n.(flag[j] < 3)$;
l_4 : $flag[i] := 3$;
l_5 : **if** $\exists j : 0 \leq j < n.(flag[j] = 1)$ **then**
$\quad l_6$: $flag[i] := 2$;
$\quad l_7$: **wait** $\exists j : 0 \leq j < n.(flag[j] = 4)$
fi;
l_8 : $flag[i] := 4$;
l_9 : **wait** $\forall j : 0 \leq j < i.(flag[j] < 2)$;
l_{10}: **critical section**;
l_{11}: **wait** $\forall j : i < j < n.(flag[j] < 2 \lor flag[j] > 3)$;
l_{12}: $flag[i] := 0$

od

and let

$$\textbf{mutex5} \equiv flag := 0; [P_0 \| P_1 \| \ldots \| P_{n-1}]. \qquad \square$$

This program satisfies the property of mutual exclusion, freedom from dead-lock, and the linear delay property provided the tests at l_3, l_5, l_7, l_9 and l_{11} are tested as **atomic** conditions, i.e., these tests must be implemented as one atomic action. Look for instance at the following sequence in which this is not the case. We assume that process P_0 does not test l_3 as an atomic statement. Suppose we have three processes P_0, P_1 and P_2. First P_1 executes l_2, next P_2 executes l_2, then P_1 passes l_3, after which P_2 passes l_3 and subsequently executes l_4 and finds the test at l_5 equal to true. Next it executes l_6 and then gets suspended at l_7. Then P_1 executes l_4, finds the test at l_5 equal to false, passes thus to l_8 and subsequently executes l_8. Then it passes l_9, and executes its **critical section** and next gets suspended at l_{11}. Then P_0 executes l_2 and checks (at l_3) if the *flag* of process P_2 is less than 3, which is true because P_2 is suspended at l_7, thus its *flag* equals 2. After this check P_2 passes l_7, because the *flag* of P_1 equals 4, and then P_2 executes l_8. Now P_1 passes l_{11}, because the *flag* of P_2 equals 4, and then P_1 executes l_{12}. Then P_2 passes l_9 (the *flag* of P_0 is still 1 and the *flag* of P_1 equals 0). So P_2 is now in its **critical section**. Then P_0 checks the *flag* of P_1 at l_3, finds its value to be 0, then checks its own *flag* (which is 1) and therefore passes to l_4. Next P_0 executes l_4, passes from l_5 to l_8, because the *flag* of P_2 equals 4 and that of P_1 equals 0. Then P_0 executes l_8 and passes l_9 because P_0 can always pass l_9. Therefore P_0 also executes its **critical section**. (We owe this scenario to [MP91c].) So the mutual exclusion property is violated. In [MP90] it is proved that when the *flag*-variables are checked in ascending order of their indices the algorithm is still correct.

We have obtained the final version of Szymanski's algorithm by observ-

ing undesirable computations in its previous approximations and by correcting
these approximations through elimination of those computations. But how
does one guarantee, without giving a formal correctness proof, that version 5
does not also display some undesirable computation? How long is one willing
to inspect version 5 before becoming convinced that this version is correct?
And, if one succeeds at all in giving a correctness proof based on behavioural
reasoning, who guarantees that no subtle error has crept in, only waiting to
be revealed by a highly complex scenario, which demonstrates that its alleged
properties are not satisfied? This applies especially when considering a version of Szymanski's algorithm in which the above-mentioned tests at l_3, etc.,
are no longer atomic, and flag variables are checked in ascending order of their
indices!

   We conclude that there is no alternative but to give formal correctness proofs
of such algorithms based on assertional reasoning. For Szymanski's algorithm
such a proof is given in Section 3.5.2, for a version in which tests are atomic.

1.4.5 Conclusion: Answers to Two Central Questions

The Stenning & Woodger bug in one of the first algorithms for concurrent
garbage collection, see Figure 1.6, was a historical landmark. For it convinced a number of people in 1976, including the designers of that algorithm
– amongst whom were some of the most brilliant programmers and most eloquent advocates of their time of the need for program verification, that the
informal style of proof, which was used in the presentation of the algorithm
[DLM+78], was no longer sufficient to guarantee correctness. David Gries
claims that if one had used the *formal* method applied in [Gri77] such a bug
would have been discovered. Leslie Lamport found a bug in this algorithm
using state-based assertional reasoning, when trying to give a proof of its correctness based on invariance properties.

   We conclude that verification is inevitable, indeed, for the development of
correct complex software for concurrent algorithms, and that one needs to give
formal proofs when software is really complex. This answers the first two
questions raised in Section 1.1.

1.4.6 Hand-Checked or Machine-Supported Verification?

So, in 1976 Stenning & Woodger's bug convinced Edsger W. Dijkstra and others that informal proofs are not convincing. Next, in 1993, even the value of
formal proofs was put in doubt when these were *hand checked*. John Rushby

and others claim [ORSvH93] that the formal proofs of all safety-critical applications they investigated were wrong. So the question becomes: Is *hand-checked* formal verification enough, or do we need *machine*-supported verification?

In view of the fact that machine-supported verification is very time consuming, Leslie Lamport and his coauthors argue in [ADH+99] that a disciplined form of hand-checked formal verification is sufficient to expose errors in a 2000-line industrial cache protocol. This style of verification by hand has been developed by Lamport and his colleagues in a series of papers, see, e.g. [AL91, AL93, AL95].

A practical argument in favour of machine-supported verification applies when correctness proofs become long and tedious, as is the case for some of the real-time algorithms discussed in the companion volume. Then, on account of their sheer multitude one does not trust one's own previous proof steps anymore *when they are merely checked by hand*, and, instead of progressing confidently with one's proof, one tends to spend more and more time on checking ever increasing lists of rather simple proof steps over and over again. When these steps are verified using a computer, this phenomenon disappears – provided one trusts the proof tool being used to a sufficient degree. This trust is only justified in case of a really mature proof tool, which has been debugged over a long period by many persons.

Especially since INTEL lost an estimated 500 million US dollars due to an error in its Pentium chip, machine-supported verification has acquired higher industrial priority. This is reported, e.g., by J Strother Moore and his colleagues in his verification of small crucial parts of an AMD chip using the ACL2 tool [KM94, MLK98], by Ed Clarke and his colleagues in their verification of crucial hardware components using algorithmic verification techniques such as model checking [CE82, QS81, QS82, CGP99], and, recently, by Alain Deutsch using machine-supported static-analysis techniques which rediscovered the very errors leading to the multi-billion US dollars ARIANE 5 disaster [LMR+98].

The higher industrial priority of machine-supported verification is illustrated by the reaction to the Pentium bug. This bug concerns an error in the floating-point division algorithm FDIV implemented in the first Pentium processor. It was reported in the New-York Times on Nov. 11, 1994. Natarajan Shankar describes the flurry of activity within the machine-supported verification community following its discovery like this [Sha01]:

Vaughan Pratt [Pra95] gives a cogent account of the discovery and diagnosis of the Pentium FDIV bug. The Pentium hardware used an SRT divider, so named for its independent inventors Sweeney, Robertson, and Tocher. This hardware algorithm is much like grade school long division. In each iteration, the divisor is multiplied by the quotient digit and subtracted from the partial remainder to obtain the new partial remainder. A lookup table is used to predict the quotient digit for the next iteration based on an approximation of the partial remainder and divisor, so that it can be computed in parallel with the partial remainder. The Pentium FDIV bug has been traced to certain incorrect entries in a lookup table that were perhaps thought to be unreachable during execution.

Randy Bryant used model-checking techniques to show how BDDs (binary decision diagrams) and BMDs (binary moment diagrams) could be used to check an invariant for FDIV [BC95, Bry95]. BDDs are notoriously bad for representing boolean functions for multiplication, but BMDs do not have this problem. Ed Clarke and Xudong Zhao showed how BMDs could be used to carry out word-level model checking of an SRT algorithm [CZ95]. Clarke, German, and Zhao used Analytica, a theorem prover built on Mathematica, to verify an SRT algorithm [CGZ96], as did Rueß, Shankar, and Srivas, using the PVS theorem prover [RSS96, RSS99]. Paul Miner extended the latter verification to show compliance with the IEEE floating-point standard [ML96]. He showed how a correct SRT lookup table could be generated using PVS within a matter of hours. Moore, Lynch and Kaufmann verified a floating point division microcode routine used in the AMD K5 processor [MLK98].

To this account J Moore adds [Moo01]:

The K5 was AMD's first Pentium-class microprocessor. We did the verification in the summer of 1995 and it was of commercial importance to AMD. The Pentium FDIV bug became widely known in November, 1994. In January, 1995, Intel announced a $475 million write-off to cover costs associated with FDIV. There was much public wringing of hands and anxiety about it in spring, 1995.

Simultaneous with that anxiety, AMD was preparing to tape out the K5 for summer, 1995. Because of management decisions changing the amount of silicon area devoted to the FPU, the FPU team had thrown out their well-tested FDIV hardware in late 1994 (nothing to do with Intel's FDIV problems) and reimplemented FDIV on the K5 in microcode. Intel's $500 million loss was obviously on the minds of the AMD folks in the Spring. They did not want to repeat it.

That is what makes our proof so important in the history of this. We did not come in after the fact and look at what might have been. We came in *before* the K5 was taped-out and looked at what *was*. We delivered a Q.E.D. to them 9 weeks after we started the project.

After the successful conclusion of the FDIV proof, David Russinoff, an AMD employee, was tasked to do K5's FSQRT. His ACL2 proof attempt uncovered a bug which had survived testing and which was fixed before tape out [Rus99].

AMD is continuing this work, with four full-time AMD employees using ACL2 all the time to verify aspects of their designs. All of the elementary floating-point operations on the AMD K7 (the "Athlon") have been mechanically verified with ACL2. Several bugs were found and fixed before tape out. None have been reported in either the fabricated K5 or Athlon (related to the formally verified operations).

But even with machine-supported verification one serious problem remains:

How to write a correct specification? This task is as hard as the verification problem.[8] A program which is proved to be correct relative to a faulty formal specification remains incorrect w.r.t. its intended purpose, whether machine checked or nor. Our conclusion is that formal methods do not give us a full 100% guarantee of the correctness of a program. They only *increase the confidence* one has in its correctness. Consequently, formal methods do not eliminate the need for testing – testing is still needed [BH95b, BH95a]!

1.5 The Approach of this Book

Next we describe the approach taken in this book.

In Section 1.5.1 this approach we characterise as a state-based dual-language approach, which is semantically-oriented as argued in Section 1.5.2. This approach is based on Floyd's inductive assertion method, which is defined in Section 1.5.3, but which is not appropriate for program development. Consequently, a change of paradigm is needed leading to Hoare logic, as discussed in Section 1.5.4. Hoare logic for sequential program constructs is compositional; why compositionality enables program derivation is explained in Section 1.6. These formalisms are extended to concurrency in Section 1.5.5. However, the resulting formalisms are again not appropriate anymore for concurrent program development since they have become noncompositional. A second change of paradigm, this time to assumption-guarantee-style formalisms, which are compositional w.r.t. concurrency, is described in Section 1.5.6. The closing Section 1.5.7 describes a noncompositional method for establishing correctness of both shared-variable concurrent and distributed network algorithms: the communication-closed-layers paradigm.

1.5.1 A State-Based Dual-Language Approach

The approach taken in this book is called *state-based*. Let us first explain this

---

[8] September 30, 1999: Mars Climate Orbiter team finds likely cause of loss in specification error. *One team used imperial units (e.g., inches, feet and pounds) while the other used metric units for a key spacecraft operation. This information was critical to the manoeuvers required to place the spacecraft in the proper Mars orbit* [NAS99].

December 3, 1999: Mars Polar Lander lost. It crashed due to a race condition in the program that steered the Lander during the last 40 metres of its descent prior to landing. This race condition was discovered by reprogramming the Lander's original landing program into JAVA, and then using static analysis tools for discovering that error. This reprogramming was necessary because the Mars Lander's original software was written in C, which is notoriously unverifiable because of its facilities for pointer arithmetic.

These failures point to the likelihood that such errors will continue to occur, as long as NASA does not exhaustively apply automatic verification tools to its software *prior to launching its vehicles.*

notion.

Recall that states are total functions from a set of variables to a set of values of these variables. In a state-based approach one uses states both to characterise the meaning of programs by sets of (action-labelled) state sequences, and to give meanings to their specifications.

However, there are significant differences in style between languages for formulating properties and specifications of a computational task, and programming languages which describe precise, unambiguous and efficient solutions on a computer which are reasonably easy to execute. The level of abstraction of the former is usually much higher than that of the latter. This certainly holds for the specification languages used in this book, which are based on first-order predicate logic. Consequently, the key issue in our mathematical theory of state-based program development and analysis is establishing the relationships between these two widely different levels of description of a computational task. This approach is, therefore, called the *dual-language* approach.

In general, the natural questions one could ask about the relationship between a programming language $\mathcal{P}$ and a specification language $\mathcal{S}$ can be classified as follows:

- **The Program Development Problem**: Given a specification $s \in \mathcal{S}$, construct a program $p \in \mathcal{P}$ which satisfies the specification.
- **The Analysis Problem**: Given a program $p \in \mathcal{P}$, find its appropriate description $s \in \mathcal{S}$.
- **The Verification Problem**: Given a specification $s \in \mathcal{S}$ and a program $p \in \mathcal{P}$, check whether they are consistent, i.e., whether p satisfies s.

As can be seen from the list of these problems, a crucial concept to all of them is that of a program p *satisfying* a specification s. Therefore, the verification problem is the most fundamental question of all, and the concepts and methodologies developed for its resolution underly the methodologies and approaches to the other problems mentioned.

Summarising, this book offers a state-based dual-language approach to the verification of concurrent and distributed systems, using specification languages based on first-order predicate logic. When this approach is *compositional*, we shall see that it can be used for formal program development.

1.5.2 A Semantic Approach

Certainly, programming languages require a precise syntax to make them amenable to computer implementation, and the same holds for specification languages. However, the aim of specific languages is primarily ease of expression and understanding by us, humans! And the same holds for high-level programming languages, for there is no single mortal who masters all the details involved in execution of these languages on even as simple a computer as a laptop. That is, one also needs high-level abstractions for understanding how a program functions. Thus our approach is based on giving meanings to both programs and their specifications, on the basis of which a precise answer can be given to the question whether a given program p satisfies a given specification s.

As we have seen before, the meaning of a concurrent program is its set of computation sequences. Therefore, the verification problem for a (concurrent) program reduces to checking whether its computation sequences satisfy the specification concerned. That is, once we know when a computation sequence satisfies a specification, the verification problem can be reduced to proving inclusion between two sets: the computation sequences generated by a given program, and the computation sequences satisfying a given specification.

More precisely, since programs manipulate data from given data domains, we will reduce the above-mentioned set-inclusion problem for a given program p and specification s in Chapter 2 to a finite set of mathematical properties which must hold in those data domains in order for p to satisfy s. Thus, using the terminology *verification conditions* for these domain properties, the field of program correctness concerns itself primarily with the question how to reduce the claim "p satisfies s" to a finite set of verification conditions which must hold in order for p to satisfy s. Observe that the finiteness of this set is the principal reason which makes it possible to give program correctness proofs at all.

Whether these verification conditions themselves are true or not, over, e.g., the domain of natural numbers, reals, lists and other data types, we consider primarily a problem whose solution belongs to the realm of mathematics, whereas the reduction of the problem whether p satisfies s to a finite set of verification conditions, and the expression of these verification conditions in given specification languages, are considered to be part of computer science.

The most direct way to generate verification conditions for programs and their specifications is based on *Floyd's inductive assertion method*. Therefore, this book is based on that approach, which will be introduced in the next section.

1.5.3 Floyd's Inductive Assertion Method

In order to analyse the behaviour of programs we represent them by extremely simple objects, called *transition diagrams,* with an equally simple semantics.

These were introduced by R. Keller [Kel76]. Yet their variety turns out to be sufficiently rich to express shared-variable concurrency and message-passing.

Transition diagrams are finite directed graphs with a distinguished entry node s and exit node t (indicating where the computations start and end, respectively), whose edges are labelled by transitions of the form $c \to f$ where c denotes a boolean state function, called *guard*, and f a state transformation used for expressing multiple assignments. A computation of transition diagram T starts in its entry node s and some initial state, and is, whenever possible, prolonged, having reached node l, $l \neq t$, in state σ, by executing some successor transition $c \to f$ of T for which $c(\sigma)$ is true and which labels some edge $\langle l, l' \rangle$ of T, resulting in reaching label l' in state $f(\sigma)$. The semantics of a transition diagram consists of the set of its *maximal* computations.

Since the observable behaviour of a sequential program construct is given by its set of pairs of initial and corresponding final states, the simplest way to specify this behaviour for a transition diagram is by providing a pair of predicates (boolean functions) $\langle \varphi, \psi \rangle$, with φ called *precondition* and ψ *postcondition,* which those initial and final states, respectively, should satisfy. Since φ and ψ describe properties of states, this specification approach is called *property-oriented.*

In order to prove that a transition diagram T satisfies a pre-postcondition pair $\langle \varphi, \psi \rangle$, we construct an *inductive assertion network*. This is a mapping Q of the nodes in T to boolean state functions satisfying certain verification conditions. These verification conditions are generated for every directed edge e of T, and are of the form $Q_l \wedge c \to Q_{l'} \circ f$, where $c \to f$ labels edge e, which leads from node l to l', and Q associates boolean state functions Q_l and $Q_{l'}$ with l and l'. Additionally, the verification conditions $\varphi \to Q_s$ and $Q_t \to \psi$ are generated. When all these verification conditions hold, it is easy to see that T satisfies the pre-postcondition pair $\langle \varphi, \psi \rangle$.

This proof method is due to Robert W. Floyd [Flo67], and is called the *inductive assertion method.*

Properly speaking, it only proves *partial correctness,* which is defined by: T is partially correct w.r.t. φ and ψ when

every computation of T which starts in an initial state satisfying precondition φ, and which terminates in T's exit node, does so in a final state satisfying postcondition ψ.

Observe that partial correctness does not imply termination. Floyd also formulated the main proof principle for establishing termination of programs, which combines the use of inductive assertion methods with so-called wellfounded orderings. These two methods, as well as their adaptations to proving *absence of runtime errors* and *blocking,* are discussed in Chapter 2.

Runtime errors arise during a computation when the static transformation f associated with a successor transition, whose guard evaluates to true, is executed in a state for which f is undefined; they occur, e.g., when executing $x := 1/0$, and $x := 1/y$ for $y = 0$.

Blocking arises when a computation, having reached a node l, $l \neq t$, cannot be prolonged by executing some successor transition, because none of the guards associated with transitions starting in l evaluates in σ to true.

Both Floyd's inductive assertion method and his method for proving termination are ideally suited for giving *soundness* and *completeness* proofs – which are given for all proof methods formulated in this work, and generalise well to shared-variable concurrency and distributed message passing.[9]

1.5.4 Hoare Logic

The inductive assertion method has no use for *program development* because of its lack of structure – an inductive assertion network for a transition diagram is not (yet) *formally* related to any of the subnetworks for its corresponding subdiagrams and, consequently, no notion of abstraction or refinement is available for the particular way these subnetworks are constructed.

To overcome this obstacle, we add sufficient structure to the inductive assertion method to use it for program development, although this leads to a change of paradigm. For in the process of adding this structure we obtain a so-called *Hoare logic,* and this logic, when confined to sequential program constructs, will turn out to be ideal for program derivation.

Adding this structure is done by:

- introducing a simple sequential programming language (with operators as sequential composition, looping constructs and guarded commands),
- defining the meaning of a program construct S by associating a transition diagram $T[\![S]\!]$ with it (whose semantics has been explained above),
- extending the algebraic structure of S to $T[\![S]\!]$ and to inductive assertion networks for $T[\![S]\!]$.

For example, for $S = S_1 ; S_2$ we have that $T[\![S]\!]$ can be written as $T[\![S_1]\!] ; T[\![S_2]\!]$, and that an inductive assertion network Q for $T[\![S]\!]$ can be written as $Q_1 ; Q_2$ with Q_i being an appropriate inductive assertion network for $T[\![S_i]\!]$, $i = 1, 2$. A

---

[9] Without such proofs, in the experience of the senior author, one can be pretty sure that the methods proposed are neither sound nor complete. And who wants to use a proof method whose conclusions are possibly wrong?

minor consequence of this set-up is that one has to work with *transition systems* instead of transition diagrams; transition systems are equivalence classes of transition diagrams w.r.t. renaming their nodes.

This structural enrichment leads to the development of a logic for reasoning about (inductive assertion networks for the transition diagrams corresponding to) programs in this language, in which every program operator has its own associated rule. And this logic turns out to be isomorphic to *Hoare logic* [Hoa69].

Before explaining the concept of Hoare logic, we formulate its single most important property (for sequential program constructs) which justifies its use for program development: Hoare logic for sequential program constructs is *compositional*, that is,

> *that a program meets its specification can be verified (in Hoare logic) on the basis of the specifications of its constituent components, without the need of additional information about the interior construction of these components.*

Why compositionality justifies (formal) program derivation, and how, is explained in Section 1.6.

Hoare logic is a formal axiom system for proving *Hoare triples*. These are of the form $\{pre\}S\{post\}$ with *pre* and *post* expressions from first-order predicate logic, called assertions, and S a (syntactically-expressed) program construct (in some programming language). Such a triple is *valid* whenever the transition diagram $T[\![S]\!]$ associated with S is partially correct w.r.t. $\mathcal{T}[\![pre]\!]$ and $\mathcal{T}[\![post]\!]$, which denote the interpretations of *pre* and *post*.

Since the observable behaviour of sequential program constructs is given by their sets of initial and corresponding final states, this behaviour can be fully specified in Hoare logic. That is, no additional information is required about the implementation of these constructs in order to formulate proof rules for them in Hoare logic. This explains why Hoare logic for sequential program constructs is compositional.

As a consequence of the set-up given above, we are able to establish a one-to-one mapping between correctness proofs in Hoare logic for programs S and the corresponding inductive assertion networks for $T[\![S]\!]$. This enables one to "lift" the soundness and completeness proofs for the inductive assertion method to similar proofs for Hoare logic. Here we use the result that the boolean functions involved in the former proofs can be expressed as first-order predicates over the standard model of the natural numbers by means of Gödel-encoding techniques [Coo78], as discussed in Chapter 5.

This set-up of Hoare logic is followed in Part IV and developed for the language of guarded commands in Chapter 9.

1.5.5 Extensions to Concurrency

Straightforward as the above development is for sequential programming constructs, the direct application of Hoare logic to program development is lost as soon as concurrency, i.e., communication between processes, enters the picture. For then the resulting Hoare logic is not compositional anymore. Again, a change of paradigm is called for, this time by switching to so-called *assumption-commitment*-type formalisms, to be discussed in the next section and in Section 1.6. But first we explain how to extend our proof to concurrency in noncompositional fashion.

The first question to answer is how to characterise concurrency, i.e., both shared-variable concurrency and message-passing, within the framework of transition diagrams.

For shared-variable concurrency this is immediate. For example, consider two transition diagrams P_1 and P_2, called *processes*. Their parallel composition $P_1 \| P_2$ is the following transition diagram:

- its nodes are pairs $\langle l_1, l_2 \rangle$ with l_i a node of P_i,
- its transitions are essentially either transitions of P_1 or transitions of P_2, i.e., of the form $(\langle l_1, l_2 \rangle, c \to f, \langle l_1', l_2' \rangle)$ with $(l_i, c \to f, l_i')$ a transition of P_i and $l_j = l_j'$, $i \neq j$, i.e., the individual transitions of P_1 and P_2 are *interleaved* inside $P_1 \| P_2$,
- its entry node is $\langle s_1, s_2 \rangle$, with s_i the entry node of P_i,
- its exit node is $\langle t_1, t_2 \rangle$, with t_i the exit node of P_i,

for $i = 1, 2$ and $j = 1, 2$.

A similar kind of definition can be given for synchronous message passing. (*Asynchronous message passing* requires the addition of buffers to the synchronous picture, where buffers communicate synchronously with processes, processes only communicate with buffers, and buffers are also described by transition diagrams.)

It is essential here that the parallel composition of transition diagrams results again in a transition diagram. This implies that the proof methods developed for sequential constructs apply in principle also to concurrency. However, there is a well-known catch: Given n parallel processes of r nodes, their parallel composition has r^n nodes – a phenomenon called *state-space explosion*. Consequently, giving a correctness proof for this parallel composition using the inductive assertion method requires an inductive assertion network consisting of r^n assertions, and checking even more verification conditions. Therefore this *global* method, as it is called, cannot be applied in practice except for very small values of r and n.

As a way out of this exponential increase in complexity of a correctness proof, historically the following strategy has been followed for proving properties of $P_1 \| \ldots \| P_n$:

(i) *For all $i = 1, \ldots, n$, give a local correctness proof Q_i for transition diagram P_i which only applies when execution of P_i takes place in isolation, i.e., is merely viewed as a sequential noncommunicating transition diagram.*

(ii) *Prove the additional properties which must be satisfied by inductive assertion network Q_i in order for it to apply also when P_i is executed in the context of $P_1 \| \ldots \| P_{i-1} \| P_{i+1} \| \ldots \| P_n$, for $i = 1, \ldots, n$.*

The problem here is that these local correctness proofs merely characterise the initial-final state behaviour of the component process P_i, whereas this characterisation does not suffice for concurrency because the interaction between concurrent processes depends on their intermediate states as well. For example, in case of shared-variable concurrency of a process, the intermediate states belong also to the observable behaviour and therefore actions upon those intermediate states by the environment also need to be specified. So, instead of "adding up" these local correctness proofs (which would have been sufficient in the absence of any interaction between parallel processes), we need a more refined dependency between the inductive assertion networks $Q_1, \ldots, Q_n$ and $P_1, \ldots, P_n$, which expresses the additional interaction by its environment upon the intermediate states of a process.

The new element required is *that the individual assertions of assertion network Q_i for process P_i should be* invariant *under execution of the transitions of all remaining processes P_j, $j \neq i$.*

The *interference freedom test,* formulated by Susan Owicki [Owi75, OG76a] for Hoare logic and Leslie Lamport [Lam77] for the inductive assertion method, guarantees that communication between P_i and P_j at intermediate points (nodes) during the execution of P_i and P_j *preserves* the assertions attached (by Q_i and Q_j) to those points.

For synchronous message passing these additional verification conditions are called *cooperation tests* [AFdR80, LG81].

It can be checked that the complexity of these methods is $O(n \times s \times r)$ in the number of verification conditions, with n the number of processes, assuming that P_i has r locations and s edges, which is quite an improvement over the global method formulated at the beginning of this section, where the complexity is $O(n \times s \times r^{n-1})$ in the number of verification conditions.

A precise formulation and the mathematical analysis of the resulting proof methods is worked out for the inductive assertion method in Chapters 3 and 4; their corresponding Hoare logics are developed in Chapters 10 and 11. These chapters also contain numerous applications of these methods, e.g., for obtaining correctness proofs of (suitably corrected versions of) the algorithms for concurrent garbage collection discussed in Section 1.4, algorithms for partitioning a set, and for mutual exclusion.

Observe that these proof methods *are not compositional.* This is because the formulation of these additional verification conditions for, say, process P_i requires information about the individual transitions of all processes P_j, $j \neq i$, to be available for $i = 1, \ldots, n$, and this constitutes *"additional knowledge about the implementation of* $P_1, \ldots, P_n$ *which is not given by their specifications."* And the latter is forbidden in case of compositional proof methods.

Consequently, these proof systems can no longer be used for formal program derivation. The fact that the behaviour of processes is now also characterised by their interaction at intermediate control points, results for the approach sketched above in a tremendous number of verification conditions. As a result it is no longer clear how to formulate an appropriate formal notion of *development* of concurrent programs from their specifications, which takes these additional verification conditions into account. This is remedied in the next section.

Please note that the latter remarks only apply to the process of *formal* program derivation from specifications. They do not apply to more heuristically-oriented methods for deriving concurrent programs. For example, consult the recent work of Wim Feijen and Netty van Gasteren [FvG99] for successful concurrent program derivation (often of new algorithms) using noncompositional techniques in heuristic fashion, as developed in the school of Edsger W. Dijkstra [Dij76, Dij82].

1.5.6 The Assume-Guarantee Paradigm

The key to formulating compositional proof methods for concurrent processes is the realisation that one has to specify not only their initial-final state behaviour, but also *their interaction at intermediate points.* This was done for shared-variable concurrency by Cliff Jones in [Jon81, Jon83] and for synchronous message passing by Jay Misra and Mani Chandy in [MC81].

The basic intuition

The basic intuition underlying the assume-guarantee paradigm can be explained by considering the very simple example of an adder component P shown in Figure 1.7 that adds two input numbers x and y and places the output in z. We owe this example to Natarajan Shankar [Sha98b].

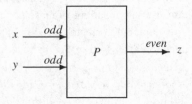

Fig. 1.7. Even number generator P.

Here x, y and z can be program variables, signals, or latches, depending on the chosen model of computation. The system containing P as its component might require its output z to be an even number, but obviously P cannot unconditionally guarantee this property of the output z. It might be reasonable to assume that the environment always provides odd number inputs at x and y, so that with this assumption it is easy to show that the output numbers at z are always even. Only local reasoning in terms of P is needed to establish that z is always even when given odd number inputs at x and y.

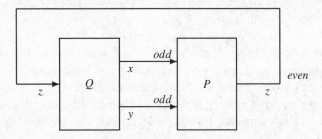

Fig. 1.8. Odd and even number generators.

If, as shown in Figure 1.8, P is now composed with another component Q that generates the inputs at x and y, then to preserve the property that only even numbers are output at z, Q must be shown to output only odd numbers at x and y. However, the demonstration that Q provides only odd numbers as outputs at x and y might require assumptions on the inputs taken by Q, where z itself might be such an input. If in showing that Q produces odd outputs at x and y, one has to assume that the z input is always even, then we have an obvious circularity and nothing can be concluded about the oddness or evenness of x, y and z. If this circularity can somehow be broken, then we have a form of well-founded mutual recursion between P and Q that admits a proof by simultaneous induction that x and y are always odd and z is always even. The circularity can be broken by noting that a z output for P is even as long as the *preceding* x and y inputs are odd, and the x and y outputs for Q are odd as long as the *preceding* z input is even. That is, using the terminology of the assume-guarantee paradigm, the guarantee that output z is even is satisfied by *P as long as the assumption that its previous inputs x and y are odd has always been satisfied before by P's environment.*

In the assume-guarantee approach for reasoning about concurrency, a property of a component process is expressed by a pair (A, G) consisting of a commitment G that the component will satisfy provided the environment of the component satisfies the assumption property A. The interpretation of (A, G) has to be carefully defined to be non-circular. Informally, a component P satisfies (A, G) if the environment of P violates A before the component P fails to satisfy G. That is, P satisfies (A, G) if at any stage of an on-going computation P's actions satisfy G as long as A is satisfied by all actions from P's environment. When two or more components, P_1 satisfying (A_1, G_1) and P_2 satisfying (A_2, G_2), are composed into a larger component $P_1 \| P_2$, the assumption A of $P_1 \| P_2$ together with property G_1 of component P_1 must be used to show that P_1's actions do not violate assumption A_2, and correspondingly, A and G_2 must be used to show that P_2 does not violate assumption A_1 [Sha98b].

And its formalisation

Jones proposed in his so-called *rely-guarantee* (R-G) formalism *to specify the interference allowed from the environment of a component during its execution without endangering fulfilment of the purpose of that component.* To this end Jones extended the format of Hoare triples with two additional predicates: a *rely* predicate, for specifying the expected behaviour of the environment, i.e., the interference allowed, and a *guarantee* predicate for expressing the task to be performed, by that component. Both these predicates are *action* predicates, i.e., they characterise *atomic transitions*.

More precisely, a rely-guarantee correctness formula has the form

$$\langle rely, guar \rangle : \{pre\} \ P \ \{post\},$$

where *pre* and *post* impose conditions upon the initial and final, respectively, states of a computation of process P, whereas *rely* and *guar* impose conditions upon environmental transitions and transitions of P itself, respectively. Validity of such an R-G formula for a process P is captured by the following intuitive characterisation of validity of an R-G correctness formula:

If

  (i) P is invoked in an initial state which satisfies pre, and

  (ii) at any moment during the computation of P all environment transitions satisfy rely,

then

  (iii) all P-transitions up to that moment satisfy guar, and

  (iv) if this computation terminates, its final state satisfies post.

A simple example of R-G-based reasoning is worked out in Section 6.5.

The proposal of Misra and Chandy is similar, be it that it applies to synchronous communication, and is called the *assumption-commitment* (A-C) formalism; a simple example is worked out in Section 6.4. A difference with the R-G formalism is that the *assumption* and *commitment* are predicates over the communication history of a component. Following Abadi and Lamport [AL93, AL95] we shall use the term *assume-guarantee* formalism (that is, paradigm) when discussing these formalisms, because they embody the same idea.

The crucial element common to both is that they specify the amount of interference which is allowed by a process *without endangering its purpose*. In the case of the A-C formalism this allowed amount is specified by an *assumption* predicate, whereas the own contribution of a process is specified by its *commitment* predicate (and postcondition). That is, in general one needs four predicates in an assume-guarantee specification: two for specifying initial-final state behaviour, and two for specifying the combination of allowed interference and desired behaviour.

As a consequence of this specification format, it turns out to be technically possible to give for each communicating process a specification of both (i) its initial and resulting final states and (ii) its full interaction with its environment. That is, this specification format allows a full characterisation of the observable behaviour of a process. This implies, in particular, that, in these formalisms, parallel composition rules can be formulated entirely in terms of those predicates without any need for additional details about the implementation of the processes concerned.

That is, the resulting proof methods are compositional! And this makes these formalisms suitable for the formal top-down derivation of concurrent processes from their specifications [Jon83, Oss83] (see Section 7.4.3 for an illustration of the systematic top-down development of a distributed priority queue).

An important application of assume-guarantee-based reasoning is given by its capacity to specify *open* systems, that is, systems which are intended to interact using certain prespecified shared variables or shared channels with the environment, without the precise implementation of that environment being known. Observe that this is consistent with the very purpose of compositional reasoning, since, because the environment of an open system is not known beforehand, *it can only be specified without giving any implementation details*, and this is exactly what compositional reasoning is about! Thus, one can summarise the above discussion by observing that the assume-guarantee paradigm is suitable for the formal top-down design (and refinement) of open concurrent systems.

It should be remarked that there are many other compositional state-based approaches to concurrency verification, see Section 1.6 for references. However, of all these approaches, this assume-guarantee paradigm is the one studied best.

Chapter 6 contains a gentle introduction to the assume-guarantee paradigm, Chapter 7 discusses the A-C formalism, and Chapter 8 analyses the R-G formalism.

Section 1.6 contains more material on compositional proof methods for concurrency.

We close Section 1.5 with Section 1.5.7 describing a promising noncompositional paradigm which has been successfully applied to proving the correctness of concurrent and distributed network algorithms and protocols, such as discussed in [Ray88]: *the communication-closed-layers paradigm*, originally proposed by Tzilla Elrad and Nissim Francez [EF82].

1.5.7 The Communication-Closed-Layers Paradigm

In Section 1.5.5 we observed that for noncompositional proof methods, which are based on interference freedom and cooperation tests, no clear notion of program derivation or program refinement exists on account of the additional complexity which is introduced by these tests within the verification process.

One way to reduce this complexity is the subject of Chapter 12. In that chapter we take the point of view that, in order to explain and clarify the final structure of a network of processes, *the structure of a correctness proof should reflect the structure of the original design process*, rather than the structure of the finally resulting network. To this end we introduce program transformation techniques that are used in combination with the Owicki & Gries style of program verification of Chapter 10. They are called *communication-closed-layer laws* (CCL).

These techniques distinguish between the "*physical structure*" and the "*logical structure*" of programs. The physical structure refers to a program S_D that has a syntactic structure that is reasonably close to the actual physical (process) architecture that will be used to execute a program. We assume here that this physical structure can be described as a collection of network nodes P_j, each of which executes a number of sequential phases $P_{0,j}, \ldots, P_{n,j}$. Schematically S_D can be described as a program of the following form:

$$S_D \overset{\text{def}}{=} [(P_{0,0}; P_{1,0}; \cdots; P_{n,0}) \parallel \cdots \parallel (P_{0,m}; P_{1,m}; \cdots; P_{n,m})].$$

The logical structure on the other hand is a program S_L that has a different syntactic structure that allows for simple verification, and appears to be *sequentially phased*, that is, has the following form:

$$S_L \overset{\text{def}}{=} [P_{0,0} \parallel \cdots \parallel P_{0,m}]; \cdots; [P_{n,0} \parallel \cdots \parallel P_{n,m}].$$

The aim of Chapter 12 is to explain under which circumstances such sequentially-phased programs S_L are actually *equivalent* to their corresponding distributed version S_D, where "equivalence" is understood as "computing the same initial-final-state relation" (stronger forms of equivalence which are preserved under parallel composition are also discussed).

A number of examples, amongst others, correctness proofs for the two-phase commit protocol and set partitioning (one of the running examples of this volume), illustrate the effectiveness of these noncompositional CCL-based techniques.

1.6 Compositionality

This section presents a detailed discussion of the concept of compositionality (in Section 1.6.2) from the viewpoint of the verify-while-develop paradigm (discussed in Section 1.6.1), supplies additional motivation for its application in the context of machine-supported verification (in Section 1.6.3), gives a detailed account of its relationship with Lamport's view of specification as a contract between client and implementor (in Section 1.6.4) which is expressed by another concept – modularity, and analyses some beliefs about the complexity of compositional reasoning in Section 1.6.5. Finally, we answer in Section 1.6.6 the third question posed in Section 1.1: Should one use compositional or noncompositional methods?

1.6.1 The Verify-While-Develop Paradigm

Most of the literature on program correctness deals with *a posteriori* program verification, i.e., the situation that *after* the program has been obtained it is proved correct, see, for instance [Man74, And91, AO91, Dah92, Fra92, Sch97]. Although a posteriori verification has been indispensable for the development of a truly mathematical theory of program correctness, it is a frustrating approach in practice, because almost all programs contain errors. Discovering that error then leads to the need for correcting the program. And the program corrected in that way contains most of the time errors again. Nevertheless one hopes that this is no nonterminating cycle. Hence the attempt at a correctness proof leads in most cases to the discovery of errors, i.e., a counterexample violating the original specification, rather than a successful proof.

This situation becomes even more serious when considering concurrent programs and systems. For then the number of cases to be verified when checking the correctness of the interaction between their individual processes grows exponentially w.r.t. the number of those processes. Consequently, checking them all becomes well-nigh impossible, except, maybe, when this process of checking has been mechanised. But even then the limits of naive machine verification are quickly reached.

It would make sense, if, rather than disproving finished programs over and over again in the course of attempting to prove them correct, one could be convinced of the correctness of a design decision *at the very moment one took that decision* during the process of top-down development of a program from its specifications – a paradigm called *"verify-while-develop"*. This paradigm requires one to verify that a program-in-the-making meets its specification by making use of specifications for its constituent parts or modules *while the implementing program text of these parts is not yet available.* This has the advantage that, since every top-down development step now requires a correctness proof based on the specifications of these parts (rather than a description of their execution mechanism), any errors made later during development of these parts which violate those specifications *do not influence the correctness of this particular development step.* Consequently, no redundant verification work is done when following this paradigm, in contrast to the situation with a posteriori program verification.

Of course, the verify-while-develop strategy is not new. It is merely a reformulation of the notion of *hierarchically-structured program development,* advocated by Edsger W. Dijkstra, Niklaus Wirth and others since the end of the sixties [Dij68c, Wir71, Dij76, Dij82, FvG99].

As we shall explain in the next section, the verify-while-develop paradigm amounts to compositional verification.

1.6.2 Compositionality: the Very Concept

The technical property which is required of program correctness methods for supporting the verify-while-develop paradigm is called *"compositionality"*, whose definition is recalled below:

> *"That a program meets its specification should be verified on the basis of specifications of its constituent components only, without additional need for information about the interior construction of those components."*

To make this verification strategy possible, programs and their components are specified using predicates *over their observable behaviour, only*. Such specifications are called *assertional*. Consequently, assertional specifications of the constituent components of a program never depend on any additional knowledge about the underlying execution mechanism of those components. Consequently, *compositional verification should be based on an assertional specification language*.

What does a compositional proof method consist of?

It consists of:

(i) *Basic techniques* for proving that a program P, which is not decomposed any further, satisfies φ.

(ii) *Compositional proof techniques* to handle the case that P is composed of parts $P_1, \ldots, P_n$, i.e., $P = op^{lang}(P_1, \ldots, P_n)$, $n \geq 1$, with op^{lang} some operator of the programming language.

For the latter kind of program operators we develop *compositional proof rules*, i.e., logical inference rules of the form:

"From P_1 *satisfies* φ_1 and ... P_n *satisfies* φ_n infer P *satisfies* φ." [Zwi89]

In order to do so we need to be more specific about assertional specifications through predicates. They should not refer to the interior construction of components. Therefore, the available information for specifying a component consists only of:

- a description of the desired observable behaviour of the component P_i (as given by the assertional specification φ_i), and
- a description of the interface $obs(P_i)$ of that component P_i.

This leads to the introduction of restrictions upon the specifications φ_i of P_i, whose purpose it is to guarantee that φ_i is invariant under independent execution of P_j, $j \neq i$. These restrictions concern the sets of observables allowed to occur within φ_i, and impose that those observables, which are involved in independent executions of P_j, $j \neq i$, are disjoint from the observables of φ_i.

Example 1.12 In the A-C rule for parallel composition (see Section 7.5.3) one imposes the following restrictions on φ_i:

- $Chan(\varphi_i) \cap Chan(P_j) \subseteq Chan(P_i)$, $i \neq j$.
  Here $Chan(\varphi_i)$ lists those communication channels, communication along which influences the value of φ_i, and $Chan(P_j)$ the communications channels occurring in P_j. This restriction expresses that those channels along which communication influences the value of φ_i, and which also occur in P_j, $j \neq i$, must be connected to P_i. That is, along such channels communication between P_i and P_j is synchronised.
- $var(\varphi_i) \cap var(P_j) = \emptyset$.
  This restriction expresses that φ_i should not involve variables whose values might be changed by P_j. □

The characteristic feature of a compositional proof rule is its so-called *compositional proof step*. This step consists essentially of a proof that φ follows from some combination of $\varphi_1, \ldots, \varphi_n$. This proof amounts to checking the validity of a finite number of implications involving the predicates occurring in $\varphi_1, \ldots, \varphi_n$ and φ, and *therefore does not involve any representation of P_i at all*!

Example 1.13 In the A-C framework for reasoning compositionally about synchronously communicating processes, a specification φ consists, essentially, of a pair $\langle A, C \rangle$ consisting of an assumption A concerning the environment of a component and a commitment C of that component. The corresponding proof rule for parallel composition of two processes features the following compositional proof step:

$$\bigwedge_{i,j=1,2,\ i \neq j} (A \wedge C_i \rightarrow A_j),$$

expressing that the assumption A concerning the environment of $P_1 \| P_2$ plus the commitment C_i of the process P_i within this network together imply the assumption of the process P_j (this takes into account that the environment of P_j is process P_i plus the environment of $P_1 \| P_2$), for $i \neq j$. □

Consequently, a compositional proof rule introduces three kinds of premises for deducing that $op^{lang}(P_1, \ldots, P_n)$ *satisfies* φ:

(i) A compositional proof (reduction) step, stating that φ follows from some combination of $\varphi_1, \ldots, \varphi_n$.

(ii) Conditions upon the observables allowed within $\varphi_1, \ldots, \varphi_n$ w.r.t. program components $P_1, \ldots, P_n$.

(iii) Compositional verification that P_i *satisfies* φ_i, $i = 1, \ldots, n$.

These considerations lead to the following definition of a *compositional proof rule for a program operator* $op^{lang}(P_1, \ldots, P_n)$:

$$\frac{for\ i = 1, \ldots, n,\ P_i\ satisfies\ \varphi_i\ and\ obs(P_i) \subseteq O_i,\quad op^{spec}(\varphi_1, \ldots, \varphi_n, \varphi; obs(P_1), \ldots, obs(P_n))}{op^{lang}(P_1, \ldots, P_n)\ satisfies\ \varphi,}$$

where $obs(P_i)$ refers to the interface of P_i, i.e., P_i's set of observables, $O_1, \ldots, O_n$ denotes given sets of observables, $\varphi_1, \ldots, \varphi_n$, and φ expresses assertional specifications, and $op^{spec}(\varphi_1, \ldots, \varphi_n, \varphi; obs(P_1), \ldots, obs(P_n))$ expresses points (i) and (ii) above[10].

Various proof methods are considered, each giving separate interpretations to φ, "P *satisfies* φ", $obs(P_i) \subseteq O_i$, op^{lang}, and op^{spec}. For each of these methods it is essential that the *basic technique* to deal with programs which are not decomposed further (although adaptation rules may be applied) are formulated and, in particular, that appropriate (meta-)predicates $op^{spec}(\varphi_1, \ldots, \varphi_n, \varphi; obs(P_1), \ldots, obs(P_n))$ for the compositional proof rules contained in the respective proof method are identified.

Although obviously for each n-ary operator op^{lang}, $n \geq 1$, one proof rule of the form above is needed, one needs additional proof rules in order to *adapt* one specification to another. These proof rules are not related to specific program constructs, but allow one to reason about specifications (and interfaces), only. They are of the following form:

$$\frac{P\ satisfies\ \varphi,\ and\ obs(P) \subseteq O,\quad op^{spec}(\varphi, \varphi'; obs(P))}{P\ satisfies\ \varphi'}$$

The most frequently used rule of this type is the rule of consequence known from Hoare logic [Hoa69]. Since these rules do not depend on the structure of

---

[10] The clause $P_i \subseteq O_i$ is added here to cover restrictions on the components, e.g., the case in shared-variable concurrency where a process is required to have exclusive write-access to a variable. Its general purpose is to be able to impose further restrictions on $P_1, \ldots, P_n$, although these are not considered here.

the actual program, but adapt its specification only, they are called *adaptation rules* [Old83b, Zwi89, ZHLdR95]. They do not refer to the internal structure of the program also and thus also qualify as compositional proof rules.

Therefore, a *compositional proof rule* is either a compositional proof rule for some program operator op^{lang} or an adaptation rule.

A proof rule is *sound* (or *valid*) whenever the truth of its premises implies the truth of its conclusions. Now a *compositional proof method* for establishing program correctness for some programming language consists of basic rules, dealing with constructs which are not decomposed any further, and compositional rules, dealing with

(i) constructs which are decomposed, and
(ii) the adaptation of specifications.

A proof method is *sound* if all its proof rules are sound.

Compositional reasoning owes its attractiveness to its application to parallel composition, since it replaces operational reasoning with a complexity *increasing exponentially* in the number of parallel components by reasoning compositionally, whose complexity increases *linearly* w.r.t. the number of those components. This is discussed further in Section 1.6.5.

Example 1.14 (The rule for sequential composition in Hoare logic is compositional) The rule for sequential composition in Hoare logic, cf. Rule 9.6, can also be formulated as:

$$\frac{\{pre_1\}P_1\{post_1\}, \{pre_2\}P_2\{post_2\}, post_1 \to pre_2, pre \to pre_1, post_2 \to post}{\{pre\}P_1 ; P_2\{post\}}$$

That this rule is compositional can be seen as follows:

* identify φ with a pair $\langle pre, post \rangle$ with *pre* and *post* predicates (that is, assertions from first-order predicate logic),
* define P *satisfies* φ by validity of $\{pre\}P\{post\}$,
* $obs(P)$ identifies the set of program variables occurring in P,
* $O_i \stackrel{\text{def}}{=} VAR$,
* $obs(P_i) \subseteq O_i$ is now satisfied,
* $op^{lang}(P_1, P_2) \stackrel{\text{def}}{=} ";"$,
* $op^{spec}(\varphi_1, \varphi_2, \varphi; obs(P_1), obs(P_2)) \stackrel{\text{def}}{=} (pre \to pre_1) \wedge (post_2 \to post) \wedge (post_1 \to pre_2)$. □

Example 1.15 (The rule for parallel composition in the assumption-commitment formalism is compositional) The assumption-commitment rule for parallel composition, Rule 7.17, is formulated as:

$$\langle A_1, C_1 \rangle : \{\varphi_1\} \, P_1 \, \{\psi_1\},$$
$$\langle A_2, C_2 \rangle : \{\varphi_2\} \, P_2 \, \{\psi_2\},$$
$$A \wedge C_1 \to A_2, A \wedge C_2 \to A_1$$
$$\overline{\langle A, C_1 \wedge C_2 \rangle : \{\varphi_1 \wedge \varphi_2\} \, P_1 \| P_2 \, \{\psi_1 \wedge \psi_2\}}$$

provided

(i) $var(A_1, C_1, \psi_1) \cap var(P_2) = \emptyset$, $var(A_2, C_2, \psi_2) \cap var(P_1) = \emptyset$, and
(ii) $Chan(A_1, C_1, \psi_1) \cap Chan(P_2) \subseteq Chan(P_1)$,
    $Chan(A_2, C_2, \psi_2) \cap Chan(P_1) \subseteq Chan(P_2)$.[11]

That this rule is compositional can be seen as follows:

- In general, identify φ with a quadruple $\langle A, C, pre, post \rangle$, where A and C are predicates from first-order predicate logic involving no program variables, and *pre* and *post* unrestricted predicates from first-order predicate logic; in this particular case, specification φ for $P_1 \| P_2$ is chosen as $\langle A, C_1 \wedge C_2, pre_1 \wedge pre_2, post_1 \wedge post_2 \rangle$ with predicates subscripted by i referring to the corresponding predicates of the specification for P_i,

- validity of P *satisfies* φ is defined by validity of $\langle A, C \rangle : \{pre\} P \{post\}$,

- $obs(P_i)$: the variables $var(P_i)$ and channels $Chan(P_i)$ involved in P_i,

- $obs(P_i) \subseteq O_i$: take $O_i \stackrel{\text{def}}{=} \overline{var(P_j)} \cup Chan(P_i)$, $i \neq j$, where $\overline{var(P_j)} \stackrel{\text{def}}{=} VAR \setminus var(P_j)$,

- $op^{lang} \stackrel{\text{def}}{=} \text{``} \| \text{''}$,

- $op^{spec}(\varphi_1, \varphi_2, \varphi; obs(P_1), obs(P_2)) \stackrel{\text{def}}{=}$
  $\bigwedge_{i \neq j} (A \wedge C_i \to A_j) \wedge$
  $\bigwedge_{i \neq j} ((var(A_i) \cup var(C_i) \cup var(post_i)) \subseteq \overline{var(P_j)}) \wedge$
  $\bigwedge_{i \neq j} ((Chan(A_i) \cup Chan(C_i) \cup Chan(post_i)) \subseteq (Chan(P_i) \cup \overline{Chan(P_j)}))$,
  with $Chan(post)$, for *post* a first-order predicate, as defined in Definition 7.10, and $i, j \in \{1, 2\}$.   □

Compositional completeness

The notion of *completeness* investigated here is that of *compositional completeness* [Zwi89]:

A proof method is compositionally complete if it is compositional and moreover complete in the following sense:

Whenever, for $P = op^{lang}(P_1, \ldots, P_n)$, P *satisfies* φ holds, there exist specifications $\varphi_1, \ldots, \varphi_n$ (and sets of observables $O_1, \ldots, O_n$) such that:

---

[11] Recall that $Chan(P_1, \ldots, P_n, \varphi, \ldots, \psi) \stackrel{\text{def}}{=} (\bigcup_{i=1}^{n} Chan(P_i)) \cup Chan(\varphi) \cup \ldots \cup Chan(\psi)$.

(a) P_i *satisfies* φ_i, and $obs(P_i) \subseteq O_i$ holds for $i = 1, \ldots, n$, and

(b) $op^{lang}(P_1, \ldots, P_n)$ *satisfies* φ is provable within the proof system under the assumption of (a).

Observe the careful formulation of part (b) above. We do *not* state that $op^{lang}(P_1, \ldots, P_n)$ *satisfies* φ can be immediately deduced from P_i *satisfies* φ_i, $i = 1, \ldots, n$, using the compositional proof rule for op^{lang}. Rather, we state this inference can be carried out using a *number* of proof rules.

For example, in case of parallel composition one can prove that, in general, no $\varphi_1, \ldots, \varphi_n$ exist which allow $op^{lang}(P_1, \ldots, P_n)$ *satisfies* φ to be deduced from P_1 *satisfies* φ_1, $\ldots$, P_n *satisfies* φ_n, without taking additional properties into account. Rather, in case of synchronous message passing, $P_1 \| P_2$ *satisfies* φ is deduced by applying a combination of rules, such as the one for parallel composition, and the prefix invariance, conjunction and consequence rules.

Semantic completeness

Observe that *nowhere* in the account above we require assertional specifications to be syntactically expressible in some logical language. The above characterisation of compositionality can be formulated using assertional specifications which consist of *boolean functions* operating upon program states (used to capture the values of variables) and sequences of communications (for capturing the communication behaviour of a component or network).

This *semantic* approach abstracts from the issue of expressibility of the predicates and the derivability of the verification conditions, which in our framework are purely set-theoretic, i.e., directly formulated in terms of operations upon sets of states and communication histories.

The attractiveness of this abstraction is that completeness is now reduced to its very essence, i.e., the *existence of appropriate boolean functions* so that the proof methods and rules *are applicable*. This notion of completeness is called *semantic completeness*.

For example, semantic completeness of our formulation of the inductive assertion method for sequential transition diagrams P is demonstrated as follows. To show that every valid correctness formula $\{\varphi\} \, P \, \{\psi\}$, where φ and ψ denote sets of states (i.e., are set-theoretic predicates), is derivable, we have to associate with every location of P an appropriate set-theoretic predicate (denoting a set of states) such that the resulting network satisfies the required verification conditions.

In the sequential case, the resulting inductive network of semantic predicates is, in fact, a finite graphical representation of the computation tree of the given transition diagram (defined w.r.t. a given initial set of states), where finiteness is obtained by labelling each location with a set of states.

For concurrent systems, completeness of our proof methods involves making those verification conditions explicit *which allows one to combine* the (compositional) characterisations of the local proofs.

Semantically complete proof methods are worked out in Chapters 2–4, in which noncompositional approaches to concurrency verification are studied, and Chapters 6–8, focussing on compositional proof methods. Consequently, in Chapters 7 and 8 we develop *semantically compositionally complete* proof methods for concurrency.

Observe that by introducing the concept of semantic completeness, *expressibility* of predicates (within a given assertion language) and *derivability* of the verification conditions (which in our framework are purely set-theoretic, i.e., directly formulated in terms of operations on sets of states) now become separate issues. This leads to the introduction of notions like relative or arithmetical completeness, which are discussed in Section 2.7, and also in Chapter 5. This chapter introduces first-order predicate logic over the standard model of the natural numbers as assertion language.

This assertion language is used in Chapters 9–12, dealing with Hoare logic. Consequently, the verification conditions in those chapters refer to properties of that standard model. This has some repercussions on the notions of completeness which are used in those chapters, since by Gödel's result [Göd31] no complete axiomatisation exists for the standard model of the natural numbers. The impact of this on our work is the following. Instead of proving completeness we shall prove *relative completeness*. By this we mean that we assume that we have an oracle at our disposal to decide whether some assertion of our assertion language is valid or not. Relative completeness means that every valid specification can be formally deduced, where we may call upon this oracle to decide the validity of assertions. The typical case where the oracle is used is for application of Hoare's consequence rule.

Since we are relying on so-called strongly arithmetical interpretations for assertions in those chapters [Cla85], our notion of completeness is better called *arithmetical completeness* [Har79]. To avoid cumbersome terminology, we usually omit the adjectives "semantic", "relative" and "arithmetical" when we discuss completeness questions. That is, these qualifications are implicitly understood.

Compositionality and the verify-while-develop paradigm

Compositional proof techniques have the advantage that they allow a systematic top-down development of programs from their specification, which is correct by construction. And this process of program derivation is exactly the *verify-while-develop paradigm!* For, as a consequence of using compositional techniques, each compositional proof (reduction) step (as defined above) can be viewed as *the verification of a design step*, which only involves reasoning about (the assertional specification of) that particular step and does not involve any future design steps. This explains why in the definition of compositional proof techniques above we stipulate that no additional knowledge about the underlying execution mechanism of the constituent components (of the to-be-verified program) is allowed. For, without that clause, reasoning about a particular design step might involve reasoning about future design steps, and we want these two stages to be independent.

This explains why compositional techniques can be viewed as the proof-theoretical analogue of Dijkstra's hierarchically-structured program development.

In Section 9.1.3 the argument that compositional verification and the verify-while-develop paradigm refer to the same concept is worked out in detail for sequential Hoare logic.

1.6.3 Compositionality and Machine-Supported Verification

The promise of the joint verify-while-develop paradigm/compositional proof-generation strategy, which is discussed above, is based on its potential for widespread application, as witnessed by the growing list of academic and industrial claims in this respect [Lar87, LT87, CLM89, Jos90, KR90, LT91, HRdR92, LS92b, Bro93b, Jos93, KL93, CMP94, DH94, GL94, Jon94, Mos94, DJS95, Hoo95, Cau96, KV96, SY96, McM97, BLO98a, BLO98b, DJHP98, HQRT98, Sha98a, McM99, NT00].

This is mainly due to the effort made in recent years towards machine-support of this form of reasoning. This effort has been caused by the following factors.

As we have seen, compositional methods enable reasoning about such systems because they reduce properties of complex systems to properties of their components which can be checked independently of their environment. Now the same applies to reasoning about complex *finite state* systems. For example, verification approaches based on the fully automatic technique of *model checking* fail to scale up gracefully because the global state space that has to be explored can grow exponentially in the number of components [GL94]. Also here compositional verification offers a solution by restricting the model checking procedure to verifying local, component-level properties, and using combinations of interactive and machine-supported theorem proving for verifying that the machine-verified local properties imply the desired global property [CLM89, Jos90, Jos93, Kle93, GL94, DJS95, KV96, McM98, Sha98a]. This is discussed in [AHK98, DJHP98, BCC98].

Secondly, complex systems, and especially safety-critical ones, are in great need of formal verification. Also, the formal verification of crucial components of such systems has acquired higher industrial priority ever since INTEL lost an estimated 500 million US dollars due to a bug in its Pentium chip. Now compositional proof methods are reported which indicate that such verification tasks are being used for medium-size examples. Also in the case of the verification of *infinite state systems*, it therefore makes sense to complement the above mentioned combination of automatic and theorem-proving-based verification techniques by compositional reasoning supported by semi-automated proof checking methods such as, PVS [ORSvH95], as reported in [Hoo95, HvR97, Sha98a], and other methods, such as ACL2 [KM94], Nqthm [BM97], the Larch Prover [GG91], Nuprl [C$^+$86] and Coq [CH88], for which we refer to the contributions of Hooman and of Shankar to [dRLP98]. Hooman and Shankar encode a *semantical* characterisation of compositional verification in PVS, thus motivating the approach followed in Chapters 6, 7 and 8. For more information concerning this topic the reader is referred to the companion volume [HdRP$^+$00].

1.6.4 Compositionality, Completeness and Modularity

In specification the compositionality principle implies a *separation of concerns* between the use of (and reasoning about) a module, and its implementation. As Lamport says [Lam83c], it provides a *contract* between programmer and implementor:

- One can program a task by the use of modules of which one only knows their specification *without any knowledge about their implementation,* and
- one can implement a module solely on the basis of satisfying its specification *without any knowledge of its use.*

This separates *programming with modules on the basis of their specifications* from *implementing a module such that its specification is satisfied.*

To succeed in this contract between programmer and implementor, all those aspects of program execution which are required to define the effect of a construct must be explicitly addressed in semantics and assertion language alike, that is, one should be able to specify the observable behaviour of such modules. And this implies that one needs at least a compositional framework. This is especially required when specifying fixed components, which can be taken ready-made from the shelf, so to say.

In order to understand the exact relationship between the compositionality principle and Lamport's view of a specification as a contract between programmer and implementor, in [Zwi89, ZHLdR95] the terminology regarding compositionality is refined by distinguishing *compositionality*, which is needed when developing a program from its specification in top-down fashion, from *modularity* (also called *modular completeness* in [Zwi89]), which is needed when constructing programs from re-usable parts with fixed proven specifications in bottom-up fashion. Similar distinctions are made in the work of Abadi and Lamport [AL93, AL95].

Thus, *compositionality* refers to a *top-down approach,* stating that for every assertional specification of a compound construct *there exist* assertional specifications for its components such that these specifications imply the original specification without further information regarding the implementation of those components. The principle of *modularity* refers to a *bottom-up approach,* and requires that, whenever a property of a compound statement follows from *"a priori" given specifications of its fixed components,* then this should be deducible in the proof system in question. As proved in [Zwi89] this amounts to requiring compositionality plus a complete, so-called, *adaptation* rule (formulated, e.g., in Section 3.5.5).

The simplest known adaptation rule is the consequence rule, familiar from, e.g., Hoare and temporal logics. In general, given the fact that a certain *given* specification φ has been proved of a *given* component C, adaptation rules state when to "plug" this proof into another proof context in which another property, say ψ, of that same component C is needed. Completeness of such a rule amounts to requiring that, whenever some requested property ψ of C is implied by the already established specification φ of C, then the adaptation rule can be applied, resulting in a proof that component C satisfies the required property ψ.

Intuitively, the problem of establishing completeness of such a rule is as follows. Of course, when a given predicate φ implies another predicate ψ, $\varphi \rightarrow \psi$ can be proved relative to the set of true properties of the domain of interest (it is such a property itself). However, things are not that simple for program specifications. For example, when does validity of one Hoare triple $\{pre\}\ S\ \{post\}$ imply validity of another such triple $\{pre'\}\ S\ \{post'\}$, regardless of the identity of S?[12]

---

[12] Observe that here we abstract from the identity of S in order to formulate a property between Hoare-style specifications rather than Hoare triples. Formally, this requires introducing variables ranging over program statements [Zwi89].

Certainly not when the implications $pre \rightarrow pre'$ and $post \rightarrow post'$ hold, as follows immediately from the definitions of valid Hoare triples given in Section 1.5.4. Requiring $pre' \rightarrow pre$ and $post \rightarrow post'$ to hold, as expressed by the consequence rule, certainly establishes that validity of $\{pre\}\ S\ \{post\}$ implies validity of $\{pre'\}\ S\ \{post'\}$, regardless of the identity of S. However, the consequence rule does not yield a solution which is complete in that there exist pairs of Hoare triples such that validity of the one implies validity of the other, regardless of the identity of S, and yet this cannot be deduced using the consequence rule. This is especially the case for Hoare triples of concurrent program constructs (as discussed in Section 3.5.1), and leads to the introduction of so-called initialisation and auxiliary-variables rules.

This problem becomes even more acute in the case of assume-guarantee formalisms. Because in that case, specifying the observable behaviour of a component requires four predicates, instead of two. For synchronous communication a solution to this problem is given in [ZHLdR95].

Consequently, also when programming solely on the basis of given, fixed, specifications, a compositional framework is required in order to convince oneself of the correctness of one's programs in a formal set-up which has both the potential for application in the large and allows modules to be specified so as to provide a contract between programmer and implementor in Lamport's sense above.

The relationship between compositional proof systems, completeness and modularity is further discussed in a paper by Trakhtenbrot [Tra].

The paper by Finkbeiner, Manna and Sipma [FMS98] presents a formalism for modular specification and deductive verification of parameterised fair transition systems, with an extension to recursion.

1.6.5 On the Complexity of Compositional Reasoning

Take an automaton with 10 states and consider the parallel composition of 80 such automata. This results in a product automaton of 10^{80} states – that is, more states than the number of electrons within our universe!

Consider now the Internet. Certainly only 80 computers operating in parallel is chicken feed; many many more are operating in parallel! As we saw above, the complexity of the product automaton is *exponential* in the number of states of the constituting automata. Consequently, a description of the Internet using an enumeration of "in principle" possible states is completely unrealistic.

This example shows that an analysis using product automata may not be appropriate for analysing the parallel composition of programs (although it sets lower bounds for worst-case complexity). After all, human beings also operate in parallel, and do not perceive their human environment as being composed of a product automaton recording the changes inside that environment.

Using compositional specification methods, the parallel composition of processes can be specified using the *conjunction* of the specification of the separate processes. Hence the complexity of this description is *linear*, rather than exponential, in the number of these specifications.

Next, assume that inside these specifications *disjunctions* are used to list various possibilities and the conditions subject to which these arise. Then, using de Morgan's law about the distribution of disjunctions over conjunctions, such a linear description may still, in the worst case, lead to the same exponential number of separate cases to be considered. So what did we gain?

Return to the analogy with humans, above. What other humans observe are not the changes of state inside their fellow human beings but rather changes in their *(inter)faces* or attitudes, from which a lot of local internal changes have been eliminated. That is, one observes the *observable behaviour* of one's fellow human beings.

Similarly, compositional specifications record changes in observable behaviour between programs (or processes), i.e., the change of externally (i.e., to other programs) visible quantities, and not the change in values of internal quantities, such as local variables, communication along local channels and the like.

This implies immediately that compositional reasoning is most successful when applied to program constructs which allow a maximal amount of hiding of these internal quantities. Observe that this is not the case for pure shared-variable concurrency when no local variables are present.

Also, as already observed, compositional specifications express the *conditions* under which such external changes occur. Now, de Morgan's law still applies w.r.t. distributing disjunctions inside (compositional) specifications over conjunctions between specifications. However, due to the fact that compositional specifications also express the conditions under which the externally observable changes occur, provided the interaction between processes is not too tight, and internal execution mechanisms can be hidden to a considerable extent, only *a manageable amount of such combinations of externally visible state changes* (of the separate processes) needs to be considered, i.e., are *consistent* – one hopes at least so few that the number of consistent combinations has a manageable complexity. And this belief is supported by current programming practice.

The assumption behind this belief is that communicating computers, operating in parallel, are invented by humans, and, since humans cannot cope with exponential complexity, any artificial artifact *which works,* and consists of parallel components, must somehow be possible to characterise using a very much lower than exponential complexity in the number of processes.

1.6.6 Compositional or Noncompositional Methods?

In this section we try to answer the last question mentioned in Section 1.1:

> *Which style of proof is more appropriate, a compositional or a noncompositional one?*

In principle every programming construct and language can be given a denotational, hence compositional, semantics, defined using the language of mathematics. In a *compositional* semantics, the semantics of a compound construct is a function of the semantics of its top-level (constituent) components.[13] Obviously, no other information about the behaviour of a construct thus characterised needs to be provided, because its denotational semantics already contains all the necessary information! Therefore, in principle, reasoning about and specifying a program can always be done compositionally, using an appropriately formalised subset of the language of mathematics as specification language.

However, in verification actually-given correctness proofs are what count, rather than stating that they might be given in principle. As it turns out, formalisms for synchronous constructs have been characterised compositionally with most success, e.g., those used for characterising the behaviour of hardware – which is synchronous, as argued, e.g., by Gérard Berry [BB91, BG88] – as the success of the assume-guarantee paradigm for such formalisms demonstrates [Sha98b].

In general, compositional approaches for synchronous constructs and languages have been a success story, e.g., for their systematic top-down development from their specifications [HdR91, Hoo95, Hoo98, Oss83, Sta85, Jon94, KR93], for their machine-supported verification [Jos93, BGA98, BCC98, BST98, KV98, MR98, Mos98, OD98, PH98, dRLP98], and for structuring the tools providing this support [DJHP98, BB91, Jos90].

Once it comes to tightly-coupled asynchronous systems, such as those based on shared-variable concurrency, e.g., mutual exclusion algorithms, compositional systems are, in general, not so successful as noncompositional proof methods. Although the rely-guarantee paradigm constitutes an important step

---

[13] In [Old91a] a distinction is made between compositional semantics, in which the semantics of a compound construct is a function of its constituent components, and *denotational* semantics, which is compositional and, additionally, gives a least or greatest fixpoint interpretation to recursively defined programming constructs.

forward in the methodology of program verification, as yet we only know of a few compositionally derived protocols which need unadulterated shared-variable concurrency for their expression, i.e., in which both reading from and writing to the same shared variable is required by more than one process [Stø90a, dBHdR97b, Din99a]. Section 8.4.3 illustrates the compositional verification of a simple mutual exclusion algorithm using the R-G method. Notice that for deriving algorithms involving tightly-coupled shared-variable concurrency, heuristic methods based on the preservation of invariants within the noncompositional framework of Owicki and Gries have been quite successful [FvG99].

Another such situation, in which compositional methods lack success, arises when programs are defined using global invariants combining local quantities which cannot be easily stated as a conjunction of local predicates, see [CM84]. An example of such an invariant is $x + y < z$, where x, y and z are local variables which occur in different processes. Another example is a distributed greatest-common-divisor algorithm due to Nissim Francez and Mickey Rodeh [FR80], the correctness of which is proved in Section 4.4.2 using a noncompositional method.

Actually, such invariants can always be formulated as a conjunction of local quantities, as shown in Example 4.22. However, this leads to a massive multiplication of information, using so-called logical variables; these are variables which do not occur in any program, but only in their specifications.

Also, compositional reasoning does not lead to improvement when the complexity of the compositional semantics of the constructs concerned is simply too high. Rob Gerth and Marly Roncken give an example of such a case in [GR90], in which a compositional semantics is displayed requiring *nine different kinds of observables!* Yet in a number of such cases noncompositional reasoning can still be successfully applied. This holds especially for *object-oriented reasoning* [dB86, GdR86, Ame87, Ger89, dB91a, dB91b, ÁMdB00].

It turns out that noncompositional methods have been quite successful for axiomatising particular forms of communication and synchronisation in existing programming languages, as in CSP [Hoa78], OCCAM [INM88], ADA [Ada83], concurrent PASCAL and other monitor-based languages and object-oriented languages such as JAVA. Apart from the compositional proof methods for CSP and OCCAM, noncompositional methods are often the only ones available with compositional versions developed at a later stage, if at all [GdR84, dB86, GdR86, Ame87, Ger89, Zwi89, dB91a, dB91b, HdR91, dBH92, ÁMdB00]. This gives us yet another incentive to study both noncompositional and compositional proof methods and emphasise their close relationship.

Summarising, compositional reasoning should be applied whenever it successfully solves the problems of specifier, prover and implementor alike – such is the case, for instance, with formalisms for synchronous constructs. However, there are many cases where the formulation of the problem at hand (developing a program preserving a certain invariant), the inherent complexity of the semantics of a program construct (e.g., one requiring nine-tuples for its compositional characterisation), or the tight coupling of the processes concerned (typical for unadulterated applications of shared-variable concurrency), prevents a practical compositional solution. This applies especially to object-oriented reasoning.

1.7 From Noncompositional to Compositional Proof Methods – a historical perspective

No survey of compositional proof methods for program correctness, in particular for establishing the correctness of concurrent programs, is complete without pointing out the fundamental contributions of Edsger W. Dijkstra to concurrent programming and program correctness in general. This concerns, especially, his insistence on developing programs hand-in-hand with their proofs, the very point of compositional correctness proofs. Quoting from the Turing Award Citation read by M.D. McIlroy at the presentation of Dijkstra's 1972 Turing Award lecture [Dij72b]:

The working vocabulary of programmers everywhere is studded with words originated or forcefully promulgated by E.W. Dijkstra – display, deadly embrace, semaphore, go-to-less programming, structured programming. But his influence on programming is more pervasive than any glossary can possibly indicate. The precious gift that this Turing Award acknowledges is Dijkstra's *style*: his approach to programming as a high, intellectual challenge; his eloquent insistence and practical demonstration that programs should be composed correctly, not just debugged into correctness; and his illuminating perception of problems at the foundations of program design. He has published about a dozen papers, both technical and reflective, among which are especially to be noted his philosophical addresses at IFIP [Dij62, Dij65a], his already classic papers on cooperating sequential processes [Dij65b, Dij68c], and his memorable indictment of the go-to-statement [Dij68b]. An influential series of letters by Dijkstra have recently surfaced as a polished monograph on the art of composing programs [Dij71].

We have come to value good programs in much the same way as we value good literature. And at the centre of this movement, creating and reflecting patterns no less beautiful than useful, stands E.W. Dijkstra.

Another quotation, from Leslie Lamport's invited talk at the ACM Symposium on Principles of Distributed Computing in 1983, strengthens the impression that Edsger W. Dijkstra should be regarded as the founding father of concurrency. In his report on Dijkstra's work on self-stabilisation [Dij74], Leslie Lamport states:

I regard this as Dijkstra's most brilliant work – at least, his most brilliant published paper. It is almost completely unknown. I regard it to be a milestone in work on fault tolerance ... I regard self-stabilisation to be a very important concept in fault tolerance, and to be a very fertile field for research.

Let us now return to the proper subject of this section: the development from noncompositional to compositional proof methods.

For a detailed description of the development of the semantics of programs and their proofs in the period 1947–1968 the reader is referred to [dB69].

The development of methods for proving the correctness of programs starts with publications by H.H. Goldstine and J. von Neumann [GvN47] and by A. Turing [Tur49].

Interestingly, the main direction in this development leads from a posteriori nonstructured program proving methods to structured compositional techniques [dR85b, HdR86].

For sequential programs this development is easy to trace. The first noncompositional method, due to R.W. Floyd's, appeared in 1967 [Flo67] (a year earlier, P. Naur illustrated in [Nau66] related ideas). This method – called the *inductive assertion method* – will be presented on the basis of labelled transition diagrams (these are directed graphs whose edges are labelled with guarded multiple assignments) in the manner of Manna & Pnueli [MP82]. This method is noncompositional because there is "little room" for program development between a specification and its ultimate atomic parts, in a manner of speaking. To use an analogy: In Floyd's approach a house is considered to consist of bricks, beams, tubes, electric wires, glass etc., rather than of a roof, walls, floors, plumbing, power supply and the like. Clearly, when designing programs one needs, mutatis mutandis, the latter higher level of abstraction.

C.A.R. Hoare reformulated this method for sequential programs in an axiomatic compositional style in 1969 [Hoa69]. Hoare observed that programs had a syntactic structure and that this structure could also be given to their correctness proofs for purposes of program development.

Also in 1969, Edsger W. Dijkstra wrote the following paragraph in [Dij69a]:

On Understanding Programs.
On a number of occasions I have stated the requirement that if we ever want to be able to compose really large programs reliably, we need a discipline such that the intellectual effort E (measured in some loose sense) needed to understand a program *does not grow more rapidly than proportional to the program length L* (measured in an equally loose sense) and that if the best we can attain is a growth of E proportional to, say, L^2, we had better admit defeat.

Since the complexity of compositional reasoning grows linearly w.r.t. the program size (as observed in the previous section), this paragraph is the first published reference within the computer science literature to the desirability of compositional reasoning. The above quotation is very general. A related argument, focussing on concurrency, appears in [Dij72a, page 75].

Within the context of predicate logic, the principle of compositionality was already formulated in 1923 by G. Frege [Fre23]. The first persons to relate Frege's notion of compositionality to logics for program proving were P. van Emde Boas and T.M.V. Janssen in [JvEB77b, JvEB77a, JvEB80].

It is not our intention here to give a full account of the rich development of verification methods for sequential program constructs. Much work has been done on Hoare logics for the verification of (recursive) procedures for an impressive variety of parameter-passing mechanisms [dB80, Apt81b] and their corresponding adaptation rules (see, e.g., [Old83b]), of **goto** constructs (see, e.g., A. de Bruin's chapter in [dB80]), the sequential theory of object orientation [Ame87], data structures (see, e.g., [Dah92]), and array- and pointer manipulation (see, e.g., [AdB94]). For the reader interested in user-oriented texts a number of excellent textbooks are available [Dij76, Gri81, Rey81, DF88, Kal90, Dah92]. But this covers merely a fraction of the important area of *formal methods*, which is devoted to the formal specification, development and verification of (sequential) program constructs. Consult our monograph [dRE98] for a comparative survey of these methods – such as, e.g., VDM [Jon90a], Z [Spi88], Hehner's method [Heh93], the Refinement Calculus [BvW90, Mor90], and Reynold's method [Rey81] – from the point of view of data refinement and the simulation techniques used for proving its correctness.

For concurrent programs both noncompositional and compositional proof methods were far more difficult to develop due to the problem of how to formalise the, in general, close interaction between processes while these are executing. For certain types of programs, such as operating systems, this close interaction is their one and only purpose. This led to their characterisation as *reactive* programs by D. Harel and A. Pnueli [HP85], that is, programs whose main rôle is to maintain an ongoing interaction with their environment, rather than to produce some final results on termination. Again, firstly noncompositional proof methods were formulated for such programs.

The first practical method for reasoning about parallel algorithms is due to Ed Ashcroft [Ash75]. This method is based on the use of *global invariants* [Ash75], and discussed in Section 10.6.

For shared-variable concurrency, the proof methods independently discovered by Owicki & Gries [OG76a] and by Lamport [Lam76, Lam77] constituted the next development. Essentially, these proof methods ramify the notion of specification by means of Hoare triples through the introduction of proof outlines, which express Ashcroft's global invariants syntactically. Proof outlines are systematically-annotated program texts in which at every control location a predicate is inserted, which characterises the program state at that point. By requiring that these predicates remain invariant under the execution of assignments in other processes – as expressed by the so-called *interference freedom test* – the influence of concurrent operations on shared variables is mathematically captured.

Thus, this method is based on the association of an assertion with each *local* node of a process, i.e., it goes back to Floyd's method.

For synchronous communication such proof systems were independently discovered by Apt, Francez and de Roever [AFdR80] and by Levin and Gries [LG81]. Here, synchronous communication was captured proof-theoretically by the so-called *cooperation test*. This test essentially requires that for communicating pairs of input-output actions – the actual fact of communication is characterised by a global invariant, basically over the separate communication histories of the various processes – the conjunction of the two predicates holding immediately before these input and output actions implies after communication (mathematically expressed as a distributed assignment) the two predicates asserted immediately after these two actions. Since only the input action can change the state of program variables, in practice this test involves checking that the input values have been appropriately specified in the postcondition of that input action.

Asynchronous message passing can be modelled using synchronous message passing by describing channels by means of processes, too. After this has been done, the communication between channels and processes can be expressed using synchronous message passing. This is worked out, amongst others, by Lynch and Tuttle [LT87] in their compositional theory of I/O automata. Of course, one would like to eliminate the names of these artificially introduced channel processes from the verification task. How this can be done is described in, e.g., [SS84]. In [dBFvHS98] de Boer, Francez, van Hulst and Stomp show that the noncompositional proof method for (synchronous) CSP of Apt, Francez, and de Roever applied to asynchronous communication allows a simple compositional formulation in which the cooperation test can be incorporated in the local verification conditions of the (sequential) components of a distributed system.

A third development, due to Amir Pnueli in 1977, led to the introduction of temporal logic in order to reason formally about fairness requirements in concurrent programs [Pnu77]. See [MP91b, MP95, MP99] for textbooks on this topic, for which Pnueli received a Turing Award in 1997.

Rob Gerth shows in [Ger84] how *transition logic* can be used to prove temporal logic properties of concurrent programs in a compositional way.

The discovery of temporal logic as a formalism for reasoning about fair computations is described in the nutshell caption for Amir Pnueli's pictures in the picture section of this book. Therein he tells that this discovery was rooted in his dissatisfaction with a previous approach, based on Nissim Francez's PhD thesis [Fra76], for reasoning about cyclic programs [FP78], which in retrospect can be viewed as being based on an encoding of temporal logic within first-order logic. The latter two publications are also interesting from another viewpoint: *They develop the first method for compositional reasoning about concurrency* using assertions to characterise the interface between concurrent processes!

The "Concurrent Hoare Logic" published by Lamport in 1980 [Lam80] *is* compositional. Unfortunately it has the disadvantage that the verification of a program against a specification is reduced to verifying the *same* specification for the components of the program. So there is no reduction in complexity of specifications. Moreover, it seems to enforce a strict top down development strategy for programs, for it would be rather surprising if, for a bottom up approach, two different and independently developed program modules had the *same* specification. And if we want to combine those modules into a larger program, then, for Lamport's system, they *must* have the same specifications. This approach is extended to synchronous message passing in [LS84b].

Early compositional proof methods for communication based parallel programming were formulated by Zhou Chao-Chen and Hoare [ZH81], and by Misra and Chandy [MC81].

Both approaches have in common that the idea of a *communication history* plays a central rôle in the specification of processes. This is also the case in Hailpern's work [HO81]. Such a history essentially describes which communications occurred in which order up to some given moment of time. Communication histories, or *traces* as they are sometimes called, are also used in [NDOG86], [Jon85], [JP87], [OH83], [Old86], [Pra86], [Rem81], [SD82], [Wid87], and, already in 1977, by Yonezawa [Yon77].

All the proof methods and systems for concurrency which are discussed above (with the exception of [FP78] and Sections 0.4 and 4.3 of [MP95]), apply to *closed* systems only, i.e., systems without any communication with processes outside of them. But who ever writes a closed system? Obviously the specification, development and verification of *open* systems is far more important, because these systems are the ones written for, e.g., operating and database systems, built into chips, and sold.

But how can one specify an open system which is intended to interact via, e.g., certain prespecified shared variables? Certainly without knowing its ultimate environment such a system cannot be verified using the method of Owicki & Gries, or any other theory mentioned above, because one does not know beforehand which interference to expect (from that environment).

A solution to that problem was worked out in [FP78] and given by Cliff Jones in [Jon81, Jon83] for shared-variable concurrency, and, for distributed communication, by Jayadev Misra and Mani Chandy in [MC81]. For both models of concurrency solutions were given by Eugene Stark in [Sta84, Sta85]. Stark also formulated the first sound and complete theory of refinement between concurrent processes specified in this way [Sta88].

Jones proposed in his so-called *rely-guarantee* (R-G) formalism *to specify the interference allowed by the environment of a component during its execution without endangering fulfilment of the purpose of that component.* Here the rely condition expresses the interference allowed, and the guarantee condition the task to be performed, by that component. An early formalisation of this paradigm, including soundness and completeness proofs, was given by Colin Stirling [Sti88]. The proposal of Misra & Chandy is similar to the R-G paradigm, be it that it applies to synchronous communication, and is called the *assumption-commitment* (A-C) formalism.

Of all the compositional approaches to the verification of concurrency, this *assume-guarantee* paradigm (as Lamport calls both these formalisms) is the one studied best [MC81, Jon83, Sou84, Pnu85, ZdBdR84, BK85, Sta85, ZdRvEB85, GdR86, Lar87, Sti88, Zwi89, Jos90, Hoo91b, PJ91, XH91, AL93, AP93, Col93, Jos93, KR93, Col94b, CMP94, DH94, XCC94, AL95, DJS95, McM97, XdRH97, HQRT98, McM98, Sha98b, McM99, NT00].

Manna and Pnueli incorporate similar ideas in Section 4.3 of [MP95] in a setting of temporal logic; additional references to compositional approaches in that setting are [MCS82, NDOG86, CMP94, Jon94].

Although the rely-guarantee and assumption-commitment paradigms were originally developed independently, it was later realised that the induction principles which they incorporate are similar [XCC94], given the appropriate compositional semantics for distributed communication and shared-variable concurrency are used. In case of distributed communication one can use, e.g., *trace-based sequences of communication records* [Hoa80, Hoa81b, FLP80], as studied in Chapter 4, and in case of shared-variable concurrency a combination of *process-indexed state sequences* and *action-indexed reactive sequences* [dBKPR91], as studied in Chapter 3, and Aczel-traces [Acz83], which are the appropriate model for the rely-guarantee paradigm and are studied in Chapter 8.

The formulation of the A-C paradigm for proving invariance properties is simpler than that for proving (the combination of invariance and) liveness properties as expressed in temporal logic. In case of invariance properties the A-C proof rule for concurrency expresses a *spiral* kind of inductive reasoning [ZdBdR84].

However, proving liveness properties such as termination and fairness requires reasoning about completed computations, and not about their prefixes as in the case of the spiral kind of reasoning above. Consequently, in the case of combinations of invariance and liveness properties, by a result of [AS85, Sch87] these properties are written as the conjunction of a maximal invariance and minimal liveness property, to which separate forms of A-C reasoning are applied [AL91]. This is worked out in, e.g., [MCS82, AL93, AP93, Col94b, CMP94, AL95].

Another promising variant of compositionality which is applied in present-day verification tools, e.g., in [BLO98a, BLO98b], is that of *compositional refinement*. This notion expresses that refinement between networks of concurrent processes can be established by proving refinement between their respective components, i.e., that refinement *commutes* w.r.t. parallel composition. In this way proving refinement between very large automata can be reduced to establishing refinement for a number of small automata. Obviously, this is a very powerful proof strategy. It occurs first in works of Gerth [Ger90] and of Zwiers, Coenen and de Roever [ZCdR92], and is worked out in a framework for dense-time temporal logic in the dissertation of Antonio Cau [Cau96, Cau00]. This thesis also describes how one can reason compositionally about *fault-tolerant* processes; this is illustrated using stable storage as example,by applying the technique of *relative* (compositional) refinement.

State-based verification methods for object-oriented languages add to the above-mentioned techniques the facility to reason formally about object creation. Now the creation of a new object implies that the domain of existing objects is extended by that object. This implies immediately that formal reasoning about object creation involves reasoning about dynamically changing networks of objects, i.e., that quantifiers within assertions are interpreted over dynamically changing domains of existing objects [Sco79]. Secondly, since newly-created objects are identified uniquely by their names, which act like pointers, the possibility of aliasing arises. This is handled on the proof-theoretical level using so-called semantic substitution [Ame87, AdB94, Mor82].

Now, the communication between objects is monitor-based, i.e., uses the remote procedure calling mechanism. Therefore, this communication can be handled proof-theoretically using the same techniques as those developed for communication in monitor-based languages [GdR86], which are based on the cooperation test. However, a new element enters the formulation of this test, namely, that of the assertional characterisation of the already mentioned dynamically changing networks of existing objects during program execution, in order to capture the synchronisation between these objects. As proved in [AdB94], first-order logic is too weak to express this characterisation, and has to be extended by allowing reasoning about finite sequences of objects (in programming jargon: arrays of objects) to do so. The resulting proof systems have been developed by Pierre America and Frank de Boer [Ame87, Ame89, dB90, dB99, dB02]. A compositional proof system for dynamic process creation appears in [dB91a].

Summarising, compositional methods enable reasoning about complex systems by reducing their properties to the properties of their components and of their interfaces. Since these components are much smaller, compositionality offers a viable solution to the problem of state-explosion associated with the *explicit* construction of the parallel composition of automata in the context of (semi-)automatic tool support for verification. This solution consists of a combination of automatic verification of the properties of components through appropriate algorithmic tools with semi-automatic verification of the mutual consistency of their interfaces using theorem provers.

For an account of the state-of-the-art in compositional verification methods for concurrency the reader is referred to [dRLP98].

Exercises

1.1   Prove that the invariant given for Example 1.4, with mutator action M_1 as indicated, is invariant, under all actions of the mutator and the collector during the marking loop.

1.2   Modify the informal argument for the correctness of the coarse grained garbage collection algorithm from Section 1.4.3 to show correctness of the following refined version:

$$M_3 \equiv\ < \text{redirect edge to the new target} >;$$
$$< \text{blacken the new target} >$$
$$C_3 \equiv C_2$$

Hint: Try to find a new (weaker) invariant which is preserved by the new mutator's actions.

Part II
The Inductive Assertion Method

2

Floyd's Inductive Assertion Method for Transition Diagrams

2.1 Objectives of Part II

The goal of this chapter and the three following ones is to develop the *inductive assertion method* attributed originally to Robert Floyd [Flo67] and Peter Naur [Nau66], and worked out later by, e.g., Zohar Manna [Man69, Man74] and Zohar Manna and Amir Pnueli [MP82, MP91b].

The inductive assertion method is a *semantic* methodology for proving state-based programs correct. Ultimately it reduces a statement of correctness of a program to a finite number of *verification conditions* in the sense that it is *sufficient* that these verification conditions hold in order for that correctness statement to be valid. Also the pure fact that such verification conditions exist is a *necessary* condition for validity of a correctness statement. Thus this method can be seen as a *generator* of a finite number of both necessary and sufficient verification conditions with the purpose of establishing various forms of correctness of a program.

Originally worked out for sequential programs, here a version is presented which extends to concurrency – both based upon shared variables (Chapter 3) and synchronous message passing (Chapter 4). The present chapter deals with an elementary form of sequential programs, that of *transition diagrams*, which provides just enough structure to give the *soundness* proof of the method – this refers to the "sufficient" part above – and its so-called *semantic completeness* proof – referring to the "necessary" part above; this set-up generalises easily to the forms of concurrency mentioned above. By semantic completeness of a method we mean that for every correct program appropriate verification conditions exist which establish its correctness. These verification conditions are first formulated in the meta-language underlying our reasoning, in this case mathematics. In Chapter 5 first-order logic over the (standard model of the) natural numbers is chosen as the formal language and shown to enable expression of these verification conditions by a technique called *Gödelisation* [Göd31, Coo78]. When these verification conditions are expressed in this formal language we call them *assertions* and first-order logic over the natural numbers our *assertion language*. We then speak about *relative* [Coo78] or *arithmetic* [Har79] *completeness*.

The importance of the method of inductive assertions for establishing correctness of programs cannot be overestimated. It provides the *semantic* foundations and, indeed, the minimal necessary structure for any other method which is based on the use of assertions to prove programs correct.

The reason for this is that it provides a *semantic analysis* of the kind of proof theory which is required for imperative state-based programming. It does so by:

(i) formulating, for every program and correctness statement considered, the basic verification conditions required for correctness to hold,

(ii) providing a simple mathematical framework for analysing soundness of the method, and

(iii) allowing a simple argument for establishing its semantic completeness by means of so-called *minimal* predicates.

So why bother formalising other methods in Part IV of this book and in the companion volume?

> *Because the inductive assertion method lacks sufficient structure.*

Ideally, one would like the structure of a correctness proof to reflect the top-down structure of a program. This has various reasons. First of all, a program proof is easier to understand that way, because as many design steps as possible are postponed until later stages.

Secondly, if one would like to replace a program part by a more efficient implementation which satisfies the same specification as that part, one would like to preserve the overall structure of the original correctness proof of that program, and just replace the proof of that old part by a proof for that new part. That is, at any stage of the proof, the part following it should be independent from the part preceding it, with specifications forming the only link between the two (i.e., no reference to any kind of text implementing a specification is allowed, and neither is any reference to any text of any surrounding program). Compositional proof systems fulfil these requirements, because compositionality *is* abstraction from the way the local proofs of correctness of the components of a program are constructed. And this abstraction leads to Hoare logics, the subject of Part IV of this book and of the companion volume, as explained below.

Such a top-down structure is absent from the inductive assertion method, because an inductive-assertion-style proof is no more than a mapping of the nodes of a transition diagram to the set of boolean state functions (predicates), and this mapping satisfies certain properties. These properties are formulated as verification conditions, each concerning the two assertions to which some pair of consecutive nodes in such a diagram is mapped. And this "successor node" structure does not reflect top-down program design.

This does not necessarily imply that the inductive assertion method cannot be equipped with a structure reflecting top-down design. For in Part III we formulate compositional proof rules for parallelism within the inductive assertion framework. And such rules can in principle also be formulated for the other program operators such as sequential composition and iteration constructs, once these are introduced for transition diagrams (as is done in Chapters 9, 10 and 11). These rules formulate how proofs about the initial-final state behaviour of the components of a diagram relate to a proof about the initial-final state behaviour of the overall diagram, that is, they expose the structure between these proofs. Consequently they are already rules from Hoare logic, for it is the very purpose of Hoare logic to expose this structure. As we shall see in Part IV, inductive-assertion-style proofs for transition diagrams even correspond to proofs in Hoare logic, and vice versa. *Thus one can regard Hoare logic as the systematic exposition of the structure in inductive-assertion-style proofs.* This structure is obtained by abstraction from the way local proofs of correctness of the components of a system are obtained, and follows the algebraic pattern of the programming operators of the programming language considered (e.g., iteration constructs, sequential or parallel composition).

Summarising, we observe the following differences between the inductive assertion method and Hoare logic. The inductive assertion method generates correctness proofs for unstructured objects, namely transition diagrams, and does so *without any abstraction* from the way local proofs for its subdiagrams are constructed. Hoare logic generates correctness proofs for structured objects, namely programs written in some programming language, and does so using rules which *do abstract* from the way the local proofs for the components of a program are generated.

The connection between Part IV and this one, Part II, is established in Chapter 5. There we prove that the predicates which are used in the semantic completeness proofs in this and the following two chapters, which are expressed there in natural language (as is customary and allowed in mathematical constructions) or by semantic means, can be formulated as first-order logic assertions over the natural numbers. This enables us at least to identify as a framework for the formulation of assertions that of first-order predicate logic over the natural numbers (other data structures are very well possible, see [TZ88]), thus providing a starting point for the process of providing more structure to correctness proofs in later parts. In particular, this expressibility result, together with the semantic completeness of the inductive assertion method, establishes its *relative* completeness. That is, every *valid* correctness statement considered can also be *proved* using the inductive assertion method once one is allowed to use valid assertions over the underlying data domain as *axioms* within these proofs [Coo78]. In the case of *arithmetical* completeness [Har79] all valid properties of the standard model of the natural numbers are also added as axioms.

2.2 Structure of this Chapter

In Section 2.3 we develop a general model of programs, that of sequential transition diagrams. Sequential transition diagrams describe the control structure of a program in terms of locations and labelled transitions. However, this view of programs is not abstract enough for our purposes for the following reasons:

(i) Usually the *observable* behaviour of a purely sequential program is defined by its initial-final state behaviour, to which locations do not belong.

(ii) In Chapter 9 we define (sequential) operations upon sequential transition diagrams. In order to define these operations correctly, they are only defined for transition diagrams with by-and-large disjoint sets of locations, i.e., these operations are *partial*. However, we would like them to be *total*, since that corresponds with their usual interpretation at the syntactic level. For example, one of these operations, sequential composition, is usually considered to be total. Consequently, the fact that sets of locations occur explicitly in the definition of sequential transition diagrams makes them a too detailed model for programs.

In order to obtain a more abstract model of programs we introduce the notion of sequential transition *systems* in Section 2.3.2. These are *equivalence classes* of sequential transition diagrams w.r.t. the *renaming* of their locations.

In Section 2.4 we introduce the notions of logical and program variables, and formulate semantic criteria for expressing that a transition system or a boolean function depends on the value of a variable. This is necessary because in Chapters 2–4 and 6–8 we do not have any syntactic notion of program or predicate available, and, consequently, do not have the syntactic notion of occurrence of a variable at our disposal. After having solved this technical problem, various kinds of specifications for programs are defined, in particular, as modalities for stating their correctness, those of *partial correctness, success* (absence of deadlock), *convergence* (absence of infinite computations), and *total correctness* (the sum of the previous modalities).

In Section 2.5 Floyd's inductive assertion method for proving partial correctness of sequential transition systems is formulated, and proved to be sound and *semantically* complete in Sections 2.6 and 2.7. Then, in Section 2.8 we define Floyd's wellfoundedness method for proving that a sequential transition system terminates, and prove its soundness and (semantic) completeness. How to prove that, e.g., a sequential transition system does not deadlock is the subject of one of the exercises at the end of this chapter (Exercise 2.12).

In Section 2.9 we extend our notion of transition diagrams from Section 2.3.1, in which labels of transitions contain *total* state transformations only, by allowing such labels also to contain *partial* state transformations, such as associated with $x := 1/0$ and $x := 1/y$. Clearly, executing $x := 1/0$, and $x := 1/y$ for $y = 0$, is undesirable because this leads to undefined results, and, therefore, to runtime errors. The corresponding correctness modality we call *absence of runtime errors*[1], which guarantees that during computations no undefined operations are applied. In this section we discuss two methods to prove this property: a direct method, and also an implicit method which reduces such proofs to proving absence of deadlock (the latter property is also called *success*).

Section 2.10 discusses the historical background of important notions such as Floyd's inductive assertion method, transition diagrams, computation step, transition relation, predicate transformers, various forms of completeness, freeze and auxiliary variables, clean termination, and the like.

2.3 Sequential Transition Diagrams and Systems

2.3.1 Sequential Transition Diagrams

First we introduce the inductive assertion method for sequential transition diagrams, basing ourselves upon Manna & Pnueli's course notes [MP82]. Transition diagrams describe the control structure of a program in terms of locations and transitions. A location represents the program counter which indicates the next instruction to be executed. A transition describes the effect of the execution of an instruction in terms of the new value of the program counter. The

---

[1] The usual name for this modality, *clean termination*[Sit74] suggests it to be a particular kind of termination, which is not the case at all. This is the reason why we give it a new name, thereby stressing that it is a *safety* property (see p. 88).

execution of an instruction itself is described in terms of a state transformation, where a state represents the contents of the memory. A state transformation consists of assigning to some memory cells the results of some operation performed on values read from the memory.

Intuitively the control structure of a program can be pictured as a labelled directed graph. The nodes in the graph are referred to as *locations*. Directed edges connect these nodes. *The entry node is a distinguished location where computation starts.* The similarly distinguished *exit* node has no outgoing edges. Each edge is labelled by an instruction of the form $c \to f$, where c denotes a total boolean condition or state function, also called *predicate*, and f denotes a total state transformation (such boolean functions will also be denoted by b):

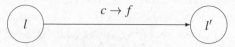

The intuitive meaning of a transition is that execution may proceed from a location l only if the current state at l satisfies the boolean condition c. In such a case we say that the transition is *enabled*. The execution of a transition then consists of applying the state transformation f to the current state. Subsequently, the execution moves to l'.

We proceed with giving a more formalised account of transition diagrams and their semantics. First we introduce formally the semantical notions of predicates and state transformations.

Definition 2.1 (Predicate, state transformation) Given a set of states Σ, with typical element σ, a predicate is a total (boolean) function assigning truth values to states. The set of predicates, with typical element φ, will be denoted by $\Phi \stackrel{\text{def}}{=} \Sigma \to Bool$, where *Bool* denotes the domain of truth values $\{tt, ff\}$. A state transformation f is simply an element of $\Sigma \to \Sigma$, i.e., the set of total functions from Σ to Σ. $\qquad \square$

For a predicate φ we introduce the notation $\models \varphi(\sigma)$ to indicate *satisfaction* of φ in σ, defined by $\varphi(\sigma) = tt$ (sometimes also the notation $\sigma \models \varphi$ will be used). Similarly, we use the notation $\models \varphi$ to express *validity* of φ, defined by: $\models \varphi(\sigma)$ for all states σ. We often use the phrases "$\varphi(\sigma)$ *holds*" and "φ *is valid*" to express, respectively, that φ is satisfied in σ and that $\models \varphi$ holds.

We have the usual lifting of the boolean operations to predicates: For example the conjunction of two predicates φ and ψ, denoted by $\varphi \wedge \psi$, is defined by $\models (\varphi \wedge \psi)(\sigma)$ if $\models \varphi(\sigma)$ and $\models \psi(\sigma)$.

Transition diagrams are mathematically defined as follows:

Definition 2.2 (Transition diagram) A transition diagram is a tuple (L, T, s, t), where L is a finite set of locations, with typical element l, T is a finite set of triples $(l, c \to f, l')$ called *transitions* with $l, l' \in L$, $c : \Sigma \to Bool$ and $f : \Sigma \to \Sigma$ total functions where Σ denotes a set of states, $s \in L$ is a distinguished location called *entry* location, and $t \in L$ is a distinguished location called *exit* location such that for no label l and instruction $c \to f$ we have that $(t, c \to f, l) \in T$. $\square$

A transition $(l, a, l') \in T$, with $a = c \to f$, we will also denote by $l \overset{a}{\to} l'$ or just $l \to l'$. Simpler variants of the general form for instructions will often be used such as c standing for a test with no state transformation, or f standing for $true \to f$, where $true$ denotes the predicate which assigns the truth value tt to every state.

In concrete examples of transition diagrams a state will be a total function assigning values to variables, i.e., $\Sigma \overset{\text{def}}{=} VAR \to VAL$, where VAR, with typical elements $x, y, z, \ldots$, denotes a set of variables, and VAL denotes the domain of values, i.e., for $y \in VAR$ one has that $\sigma(y)$ denotes the value of variable y in state σ, and this value belongs to VAL. A state transformation will then denote an assignment of the form $(y_1, \ldots, y_n) := (g_1, \ldots, g_n)$, or $\bar{y} := \bar{g}$, for short, where $g_i : \Sigma \to VAL$ denotes a total semantic function for computing a value from VAL, called *value* expression, y_i is a variable belonging to VAR, $i = 1, \ldots, n$, and the variables y_i in $\bar{y}$ are different from each other. Note that in general it is not the case that $VAR = \{y_1, \ldots, y_n\}$; usually only a few variables of VAR are changed in such a state transformation.

The semantics of an assignment is given by the following definition:

Definition 2.3 (Semantic assignment) First we define the *variant* of a state σ with respect to a sequence of distinct program variables $\bar{x} = (x_1, \ldots, x_n)$ and a corresponding sequence of values $\bar{d} = (d_1, \ldots, d_n)$, denoted by $(\sigma : \bar{x} \mapsto \bar{d})$,

$$(\sigma : \bar{x} \mapsto \bar{d})(y) = \begin{cases} d_i & \text{if } y \equiv x_i, \\ \sigma(y) & \text{if } y \not\equiv x_i, \text{ for } i = 1, \ldots, n, \end{cases}$$

where $\equiv$ denotes syntactic equality. Semantically an assignment $\bar{y} := \bar{g}$ denotes the state transformation: $(\bar{y} := \bar{g})(\sigma) = (\sigma : \bar{y} \mapsto \bar{d})$, where $\bar{d} = (g_1(\sigma), \ldots, g_n(\sigma))$. $\square$

Since f and g are total functions, this definition does not model the effect of executing undefined or partially defined operations such as $x := 1/0$ or $x := 0/y$; extending our model to such operations is the subject of Section 2.9.

Now we are able to define formally the semantics *Comp* $[\![P]\!]$ of transition diagrams: For a transition diagram P, an *execution sequence (or computation*

η *starting in* σ_0 is a sequence of *configurations*

$$\eta : \langle l_0; \sigma_0 \rangle \longrightarrow \langle l_1; \sigma_1 \rangle \longrightarrow \langle l_2; \sigma_2 \rangle \longrightarrow \ldots$$

such that $l_0 \equiv s$, and:

- For each *computation step* $\langle l_i; \sigma_i \rangle \longrightarrow \langle l_{i+1}; \sigma_{i+1} \rangle$ in this sequence there is a transition of P of the form

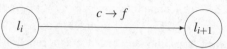

such that $c(\sigma_i) = tt$ and $\sigma_{i+1} = f(\sigma_i)$. Note that our transition diagrams may be nondeterministic since two different transitions may depart from a single location with conditions that are not necessarily disjoint.
- This sequence cannot be extended; i.e., if the sequence is finite, its last configuration has no possible successors.

Consequently, such an execution sequence satisfies one of the following cases:

(i) The sequence is finite, and its last configuration is of the form $\langle t; \sigma \rangle$. Such a sequence is called a *terminating* sequence, and we define the value of the sequence η as:

$$val(\eta) \stackrel{def}{=} \sigma, \text{ with } \sigma \in \Sigma.$$

(ii) The sequence is finite, but its last configuration is of the form $\langle l; \sigma \rangle$, $l \not\equiv t$. This must therefore be a deadlock state such that for no transition departing from l there exists a condition c with $c(\sigma) = tt$. Such a sequence is called a *failing* sequence, and we define its value as:

$$val(\eta) \stackrel{def}{=} fail.$$

(iii) The sequence is infinite. Such a sequence is called *divergent*, and we define its value as:

$$val(\eta) \stackrel{def}{=} \bot.$$

The values *fail* and $\bot$ are special symbols used to denote failure and divergence, respectively, and are not contained in Σ.

Denote by *Comp* $[\![P]\!] \sigma$ the set of all computations of P starting with the initial state σ. We define the *meaning* of the transition diagram P as a function $\mathcal{M}[\![P]\!]$:

$$\mathcal{M}[\![P]\!]\sigma \stackrel{def}{=} \{val(\eta) \mid \eta \in Comp\ [\![P]\!]\sigma\}.$$

Thus the meaning of a transition diagram P is a function which for a given initial state σ gives the set of all possible outcomes, including the possibility of failing and of divergent computations ($fail \in \mathcal{M}[\![P]\!]\sigma$ or $\perp \in \mathcal{M}[\![P]\!]\sigma$).

It is customary to write $\mathcal{M}[\![P]\!](\sigma)$ in order to emphasise that $\mathcal{M}$ is a mapping which for each transition system P yields a function $\mathcal{M}[\![P]\!]$ describing the initial-final state, failure and divergent behaviour of the computations of P:

$$\mathcal{M}[\![P]\!] : \Sigma \to 2^{\Sigma \cup \{\perp, fail\}}.$$

2.3.2 Transition Systems

The *val* function used to define the $\mathcal{M}[\![P]\!]$ semantics ignores the actual locations of execution sequences. The only aspect that remains is whether the last location is the exit location or not, and whether the computation is infinite. Therefore the meaning $\mathcal{M}[\![P]\!]$ of a transition diagram P does not depend on the particular names of the locations in a transition diagram. Informally, two transition diagrams are equivalent if they are the same up to a renaming of the locations, where the renaming should respect the start and exit locations. Assume that we have two transition diagrams $P \equiv (L, T, s, t)$ and $P' \equiv (L', T', s', t')$, with the same state space Σ. A renaming that transforms the names of the nodes of P into those of P' can be formalised as a *bijection* ϕ between L and L' that respects the entry and exit locations and the T relation:

Definition 2.4 (Equivalence of transition diagrams) We call two transition diagrams, $P \stackrel{def}{=} (L, T, s, t)$ and $P' \stackrel{def}{=} (L', T', s', t')$, *equivalent* , if there exists a bijection $\phi : L \to L'$ such that

- $s' = \phi(s)$,
- $t' = \phi(t)$, and
- $(l, a, m) \in T$ if and only if $(\phi(l), a, \phi(m)) \in T'$. $\square$

Observe that renaming is an equivalence relation.

Definition 2.5 (Transition systems and programs) A *transition system* is an equivalence class of transition diagrams. Such an equivalence class is also called a *program*. $\square$

Let P be a program, i.e., an equivalence class of transition diagrams. As remarked above, all transition diagrams in this class have the same meaning. Hence we can define the meaning of the program by taking the meaning of an arbitrary element from the equivalence class.

In the sequel, when dealing with transition systems we will often use transition diagrams that represent these equivalence classes instead. We say for instance: "let program P be represented by (L, T, s, t)", or even "let program $P \stackrel{\text{def}}{=} (L, T, s, t)$". One should check in such cases that the results are independent from the choice of the representatives. This is usually left to the reader.

Example 2.6 Consider program $P = (L, T, s, t)$ with

- $L = \{s, l, t\}$ and
- $T = \{(s, true \to f_0, l), (l, c_1 \to f_1, l), (l, c_2 \to f_2, t)\}$, where

$$c_1(\sigma) = tt \text{ iff } \sigma(y) > 0, c_2(\sigma) = tt \text{ iff } \sigma(y) = 0,$$
$$f_0(\sigma) = (\sigma : y, z \mapsto \sigma(x), 0),$$
$$f_1(\sigma) = (\sigma : y, z \mapsto \sigma(y) - 1, \sigma(y) + \sigma(z)), \text{ and}$$
$$f_2(\sigma) = \sigma,$$

where $\sigma \in \Sigma$, with $\Sigma \stackrel{\text{def}}{=} \{x, y, z\} \to \mathcal{Z}$, and $\mathcal{Z}$ denoting the set of integers.

Graphically, P can be represented as the transition diagram in Figure 2.1 below.

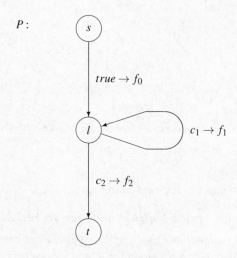

Fig. 2.1. A simple transition diagram.

It is easy to check that, if $\sigma(x) \geq 0$, then $\mathcal{M} \llbracket P \rrbracket \sigma = \{(\sigma : y, z \mapsto 0, \sum_{i=0}^{\sigma(x)} i)\}$ and that, if $\sigma(x) < 0$, then $\mathcal{M} \llbracket P \rrbracket \sigma = \{fail\}$.   □

Using Definition 2.3 of semantic assignment, we obtain that in the example above f_0 can be expressed as $(y, z) := (\lambda\sigma.\sigma(x), \lambda\sigma.0)$ and f_1 as $(y, z) := (\lambda\sigma.\sigma(y) - 1, \lambda\sigma.(\sigma(y) + \sigma(z)))$ (here the λ-notation is used to express functions, e.g., $\lambda\sigma.(\sigma(y) - 1)$ denotes the function which assigns the value of $\sigma(y) - 1$ to state σ). These assignments we abbreviate, respectively, to $(y, z) := (x, 0)$ and $(y, z) := (y - 1, y + z)$, thus suppressing any mentioning of σ. Similarly, condition c_1 will be abbreviated to $(y > 0)$ and c_2 to $(y = 0)$. Parentheses are dropped whenever this does not lead to confusion. This notation is formalised in Chapter 5.

Now P can be represented as in Figure 2.2 below, using the above abbreviations and the additional ones introduced in Section 2.3.1. Whenever this is convenient, we will stick to these abbreviations in the remainder of this book.

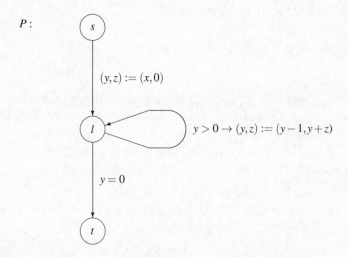

Fig. 2.2. A more convenient notation for the simple transition diagram.

2.4 Specification and Correctness Statements

2.4.1 Specifications, Logical Variables and Program Variables

A *specification* for a program P is given by a pair of predicates $< \varphi, \psi >$. The predicate φ is called the *precondition* for P, and ψ is called the *postcondition* for P.

Intuitively speaking a program P is correct w.r.t. a specification $< \varphi, \psi >$ if, for all initial states σ_0 such that $\models \varphi(\sigma_0)$, and for all final states $\sigma \in \mathcal{M} \llbracket P \rrbracket \sigma_0$, one has that $\models \psi(\sigma)$. Observe, since $fail, \bot \notin \Sigma$, that this definition only applies to final states $\sigma \in \Sigma$, i.e., to the case that P terminates for σ_0. So it can be alternatively formulated by:

For all $\sigma_0, \sigma \in \Sigma$, if, for initial state σ_0, P terminates in final state σ, then $\models \varphi(\sigma_0)$ implies $\models \psi(\sigma)$.

Thus, for example, a specification for a program for extracting roots of real numbers up to a given accuracy may be $< \varphi, \psi >$, where:

$$\varphi : \Sigma \to Bool, \varphi(\sigma) \stackrel{\mathrm{def}}{=} tt \text{ if } \sigma(y_1) \geq 0,$$

$$\psi : \Sigma \to Bool, \psi(\sigma) \stackrel{\mathrm{def}}{=} tt \text{ if } |\sigma(y_2)^2 - \sigma(y_1)| \leq 10^{-7}$$

and Σ is instantiated as the set of mappings assigning reals to variables. In general we will make in the rest of this chapter and the following ones informal use of an assertion language to denote predicates. This assertion language will be formalised in Chapter 5. As an example, φ and ψ are denoted by the assertions $y_1 \geq 0$ and $|y_2^2 - y_1| \leq 10^{-7}$. Note that in our specification we freely use functions and relations specific to the domain of application, in this case the real numbers.

In this example, y_1 is the input variable and the initial value of y_2 is irrelevant. On the other hand on termination y_2 is the output variable and is expected to hold an approximation to the square root of y_1. The input predicate in this case restricts the range of inputs, for which the program is supposed to perform correctly, to nonnegative numbers. Given that a program P is correct w.r.t. $< \varphi, \psi >$, as above, then the *interpretation* of this fact (saying that P computes the square root of y_1) depends on the assumption that y_1 is not modified anywhere in the program. This assumption can be verified by examining the text of the program and ensuring that no assignment to y_1 is made.

Observe that program P' given by:

$$P' : \qquad \underbrace{s} \xrightarrow{\quad (y_1, y_2) := (0,0) \quad} \underbrace{t}$$

is also correct with respect to the specification above. But certainly this program *cannot be interpreted as computing in program variable y_2 the square root of the initial value of program variable y_1!*

In this example we conveniently had y_1 available at the last state in order to compare y_2^2 to it. In other cases we may assign new values to the input variables during the computation. In order to be able to relate the final state to the initial state and also to eliminate the need for independently verifying that input values are not modified, it is possible to use specifications parameterised by so-called *logical variables*. These variables are not allowed to occur in any program but are still considered to be part of the state. Thus we assume that the set of variables is partitioned into a set of program variables, namely those variables which are allowed to occur in programs, and a set of logical variables. Formally, $VAR = Pvar \cup Lvar$, where $Pvar$ denotes the set of program variables, $Lvar$ denotes the set of logical variables, and $Pvar \cap Lvar = \emptyset$. Since logical variables do not occur in any program, their values (1) are not subject to change under transitions, and, hence, (2) are not changed upon termination w.r.t. their values in the initial state. Thus they serve to remember the values of input variables in the initial state.

Consider again a program for computing the square root of a nonnegative real number. This time we assume that the program has a single program variable y that satisfies $y \geq 0$ on entry to the program, and is expected on termination to contain as output the square root of the input.

An appropriate parameterised specification in this case is given by

$$< \varphi(v,y), \psi(v,y) >$$

where:

$$\varphi(v,y) : y = v \wedge v \geq 0,$$
$$\psi(v,y) : |y^2 - v| \leq 10^{-7}.$$

Here v is assumed to be a logical variable. As was said above, logical variables do not occur in any program. But since we do not deal with any syntactic notion of program in Part II, we must still formulate a semantic criterion expressing this fact.

We express this semantic criterion in terms of the concept of the variables *involved* in a state transformation and a predicate, respectively.

Formally a function $f : \Sigma \to \Sigma$ involves the variables $\bar{x}$ if

- $\forall \sigma, \sigma' \in \Sigma.\ \sigma(\bar{x}) = \sigma'(\bar{x}) \Rightarrow f(\sigma)(\bar{x}) = f(\sigma')(\bar{x})$
- $\forall \sigma \in \Sigma, y \in Pvar \setminus \bar{x}.\ f(\sigma)(y) = \sigma(y).$

The first condition expresses that if two states σ and σ' agree with respect to the variables $\bar{x}$, then so do their images under f. The second condition expresses that any other variable is not changed by f.[2]

---

[2] These two concepts have been introduced in [Sch77] as *aloofness* and *stability*, respectively, to express that f transforms $\sigma|\bar{x}$, i.e., σ restricted to the variables $\bar{x}$.

A predicate $\varphi : \Sigma \to Bool$ involves at most the variables $\bar{x}$ if

- $\forall \sigma, \sigma' \in \Sigma.\ \sigma(\bar{x}) = \sigma'(\bar{x}) \Rightarrow \varphi(\sigma) = \varphi(\sigma')$.

This condition expresses that the outcome of φ depends at most on the variables $\bar{x}$.

For $\bar{x}$ we will use the notations $f(\bar{x})$ and $\varphi(\bar{x})$ to indicate that f and φ involve the variables $\bar{x}$. Note that for any function f which involves $\bar{x}$ we also have that f involves $\bar{y}$, for any $\bar{x} \subseteq \bar{y}$ (and a similar remark applies to predicates). Moreover we have that if f involves the variables $\bar{x}$ and $\bar{y}$ then f involves $\bar{x} \cap \bar{y}$ (and similarly for predicates). This we can prove as follows: Let σ and σ' be such that $\sigma(\bar{x} \cap \bar{y}) = \sigma'(\bar{x} \cap \bar{y})$. Let $\bar{z} = \bar{y} \setminus \bar{x}$ and $\sigma'' = (\sigma : \bar{z} \mapsto \sigma'(\bar{z}))$. So we have that $\sigma(\bar{x}) = \sigma''(\bar{x})$ and $\sigma''(\bar{y}) = \sigma'(\bar{y})$. Since f involve the variables $\bar{x}$ and $\bar{y}$ it then follows that $f(\sigma)(u) = f(\sigma'')(u) = f(\sigma')(u)$, for $u \in \bar{x} \cap \bar{y}$. In other words, $f(\sigma)(\bar{x} \cap \bar{y}) = f(\sigma')(\bar{x} \cap \bar{y})$. Next let $u \notin \bar{x} \cap \bar{y}$, that is, $u \notin \bar{x}$ or $u \notin \bar{y}$. Since f involves the variables $\bar{x}$ and $\bar{y}$ it thus follows that $f(\sigma)(u) = \sigma(u)$. A similar argument applies to predicates. Although this proves that sets of involved variables of f and φ are closed under finite intersection, it does not necessarily imply that they are closed under infinite intersection, as the following example shows.

Example 2.7 Let $VAR = \{x_1, \ldots, x_n, \ldots\}$ and the predicate φ be defined as follows:

$$\varphi(\sigma) = \begin{cases} tt & \text{if } \exists i. \forall j, k \geq i. \sigma(x_j) = \sigma(x_k), \\ ff & \text{otherwise.} \end{cases}$$

It follows that φ involves $VAR \setminus \{x_1, \ldots, x_n\}$, for any n. But the infinite intersection of the sets $VAR \setminus \{x_1, \ldots, x_n\}$ is empty and clearly it is not the case that φ involves the empty set. (A similar counterexample applies to functions.) $\square$

Consequently we restrict ourselves to functions f and predicates φ for which there exists a *finite* set of variables which are involved in f and φ. Since any intersection with a finite set can be reduced to a finite intersection, the *smallest* sets of variables involved in f and φ are well-defined. From now on we will call these smallest sets the sets of variables involved in f and φ, denoted by $var(f)$ and $var(\varphi)$ respectively.

Note that $var(f)$ will contain both the so-called *read* and *write* variables of f, that is, those variables which are read by f and those variables which can be changed by f. The *read-only* variables of a state transformation f, denoted by $read(f)$, are those variables $\bar{x} \subseteq var(f)$ which are unchanged by f. Formally,

$$\forall \sigma \in \Sigma.\ f(\sigma)(\bar{x}) = \sigma(\bar{x}).$$

The write variables of f, denoted by $write(f)$, can then be formally defined as the remaining variables of $var(f)$.

For every program P we require that every state transformation f and boolean condition c of P satisfies that $var(f) \subseteq Pvar$ and $var(c) \subseteq Pvar$. This requirement then formalises the condition that logical variables do not occur in any program. We will use the phrase 'the variable x occurs in the state transformation f (condition c)' for $x \in var(f)$ ($x \in var(c)$). By $var(P)$, for a program P, we denote the variables occurring in its state transformations and boolean conditions. For programs we then use the phrase 'the variable x occurs in P' for $x \in var(P)$. Observe that this notion of occurrence of a variable in a transition system (or diagram) P is different from that in a syntactic representation of P. This is explained below.

Example 2.8 First consider the state transformation f expressed by $(x,y) := (x+3, y+7)$. Clearly f involves $\{x,y\}$.

Secondly, consider $id \stackrel{\text{def}}{=} \lambda\sigma.\sigma$, describing the usual meaning of **skip**. The set of program variables involved in id is the empty set, since for all $y \in Pvar$ one has that:

$$\forall \sigma \in \Sigma.\; id(\sigma)(y) = \sigma(y).$$

Now the objective for introducing such definitions is to approximate at a semantic level the syntactic notion of (program) variables *occurring* in the syntactic definition of some construct. This example therefore demonstrates why the notion "f involves $\bar{x}$" does not fully characterise that syntactic concept. This becomes clear when considering some syntactic representation of the program P manipulating, e.g., the program variables $\{x,y,z\}$. Within such a syntactic representation of P **skip** can be characterised by the assignment $(x,y,z) := (x,y,z)$, in which the variables x,y and z occur. The meaning of **skip** continues to be id, involving the empty set of variables.   □

2.4.2 Correctness Statements

Given a precondition φ, a computation whose initial state satisfies φ is called a φ-*computation*.

The main verification questions we would ask about a program P and a specification $< \varphi, \psi >$ are the following:

- **Partial Correctness.** A program P is *partially correct* with respect to a specification $< \varphi, \psi >$ if every terminating φ-computation also terminates in a state satisfying ψ, i.e., for all σ and σ' in Σ,

$$\text{if} \models \varphi(\sigma) \text{ and } \sigma' \in \mathcal{M} [\![P]\!] \sigma \text{ then} \models \psi(\sigma').$$

As notation for this property, the triple $\models \{\varphi\} \ P \ \{\psi\}$ will be used.

- **Success.** A program P is successful under φ (φ-successful) if there are no failing φ-computations. That is, for all σ in Σ,

$$\models \varphi(\sigma) \text{ implies } fail \notin \mathcal{M} [\![P]\!] \sigma.$$

- **Convergence.** A program P is *convergent* under φ (φ-convergent) if there are no divergent φ-computations. That is, for all σ in Σ,

$$\models \varphi(\sigma) \text{ implies } \bot \notin \mathcal{M} [\![P]\!] \sigma.$$

- **Total Correctness.** A program P is *totally correct* w.r.t. a specification $< \varphi, \psi >$ if every φ-computation terminates in a state satisfying ψ. This is equivalent to P being both φ-successful, φ-convergent and partially correct w.r.t. $< \varphi, \psi >$, i.e., the following properties hold for all σ and σ' in Σ:

  - $\models \varphi(\sigma)$ implies $\{\bot, fail\} \cap \mathcal{M} [\![P]\!] \sigma = \emptyset$,
  - $\models \varphi(\sigma)$ and $\sigma' \in \mathcal{M} [\![P]\!] \sigma$ imply $\models \psi(\sigma')$.

Notation: $\models [\varphi] \ P \ [\psi]$.

Even though it seems that total correctness is the natural concept to be proved for sequential programs, it is established in separate steps that prove first partial correctness, and then success and convergence. Since different methods are used to establish each of these properties, see Sections 2.5 and 2.8, their introduction as independent concepts is justified.

Note that partial correctness relative to $< \varphi, \psi >$ allows divergent and failing φ-computations, but no φ-computations which terminate in a state falsifying ψ.

We shall give proof methods for partial correctness and convergence in Sections 2.5 and 2.8. Establishing success is part of the exercises.

One may wonder why the above list of verification modalities does not contain a property such as *absence of runtime errors* (sometimes called *clean termination* in the literature). Runtime errors are associated with executing $x := 1/0$, and $x := 1/y$ when $y = 0$. The absence of this modality in the present section is due to the fact that, in the framework discussed in Section 2.3.1, transitions are labelled using *total* boolean state functions and *total* state transformations. In Section 2.9 our formalism is extended by including partial state functions, consequently allowing such runtime errors during program execution. The subject proper of that section is then how to prove absence of runtime errors.

Partial correctness and success of a program are instances of so-called *safety* properties. The term "safety", originally introduced by Lamport in [Lam77], refers to the fact that during execution of a program *"no bad things happen"*, e.g., the property that *fail* never occurs as an intermediate state in any of its computations (an indication of the fact that a successor state is always defined) is a safety property. That is, a safety property of a program refers to the fact that this program maintains some invariant property which excludes such "bad" things from happening.

Convergence of a program is an instance of a so-called *liveness* property. The term "liveness", also introduced in [Lam77], refers to the fact that *"good things eventually happen"*, e.g., in every computation of a given program a certain location (such as, e.g., its end location, or exit label) is eventually reached, or a given program terminates provided some kind of so-called *fairness property* is satisfied. Fairness properties are also examples of liveness properties and will be discussed in Section 3.2.

Safety and liveness properties were introduced by Lamport in order to classify the properties of concurrent programs.

2.5 A Proof Method for Partial Correctness

2.5.1 Definition plus Example

The proof method presented here for establishing partial correctness is called the *inductive assertion method* [Flo67].

Given a program $P = (L, T, s, t)$, we define the following concepts:

- An *assertion network for P* is a function Q which associates to each location $l \in L$ a predicate Q_l, sometimes expressed by $Q(l)$.
- Given an assertion network Q for P and a transition $\pi = (l, a, l')$, with $a = c \rightarrow f$, define the *verification condition* V_π along π by

$$V_\pi \stackrel{\text{def}}{=} Q_l \wedge c \rightarrow Q_{l'} \circ f.$$

The operation $\circ$ denotes functional composition, that is, $f \circ g$ denotes the function resulting from applying f after g. We use the binding convention that the operator $\circ$ binds stronger than the boolean operators, and that $\wedge$ has priority over $\rightarrow$. For later use we define $V(P, Q)$ as *the set of verification conditions associated by Q with P:*

$$V(P, Q) \stackrel{\text{def}}{=} \{Q_l \wedge c \rightarrow Q_{l'} \circ f | (l, c \rightarrow f, l') \in T\}.$$

- An assertion network for P is said to be *inductive* if all verification conditions in $V(P, Q)$ are valid.
- An assertion network Q for P is said to be an *invariant network* if for every computation $\langle l_0; \sigma_0 \rangle \longrightarrow \langle l_1; \sigma_1 \rangle \longrightarrow \ldots$ of P with $l_0 = s$ and $\models Q_s(\sigma_0)$ we have that $\models Q_{l_i}(\sigma_i)$.
- An inductive assertion network Q is called *consistent* or *correct* w.r.t. $\langle \varphi, \psi \rangle$ if the additional verification conditions $\models \varphi \to Q_s$ and $\models Q_t \to \psi$ hold.

In many of the examples in this book we use as a particular convention that the set of labels L is enumerated in order to facilitate the definition of assertion networks by associating label l_i with predicate Q_i. In this set up, $l_0 = s$ and the label with the highest index l_n stands for exit node t.

Example 2.9 To illustrate these concepts let us consider Figure 2.3 showing the program *Introot* for computing the integer square root of a nonnegative integer input y_1, and assigning it to y_2, where l_0 represents s, and l_3 represents t.

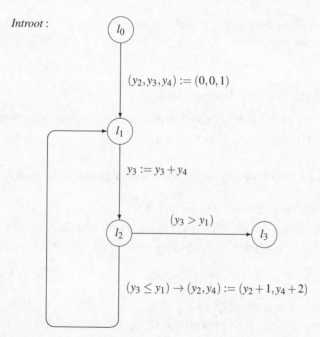

Fig. 2.3. The program *Introot* for finding the integer root of y_1 and outputting the value of this root in y_2.

Assume the assertion network Q associates the predicates Q_0, Q_1, Q_2, Q_3

with the locations l_0, l_1, l_2, l_3, respectively. Corresponding to the four transitions

$$\pi_1 : l_0 \to l_1$$
$$\pi_2 : l_1 \to l_2$$
$$\pi_3 : l_2 \to l_1$$
$$\pi_4 : l_2 \to l_3$$

there are four verification conditions to be checked. Consider first π_1. Its verification condition is given by:

$$V_{\pi_1} : \quad Q_0(y_1, y_2, y_3, y_4) \to Q_1(y_1, 0, 0, 1).$$

Analogously, the verification conditions for the other transitions are derived:

$$V_{\pi_2} : \quad Q_1(y_1, y_2, y_3, y_4) \to Q_2(y_1, y_2, y_3 + y_4, y_4)$$
$$V_{\pi_3} : \quad Q_2(y_1, y_2, y_3, y_4) \wedge (y_3 \leq y_1) \to Q_1(y_1, y_2 + 1, y_3, y_4 + 2)$$
$$V_{\pi_4} : \quad Q_2(y_1, y_2, y_3, y_4) \wedge (y_3 > y_1) \to Q_3(y_1, y_2, y_3, y_4). \qquad \square$$

Next we formulate Floyd's inductive assertion method for proving transition diagrams partially correct.

2.5.2 Floyd's Inductive Assertion Method

To prove $\models \{\varphi\} \, P \, \{\psi\}$, i.e., that a transition system P is partially correct w.r.t. a given specification $< \varphi, \psi >$, we use:

Definition 2.10 (Floyd's inductive assertion method)

  (i) Give an assertion network Q for P.

  (ii) Prove that this assertion network is inductive, that is, for each transition (l, a, l') of P prove validity of its associated verification condition

$$Q_l \wedge c \to Q_{l'} \circ f,$$

  assuming that $a = c \to f$.

  (iii) Prove that Q is consistent with $\langle \varphi, \psi \rangle$, i.e., that the additional verification conditions $\models \varphi \to Q_s$ and $\models Q_t \to \psi$ are valid. $\qquad \square$

Example 2.11 (Continuation of Example 2.9) Consider the program *Introot* for integer root finding. We prove $\models \{y_1 \geq 0\}$ *Introot* $\{y_2^2 \leq y_1 < (y_2 + 1)^2\}$

using Floyd's method. Take the assertion network defined by:

$$Q_0(\bar{y}) \overset{\text{def}}{=} y_1 \geq 0$$
$$Q_1(\bar{y}) \overset{\text{def}}{=} (y_2^2 \leq y_1) \wedge (y_3 = y_2^2) \wedge (y_4 = 2 * y_2 + 1)$$
$$Q_2(\bar{y}) \overset{\text{def}}{=} (y_2^2 \leq y_1) \wedge (y_3 = (y_2 + 1)^2) \wedge (y_4 = 2 * y_2 + 1)$$
$$Q_3(\bar{y}) \overset{\text{def}}{=} y_2^2 \leq y_1 < (y_2 + 1)^2.$$

We first show that this network is inductive.

Substituting the predicates Q_0 and Q_1 into V_{π_1} we must prove its validity:

$$\models (y_1 \geq 0) \to (0 \leq y_1) \wedge (0 = 0) \wedge (1 = 0 + 1)$$

is trivially valid.

Similarly for V_{π_2}:

$$\models (y_2^2 \leq y_1) \wedge (y_3 = y_2^2) \wedge (y_4 = 2 * y_2 + 1) \to$$
$$(y_2^2 \leq y_1) \wedge (y_3 + y_4 = (y_2 + 1)^2) \wedge (y_4 = 2 * y_2 + 1).$$

Notice that $y_2^2 \leq y_1$ and $y_4 = 2 * y_2 + 1$ appear both in the antecedent and the consequent. Hence we show:

$$\models (y_3 = y_2^2) \wedge (y_4 = 2 * y_2 + 1) \to (y_3 + y_4 = (y_2 + 1)^2).$$

Substituting y_2^2 for y_3 and $2 * y_2 + 1$ for y_4 in the consequent we obtain

$$y_2^2 + 2 * y_2 + 1 = (y_2 + 1)^2,$$

which is obviously correct.

Next consider the validity of V_{π_3}:

$$\models (y_2^2 \leq y_1) \wedge (y_3 = (y_2 + 1)^2) \wedge (y_4 = 2 * y_2 + 1) \wedge (y_3 \leq y_1) \to$$
$$((y_2 + 1)^2 \leq y_1) \wedge (y_3 = (y_2 + 1)^2) \wedge (y_4 + 2 = 2 * (y_2 + 1) + 1).$$

One has that $((y_2 + 1)^2 \leq y_1)$ in the consequent follows from $y_3 = (y_2 + 1)^2$ and $y_3 \leq y_1$ in the antecedent, and hence this is a valid statement.

Finally, consider the validity of V_{π_4}:

$$\models (y_2^2 \leq y_1) \wedge (y_3 = (y_2 + 1)^2) \wedge (y_4 = 2 * y_2 + 1) \wedge (y_3 > y_1) \to$$
$$(y_2^2 \leq y_1 < (y_2 + 1)^2).$$

The first conjunct of the consequent is $y_2^2 \leq y_1$ which already appears in the antecedent. The second conjunct $y_1 < (y_2 + 1)^2$ is a consequence of $y_3 = (y_2 + 1)^2$ and $y_3 > y_1$ – both appearing in the antecedent.

This establishes that Q_0, Q_1, Q_2, Q_3 as defined above constitute an inductive assertion network and hence by Lemma 2.13 below are also *invariant assertions* (forming an invariant network). Thus, whenever an execution which started with $y_1 \geq 0$ reaches the point l_2 in the program,

$$Q_2 \stackrel{\text{def}}{=} (y_2^2 \leq y_1) \wedge (y_3 = (y_2 + 1)^2) \wedge (y_4 = 2 * y_2 + 1)$$

must be true invariantly of the current values of the program variables. And, if we ever reach l_3, we are assured by Q_3 that y_1 lies between y_2^2 and $(y_2 + 1)^2$ or equals y_2^2, in other words, y_2 is the best integer approximation from below to the square root of y_1, i.e., $y_2 = \lfloor \sqrt{y_1} \rfloor$. In order to prove $\models \{y_1 \geq 0\} Introot \{y_2^2 \leq y_1 < (y_2 + 1)^2\}$ we must additionally prove $\models y_1 \geq 0 \rightarrow Q_0$ and $\models Q_3 \rightarrow y_2^2 \leq y_1 < (y_2 + 1)^2$, which are in this case obviously true.   □

In general, if a proof method is presented to establish properties of systems, then there are two basic questions which have to be considered.

- Is the proof method *sound*, that is, does *every* property which is proved using the method always hold? That is, is it a *valid* property?
- Is the method *complete*, that is, is it adequate for proving *any* valid property of the system?

We shall prove in the following sections that Floyd's inductive assertion method for sequential programming is sound and that it is complete in a restricted sense (since by Gödel's theorem no proof system for establishing validity of verification conditions exists).

2.6 Soundness

First we prove soundness of the inductive assertion method, i.e.,

Theorem 2.12 (Soundness of the inductive assertion method)
Let $P = (L, T, s, t)$. If Q is an inductive assertion network for P, $\models \varphi \rightarrow Q_s$, and $\models Q_t \rightarrow \psi$, then P is partially correct w.r.t. $< \varphi, \psi >$, i.e., $\models \{\varphi\}\ P\ \{\psi\}$ holds.

The proof of this theorem follows from Lemmas 2.13 and 2.14.

Lemma 2.13 Let $P = (L, T, s, t)$. If Q is an inductive assertion network for P then this assertion network is invariant for P.

Proof Consider an execution sequence $\langle l_0; \sigma_0 \rangle \longrightarrow \langle l_1; \sigma_1 \rangle \longrightarrow \ldots$ of P, with $l_0 = s$ and $\models Q_s(\sigma_0)$. From the definition of execution sequence there exists a sequence of instructions $c_0 \rightarrow f_0, c_1 \rightarrow f_1, \ldots$ such that for every $j \geq 0$, $(l_j, c_j \rightarrow f_j, l_{j+1}) \in T$, $c_j(\sigma_j) = tt$, and $\sigma_{j+1} = f_j(\sigma_j)$. We prove by induction on j that $Q_j(\sigma_j) = tt$, where Q_j denotes the predicate associated with location l_j. The case that $j = 0$ follows immediately from $\models Q_s(\sigma_0)$. Next we assume that we already have $Q_j(\sigma_j) = tt$. Let $\pi_{j+1} \overset{\text{def}}{=} (l_j, c_j \rightarrow f_j, l_{j+1})$. Since the network is inductive, we know that the validity of $V_{\pi_{j+1}}$ holds for σ_j. Thus we have that

$$\models (Q_j \wedge c_j \rightarrow (Q_{j+1} \circ f_j))(\sigma_j),$$

by our induction hypothesis $Q_j(\sigma_j) = tt$. Since the computation starting with σ_j at l_j did follow the transition π_{j+1}, the necessary condition for the existence of a π_{j+1} transition, c_j, must certainly hold. Thus we conclude that $(Q_{j+1} \circ f_j)(\sigma_j)$ must also hold. On the other hand, σ_{j+1} is the state obtained from σ_j by the transition π_{j+1} so that $\sigma_{j+1} = f_j(\sigma_j)$. Consequently it follows that $Q_{j+1}(\sigma_{j+1}) = tt$. $\qquad\square$

Lemma 2.14 follows easily from the definitions.

Lemma 2.14 Let $P = (L, T, s, t)$. If Q is an invariant network for P, and $\models \varphi \rightarrow Q_s$ and $\models Q_t \rightarrow \psi$ hold, then P is partially correct w.r.t. $< \varphi, \psi >$, i.e., $\models \{\varphi\} P \{\psi\}$ holds. $\qquad\square$

Let us step back for an overview of the advantages offered by the inductive assertion method. At first glance it seems that we have complicated matters. Starting with the need to prove that all φ-computations satisfy ψ when they reach the exit location t, we have complicated the task by, e.g., also requiring a proof that when such computations reach any other location l, they must satisfy Q_l. On the other hand, in general the $\varphi - \psi$ relationship has to be established for an *infinite* number of computations including a computation that goes exactly once around some loop, one that goes twice around that loop, etc. We have to consider more assertions to be verified, but over a *finite* number of transitions.

It is important to observe that the converse of Lemma 2.13 does not generally hold. A network may be invariant without being inductive. This is worked out in Exercise 2.10.

2.7 Semantic Completeness of the Inductive Assertion Method

Next we consider completeness of the inductive assertion method, i.e., we prove:

Theorem 2.15 (Semantic completeness)

Let $P = (L, T, s, t)$. If P is partially correct w.r.t. $< \varphi, \psi >$ then there exists an inductive assertion network Q for P s.t. $\models \varphi \rightarrow Q_s$ and $\models Q_t \rightarrow \psi$ hold. Moreover, for any invariant assertion network Ψ for P with $\models \varphi \rightarrow \Psi_s$ one has $\models Q_l \rightarrow \Psi_l$ for all $l \in L$.

Proof Assume P is partially correct w.r.t. $< \varphi, \psi >$. Then apply the inductive assertion method as follows:

- Let Q be the following assertion network for P: For each $l \in L$, we define a predicate Q_l such that for all $\sigma \in \Sigma$, $\models Q_l(\sigma)$ *iff there exists a state* σ' *s.t.* $\models \varphi(\sigma')$ *and* $\langle s; \sigma' \rangle \longrightarrow^* \langle l; \sigma \rangle$. Here $\longrightarrow^*$ denotes the reflexive and transitive closure of the transition relation $\longrightarrow$ between configurations. By the definition of invariance of a network we immediately obtain for each invariant assertion network Ψ for P that if $\models \varphi \rightarrow \Psi_s$ holds, then $\models Q_l \rightarrow \Psi_l$ holds, for each $l \in L$.

- We show that Q as defined above is an inductive assertion network. Consider a transition $\pi = (l, a, l')$, with $a = c \rightarrow f$. We have to prove $\models Q_l \wedge c \rightarrow Q_{l'} \circ f$. Let σ be a state such that $\models Q_l(\sigma)$ and $\models c(\sigma)$. From $\models Q_l(\sigma)$ we obtain that $\langle s; \sigma' \rangle \longrightarrow^* \langle l; \sigma \rangle$, for some initial state σ' which satisfies φ. Since $\models c(\sigma)$ there exists a computation step $\langle l; \sigma \rangle \longrightarrow \langle l'; f(\sigma) \rangle$. So we have $\langle s; \sigma' \rangle \longrightarrow^* \langle l'; f(\sigma) \rangle$, and thus by definition of $Q_{l'}$ we conclude $\models Q_{l'}(f(\sigma))$.

- We prove $\models \varphi \rightarrow Q_s$ and $\models Q_t \rightarrow \psi$.

  – Consider σ s.t. $\models \varphi(\sigma)$ holds. Since $\langle s; \sigma \rangle \longrightarrow^* \langle s; \sigma \rangle$, it follows immediately from the definition of Q_s that $\models Q_s(\sigma)$ holds.

  – Let σ be such that $\models Q_t(\sigma)$. From the definition of Q_t it then follows that $\sigma \in \mathcal{M}[\![P]\!](\sigma')$, for some σ' such that $\models \varphi(\sigma')$. Since P is partially correct w.r.t. $< \varphi, \psi >$ this leads to $\models \psi(\sigma)$. $\square$

In the above proof the so-called *reachability* predicates Q_l are characterised mathematically, and not by means of assertions in, e.g., first-order predicate logic. When formalising the inductive assertion method within some logical system such as Hoare logic in Chapter 9 – a necessary prerequisite for machine-checked proofs – it is mandatory to express Q_l by such an assertion. This is done by encoding computations within the standard model of the natural numbers using a technique called *Gödel encoding* [Göd31], which is the subject of Chapter 5. This explains why we are especially interested in transition diagrams over an underlying data domain which contains this standard model (or, alternatively, in proof methods in which all valid properties in this standard model have been added as axioms). Unfortunately, there exists no complete formal system for proving the verification conditions for such diagrams (this is explained below), and consequently there is no hope of obtaining a complete formal system for proving the correctness of such diagrams. (By a proof in a formal proof system we understand a finite sequence of formulae each of which is either an axiom of that system or obtained by applications of one of its inference rules to formulae which occur earlier in that sequence.)

These considerations lead to the introduction of new, restricted, notions of completeness which can be achieved, and which are discussed below.

- In the above proof we have established *semantic completeness*, i.e., we have proved the existence of an assertion network Q such that all the associated verification conditions, plus $\models \varphi \to Q_s$ and $\models Q_t \to \psi$ hold. We did not express those predicates as assertions from first-order predicate logic. Rather, we gave a semantical (or extensional) description of their meaning. In Chapter 5 we shall demonstrate that the predicates Q_l defined in the completeness proof can be expressed as first-order assertions over the natural numbers, by encoding finite computation sequences into natural numbers. The resulting assertions are called φ-*minimal* (or φ-*reachable*) because by Theorem 2.15 and Lemma 2.13 they are also the *strongest possible* predicates – i.e., with the *smallest* denotations – which form an inductive assertion network Ψ for which $\models \varphi \to \Psi_s$ and $\models \Psi_t \to \psi$ hold. The predicate associated with a location l is also called the *strongest l-condition* of P w.r.t. the precondition φ, with notation $SP_l(\varphi, P)$. As a particular convention $SP_t(\varphi, P)$ is also called the *strongest postcondition* of P w.r.t φ, which is usually written as $SP(\varphi, P)$. This notion figures frequently in completeness proofs [dB80, Dij76, Apt81a].

- It is important to observe that Theorem 2.15 does not claim that one can *prove* the verification conditions for P w.r.t. Q and prove $\models \varphi \to Q_s$ and $\models Q_t \to \psi$ within a formal proof system, e.g., using the axioms and rules for first-order predicate logic over the natural numbers. It merely states that these verification conditions and these implications are *valid*. By Gödel's incompleteness result [Göd31], no complete proof system exists for proving these verification conditions over the natural numbers. This can be understood as follows.

Consider the trivial program over the natural numbers in Figure 2.4 with the specification $< true, \psi >$. This program is partially correct w.r.t. $< true, \psi >$ iff $\models \psi$ holds. The only verification condition is $true \to \psi$, which is equivalent to ψ. Completeness in this case would require that if ψ is valid, i.e., $\models \psi$ holds, then it is provable in some deductive system. However,

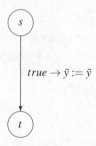

Fig. 2.4. A trivial program.

in view of Gödel's incompleteness theorem, no deductive system can exist which ensures provability of every valid statement over the natural numbers.

Thus, if we choose the natural numbers (or any other domain which is at least as powerful as Peano arithmetic) as the domain, we have to give up any hope of being able to present a deductive formalism in which all possible verification conditions can be proven, and must be satisfied with the requirement that the verification conditions are valid statements.

Now, the following question arises: Why do we not choose a less powerful domain than Peano arithmetic, say, Presburger arithmetic?

The point is that in order to be able to express the strongest l-conditions, we need to encode finite sequences of states over the natural numbers into natural numbers. This is usually done by means of Gödel encoding. In our case, however, we have the additional difficulty that this encoding has to be carried out within the fixed formal language. It is a well-known fact that one needs at least Peano arithmetic in order to enable Gödel encoding.

- As stated above, in Chapter 5 we construct for every Q_l a corresponding assertion from first-order predicate logic which has the same meaning as Q_l. Having obtained such assertions, we have established another kind of completeness, called *relative* completeness. Relative completeness of a proof method implies that there exist proofs for every valid correctness statement, provided all valid assertions *over the underlying data domain* (or interpretation), *which is assumed to contain the standard model of the natural numbers*, are assumed as axioms.

This implies in the case of Theorem 2.15 that we may assume that every (valid) verification condition plus the (valid) implications $\varphi \to Q_0$ and $Q_t \to \psi$ can be used as axioms!

What then is the difference between relative completeness and semantic completeness? Usually, semantic completeness applies to a rule, or a verification algorithm such as Floyd's method, and establishes that certain auxiliary quantities required for applying that rule – here: a suitable induction assertion network – indeed exist.

Relative completeness applies to formal systems equipped with a syntactically defined notion of well-formed formulae (wff), a formally defined notion of interpretation and truth of wffs, plus a proof system intended to establish the truthfulness of its wffs. And it applies precisely when such a proof system is complete in the sense that it does *reduce* the properties at hand, here (valid) *correctness statements*, to the *validity of certain assertions over the underlying interpretation*, and this underlying interpretation is assumed to contain the natural numbers. This is because relative complete proof systems are successful in performing this reduction.

- But which notion of completeness does one apply when the underlying interpretation does not contain the natural numbers? David Harel [Har79] introduced the notion of *arithmetical completeness* to cover that case, in which all valid properties of the natural numbers are added as axioms, regardless of whether these properties belong to the underlying interpretation of a program or not.

These notions of completeness *separate* the issue of the dynamic nature of program behaviour due to assignments and control flow, *which is the main concern of the computer scientist,* from the task of finding proper formalisation for important interpretations, *which has been the occupation of mathematical logicians* for some time. They are called relative or arithmetical completeness, since it is assumed that if somebody will provide the necessary information about the interpretation, i.e., the set of all true properties, *including those of the natural numbers,* then *relative to this knowledge* we can conduct our proof.

One should not overemphasise the importance of the completeness theorem, since, assuming the result of Chapter 5 is at our disposal, we have only established relative (or arithmetical) completeness. Its true significance may be interpreted as saying that if we have failed to prove the partial correctness of a program using the inductive assertion method, it is not because the method is inadequate but because either we have not been clever enough in devising the appropriate assertions, or the program is not really partially correct.

In particular, we would like to stress that the completeness theorem gives no clue about choosing appropriate assertion networks. Even though it does appear to define an invariant network, this network is proved to be consistent with $< \varphi, \psi >$ on the basis of the knowledge that P is partially correct with respect to $< \varphi, \psi >$. Without this knowledge we have to prove $\models Q_l \rightarrow \psi$, which is as hard as proving partial correctness.

2.8 Proving Convergence

A program is called convergent, if it does not have any infinite computations, that is, it either terminates or becomes deadlocked, but will never go on forever. Of course, in general we can only expect a program to converge when started from certain initial states. Let φ be a precondition. We define a program to be φ-convergent, if it does not admit infinite φ-computations. In this section, we look at methods for proving that a program is convergent.

The importance of this notion is that in order to prove a program to be totally correct, in the present framework one has to prove that it is both partially correct and convergent and has no failing computations, i.e., it is successful.[3]

2.8.1 Wellfounded Sets

The basic idea for proving convergence is to show that *there is a bound on the remaining computation steps from any state that the program reaches*. This notion of bound is formalised by the concept of *wellfounded* set in mathematics.

Let W be a set and $\prec$ a binary relation on $W \times W$. We say $\prec$ is an ordering if it is:

   (i) *Irreflexive,* i.e., $a \not\prec a$ for any $a \in W$,
  (ii) *Asymmetric,* i.e., $a \prec b$ implies $b \not\prec a$ for any $a, b \in W$,
 (iii) *Transitive,* i.e., $a \prec b$ and $b \prec c$ implies that $a \prec c$ for any $a, b, c \in W$.

Note that conditions (i) and (iii) imply condition (ii) (which in its turn implies condition (i)). Such an ordering can be partial in the sense that there may exist pairs of unrelated elements in the set. The partially ordered set $(W, \prec)$ is called *wellfounded* if there exists no infinitely descending sequence in $(W, \prec)$:

$$\ldots \prec w_2 \prec w_1 \prec w_0, \text{ with } w_i \in W.$$

Such a chain will also be written as $w_0 \succ w_1 \succ w_2 \succ \ldots$. One of the simplest wellfounded sets is the set of nonnegative integers $N = \{0, 1, 2, \ldots\}$, with the ordering of the "less than" relation '$<$'. As we shall see, we (only) use this set in the completeness proof in this chapter. Hence, in principle, it suffices to use nonnegative integers to prove that the kind of program we study here is convergent. Nevertheless, forcing the use of nonnegative integers in practice often leads to complicated assertions and ranking functions, a notion introduced later. Therefore, and for proving convergence of concurrent programs in

---

[3] When considering frameworks in which runtime errors also occur, one has to prove additionally the absence of runtime errors, as discussed in Section 2.9.

later chapters, other sorts of wellfounded sets are used, too. One such example is the product of two (simpler) wellfounded sets with the lexicographical order. More precisely, let $(W_1, \prec_1)$ and $(W_2, \prec_2)$ be two wellfounded sets, then the partially ordered set $(W, \prec)$ defined by

$$W \overset{\text{def}}{=} W_1 \times W_2 \text{ and}$$
$$(m_1, n_1) \prec (m_2, n_2) \overset{\text{def}}{=} (m_1 \prec_1 m_2) \vee ((m_1 = m_2) \wedge (n_1 \prec_2 n_2)),$$

is also wellfounded. The proof is left as an exercise. This construction can be easily extended to the product of an arbitrary (finite) number of wellfounded sets. This associated partial order is called *lexicographical ordering*.

2.8.2 A Proof Method for Convergence

In this section we give a proof method for establishing convergence of a program. This method builds directly on the one for partial correctness developed in the previous sections.

Definition 2.16 (Floyd's wellfoundedness method) Given a transition diagram $P = (L, T, s, t)$, in order to verify that it is φ-convergent with respect to a precondition φ we use Floyd's *wellfoundedness* method for proving convergence (i.e., either termination or deadlock) of sequential programs as formulated below:

(i) Find an assertion network Q, show that it is inductive, and that $\models \varphi \rightarrow Q_s$ holds.

(ii) Choose a wellfounded set $(W, \prec)$ and a network $\rho \overset{\text{def}}{=} \{\rho_l \mid l \in L\}$ of *partially* defined *ranking functions* $\rho_l : \Sigma \rightarrow W$ for every $l \in L$, and prove points (iii) and (iv) below:

(iii) Q_l implies that ρ_l *is defined*, i.e., for every σ,

$$\models Q_l(\sigma) \text{ implies } \rho_l(\sigma) \in W.$$

(iv) Every transition $l \overset{a}{\rightarrow} l'$, with $a = c \rightarrow f$, *decreases* the ranking function, i.e.,

$$\models Q_l \wedge c \rightarrow \rho_l \succ (\rho_{l'} \circ f).$$

Here $\rho_l \succ (\rho_{l'} \circ f)$ denotes the predicate defined by

$$(\rho_l \succ (\rho_{l'} \circ f))(\sigma) \overset{\text{def}}{=} tt \text{ iff } \rho_l(\sigma) \succ \rho_{l'}(f(\sigma)). \qquad \square$$

Example 2.17 As a first step, consider proving convergence of the following simple program in Figure 2.5 with respect to the trivial precondition *true*. To make it a little more interesting, we assume that x belongs to the set of real numbers, which is not wellfounded w.r.t. the "less than" relation '$<$'.

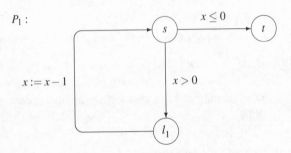

Fig. 2.5. A terminating program over the real numbers.

The assertion network is chosen as:

$$Q_s(x) \stackrel{\text{def}}{=} true$$
$$Q_1(x) \stackrel{\text{def}}{=} x > 0$$
$$Q_t(x) \stackrel{\text{def}}{=} true.$$

Next we consider the ranking function network. We have to map real numbers to a wellfounded set. Let $nni(x)$ be the function which returns the next nonnegative integer for a real number x (so for $-\sqrt{2}$ and π, it returns 0 and 4, respectively). The ranking function network defined over the lexicographical ordering $N \times N$ of nonnegative integers N is as follows:

$$\rho_s(x) \stackrel{\text{def}}{=} (nni(x), 1)$$
$$\rho_1(x) \stackrel{\text{def}}{=} (nni(x), 0)$$
$$\rho_t(x) \stackrel{\text{def}}{=} (0, 0).$$

Checking validity of the verification conditions is trivial; the ranking functions are always defined, and decrease along each transition, as shown below:

$\pi_1 : s \to l_1,$ the first component of the ranking function does not increase, whereas the second decreases by one,

$\pi_2 : l_1 \to s,$ the first component of the ranking function decreases at least by one when $x > 0$, and

$\pi_3 : s \to t,$ the first component of the ranking function does not increase, whereas the second decreases by one.   □

Example 2.18 Consider again the integer root-finding program from Examples 2.9 and 2.11. Now we want to show that it is convergent with respect to the precondition $\varphi \stackrel{\text{def}}{=} y_1 \geq 0$. We take the same assertion network as before, namely,

$$Q_0(\bar{y}) \stackrel{\text{def}}{=} y_1 \geq 0$$
$$Q_1(\bar{y}) \stackrel{\text{def}}{=} (y_2^2 \leq y_1) \wedge (y_3 = y_2^2) \wedge (y_4 = 2 * y_2 + 1)$$
$$Q_2(\bar{y}) \stackrel{\text{def}}{=} (y_2^2 \leq y_1) \wedge (y_3 = (y_2 + 1)^2) \wedge (y_4 = 2 * y_2 + 1)$$
$$Q_3(\bar{y}) \stackrel{\text{def}}{=} y_2^2 \leq y_1 < (y_2 + 1)^2.$$

We already proved in Example 2.11 that it is inductive. The initial condition $\models \varphi \rightarrow Q_0$ holds trivially. Next we choose as wellfounded set the lexicographically ordered product $N \times N \times N$ over the set of nonnegative integers N, and define the ranking functions as follows:

$$\rho_0(\bar{y}) \stackrel{\text{def}}{=} (y_1 + 1, 0, 0)$$
$$\rho_1(\bar{y}) \stackrel{\text{def}}{=} (y_1 - y_3, y_1 - y_2, 2)$$
$$\rho_2(\bar{y}) \stackrel{\text{def}}{=} (max(y_1 - y_3, 0), y_1 - y_2, 1)$$
$$\rho_3(\bar{y}) \stackrel{\text{def}}{=} (0, 0, 0).$$

We now show that Q_i implies that ρ_i is defined. The only problematic cases are ρ_1 and ρ_2, because the expressions $y_1 - y_3$ and $y_1 - y_2$ may not be defined over the set of nonnegative integers. First, look at ρ_1. We immediately have $y_1 \geq y_2^2 = y_3$ from Q_1. It is also obvious that $y_1 \geq y_2$ follows from $y_1 \geq y_2^2$. Secondly, consider ρ_2. From Q_2, it follows that $y_1 \geq y_2$ holds for the same reason.

What remains to be proved is that the ranking functions decrease along every transition. This is proved as follows:

$\pi_1 : l_0 \rightarrow l_1$,   the first component of the ranking function decreases at least by one,

$\pi_2 : l_1 \rightarrow l_2$,   the first and second components of the ranking function do not increase, whereas the third decreases by one,

$\pi_3 : l_2 \rightarrow l_1$,   the first component of the ranking function does not increase, whereas the second decreases by one,

$\pi_4 : l_2 \rightarrow l_3$,   the first and second components of the ranking function do not increase, whereas the third decreases by one. $\square$

2.8.3 Soundness and Semantic Completeness

Next we prove soundness and semantic completeness of the method.

Theorem 2.19 (Soundness)

Let $P = (L, T, s, t)$. If Q is an inductive assertion network for P, ρ is a ranking function network over the wellfounded set $(W, \prec)$ satisfying points (iii) and (iv) of Definition 2.16, and $\models \varphi \rightarrow Q_s$, then P is φ-convergent.

Proof Proving soundness is straightforward. Just consider an arbitrary φ-computation

$$\eta : \langle l_0; \sigma_0 \rangle \longrightarrow \langle l_1; \sigma_1 \rangle \longrightarrow \dots,$$

with $l_0 = s$, then inductiveness of Q implies that Q is invariant, and hence $\models \varphi \rightarrow Q_s$ implies, using conditions (iii) and (iv) of Definition 2.16, that $\rho_{l_0}(\sigma_0), \rho_{l_1}(\sigma_1), \dots$ are all defined. Furthermore, the chain

$$\rho_{l_0}(\sigma_0) \succ \rho_{l_1}(\sigma_1) \succ \dots$$

is decreasing. Due to the wellfoundedness of W, the above chain is finite, and, hence, η is also finite. $\square$

The completeness proof is more complicated. Define a tree to be of *finite degree* if each of its nodes has no more than a finite number of direct descendant nodes (children). First, we prove the following lemma due to König [Kön32].

Lemma 2.20 (König's lemma) An infinite tree of finite degree must have an infinite path.

Proof Let n_0 be the root of an infinite tree T of finite degree. Let the descendants of n_0 be $n_1, \dots, n_m$. Each node $n_i, i = 1, \dots, m$ is the root of a subtree T_i. Since the number of nodes in the complete tree is infinite and there are finitely many T_i's, at least one of them must contain an infinite number of nodes. Let n_{i_1} be the root of a subtree T_{i_1} which is infinite. We now repeat the argument with respect to n_{i_1} and its immediate descendants $n'_1, \dots, n'_t$. At least one of them must be the root of an infinite tree. Let us denote it by n_{i_2}. Repeating the argument we trace in the tree T a path

$$n_0, n_{i_1}, n_{i_2}, \dots$$

of nodes each of which is the root of an infinite tree. The process will never terminate since we are continuously examining roots of infinite subtrees. Consequently the traced path is an infinite path in T. $\square$

An immediate corollary of König's lemma is that *a tree of finite degree which has no infinite paths must be finite*. In other words, in such a case there exists a constant such that all paths in the tree are not longer than that constant. We need this result to define the ranking functions.

Theorem 2.21 (Semantic completeness)
If P is φ-convergent, then there exist assertion and ranking-function networks satisfying the verification conditions for proving convergence.

Proof Let $P = (L, T, s, t)$. We choose the same assertion network Q as in the semantic completeness proof of the partial correctness method, namely, the one consisting of semantic φ-minimal predicates. By Theorem 2.15, it is inductive, and $\models \varphi \to Q_s$ holds.

As wellfounded set we choose $(N, <)$, and define the ranking functions $\rho_l : \Sigma \to W$ as

$$\rho_l(\sigma) \stackrel{\text{def}}{=} \text{the length of the longest computation path starting at } l \text{ in state } \sigma.$$

The two extra conditions, namely, that the minimal predicate Q_l implies that the ranking function ρ_l is defined, and that the ranking functions decrease along each transition, remain to be shown.

Obviously, if there exists an infinite computation starting at l with state σ then $\rho_l(\sigma)$ is undefined. König's lemma ensures that in the other case, namely, when there is no infinite computation starting at l with σ, $\rho_l(\sigma)$ is indeed defined. To see this, *we construct the computation tree starting from l with σ.* The nodes of the tree are the configurations in the computation, and one node is an immediate descendant of another if and only if it is a configuration which is the result of one transition from the latter. To see why this construction leads to a tree, note that there is always at least one node, namely, the root $\langle l; \sigma \rangle$. The degree of this tree is finite, because one configuration can only lead to a finite number of direct descendant (follow-up) configurations in one step. (This follows from the finiteness of T.) By the assumption that there are no infinite computations from $\langle l; \sigma \rangle$, the tree also does not have infinite paths. Therefore, by König's lemma the tree is finite, and, consequently, $\rho_l(\sigma)$ is defined. To establish the first verification condition, we now only need to show that, when the minimal predicate Q_l holds in state σ, there are no infinite computations from $\langle l; \sigma \rangle$. By the definition of Q_l, there exists a partial computation η starting from a state which satisfies φ and reaching l with σ. Clearly, the partial computation η can be continued by any computation η' starting from $\langle l; \sigma \rangle$. Since P is φ-convergent, this implies that any computation from $\langle l; \sigma \rangle$ is also finite.

Establishing the second condition now becomes straightforward, because it is easy to see that by the definition of ρ_l the value of the defined ranking function decreases by at least one along each transition.

We have shown semantic completeness of the method by using the same assertion network as before and constructing a particular ranking-function network, which satisfies the verification conditions (iii) and (iv) of Definition 2.16.

$\square$

The kind of completeness shown here is *semantic* completeness, because we (i) define the ranking functions ρ_l mathematically, by giving an existence proof (and not by expressing them, e.g., using first-order predicate logic), and (ii) prove that the verification conditions for proving convergence are valid mathematically, i.e., we did not prove the implications within some formal system. Formalising these quantities in an assertion language requires at least the expressive power of the μ-calculus [HP72], and therefore goes beyond first-order predicate logic.

We conclude this chapter with an alternative proof method for convergence which is based on a network of ranking functions only.

Definition 2.22 (Wellfoundedness method) To prove φ-convergence of $P = (L,T,s,t)$:

(i) Choose a wellfounded set $(W, \prec)$ and a network $\rho \stackrel{\text{def}}{=} \{\rho_l \,|\, l \in L\}$ of *partially* defined *ranking functions*

$$\rho_l : \Sigma \to W \quad \text{for every } l \in L,$$

and prove points (ii) and (iii) below:

(ii) For every state σ, $\models \varphi(\sigma)$ implies that $\rho_s(\sigma)$ is defined, i.e., $\rho_s(\sigma) \in W$.

(iii) Every transition $l \stackrel{a}{\to} l'$, with $a = c \to f$, *decreases* the ranking function, i.e., $\models c(\sigma)$ and $\rho_l(\sigma) \in W$ implies that $\rho_{l'}(f(\sigma)) \in W$ and $\rho_l(\sigma) \succ \rho_{l'}(f(\sigma))$. $\square$

The proofs of the soundness and completeness of the above method for convergence are left as Exercises 2.18 and 2.19.

2.9 Proving Absence of Runtime Errors

Finally, we extend our notion of transition diagrams (and systems) by allowing them to contain partial state transformations. In particular, we consider the case that state transformations f occurring in instructions $c \to f$, which label an edge of a transition diagram, are partial, such as, e.g., the state transformations associated with $x := 1/0$ and $x := 1/y$. Clearly, executing $x := 1/0$, and

$x := 1/y$ for $y = 0$, is undesirable because this leads to an undefined result, and, therefore, to runtime errors.

Consequently, in addition to the four modalities of program correctness defined in Section 2.4.2, we introduce a fifth one, called *absence of runtime errors*, and discuss two methods to prove this modality for a given program (and given precondition). Observe, that as a consequence of it being possible to model runtime errors in our formalism, total correctness amounts to the *sum* of partial correctness, convergence, success, and absence of runtime errors. That is, in order to prove total correctness of a program P w.r.t. precondition φ and postcondition ψ, one has to prove that P is partially correct w.r.t. precondition φ and postcondition ψ, is φ-convergent, and displays neither deadlocks nor runtime errors when started in φ.

The possibility that a transition is enabled and yet leads to an undefined result generates two different notions of nondeterminism for transition diagrams, *angelic* and *demonic* nondeterminism [Bro86].

In general, the words "angelic" and "demonic" refer to the existence of, respectively, a helper – an angel – and an opponent – a demon, w.r.t. winning a certain game.

The helper aims to find a winning strategy for that game, whereas the opponent tries to systematically sabotage the player in order to make him lose.

In this section, a move of the game consists of prolonging a given finite prefix in the end state of which at least one transition is enabled, by executing some enabled transition. The game is lost when this leads to an undefined result, and won when no more transitions are enabled and, therefore, a maximal sequence has been obtained, i.e., a computation (or execution sequence) in the terminology of Section 2.3.1. Recall that a computation is either terminating (i.e., ends in the exit location), failing (i.e., blocked) or infinite.

Consequently, in every reachable location, the angelic helper tries to select those enabled transitions for execution which are prefixes of such maximal sequences (i.e., computations in the latter sense), whereas the demonic adversary tries to select from the enabled transitions those for execution which lead to undefined results or to prefixes of partial execution sequences in whose end states only enabled transitions leading to undefined results are left.

Angelic nondeterminism is the usual notion of nondeterminism in automata theory.

In contrast, demonic nondeterminism is the appropriate notion in the context of program verification. This can be seen as follows. For example, how does one express that in a nondeterministic program no runtime errors occur? Not by claiming the existence of a computation (in the sense of Section 2.3.1) since that does not preclude the existence of prefixes of computations which lead to runtime errors! For in programming nondeterministic choices are usually resolved by schedulers, and there is no guarantee that such schedulers are angelic. However, one can express absence of runtime errors by requiring the nonexistence of a successful demonic scheduler, or, alternatively, that all demonic schedulers are not successful.

Next we relativise the above account w.r.t. a precondition φ.

Definition 2.23 (Absence of runtime errors) Given a transition diagram P and a precondition φ, whenever no φ-computation of P ever reaches a location in which an enabled transition is undefined, one speaks of *absence of* (or *freedom from*) *runtime errors of P in* φ.   □

We present two methods for proving φ-absence of runtime errors, one direct method obtained by modifying Floyd's inductive assertion method (Definition 2.10), and one implicit method which reduces proofs of absence of runtime errors to proofs of success.

2.9.1 A Direct Method for Proving Absence of Runtime Errors

Obtaining the first method for proving φ-absence of runtime errors is at first sight straightforward. Just modify the second clause of Definition 2.10 of Floyd's method by also proving

$$\models Q_l \wedge c \rightarrow Def(f),$$

where $Def(f)$ denotes a predicate expressing the domain of definition of f, and delete in its third clause the condition $\models Q_l \rightarrow \psi$.

However, how does one evaluate the verification condition $\models false \rightarrow true \circ (x := 1/0)$? Here the difficulty is that $true \circ (x := 1/0)$ denotes a nowhere-defined function.

In general, the possibility of state transformations f being partial functions leads to the occurrence of partially-defined boolean functions, when applying Floyd's method, and this forces one to modify the definitions of the boolean connectives accordingly, because these occur in the formulation of verification conditions.

Since a boolean function $\varphi : \Sigma \rightarrow Bool$, with $Bool \stackrel{\text{def}}{=} \{tt, ff\}$, can now be partial – e.g., consider $true \circ (x := 1/0)$, one distinguishes between three cases: that $\varphi(\sigma) = tt$, $\varphi(\sigma) = ff$ and $\varphi(\sigma)$ is undefined, for $\sigma \in \Sigma$; the latter case we abbreviate by $\varphi(\sigma) = \bot$, with "$\bot$" pronounced as "bottom". That is, instead of dealing with *partial* functions to *Bool*, we model them using *total* functions to $Bool_\perp$, with $Bool_\perp \stackrel{\text{def}}{=} \{tt, ff, \perp\}$, where $\varphi(\sigma) = \perp$ in the total-function view of φ iff $\varphi(\sigma)$ is undefined in the partial-function view of φ.

The meanings of $\neg$, $\rightarrow$, $\wedge$ and $\vee$ in this total-function view are given by:

(i) definition of "$\neg$":

$\neg$	tt	ff	$\perp$
	ff	tt	$\perp$

(ii) definition of "$\rightarrow$":

$\rightarrow$	tt	ff	$\perp$
tt	tt	ff	$\perp$
ff	tt	tt	tt
$\perp$	tt	$\perp$	$\perp$

(iii) definition of "$\wedge$":

$\wedge$	tt	ff	$\perp$
tt	tt	ff	$\perp$
ff	ff	ff	ff
$\perp$	$\perp$	ff	$\perp$

(iv) definition of "$\vee$":

$\vee$	tt	ff	$\perp$
tt	tt	tt	tt
ff	tt	ff	$\perp$
$\perp$	tt	$\perp$	$\perp$

The motivation for these definitions is twofold:

(i) It defines $tt \vee \perp = \perp \vee tt = tt$. When generalised to existential quantifiers this lets such reasonable predicates as $\exists x(1/x = 1)$ denote tt.

(ii) By ordering $Bool_\perp$ as follows: $\perp \sqsubseteq tt$, $\perp \sqsubseteq ff$, $Bool_\perp$ becomes a so-called *complete partial order* (cpo). In this structure we want $\wedge$, $\vee$ and $\rightarrow$ to denote monotone functions in their arguments, where f is *monotone* if:

$$a \sqsubseteq b \Rightarrow f(a) \sqsubseteq f(b).$$

It can be checked that requirements (i) and (ii) above determine the meanings of these propositional connectives uniquely, and that they coincide with the ones given above them. Consult, e.g., [dRE98, Chapter 8], for more details on this topic.

Next we face the choice between partial and total inductive assertions. Here we choose them to be total $\{tt, ff\}$-valued functions φ, $\varphi : \Sigma \rightarrow Bool$. That is, the predicates Q_l used for reasoning about transition diagrams in the inductive assertion approach are *total $\{tt, ff\}$-valued boolean functions,* even in the presence of runtime errors during the execution of transition diagrams. Observe that this is consistent with the five modalities of program correctness which we want to prove. For example, partial correctness means that only in the case of termination has some predicate to hold; and, since in that case the resulting state is well-defined, that predicate can be chosen to be total and $\{tt,ff\}$-valued. Or, in the case of success, one has to prove absence of blocking when the execution is started in a given precondition, which must, therefore, yield a well-defined starting state, and, hence, can be chosen to be total and $\{tt,ff\}$-valued. Similar arguments apply to the other modalities. Again, more information about this subject can be found in, e.g., Chapter 8 of [dRE98].

Given the formal framework as defined above, we modify Definition 2.10 of Floyd's inductive assertion network as follows in order to obtain a method of proving absence of runtime errors in φ of transition diagrams P.

Definition 2.24 (Floyd's inductive assertion method including absence of runtime errors)

  (i)   Consider a total $\{tt,ff\}$-valued boolean function φ.
 (ii)   Choose the predicates Q_l in its first clause to be total and $\{tt,ff\}$-valued.
(iii)   Replace its second clause by:
        Prove that Q is inductive *and implies freedom from runtime errors* of P, that is, for each transition (l,a,l') of P, prove the validity of

$$\models Q_l \wedge c \to (Q_{l'} \circ f) \wedge Def(f),$$

        with $Def(f)$ as above, assuming that $a = c \to f$.
(iv)   Prove that Q is consistent w.r.t. precondition φ, i.e., replace its third clause by requiring the proof of $\models \varphi \to Q_s$.   □

This method verifies explicitly whether the applied state transformations in P are well-defined. Consequently, soundness of the method is obvious. Its semantic completeness can be proved using the reachability predicates Q_l from Theorem 2.15 as the assertion network.

2.9.2 An Implicit Method for Proving Absence of Runtime Errors

The second method for establishing absence of runtime errors reduces proving absence of runtime errors to proving success (i.e., absence of blocking or deadlock) of P in φ, i.e., the property that each nonterminal configuration of P, which is reachable from an initial state satisfying φ, always has a well-defined successor.

How to prove the latter is the subject of Exercise 2.12. Notice that both success and absence of runtime errors are notions involving demonic nondeterminism.

This reduction is based on a transformation $T(P)$ of P which satisfies the following property:

> *Whenever P is φ-successful, the following holds:*
> *P is free from runtime errors in* φ $\iff$ *$T(P)$ is φ-successful.*

It follows that one can obtain a proof method for runtime-error freedom by:

(i) transforming P into a transition diagram P' which is by construction free from blocking, i.e., successful, and which displays the same behaviour w.r.t. runtime errors as P, and

(ii) proving that $T(P')$ is φ-successful.

Next we define P' and $T(P)$, using P.

Given a candidate transition diagram P of which one would like to prove runtime-error freedom, transform P to P' by adding to every non-exit location l of P the transition $(l, (\bigwedge_{i=1}^{n} \neg c_i) \to id, t)$, where $c_1, \ldots, c_n$ is the list of guards of transitions starting in l, and t is the exit location of P.

It is easy to see that P' can never block, i.e., is successful in every precondition.

$T(P)$ is obtained from P by executing the following transformation in each of P's locations.

Whenever, for $n > 0$, n transitions labelled $c_1 \to f_1, \ldots, c_n \to f_n$ leave l, replace in each of them guard c_i by

$$c_i \wedge Def(f_i) \wedge \bigwedge_{\substack{j=1,\ldots,n \\ j \neq i}} (c_j \to Def(f_j)),$$

where $Def(f)$ generally denotes a total predicate expressing the domain of definition of f, i.e., $Def(f)(\sigma) = tt$ iff $f(\sigma)$ yields a well-defined result, for $\sigma \in \Sigma$.

Example 2.25

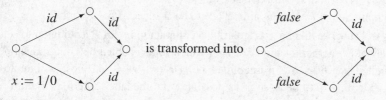

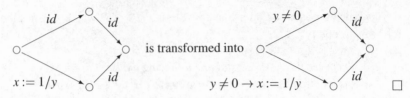

Consequently, in order to prove freedom from runtime errors of P in φ, one should prove that $T(P')$ is successful in φ.

The following lemma remains to be proved.

Lemma 2.26 If P is φ-successful then:

$$P \text{ is free from runtime errors in } \varphi \iff T(P) \text{ is successful in } \varphi.$$

Proof Assume P to be φ-successful.

$\Rightarrow$: Suppose this direction of the implication does not hold, i.e., P is free from runtime errors in φ, whereas $T(P)$ is not φ-successful.

Then there exists a partial φ-computation η of $T(P)$, leading up to state σ, and some internal location l of $T(P)$ which has no successor configuration.

Since by construction of T, whenever $c' \to f$ labels a transition of $T(P)$, the original label of that transition in P is $c \to f$ with c' implying c, η is also a partial φ-computation of P. Since, by assumption, P is both φ-successful and free from runtime errors in φ, η can be prolonged along each enabled transition leaving l, and there is at least one such transition.

But this implies that $\sigma \in Def(f_i)$ and $c_i(\sigma) = tt$, with $c_i \to f_i$ labelling the enabled transitions leaving l in P, for $i = 1, \ldots, m$, i.e.,

$$\left(c_i \wedge Def(f_i) \wedge \bigwedge_{\substack{j=1,\ldots,n \\ j \neq i}} (c_j \to Def(f_j))\right)(\sigma) = tt, i = 1, \ldots, m, \text{ for } m \geq 1.$$

Hence $c_1 \to f_1, \ldots, c_n \to f_n$ is the (possibly reordered) list of all transitions leaving l in P, of which the first m ones are enabled in σ. But this implies that there exists at least one successor state of σ in location l of $T(P)$. This is a contradiction.

$\Leftarrow$: From the above one sees that every φ-computation of $T(P)$ is a φ-computation of P. Now assume $T(P)$ to be φ-successful.

And suppose there exists a partial φ-computation η' of P leading up to state σ at some internal location l of P in which some enabled outgoing transition, labelled by, say, $c \to f$, is undefined, i.e., $Def(f)(\sigma) = ff$. Choose without loss of generality η' to be as short as possible w.r.t. the latter criterion. Then η' is also a partial φ-computation of $T(P)$, which by assumption can be prolonged within $T(P)$.

This implies that there is some transition of $T(P)$, say, labelled by $c_k' \to f_k$, enabled in σ at l. The guard of this transition has the form

$$c_k' \equiv c_k \wedge Def(f_k) \wedge \bigwedge_{\substack{j=1,\ldots,n \\ j \neq i}} (c_j \to Def(f_j)),$$

and also $c_k'(\sigma) = tt$.

Since $c \to f$ occurs as, say, $c_p \to f_p$ in the list of transitions leaving l, and $c(\sigma) = c_p(\sigma) = tt$, this implies $Def(f_p)(\sigma) = Def(f)(\sigma) = tt$. This is a contradiction. $\qquad\square$

2.10 Historical Notes

The inductive assertion method, as well as the wellfoundedness method for proving convergence of programs, were formulated by Robert W. Floyd in [Flo67]. Floyd refers in this paper to earlier ideas of Alan Perlis and Saul Gorn, stating that these concepts "have made their earliest appearance in an unpublished paper by Gorn". This is the more striking because Amir Pnueli attributes his discovery of the relevance of temporal logic to computer science [Pnu77] to a remark also made by Saul Gorn.

Peter Naur gave an illustration of what became known as the inductive assertion method in [Nau66] by giving an invariant network of assertions for a program written in ALGOL 60 (for computing the maximal value of an array of numbers), choosing these in such a way that subsequent assertions justify each other, i.e., are inductive.

Subsequently, Floyd's approach was extended by his first student, Zohar Manna, in [Man69, Man74]. Amir Pnueli generalised this approach together with Manna to concurrent-program proving through the use temporal logic [MP82, MP89, MP91b, MP95, MP99].

Traditionally, Robert M. Keller [Kel76] is regarded as the inventor of our notion of transition diagram, in which a distinction is made between *control states* (i.e., our concept of locations) and *data states* (i.e., our concept of program states). However, actually, our notion is a nontrivial restriction of Keller's, since the latter resembles that of Petri nets as they occur in the work of Holt and Commoner [HC70], and, therefore, goes ultimately back to Carl Petri's work [Pet62, Pet63].

Keller also discusses various induction principles for proving programs correct, and applies these, amongst others, to proving absence of deadlock (or blocking), which is also called success in our approach.

Our notion of a computation step, used for defining the operational semantics of our notion of programs, is an instance of the more fundamental notion of *transition relations*, also already appearing in Keller's work [Kel76]. In subsequent chapters we shall use various forms of so-called *"Structural Operational Semantics"* to define a compositional semantics for concurrent programs. This format was invented by Gordon Plotkin [Plo81, Plo82]. A discussion of the relationship between transition relations and various programming logics is given in [Arn94]; this publication emphasises pre-1991 work by French researchers. For a recent authoritative discussion of transition relations, and the formats used for defining them, see [BPS01].

The advantages of a strict separation between semantic notions in programming theory and their corresponding syntactic expressions we learned from Jaco de Bakker [dB80], who attributes this distinction to the work of Dana Scott and Christopher Strachey [Str66, dBS69, SS71].

The notion of logical variables, also called *freeze* variables, goes back to [HPS77].

In Chapter 3 we shall encounter another kind of variable, so-called *auxiliary* variables, which is used to encode the control flow in proof methods for parallel programs, and which is needed to formulate semantically-complete proof methods for concurrency. Some authors mention Maurice Clint [Cli73] as their inventor, but, actually they are already begin applied in work by Peter Lucas [Luc68].

The notions of relative and arithmetical completeness are introduced in, respectively, [Coo78] and [Har79]. we refer to [Apt81b] for a discussion of the relationship between these notions of completeness and syntactic completeness as they occur in logic.

The notion of semantic completeness, considered as a separate concept, seems to be more recent. It is mentioned, e.g., in [GFMdR81, dB94], although it is implicit in various earlier papers on completeness proofs within programming theory, e.g., [dBM75].

Why syntactic expressibility of the wellfoundedness method for proving program convergence requires assertion languages stronger than first-order predicate logic, such as, e.g., the μ-calculus, is argued in a fundamental paper by Peter Hitchcock and David Park [HP72].

The rôle of strongest postcondition, weakest precondition, weakest liberal precondition, box, diamond and various other (synonyms for) operators in (completeness proofs for) proof methods for establishing program correctness is discussed in a masterful publication of K.R. Apt [Apt81b]. These operators are all instances of *predicate transformers*, introduced by E.W. Dijkstra in [Dij75a], where they are used to characterise the semantics of programming language constructs using functions mapping predicates to predicates, rather than by means of functions mapping states to states, called state transformers.

Other early references to concepts which were later called predicate transformers are contained in [dBdR72, HP72, dBM75, dR76, Dij76, Pra76, Plo79, Har79, Bac80, Zwi89]. Vaughan Pratt's work [Pra76] led to a separate strand of results, called *dynamic logic*, culminating in David Harel's dissertation [Har78]. The emphasis in dynamic logic is on decidability, complete axiomatisation, and total correctness.

Consult Chapter 10 of [dRE98] for an overview of concepts related to predicate transformers.

Clean termination appears first in [Sit74] as a separate concept; we use the term freedom from runtime errors for this concept.

Exercises

2.1   Give the transition diagrams for the following PASCAL-like program fragments:

      (a) **if** b **then** S_1 **else** S_2 **fi**

      (b) **while** b **do** S **od**

2.2   Prove that if predicate φ involves both a set of variables $\bar{x}$ and a set of variables $\bar{y}$, then φ involves $\bar{x} \cap \bar{y}$.

2.3   Let $VAR = \{x_1, \ldots, x_n, \ldots\}$ and the predicate φ be defined as follows:

$$\varphi(\sigma) = \begin{cases} tt & \text{if } \exists i. \forall j, k \geq i. \sigma(x_j) = \sigma(x_\kappa), \\ f\!f & \text{otherwise.} \end{cases}$$

Prove that φ involves $VAR \setminus \{x_1, \ldots, x_n\}$, for any n. The infinite intersection of the sets $VAR \setminus \{x_1, \ldots, x_n\}$ is empty. Check that it is not the case that φ involves the empty set. Hence the notion "to involve" is not closed w.r.t. infinite intersections.

2.4   Determine the set of programs that are partially correct w.r.t., respectively:

      (a) $< true, true >$ (c) $< true, false >$

      (b) $< false, true >$ (d) $< false, false >$.

2.5   Give examples of a proof method (or proof rule) which is incomplete, i.e., not semantically complete, and of one which is unsound.

2.6   Let P be the following program:

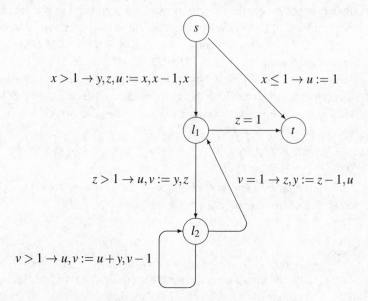

$\varphi \stackrel{\text{def}}{=} (x \geq 0)$ and $\psi \stackrel{\text{def}}{=} (u = x!)$. Prove $\models \{\varphi\} P \{\psi\}$.

2.7   Let P be the following program:

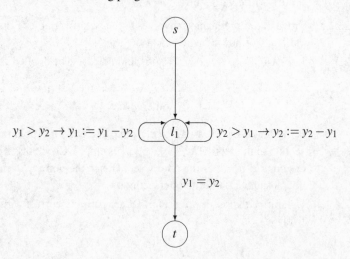

$\varphi \stackrel{\text{def}}{=} (y_1 = x_1) \wedge (y_2 = x_2) \wedge (y_1 > 0) \wedge (y_2 > 0)$ and $\psi \stackrel{\text{def}}{=} y_1 = GCD(x_1, x_2)$. Prove $\models \{\varphi\} P \{\psi\}$.

2.8   Let $P = (L, T, s, t)$ be a given program. Given assertion networks Q and Q' for P, Q' is called *generalisation of Q* if for every $l \in L$, $Q_l \to Q'_l$ is a valid predicate.

Prove or disprove the following hypothesis:

Any generalisation of an invariant network is invariant.

2.9   Consider two isomorphic state spaces Σ and Σ'. Let χ be the isomorphism from Σ onto Σ'. χ induces two functions $\chi_P : (\Sigma \to Bool) \to (\Sigma' \to Bool)$ and $\chi_T : (\Sigma \to \Sigma) \to (\Sigma' \to \Sigma')$ as follows:

- $\chi_P(\varphi)(\sigma') = \varphi(\chi^{-1}(\sigma'))$, for every predicate $\varphi : \Sigma \to Bool$ and state $\sigma' \in \Sigma'$.

- $\chi_T(f) = \chi \circ f \circ \chi^{-1}$, for every state transition $f : \Sigma \to \Sigma$.

For a program $P = (L, T, s, t)$ we define program $\chi(P) \stackrel{\text{def}}{=} (L, T', s, t)$ and $T' \stackrel{\text{def}}{=} \{(l, \chi(c) \to \chi(f), l') \mid (l, c \to f, l') \in T\}$.
Prove or disprove:

- For all predicates φ and ψ from Σ into $Bool$, $\models \{\varphi\}P\{\psi\}$ iff $\models \{\chi(\varphi)\}\chi(P)\{\chi(\psi)\}$.
- For each inductive (invariant) network Q for P the network for $\chi(P)$ that associates $\chi_P(Q_l)$ for each $l \in L$ is inductive (invariant).

2.10   Prove or disprove the following hypothesis: Every invariant network is inductive.

2.11   We consider a program for computing integer powers of an arbitrary real number. The method used is essentially based on the binary representation of integers as follows:

Let $b = \sum_{i=0}^{k} b_i 2^i$ be the binary representation of the integer b. Then

$$a^b = a^{\sum_{i=0}^{k} b_i 2^i} = \prod_{i=0}^{k} a^{2^i b_i}.$$

Observe that the sequence of a^{2^i}, $i = 0, 1, 2, \ldots, k$ can be obtained by starting with a and then successively squaring the previous element

$$a, a^2, a^4, a^8, \ldots, a^{2^i}, \ldots.$$

Also, since b_i is either 0 or 1, the product above can be interpreted as "multiply all a^{2i} for which $b_i = 1$".

The sequence $b_i, i = 0, 1, 2, \ldots, k$, can be obtained by successively dividing b by 2 and checking if the result is odd. On a binary machine divisions by 2 can be efficiently performed by right shifts. Altogether, the complexity of the algorithm is $log_2 b$, which is quite efficient.

The method of computation explained above is implemented in this program:

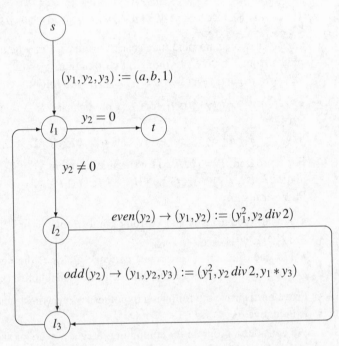

The variable y_1 holds the current value of a^{2^i} and is squared on each execution of the loop. The variable y_2 is initialised to b and is successively divided by 2 in order to obtain the sequence $b_0, b_1, b_2, \ldots$. The variable y_3 accumulates the product of all the a^{2^i} such that $b_i = 1$.

Let $\varphi \stackrel{\text{def}}{=} (b \geq 0)$ and $\psi \stackrel{\text{def}}{=} (y_3 = a^b)$. Prove $\models \{\varphi\} P \{\psi\}$.

2.12   A program P is φ-*successful*, if for every execution η of P, starting in a state satisfying φ, $val(\eta) \neq fail$ holds. Give a method based on Floyd's inductive assertion method for proving that a program P is φ-successful for some given formula φ. Show soundness and semantic completeness of your method.

2.13   An ordering $\prec \subseteq W \times W$ on W is *total* iff $\forall x, y \in W. x \neq y \Rightarrow x \prec y \lor y \prec x$. An element $x \in W$ is called *least* element in W w.r.t. $\prec$ iff $\forall y \in W. x \prec y \lor x = y$. Prove or disprove the following hypothesis: A total ordering over W is wellfounded iff each non-empty subset N of W has a least element.

2.14 The "less than"-relation $\prec_N \subseteq N \times N$ is an irreflexive, transitive ordering on N, which is total and wellfounded. On the basis of this relation we define the following orderings:

    (i) $\prec_{lex(k)} \subseteq N^k \times N^k : (n_1, \ldots, n_k) \prec_{lex(k)} (m_1, \ldots, m_k) \iff$
$$\exists 1 \leq i \leq k. \forall 1 \leq j < i. n_j = m_j \wedge n_i \prec_N m_i$$

    (ii) $\prec_{lex(N)} \subseteq \bigcup_{k \in N \setminus \{0\}} N^k \times \bigcup_{k \in N \setminus \{0\}} N^k$
$$\prec_{lex(N)} := \bigcup_{k \in N \setminus \{0\}} \prec_{lex(k)}$$

    (iii) $\prec_{lex} \subseteq \bigcup_{k \in N \setminus \{0\}} N^k \times \bigcup_{k \in N \setminus \{0\}} N^k :$
$(n_1, \ldots, n_r) \prec_{lex} (m_1, \ldots, m_s) \iff \exists i \in N \setminus \{0\}. \forall 1 \leq j < i.$
$(n_j = m_j \wedge n_i \prec_N m_i) \vee (r \prec_N s \wedge \forall 1 \leq j \leq r. (n_j = m_j))$

Prove or disprove the following hypotheses:

    (a) $\prec_{lex(k)} \subseteq N^k \times N^k$ is wellfounded.

    (b) $\prec_{lex(N)} \subseteq \bigcup_{k \in N \setminus \{0\}} N^k \times \bigcup_{k \in N \setminus \{0\}} N^k$ is wellfounded.

    (c) $\prec_{lex} \subseteq \bigcup_{1 \leq k \leq n} N^k \times \bigcup_{1 \leq k \leq n} N^k$ is wellfounded for arbitrary $n \in N$.

    (d) $\prec_{lex} \subseteq \bigcup_{k \in N \setminus \{0\}} N^k \times \bigcup_{k \in N \setminus \{0\}} N^k$ is wellfounded.

2.15 Decide whether the program in Exercise 2.6 is convergent or not; if it is convergent, give a proof using the method in Section 2.8; if not, give an infinite computation.

2.16 Define the weakest l-condition operator of P w.r.t. postcondition ψ, $wp_l(P, \psi)(\sigma)$, by "for all computation sequences of P which start in configuration $\langle l; \sigma \rangle$ and lead to $\langle t; \sigma' \rangle$ one has $\models \psi(\sigma')$."

    (a) Prove that $\{wp_l(P, \psi) \mid l \in L\}$ is an inductive assertion network for P, and that when P is partially correct w.r.t. φ and ψ, i.e., $\models \{\varphi\} P \{\psi\}$ holds, one has $\models \varphi \rightarrow wp_s(P, \psi)$ and $\models wp_t(P, \psi) \rightarrow \psi$. Consequently one could also have based the completeness proof on such weakest l-condition operators.

    (b) Does the following also hold: For any invariant assertion network $\{Q_l \mid l \in L\}$ for $P \models wp_l(P, Q_l) \rightarrow Q_l$ holds? If the answer is yes, prove this; if the answer is no, give a counterexample.

2.17   (a) Using the notation of the previous exercise, prove that the validity of the verification conditions as defined in Section 2.5.1 can be alternatively characterised by

$$\models Q_l \wedge c \rightarrow wp_l (l \xrightarrow{c \to f} l', Q_{l'}),$$

where $l \xrightarrow{c \to f} l'$ stands for the program starting in l and ending in l' with a single transition $(l, c \to f, l')$. Hint: prove $\models (c \to Q_{l'} \circ f) \leftrightarrow wp_l(l \xrightarrow{c \to f} l', Q_{l'})$.

(b) Similarly, prove that the validity of the verification condition

$$\models Q_l \wedge c \to Q_{l'} \circ f$$

can be equivalently characterised by

$$\models SP(Q_l, l \xrightarrow{c \to f} l') \to Q_{l'}.$$

2.18   Prove the soundness of the alternative method for convergence described in Definition 2.22.

2.19   Prove the completeness of the alternative method for convergence described in Definition 2.22. *Hint*: Define ρ_l as follows:

$\rho_l(\sigma) \stackrel{\text{def}}{=}$ the length of the longest computation path starting at l in σ, if the configuration $\langle l; \sigma \rangle$ is reachable from an initial state satisfying precondition φ, otherwise undefined.

2.20   Given transition diagram P, reduce freedom of runtime errors of P to partial correctness of P.

Hint: Transform P by adding to every non-exit location l of P a transition which sets some predefined and preset variable b to *false* whenever there are enabled transitions in l which lead to an undefined result.

2.21   Prove soundness and semantic completeness of the direct method for proving absence of runtime errors given by Definition 2.24.

3

The Inductive Assertion Method for Shared-Variable Concurrency

3.1 Objective and Structure of this Chapter

Our next goal is to generalise the inductive assertion method for sequential transition diagrams to shared-variable concurrency.

First, concurrent execution is characterised in Section 3.2 by the so-called *"interleaving"* model. This model consists of sequences of nondeterministically-interleaved *atomic* actions of the processes which are composed in parallel. Atomic actions are transitions which are executed without any interference from the environment. Section 3.3 contains a discussion of alternative characterisations involving *"true"* concurrency, and Section 3.4 discusses how to generalise Floyd's approach to this interleaving model.

In Section 3.5 the inductive assertion method is generalised to the concurrent execution of sequential transition diagrams which communicate by means of shared variables, i.e., to shared-variable concurrency.

To this end the language of transition diagrams is extended with a parallel composition operator. The semantics of this operator consists of the set of all maximal interleaved computation sequences of atomic actions from its argument processes, where an atomic action consists of the execution of a single enabled transition in a transition diagram. Specifically, the inductive assertion method is extended to shared-variable concurrency by:

(i) Characterising the parallel composition of such sequential transition diagrams by a single new sequential transition diagram whose set of nodes is the Cartesian product $L_1 \times \ldots \times L_n$ of the nodes L_i of its component diagrams, and whose transitions consist of the individual transitions in these diagrams.

(ii) Associating an assertion network with $L_1 \times \ldots \times L_n$.

(iii) Defining verification conditions for each transition in this new diagram.

119

Since the resulting method generates a set of verification conditions whose size is *exponential* in the number of processes, as an alternative a more manageable proof method is adopted which is based on local inductive assertion networks which additionally satisfy the *interference freedom test* formulated by Susan Owicki and David Gries [OG76a]; in [Lam76, Lam77] a similar condition is formulated. The resulting method is called the proof method of Owicki & Gries. It is illustrated in Section 3.5.2 by correctness proofs for Lamport's ticket algorithm and Szymanski's mutual exclusion algorithm (discussed in Section 1.4.4), and proved sound in Section 3.5.3.

In order to obtain a *semantically* complete proof method the concept of *auxiliary variables* is introduced. These variables do not influence the flow of control inside a program, and therefore neither occur in its boolean tests (inside transitions), nor in its assignments to non-auxiliary variables. Yet their presence enables one to record the flow of control sufficiently precisely as to allow for the expression of inductive assertion networks in a complete manner.

Because of the additional interference freedom test the proof method presented by Owicki & Gries is noncompositional, since it refers to the structure of the associated component transition diagrams, and not to their initial-final-state behaviour. The noncompositional reasoning pattern shows itself clearly in the original completeness proof of [Owi75]. The local assertions of a component in this completeness proof are defined in terms of an *operational* semantics of the particular given parallel program. This operational semantics does not provide a semantics of a separate component of a program. It is based on the above view of a parallel program as a monolithic nondeterministic transition diagram. Moreover, it can be shown that this operational semantics does not allow a compositional description of the behaviour of a parallel program in terms of its components. Consequently the main technical ingredient of this completeness proof used to be the so-called *merging* lemma, which is discussed in Section 3.9.1. This lemma states the conditions under which the local assertions in the separate processes can be combined into a global assertion about their parallel composition; Krzysztof Apt was the first one to formulate such lemmas explicitly[Apt83, Apt81a].

An interesting new observation [dB94] is that these conditions are implied by the existence of a *compositional* semantics for the parallel composition of processes, as also shown in Section 3.9.1. Moreover, the use of a compositional semantics allows for a new completeness proof in which only purely local information about the behaviour of a component in isolation is used without using *any* environmental information regarding the particular given parallel program in which it occurs. This approach is followed in Sections 3.5.4 and 3.5.6. Section 3.5.4 contains a general discussion of such proofs, whereas

Section 3.5.6 contains the completeness proof proper. In Section 3.5.7 we also present a second version of this new completeness proof which does not require annotation of boolean tests with assignments to auxiliary variables (this is the strategy followed in the syntactically-oriented completeness proofs given in [Owi75, Owi76, Apt81a, Apt83]). As such this new completeness proof can be shown to encode a compositional reasoning pattern, which, when isolated, gives rise to a compositional proof method! This compositional proof method is worked out in Chapter 8.

After this, a modular proof method for convergence of concurrent programs is introduced in Section 3.6. Similarly to the above, first a global monolithic proof method is sketched, the complexity of which forces one to look for an alternative. This alternative is obtained by defining a product for which decrease of its tuples is defined by a local decrease in one or more of its components without an increase in its remaining components. The resulting method is proved sound and semantically complete. However, the (compositional) completeness proof of the Owicki & Gries method for proving partial correctness as described in Section 3.5.6 *cannot* be extended to a completeness proof of the modular method for proving convergence. This is because the local predicates used in the former describe the behaviour of a process with respect to *any* environment. However, convergence of a process depends on a *particular* environment. Therefore, our third completeness proof in Section 3.6.3 is based on *reachability* predicates, taking that particular environment into account.

We show how to prove absence of deadlock in Section 3.7, and describe in Section 3.8 how to reduce proofs of absence of runtime errors to proofs of absence of deadlock. Finally, Section 3.9 discusses the history of proof methods for shared-variable concurrency and their central concepts, and Leslie Lamport's view upon such methods. A list of exercises is presented at the end of this chapter. Relative completeness of the method of Owicki & Gries is proved in Chapter 5.

3.2 A Characterisation of Concurrent Execution

In this section a model is developed for characterising the influence upon the program state of the execution of concurrent programs P that operate upon shared variables. Such a program $P \equiv P_1 \| \ldots \| P_n$ consists of one or more processes $P_1, \ldots, P_n$ which communicate with each other by reading and updating the values of so-called *shared* variables. Shared variables of $P_1, \ldots, P_n$ are variables which are accessed by two or more processes – whence the name "shared"; the remaining variables of $P_1, \ldots, P_n$ are called *local*, because they are accessed by merely one process P_i, $i = 1, \ldots, n$.

We characterise *concurrency* in this chapter as follows.

During program execution several processes may *compete* in accessing the same shared variable. Since ultimately such a shared variable models a particular memory location, and in current computers more than one process cannot simultaneously access the same memory location, the outcome of such a competition is that accesses to the same shared variable are linearly ordered, or interleaved, as the lingo goes. This explains why two enabled actions, whose execution requires them to access the same shared variable, are said to be in *conflict*. Another aspect of concurrency is *independent* simultaneous execution whenever the shared variables, which are accessed, are all different. Besides these two elements – *competition* for access to the same variable, and *independent* operation on disjoint sets of variables – a third element which characterises execution of concurrent programs in this chapter is that each process involved has a positive, although arbitrary, speed of execution, unless it is terminated, deadlocked or waiting to obtain access to a shared variable, in which case we postulate that access is eventually granted after waiting long enough. By convention this also includes accesses to local variables, implying that every enabled action operating on purely local variables will be eventually executed.

This abstraction from the particular execution speed of a process is characteristic for models of program execution where the duration of program execution is not measured. (In other models, e.g., for real-time processes, this duration is a central element in their semantics.) For instance, in general it is not considered to be acceptable that during execution of a concurrent program one particular infinite process monopolises all accesses to a certain shared variable in case other processes also try to access this variable. For, if this were to be allowed, what would be the sense of the remaining processes which were supposed to be operating concurrently with that one monopolising process? Should that not be regarded as a scheduling error? These observations lead to postulating so-called *fairness* requirements in Section 3.2.2, whose formalisation inside temporal logic earned Amir Pnueli a Turing Award [Pnu77].

3.2.1 Basic Requirements and Atomic Actions

In a first approximation, the execution of a concurrent program therefore satisfies the following two requirements:

Requirement 1: More than one process cannot have simultaneous access to the same shared variable.

Requirement 2: The execution speed of every nonterminated and nondead-

locked process is positive and arbitrary, unless it is waiting for access
to a shared variable, in which case by waiting long enough access is
eventually granted and the process resumes execution.

Next we introduce the notion of an *atomic action* using a purely textual
representation of programs in case their representation as a transition system
is unambiguous. This is the case for, e.g, $R_1 : x := 1$ and $R_2 : x := 2$. What is
the effect of executing $R_1 \| R_2$? By **Requirement 1**, R_1 and R_2 cannot access
x simultaneously. However, the result of $R_1 \| R_2$ is by no means fixed, for this
depends, as we shall see below, upon the way $x := 1$ and $x := 2$ are executed.
First consider the following two-bit implementation of these actions:

$$R_1 : x := 1 \Longleftrightarrow \textit{first bit of} (x) := 1; \textit{second bit of} (x) := 0, \text{ and}$$
$$R_2 : x := 2 \Longleftrightarrow \textit{first bit of} (x) := 0; \textit{second bit of} (x) := 1,$$

where, for $i = 0, 1$, *first bit of* $(x) := i$ and *second bit of* $(x) := i$ are regarded as
single uninterruptable actions. Such uninterruptable actions are called atomic,
because during their execution no interference by other actions from other processes takes place together with their execution. That is, during execution of
an atomic action the set of objects manipulated by that action (i.e., whose values are read or changed) and the set of objects manipulated by other actions
from other processes are *disjoint*. In the case of R_1 and R_2 the atomic accesses
to the shared variable x concern single bits.

Executing R_1 and R_2 concurrently may now lead to $x = 3$ – which is the
effect of executing the following interleaving of their atomic actions:

$$\textit{first bit of} (x) := 0; \textit{first bit of} (x) := 1;$$
$$\textit{second bit of} (x) := 0; \textit{second bit of} (x) := 1$$

– or to $x = 2$ – the effect of executing:

$$\textit{first bit of} (x) := 1; \textit{first bit of} (x) := 0;$$
$$\textit{second bit of} (x) := 0; \textit{second bit of} (x) := 1.$$

Other possible interleavings lead to $x = 0$ or $x = 1$.

Secondly consider an alternative implementation of $x := 1$ and $x := 2$ for
which $x := 1 \| x := 2$ leads to a different result:

$$R_1' : x := 1 \Longleftrightarrow \textit{first byte of} (x) := 00000001;$$
$$\textit{second byte of} (x) := 00000000$$
$$R_2' : x := 2 \Longleftrightarrow \textit{first byte of} (x) := 00000010;$$
$$\textit{second byte of} (x) := 00000000,$$

assuming a word-size for x of two bytes, and *first byte of* $(x) := i$ and *second byte of* $(x) := j$ to be atomic. That is, the atomic accesses to shared variable x concern in the case of R'_1 and R'_2 single bytes.

Now the effect of executing $R'_1 \| R'_2$ is $x = 1$ or $x = 2$, which is different from that of $R_1 \| R_2$ which possibly leads to $x = 3$.

These examples indicate that *to characterise the meaning of a concurrent program one has to specify its atomic actions.*

In the remainder of this section (3.2) we do this by reformulating **Requirement 1** as follows by making a specific choice of atomic actions:

Requirement 1: All accesses to the same shared variable are linearly ordered. There are two ways to access a (shared) variable: by reading its value and by writing its value. In case of reading a value this is considered to be an atomic action, i.e., to take place without being influenced by other processes. When writing a value, this is also considered to be atomic.

Consequently, the atomic accesses of shared variables in the remainder of this section concern the full size of words used for implementing them.

Example 3.1 For $P \equiv (x := 0 \| (x := 1; x := 2))$, $\models \{true\}\ P\ \{x = 0 \lor x = 2\}$ holds, for execution of P amounts to execution of one of the following sequences of atomic actions, as follows from the two requirements above:

$$x := 0; x := 1; x := 2, \ x := 1; x := 0; x := 2, \ \text{or}\ x := 1; x := 2; x := 0.$$

$\square$

Example 3.2 Let $Q_1 \equiv x := x + 1$, $Q_2 \equiv x := x + 1$ and $Q \equiv Q_1 \| Q_2$. Then $\models \{x = 0\}\ Q\ \{x = 2\}$ need not hold, because execution of Q is not equivalent to the sequential execution of $x := x + 1; x := x + 1$, since $x := x + 1$ is not atomic according to **Requirement 1**, reformulated as above. This is explained below. Assume execution of $x := x + 1$ by Q_i to be equivalent to execution of $ti := x; ti := ti + 1; x := ti$ with ti standing for a local register of Q_i (here modelled by a local variable), $i = 1, 2$, and $ti := x$, $ti := ti + 1$ and $x := ti$ considered as atomic actions (this will be justified by Theorem 3.3 below). Note that this interpretation of the execution of $x := x + 1$ is consistent with **Requirement 1**.

Now a counterexample to the partial correctness formula above is provided by the following interleaving of $ti := x; ti := ti + 1; x := ti$, for $i = 1, 2 : t1 := x; t2 := x; t2 := t2 + 1; x := t2; t1 := t1 + 1; x := t1$, which results in $x = 1$ as postcondition, when started in $x = 0$.

Listing the remaining possible interleavings of $t1 := x; t1 := t1 + 1; x := t1$ and $t2 := x; t2 := t2 + 1; x := t2$ then leads to establishing $\models \{x = 0\}\ Q\ \{x = 1 \vee x = 2\}$. $\square$

In the examples above we have analysed the behaviour of some trivial concurrent programs by listing all interleavings of their atomic actions, while preserving the relative order of these actions inside the individual processes. Due to the prohibitively high number of these interleavings this does not lead to a realistic method for the analysis of concurrent programs. However, the net effect of many interleavings upon the variables of a program is the same. For instance, in Example 3.2 execution of $t1 := x; t2 := x; t2 := t2 + 1; x := t2; t1 := t1 + 1; x := t1$ and of $t1 := x; t1 := t1 + 1; t2 := x; t2 := t2 + 1; x := t2; x := t1$ has the same net effect upon $x, t1$ and $t2$. One therefore looks for ways of reducing the number of different interleavings of processes by considering only certain representative normal forms. These are provided by Reynolds' criterion in combination with the generalised criterion below.[1]

Theorem 3.3 (Reynolds' criterion)
When **Requirements 1** and **2** are satisfied, concurrent execution of $P_1, \ldots, P_n$ has the same net effect on the program state as the nondeterministic interleavings of their tests and assignments, provided every assignment and test contains at most one occurrence of a shared variable.

Proof Let every test T_i and assignment AS_i in P_i contain at most one occurrence of a shared variable, $i = 1, \ldots, n$. This occurrence identifies a read or write action. Then execution of AS_i consists of a number of actions l_i^j upon the local variables of P_i – these are called *local* actions – plus one access SV_i to a shared variable of P_i, if any, which consists of a read or write action upon that shared variable. Hence the execution of AS_i can be characterised by the execution of the sequence of actions $l_i^1 \ldots l_i^q\, SV_i l_i^{q+1} \ldots l_i^m$ for suitable l_i^j, q and m.

Now certainly other actions A_k in other processes $P_k, k \neq i$, can take place during execution of such a local action l_i^j in P_i. However, such other actions A_k do not influence the execution of l_i^j *because the variables occurring in A_k and l_i^j are disjoint*. In fact, l_i^j commutes with such actions: $A_k; l_i^j \approx l_i^j; A_k$, for l_i^j a local action in P_i and A_k any action in $P_k, k \neq i$.

Consequently, no matter how AS_i, i.e., $l_i^1 \ldots l_i^q SV_i l_i^{q+1} \ldots l_i^m$, is interleaved by the actions of other processes, since the l_i^j commute with those actions, the effect of executing AS_i is as if all its local actions $l_i^1 \ldots l_i^q$ take place immediately

---

[1] Theorem 3.3 has been first formulated by John Reynolds, according to Owicki and Gries [OG76a].

before SV_i, and all its remaining local actions $l_i^{q+1} \ldots l_i^m$ immediately after SV_i. That is, the *effect* of executing AS_i is *as if* AS_i *has been executed as an atomic action*. Therefore AS_i may be regarded as atomic.

When AS_i contains no occurrence of a shared variable it consists of local actions only and can therefore be trivially regarded as atomic. And to a boolean test containing at most one occurrence of a shared variable a similar argument applies.

Finally we point out why **Requirement 2** is essential for this theorem to hold. For without **Requirement 2** it might be the case that one infinite process monopolises all accesses to shared variables, i.e., *none* of the other processes ever gets its turn when requesting access. In that case also none of their assignments and tests would be executed, and hence the basis for characterising concurrency by means of interleaving would disappear. Another possibility is that without **Requirement 2** the above action AS_i might only be partially executed, say stopping at execution of l_i^{q+1}. Since l_i^{q+1} remains enabled, **Requirement 2** implies that it will be eventually executed, thereby excluding this possibility.

$\square$

Let a *critical reference* of $P_1, \ldots, P_n$ denote an occurrence of a shared variable (of $P_1, \ldots, P_n$). Furthermore, let every test and assignment of P_i contain at most one critical reference. In the above proof of Theorem 3.3 we analyse the case of given assignments (or tests) containing at most one critical reference. Conversely, given (1) a finite number of assignments, or (2) a finite number of tests, one might combine these into bigger groups, using sequential composition and propositional operations, respectively, as long as each of these groups contains at most one critical reference. An example of such a combination is obtained by combining $ti := x$ and $ti := ti + 1$ from Example 3.2 into the bigger unit $ti := x; ti := ti + 1$. This unit still contains one critical reference.

The above proof still applies to these bigger groups.

In this way the so-called *"grain of interleaving"* is enlarged, decreasing the number of interleaved sequences of atomic actions to consider when analysing a concurrent program. This is of vital importance for obtaining a practical method for analysing the correctness of such programs.

Thus one obtains:

Corollary 3.4 (Generalised criterion) Join in every process P_i (1) a finite number of assignments together using sequential composition, or (2) a finite number of tests together using propositional operations, as long as the resulting groups each contain at most one critical reference. Then nondeterministic interleaved execution of those groups is equivalent with (i.e., has the same net effect upon the program state as) concurrent execution of $P_1 \parallel \ldots \parallel P_n$ provided **Requirements 1** and **2** are fulfilled. □

Example 3.5 Let A and B denote operations upon shared variables and upon disjoint sets of local variables. Let $\boxed{1 : \text{local}}$ denote an operation upon A's local variables only, $\boxed{S1 : \text{shared}}$ denote an operation upon both A's local and shared variables containing only one critical reference, and let $\boxed{S2 : \text{shared}}$ denote a similar operation upon B's local variables (which are disjoint from A's local variables) and the (commonly) shared variables containing (at most) one critical reference, then one has the following equivalence, as pictured in Figure 3.1.

$$\left[\overbrace{\boxed{1 : \text{local}}; \boxed{S1 : \text{shared}}}^{A} \parallel \overbrace{\boxed{S2 : \text{shared}}}^{B} \right] \approx \text{ (by Reynolds' criterion)}$$

$$\{ \boxed{S2}; \boxed{1}; \boxed{S1} \, , \, \boxed{1}; \boxed{S2}; \boxed{S1} \, , \, \boxed{1}; \boxed{S1}; \boxed{S2} \} \approx \{A;B \, , \, B;A\}$$

Fig. 3.1. An illustration of the generalised criterion.

Here $\boxed{1}; \boxed{S2} \approx \boxed{S2}; \boxed{1}$ follows from the fact that the local variables in $\boxed{1}$ are disjoint from the variables of $\boxed{S2}$, where $\boxed{1}$, $\boxed{S1}$ and $\boxed{S2}$ abbreviate the operations described above.

In this example "$\approx$" denotes equivalence as far as the net effect on the values of program variables, i.e., initial-final-state behaviour, is concerned. □

When several processors are involved in executing $P_1 \parallel \ldots \parallel P_n$, the set of all nondeterministic interleavings of the sequences of atomic actions of $P_1, \ldots, P_n$ need not faithfully model concurrent execution of $P_1, \ldots, P_n$ when some P_i are diverging, since not necessarily all of these interleavings are realistic when one infinite process monopolises access to certain shared variables, access to which is also requested by other processes. We excluded this situation by requiring *fairness* of the accessing mechanism by imposing **Requirement 2**.

But there exist simpler undesirable cases. Without **Requirement 2**, one might claim that the concurrent execution of two infinite processes which only operate on local variables would be modelled by a set of interleaved sequences to which also the infinite execution sequences of only one of these processes would belong. That is, in such an obviously *unfair* sequence no operation of the other process, assumed to be concurrently operating together with the modelled one, would appear! That situation is also ruled out by **Requirement 2**.

3.2.2 The Need for Fairness Assumptions

We are about to add as a new feature to our model of concurrency that of *programmed* atomic execution of certain statements, i.e., that the implementing process must prevent interfering environmental actions from occurring during the atomic execution of such statements. The introduction of this concept requires a more refined analysis of the issue of *fairness* than that provided by **Requirement 2**.

Before explaining this point, two additional aspects of concurrent programming are first incorporated within our model of concurrency:

(1) the different meaning of boolean tests in traditional sequential programming languages, such as PASCAL, and in concurrent programming, and

(2) the additional use of indivisible atomic operations to express synchronisation between concurrent processes.

Ad (1):

- In sequential programming boolean tests serve to decide between two possibilities for *advancing* control flow; e.g., the value of b in **if** b **then** S **fi** determines whether S is executed or passed.

- In concurrent programming boolean tests often serve as *traffic lights which are repeatedly tested to decide whether or not control flow advances*. In fact, this aspect of concurrency has already been incorporated into our model of sequential transition diagrams of the previous chapter by allowing a transition $c(\bar{y}) \rightarrow \bar{y} := f(\bar{y})$ to be passed only when c is enabled.

  Using boolean tests as traffic lights is motivated by the need to synchronise concurrent processes in the case of shared-variable concurrency. Because the presence of a concurrent context consisting of other processes may cause a test which previously evaluated to false later to evaluate to true due to interference by that context, as illustrated in Sections 1.3 and 1.4. Synchronisation by means of such tests is called *conditional* synchronisation.

Ad (2):

- Let $\langle S \rangle$ signify that statement S is executed indivisibly, i.e., without interfering actions from other processes. Then one has that, e.g.,

$$\models \{x = 0\}\ \langle x := x + 1\rangle \parallel \langle x := x + 1\rangle\ \{x = 2\}$$

holds, because the interleaving illustrated in Example 3.2, which leads to postcondition $x = 1$, breaks each of the two occurrences of $x := x + 1$ into two parts, say, A and B of which first both A-parts are executed. Consequently in that case the execution of these two occurrences of $x := x + 1$ interfere with each other. This is exactly the situation forbidden in the case of $\langle x := x + 1 \rangle$. Therefore, only those interleavings are left which result in postcondition $x = 2$.

- A frequent use of such atomic operations is made in cases of transitions. In Chapter 2 we introduced transitions of the form shown in Figure 3.2.

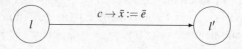

Fig. 3.2. A transition.

Now consider concurrent execution of the two transitions shown in Figure 3.3.

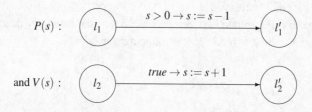

Fig. 3.3. Semaphore.

Does one mean that $s := s - 1$ and $s := s + 1$ have the same granularity as $x := x + 1$ in Example 3.2, or are $P(s)$ and $V(s)$ executed as atomic actions?

We shall opt for the latter, i.e., expressed in our pseudo language we shall consider only transitions of the form

$$P(s) : \langle s > 0 \rightarrow s := s - 1 \rangle \text{ and } V(s) : \langle s := s + 1 \rangle.$$

Now when $s > 0$ evaluates to false, execution of $P(s)$ waits in front of this instruction (rather than passing it as would otherwise have been the case when considering $\langle \textbf{if } s > 0 \textbf{ then } s := s_1 \textbf{ fi} \rangle$).

Traditionally, $P(s)$ and $V(s)$ are called *semaphore* operations upon the "semaphore" s if these are the only instructions involving the integer variable s. This model for synchronisation between concurrent processes by means of shared-variables has been introduced by Edsger W. Dijkstra in order to introduce levels of abstraction in his description of the THE multi-programming system [Dij68c]. In this way he separated the implementation of semaphore instructions (using mutual exclusion algorithms) at a lower level of abstraction from their usage for synchronisation purposes within his description of the THE system at a higher level of abstraction.

Consequently, in concurrent programming $P(s)$ need not be passed in case it happens that $s > 0$ is always *tested* at those moments when it yields *false*.

A consequence of incorporating semaphore operations into our model is that one may object that now **Requirement 2**: "The execution speed of every nonterminated (and nondeadlocked) process is arbitrary and positive", is no longer satisfied. The problem is as follows.

Consider the program

$$\{s = 1\}(Q_1 : \textbf{while } true \textbf{ do } P(s); V(s) \textbf{ od } \|$$
$$Q_2 : \textbf{while } true \textbf{ do } P(s); V(s) \textbf{ od})$$

executed in initial state $s = 1$.

In order to differentiate between occurrences of the same constructs in Q_1 and in Q_2 we distinguish them by introducing subscripts:

$$\{s = 1\}(Q_1 : \textbf{while } true_1 \textbf{ do } P_1(s); V_1(s) \textbf{ od } \|$$
$$Q_2 : \textbf{while } true_2 \textbf{ do } P_2(s); V_2(s) \textbf{ od}).$$

Now, starting in $s = 1$, the sequence $(true_1 ; P_1(s); V_1(s))^\infty$ is a computation sequence of $Q_1 \| Q_2$ in which $P_2(s)$ is never executed, thereby violating **Requirement 2**.

But is this true? It may have been the case that the test $s >_2 0$ in $P_2(s)$ has always been evaluated *in between* executions of $P_1(s)$ and $V_1(s)$. This situation one may express by the sequence $(true_1 ; P_1(s); \neg(s >_2 0); V_1(s))^\infty$, where $\neg(s >_2 0)$ indicates that the test $s > 0$ in Q_2 evaluates to *false*, and hence its negation can always be passed. Yet one may still maintain that **Requirement 2** is not violated because the attempt at advancing flow of control in Q_2 has been made infinitely often.

Is this position realistic?

Let us make the extra assumption that $P(s)$ operations are executed on separate processors with similar properties. Then one may object that

$$(true_1 ; P_1(s); \neg(s >_2 0); V_1(s))^\infty$$

is:

an infinite sequence in which the test $s >_2 0$ in $P_2(s)$ happens to be evaluated only when $s = 0$ happens to be true, whereas $s >_2 0$ is also infinitely often true at other positions in that sequence!

During truly concurrent execution (as is the case when several processors are involved), this sequence should not occur when $P(s)$ operations test $s > 0$ at *random* moments (as permitted by the arbitrariness of execution speeds – **Requirement 2**) since then the probability that a situation arises in which $s = 0$ holds at an infinite number of randomly selected *consecutive* moments is zero.

This discrepancy between the interleaving model and concurrent execution on several processors is removed by imposing stronger fairness assumptions. An example of such an assumption is **Requirement 3**:

Requirement 3: If an occurrence of an operation is infinitely often enabled in an execution sequence (i.e., its associated test is infinitely often true) then it is eventually performed.

Remark 3.6 This requirement rules $(true_1 ; P_1(s); \neg(s >_2 0); V_1(s))^\infty$ out as a legitimate sequence because there exists a computation, namely,

$$((s >_2 0); true_1 ; (s >_2 0); P_1(s); \neg(s >_2 0); V_1(s))^\infty, \tag{3.1}$$

in which $s >_2 0$ is infinitely often true, hence $P_2(s)$ is infinitely often enabled, and yet $P_2(s)$ is never passed. Therefore the former sequence is illegitimate.

Consequently only those finite prefixes of (3.1) are allowed which are prolonged to infinite sequences in which $P_2(s)$ occurs at least once, after passing of which the same argument applies again; therefore $P_2(s)$ should in fact occur infinitely often.

Thus one sees that by **Requirement 3** only those execution sequences are allowed in which both $P_1(s)$ and $P_2(s)$ are executed infinitely often. □

Example 3.7 Under this fairness assumption the transition diagram $Q_1 \parallel Q_2$, shown in Figure 3.4, starting in a state in which both x and s have the value 1, terminates.

Here, transitions of $Q_1 \parallel Q_2$ are either transitions of Q_1 or of Q_2, which are by definition regarded as atomic. □

The formalisation of fairness assumptions belongs to the domain of temporal logic for which excellent texts already exist [MP91b, MP95, MP99].

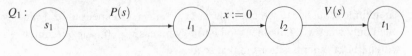

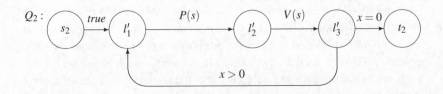

Fig. 3.4. A program terminating subject to satisfaction of **Requirement 3**.

3.3 Is this Characterisation of Concurrent Execution Justified?

In principle, an interleaving semantics models a uniprocessor implementation where at most one process may perform an action at every point in a computation. Such a semantics allows, in principle, that one infinite process monopolises (the resources of) that uniprocessor. In order to disallow such a case, fairness assumptions, such as **Requirements 2** and **3** above, are introduced; these forbid such monopolisation depending on various conditions upon the enabledness of the remaining processes. However, in certain cases a more careful analysis is needed for a truthful modelling of concurrency.

Imagine a nondeterministic interleaving of the atomic actions of a symphony of Mozart; obviously the result is a cacophony.

Thus, if one's goal is "to yeeld to sweet Musick", then the nondeterministic interleaving of atomic actions is not justified as a model for concurrency, because in symphonic music it is the overlapping of atomic actions in time which matters, in combination with their synchronisation by a conductor.[2]

Petri net theory supports the point of view that concurrency adds an essentially new element to the concept of computation [Pet62, Pet63, Rei85, Rei98]. In fact, we adopted from Petri net theory the notions of "conflict" and "true concurrency" by which we introduced concurrency in this chapter. In Petri net theory the term "concurrency" is reserved for "true concurrency". Truly concurrent events are *mutually independent*. For example, a black hole swallowing a star is truly concurrent to your reading this note (assuming the universe has no conductor).

Petri net theory is an instance of a theory which models concurrency by means of *partial orders*. Let us introduce the term *events* for the various actions

---

[2] This has been pointed out by Wolfgang Reisig.

executed during execution of a concurrent program. In a truthful modelling of concurrency the events occurring during a computation are partially ordered. This results in *the representation of a computation by means of a partial order* and, consequently, the behaviour of a program by *a set of partial orders*. For example, an output event in one process occurs before the corresponding input event in another process, and successive events in purely sequential local computations inside a process occur after each other; the partial order concerned is then the transitive closure of these events. This partial order reflects the dependency of events upon each other – whether they are dependent (in case of access to a commonly shared variable), or independent (such as actions involving disjoint sets of local variables), or *scheduled* to be dependent (e.g., in the case of execution of a concurrent program on only one processor). Such a partial order can be represented within the context of interleaved sequences by introducing a symmetric and reflexive binary relation on events – called *dependency relation D* – in order to model this dependency. When two events a and b are independent, this is modelled by $(a,b) \notin D$. The interleaving sequence $\sigma\, ab\, \sigma'$ is then considered to be equivalent to $\sigma\, ba\, \sigma'$. The resulting equivalence classes are called *traces*, cf. [Maz89]. The book [dBdRR89] represents an introduction to the topic of how concurrency should be modelled depending on the criteria used.

Above we gave a rather outlandish example of the need for modelling concurrency by means of partial orders. An example which is much closer to our topic is that of the independent infinite execution of two processes P and Q in

$$P: \ \textbf{while } \textit{true } \textbf{do } x := x + 1 \textbf{ od } \| \ Q: \ \textbf{while } \textit{true } \textbf{do } y := y + 1 \textbf{ od}.$$

Certainly P does not interfere with the actions of Q, and vice versa. Yet although neither P nor Q contains any critical reference to any commonly shared variable, Corollary 3.4 (the generalised criterion) does not hold for the simple reason that concatenating two infinite sequences leads to disappearance of one of them. Yet the intention of Corollary 3.4 can still be captured by adopting the partial order model, for what is wrong with representing the behaviour of $P\|Q$ by a set of partial orders, each consisting of two *independent infinite* suborders?

Although such examples suggest adoption of more sophisticated models than those of interleaving sequences, the problem with the former ones is that their structure is so much more complicated. We quote from Olderog's masterful monograph ([Old91a], Section 4: *Problems with Nets*, page 34; see also Section 6, page 70 ff.):

Petri nets are able to distinguish clearly the basic concepts of processes. The graphical representation of nets visualises these concepts. Therefore we selected nets for our very detailed, machine-like view of processes. But is this view of processes satisfactory? The answer is "no" because there are at least two serious problems with it:

(i) **Compositionality.** Missing is a convenient way of composing or decomposing larger nets from, or into, smaller ones by a set of high-level operations.

(ii) **Abstraction.** Missing is a way of abstraction from internal actions τ, i.e., processes are not yet treated as "black boxes" where only the communication behaviour is important. Both compositionality and abstraction are necessary to manage the behavioural complexity of processes.

Since compositionality is one of the key concepts used in this book to overcome the exponential complexity of reasoning about concurrent processes, and this is done on the basis of the interleaving model, we adopt Lamport's position, below.

Lamport writes in "What good is temporal logic" [Lam83c] on this topic:[3]

Computer scientists often feel that something is lost by sequentialising a concurrent program ... and that one should use a partial ordering among actions, instead. However, as long as we consider [the effect upon the state variables] only, there is no loss of generality in considering totally-ordered sequences of atomic actions. Our model includes all possible sequences, and [from the point of view of the effect upon the program state] a partial ordering is completely equivalent with the set of all total orderings consistent with it.[4] The real assumption implicit in the model is the existence of atomic actions.

This assumption is made in virtually all formal models of concurrency ...

In this text we shall make the same assumption. The discussion concerning partially-ordered computations will be continued in Chapter 12, in which a number of proof methods based on partial-order reasoning, so-called communication-closed-layers laws, are presented.

3.4 The Generalisation of Floyd's Approach to Nondeterministic Interleavings

The essence of Floyd's inductive assertion method is the observation that a partial-correctness proof can be reduced to checking *finitely* many verification

---

[3] This quotation is modified because the original text contains some not yet explained terminology.

[4] As pointed out by Wolfgang Reisig, this argument is wrong. He writes: "Of course, a partial order can be recomputed from the set of all its total extensions. But the behaviour of a program consists of a *set* of partial orders. Given the set of all total-order extensions of elements of a set of partial orders, can one then recompute the original partial orders? No. Or sometimes. For instance, this is the case when you additionally know the Mazurkiewicz dependency relation (introduced on page 133)."

conditions, i.e., for every transition $l \xrightarrow{a} l'$: if execution arrives at l, the associated predicate Q_l holds, and if the action a is executed, then $Q_{l'}$ holds at l'. This observation is based upon the fact that every execution sequence is equivalent with a sequence of transitions taken from a fixed, finite, collection.

Since concurrent execution is now modelled by nondeterministic interleavings of atomic actions, the incorporation of concurrency within Floyd's method dictates that every nondeterministic interleaving of atomic actions should be described using such transitions. That is, *execution of a transition should correspond to an atomic action.*

Thus, execution of $P_1 \parallel \ldots \parallel P_n$ should be characterised by the interleaved execution of such transitions from a fixed, finite, collection. Furthermore, during execution of a local transition contained in P_i no execution is modelled in P_j, for $j \neq i$. This implies that a global transition of $P_1 \parallel \ldots \parallel P_n$ contained in P_i is characterised by two n-tuples of *composite* locations, beginning in an n-tuple $\langle l_1, \ldots, l_i, \ldots, l_n \rangle$ and ending in an n-tuple $\langle l_1, \ldots, l_i', \ldots, l_n \rangle$ with $l_1, \ldots, l_n$ and l_i' locations in $P_1, \ldots, P_n$ and P_i, and local transition $l_i \xrightarrow{a} l_i'$ in P_i containing at most one critical reference. In case action a is obvious from the context, $l \xrightarrow{a} l'$ is abbreviated to $l \rightarrow l'$. Composite locations will also be called *global* locations in the following.

Example 3.8 Let x be shared and y be local. Consider the concurrent program fragment illustrated in Figure 3.5. According to the above, in order to describe

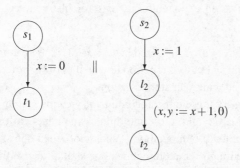

Fig. 3.5. A simple fragment of a shared variable concurrent program.

the execution of this fragment one has to introduce:

(i) composite locations: $\langle s_1, s_2 \rangle$, $\langle s_1, l_2 \rangle$, $\langle s_1, t_2 \rangle$, $\langle t_1, s_2 \rangle$, $\langle t_1, l_2 \rangle$, $\langle t_1, t_2 \rangle$

(ii) global transitions:
$$\underbrace{(\langle s_1, s_2 \rangle, \langle t_1, s_2 \rangle)}_{s_2 \text{ fixed}}, \underbrace{(\langle s_1, l_2 \rangle, \langle t_1, l_2 \rangle)}_{l_2 \text{ fixed}}, \underbrace{(\langle s_1, t_2 \rangle, \langle t_1, t_2 \rangle)}_{t_2 \text{ fixed}}, \ldots$$

This leads to the transition diagram in Figure 3.6. Instead of 3 instructions

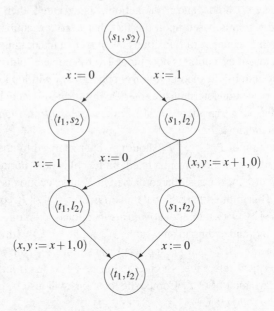

Fig. 3.6. Parallel composition reduced to a sequential diagram.

between 5 nodes, one has to consider 7 instructions between 6 nodes, which in general leads to an exponential increase of instructions and nodes to be considered. □

Note that we have now considered $(x, y := x + 1, 0)$ as an atomic action. This contrasts with the generalised criterion in which only *one* reference to a shared variable is allowed within an atomic action.

We can still unify these opposing points of view by stating that, once their corresponding guards hold, these multiple assignments are executed as *indivisible, atomic* units of computation. When more than one shared variable is involved in executing such atomic units, one should realise that such instructions are not amongst the atomic instructions on present day computers, and that mutual exclusion algorithms are required for their implementation (see Section 1.4.2 for such an algorithm). This adds up to saying that *if one wants to model concurrent executions of programs without the prior assumption of using mutual exclusion algorithms to guarantee atomicity of the individual transitions, one should restrict oneself to programs satisfying Reynolds' criterion.*

We continue in the next section with the development of a formal verification theory for concurrent programs operating upon shared variables, based on the assumption that transitions $(l, c \to f, l')$ are executed as single atomic actions.

3.5 Concurrent Transition Systems with Shared Variables

3.5.1 The Proof Method of Owicki & Gries

We generalise the inductive assertion method to concurrent transition systems that communicate by means of shared variables. From now on, primitive boolean and state functions are considered to be total, i.e., we base this section on Sections 2.3–2.8, unless stated otherwise. In Section 3.8 we lift this restriction and allow the occurrence of runtime errors. The subject proper of that section is then how to prove absence of runtime errors.

First we define the parallel composition of transition diagrams by means of a transition diagram itself.

Definition 3.9 (Parallel composition) Given transition diagrams $P_i \equiv (L_i, T_i, s_i, t_i)$, $i = 1, \ldots, n$, we define their parallel composition as the product transition diagram $P \equiv (L, T, s, t)$, also denoted by $P_1 \| \ldots \| P_n$, where:

- $L = L_1 \times \ldots \times L_n$
- $T = \{(l, a, l') \mid l = \langle l_1, \ldots, l_i, \ldots, l_n \rangle, l' = \langle l'_1, \ldots, l'_i, \ldots, l'_n \rangle,$
  $\qquad\qquad$ such that $(l_i, a, l'_i) \in T_i, l_j = l'_j, j \neq i\}$
- $s = \langle s_1, \ldots, s_n \rangle$
- $t = \langle t_1, \ldots, t_n \rangle.$ $\qquad\qquad\qquad\qquad\qquad\qquad\qquad\qquad\square$

We can generalise Definition 3.9 to the parallel composition of transition systems by observing that the above definition does not impose any restriction on the names of the nodes involved. Mathematically this amounts to the observation that renaming is a congruence w.r.t. the operation of parallel composition defined above, and that therefore this operation can be extended to the equivalence classes generated by the renaming relation.

In the following we will define all our operations on diagrams. However, in case it is obvious that the renaming relation is a congruence w.r.t. these operations, we will no longer mention their extension to the equivalence classes generated by this relation.

Lemma 3.10 (Associativity and commutativity of parallel composition) Parallel composition of transition systems is associative and commutative. That is, for transition systems P_1, P_2, and P_3, $[[P_1 \| P_2] \| P_3]$ is one-to-one (i.e., isomorphic) to $[P_1 \| [P_2 \| P_3]]$, and $[P_1 \| P_2]$ is one-to-one (i.e., isomorphic) to $[P_2 \| P_1]$.

Proof Left as an exercise [Han00].   □

As a consequence of Lemma 3.10, one can drop brackets inside $P_1 \| \ldots \| P_n$-terms.

Applying the global method

Thus, all definitions based on the notion of transition diagrams in the previous chapter also apply to the parallel composition of transition diagrams (or systems) in the present chapter. In particular, the execution of $P_1 \| \ldots \| P_n$ starts in $s = \langle s_1, \ldots, s_n \rangle$, that is, in all entry nodes of its constituent processes $P_1, \ldots, P_n$. Then execution proceeds by subsequently taking an enabled transition in *one* of the processes $P_1, \ldots, P_n$. This can take place infinitely often, or until all processes are blocked because there are no enabled transitions left, or until a number of processes have terminated and the remaining ones are blocked, or until the program terminates. In the last case all processes have reached their exit nodes and hence $P_1 \| \ldots \| P_n$ has reached $t = \langle t_1, \ldots, t_n \rangle$. Otherwise, if a process P_i is no longer enabled and yet t has not been reached, $P_1 \| \ldots \| P_n$ is said to be *blocked,* and a *deadlock* has been reached.

Note that parallelism is defined by an interleaving of the individual transition of the processes $P_1, \ldots, P_n$. In particular we draw attention to the fact that now the local transitions in the processes $P_i,$, $i = 1, \ldots, n$, are executed *atomically.* In the previous section we have pointed out that only when such local transitions require the calculation of at most one critical reference does this model assignments as they occur in present-day computers. In case more than one critical reference is involved, implementation of (atomic execution of transitions in) our model requires the introduction of mutual exclusion algorithms (on the level of software or hardware).

As in Section 2.3, the function *val* is defined as follows, where η denotes a maximal execution sequence of $P_1 \| \ldots \| P_n$:

$$val(\eta) \stackrel{\text{def}}{=} \begin{cases} \sigma, \text{ in case } \eta \text{ terminates in } t, \text{ and the last state of } \eta \text{ is } \sigma, \\ fail, \text{ in case } \eta \text{ ends in } l, \ l \neq t, \text{ to indicate a deadlocked} \\ \qquad \text{(or blocked) computation, and} \\ \bot, \text{ in case } \eta \text{ is infinite.} \end{cases}$$

Define *Comp* $[\![P_1 \| \ldots \| P_n]\!] \sigma$ as the set of computations of $P_1 \| \ldots \| P_n$ starting in initial state σ, and the *meaning* of $P_1 \| \ldots \| P_n$ as the function:

$$\mathcal{M} [\![P_1 \| \ldots \| P_n]\!] \sigma \stackrel{def}{=} \{val(\eta) \mid \eta \in Comp [\![P_1 \| \ldots \| P_n]\!] \sigma\}.$$

Hence $\mathcal{M} [\![P_1 \| \ldots \| P_n]\!] \sigma$ may contain proper states, and the symbols *fail* and

$\perp$ corresponding with nontermination, i.e., with a deadlock and divergence, respectively, which are not considered as proper program states.

The definition of partial correctness from the previous chapter applies immediately to the parallel composition of transition diagrams (or systems) because it results by Definition 3.9 in a particular instance of a transition diagram (or system) according to Definition 2.5.

In particular, a program $P_1 \parallel \dots \parallel P_n$ is *partially correct* w.r.t. a specification $< \varphi, \psi >$ iff for all states σ, σ', if $\models \varphi(\sigma)$ and $\sigma' \in \mathcal{M}[\![P_1 \parallel \dots \parallel P_n]\!](\sigma)$ then $\models \psi(\sigma')$ holds. This is also expressed by $\models \{\varphi\}P_1 \parallel \dots \parallel P_n\{\psi\}$.

The definitions of success, convergence and total correctness carry over, similarly.

Since the parallel composition of (sequential) transition diagrams is itself a sequential transition diagram, which describes all possible interleavings of the parallel components, we can simply apply the inductive assertion method to concurrent systems. This leads to a *global* proof method where an assertion has to be found for every global location in $P_1 \parallel \dots \parallel P_n$. If every process P_i has r locations and s edges then $P_1 \parallel \dots \parallel P_n$ has r^n global locations and $n \times s$ edges. For every edge there are r^{n-1} global locations from which it can start, thus also r^{n-1} verification conditions. Thus for $P_1 \parallel \dots \parallel P_n$ we have to prove $n \times s \times r^{n-1}$ verification conditions, which is exponential in the number of programs. Consequently this method has no practical value.

Basic intuition of the method of Owicki & Gries

Let us try to improve this situation by deriving predicates associated with global locations from predicates attached to local locations. First these local predicates in P_i are proved to be *locally correct*, i.e., partially correct for the sequential execution of P_i when P_i is considered in isolation as a separate process. We investigate what must be added to these proofs in order to achieve partial correctness of $P_1 \parallel \dots \parallel P_n$.

Let $P \equiv P_1 \parallel \dots \parallel P_n$. Associate predicates to *local* locations of P instead of to its global locations: assume that for every *local* location l_i in P_i there exists a predicate Q_{l_i}. In order to apply the inductive assertion method, Definition 2.10, associate with every global location $l = \langle l_1, \dots, l_n \rangle$ of P (where l_i denotes a location of P_i) the predicate $Q_l \equiv Q_{l_1} \wedge \dots \wedge Q_{l_n}$; the resulting inductive assertion network is called $Q_1 \times \dots \times Q_n$. Next this assertion network is shown to be inductive by proving the verification conditions for all steps. That is, for each transition $b \to f$ leading from $l = \langle l_1, \dots, l_n \rangle$ to $l' = \langle l_1', \dots, l_n' \rangle$ we have to prove

$$\models Q_l \wedge b \to Q_{l'} \circ f,$$

i.e.,

$$\models (Q_{l_1} \wedge \ldots \wedge Q_{l_n} \wedge b) \to (Q_{l'_1} \wedge \ldots \wedge Q_{l'_n}) \circ f.$$

By the definition of a transition in a parallel composition, l differs from l' in at most only one local location. Suppose this step is a transition in P_i. Then $l_j \equiv l'_j$, for $i \neq j$, and hence $Q_{l_j} = Q_{l'_j}$. We shall demonstrate that it is sufficient to prove:

(i) $\models Q_{l_i} \wedge b \to Q_{l'_i} \circ f$,
   i.e., the *local* verification condition in P_i, and

(ii) $\models Q_{l_j} \wedge Q_{l_i} \wedge b \to Q_{l_j} \circ f$, for all $j \neq i$,
   that is, all predicates Q_{l_j} associated with other processes P_j, with $j \neq i$, are *invariant* under execution of this particular transition in P_i. In other words, *executing a transition in P_i does not interfere with the validity of the local assertions Q_{l_j} chosen in the other processes.*

This can be understood as follows:

$Q_l \wedge b =$	(by definition and propositional logic)
$(\bigwedge_{j \neq i} Q_{l_j} \wedge Q_{l_i} \wedge b) \wedge (Q_{l_i} \wedge b) \to$	(by (i) and (ii) above)
$(\bigwedge_{j \neq i} Q_{l_j} \circ f) \wedge Q_{l'_i} \circ f =$	(by definition and propositional logic)
$Q_{l'} \circ f.$	

Consequently, the combination of conditions (i) and (ii) above leads to a sound proof method.

Condition (i) implies that process P_i is partially correct w.r.t. $< Q_{s_i}, Q_{t_i} >$ *in isolation*. We say that P_i is *locally correct* w.r.t. $< Q_{s_i}, Q_{t_i} >$, for $i = 1, \ldots, n$. Condition (ii) corresponds to the *interference freedom test* of Owicki & Gries [OG76a].

This leads to a more efficient method for proving partial correctness of $P_1 \parallel \ldots \parallel P_n$: first prove partial correctness for every process P_i in isolation, and then check interference freedom. In order to compute the complexity of this new method, again suppose that P_i has r locations and s edges. Now we have to find $n \times r$ local assertions and then we must prove for every edge

- local correctness: 1 verification condition, and
- interference freedom: there are $(n-1) \times r$ assertions in the other processes, so $(n-1) \times r$ verification conditions.

Since there are $n \times s$ edges in $P_1 \parallel \ldots \parallel P_n$, we obtain $n \times s \times (1 + (n-1) \times r)$ verification conditions. Clearly this improves upon the global method, which required $n \times s \times r^{n-1}$ verification conditions, and reflects the so-called *state explosion* associated with parallel composition.

Example 3.11 Consider program $P \equiv P_1 \parallel P_2$ as in Figure 3.7.

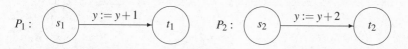

Fig. 3.7. A very simple concurrent program.

We prove that P is partially correct w.r.t. specification $< y = 0, y = 3 >$, i.e., $\models \{y = 0\} P \{y = 3\}$. Take the assertion network Q defined in Figure 3.8.

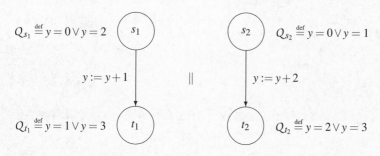

Fig. 3.8. And its associated inductive assertion network.

(i) It is easy to check that P_i is partially correct w.r.t. $< Q_{s_i}, Q_{t_i} >$, for $i \in \{1, 2\}$.

(ii) Verify interference freedom:

- We show that Q_{s_1} and Q_{t_1} are invariant under $y := y + 2$, as follows.

    – Assume $Q_{s_1} \wedge Q_{s_2}$ holds. Then $y = 0$, and thus after executing $y := y + 2$ we have that $Q_{s_1} \equiv y = 0 \vee y = 2$ holds.

    – Assume $Q_{t_1} \wedge Q_{s_2}$ holds. Then $y = 1$, and thus after executing $y := y + 2$ we have that $Q_{t_1} \equiv y = 1 \vee y = 3$ holds.

- Similarly, Q_{s_2} and Q_{t_2} are invariant under $y := y + 1$.

(iii) • $\models y = 0 \rightarrow Q_s$, since $Q_s \equiv Q_{s_1} \wedge Q_{s_2}$ and $\models Q_{s_1} \wedge Q_{s_2} \leftrightarrow y = 0$, and

- $\models Q_t \rightarrow y = 3$, since $Q_t \equiv Q_{t_1} \wedge Q_{t_2}$ and $\models Q_{t_1} \wedge Q_{t_2} \leftrightarrow y = 3$. $\square$

Incompleteness of the proposed method

Example 3.12 (Incompleteness of the proposed method) Consider $P \equiv P_1 \parallel P_2$ as in figure 3.9.

Fig. 3.9. An even simpler concurrent program.

The aim is to prove that P is partially correct w.r.t. specification $< y = 0, y = 2 >$. Analogously to the previous example, we investigate whether the assertion network given in Figure 3.10 is interference free.

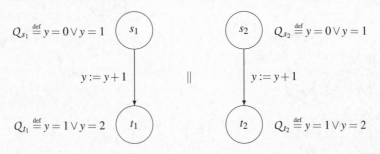

Fig. 3.10. And a failed attempt at defining an interference free inductive assertion network for it.

Clearly P_i is partially correct w.r.t. $< Q_{s_i}, Q_{t_i} >$, for $i \in \{1, 2\}$. These predicates, however, are not interference free. For instance, assume that $Q_{s_1} \wedge Q_{s_2}$ holds. Then $y = 0 \vee y = 1$, and thus after executing $y := y + 1$ we have that $y = 1 \vee y = 2$ holds. Hence $Q_{s_1} \equiv y = 0 \vee y = 1$ is *not* invariant under execution of $y := y + 1$ in P_2.

A second problem is that $Q_{t_1} \wedge Q_{t_2}$ does not imply $y = 2$.

It is even impossible to find assertions that prove specification $< y = 0, y = 2 >$ for P using program variable y only! In order to show this, suppose we have Q_{s_i} and Q_{t_i} which are locally correct for P_i and, moreover, $\models y = 0 \rightarrow Q_{s_1} \wedge Q_{s_2}$, and $\models Q_{t_1} \wedge Q_{t_2} \rightarrow y = 2$. From the first implication, $\models y = 0 \rightarrow Q_{s_1} \wedge Q_{s_2}$, we obtain that Q_{s_1} and Q_{s_2} hold for a state which assigns the value 0 to y. Since we assumed local correctness, this implies that Q_{t_1} and Q_{t_2} hold for a state which assigns the value 1 to y, thus $\models y = 1 \rightarrow Q_{t_1} \wedge Q_{t_2}$. This, however, leads to a contradiction with the second implication, $\models Q_{t_1} \wedge Q_{t_2} \rightarrow y = 2$.   □

Noncompositionality of the $\mathcal{M}$ semantics

This is the right point to reflect upon what is going on. In the last chapter we proposed a proof method for sequential programs, Floyd's inductive assertion method, and proved it to be *complete* in a semantic sense, i.e., the required predicates could always be found (although by Gödel's incompleteness theorem formal proofs for establishing validity of the verification conditions need not always exist). In the present chapter we propose a similar method, which consists of a reduction of concurrent program proving to sequential program proving, and, since the latter is complete, the former "generalised one" is complete, too. But that method has a drawback: the number of verification conditions whose validity must be proved is exponential in the number of processes inside a concurrent program. So we are led to the present method, based on (1) local verification proofs, and (2) interference freedom checks, which, as we have seen, is *incomplete*.

As such the present method intrinsically involves a so-called *compositional* way of reasoning since it allows one to obtain a proof of correctness of an entire system from local correctness proofs of its components.

We show next that our semantics function $\mathcal{M}$ is *not* compositional w.r.t. parallel composition in that $\mathcal{M}[\![P_1\|\ldots\|P_n]\!]$ cannot be defined as a function of $\mathcal{M}[\![P_i]\!], i = 1, \ldots, n$.

Consider the parallel programs $P_1\|P_2$ and $Q_1\|P_2$ defined in Figure 3.11.

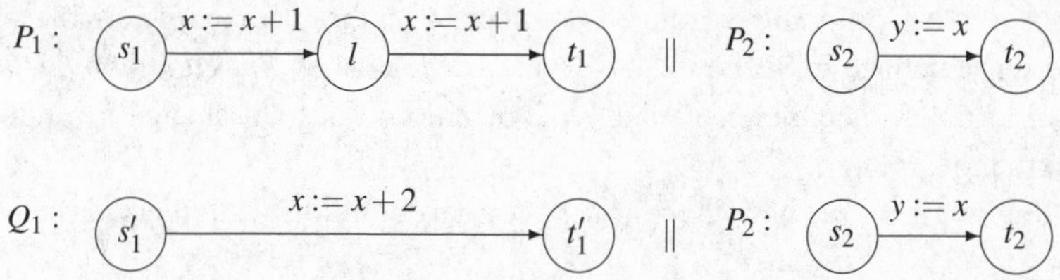

Fig. 3.11. Two parallel programs, $P_1\|P_2$ and $Q_1\|P_2$ which have different $\mathcal{M}$-semantics although $\mathcal{M}[\![P_1]\!] = \mathcal{M}[\![Q_1]\!]$.

It is clear that $\mathcal{M}[\![P_1]\!] = \mathcal{M}[\![Q_1]\!]$, yet $\mathcal{M}[\![P_1\|P_2]\!] \neq \mathcal{M}[\![Q_1\|P_2]\!]$ because due to the definition of interleaving semantics the single transition of P_2 can be wedged in between the execution of $(s_1, x := x+1, l)$ and $(l, x := x+1, t_1)$ in P_1, whereas this is not possible in case of Q_1, resulting in a different value of y. This is due to the fact that $\mathcal{M}[\![P_1]\!]$ *does not express the possibility to interleave at location l!* Only the functional behaviour of P_1 when regarded in isolation *disregarding* that interleaving potential is recorded by $\mathcal{M}$. Hence, in general, $\mathcal{M}[\![P_1\|P_2]\!]$ cannot be expressed as a function $\bar{\|}$ of $\mathcal{M}[\![P_i]\!], i = 1, 2$.

This creates a discrepancy. The proof method developed up to now aims at reducing reasoning about $P_1 \| \ldots \| P_n$ to reasoning about its separate components P_i, whereas the very semantics $\mathcal{M}$ which we use does not express the semantics of parallel composition $\mathcal{M}[\![P_1 \| \ldots \| P_n]\!]$ as a function $\bar{\|}$ of the semantics $\mathcal{M}[\![P_i]\!]$ of its separate components!

In Section 3.5.4 we analyse how this source of incompleteness can be removed. This will be done in a uniform manner depending on the behaviour of P_i only, and not on any particular environment for P_i, by the introduction of a semantics $\mathcal{R}$ which is compositional w.r.t. parallelism and by incorporating this semantics in the proof procedure for parallelism. For *closed* programs, i.e., programs with no environment, $\mathcal{R}$ and $\mathcal{M}$ yield consistent results.

Formulating a complete version

The solution of Owicki and Gries to the particular form of incompleteness signalled in Example 3.12 above is the introduction of *auxiliary* variables that do not occur in the original transitions of a program but are added to their assignments in order to be able to *express assumptions about the other components*. These variables are not allowed in conditions inside transitions. Furthermore, auxiliary variables should not occur in the original assignments of the program – they only occur in assignments to auxiliary variables themselves, and thus the values of the program variables are also not affected by adding auxiliary variables. Within our semantic set up this is expressed by requiring that conditions c in our original program do not depend on these auxiliary variables, in the sense defined in Section 2.4.1. Hence *auxiliary variables do not influence control flow*, since the enabledness of transitions does not change by adding auxiliary variables.

Summarising, we have the following formal definition of auxiliary variables:

Definition 3.13 (Auxiliary variables) A set of program variables $\bar{z} = z_1, \ldots, z_n$ is a set of auxiliary variables of a program P if

- for any boolean condition c of P, $\bar{z} \cap var(c) = \emptyset$,
- for any state transformation f of P there exist state transformations g and h such that $f = g \circ h$, $\bar{z} \cap var(g) = \emptyset$, and the write variables of h are among $\bar{z}$.

(For the definition of $var(f)$ and the write variables of a function f we refer to Section 2.4.1.)   □

Observe that the above second condition expresses that every state transformation f of P can be decomposed in a state transformation g which does not involve the auxiliary variables and a state transformation h which changes only the auxiliary variables. Note also that logical variables trivially satisfy this definition.

Now, the test for interference freedom allows one to check the consistency of the introduced assumptions when these are expressed in terms of the program variables and the auxiliary variables.

Example 3.14 (Continuation of Example 3.12) In our example we can use two auxiliary variables z_1 and z_2 to encode the location which the control flow of a process has reached: $z_i = 0$ iff P_i is at location s_i, and $z_i = 1$ iff P_i is at location t_i. Therefore we augment the program with assignments to these auxiliary variables, resulting in $P' \equiv P_1' \parallel P_2'$ as in Figure 3.12.

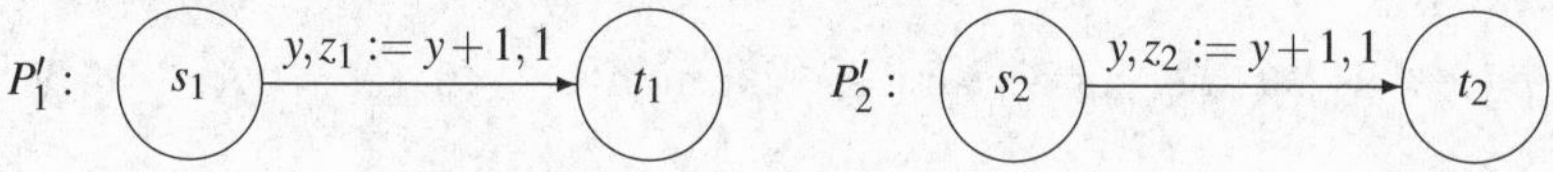

$$P_1': \quad \left(s_1\right) \xrightarrow{\;y, z_1 := y+1, 1\;} \left(t_1\right) \qquad P_2': \quad \left(s_2\right) \xrightarrow{\;y, z_2 := y+1, 1\;} \left(t_2\right)$$

Fig. 3.12. Adding auxiliary variables z_1 and z_2 to the program from Figure 3.9.

In the predicates defined in Figure 3.13 these auxiliary variables are used to express the relation between the values of y and the locations of the other process.[5]

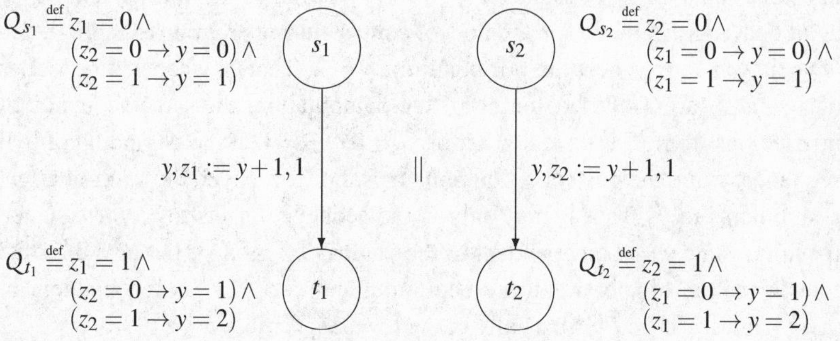

$$Q_{s_1} \stackrel{\text{def}}{=} z_1 = 0 \wedge \qquad\qquad Q_{s_2} \stackrel{\text{def}}{=} z_2 = 0 \wedge$$
$$(z_2 = 0 \to y = 0) \wedge \quad \left(s_1\right) \qquad \left(s_2\right) \qquad (z_1 = 0 \to y = 0) \wedge$$
$$(z_2 = 1 \to y = 1) \qquad\qquad\qquad\qquad\qquad\qquad (z_1 = 1 \to y = 1)$$

$$y, z_1 := y+1, 1 \qquad \parallel \qquad y, z_2 := y+1, 1$$

$$Q_{t_1} \stackrel{\text{def}}{=} z_1 = 1 \wedge \qquad\qquad Q_{t_2} \stackrel{\text{def}}{=} z_2 = 1 \wedge$$
$$(z_2 = 0 \to y = 1) \wedge \quad \left(t_1\right) \qquad \left(t_2\right) \qquad (z_1 = 0 \to y = 1) \wedge$$
$$(z_2 = 1 \to y = 2) \qquad\qquad\qquad\qquad\qquad\qquad (z_1 = 1 \to y = 2)$$

Fig. 3.13. The use of auxiliary variables in predicates allows for the expression of interference free assertion networks.

We prove that this modified program P' is partially correct with respect to the specification $< y = 0 \wedge z_1 = 0 \wedge z_2 = 0, y = 2 >$:

---

[5] In fact, we have introduced again, through the back door, a number of (sub-)assertions, the value of which is exponential in the number of processes. This problem will be solved by giving an alternative solution in Sections 3.5.4 and 3.5.6, which is based on the notion of *communication interface* of a process.

(i) Local correctness of P_1' and P_2' is straightforward.
(ii) Interference freedom:

- Assume $Q_{s_1} \wedge Q_{s_2}$ holds, that is, $z_1 = 0 \wedge z_2 = 0 \wedge y = 0$ holds. Then after executing $y, z_2 := y + 1, 1$ we have $z_1 = 0 \wedge z_2 = 1 \wedge y = 1$, and thus Q_{s_1} holds.
- Assume $Q_{t_1} \wedge Q_{s_2}$ holds, that is, $z_1 = 1 \wedge z_2 = 0 \wedge y = 1$ holds. Then after executing $y, z_2 := y + 1, 1$ we have $z_1 = 1 \wedge z_2 = 1 \wedge y = 2$, and thus Q_{t_1} holds.
- Symmetrically, Q_{s_2} and Q_{t_2} are invariant under $y, z_1 := y + 1, 1$.

(iii) Clearly, $\models y = 0 \wedge z_1 = 0 \wedge z_2 = 0 \rightarrow Q_{s_1} \wedge Q_{s_2}$ and $\models Q_{t_1} \wedge Q_{t_2} \rightarrow y = 2$.

Hence P' is partially correct w.r.t. specification $< y = 0 \wedge z_1 = 0 \wedge z_2 = 0, y = 2 >$.   □

However, we started out wishing to prove P to be partially correct w.r.t. $< y = 0, y = 2 >$! So, *how does one argue that the former, a statement about P' involving z_1, z_2 and y, implies the latter, a statement involving P and only y?*

P''s partial correctness w.r.t. $< y = 0 \wedge z_1 = 0 \wedge z_2 = 0, y = 2 >$ means that every terminating $(y = 0 \wedge z_1 = 0 \wedge z_2 = 0)$-computation terminates in a state satisfying $y = 2$. Then also every terminating $(y = 0)$-computation terminates in a state satisfying $y = 2$, since (1) z_1 and z_2 do not occur in tests, and hence do not have any influence on the flow of control during program execution, and (2) neither z_1 nor z_2 occur in postcondition $y = 2$. That is, whatever the values of z_1 and z_2 are at the beginning of the computation, the same sequence of instructions from P_1 is executed as for $z_1 = 0 \wedge z_2 = 0$ at the beginning of that sequence, while the postcondition remains valid. Moreover, they do not affect assignments to y. That is, not only is the sequence of instructions executed for initial state $y = 0$ independent of the values of z_1 and z_2, but also the state transformation of y between the beginning and end of P' is independent of these values. Hence P' is partially correct w.r.t. specification $< y = 0, y = 2 >$.

This argument summarises soundness of the following *initialisation rule*, because we can initialise the auxiliary variables z_1 and z_2 both to 0 so that the old precondition $y = 0 \wedge z_1 = 0 \wedge z_2 = 0$ results in a new precondition $y = 0$ for P', while preserving partial correctness of P'.

Rule 3.1 (Initialisation rule)

$$\frac{\{\varphi\}\, P\, \{\psi\}}{\{\varphi \circ f\}\, P\, \{\psi\}},$$

where f is a function such that its write variables constitute a set of auxiliary variables for P which do not occur in ψ.

Here the format

$$\frac{\{\varphi_1\}\, P_1\, \{\psi_1\}}{\{\varphi_2\}\, P_2\, \{\psi_2\}}$$

is used to express the rule that $\models \{\varphi_1\}\, P_1\, \{\psi_1\}$ *implies* $\models \{\varphi_2\}\, P_2\, \{\psi_2\}$. If the latter is the case, the rule is called *sound*. Soundness of the initialisation rule is proved in Section 3.5.3 (see Lemma 3.22).

Example 3.15 (Continuation of Example 3.12) In more detail, with Q_{s_i} as in Figure 3.13 above, the following equivalences hold:

$$
\begin{aligned}
&Q_{s_1} \wedge Q_{s_2}\\
\leftrightarrow\ & z_1 = 0 \wedge (z_2 = 0 \to y = 0)\ \wedge (z_2 = 1 \to y = 1)\wedge\\
& z_2 = 0 \wedge (z_1 = 0 \to y = 0)\wedge (z_1 = 1 \to y = 1)\\
\leftrightarrow\ & \text{(by propositional logic)}\ z_1 = 0 \wedge z_2 = 0 \wedge y = 0.
\end{aligned}
$$

Choosing $(z_1, z_2) := (0,0)$ for f, one has

$$\models (z_1 = 0 \wedge z_2 = 0 \wedge y = 0) \circ f \leftrightarrow y = 0.$$

Now, using these two results and given that

$$\{z_1 = 0 \wedge z_2 = 0 \wedge y = 0\}\, P'\, \{y = 2\}$$

holds for P' as above, the initialisation rule states:

$$\frac{\{z_1 = 0 \wedge z_2 = 0 \wedge y = 0\}\, P'\, \{y = 2\}}{\{y = 0\}\, P'\, \{y = 2\}}$$

and therefore (soundness of this rule) leads to

$$\models \{y = 0\}\, P'\, \{y = 2\}.$$

Please, observe that $\models y = 0 \to z_1 = 0 \wedge z_2 = 0 \wedge y = 0$ does not hold. Hence, one needs an *extra* rule to justify the step from $\models \{z_1 = 0 \wedge z_2 = 0 \wedge y = 0\}\, P'\, \{y = 2\}$ to $\models \{y = 0\}\, P'\, \{y = 2\}$. This justifies the initialisation rule, applied above. $\qquad\square$

This raises as the next question how to get rid of P' in $\models \{y = 0\}\, P'\, \{y = 2\}$, for it is our intention to prove $\models \{y = 0\}\, P\, \{y = 2\}$!

Since every $(y = 0)$-computation in P has a *corresponding* $(y = 0)$-computation in P' which assigns the same values to y, we also obtain that P is partially correct w.r.t. $< y = 0, y = 2 >$.

This second argument summarises application of Owicki & Gries' so-called *auxiliary variables rule*, stating that a correctness statement about P' in the postcondition of which no auxiliary variables occur implies the similar statement about P, where P is obtained from P' by removing auxiliary variables.

Rule 3.2 (Owicki & Gries' auxiliary variables rule) Let $\bar{z}$ be a set of auxiliary variables of P'. Then

$$\frac{\{\varphi\}\,P'\,\{\psi\}}{\{\varphi\}\,P\,\{\psi\}}$$

provided $\bar{z} \cap var(\psi) = \emptyset$ and P is obtained from P' by restricting the state transformations of P' to all the variables excluding the auxiliary variable set $\bar{z}$. More precisely, let f be a state transformation of P' such that $f = g \circ h$, where g does not involve $\bar{z}$ and the write variables of h are among $\bar{z}$, then g is the corresponding state transformation of P.

Soundness of this rule follows from Lemma 3.23.

Example 3.16 (Continuation of Example 3.12) In the case of our example, application of the auxiliary variables rule amounts to

$$\frac{\{y=0\}\ (y,z_1) := (y+1,1)\,\|\,(y,z_2) := (y+1,1)\ \{y=2\}}{\{y=0\}\ y := y+1\,\|\,y := y+1\ \{y=2\}},$$

where the above assignments stand for the corresponding transition diagrams from Figures 3.9 and 3.12. Consequently its soundness gives that from

$$\models \{y=0\}\,P'\,\{y=2\}$$

one derives

$$\models \{y=0\}\,P\,\{y=2\},$$

with P as defined in Example 3.12.   □

The general formulation of the proof method of Owicki & Gries [OG76a] is given below.

Definition 3.17 (The proof method of Owicki & Gries) Consider $P \equiv P_1 \,\|\, \dots \,\|\, P_n$. To prove $\{\varphi\}P\{\psi\}$ we introduce the *proof method of Owicki & Gries*:

(i) Augment P_i by introducing auxiliary variables; every action $b \to f$ can be extended as follows: $b \to f \circ g$, where g is a state transformation such that its write variables are among the auxiliary variables $\bar{z}$ where

$\bar{z} \cap var(\varphi, P, \psi) = \emptyset$. This leads to an augmented transition diagram $P' \equiv P'_1 \| \ldots \| P'_n$.

(ii) Associate a predicate Q_l with every location l of P'_i.

(iii) Prove *local correctness* of every P'_i: For every transition $l \xrightarrow{a} l'$ of P'_i, assuming $a \equiv b \to f$, we prove

$$\models Q_l \wedge b \to Q_{l'} \circ f.$$

(iv) Prove *interference freedom*, that is, for every transition $l \xrightarrow{a} l'$ of P'_i, and for every predicate $Q_{l'''}$ associated to a location l'' of P'_j, with $j \neq i$, assuming $a \equiv b \to f$,[6] we prove

$$\models Q_l \wedge Q_{l''} \wedge b \to Q_{l''} \circ f.$$

(v) Prove

- $\models \varphi \to (\bigwedge_{i=1}^n Q_{s_i}) \circ h$, for some state transformation h whose write variables $write(h)$ belong to the set of auxiliary variables $\bar{z}$, and where s_i denotes the initial location of P'_i, and
- $\models (\bigwedge_{i=1}^n Q_{t_i}) \to \psi$, where t_i denotes the final location of P'_i. □

Let us trace how the proof method of Owicki & Gries has been applied in case of our example. Step (i) corresponds with the transformation of P in Figure 3.9 to P' as in Figure 3.12. Step (ii) is given by Figure 3.13, step (iii) is straightforward, and step (iv) has been checked above. The first part of step (v) is trivial, since $\varphi \equiv y = 0$ and

$$\models \bigwedge_i Q_{s_i} \circ h \leftrightarrow \bigwedge_i Q_{s_i} \circ (z_1, z_2) := (0, 0) \leftrightarrow 0 = 0 \wedge 0 = 0 \wedge y = 0 \leftrightarrow y = 0,$$

choosing $(z_1, z_2) := (0, 0)$ for h; the second part of step (v) amounts to proving the validity of

$$\models z_1 = 1 \wedge z_2 = 1 \wedge y = 2 \to y = 2,$$

which is trivial.

Observe that when $n = 1$ this proof method still makes sense (and, by the results of the next two sections, is even sound and semantically complete).

So what has been accomplished up until now? Since we do not as yet have a compositional semantics to base our proof method upon, there is no way out for obtaining a formulation of Owicki & Gries' method (which is also complete) but to use brute force by proving properties of $P_1 \| \ldots \| P_n$ in a somewhat ad-hoc manner via the introduction of:

---

[6] The intention is here that $b \to f$ identifies a label occurring in P', i.e., it is of the form $b \to f' \circ g$ with $b \to f'$ occurring in P.

- appropriately-changed auxiliary programs P_i' derived from P_i,
- assertion networks for P_i' whose predicates also depend on the behaviour of the environmental processes P_j of P_i, and which hence record the progress of computation in $P_j, j \neq i$ – note that this is the very reason why the assertion networks defined in Figure 3.10 are not interference free and no such network can be found depending on P_i's free variables only – and
- explicit rules for transforming correctness proofs for $P_1' \| \ldots \| P_n'$ into proofs about $P_1 \| \ldots \| P_n$ and the particular correctness statement $\{\varphi\}P_1 \| \ldots \| P_n\{\psi\}$ concerned.

3.5.2 Examples

In this section we illustrate the method of Owicki & Gries by proving mutual exclusion of different algorithms. First we investigate the general structure of mutual exclusion algorithms where two processes should be coordinated, leading to the development of Dijkstra's mutual exclusion algorithm [Dij65b, Dij68a] and a proof of its correctness using the method of Owicki & Gries. Then the problem is generalised to n-process solutions as tackled by the so-called Ticket Algorithm and Szymanski's mutual exclusion algorithm. The Ticket Algorithm is one of the simplest of the n-process solutions to the critical section problem. It is taken from Section 3.3 of Andrews' beautiful monograph [And91] (which is still a joy to read). An attempt at an informal explanation why Szymanski's algorithm preserves mutual exclusion appears in Section 1.4.4 of this book.

The mutual exclusion property we want to establish for these algorithms cannot be expressed directly as a partial-correctness formula. Consequently, we do not use the whole of the method of Owicki & Gries, since that proves partial-correctness formulae of the $\{pre\}P_1 \| \ldots \| P_n\{post\}$-type, but only part of it. We only need the notion of inductive assertion networks in the way these are constructed according to the method of Owicki & Gries, since these express properties which hold at the locations of processes. We shall prove that these properties, when applied to the locations of the critical sections of each process, imply mutual exclusion.

In general, the mutual exclusion problem is present in a system of concurrently executing processes where some common resources can only be used by one process at-a-time. For simplicity, we model these processes as infinite loops alternating between a *critical section* and a *non-critical section*. The general idea to enforce this property is to introduce *pre- and postprotocols* to the involved processes to ensure mutual exclusion.

In order to model mutual exclusion algorithms in terms of transition diagrams for two processes we use the following conventions.

- For each process P_i, $i = 1, 2$ we introduce a boolean variable cs_i as *observable*, with the intention that the value of cs_i is *tt* if and only if P_i is in its critical section.
- A program never starts in its critical section; we thus identify the beginning of the noncritical section with the entry location.
- Infinitely looping programs never reach their exit location; this explains the transition $(s, false \rightarrow id, t)$.

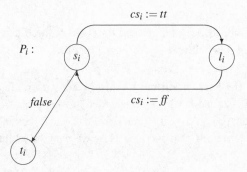

Fig. 3.14. General structure of a mutual exclusion algorithm.

We first consider systems which are composed of two concurrent processes P_1 and P_2. We say that they *satisfy the mutual exclusion property* if their parallel execution $P_1 \| P_2$ ensures that $\neg(cs_1 \wedge cs_2)$ always holds, i.e., P_1 and P_2 are never in their critical sections simultaneously – for the transition diagrams as in Figure 3.14 this obviously does not hold.

Example 3.18 Consider the following approach: For each process P_1 and P_2 a (boolean) variable req_i, $i = 1, 2$ is introduced to indicate that process P_i requests access to its critical section. These variables are shared, but process P_i has exclusive write-access to its own request flag req_i. Process P_j, $i \neq j$, can read req_i, but it cannot change the value of req_i.

To be sure that mutual exclusion holds we require that no process enters the critical section while the other process has already requested entrance to its critical section. Although we have satisfied the mutual exclusion requirement (not formally proven), this "solution" suffers from the possibility of running into a "deadlock" situation when P_i sets its request flag and does not enter the

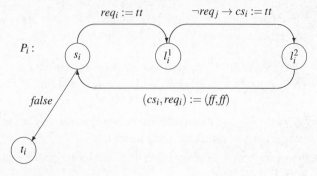

Fig. 3.15. A deadlock solution.

critical section immediately, but instead P_j sets its request flag; then both req_1 and req_2 are *true* and neither P_1 nor P_2 can proceed.   □

Example 3.19 (Dijkstra's Mutual Exclusion Algorithm) To avoid this possibility of deadlock, another location is added to each process, setting req_i to *ff* during a certain period so that P_j can reach its critical section and set its flag req_j to *ff* after executing that section. Now we want to establish that $P_1 \| P_2$

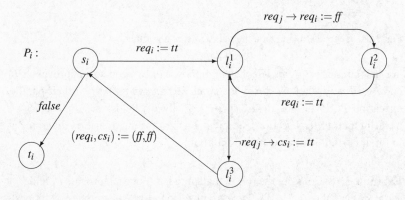

Fig. 3.16. Dijkstra's mutual exclusion algorithm.

in Figure 3.16 satisfies the mutual exclusion property. Since the transition diagram resulting from parallel composition in terms of their product would consist of 25 location and 60 transitions, we give a proof using the method of Owicki and Gries to reduce the required effort.

Proof We have the following assertion network Q_i for P_i, $i = 1, 2$, where

$j = 1, 2, i \neq j$.

$$Q(s_i) \stackrel{\text{def}}{=} \neg cs_i \wedge \neg req_i \wedge (cs_j \to req_j) \wedge (\neg(cs_i \wedge cs_j))$$
$$Q(l_i^1) \stackrel{\text{def}}{=} \neg cs_i \wedge req_i \wedge (cs_j \to req_j) \wedge (\neg(cs_i \wedge cs_j))$$
$$Q(l_i^2) \stackrel{\text{def}}{=} \neg cs_i \wedge \neg req_i \wedge (cs_j \to req_j) \wedge (\neg(cs_i \wedge cs_j))$$
$$Q(l_i^3) \stackrel{\text{def}}{=} cs_i \wedge req_i \wedge (cs_j \to req_j) \wedge (\neg(cs_i \wedge cs_j))$$
$$Q(t_i) \stackrel{\text{def}}{=} false$$

Local correctness: We have to check the following local verification conditions of which only the fourth one is nontrivial.

- $\models Q(s_i) \to Q(l_i^1) \circ (\lambda\sigma.(\sigma : req_i \mapsto tt))$.
- $\models Q(l_i^1) \wedge req_j \to Q(l_i^2) \circ (\lambda\sigma.(\sigma : req_i \mapsto ff))$.
- $\models Q(l_i^2) \to Q(l_i^1) \circ (\lambda\sigma.(\sigma : req_i \mapsto tt))$.
- $\models Q(l_i^1) \wedge \neg req_j \to Q(l_i^3) \circ (\lambda\sigma.(\sigma : cs_i \mapsto tt))$.

  Here we have to particularly check that our invariant $\neg(cs_i \wedge cs_j)$ is maintained. Now $Q(l_i^1) \wedge \neg req_j$ implies that $(cs_j \to req_j) \wedge \neg req_j$ and therefore $\neg cs_j$. Since cs_j is not changed by this transition, we have established that $\neg(cs_i \wedge cs_j)$ holds in l_i^3.

- $\models Q(l_i^3) \to Q(s_i) \circ (\lambda\sigma.(\sigma : cs_i, req_i \mapsto ff, ff))$.
- $\models Q(s_i) \wedge false \to Q(t_i)$.

Interference freedom: We only consider the interesting case in which the transition from l_i^1 to l_i^3 is taken in P_i and prove that the assertion network associated with the locations of P_j remains interference free.

- $\models Q(l_i^1) \wedge Q(s_j) \wedge \neg req_j \to Q(s_j) \circ (\lambda\sigma.(\sigma : cs_i \mapsto tt))$.

  The only crucial clause is $\neg(cs_1 \wedge cs_2)$. Since $Q(s_j)$ implies $\neg cs_j$ and cs_j is not changed by this particular transition, $Q(s_j)$ holds afterwards.

- $\models Q(l_i^1) \wedge Q(l_j^1) \wedge \neg req_j \to Q(l_j^1) \circ (\lambda\sigma.(\sigma : cs_i \mapsto tt))$.

  Now since $Q(l_j^1)$ implies req_j, we conclude from the premise that $req_j \wedge \neg req_j$ has to hold to enable the transition in this particular case. This turns out to be false, and hence the verification condition above is satisfied trivially.

- $\models Q(l_i^1) \wedge Q(l_j^2) \wedge \neg req_j \to Q(l_j^2) \circ (\lambda\sigma.(\sigma : cs_i \mapsto tt))$.

  Since $Q(l_j^2)$ is the same as $Q(s_j)$ this condition is already proven above.

- $\models Q(l_i^1) \wedge Q(l_j^3) \wedge \neg req_j \to Q(l_j^3) \circ (\lambda\sigma.(\sigma : cs_i \mapsto tt))$.

  Again, $Q(l_j^3)$ implies req_j, and analogously to the case of $Q(l_j^1)$ this verification condition is satisfied trivially.

- $\models Q(l_i^1) \land Q(t_j) \land \neg req_j \to Q(t_j) \circ (\lambda\sigma.(\sigma : cs_i \mapsto tt))$.

Since $Q(t_j) \equiv false$, this verification condition holds trivially.

We have to check 60 verification conditions for the interference test and 12 local verification conditions – but due to the symmetry of the processes only half of them have to be actually carried out. This is an improvement over the direct product. Additionally, the verification conditions for the Owicki & Gries method are better structured and usually simpler than those for the product of the processes.

The proof above indicates that $P_1 \| P_2$ satisfies the mutual exclusion property, since every assertion implies $\neg(cs_1 \land cs_2)$. □

Example 3.20 **(Correctness of the ticket algorithm)** We prove in this example that the ticket algorithm

$$\textbf{ticket} \equiv num := 1 ; next := 1 ; turn := 0 ; [P_0 \| P_1 \| \ldots \| P_{n-1}],$$

where each P_i has the structure as presented in Figure 3.17, satisfies mutual exclusion, i.e., there exists no computation of **ticket** leading to a state with more than one process at location l_4. Note, that the array assignment $turn := 0$ means that 0 is assigned to each component of the array.

Proof Let I be the formula

$$next \geq 1 \land \forall k, l : 1 \leq k \neq l \leq n. \; turn[k] < num \land$$
$$(turn[k] = 0 \lor turn[k] \neq turn[l]).$$

The assertion network of Figure 3.18 for each $P[i]$ shows that I is a global invariant. First observe that I holds initially, because $next$ and num are initialised to 1 and the $turn$-array is initialised to 0. Now, we prove local correctness and interference freedom of the given assertion network.

Local correctness: First we observe that the critical and noncritical sections do not change the variables needed for implementing mutual exclusion, i.e., they do not change the values of num, $next$, and $turn$. Therefore, I and $I \land turn[i] = next$, respectively, are inductive w.r.t. the transitions representing the critical and noncritical sections, respectively. For the transition leading from l_3 to l_4, i.e., leading into the critical section, we have the trivial proof obligation:

$$\models I \land turn = next \to I \land turn = next.$$

The only interesting transition is the one leading from l_2 to l_3, where the value of num is assigned to $turn[i]$ and num is incremented by 1 in one atomic step.

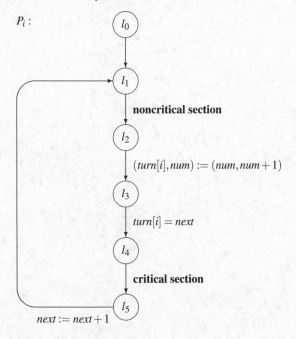

$P_i:$

noncritical section

$(turn[i], num) := (num, num + 1)$

$turn[i] = next$

critical section

$next := next + 1$

Fig. 3.17. Ticket algorithm.

Here we have to show:

$$\models I \rightarrow I \circ (\lambda\sigma.(\sigma : turn[i], num \mapsto \sigma(num), \sigma(num) + 1)), \text{ i.e.,}$$

one has to prove

$$\models I \rightarrow next \geq 1 \wedge \forall k, l : 1 \leq k \neq l \leq n.$$
$$((k \neq i \rightarrow turn[k] < num + 1)$$
$$\wedge (k = i \rightarrow num < num + 1)$$
$$\wedge (k \neq i \wedge l \neq i \rightarrow turn[k] = 0 \vee turn[k] \neq turn[l])$$
$$\wedge (k = i \vee l = i \rightarrow num = 0 \vee k = i \vee turn[k] = 0 \wedge l = i \vee$$
$$num \neq turn[l] \wedge k = i \vee turn[k] \neq num \wedge l = i)).$$

For processes with process indices k and l different from i one can conclude:

$$\models \forall k, l : 1 \leq k \neq l \leq n. \ turn[k] < num \wedge (turn[k] = 0 \vee turn[k] \neq turn[l]) \rightarrow$$
$$\forall k, l : 1 \leq k \neq l \leq n. \ (k \neq i \wedge l \neq i) \rightarrow$$
$$turn[k] < num + 1 \wedge (turn[k] = 0 \vee turn[k] \neq turn[l]).$$

For process P_i we have:

$$\models I \rightarrow num < num + 1 \wedge \forall k : 1 \leq k \leq n. \ turn[k] < num.$$

P_i :

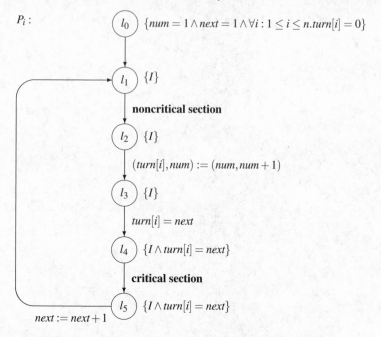

Fig. 3.18. Assertion network of the ticket algorithm.

Combining these two implications proves that the transition from l_2 to l_3 preserves I.

The last transition to be checked is the one incrementing the variable *next*. Since I just constrains *next* in stating that it has a positive value, the transition preserves I trivially.

This completes the proof of local correctness of I.

Interference Freedom: Next we show that the given assertion network for $P[i]$, $1 \le i \le n$, is interference free. First observe that the global invariant I is obviously interference free. We have only to show that $turn[i] = next$ is interference free when $P[j]$, for $j \ne i$, executes either $(turn[j], num) := (num, num + 1)$ or $next := next + 1$. The first transition does not change the *turn* value of another process, and neither does it change *next*. So, it remains to show that $turn[i] = next$ is interference free when $P[j]$, for $j \ne i$, executes $next := next + 1$, i.e.:

$$\models I \wedge turn[i] = next \wedge turn[j] = next \rightarrow$$
$$turn[i] = next \circ (\lambda\sigma.(\sigma : next \mapsto \sigma(next) + 1)).$$

It suffices to observe that the above premise implies *false* because it implies that $turn[i] = turn[j] \geq 1$, which contradicts I (note that $i \neq j$ and observe the use of $next \geq 1$).

So, we have established interference freedom and proved that I is a global invariant. Together with the information that the $turn$ value of a process equals $next$ inside the critical section this implies mutual exclusion. $\qquad\square$

Example 3.21 (Correctness of Szymanski's mutual exclusion algorithm)
Szymanski's mutual exclusion algorithm [Szy88] as presented in Example 1.6 is correct, i.e.,

$$\mathbf{mutex} \equiv flag := 0 \; ; \; [P_0 \| P_1 \| \dots \| P_{n-1}]$$

with

$P_i \equiv l_0 \; : \; \mathbf{loop\ forever\ do}$
$\qquad\qquad l_1 \; : \; \mathbf{noncritical\ section};$
$\qquad\qquad l_2 \; : flag[i] := 1;$
$\qquad\qquad l_3 \; : \mathbf{wait} \; \forall j : 0 \leq j < n.(flag[j] < 3);$
$\qquad\qquad l_4 \; : flag[i] := 3;$
$\qquad\qquad l_5 \; : \mathbf{if} \; \exists j : 0 \leq j < n.(flag[j] = 1) \; \mathbf{then}$
$\qquad\qquad\qquad l_6 : \; flag[i] := 2;$
$\qquad\qquad\qquad l_7 : \; \mathbf{wait} \; \exists j : 0 \leq j < n.(flag[j] = 4);$
$\qquad\qquad \mathbf{fi};$
$\qquad\qquad l_8 \; : flag[i] := 4;$
$\qquad\qquad l_9 \; : \mathbf{wait} \; \forall j : 0 \leq j < i.(flag[j] < 2);$
$\qquad\qquad l_{10}: \mathbf{critical\ section};$
$\qquad\qquad l_{11}: \mathbf{wait} \; \forall j : i < j < n.(flag[j] < 2 \vee flag[j] > 3);$
$\qquad\qquad l_{12}: flag[i] := 0$
$\qquad\quad \mathbf{od}$

satisfies the mutual exclusion property, i.e., there exists no computation of **mutex** leading to a state with more than one process being at control location l_{10}.

Proof Since Chapter 3 discusses correctness of transition diagrams and not of linear text programs, first the above program text should be converted to a corresponding transition diagram (see Figure 3.19). We prove the mutual exclusion property of Szymanski's algorithm using the above proof method of Owicki & Gries. Note that since **wait** b abbreviates a transition whose condition is b, b is regarded as an atomic test. In the presentation of the algorithm in Section 1.4.4 its correctness was explained using incorrect intermediate approximations. In each approximation the errors of the preceding version were

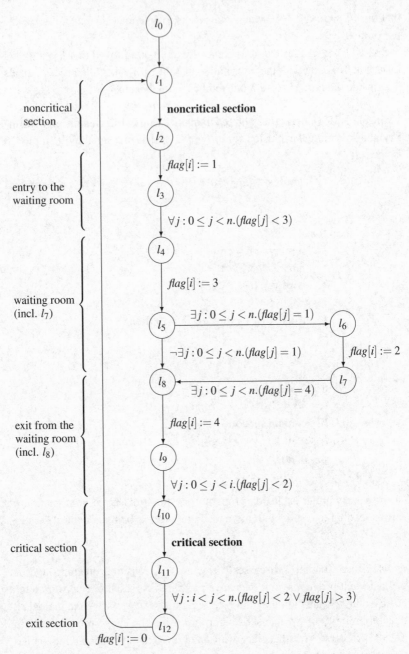

Fig. 3.19. Szymanski's algorithm.

corrected. This way of presentation makes it easier to understand such distributed algorithms, but, of course, it represents no proof of correctness.

Before we start with a formal proof of this algorithm, recall its informal justification due to Szymanski [Szy90]:

The idea behind the algorithm is simple. The prologue section simulates a waiting room with a door. All processes requesting entry to the critical section at roughly the same time gather first in the waiting room. Then, when there are no more processes requesting entry, processes inside the waiting room shut the door and move to the exit from the waiting room. From there, one by one, they enter their critical sections in the order of their numbering. Any process requesting access to its critical section at that time has to wait in the initial part of the prologue section (at the entry to the waiting room).

The door to the waiting room is initially opened. The door is closed when a process inside the waiting room does not see any new processes requesting entry. The door is opened again when the last process inside the waiting room leaves the exit section of the algorithm.

We give a proof for mutual exclusion of this algorithm using the proof method of Owicki & Gries, basing this proof on Z. Manna and A. Pnueli's [MP91c].[7] To be able to refer to the current control location of each process, we augment each process P_i by introducing auxiliary variables $cl[i]$ ranging over the finite domain $\{l_1, \ldots, l_{12}\}$. The values assigned to these variables correspond with the labels in the presentation below (except for l_0 which is of no interest for our purposes). Each transition in the transition diagram of Figure 3.19 is augmented by such an assignment. P_i' denotes the transition diagram corresponding to the following linear text program:

l_0 : **loop forever do**
      l_1 : **noncritical section**; $cl[i] := l_2$;
      l_2 : $flag[i], cl[i] := 1, l_3$;
      l_3 : **wait** $\forall j : 0 \leq j < n.(flag[j] < 3)$; $cl[i] := l_4$;
      l_4 : $flag[i], cl[i] := 3, l_5$;
      l_5 : **if** $\exists j : 0 \leq j < n.(flag[j] = 1)$ **then**
               $cl[i] := l_6$;
           l_6 : $flag[i], cl[i] := 2, l_7$;
           l_7 : **wait** $\exists j : 0 \leq j < n.(flag[j] = 4)$;
               $cl[i] := l_8$;
        fi; $cl[i] := l_8$;
      l_8 : $flag[i], cl[i] := 4, l_9$;

---

[7] In our proof boolean expressions in tests are evaluated atomically, by definition. Since this is, in general, not realistic, [MP91c] also refers to a correctness proof for the case that boolean expressions are evaluated non-atomically, in a scanning order of increasing values of indices. It is also proved in [MP90] that the algorithm is incorrect for any different scanning order.

l_9 : **wait** $\forall j : 0 \leq j < i.(flag[j] < 2)$; $cl[i] := l_{10}$;
l_{10}: **critical section**; $cl[i] := l_{11}$;
l_{11} : **wait** $\forall j : i < j < n.(flag[j] < 2 \vee flag[j] > 3)$;
    $cl[i] := l_{12}$;
l_{12}: $flag[i], cl[i] := 0, l_1$;

od

So, we obtain a new transition diagram **mutex'**:

$$\textbf{mutex}' \equiv flag := 0 \; ; \; cl := l_1 \; ; \; [P'_0 \| P'_1 \| \ldots \| P'_{n-1}],$$

where the assignments to the arrays, $flag := 0$ and $cl := l_1$, mean that each component of the array is set to the value 0 or l_1, respectively.

Next, we give an assertion network for each process. Since Szymanski's algorithm is parameterised, it is quite natural to use assertion networks parameterised by process index i. To be able to give the assertion networks in a compact form, we introduce some notation to abbreviate assertions, as used in [MP91c]. First, we define certain sets of process indices. Let us denote the set of processes having set the value of their flag variable to k by:

$$F_k \stackrel{\text{def}}{=} \{i | 0 \leq i < n, flag[i] = k\}.$$

Furthermore, let us denote the set of processes being at control location l_j by:

$$L_j \stackrel{\text{def}}{=} \{i | 0 \leq i < n, cl[i] = l_j\}.$$

Note that these are useful notations since we have a distributed algorithm with similar components. We will also use abbreviations like $L_{i,j,k}$ and $F_{1..3}$ for $L_i \cup L_j \cup L_k$ and $F_1 \cup F_2 \cup F_3$.

Secondly, we give a simple assertion network with an obvious proof of local correctness and interference freedom to establish some invariants connecting the flag values of the processes with their control locations:

l_0 : **loop forever do**
    $\{flag[i] = 0 \wedge cl[i] = l_1\}$
l_1 : **noncritical section**; $cl[i] := l_2$;
        $\{flag[i] = 0 \wedge cl[i] = l_2\}$
l_2 : $flag[i], cl[i] := 1, l_3$;
        $\{flag[i] = 1 \wedge cl[i] = l_3\}$
l_3 : **wait** $\forall j : 0 \leq j < n.(flag[j] < 3)$; $cl[i] := l_4$;
        $\{flag[i] = 1 \wedge cl[i] = l_4\}$
l_4 : $flag[i], cl[i] := 3, l_5$;
        $\{flag[i] = 3 \wedge cl[i] = l_5\}$
l_5 : **if** $\exists j : 0 \leq j < n.(flag[j] = 1)$ **then**

$$cl[i] := l_6;$$
$$\{flag[i] = 3 \wedge cl[i] = l_6\}$$
$$l_6 : flag[i], cl[i] := 2, l_7;$$
$$\{flag[i] = 2 \wedge cl[i] = l_7\}$$
$$l_7 : \textbf{wait } \exists j : 0 \le j < n.(flag[j] = 4);$$
$$cl[i] := l_8;$$
$$\{flag[i] = 2 \wedge cl[i] = l_8\}$$
$$\textbf{fi}; cl[i] := l_8;$$
$$\{(flag[i] = 2 \vee flag[i] = 3) \wedge cl[i] = l_8\}$$
$$l_8 : flag[i], cl[i] := 4, l_9;$$
$$\{flag[i] = 4 \wedge cl[i] = l_9\}$$
$$l_9 : \textbf{wait } \forall j : 0 \le j < i.(flag[j] < 2); cl[i] := l_{10};$$
$$\{flag[i] = 4 \wedge cl[i] = l_{10}\}$$
$$l_{10} : \textbf{critical section}; cl[i] := l_{11};$$
$$\{flag[i] = 4 \wedge cl[i] = l_{11}\}$$
$$l_{11} : \textbf{wait } \forall j : i < j < n.(flag[j] < 2 \vee flag[j] > 3);$$
$$cl[i] := l_{12};$$
$$\{flag[i] = 4 \wedge cl[i] = l_{12}\}$$
$$l_{12} : flag[i], cl[i] := 0, l_1;$$
$$\{flag[i] = 0 \wedge cl[i] = l_1\}$$
$$\textbf{od}$$

Using this assertion network for each process we conclude the following invariants:

$$F_0 = L_{1,2}, F_1 = L_{3,4}, F_2 \subseteq L_{7,8}, F_3 \subseteq L_{5,6,8}, F_4 = L_{9..12}.$$

The two subset relations for $flag[i] = 2$ and $flag[i] = 3$ are due to the fact that at control location l_8 one may have both flag values. Since this is the only location where the flag values are not determined, we can be more precise and establish also:

$$L_5 \subseteq F_3, L_6 \subseteq F_3, L_7 \subseteq F_2, L_8 \subseteq F_{2,3}.$$

As a next step, we want to formalise the explanation of Szymanski and justify it intuitively. All processes requiring entry to their critical section gather first in the waiting room. The first one passing the test labelled l_5 negatively locks the doorway, i.e., there is no process at l_4 on its way to the waiting room and no other process will reach l_4. This is expressed by:

$$I_1 : (L_{8..12} \ne \emptyset) \to (L_4 = \emptyset).$$

This is justified by the fact that the first process reaching l_8 has checked that no process is left with flag value 1 at l_3 or l_4. Of course a process may reach l_3 unconditionally, but there it finds a process whose flag value is 3 at least, and therefore cannot pass to l_4. This can be formalised by:

$$I_2 : (L_{8..12} \neq \emptyset) \to (L_{8..12} \cap F_{3,4} \neq \emptyset).$$

If all processes requiring entry are in the waiting room they leave the waiting room one by one and enter their critical section in order of their process number. This implies that, if there is a process in the critical section, then there are no processes left in the waiting room or the critical section with a lower process number:

$$I_3 : ((k < i) \wedge (i \in L_{10..12})) \to (k \notin L_{5..12}).$$

Note that this implies mutual exclusion. For if there are two processes in their critical sections, they have different process indices. The one with the lower process index would violate I_3. So, mutual exclusion is established with the help of I_3.

The test at l_{11} was introduced to guarantee linear delay. So, we want to establish that when a process passes this test the waiting room is empty and all processes have queued up to enter their critical section, i.e., their flag value is 4:

$$I_4 : ((i \in L_{12}) \wedge (k \in L_{5..12})) \to (k \in F_4).$$

Since we expect the above formulae to be invariants, we take them as assertions at every location. Note that I_3 and I_4 simplify to *true* for all locations not fulfilling the premises. Furthermore, the already established invariants will be used to prove local correctness and interference freedom of the following assertion network whenever needed:

l_0 : **loop forever do**

    l_1 : **noncritical section**; $cl[i] := l_2$;

        $\{I_1 \wedge I_2\}$

    l_2 : $flag[i], cl[i] := 1, l_3$;

        $\{I_1 \wedge I_2\}$

    l_3 : **wait** $\forall j : 0 \leq j < n.(flag[j] < 3)$; $cl[i] := l_4$;

        $\{I_1 \wedge I_2\}$

    l_4 : $flag[i], cl[i] := 3, l_5$;

        $\{I_1 \wedge I_2\}$

    l_5 : **if** $\exists j : 0 \leq j < n.(flag[j] = 1)$ **then**

        $cl[i] := l_6$;

        $\{I_1 \wedge I_2\}$

$$l_6 : \mathit{flag}[i], cl[i] := 2, l_7;$$
$$\{I_1 \wedge I_2\}$$
$$l_7 : \mathbf{wait} \; \exists j : 0 \leq j < n.(\mathit{flag}[j] = 4);$$
$$cl[i] := l_8;$$
$$\{I_1 \wedge I_2\}$$
$$\mathbf{fi}; \; cl[i] := l_8; \; \{I_1 \wedge I_2\}$$
$$l_8 \; : \mathit{flag}[i], cl[i] := 4, l_9;$$
$$\{I_1 \wedge I_2\}$$
$$l_9 \; : \mathbf{wait} \; \forall j : 0 \leq j < i.(\mathit{flag}[j] < 2); cl[i] := l_{10};$$
$$\{I_1 \wedge I_2 \wedge \forall k < i.k \notin L_{5..12}\}$$
$$l_{10} : \mathbf{critical \; section}; \; cl[i] := l_{11};$$
$$\{I_1 \wedge I_2 \wedge \forall k < i.k \notin L_{5..12}\}$$
$$l_{11} : \mathbf{wait} \; \forall j : i < j < n.(\mathit{flag}[j] < 2 \vee \mathit{flag}[j] > 3);$$
$$cl[i] := l_{12};$$
$$\{I_1 \wedge I_2 \wedge \forall k < i.k \notin L_{5..12}$$
$$\wedge \forall k.k \in L_{5..12} \rightarrow k \in F_4\}$$
$$l_{12} : \mathit{flag}[i], cl[i] := 0, l_1;$$
$$\{I_1 \wedge I_2\}$$

od

Remark: To show a property for a distribute algorithm parameterised by n we have to show the property for an arbitrarily chosen but fixed value of n. Therefore, expressions like $F_{3,4} \neq \emptyset$ can be formulated as

$$\exists i \in \{0, \ldots, n-1\}.\mathit{flag}[i] = 3 \vee \mathit{flag}[i] = 4.$$

For a fixed value of n this formula can be written without quantification. Thus, $F_{3,4} \neq \emptyset$ is indeed an assertion and can be used in an assertion network.

Local correctness: The invariants I_1 and I_2 are inductive for transitions not changing the sets $L_{8..12}$, L_4 and $F_{3,4}$. Let process index i satisfy $i \in \{0, \ldots, n - 1\}$. Consider the transition from l_5 to l_8:

$$\models (I_1 \wedge I_2 \wedge (L_5 \subseteq F_3) \wedge (F_1 = L_{3,4})) \circ (\lambda \sigma.(\sigma : cl[i] \mapsto l_5))$$
$$\wedge \neg \exists j : 0 \leq j < n.(\mathit{flag}[j] = 1)$$
$$\rightarrow (I_1 \wedge I_2) \circ (\lambda \sigma.(\sigma : cl[i] \mapsto l_8)).$$

In the following we abbreviate the semantic substitution of constants

$$\varphi \circ (\lambda \sigma.(\sigma : x_1, \ldots, x_n \mapsto c_1, \ldots, c_n))$$

by $\varphi[\bar{c}/\bar{x}]$, where $\bar{c}$ is a vector of length n of constants. The other transition reaching l_8 starts at l_7; there we have:

$$\models (I_1 \wedge I_2 \wedge (F_4 = L_{9..12}))[l_7/cl[i]] \wedge \exists j : 0 \le j < n.(flag[j] = 4)$$
$$\rightarrow (I_1 \wedge I_2)[l_8/cl[i]].$$

The transition leading from l_3 to l_4 may change the set L_4 from empty to nonempty, but:

$$\models (I_1 \wedge I_2)[l_3/cl[i]] \wedge \forall j : 0 \le j < n.(flag[j] < 3) \rightarrow (L_{8..12} = \emptyset)[l_4/cl[i]],$$

so I_1 and I_2 then hold trivially.

The transition from location l_8 to l_9 changes the flag value to 4. This may increase $F_{3,4}$, but it leaves $F_{3,4} \cap L_{8..12}$ nonempty, anyway. The transition to l_9 does not change the flag value, so I_1 and I_2 are not affected by that transition, since control still remains in $\{l_8, \dots, l_{12}\}$. For the transition leading to l_{10} it suffices to show that $\forall k : k < i.k \notin L_{5..12}$ holds. This is true due to the following:

$$\models \forall j : 0 \le j < i.(flag[j] < 2) \wedge (F_{0,1} = L_{1..4}) \rightarrow \{0, \dots, i-1\} \subseteq L_{1..4}.$$

The critical section does not change any original protocol variables. The wait statement at l_{11} also does not affect any variables. It remains to establish $\models \forall k.k \in L_{5..12} \rightarrow k \in F_4$. With $F_{2,3,4} = L_{5..12}$ we get:

$$\models \forall j : i < j < n.(flag[j] < 2 \vee flag[j] > 3) \wedge F_{2,3,4} = L_{5..12}$$
$$\rightarrow \forall k.k \in L_{5..12} \rightarrow k \in F_4.$$

The last transition of the process, which leads back to the noncritical section, may change $L_{8..12}$ to empty, and consequently makes $I_1 \wedge I_2$ true. If any processes are left in $L_{8..12}$, we have to prove I_2, i.e., that one of them has a flag value of 3 or 4. By I_4, $\models \forall k.k \in L_{5..12} \rightarrow k \in F_4$ holds, so we get a guaranteed flag value of 4.

This establishes the proof of local correctness.

Interference freedom: Since I_1 and I_2 are part of each assertion at all locations of the network, to show interference freedom for them falls to proving local correctness. It suffices to prove that for a process i with $i \in L_{10..12}$ that $\forall k : k < i.k \notin L_{5..12}$ and for $i \in L_{12}$ that $\forall k.k \in L_{5..12} \rightarrow k \in F_4$ cannot be violated by another process. By I_1 we get $L_4 = \emptyset$, so no other process can enter $L_{5..12}$. Since we have, by I_3, mutual exclusion not only at l_{10} but also at l_{11} and l_{12}, no process can change its flag value from 4 to 0 at l_{12} accept for process i.

This concludes the proof of interference freedom, and thereby the proof of the mutual exclusion property of Szymanski's algorithm.   □

3.5.3 Soundness of the Owicki & Gries Proof Method

In order to prove the soundness of the Owicki & Gries proof method we first prove the soundness of the initialisation and the auxiliary variables rules. These rules also apply to the proof method of Apt, Francez & de Roever in Chapter 4, since they are also used there to reason about sequential transition diagrams. Consequently, properly speaking they should have been part of Chapter 2. However, then their motivation would have been missing, which is the reason why we discuss them here.

Lemma 3.22 (Initialisation rule) Let h be a total function such that the set of write variables of h consists of auxiliary variables of P which do not occur in ψ, then $\models \{\varphi\}P\{\psi\}$ implies $\models \{\varphi \circ h\}P\{\psi\}$.

Proof First note that $\varphi \circ h$ is a total boolean function because both φ and h are total and φ is boolean. Next, let $\bar{z} = write(h)$ and $c \to f$ be a transition of P. Then $f = f_1 \circ f_2$, for some f_1 and f_2 such that $\bar{z} \cap var(f_1) = \emptyset$ and the write variables of f_2 are only among $\bar{z}$. Since $\bar{z}$ is a collection of auxiliary variables of P, for every pair of states σ and σ' such that $\sigma(x) = \sigma'(x)$, for all $x \in VAR \setminus \bar{z}$, we have that $\sigma \models c$ if and only if $\sigma' \models c$, because c does not involve the variables of $\bar{z}$. Moreover, for all $x \in VAR \setminus \bar{z}$, we have that $f(\sigma)(x) = f_1(\sigma)(x) = f_1(\sigma')(x) = f(\sigma')(x)$, because the write variables of f_2 are only among $\bar{z}$ and f_1 does not involve the variables of $\bar{z}$. Now let $\sigma \models \varphi \circ h$ and σ' be a final state of a terminating computation of P starting from σ. By a straightforward induction on the length of the computation, using the above observation, we derive that there exists an execution of P starting from $h(\sigma)$ and resulting in a state σ'' such that $\sigma'(x) = \sigma''(x)$, for all $x \in VAR \setminus \bar{z}$. So, since $h(\sigma) \models \varphi$, we infer by $\models \{\varphi\}P\{\psi\}$ that $\sigma'' \models \psi$. But the variables of $\bar{z}$ do not occur in ψ so we also conclude that $\sigma' \models \psi$. $\qquad\square$

Lemma 3.23 (Auxiliary variables rule) Let $\bar{z}$ be a set of auxiliary variables of P', and P be obtained from P' by restricting all state transformations of P' to all variables excluding $\bar{z}$. Furthermore let ψ be a predicate in which no variable of $\bar{z}$ occurs. Then $\models \{\varphi\}P'\{\psi\}$ implies $\models \{\varphi\}P\{\psi\}$.

Proof Let $c \to f$ be a transition of P and $c \to f \circ g$ be the corresponding transition of P'. Since c and g are total functions, and g only changes the values of variables belonging to $\bar{z}$, the effect of executing $c \to f$ in some state σ such that $c(\sigma) = tt$ is well-defined iff executing $c \to f \circ g$ in σ is well-defined, since f does not involve $\bar{z}$. We have that f does not involve the auxiliary variables $\bar{z}$ and that the write variables of g are among $\bar{z}$. For every pair of states σ and σ'

such that $\sigma(x) = \sigma'(x)$, for every $x \in VAR \setminus \bar{z}$, it follows that $\sigma \models c$ if and only if $\sigma' \models c$ and that $f(\sigma)(x) = f \circ g(\sigma)(x)$ is well-defined whenever $f(\sigma)(x)$ is well-defined, for all $x \in VAR \setminus \bar{z}$. Now let $\sigma \models \varphi$ and σ' be the final state of a terminating computation of P starting from σ. By a straightforward induction on the length of the computation we derive, using the above observations, that there exists a final state σ'' of an execution of P' starting from σ such that $\sigma'(x) = \sigma''(x)$, for every $x \in VAR \setminus \bar{z}$. So by $\models \{\varphi\}P'\{\psi\}$ we infer that $\sigma'' \models \psi$ and, thus, since σ' and σ'' only differ with respect to the values of the variables $\bar{z}$, and the variables of $\bar{z}$ do not occur in ψ, we conclude that $\sigma' \models \psi$. □

Observe that had we allowed undefined, or partially defined, operations upon auxiliary variables, then the auxiliary variables rule would have been unsound, as the valid triple

$$\models \{true\} \; (x, y := 1/0, 0) \; \{y = 2\}$$

demonstrates. Certainly x is an auxiliary variable of $(x, y) := (1/0, 0)$. However, removing the auxiliary variable component from that assignment does not result in a valid triple, since $\not\models \{true\} \; y := 0 \; \{y = 2\}$. This observation – first given in [McC89] – has been pointed out to us by Fred B. Schneider.

Assume that a proof using Owicki & Gries' proof method, that is satisfying points (i) through (v) of Definition 3.17 above, has been given for $\{\varphi\} P \{\psi\}$. Then we want to be convinced that this is a valid procedure, i.e., that this proof method is *sound*, and that $\models \{\varphi\} P \{\psi\}$ holds.

Theorem 3.24 (Soundness)
The proof method of Owicki & Gries as formulated in Definition 3.17 is sound.

Proof We will prove that $\models \{\varphi\}P\{\psi\}$ holds. Let P' be obtained from $P \equiv P_1 \| \ldots \| P_n$ as described in point (i) of Definition 3.17, with $\bar{z}$ a list of the newly introduced auxiliary variables. Furthermore let Q_l be associated with $l \in L_i$ for $i = 1, \ldots, n$ such that points (ii), (iii), (iv) and (v) of Definition 3.17 are satisfied.

We need to prove that $\models \{\varphi\}P_1 \| \ldots \| P_n\{\psi\}$ holds, where φ and ψ in particular satisfy the following clause of Definition 3.17:

(v) There exists a function h whose write variables belong to $\bar{z}$ such that $\models \varphi \to \bigwedge_{i=1}^{n} Q_{s_i} \circ h$ and $\models \bigwedge_{i=1}^{n} Q_{t_i} \to \psi$ hold.

It suffices to prove $\models \{\bigwedge_{i=1}^{n} Q_{s_i}\} \; P'_1 \| \ldots \| P'_n\{\psi\}$ using the soundness of Floyd's inductive assertion method. The soundness of the initialisation rule then gives us

$$\models \{\bigwedge_{i=1}^{n} Q_{s_i} \circ h\} P_1' \| \dots \| P_n' \{\psi\},$$

and so $\models \{\varphi\} P_1' \| \dots \| P_n' \{\psi\}$ follows using (v). Using the soundness of the auxiliary variables rule we conclude that $\models \{\varphi\} P_1 \| \dots \| P_n \{\psi\}$.

We still have to prove $\models \{\bigwedge_{i=1}^{n} Q_{s_i}\} P_1' \| \dots \| P_n' \{\psi\}$. By associating $\bigwedge_{i=1}^{n} Q_{l_i}$ with global label $\langle l_1, \dots, l_n \rangle \in L_1 \times \dots \times L_n$ it follows from the discussion in Section 3.5.1 above, that

(i) local correctness of $\{Q_l | l \in L_i\}$ w.r.t. P_i', i.e., $\{Q_l | l \in L_i\}$ is an inductive assertion network for P_i', $i = 1, \dots, n$, and

(ii) the interference freedom test, i.e., Q_l for $l \in L_i$ is invariant under transitions of P_j', $j \neq i$,

both imply that $Q_1 \times \dots \times Q_n$ is an inductive assertion network for $P_1' \| \dots \| P_n'$. Moreover point (v) above holds. Hence one can apply Floyd's inductive assertion method, and by the soundness of that method (Theorem 2.12)

$$\models \{\bigwedge_{i=1}^{n} Q_{s_i}\} P_1' \| \dots \| P_n' \{\psi\}$$

follows. $\qquad\qquad\qquad\qquad\qquad\qquad\qquad\qquad\qquad\qquad\qquad\qquad\qquad\qquad$ □

3.5.4 Completeness of the Proof Method of Owicki & Gries: Introduction

Given $\models \{\varphi\} P_1 \| \dots \| P_n \{\psi\}$, semantic completeness of the proof method of Owicki & Gries consists of constructing assertion networks for each of the processes P_i, $i = 1, \dots, n$, such that these satisfy the verification conditions listed in points (i) through (v) of this method w.r.t. precondition φ and postcondition ψ, and therefore allow us to derive $\{\varphi\} P_1 \| \dots \| P_n \{\psi\}$ using that method.

Basic intuition

The basic intuition in this completeness proof is simple and reflects the following extension of the completeness proof for the sequential case:

Associate with every location $l \in P_i$ a φ-minimal predicate $\varphi_l(\sigma)$, which expresses that some computation of $P_1 \| \dots \| P_n$, whose initial state satisfies φ, reaches node l in state σ. Then local correctness, i.e., inductiveness of the resulting assertion network for each P_i, follows as in the sequential case. Now the interference freedom test (IFT) is also satisfied once the following *merging* lemma holds. This lemma stipulates that, whenever there exist two *separate* φ-computations which reach P_i in l and P_j in l'

in the same state σ, then there also exists a *single* φ-computation which reaches l and l' at the same time, i.e., the *pair* $\langle l, l' \rangle$, in state σ. Since prolonging this single computation by a transition τ of P_j, which starts in $l' \in L_j$ and results in state σ', does not move P_i away from l, one has that $\varphi_l(\sigma')$ still holds, i.e., $\models \varphi_l \wedge \varphi_{l'} \wedge b \to \varphi_l \circ f$ holds, with τ of the form $(l', b \to f, l'')$. And this expresses exactly the interference freedom test!

A similar argument holds for proving $\models \bigwedge_i \varphi_{t_i} \to \psi$: By generalising the merging lemma to n processes one sees that $\bigwedge_i \varphi_{t_i}(\sigma)$ implies that there exists a *single* φ-computation of $P_1 \| \ldots \| P_n$ which ends in the n-tuple of end labels $\langle t_1, \ldots, t_n \rangle$ in state σ. Since this single computation is a terminating one, by the assumption of $\models \{\varphi\} P_1 \| \ldots \| P_n \{\psi\}$ also $\psi(\sigma)$ holds.

Regrettably, in the simple formulation given above, the merging lemma does not always hold. Already Exercise 3.19 illustrates a case for which $\models \varphi_{t_1} \wedge \varphi_{t_2} \to \varphi_{\langle t_1, t_2 \rangle}$ does not hold. Yet it is possible to obtain a correct formulation of this lemma by including the computation history in the state, e.g., the merging lemma holds for the assertion network from Figure 3.13.

We return to this basic intuition and a correct formulation and proof of the merging lemma 3.63 in Section 3.9.1 which concerns the historical development of the method of Owicki & Gries, since it captures the original intuition behind Susan Owicki's first completeness proofs [Owi75, Owi76, Apt81a].

Next observe that $\varphi_l(\sigma)$ above postulates the existence of a *global* computation, namely of $P_1 \| \ldots \| P_n$, reaching label l in P_i. As argued below, when proving partial correctness it suffices to develop a compositional completeness proof based on *local* assertion networks for the processes P_i which depend solely on P_i, regardless of the context in which P_i is operating, $i = 1, \ldots, n$. Subsequently such compositional completeness proofs are given in two versions. In the first version, discussed in Section 3.5.6, all transitions of the form $b \to g$ are annotated, including transitions only consisting of a boolean test, whereas in the second version, discussed in Section 3.5.7, annotating the latter kind of transitions is not allowed and only assignments can be annotated. The latter version is required to prove completeness of Hoare logics for certain shared-variable-based languages for concurrency in which boolean tests are not annotated [Apt81a].

An interesting aspect of these new completeness proofs is that the local assertion networks thus generated trivially satisfy the interference freedom test, because their predicates specify the meaning of a component in terms of its interaction with an *arbitrary* parallel environment. This observation suggests a compositional proof method for partial correctness which is based on inductive assertions, and is discussed in Section 8.3.

We return to completeness issues in Section 3.6.3 when discussing methods for proving termination. As we shall see, the assertion networks in the completeness proof of our local method for proving *termination* crucially depend on the environment of a process, *since a process terminates because its environment allows it to do so.* This is in contrast to proof methods for partial correctness, in which that environment does not need to be taken into account. When proving termination, the φ_l assertions mentioned in the basic intuition remain the only possibility for generating assertion networks satisfying the various conditions imposed in Definition 3.59.

Completeness via the introduction of instruction counters

The main problem with the basic intuition sketched above is to determine which parameters these φ-minimal predicates depend on, and how to express these predicates formally.

Already in Example 3.12 we saw that when $VAR = \{y\}$ such predicates cannot be expressed as functions of y (or σ) alone. More precisely, the problem with the $y = 0$-minimal inductive assertion network Q for P_i, when P_i as in Figure 3.9 is considered in isolation, is that the predicates $\{Q_{s_i}, Q_{t_i}\}$ constituting this network only depend on the value of y. For example, the strongest t_i-condition Q_{t_i} of P_i w.r.t. $y = 0$ (i.e., the strongest postcondition), as defined in Section 2.7, expresses that "there exists a computation of P_i starting in a state satisfying $y = 0$ and ending after executing $y := y + 1$". This predicate is expressed by $\varphi_{t_i} \stackrel{\text{def}}{=} \exists v. v = 0 \wedge y = v + 1$. Since $\models \exists v. v = 0 \wedge y = v + 1 \leftrightarrow y = 1$, φ_{t_i} expresses the predicate $y = 1$ and clearly $y = 1$ is not interference free under the execution of $y := y + 1$ in the other process. Also $\models \varphi_{t_1} \wedge \varphi_{t_2} \rightarrow y = 2$ does not hold. Hence this strongest t_i-condition φ_{t_i} does not express the intended φ-minimal predicate φ_{t_i} defined above.

This leads to the idea of *expressing the effects of concurrent execution in other processes explicitly by introducing new, auxiliary, variables, such as z_1 and z_2 in Figure 3.12, whose values record the progress of computation in those other processes.* By simulating the effects of the local instruction counter of P_i by means of auxiliary variable z_i, such as is done above for $n = 2$ in Figure 3.12, one obtains all the expressive power needed. By just enumerating the effects upon program variables of every combination of instruction counter values z_j in other processes $P_j, j \neq i$, one can express φ_l (how to construct such expressions effectively using the canonical technique of Gödel encoding is explained in Chapter 5).

However, if every P_i has r locations, this requires $n * r^n$ cases to be distinguished to express the $n*r$ predicates required for the Owicki & Gries method. Consequently, this way of establishing completeness has no practical value. Note that this kind of completeness proof is based on generating an assertion for every combination of instruction counters, i.e., for every global location $l \in L_1 \times \ldots \times L_n$, and therefore simply encodes the global approach which we considered first in Section 3.5.1 and rejected on complexity grounds.

The problem with this method is, that, by recording the values of the instruction counters, too many distinctions are introduced which one does not want to observe at all!

This observation relates to an even more compelling reason for rejecting this approach, even for examples whose complexity is not that forbidding. For example, the completeness proof based on introducing instruction counters makes an explicit difference between the two programs given in Figure 3.20.

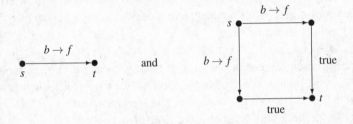

Fig. 3.20. Two semantically equivalent programs which cannot be distinguished in any concurrent context.

In general, location counters distinguish between transition diagrams which have *semantically equivalent control structures* such as a loop and its unfoldings, see Figure 3.21.

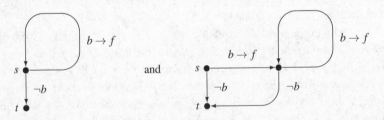

Fig. 3.21. Another pair of programs, indistinguishable in any concurrent context: a loop and its unfolding.

Figures 3.20 and 3.21 each illustrate a pair of programs *which are equivalent when placed in any possible concurrent environment.*

Therefore, from a semantical point of view, one wants to be able to substitute the one element of these pairs for the other one. And obviously, when specifying each of these programs, the specifications of two semantically indistinguishable programs should be the same. This is not the case when simulating location counters as sketched above.

A third disadvantage of this method is that the free auxiliary variables of the predicates, which are introduced above to express an inductive assertion network for P_i, depend on P_i's environment. That is, every new context for P_i requires another network. This is not practicable, for in the case of a library of ready-made modules one needs to have fixed specifications for these modules at one's disposal (which should not be rewritten for any new concurrent environment).

Completeness by formalising the notion of communication interface

Therefore, we aim at obtaining a specification for such a component which can be used in deriving properties in any concurrent environment, i.e., no matter what the concurrently executing processes in its environment are. This strategy enables one to set up a library of "minimal" specifications which characterise the behaviour of a reusable component in any arbitrary context and, hence, do not require new proofs for new specifications due to some change of environment.

To succeed in this strategy, it is first of all necessary to determine exactly what one wants to observe about a concurrent process. These quantities are called the *observable behaviour*, of a process, and consist of:

(i) Its *initial* and *final state*; by convention, in the case of partial correctness a final state is only observable when a process terminates[8].

(ii) Its *communication interface*, which records the communication behaviour of a process regardless of any particular environment, i.e., with respect to all possible environments.

In the shared-variables model the communication interface of a process in isolation consists of recording the effect of each possible basic computation step in that process, *given an arbitrary initial state for that step* (since one does not know beforehand whether steps from other processes are interleaved before that step). In the context of the interleaving models considered here, this amounts to recording all possible sequences of *disconnected* individual computation steps, in which arbitrary interferences due to some envi-

---

[8] In case of a semantics for total correctness, the nondeterministic presence or absence of infinite computations must also be recorded; then the "⊥" (bottom) final state, indicating the presence of such an infinite computation, is also an observable.

ronment are modelled by *"gaps"*, as explained below. Such sequences are introduced in [dBKPR91] as a general model for asynchronous communication. These so-called *"reactive"* sequences abstract from any information concerning the location counters in our interface. For example, the global computation $(l_0, \sigma_0) \rightarrow (l_1, \sigma_1) \rightarrow \ldots \rightarrow (l_n, \sigma_n)$ of $P_1 \| P_2$ can be modelled by the *"connected"* sequence of computation steps $\langle \sigma_0, \sigma_1 \rangle \langle \sigma_1, \sigma_2 \rangle \ldots \langle \sigma_{n-1}, \sigma_n \rangle$ in which "connected" means that the second element of any pair equals the first element of its succeeding pair, if any. However, from the point of view of P_1, only the *projection* of this sequence is generated, which consists of the reactive subsequence $\langle \sigma_{i_0}, \sigma_{i_1} \rangle \langle \sigma_{i_2}, \sigma_{i_3} \rangle \ldots \langle \sigma_{i_{(k-1)}}, \sigma_{i_k} \rangle$ of its own computation steps, in which $\sigma_{i_{(2k-1)}}$ and $\sigma_{i_{2k}}$ are not necessarily the same, because the sequence of steps from $\sigma_{i_{(2k-1)}}$ to $\sigma_{i_{2k}}$ has been carried out by P_2 and therefore constitutes a *"gap"* in the behaviour. This suggests the terminology of a *disconnected* sequence.

Let a *closed* system $P_1 \| \ldots \| P_n$ be a system in which interleaving with any concurrent environment is no longer intended. In the case of such a closed system $P_1 \| \ldots \| P_n$ an interleaving for $i = 1, \ldots, n$ of the individual reactive sequences of each P_i results in a connected reactive sequence, i.e., a sequence without gaps, this represents a *global computation* of $P_1 \| \ldots \| P_n$. Note that the set of such computations of $P_1 \| \ldots \| P_n$ can be obtained as a *function* of the set of reactive sequences of its components P_i.

Similarly, when $P_i \| P_j$ is not closed, the set of reactive sequences of $P_i \| P_j$ is obtained by interleaving the individual reactive sequences of P_i and P_j. Therefore, the set of reactive sequences $\mathcal{R}[\![P]\!]$ of a process P yields a semantics which is compositional w.r.t. parallelism: Let $P \equiv P_1 \| \ldots \| P_n$, then $\mathcal{R}[\![P]\!] \stackrel{\text{def}}{=} \mathcal{R}[\![P_1]\!] \tilde{\|} \ldots \tilde{\|} \mathcal{R}[\![P_n]\!]$, where $\tilde{\|}$ denotes the operation of interleaving (given in Definition 3.33).

The next problem we face is how to base our logic for shared-variable concurrency on such sequences. That is, how to encode these reactive sequences by means of auxiliary variables.

As a first attempt to solve this problem, assume that one records for every process P_i its reactive sequence of previous disconnected steps in a local auxiliary variable h_i. This forces us to introduce a *compatibility* predicate *compat* $(h_1, \ldots, h_n)$ for $P_1 \| \ldots \| P_n$ to express the postcondition of $P_1 \| \ldots \| P_n$, which checks whether there exists a single connected interleaving of computation steps for the closed system $P_1 \| \ldots \| P_n$. For when a computation of a closed program $P_1 \| \ldots \| P_n$ terminates, this is equivalent to the existence of a global terminating computation of $P_1 \| \ldots \| P_n$, that is, the existence of a connected interleaving of the computation steps of $P_1 \| \ldots \| P_n$. Since these steps are recorded locally in P_i in the variable h_i, this is equivalent to the existence of a connected interleaving h of the values of $h_1, \ldots, h_n$ upon termination of $P_1 \| \ldots \| P_n$, i.e., the existence of a connected sequence of steps h such that the projection $\text{proj}_i(h)$ of h on the steps of P_i yields the value of h_i. Hence, *compat* $(h_1, \ldots, h_n) \stackrel{\text{def}}{=} \exists h. \bigwedge_{i=1}^{n} \text{proj}_i(h) = h_i$. This predicate has been introduced by Soundararajan [Sou84]. However, in order to compute the value of *compat* $(h_1, \ldots, h_n)$ one needs a constructive definition of *compat* which requires recursion. Therefore, *compat* cannot be expressed using only first-order operators (unless one introduces a second-order element via the back door by using Gödel encoding of these sequences into the standard model of the natural numbers – but that we consider too contrived a solution for the simple purpose here).

A second attempt consists of introducing *one global auxiliary variable h* for $P_1 \| \ldots \| P_n$ which records the necessarily connected interleaving of computation steps of the individual processes, because h is updated in the order in which the flow-of-control selects a next computation step, and therefore records a connected sequence of computation steps. However, this has the disadvantage that now one cannot identify the individual contributions (steps) of the processes P_i for which one has to prove that they are generated by the particular program text of P_i!

This leads to a third attempt in which connected sequences of steps $\langle \sigma_k \stackrel{i}{\to} \sigma_{k+1} \rangle$ are recorded in h, with i identifying the active process P_i, i.e., the process making the step $\langle \sigma_k, \sigma_{k+1} \rangle$. A more concise representation of this strategy is obtained by recording the sequences of pairs (i, σ), in which i identifies that process P_i operates on state σ, resulting in state σ' contained in the next pair (j, σ') *under the assumption of connectedness*.

We incorporate shared-variable concurrency as follows into our definition of the *strongest l-condition $SP_l'(\varphi, P)$ of P with respect to precondition φ*, which is independent of the environment of P. First we extend program state σ with (the value of) connected sequence h, thus obtaining (σ, h). Next we define $SP_l'(\varphi, P)$ as:

> The set of all pairs (σ, h) such that the initial state σ' recorded in h satisfies φ, and the sequence of steps obtained by *projecting h onto P* generates a sequence of (in general disconnected) computation steps of P leading up to state σ at l. In case h denotes the empty history, σ itself should satisfy φ.

Here the projection of h onto P is obtained by dropping all pairs (j, σ) from h with j not belonging to the indices of (processes inside) P. Note that $SP_l'(\varphi, P)$ represents the analogue of φ-minimal predicates φ_l for concurrency, obtained by recording the contribution of process P to any possible computation which starts in φ. These predicates $SP'_l(\varphi, P)$ form for each process P an inductive assertion network, because making a computation step in P from l to l' corresponds to adding the P-indexed initial state of that step to h, which is consistent with its projection on P. They are also *by definition* interference free, since *making a step elsewhere leaves the projection of h onto the process itself unchanged*. This leads to the following property of SP'_l w.r.t. parallel composition[9]:

$$\models \bigwedge_{i=1}^{n} SP'_{l_i}(\varphi, P_i) \rightarrow SP'_{\langle l_1, \ldots, l_n \rangle}(\varphi, P_1 \| \ldots \| P_n).$$

This is proved in Section 3.5.6.

Observe that the SP'-semantics is just a reformulation of the "gapped" reactive-sequences semantics (in which every step is identified by the index of its active process) in order to model parallelism by means of projection instead of interleaving. Hence this definition of SP' does not impose any restrictions on the kind of process identifiers occurring in $SP'_l(\varphi, P)$. However, as demonstrated in the following example, when constructing a proof outline in an actual correctness proof for the *closed* network $P \equiv P_1 \| \ldots \| P_n$ we do need such a restriction. Then we associate with each location l of a component P_i the predicate $SP'_l(\varphi, P_i)$ with the restriction that it *only* refers to identifiers of the components of P, because this is the only way to capture properties of a closed network semantically.

Note that the above definition of $SP'_l(\varphi, P)$ applies only to transition diagrams, and not to transition systems.

Example 3.25 Let us see how this definition of $SP'_l(\varphi, P)$ works when applied to program $P_1 \| P_2$ in Figure 3.9. The set of global $(y = 0)$-computations of $P_1 \| P_2$ is

$$\{ (\langle s_1, s_2 \rangle; \sigma_{y=0}) \rightarrow (\langle t_1, s_2 \rangle; \sigma_{y=1}) \rightarrow (\langle t_1, t_2 \rangle; \sigma_{y=2}),$$
$$(\langle s_1, s_2 \rangle; \sigma_{y=0}) \rightarrow (\langle s_1, t_2 \rangle; \sigma_{y=1}) \rightarrow (\langle t_1, t_2 \rangle; \sigma_{y=2}) \},$$

which is described by the computation histories $h_1 = (1, \sigma_{y=0}) \cdot (2, \sigma_{y=1})$ and $h_2 = (2, \sigma_{y=0}) \cdot (1, \sigma_{y=1})$, where $\sigma_{y=j}$ expresses a state mapping y to $j, j \in N$.

Locally, the view of P_i in isolation at location t_i is quite different. This view merely expresses that the only instruction of $P_i, y := y + 1$, has been executed. It is described by a pair (i, σ), indicating that process P_i has made a move in

---

[9] This property is discussed in the technical note on page 185, where also a counterexample to the reverse implication is given. This counterexample is possible because the reactive sequence semantics $\mathcal{R}[\![P]\!]$ does not record the identity of the active process making a step. If this information had been included, SP'_l would have been compositional w.r.t. parallel composition.

state σ, and by the fact that only one pair of form (i, σ) occurs in the sequence of pairs h describing a possible history of the overall system $P_1 \| P_2$.

That globally $y := y + 1$ has been executed by P_i, for $i = 1, 2$, within the context of $P_1 \| P_2$ is characterised by the following facts:

(i) Any process $P_j, j \neq i$, whose transition is interleaved immediately after P_i, does so in a state of the form $(\sigma : y \mapsto 1 + \sigma(y))$, resulting in a sequence h of the form $\ldots (i, \sigma) \cdot (j, (\sigma : y \mapsto 1 + \sigma(y))) \ldots$, and this is the only part of h containing (i, σ).

(ii) When the overall system terminates, this results in a final state σ', where $\sigma' = (\sigma : y \mapsto 1 + \sigma(y))$, with (i, σ) the last and only pair in h of this form.

(iii) Since precondition $y = 0$ is also imposed, the initial state of h should satisfy $y = 0$, i.e., h starts in some pair $(j, \sigma_{y=0})$.

Hence $SP'_{t_i}(y = 0, P_i) = \{(\sigma', h) \mid h$ satisfies clauses (i) and (iii) above, and σ' satisfies clause (ii), i.e., $\sigma' = (\sigma : y \mapsto 1 + \sigma(y))$, where σ denotes the last state inside $h\}$. That $SP'_{t_i}(y = 0, P_i)$ is interference free follows from clause (i) and the definition of SP'_{t_i}.

Now the main point of this example is that, without imposing any additional restrictions on $SP'_{t_i}(y = 0, P_i)$,

$$\models \bigwedge_{i=1,2} SP'_{t_i}(y = 0, P_i) \rightarrow y = 2$$

does *not* hold!

For, since SP'_{t_i} is not restricted to histories with the process identifiers P_1 and P_2, possible contributions of a P_3 in which, e.g., a transition $y := y + 666$ occurs, are also captured! Thus, a possible history $h' = (1, \sigma_{y=0}) \cdot (3, \sigma_{y=1}) \cdot (2, \sigma_{y=667})$ is allowed and $(\sigma_{y=668}, h')$ is a legal final state at t_i, satisfying clauses (i)–(iii). But if we restrict SP'_{t_i} to histories over P_1 and P_2 only, we have validity of

$$\models \bigwedge_{i=1,2} SP'_{t_i}(y = 0, P_i) \rightarrow y = 2.$$

For then one has that

$$SP'_{t_i}(y = 0, P_i) = \{(\sigma_{y=1}, (i, \sigma_{y=0})),$$
$$(\sigma_{y=2}, (j, \sigma_{y=0}) \cdot (i, \sigma_{y=1})),$$
$$(\sigma_{y=2}, (i, \sigma_{y=0}) \cdot (j, \sigma_{y=1})), \ldots,$$
$$(\sigma_{y=27}, (i, \sigma_{y=0}) \cdot (j, \sigma_{y=1})), \ldots,$$
$$(\sigma_{y=99}, (j, \sigma_{y=0}) \cdot (i, \sigma_{y=66}) \cdot (j, \sigma_{y=67})), \ldots |$$
with $j = 1$ when $i = 2$, and $j = 2$ when $i = 1\}$.

Hence one has that:

- $\bigwedge_{i=1,2} SP'_{t_i}(y = 0, P_i)$ implies by (i) that *only two* transitions $y := y + 1$ have been executed (i.e., without any contributions from outside of P_1 and P_2), one by P_1 and one by P_2,
  - which are interleaved arbitrarily,
  - which start in $y = 0$ by clause (iii), and
  - which end in $y = 2$ by clause (ii).

A compositional correctness proof along the lines of this example is given in Example 8.9.   □

This generic characterisation of a process can now be used in a modular setting in which one programs with the specification of a module, rather than its actual programming text. The only restriction on this idealised way of presenting things is that we have to know the names or subscripts of processes which constitute a network, e.g., whether we have a two-process network of the form $P_1 \| P_2$ or $P_1 \| P_{666}$ (in case in the end only two processes are involved), in order to be able to *identify* the actions of the other process(es) in our generic predicates. The resulting setting is still modular in that we do not need to know anything else, i.e., the characterisation of P_i so obtained refers to the other processes inside the network through their names (or subscripts), but does not require any information regarding their specification or internal functioning.

As a result of this set up, we are able to characterise the behaviour of a single process w.r.t. a given fixed precondition φ, independently of its particular environment of concurrent processes, insofar only as the contribution of this process in terms of its own state-changes is recorded; yet it depends on its environment in that the latter determines the additional interleavings which are added to this contribution. Note that this does not result as yet in a really modular approach in which we specify the behaviour of a module *irrespective of a fixed precondition*, which is needed for obtaining a library of correctly specified modules. Technically this problem is solved in Section 3.5.5 below by the introduction of a (complete) adaptation rule.

3.5.5 Technical Note: An Adaptation Rule

A modular approach, which is independent from any particular precondition, can be realised by observing that the following *rule of adaptation* [Old83b] holds:

$$\models \{\varphi\} \, P \, \{\psi\} \text{ iff } \models \{\bar{x} = \bar{x}_0 \wedge h = t'\} \, P \, \{\varphi \rightsquigarrow \psi\},$$

where the logical variables occurring in φ and ψ are $(\bar{y}_0, t)$, logical variables $(\bar{x}_0, t')$ are disjoint from $(\bar{y}_0, t)$, and $\varphi \leadsto \psi$ denotes the semantic equivalent of

$$\forall \bar{y}_0, t. \varphi[\bar{x}_0 / \bar{x}, t' / h] \to \psi.$$

This semantic equivalent is expressed by $\forall \bar{y}_0, t. \varphi \circ f \to \psi$, where f expresses the substitution $[\bar{x}_0 / \bar{x}, t' / h]$ by $f(\sigma) \stackrel{\text{def}}{=} (\sigma : \bar{x} \mapsto \sigma(\bar{x}_0), h \mapsto \sigma(t'))$, and quantification is defined by: for $\varphi : \Sigma \to Bool$, $(\forall x. \varphi)(\sigma) = tt$ iff $\varphi((\sigma : x \mapsto d)) \stackrel{\text{def}}{=} tt$ for all $d \in VAL$.

By noting that one can systematically choose one's logical variables in pre- and postconditions to be disjoint from $(\bar{x}_0, t')$, one obtains a characterisation of *every* specification $\{\varphi\} P \{\psi\}$ in terms of the fixed precondition $\bar{x} = \bar{x}_0 \wedge h = t'$. As a result, our technique can be generalised to any precondition φ by instantiating it to $\bar{x} = \bar{x}_0 \wedge h = t'$ and replacing ψ by $\varphi \leadsto \psi$. This explains why we call such rules adaptation rules. Consult [Old83b] for a comprehensive study of such rules for sequential programming. For shared-variable concurrency, such a rule is the subject of Exercise 8.11, and for synchronous message passing it is formulated in [ZHLdR95].

3.5.6 Completeness of the Method of Owicki & Gries: a Compositional Approach

To establish the fact that $\models \{\varphi\} P_1 \| \ldots \| P_n \{\psi\}$ implies that $\{\varphi\} P_1 \| \ldots \| P_n \{\psi\}$ can be derived using the method of Owicki & Gries, one needs to define an appropriate assertion network.

As seen previously, the predicates of this network consist of strongest l-conditions of P_i w.r.t. precondition φ at label l, which are defined using a compositional semantics based on process-indexed sequences of states.

In order to define these concepts formally, we go through the same stages as in the previous section, but now in a formal setting. Thus we first formalise a simple, noncompositional, notion of initial-final-state behaviour $O[\![P]\!]$ of a transition system P in a sequential setting, specialise this notion to the initial-final-state behaviour $O_l[\![P]\!]$ at label l of P, and define strongest postconditions $SP(\varphi, P)$ and strongest l-conditions $SP_l(\varphi, P)$ w.r.t. this simple semantics. Due to the noncompositionality of this semantics w.r.t. concurrency these predicates are not interference free.

To obtain compositionality, we formally introduce *reactive sequences* in order to give a compositional characterisation $\mathcal{R}_l[\![P]\!]$ of $O_l[\![P]\!]$. Using the compositional semantics $\mathcal{R}_l[\![P]\!]$ for shared-variable concurrency, a new notion of strongest postcondition, expressed by $SP'_l(\varphi, P)$ is defined. More precisely, first we consider the set of pairs $\langle \sigma, \theta \rangle$ with θ denoting a sequence of process-indexed states and σ the final state of the computation thus characterised, such that the projection $\theta[P](\sigma)$ of $\langle \sigma, \theta \rangle$ on P results in a sequence of state pairs describing transitions of P, i.e., such that $\theta[P](\sigma) \in \mathcal{R}_l [\![P]\!]$. Next the $SP'_l(\varphi, P)$ semantics is obtained by restricting this set to pairs $\langle \sigma, \theta \rangle$ of which the first state of θ satisfies φ in case θ is nonempty, and $\sigma \models \varphi$, if θ is empty.

Finally we prove that this choice of assertions satisfies the requirements imposed by the method of Owicki & Gries.

Strongest postcondition operators: sequential case

Definition 3.26 One defines the initial-final-state behaviour of transition system P by:

$$O[\![P]\!] \stackrel{\text{def}}{=} \{(\sigma, \sigma') \mid \langle s; \sigma \rangle \to^* \langle t; \sigma' \rangle\},$$

where $\to^*$ denotes the reflexive transitive closure of the computation-step relation $\to$ between configurations defined in Section 2.3, where s and t are the entry and exit labels of a diagram representing P. $\square$

Note that for all programs P one has that

$$O[\![P]\!] = \{(\sigma, \sigma') \mid \sigma' \in \mathcal{M}[\![P]\!]\sigma \text{ and } \sigma, \sigma' \in \Sigma\}.$$

For an always terminating program P one even has

$$\mathcal{M}[\![P]\!]\sigma = \{\sigma' \mid (\sigma, \sigma') \in O[\![P]\!]\}.$$

Next we define the initial-final-state behaviour at a location l of a transition diagram P. Observe that we have to switch from transition systems to transition diagrams because labels can only be identified by their names in transition diagrams.

Definition 3.27 Given a location l of P, define:

$$O_l [\![P]\!] \stackrel{\text{def}}{=} \{(\sigma, \sigma') \mid \langle s; \sigma \rangle \to^* \langle l; \sigma' \rangle\}.$$ $\square$

Note that $O[\![P]\!] = O_t [\![P]\!]$.

To relate these semantic notions to predicates, we introduce the notions of *strongest postcondition and strongest l-condition,* respectively, of a transition diagram P w.r.t. a precondition φ and a label $l \in P$.

Definition 3.28 (Strongest postcondition) Given a transition system P and a precondition φ, the strongest postcondition of P with respect to φ, expressed by $SP(\varphi, P)$, is defined as:

$$SP(\varphi, P) \stackrel{\text{def}}{=} \{\sigma' \mid \text{there exists } \sigma \text{ such that } (\sigma, \sigma') \in O[\![P]\!] \text{ and } \sigma \models \varphi\}.$$ $\square$

We have the following basic property of strongest postcondition semantics.

Lemma 3.29 (Characterising property of *SP*) For any transition system P and predicate φ one has

$$\models \{\varphi\} \; P \; \{SP(\varphi, P)\}$$

and whenever $\models \{\varphi\} \; P \; \{\psi\}$ then $\models SP(\varphi, P) \to \psi$.

Proof Exercise. □

Definition 3.30 Given a transition diagram P, a location l of P, and a precondition φ, the strongest l-condition of P w.r.t. φ, expressed by $SP_l(\varphi, P)$, is defined as:

$$SP_l(\varphi, P) \stackrel{\text{def}}{=} \{\sigma' \mid \text{there exists } \sigma \text{ such that } (\sigma, \sigma') \in O_l[\![P]\!] \text{ and } \sigma \models \varphi\}. \quad \square$$

Observe that $SP_t(\varphi, P) = SP(\varphi, P)$. That SP_l is not compositional w.r.t. $\|$ can be seen as follows. Let $P \equiv P_1\|\dots\|P_n$. By Lemma 3.29, $\models \{\varphi\} \; P \; \{SP(\varphi, P)\}$ and $\models \{\varphi\} \; P \; \{\psi\}$ imply $\models SP(\varphi, P) \to \psi$. To derive $\{\varphi\} \; P \; \{SP(\varphi, P)\}$ we consider inductive assertion networks for $\{\varphi\} \; P_i \; \{SP(\varphi, P_i)\}$, P_i being a component of $P, i = 1, \dots n$. However, in general $\bigwedge_i SP(\varphi, P_i)$ does not imply $SP(\varphi, P)$. This is the lesson of Example 3.12, since for P_i as defined in Figure 3.9, one has that $SP(y = 0, P_i)$ is equivalent to $y = 1$, whereas for $P \equiv P_1\|P_2$, $SP(y = 0, P)$ is equivalent to $y = 2$ (see the discussion at the beginning of Section 3.5.4). Hence $\not\models \bigwedge_i SP(\varphi, P_i) \to SP(\varphi, P_1\|\dots\|P_n)$.

Reactive sequences

Next we investigate a definition of strongest l-condition in terms of a compositional semantics $\mathcal{R}_l$ based on reactive sequences. The additional information to make SP_l compositional will be encoded by auxiliary variables.

For the formal definition of reactive sequences we introduce the following alternative representation of a transition step.

Definition 3.31 (Reactive sequences) $l \stackrel{\langle \sigma, \sigma' \rangle}{\longrightarrow} l'$ iff $\langle l; \sigma \rangle \to \langle l'; \sigma' \rangle$. The following axiom and rule allow us to compute the reflexive, transitive closure of $\stackrel{\langle \sigma, \sigma' \rangle}{\longrightarrow}$ and generate so-called reactive sequences, i.e., sequences of pairs of states:

$$l \stackrel{\varepsilon}{\to} l$$

and

$$\frac{l \xrightarrow{w} l', l' \xrightarrow{w'} l''}{l \xrightarrow{w \cdot w'} l''}.$$

Here w and w' denote reactive sequences, ε the empty sequence, and the operation of concatenation is denoted by "$\cdot$".   □

A reactive sequence models a computation of a transition diagram which takes into account possible interleavings by (other) parallel processes. These possible interleavings are made room for by "gaps", that is, subsequent pairs are such that the final state of the preceding pair differs from the initial state of the following pair, allowing for the insertion of interleaved pairs.

Now one can define the following compositional characterisation of $O_l \llbracket P \rrbracket$.

Definition 3.32 $\mathcal{R}_l \llbracket P \rrbracket \overset{\text{def}}{=} \{w \mid s \xrightarrow{w} l\}$.   □

Note that $O_l \llbracket P \rrbracket$ is obtained from $\mathcal{R}_l \llbracket P \rrbracket$ by taking the initial state of the first pair and the final state of the last pair of *connected* sequences. Here connectedness means the absence of gaps in sequences, i.e., the final state of a preceding pair is the initial state of the next pair.

Next we need a definition of the interleaving operator $\tilde{\|}$ between sequences over some alphabet A.

Definition 3.33 (Interleaving) Let $a = a_k \ldots a_{k'}$, and $b = b_l \ldots b_{l'}$, be finite sequences over some alphabet A, with $k' \geq k - 1$, and $l' \geq l - 1$, and with $a = \varepsilon$ if $k' = k - 1$ and $b = \varepsilon$ if $l' = l - 1$. Then the operation of *interleaving* $\tilde{\|}$ the finite sequences a and b is defined as follows:

$$a \tilde{\|} b \overset{\text{def}}{=} \begin{cases} \{a\}, \text{if } b = \varepsilon, \\ \{b\}, \text{if } a = \varepsilon, \\ \{a_k \cdot (a_{k+1} \ldots a_{k'} \tilde{\|} b)\} \cup \{b_l \cdot (a \tilde{\|} b_{l+1} \ldots b_{l'})\}, \text{otherwise,} \end{cases}$$

where for $a_i \in A$ and $s = s_1 \ldots s_m$, $a_i \cdot \{s \mid s \text{ satisfies } p\} \overset{\text{def}}{=} \{a_i \cdot s \mid s \text{ satisfies } p\}$, and $a_i \cdot s \overset{\text{def}}{=} a_i s_1 \ldots s_m$.   □

The interleaving operator can be extended to sets of sequences by defining their pointwise extension $S \tilde{\|} T \overset{\text{def}}{=} \{s \tilde{\|} t \mid s \in S, t \in T\}$, and is commutative and associative, as, e.g., proved in [BK84].

Next we observe that $\mathcal{R}_l \llbracket P \rrbracket$ is compositional w.r.t. parallel composition.

Theorem 3.34 (Compositionality of interleaving)
Let $l = \langle l_1, \ldots, l_n \rangle$ be a location of $P \equiv P_1 \| \ldots \| P_n$, then

$$\mathcal{R}_l \llbracket P \rrbracket = \mathcal{R}_{l_1} \llbracket P_1 \rrbracket \, \tilde{\|} \ldots \tilde{\|} \mathcal{R}_{l_n} \llbracket P_n \rrbracket,$$

where $\tilde{\|}$ denotes the operation of interleaving. $\qquad\square$

This theorem follows immediately from the definition of $\mathcal{R}$. Observe that $\mathcal{R}_l \llbracket P \rrbracket$ extends and generalises the information given by $O_l \llbracket P \rrbracket$. This is an example of a general principle that *compositional semantics are obtained from noncompositional ones by adding missing information in order to reconstruct the functional dependency between the semantics of a construct and the semantics of its components.*

Strongest postcondition operators: concurrent case

Next we define a strongest postcondition semantics based on the compositional semantics $\mathcal{R}$. To this end we introduce histories which record the sequence of state changes together with the active components responsible for these changes. Formally:

Definition 3.35 (Computation history) Given a set of process indices $(i \in)I$, a history θ is a sequence of indexed states (i, σ) indicating that process P_i makes a computation step in state σ. $\qquad\square$

Remark 3.36 Given a sequence s and an element v, $s \cdot v$ denotes the sequence resulting from appending v to s. $\qquad\square$

We also need the following projection operator which, given some set of sequential components and a final state, transforms a history into a reactive sequence consisting of all the computation steps involving one of the given components.

Definition 3.37 (Projection operator) We introduce the projection operator $\theta[I](\sigma)$ to denote the sequence of pairs of states which correspond to transitions of processes with indices from the set I:

$$\varepsilon[I](\sigma) \stackrel{\text{def}}{=} \varepsilon$$

$$(\theta \cdot (i, \sigma'))[I](\sigma) \stackrel{\text{def}}{=} \begin{cases} \theta[I](\sigma') \cdot \langle \sigma', \sigma \rangle, & \text{if } i \in I, \\ \theta[I](\sigma'), & \text{otherwise.} \end{cases} \qquad\square$$

When the index set I contains the indices occurring in θ, then $\theta[I](\sigma)$ is connected. In that case the pair $\langle \sigma, \theta \rangle$ represents a connected reactive sequence with additional information about the identity of the active components. Let $\theta = (i_0, \sigma_0) \cdot \ldots \cdot (i_k, \sigma_k) \cdot \ldots \cdot (i_l, \sigma_l)$. Then process $P_{i_m}, 0 \le m \le l$, transforms state σ_m into σ_{m+1}, where $\sigma_{l+1} = \sigma$.

Given a parallel program $P \equiv P_1 \parallel \cdots \parallel P_n$ we will identify below the set of indices $\{1, \ldots, n\}$ with the program P itself and the index i with its component P_i; correspondingly, one has notation $\theta[P](\sigma)$ for $\theta[\{1, \ldots, n\}](\sigma)$ and $\theta[P_i](\sigma)$ for $\theta[\{i\}](\sigma)$.

We are now able to introduce the strongest postcondition semantics based on the compositional semantics $\mathcal{R}$.

Definition 3.38 (Strongest l-condition for shared-variable concurrency)
We associate with a location l of a transition system P the strongest l-condition of P based on the semantics $\mathcal{R}$:

$$SP'_l(\varphi, P) \stackrel{\text{def}}{=} \{\langle \sigma, \theta \rangle \mid \theta[P](\sigma) \in \mathcal{R}_l[\![P]\!] \text{ and } \sigma' \models \varphi, \text{ with } \sigma' = Init(\sigma, \theta)\},$$

where

$$Init(\sigma, \theta) \stackrel{\text{def}}{=} \begin{cases} \text{the initial state of } \theta, & \text{if } \theta \text{ is non-empty,} \\ \sigma, & \text{otherwise.} \end{cases} \qquad \square$$

Note that if we restrict ourselves to histories referring only to the components of P, we have that

$$SP_l(\varphi, P) = \{\sigma \mid \text{there exists history } \theta \text{ referring only to the} \\ \text{components of } P \text{ s.t. } \langle \sigma, \theta \rangle \in SP'_l(\varphi, P)\}.$$

Semantic completeness of the method of Owicki & Gries

In order to view the strongest l-condition of P as defined above as a state predicate (i.e., a predicate upon (program) states), we include histories of indexed states in the domain of values $\mathcal{D}$. A pair $\langle \sigma, \theta \rangle$ is then interpreted as a state which assigns the history θ to a distinguished history variable h, with all the other variables being assigned a value by σ.

Remark 3.39 For the sake of readability we express the application of a state-transformation f to a pair $\langle \sigma, \theta \rangle$ by $f(\sigma, \theta)$. $\qquad \square$

Now we can prove completeness by associating with a location l of a component P_i of a parallel system $P \equiv P_1 \parallel \ldots \parallel P_n$ the predicate $SP'_l(\varphi, P_i)$, *where we implicitly restrict ourselves to histories referring only to components of P*. In order to prove local correctness and interference freedom we augment the transition system as follows (we assume that the variable h does not already occur in P): Every transition $l \xrightarrow{a} l'$ in P_i, with $a = b \rightarrow f$, is transformed in a transition with action $b \rightarrow f \circ g$, where g is the (total) state transformation such that $g(\sigma, \theta) \stackrel{\text{def}}{=} \langle \sigma, \theta \cdot (i, \sigma) \rangle$, i.e., g only involves h. The resulting transition system is expressed by $P' \equiv P'_1 \| \ldots \| P'_n$. Note that we therefore associate with *each* location l of P'_i the predicate $SP'_l(\varphi, P_i)$, that is, the predicates of P'_i are defined in terms of P_i. In the following we show that the resulting assertion networks for P' are locally correct and free from interference.

Lemma 3.40 (Local correctness) Let P be a transition system in which the variable h does not already occur. For every transition $l \xrightarrow{a} l'$ of P' (the transition system P augmented with updates to the history variable h, as described above), we have

$$\models SP'_l(\varphi, P) \wedge b \rightarrow SP'_{l'}(\varphi, P) \circ f,$$

assuming $a = b \rightarrow f$.

Proof Let $f(\sigma, \theta) = \langle \sigma', \theta' \rangle$. Note that $\theta' = \theta \cdot (i, \sigma)$, where i denotes the index of the active component of P', since f includes an update to the history variable as described above. Now, let $\langle \sigma, \theta \rangle \models SP'_l(\varphi, P) \wedge b$. Thus $\theta[P](\sigma) \in \mathcal{R}_l[\![P]\!]$. Since $\sigma \models b$ we derive that $\theta'[P](\sigma') = \theta[P](\sigma) \cdot \langle \sigma, \sigma' \rangle \in \mathcal{R}_{l'}[\![P]\!]$. Thus we conclude $\langle \sigma', \theta' \rangle \models SP'_{l'}(\varphi, P)$, or, equivalently, $\langle \sigma, \theta \rangle \models SP'_{l'}(\varphi, P) \circ f$. □

Lemma 3.41 (Interference freedom) Let P and Q be two transition systems in which the variable h does not occur. Let $l \xrightarrow{a} l'$ be a transition of P' (the transition system P augmented with updates to the history variable h, as described above) and l'' be a location of Q, then:

$$\models SP'_{l''}(\varphi, Q) \wedge SP'_l(\varphi, P) \wedge b \rightarrow SP'_{l''}(\varphi, Q) \circ f,$$

assuming $a = b \rightarrow f$.

Proof Actually we have already that

$$\models SP'_{l''}(\varphi, Q) \rightarrow SP'_{l''}(\varphi, Q) \circ f.$$

Let $\langle \sigma, \theta \rangle \models SP'_{l''}(\varphi, Q)$. By definition of SP' we have that $\theta[Q](\sigma) \in \mathcal{R}_{l''}[\![Q]\!]$. Moreover, we have that $f(\sigma, \theta) = \langle \sigma', \theta' \rangle$, where $\theta' = \theta \cdot (i, \sigma)$, with i the index of the active component of P'; and thus $\theta'[Q](\sigma') = \theta[Q](\sigma)$. From this we conclude $\langle \sigma', \theta' \rangle \models SP'_{l''}(\varphi, Q)$, i.e., $\langle \sigma, \theta \rangle \models SP'_{l''}(\varphi, Q) \circ f$. □

Next we establish the remaining clauses of the method of Owicki & Gries.

Lemma 3.42 (Initialisation) Let $P \equiv P_1 \| \ldots \| P_n$ such that the variable h does not occur in P, and s_i denote the initial location of P_i. For any φ which does not refer to the variable h we have

$$\models \varphi \to \bigwedge_{i=1}^{n} SP'_{s_i}(\varphi, P_i) \circ f,$$

where $f(\sigma, \theta) \stackrel{\text{def}}{=} \langle \sigma, \varepsilon \rangle$. (Here "$\wedge$" is assumed to bind stronger than "$\circ$", which binds in turn stronger than "$\to$".)

Proof Exercise. □

Lemma 3.43 (Finalisation) Let $P \equiv P_1 \| \ldots \| P_n$, let the variable h not occur in P, and t_i denote the final location of P_i. Furthermore suppose that $\models \{\varphi\}P\{\psi\}$, where h does neither occur in φ nor in ψ. We have, restricting to histories which contain only references to components of P,

$$\models \bigwedge_{i=1}^{n} SP'_{t_i}(\varphi, P_i) \to \psi.$$

Proof Let $\langle \sigma, \theta \rangle \models \bigwedge_i SP'_{t_i}(\varphi, P_i)$, and θ only refer to the components of P. It follows that $\theta[P_i](\sigma) \in \mathcal{R}_{t_i}[\![P_i]\!]$ for every $i \in \{1, \ldots, n\}$. Thus we obtain by the compositionality of $\mathcal{R}$ that $\theta[P](\sigma) \in \mathcal{R}_t[\![P]\!]$, where t denotes the final location of P, i.e., $t = \langle t_1, \ldots, t_n \rangle$. Next we observe that $\theta[P](\sigma)$ is a *connected* reactive sequence, since θ is assumed to contain only references to components of P. Thus it follows that $\sigma \in \mathcal{M}[\![P]\!]\sigma'$, where σ' is the initial state of $\theta[P](\sigma)$. Note furthermore that $\sigma' \models \varphi$, so we conclude by $\models \{\varphi\}P\{\psi\}$, that $\sigma \models \psi$ (and so, since h does not occur in ψ, $\langle \sigma, \theta \rangle \models \psi$). □

Therefore we conclude:

Theorem 3.44 (Semantic completeness – 1st version)
The proof method of Owicki & Gries is semantically complete. □

It is interesting to observe that in the above completeness proof the compositionality of $\mathcal{R}$ is only used in the 'finalisation' lemma, namely in order to establish $\models \bigwedge_i SP'_{t_i}(\varphi, P_i) \to SP'_{\langle t_1, \ldots, t_n \rangle}(\varphi, P)$. Actually one has the following property, needed for later reference.

Lemma 3.45 With P as above, let $l = \langle l_1, \ldots, l_n \rangle$ be a location of P. Then

$$\models \bigwedge_{i=1}^{n} SP'_{l_i}(\varphi, P_i) \to SP'_l(\varphi, P). \qquad \square$$

Technical note: How to obtain compositionality of SP'

As observed above, the compositionality of $\mathcal{R}_l$ with respect to $\|$ implies that $\models \bigwedge_{i=1}^{n} SP'_{l_i}(\varphi, P_i) \rightarrow SP'_l(\varphi, P)$ holds, where $l = \langle l_1, \ldots, l_n \rangle$ is a location of $P \equiv P_1 \| \ldots \| P_n$. However, the inverse inclusion does not hold in general since $\theta[P](\sigma) \in \mathcal{R}[\![P]\!]$ does not necessarily imply that the indices in θ indicate the actual active components. For example, consider a system P consisting of two components P_1 and P_2 such that P_1 contains only a transition labelled with the instruction $x := 0$ and P_2 contains only a transition labelled with the instruction $x := 1$. Let $x = n$ denote a state in which x has the (integer) value n. Consider the history $\theta = (1, x = n) \cdot (2, x = 1)$. It follows that $\theta[P](x = 0) = \langle x = n, x = 1 \rangle \cdot \langle x = 1, x = 0 \rangle$. However, $\theta[P_1](x = 0) = \langle x = n, x = 1 \rangle$ is not a reactive sequence of P_1.

Full compositionality of SP' can be obtained by also including in the semantics $\mathcal{R}$ indices indicating for each computation step which component was involved. This approach is followed in Chapter 12.

3.5.7 An Alternative Completeness Proof

It is interesting to observe that in the above completeness proof *all* transitions are annotated with updates to the history variable, including transitions which are labelled by booleans only, i.e., transitions which are labelled with actions of the form $b \rightarrow f$, where f denotes the identity function; such transitions are called boolean tests. In Chapter 10 we extend the Owicki & Gries proof method to a parallel programming language based on assignments and control structures like sequential composition, guarded nondeterministic selection and guarded loops. Now it is usual in the literature [Apt81a, Owi75] that in such extended proof methods only assignments are annotated by auxiliary variables. No such annotation is allowed for a boolean test within a guarded selection or loop. Still we would like to be able to reduce both the soundness and completeness proofs of such proof methods to the soundness and completeness proofs of the corresponding proof methods for transition diagrams. This reduction can be obtained in principle by translating a concurrent program into a transition diagram. In such a translation a boolean test of a conditional is naturally translated into a boolean transition. So if we want to 'translate' the proof of the correctness of a transition diagram into a correctness proof of its corresponding program, we cannot always allow annotation of boolean transitions.

An alternative completeness proof, which introduces updates to the history variable only for the non-boolean transitions, can be based on a slight modification of the definition of the strongest l-condition SP'_l. Such a modification is needed to compensate for the loss of information caused by not explicitly recording the boolean transitions. For example, Lemma 3.40 would no longer hold without such a modification. The basic idea of the modification is simply to state the existence of an *extension* of the history which takes the boolean transitions into account. Such extensions are defined as follows.

Definition 3.46 We define the following *stuttering* relation between possibly extended states: Let I be a set of process indices, then $\langle \sigma, \theta \rangle \to_I \langle \sigma', \theta' \rangle$ if $\sigma = \sigma'$ and θ' is obtained by either appending (i, σ), for some $i \in I$, to θ, or prefixing an element (j, σ'') of θ by (i, σ''). □

Example 3.47 Consider the state $\langle \sigma, \theta \rangle$, with $\theta = (i_0, \sigma_0) \cdot \ldots \cdot (i_k, \sigma_k) \cdot \ldots \cdot (i_l, \sigma_l)$. So process $i_m, 0 \leq m \leq l$, transforms state σ_m into σ_{m+1}, where $\sigma_{l+1} = \sigma$. Appending θ then with an element (j, σ) would introduce a computation step by process j which transforms σ into σ, and which thus may correspond with a boolean transition of j. Similarly, prefixing an element (i_k, σ_k) with (j, σ_k) (thus obtaining the history $(i_0, \sigma_0) \cdot \ldots \cdot (i_{k-1}, \sigma_{k-1}) \cdot (j, \sigma_k) \cdot (i_k, \sigma_k) \cdot \ldots \cdot (i_l, \sigma_l)$, in case $k > 0$, and $(j, \sigma_0) \cdot (i_0, \sigma_0) \cdot \ldots \cdot (i_l, \sigma_l)$, otherwise), corresponds to the introduction of a computation step by process j which transforms σ_k into itself again. Note that the computation steps of the old history are not affected by the insertion. □

The reflexive transitive closure of the above defined relation $\to_I$ we denote by $\to_I^*$. Given a program P we will also use the notation $\to_P$, which stands for $\to_I$, where I denotes the set of indices of the parallel processes of P.

Definition 3.48 Let l be a location of the transition system P. We introduce the following modification of the definition of $SP_l'(\varphi, P)$, which we denote by $SP_l^\tau(\varphi, P)$:

$$SP_l^\tau(\varphi, P) \stackrel{\text{def}}{=} \{ \langle \sigma, \theta \rangle \mid \text{there exists } \theta' \text{ such that}$$
$$\langle \sigma, \theta \rangle \to_P^* \langle \sigma, \theta' \rangle \text{ and } \langle \sigma, \theta' \rangle \in SP_l'(\varphi, P) \}. \quad □$$

So $SP_l^\tau(\varphi, P)$ holds in $\langle \sigma, \theta \rangle$ if θ can be extended by stuttering steps (which correspond to boolean transitions) to a history θ' such that the 'old' strongest l-condition $SP_l'(\varphi, P)$ holds in $\langle \sigma, \theta' \rangle$.

Let $P \equiv P_1 \| \ldots \| P_n$ be such that $\models \{\varphi\} P \{\psi\}$. We prove the derivability of $\{\varphi\} P \{\psi\}$ by associating with a location l of a component P_i the predicate $SP_l^\tau(\varphi, P_i)$, where we implicitly restrict ourselves to histories referring only to components of P. We augment the transition system P as follows (we assume that the variable h does not already occur in P): Every transition $l \stackrel{a}{\to} l'$ in

P_i, with $a = b \to f$, where f is *not* the identity function, is transformed in a transition with action $b \to f \circ g$, where g is the state transformation such that $g(\sigma, \theta) \stackrel{\text{def}}{=} \langle \sigma, \theta \cdot (i, \sigma) \rangle$, i.e., g only involves an update to h. The resulting transition system is denoted by $P' \equiv P'_1 \| \ldots \| P'_n$. Note that boolean transitions are not annotated. In the following we show that the resulting assertion networks for P' are locally correct and free from interference.

Lemma 3.49 (Local correctness) Let P be a transition system in which the variable h does not already occur. For every transition $l \stackrel{a}{\to} l'$ of P' (the transition system P augmented with updates to the history variable h, as described above), we have

$$\models SP_l^{\tau}(\varphi, P) \wedge b \to (SP_{l'}^{\tau}(\varphi, P) \circ f),$$

assuming $a = b \to f$.

Proof First we consider the case of a boolean transition, i.e., $a = b \to f$, where f is the identity function (note that such a transition stems from the original transition system P). So we have to show that

$$\models SP_l^{\tau}(\varphi, P) \wedge b \to SP_{l'}^{\tau}(\varphi, P).$$

To this end let $\langle \sigma, \theta \rangle \models SP_l^{\tau}(\varphi, P) \wedge b$. So there exists θ' such that $\langle \sigma, \theta \rangle \to_i^* \langle \sigma, \theta' \rangle$, where i denotes the active component of P, and $\langle \sigma, \theta' \rangle \models SP_l'(\varphi, P)$. By Lemma 3.40 we derive that $\langle \sigma, \theta'' \rangle \models SP_{l'}'(\varphi, P)$, where $\theta'' = \theta' \cdot (i, \sigma)$. Next observe that $\langle \sigma, \theta \rangle \to_i^* \langle \sigma, \theta'' \rangle$. Thus we conclude that $\langle \sigma, \theta \rangle \models SP_{l'}^{\tau}(\varphi, P)$.

Next we treat the case that f is not the identity function: Let $f(\sigma, \theta) = \langle \sigma', \theta' \rangle$. Note that $\theta' = \theta \cdot (i, \sigma)$, where i denotes the index of the active component of P'. Now, let $\langle \sigma, \theta \rangle \models SP_l^{\tau}(\varphi, P) \wedge b$. It follows that $\langle \sigma, \theta'' \rangle \models SP_l'(\varphi, P)$, for some θ'' such that $\langle \sigma, \theta \rangle \to_i^* \langle \sigma, \theta'' \rangle$. By Lemma 3.40 we derive that $\langle \sigma', \theta''' \rangle \models SP_{l'}'(\varphi, P)$, where $\theta''' = \theta'' \cdot (i, \sigma)$. Next observe that $\langle \sigma', \theta' \rangle \to_i^* \langle \sigma', \theta''' \rangle$, so $\langle \sigma', \theta' \rangle \models SP_{l'}^{\tau}(\varphi, P)$, that is, $\langle \sigma, \theta \rangle \models SP_{l'}^{\tau}(\varphi, P) \circ f$. $\square$

Lemma 3.50 (Interference freedom) Let P and Q be two parallel transition systems in which the variable h does not occur. Let $l \stackrel{a}{\to} l'$ be a transition of P' (the transition system P augmented with updates to the history variable h, as described above) and l'' be a location of Q, then:

$$\models SP_{l''}^{\tau}(\varphi, Q) \wedge SP_l^{\tau}(\varphi, P) \wedge b \to (SP_{l''}^{\tau}(\varphi, Q) \circ f),$$

assuming $a = b \to f$.

Proof First observe that the lemma holds trivially in case of a boolean transition. So consider the case that f is not the identity function. We will show that in fact $\models SP^{\tau}_{l''}(\varphi, Q) \to SP^{\tau}_{l''}(\varphi, Q) \circ f$. Let $\langle \sigma, \theta \rangle \models SP^{\tau}_{l''}(\varphi, Q)$. So there exists θ' such that $\langle \sigma, \theta \rangle \to^*_i \langle \sigma, \theta' \rangle$ and $\langle \sigma, \theta' \rangle \models SP_{l''}(\varphi, Q \parallel P)$, where i denotes the active component of P. Let $f(\sigma, \theta') = \langle \sigma', \theta'' \rangle$, where $\theta'' = \theta' \cdot (i, \sigma)$. Next we observe that $\langle \sigma', \theta \cdot (i, \sigma) \rangle \to^*_i \langle \sigma', \theta'' \rangle$. Thus it follows that $\langle \sigma', \theta \cdot (i, \sigma) \rangle \models SP^{\tau}_{l''}(\varphi, P')$, that is, $\langle \sigma, \theta \rangle \models SP^{\tau}_{l''}(\varphi, P') \circ f$. □

Lemma 3.51 (Initialisation) Let $P \equiv P_1 \parallel \ldots \parallel P_n$ such that the variable h does not occur in P, and s_i denote the initial location of P_i. We have:

$$\models \varphi \to \bigwedge_{i=1}^{n} SP^{\tau}_{s_i}(\varphi, P_i) \circ f,$$

where $f(\sigma, \theta) = \langle \sigma, \varepsilon \rangle$.

Proof Exercise.   □

Lemma 3.52 (Finalisation) Let $P \equiv P_1 \parallel \ldots \parallel P_n$, be such that the variable h does not occur in P, and t_i denote the final location of P'_i (the transition system P_i augmented with updates to the history variable h, as described above). Furthermore suppose that $\models \{\varphi\}P\{\psi\}$, where h does neither occur in φ nor in ψ. We have, restricting to histories which contain only references to components of P,

$$\models \bigwedge_i SP^{\tau}_{t_i}(\varphi, P_i) \to \psi.$$

Proof Exercise.   □

These lemmas also establish the semantic completeness of the method of Owicki & Gries when one is only allowed to augment assignments, as stated below.

Theorem 3.53 (Semantic completeness – 2nd version)
The proof method of Owicki & Gries is also semantically complete when one is only allowed to augment transitions which are not in the form $b \to id$.   □

3.6 Proving Convergence for Shared-Variable Concurrency

As mentioned before, diagram $P_1 \parallel \ldots \parallel P_n$ is φ-convergent if it does not admit infinite φ-computations. In this section, we extend the method for proving convergence of sequential transition diagrams from the last chapter to the parallel composition of such diagrams operating upon shared variables. We shall do this along the same lines as we have done in generalising Floyd's inductive assertion method for proving partial correctness of sequential diagrams to the Owicki & Gries method for proving partial correctness of concurrent shared-variable diagrams, as worked out in the previous sections.

3.6.1 A Global Method

Since the semantics of a concurrent transition diagram is given by constructing an equivalent sequential transition diagram (up to observations based on interleaving), one immediately gets a global method for proving convergence by adapting Floyd's wellfoundedness method (Definition 2.16) to the resulting diagram.

Definition 3.54 (Global method for proving convergence) Let L be the set of *global* locations $l \in L$ of $P \equiv P_1 \parallel \ldots \parallel P_n$. To prove that P is φ-convergent:

(i) Find an assertion network Q for the *global* locations of P, and prove that it is inductive, and that $\models \varphi \to Q_s$ holds, where s denotes the initial location of P.

(ii) Choose a wellfounded set $(W, \prec)$ and a network of partially-defined ranking functions ρ for the global locations of P such that

$$\rho_l : \Sigma \to W \text{ for every } l \in L.$$

(iii) Prove *local consistency,* of Q_l and ρ_l, i.e., that, for every $l \in L$, Q_l implies that ρ_l is defined, i.e., for every $\sigma \in \Sigma$,

$$\sigma \models Q_l \Rightarrow \rho_l(\sigma) \in W$$

holds.[10]

(iv) Prove that for $l, l' \in L$, every transition $l \xrightarrow{a} l'$ of P, with $a = b \to f$, decreases the ranking function, i.e.,

$$\models Q_l \wedge b \to \rho_l \succ (\rho_{l'} \circ f). \qquad \Box$$

Soundness and semantic completeness of this global method for proving convergence follow from the corresponding proofs for the sequential method and from the definition of the semantics of the parallel composition of diagrams. Similar to the case of partial correctness, the global method requires too many verification conditions. Therefore, we wish to improve on that by

[10] The "$\Rightarrow$" symbol denotes implication in our meta language.

examining a more localised approach. Our task is again to find a way to formulate the verification conditions for the whole program in terms of verification conditions for its composing processes.

3.6.2 A Local Method

Looking at the problem from another angle, we assume that for each process P_i there exists a local assertion network and a network of local ranking functions to a wellfounded set $(W_i, \prec_i)$. Our task is to find verification conditions for (global) convergence in terms of these local quantities. Since we have the global method already at our disposal, we look at whether we can derive a global proof for convergence from these local conditions. Now there are two networks to be constructed: one consisting of assertions, and one of ranking functions.

The global assertion network can be derived in the same way as we have done for proving partial correctness: for a global location $l = \langle l_1, \ldots l_n \rangle$, define

$$Q_l \stackrel{\text{def}}{=} Q_{l_1} \wedge \ldots \wedge Q_{l_n}.$$

The following two conditions, namely, local correctness (LC) and the interference freedom test (IFT):

$$\models Q_l \wedge b \to Q_{l'} \circ f, \tag{LC},$$

$$\models Q_l \wedge Q_{l'''} \wedge b \to Q_{l'''} \circ f, \tag{IFT},$$

for any transition $l \stackrel{a}{\to} l'$ of P_i, with $a = b \to f$ and location l'' of P_j, for $j \neq i$, ensure that the network is inductive by Theorem 3.24.

Definition 3.55 (Componentwise order) Let $W \stackrel{\text{def}}{=} W_1 \times \ldots \times W_n$ and $(W_i, \prec_i)$ be wellfounded sets, $i = 1, \ldots n$. For
$(w_1, \ldots, w_n), (w'_1, \ldots, w'_n) \in W$, define the componentwise order as follows:

$$(w_1, \ldots, w_n) \prec (w'_1, \ldots, w'_n) \text{ iff } \exists i. w_i \prec_i w'_i \text{ and } \forall j \neq i. w_j \preceq_j w'_j. \qquad \square$$

We leave it as an exercise to prove that $(W, \prec)$ is also a wellfounded set.

For global location $l = \langle l_1, \ldots, l_n \rangle$, we define

$$\rho_l \stackrel{\text{def}}{=} (\rho_{l_1}, \ldots, \rho_{l_n}).$$

To prove that this function indeed decreases along the transitions of P, the following two additional conditions on local correctness and the interference-freedom test for the ranking functions suffice:

$$\models Q_l \wedge b \to \rho_l \succ_i (\rho_{l'} \circ f), \tag{LC},$$

$$\models Q_l \wedge Q_{l''} \wedge b \rightarrow \rho_{l''} \succeq_j (\rho_{l''} \circ f), \qquad \text{(IFT)},$$

for any transition $l \xrightarrow{a} l'$ of P_i, with $a = b \rightarrow f$, and location l'' of P_j, for $j \neq i$.

Example 3.56 As a first step, we show that the following simple program $P_1 \| P_2$ is convergent.

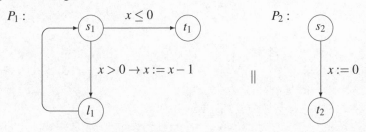

Let the value of x be a natural number. Define all the assertions to be simply *true* and the ranking-function network as follows:

$$\rho_{s_1}(x) \stackrel{\text{def}}{=} (x,1) \qquad\qquad \rho_{s_2}(x) \stackrel{\text{def}}{=} 1$$
$$\rho_{l_1}(x) \stackrel{\text{def}}{=} (x,2) \qquad\qquad \rho_{t_2}(x) \stackrel{\text{def}}{=} 0$$
$$\rho_{l_1'}(x) \stackrel{\text{def}}{=} (0,0),$$

where the wellfounded set for the first ranking-function network is the lexicographical ordering of $N \times N$ over $(N, <)$, and for the second ranking-function network is $(N, <)$ itself. Local correctness and interference freedom are both trivially satisfied. $\qquad\square$

Example 3.57 The program given in Figure 3.22 is concerned with finding the first positive number in an integer array $a[1, \dots, N]$. This program was suggested in [OG76a], and consists of the following two parallel processes, searching separately for the odd and even positions within the array. Two variables *otop* and *etop* store the odd and even indices of the currently found positive number, where *otop* and *etop* have $N + 1$ as initial value. Two search pointers i and j are introduced. Obviously, a process can stop if its pointer is already greater than or equal to the minimum value $min(otop, etop)$ of *otop* and *etop*.

For process P_1, we select the following assertion and ranking-function networks:

$$Q_{s_1} \stackrel{\text{def}}{=} otop = N + 1 \qquad\qquad \rho_{s_1} \stackrel{\text{def}}{=} (N+1, 0)$$
$$Q_{l_1} \stackrel{\text{def}}{=} true \qquad\qquad \rho_{l_1} \stackrel{\text{def}}{=} (max(otop - i, 0), 1)$$
$$Q_{l_1'} \stackrel{\text{def}}{=} otop > i \qquad\qquad \rho_{l_1'} \stackrel{\text{def}}{=} (max(otop - i, 0), 0)$$
$$Q_{t_1} \stackrel{\text{def}}{=} true \qquad\qquad \rho_{t_1} \stackrel{\text{def}}{=} (0, 0),$$

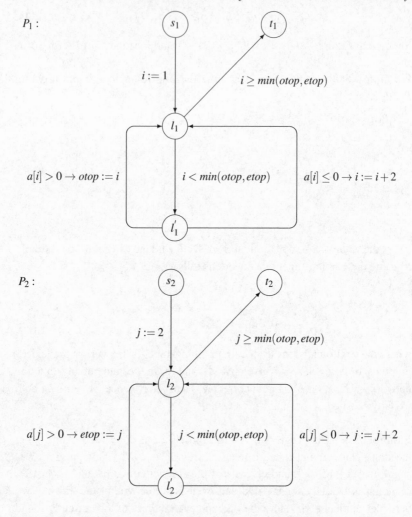

Fig. 3.22. A program for finding the first positive number in an array.

where the wellfounded set for P_1 is the lexicographical order of $N \times N$ over the sets of nonnegative numbers $(N, <)$. The verification conditions for the assertion network are trivial to establish. As for the ranking-function network, we are required to prove that the ranking functions decrease along each transition of P_1:

$s_1 \to l_1$,   the first component of the ranking function decreases at least by one,

$l_1 \rightarrow l'_1$, the first components of the ranking function do not increase, whereas the second decreases by one,

$l'_1 \rightarrow l_1$, there are two transitions leading from l'_1 to l_1, and in both cases the first component of the ranking function decreases,

$l_1 \rightarrow t_1$, the first components of the ranking function do not increase, whereas the second decreases by one.

Since process P_2 does not modify the variables occurring in the definition of P_1's ranking functions, the verification conditions concerning interference freedom trivially hold.

A similar construction of assertion and ranking-function networks, as well as a similar way of reasoning for establishing the related verification conditions can be applied to process P_2. □

Recall that auxiliary variables are needed for making the partial-correctness method complete. For the same reason, auxiliary variables are also necessary in general for proving convergence. We illustrate this by the following example.

Example 3.58 It is obvious that the program shown in Figure 3.23 is convergent under the precondition $x = 0$, but this fact is not possible to prove by the proposed method without introducing auxiliary variables. We prove this by demonstrating that if an assertion network and a ranking-function network as-

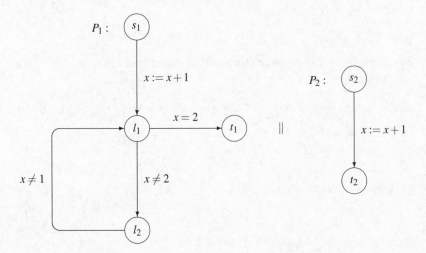

Fig. 3.23. A program which is convergent under the precondition $x = 0$.

sociated with process P_i only use program variables, here x, then not all the verification conditions can be satisfied.

We first show that Q_{l_1} implies $x = 1 \lor x = 2$. Then local correctness requires that the values of the ranking functions decrease along the two transitions between l_1 and l_2, and, since neither of them modifies the value of x, we have

$$\models Q_{l_1}(x) \land x \neq 2 \rightarrow \rho_{l_1}(x) > \rho_{l_2}(x) \tag{3.2}$$

$$\models Q_{l_2}(x) \land x \neq 1 \rightarrow \rho_{l_2}(x) > \rho_{l_1}(x). \tag{3.3}$$

It also requires that

$$\models Q_{l_1}(x) \land x \neq 2 \rightarrow Q_{l_2}(x) \tag{3.4}$$

holds due to inductiveness along the transition from l_1 to l_2. Therefore, from (3.2), (3.3) and (3.4), it follows that

$$\models Q_{l_1}(x) \land x \neq 2 \land x \neq 1 \rightarrow (\rho_{l_1}(x) > \rho_{l_2}(x)) \land (\rho_{l_2}(x) > \rho_{l_1}(x)), \tag{3.5}$$

which is equivalent to

$$\models Q_{l_1}(x) \rightarrow (x = 1 \lor x = 2). \tag{3.6}$$

We then have

$$\models Q_{s_1}(x) \rightarrow (x = 0 \lor x = 1) \tag{3.7}$$

from local correctness concerning the transition from s_1 to l_1. From the initial condition, we have

$$\models x = 0 \rightarrow Q_{s_1}(x) \land Q_{s_2}(x). \tag{3.8}$$

By the interference freedom condition, $Q_{s_1}(x)$ should not be invalidated by the assignment in P_2:

$$\models Q_{s_1}(x) \land Q_{s_2}(x) \rightarrow Q_{s_1}(x+1). \tag{3.9}$$

Hence, it follows from (3.8) and (3.9) that

$$\models x = 0 \rightarrow Q_{s_1}(x+1), \tag{3.10}$$

and this is equivalent to

$$\models x = 1 \rightarrow Q_{s_1}(x). \tag{3.11}$$

Combining (3.7), (3.8) and (3.11), we have

$$\models Q_{s_1}(x) = (x = 0 \lor x = 1). \tag{3.12}$$

Reasoning similarly to (3.11) shows that

$$\models x = 1 \rightarrow Q_{s_2}(x) \tag{3.13}$$

holds. However, (3.12), (3.13) and (3.9) would lead to

$$\models (x = 0 \lor x = 1) \land x = 1 \rightarrow (x + 1 = 0 \lor x + 1 = 1), \tag{3.14}$$

which obviously is not true, hence a contradiction follows. □

This leads to the following semantically-complete local method for proving convergence.

Definition 3.59 (A local method for proving convergence) Consider $P \equiv P_1 \| \dots \| P_n$. To prove that P converges (i.e., terminates or deadlocks) w.r.t. precondition φ, we define the following local method for proving convergence of the parallel composition of transition diagrams P_i:

  (i) Augment P by introducing auxiliary variables; every action $b \rightarrow f$ can be extended as follows: $b \rightarrow f \circ g$, where $g(\bar{z})$ is a state transformation involving only the auxiliary variables $\bar{z}$ not occurring in P or φ. This leads to an augmented transition system $P' \equiv P'_1 \| \dots \| P'_n$.

  (ii) Associate a predicate Q_l with every location l of P'_i. Choose a well-founded set $(W_i, \prec_i)$ and a network of partial ranking functions $\rho \stackrel{\text{def}}{=} \{\rho_l \mid l \in P'_i\}$. Prove that the assertion and ranking functions are *locally* consistent, namely, predicate Q_l implies that ranking function ρ_l is defined:

$$\models Q_l(\sigma) \Rightarrow \rho_l(\sigma) \in W_i, \text{ for } \sigma \in \Sigma.$$

  (iii) Prove *local correctness* of every P'_i. This involves proving two properties: that the local assertion network of P'_i is inductive, and that the ranking functions decrease along every local transition. That is, for every transition $l \xrightarrow{a} l'$ of P'_i, with $a = b \rightarrow f$, we have to prove:

  - $\models Q_l \land b \rightarrow Q_{l'} \circ f$
  - $\models Q_l \land b \rightarrow \rho_l \succ_i (\rho_{l'} \circ f)$ $\left.\right\}$ (LC).

  (iv) Prove *interference freedom* of both the local assertion networks and the local networks of ranking functions, where the latter amounts to showing that the ranking functions in one process do not increase due to transitions in other processes. That is, for every transition $l \xrightarrow{a} l'$ of P'_i, with $a = b \rightarrow f$, and location l'' of P'_j, for $j \neq i$, prove that:

  - $\models Q_l \land Q_{l''} \land b \rightarrow Q_{l''} \circ f$
  - $\models Q_l \land Q_{l''} \land b \rightarrow \rho_{l''} \succeq_j (\rho_{l''} \circ f)$ $\left.\right\}$ (IFT).

(v) Prove that:

- $\models \varphi \to (\bigwedge_i Q_{s_i}) \circ f$ for some state transformation f whose write variables belong to the set of auxiliary variables $\bar{z}$. Here s_i denotes the initial location of P_i'. $\qquad\square$

3.6.3 Soundness and Semantic Completeness of the Local Method for Proving Convergence

Recall that convergence is defined as absence of an infinite computation. In the present setting (where total state functions are used to characterise assignments) convergence therefore implies either termination or deadlock.

Soundness of the local method for proving convergence follows in a straightforward manner from the soundness of the global method:

Theorem 3.60 (Soundness)
The local method for proving convergence given in Definition 3.59 is sound.

Proof It is easy to prove that if the verification conditions for the local method for proving φ-convergence of $P_1 \parallel \ldots \parallel P_n$ are satisfied then there exists an assertion network and a ranking-function network satisfying the verification conditions for the global method, as formulated in Definition 3.54, for proving $Q_{s_1} \wedge \ldots \wedge Q_{s_n}$-convergence of $P_1' \parallel \ldots \parallel P_n'$, where P_i' denotes an augmented transition system and Q_{s_i} denotes the initial assertion of the local network of P_i'. Simply define $Q_l \stackrel{\text{def}}{=} \bigwedge_i Q_{l_i}$, for every location $l = \langle l_1, \ldots, l_n \rangle$ of $P_1' \parallel \ldots \parallel P_n'$ and $\rho_l \stackrel{\text{def}}{=} \langle \rho_{l_1}, \ldots, \rho_{l_n} \rangle$, defining $(W, \prec)$ componentwise as in Definition 3.55 from $(W_1, \prec_1), \ldots, (W_n, \prec_n)$. It remains to be shown that $Q_{s_1} \wedge \ldots \wedge Q_{s_n}$-convergence of $P_1' \parallel \ldots \parallel P_n'$ implies that $P_1 \parallel \ldots \parallel P_n$ is φ-convergent. Let $\langle l_0; \sigma_0 \rangle \to \ldots \langle l_k; \sigma_k \rangle \to \ldots$ be an infinite computation of $P_1 \parallel \ldots \parallel P_n$ such that $\sigma_0 \models \varphi$. Define σ_k' as follows: $\sigma_0' \stackrel{\text{def}}{=} f(\sigma_0)$, where f is some state transformation which involves only the auxiliary variables $\bar{z}$ and for which $\models \varphi \to (\bigwedge Q_{s_i} \circ f)$, and $\sigma_{k+1}' \stackrel{\text{def}}{=} f_k(\sigma_k')$, where $c_k \to f_k$ is the transition of $P_1' \parallel \ldots \parallel P_n'$ corresponding with the k-th transition of the given computation of $P_1 \parallel \ldots \parallel P_n$. It follows that $\langle l_0; \sigma_0' \rangle \to \ldots \langle l_k; \sigma_k' \rangle \to \ldots$ is an infinite computation of $P_1' \parallel \ldots \parallel P_n'$ (note that σ_k' differs from σ_k only with respect to the auxiliary variables $\bar{z}$). Moreover we have that $\sigma_0' \models \bigwedge_i Q_{s_i}$, since $\models \varphi \to (\bigwedge Q_{s_i} \circ f)$. This contradicts the $Q_{s_0} \wedge \ldots \wedge Q_{s_n}$-convergence of $P_1' \parallel \ldots \parallel P_n'$. $\qquad\square$

Next we prove semantic completeness. Assume $P \equiv P_1 \parallel \ldots \parallel P_n$ is φ-convergent, then our task is to find a proof using the proposed local verification method. However, the (compositional) completeness proof of the Owicki

& Gries method for proving partial correctness, as described in Section 3.5.6, *cannot* be extended with appropriate ranking functions to a completeness proof of the local method for proving convergence. This is because the (local) predicates used in the compositional completeness proof describe the behaviour of a process with respect to *any* environment. However, convergence of a process clearly depends on a *particular* environment. Therefore we first construct an alternative completeness proof for proving partial correctness which is based on so-called *reachability* predicates, which do take the particular given environment of a process into account.

A third completeness proof of the method of Owicki & Gries based on reachability predicates

As the first step of this third completeness proof for partial correctness, let $P \equiv P_1 \| \ldots \| P_n$ such that $\models \{\varphi\}P\{\psi\}$, i.e., P is partially correct w.r.t. $< \varphi, \psi >$. In the following we assume the program P, and the predicates φ and ψ, to be fixed. Moreover, for the sake of convenience and readability we introduce the following notation: The i-th component of a location l of P is denoted by $l(i)$.

Definition 3.61 (Reachability predicates) Given locations $l_1, \ldots, l_k$, with l_i belonging to P_{f_i} ($f_i \neq f_j$, for $i \neq j$) define the reachability predicate $\varphi_{\langle l_1, \ldots, l_k \rangle}$ as follows:

$\langle \sigma, \theta \rangle \models \varphi_{\langle l_1, \ldots, l_k \rangle}$ if there exists a location l of P such that for $1 \leq i \leq k$, $l(f_i) = l_i$, and for $1 \leq i \leq n$, $\theta[P_i](\sigma) \in \mathcal{R}_{l(i)}[\![P_i]\!]$. Moreover, we require that $\sigma' \models \varphi$, where σ' is the initial state of $\theta[P](\sigma)$. ☐

By the compositionality of $\mathcal{R}_l$ (as stated in Theorem 3.34) we have that $\theta[P_i](\sigma) \in \mathcal{R}_{l(i)}[\![P_i]\!]$, for $1 \leq i \leq n$, implies that $\theta[P](\sigma) \in \mathcal{R}_l[\![P]\!]$. If we assume furthermore that θ refers only to components of P, the definition of the truth of the reachability predicate $\varphi_{\langle l_1, \ldots, l_k \rangle}$ in an (extended) state $\langle \sigma, \theta \rangle$ then amounts to stating the existence of a computation of P, which satisfies the following requirements:

(i) its state changes are recorded in Θ,

(ii) it starts in a state satisfying φ, and

(iii) it reaches a configuration $\langle l; \sigma \rangle$ of P such that $l(f_i) = l_i$, for $i = 1, \ldots, k$, that is, each component $P_{f_i}, 1 \leq i \leq k$, reaches its corresponding location l_i.

Here an example helps. Consider $P \equiv P_1 \| P_2 \| P_3 \| P_4$, and l_1, l_2 such that l_1 is a location of P_2, l_2 is a location of P_3, and $k = 2$, i.e., $f_1 = 2$ and $f_2 = 3$. Then the reachability predicate $\varphi_{\langle l_1, l_2\rangle}$ expresses that there exists a partial computation of P starting in φ and ending in l such that $l(2) = l_1$ and $l(3) = l_2$.

The formulation of the reachability predicates in terms of the compositional semantics $\mathcal{R}$ allows, as we will see below, a simple proof of the interference freedom test.

We prove local correctness and interference freedom of the reachability predicates with respect to $P' \equiv P'_1 \parallel \ldots \parallel P'_n$, the augmented program. In P'_i every transition $l \xrightarrow{a} l'$ in P_i, with $a = b \rightarrow f$, is transformed in a transition with action $b \rightarrow f \circ g$, where g is the state transformation such that $g(\sigma, \theta) = \langle \sigma, \theta \cdot (i, \sigma)\rangle$. So we associate with each location l of P'_i the predicate φ_l, which basically states that there exists a computation of P (the original program) in which the component P_i reaches its location l.

Lemma 3.62 (Local correctness) For every transition $l \xrightarrow{a} l'$ of P'_i, with $a = b \rightarrow f$, we have

$$\models \varphi_l \wedge b \Rightarrow (\varphi_{l'} \circ f).$$

Proof Let $\langle \sigma, \theta\rangle \models \varphi_l \wedge b$. Let $f(\sigma, \theta) = \langle \sigma', \theta'\rangle$. Note that $\theta' = \theta \cdot (i, \sigma)$. By definition of the reachability predicates there exists a location $\bar{l}$ of P such that $\bar{l}(i) = l$, $\theta[P_j](\sigma) \in \mathcal{R}_{\bar{l}(j)}[\![P_j]\!]$, for $1 \leq j \leq n$, and $\sigma'' \models \varphi$, with σ'' the initial state of $\theta[P](\sigma)$. Let $\bar{l}'$ be the location of P such that $\bar{l}'(j) = \bar{l}(j)$, for $j \neq i$, and $\bar{l}'(i) = l'$. Since $\sigma \models b$ we derive that $\theta'[P_j](\sigma') \in \mathcal{R}_{\bar{l}'(j)}[\![P_j]\!]$, for $1 \leq j \leq n$ (note that for $j \neq i$, $\theta'[P_j](\sigma') = \theta[P_j](\sigma) \in \mathcal{R}_{\bar{l}(j)}[\![P_j]\!] = \mathcal{R}_{\bar{l}'(j)}[\![P_j]\!]$, and $\theta'[P_i](\sigma') = \theta[P_i](\sigma) \cdot \langle \sigma, \sigma'\rangle \in \mathcal{R}_{\bar{l}'(i)}[\![P_i]\!]$). Thus we conclude that $\langle \sigma', \theta'\rangle \models \varphi_{l'}$, or, equivalently, $\langle \sigma, \theta\rangle \models \varphi_{l'} \circ f$. $\square$

For interference freedom we need the following compositional characterisation of the reachability predicates:

Lemma 3.63 (Merging lemma) Let k satisfy $1 \leq k \leq n$, and, for $1 \leq i \leq k$, let l_i be a location of P_{f_i} such that $f_i \neq f_j$ for $1 \leq i \neq j \leq k$. We have $\models \bigwedge_{i=1}^k \varphi_{l_i} \rightarrow \varphi_{\langle l_1, \ldots, l_k\rangle}$.

Proof Let $\langle \sigma, \theta\rangle \models \bigwedge_{i=1}^k \varphi_{l_i}$. So for every $1 \leq i \leq k$ there exists a location l'_i of P such that $l'_i(f_i) = l_i$, and $\theta[P_j](\sigma) \in \mathcal{R}_{l'_i(j)}[\![P_j]\!]$, for $1 \leq j \leq n$. Define a location l of P as follows:

$$l(j) = l'_i(j), \ j = f_i, i = 1, \ldots, k,$$
$$= l'_1(j), \text{ otherwise.}$$

By *mere definition* we have, for $1 \leq i \leq n$, $\theta[P_i](\sigma) \in \mathcal{R}_{l(i)}[\![P]\!]$, that is, $\langle \sigma, \theta\rangle \models \varphi_{\langle l_1, \ldots, l_k\rangle}$. $\square$

Observe that since $\models \varphi_{\langle l_1,\dots,l_k\rangle} \to \varphi_{l_i}$, for $1 \le i \le k$, we actually also have that $\models \bigwedge_{i=1}^{k} \varphi_{l_i} \leftrightarrow \varphi_{\langle l_1,\dots,l_k\rangle}$.

Lemma 3.64 (Interference freedom) Let $l \xrightarrow{a} l'$, with $a = b \to f$, be a transition of P_i' and l'' be a location of P_j ($i \ne j$), then

$$\models \varphi_l \wedge \varphi_{l''} \wedge b \Rightarrow (\varphi_{l''} \circ f).$$

Proof Let $\langle \sigma, \theta \rangle \models \varphi_l \wedge \varphi_{l''} \wedge b$ and $f(\sigma, \theta) = \langle \sigma', \theta' \rangle$. Note that $\theta' = \theta \cdot (i, \sigma)$. By Lemma 3.63, we have $\langle \sigma, \theta \rangle \models \varphi_{\langle l, l'' \rangle} \wedge b$. So there exists a location $\bar{l}$ of P such that $\bar{l}(i) = l$, $\bar{l}(j) = l''$, and $\theta[P_k](\sigma) \in \mathcal{R}_{\bar{l}(k)} [\![P_k]\!]$, for $1 \le k \le n$. Let $\bar{l}'$ be the location of P such $\bar{l}'(i) = l'$ and $\bar{l}'(k) = \bar{l}(k)$, $k \ne i$. It follows that $\theta'[P_k](\sigma') \in \mathcal{R}_{\bar{l}'(k)} [\![P_k]\!]$, for $1 \le k \le n$. Actually, observe that for $k \ne i$ we have $\theta'[P_k](\sigma') = \theta[P_k](\sigma) \in \mathcal{R}_{\bar{l}(k)} [\![P_k]\!] = \mathcal{R}_{\bar{l}'(k)} [\![P_k]\!]$, and, since $\sigma \models b$, we moreover have $\theta'[P_i](\sigma') = \theta[P_i](\sigma) \cdot \langle \sigma, \sigma' \rangle \in \mathcal{R}_{\bar{l}'(i)} [\![P_i]\!]$. So we derive that $\langle \sigma', \theta' \rangle \models \varphi_{l''}$, that is $\langle \sigma, \theta \rangle \models \varphi_{l''} \circ f$. $\qquad\square$

Note that in both the proofs of local correctness and interference freedom we did not yet use the compositionality of $\mathcal{R}$! The compositionality of $\mathcal{R}$ is only used in the *finalisation* lemma:

Lemma 3.65 (Finalisation) We have $\models \bigwedge_{i=1}^{n} \varphi_{t_i} \to \psi$, where t_i denotes the exit location of P_i.

Proof Let $\langle \sigma, \theta \rangle \models \bigwedge_{i=1}^{n} \varphi_{t_i}$. By the above we have that $\langle \sigma, \theta \rangle \models \varphi_{\langle t_1,\dots,t_n \rangle}$. So there exists a location l of P such that, for $1 \le i \le n$, $l(i) = t_i$, $\theta[P_i](\sigma) \in \mathcal{R}_{t_i} [\![P_i]\!]$, and $\sigma' \models \varphi$, where σ' is the initial state of $\theta[P](\sigma)$. By the compositionality of $\mathcal{R}$ it then follows that $\theta[P](\sigma) \in \mathcal{R}_l [\![P]\!]$. Since θ by assumption only refers to the components of P it follows that $\sigma \in \mathcal{M} [\![P]\!] \sigma'$ (note that $\theta[P](\sigma)$ is a connected reactive sequence and as such records the state changes of a computation of P). Now $\models \{\varphi\}P\{\psi\}$ and $\sigma' \models \varphi$ imply $\sigma \models \psi$. The history variable h is assumed not to occur in ψ, so we conclude that $\langle \sigma, \theta \rangle \models \psi$. $\qquad\square$

Finally, the initialisation lemma concludes the completeness proof:

Lemma 3.66 (Initialisation) We have

$$\models \varphi \to \bigwedge_i \varphi_{s_i} \circ f,$$

where s_i denotes the initial location of P_i and $f(\sigma, \theta) = \langle \sigma, \varepsilon \rangle$, that is, f initialises the global history to the empty sequence.

Proof Left as an exercise.   □

Hence we obtained a third proof for Theorem 3.44.

Semantic completeness of the local method for proving convergence

Now we also assume that $P \equiv P_1 \parallel \ldots \parallel P_n$ is φ-convergent; then we use the assertion network based on the reachability predicates for the parallel system P augmented with updates to the history variable, as described above in the alternative completeness proof for the partial correctness method. What remains is to find a ranking-function network for each P_i', i.e., the augmented P_i, and to show that the corresponding verification conditions are satisfied.

Intuitively, for a local location l of P_i', the ranking function ρ_l gives for any (extended) state the distance which P_i' has from convergence at that point. Therefore, the set of natural numbers $(N, <)$ is chosen as the wellfounded set. One problem which we did not have in the sequential case is that now we do not know what locations other processes are at, and, therefore, we have to take all possibilities for such locations into account. So we consider the finite set of global locations $\bar{l}$ such that the i-th component, denoted by $\bar{l}(i)$ equals the given local location l of P_i'. Suppose now that for such a global location $\langle l_1, \ldots, l_n \rangle$ we have that $\langle \sigma, \theta \rangle \models \varphi_{l_1}, \ldots, \langle \sigma, \theta \rangle \models \varphi_{l_n}$, for some (extended) state $\langle \sigma, \theta \rangle$ (φ_{l_i} denotes the reachability predicate associated with l_i). By the merging lemma (Lemma 3.63) it follows that the configuration consisting of the global location $\langle l_1, \ldots, l_n \rangle$ and the state $\langle \sigma, \theta \rangle$ is a configuration which is reachable from an initial state satisfying φ. Consequently by a reasoning similar to that in Section 2.8.3 on completeness of the method for proving convergence of sequential programs, it follows that all computations starting from this configuration are finite (because, if not, one could obtain an infinite computation by adding the initial computation leading up to this configuration).

In order to formalise the argument above we introduce the following definitions.

Definition 3.67 Let t be a computation tree of P' starting from a certain global location and state, and define $|t|$ to be the length of the longest path in t, when such a path exists, otherwise $|t|$ is undefined. For T a finite set of computation trees of P' we define $|T| = max(\{|t| \mid t \in T\})$, if $|t|$ is defined for every $t \in T$, otherwise $|T|$ is undefined. (For X a finite set of natural numbers, $max(X)$ gives the maximum element of X. Note that $max(\emptyset)$ is undefined.)   □

Definition 3.68 Let l be a location of P_i'. Then we define the ranking function

ρ_l by

$$\rho_l(\sigma, \theta) \stackrel{\text{def}}{=} |T_l(\sigma, \theta)|,$$

where $T_l(\sigma, \theta)$ denotes the (finite) set of all possible computation trees of P' starting in state $\langle \sigma, \theta \rangle$ at a global location $\langle l_1, \ldots, l_n \rangle$ such that $l_i = l$ and $\langle \sigma, \theta \rangle \models \varphi_{l_j}$, for $j \neq i$. $\qquad \square$

The rest of this section is devoted to checking that the relevant conditions concerning the so-defined ranking functions are satisfied.

Lemma 3.69 (Well-definedness of the ranking functions) Let l be a location of P_i'. Then we have for any state $\langle \sigma, \theta \rangle$ that $\langle \sigma, \theta \rangle \models \varphi_l$ implies that $\rho_l(\sigma, \theta)$ is defined.

Proof See the above discussion. $\qquad \square$

Next we prove local correctness of the ranking functions.

Lemma 3.70 (Local correctness of the ranking functions) For every transition $l \stackrel{a}{\to} l'$ of P_i', with $a = b \to f$, we have that

$$\models \varphi_l \wedge b \to \rho_l > (\rho_{l'} \circ f).$$

Proof Let $\langle \sigma, \theta \rangle \models \varphi_l \wedge b$ and $f(\sigma, \theta) = \langle \sigma', \theta' \rangle$. Note that $\theta' = \theta \cdot (i, \sigma)$. It follows from the inductiveness of the assertion network that $\langle \sigma, \theta \rangle \models \varphi_{l'} \circ f$, and that therefore $\rho_{l'}(\sigma', \theta')$ is also defined. Since $\langle \sigma, \theta \rangle \models b$, we have for any global location $\bar{l} = \langle l_1, \ldots, l_n \rangle$ with $l_i = l'$, that $\langle \bar{l}'; \langle \sigma, \theta \rangle \rangle \to \langle \bar{l}; \langle \sigma', \theta' \rangle \rangle$, where $\bar{l}' = \langle l_1', \ldots, l_n' \rangle$ with $l_j' = l_j$, for $j \neq i$, and $l_i' = l$. Moreover, note that, for $j \neq i$, we have $\theta \cdot (i, \sigma)[P_j](\sigma') = \theta[P_j](\sigma)$, and so, by Definition 3.61 of φ_{l_j}, $\langle \sigma', \theta' \rangle \models \varphi_{l_j}$ if and only if $\langle \sigma, \theta \rangle \models \varphi_{l_j}$. Thus we derive that every computation tree of $T_{l'}(\sigma', \theta')$ is a subtree of a computation tree of $T_l(\sigma, \theta)$, and so we have that $|T_l(\sigma, \theta)| > |T_{l'}(\sigma', \theta')|$. That is, $\rho_l(\sigma, \theta) > \rho_{l'}(\sigma', \theta')$. $\qquad \square$

Finally, we prove interference freedom of the ranking functions:

Lemma 3.71 (Interference freedom of the ranking functions) For every transition $l \stackrel{a}{\to} l'$ in P_i', with $a = b \to f$, and for every location l'' of P_j', $j \neq i$, we have

$$\models \varphi_l \wedge \varphi_{l''} \wedge b \to \rho_{l''} \geq (\rho_{l''} \circ f).$$

Proof Let $\langle \sigma, \theta \rangle \models \varphi_l \wedge \varphi_{l''} \wedge b$ and $f(\sigma, \theta) = \langle \sigma', \theta' \rangle$. Note that $\theta' = \theta \cdot (i, \sigma)$. It follows from the interference freedom of the assertion network that $\langle \sigma', \theta' \rangle \models \varphi_{l''}$, and therefore $\rho_{l''} \circ f$ is defined in $\langle \sigma, \theta \rangle$. Let $\bar{l} = \langle l_1, \dots, l_n \rangle$ be a global location such that $l_j = l''$ and $\langle \sigma', \theta' \rangle \models \varphi_{l_k}, k \neq j$. Note that, as already remarked above, by the interference freedom of the assertion network, we have also that $\langle \sigma', \theta' \rangle \models \varphi_{l_j}$. It follows by the merging Lemma 3.63 that the configuration $\langle \bar{l}, \langle \sigma', \theta' \rangle \rangle$ is reachable form an initial state satisfying φ. Since $\theta' = \theta \cdot (i, \sigma)$, there exists a reachable configuration $\langle \bar{l}'; \langle \sigma, \theta \rangle \rangle$ such $\bar{l}'(k) = \bar{l}(k), k \neq i$, and $\langle \bar{l}'; \langle \sigma, \theta \rangle \rangle \rightarrow \langle \bar{l}; \langle \sigma', \theta' \rangle \rangle$. Thus we have argued that every computation tree of $T_{l''}(\sigma', \theta')$ is a subtree of a computation tree of $T_{l''}(\sigma, \theta)$, and thus we derive that $\rho_{l''}(\sigma, \theta) \geq \rho_{l''}(\sigma', \theta')$ (in fact, $\rho_{l''}(\sigma, \theta) > \rho_{l''}(\sigma', \theta')$). $\qquad\square$

We conclude this discussion on convergence with a formulation of an alternative local proof method for convergence based only on local networks of ranking functions. This proof method generalises the alternative proof method for convergence of sequential transitions diagrams formulated in Definition 2.22.

Definition 3.72 (An alternative local proof method for convergence) Consider $P \equiv P_1 \| \dots \| P_n$. To prove that P converges w.r.t. precondition φ, we define the following local method for proving convergence of concurrent shared variable programs:

(i) Augment P_i by introducing auxiliary variables; every action $b \rightarrow f$ can be extended as follows: $b \rightarrow f \circ g$, where $g(\bar{z})$ is a state transformation involving only the auxiliary variables $\bar{z}$ not occurring in P or φ. This leads to an augmented transition system $P' \equiv P'_1 \| \dots \| P'_n$.

(ii) Choose for every component P'_i a wellfounded set $(W_i, \prec_i)$ and a network of partial ranking functions $\rho \stackrel{\text{def}}{=} \{\rho_l \mid l \in P'_i\}$. Prove that the ranking functions decrease along every local transition. That is, for every transition $l \xrightarrow{a} l'$ of P'_i, with $a = b \rightarrow f$, we have to prove: If $\rho_l(\sigma) \in W$ and $\models b(\sigma)$ then $\rho_{l'} \circ f(\sigma) \in W$ and $\rho_l(\sigma) \succ_i \rho_{l'} \circ f(\sigma)$, for any state σ.

(iii) Prove *interference freedom* of the local networks of ranking functions. This amounts to showing that the ranking functions in one process do not increase due to transitions in other processes. That is, for every transition $l \xrightarrow{a} l'$ of P'_i, with $a = b \rightarrow f$, and location l'' of P'_j, for $j \neq i$, prove that: If $\rho_l(\sigma), \rho_{l''}(\sigma) \in W$ and $\models b(\sigma)$ then $\rho_{l''} \circ f(\sigma) \in W$ and $\rho_{l''}(\sigma) \succeq_j \rho_{l''} \circ f(\sigma)$, for any state σ.

(iv) Prove that for some state transformation f whose write variables belong to the set of auxiliary variables $\bar{z}$ we have that: $\models \varphi(\sigma)$ implies $\rho_{s_i} \circ f(\sigma) \in W$, for any σ.   □

The soundness and completeness proofs of the above method are left as exercises.

3.7 Proving Deadlock Freedom

In the preceding sections, we have not looked at the problem of deadlock or blocking. Let us first introduce some terminology.

A transition is said to be *enabled* if its boolean condition is satisfied. A process is said to be *blocked* at a certain location if it has not terminated and none of its transitions are enabled there. When blocked, a process waits until some other process causes one of its transitions (i.e., of the former process) to become enabled. For concurrent programs, it is not harmful to allow some of its processes to be blocked from time to time, and actually such blocking is essential to the correct functioning of some algorithms – this is called synchronisation. However, if adequate care is not exercised, it might happen that at a certain point all the processes of a system become blocked. Then no process can make a move anymore, and the system is said to be *deadlocked*. When we looked at proving partial correctness and convergence, we considered deadlocked behaviour as acceptable. However, in general, deadlock is clearly undesirable, for almost all the concurrent programs that we are aware of are either supposed to terminate normally or run forever, that is, they should never end up in deadlock. In this section a method for verifying deadlock freedom is investigated, that is, for proving that deadlock does not occur. Sometimes deadlock freedom is also called absence of blocking, or success.

Suppose the program under consideration is $P_1 \parallel \cdots \parallel P_n$, its precondition is φ, and for each process P_i there exists a local assertion network Q_i which satisfies steps (i) through (iv) of the Owicki & Gries method plus the first clause of step (v). Process P_i can only be blocked in state σ at local location l from which there are m transitions with boolean conditions $c_1, \cdots, c_m$ respectively, if

$$b_l \stackrel{\text{def}}{=} Q_l \wedge \neg(c_1 \vee \cdots \vee c_m)$$

holds in σ. The complete program $P_1 \parallel \cdots \parallel P_n$ is blocked, if some of its processes have terminated, while the remaining processes (at least one) are blocked. Let L_i be the set of locations of P_i and t_i be its exit location. Introducing the predicate

$$B_i \stackrel{\text{def}}{=} \bigvee_{l \in L_i \setminus \{l_{t_i}\}} b_l,$$

deadlock can only occur in a state σ if

$$\models (\bigwedge_{i=1}^{n} (Q_{t_i} \vee B_i) \wedge (\bigvee_{i=1}^{n} B_i))(\sigma)$$

holds. This is quite obvious, since for any process P_i, either it has terminated or is blocked when deadlock occurs, so $Q_{t_i}(\sigma)$ or $B_i(\sigma)$ holds, respectively. Moreover, at least one of the processes P_j is blocked, therefore $B_j(\sigma)$ holds. To this end, it is easy to see that the following deadlock-freedom condition (DFC) due to Owicki & Gries [OG76b]:

$$\models (\bigwedge_{i=1}^{n} (Q_{t_i} \vee B_i) \wedge (\bigvee_{i=1}^{n} B_i)) = false \qquad \text{(DFC)}$$

ensures that deadlock will not occur.

Example 3.73 We prove that the following program is deadlock free.

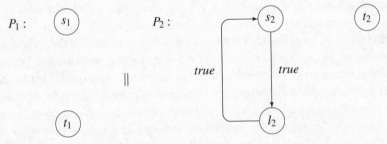

Process P_1 can never execute any transition (not even a transition to terminate), so it is always blocked. Process P_2 executes its loop infinitely, therefore, the complete program is deadlock free. We choose the assertion networks as below:

$$Q_{s_1} \stackrel{\text{def}}{=} true, \qquad\qquad Q_{s_2} \stackrel{\text{def}}{=} true,$$
$$Q_{t_1} \stackrel{\text{def}}{=} true, \qquad\qquad Q_{l_2} \stackrel{\text{def}}{=} true,$$
$$\qquad\qquad\qquad\qquad Q_{t_2} \stackrel{\text{def}}{=} false.$$

It is easy to see that they are inductive. The deadlock-freedom condition DFC in this case requires us to prove

$$\models (Q_{t_1} \vee B_1) \wedge (Q_{t_2} \vee B_2) \wedge (B_1 \vee B_2) = false$$

and this is trivial as the second conjunct evaluates to $false$. $\square$

For establishing semantic completeness of this method, we again need to employ auxiliary variables in defining the necessary predicates. Auxiliary variables do not change the control flow of the program, and therefore do not alter the possibility regarding deadlock.

In summary, the method for proving deadlock freedom is very similar to the method for proving partial correctness (Definition 3.17); the only difference is that now instead of proving $\models Q_{J_1} \wedge \ldots \wedge Q_{J_n} \rightarrow \psi$, we prove the deadlock-freedom condition.

Definition 3.74 (Proof method of Owicki & Gries for deadlock freedom)
In order to prove that a concurrent program is deadlock free relative to some precondition φ, prove steps (i) to (v) of the Owicki & Gries method given in Definition 3.17 except that the second clause of point (v) is replaced by the deadlock-freedom condition:

$$\models (\bigwedge_{i=1}^{n}(Q_{J_i} \vee B_i) \wedge (\bigvee_{i=1}^{n}B_i)) = false. \tag{DFC}$$

$\square$

Theorem 3.75 (Soundness and semantic completeness)
The method for proving deadlock freedom relative to a precondition φ as defined above is both sound and semantically complete.

Proof Soundness has already been argued in this section, so we only present the completeness result in some detail.

As just pointed out, auxiliary variables do not change the possibility regarding deadlock. Hence, to prove that $P_1 \parallel \ldots \parallel P_n$ is deadlock free, we only have to prove the same result for the program $P_1' \parallel \ldots \parallel P_n'$ augmented with history variables. We choose again the same assertion network as in the (compositional) completeness proof of partial correctness, i.e., with every location l of P_i we associate the predicate $SP_l'(\varphi, P_i)$. We prove the claim by showing that if the DFC does not hold, then $P_1' \parallel \ldots \parallel P_n'$ is not deadlock free.

So, suppose there exist a state and history pair $\langle \sigma, \theta \rangle$ such that

$$\models (\bigwedge_{i=1}^{n}(SP_{t_i}'(\varphi, P_i) \vee B_i) \wedge (\bigvee_{i=1}^{n}B_i))(\langle \sigma, \theta \rangle)$$

holds, then for every $1 \leq i \leq n$, $(SP_{t_i}'(\varphi, P_i) \vee B_i)(\langle \sigma, \theta \rangle)$ holds. By Lemma 3.45 there exists a location l of P' such that each process P_i is either terminated or deadlocked; moreover, from this configuration no transitions are enabled. By the fact that $\bigvee_{i=1}^{n}B_i(\langle \sigma, \theta \rangle)$ holds, at least one process has not terminated. Hence program $P_1' \parallel \ldots \parallel P_n'$ is deadlocked at $\langle l; (\sigma, \theta) \rangle$. $\square$

3.8 Proving Absence of Runtime Errors

As in Section 2.9, we give up the assumption that the primitive state transformations which occur in our theory are total, and consider in this section the problem of proving absence of runtime errors also for shared-variable concurrency. Since the boolean functions which occur in verification conditions can now be partial, we adopt the framework of three-valued propositional logic from Section 2.9.1.

As before, there are at least two methods for solving this problem: one direct method, which is the subject of Exercise 3.27, and an implicit method which reduces this problem to proving success (i.e., absence of deadlock or blocking) of suitably-transformed concurrent programs. However, in contrast to Chapter 2, where auxiliary variables were not an issue, one must now require that *all state transformations h, whose write variables are auxiliary variables, are total, including those state transformations f which appear in the formulation of the initialisation rule*. Otherwise, both the auxiliary variables and initialisation rules would become unsound (as indicated in Section 3.5.3).

One would like to prove absence of runtime errors of $P_1 \| \ldots \| P_n$ componentwise, in order to preserve the modular character of the Owicki-Gries-style methods. This is done by reducing the proof of absence of runtime errors of $P_1 \| \ldots \| P_n$ to proving absence of deadlock (or blocking), also called success, of $U(P_1') \| \ldots \| U(P_n')$, with $U(P)$ defined below and P_i' as in Section 2.9.

Definition 3.76 ($U(P)$) Let P be a transition diagram, and $sink_P$ be a fresh, new location not occurring in P. $U(P)$ is obtained as follows:

  (i) Every transition of P is contained in $U(P)$.
  (ii) For each location l of P, whenever $c_1 \to f_1, \ldots, c_n \to f_n$ are the transitions leaving l, add transition

$$(l, \bigwedge_{i=1}^{n} c_i \wedge \neg Def(f_i), sink_P)$$

  to $U(P)$.

Here $Def(f)$ denotes a total predicate for the domain of definition of f.   □

Notice that whenever P displays runtime errors, $U(P)$ has the nondeterministic possibility to deadlock, and, hence, is not successful.

Next we argue the correctness of this reduction of runtime-error freedom to absence of deadlock.

First of all, establish the following property.

Lemma 3.77 Let $U(P)$ be defined as above, and $P_1 \| \ldots \| P_n$ be φ-successful, then:

$P_1 \| \ldots \| P_n$ is runtime-error free in φ $\iff$ $U(P_1) \| \ldots \| U(P_n)$ is φ-successful.

Proof Exercise. □

Secondly, transform $P_1 \| \ldots \| P_n$ to transition diagram $P'_1 \| \ldots \| P'_n$. Then $P'_1 \| \ldots \| P'_n$ is φ-successful by construction, and yet displays the same runtime errors as $P_1 \| \ldots \| P_n$.

Now apply Lemma 3.77 to $P'_1 \| \ldots \| P'_n$. Using the latter two properties of $P'_1 \| \ldots \| P'_n$ one deduces:

$P_1 \| \ldots \| P_n$ *is runtime-error free in* φ $\iff$ $U(P'_1) \| \ldots \| U(P'_n)$ *is* φ-*successful.*

Finally observe that, since the definition of the proof method of Owicki & Gries for deadlock freedom (Definition 3.74) preserves the modular character of Owicki-Gries-style proofs, so does the proof of runtime-error freedom of $P_1 \| \ldots \| P_n$ in φ using the above property.

Example 3.78 Prove freedom of runtime errors of $P_1 \| P_2$, given below, in predicate $y \neq 0$.

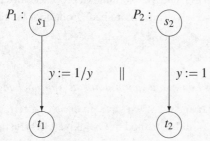

First, observe $P'_1 \equiv P_1$ and $P'_2 \equiv P_2$.

Next, prove $y \neq 0$-success of $U(P_1) \| U(P_2)$, given below, using the method of Definition 3.74.

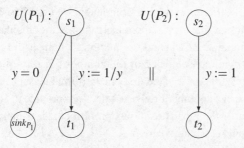

Choosing $Q_{s_1} \stackrel{\text{def}}{=} y \neq 0$, $Q_{sink_{P_1}} \stackrel{\text{def}}{=} false$, $Q_{l_1} \stackrel{\text{def}}{=} true$, then $b_{s_1} \equiv Q_{s_1} \wedge \neg(y = 0 \vee true) = false$ and $b_{sink_{P_1}} \equiv Q_{sink_{P_1}} \wedge \ldots = false$. Also choose $Q_{s_2} = Q_{l_2} \stackrel{\text{def}}{=} y \neq 0$, then $b_{s_2} \equiv Q_{s_2} \wedge \neg true = false$. The assertion network so defined is locally correct and interference free.

Also $B_1 \equiv b_{s_1} \vee b_{sink_{P_1}} = false = b_{s_2} \equiv B_2$.

Consequently, $\models (Q_{l_1} \vee B_1) \wedge (Q_{l_2} \vee B_2) \wedge (B_1 \vee B_2) = false$.   □

3.9 Historical Notes

Characteristic for this chapter are its completeness proofs based on a compositional semantics and its use of auxiliary variables. Section 3.9.1 provides some general background to the history of completeness proofs for shared-variable concurrency.

The use of auxiliary variables in proofs about shared-variable concurrency raised some controversy at the time of their introduction in Susan Owicki's thesis [Owi75]. Leslie Lamport is one of the main exponents against their use – albeit in a restricted setting, since they appear in his own work [AL91]. Some of his many impressive contributions to proof methods for concurrency as well as his arguments against the use of such variables are discussed in Section 3.9.2 (his contributions to the theory of simulation proofs are discussed in [dRE98]).

In Section 3.9.3 we give some more background for the remaining concepts in this chapter.

3.9.1 The Merging Lemma, a Combinatorial Approach to Completeness

In the Sections 3.5.6 and 3.6.3 we have given two different proofs of the semantic completeness of the method of Owicki & Gries, using a compositional semantics. However, looking back upon the history of such proofs, Krzysztof Apt in [Apt83, Apt81a], based them directly on the (noncompositional) operational semantics $Comp[\![P]\!]$, for $P \equiv P_1 \| \cdots \| P_n$. The completeness proofs in [Apt83, Apt81a] are inspired by Susan Owicki's original proof in [Owi75]. One of the main differences with a completeness proof based on a compositional semantics is that Apt's approach requires a combinatorial proof of the merging Lemma 3.63 (whereas the merging lemma as formulated in Section 3.5.4 is a trivial consequence of the compositionality of the underlying semantics). Krzysztof Apt was the first one to formulate such a lemma explicitly. Moreover such a combinatorial proof does not provide insight into the full reasoning power of the Owicki & Gries proof method, namely that it allows for a compositional reasoning pattern.

In order to give a third completeness proof, which is directly based on the operational semantics *Comp*, we start again with the basic intuition as formulated in Section 3.5.4, and introduce as before a single auxiliary variable h which is common to all processes P_i of a concurrent program P and which records the sequence of pairs $\langle i, \sigma \rangle$ where i identifies the process P_i whose turn it is to execute the following instruction in state σ. To record this history, every instruction $c \to f$ in every process P_i $(i = 1, \ldots, n)$ is changed into $c \to f \circ (h := h \cdot (i, \bar{y}))$, with $\bar{y}$ expressing the vector of program variables of $P_1 \| \ldots \| P_n$, and ε the empty history. These changes result in processes $P_1', \ldots, P_n'$. The reachability predicates are now defined formally as follows:

Definition 3.79 (Reachability predicates) Let $1 \le k \le n$ and, for $1 \le i \le k$, $l_i \in L_{f_i}$ (for $1 \le i \ne j \le k$ it is assumed that $f_i \ne f_j$). We define

$\langle \sigma, \theta \rangle \models \varphi_{\langle l_1, \ldots, l_k \rangle}$ if there exists a computation $\eta \in Comp[\![P]\!]$ which starts in a state $\langle \sigma', \varepsilon \rangle$ which satisfies φ and which ends in a configuration $\langle l'; \langle \sigma, \theta \rangle \rangle$ such that $l' = \langle l_1', \ldots, l_n' \rangle$, with $l_{f_i}' = l_i$, for $i = 1, \ldots, k$. $\square$

Thus the difference with Definition 3.61 is that there the reachability predicates are defined in terms of the compositional semantics $\mathcal{R}$, whereas here they are defined directly in terms of the operational semantics of P.

As before, the crucial question in the basic intuition for completeness proofs, as formulated in Section 3.5.4, is:

Does $\models \bigwedge_{j=1}^{k} \varphi_{l_j} \to \varphi_{\langle l_1, \ldots, l_k \rangle}$ hold, where $l_j \in L_{i_j}$ for $j = 1, \ldots, k$? (Notice that for $k = 2$ and $k = n$ this was the assumption in the basic intuition.)

The *merging lemma* states that such is the case. That this lemma is not altogether trivial is shown in the example below, in which we argue that φ_l also characterises other computations leading up to different labels of P_i', although they result in the same state. Consequently it is no longer clear, for $l \in L_i$ and $l' \in L_j$, that $\varphi_l \wedge \varphi_{l'}$ expresses that there exists a computation reaching *both l and l'* in the same state, for, in principle it might be the case that this expression implies the existence of computations reaching other pairs of labels of P_i' and P_j'. And then the interference freedom test might hold no longer!

Example 3.80

a) Consider program $P' \equiv P_1' \| P_2'$ with P_i' as in Figure 3.24, $i = 1, 2$.

Note that the instructions labelling edges (s_i, l_i) and (s_i, l_i') in Figure 3.24 are the same. This implies immediately that one cannot deduce from the values of the program variables and the history variable

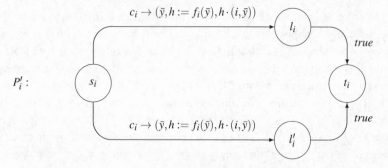

Fig. 3.24. A nondeterministic process featuring two observationally indistinguishable paths.

h whether the (s_i, l_i) or (s_i, l_i') transition has been taken. This demonstrates that, although state and history of the computation are observable, *the locations reached in each transition of this computation are not uniquely determined by the values of the program variables and the history variable h*, i.e., *these two different branches are observationally indistinguishable*.

Now, if one associates, for $i = 1, 2$, φ-reachability predicates φ_{l_i} with label l_i and $\varphi_{l_i'}$ with label l_i', then the conjunction $\varphi_{l_1} \wedge \varphi_{l_2}$ implies that:

(a) There exists a computation η_1 of P_1' reaching l_1 which also contains a computation step of P_2' (since otherwise φ_{l_2} could not have held for the same value of h), but one does not know whether this step corresponds with an (s_2, l_2) or (s_2, l_2') transition.

(b) Similarly, there exists a computation η_2 of P_2' demonstrating an analogous kind of ambiguity.

Consequently, computations η_1 and η_2 may have reached, respectively, P_2' in l_2' and P_1' in l_1'. That is, in general it does not follow straightforwardly that $\varphi_{l_1} \wedge \varphi_{l_2}$ implies $\varphi_{\langle l_1, l_2 \rangle}$.

Yet, since it is unobservable which steps, i.e., (s_i, l_i) or (s_i, l_i'), have been made, it is clear that, if there exists a computation reaching l_1 and l_2', there also exists a computation reaching l_1 and l_2 (in the same state). The merging lemma states in general that comparable differences w.r.t. reaching certain labels in other processes, which cannot be distinguished through the values of the program variables and the history variable h, can be similarly resolved, resulting in a computation reaching both these labels.

b) Consider program $P_1' \| P_2'$ with P_i', for $i = 1, 2$, as given in Figure 3.25. This program displays the same phenomenon as above; it features several observationally indistinguishable computations.

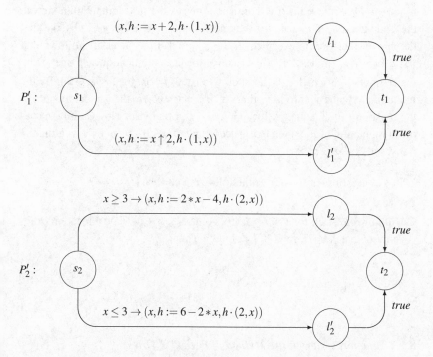

Fig. 3.25. Another concurrent program featuring observationally indistinguishable computations.

The reader may wish to check that the merging lemma holds for $P_1' \parallel P_2'$ as in Figure 3.25 using the following preconditions $\varphi : x = 2, x \neq 2$ and *true*. $\quad\square$

Now we prove on the basis of the operational semantics *Comp* that histories of the form $\langle (i_0, \sigma_0) \dots (i_m, \sigma_m) \rangle$ are sufficient to obtain a valid merging lemma.

Lemma 3.81 (Merging lemma) Let l_i be a location of P_i', $1 \leq i \leq n$. We have $\models \bigwedge_{i=1}^{n} \varphi_{l_i} \rightarrow \varphi_{\langle l_1, \dots, l_n \rangle}$.

Proof Let $\langle \sigma, \theta \rangle \models \varphi_{l_i}$, for $1 \leq i \leq n$. The proof proceeds by induction on the length of θ.

Basic step: Let $\theta = \varepsilon$, which implies that location l_i equals the initial location of P'_i. Then $\langle \sigma, \theta \rangle \models \varphi_{\langle l_1, \dots, l_n \rangle}$ clearly holds.

Induction step: Let $\theta = \theta' \cdot (j, \sigma')$, for some j and σ'. Let $l'_j \xrightarrow{a} l_j$, with $a = c \to f$, be the transition corresponding to the last computation step in the computation of P' which exists according to $\langle \sigma, \theta \rangle \models \varphi_{l_j}$ (observe that the above transition is executed in the state $\langle \sigma', \theta' \rangle$). It easily follows that $\langle \sigma', \theta' \rangle \models \bigwedge_{1 \leq i \neq j \leq n} \varphi_{l_i} \wedge \varphi_{l'_j}$ (just remove the last computation step of P'_j from the computations which exist according to $\langle \sigma, \theta \rangle \models \varphi_{l_i}$, for $1 \leq i \leq n$,). By the induction hypothesis it follows that $\langle \sigma', \theta' \rangle \models \varphi_{\bar{l}}$, where the i-th component of the location $\bar{l}$ of P' equals l_i for $i \neq j$, and l'_j, otherwise. Now simply extend the computation of P' which exists according to $\langle \sigma', \theta' \rangle \models \varphi_{\bar{l}}$ by executing the transition $l'_j \xrightarrow{a} l_j$ of P'_j. $\qquad\square$

It is straightforward to derive the following corollary:

Corollary 3.82 Let, for $1 \leq i \leq k$ (for some $1 \leq k \leq n$), l_i be a location of P'_{f_i} (assuming that $f_i \neq f_j$, for $1 \leq i \neq j \leq k$). Then

$$\models \bigwedge_{i=1}^{k} \varphi_{l_i} \to \varphi_{\langle l_1, \dots, l_k \rangle}. \qquad\square$$

3.9.2 Lamport's View of the Method of Owicki & Gries

A method very much related to the method of Owicki & Gries for proving invariance properties (such as partial correctness, absence of deadlock or runtime errors) has been formulated independently by Leslie Lamport [Lam77]. In a sense, Lamport's formulation is even closer to our presentation in this chapter in that he bases his proof method, too, on transition diagrams, because this makes the atomic actions explicit [Lam99], whereas Owicki & Gries present their method in the context of Hoare logic [OG76a], as worked out in Chapter 10. A difference between the method of Owicki & Gries and that of Lamport is that Lamport uses *location predicates* (which he calls "token positions") instead of auxiliary variables. Location predicates are introduced in Section 10.4.3 and applied in Section 10.6 to prove (relative) completeness of the method of Owicki & Gries in a setting of Hoare logic. In particular, we use location predicates to obtain a decomposition lemma for inductive assertion networks for shared-variable concurrency which have a certain standard form, reflecting Lamport's view on *"The Hoare Logic of Concurrent Programs"* [Lam80].

In [Lam88] Lamport explains his viewpoint that location predicates are "better" than auxiliary variables (which he calls *fictitious* or *dummy* variables). In Section 3.5.4 we listed some disadvantages of using location predicates: Their number is exponential in the number of processes, their lack of abstractness (using location predicates one can distinguish programs with identical observable behaviour), and their unsuitability for specifying open programs (as needed for obtaining a library of formally-specified modules). Lamport especially rejects the use of history variables (which are auxiliary variables of a certain type) in correctness proofs for practical applications, although these variables turn out to be essential in his later work [AL91]. We use history variables in completeness proofs and for formulating compositional proof methods. In his own words [Lam99]:

Dummy variables were more than just an ugly hack to avoid control variables. They also allowed you to capture history. Adding history variables makes it possible to introduce behavioral reasoning into an assertional proof. (In the limit, you can add a variable that captures the entire history and clothe a completely behavioral proof in an assertional framework.) What a program does next depends on its current state, not on its history. Therefore, a proof that is based on a history variable does not capture the real reason why a program works. I have always found that proofs that do not use history variables teach you more about the algorithm. (In more recent work, when the correctness conditions themselves are in terms of history, the use of history variables is often necessary.)

However, the authors of this volume regard this as an issue which is separate from that of proving completeness. We use history variables in completeness proofs in order to prove that no axioms and proof rules have been "forgotten". Chapters 7 and 8 list a number of such "forgotten" axioms and rules which did not appear in the original presentations of the proof methods concerned [MC81, Jon81, Jon83], such as the *prefix-invariance axiom* in Chapter 7 and the *auxiliary-variables rule* in Chapter 8. Consequently, it is simple to generate examples which cannot be proved correct using these methods in their original formulation, see, e.g., Example 7.19. We attach considerable weight to formulating complete proof methods, because one should either describe complete proof methods or, at least, mention which proof methods are incomplete. Otherwise, a student who does not succeed in applying some proof methods might attribute this to her or his own inability, whereas the real reason for this apparent lack of success might be that such a proof cannot be given at all, due to incompleteness of the proof method! In case the student knows this proof method to be complete, she or he also knows that either such a proof exists or that what she or he wants to prove is invalid. This knowledge can act as a guideline towards finding a solution.

3.9.3 More Background

This section presents a very brief history of some concepts in the theory of shared-variable concurrency. Consult [And91] for more material on synchronisation primitives, and [Ray86] for the early history of mutual exclusion algorithms.

In 1959, Edsger W. Dijkstra develops the first synchronisation primitives for shared-variable concurrency, as part of an operating system for the Electrologica X1 computer [Dij59].

The next fundamental contribution is made in 1962 by Carl Adam Petri, who introduces Petri nets to express and reason about concurrency as an independent concept [Pet62, Pet63], and introduces the notions of pre- and postconditions.

In 1965, Dijkstra publishes the first mutual exclusion algorithm [Dij65b], based upon ideas of T.J. Dekker, and he revolutionises in 1968 the way operating systems are built [Dij68c] by presenting the THE operating system for the Electrologica X8 computer. This system is based upon the so-called *onion model*, consisting of layers of abstraction, in which each next layer builds upon operations, such as the P and V synchronisation primitives, which are defined in a previous layer. Dijkstra's contributions to the field are extensively discussed in Section 1.7.

In 1971, Hans Bekić publishes the first mathematical theory of concurrency [Bek71], followed in 1973 by Robin Milner's mathematical model of computing agents [Mil73].

In 1976, Gordon Plotkin [Plo76] formulates the first powerdomain for modelling concurrency, extending Dana Scott's theory of reflexive domain equations with a parallel composition operator which is modelled using constructive power domains. His model of *renewals* characterises the interleaving model by infinite-order relations. A simpler version of such a domain is formulated by Michael Smyth [Smy78] in 1978. Later, Plotkin edits his so-called Pisa lecture notes about this topic [Plo83].

In 1977, Amir Pnueli introduces temporal logic [Pnu77] for formulating fairness principles in order to distinguish formally between various proposals for synchronisation principles based on semaphores. He does so in a formalism based on transition diagrams, using temporal logic as a specification language.

Also in 1977, Antoni Mazurkiewicz introduces trace theory as a tool for analysing the behaviour of Petri nets [Maz77]. This theory of Mazurkiewicz traces, as they are later called, develops into the first satisfactory theory of partial-order reasoning [Maz89].

In 1983, Peter Aczel formulates a compositional semantics for specifying open shared-variable networks using the Rely-Guarantee style, in a letter to Cliff Jones [Acz83]; this is the origin of the concept of Aczel traces.

Already in 1984 one finds in, e.g., a paper by Rob Gerth [Ger84] a formulation of the reactive-sequences model, although not in a version which is fully abstract.

Past-time temporal logic is developed in 1985 by Orna Lichtenstein, Amir Pnueli and Leonore Zuck [LPZ85]. Besides resulting in an increase in expressive power of linear time temporal logic, the need for which was already argued in previous work by Koymans et al. [KVdR83], this development results in an integration within temporal logic of arguments which in our approach require the introduction of auxiliary variables. In Section 12.5 instances of this integration are discussed.

In 1991, Zohar Manna and Amir Pnueli publish the most fundamental paper of their series of contributions to the development of linear time temporal logic [MP91a]. This paper contains soundness and completeness proofs for the full version of linear-time temporal logic, including both past- and future-time modalities. This leaves [MP84] as the most accessible introduction to the application of linear time temporal logic to the verification of concurrent programs.

Also in 1991, a paper by Frank de Boer, Joost Kok, Catuscia Palamidessi, and Jan Rutten [dBKPR91] marks the development of the first fully-abstract model for shared-variable concurrency, reactive sequences, to be followed in 1993 by a similar result by Stephen Brookes [Bro93a, Bro96]. Compositional proof systems which characterise this fully abstract semantics and generalise it to a multi-step model for real-time shared-variable concurrency are described in, respectively, [dBHdR97a] and [dBTdRvH96].

The interest in verification techniques based on partial-order reasoning about concurrency, of which Petri nets were the first example, has continued to develop through the years – see, e.g., Chapter 12 of this book for a recent account of such techniques. Chapters 10–12 of Wolfgang Reisig's monograph on the theory of Petri nets [Rei98] offer a fresh look upon the use and formulation of fairness principles, challenging the distinction between weak and strong fairness principles made in [MP91b, MP95, MP99]. Reisig maintains that there is only one fairness principle.

In [RF00] Reisig challenges Lamport's arguments about concurrent runs, and develops a *Temporal Logic of Distributed Actions* (TLDA), extending TLA with a logic for expressing important properties of distributed systems that cannot be expressed in TLA.

In [FvG99], Wim Feijen and Netty van Gasteren present a methodology for developing multiprograms – their terminology for parallel programs – on the basis of a wealth of carefully selected examples. Any lover of the field of concurrent programming will celebrate the advent of this work, in which around 35 years of experience in teaching multiprogramming in the style of Edsger W. Dijkstra at the Eindhoven University of Technology is accumulated.

Exercises

3.1   In Corollary 3.4 we restrict the process of combining smaller units of interleaving – atomic actions – into bigger ones to a finite number of such units. What happens when this restriction is dropped? Does Corollary 3.4 still hold?

3.2   Prove Lemma 3.10.

3.3   Let $P \equiv P_1 \parallel P_2 \parallel P_3$:

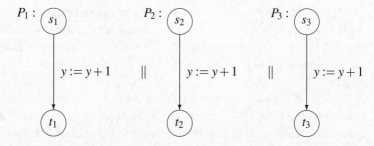

Prove $\models \{y = 0\}P\{y = 3\}$.

3.4   Consider the variant of Peterson's mutual exclusion algorithm shown in Figure 3.26 ($F \equiv false$, $T \equiv true$). Let $P \equiv P_1 \parallel P_2$ be the the program with precondition $\neg enter_1 \wedge \neg enter_2 \wedge x = 1$.

The intention is that b_3 and a_3 represent a transition to a critical section. After executing b_3 process P_1 should first release the critical section by executing b_4 before P_2 can perform a_3. The transitions b_1 and b_2 represent the requesting procedure of P_1 to enter the critical section. Thus the sequence b_3, a_3, b_4, a_4 should not be possible in a computation, and hence, it should not be possible to reach l_1^1 and l_1^2 with $x = 2$. Observe that with a method for partial correctness we cannot prove that a program terminates. Nontermination (i.e., divergence or deadlock), however, can be expressed by the specification $\langle \varphi, false \rangle$. This leads to the following exercise:

Prove $\models \{\neg enter_1 \wedge \neg enter_2 \wedge x = 1\}P\{false\}$.

3.5   Let P and P' be equivalent programs, i.e., $\mathcal{M}[\![P]\!] = \mathcal{M}[\![P']\!]$. Consider a program S and predicates φ and ψ.

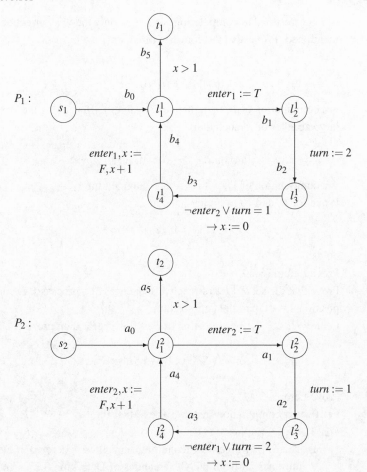

Fig. 3.26. A variant of Peterson's mutual exclusion algorithm.

Prove or disprove

$$\models \{\varphi\}P \parallel S\{\psi\} \text{ implies } \models \{\varphi\}P' \parallel S\{\psi\}.$$

What can you deduce from this exercise concerning verification and design of parallel programs?

Here P, P' and S are considered to be programs communicating through shared variables.

3.6   Let $P \equiv P_1 \parallel \cdots \parallel P_N$ be a concurrent program with shared variables. Let P' be a program obtained from P as described in point (i) of the Owicki & Gries method. Then Lemma 3.23 states that computations

of P' correspond to computations of P, i.e., only the "$\Rightarrow$" direction is mentioned. Prove also the converse direction:
if

$$\langle l_0; \bar{\eta}_0 \rangle \overset{e_1}{\to} \langle l_1; \bar{\eta}_1 \rangle \overset{e_2}{\to} \cdots$$

is a computation of P, then there exist values $\bar{\mu}_0, \bar{\mu}_1, \ldots$ for the auxiliary variables of P' such that

$$\langle l_0; (\bar{\eta}_0, \bar{\mu}_0) \rangle \overset{e_1'}{\to} \langle l_1; (\bar{\eta}_1, \bar{\mu}_1) \rangle \overset{e_2'}{\to} \cdots$$

is a computation of P', with $e_1', e_2', \ldots$ augmenting $e_1, e_2, \ldots$.

3.7   Prove for P_1 and P_2 in Figure 3.9 that

$$\models SP(y = 0, P_i) \leftrightarrow (y = 1)$$

holds.

3.8   Prove Lemma 3.29.

3.9   Prove that the set $\mathcal{R}\,[\![P]\!]$ of reactive sequences of a process P is compositional w.r.t. parallel composition.

3.10   Let $l = \langle l_1, \ldots, l_n \rangle$ be a location of $P \equiv P_1 \| \ldots \| P_n$, then prove

$$\models \bigwedge_{i=1}^{n} SP_{l_i}'(\varphi, P_i) \to SP_l'(\varphi, P).$$

3.11   Prove Lemma 3.42.

3.12   Let θ be a computation history. Prove that $\theta[P_i](\sigma) \in \mathcal{R}_{l_i}\,[\![P_i]\!]$, for $i \in \{1, \ldots, n\}$, implies $\theta[P_1 \| \ldots \| P_n](\sigma) \in \mathcal{R}_{\langle l_1, \ldots, l_n \rangle}\,[\![P_1 \| \ldots \| P_n]\!]$.

3.13   a) The SP_l strongest postcondition semantics is derived in Definition 3.28 from the O_l semantics of Definition 3.27. Analogously, one can introduce an O_l' semantics from which the SP_l' semantics of Definition 3.38 is deduced by imposing that $Init(\sigma, \theta) \models \varphi$ holds, when defining $SP_l'(\varphi, P)$. Define O_l'.

b) Prove that for $l = \langle l_1, \ldots, l_n \rangle$, a location of $P \equiv P_1 \| \ldots \| P_n$,

$$\models \bigcap_{i=1}^{n} O_{l_i}'\,[\![P_i]\!] \subseteq O_l'\,[\![P]\!].$$

c) Prove that the reverse inclusion does not hold (a hint is given in the technical note following Theorem 3.44).

3.14   Let $l = \langle l_1, \ldots, l_n \rangle$ be a location of $P \equiv P_1 \| \ldots \| P_n$, then prove

$$\models \bigwedge_{i=1}^{n} SP_{l_i}^{\tau}(\varphi, P_i) \to SP_l^{\tau}(\varphi, P).$$

3.15 Prove that the partially ordered set $(W, \prec)$ in the completeness proof of Section 3.6 is a wellfounded one.

3.16 The program in Example 3.58 converges with respect to the pre–condition $x = 0$. As pointed out earlier, auxiliary variables have to be used in the proof. A similar program, given below, converges with respect to the same precondition $x = 0$, but its proof can be given without using auxiliary variables. Prove this.

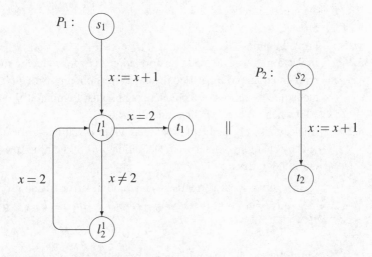

3.17 Prove Lemma 3.66.

3.18 Prove the soundness of the alternative method for convergence described in Definition 3.72.

3.19 Prove the completeness of the alternative method for convergence described in Definition 3.72. *Hint*: Augment the given program $P \equiv P_1 \parallel \cdots \parallel P_n$ with history variables and use the same ranking functions as defined in Definition 3.68.

3.20 Determine whether the variant of Peterson's mutual exclusion algorithm in Exercise 3.4 is deadlock free; if it is deadlock free, find a proof by the method proposed in Section 3.7; if not, find a deadlocked computation.

3.21 Prove that the method for proving deadlock freedom in Section 3.7 is not complete without using auxiliary variables.

3.22 Show, by means of counterexamples, that the merging lemma does not hold when the following histories are used:

(a) A history only records the initial states of the variables for each step. Thus a history is a sequence of states: $\langle \bar{\eta}_0, \bar{\eta}_1, \ldots,$

$\bar{\eta}_m\rangle$ and each label $c(\bar{y}) \rightarrow [\bar{y} := f(\bar{y})]$ is transformed into $c(\bar{y}) \rightarrow [\bar{y}, h := f(\bar{y}), h \cdot \bar{y}]$.

(b) A history is a sequence of process numbers, $\langle i_0, \dots, i_m \rangle$, recording the number of the process that performs the step. Each label $c(\bar{y}) \rightarrow [\bar{y} := f(\bar{y})]$ in P_i becomes $c(\bar{y}) \rightarrow [\bar{y}, h := f(\bar{y}), h \cdot i]$.

3.23   Check that the merging lemma holds for $P_1' \| P_2'$ as in Figure 3.25 w.r.t. the preconditions $x = 2, x \neq 2$ and *true*.

3.24   Prove Corollary 3.82.

3.25   Prove Lemma 3.77.

3.26   In Section 2.9 we defined transformation $T(P)$ for reducing runtime-error-freedom proofs of P to deadlock-freedom proofs of $T(P')$. Demonstrate by means of a counterexample that Lemma 3.77 does not hold when we use $T(P)$ instead of $U(P)$.

3.27   One can also give a direct proof method for φ-runtime-error freedom of P by changing point (iii) in Definition 3.17 of the proof method of Owicki & Gries to:

(iii) *Prove* local correctness *and* runtime-error freedom *of every* P_i': For every transition $l \xrightarrow{a} l'$ of P_i', with $a \equiv b \rightarrow f$, prove

$$\models Q_l \wedge b \rightarrow (Q_{l'} \circ f) \wedge Def(f),$$

and dropping the second clause from point (v); also requiring g in point (i) and h in point (v) to be total.

Prove that the resulting method is sound and semantically complete.

4

The Inductive Assertion Method for Synchronous Message Passing

4.1 Objective and Introduction

In the previous chapter, the inductive assertion method has been generalised to concurrent programs which interact by means of shared variables. We have developed the proof method of Owicki & Gries and proved it to be sound and semantically complete. In this chapter we develop along the same lines the proof methods of Apt, Francez & de Roever [AFdR80] and of Levin & Gries [LG81] for distributed processes which communicate by means of synchronous message passing [Hoa78], proving their soundness and semantic completeness. Similarly as in the previous chapter, these completeness proofs are based on a compositional semantics, and form the starting point for the formulation of compositional proof methods for synchronous message passing in Part III.

Moreover, methods for proving φ-convergence and absence of deadlock and runtime errors, relative to a precondition φ, will be formulated, and also these will be proved sound and semantically complete. Similarly as in the previous chapter, a connection will be made between the existence of a compositional semantics for (our form of) distributed processes, and the merging lemma.

That we speak in this chapter of *distributed* rather than *concurrent* programming has to do with the following distinction. In the previous chapter we used the term "concurrent programming" to refer to parallel processing with communication through one *common shared* memory, i.e., whereas processes are considered as separate entities, their memory is considered as a single monolithic entity. In contrast, distributed processes operate upon separate (their own) memories, and are, therefore, associated with different geographical locations. Their interaction takes place through channels along which messages are sent, in which case one speaks of *outputs*, or received, and then we speak of *inputs*.

The difference between synchronous and asynchronous communication refers to the distinction whether message exchange requires *coordination* between sender and receiver of a message (sometimes called a *handshaking* mechanism), *or not*. In cases of *asynchronous* communication, processes send messages regardless of the state of the receivers of those messages, i.e., it might even be the case that a sent message does not arrive, or will never be received, by any process, at all. In this chapter *synchronous* communication of messages refers to the situation where message communication only takes place when both the sending process is ready to send a message and the receiving process of that message is known and ready to receive that message, after which that message is exchanged (this is called a "handshake"). The implicit assumption here is that communication requires one sender and one receiver (and not *more* as is the case with multi-party interactions), and in this book takes place along *unidirectional* channels which are one-to-one, i.e., each communication channel has a fixed direction of communication and connects exactly two processes. These restrictions lead to a simple compositional semantics, and as such play an important rôle in the completeness proof of the proof system.

Apart from the proof method of Apt, Francez & de Roever [AFdR80], for proving properties of transition systems for synchronous message passing, we also investigate another method, that of Levin & Gries [LG81], which was invented independently and, besides using cooperation tests, also uses interference freedom tests. The latter method evolved from the work of Owicki & Gries, whereas the former aims at formulating a proof method using a notion of consistency between the various local assertion networks which characterises distributed rather than concurrent programming on the level of assertions. The proof method of Levin & Gries is based on the use of shared variables as auxiliary variables and as such does not capture the distinction between geographical separation of processes and access to a common shared memory. In the former method, we model this difference when proving partial correctness by introducing for synchronous communication additional auxiliary variables which are *local* to each process in question – the need for auxiliary variables is proved along similar lines as those in the previous chapter. The price we have to pay for this is the need to introduce a *global*, so-called, *communication* invariant *I* between these newly introduced local auxiliary variables. Such an invariant is not needed in the method of Levin & Gries.

Similarly to the method of Owicki & Gries, the method of Apt, Francez & de Roever consists of two stages: a first stage for constructing local proofs and a second stage for checking the consistency of these local proofs. In the method of Apt, Francez & de Roever, this second step uses a global *communication* invariant (mentioned above) in order to check for consistency of the local proofs by means of so-called *cooperation* tests. As observed previously, the proof methods of Owicki & Gries and of Apt, Francez & de Roever are both noncompositional, because they are based on the internal structure of processes.

4.2 Structure of this Chapter

In Section 4.3 we develop a syntax and semantics for synchronous processes. In Section 4.4 a method for proving partial correctness of such processes is formulated, that of Apt, Francez & de Roever (AFR-method), introducing the notion of the *cooperation* test; soundness of this method is proved along similar lines to those in Chapter 3. We also develop the method of Levin & Gries [LG81], which, besides using cooperation tests, also uses interference freedom tests. In Section 4.4.2 the AFR-method is applied to proving correctness of a distributed greatest common divisor algorithm for n natural numbers [FR80].

In Section 4.5 semantic completeness is proved for the methods of Apt, Francez & de Roever and of Levin & Gries, using compositional semantics for synchronous communication. Sections 4.7 and 4.8 formulate and concern similar results as Sections 4.4 and 4.5, but in those cases for proving convergence and absence of deadlock. Section 4.9 considers two methods for proving the absence of runtime errors, and Section 4.10 provides some background for the material discussed in this chapter. A list of exercises is given at the end of this chapter. *Relative* completeness of the AFR-method is proved in Chapter 5.

4.3 Syntax and Semantics of Synchronous Transition Diagrams

We consider synchronous transition diagrams $P_1 \| \ldots \| P_n$ in which the components $P_1, \ldots, P_n$, called processes, do not share variables. These diagrams are inspired by Tony Hoare's language proposal Communicating Sequential Processes [Hoa78]. The processes which constitute those diagrams communicate by means of synchronous message passing along unidirectional channels which connect *at most* two different processes. These components are called sequential synchronous (transition) diagrams and are defined below. The term synchronous diagram is reserved for their parallel composition $P_1 \| \ldots \| P_n$, which includes sequential synchronous diagrams for $n = 1$ as a special case. Unless stated otherwise, primitive boolean and state functions are considered to be total. Only in Section 4.9 do we remove this restriction when discussing methods for proving the absence of runtime errors.

Let *CHAN* be a set of channel names, with typical elements $C, D \ldots$. For $C \in CHAN$, e a semantic expression, i.e., $e : \Sigma \to VAL$, where *VAL* denotes the given underlying domain of values, and x a variable, execution of *output* statement $C!e$ has to wait for execution of a corresponding *input* statement $C?x$, and, similarly, execution of an input statement has to wait for execution of a corresponding output statement. If there exists a computation of $P_1||\ldots||P_n$ in which both an input statement $C?x$ and an output statement $C!e$ are simultaneously executed, this implies that communication can take place and the value of e is assigned to x. Then one speaks of a *semantically-matching communication pair*. When formulating our proof method, we also need the concept of a *syntactically*-matching communication pair. This is a pair consisting of occurrences of an output statement $C!e$ and an input statement $C?x$ which refer to the same communication channel (in this case C), *irrespective of whether these communicate or not*. We often refer to an input or output statement as an *io-statement* or *communication* statement. Labels on edges in P_i can have the following form:

(i) A boolean condition b followed by a state transformation f:

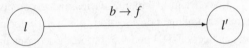

Transitions of this form are called *internal* transitions.

(ii) A guarded io-statement followed by a state transformation. There are two possibilities:

a)
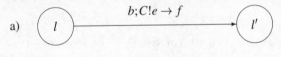

b)
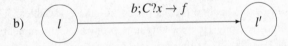

We call these transitions *communication* or *input-output* transitions. We extend the definitions of semantically- and syntactically-matching communication pairs to pairs of such transitions of which the communication statements satisfy the conditions listed above.

We assume that each sequential synchronous diagram P is associated with a set of program variables such that every condition, state transformation, expression, and input statement occurring in P involves only those program variables. We call sequential synchronous diagrams $P_1,\ldots,P_n$ *disjoint* if their associated sets of program variables are mutually disjoint, and every channel occurring in $P_1, \ldots, P_n$ is unidirectional and connects two different processes. In the companion volume we shall assume that only disjoint processes are composed in parallel. Below we define the *closed* product $P_1 \parallel \ldots \parallel P_n$ of such diagrams, in which only the communication capabilities of those io-statements are resolved, concerning channels connecting two processes which both occur amongst $P_1, \ldots, P_n$.

Definition 4.1 (Closed product of synchronous sequential transition diagrams) Given disjoint sequential synchronous transition diagrams $P_1, \ldots, P_n$, with $P_i \equiv (L_i, T_i, s_i, t_i)$, we define the closed product P of $P_1 \parallel \ldots \parallel P_n$ as the following transition diagram (L, T, s, t):

- $L \equiv L_1 \times \ldots \times L_n$ is the set of locations of P,
- $l \overset{a}{\to} l'$ is a transition in T iff

  (i) $l = \langle l_1, \ldots, l_i, \ldots, l_n \rangle$ and $l' = \langle l_1, \ldots, l_i', \ldots, l_n \rangle$, with $l_i \overset{a}{\to} l_i'$ an internal transition of T_i, or

  (ii) $l = \langle l_1, \ldots, l_i, \ldots, l_j, \ldots, l_n \rangle$ and $l' = \langle l_1, \ldots, l_i', \ldots, l_j', \ldots, l_n \rangle$, $i \neq j$, with $(l_i \overset{a_i}{\to} l_i') \in T_i$, $(l_j \overset{a_j}{\to} l_j') \in T_j$, $a_i \equiv b; C!e \to f$, $a_j \equiv b'; C?x \to g$, and $a \equiv b \wedge b' \to f \circ g \circ (x := e)$; this is called a communication step. The assignment $x := e$, where $e : \Sigma \mapsto VAL$, for some domain of values VAL, denotes the following state-transformation $(x := e)(\sigma) \overset{\text{def}}{=} (\sigma : x \mapsto e(\sigma))$,

- $s \equiv \langle s_1, \ldots, s_n \rangle$,
- $t \equiv \langle t_1, \ldots, t_n \rangle$.   □

Communication between $a_i \equiv b; C!e \to f$ and $a_j \equiv b'; C?x \to g$ is modelled in three stages. First the boolean function $b \wedge b'$ is evaluated; when the result is tt, $x := e$ is executed, and finally f and g are applied in any order, because they operate on disjoint state spaces. Note that the closed parallel composition of sequential synchronous diagrams therefore gives rise to a transition diagram as defined in Chapter 2, and so the definitions from Chapter 2 apply for defining the semantics $\mathcal{M}$ of the parallel composition of synchronous transition diagrams, their specifications, partial correctness, φ-convergence, φ-success and total correctness.

We emphasise here that the closed product is a simple transition diagram in which no io-statements occur. As such communications with the outside world are no longer offered. For example, the closed product of $C!0 \parallel D?x$ does not contain any transitions, and models that this system when it is executed on its own will deadlock. In a compositional semantics, however, we will need an *open* interpretation of synchronous transition diagrams. For example, we want to be able to compose $C!0 \parallel D?x$ in parallel with a diagram which offers corresponding inputs and outputs. Therefore an open interpretation of the communications in $C!0 \parallel D?x$ is required in which the communication capabilities of $C!0$ and $D?x$ are postponed, i.e., are not yet resolved. This open interpretation of networks requires the channels to be uni-directional and also one-to-one, and will be discussed in Section 4.5.1.

For all channels C, variables x and semantic expressions e, we use the following abbreviations:

(i) when $b = true$ or $f = id_\Sigma$, $b;C?x \to f$ is abbreviated to, respectively, $C?x \to f$ or $b;C?x$,

(ii) these conventions can be combined, and

(iii) they also apply to $b;C!e \to f$.

Example 4.2 (Partitioning a set) Given two disjoint finite sets of integers S and T, $S \cup T$ must be partitioned into two subsets S' and T' such that $|S'| = |S|$, $|T'| = |T|$, and every element of S' is smaller than any element of T'. The program is inspired by Dijkstra [Dij77]. $P \equiv (P_1 \parallel P_2)$ is given in Figures 4.1 and 4.2, with $S \neq \emptyset \wedge S \cap T = \emptyset \wedge x \neq mx \wedge y \neq mn$ as precondition, with channel C directed from P_1 to P_2, and channel D from P_2 to P_1.

Let S and T denote set variables. Intuitively, P_1 and P_2 exchange the current maximum of S, $max(S)$, with the current minimum of T, $min(T)$, until the same element has been exchanged two or three times. This indicates that

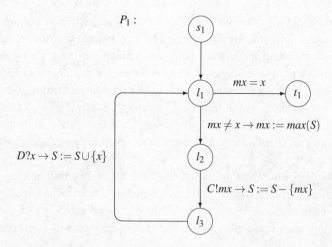

Fig. 4.1. Set-partitioning program P_1

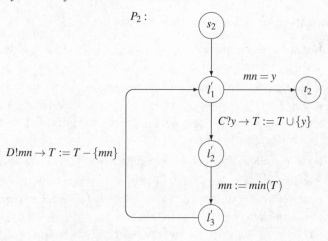

Fig. 4.2. Set-partitioning program P_2

the condition for termination $max(S) < min(T)$ has been reached. Then the processes terminate.

$\square$

4.4 Proof Methods for Partial Correctness

4.4.1 The Proof Method of Apt, Francez & de Roever

Partial correctness of a synchronous diagram $P \equiv P_1 \parallel \ldots \parallel P_n$ w.r.t. a specification $< \varphi, \psi >$ can be proved by constructing an inductive assertion network $\{Q_l \mid l \in L\}$ for P (here L denotes the set of locations of P) such that $\models \varphi \rightarrow Q_s$ and $\models Q_t \rightarrow \psi$ hold. Analogous to concurrent programs with shared variables this leads to a number of verification conditions which are exponential in the number of parallel processes. Similarly, we try to improve upon this by attaching predicates to local locations. We associate a predicate Q_{l_i} with every local location l_i in P_i such that Q_{l_i} does not involve any of the variables of the other components P_j, $j \neq i$. Then with every global location $l \equiv \langle l_1, \ldots, l_n \rangle$ in P the predicate $Q_l \stackrel{\text{def}}{=} Q_{l_1} \wedge \ldots \wedge Q_{l_n}$ is associated.

This assertion network is shown to be inductive by proving the verification conditions along each verification path. That is, for every transition $l \xrightarrow{a} l'$ of P, with $a \equiv b \rightarrow f$, we should prove

$$\models Q_l \wedge b \rightarrow Q_{l'} \circ f.$$

Thus, with $l = \langle l_1, \ldots, l_n \rangle$ and $l' = \langle l'_1, \ldots, l'_n \rangle$, we have to prove

$$\models (Q_{l_1} \wedge \ldots \wedge Q_{l_n} \wedge b) \rightarrow (Q_{l'_1} \wedge \ldots \wedge Q_{l'_n}) \circ f.$$

Observe that this verification condition can be of two kinds:

(i) It stems from an internal transition of P_i. Then $Q_{l_j} = Q_{l'_j}$, for $j \neq i$, and thus we have to prove:

- $\models (Q_{l_i} \wedge b) \rightarrow Q_{l'_i} \circ f$, i.e., local correctness.
- $\models (Q_{l_j} \wedge Q_{l_i} \wedge b) \rightarrow Q_{l_j} \circ f$, for $j \neq i$, i.e., interference freedom. However, since Q_{l_j} does not involve the variables of P_i, this implication is trivially satisfied.

(ii) It stems from a communication step between P_i and P_j; so there exist transitions $l_i \xrightarrow{a_i} l'_i$ and $l_j \xrightarrow{a_j} l'_j$ of P_i and P_j, with $a_i \equiv b; C!e \rightarrow f$ and $a_j \equiv b'; C?x \rightarrow g$ such that $a \equiv b \wedge b' \rightarrow f \circ g \circ (x := e)$. Let h denote the transformation $f \circ g \circ (x := e)$. Then, for $k \neq i, k \neq j$, we have $Q_{l_k} = Q_{l'_k}$ and a does not change the variables of P_k. Thus $\models Q_{l_k} \rightarrow Q_{l'_k} \circ h$. It remains to prove

$$\models Q_{l_i} \wedge Q_{l_j} \wedge b \wedge b' \rightarrow (Q_{l'_i} \wedge Q_{l'_j}) \circ h.$$

Definition 4.3 (First try to formulate an inductive assertion method for synchronous communication) In order to prove partial correctness of synchronous diagram $P_1 \parallel \dots \parallel P_n$ w.r.t. $< \varphi, \psi >$ find local predicates Q_l (associated with the local locations l of P_i and which do not involve any of the variables of the other components) and prove:

(i) the local verification conditions of P_i w.r.t. $\{Q_l \mid l \text{ is a location of } P_i\}$,
(ii) for every pair of syntactically-matching input-output transitions $l_i \xrightarrow{a_i} l'_i$ of P_i and $l_j \xrightarrow{a_j} l'_j$ of P_j, with $a_i \equiv b; C!e \rightarrow f$ and $a_j \equiv b'; C?x \rightarrow g$:

$$\models Q_{l_i} \wedge Q_{l_j} \wedge b \wedge b' \rightarrow (Q_{l'_i} \wedge Q_{l'_j}) \circ h,$$

where $h \stackrel{\text{def}}{=} f \circ g \circ (x := e)$,
(iii) $\models \varphi \rightarrow Q_{s_1} \wedge \dots \wedge Q_{s_n}$, with s_i the initial location of P_i, and $\models Q_{t_1} \wedge \dots \wedge Q_{t_n} \rightarrow \psi$, with t_i the final location of P_i. $\square$

Observe that in the above we proved inductiveness of the global assertion network

$$\{Q_l \mid l \in L_1 \times \dots \times L_n\},$$

and, hence, by soundness of the inductive assertion method (Theorem 2.12), also soundness of the method of Definition 4.3.

The second requirement in Definition 4.3 corresponds to the *cooperation test* from the proof system of Apt, Francez & de Roever for CSP. Their methodology consists essentially of two phases. In the first phase, covered by the first requirement, the local steps of the processes are proved correct and nothing is verified for the communication actions. This is called proving *local correctness*. In the second phase the communication actions are verified. This raises a problem, since we have no syntactic means at our disposal to determine which syntactically-matching pairs actually do communicate (recall that a *syntactically-matching pair of communication transitions* is a pair of occurrences of transitions with labels $b_1; C!e \rightarrow f_1$ and $b_2; C?x \rightarrow f_2$, irrespective of whether these transitions communicate or not). For we only need to prove something about actually occurring communication steps. Hence we shall resort to assertional means to express which pairs are *semantically matching*, i.e., do actually communicate, and which pairs do not. The difference between syntactically- and semantically-matching pairs is illustrated in the following example.

Example 4.4 Consider Figure 4.3 where t_1, t_2, t_3 and t_4 are names of the tran-

Fig. 4.3. Illustrating the difference between syntactically- and semantically-matching pairs.

sitions. There are four syntactically-matching pairs: (t_1, t_3), (t_1, t_4), (t_2, t_3) and (t_2, t_4), whereas only two of them match semantically, namely, (t_1, t_3) and (t_2, t_4). □

Observe that the cooperation test gives a verification condition for every syntactically-matching pair of communication transitions, although some of them may not match semantically. First we illustrate how the cooperation test works. In Example 4.7 we show a problem with this method. It is incomplete.

Example 4.5 Consider program $P_1 \| P_2 \| P_3$ plus associated local assertion networks as illustrated in Figure 4.4. Let $l_0 \equiv s$, $l_t \equiv t$, $l_0' \equiv s'$, $l_t' \equiv t'$, $l_0'' \equiv s''$, and $l_t'' \equiv t''$. $P_1 \| P_2 \| P_3$ is partially correct w.r.t. specification $< true, x_1 = 0 \wedge x_2 = 1 \wedge x_3 = 3 >$. This can be proved as follows.

- There is only one local verification condition. For the transition with label $x_1 := 0$ we have to prove

$$\models Q_{l_0}(x_1) \rightarrow Q_{l_1}(0),$$

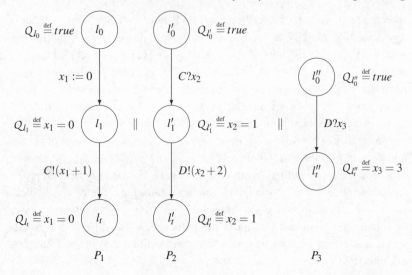

Fig. 4.4. Program $P_1\|P_2\|P_3$ plus associated assertion networks.

which is fulfilled since $\models true \to 0 = 0$.

- For the cooperation test we have to prove for channel C

$$\models (Q_{l_1} \wedge Q_{l'_0})(x_1, x_2, x_3) \to (Q_{l_t} \wedge Q_{l'_1})(x_1, x_1 + 1, x_3),$$

which holds, since $\models (x_1 = 0 \wedge true) \to (x_1 = 0 \wedge x_1 + 1 = 1)$, and for channel D

$$\models (Q_{l'_1} \wedge Q_{l''_0})(x_1, x_2, x_3) \to (Q_{l'_t} \wedge Q_{l''_t})(x_1, x_2, x_2 + 2),$$

which holds, since $\models (x_2 = 1 \wedge true) \to (x_2 = 1 \wedge x_2 + 2 = 3)$.

- That point (iii) of Definition 4.3 holds, i.e., $\models true \to Q_{l_0} \wedge Q_{l'_0} \wedge Q_{l''_0}$ and $\models Q_{l_t} \wedge Q_{l'_t} \wedge Q_{l''_t} \to x_1 = 0 \wedge x_2 = 1 \wedge x_3 = 3$, follows from the definition of the assertions concerned.   □

Next we illustrate a case where logical variables are needed to express local assertions.

Example 4.6 (The need for logical variables) Consider $R \equiv R_1 \parallel R_2$ as in Figure 4.5.

We would like to prove $\models \{true\}\ R_1 \| R_2\ \{x = y\}$. Due to the restriction that the assertion network $\{Q_{s_1}, Q_{l_1}\}$ should not involve the variables of R_2, i.e., y, one cannot choose Q_{l_1} as $x = y$. However, this choice is not forced upon us, according to Definition 4.3. All one needs is to find predicates Q_{l_1} and Q_{l_2}

Fig. 4.5. A simple synchronous diagram.

such that $\models Q_{t_1} \wedge Q_{t_2} \to x = y$. These can be found using logical variables, i.e., variables not occurring in any program text and therefore not involved in any process; they are introduced in Section 2.4.1. Let y_0 be a logical variable, then our local assertions can be chosen as in Figure 4.6 below.

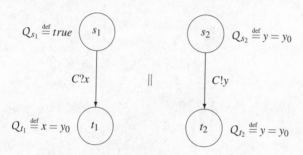

Fig. 4.6. Program $R_1 \| R_2$ plus associated assertion network.

Note that $\{ Q_{s_1}, Q_{t_1} \}$ does not involve any program variable of R_2, and neither does $\{ Q_{s_2}, Q_{t_2} \}$ involve any program variable of R_1. Next, we prove that $\models \{true\}\ R_1 \| R_2\ \{x = y\}$ holds:

- There are no local verification conditions to be checked.
- There is only one cooperation test, namely

$$\models (true \wedge y = y_0)(x, y) \to (x = y_0 \wedge y = y_0)(y, y),$$

  which holds, because $\models y = y_0 \to y = y_0$.
- Point (iii) of Definition 4.3 raises a problem since $\not\models true \to true \wedge y = y_0$. Note that we do have that $\models x = y_0 \wedge y = y_0 \to x = y$ holds. However, y_0 being a logical variable allows application of the initialisation Rule 3.1 of Chapter 3, since any set of logical variables satisfies Definition 3.13 (because it is a set of auxiliary variables for any program P). Consequently, by the initialisation rule $\{y = y_0\}\ R_1 \| R_2\ \{x = y\}$ implies

$$\{y = y_0 \circ f\}\ R_1 \| R_2\ \{x = y\}$$

for $f(\sigma) \stackrel{\text{def}}{=} (\sigma : y_0 \mapsto \sigma(y))$, which implies $\{true\}\ R_1 \| R_2\ \{x = y\}$. $\qquad\square$

In the following example we show that there is a serious problem: the method sketched above is not complete.

Example 4.7 (Incompleteness of the method of Definition 4.3) Consider again $P_1 \| P_2$ in Figure 4.3, where $l_0 \equiv s$, $l_t \equiv t$, $l_0' \equiv s'$, and $l_t' \equiv t'$. With every local location we associate an assertion as shown in Figure 4.7.

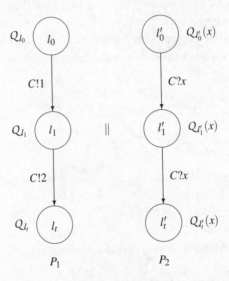

Fig. 4.7. Adding assertions to program $P_1 \| P_2$ from Figure 4.3.

Clearly $P_1 \| P_2$ is partially correct w.r.t. specification $< true, x = 2 >$. This cannot be proved, however, with the method described above. To show this, assume we have associated with all locations in the program predicates that satisfy the requirements of the method. Since predicates for P_1 may only refer to program variables of P_1, and there are no program variables in P_1, the predicates Q_{l_0}, Q_{l_1}, and Q_{l_t} do not contain free program variables and, as shown below, are identical to *true*. Similarly, $Q_{l_0'}(x)$, $Q_{l_1'}(x)$, and $Q_{l_t'}(x)$ may only refer to program variable x.

From point (iii) of the method we obtain

$$\models \quad true \to Q_{l_0} \wedge Q_{l_0'}(x), \text{ and} \tag{4.1}$$
$$\models \quad Q_{l_t} \wedge Q_{l_t'}(x) \to x = 2. \tag{4.2}$$

According to point (ii), the cooperation test, the verification conditions for all syntactically-matching pairs should be valid. Thus one has validity of the following conditions:

$$\models \quad Q_{l_0} \wedge Q_{l_0'}(x) \rightarrow Q_{l_1} \wedge Q_{l_1'}(1), \tag{4.3}$$

$$\models \quad Q_{l_0} \wedge Q_{l_1'}(x) \rightarrow Q_{l_1} \wedge Q_{l_t'}(1), \tag{4.4}$$

$$\models \quad Q_{l_1} \wedge Q_{l_0'}(x) \rightarrow Q_{l_t} \wedge Q_{l_1'}(2), \text{ and} \tag{4.5}$$

$$\models \quad Q_{l_1} \wedge Q_{l_1'}(x) \rightarrow Q_{l_t} \wedge Q_{l_t'}(2). \tag{4.6}$$

From (4.1) we obtain $\models Q_{l_0} \wedge Q_{l_0'}(x)$, and by (4.3) this leads to $\models Q_{l_1}$ and $\models Q_{l_1'}(1)$. Then by (4.6) we obtain that $\models Q_{l_t}$ holds. Since $\models Q_{l_0}$ holds and $\models Q_{l_1'}(1)$ is also *true*, (4.4) implies that $\models Q_{l_t'}(1)$ holds. Hence, $\models Q_{l_t} \wedge Q_{l_t'}(1)$ is *true*, that is, if $x = 1$ then $\models Q_{l_t} \wedge Q_{l_t'}(x)$ holds. Thus $\models x = 1 \rightarrow Q_{l_t} \wedge Q_{l_t'}(x)$ holds. But then (4.2) would imply, by transitivity of implication, that $\models x = 1 \rightarrow x = 2$. This is a contradiction. $\qquad\square$

Two solutions are given for this problem:

(i) Use *shared* auxiliary variables to relate local locations in different processes by expressing that certain combinations of locations will not occur during execution. (Observe that this is similar to the use of auxiliary variables in the method of Owicki & Gries.) In the case of Example 4.7 we can use a shared auxiliary variable k, *which counts the number of C-communications,* and the corresponding assertions, as illustrated in Figure 4.8, where $l_0 \equiv s$, $l_t \equiv t$, $l_0' \equiv s'$, and $l_t' \equiv t'$.

Then the semantically matching pairs cooperate:

$$\models (Q_{l_0} \wedge Q_{l_0'})(x,k) \rightarrow (Q_{l_1} \wedge Q_{l_1'})(1,1) \quad \text{and}$$
$$\models (Q_{l_1} \wedge Q_{l_1'})(x,k) \rightarrow (Q_{l_t} \wedge Q_{l_t'})(2,2).$$

Now the other, not semantically-matching, communication pairs pass the cooperation test because the conjunction of their preconditions evaluates to *false*:

$$\models (Q_{l_0} \wedge Q_{l_1'})(x,k) \rightarrow (Q_{l_1} \wedge Q_{l_t'})(1,2)$$

since $\models k = 0 \wedge k = 1 \wedge x = 1 \rightarrow \textit{false}$, and

$$\models (Q_{l_1} \wedge Q_{l_0'})(x,k) \rightarrow (Q_{l_t} \wedge Q_{l_1'})(2,1)$$

since $\models k = 1 \wedge k = 0 \rightarrow \textit{false}$.

This approach leads to the method of Levin & Gries [LG81]. A systematic development of this method calls for defining a product of synchronous transition diagrams whose state spaces are no longer disjoint, since auxiliary variables now may be shared. Consequently, in

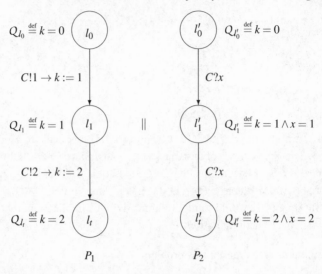

Fig. 4.8. Adding shared auxiliary variables plus corresponding assertions to program $P_1 \| P_2$ from Figure 4.3.

addition to the cooperation test, this method again introduces the interference freedom test. This is illustrated in Figure 4.8 and further discussed in Section 4.4.3

(ii) Use of the interference freedom test is avoided in the AFR-method where only *local* auxiliary variables are used. In that method every process has its own set of local programming and local auxiliary variables, and assertions associated with a process should only refer to these local variables. Therefore, parallel composition remains formulated as in Definition 4.1.

In case of Example 4.7, the use of two auxiliary local counters k_1 and k_2 leads to program $P_1' \| P_2'$ plus associated assertions as illustrated in Figure 4.9, where $l_0 \equiv s$, $l_t \equiv t$, $l_0' \equiv s'$, and $l_t' \equiv t'$.

This, however, does not solve the problem that the conjunction of preconditions for a not semantically-matching pair, e.g., $Q_{l_0} \wedge Q_{l_1'} \equiv k_1 = 0 \wedge k_2 = 1 \wedge x = 1$, does not evaluate to *false*. Therefore, a *global invariant* I (also called communication invariant) is introduced to relate the values of the local auxiliary variables in the various processes. *This invariant can be used to express which combinations of values for the local auxiliary variables occur*

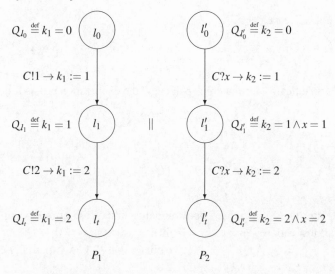

Fig. 4.9. Adding local auxiliary variables plus corresponding assertions to $P_1 \| P_2$ from Figure 4.3.

during execution, and thus to indicate which combination of locations, and corresponding communications, occur during execution.

In our example above we use the global invariant $I \stackrel{\text{def}}{=} k_1 = k_2$ to express that both processes have performed the same number of C-communications at any point during an execution. Of course we have to show that I is indeed invariant and that it holds prior to executing $P_1' \parallel P_2'$. Since the auxiliary variables are only added to communication steps, I is trivially invariant under local steps. In order to prove that I is invariant under all communication steps, one adds I as follows to the cooperation test.

For every communication step leading from l_1 and l_1' to l_2 and l_2', prove:

$$\models (Q_{l_1} \wedge Q_{l_1'} \wedge I) \rightarrow (Q_{l_2} \wedge Q_{l_2'} \wedge I) \circ h,$$

where h is the state transformation corresponding to the communication.

In the case of our example this leads to four verification conditions.

For the semantically-matching communication pairs, we have to check

$$\models (Q_{l_0} \wedge Q_{l_0'} \wedge I)(x, k_1, k_2) \rightarrow (Q_{l_1} \wedge Q_{l_1'} \wedge I)(1, 1, 1),$$

which holds because $\models (k_1 = 0 \wedge k_2 = 0 \wedge k_1 = k_2) \rightarrow (1 = 1 \wedge 1 = 1 \wedge 1 = 1)$ is *true*, and

$$\models (Q_{l_1} \wedge Q_{l_1'} \wedge I)(x, k_1, k_2) \rightarrow (Q_{l_t} \wedge Q_{l_t'} \wedge I)(2, 2, 2),$$

which holds because

$$\models (k_1 = 1 \wedge k_2 = 1 \wedge x = 1 \wedge k_1 = k_2) \rightarrow (2 = 2 \wedge 2 = 2 \wedge 2 = 2 \wedge 2 = 2)$$

is *true*.

The semantically-not-matching pairs pass the cooperation test as follows:

$$\models (Q_{l_0} \wedge Q_{l_1'} \wedge I) \rightarrow (Q_{l_1} \wedge Q_{l_1'} \wedge I)(1,1,2)$$

since $\models (k_1 = 0 \wedge k_2 = 1 \wedge x = 1 \wedge k_1 = k_2) \rightarrow false$, and

$$\models (Q_{l_1} \wedge Q_{l_0'} \wedge I) \rightarrow (Q_{l_1} \wedge Q_{l_1'} \wedge I)(2,2,1)$$

since $\models (k_1 = 1 \wedge k_2 = 0 \wedge k_1 = k_2) \rightarrow false$.

It remains to establish that I holds initially. In the case of our example this is trivial: just choose $k_1 = 0 \wedge k_2 = 0$, then $\models k_1 = 0 \wedge k_2 = 0 \rightarrow Q_{l_0} \wedge Q_{l_0'} \wedge I$ holds. Since $\models Q_{l_t} \wedge Q_{l_t} \rightarrow x = 2$, we obtain that $P_1' \parallel P_2'$ is partially correct w.r.t. $< k_1 = 0 \wedge k_2 = 0 \wedge k_1 = k_2, x = 2 >$.

Next we discuss how to derive from this result that $\{true\}\ P_1 \parallel P_2\ \{x = 2\}$ holds, using the initialisation and auxiliary variables rules from Chapter 3.

As in Example 3.12 of the previous chapter, we observe that the value of x during any execution is not affected by the auxiliary variables k_1 and k_2, since these variables do not occur in the conditions and the assignments to x. Hence the postcondition $x = 2$ does not depend on the initial values of k_1 and k_2, and is established by the initialisation rule for any arbitrary initial value of k_1 and k_2, as long as $k_1 = k_2$ holds. This justifies choosing 0 as the value for k_1 and for k_2 in the precondition, and leads to: $P_1' \parallel P_2'$ is partially correct w.r.t. $< true, x = 2 >$, since $\models true \leftrightarrow 0 = 0 \wedge 0 = 0 \wedge 0 = 0$, by soundness of the initialisation rule. Similarly to Lemma 3.23, we observe that for any execution of $P_1' \parallel P_2'$ there exists a corresponding execution of $P_1 \parallel P_2$ with the same value for x in the final state. Hence $\models \{true\}P_1 \parallel P_2\{x = 2\}$ holds by soundness of the auxiliary variables rule.

This leads to the following formulation of the AFR-method.

Definition 4.8 (Proof method of Apt, Francez & de Roever) The proof method of Apt, Francez & de Roever (AFR-method) is formulated as follows.

Given synchronous transition diagram $P \equiv P_1 \parallel \ldots \parallel P_n$ with locations $L \equiv L_1 \times \ldots \times L_n$.

Prove as follows that P is partially correct w.r.t. specification $< \varphi, \psi >$:

(i) Augment P_i by introducing auxiliary variables; every input-output transition $\alpha \rightarrow f$ is extended as follows: $\alpha \rightarrow f \circ g$, where g is a state transformation such that its write variables are amongst the auxiliary variables $\bar{z}^i$, which should not occur in P, φ and ψ; furthermore the auxiliary variables $\bar{z}^i$ associated with the components P_i are required to be mutually disjoint for $i = 1, \dots, n$. This leads to an augmented synchronous transition diagram $P' \equiv P'_1 \parallel \dots \parallel P'_n$.

(ii) Associate a predicate Q_l with every location l of P'_i, where Q_l does not involve any of the variables of P'_j, $j \neq i$.

(iii) Prove *local correctness* of every P'_i: for every internal transition $l \overset{a}{\rightarrow} l'$ of P'_i, assuming $a \equiv b \rightarrow f$, we have to prove

$$\models Q_l \wedge b \rightarrow Q_{l'} \circ f.$$

(iv) Choose a predicate $I(\bar{z})$, called *global invariant*, involving only the auxiliary variables $\bar{z} \equiv \bigcup_i \bar{z}^i$. Then prove *the cooperation test*, verify for every pair of transitions $l_1 \overset{a}{\rightarrow} l_2$ of P'_i and $l'_1 \overset{a'}{\rightarrow} l'_2$ of P'_j, with $j \neq i$, $a \equiv b; C!e \rightarrow f$ and $a' \equiv b'; C?x \rightarrow g$, that

$$\models I \wedge Q_{l_1} \wedge Q_{l'_1} \wedge b \wedge b' \rightarrow (I \wedge Q_{l_2} \wedge Q_{l'_2}) \circ h,$$

where $h \overset{\text{def}}{=} f \circ g \circ (x := e)$.

(v) Prove that

- $\models \varphi \rightarrow (I \wedge \bigwedge_i Q_{s_i}) \circ f$, for some state transformation f whose write variables belong to the set of auxiliary variables $\bar{z}$ (s_i denotes the initial location of P'_i), and

- $\models I \wedge \bigwedge_i Q_{t_i} \rightarrow \psi$, where t_i denotes the final location of P'_i. $\square$

Observe that at the beginning of this section we argued soundness of our first attempt at formulating an inductive assertion method for synchronous communication, by demonstrating that the associated global assertion network, consisting of global assertions $Q_l \overset{\text{def}}{=} Q_{l_1} \wedge \dots \wedge Q_{l_n}$, is inductive. All that we have argued above is, essentially, that this method, introduced in Definition 4.3, is incomplete, requires an extension with local auxiliary variables and a global invariant I, then results again in an inductive assertion network by redefining $Q_l \overset{\text{def}}{=} Q_{l_1} \wedge \dots \wedge Q_{l_n} \wedge I$ and by adapting the formulation of the cooperation test, and, hence, is again sound by Theorem 2.12. Soundness of the AFR-method then follows in exactly the same way as the soundness of the proof method for concurrent systems with shared variables, using the soundness of the initialisation rule and the rule for auxiliary variables.

In the next section, we give an invariance proof for establishing correctness of a distributed greatest common divisor algorithm of n positive numbers, which is due to Nissim Francez and Mickey Rodeh [FR80]. This invariance proof is based on a generalisation of the AFR-method in that the global invariant is allowed to involve non-auxiliary program variables, which are only updated during io-transitions.

The method of Levin & Gries is formulated, and proved to be sound, in Section 4.4.3.

Section 4.5 contains a semantic completeness proof of the AFR-method.

4.4.2 Example

We consider a synchronous diagram $P \equiv P_1 \| \dots \| P_n$ which computes the greatest common divisor of n numbers, $gcd(k_1, \dots, k_n)$, $k_i > 0$, $i = 1, \dots, n$. This program, presented in Figure 4.10, has the property that when all processes have finished computing that value, the program is blocked in a deadlock state, since no process "knows" that all other processes have also finished computing.

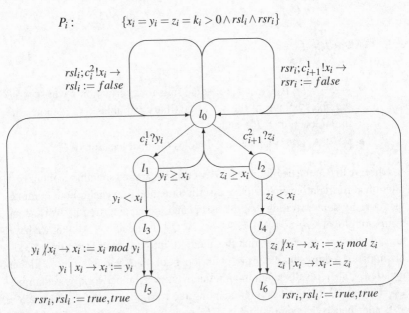

Fig. 4.10. Structure of P_i for $i \le n$.

Using such an example, we are able to show that our proof method can deal with more general invariance (or safety) properties than just partial correctness.

The program P consists of n parallel processes arranged in a ring configuration, where each process P_i communicates with its own immediate neighbours

P_{i-1}, P_{i+1} (+ and − are interpreted cyclically over $\{1, \ldots, n\}$). The corresponding communication channels are presented in Figure 4.11.

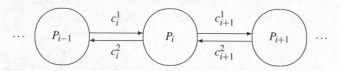

Fig. 4.11. Channels of P_i for $i \leq n$.

Each process has a local variable x_i which initially has the value k_i. Each process P_i sends the value of its own variable x_i to each immediate neighbour, and uses flags rsl_i (ready to send left) and rsr_i (ready to send right) to avoid sending the value of x_i again before it is modified. Other tasks of P_i are to receive copies of the values of x_{i-1} in y or of x_{i+1} in z. When such a number is received from a neighbour process, it is compared to the value of x_i. If x_i is larger, it is updated according to Euclid's rule, and the rsl_i and rsr_i flags are set to true. Otherwise, nothing happens.

Since the program deadlocks upon reaching the final state, no postcondition is claimed for the whole program. Rather, we show how to express in our formalism our above claim about the state at the instant of blocking.

Proof By applying Reynolds' generalised criterion we can simplify the process presented in Figure 4.10 without changing its state-transformation behaviour, by integrating local steps into communication steps. Then, we obtain a transition diagram as presented in Figure 4.12.

In the following, LI_i expresses the loop invariant of P_i, which serves as the precondition and postcondition for the body of the main loop and which is therefore expected to hold at l_0.

As the global invariant GI we define:

$$GI \overset{\text{def}}{=} \bigwedge_{i=1}^{n} ((\neg rsl_i \to z_{i-1} = x_i) \wedge (\neg rsr_i \to y_{i+1} = x_i))$$
$$\wedge gcd(x_1, \ldots, x_n) = gcd(k_1, \ldots, k_n)$$

GI establishes the correct sending and receiving relationship between any triple of consecutive processes P_{i-1}, P_i, P_{i+1}, and also establishes that all the indicated changes in the values of the x_i's preserve $gcd(k_1, \ldots, k_n)$. Observe that GI is not a global invariant in the sense of Definition 4.8, since GI also involves non-auxiliary program variables. Yet, since GI involves program variables which are only updated during io-transitions, the cooperation test guarantees that GI is preserved over all communications. Since the transition diagram in Figure 4.10 has no local transitions, this implies GI is preserved over all transitions.

The loop invariant LI_i is expressed only in terms of local variables (of P_i), and describes the sequential behaviour of the loop body:

$$LI_i \stackrel{\text{def}}{=} y_i \geq x_i \wedge z_i \geq x_i.$$

The instant where a process is about to execute the loop body and finds itself blocked is characterised by

$$BL_i \stackrel{\text{def}}{=} (LI_i \wedge \neg rsl_i \wedge \neg rsr_i).$$

Therefore we have to prove the following property:

$$(GI \wedge \bigwedge_{i=1}^{n} BL_i) \rightarrow (\bigwedge_{i=1}^{n} x_i = gcd(k_1, \ldots, k_n)). \qquad (*)$$

Validity of $(*)$ implies that the conclusion indeed holds at the instant of total blocking provided it occurs.

Next we establish $(*)$. Suppose that $GI \wedge \bigwedge_{i=1}^{n} BL_i$ holds. Now we infer from $GI \wedge \bigwedge_{i=1}^{n} (\neg rsl_i \wedge \neg rsr_i)$ that

$$\bigwedge_{i=1}^{n} x_i = z_{i-1} = y_{i+1} \qquad (4.7)$$

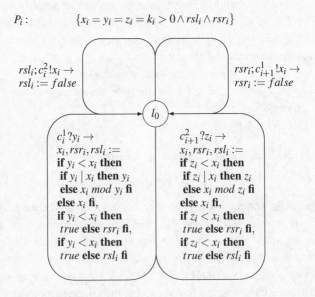

$$P_i: \qquad \{x_i = y_i = z_i = k_i > 0 \wedge rsl_i \wedge rsr_i\}$$

Fig. 4.12. Structure of P_i for $i \leq n$.

holds.

Furthermore we have $\bigwedge_{i=1}^{n} LI_i$, i.e.,

$$\bigwedge_{i=1}^{n} (y_i \geq x_i \wedge z_i \geq x_i). \tag{4.8}$$

Using (4.7) and (4.8) we get

$$x_i \geq z_i = x_{i+1} \text{ and } x_{i+1} \geq y_{i+1} = x_i, \text{ for } i = 1, \ldots, n-1,$$

which together imply that

$$x_i = x_{i+1}, \text{ for } i = 1, \ldots, n-1, \tag{4.9}$$

and therefore

$$x_1 = x_2 = \ldots = x_n. \tag{4.10}$$

Finally, (4.10) and $gcd(x_1, \ldots, x_n) = gcd(k_1, \ldots, k_n)$ imply the required conclusion,

$$\bigwedge_{i=1}^{n} x_i = gcd(k_1, \ldots, k_n).$$

We are left with the problem of verifying that GI is a global invariant and that LI_i is a local loop invariant.

Using the AFR-method, the latter normally involves ordinary sequential reasoning to establish local correctness for an assertion network. In this example, in which each process has only one location, the assertion network is the one associating LI_i with l_0 in each process P_i. Hence, this proves local correctness is trivial since P_i in Figure 4.12 does not have any purely local transitions. Since we are not interested in establishing partial correctness we do not have to check the termination requirement of point (v) in the AFR-method. So, the AFR-method reduces to checking the initial requirement of point (v) and the cooperation of the processes (point (iv)).

(i) Initially, $\bigwedge_{i=1}^{n} (\neg rsl_i \wedge \neg rsr_i)$ is false, and, therefore, the first two (parameterised) clauses of GI are trivially true. Also, $\bigwedge_{i=1}^{n} x_i = k_i$ trivially implies the third clause. LI_i holds initially for each process P_i because the processes start with x_i, y_i and z_i being equal. Hence, the initial requirement of point (v) in the AFR-method is valid since no auxiliary variables are needed, and, therefore, no auxiliary variables need to be initialised.

(ii) Proving the cooperation test for P involves checking the cooperation of two pairs of syntactically-matching communications per process. One pair of matching communication transitions is the one consisting of the left alternative for an input statement of some P_i and the right alternative for an input statement of P_{i-1}. Hence, we have to show

$$\models \{rsl_i \wedge LI_i \wedge LI_{i-1} \wedge GI\}$$
$$c_i^2!x_i \to \underbrace{rsl_i := false}_{A}$$
$$\|$$
$$c_i^2?z_{i-1} \to \underbrace{rsl_{i-1}, rsr_{i-1}, x_{i-1} := \dots}_{B}$$
$$\{LI_i \wedge LI_{i-1} \wedge GI\}.$$

The variables changed are rsl_i, rsl_{i-1}, rsr_{i-1}, z_{i-1}, and x_{i-1}. By the cooperation test, this reduces to proving

$$\models rsl_i \wedge LI_i \wedge LI_{i-1} \wedge GI \to (LI_i \wedge LI_{i-1} \wedge GI) \circ (A; B) \circ z_{i-1} := x_i.$$

We split this proof into two parts. First one proves

$$\models rsl_i \wedge LI_i \wedge LI_{i-1} \wedge GI$$
$$\to (LI_i \wedge y_{i-1} \geq x_{i-1} \wedge GI \wedge z_{i-1} = x_i) \circ z_{i-1} := x_i,$$

which is obvious, and then

$$\models LI_i \wedge y_{i-1} \geq x_{i-1} \wedge GI \wedge z_{i-1} = x_i \to (LI_i \wedge LI_{i-1} \wedge GI) \circ (A; B).$$

Intuitively, the intermediate assertion above can be thought of as the postcondition of

$$c_i^2!x_i \| c_i^2?z_{i-1}.$$

Now, $x_i = z_{i-1}$ implies, by known facts about the *gcd* function, that

$$gcd(x_1, \dots, x_n) = gcd(k_1, \dots, k_n)$$

remains true after executing $A; B$. Establishing $LI_i \wedge LI_{i-1}$ after executing $A; B$ (after $z_{i-1} := x_i$) is obvious.

Hence, this matching pair of communications satisfies the cooperation test.

The remaining pair of matching communication transitions is the right input alternative of P_i and the left output alternative of P_{i+1}; its cooperation is verified similarly. $\square$

4.4.3 Technical Note: The Proof Method of Levin & Gries

As already illustrated in Figure 4.8, in order to apply the method of Levin & Gries, one has to annotate the program with assignments to *global auxiliary variables*, i.e., variables which are shared by the processes constituting the network. By dropping the restriction that the variable sets of different processes are disjoint we run into the danger that inconsistencies may arise when annotating these programs; e.g., it might be possible to update an auxiliary variable both in the input transition and in the output transition of a matching pair of communications – which assignment should be the correct one? We thus restrict annotations to communication statements only, and in such a fashion that each auxiliary variable is updated only once in a communication step. We fulfil these requirements by annotating output statements only (without losing completeness of this method, as we shall see).

Definition 4.9 (Proof method of Levin & Gries) The proof method of Levin & Gries is formulated below.

Given synchronous transition diagram $P \equiv P_1 \parallel \ldots \parallel P_n$ with locations $L \equiv L_1 \times \ldots \times L_n$.

Prove as follows that P is partially correct w.r.t. specification $< \varphi, \psi >$:

(i) Augment P_i by introducing auxiliary variables; every output transition $\alpha \to f$ is extended as follows: $\alpha \to f \circ k$, where k is a state transformation such that its write variables are amongst the auxiliary variables $\bar{z}$, which should not occur in P, φ and ψ. This leads to an augmented synchronous transition diagram $P' \equiv P'_1 \parallel \ldots \parallel P'_n$.

(ii) Associate with every location l of P'_i a predicate Q_l which does not involve any of the program variables of P_j, $j \neq i$, i.e., Q_l may only refer to the program variables of P_i, to auxiliary variables and to logical variables.

(iii) Prove *local correctness* of every P'_i: For every internal transition $l \xrightarrow{a} l'$ of P'_i, assuming $a \equiv b \to f$, we prove

$$\models Q_l \wedge b \to Q_{l'} \circ f.$$

(iv) Prove *the cooperation test*, that is, verify for every pair of transitions $l_1 \xrightarrow{a} l_2$ of P'_i and $l'_1 \xrightarrow{a'} l'_2$ of P'_j, with $j \neq i$, $a \equiv b; C!e \to f \circ k$ and $a' \equiv b'; C?x \to g$, that

$$\models Q_{l_1} \wedge Q_{l'_1} \wedge b \wedge b' \to (Q_{l_2} \wedge Q_{l'_2}) \circ f',$$

where $f' \stackrel{\text{def}}{=} f \circ g \circ k \circ (x := e)$.

(v) Prove *interference freedom*, that is, verify for every pair of transitions $l_1 \xrightarrow{a} l_2$ of P_i' and $l_1' \xrightarrow{a'} l_2'$ of P_j', with $j \neq i$, $a \equiv b; C!e \rightarrow f \circ k$ and $a' \equiv b'; C?x \rightarrow g$, and for all predicates Q_l associated with locations l of process P_m', $m \neq i$, $m \neq j$, that

$$\models Q_{l_1} \wedge Q_{l_1'} \wedge Q_l \wedge b \wedge b' \rightarrow Q_l \circ f',$$

where $f' \stackrel{\text{def}}{=} f \circ g \circ k \circ (x := e)$.

(vi) Prove

- $\models \varphi \rightarrow (\bigwedge_i Q_{s_i}) \circ f$, for some state transformation f whose write variables belong to the set of auxiliary variables $\bar{z}$ (s_i denotes the initial location of P_i'), and

- $\models \bigwedge_i Q_{t_i} \rightarrow \psi$, where t_i denotes the final location of P_i'. $\qquad\square$

Note that we have to test for interference freedom only for communication steps, as the shared variables of the program (i.e., the auxiliary variables) are updated only in augmentations of communication statements.

Since $P_1' \| \ldots \| P_n'$ is no longer a synchronous transition diagram in the sense of Definition 4.1, because $P_1', \ldots, P_n'$ are no longer disjoint, a new definition of the semantics of this extended notion of synchronous transition diagram is needed.

Definition 4.10 (Extended synchronous product of transition diagrams) Given sequential synchronous transition diagrams $P_1, \ldots, P_n$, with $P_i = (L_i, T_i, s_i, t_i)$, s.t. the communication channels of $P_1, \ldots, P_n$ connect $P_1, \ldots, P_n$ only, and $P_1, \ldots P_n$ only share auxiliary variables from the set $\bar{z}$ as in Definition 4.9, we define their parallel composition $P \equiv P_1 \| \ldots \| P_n$ as the following product $P \equiv (L, T, s, t)$:

- $L \equiv L_1 \times \ldots \times L_n$ is the set of locations of P,
- $l \xrightarrow{a} l'$ is a transition in T iff

  (i) $l \equiv \langle l_1, \ldots, l_i, \ldots, l_n \rangle$ and $l' \equiv \langle l_1, \ldots, l_i', \ldots, l_n \rangle$, with $l_i \xrightarrow{a} l_i'$ an internal transition of T_i, or

  (ii) $l \equiv \langle l_1, \ldots, l_i, \ldots, l_j, \ldots, l_n \rangle$ and $l' \equiv \langle l_1, \ldots, l_i', \ldots, l_j', \ldots, l_n \rangle$, $i \neq j$, with $(l_i \xrightarrow{a_i} l_i') \in T_i$, $(l_j \xrightarrow{a_j} l_j') \in T_j$, $a_i \equiv b; C!e \rightarrow f \circ k$, $a_j \equiv b'; C?x \rightarrow g$, and $a \equiv b \wedge b' \rightarrow f \circ g \circ k \circ (x := e)$,

- $s \equiv \langle s_1, \ldots, s_n \rangle$,
- $t \equiv \langle t_1, \ldots, t_n \rangle$. $\qquad\square$

Recall that the introduction of shared auxiliary variables does not change the flow of control of the program, and that $P_1 \| \ldots \| P_n$ is a sequential transition diagram.

Remark 4.11 Note also that we have to consider carefully the order of the changes to the state as the result of a communication step. While the local assignments f and g of the original processes P_i and P_j only involve local variables of their respective process, i.e., $var(f) \cap var(g) = \emptyset$, the assignment k to the auxiliary variables may involve other auxiliary variables as well as local program variables of the process it occurs in. Our intention is that this assignment is executed on the basis of the state as it is while executing the communication, i.e., the pre-communication state of the sending process, before the local assignment f is executed (as variables updated by f may be involved in the assignment to auxiliary variables). Thus we have to apply k before f in the definition of a communication step.

Example 4.12 We use the method of Levin & Gries to give a proof that the program $P_1 \| P_2$ of Example 4.2 is partially correct w.r.t. φ and ψ, where

$$\varphi \stackrel{\text{def}}{=} S_0 \cap T_0 = \emptyset \wedge S = S_0 \wedge T = T_0 \wedge S_0 \neq \emptyset \wedge x \neq mx \wedge y \neq mn$$

and

$$\psi \stackrel{\text{def}}{=} S \cap T = \emptyset \wedge S \cup T = S_0 \cup T_0 \wedge max(S) < min(T) \wedge |S_0| = |S| \wedge |T_0| = |T|.$$

By convention, $min(\emptyset) \stackrel{\text{def}}{=} +\infty$ and $max(\emptyset) \stackrel{\text{def}}{=} -\infty$.

In our first step we augment the output statements with assignments to auxiliary variables. The variable mxS collects all values sent via channel C, and the variable mnT collects all values sent via channel D. The variable $last$ records the last value sent via D and "connects" the value sent and the value received in the assertions.

Next we have to construct assertion networks for the augmented transition diagrams P_1' and P_2'. For brevity of notation we define invariants I_1 and I_2 which occur in the respective assertion networks. These express that S_0 and T_0 are disjoint, that no new elements outside of S_0 or T_0 are inserted into S or T, and also express how the actual set S is constructed by the algorithm.

$$I_1 \stackrel{\text{def}}{=} S_0 \cap T_0 = \emptyset \wedge S \subseteq S_0 \cup T_0 \wedge S = (S_0 - mxS) \cup mnT.$$
$$I_2 \stackrel{\text{def}}{=} S_0 \cap T_0 = \emptyset \wedge T \subseteq S_0 \cup T_0.$$

We have the following assertion network for P_1':

$$Q_{s_1} \stackrel{\text{def}}{=} S_0 \cap T_0 = \emptyset \wedge S = S_0 \wedge S_0 \neq \emptyset \wedge x \neq mx \wedge mxS = \emptyset \wedge |mnT| = |mxS|$$

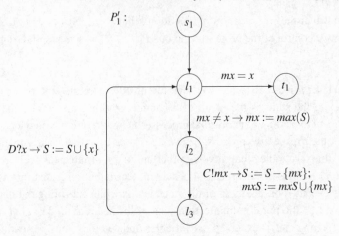

Fig. 4.13. Set-partitioning program P_1'

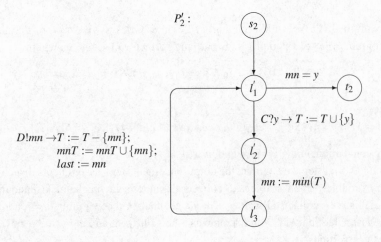

Fig. 4.14. Set-partitioning program P_2'

$Q_{I_1} \overset{\text{def}}{=} |mnT| = |mxS| \wedge |S| = |S_0| \wedge I_1 \wedge (mxS = \emptyset \rightarrow x \neq mx) \wedge$
$\qquad (mxS \neq \emptyset \rightarrow (mx > max(S - \{x\}) \wedge mx \in mxS \wedge x \in mnT \wedge last = x))$

$Q_{I_2} \overset{\text{def}}{=} |mnT| = |mxS| \wedge mx = max(S) \wedge |S| = |S_0| \wedge I_1 \wedge mx \in S$

$Q_{I_3} \overset{\text{def}}{=} |mnT| = |mxS| - 1 \wedge |S| = |S_0| - 1 \wedge I_1 \wedge$
$\qquad mxS \neq \emptyset \wedge mx > max(S) \wedge mx \in mxS$

$Q_{I_1} \overset{\text{def}}{=} S_0 \cap T_0 = \emptyset \wedge |mnT| = |mxS| \wedge S = (S_0 - mxS) \cup mnT \wedge mx = x \wedge$
$\qquad |S| = |S_0| \wedge S \subseteq S_0 \cup T_0 \wedge x \in S \wedge mx > max(S - \{x\}) \wedge last = x.$

Similarly, we have as the assertion network for P_2':

$$Q_{s_2} \overset{\text{def}}{=} \ S_0 \cap T_0 = \emptyset \wedge T = T_0 \wedge T_0 \neq \emptyset \wedge y \neq mn \wedge mnT = \emptyset \wedge$$
$$|mnT| = |mxS|$$

$$Q_{l_1'} \overset{\text{def}}{=} \ |mnT| = |mxS| \wedge |T| = |T_0| \wedge I_2 \wedge (mnT = \emptyset \to y \neq mn) \wedge$$
$$(mnT \neq \emptyset \to (mn < min(T) \wedge mn \in mnT \wedge last = mn)) \wedge$$
$$T = (T_0 \cup mxS) - mnT$$

$$Q_{l_2'} \overset{\text{def}}{=} \ |mnT| = |mxS| - 1 \wedge |T| = |T_0| + 1 \wedge I_2 \wedge y \in mxS \wedge$$
$$T = ((T_0 \cup mxS) - mnT) \cup \{y\}$$

$$Q_{l_3'} \overset{\text{def}}{=} \ |mnT| = |mxS| - 1 \wedge |T| = |T_0| + 1 \wedge I_2 \wedge mn = min(T) \wedge$$
$$y \in mxS \wedge T = ((T_0 \cup mxS) - mnT) \cup \{y\}$$

$$Q_{l_2} \overset{\text{def}}{=} \ S_0 \cap T_0 = \emptyset \wedge |mnT| = |mxS| \wedge T = (T_0 \cup mxS) - mnT \wedge mn = y \wedge$$
$$|T| = |T_0| \wedge T \subseteq S_0 \cup T_0 \wedge mn \in mnT \wedge mn < min(T) \wedge last = mn.$$

In order to prove local correctness of these assertion networks we have to check the following verification conditions, which is straightforward,

$$\models Q_{s_1} \to Q_{l_1}$$
$$\models Q_{l_1} \wedge mx \neq x \to Q_{l_2}[max(S)/mx]$$
$$\models Q_{l_1} \wedge mx = x \to Q_{l_1}$$

$$\models Q_{s_2} \to Q_{l_1'}$$
$$\models Q_{l_2'} \to Q_{l_3'}[min(T)/mn]$$
$$\models Q_{l_1'} \wedge mn = y \to Q_{l_2},$$

using the notation $\varphi[e/x] \overset{\text{def}}{=} \varphi \circ (\lambda\sigma.(\sigma : x \mapsto e(\sigma)))$ introduced in Chapter 3.

We have two pairs of syntactically-matching communications (which are also semantically matching), and have to check for the cooperation test

$$\models Q_{l_2} \wedge Q_{l_1'} \to Q_{l_3} \wedge Q_{l_2'} \circ f_1,$$

with $f_1(\sigma) \overset{\text{def}}{=} (\sigma : T, S, y, mxS \mapsto \sigma(T) \cup \{\sigma(mx)\}, \sigma(S) - \{\sigma(mx)\}, \sigma(mx),$
$\sigma(mxS) \cup \{\sigma(mx)\})$,

$$\models Q_{l_3} \wedge Q_{l_3'} \to Q_{l_1} \wedge Q_{l_1'} \circ f_2,$$

and $f_2(\sigma) \overset{\text{def}}{=} (\sigma : T, S, x, mnT, last \mapsto \sigma(T) - \{\sigma(mn)\}, \sigma(S) \cup \{\sigma(mn)\}, \sigma(mn),$
$\sigma(mnT) \cup \{\sigma(mn)\}, mn)$.

We prove the first verification condition by assuming that $\sigma \models Q_{l_2} \wedge Q_{l_1'}$. We show first that $\sigma' \models Q_{l_3}$, where $\sigma' \overset{\text{def}}{=} f_1(\sigma)$. Since $\sigma \models |mnT| = |mxS|$ and a new value is send along channel C, we indeed have that $\sigma' \models |mnT| =$

$|mxS| - 1$. We remove one element from S; hence, $\sigma \models |S| = |S_0|$ leads to $\sigma' \models |S| = |S_0| - 1$ (the logical variable S_0 does not change its value, i.e., $\sigma(S_0) = \sigma'(S_0)$). The invariant I_1 is maintained by the state transformation f_1; obviously $\sigma' \models mxS \neq \emptyset$ and $\sigma' \models mx \in mxS$. Since $\sigma \models mx = max(S)$ we have

$$\sigma'(mx) = \sigma(mx) > max(\sigma'(S)) = max(\sigma(S) - \{\sigma(mx)\}),$$

i.e., $\sigma' \models mx > max(S)$.

We already have $\sigma \models |mnT| = |mxS| - 1$, and similarly as above $\sigma \models |T| = |T_0| + 1$, and $\sigma' \models I_2$. From $\sigma \models T = ((T_0 \cup mxS) - mnT)$ we deduce that $\sigma' \models T = ((T_0 \cup mxS) - mnT) \cup \{y\}$. Since $\sigma'(mxS) = \sigma(mxS) \cup \{\sigma(mx)\}$ and $\sigma'(y) = \sigma(mx)$ we conclude $\sigma' \models y \in mxS$, i.e., $\sigma' \models Q_{l_2'}$.

Since there are only two processes, and assignments to auxiliary variables are only added to io-statements, we do not have to perform any interference freedom tests.

Finally, choosing $f(\sigma) \stackrel{\text{def}}{=} (\sigma : mxS, mnT \mapsto \emptyset, \emptyset)$, we establish

$$\models \varphi \rightarrow (Q_{s_1} \wedge Q_{s_2}) \circ f.$$

The last implication

$$\models Q_{t_1} \wedge Q_{t_2} \rightarrow \psi$$

is proved as follows. Since $S \subseteq S_0 \cup T_0$ and $T \subseteq S_0 \cup T_0$, we have $S \cup T \subseteq S_0 \cup T_0$. We also have $S \cup T = ((S_0 - mxS) \cup mnT) \cup ((T_0 \cup mxS) - mnT) \supseteq (S_0 - mxS) \cup T_0 \cup mxS \supseteq S_0 \cup T_0$, hence $S_0 \cup T_0 = S \cup T$. Since $S_0 \cap T_0 = \emptyset$ we have $|S_0 \cup T_0| = |S_0| + |T_0| = |S| + |T|$. Now assume that $S \cap T \neq \emptyset$; then $|S \cup T| < |S| + |T|$. But since $S_0 \cup T_0 = S \cup T$ we obtain a contradiction: $|S \cup T| < |S| + |T| = |S_0 \cup T_0| = |S \cup T|$. Consequently $S \cap T = \emptyset$ follows. From Q_{t_1} and Q_{t_2} we have immediately $|S| = |S_0|$ and $|T| = |T_0|$.

From $mx = x \wedge mx \in mnT \wedge mx > max(S - \{x\})$ we infer that $x \in S$ and $x = mx = max(S)$.

From $mn = y \wedge mn \in mnT \wedge T = (T_0 \cup mxS) - mnT$ we infer $mn \notin T$. Since $S \cup T = S_0 \cup T_0$ this implies $mn \in S$. Now $mn < min(T)$ and, moreover, $x = last = mn$. Consequently, $max(S) = mx = mn < min(T)$.

Having applied the proof method of Levin & Gries successfully, we can indeed claim that $P_1 \| P_2$ is correct w.r.t. $< \varphi, \psi >$.   □

Soundness of the proof method of Levin & Gries follows along the same lines as soundness of the AFR-method. For every location $l \equiv \langle l_1, \dots, l_n \rangle$ of the transition diagram $P \equiv P_1 \| \dots \| P_n$ obtained in Definition 4.10, we define $Q_l \stackrel{\text{def}}{=} Q_{l_1} \wedge \dots \wedge Q_{l_n}$, and from the considerations at the beginning of Section 4.4, together with the interference freedom test, it follows that $Q \stackrel{\text{def}}{=} \{Q_l | l \in L\}$ is inductive. Since P is a sequential transition diagram, by Theorem 2.12, and by soundness of the initialisation rule and the auxiliary variable rule as proved in Chapter 3 we conclude soundness of this method.

4.5 Semantic Completeness

4.5.1 Compositional Semantics of Synchronous Transition Diagrams

We want to apply a similar methodology for proving completeness in a compositional way as presented in Chapter 3. However, here the problem arises that we cannot even define the initial-final state behaviour of a location of a component of a parallel diagram in isolation, since input-output transitions are defined only in terms of the context of a parallel composition. Therefore we first define a *labelled* transition relation which also provides a semantics for input-output transitions, when considered in isolation, by defining their communication capabilities.

Definition 4.13 Let $P \equiv (L, T, s, t)$ be a sequential synchronous transition diagram. We define

$$\langle l; \sigma \rangle \xrightarrow{\langle \rangle} \langle l'; \sigma' \rangle$$

for $\sigma \models b$ and $\sigma' = f(\sigma)$, in case of an internal transition $l \xrightarrow{a} l' \in T$, with $a \equiv b \to f$, and where "$\langle \rangle$" expresses the empty sequence of communications.

In the case of an output transition $l \xrightarrow{a} l' \in T$, $a \equiv b; C!e \to f$, we have

$$\langle l; \sigma \rangle \xrightarrow{\langle (C, v) \rangle} \langle l'; \sigma' \rangle$$

if $\sigma \models b(\sigma)$, where $v = e(\sigma)$ and $\sigma' = f(\sigma)$.

In the case of an input transition $l \xrightarrow{a} l' \in T$, with $a \equiv b; C?x \to f$, we define

$$\langle l; \sigma \rangle \xrightarrow{\langle (C, v) \rangle} \langle l'; \sigma' \rangle$$

if $\models b(\sigma)$, where $\sigma' = f(\sigma : x \mapsto v)$, for v an *arbitrary* value in *VAL*.

Furthermore, we have the following rules for computing the reflexive and transitive closure:

$$\langle l; \sigma \rangle \xrightarrow{\langle \rangle} \langle l; \sigma \rangle$$

and

$$\frac{\langle l; \sigma \rangle \xrightarrow{\theta} \langle l'; \sigma' \rangle \quad \langle l'; \sigma' \rangle \xrightarrow{\theta'} \langle l''; \sigma'' \rangle}{\langle l; \sigma \rangle \xrightarrow{\theta \cdot \theta'} \langle l''; \sigma'' \rangle}.$$

Here θ and θ' denote sequences of communications, where a communication is represented by a pair of the form (C, v), called *communication record*, with C a channel and v a value. (The operation of concatenation is denoted by '$\cdot$'; we will frequently use, e.g., $\theta \cdot (C, v)$ to abbreviate $\theta \cdot \langle (C, v) \rangle$.) $\square$

One of the main points in the above definition is that an input transition is modelled by *guessing* locally the value received (in case the corresponding boolean guard is true) and assigning it to the specified local variable, after which the corresponding local state transformation is executed. The information about the communication, i.e., the guessed value and the channel involved, is attached to the transition itself in the form of a communication record. As we will see below, this information can be used in a parallel context to select the 'right' guesses, i.e., those guesses which correspond with the actual value sent.

Using the above transition relation we can now define the semantics of a *sequential* synchronous transition diagram, in which the value received in an input transition is selected by local guessing.

Definition 4.14 Let P be a sequential synchronous transition diagram, and l occur in P. We define

$$O_l(P) \stackrel{\text{def}}{=} \{(\sigma, \sigma', \theta) \mid \langle s; \sigma \rangle \stackrel{\theta}{\longrightarrow} \langle l; \sigma' \rangle\}.$$

Note that we can now define the initial-final state semantics of P as $O_l(P)$, also simply expressed as $O(P)$. $\square$

For a sequence of communications θ and a set of channels $cset \in CHAN$, we define the *projection* of θ onto $cset$, expressed by $\theta{\downarrow}cset$, as the sequence obtained from θ by deleting all records with channels not in $cset$.

Definition 4.15 (Projection of a sequence of communications to a set of channels) One can define $\theta{\downarrow}cset$, the projection of θ onto a set of channels $cset$, by induction on the length of θ:

$$\langle \rangle {\downarrow} cset \stackrel{\text{def}}{=} \langle \rangle,$$

$$(\langle (C, \mu) \rangle \cdot \theta'){\downarrow}cset \stackrel{\text{def}}{=} \begin{cases} \langle (C, \mu) \rangle \cdot \theta'{\downarrow}cset, & \text{if } C \in cset, \\ \theta'{\downarrow}cset, & \text{otherwise.} \end{cases} \qquad \square$$

Also we need to define the set of channels occurring in a trace θ.

Definition 4.16 (Channels occurring in a trace) The set of channels occurring in a sequence of communications, or *trace* θ, notation $Chan(\theta)$, is defined by

- $Chan(\langle\rangle) \overset{\text{def}}{=} \emptyset$
- $Chan(\theta \cdot (C,\mu)) \overset{\text{def}}{=} Chan(\theta) \cup \{C\}.$ □

In the following definition we extend the above semantics to a parallel composition of sequential synchronous diagrams.

Definition 4.17 (Compositional semantics of synchronous diagrams) Let $P \equiv P_1 \| \ldots \| P_n$ and $l = \langle l_1, \ldots, l_n \rangle$, l_i occurring in P_i. We define

$$O_l(P) \overset{\text{def}}{=} \{(\sigma, \sigma', \theta) \mid (\sigma, \sigma'_i, \theta_i) \in O_{l_i}(P_i), \, i = 1, \ldots, n\},$$

where

$$\sigma'(x) \overset{\text{def}}{=} \begin{cases} \sigma'_i(x), \text{ if } x \in var(P_i), \text{ for some } i = 1, \ldots, n, \\ \sigma(x), \text{ if } x \notin var(P_i), \text{ for all } i = 1, \ldots, n, \end{cases}$$

and θ_i denotes the projection $\theta{\downarrow}Chan(P_i)$ of θ along the channels of P_i. Similarly as above, the initial-final state semantics of a system of synchronous diagrams $P_1\|\ldots\|P_n$ is given by $O_l(P_1\|\ldots\|P_n)$, which is also expressed by $O(P_1\|\ldots\|P_n)$. □

Alternatively, one could have defined the parallel operator by giving the definition of $P_1\|P_2$, proved its associativity and commutativity, and then observed that the meaning of $(\ldots((P_1\|P_2)\|P_3)\ldots P_n)$ amounts to the one given above. This approach is followed in [Han00].

Below we will refer to the compositional semantics defined above only as O. We observe that in the above definition the requirement that the local histories θ_i can be obtained as the projection of one global history θ guarantees that an input on a channel indeed can be synchronised with a corresponding output. The following example illustrates this point.

Example 4.18 Consider the following parallel diagram:

Now the process P_2 generates histories of the form $\langle (C,v), (C,w) \rangle$, where v and w are arbitrary values. On the other hand P_1 generates the history $\langle (C,1), (C,2) \rangle$. The requirement of the existence of a global history such that both the local histories of P_1 and P_2 can be obtained from it by projection along channel C thus restricts the choice of possible histories of P_2 to the 'right' one: $\langle (C,1), (C,2) \rangle$.

Consider next the diagram

$$P_1 : \quad \boxed{s_1} \xrightarrow{C!1} \boxed{l} \xrightarrow{D!2} \boxed{t_1} \quad \| \quad P_2 : \quad \boxed{s_2} \xrightarrow{D?x} \boxed{l'} \xrightarrow{C?x} \boxed{t_2}$$

This diagram obviously deadlocks. This is also reflected by the fact that there exists no global history θ such that θ projected along the channels C and D equals each of the local histories of P_1 and P_2 (the local history of P_1 starts with a communication statement along C followed by one along D, whereas the local history of P_2 reverses the order of these communications). $\qquad\square$

The semantics $O_l(P)$ also applies to the parallel composition $P_1 \| \ldots \| P_n$ of sequential synchronous diagrams $P_1, \ldots, P_n$ in case the channels along which these processes communicate are *not* restricted to connecting processes from only the set $P_1, \ldots, P_n$. In this case $P_1 \| \ldots \| P_n$ is called an *open* network. In the other case, in which every channel occurring in $P_1, \ldots, P_n$ connects exactly two different processes from $P_1, \ldots, P_n$, $P_1 \| \ldots \| P_n$ is called *closed*.

It is important to realise that the above compositional semantics is consistent with our basic assumption that any communication involves only one sender and one receiver, under the condition that the channels are both uni-directional and one-to-one.

In fact, this semantics allows the generalisation of the one-to-one condition to channels with one sender and multiple receivers, while preserving unidirectionality. Consider, e.g., the network $C?x \| C?y \| C!0$, in which C connects two consumers with one producer. The above compositional semantics would generate for this network a global history which in fact models a multi-party communication interaction, i.e., the input produced is received by both consumers.

However, the condition of unidirectionality of the channels is necessary for this semantics to be consistent. Consider, e.g., the following network:

$$P_1 : \quad \boxed{s_1} \xrightarrow{C?x} \boxed{l} \xrightarrow{C!0} \boxed{t_1} \quad \| \quad P_2 : \quad \boxed{s_2} \xrightarrow{C?y} \boxed{l'} \xrightarrow{C!0} \boxed{t_2}$$

This network satisfies the one-to-one condition, since it connects exactly two processes, but violates unidirectionality of C. Both processes P_1 and P_2 act as producer and consumer with respect to C. It is easy to see that $O_t(P_1 \| P_2)$ is nonempty, for $t = \langle t_1, t_2 \rangle$. This is due to the fact that the communication history does not indicate the direction of the communications, and consequently does not capture the different rôles of $C?x$ and $C!0$. However, according to our definition of closed product this diagram clearly deadlocks. Consequently the compositional semantics defined above is not correct with respect to the definition of closed product.

The following theorem states the correctness of the compositional semantics of a synchronous diagram $P \equiv P_1 \parallel \cdots \parallel P_n$, which does not contain any *external* channels, with respect to the initial-final state semantics $\mathcal{M} \llbracket P \rrbracket$. Here P denotes the closed product $P_1 \parallel \cdots \parallel P_n$. Its external channels are those channels which occur in some component P_i and which do not occur in the other components. The *internal* channels of such a system are those channels which connect two processes of that system.

Theorem 4.19 (Correctness of the compositional semantics)

Let $P_1 \parallel \cdots \parallel P_n$ be a synchronous diagram which does not contain external channels. We have that

$$\sigma' \in \mathcal{M} \llbracket P \rrbracket \sigma \quad \textit{iff} \quad \begin{array}{l} \textit{there exists a sequence of communications } \theta \\ \textit{such that } (\sigma, \sigma', \theta) \in O_t(P), \end{array}$$

where P denotes the closed product $P_1 \parallel \cdots \parallel P_n$ and t denotes the exit location of P.

Proof Let, for a location l of P, $\mathcal{M}_l \llbracket P \rrbracket \sigma$ denote all the resulting states of partial computations of P (viewed as a sequential transition diagram as formulated in Definition 4.1) which reach location l (note: $\mathcal{M} \llbracket P \rrbracket \sigma = \mathcal{M}_t \llbracket P \rrbracket \sigma$).

We first prove, for any location l of P, that the existence of a history θ such that $(\sigma, \sigma', \theta) \in O_l(P)$ implies $\sigma' \in \mathcal{M}_l \llbracket P \rrbracket \sigma$. Let $l = \langle l_1, \ldots, l_n \rangle$. By the Definitions 4.13 and 4.17 we have that $(\sigma, \sigma', \theta) \in O_l(P)$ iff $\langle s_i; \sigma \rangle \xrightarrow{\theta_i} \langle l_i; \sigma_i' \rangle$, for $i = 1, \ldots, n$, where s_i denotes the initial location of P_i, θ_i denotes the projection of θ along the channels of P_i, and σ_i' is obtained from σ' by assigning to the variables not belonging to process P_i their corresponding values in σ. If $\theta \neq \langle \rangle$ let the last communication of θ involve the channel C, with P_k and P_j the processes connected by C. Let $\theta = \theta' \cdot (C, v)$ and, for $i = 1, \ldots, n$, θ_i' denote the projection of θ' along the channels of P_i.

We proceed by induction on the sum of the lengths of the local computations

$$\langle s_i; \sigma \rangle \xrightarrow{\theta_i} \langle l_i; \sigma_i' \rangle.$$

For the starting location $s = \langle s_1, \ldots, s_n \rangle$ all local computations have a length of 0, $(\sigma, \sigma, \langle \rangle) \in O_s(P)$ and $\sigma \in \mathcal{M}_s \llbracket P \rrbracket \sigma$.

We consider the different possibilities for the last transition that has *globally* taken place, separately – either it has been a local step of one process P_r or it has been the communication step along C.

Suppose first that there is an r, $1 \leq r \leq n$ such that the local computation of P_r ends with an internal transition, i.e., $\langle s_r; \sigma \rangle \xrightarrow{\theta_r} \langle l_r''; \tau \rangle \xrightarrow{\langle \rangle} \langle l_r; \sigma_r' \rangle$, for some location l_r'' of P_r and state τ.

Let σ'' be obtained from σ' by assigning to all the variables of P_r their corresponding values in τ, i.e.,

$$\sigma''(x) \stackrel{\text{def}}{=} \begin{cases} \tau(x) & \text{if } x \in var(P_r), \\ \sigma'(x) & \text{if } x \notin var(P_r). \end{cases}$$

Moreover, let σ''_i, for $i = 1, \dots, n$, be obtained from σ'' by assigning to the variables not belonging to process P_i their corresponding values in σ. We observe that $\sigma''_r = \tau$ and $\sigma''_i = \sigma'_i$, for $i \neq r$. Let $l''_i \stackrel{\text{def}}{=} l_i$, for $i \neq r$ and let $l'' \stackrel{\text{def}}{=} \langle l''_1, \dots, l''_n \rangle$. For $i = 1, \dots, n$, there exist computations $\langle s_i; \sigma \rangle \stackrel{\theta_i}{\longrightarrow} \langle l''_i; \sigma''_i \rangle$, hence $(\sigma, \sigma'', \theta) \in O_{l''}(P)$.

Since we have that the sum of the lengths of the following local computations $\langle s_i; \sigma \rangle \stackrel{\theta_i}{\longrightarrow} \langle l''_i; \sigma''_i \rangle$, $i = 1, \dots, n$, is one smaller than the sum of the lengths of the computations leading to l, we can apply the induction hypothesis: $\sigma'' \in \mathcal{M}_{l''} \llbracket P \rrbracket \sigma$, from which we derive by the internal transition $\langle l''_r; \sigma''_r \rangle \stackrel{\langle\rangle}{\longrightarrow} \langle l_r; \sigma'_r \rangle$ and Definition 4.1 that $\sigma' \in \mathcal{M}_l \llbracket P \rrbracket \sigma$.

Suppose now that both the local computations of P_k and P_j end with a communication. Since both θ_k and θ_j are projections of θ along the channels of P_k and P_j, respectively, we have that

- for some state τ_k and location l''_k of P_k, $\langle s_k; \sigma \rangle \stackrel{\theta'_k}{\longrightarrow} \langle l''_k; \tau_k \rangle$ and $\langle l''_k; \tau_k \rangle \stackrel{\langle(C,v)\rangle}{\longrightarrow} \langle l_k; \sigma'_k \rangle$, with $\theta_k = \theta'_k \cdot (C, v)$, and, similarly,
- for some state τ_j and location l''_j of P_j, $\langle s_j; \sigma \rangle \stackrel{\theta'_j}{\longrightarrow} \langle l''_j; \tau_j \rangle$ and $\langle l''_j; \tau_j \rangle \stackrel{\langle(C,v)\rangle}{\longrightarrow} \langle l_j; \sigma'_j \rangle$, with $\theta_j = \theta'_j \cdot (C, v)$.

Let σ'' be obtained similarly as above from σ' by assigning to all the variables of P_k and P_j their corresponding values in τ_k and τ_j, respectively.

Moreover, let σ''_i, for $i = 1, \dots, n$, be obtained from σ'' by assigning to the variables not belonging to process P_i their corresponding values in σ. We observe that $\sigma''_k = \tau_k$, $\sigma''_j = \tau_j$ and $\sigma''_i = \sigma'_i$, for $i \neq k$, $i \neq j$.

Let $l''_i \stackrel{\text{def}}{=} l_i$, for $i \neq k$, $i \neq j$ and let $l'' \stackrel{\text{def}}{=} \langle l''_1, \dots, l''_n \rangle$. There exist computations $\langle s_i; \sigma \rangle \stackrel{\theta'_i}{\longrightarrow} \langle l''_i; \sigma''_i \rangle$, for all $i = 1, \dots, n$. Consequently, $(\sigma, \sigma'', \theta') \in O_{l''}(P)$. Since the sum of the lengths of these local computations is smaller than the sum of the lengths of the computations leading to location l, we can apply the induction hypothesis: $\sigma'' \in \mathcal{M}_{l''} \llbracket P \rrbracket \sigma$, from which we derive by Definition 4.1 and the transitions $\langle l''_k; \sigma''_k \rangle \stackrel{\langle(C,v)\rangle}{\longrightarrow} \langle l_k; \sigma'_k \rangle$ and $\langle l''_j; \sigma''_j \rangle \stackrel{\langle(C,v)\rangle}{\longrightarrow} \langle l_j; \sigma'_j \rangle$ that $\sigma' \in \mathcal{M}_l \llbracket P \rrbracket \sigma$.

Conversely, that $\sigma' \in \mathcal{M}_l \llbracket P \rrbracket \sigma$ implies $(\sigma, \sigma', \theta) \in O_l(P)$ for some θ, can be proved by a straightforward induction on the length of the computation of

P (viewed as a sequential transition diagram). The proof itself is left as an exercise.   □

4.5.2 Semantic Completeness of the AFR-Method

Finally we are ready to establish semantic completeness of the AFR-method. Based on the compositional semantics O we define the following minimal predicates.

Definition 4.20 (Strongest l-condition for synchronous communication) We associate with a location l of a transition diagram P the strongest l-condition with respect to a given precondition φ:

$$SP_l(\varphi, P) \stackrel{\text{def}}{=} \{\sigma \mid \text{there exist } \sigma', \theta \text{ such that } \sigma' \models \varphi \text{ and } (\sigma', \sigma, \theta) \in O_l(P)\}. \quad \square$$

Let $P \equiv P_1 \| \cdots \| P_n$ be a closed system, and $\{\varphi\}P\{\psi\}$ be a valid correctness formula.

We encode the above semantics O by introducing for each component P_i of P a history variable h_i, denoting a finite sequence of communication records $\langle (C_1, v), \ldots, (C_k, v_k) \rangle$, and by transforming an input-output transition $l \stackrel{a}{\rightarrow} l'$ into a transition with action $a' \stackrel{\text{def}}{=} b; C!e \rightarrow f \circ g$, where $g(\sigma) \stackrel{\text{def}}{=} (\sigma : h_i \mapsto \sigma(h_i) \cdot (C, e(\sigma)))$ in the case $a \equiv b; C!e \rightarrow f$, and into a transition with action $a' \equiv b; C?x \rightarrow f \circ g$, where $g(\sigma) \stackrel{\text{def}}{=} (\sigma : h_i \mapsto \sigma(h_i) \cdot (C, \sigma(x)))$ in the case $a \equiv b; C?x \rightarrow f$ (here '$\cdot$' denotes the append operation). Observe that evaluation of a' in σ with $\models b(\sigma)$ results in evaluating the $f \circ g$-part of a' in state $(\sigma : x \rightarrow v)$, for arbitrary values v, according to Definition 4.13. This models that x has received its value in the $b; C?x$-part of a', i.e., prior to executing $f \circ g$. Let $P' \equiv P_1' \| \ldots \| P_n'$ denote the augmented transition diagram thus obtained (which is also closed).

The semantics of P_i' records its own sequence of communications θ_i, according to its O-semantics, in auxiliary variable h_i, as stated below.

Lemma 4.21 For $(\sigma, \sigma', \theta_i) \in O_{l_i}(P_i')$,

$$(\sigma(h_i) = \langle \rangle \wedge (\langle s; \sigma \rangle \stackrel{\theta_i}{\rightarrow} \langle l_i; \sigma' \rangle)) \Rightarrow \sigma'(h_i) = \theta_i.$$

Proof By induction on the length of the computation history θ_i.   □

Since O is correctly defined from an operational point of view, as proved in Theorem 4.19, we conclude that h_i records the correct communication history of process P_i.

After we have encoded the local communication histories θ_i into the history variables h_i by transforming P_i to P_i', we would like to associate with each location l_i of P_i' the predicate $SP_{l_i}(\varphi, P_i')$. However, since φ may involve variables of the other components, this choice of predicates is not allowed. To overcome this problem we introduce new logical variables $\bar{z}^i$, so-called *freeze* variables, corresponding to the variables $\bar{x}^i$ of P_i, and define

$$\varphi_i \stackrel{\text{def}}{=} \varphi \circ k \wedge \bar{z}^i = \bar{x}^i \wedge h_i = \langle \rangle,$$

where $k(\sigma) \stackrel{\text{def}}{=} (\sigma : \bar{x} \mapsto \sigma(\bar{z})), \bar{z} = \bar{z}^1, \ldots, \bar{z}^n$ and $\bar{x} = \bar{x}^1, \ldots, \bar{x}^n$.

So φ_i replaces in φ all the program variables $\bar{x}$ of P by their corresponding freeze variables $\bar{z}$ and identifies the freeze variables $\bar{z}^i$ with the corresponding local variables $\bar{x}^i$ of P_i (we define for sequences of variables $\bar{u} = (u_1, \ldots, u_m)$ and $\bar{v} = (v_1, \ldots, v_m)$, $\models \bar{u} = \bar{v}(\sigma)$ iff $\sigma(u_i) = \sigma(v_i)$, $1 \leq i \leq m$). Additionally φ_i initialises the history variable h_i to the empty sequence (denoted by $\langle \rangle$).

Let $\bar{u}$ be a set of program variables disjoint from $\bar{x}$ such that φ only involves the variables $\bar{x}$ and $\bar{u}$. It is not so difficult to check that $SP_{l_i}(\varphi_i, P_i')$ only involves the newly introduced freeze variables $\bar{z}$, the program variables of P_i', and the variables $\bar{u}$. Thus we derive that $SP_{l_i}(\varphi_i, P_i')$ does not involve the variables of the remaining components. This justifies the association of $SP_{l_i}(\varphi_i, P_i')$ with location l_i of P_i'.

The following example illustrates the need for freeze variables.

Example 4.22 Consider the correctness assertion

$$\{x_1 = x_2\} x_1 := x_1 + 1 \parallel x_2 := x_2 + 1 \{x_1 = x_2\}.$$

We cannot prove this assertion without introducing logical freeze variables because, according to Definition 4.8, in the local assertion network for $x_1 := x_1 + 1$ we are not allowed to refer to x_2, and vice versa. The solution is, of course, to use logical variables z_1 and z_2 for freezing the values of x_1 and x_2: $\{z_1 = z_2 \wedge x_1 = z_1\} x_1 := x_1 + 1 \{z_1 = z_2 \wedge x_1 = z_1 + 1\}$ and $\{z_1 = z_2 \wedge x_2 = z_2\} x_2 := x_2 + 1 \{z_1 = z_2 \wedge x_2 = z_2 + 1\}$. Also note that, e.g., $\sigma \models z_1 = z_2 \wedge x_1 = z_1$ iff $\sigma \models (x_1 = x_2) \circ k \wedge x_1 = z_1$, with k as defined above.

Since this example does not involve communication, we omitted the $h_i = \langle \rangle$-part from the definition of φ_i. $\qquad \square$

Next we introduce the global invariant $I(h_1, \ldots, h_n)$.

Definition 4.23 (Global invariant) Let $I(h_1, \ldots, h_n)$ be the predicate such that

$$\sigma \models I(h_1, \ldots, h_n) \text{ iff there exists } \theta \text{ such that}$$
$$\sigma(h_i) = \theta_i \text{ for every } i \in \{1, \ldots, n\},$$

where θ_i denotes the projection of θ along the channels of P_i.   □

The global invariant $I(h_1, \ldots, h_n)$ thus ensures the *compatibility* of the histories $h_1, \ldots, h_n$, i.e., that every value recorded as received is also recorded as being sent.

Intuitively, I characterises the *frontier of communication* of a network $P_1 \parallel \cdots \parallel P_n$. That is, if $\sigma \models I(h_1, \ldots, h_n)$ for a network $P_1 \parallel \cdots \parallel P_n$, then inside every process P_i $\sigma(h_i)$ expresses the communication history of P_i. This allows one to determine locally how far a global computation of a network has proceeded inside its processes.

We have the following compositional characterisation of the strongest post-condition operator defined above. This characterisation holds for both open and closed networks.

Theorem 4.24

Let $P \equiv P_1 \parallel \cdots \parallel P_n$, for some $n \geq 2$, be a synchronous diagram. We express the diagram P modified with updates to the history variables $h_1, \ldots, h_n$ by $P' \equiv P'_1 \parallel \cdots \parallel P'_n$. Let $l \equiv \langle l_1, \ldots, l_n \rangle$, with l_i a location of P'_i. We then have

$$\models I(h_1, \ldots, h_n) \wedge \bigwedge_i SP_{l_i}(\varphi_i, P'_i) \leftrightarrow SP_l(\bigwedge_i \varphi_i, P').$$

(Here the index i is implicitly assumed to range over $\{1, \ldots, n\}$.)

Proof Let $\sigma \models I \wedge \bigwedge_i SP_{l_i}(\varphi_i, P'_i)$. By the definition of SP it follows that there exist states σ_i and histories θ_i, such that $(\sigma_i, \sigma, \theta_i) \in O_{l_i}(P'_i)$ and $\sigma_i \models \varphi_i$. Since φ_i stipulates that $\sigma_i(h_i) = \langle\rangle$, we have by Lemma 4.21 that $\theta_i = \sigma(h_i)$. Let σ' be such that σ', σ_i agree w.r.t. the variables of P'_i, for $1 \leq i \leq n$, and σ', σ agree w.r.t. the remaining (logical) variables, and hence also agree with $\sigma_1, \ldots, \sigma_n$ w.r.t. these variables. It follows that $\sigma' \models \bigwedge_i \varphi_i$ and $(\sigma', \sigma'_i, \theta_i) \in O_{l_i}(P'_i)$, where σ'_i is obtained from σ by assigning to all the variables not belonging to P'_i their corresponding value in σ'. Since $\sigma \models I$ and $\theta_i = \sigma(h_i)$ we have that there exists a history θ such that θ_i equals the projection of θ along the channels of P'_i. By the compositionality of O we then derive that $(\sigma', \sigma, \theta) \in O_l(P')$. In other words: $\sigma \in SP_l(\bigwedge_i \varphi_i, P')$.

To prove the other direction, let $\sigma \models SP_l(\bigwedge_i \varphi_i, P')$. So for some state σ' such that $\sigma' \models \bigwedge_i \varphi_i$ we have that $(\sigma', \sigma, \theta) \in O_l(P')$, for some θ. By the compositionality of O we derive that $(\sigma', \sigma_i, \theta_i) \in O_{l_i}(P'_i)$, where θ_i denotes the projection of θ along the channels of P'_i and σ_i is obtained from σ by assigning to all the variables not belonging to P'_i their corresponding value in σ'. Thus by definition of SP and the fact that σ and σ_i by definition agree w.r.t. the variables of P'_i and the remaining variables of φ_i, we have that $\sigma \models SP_{l_i}(\varphi_i, P'_i)$.

Moreover since $\sigma'(h_i) = \langle \rangle$, for $1 \leq i \leq n$, we have by construction of P_i' that $\sigma(h_i) = \sigma_i(h_i) = \theta_i$, $1 \leq i \leq n$, i.e., $\sigma \models I$.   □

Local correctness of a component is straightforward:

Lemma 4.25 (Local correctness) For each internal transition $l \overset{a}{\to} l'$ of a transition system P_i', with $a \equiv b \to f$, we have

$$\models SP_l(\varphi_i, P_i') \wedge b \to SP_{l'}(\varphi_i, P_i') \circ f.$$

Proof Left as an exercise.   □

Lemma 4.26 (Cooperation test) Let $l_1 \overset{a}{\to} l_2$ occur in P_i' and $l_1' \overset{a'}{\to} l_2'$ in P_j', with $a \equiv b; C!e \to f$ and $a' \equiv b'; C?x \to g$. Furthermore, let $I(h_1, \ldots, h_n)$ be the compatibility predicate defined above. We then have

$$\models I \wedge SP_{l_1}(\varphi_i, P_i') \wedge SP_{l_1'}(\varphi_j, P_j') \wedge b \wedge b'$$
$$\to (I \wedge SP_{l_2}(\varphi_i, P_i') \wedge SP_{l_2'}(\varphi_j, P_j')) \circ f',$$

where $f' \overset{\text{def}}{=} (f \circ g \circ (x := e))$.

Proof In fact we prove the following implications:

$$\models I \to I \circ f', \quad \models SP_{l_1}(\varphi_i, P_i') \wedge b \to SP_{l_2}(\varphi_i, P_i') \circ f'$$

and

$$\models SP_{l_1'}(\varphi_j, P_j') \wedge b' \to SP_{l_2'}(\varphi_j, P_j') \circ f'.$$

In order to prove the validity of $I \to I \circ f'$, let $\sigma \models I$ and $f'(\sigma) = \sigma'$. By the construction of P_i' and P_j' it follows that $\sigma'(h_i) = \sigma(h_i) \cdot (C, v)$ and $\sigma'(h_j) = \sigma(h_j) \cdot (C, v)$, where $v = e(\sigma)$. Moreover $\sigma'(h_k) = \sigma(h_k)$, for $k \neq i, j$. Thus by definition of I it follows immediately that $\sigma' \models I$.

Next we prove that $\models SP_{l_1}(\varphi_i, P_i') \wedge b \to SP_{l_2}(\varphi_i, P_i') \circ f'$. Let $\sigma \models SP_{l_1}(\varphi_i, P_i') \wedge b$. So there exist σ' and θ such that $\sigma' \models \varphi_i$ and $(\sigma', \sigma, \theta) \in O_{l_1}(P_i')$. By definition of O it follows immediately that $(\sigma', f(\sigma), \theta \cdot (C, v)) \in O_{l_2}(P_i')$, where $v = e(\sigma)$. By definition of SP we thus derive that $f(\sigma) \models SP_{l_2}(\varphi_i, P_i')$. Since $SP_{l_2}(\varphi_i, P_i')$ only involves the variables of P_i' and the freeze variables $\bar{z}$, we thus may conclude that $f'(\sigma) \models SP_{l_2}(\varphi_i, P_i')$, that is, $\sigma \models SP_{l_2}(\varphi_i, P_i') \circ f'$.

In order to prove the validity of the last implication, let $\sigma \models SP_{l_1'}(\varphi_j, P_j')$. So there exist σ' and θ such that $\sigma' \models \varphi_j$ and $(\sigma', \sigma, \theta) \in O_{l_1'}(P_j')$. By definition of O it follows that $(\sigma', g(\sigma : x \mapsto v), \theta \cdot (C, v)) \in O_{l_2'}(P_j')$, for any value v. So in particular we have that $(\sigma', g(\sigma : x \mapsto v), \theta \cdot (C, v)) \in O_{l_2'}(P_j')$, for $v = e(\sigma)$,

from which we derive by definition of SP that $g \circ x := e(\sigma) \models SP_{l'_2}(\varphi_i, P'_j)$.
Since $SP_{l'_2}(\varphi_j, P'_j)$ only involves the variables of P'_j we thus may conclude that
$f'(\sigma) \models SP_{l'_2}(\varphi_j, P'_j)$, that is, $\sigma \models SP_{l'_2}(\varphi_j, P'_j) \circ f'$. $\square$

We conclude the completeness proof with the remaining clauses.

Lemma 4.27 (Initialisation) We have

$$\models \varphi \to (I \wedge \bigwedge_i SP_{s_i}(\varphi_i, P'_i) \circ f),$$

where f assigns to history variable h_i the empty sequence $\langle\rangle$ and assigns to
every freeze variable z the value of its corresponding (program) variable x.

Proof Let $\sigma \models \varphi$. It follows that $f(\sigma) \models \varphi_i$ (note that h_i is assumed not to
occur in φ). Furthermore we have that $(f(\sigma), f(\sigma), \langle\rangle) \in O_{s_i}(P'_i)$, so we have
that $f(\sigma) \models \bigwedge_i SP_{s_i}(\varphi_i, P'_i)$. Since $f(\sigma)(h_i)$ equals the empty sequence $\langle\rangle$ it
trivially follows that $f(\sigma) \models I$. $\square$

Lemma 4.28 (Finalisation) We have

$$\models I \wedge \bigwedge_i SP_{t_i}(\varphi_i, P'_i) \to \psi.$$

Proof Let $\sigma \models I \wedge \bigwedge_i SP_{t_i}(\varphi_i, P'_i)$. By Theorem 4.24 we derive that $\sigma \models$
$SP_t(\bigwedge_i \varphi_i, P')$, where t denotes the final label of P'. By definition of SP we
thus have for some state σ' and sequence of communications θ that $\sigma' \models \bigwedge_i \varphi_i$
and $(\sigma', \sigma, \theta) \in O_t(P)$. Since $P'_1 \| \ldots \| P'_n$ contains no external channels, by the
correctness of O (Theorem 4.19) we obtain that $\sigma \in \mathcal{M}[\![P']\!]\sigma'$. Furthermore
observe that since $\bigwedge_i \varphi_i$ implies φ, $\sigma' \models \varphi$. Now the validity of $\{\varphi\}P\{\psi\}$ implies that of $\{\varphi\}P'\{\psi\}$, since the auxiliary variables h_i do not occur in φ, ψ.
So we conclude that $\sigma \models \psi$. $\square$

As a consequence we have proved the following theorem.

Theorem 4.29 (Semantic Completeness)
The proof method of Apt, Francez & de Roever is semantically complete. $\square$

4.5.3 Technical Note: Semantic Completeness of the Method of Levin & Gries

For proving semantic completeness of the method of Levin & Gries we essentially apply the same methodology for proving completeness using a composi-

tional semantics as presented for the AFR-method, and prove completeness of the method of Levin & Gries following steps (i)–(vi) of Definition 4.9.

Let $P \equiv P_1 \parallel \cdots \parallel P_n$ be a closed system, and $\{\varphi\}P\{\psi\}$ a valid correctness formula. We encode the semantics O of P by adding only one *global* auxiliary variable h to the program P. This auxiliary variable records the *global* history. We transform every output transition $(l, b; C!e \to f, l')$ into a transition (l, a', l') with action $a' \equiv b; C!e \to f \circ k$, where $k(\sigma) \stackrel{\text{def}}{=} (\sigma : h \mapsto \sigma(h) \cdot (C, e(\sigma)))$. The resulting augmented program $P_1' \parallel \ldots \parallel P_n'$ will be denoted by P'. As before, we implicitly assume that the domain of values contains histories. Observe that the semantics of P' is given by Definition 4.10.

In order to obtain a compositional semantics for the separate processes P_i' in isolation, we use the same *labelled* transition relation as defined in Definition 4.13 for providing a semantics of input-output transitions; but we also have to adapt Definition 4.14 to the case of the *shared* auxiliary variable h. Note that Definition 4.14 only records the local state changes since the underlying model deals with disjoint sets of variables. For our annotated system we have to ignore the global variable h in our local semantics, since the value of this global variable can in general only be determined globally.

Definition 4.30 Let $P \equiv P_1 \parallel \cdots \parallel P_n$, $P' \equiv P_1' \parallel \ldots \parallel P_n'$ be augmented transition diagrams as constructed above, and l occur in P_i'. We define

$$O_l(P_i') \stackrel{\text{def}}{=} \{(\sigma \mid_{var(P)}, \sigma' \mid_{var(P)}, \theta_i) \mid \langle s; \sigma \rangle \xrightarrow{\theta_i} \langle l; \sigma' \rangle\}.$$

Here $\sigma \mid_{var(P)}$ expresses the restriction of σ' to the original state space, i.e., $\Sigma \setminus \{h\}$, and the labelled transition relation is given by Definition 4.13. $\qquad \square$

The semantics of the closed system $P' \equiv P_1' \parallel \ldots \parallel P_n'$ is described similarly to Definition 4.17.

Definition 4.31 Let $P' \equiv P_1' \parallel \ldots \parallel P_n'$, $l \equiv \langle l_1, \ldots l_n \rangle$, and l_i occur in P_i'.

$$O_l(P') \stackrel{\text{def}}{=} \{((\sigma : h \mapsto \langle \rangle), (\sigma' : h \mapsto \theta)) \mid (\sigma, \sigma_i', \theta_i) \in O_{l_i}(P_i')\},$$

where $\theta_i = \theta \downarrow Chan(P_i')$, and, since only the program variables of P_i' are subject to change in $O_{l_i}(P_i')$, the global state σ' is the 'collection' of the changes σ_i' to the disjoint sets of program variables. Formally one has:

$$\sigma'(x) \stackrel{\text{def}}{=} \sigma_i'(x) \text{ for } i = 1, \ldots, n \text{ and } x \in var(P_i). \qquad \square$$

The crucial question for the local semantics is where to mention the value of the history variable h. Notice that for all computations of P' the projection of the value of history variable h corresponds with the value of the history of the O semantics for each process P_i' of Definition 4.30, similarly to Lemma 4.21.

In fact we have:

Theorem 4.32 (Correctness of the compositional semantics)
Let $P' \equiv P_1' \| \dots \| P_n'$ denote the closed product of the augmented processes $P_1', \dots, P_n'$ and t denote the exit location of P'. Then we have

$$\sigma' \in \mathcal{M} \llbracket P' \rrbracket \sigma \text{ iff } (\sigma, \sigma') \in O_t(P').$$

Proof The proof follows the same lines as the proof of Theorem 4.19 and is proved by induction on the sum of the lengths of the local computations. $\square$

As with the proof method of Apt, Francez & de Roever, we want to associate with each location l of P_i' a strongest postcondition w.r.t. precondition $\varphi \wedge h = \langle \rangle$. Again since φ may involve the variables of other components we have to introduce logical (freeze) variables $\bar{z}^i$ corresponding to the variables $\bar{x}^i$ of P_i, and define $\varphi_i \stackrel{\text{def}}{=} \varphi \circ g \wedge \bar{z}^i = \bar{x}^i \wedge h = \langle \rangle$, as on page 256.

In order to obtain sufficient information about the history for a sequential process only the projection onto the involved channels is needed; yet since h is a *global* variable, each process records the value of h only in so far as it is consistent with that projection. This is reflected in the definition of the strongest postcondition of a sequential process which refers to the local variables of a process and to the value of the global history variable.

Definition 4.33 We associate with a location l of a sequential synchronous transition diagram P_i' the strongest l-condition with respect to a given precondition φ_i:

$$SP_l(\varphi_i, P_i') \stackrel{\text{def}}{=} \{(\sigma : h \mapsto \theta) \mid \text{ there exists } \sigma' \text{ such that } \sigma' \models \varphi_i$$
$$\text{and } (\sigma', \sigma, \theta{\downarrow}Chan(P_i')) \in O_l(P_i')\}. \qquad \square$$

The value of h in $SP_l(\varphi_i, P_i')$ is therefore only determined by its projection upon the channels of P_i'.

In order to prove completeness, we annotate the processes P_i' using the assertion networks $SP_l(\varphi_i, P_i')$ for $l \in L_i$ and check steps (iii)–(vi) of Definition 4.9.

Local correctness of an annotated component is still straightforward.

Lemma 4.34 (Local correctness) For every internal transition $l \stackrel{a}{\to} l'$ of a transition system P_i', with $a \equiv b \to f$, we have

$$\models SP_l(\varphi_i, P_i') \wedge b \to SP_{l'}(\varphi_i, P_i') \circ f$$

Proof Let $\sigma \models SP_l(\varphi_i, P_i')$ and $\sigma \models b$.

By definition of $SP_l(\varphi_i, P_i')$ there exist σ' and θ such that $\sigma' \models \varphi_i$ and $(\sigma', \sigma, \theta \downarrow Chan(P_i)) \in O_l(P_i'))$. By Definition 4.30 of O, we have that $(\sigma', f(\sigma), \theta \downarrow Chan(P_i)) \in O_{l'}(P_i')$. Again by definition of $SP_{l'}(\varphi_i, P_i')$ we have that $(f(\sigma) : h \mapsto \theta) \models SP_{l'}(\varphi_i, P_i')$, and since f does not involve h and $\sigma(h) = \theta$, $f(\sigma) \models SP_{l'}(\varphi_i, P_i')$. $\square$

The effect of synchronous communication is dealt with using the cooperation test.

Lemma 4.35 (Cooperation Test) Let $l_i \xrightarrow{a} l_i'$ occur in P_i' and $l_j \xrightarrow{a'} l_j'$ in P_j', with $a \equiv b; C!e \to f \circ k$ and $a' \equiv b'; C?x \to g$. Then we have

$$\models SP_{l_i}(\varphi_i, P_i') \wedge SP_{l_j}(\varphi_j, P_j') \wedge b \wedge b' \to (SP_{l_i'}(\varphi_i, P_i') \wedge SP_{l_j'}(\varphi_j, P_j')) \circ f'$$

where $f' \stackrel{\text{def}}{=} (f \circ g \circ k \circ x := e)$.

Proof First we prove $\models SP_{l_i}(\varphi_i, P_i') \wedge b \to SP_{l_i'}(\varphi_i, P_i') \circ f'$.

Let $\sigma \models SP_{l_i}(\varphi_i, P_i') \wedge b$.

Then there exist σ' and θ such that

$$\sigma' \models \varphi_i \text{ and } (\sigma', \sigma_i \mid_{var(P)}, \theta \downarrow Chan(P_i')) \in O_{l_i}(P_i'),$$

where

$$\forall x \in var(P).\sigma_i(x) \stackrel{\text{def}}{=} \begin{cases} \sigma(x) & \text{if } x \in var(P_i'), \\ \sigma'(x) & \text{if } x \notin var(P_i') \end{cases}$$

By Definitions 4.13 and 4.30 we have that $(\sigma', f(\sigma_i), \theta \downarrow Chan(P_i') \cdot (C, e(\sigma))) \in O_{l_i'}(P_i')$.

Thus we have $(f(\sigma) : h \mapsto \theta \cdot (C, e(\sigma))) \in SP_{l_i'}(\varphi_i, P_i')$, i.e., $(f \circ k)(\sigma) \models SP_{l_i'}(\varphi_i, P_i')$.

Since $SP_{l_i'}(\varphi_i, P_i')$ involves only the local variables of P_i' and h, and neither g nor $(x := e)$ involve these local variables of P_i' or the auxiliary variable h we conclude that $f'(\sigma) \models SP_{l_i'}(\varphi_i, P_i')$, that is, $\sigma \models SP_{l_i'}(\varphi_i, P_i') \circ f'$.

Next we prove $\models SP_{l_j}(\varphi_j, P_j') \wedge b' \to SP_{l_j'}(\varphi_j, P_j') \circ f'$.

Let $\sigma \models SP_{l_j}(\varphi_j, P_j')$. There exist σ' and θ such that

$$\sigma' \models \varphi_j \text{ and } (\sigma', \sigma_j \mid_{var(P)}, \theta \downarrow Chan(P_j')) \in O_{l_j}(P_j').$$

where $\sigma_j(x)$ is defined analogously to the case above. By Definitions 4.13 and 4.30 we have that $(\sigma', g(\sigma : x \mapsto v), \theta \downarrow Chan(P_j') \cdot (C, v)) \in O_{l_j'}(P_j')$ for an arbitrary value v. In particular for $v = e(\sigma)$ we conclude that $g \circ (x := e)(\sigma : h \mapsto \theta \cdot (C, e(\sigma))) \models SP_{l_j'}(\varphi_j, P_j')$. Since $SP_{l_j'}(\varphi_j, P_j')$ involves only the variables of P'_j, and f involves none of these variables, $f'(\sigma) \models SP_{l'_j}(\varphi_j, P'_j)$, as was to be shown. $\qquad\square$

Since our formulation of $SP_l(\varphi_i, P'_i)$ refers to program variables and the value of h without projection, we need an interference freedom test to cope with the problems caused by the shared variable h.

Lemma 4.36 (Interference Freedom) Let $l_i \xrightarrow{a} l'_i$ occur in P'_i and $l_j \xrightarrow{a'} l'_j$ in P'_j, with $a \equiv b; C!e \to f \circ k$ and $a' \equiv b'; C?x \to g$. Let l be a location of P_m, $m \neq j, m \neq i$. Then

$$\models SP_{l_i}(\varphi_i, P'_i) \wedge SP_{l_j}(\varphi_j, P'_j) \wedge SP_l(\varphi_m, P'_m) \wedge b \wedge b' \to (SP_l(\varphi_m, P'_m)) \circ f',$$

where $f' \stackrel{\text{def}}{=} (f \circ g \circ k \circ x := e)$.

Proof It is sufficient to prove $\models SP_l(\varphi_m, P'_m) \to (SP_l(\varphi_m, P'_m)) \circ f'$.

Let $\sigma \models SP_l(\varphi_m, P'_m)$. There exist σ' and θ such that

$$\sigma' \models \varphi_m \text{ and } (\sigma', \sigma_m \mid_{var(P)}, \theta \downarrow Chan(P'_m)) \in O_l(P'_m),$$

where $\sigma_m(x)$ is defined analogously to the case above.

Since $(\theta \cdot (C, v)) \downarrow Chan(P'_m) = \theta \downarrow Chan(P'_m)$ holds for arbitrary v (because $C \notin Chan(P'_m)$), we conclude also that $(\sigma', \sigma_m \mid_{var(P)}, \theta \cdot (C, e(\sigma)) \downarrow Chan(P'_m)) \in O_l(P'_m)$ and $k(\sigma) \in SP_l(\varphi_m, P'_m)$. Since $SP_l(\varphi_m, P'_m)$ only involves the variables of P'_m, neither g nor f involves the variables of P'_m, and P'_m does not involve x, we conclude that $f'(\sigma) \models SP_l(\varphi_m, P'_m)$. $\qquad\square$

We conclude the completeness proof with the remaining clauses.

Lemma 4.37 (Initialisation) We have

$$\models \varphi \to (\bigwedge_i SP_{s_i}(\varphi_i, P'_i) \circ f),$$

where f assigns to history variable h the empty sequence $\langle \rangle$, and assigns to every freeze variable z the value of its corresponding (program) variable x.

Proof Let $\sigma \models \varphi$. It follows that $f(\sigma) \models \varphi_i$. Furthermore we have that $(f(\sigma), f(\sigma), \langle \rangle) \in O_{s_i}(P'_i)$, so we have that $f(\sigma) \models \bigwedge_i SP_{s_i}(\varphi_i, P'_i)$. $\qquad\square$

Lemma 4.38 (Finalisation) We have

$$\models \bigwedge_i SP_{t_i}(\varphi_i, P'_i) \to \psi.$$

Proof Let $\sigma \models \bigwedge_i SP_{t_i}(\varphi_i, P_i')$. By Definition 4.33 of *SP* there exist states σ_i such that $(\sigma_i, \sigma, \theta \downarrow Chan(P_i')) \in O_{t_i}(P_i')$ and $\sigma_i \models \varphi_i$, where $\theta = \sigma(h)$. Note that φ_i stipulates that $\sigma_i(h) = \langle \rangle$ for all $i = 1, \ldots, n$.

We define σ' as follows:

$$\sigma'(x) \stackrel{\text{def}}{=} \begin{cases} \sigma_i(x) & \text{if } x \in var(P_i), \\ \sigma(x) & \text{if } x \in Lvar, \\ \langle \rangle & \text{if } x = h. \end{cases}$$

It follows that $\sigma' \models \bigwedge_i \varphi_i$ and $(\sigma', \sigma_i', \theta \downarrow Chan(P_i')) \in O_{t_i}(P_i')$, where σ_i' is obtained from σ by assigning to all the variables not belonging to P_i' their corresponding value in σ'. Then, by Definition 4.31 we have that $(\sigma', \sigma) \in O_t(P')$ where t denotes the final label of P'.

We thus have some state σ' such that $\sigma' \models \bigwedge_i \varphi_i$ and $(\sigma', \sigma) \in O_t(P')$. Since P' contains no external channels, by the correctness of O we obtain that $\sigma \in \mathcal{M}[\![P']\!] \sigma'$. Furthermore observe that since $\bigwedge_i \varphi_i$ implies φ, $\sigma' \models \varphi$. Since the validity of $\{\varphi\} P \{\psi\}$ implies that of $\{\varphi\} P' \{\psi\}$, we conclude that $\sigma \models \psi$. $\Box$

As a consequence we have proved the following theorem.

Theorem 4.39
The proof method of Levin & Gries is semantically complete. $\Box$

4.6 Technical Note: Modifications Towards Compositionality

Now that we have developed a sound and semantically complete proof system we observe that we can give a proof for a synchronous transition diagram only if the entire composed transition diagram is available in order to determine the corresponding assertion networks for each single sequential synchronous transition diagram and then check for cooperation and interference freedom. However, our very aim is to develop a *compositional* proof system where we can give proofs for each process in isolation and combine them to a distributed program *without precise knowledge about the internal details of each process*. On the basis of the proof system developed by Levin & Gries and the foundations of its completeness proof we can restrict ourselves in the use of auxiliary variables to a *single global history variable* only and simplify proofs by removing the interference freedom test and the cooperation test due to restrictions on the assertions allowed in the inductive assertion networks for the components.

Observe that the proof system given in the previous section is not compositional, since the rule for parallel composition contains both a cooperation and an interference freedom test, each of which requires the complete program text of the processes involved to be known.

In this section we discuss how this noncompositional method can be adapted to obtain a compositional proof system. In general, proofs in the methods described in [AFdR80, LG81] will use different auxiliary variables for different programs. The first idea is to use the same auxiliary variable for the proofs of all programs. This is justified by the completeness proof given in Section 4.6.3, discussing semantic completeness of the method of Levin & Gries. This completeness result shows that any valid correctness formula for a parallel program can be proved by adding a single, global, history variable h to the program. This variable records the global communication history of the whole program during its execution.

Definition 4.40 In order to prove that P is partially correct w.r.t. specification $< \varphi, \psi >$ we change point (i) of Definition 4.9 as follows:

(i) Augment P_i by introducing a single auxiliary variable h; every output transition $b; C!e \to f$ is extended as follows: $b; C!e \to f \circ k$, where $k(\sigma) \stackrel{\text{def}}{=} (\sigma : h \mapsto h \cdot (C, e(\sigma)))$. This leads to an augmented synchronous transition diagram $P' \equiv P'_1 \parallel \ldots \parallel P'_n$. $\qquad\square$

We show next that we can remove the interference freedom and the cooperation tests from the method of Levin & Gries, once this single auxiliary variable is used.

4.6.1 Removing the Cooperation Test

Recall that the cooperation test has been introduced to verify the postconditions of io-statements in the local proof of a process. These assertions represent assumptions about the communication behaviour of the environment of this process. We can impose some restrictions on these assertions associated with a location after a communication step. After an output transition $b; C!e \to f \circ g$ both f (which is local to that process) and g (which only changes h) should be taken into account when evaluating the assertion after the transition. The case of an input transition is more complicated. In order to verify local correctness of an input transition we have to formulate the assertion associated with the location reached by this transition in such a way that the verification condition holds for any possible value received from the environment. This is achieved by changing in Definition 4.40 the requirements for proving local correctness of process P'_i.

Definition 4.41 Change Definition 4.40 by replacing point (iii) taken from Definition 4.9 as follows:

(iii) Prove *local correctness* of every P_i':

- For every internal transition $l \xrightarrow{a} l'$ of P_i', assuming $a \equiv b \to f$, we prove

$$\models Q_l \wedge b \to Q_{l'} \circ f.$$

- For $l \xrightarrow{a} l'$ an output transition of P_i', i.e., $a \equiv b; C!e \to f \circ g$, for some boolean b, channel C, state-transformation f and history update $g(\sigma) \overset{\text{def}}{=} (\sigma : h \mapsto \sigma(h) \cdot (C, e(\sigma)))$, one has

$$\models Q_l \wedge b \to Q_{l'} \circ (f \circ g).$$

- For $l \xrightarrow{a} l'$ an input transition of P_i', i.e., $a \equiv b; C?x \to f$, for some boolean b, channel C and state-transformation f, one has

$$\models Q_l \wedge b \to \forall x. Q_{l'} \circ (f \circ g),$$

where $g(\sigma) \overset{\text{def}}{=} (\sigma : h \mapsto \sigma(h) \cdot (C, \sigma(x)))$.   □

In general, we can prove that, when using the proof method of Levin & Gries restricted as above, the cooperation test is *always* fulfilled.

Proof Suppose that $l_1 \xrightarrow{a} l_2$ is a transition of P_i' and $l_1' \xrightarrow{a'} l_2'$ is a transition of P_j', with $j \neq i$, $a \equiv b; C!e \to f \circ k$ and $a' \equiv b'; C?x \to g$.

Then

$$\models Q_{l_1} \wedge b \to Q_{l_2} \circ (f \circ k),$$

and

$$\models Q_{l_1'} \wedge b' \to \forall v Q_{l_2'} \circ (g \circ \zeta),$$

where $\zeta(\sigma) \overset{\text{def}}{=} (\sigma : h \mapsto \sigma(h) \cdot (C, \sigma(x)))$.

In particular, we have for $x = e(\sigma)$

$$\models Q_{l_1'} \wedge b' \to Q_{l_2'} \circ (g \circ \zeta),$$

where $\zeta(\sigma) \overset{\text{def}}{=} (\sigma : x, h \mapsto e(\sigma), \sigma(h) \cdot (C, e(\sigma))) = (k \circ (x := e))(\sigma)$.

Since $x \in var(P_j')$, x does not occur in assertions of P_i', and neither do $var(g)$, hence we also have

$$\models Q_{l_1} \wedge b \to Q_{l_2} \circ (f \circ g \circ k \circ (x := e)).$$

Similarly, $var(f) \cap var(P_j') = \emptyset$ and we have

$$\models Q_{l_1'} \wedge b' \to Q_{l_2'} \circ (f \circ g \circ k \circ (x := e)).$$

Combining these implications we have

$$\models Q_{l_1} \wedge Q_{l_1'} \wedge b' \wedge b \rightarrow Q_{l_2} \wedge Q_{l_2'} \circ (f \circ g \circ k \circ (x := e)),$$

as required for the cooperation test. □

4.6.2 Removing the Interference Freedom Test

The main idea for removing the interference freedom test is to use projections on the history variable.

Recall that the interference freedom test is required because variable h denotes the communication history of the complete diagram and h might occur in the assertions of each process. Hence these assertions can refer to the global trace of the complete diagram. For instance, a process that only communicates on channels A and B is allowed to use h in its assertions, and thus can state properties about a channel C connecting other processes. This can be avoided by the following requirement:

> In a proof for a program $P_1 \| \cdots \| P_n$ the assertions associated with the locations of process P_i only refer to h by means of projections onto channels of P_i, that is, any assertion Q_l associated with a location l of P_i depends at most on $h{\downarrow}cset$ with $cset \subseteq Chan(P_i)$, for $i = 1, \dots, n$.

By this restriction each process only uses its own view of the global history. What it asserts about the global trace is directly under its control and cannot be changed by other processes without participation of the process itself. To avoid interference by assignments in other processes we impose the following requirement.

> In a proof for a diagram $P_1 \| \cdots \| P_n$ all program variables occurring in assertions associated with locations of process P_i are program variables of P_i, for $i = 1, \dots, n$. Thus if $x \in var(P_1 \| \dots \| P_n)$ and x occurs in the assertion network for process P_i then $x \in var(P_i)$, for $i = 1, \dots, n$, i.e., $x \notin var(P_j)$ for $j \neq i$.

Since processes do not share variables, this requirement implies that an assertion network for one process does not refer to program variables of other processes.

Next we argue that due to these two requirements the interference freedom test is trivially satisfied and hence not needed. By the restriction above, the only variable (in the assertion network of a process) that might change by executing statements in other processes is history variable h.

Proof To prove interference freedom, let $l_1 \xrightarrow{a} l_2$ be a transition of P_i' and $l_1' \xrightarrow{a'} l_2'$ be a transition of of P_j', with $j \neq i$, $a \equiv b;C!e \to f \circ k$ and $a' \equiv b';C?x \to g$, and predicate Q_l is associated with a location l of process P_m', $m \neq i$, $m \neq j$. Assume that

$$\sigma \models Q_{l_1} \wedge Q_{l_1'} \wedge Q_l \wedge b \wedge b',$$

then we have to prove that

$$\sigma \models Q_l \circ (f \circ g \circ k \circ (x := e)).$$

Since $var(f) \subseteq var(P_i)$, $var(g) \subseteq var(P_j)$ and $x \in var(P_j)$ we have from the fact that $var(P_m) \cap var(P_i) = \emptyset$ and $var(P_m) \cap var(P_j) = \emptyset$ immediately that

$$\sigma \models Q_l \circ (f \circ g \circ (x := e)).$$

The only crucial operation is the extension of the shared history variable h by k, since $k(\sigma) = (\sigma : h \mapsto \sigma(h) \cdot (C, e(\sigma)))$.

Q_l depends at most on $h \downarrow cset$ with $cset \subseteq Chan(P_m')$.

Since channel C connects P_i and P_j and a channel connects at most two processes, we have $C \notin Chan(P_m)$, and thus $C \notin cset$. But then the value of Q_l is not affected by the assignment $h := h \cdot (C, e)$, since $h \downarrow cset = (h \cdot (C, e(\sigma))) \downarrow cset$ and hence Q_l remains valid under the C-communication.   □

4.6.3 Towards a Compositional Method

Summarising, we have removed the interference freedom test and the cooperation test as follows:

(i) Always use a single auxiliary variable h which records the global communication history of the program. Therefore each output statement $b;C!e \to f$ in the program is transformed into $b;C!e \to f \circ g$, where $g(h) \stackrel{\text{def}}{=} h \cdot (C, e)$.

(ii) Require that assertions in an assertion network of a process refer only to program variables of the process itself and to h by means of projections onto the channels of that process.

(iii) Require the assertion associated with a location immediately after an input transition to be valid for all possible values sent by the environment.

Using Definition 4.9 we obtain

Rule 4.1   There exist inductive assertion networks Q_i for P_i',
which prove local correctness of P_i', $i = 1, \ldots, n$,

$$\frac{\varphi \to \bigwedge_{i=1}^n Q_{s_i}, \ \bigwedge_{i=1}^n Q_{J_i} \to \psi}{\{\varphi\} \ P_1 \| \cdots \| P_n \ \{\psi\}}$$

provided

- each output transition $b; C!e \to f$ is annotated by an assignment g to h where $g(h) \stackrel{\text{def}}{=} h \cdot (C, e)$.
- all program variables occurring in an assertion network of P_i' are program variables of P_i', for $i = 1, \ldots, n$, and
- history variable h occurs in an assertion network for P_i' only in the form $h\downarrow cset$ with $cset \subseteq Chan(P_i')$, for $i = 1, \ldots, n$.

Note that the resulting method leaves no freedom of choice for the auxiliary variables used and the operations performed upon them. We have a canonical annotation scheme which is not subject to change throughout the verification process.

By always using the same, standard, auxiliary variable there is no need to augment programs explicitly with assignments to this auxiliary variable. We can remove the actual task of annotating programs with canonical assignments to h by using a logical variable h which can be updated implicitly in the semantics of programs, as a consequence of which no auxiliary variables rule is needed to remove them.

Observe that in Rule 4.1 only the pre- and postconditions of the assertion networks are used, i.e., we do not refer anymore to the internal details of the processes P_i when applying Rule 4.1. Thus we have succeeded in the development of a compositional rule out of the method of Levin & Gries. In Chapter 7 we develop a compositional proof rule for parallel composition directly out of the compositional semantics introduced in Section 4.5.1 which is similar to Rule 4.1.

4.7 A Modular Method for Proving Convergence

In this section, we investigate how to extend the AFR-method to proving φ-convergence of distributed processes communicating by synchronous message passing, in the same way as the Owicki & Gries method is extended to proving φ-convergence of shared-variable concurrent programs in Section 3.6.

We use the same notations as in the previous sections: for example, the program P concerned is $P_1 \| \ldots \| P_n$; the augmented program P' is $P_1' \| \ldots \| P_n'$, etc. Basically, to every local location l in P_i', we associate a ranking-function ρ_l

in such a way that any local transition from P'_i decreases the ranking function, and any communication transition between P'_i and P'_j decreases the pair of ranking functions for P'_i and P'_j according to the componentwise order given in Definition 3.55. When these conditions are satisfied, it follows that there exists a network of global ranking functions (composed of the local ranking functions in the same way as in the shared variable case), which decreases along any transition of P' according to the componentwise order; hence, convergence is guaranteed.

Definition 4.42 (A proof method for convergence à la AFR) Given $P \equiv P_1 \parallel \ldots \parallel P_n$ with locations $L \equiv L_1 \times \ldots \times L_n$.

Prove as follows that P is convergent w.r.t. precondition φ:

(i) Same as the clauses of Definition 4.8 (except for the last point of clause (v) which is deleted).

(ii) Choose wellfounded sets $(W_i, \prec_i)$, $i = 1, \ldots, n$, and a network of ranking-functions $\rho \stackrel{\text{def}}{=} \{\rho_l \mid l \in L_i\}$, satisfying the following conditions. It is required that ρ_l ($l \in L_i$) does not involve variables of the other components. Prove that the assertion and ranking-function networks are *locally* consistent, namely, assertion Q_l implies that ranking-function ρ_l is defined: For every state σ,

$$\sigma \models Q_l \Rightarrow \rho_l(\sigma) \in W_i.$$

And moreover, for every internal transition $l \xrightarrow{a} l'$ of P'_i, with $a \equiv b \to f$ prove that

$$\models Q_l \wedge b \to \rho_l \succ_i (\rho_{l'} \circ f).$$

(iii) Prove that the local ranking functions *cooperate*: i.e., for every pair of transitions $l_1 \xrightarrow{a} l_2$ of P'_i and $l'_1 \xrightarrow{a'} l'_2$ of P'_j, with $j \neq i$, $a \equiv b;C!e \to f$ and $a' \equiv b';C?x \to g$, or vice versa, prove that

$$\models (Q_{l_1} \wedge Q_{l'_1} \wedge I \wedge b \wedge b') \to [(\rho_{l_1}, \rho_{l'_1}) \succ (\rho_{l_2} \circ h, \rho_{l'_2} \circ h)],$$

where $h \stackrel{\text{def}}{=} f \circ g \circ x := e$ and $(W_i \times W_j, \prec)$ is the componentwise order over $(W_i, \prec_i)$ and $(W_j, \prec_j)$. $\qquad\square$

Example 4.43 Consider program $P_1 \parallel P_2$ in Figure 4.15. When the program is executed, the value in y is first passed to x, and then the loop is performed until the value in x is less than or equal to 0. Obviously, the program converges for any real number value of y, but to make things simple, we assume it is a natural number. This can be captured formally by precondition $y \in N$.

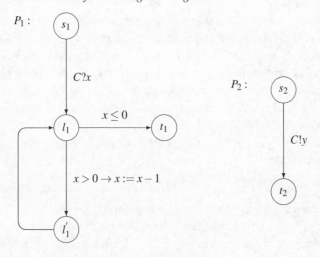

Fig. 4.15. An example program for proving convergence.

Process P_2 is trivial, as it contains no loop, and, therefore, we concentrate on process P_1. We select the following assertion and ranking-function networks:

$$\varphi_{s_1} \stackrel{\text{def}}{=} true \qquad \rho_{s_1} \stackrel{\text{def}}{=} (1, 0, 0)$$
$$\varphi_{l_1} \stackrel{\text{def}}{=} x \in \mathbf{N} \qquad \rho_{l_1} \stackrel{\text{def}}{=} (0, x, 1)$$
$$\varphi_{l_1'} \stackrel{\text{def}}{=} x \in \mathbf{N} \qquad \rho_{l_1'} \stackrel{\text{def}}{=} (0, x, 2)$$
$$\varphi_{t_1} \stackrel{\text{def}}{=} true \qquad \rho_{t_1} \stackrel{\text{def}}{=} (0, 0, 0),$$

where the wellfounded set is the lexicographical ordering of $\mathbf{N} \times \mathbf{N} \times \mathbf{N}$ over the set of natural numbers $(\mathbf{N}, <)$.

The proof obligations for the assertional network are trivial to check, and it is also straightforward to see that the ranking-function network is consistent with it. It is easy to show that the ranking functions decrease along every transition. □

4.7.1 Soundness and Semantic Completeness

Theorem 4.44 (Soundness)
The modular method for proving convergence formulated in Definition 4.42 is sound.

Proof It is easy to prove that, if the verification conditions for the local method for proving φ-convergence of $P_1 \parallel \ldots \parallel P_n$ are satisfied, then there exists an assertion network and a ranking-function network satisfying the verification conditions of the method of Definition 2.22, for proving $Q_{s_0} \land \ldots \land Q_{s_n}$-convergence of $P'_1 \parallel \ldots \parallel P'_n$, where P'_i denotes the augmented transition system and Q_{s_i} denotes the initial assertion of the local network of P'_i. Simply define $Q_l \overset{\text{def}}{=} \bigwedge_i Q_{l_i}$, for every location $l \equiv \langle l_1, \ldots, l_n \rangle$ of $P'_1 \parallel \ldots \parallel P'_n$ and $\rho_l \overset{\text{def}}{=} \langle \rho_{l_1}, \ldots, \rho_{l_n} \rangle$, defining $(W, \prec)$ componentwise as in Definition 3.55 from $(W_1, \prec_1), \ldots, (W_n, \prec_n)$. It remains to be shown that $Q_{s_0} \land \ldots \land Q_{s_n}$-convergence of $P'_1 \parallel \ldots \parallel P'_n$ implies that $P_1 \parallel \ldots \parallel P_n$ is φ-convergent, which is left as an exercise.   □

A completeness proof for partial correctness based on reachability predicates

Next we discuss the semantic completeness proof. Let $P \equiv P_1 \parallel \cdots \parallel P_n$ be φ-convergent. We have to find local assertion networks and ranking networks which satisfy the clauses of the local method. Unfortunately, we cannot use the (local) predicates used in the compositional completeness proof of the proof method for partial correctness, since they describe the behaviour of a process with respect to *any* environment. This is caused by the fact that termination of a process depends on a *particular* environment. Therefore, as in Chapter 3, we first develop an alternative completeness proof for partial correctness based on *reachability predicates*. To this end we augment P_i with updates to the history variable h_i. Let $P' \equiv P'_1 \parallel \cdots \parallel P'_n$ denote the augmented program. Furthermore let $\bar{z}$ be a sequence of fresh variables corresponding to the variables of P'. We define $\varphi' \overset{\text{def}}{=} \varphi \land \bar{z} = \bar{x}$. Thus the variables $\bar{z}$ are used to 'freeze' the initial state. Observe that φ-convergence of P implies φ'-convergence of P'.

Definition 4.45 (Reachability predicates) Given locations $l_1, \ldots, l_k$, where l_i is a location of P'_{f_i} ($f_i \neq f_j$ for $i \neq j$), we define the reachability predicate $\varphi_{\langle l_1, \ldots, l_k \rangle}$ as follows:

> $\sigma \models \varphi_{\langle l_1, \ldots, l_k \rangle}$ iff there exists a computation of P' starting from a state satisfying φ' and which reaches a configuration $\langle l; \sigma' \rangle$ such that $l \equiv \langle l(1), \ldots, l(n) \rangle$ with $l(f_i) = l_i$, and σ and σ' agree w.r.t. the variables $\bar{z}$ and the variables of P'_{f_i}, for $1 \leq i \leq k$.   □

We associate with each location l of P'_i the reachability predicate φ_l. It follows immediately from the above definition that φ_l, with l a location of P'_i, does not involve the variables of the other components, since for any states σ and σ' which agree w.r.t. the variables of $\bar{z}$ and the variables of P'_i, we have that $\sigma \models \varphi_l$ iff $\sigma' \models \varphi_l$. We next have to show that the resulting assertion networks of P'_i satisfy the local verification conditions and the cooperation test w.r.t. the following global invariant I:

Definition 4.46 Let I be the predicate for which $\sigma \models I$ iff there exists a computation of P' starting from a state satisfying φ' which reaches a state σ' such that σ and σ' agree with respect to the variables $\bar{z}$ and the history variables $h_1, \ldots, h_n$. $\qquad \square$

It follows immediately from the above definition that I only involves variables $\bar{z}$ and the history variables $h_1, \ldots, h_n$. For states σ and σ' which agree w.r.t. the variables $\bar{z}$ and $h_1, \ldots, h_n$, we have $\sigma \models I$ iff $\sigma' \models I$.

Lemma 4.47 (Local correctness) Let $l \xrightarrow{a} l'$, with $a \equiv b \to f$, be an internal transition of P'_i. We have that

$$\models \varphi_l \wedge b \to \varphi_{l'} \circ f.$$

Proof Let $\sigma \models \varphi_l \wedge b$. So there exists a computation of P' starting from a state satisfying φ' which reaches a configuration $\langle l_1; \sigma' \rangle$ such that $l_1(i) = l$ and σ and σ' agree w.r.t. the variables $\bar{z}$ and the variables of P'_i. Since $\sigma \models b$ (and so $\sigma' \models b$) there exists a transition $\langle l_1; \sigma' \rangle \to \langle l_2; f(\sigma') \rangle$, with $l_2(i) = l'$ and $l_2(j) = l_1(j)$, for $j \neq i$. Note that $f(\sigma)$ and $f(\sigma')$ agree with respect to the variables $\bar{z}$ and the variables of P'_i, thus we have that $f(\sigma) \models \varphi_{l'}$. $\qquad \square$

In order to prove the cooperation test we need the following merging lemma (corresponding to the merging Lemma 3.63 for shared-variable systems):

Lemma 4.48 (Merging lemma) Let k be such that $1 \leq k \leq n$, and, for $1 \leq i \leq k$, let l_i be a location of P'_{f_i} ($f_i \neq f_j$, $1 \leq i \neq j \leq k$). We have $\models I \wedge \bigwedge_{i=1}^{k} \varphi_{l_i} \to \varphi_{\langle l_1, \ldots, l_k \rangle}$.

Proof Let $\sigma \models I \wedge \bigwedge_{i=1}^{k} \varphi_{l_i}$. By the definition of the reachability predicates φ_{l_i} there exists for $1 \leq i \leq k$ a computation η_i of P' starting from a state satisfying φ' and which reaches a global configuration $\langle l'_i; \sigma_i \rangle$ such that $l'_i(f_i) = l_i$ and σ and σ_i agree w.r.t. the variables $\bar{z}$ and the variables of P'_{f_i}. By the definition of I there exists a computation of P' starting from a state satisfying φ' which reaches a configuration $\langle l'; \sigma' \rangle$ such that σ and σ' agree w.r.t. the variables $\bar{z}$ and the history variables $h_1, \ldots, h_n$. Since $\varphi' \equiv \varphi \wedge \bar{z} = \bar{x}$, we may assume without loss of generality that the computations η_i, for $1 \leq i \leq k$, and η all start from the same initial state σ_0 in which the values of the program variables $\bar{x}$ are given by $\sigma(\bar{z})$ (note that σ and σ_i agree w.r.t. the variables $\bar{z}$ and, since the variables $\bar{z}$ are not affected by P'_{f_i}, σ_i and the initial state of η_i agree w.r.t. $\bar{z}$, moreover we are given that the initial state of η_i satisfies $\bar{z} = \bar{x}$). By the compositionality of O we have that, for $1 \leq i \leq k$, $(\sigma_0, \sigma'_i, \sigma_i(h_i)) \in O_{l_i}(P'_{f_i})$, where σ'_i is obtained from

σ_i by assigning to all the variables not belonging to P'_{f_i} their corresponding values in σ_0. Now let l'' be a location of P' such that $l''(f_j) = l_j$, for $1 \leq j \leq k$, and $l''(j) = l'(j)$, for the remaining components of P'. Moreover, let σ'' be such that σ'' and σ agree w.r.t. the variables of P'_{f_i}, for $1 \leq i \leq k$, and σ'' and σ' agree with respect to the variables of the remaining components. It follows that $(\sigma_0, \sigma''_i, \sigma''(h_i)) \in O_{l''(i)}(P'_i)$, for $1 \leq i \leq n$, where σ''_i is obtained from σ'' by assigning to the variables not belonging to P'_i their corresponding values in σ_0. Since $\sigma \models I$ and $\sigma(h_i) = \sigma''(h_i)$, for $1 \leq i \leq n$, it follows that there exists a history θ such that $\sigma(h_i) = \theta_i$, for $1 \leq i \leq n$, where θ_i denotes the projection of θ onto the channels of P'_i. By the compositionality of O we infer that $(\sigma_0, \sigma'', \theta) \in O_{l''}(P')$, from which we conclude that $\sigma \models \varphi_{\langle l_1, \ldots, l_k \rangle}$. □

Lemma 4.49 (Cooperation test) For every pair of transitions $l_1 \overset{a}{\to} l_2$ of P'_i and $l'_1 \overset{a'}{\to} l'_2$ of P'_j, with $j \neq i$, $a \equiv b; C!e \to f$ and $a' \equiv b'; C?x \to g$, or vice versa, we have that

$$\models I \wedge \varphi_{l_1} \wedge \varphi_{l'_1} \wedge b \wedge b' \to (I \wedge \varphi_{l_2} \wedge \varphi_{l'_2}) \circ h,$$

where $h \overset{\text{def}}{=} f \circ g \circ x := e$.

Proof Follows in a straightforward manner from the above merging lemma.

□

Finally we have the following initialisation lemma:

Lemma 4.50 (Initialisation lemma) Let $f(\sigma)(h_i) \overset{\text{def}}{=} \langle \rangle$, for $1 \leq i \leq n$, and $f(\sigma)(x) \overset{\text{def}}{=} \sigma(x)$, for the remaining variables. Then

$$\models \varphi \to (I \wedge \bigwedge_i \varphi_{s_i}) \circ f.$$

Proof Left as an exercise.

□

Completeness of the modular method for proving convergence

In order to apply the local proof method for convergence we introduce on top of the assertion networks consisting of the above reachability predicates similar ranking functions as defined in Chapter 3 in Definition 3.68.

Definition 4.51 Let l be a location of P'_i. Then we define the ranking-function ρ_l by

$$\rho_l(\sigma) \overset{\text{def}}{=} |T_l(\sigma)|,$$

where $T_l(\sigma)$ denotes the set of all possible computation trees of P' starting in a φ'-reachable configuration $\langle l'; \sigma' \rangle$ such that $l'(i) = l$ and σ and σ' agree w.r.t. the variables $\bar{z}$ and the variables of P'_i. $\qquad \square$

From the above definition it immediately follows that ρ_l, with l a location of P'_i, does not involve the variables of the other components. The rest of this section is devoted to checking that the relevant conditions concerning the so-defined ranking functions are satisfied.

Lemma 4.52 (Well-definedness of the ranking functions) Let l be a location of P'_i. Then we have for any state σ: If $\sigma \models \varphi_l$ then $\rho_l(\sigma)$ is defined.

Proof Follows immediately from the φ'-convergence of P' and the use of the 'freeze' variables $\bar{z}$ which fix the initial state (φ'-convergence of P' and the use of the freeze variables $\bar{z}$ together guarantee that there are only a finite number of φ'-reachable configurations $\langle l'; \sigma' \rangle$ such that σ and σ' agree with respect to the variables $\bar{z}$ and the variables of P'_i, and φ'-convergence of P' then ensures that the computation tree starting from such a configuration is finite). $\qquad \square$

Next we prove the local correctness of the ranking functions.

Lemma 4.53 (Local correctness of the ranking functions) For every internal transition $l \xrightarrow{a} l'$ of P'_i, with $a \equiv b \to f$, we have that

$$\models \varphi_l \wedge b \to \rho_l \succ_i (\rho_{l'} \circ f).$$

Proof Let $\sigma \models \varphi_l \wedge b$. First observe that by Lemma 4.52 and the validity of $\varphi_l \wedge b \to \varphi_{l'} \circ f$ we know that $\rho_l(\sigma)$ and $\rho_{l'} \circ f(\sigma)$ are indeed defined. Let η be a computation of P' starting in a state satisfying φ' and which reaches a configuration $\langle l_1; \sigma' \rangle$ such that $l_1(i) = l'$ and $f(\sigma)$ and σ' agree w.r.t. the variables of $\bar{z}$ and the variables of P'_i. By $\sigma \models \varphi_l$ there exists a computation η' of P' starting in a state satisfying φ' and which reaches a configuration $\langle l_2; \sigma'' \rangle$ such that $l_2(i) = l$ and σ and σ'' agree w.r.t. the variables of $\bar{z}$ and the variables of P'_i. Observe that by the use of the freeze variables $\bar{z}$ we may assume that both computations η and η' start from the same state, say σ_0. Let l'' be the location of P' such that $l''(j) = l_1(j)$, for $j \neq i$ and $l''(i) = l$. Furthermore let σ''' be such that σ and σ''' agree w.r.t. the variables of P'_i, and σ' and σ''' agree w.r.t. the remaining variables. By the compositionality of O it then follows from the above computations η and η' that $(\sigma_0, \sigma'''_j, \sigma'''(h_j)) \in O_{l''(j)}(P'_j)$, for $1 \leq j \leq n$, where σ'''_j is obtained from σ''' by assigning to all the variables not belonging to P'_j their corresponding values of σ_0. Using again the compositionality of O

we thus derive $\langle l''; \sigma''' \rangle$ is a φ'-reachable configuration. Since σ and σ''' agree w.r.t. the variables of P_i' there exists a transition $\langle l''; \sigma''' \rangle \to \langle l_1, f(\sigma''') \rangle$. Note that $f(\sigma''') = \sigma'$, consequently we have shown that every tree of $T_{l'}(f(\sigma))$ is a subtree of a tree of $T_l(\sigma)$, i.e., $\rho_l(\sigma) \succ_i \rho_{l'}(f(\sigma))$. $\square$

Finally, we prove the cooperation test.

Lemma 4.54 (Cooperation test) Let $l_1 \overset{a}{\to} l_2$ be a transition of P_i' and $l_1' \overset{a'}{\to} l_2'$ a transition of P_j', with $j \neq i$, $a \equiv b; C!e \to f$ and $a' \equiv b'; C?x \to g$, or vice versa, then

$$\models I \wedge \varphi_{l_1} \wedge \varphi_{l_1'} \wedge b \wedge b' \to [(\rho_{l_1}, \rho_{l_1'}) \succ (\rho_{l_2} \circ h, \rho_{l_2'} \circ h)],$$

where $h \overset{\text{def}}{=} f \circ g \circ x := e$ and $(W_i \times W_j, \prec)$ is the componentwise order over $(W_i, \prec_i)$ and $(W_j, \prec_j)$.

Proof Let $\sigma \models I \wedge \varphi_{l_1} \wedge \varphi_{l_1'} \wedge b \wedge b'$. By Lemma 4.47 and Lemma 4.52 we have that $\rho_{l_1}(\sigma)$ and $\rho_{l_2}(\sigma)$ are defined. Moreover by the merging lemma it easily follows that $\rho_{l_2} \circ h(\sigma)$ and $\rho_{l_2'} \circ h(\sigma)$ are defined too. Next we show that

$$\models \varphi_{l_1} \wedge b \to \rho_{l_1} \succ_i \rho_{l_2} \circ h \text{ and } \models \varphi_{l_1'} \wedge b' \to \rho_{l_1'} \succ_j \rho_{l_2'} \circ h.$$

We prove the first implication (the second being similar). Let $\sigma \models \varphi_{l_1} \wedge b$. We show that $\rho_{l_1}(\sigma) \succ_i \rho_{l_2}(f(\sigma))$ (note that since ρ_{l_2} does not involve the variables of the other components we have that $\rho_{l_1} \succ_i \rho_{l_2} \circ h$ is equivalent to $\rho_{l_1} \succ_i \rho_{l_2} \circ f$). Let $\langle l; \sigma' \rangle$ be a φ'-reachable configuration starting from a state σ_0 satisfying φ' such that $l(i) = l_2$ and σ' and $f(\sigma)$ agree w.r.t. the variables $\bar{z}$ and the variables of P_i'. Let $\langle l'; \sigma'' \rangle$ be the intermediate configuration of the computation leading to $\langle l; \sigma' \rangle$, such that P_i' and P_j' are about to communicate along channel C and $\sigma''(h_i) = \sigma(h_i)$. Let l'' be such that $l''(j) = l'(j)$, for $j \neq i$, and $l''(i) = l_1$. Furthermore let σ''' be such that σ and σ''' agree w.r.t. the variables of P_i' and σ'' and σ''' agree w.r.t. the remaining variables. By $\sigma \models \varphi_{l_1}$ and the use of the freeze variables $\bar{z}$ it then follows from the compositionality of O that $(\sigma_0, \sigma_j''', \sigma'''(h_j)) \in O_{l'''(j)}(P_j')$, for $1 \leq j \leq n$, where σ_j''' is obtained from σ''' by assigning to the variables not belonging to P_j''' their corresponding values in σ_0. By the compositionality of O again we thus derive that $(\sigma_0, \sigma''', \theta) \in O_{l'''}(P')$, where θ is such that the projection of θ along the channels of P_i' equals $\sigma'''(h_j)$, for $1 \leq j \leq n$ (note that the histories in σ''' are compatible since $\sigma'''(h_i) = \sigma''(h_i)$, $1 \leq i \leq n$). Next we observe that from $\langle l''; \sigma''' \rangle$ we can make a transition consisting of a communication between P_i' and P_j' over channel C resulting in $\langle l; \sigma' \rangle$. Thus we have shown that every tree of $T_{l_2}(f(\sigma))$ is a subtree of a tree of $T_{l_1}(\sigma)$. $\square$

The above argument is summarised by the following theorem.

Theorem 4.55 (Completeness)
The modular method for proving convergence formulated in Definition 4.42 is complete. □

4.8 Verifying Deadlock Freedom

An internal transition can occur if and only if its guard holds; a communication transition can occur if and only if the guards of both transitions involved hold and these two transitions match (namely, one is an input and another one is an output, both along the same channel). A system will never deadlock if at any (non-terminal) configuration during the execution either a local or a communication transition can take place. For a global configuration $\langle l; \sigma \rangle$, in which at least one local location is not the terminal one, define predicate $Live(l)$ as

$$\sigma \models Live(l) \stackrel{\text{def}}{=} \text{there is a transition enabled from } \langle l; \sigma \rangle.$$

Note that above we have only given a semantical characterisation of this predicate. When the program is available, $Live$ can be defined using the syntactical information contained in it. Considering Example 4.43 for instance, this yields the following results:

$Live(s_1, s_2) = true$, the communication matches,
$Live(s_1, t_2) = false$, no matching communications, no internal transitions,
$\left.\begin{array}{l} Live(l_1, s_2) = true, \\ Live(l_1, t_2) = true, \end{array}\right\}$ one internal transition is always enabled,
$\left.\begin{array}{l} Live(l_1', s_2) = true, \\ Live(l_1', t_2) = true, \end{array}\right\}$ the internal transition is always enabled,
$\left.\begin{array}{l} Live(t_1, s_2) = false, \\ Live(t_1, t_2) = false, \end{array}\right\}$ no matching communications, no internal transitions.

For the sake of convenience in formulating the deadlock-freedom conditions, let

$$Live(t) \stackrel{\text{def}}{=} true$$

regarding the (global) terminal location t. Let $P \equiv P_1 \| \cdots \| P_n$. Suppose there exists an assertion network which associates to each local location l of P_i a predicate Q_l and a global invariant I. It follows from the soundness theorem that $Q_{l_1} \wedge \ldots \wedge Q_{l_n} \wedge I$ holds at global location $\langle l_1, \ldots, l_n \rangle$. Therefore, if one can prove

$$\models Q_1 \wedge \ldots \wedge Q_n \wedge I \to Live(l_1, \ldots, l_n),$$

then deadlock will not occur. This leads to the following method for proving deadlock freedom.

Definition 4.56 (A proof method for deadlock freedom à la AFR) Given $P \equiv P_1 \parallel \ldots \parallel P_n$ with locations $L \equiv L_1 \times \ldots \times L_n$.

Prove as follows that P is deadlock free w.r.t. precondition φ:

   (i) Same as points (i), (ii), (iii) and (iv) in Definition 4.8.

  (ii) Verify the *deadlock-freedom condition* for every global label $\langle l_1, \ldots, l_n \rangle$ of P':

$$\models Q_{l_1} \wedge \ldots \wedge Q_{l_n} \wedge I \to Live(l).$$

 (iii) Prove that for some state-transformation f whose write variables belong to the set of auxiliary variables $\bar{z}$ that

$$\models \varphi \to (I \wedge \bigwedge_i Q_{s_i}) \circ f,$$

where s_i denotes the initial location of P_i'.   □

Consider Example 4.43 again. The only non-trivial case in checking the deadlock-freedom condition is the one with global locations $\langle s_1, t_2 \rangle$ and $\langle t_1, s_2 \rangle$ (since *Live* holds trivially at all the other locations). Because $Live(s_1, t_2)$ and $Live(t_1, s_2)$ are both *false*, we have to find assertion networks $\{Q_l \mid l \in L_1\}$ and $\{Q_l \mid l \in L_2\}$, as well as a global invariant I, such that

$$\not\models Q_{s_1} \wedge Q_{t_2} \wedge I$$
$$\not\models Q_{t_1} \wedge Q_{s_2} \wedge I.$$

For this purpose, one can introduce two local auxiliary variables k_1 and k_2 to count the communication steps, and augment the program as follows:

Example 4.57 Consider program $P_1 \parallel P_2$ in Figure 4.16. The global invariant and the assertion networks can be chosen as:

$$I \stackrel{\text{def}}{=} k_1 = k_2 \qquad Q_{s_1} \stackrel{\text{def}}{=} k_1 = 0 \qquad\qquad Q_{s_2} \stackrel{\text{def}}{=} k_2 = 0$$
$$Q_{t_1} \stackrel{\text{def}}{=} x \in N \wedge k_1 = 1 \qquad Q_{t_2} \stackrel{\text{def}}{=} k_2 = 1.$$
$$Q_{t_1'} \stackrel{\text{def}}{=} x \in N \wedge k_1 = 1$$
$$Q_{t_1} \stackrel{\text{def}}{=} k_1 = 1$$

It is easy to see that the deadlock-freedom condition as well as the other proof obligations are satisfied.   □

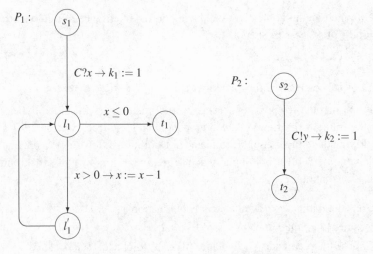

Fig. 4.16. An example program for checking deadlock freedom.

This method is both sound and semantically complete.

Theorem 4.58 (Soundness and semantic completeness)
The method for proving deadlock freedom formulated in Definition 4.56 is
both sound and semantically complete.

Proof Left as an exercise.   □

4.9 Proving Absence of Runtime Errors

In this section we give up our assumption that the primitive state transformations which occur in our theory are total functions, and consider the problem
of proving the absence of runtime errors of distributed programs $P_1 \| \ldots \| P_n$
which communicate by synchronous message passing.

As in Section 3.8, we must now require that certain primitive state transformations in our theory are total, since, otherwise, the auxiliary variables and
initialisation rules would become unsound. In particular, we require *all state
transformations whose write variables are auxiliary variables to be total, including those state transformations f which happen to occur in the formulation
of the initialisation rule.*

We sketch two methods for proving absence of runtime errors, one direct
method which is obtained by modifying the AFR-method in Section 4.9.1, and

one implicit method obtained by reducing proofs of absence of runtime errors to proofs of success in Section 4.9.2.

4.9.1 A Direct Method for Proving Absence of Runtime Errors

The first method for proving absence of runtime errors is obtained by adopting the framework of three-valued propositional logic from Section 2.9.1 and modifying the AFR-method formulated in Definition 4.8 in order to obtain the following method for proving absence of runtime errors in φ of synchronous transition diagram $P_1 \| \ldots \| P_n$:

- Consider a total $\{tt,ff\}$-valued boolean function φ.
- Require function g in clause (i) to be total.
- Choose the predicates Q_l in clause (ii) to be total and $\{tt,ff\}$-valued.
- Replace clause (iii) by:
  Prove local correctness *and freedom from local runtime errors* of every P_i'; for every internal transition $l \xrightarrow{a} l'$ of P_i', assuming $a \equiv b \to f$, we have to prove

  $$\models Q_l \wedge b \to (Q_{l'} \circ f) \wedge Def(f),$$

  where $Def(f)$ denotes a total $\{tt,ff\}$-valued predicate expressing the domain of definition of f.
- Require in clause (iv) the global invariant $I(\bar{z})$ to be total, and replace the verification condition by:

  $$\models I \wedge Q_{l_1} \wedge Q_{l_1'} \wedge b \wedge b' \to Def(h) \wedge (I \wedge Q_{l_2} \wedge Q_{l_2'}) \circ h,$$

  with $h \overset{\text{def}}{=} f \circ g \circ x := e$, and $Def(h)$ defined as above.
- Replace clause (v) by:
  Prove $\models \varphi \to (I \wedge \bigwedge_i Q_{s_i}) \circ f$, for some total state transformation f whose write variables belong to the set of auxiliary variables $\bar{z}$ (and s_i denotes the initial location of P_i').   □

This method verifies explicitly whether the applied state transformations in $P_1' \| \ldots \| P_n'$ are well-defined. In particular, it views a communication as a distributed assignment whose definedness should be proved explicitly. Consequently, soundness of the method is obvious.

Its semantic completeness can be proved using the $SP_l(\varphi_{i'}, P_i')$-predicates from Section 4.5.2 as the inductive assertion network for P_i', $i = 1, \ldots, n$, choosing I as in Definition 4.23 and choosing f as in Lemma 4.27.

4.9.2 An Implicit Method for Proving Absence of Runtime Errors

The second method for proving absence of runtime errors reduces absence of runtime errors to success, similarly as in Sections 2.9 and 3.8, but now for synchronously-communicating transition diagrams. As before, the method is based on transforming synchronous transition diagrams P into $W(P)$, using a transformation W which is defined below, and which satisfies the following property.

Lemma 4.59 Let P denote a synchronous transition diagram and $W(P)$ be as defined below. If $P_1 \| \ldots \| P_n$ is φ-successful, then:

$$P_1 \| \ldots \| P_n \text{ displays no runtime errors in precondition } \varphi$$
$$\iff W(P_1) \| \ldots \| W(P_n) \text{ is } \varphi\text{-successful.} \qquad \square$$

To obtain a proof method from this property, as before one transforms $P_1 \| \ldots \| P_n$ to another program $P_1' \| \ldots \| P_n'$, which displays the same runtime-error behaviour as $P_1 \| \ldots \| P_n$, but which by definition does not block. P_i' is obtained from P_i by adding to every location l_i of P_i the transition (l_i, id, t_i), with t_i denoting the exit location of P_i, $i = 1, \ldots, n$.

Consequently, by applying Lemma 4.59, one obtains the following method for proving that $P_1 \| \ldots \| P_n$ displays no runtime errors when started in precondition φ:

Prove that $W(P_1') \| \ldots \| W(P_n')$ is φ-successful.

All that remains is to define $W(P)$.

Essentially, $W(P)$ is obtained from P by executing in every non-exit location l of P a local transformation which strengthens the guards of every transition of P starting in l, along the lines given in Section 2.9, i.e., by guaranteeing that a guard is true in $W(P)$ iff all enabled transitions starting in l yield well-defined results in P.

However, the latter is difficult to express directly for transitions of the form $(l, b; C?x \to f, l')$, for how does one express *locally* that these are enabled?

The solution is to transform such transitions first by splitting them into two transitions $(l, b; C?x \to id, l'')$ and (l'', f, l'), for some fresh new location l'' not yet considered (with every split introducing a new location). Since transitions labelled by $(b; C?x \to id)$ display no runtime errors (since id is total), they do not contribute any verification conditions when proving the absence of runtime errors.

After applying this transformation, the remainder of the definition of $W(P)$ is straightforward.

For every process P_i and every node l, $l \neq t_i$, execute the following transformation upon the guards of all transitions which start in l, $i = 1, \ldots, n$.

These transitions are of the following three types:

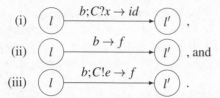

(i) $l \xrightarrow{\quad b; C?x \to id \quad} l'$,

(ii) $l \xrightarrow{\quad b \to f \quad} l'$, and

(iii) $l \xrightarrow{\quad b; C!e \to f \quad} l'$.

Transitions of type (ii) generate a $b \wedge Def(f)$-conjunct in their own transformed guards, and a $(b \to Def(f))$-conjunct in the transformed versions of the guards of the remaining transitions which start in l.

Transitions of type (iii) generate a $b \wedge Def(f) \wedge Def(e)$-conjunct in their own transformed guards, and a $(b \to Def(f) \wedge Def(e))$-conjunct in the transformed versions of the guards of the remaining transitions starting in l.

Observe that transitions of type (i) do not contribute conjuncts to the transformed guards of other transitions; yet their guards are possibly transformed as a result of conjuncts contributed by transitions of types (ii) and (iii).

Call the resulting transformation $W(P)$.

An example will help.

Example 4.60 Figures 4.17 and 4.18 show a synchronous transition diagram P and its resulting transformation $W(P)$. $\qquad \square$

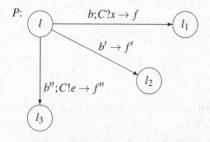

Fig. 4.17. A synchronous transition diagram P.

4.10 Historical Notes

An interesting question is whether there exists in some formal sense a difference in *expressive* power between concurrent and distributed processes. We

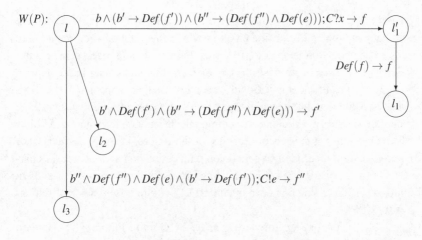

Fig. 4.18. The resulting transformation $W(P)$.

only mention here that a concurrent program can be converted into an equivalent distributed one by introducing a new process for each shared variable with separate channels for read and write requests [Mil80]. In [dBP94] it is shown that, on the basis of a refinement of a notion of expressiveness first introduced in [Sha89], one can prove that the converse does not hold in general. Of interest in this context is also the expressiveness result of [Bou88] which relates different forms of non-determinism in synchronous communication.

Next, we discuss the history of work on Communicating Sequential Processes and related programming languages for synchronous communication.

In 1978 and 1979, Tony (C.A.R.) Hoare and Robin (A.J.R.G.) Milner publish two formalisms for distributed computation, respectively, a programming language called Communicating Sequential Processes (CSP) [Hoa78], and a calculus for communicating systems (CCS) [Mil80]. Hoare refers to previous unpublished work of Edsger W. Dijkstra as one of his sources for inspiration, whereas Milner refers to previous work by Hans Bekić [Bek71] and Carl Adam Petri [Pet62, Pet63]. These two publications mark the beginning of two schools of research in concurrency theory, each dominating different parts of the field. This may be the reason why, when this book was produced, no balanced survey had appeared listing the complementary strengths and weaknesses of the formalisms developed in these schools, let alone any comparison between the state-based approach to concurrent program specification and verification (as worked out in, e.g., this book, and in [MP91b, MP95, MP99]) and the process-algebraic approach based on laws and calculi, initiated by Tony Hoare, Robin Milner, Jan Bergstra, Matthew Hennessy, Jan-Willem Klop and coworkers, see, e.g., [Mil80, BK84, Hoa85a, Hen88, Mil89, BPS01]. Yet there are many examples of specifications in which the algebraic/automata-based style of specification is superior to a state-based one, and vice-versa, a state-based style of specification is superior to an algebraic/automata-based one.

In 1979, the first compositional semantics for CSP appears [FHLdR79], based on a domain of finite and infinite trees with *two* kinds of nodes in order to model, respectively, willingness to communicate and nondeterministic choice. The realisation that the sets of branches of these trees, i.e., their sequences of communication records (also called communication histories or *traces*) characterise the semantics of communicating processes more abstractly, leads in 1980 to [FLP80], which is developed in [FLP84] into a fully abstract semantics for CSP.

In 1981, a major step forward is made by Gordon Plotkin's "Structured Operational Semantics" for CSP [Plo81, Plo82], demonstrating that also the operational semantics of concurrency can be formulated in a compositional way. All soundness and completeness proofs for Hoare-style proof methods for compositional formalisms for concurrency are based on this discovery.

Also in 1981, Tony Hoare publishes his first calculus of total correctness for CSP [Hoa81a], to be followed in 1982 by Ruurd Kuiper and Willem-Paul de Roever's paper [KdR82] on fairness assumptions for a temporal-logic-based framework for CSP.

For a discussion of the literature on compositional trace- and state-based proof theories for communicating processes we refer to Sections 1.7 and 7.6.

In 1982 and 1983, two theses appear on fully abstract compositional semantics for different aspects of CSP, together with their corresponding proof theories: those of Bill Roscoe [Ros82] and Steve Brookes [Bro83]. This work culminates in [BHR84] in a failure-divergence semantics for CSP. Tony Hoare's monograph [Hoa85a] presents an introduction to CSP-related research at the Programming Research Group at Oxford University until the mid-1980s, in which properties of CSP programs are deduced using algebraic laws.

In 1983, Ernst-Rüdiger Olderog and Tony Hoare publish an in-depth survey of the various existing compositional semantics of CSP-like languages, classifying these according to the properties one intends to specify [OH83, OH86]. In these papers the different semantic models for CSP based on channel histories, communication traces, ready sets and failure sets are incrementally developed using the concept of observation space. Consistency of the denotational and operational definitions of these models is shown.

Also in 1983, soundness and completeness proofs for a version of the AFR proof system for CSP are published by Krzysztof R. Apt [Apt83].

From 1985, the focus of research on semantics and proof theory for CSP-like languages includes a second aspect: that of real-time. Initiated by [KSdR$^+$85], many proposals for the semantics and proof theory of real-time versions of CSP, and their supporting tools, including full-abstractness proofs, see, e.g. [RR86, GB87, HGdR87, RR88, Sch89, GR90, Jac91, DS92, Dav93], culminating in a framework in which properties of timed CSP programs can be deduced using temporal logic and model checking, and through so-called *timewise* refinement [SDJ$^+$92]. Subsequently, more advanced model-checking tools are developed for CSP by Bill Roscoe and coworkers [Ros94a]. His monograph [Ros98] gives an overview of recent developments in the semantics and proof theory for untimed and timed CSP, such as algebraic semantics, the use of abstraction and tools, and deadlock prevention. A modern textbook on timed and untimed CSP, with special emphasis on timewise refinement, is Steve Schneider's [Sch99b]. Our survey of work on CSP, by-and-large done at Oxford during the Hoare era, closes by mentioning the book "Unifying Theories of Programming" [HH98] by Jifeng He and Tony Hoare.

Stepwise refinement of distributed systems and protocols is the subject of many papers by Simon S. Lam and A. Udaya Shankar, of which we mention [LS84a, LS90, LS92a, LS94, SL87, SL90]. Amongst others, they introduce the notion of conditional refinement in the context of formally deriving protocols and fault-tolerant algorithms [SL90, LS90].

Next we discuss noncompositional proof theories for CSP-like programming languages. Compositional proof theories for such languages are discussed in Chapter 7.

The two-stage approach to proving properties about synchronous communication has been applied to other forms of communication and synchronisation mechanisms for distributed processes. First of all, it has been applied to asynchronous communication by, amongst others, R.D. Schlichting & F.B. Schneider [SS84]. They introduce additional processes for communication channels (queues), in order to model asynchronous communication between processes by synchronous communication with these channel processes, and eliminate the identities of these channel processes from the verification conditions generated by the cooperation tests.

Originally, the method of Apt, Francez & de Roever was developed as a proof theory for Hoare's language Communicating Sequential Processes (CSP) [Hoa78]. Afterwards this two-stage approach involving cooperation tests was used to obtain a proof system for the concurrency fragment of ADA [GdR84], and to proof systems for Brinch-Hansen's Language Distributed Processes [GdRR82] and for monitor-based languages in general [Ger89]. An overview of these results is presented in [dR85a], focussing on applications of the cooperation test. Soundness and relative completeness proofs for these systems are considered in [Ger89, GdR86]. An introduction to and survey of proof systems based on the cooperation test, involving also synchronous multi-party interactions and a characterisation of asynchronous communication, is given in Chapter 8 of Nissim Francez' book [Fra92] on program verification. Subsequently, this two-stage approach to the proof theory of synchronous communication has been applied to the verification of object-oriented programs in [AdB94, dB86, dB91b, dB91a], requiring a different assertion language for the second stage which involves reasoning about dynamically-evolving networks of object-oriented processes; the resulting proof methods have been proved sound and semantically complete.

Exercises

4.1   Prove that $P_1 \parallel P_2$ in Figure 4.19 is partially correct w.r.t. $\langle true, x = y \rangle$.

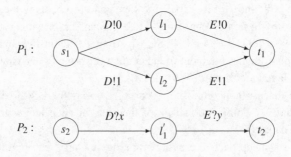

Fig. 4.19. Program $P_1 \parallel P_2$ for Exercise 4.1.

4.2   Prove that $P_1 \parallel P_2$ in Figure 4.20 is partially correct w.r.t. $\langle true, x+1 = y \rangle$.

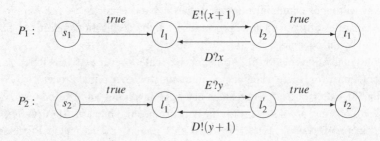

Fig. 4.20. Program $P_1 \parallel P_2$ for Exercise 4.2.

4.3   Prove that $P_1 \parallel P_2 \parallel P_3$ in Figure 4.21 is partially correct w.r.t. $\langle true,$
        $y = 1 \rangle$.

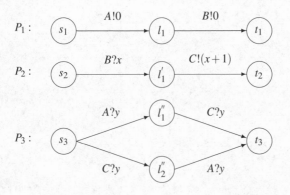

Fig. 4.21. Program $P_1 \parallel P_2 \parallel P_3$ for Exercise 4.3.

4.4   **Partitioning a set**

        Given two disjoint sets of integers S_0 and P_0, $S_0 \cup P_0$ has to be parti-
        tioned into two subsets S and P such that $|S| = |S_0|$, $|P| = |P_0|$, and
        every element of S is smaller than any element of P.

        Consider program P_1 in Figure 4.22 and program P_2 in Figure 4.23.
        Use the AFR-method to prove that $P_1 \parallel P_2$ is partially correct w.r.t. φ
        and ψ, where $\varphi \overset{\text{def}}{=} S_0 \cap P_0 = \emptyset \wedge S = S_0 \wedge P = P_0 \wedge S_0 \neq \emptyset \wedge x \neq mx \wedge y \neq$
        mn and $\psi \overset{\text{def}}{=} S \cap P = \emptyset \wedge S \cup P = S_0 \cup P_0 \wedge max(S) < min(P) \wedge |S_0| =$
        $|S| \wedge |P_0| = |P|$. By convention, $min(\emptyset) \overset{\text{def}}{=} +\infty$ and $max(\emptyset) \overset{\text{def}}{=} -\infty$.

4.5   This exercise is similar to the above, but uses a different program,
        as given in Figure 4.24. This program needs only two exchanges
        of the current maximum of S, $max(S)$, with the current minimum of
        P, $min(P)$, in order to terminate. Prove partial correctness of this
        program w.r.t. appropriate pre- and postconditions.

4.6   Prove that $P_1 \parallel P_2$ in Figure 4.25 is partially correct w.r.t.

$$\langle x + y < u \wedge x = z, x + y < u \rangle.$$

4.7   Prove Lemma 4.21, i.e., that the semantics of the augmented sys-
        tem records its own sequence of communications according to the
        O-semantics. Formally, prove that for $(\sigma, \sigma', \theta_i) \in O_{l_i}(P_i')$,

$$(\sigma(h_i) = \langle \rangle \wedge (\langle s; \sigma \rangle \overset{\theta_i}{\to} \langle l_i; \sigma' \rangle)) \Rightarrow \sigma'(h_i) = \theta_i$$

        holds.

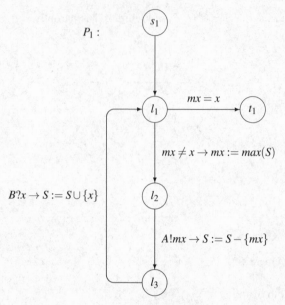

Fig. 4.22. Set-partitioning program P_1 for Exercise 4.4.

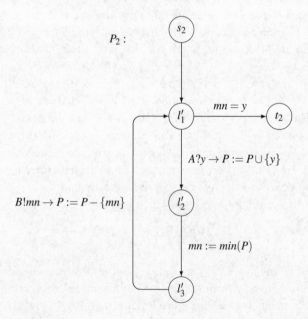

Fig. 4.23. Set-partitioning program P_2 for Exercise 4.4.

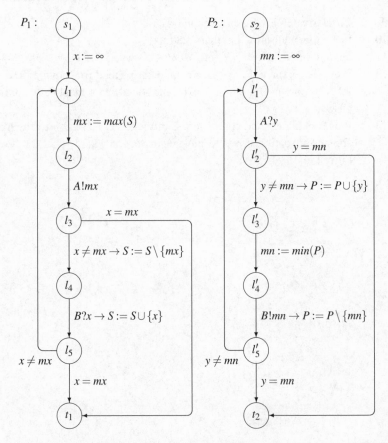

Fig. 4.24. Set-partitioning program $P_1 \parallel P_2$ for Exercise 4.5.

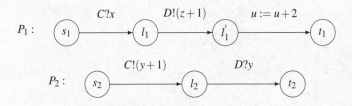

Fig. 4.25. Program $P_1 \parallel P_2$ for Exercise 4.6.

4.8   Let $\mathcal{M}_l \llbracket P \rrbracket \sigma$ denote the resulting states of partial computations of P (viewed as a sequential diagram as defined in Section 4.3) reaching the location l. Prove by induction on the length of the computation $\langle s; \sigma \rangle \to^* \langle l; \sigma' \rangle$ of P that $(\sigma, \sigma', \theta) \in O_l(P)$, for some θ.

4.9   Check Example 4.6 using Lemma 4.26.

4.10   Prove the finalisation Lemma 4.28 fully.

4.11   Prove Lemma 4.50.

4.12   Prove Theorem 4.58, that is, the modular method for proving dead-lock freedom in Definition 4.56 is both sound and semantically complete.

4.13   Prove soundness and completeness of the direct method for proving absence of runtime errors formulated in Section 4.9.1.

4.14   Prove Lemma 4.59.

5

Expressibility and Relative Completeness

5.1 Objective

This chapter constitutes a link between the previous chapters, in which a *mathematical* analysis of program verification has been given, and the chapters in Part IV, in which this analysis is expressed *syntactically* using the formalism of *Hoare logic*. The nature of this link is that of an *expressibility* result. We derive under which conditions the mathematical entities used in the soundness and semantic completeness proofs of the previous chapters can be expressed within first order predicate logic, i.e., as *assertions*. This result allows us to carry these proofs over from the semantic level represented by the inductive assertion method to the syntactic level of Hoare logic. In other words, the soundness and *relative* completeness proofs for the Hoare logics developed in Part IV of this book are directly based on the corresponding soundness and *semantic* completeness proofs developed for the inductive assertion method in Part II. This "bridge" constitutes one of the distinguishing methodological features of this book, and represents in the opinion of its authors a significant conceptual advance because soundness and completeness proofs are much easier to understand at the semantic level.

More precisely, in the previous chapters we have considered sequential and concurrent programs that are represented as transition diagrams. Proof methods for partial correctness for various computational models, based on Floyd's inductive assertion method, have been provided. In the case of shared-variable concurrency the interference freedom test has been added to ensure soundness of the method, whereas in the case of distributed concurrency a cooperation test is needed. All three proof methods are exclusively based on semantic notions and have been proved semantically complete. The word "semantic" refers to the fact that we do not express the predicates used when the methods are applied in any specific assertion language, but express them in the metalanguage (here, that of mathematics).

The purpose of this chapter is twofold. The first purpose is to provide the semantic notions used in the proof methods with syntactic counterparts and to prove that these syntactic notions express the corresponding semantic ones. The second purpose is to prove that under some restrictions we have a stronger completeness result than semantic completeness. We prove that if we use an assertion language which is at least as powerful as Peano arithmetic, and consider programs that only contain conditions and state transformations which have their syntactic counterparts in the assertion language, then we can express the predicates used in the completeness proofs of Chapters 2, 3, and 4 in the assertion language. This result is known as *relative completeness*, where the word "relative" refers to the fact that we assume all tautologies of the domain underlying the considered interpretation are axioms.

5.2 Structure of this Chapter

Section 5.3 introduces syntactic transition diagrams to express the semantic notion of transition diagrams, and defines the assertion language of first-order logic syntactically. In Section 5.4 the partial correctness of syntactic transition diagrams is defined and a syntactic version of Floyd's inductive assertion method introduced for such syntactic diagrams. In Section 5.5 the relative completeness is proved of this version of Floyd's method, by proving the expressibility of φ-minimal predicates through Gödel encodings which use the standard model of the natural numbers.

In Sections 5.6 and 5.7 this relative completeness result is generalised to, respectively, syntactic formulations of the methods of Owicki & Gries and of Apt, Francez & de Roever. In Section 5.8 we discuss the history of material discussed in this chapter. Some exercises can be found at the end of this chapter.

5.3 Syntactic Notions

In Chapter 2 programs are represented as transition diagrams (L, T, s, t) with L a set of locations, T a set of transitions of the form $(l, c \rightarrow f, l')$ with $l, l' \in L$, c a predicate over Σ, with Σ a set of states, and f a state transformation over Σ, and s, t indicating start and exit locations. In this section we define a syntax for instructions $c \rightarrow f$. For guards c we use boolean expressions and for state transformations f assignments of the form $x_1, \ldots, x_n := e_1, \ldots, e_n$. The notation $x_1, \ldots, x_n := e_1, \ldots, e_n$ has already been introduced in Chapter 2 as abbreviation; we show that our definition of $x_1, \ldots, x_n := e_1, \ldots, e_n$ in the present chapter is in accordance with this abbreviation. Throughout this chapter we assume as given a set *Pvar* of program variables and a set *Lvar* of logical variables with $Pvar \cap Lvar = \emptyset$, and define $VAR \stackrel{\text{def}}{=} Pvar \cup Lvar$ as in Section 2.4.1. The need for logical variables has been discussed in Chapter 2, where we formulated conditions to ensure that the meaning of a program does not depend on the values of the logical variables and that the execution of a program does not affect logical variables. We show that the syntax of instructions we define in this chapter implies these conditions.

5.3.1 Expressions and Boolean Expressions

The set *Exp* of expressions, with typical elements $e, e_1, \ldots$ is defined by the following BNF-form:

$$e ::= 0 \mid 1 \mid \ldots \mid x \mid e_1 + e_2 \mid e_1 * e_2 \mid e_1 \uparrow e_2 \mid f(e_1, \ldots, e_n),$$

with $0, 1, \ldots$ constant symbols, $x \in VAR$, f a function symbol of arity n, and $n \geq 0$.

For an expression e in *Exp*, we denote by $var(e)$ the set of variables which occur in e.

The set *PExp* of program expressions is the set of all $e \in Exp$ which do not contain variables in *Lvar*. *PExp* is defined by the same BNF-form as *Exp* except that variable x is required to belong to *Pvar*.

As syntax for guards c in instructions $c \to f$ we define boolean expressions. The set *BExp* of boolean expressions, with typical elements $b, b_1, \ldots$, is given by:

$$b ::= true \mid e_1 = e_2 \mid \neg b \mid b_1 \vee b_2 \mid R(e_1, \ldots, e_n),$$

with $e_1, e_2, \ldots, e_n \in PExp$ and R a relation symbol of arity n, $n \geq 0$.

Note that because we only allow expressions in *PExp* to occur in boolean expressions, the latter do not contain logical variables.

Meanings of expressions and boolean expressions depend on the domain of interpretation and on the meanings assigned to the constant, function, and relation symbols. An *interpretation* I is a pair (VAL, I_0) with *VAL* a non-empty set, called domain of interpretation, and I_0 a mapping that assigns to each constant symbol μ a value $I_0(\mu)$ in *VAL*, to $+$, $*$, and $\uparrow$ functions $I_0(+)$, $I_0(*)$, and $I_0(\uparrow)$ from VAL^2 into *VAL*, to each function symbol of arity n a function $I_0(f) : VAL^n \to VAL$, and to each relation symbol R of arity n a relation $I_0(R) \subseteq$

VAL^n. In the remainder of this chapter we simply write μ, $+$, and $*$ for $I_0(\mu)$, $I_0(+)$, and $I_0(*)$, respectively.

Definition 5.1 Meanings of expressions and boolean expressions are defined by functions $\mathcal{E}_I : Exp \to (\Sigma \to VAL)$ and $\mathcal{B}_I : BExp \to (\Sigma \to \{tt, ff\})$, respectively, with $\Sigma = VAR \to VAL$. Both $\mathcal{E}_I$ and $\mathcal{B}_I$ are inductively defined:

- $\mathcal{E}_I \llbracket \mu \rrbracket \sigma \overset{\text{def}}{=} \mu$
- $\mathcal{E}_I \llbracket x \rrbracket \sigma \overset{\text{def}}{=} \sigma(x)$
- $\mathcal{E}_I \llbracket e_1 \Delta e_2 \rrbracket \sigma \overset{\text{def}}{=} \mathcal{E}_I \llbracket e_1 \rrbracket \sigma \Delta \mathcal{E}_I \llbracket e_2 \rrbracket \sigma$, where Δ stands for either $+$, $*$, or $\uparrow$
- $\mathcal{E}_I \llbracket f(e_1, \ldots, e_n) \rrbracket \sigma \overset{\text{def}}{=} I_0(f)(\mathcal{E}_I \llbracket e_1 \rrbracket \sigma, \ldots, \mathcal{E}_I \llbracket e_n \rrbracket \sigma)$
- $\mathcal{B}_I \llbracket true \rrbracket \sigma \overset{\text{def}}{=} tt$
- $\mathcal{B}_I \llbracket e_1 = e_2 \rrbracket \sigma \overset{\text{def}}{=} \begin{cases} tt & \text{, if } \mathcal{E}_I \llbracket e_1 \rrbracket \sigma = \mathcal{E}_I \llbracket e_2 \rrbracket \sigma, \\ ff & \text{, if } \mathcal{E}_I \llbracket e_1 \rrbracket \sigma \neq \mathcal{E}_I \llbracket e_2 \rrbracket \sigma \end{cases}$
- $\mathcal{B}_I \llbracket \neg b \rrbracket \sigma \overset{\text{def}}{=} \begin{cases} tt & \text{, if } \mathcal{B}_I \llbracket b \rrbracket \sigma = ff, \\ ff & \text{, if } \mathcal{B}_I \llbracket b \rrbracket \sigma = tt \end{cases}$
- $\mathcal{B}_I \llbracket b_1 \vee b_2 \rrbracket \sigma \overset{\text{def}}{=} \begin{cases} tt & \text{, if } \mathcal{B}_I \llbracket b_1 \rrbracket \sigma = tt \text{ or } \mathcal{B}_I \llbracket b_2 \rrbracket \sigma = tt, \\ ff & \text{, if } \mathcal{B}_I \llbracket b_1 \rrbracket \sigma = ff \text{ and } \mathcal{B}_I \llbracket b_2 \rrbracket \sigma = ff \end{cases}$
- $\mathcal{B}_I \llbracket R(e_1, \ldots, e_n) \rrbracket \sigma \overset{\text{def}}{=} \begin{cases} tt & \text{, if } (\mathcal{E}_I \llbracket e_1 \rrbracket \sigma, \ldots, \mathcal{E}_I \llbracket e_n \rrbracket \sigma) \in I_0(R), \\ ff & \text{, if } (\mathcal{E}_I \llbracket e_1 \rrbracket \sigma, \ldots, \mathcal{E}_I \llbracket e_n \rrbracket \sigma) \notin I_0(R). \end{cases}$ $\quad\square$

Since program expressions and boolean expressions do not contain logical variables, their meanings do not depend on the values assigned to these variables. We have the following:

Lemma 5.2 For every expression $e \in PExp$ and boolean expression $b \in BExp$ and every state σ and σ',

(i) $(\forall x \in Pvar. \, \sigma(x) = \sigma'(x)) \Rightarrow \mathcal{E}_I \llbracket e \rrbracket \sigma = \mathcal{E}_I \llbracket e \rrbracket \sigma'$ and
(ii) $(\forall x \in Pvar. \, \sigma(x) = \sigma'(x)) \Rightarrow \mathcal{B}_I \llbracket b \rrbracket \sigma = \mathcal{B}_I \llbracket b \rrbracket \sigma'$.

Proof By induction on the structures of e and b, respectively. $\quad\square$

5.3.2 Assignments

An instruction $c \to f$ is determined by its boolean condition c and its state transformation f. For condition c we have introduced boolean expressions as syntax; for state transformations we introduce *assignments*.

Let $x_1, \ldots, x_n$ be distinct variables in $Pvar$, $x_i \neq x_j$ for $i \neq j$, and $e_1, \ldots, e_n$ be expressions in $PExp$. An assignment has the form $x_1, \ldots, x_n := e_1, \ldots, e_n$

with $n \geq 1$. The meaning of an assignment $x_1, \ldots, x_n := e_1, \ldots, e_n$ is a state transformation

$$\mathcal{A}_I \llbracket x_1, \ldots, x_n := e_1, \ldots, e_n \rrbracket : \Sigma \to \Sigma$$

with

$$\mathcal{A}_I \llbracket x_1, \ldots, x_n := e_1, \ldots, e_n \rrbracket \sigma = (\sigma : x_1, \ldots, x_n \mapsto \mathcal{E}_I \llbracket e_1 \rrbracket \sigma, \ldots, \mathcal{E}_I \llbracket e_n \rrbracket \sigma).$$

A *syntactic instruction* has the form $b \to x_1, \ldots, x_n := e_1, \ldots, e_n$, where b is a boolean expression in *PExp* and $x_1, \ldots, x_n := e_1, \ldots, e_n$ is an assignment. Henceforth, we simply say instruction instead of syntactic instruction, provided it is clear from the context that the syntactic version is meant.

Notice that the definition in Chapter 2 for the semantics of $(x_1, \ldots, x_n := e_1, \ldots, e_n)$ is in accordance with the semantic function $\mathcal{A}_I$ defined above, when $\lambda \sigma . \mathcal{E}_I \llbracket e_1 \rrbracket \sigma, \ldots, \lambda \sigma . \mathcal{E}_I \llbracket e_n \rrbracket \sigma$ are considered as value expressions.

In Section 2.4.1 we have formulated conditions on boolean conditions and state transformations to ensure that the meaning of a program does not depend on the values of the logical variables and that the execution of a program does not affect the logical variables. We now show that the syntax of instructions defined above implies these conditions, i.e., that we have

(i) $\forall \sigma, \sigma' \in \Sigma. \ (\forall x \in Pvar. \ \sigma(x) = \sigma'(x)) \Rightarrow \mathcal{B}_I \llbracket b \rrbracket \sigma = \mathcal{B}_I \llbracket b \rrbracket \sigma'$,
(ii) $\forall \sigma, \sigma' \in \Sigma. \ (\forall x \in Pvar. \ \sigma(x) = \sigma'(x)) \Rightarrow$
$\forall x \in Pvar. (\mathcal{A}_I \llbracket x_1, \ldots, x_n := e_1, \ldots, e_n \rrbracket \sigma)(x) =$
$(\mathcal{A}_I \llbracket x_1, \ldots, x_n := e_1, \ldots, e_n \rrbracket \sigma')(x)$, and
(iii) $\forall \sigma \in \Sigma. \forall x \in Lvar. (\mathcal{A}_I \llbracket x_1, \ldots, x_n := e_1, \ldots, e_n \rrbracket \sigma)(x) = \sigma(x)$.

It is easy to see that (i) and (ii) follow from Lemma 5.2 and that (iii) follows from the definitions of $\mathcal{A}$ and state variant.

The next question that arises is whether we can really represent each instruction in our syntax. The answer is no. The point is that in the previous chapters we allow predicates that depend on infinitely many program variables as boolean conditions and allow state transformations that depend on and affect infinitely many such variables. Neither such predicates nor such state transformations can be expressed in our syntax. These remarks lead to the following definition:

Definition 5.3 (Syntactic transition diagrams) We define a *syntactic transition diagram*, STD for short, as a tuple (L, ST, s, t) with L, s, and t as in Definition 2.2 and ST a set of triples $(l, b \to \bar{x} := \bar{e}, l')$ called *syntactic transitions* with $l, l' \in L$, $b \in BExp$, and $\bar{x} := \bar{e}$ an assignment. $\qquad \square$

Each STD S induces a program P_S by interpreting all instructions $b \to \bar{x} := \bar{e}$ of S, i.e., if $S \equiv (L, ST, s, t)$ then we obtain a program $P_S \equiv (L, T, s, t)$ with

$$T \stackrel{\text{def}}{=} \{ (l, \mathcal{B}_I \llbracket b \rrbracket) \to \mathcal{A}_I \llbracket \bar{x} := \bar{e} \rrbracket, l') \mid (l, b \to \bar{x} := \bar{e}, l') \in ST \}.$$

We define the meaning $\mathcal{M}_I \llbracket S \rrbracket$ of an STD S by $\mathcal{M}_I \llbracket S \rrbracket \stackrel{\text{def}}{=} \mathcal{M} \llbracket P_S \rrbracket$. In the examples of the previous chapters we used expressions such as $y_1 > 0$ and $y_3 > y_1$ as abbreviations of predicates φ and ψ with $\varphi(\sigma) = tt$ iff $\sigma(y_1) > 0$ and $\psi(\sigma) = tt$ iff $\sigma(y_3) > \sigma(y_1)$. Note that we can regard ">" as a binary relation symbol and that if we fix an interpretation that assigns to ">" its standard meaning, we have $\varphi = \mathcal{B}_I \llbracket y_1 > 0 \rrbracket$ and $\psi = \mathcal{B}_I \llbracket y_3 > y_1 \rrbracket$.

In general we can consider the transition diagrams used in most examples as STDs, and we have that this view is consistent with the definitions above in the sense that for each STD S the induced program P_S is the program for which S is an abbreviation according to the previous chapters.

5.3.3 Assertion Language

The set $\mathcal{A}ss$ of assertions, with typical elements $\phi, \phi_1, \ldots,$ is defined by:

$$\phi ::= true \mid e_1 = e_2 \mid R(e_1, \ldots, e_n) \mid \neg \phi \mid \phi_1 \vee \phi_2 \mid \forall x. \phi \mid (\phi),$$

with $e_1, e_2, \ldots, e_n \in Exp$, $x \in Lvar$, and $n \geq 0$.

Henceforth, we use the standard abbreviations, such as $\phi_1 \to \phi_2 \equiv \neg \phi_1 \vee \phi_2$, $\phi_1 \wedge \phi_2 \equiv \neg(\neg \phi_1 \vee \neg \phi_2)$, $\exists x. \phi \equiv \neg \forall x. \neg \phi$, etc.

Let $var(\phi)$ denote the set of variables that occur free in ϕ. Given a sequence $\bar{x}$ of distinct variables and a sequence $\bar{e}$ of expressions with the same length as $\bar{x}$, we use $e_0[\bar{e}/\bar{x}]$ to denote the expression that is obtained from e_0 by substituting $e \in \bar{e}$ for each corresponding $x \in \bar{x}$ in expression e_0. Formally, one has the following definition of substitution.

Definition 5.4 (Substitution) Let $\bar{x}$ denote the list $x_1, \ldots, x_n$ of distinct variables and $\bar{e}$ denote the list $e_1, \ldots, e_n$ of expressions.

- $\mu[\bar{e}/\bar{x}] \stackrel{\text{def}}{=} \mu$, for every constant symbol μ,
- $x[\bar{e}/\bar{x}] \stackrel{\text{def}}{=} \begin{cases} e_i & \text{, if there exists } i \text{ with } x_i \equiv x, \\ x & \text{, otherwise} \end{cases}$
- $(e_0 \Delta e_1)[\bar{e}/\bar{x}] \stackrel{\text{def}}{=} e_0[\bar{e}/\bar{x}] \Delta e_1[\bar{e}/\bar{x}]$, where Δ is either $+$, $*$, or $\uparrow$, and
- $f(e_0, \ldots, e_n)[\bar{e}/\bar{x}] \stackrel{\text{def}}{=} f(e_0[\bar{e}/\bar{x}], \ldots, e_n[\bar{e}/\bar{x}])$. $\qquad \square$

We then have the following lemma relating substitutions and variants for expressions:

Lemma 5.5 For each expression e, distinct variables $x_1 \ldots, x_n$, and expressions $e_1, \ldots, e_n$,

$$\mathcal{E}_I \llbracket e[e_1, \ldots, e_n/x_1, \ldots, x_n] \rrbracket \sigma =$$
$$\mathcal{E}_I \llbracket e \rrbracket (\sigma : x_1, \ldots, x_n \mapsto \mathcal{E}_I \llbracket e_1 \rrbracket \sigma, \ldots, \mathcal{E}_I \llbracket e_n \rrbracket \sigma).$$

Proof By induction on the structure of e. $\qquad\qquad\square$

Next, we define $\phi[e/x]$, denoting the substitution of each *free* occurrence of x by e within ϕ, provided this does not lead to the binding of free variables of e by quantifiers in ϕ.

Definition 5.6 (Substitution continued)

- $true[e/x] \stackrel{\text{def}}{=} true$,
- $(e_1 = e_2)[e/x] \stackrel{\text{def}}{=} e_1[e/x] = e_2[e/x]$,
- $R(e_1, \ldots, e_n)[e/x] \stackrel{\text{def}}{=} R(e_1[e/x], \ldots, e_n[e/x])$,
- $(\neg\phi)[e/x] \stackrel{\text{def}}{=} \neg(\phi[e/x])$,
- $(\phi_1 \vee \phi_2)[e/x] \stackrel{\text{def}}{=} \phi_1[e/x] \vee \phi_2[e/x]$,
- $(\forall y.\phi)[e/x] \stackrel{\text{def}}{=} \begin{cases} \forall y.\phi \,, \text{ if } y \equiv x \\ \forall y.\phi[e/x] \,, \text{ if } y \not\equiv x \wedge y \notin var(e) \\ \forall y'.\phi[y'/y][e/x] \,, \text{ if } y \not\equiv x \wedge y \in var(e) \,\wedge \\ \qquad\qquad y' \notin (var(\phi) \cup var(e)) \wedge y' \not\equiv x, \end{cases}$
- $(\phi)[e/x] \stackrel{\text{def}}{=} (\phi[e/x])$. $\qquad\qquad\square$

This definition can be generalised to sequences of variables and expressions.

To assign meanings to assertions we assume as given an interpretation I as in Section 5.3.1.

Definition 5.7 The meaning of an assertion ϕ is a predicate $\mathcal{T}_I \llbracket \phi \rrbracket : \Sigma \to \{tt, ff\}$ which is defined as follows:

- $\mathcal{T}_I \llbracket true \rrbracket \sigma \stackrel{\text{def}}{=} tt$
- $\mathcal{T}_I \llbracket e_1 = e_2 \rrbracket \sigma \stackrel{\text{def}}{=} \begin{cases} tt \,, \text{ if } \mathcal{E}_I \llbracket e_1 \rrbracket \sigma = \mathcal{E}_I \llbracket e_2 \rrbracket \sigma, \\ ff \,, \text{ if } \mathcal{E}_I \llbracket e_1 \rrbracket \sigma \neq \mathcal{E}_I \llbracket e_2 \rrbracket \sigma \end{cases}$
- $\mathcal{T}_I \llbracket \neg\phi \rrbracket \sigma \stackrel{\text{def}}{=} \begin{cases} tt \,, \text{ if } \mathcal{T}_I \llbracket \phi \rrbracket \sigma = ff, \\ ff \,, \text{ if } \mathcal{T}_I \llbracket \phi \rrbracket \sigma = tt \end{cases}$
- $\mathcal{T}_I \llbracket \phi_1 \vee \phi_2 \rrbracket \sigma \stackrel{\text{def}}{=} \begin{cases} tt \,, \text{ if } \mathcal{T}_I \llbracket \phi_1 \rrbracket \sigma = tt \text{ or } \mathcal{T}_I \llbracket \phi_2 \rrbracket \sigma = tt, \\ ff \,, \text{ if } \mathcal{T}_I \llbracket \phi_1 \rrbracket \sigma = ff \text{ and } \mathcal{T}_I \llbracket \phi_2 \rrbracket \sigma = ff \end{cases}$
- $\mathcal{T}_I \llbracket R(e_1, \ldots, e_n) \rrbracket \sigma \stackrel{\text{def}}{=} \begin{cases} tt \,, \text{ if } (\mathcal{E}_I \llbracket e_1 \rrbracket \sigma, \ldots, \mathcal{E}_I \llbracket e_n \rrbracket \sigma) \in I_0(R), \\ ff \,, \text{ if } (\mathcal{E}_I \llbracket e_1 \rrbracket \sigma, \ldots, \mathcal{E}_I \llbracket e_n \rrbracket \sigma) \notin I_0(R) \end{cases}$

- $\mathcal{T}_I \, [\![\forall x.\phi]\!] \, \sigma \stackrel{\text{def}}{=} \begin{cases} tt & \text{, if } \mathcal{T}_I \, [\![\phi]\!] \, (\sigma : x \mapsto \mu) = tt, \text{ for all } \mu \in VAL, \\ ff & \text{, otherwise} \end{cases}$

- $\mathcal{T}_I \, [\![(\phi)]\!] \, \sigma \stackrel{\text{def}}{=} \mathcal{T}_I \, [\![\phi]\!] \, \sigma.$ $\square$

Note that *BExp* is a subset of $\mathcal{A}ss$ and that $\mathcal{B}_I$ and $\mathcal{T}_I$ coincide on *BExp*. We often write $\sigma \models_I \phi$ or $\models_I \phi(\sigma)$ for $\mathcal{T}_I \, [\![\phi]\!] \, \sigma = tt$. Validity of an assertion ϕ in an interpretation I, denoted by $\models_I \phi$, is defined by $\sigma \models_I \phi$, for all $\sigma \in \Sigma$.

We often do not write the index I when it is clear from the context which interpretation is meant.

We have the following lemma that relates substitutions and state variants for assertions:

Lemma 5.8 (Substitution lemma) For each assertion ϕ, expression e, and variable x,

$$\mathcal{T}_I \, [\![\phi[e/x]]\!] \, \sigma = \mathcal{T}_I \, [\![\phi]\!] \, (\sigma : x \mapsto \mathcal{E}_I \, [\![e]\!] \, \sigma).$$

Proof By induction on the structure of ϕ using Lemma 5.5. $\square$

Also this lemma can be generalised to sequences of expressions and variables, leading to:

$$\mathcal{T}_I \, [\![\phi[e_1, \dots, e_n / x_1 \dots, x_n]]\!] \, \sigma = \\ \mathcal{T}_I \, [\![\phi]\!] \, (\sigma : x_1 \dots, x_n \mapsto \mathcal{E}_I \, [\![e_1]\!] \, \sigma, \dots, \mathcal{E}_I \, [\![e_n]\!] \, \sigma).$$

Henceforth, we also refer to this generalised result as Lemma 5.8.

As a consequence we have:

Lemma 5.9 For every assertion ϕ, assignment $\bar{x} := \bar{e}$, and state σ,

$$\sigma \models_I \phi[\bar{e}/\bar{x}] \text{ iff } \sigma \models \mathcal{T}_I \, [\![\phi]\!] \circ \mathcal{A}_I \, [\![\bar{x} := \bar{e}]\!].$$

Proof Follows from the definition of $\mathcal{A}_I$ and Lemma 5.8. $\square$

5.4 Partial Correctness of Syntactic Transition Diagrams

Definition 5.10 For assertions ϕ and ψ, we call a syntactic transition diagram S *partially correct with respect to* $< \phi, \psi >$ *in* I, expressed by $\models_I \{\phi\} S \{\psi\}$, if P_S is partially correct w.r.t. $< \mathcal{T}_I \, [\![\phi]\!], \mathcal{T}_I \, [\![\psi]\!] >$, i.e., $\models \{\mathcal{T}_I \, [\![\phi]\!]\} P_S \{\mathcal{T}_I \, [\![\psi]\!]\}$ holds. When interpretation I is clear from the context, we write $\models \{\phi\} S \{\psi\}$.
     $\square$

An immediate consequence of this definition is that Floyd's inductive assertion method can be adapted to proving partial correctness of programs w.r.t. specifications $< \phi, \psi >$ with $\phi, \psi \in \mathcal{A}ss$. However, our formulation of Floyd's inductive assertion method in Chapter 2 is based on semantic notions since an assertion network associates predicates to locations, and predicates are semantic objects.[1] Since we are now interested in proving partial correctness of STDs w.r.t. $< \phi, \psi >$ with $\phi, \psi \in \mathcal{A}ss$, this suggests the reformulation of this method using assertions instead of predicates. Therefore, we introduce the following notions.

Definition 5.11 Given an STD $S \equiv (L, ST, s, t)$ and a specification $< \phi, \psi >$ with $\phi, \psi \in \mathcal{A}ss$.

- A *syntactic assertion network* $\mathcal{AN}$ for S is a function that associates to each location $l \in L$ an assertion $\mathcal{AN}(l) \in \mathcal{A}ss$.
- The set of assertional verification conditions associated to S by $\mathcal{AN}$, denoted by $SV(S, \mathcal{AN})$, is the set containing for each transition $(l, b \rightarrow \bar{x} := \bar{e}, l')$ of S the *assertional verification condition* $(\mathcal{AN}(l) \wedge b) \rightarrow \mathcal{AN}(l')[\bar{e}/\bar{x}]$.
- A syntactic assertion network $\mathcal{AN}$ for S is called *inductive*, if $\models_I vc$ holds for each $vc \in SV(S, \mathcal{AN})$.
- We call $\mathcal{AN}$ *consistent* w.r.t. $< \phi, \psi >$, if $\models_I \phi \rightarrow \mathcal{AN}(s)$ and $\models_I \mathcal{AN}(t) \rightarrow \psi$. $\qquad \square$

In the definition above we have introduced the notion of syntactic inductive assertion networks; in Chapter 2 we have introduced a similar notion for semantic assertion networks. The following lemma relates both notions:

Lemma 5.12 Let $S \equiv (L, ST, s, t)$ and $\mathcal{AN}$ be a syntactic inductive assertion network for S. Then the assertion network Q for P_S with $Q_l \stackrel{\text{def}}{=} \mathcal{T}_I [\![\mathcal{AN}(l)]\!]$, for $l \in L$, is inductive, too.

Furthermore, if Q is a semantic inductive assertion network for P_S, and for each $l \in L$, there is an assertion $\mathcal{AN}(l)$ with $\mathcal{T}_I [\![\mathcal{AN}(l)]\!] = Q_l$, then the syntactic assertion network $\mathcal{AN}$ that associates $\mathcal{AN}(l)$ to each $l \in L$ is inductive, too.

Proof It suffices to prove that $\models_I (\mathcal{AN}(l) \wedge b) \rightarrow \mathcal{AN}(l')[\bar{e}/\bar{x}]$ holds iff for every state σ, $\sigma \models \mathcal{T}_I [\![\mathcal{AN}(l)]\!]$ and $\sigma \models \mathcal{B}_I [\![b]\!]$ implies $\sigma \models \mathcal{T}_I [\![\mathcal{AN}(l')]\!] \circ \mathcal{A}_I [\![\bar{x} := \bar{e}]\!]$. Now, this follows from Lemma 5.9 and the fact that for each $\phi \in \mathcal{A}ss$ and $\sigma \in \Sigma$, $\sigma \models_I \phi$ iff $\sigma \models \mathcal{T}_I [\![\phi]\!]$. $\qquad \square$

---

[1] Hence, in retrospect it would have been more appropriate to have used the term *predicate network* for the assertion networks of Chapters 2, 3, and 4.

Definition 5.13 (Floyd's inductive assertion method – syntactic formulation) We assume as given an STD $S \equiv (L, ST, s, t)$ and a specification $< \phi, \psi >$ with $\phi, \psi \in \mathcal{A}ss$. Now the syntactic formulation of Floyd's inductive assertion method consists of the following steps:

- Give a syntactic assertion network $\mathcal{A}\mathcal{N}$ for S.
- Prove that this syntactic assertion network is inductive.
- Prove that $\mathcal{A}\mathcal{N}$ is consistent w.r.t. $< \phi, \psi >$. $\square$

Theorem 5.14

Floyd's inductive assertion method for STDs is sound.

Proof Follows from Lemma 5.12, the fact that $\mathcal{A}\mathcal{N}$ is consistent with respect to $< \phi, \psi >$ iff $\mathcal{T}_I[\![\mathcal{A}\mathcal{N}]\!]$ is consistent w.r.t. $< \mathcal{T}_I[\![\phi]\!], \mathcal{T}_I[\![\psi]\!] >$, and $\models_I \{\phi\}S\{\psi\}$ iff $\models \{\mathcal{T}_I[\![\phi]\!]\}P_S\{\mathcal{T}_I[\![\psi]\!]\}$. $\square$

5.5 Relative Completeness of Floyd's Inductive Assertion Method

In Chapter 2 the completeness of the inductive assertion method has been discussed. In the proof presented semantic completeness has been established. That means,

(i) we showed that there exist, mathematically speaking, predicates satisfying the properties required for using the method, and

(ii) we did not provide a proof system for the underlying domain.

The predicates used in the proof, i.e., the ϕ-minimal predicates C_l, are defined by verbal description. The definition of these predicates, although exact and unambiguous, describes the semantics of C_l at the level, and in terms, of the language we used to give our definitions and to write down our mathematical proofs, i.e., at a meta-level w.r.t. the program correctness theory we are developing. Therefore, it is important to know whether they are expressible in our assertion language $\mathcal{A}ss$. Since the notion of *expressibility* is important for the rest of the discussion we introduce the following :

Definition 5.15 A predicate ϕ is called *expressible* in an assertion language L with interpretation I, if there exists an assertion $\psi \in L$ such that $\sigma \models_I \psi$ iff $\sigma \models \phi$, for every state σ. $\square$

We show below that the ϕ-minimal predicates are in general not expressible in our assertion language $\mathcal{A}ss$, as soon as we have an interpretation with a domain VAL with $|VAL| \geq 2$ and $|Pvar| = \infty$. Actually, we prove a stronger result, namely that there exists a program P and a specification $< \varphi, \psi >$ such that P is partially correct w.r.t. $< \varphi, \psi >$ and that there does not exist any inductive assertion network Q for P that is consistent w.r.t. $< \varphi, \psi >$ such that Q_l is expressible, for each label l of P.

Assume $|Pvar| = \infty$ and consider an interpretation I with a domain VAL containing at least two different elements 0 and 1. Let *true* denote the predicate that assigns *tt* to each state. Consider the program $P \equiv (\{s,t\}, \{(s, true \rightarrow f,t)\}, s, t)$ with $f(\sigma)(x) = 0$ for each $x \in Pvar$. Let c denote the predicate satisfying $c(\sigma) = tt$ iff $\sigma(x) = 0$, for each $x \in Pvar$. It is easy to prove that $\models \{true\} P \{c\}$ holds. We prove that there does not exist any inductive assertion network Q for P that is consistent w.r.t. $< true, c >$ such that Q_l is expressible in $\mathcal{A}$ss with I. To do so it suffices to prove that for no assertion $\phi \in \mathcal{A}$ss both $\models \mathcal{T}_I [\![\phi]\!] \circ f$ and $\models \mathcal{T}_I [\![\phi]\!] \rightarrow c$ hold.

Let ϕ be such that $\models \mathcal{T}_I [\![\phi]\!] \circ f$ and $\models \mathcal{T}_I [\![\phi]\!] \rightarrow c$. From $\models \mathcal{T}_I [\![\phi]\!] \circ f$ we have $\sigma \models \mathcal{T}_I [\![\phi]\!]$, for any σ satisfying $\sigma(x) = 0$ for all $x \in Pvar$. On the other hand, $\models \mathcal{T}_I [\![\phi]\!] \rightarrow c$ implies for any σ, if $\sigma \models \mathcal{T}_I [\![\phi]\!]$, then $\sigma(x) = 0$, for each $x \in Pvar$.

Hence, $\sigma \models \mathcal{T}_I [\![\phi]\!]$ iff $\sigma(x) = 0$ for each $x \in Pvar$. $\hfill (\dagger)$

Since $\phi \in \mathcal{A}$ss holds, there exists a variable $y \in Pvar$ with $y \notin var(\phi)$. Therefore, for each $\sigma \in \Sigma$, $\sigma \models \mathcal{T}_I [\![\phi]\!]$ iff $(\sigma : y \mapsto 1) \models \mathcal{T}_I [\![\phi]\!]$. This contradicts $(\dagger)$.

Fortunately, for programs containing boolean expressions as guards and state transformations f which are expressible in $\mathcal{A}$ss it turns out that, if φ is expressible, then the φ-minimal predicates are expressible in $\mathcal{A}$ss using an arithmetical interpretation, i.e., with an interpretation that has the natural numbers as domain and that gives a standard interpretation to arithmetical operations. This, in particular, implies that for STDs and specifications $< \varphi, \psi >$ with expressible φ, the φ-minimal predicates are expressible.

Next, we need to define when a state transformation is expressible, because we must characterise the effect upon the state of executing assignments s.a. $x := x + 1$ in terms of pre- and postassertions. For example, how does one characterise the program $x := x + 1$? By $\{x = v\} x := x + 1 \{x = v + 1\}$ where $v \in Lvar$, because one can prove that for any assertion ψ s.t. $\models \{x = v\} x := x + 1 \{\psi\}$ holds, also $\models x = v + 1 \rightarrow \psi$ holds. That is, $x = v + 1$ expresses the $x = v$-minimal predicate $SP(x = v, x := x + 1)$ of $x := x + 1$ w.r.t. $x = v$. This can be understood as follows. Consider an assertion ψ with $\models \{x = v\} x := x + 1 \{\psi\}$. Thus, for any state σ, if $\sigma \models_I x = v$, then $(\sigma : x \mapsto \sigma(x) + 1) \models_I \psi$. Consider an arbitrary state σ with $\sigma(x) = \sigma(v) + 1$. Then, $(\sigma : x \mapsto \sigma(x) - 1) \models_I x = v$. Hence, $\sigma \models_I \psi$. Thus, $\models_I x = v + 1 \rightarrow \psi$. Since $\models \{x = v\} x := x + 1 \{x = v + 1\}$ holds, $x = v + 1$ is the strongest postassertion of $x = v$ w.r.t. $x := x + 1$.

In general this leads to the following definition:

Definition 5.16 A state transformation f that only depends on $\{y_1, \dots, y_n\}$ and only affects variables in $\{y_1, \dots, y_n\}$ is called *expressible* in Ass, if there exists an assertion $\tilde{f} \in Ass$ such that $var(\tilde{f}) = \{y_1, \dots, y_n, y_1', \dots, y_n'\}$, where $y_1', \dots, y_n' \in Lvar$, and for all $\sigma, \sigma' \in \Sigma$:

$$\sigma' = f(\sigma) \quad \text{iff} \quad (\sigma : y_1', \dots y_n' \mapsto \sigma'(y_1), \dots, \sigma'(y_n)) \models_I \tilde{f} \text{ and}$$
$$\sigma(x) = \sigma'(x) \text{ for each } x \notin \{y_1, \dots, y_n\}. \qquad \square$$

Example 5.17 Thus, according to this definition the assignment $x := x + 1$ is expressible, since the assertion $x = v \to x' = v + 1$, where $v \in Lvar$, satisfies the conditions for this assignment. Indeed, every assignment $x_1, \dots, x_n := e_1, \dots, e_n$ is expressible, since the assertion $(x_1 = v_1 \wedge \dots \wedge x_n = v_n) \to (x_1' = e_1[v_1, \dots, v_n/x_1, \dots, x_n] \wedge \dots \wedge x_n' = e_n[v_1, \dots, v_n/x_1, \dots, x_n])$ satisfies the conditions of the definition for this assignment. $\qquad \square$

In fact, it is not really relevant for the remainder of this section that state transformations are functions, that is, *we can prove relative completeness of Floyd's inductive assertion method for transition diagrams where the instructions define relations rather than functions.* Therefore, we introduce the following definition:

Definition 5.18 An *extended transition diagram* consists of the same components as a transition diagram except that transitions are of the form (l, R, l'), where l and l' are locations and R is a function from $\Sigma \times \Sigma \to Bool$.

Let $\bar{x}$ be a finite set of variables in $Pvar$. A *syntactic extended transition diagram* which is based on $\bar{x}$ consists of the same components as a syntactic transition diagram except that transitions have the form (l, ρ, l'), where l and l' are locations and ρ is an assertion with $var(\rho) = \bar{x} \cup \bar{x}'$ with $\bar{x}' \subseteq Lvar$. $\qquad \square$

The semantics of extended transition diagrams is defined in the same manner as for transition diagrams except that now we have the following definition of a step for a transition (l, R, l'):

$$\langle l; \sigma \rangle \longrightarrow \langle l'; \sigma' \rangle \text{ iff } R(\sigma, \sigma') = tt.$$

In the same way that syntactic transition diagram can be associated with a transition diagram an extended syntactic transition diagram can also be associated with an extended transition diagram by replacing each syntactic transition (l, ρ, l') by a transition (l, R, l') such that $R(\sigma, \sigma') = tt$ iff $(\sigma : \bar{x}' \mapsto \sigma'(\bar{x})) \models \rho$ and $\sigma'(y) = \sigma(y)$, for every variable y not in $\bar{x}$.

In Exercise 5.1 we ask the reader to extend Floyd's inductive assertion method to cover extended transition diagrams and to prove its soundness and semantic completeness. Henceforth, we will refer to the extended method as *Floyd's inductive assertion method for extended syntactic transition diagrams*.

The general problem we face in proving relative completeness of Floyd's inductive assertion method is to express conditions on sequences of states using assertions from $\mathcal{A}$ss. Following [Coo78], this will be done using Gödel encoding [Göd31] and leads to the following theorem.

Theorem 5.19 (Relative completeness of Floyd's inductive assertion method)
Floyd's inductive assertion method for extended syntactic transition diagrams is relatively complete if the formal assertion language contains first order predicate logic over the standard model of the natural numbers. □

This theorem is proved in the next section.

5.5.1 Expressibility of φ-Minimal Predicates

In this section we assume an interpretation $I = (VAL, I_0)$ of $\mathcal{A}$ss such that $N = VAL$, $I_0(n)$ is the natural number n, and $I_0(+)$, $I_0(*)$, $I_0(\uparrow)$ are the standard addition, multiplication, and exponentiation operations of the natural numbers, respectively.

Because in the following account the difference between *syntax* and *semantics* is very important, we always use outside the formal logic (syntax) meta-symbols when reasoning semantically, thus $\Rightarrow$ instead of $\rightarrow$, and $\exists\!\!\!\exists$ instead of $\exists$, etc.

Let $S \equiv (L, ST, s, t)$ be an extended syntactic transition diagram which is based on $\bar{y}$. Without loss of generality we assume $L \subset N$. Now, for a location i of S the φ-minimal predicate C_i has been defined as follows in Chapter 2:

$$C_i(\sigma) \stackrel{\text{def}}{=} \text{there exists a state } \sigma_0 \text{ with } \sigma_0 \models \varphi \text{ and } \langle s; \sigma_0 \rangle \longrightarrow^* \langle i; \sigma \rangle$$

Using the definition of computation sequence and meta-symbols we get[2]:

$$\begin{aligned}
C_i(\sigma) \quad \stackrel{\text{def}}{=} \quad &\exists\!\!\!\exists k. \exists\!\!\!\exists \text{nodes } i_0, \dots, i_k. \exists\!\!\!\exists \text{states } \sigma_0, \dots, \sigma_k. \\
&i_0 = s \wedge i_k = i \wedge \varphi(\sigma_0) = tt \wedge \sigma_k = \sigma \wedge \\
&\forall\!\!\!\forall 0 \leq j < k. \exists\!\!\!\exists \text{edge } ed \text{ from } i_j \text{ to } i_{j+1} \text{ with label } \rho \text{ such that} \\
&\sigma \models_I \rho[\sigma_j(\bar{y})/\bar{y}, \sigma_{j+1}(\bar{y})/\bar{y}'] \wedge \\
&\sigma_j(x) = \sigma_{j+1}(x), \text{ for every } x \notin \bar{y}.
\end{aligned}$$

Our task is to find a formula in $\mathcal{A}$ss, i.e., an assertion, whose semantics is equivalent to that of the predicate in the right hand side (r.h.s.) of the definition

---

[2] Recall that we identify constant symbols with their interpretations (see page 294).

above. The idea is to obtain this formula from the definition of C_i by replacing the meta-symbols by symbols of our formal assertion language with the same semantics.

To achieve this we have to do the following:

(i) Remove the references to the states, i.e., to $\sigma_0, \ldots, \sigma_k$, and the infinite conjunction $\sigma_j(x) = \sigma_{j+1}(x)$, for every $x \notin \bar{y}$.

(ii) Remove the references to the state transition graph, i.e., to the nodes $i_0, \ldots, i_k$ and edges ed.

(iii) Replace the unbounded formula:

$$\exists k. \exists \text{ nodes } i_0, \ldots, i_k. \exists \text{ state vectors } \sigma_0, \ldots, \sigma_k$$

by an equivalent formula whose length is independent of the length of the computation which it characterises, and determined only by the syntax of S.

(iv) Remove the vectors.

(v) Remove the reference to φ.

We proceed as follows:

For (i) To solve this, we observe that the predicate C_i is equivalent to the following predicate:

$\exists k. \exists \text{nodes } i_0, \ldots, i_k. \exists \text{vectors of values } \bar{\mu}_0, \ldots, \bar{\mu}_k$ of the same length as $\bar{y}$ such that $i_0 = s \wedge i_k = i \wedge \sigma \models \varphi[\bar{\mu}_0/\bar{y}] \wedge \sigma \models \bar{y} = \bar{\mu}_k$
$\forall 0 \leq j < k. \exists \text{edge } ed$ from i_j to i_{j+1} with label ρ such that
$\sigma \models_I \rho[\bar{\mu}_j/\bar{y}, \bar{\mu}_{j+1}/\bar{y}']$.

Then, we replace the state σ over the value domain by the syntactic vector variables $\bar{y}$ that will be free in the formula. We also replace the vectors of values $\bar{\mu}_0, \ldots, \bar{\mu}_k$ by the syntactic vector variables $\bar{y}_0, \ldots, \bar{y}_k$. Thus, using $|\bar{y}_j|$ to denote the length of the vector $\bar{y}_j$ and $|\bar{y}|$ to denote the length of the vector $\bar{y}$ we obtain the formula:

$\exists k. \exists \text{nodes } i_0, \ldots, i_k. \exists \bar{y}_0, \ldots, \bar{y}_k$ such that $(\forall 0 \leq j \leq k. |\bar{y}_j| = |\bar{y}|) \wedge$
$i_0 = s \wedge i_k = i \wedge \sigma \models \varphi[\bar{\mu}_0/\bar{y}] \wedge \sigma \models \bar{y} = \bar{\mu}_k$
$\forall 0 \leq j < k. \exists \text{edge } ed$ from i_j to i_{j+1} with label ρ such that
$\sigma \models_I \rho[\bar{y}_j/\bar{y}, \bar{y}_{j+1}/\bar{y}']$.

For (iv) This is easy, because all the vectors have the same fixed length, namely the total number of program variables used in the program concerned. Thus we can always write $y_1, \ldots, y_n$ for $\bar{y}$.

For (v) This is also easy, because we assumed that φ is expressible in $\mathcal{A}$ss, i.e., there exists an assertion $\tilde{\varphi} \in \mathcal{A}$ss with $\mathcal{T}_I \llbracket \tilde{\varphi} \rrbracket = \varphi$. Henceforth, we write φ for $\tilde{\varphi}$.

For (ii) We use the fact that the program is finite and that the number of edges and labels is fixed. We enumerate all edges between locations j and j' beginning at 0 and define $E_{j,j',k}$ for the edge *ed* with number k from j to j' as follows:

$$E_{j,j',k} \overset{\text{def}}{=} l = j \wedge m = j' \wedge \rho_k, \text{ provided } ed \equiv (j, \rho_k, j').$$

In fact $l = j \wedge m = j' \wedge \rho_k$ is not a formula but rather a formula scheme which gives us a formula when j and j' are instantiated by specific numbers in L. The obtained formula contains l and m as free variables. Using the fact that an existential quantification over a finite number of objects can be written as a disjunction, we define the assertion E in $\mathcal{A}$ss as follows:

$$E \overset{\text{def}}{=} E_{i_1,j_1,0} \vee \ldots \vee E_{i_1,j_1,k_1} \vee E_{i_2,j_2,0} \vee \ldots \vee E_{i_2,j_2,k_2} \ldots,$$

where the pairs (i_r, j_r) are exactly those for which there are $(k_r + 1)$ edges from i_r to j_r in the program.

Lemma 5.20 For every state σ and σ' and location j and j', we have $\sigma \models_I E[\sigma'(\bar{y})/\bar{y}', j/l, j'/m]$ iff there is a transition (j, ρ, j') in S such that $\langle j; \sigma \rangle \rightarrow \langle j'; \sigma' \rangle$ is a legal computation step. $\qquad \square$

Using the formula E we now can express that a sequence

$$\langle i_0; \sigma_0 \rangle \rightarrow \langle i_1; \sigma_1 \rangle \rightarrow \ldots \rightarrow \langle i_k; \sigma_k \rangle$$

is a legal computation sequence by the following formula in $\mathcal{A}$ss:

$$\forall j.((0 \leq j \wedge j < k) \rightarrow E[\sigma_j(\bar{y})/\bar{y}, \sigma_{j+1}(\bar{y})/\bar{y}', i_j/l, i_{j+1}/m]).$$

The relation symbols "$\leq$" and "$<$" can either be considered as relation symbols of $\mathcal{A}$ss and then they are assigned their standard meanings by I or they can be introduced as abbreviations with $x < y \equiv \exists z. \neg(z = 0) \wedge x + z = y$ and $x \leq y \equiv x < y \vee x = y$, respectively. We also use $\forall j.0 \leq j < k.E[\sigma_j(\bar{y})/\bar{y}, \sigma_{j+1}(\bar{y})/\bar{y}', i_j/l, i_{j+1}/m]$ as an abbreviation of the formula above.

For (iii) This is a serious problem that we solve by coding. A list of numbers $m_0, \ldots, m_k$ from N can be represented by a single number m. Take for instance the following method:

$$m = \Pi_{i=0}^k p_i^{m_i+1}, \text{ where } p_i \text{ is the i-th prime } (p_0 = 2).$$

Because of the uniqueness of prime factorisation, given such an m we can regain the original list of numbers. One has to encode $n+1$ such sequences in order to code the quantification "$\exists k.\exists l^0,\dots,l^k.\exists \bar{y}_0,\dots,\bar{y}_k$" as a formula of fixed finite length, independent of k, where n denotes the number of program variables. This technique is illustrated in the following figure:

$$
\begin{array}{ccccc}
i_0 & \dots & i_k & \leftarrow & \tilde{v}_0 \\
y_{01} & \dots & y_{k1} & \leftarrow & \tilde{v}_1 \\
\vdots & & \vdots & & \vdots \\
\vdots & & \vdots & & \vdots \\
y_{0n} & \dots & y_{kn} & \leftarrow & \tilde{v}_n \\
\uparrow & & \uparrow & & \\
\bar{y}_0 & & \bar{y}_k & &
\end{array}
$$

Suppose $\mathcal{A}ss$ is extended with predicate $seq(x)$ and Exp is extended with functions $len(x)$ and $proj(x,y)$ whose meaning is defined as follows at the meta-level:

$$seq(x) \stackrel{\text{def}}{=} \exists k.\exists x_0 \dots x_k.x = \Pi_{i=0}^{k} p_i^{x_i+1},$$

$len(x) = y \stackrel{\text{def}}{=}$ "p_y is the first prime that is not a divisor of x",

$$proj(x,y) \stackrel{\text{def}}{=} \begin{cases} \text{the greatest } k \text{ such that} \\ \quad p_x^{k+1} \text{ is a divisor of } y & , \text{if } x < len(y), \\ 0 & , \text{otherwise.} \end{cases}$$

Then $seq(x)$ expresses that x codes a list, $seq(x) \wedge len(x) = n$ expresses that x codes a list of length n and finally the expression $seq(x) \wedge j < len(x) \wedge proj(j,x) = n$ expresses that n is the number with index j from the list coded in x.

Using this notation one can rewrite C_i, namely by letting $\tilde{v}_i$ code the list $y_{0i},\dots,y_{ki}$ for $1 \leq i \leq n$ and $\tilde{v}_0$ code the list of numbers associated with $i_0,\dots,i_k$.

The syntactic expression of the φ-minimal predicate C_i now becomes:

$\exists k.\exists \tilde{v}_0 \dots \tilde{v}_n.$

$\bigwedge_{j=0}^{n} (seq(\tilde{v}_j) \wedge len(\tilde{v}_j) = k+1) \wedge$

$proj(0,\tilde{v}_0) = s \wedge proj(k,\tilde{v}_0) = i \wedge$

$\varphi[proj(0,\tilde{v}_1)/y_1,\dots,proj(0,\tilde{v}_n)/y_n] \wedge$

$\bigwedge_{j=1}^{n} proj(k,\tilde{v}_j) = y_j \wedge$

$\forall j.0 \leq j < k.E[proj(j,\tilde{v}_1)/y_1,\dots,proj(j,\tilde{v}_n)/y_n,$

$$proj(j+1,\tilde{v}_1)/y_1',\dots,proj(j+1,\tilde{v}_n)/y_n',$$
$$proj(j,\tilde{v}_0)/l,proj(j+1,\tilde{v}_0)/m].$$

Note that $\exists \tilde{v}_0 \dots \tilde{v}_n$ is no longer dependent on k. The only problem left is that "seq", "len" and "$proj$" do not occur as primitives in $\mathcal{A}$ss. This is solved by the following lemma:

Lemma 5.21 There are assertions SEQ, LEN and PROJ in $\mathcal{A}$ss such that

$$seq(x) \quad\quad \Leftrightarrow \quad \models \text{SEQ}(x),$$
$$len(x) = y \quad \Leftrightarrow \quad \models \text{LEN}(x,y), \text{ and}$$
$$proj(x,y) = z \quad \Leftrightarrow \quad \models \text{PROJ}(x,y,z).$$

Proof Define first the following auxiliary formulae in $\mathcal{A}$ss:

$$\text{DIV}(x,y) \quad\equiv\quad \exists z.x*z = y,$$
$$\text{PRIME}(y) \quad\equiv\quad y > 1 \wedge \forall x.\text{DIV}(x,y) \rightarrow (x = 1 \vee x = y), \text{ and}$$
$$\text{PR\_SUC}(x,y) \quad\equiv\quad \text{PRIME}(x) \wedge \text{PRIME}(y) \wedge x < y \wedge$$
$$\forall z.(x < z \wedge z < y) \rightarrow \neg\text{PRIME}(z).$$

Obviously, the following equivalences hold:

"x is a divisor of y" $\quad\quad\quad\quad\quad \Leftrightarrow \quad \models \text{DIV}(x,y),$

"y is a prime number" $\quad\quad\quad\quad\quad \Leftrightarrow \quad \models \text{PRIME}(y) \text{ and}$

"x and y are successive prime numbers" $\quad \Leftrightarrow \quad \models \text{PR\_SUC}(x,y).$

It is more difficult to see that the predicate "$p_x = y$", that is, the x-th prime number is y, can be defined in $\mathcal{A}$ss. We define the assertion $\text{PN}(x,y)$ as follows:

$$\text{PN}(x,y) \equiv \text{PRIME}(y) \wedge \exists z.\neg\text{DIV}(2,z) \wedge \tag{5.1}$$

$$(\forall u \forall v.u \leq y \wedge v \leq y.\text{PR\_SUC}(u,v) \rightarrow$$

$$\forall i.(\text{DIV}(u \uparrow i,z) \wedge \neg\text{DIV}(u \uparrow (i+1),z)) \rightarrow \tag{5.2}$$

$$\text{DIV}\,(v \uparrow (i+1),z) \wedge \neg\text{DIV}(v \uparrow (i+2),z)) \wedge$$

$$\text{DIV}(y \uparrow x,z) \wedge \neg\text{DIV}(y \uparrow (x+1),z) \tag{5.3}$$

and we prove that $\text{PN}(x,y)$ indeed expresses "$p_x = y$".

a) Let $p_k = m$, then $\models \text{PN}(k,m)$ too. Choose $z = \Pi_{j=0}^{k} p_j^j$.

b) Assume $\models \text{PN}(k,m)$. Then $\text{PRIME}(m)$, say $m = p_l$, and there is a z, for which $z = \Pi_{j=0}^{l} p_j^{z_j}$ (prime factorisation of z), with $\neg\text{DIV}(2,z)$. Thus $z_0 = 0$. If $p_1 \leq m$, then with the help of 5.2 (take $i = 0, u = p_0, v = p_1$):

$$\text{DIV}\,(p_1,z) \wedge \neg\text{DIV}(p_1^2,z), \text{ thus } z_1 = 1.$$

In general, if $p_j \leq m$ then one proves with the help of 5.2: $z_j = j$. Because $m = p_l$ the following especially holds: $z_l = l$.
5.3 delivers

$$\text{DIV}(m^k, z) \land \neg \text{DIV}(m^{k+1}, z), \text{ i.e.,}$$

$\text{DIV}(p_l^k, z) \land \neg \text{DIV}(p_l^{k+1}, z)$, thus $k = z_l = l$, so that $m = p_k$.

(end of proof for case PN)

We are now able to define SEQ, LEN and PROJ in $\mathcal{A}$ss:

$$\text{SEQ}(x) \equiv \exists y. \text{PRIME}(y) \land \forall z \geq y. \text{PRIME}(z) \to \neg \text{DIV}(z, x) \land$$
$$\forall z < y. \text{PRIME}(z) \to \text{DIV}(z, x).$$
$$\text{LEN}(x, y) \equiv \exists v. \text{PRIME}(v) \land \text{PN}(y, v) \land \neg \text{DIV}(v, x) \land$$
$$\forall u < v. \text{PRIME}(u) \to \text{DIV}(u, x).$$

Note that, since the length of $(m_0, \ldots, m_k)$ is $k+1$ and $x = p_0^{m_0+1} \ldots p_k^{m_k+1}$, then if you consider p_{k+1} index $k+1$ indicates the length of the row.

$$\text{PROJ}(x, y, z) \equiv (z = 0 \land \forall u. \text{LEN}(y, u) \to x \geq u) \lor \qquad (5.4)$$
$$(\exists u. \text{LEN}(y, u) \land x < u \land \exists v. \text{PN}(x, v) \land \qquad (5.5)$$
$$\text{DIV}(v \uparrow (z+1), y) \land \neg \text{DIV}(v \uparrow (z+2), y)).$$

Note that z is the number with index x coded in row y. The first disjunct applies when index $x \geq$ length of y and the second disjunct when $x < $ length of $y(= u)$ and the x-th prime number is v and $(v \uparrow (z+1)$ is a divisor of y) but $\neg(v \uparrow (z+2)$ is a divisor of y). $\qquad \square$

Thus, using the disjoint lists $\bar{z} = z_1, \ldots, z_n$ and $\bar{w} = w_1, \ldots, w_n$ of fresh logical variables, the φ-minimal predicate C_i can be expressed as the following assertion in $\mathcal{A}$ss:

$$\exists k. \exists \tilde{v}_0 \ldots \tilde{v}_n.$$
$$\bigwedge_{j=0}^{n} (\text{SEQ}(\tilde{v}_j) \land \text{LEN}(\tilde{v}_j, k+1)) \land \text{PROJ}(0, \tilde{v}_0, s) \land \text{PROJ}(k, \tilde{v}_0, i) \land$$
$$(\forall \bar{z}. \bigwedge_{j=1}^{n} \text{PROJ}(0, \tilde{v}_j, z_j) \to \varphi[\bar{z}/\bar{y}]) \land \bigwedge_{j=1}^{n} \text{PROJ}(k, \tilde{v}_j, y_j) \land$$
$$\forall j. 0 \leq j < k. \forall \bar{z} \bar{w} v v'.$$
$$(\bigwedge_{s=1}^{n} (\text{PROJ}(j, \tilde{v}_s, z_s) \land \text{PROJ}(j+1, \tilde{v}_s, w_s)) \land$$
$$\text{PROJ}(j, \tilde{v}_0, v) \land \text{PROJ}(j+1, \tilde{v}_0, v'))$$
$$\to E[\bar{z}/\bar{y}, \bar{w}/\bar{y}', v/l, v'/m].$$

We have proved that the inductive assertion method is relatively complete for programs which only contain conditions and state transformations that are expressible in $\mathcal{A}$ss, provided the interpretation of $\mathcal{A}$ss contains the standard model of the natural numbers. This finishes our proof of Theorem 5.19.

For obtaining relative completeness of Floyd's inductive assertion method of Chapter 2, the corollary below suffices, in which only syntactic transition diagrams are considered; extended syntactic transition diagrams are only needed to establish the relative completeness of the Apt, Francez & de Roever method of Chapter 4.

Corollary 5.22 Floyd's inductive assertion method for syntactic transition diagrams is relatively complete if the formal assertion language contains at least first order predicate logic over the standard model of the natural numbers.

Proof It suffices to prove that assignments are expressible in $\mathcal{A}$ss. Consider an assignment $x_0, \ldots, x_n := e_0, \ldots, e_n$. Let $\psi \stackrel{\text{def}}{=} (v_0 = e_0 \wedge \ldots \wedge v_n = e_n)$, with $v_0, \ldots, v_n \in Lvar$. We prove that for any σ and σ' with $\sigma(y) = \sigma'(y)$, for every $y \notin \{x_0, \ldots, x_n\}$, $\sigma' \in \mathcal{A}_I \llbracket x_0, \ldots, x_n := e_0, \ldots, e_n \rrbracket \sigma$ iff $(\sigma : v_0, \ldots, v_n \mapsto \sigma'(x_0), \ldots, \sigma'(x_n)) \models_I \psi$.

In the proof we abbreviate $\mathcal{E}_I \llbracket e_0 \rrbracket \sigma, \ldots, \mathcal{E}_I \llbracket e_n \rrbracket \sigma$ by $\mathcal{E}_I \llbracket \bar{e} \rrbracket \sigma$, $x_0, \ldots, x_n$ by $\bar{x}$, and $v_0, \ldots, v_n$ by $\bar{y}'$.

By definition of $\mathcal{A}_I$, we have $\sigma' = \mathcal{A}_I \llbracket \bar{x} := \bar{e} \rrbracket \sigma$ iff $\sigma' = (\sigma : \bar{x} \mapsto \mathcal{E}_I \llbracket \bar{e} \rrbracket \sigma)$. Since $\sigma(y) = \sigma'(y)$, for $y \notin \{\bar{x}\}$, we obtain by Lemma 5.8, $\sigma' = \mathcal{A}_I \llbracket \bar{x} := \bar{e} \rrbracket \sigma$ iff $(\sigma' : \bar{x}, \bar{y}' \mapsto \mathcal{E}_I \llbracket \bar{e} \rrbracket \sigma, \mathcal{E}_I \llbracket \bar{e} \rrbracket \sigma) \models_I (\bar{x} = \bar{e})[\bar{y}'/\bar{x}]$. Thus, $\sigma' = \mathcal{A}_I \llbracket \bar{x} := \bar{e} \rrbracket \sigma$ iff $(\sigma : \bar{y}' \mapsto \mathcal{E}_I \llbracket \bar{e} \rrbracket \sigma) \models_I \bar{y}' = \bar{e}$. $\square$

We mention that if we do not have the usual interpretation of the natural numbers, for instance, we have Presburger arithmetic, then the inductive assertion method is not relatively complete but only semantically complete.

5.6 Relative Completeness of the Method of Owicki & Gries

In the previous sections we have provided the semantic notions introduced in Chapter 2 with syntactic counterparts and proved relative completeness of Floyd's inductive assertion method for syntactic transition diagrams. In this section, we prove relative completeness of the method of Owicki & Gries introduced in Chapter 3. Recall that the parallel composition of transition diagrams as defined in Chapter 3 is again a transition diagram. Therefore, we can use the same syntactic notions introduced in the previous sections to define the parallel composition of syntactic transition diagrams.

Let us formulate a syntactic version of the method of Owicki & Gries. To do so, we first define a notion of auxiliary variables for syntactic transition diagrams.

Definition 5.23 Consider two STDs S and S'. Then, we say that S' is obtained from S by introducing the auxiliary variables $\bar{z}$, if the following conditions are satisfied:

- for every guard b appearing in S, $var(b) \cap \bar{z} = \emptyset$,
- for every assignment $\bar{x} := \bar{e}$ appearing in S, $(\bar{x} \cup var(\bar{e})) \cap \bar{z} = \emptyset$, and
- there exists a bijective function associating to each transition $(l, b \to \bar{x} := \bar{e}, l')$ of S' a transition $(l, b \to \bar{x}' := \bar{e}', l')$ of S such that either $\bar{x} = \bar{x}'$ and $\bar{e} = \bar{e}'$, or $\bar{x} := \bar{e}$ has the form $\bar{x}', \bar{x}'' := \bar{e}', \bar{e}''$ with $\bar{x}'' \subseteq \bar{z}$. $\qquad\square$

It is a routine exercise to prove that if $\bar{z}$ is a set of auxiliary variables for an STD S, then $\bar{z}$ is a set of auxiliary variables for the program P_S.

We can now define a syntactic version of the method of Owicki & Gries.

Definition 5.24 (The method of Owicki & Gries – syntactic formulation)
Consider a parallel composition $S \equiv S_1 \parallel \ldots \parallel S_n$ of STDs and a specification $< \phi, \psi >$ with $\phi, \psi \in \mathcal{A}ss$.

The syntactic formulation of the method of Owicki & Gries to prove partial correctness of S w.r.t. $< \phi, \psi >$ consists of the following steps:

(i) Augment S_i by introducing auxiliary variables leading to $S' \equiv S'_1 \parallel \ldots \parallel S'_n$.

(ii) Give a syntactic assertion network $\mathcal{AN}_i$ for each S'_i, for $i = 1, \ldots, n$.

(iii) For each $i = 1, \ldots, n$, prove that $\mathcal{AN}_i$ is inductive.

(iv) Prove interference freedom, that is, for every distinct i and j in $\{1, \ldots, n\}$, for every transition $(l, b \to \bar{x} := \bar{e}, l')$ of S'_i and every location l'' of S'_j, we have:

$$\models_I (\mathcal{AN}_i(l) \wedge \mathcal{AN}_j(l'') \wedge b) \to \mathcal{AN}_j(l'')[\bar{e}/\bar{x}].$$

(v) Prove that

- $\models_I \exists \bar{v}.(\phi \to \bigwedge_i \mathcal{AN}_i(s_i)[\bar{v}/\bar{z}])$, where s_i denotes the initial location of S'_i and $\bar{v}$ is a set of variables not occurring in S'.
- $\models_I (\bigwedge_i \mathcal{AN}_i(t_i)) \to \psi$, where t_i denotes the final location of S'_i. $\quad\square$

Soundness of the syntactic formulation of the method of Owicki & Gries follows immediately from the soundness of the semantic formulation and Lemma 5.8. Thus, we have:

Theorem 5.25
The method of Owicki & Gries for parallel syntactic transition diagrams is sound. $\qquad\square$

In the remainder of this section we prove relative completeness of the syntactic formulation of the method of Owicki & Gries. Clearly, it suffices to prove that for every STD S the strongest l-condition of P_S based on $\mathcal{R}$, i.e., the predicate $SP'_l(\varphi, P_S)$, is expressible in our assertion language $\mathcal{A}ss$.

Thus, assume we are given a parallel composition $S \equiv S_1 \parallel \ldots \parallel S_n$ of STDs and let P_i denote the program associated to S_i. Let $\bar{x} = x_1, \ldots, x_k$ be the set of variables which occur in S. Let h be a variable in $Pvar \setminus \bar{x}$ that ranges over $(\{1, \ldots, n\} \times N^k)^*$. We assume that we have the expression $h \frown (i, x_1, \ldots, x_k)$ in $\mathcal{A}ss$ and that $\mathcal{E}_I[\![h]\!] \frown (i, \sigma(x_1), \ldots, \sigma(x_k)) = \mathcal{E}_I[\![h]\!] \cdot (i, \sigma(x_1), \ldots, \sigma(x_k))$, where $\cdot$ denotes the concatenation of sequences. Then, we augment S_i by the auxiliary variable h as follows: every instruction $b \to \bar{x} := \bar{e}$ is transformed into $b \to \bar{x}, h := \bar{e}, h \frown (i, x_1, \ldots, x_k)$.

In order to express $SP'_l(\varphi, P_i)$, we show how to express $\mathcal{R}_l[\![P_i]\!]$ and $\theta[P_i](\sigma)$ in $\mathcal{A}ss$. To do so, we give alternative definitions for $\mathcal{R}_l[\![P_i]\!]$, respectively, $\theta[P_i](\sigma)$, which are equivalent to Definitions 3.32 and 3.37, respectively.

Definition 5.26 Let $w = (\sigma_1, \sigma'_1) \ldots (\sigma_m, \sigma'_m)$ be a sequence of pairs of states with $m \geq 0$. Then, $w \in \mathcal{R}'_l[\![P_i]\!]$ iff there exists a sequence $l_1, \ldots, l_{m+1}$ of locations with $l_1 = s$ and $l_{m+1} = l$ such that $l_i \xrightarrow{\langle \sigma_i, \sigma'_i \rangle} l_{i+1}$, for every $i = 1, \ldots, m$. $\qquad \square$

By induction on the length of w it can easily be proved that this definition is equivalent to Definition 3.32, i.e., $\mathcal{R}'_l[\![P_i]\!] = \mathcal{R}_l[\![P_i]\!]$. The advantage of this definition is that it is not recursive and can easily be expressed in $\mathcal{A}ss$. Indeed, using Lemma 5.20 and Lemma 5.21, we can construct an assertion $\alpha_{i,l}$ with $var(\alpha_{i,l}) = \{\tilde{\theta}_i\}$ such that for every state σ we have $\mathcal{T}_I[\![\alpha_{i,l}]\!]\sigma = tt$ iff $\sigma(\tilde{\theta}_i) \in \mathcal{R}'_l[\![P_i]\!]$.

Definition 5.27 Let $\theta = (i_0, \sigma_0) \ldots (i_m, \sigma_m)$ be a sequence of pairs each consisting of an index in $\{1, \ldots, n\}$ and a state. Let w be a sequence of pairs of states and let σ be a state. Let $\sigma_{m+1} = \sigma$. Then $pr_i(\theta, \sigma) = w$ iff one of the following conditions is satisfied:

- $w = \varepsilon$ and for all $j \in \{0, \ldots, m\}$ we have $i_j \neq i$, or
- $w = (\sigma'_0, \sigma''_0) \ldots (\sigma'_k, \sigma''_k)$ with $k \geq 0$ and there exists a maximal and ordered subsequence $j_0, \ldots, j_k$ such that $i_{j_0} = \ldots = i_{j_k} = i$ and for every $u = 0, \ldots, k$ we have $\sigma'_u = \sigma_{i_{j_u}}$ and $\sigma''_u = \sigma_{i_{j_u+1}}$. $\qquad \square$

It is easy to see that using the projection function and the relation $<$ one can express in $\mathcal{A}ss$ that a sequence of natural numbers in $\{1, \ldots, n\}$ is a maximal and ordered subsequence of $i_0, \ldots, i_m$. Thus, one can write an assertion β_i with

$var(\beta_i) = \{\tilde{\theta}_i, h\}$ that expresses $pr_i(\theta, \sigma)$, that is, which satisfies for every state σ, $\mathcal{T}_I [\![\beta_i]\!] \sigma = tt$ iff $\sigma(\tilde{\theta}_i) = \sigma(h)[P_i](\sigma)$. The equivalence of Definition 5.27 with Definition 3.37 can be proved by induction on the length of w. Now, using the assertions $\alpha_{i,l}$ and β_i one can express $SP_l'(\varphi, P_i)$ as follows:

$$\exists \tilde{\theta}_i. \beta_i \wedge \alpha_{i,l} \wedge$$
$$(\text{LEN}(h, 0) \to \varphi) \wedge$$
$$\neg \text{LEN}(h, 0) \to$$
$$\forall x_1', \dots, x_n'. \forall y. (\text{PROJ}(1, h, y) \wedge \bigwedge_i \text{PROJ}(i, y, x_i')) \to \varphi[x_i'/x_i],$$

where the latter two conjuncts express the condition $Init(\sigma, \theta) \models \varphi$.

Remember that in this section we made the assumption that $\mathcal{A}ss$ contains a variable h which is interpreted over $(\{1, \dots, n\} \times N^k)^*$ and that we have a function symbol for concatenation of finite lists. These assumptions are in fact not essential, since by the results of the previous section tuples and finite sequences of values in N can be encoded in N.

Thus, we have the following theorem:

Theorem 5.28
The method of Owicki & Gries for parallel syntactic transition diagrams is relatively complete, provided the formal assertion language includes at least Peano arithmetic. □

5.7 Relative Completeness of the Method of Apt, Francez & de Roever

The method of Apt, Francez & de Roever allows us to prove partial correctness of synchronous transition diagrams that communicate using synchronous message passing and do not share variables. In this section, we define syntactic synchronous transition diagrams and formulate a syntactic version of the method of Apt, Francez & de Roever. Then, we show that also this method is relatively complete, provided the formal assertion language includes at least Peano arithmetic.

We first extend our formal assertion language with a set *CHAN* of channel names. Then, we define *syntactic communication instructions* as follows.

Definition 5.29 A *syntactic communication instruction* is either a *syntactic input instruction* or a *syntactic output instruction*, where

- a *syntactic input instruction* has the form $b; C?x \to \bar{x} := \bar{e}$, where $b \in BExp$, $C \in CHAN$, $x \in Pvar$, and $\bar{x} := \bar{e}$ is an assignment, and
- a *syntactic output instruction* has the form $b; C!e \to \bar{x} := \bar{e}$, where b, C, and $\bar{x} := \bar{e}$ are as above and $e \in PExp$. □

A *syntactic process* is defined in the same way as an STD except that its transitions are of the form $(l, inst, l')$ where *inst* is either an ordinary syntactic instruction or a syntactic communication instruction. A transition $(l, inst, l')$ is called *external*, if *inst* is a communication instruction; otherwise, it is called *internal*.

A syntactic synchronous transition diagram (SSTD for short) $S_1 \parallel \ldots \parallel S_n$ is given by a set of syntactic processes $S_1, \ldots, S_n$ such that no variable in *Pvar* occurs in two different processes. Moreover, we put the same restrictions on the use of channels as in Chapter 4. It is obvious how to associate a synchronous diagram P_S to an SSTD S. This defines a semantics for SSTDs as well as a corresponding notion of partial correctness, that is, we say that an SSTD S is partially correct w.r.t. $\langle \phi, \psi \rangle$ in interpretation I iff P_S is partially correct w.r.t. $< \mathcal{T}_I [\![\phi]\!], \mathcal{T}_I [\![\psi]\!] >$.

Next, we define a syntactic formulation of the method of Apt, Francez & de Roever:

Definition 5.30 (The method of Apt, Francez & de Roever – syntactic formulation) Given an SSTD $S \equiv S_1 \parallel \ldots \parallel S_n$. Prove as follows that S is partially correct w.r.t. $\langle \phi, \psi \rangle$:

 (i) Augment S_i by introducing auxiliary variables $\bar{z}^i$ which do not occur in S, ϕ or ψ: an assignment $\bar{x} := \bar{e}$ of a communication instruction can be replaced by $\bar{x}, \bar{z}^i := \bar{e}, \bar{e}'$. Let S_i' be the process so obtained, $S' \equiv S_1' \parallel \ldots \parallel S_n'$, and $\bar{z} = \bigcup_{i=1}^n \bar{z}^i$.

 (ii) Give a syntactic assertion network $\mathcal{AN}_i$ for each S_i' such that no program variable of S_i' occurs freely in an assertion $\mathcal{AN}_j$, for $i \neq j$. Note that this condition does not prevent the same *logical* variable from occurring freely in both $\mathcal{AN}_i$ and $\mathcal{AN}_j$.

 (iii) Prove local correctness of every assertion network $\mathcal{AN}_i$, that is, for every internal transition $(l, b \to \bar{x} := \bar{e}, l')$ of S_i', prove

$$\models_I \mathcal{AN}_i(l) \wedge b \to \mathcal{AN}_i(l')[\bar{e}/\bar{x}].$$

 (iv) Prove the cooperation test, that is, give an assertion I with free variables in $\bar{z}$ that satisfies the following condition for every pair of transitions $(l_1, b; C!e \to \bar{x} := \bar{e}, l_2)$ of S_i' and $(l_1', b'; C?x \to \bar{x}' := \bar{e}', l_2')$ of S_j':

$$\models_I (I \wedge \mathcal{AN}_i(l_1) \wedge \mathcal{AN}_j(l_1') \wedge b \wedge b') \to (I \wedge \mathcal{AN}_i(l_2) \wedge \mathcal{AN}_j(l_2'))[\bar{e}/\bar{x}, \bar{e}'/\bar{x}'][e/x].$$

 (v) Prove:

- the initialisation condition, that is,

$$\models_I \exists \bar{w}.\exists \bar{v}.(\varphi \to (I \wedge \bigwedge_i \mathcal{AN}_i(s_i))[\bar{v}/\bar{z}]),$$

where s_i denotes the initial location of S_i', $\bar{w}$ is the set of logical variables which do not occur in φ, and $\bar{v}$ is a set of fresh logical variables which do not occur in S' and φ, and

- the finalisation condition, that is,

$$\models_I (I \wedge \bigwedge_i \mathcal{AN}_i(t_i)) \to \psi,$$

where t_i denotes the final location of S_i'.   □

As in the case of the method of Owicki & Gries the soundness of the syntactic version of the method of Apt, Francez & de Roever (AFR for short) follows from the soundness of its semantic formulation and Lemma 5.8. Thus, we have

Theorem 5.31
The (syntactic version of the) method of Apt, Francez & de Roever for distributed syntactic transition diagrams is sound.   □

We consider now the relative completeness of this method. Assume we are given a closed synchronous transition diagram $P \equiv P_1 \parallel \ldots \parallel P_n$. In order to prove partial correctness of P w.r.t. $\langle \varphi, \psi \rangle$, we extend each P_i by introducing a new variable h_i which is then used to trace the communications of P_i. The synchronous transition diagram so obtained is denoted by P_i'. Next recall that in the completeness proof one cannot associate strongest postcondition $SP_l(\varphi, P_i')$ to l because in general φ depends on free variables from all the processes P_j', i.e., also from processes P_j' with $i \neq j$. So assuming φ to be expressed by $\bar{\varphi}$ this implies that in general $\bar{\varphi}$ contains free variables from processes P_j' with $i \neq j$, whereas by step (ii) of Definition 5.30 $\mathcal{AN}_i(l)$ is not allowed to contain program variables from P_j' with $i \neq j$. A possible solution to this problem is to "freeze" the initial values of the program variables in logical variables and substitute these logical variables for their corresponding program variables inside $\bar{\varphi}$. At the semantic level this corresponds to predicate φ_i of the semantic completeness proof, which is therefore expressed by $\bar{\varphi}_i \stackrel{\text{def}}{=} \bar{\varphi}[\bar{w}/\bar{x}] \wedge \bar{w}^i = \bar{x}^i \wedge h_i = \langle \rangle$, where $\bar{w}$ is a set of fresh logical variables, and we take the initialisation of h_i into account. Note that $\models_I (\bigwedge_{i=1}^{n} \bar{\varphi}_i) \to \bar{\varphi}$ but that the converse does not hold in general. The conclusion from this discussion is that in the semantic completeness proof, we associate the strongest l-condition $SP_l(\bar{\varphi}_i, P_i')$ to location l.

Observe that instead of using logical variables to freeze the initial values of the initial variables we could use auxiliary variables which are not modified during execution of the processes P_i'. This would simplify the initialisation condition.

Now, to prove relative completeness of the method of Apt, Francez & de Roever, it suffices to show that the predicates $SP_l(\bar{\varphi}_i, P_i')$ as well as the global invariant I defined in Definition 4.23 are expressible in our assertion language, provided it contains Peano arithmetic.

Let us assume that our assertion language contains variables which range over sequences of communications and that it includes the usual operations on sequences. We have already discussed that such an assumption is not essential, if we assume that our assertion language contains Peano arithmetic. In that case it is not difficult to see that the predicate I is expressible in our assertion language. Thus, it remains to show that $SP_l(\bar{\varphi}_i, P_i')$ is expressible in Ass. To do so, we transform P_i' into an extended transition diagram $\widehat{P}_i$ which does not contain communications and is such that $SP_l(\bar{\varphi}_i, P_i')$ is equivalent to the $\bar{\varphi}_i$-minimal predicate of $\widehat{P}_i$ at l. Since we know that the $\bar{\varphi}_i$-minimal predicate is expressible in Ass we also obtain that $SP_l(\bar{\varphi}_i, P_i')$ is expressible in Ass, and, hence, establish the relative completeness of AFR.

Consider an SSTD $S \equiv S_1 \parallel \dots \parallel S_n$ in which the variables $h_1, \dots, h_n$ do not occur. Let S_i' be the SSTD obtained from S_i by applying the following transformations:

- Replace each input instruction $b; C?x \to \vec{x}^i := \vec{e}^i$ by the input instruction $b; C?x \to \vec{x}^i, h_i := \vec{e}^i, h_i \cdot (C, x)$.
- Replace each output instruction $b; C!e \to \vec{x}^i := \vec{e}^i$ by the output instruction $b; C!e \to \vec{x}^i, h_i := \vec{e}^i, h_i \cdot (C, e)$.

It is not difficult to check that $P_{S_i'} = P_{S_i}'$, where P_{S_i}' is the augmented program obtained from P_{S_i} by adding the history variable h_i as explained in the semantic completeness proof of AFR in Chapter 4.

The extended transition diagram $\widehat{S}_i$ is then obtained from S_i' by applying the following transformations:

- Replace each input instruction $b; C?x \to \vec{x}^i, h_i := \vec{e}^i, h_i \cdot (C, x)$ by the instruction $b \to \exists v. (\vec{x}'^i = \vec{e}^i[v/x] \wedge h_i' = h_i \cdot (C, v))$, where v is a logical variable.
- Replace each output instruction $b; C!e \to \vec{x}^i, h_i := \vec{e}^i, h_i \cdot (C, e)$ by the instruction $b \to \vec{x}^i, h_i := \vec{e}^i, h_i \cdot (C, e)$.

The relationship between S_i' and $\widehat{S}_i$ is given by the following lemma, which can easily be proved by induction.

Lemma 5.32 For every state σ and σ' with $\sigma(h_i) = \langle\rangle$,

$$\langle s;\sigma\rangle \xrightarrow{\sigma'(h_i)} \langle l;\sigma'\rangle \text{ iff } \langle s;\sigma\rangle \longrightarrow^* \langle l;\sigma'\rangle,$$

where $\langle s;\sigma\rangle \xrightarrow{\sigma'(h_i)} \langle l;\sigma'\rangle$ refers to the operational semantics of synchronous communication as given by Definition 4.13 and $\langle s;\sigma\rangle \longrightarrow^* \langle l;\sigma'\rangle$ refers to the operational semantics of extended sequential transition diagrams given in Section 5.5. $\square$

Using Lemma 5.32, we have that $SP_l(\bar{\varphi}_i, P'_{S_i})$ is equivalent to the $\bar{\varphi}_i$-minimal predicate of $\widehat{P'_{S_i}}$ at l, which we denote by $C_l(\bar{\varphi}_i, \widehat{S}_i)$.

Lemma 5.33 For every state σ, $\sigma \in SP_l(\bar{\varphi}_i, P'_{S_i})$ iff $\sigma \in C_l(\bar{\varphi}_i, \widehat{S}_i)$.

Proof Since we have $P'_{S_i} = P_{S'_i}$, it suffices to prove $\sigma \in SP_l(\bar{\varphi}_i, P_{S'_i})$ iff $\sigma \in C_l(\bar{\varphi}_i, \widehat{S}_i)$. Thus, consider a state σ. By definition of SP_l, we have $\sigma \in SP_l(\bar{\varphi}_i, P_{S'_i})$ iff there exists a state σ' and a communication sequence θ such that $\langle s;\sigma'\rangle \xrightarrow{\theta} \langle l;\sigma\rangle$ and $\sigma' \models_I \bar{\varphi}_i$. By Lemma 5.32, we have $\theta = \sigma'(h_i)$, and we obtain $\sigma \in SP_l(\bar{\varphi}_i, P_{S'_i})$ iff there exists a state σ' such that $\langle s;\sigma'\rangle \longrightarrow^* \langle l;\sigma\rangle$ and $\sigma' \models_I \bar{\varphi}_i$. Therefore, by the definition of $C_l(\bar{\varphi}_i, \widehat{S}_i)$, $\sigma \in SP_l(\bar{\varphi}_i, P_{S'_i})$ iff $\sigma \in C_l(\bar{\varphi}_i, \widehat{S}_i)$. $\square$

Since $C_l(\bar{\varphi}_i, \widehat{S}_i)$ is expressible in $\mathcal{A}$ss, we obtain the following result.

Theorem 5.34
The (syntactic version of the) method of Apt, Francez & de Roever for distributed transition diagrams with synchronous message passing is relatively complete, provided the formal assertion language includes at least Peano arithmetic. $\square$

5.8 Historical Notes

Stephen Cook introduces the notion of relative completeness in [Coo78], and proves that the Hoare logic of while programs [Hoa69] is relatively complete. In an appendix of [dB80], Jeffery I. Zucker extends this result to arrays of integers. In [TZ88] John V. Tucker and Jeff Zucker extend Cook's result to iteration and recursion in the presence of arithmetic, booleans, arrays and errors in a setting of abstract computability, using a weak second-order assertion language. [Apt81b] is an excellent survey of material directly relevant to the subject of this chapter.

Exercises

5.1   Generalise Floyd's inductive assertion method to extended transition diagrams and show the soundness as well as the semantic completeness of the extended method.

5.2   Consider the assertion language Ass' where expressions are defined as follows:

$$e ::= 0 \mid 1 \mid \ldots \mid x \mid e_1 + e_2.$$

Assume that constants are interpreted as natural numbers and $+$ as addition.

Write a transition diagram which satisfies the specification $\langle x = v, y = x \cdot x \wedge x = v \rangle$. Thus, the transition diagram squares the value of x and stores it in y. Prove that the $\bar{\varphi}$-minimal predicates of this STD cannot be expressed in Ass'.

Picture Gallery

Who are the main researchers in the field of concurrency verification mentioned in this book? What do they look like? And what do they themselves consider as their main contributions? Some of them were willing to help us in our attempt to answer these questions. This resulted in the following collection of photographs and nutshell captions. Twelve of these pioneers have already been portrayed in [dRE98] because of their important work on refinement; their pictures are repeated here but without captions and in a smaller format.

Manfred Broy, Edsger Dijkstra, and David Gries
At the 1994 Marktoberdorf Summer School. Manfred Broy contributed to this book several pictures from his archive.

Martín Abadi

Hans Bekić

Eric C.R. Hehner

Sir C.A.R. Hoare

Cliff B. Jones

Bengt Jonsson

Leslie Lamport

Nancy A. Lynch

Antoni Mazurkiewicz

Robin Milner

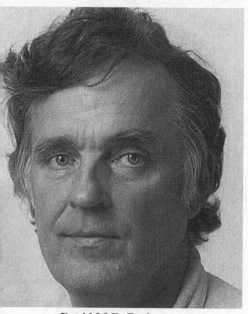

David M.R. Park

Eugene W. Stark

Gérard Berry

Gérard Berry, one of the more prominent computer scientists in the south of France, is known for a number of important results, for whose (re)discovery he used to give credit to his colleagues.

For example, the rather esoteric concept of stable functions in domain theory was reinvented by Jean-Yves Girard, who characterised this concept by: "The small category of stable domains modulo stable inclusion is a point in itself". Similarly, Gérard's formulation of the perfect synchrony hypothesis [BG88] he contributes to Isaac Newton and Hergé. Finally, the deepest result in mathematical semantics which he found is the full abstraction of constructive logic with respect to electricity [Ber99]. The crux of this result is the proof of the absence of a solution of Shakespeare's equation "To be = To be or not to be". The proof was dug out of Janos Brzozowski's work on asynchronous circuits.

In his free time, Gérard likes to sail with his family in the Mediterranean, or to walk towards the exact middle of nowhere. In his non-free time, he tries to develop the core technology on the basis of which the Esterel Technologies start-up company will become a major player in the field of real-time circuits and software.

Frank de Boer

During his study of philosophy, the courses on mathematical logic given by
Johan van Benthem inspired Frank de Boer to pursue a scientific career in program verification. After Frank finished his Master's, Jaco de Bakker offered
him a research position in ESPRIT Project 415. In his thesis [dB91b] Frank
developed the first sound and relatively complete proof system for an object-
oriented language (POOL). Subsequently, he developed semantics for concurrent constraint programming languages, culminating in a fully-abstract model
based on reactive sequences [dBKPR91]. Currently, he is working on the semantics and proof theory of real-time extensions of concurrent constraint programming and coordination languages, the development of assertional methods for UML, and the application of theorem provers and model-checking techniques to assertional proof methods. Frank is a self-taught player of the guitar,
with a marked preference for Baroque music.

Since the start of their career at the C.W.I., Frank and his buddy Jan Rutten
play squash every Thursday evening, after which, in the pub, their picture is
taken and they start to booze. This series of pictures will be published once the
coroner has been informed of the final match.

Manfred Broy

Initially interested in functional programs, their specification, transformation and verification, Manfred Broy believes that good concepts in Computing Science have nice and tractable theories. He is convinced that a denotational model for programming concepts is a key for their specification and verification, and that such models and their logic are to be expressed by simple mathematical concepts. Consequently, he tries to extend these ideas to distributed interactive systems with a strong emphasis on modularity, causality, and the idea of input and output.

Today, as a full professor of Computing Science at the Technical University of Munich, he believes that theory is a valuable input for the practice of software and systems engineering. He studies system models, specification and refinement of system components, specification techniques, development methods and verification. He leads a research group working in a number of industrial projects that apply mathematically-based techniques to practical problems, and that combine practical approaches to software engineering with mathematical rigour.

In his spare time he enjoys sitting in the sun with his family, swimming, and having a glass of good wine.

In 1994 Manfred Broy and Ernst-Rüdiger Olderog were jointly awarded the Leibniz Prize of the Deutsche Forschungsgemeinschaft. It is the highest German research prize for younger scientists given once a year to about 15 recipients in all disciplines.

K. Mani Chandy

Mani Chandy finished his Bachelor's in Electrical Engineering at the Indian Institute of Technology, Madras, and studied, subsequently, at the Polytechnic Institute of Brooklyn and MIT. His main interest in Computer Science concerns methods for reasoning about concurrent programs. Together with Jayadev Misra he wrote *Parallel Program Design: A Foundation* [CM88] on UNITY, a formalism for the logical design and formal development of concurrent programs. More recently, he wrote an introductory textbook for parallel programming [CT91], collaborated in editing a book on specifications of parallel algorithms [BCJ94], and published, together with Beverly Sanders, on predicate transformers for reasoning about concurrent computations [CS95b].

His present research focusses on modularisation mechanisms for concurrent programming, such as component-based design and their compositional formalisation [CC99].

Model Checking

Model Checking is an algorithmic method for verifying the correctness of finite-state systems, usually with respect to specifications written in Temporal Logic. In contrast to earlier approaches to verification which emphasised syntactic proofs, model checking exploits the basic model theory of Kripke structures, and is therefore amenable to efficient automation. Today model checking is the most successful formal technique in industry for verifying hardware and software. Model Checking was independently discovered on both sides of the Atlantic in the early 1980's.

In the United States, the idea was proposed, and the term "model checking" coined, in the dissertation of E. Allen Emerson [Eme81], whose advisor was Edmund M. Clarke; [CE82] is its conference presentation. In his thesis Emerson also introduced the branching-time temporal logic CTL. In France it appeared in the dissertation of Jean-Pierre Queille [Que82], with Joseph Sifakis as advisor; [QS82] is the corresponding conference version of their ideas. Consult [CGP99] for an authoritative introduction to Model Checking. Emerson and Clarke received, together with Randy Bryant and Clarke's former student Ken McMillan, the Paris Kanellakis Theory and Practice Award from the ACM "for the invention of symbolic model checking" in 1998. The pictures show Ed Clarke at CAV 2000, Allen Emerson also at CAV 2000, Joseph Sifakis at the 1998 Marktoberdorf Summer School, and Jean-Pierre Queille in 1999.

Ed Clarke

Allen Emerson

Jean-Pierre Queille   **Joseph Sifakis**

Edsger W. Dijkstra

It is generally accepted that few men have influenced the development of computer science more than Edsger W. Dijkstra. What is less well known is that, historically, he was also the first person become a programmer in the Netherlands, and that his monumental career had been predicted. In his own words [Dij72b]:

I entered the programming profession officially on the first spring morning of 1952, and as far as I have been able to trace, was the first Dutchman to do so in my country.

After having programmed for some three years, I had a discussion with van Wijngaarden, who was then my boss at the Mathematical Centre in Amsterdam – a discussion for which I shall remain grateful to him as long as I live.

The point was that I was supposed to study theoretical physics at the University of Leiden simultaneously, and as I found the two activities harder and harder to combine, I had to make up my mind, either to stop programming and become a real, respectable theoretical physicist, or [...] to become ... yes what? A programmer? But was that a respectable profession? After all, what was programming? Where was the sound body of knowledge that could support it as an intellectually respectable discipline? I remember quite vividly how I envied my hardware colleagues, who, when asked about their professional competence, could at least point out that they knew everything about vacuum tubes, amplifiers and the rest, whereas I felt that, when faced with that question, I would stand empty-handed.

Full of misgivings, I knocked on van Wijngaarden's office door, asking him whether I could speak to him for a moment; when I left his office a number of hours later, I was another person.

After having patiently listened to my problems, he agreed that up till that moment there was not much of a programming discipline, but then he went on to explain quietly that automatic computers were here to stay, that we were just at the beginning, and could I not be one of the persons called to make programming a respectable discipline in the years to come?

Van Wijngaarden's words on Dijkstra's calling turned out to be prophetic.

Peter van Emde Boas and Theo Janssen

This picture, taken by Michael van Emde Boas in 2000, shows Peter van Emde Boas on the left and Theo Janssen on the right. Peter and Theo introduced Frege's principle of compositionality to the field of Computer Science [JvEB77b, JvEB77a, JvEB80]. Peter is a true polymath. His research interests include set-theoretical topology (from 1964 to 1969), algebra (from 1965 to 1971), complexity theory (since 1971), semantics (since 1972), mathematical linguistics (since 1976), database theory and information systems (since 1983), and the foundations of artificial intelligence (since 1985). He is a notorious participant in conferences and seminars, always asking embarrassingly relevant questions, and taking snapshots. The resulting archive, consisting of approximately 40,000 pictures of mathematicians, computer scientists and other researchers, formed a major source of material during his 10 years of service as EATCS Bulletin picture editor (from 1979 to 1989). Peter and his wife Ghica, who worked for IBM for 30 years, recently founded the start-up company Bronstee.com Software and Services, specialising in the development of code generation tools for object-oriented systems. Theo Janssen's dissertation [Jan86a, Jan86b] is a paradigm of classical scholarship, in which he applies Montague grammars and Montague logic to the formal analysis of concepts in the field of semantics of natural and programming languages, such as the reference concept. He showed that the philosophical principle of compositionality can be formalised in an algebraic way. During his scientific career he worked on a variety of subjects, with compositionality as the leading theme [Ros94b, Jan84, JvEB77b, JvEB77a, Jan98, Jan01, Jan97].

Theo likes to hike along long-distance footpaths.

Robert W. Floyd

Although the development of methods for proving the correctness of programs started earlier [GvN47, Tur49], *practical* program verification starts with Robert W. Floyd's paper *"Assigning meanings to programs"* [Flo67], in which he describes the inductive assertion method for proving invariance properties of programs, as well as the wellfoundedness method for proving their convergence.

However, Robert Floyd's impact on computer science is much greater. In the citation read at the presentation of Robert W. Floyd's 1978 Turing Award lecture [Flo79], he emerges as one of the pioneers of Computer Science:

In making the selection, ... the Turing Award Subcommittee cites Professor Floyd for "helping to found the following important subfields of computer science: the theory of parsing, the semantics of programming languages, automatic program verification, automatic program synthesis, and analysis of algorithms."

His study of computing began in 1956, when as a night operator for an IBM 650, he found time to learn about programming between loads of cardhoppers. Floyd implemented one of the first Algol 60 compilers. In the process, he did some early work on compiler optimisation. Subsequently, Floyd systematised the parsing of programming languages. To achieve this he originated the precedence method, the bounded context method, and the production language method of parsing.

In 1966 he presented a mathematical method for proving the correctness of programs. He has offered, over the years, a number of fast, useful algorithms. In addition, Floyd determined the limiting speeds for digital addition and permuting information in computer memory.

Nissim Francez

This picture, dating from 1981, shows Nissim Francez on the right and Willem-Paul de Roever on the left. Nissim developed in his 1976 dissertation the first assume-guarantee-style method for proving liveness properties of reactive systems, a momentous achievement indeed! Apart from his contribution to the AFR-method, his other discoveries include the formulation of the concept of distributed termination and the use of the superposition principle for detecting it [Fra79, Fra80, FR82], and the formulation of the notion of communication-closed layers and an associated proof principle [EF82], for which he credits Tzilla Elrad, since these originate from her Ph.D. thesis. Nissim is a prolific writer, with a number of textbooks on program verification [Fra86, Fra92] to his name, and a book on multi-party interactions co-authored with Ira Forman [FF96]. His present interest concerns the formalisation of natural languages.

Gottlob Frege

Gottlob Frege (1848-1925) was a mathematician at the university of Jena, and the founder of modern logic. An important contribution in this respect is his *Begriffsschrift* [Fre79]. In the traditional Aristotelian logic there were no quantifiers. Frege invented them and thus modern first-order logic.

The principle of compositionality – the meaning of a compound expression is a function of the meanings of its parts and of the way in which these are combined – is also known under the name "Frege's principle". The most well-known fragment of Frege which reminds one of compositionality is the first sentence of *Gedankengefüge* [Fre23] :

It is astonishing what language can do. With a few syllables it can express an incalculable number of thoughts, so that even a thought grasped by a terrestrial being for the very first time can be put into a form of words which will be understood by someone to whom the thought is entirely new. This would be impossible, were we not able to distinguish parts in the thoughts corresponding to the image of the structure of the thoughts.

It is questionable, however, whether Frege himself adhered to the principle of compositionality. In the beginnings of *Grundlagen* [Fre84] he presents a principle that is known as "the contextuality principle", but is also known in certain philosophical circles as "Frege's principle". The contextuality principle reads "never ask for the meaning of a word in isolation, but only in the context of a sentence", which amounts to the exact opposite of the compositionality principle! For a discussion of Frege's relation to "Frege's principle" consult Theo Janssen's thesis [Jan01].

David Gries

David Gries's interests are both in the teaching of, and research in, programming methodology, in particular formal program development, programming
languages, their semantics, and logic [Gri81]. He writes:

I received a Master's degree from Illinois in 1963. My assistantship was to help Manfred Paul and Rüdiger Wiehle write a full Algol compiler for the IBM7090 computer –
it was fun, figuring out how to implement recursion efficiently before there were many
papers on the topic. I received my doctorate under F.L. Bauer and Joseph Stör from the
Munich Institute of Technology, Germany, in June 1966.

I am better known for my text writing and my contributions to education than for the
wonderfulness of my research (although I made some contributions). I have received
several awards for contributions to education: e.g., the 1994 ACM Karl Karlstrom
Award, the 1994 IEEE Taylor L. Booth Award, and 1995 the AFIPS education award.

I am proud of all my Ph.D. students, but two stand out. Susan Owicki's thesis laid the
foundation for correctness proofs of parallel programs, with the notion of *interference-
freeness*. And T.V. Raman's thesis won the ACM best-dissertation award for 1993–94.
Raman designed and implemented a system for "speaking" any TEX/LATEX document,
including technical articles and books, used to produce audio cassettes for the blind.

His latest endeavour is a college-level livetext on programming, called Pro-
gramLive, written with his son Paul, who teaches Computer Science at the
University of Toronto. It is called a livetext because it has over 250 recorded
3–5 minute long lectures with synchronised animations that appear in a win-
dow on the monitor. He follows the teachings of Sathya Sai Baba and has been
teaching Computer Science since the 1980s during visits to the Sri Sathya Sai
Institute of Higher Learning (deemed University) in Puttaparthy, India.

Jozef Hooman

Jozef Hooman's dissertation concerns the specification and compositional verification of real-time systems [Hoo91b], which he extended in later work to distributed systems and fault tolerance. Gradually, his research has shifted towards the application of formal methods, to hybrid systems and to distributed real-time protocols. Initially, these applications were verified by hand, but the increasing complexity of the case studies revealed the need for tool support. Since 1993 he has applied the interactive theorem prover PVS to a large number of case studies, in particular, the formal specification and analysis of the requirements of command and control systems, the formalisation of a coordination paradigm, and the verification of concurrency control protocols. His current research involves the formalisation and verification of the design process of concurrent real-time software using UML.

Jozef is a competitive sportsman, an accomplished table-tennis player, and the favourite training partner of his wife Mirjam Kloppenburg. She has repeatedly been table tennis champion of the Netherlands and of Europe, and has participated three times for the Netherlands in the Olympic Games. The picture shows the Hooman couple on their honeymoon.

Zohar Manna

Zohar Manna is one of the pioneers in the field of deductive verification of programs and their synthesis from specifications. As early as 1969 he published a paper on the correctness of programs [Man69], and in 1974 the first textbook on program correctness, on topics such as the deductive verification of programs, their denotational semantics, and program schematology [Man74]. Subsequently, he did research in program synthesis together with Richard Waldinger from SRI, resulting in two books on the logical basis of computer science [MW85, MW90].

In 1973 he teamed up with Amir Pnueli. After Amir's 1977 paper, this successful team started developing the foundations of deductive verification of concurrent programs using Linear-Time Temporal Logic (LTL) as specification language, culminating in the publication of the basic textbooks in the field [MP91b, MP95, MP99].

Zohar and his team are currently involved in developing the tool STeP (for Stanford Theorem Prover) for automating the verification of LTL specifications of concurrent programs, which includes both a proof system, a theorem prover, a model-checking tool, and visual proof aids [BBC⁺95].

Zohar and his wife Nitza are ardent folkdancers and known for their predilection for visiting exotic places all over the world. The picture shows Nitza and Zohar at CAV 2000.

Jayadev Misra

Jayadev Misra received his Bachelor's at the Indian Institute of Technology, Kanpur, one of the world's breeding places for talented computer scientists. His research interests are in the area of concurrent programming, with emphasis on rigorous methods for improving the programming process. He has published extensively, and is the coauthor, with Mani Chandy, of *Parallel Program Design: A Foundation* [CM88].

His latest monograph is *A Discipline of Multiprogramming* [Mis01]. In its preface he describes its contents as follows:

For every complex problem, there is a solution that is simple, neat and wrong, so noted H. L. Mencken in *Prejudices, second series (1920)*. It is with great trepidation, therefore, that I propose a simple, and mostly neat, solution for designing distributed applications. The solution consists of a programming model, similar to object-oriented programming, that imposes a strict discipline on the form of the constituent objects and interactions among them. Additionally, concerns of concurrency are eliminated from the model and introduced only during implementation. The programmers do not have to deal with concurrency explicitly, and that, I believe, is essential for a discipline of multiprogramming.

In this book he argues that a few simple constructs are adequate for programming a variety of distributed applications that might be suitable for the Internet; one important class of such applications is transaction processing.

Ernst-Rüdiger Olderog

The scientific depth of Ernst-Rüdiger Olderog's Master's thesis [LO80, Old81] is befitting a doctoral thesis. The brilliance of his Ph.D. thesis [Old83a, Old84a, Old84b] would have earned him a professorship everywhere but in Germany, the country where he lives. And his Habilitations-Schrift [Old91a] – the Habil-itation is the German qualification for lecturing at a University – is one of the first books describing semantic integration in a multi-paradigm setting (in this case, consisting of Petri nets, process algebra and Zwiers' trace logic). Being a modest person, part of the "blame" for this overkill rests with his supervisor and friend Hans Langmaack, the nestor of formal methods in Germany. Sub-sequently, Olderog collaborated, in the context of a project on the design of provably-correct systems [HHF+94, MO97, SO99, Sch99a], on the semantic integration of, and the transformations between, a number of formalisms for real-time concurrency, down to the level of machine code. He writes:

I remain fascinated by the topic of system design through various levels of abstraction, but now for more realistic settings. With my research team at Oldenburg University we have obtained a design trajectory from graphic descriptions of real-time require-ments via a new model of real-time automata down to correct software for real-time controllers running on Programmable Logic Controllers (PLCs). The whole approach is tool-supported. In my free time I like to cycle and walk in the countryside, in partic-ular in the beautiful scenery of Eastern Holstein with its gentle hills and woods, tufted ponds and reedy lakes, and the Baltic Sea, nearby.

Susan Owicki

In her dissertation [Owi75] Susan Owicki presented a proof system for shared-variable concurrency, together with the first fully-worked-out soundness and completeness proofs in that field – an exceptional accomplishment by 1975 standards, taking into account the fact that she presented the first *practical* method for verifying concurrency, that the value of such proofs were still under debate, and that they turned out to be considerably more complex than similar proofs for sequential constructs. The corresponding paper [OG76a], written together with her thesis advisor David Gries, received the 1977 ACM Programming Systems and Languages Paper Award. In the following 10 years she published widely on concurrent program verification, developing compositional techniques for protocol verification together with Brent Hailpern [HO81, HO83] as early as 1981, and was coauthor of a number of classic references in the field, such as [OL82, NDOG86]. In the following 10 years she switched her research direction to distributed systems and operating systems, resulting in several awards. Presently, she is associate director of InterTrust Technologies, and has posed herself a new challenge: she received her M.A. in Counseling Psychology in 1999, and is now accumulating supervised work in order to become a therapist by working (unpaid) as an intern at an agency in San Jose that specialises in domestic violence. Her husband Jack is an interdisciplinary scientist who consults for biotechnology firms, having drug discovery as a special area of expertise.

Amir Pnueli

Although Amir Pnueli is widely known for originating the temporal logic approach to verifying concurrent programs [Pnu77], for which he received the Turing Award in 1996, his influence on Computer Science is much greater.

Writing his dissertation *Tides in Simple Basins* in numerical mathematics [Pnu67], supervised by the late Chaim Leib Pekeris [PP68a, PP68b], Amir realised that he spent more time on programming, not necessarily related to his thesis, than on the research itself. Consequently, he decided to enter the field of Computer Science. His stay at Stanford University led to collaboration with Zohar Manna, and resulted in, e.g., [MP82, MP89, MP91a, MP91b, MP95, MP99].

Amir's seminal paper [Pnu77] had a decisive influence on program verification in general, eventually leading to the algorithmic verification of finite-state systems, which in turn caused program verification to be accepted by such key organisations as BULL, IBM, INTEL, NASA, and Siemens. Subsequently he opened up more areas in Computer Science, such as modelling and verification of hybrid systems [MMP92], and runtime compiler validation [PSS98], which constitutes his present interest. Although it is not generally known, he is also an accomplished systems programmer and an entrepreneur, having initiated various software ventures. His description of the way he stumbled upon temporal logic is characteristic of the way great ideas are born:

Nissim Francez, in his thesis, proposed a compositional approach to the verification of concurrent programs, which is the precursor of temporal reasoning as we know it today. The only problem was that we used first-order logic with explicit reference to time instances by parameters $t_1, t_2, \ldots$, which made the whole thing very cumbersome to read and comprehend.

Then I went on a sabbatical to the University of Pennsylvania at Philadelphia. In a colloquium I described the results obtained in Nissim's thesis but also frankly complained about the awkwardness of the notation. After the seminar, Saul Gorn, who was one of the old-timers of Computer Science and a very wise man, but notoriously cryptic and difficult to understand, came to me with a book: *'The Logic of Command* published by Springer Verlag in the series *Library of Exact Philosophy*. Saul said "I believe this is what you are looking for".

I started reading the book, and it did not take me more than 5 pages to find out that the material had no relevance to programs and their specification at all. Giving up and closing the book, I noticed that on the back cover of the book there was a list of additional books published in the same series, including the book *Temporal Logic* by Rescher and Urquhart. Since I was in a reading mood, I went to the library and borrowed this one. It also did not take me more than 5 pages to realize the extreme relevance of this text to what I had in mind. This started my interest in Temporal Logic as a language for the specification of reactive systems.

The pictures display Amir in 1981, and when he received the Israel Prize in the category Exact Sciences in the year 2000.

Amir Pnueli in 1981 ...

... and 20 years, several awards, prizes, and honorary doctorates later

The PVS team

The family of proof systems presented in this book has been implemented using the PVS tool, designed and built principally by Sam Owre and Natarajan Shankar as part of a team at SRI led by John Rushby [ORS92]. In Shankar's words [Sha01]:

In the 1980s, theorem proving support for verification came in the form of LCF-style interactive proof checkers that had expressive logics but very little automation, or in the form of batch-oriented automatic theorem provers like Nqthm where the automation was sometimes impressive but quite difficult to control or predict. None of these systems adequately addressed the problem of efficient proof construction. We felt that what was needed was a system combining a rich specification logic with an interactive but programmable theorem prover having a high level of built-in automation. John Rushby somehow convinced SRI's management to fund the development of such a system, which he christened PVS. Sam Owre worked his magic to weave the bits and pieces of code into a coherent system. PVS was first released in 1993, and has since been substantially improved and extended, largely due to suggestions by its users. Some of the crucial extensions include the embedding of a model checker, an automatic abstraction scheme for approximating infinite-state problems by finite-state ones, and a fast evaluation mechanism for executable PVS functions.

Prior to switching to Computer Science at the University of Texas, Shankar studied electrical engineering at the Indian Institute of Technology in Madras. A book based on his 1986 dissertation (supervised by Bob Boyer and J Moore) has been published under the title *Metamathematics, Machines, and Gödel's Proof* [Sha94]. Shankar is currently pursuing the integration of enumerative and deductive verification methods, and enjoys teaching whenever the opportunity arises. John Rushby received his Ph.D. degree in Computer Science at the University of Newcastle upon Tyne in 1977. He joined SRI in 1983 and is primarily interested in the design and assurance of "critical systems". Sam Owre obtained a Master's degree in Mathematics from UCLA in 1975 and has been at SRI since 1989. He has over twenty years of system building experience, and his credits include Muse, PVS, and InVest.

John Rushby, Patrick Lincoln, Sam Owre, Judy Crow, Hassen Saïdi, Natarajan Shankar, Harald Rueß, and David Stringer-Calvert

Natarajan Shankar at CAV 99

Corinne and Willem-Paul de Roever (in 1989)

Willem-Paul de Roever's research concerns formal methods and tools for the verification and development of concurrent and real-time programs. Inspired by de Bakker and Scott's work [dBS69], and the presentations at the 1971 Marktoberdorf Summer School, he made substantial contributions to the introduction of predicate transformers and the use of the relational μ-calculus for proving program correctness [dR76]. It has now been shown [FM98] that his 1975 Ph.D. thesis contains the oldest sound and complete axiomatisation of the relational calculus within computer science. During the eighties he contributed to the first fully abstract semantics for distributed real-time computing [HGdR87] and Statecharts [HGdR88]. From 1985 onwards his research has been guided by the compositionality principle, leading, as a result of his interest in refinement, to the important notion of *compositional* refinement [Ger90, ZCdR92]. Willem-Paul is highly critical of the manner in which the fruits of research in Computer Science find their place in literature – too much fragmentation into different schools and communities, with a severe lack of mutual understanding at a higher level. This results in frequent rediscovery of essential results, a phenomenon which is hard to counteract, given the speed required to provide timely feedback to the authors in our frenzied publication culture. The proposed remedy: integration of essential ideas, and synthesis, placing these contributions, including those of the authors, in the overall picture. Willem-Paul's hobby is birdwatching. His wife, Corinne, is a social worker, active in the field of resocialisation of prisoners and families of children at risk. One of his sons has founded the start-up company Newfoundland Interactive Technology, focussing, amongst other things, on building systems for electronic auctioning.

The Synchronous Approach

Synchronous languages are used for the design and development of safety-critical reactive and real-time systems [BB91, HP98]. Their full power enfolds once the graphical ease of expression of hierarchy and concurrency of Statecharts – invented by David Harel [Har87] – is combined with the semantic simplicity of Esterel, Lustre, and Signal, which all have the same underlying semantic model [Hal93]. Esterel is a textual synchronous programming language developed by Gérard Berry and his team [BG88, BBF⁺00], and is dedicated to software or hardware control-dominated systems. Lustre and Signal are both dataflow synchronous languages [BCGH94], with Lustre having been developed by Paul Caspi and Nicolas Halbwachs [HCP91], and Signal by Albert Benveniste and Paul le Guernic [BGJ91]. Signal has multiple clocks, and thus enables the design and implementation of truly distributed software. The language of Statecharts is incorporated into the tools StateMate and Rhapsody. The first version of StateMate was built by a team that included Rivi Sherman, Michal Politi, David Harel, and Amir Pnueli, to cope, originally, with the complex task of designing software for the LAVI fighter, built by Israel Aircraft Industries. Judged by the yardstick that new development methods in software engineering are successful only when they lead to at least an order of magnitude of improvement, the synchronous-languages approach is an outstanding success. Their application cuts down the error ratio during test phases, and increases the average number of lines produced per day per designer, by a factor higher than 10 [HLN⁺90, Sca97, DD99].

Albert Benveniste

Paul Caspi

Paul le Guernic

Nicolas Halbwachs

David Harel

Job Zwiers

Job Zwiers published the first book on compositional proof theories for distributed networks [Zwi89]. Subsequently, he pioneered compositional proof theories for various other forms of concurrency, generalised He, Hoare and Sanders' theory of pre- and post-specifications to concurrency [ZdR89, Zwi90], and coauthored an early paper on compositional refinement [ZCdR92].

Subsequently, together with Mannes Poel and Wil Janssen, he concentrated on developing an algebraic framework for the communication-closed-layers paradigm in the context of causally-ordered computations, and on formulating verification conditions for action refinement in this setting, obtaining a completeness result in [ZJ94]. More recently, he contributed to the specification and design of a controller for the storm-surge barrier in the Rhine estuary near Rotterdam, the so-called Maeslant Kering.

His present interest concerns the development of software agents, in a setting of virtual reality, for advising visitors to the music centre of Enschede, the Netherlands, the city where he lives.

Job likes to play the violin. His wife Elisabeth is a professional opera singer.

Amir Pnueli with Joseph Sifakis at CAV 89

Picture made by David Harel
David Harel writes:

I do photography as a hobby, and people should know that scientists have hobbies too ... How about having a photo with me behind the lens instead of in front of it?

Robin Milner at the ceremony during which he was granted an honorary degree from the University of Bologna, as part of ICALP'97.

Leslie Lamport in action at the Marktoberdorf Summer School in 1998.

Peter van Emde Boas

The photographer of computer scientists par excellence.[3] Peter contributed
several pictures from his extensive archive to [dRE98] and this book.

[3] On a picture by Henk Thomas, which appeared in *Folia Civitatis,* 15, November 30, 1990,
page 9.

Part III

Compositional Methods based on Assertion Networks

6

Introduction to Compositional Reasoning

6.1 Motivation

Large-scale concurrent systems are usually defined by composing together a number of components or subsystems. Traditional verification methods are noncompositional and require a global examination of the entire system. In the *deductive* approach to verification, which is the subject of this book, this means that a property such as an invariant has to be verified with respect to each transition of all of the components in the system. Clearly, noncompositional methods do not scale up well for verifying really large systems.

Verification approaches based on algorithmic verification methods, such as *model checking*, also fail to scale up well since the global state space that has to be explored can grow exponentially in the number of components. The purpose of a *compositional* verification approach is therefore to shift the burden of verification from the global level to the local, component level so that global properties are established by composing together independently verified component properties [Sha98b].

Under *compositional* proof methods, we include any method of proof by which the specification of a system can be inferred from specifications of its constituents, without additional information about their internal structure. The two main questions that have to be addressed in forming a viable compositional theory are:

- How can a global specification be decomposed into local specifications such that satisfaction of the global specification can be inferred from satisfaction of these local specifications?

- After having applied this process of specification decomposition recursively until specifications of basic components are obtained, how can basic components be found satisfying these specifications?

Compositional reasoning owes its attractiveness to its application to parallel composition. For it replaces operational noncompositional reasoning, with a complexity *increasing exponentially* in the number of parallel components, by reasoning compositionally on the basis of given specifications, and the complexity of this way of reasoning increases *linearly* w.r.t. the number of those specifications. This is the main reason why compositional verification methods, especially when combined with (state-space reducing) abstraction techniques, show promise of scaling up to really large systems. For in the literature more and more examples appear in which large systems are verified by combining algorithmic (model checking) verification methods with a compositional deductive verification technology, in which the local specifications are verified by algorithmic methods and specification decomposition and recomposition are done using a compositional deductive technology [HP99]. To increase the degree of confidence in such mixed technologies, the deductive parts are machine-checked semi-automatically using special-purpose theorem provers, such as PVS [ORS92, ORSvH95].

There are two strategies for the latter when using PVS. In the first one, the parallel processes involved are mapped on a representation of their compositional semantics within PVS, their proof rules are formulated (and proved sound) within the PVS framework, and then the theorem proving facilities of PVS are used to deduce the desired properties semi-automatically. In the second strategy, a special purpose deductive tool, see, e.g., [BLO98b, BBC+95], is built, which reduces the to-be-proved specification to a set of verification conditions (generated according to the deductive method) that can be proved using PVS. For this it is important to know *which kind* of verification conditions are generated by the deductive rules, and *how* they are generated. Expressing them in a formal language now becomes a less important issue.

These are some of the reasons why the authors of this monograph have opted for a semantic (rather than syntactic) approach to deductive compositional verification in this Part III. Another reason for adopting such a semantic approach is that, especially for compositional verification methods, soundness and completeness proofs are easier to give (and to understand) in a semantic framework. In fact these proofs constitute one of the main new features of this monograph.

This does not imply that such a semantic approach should always be preferred. As soon as real examples need to be verified compositionally, see Section 7.4.3, the disadvantage of a semantic set-up also becomes apparent, since in such a set-up, programs are represented by transition diagrams. For more complicated programs this is not feasible, and then a syntactic approach should be adopted, for which we refer to the companion volume.

6.2 Introduction to Part III and to this Chapter

Part III of this monograph focusses on the *semantic foundations* of the main compositional partial-correctness proof methods for concurrency which are currently in use. These are the *assumption-commitment* (A-C) method for verifying synchronous distributed message passing systems, which has been invented by Misra & Chandy [MC81] and is studied in Section 7.5, and the *rely-guarantee* (R-G) method for verifying shared-variable concurrency, which has been invented by Jones [Jon81, Jon83] and is studied in Section 8.4.

Let us first clarify these three notions.

The reasons why we study a semantic rather than a syntactic approach to deductive compositional program verification have been explained above. When we speak about "semantic foundations" or "the semantic approach to deductive program verification", the following is meant:

- No attention is paid to how the predicates which occur in the formulation of these proof methods are expressed within any particular language (their expression in first-order predicate logic over a domain including that of the natural numbers is straightforward using the techniques from Chapter 5).
- The systems, which we prove correctness of, are built from transition diagrams using sequential and/or parallel composition as operations.
- We prove soundness and semantic completeness of these proof methods.

Secondly, we explain why we focus on the A-C and R-G paradigms. Existing compositional methods can be classified as follows:

- Either a process or system is characterised regardless of any assumption about the behaviour of its parallel environment; we shall encounter several instances of such methods (in Sections 7.4 and 8.3).
- Or a process or system is characterised only in so far as its environment satisfies certain assumptions (i.e., when these assumptions are violated nothing about the behaviour of that process is claimed).

The first class can be seen as a special instance of the latter by choosing the predicate *true* as the assumption about the environment (thus expressing that no assumptions are made about the environment). Now for synchronous distributed message passing the resulting compositional proof method, which is based on assumptions about the environment, is the assumption-commitment paradigm, whereas for shared-variable concurrency it is the rely-guarantee paradigm. These are by far the most successful approaches to the compositional verification of concurrency.

Part III consists of three chapters.

This chapter focusses on the similarities between the A-C and R-G paradigms, which are explained in Section 6.3; a simple example of an even number generator will be used to illustrate them. Because of these similarities these two paradigms are also called *assume-guarantee* paradigms. In the subsequent Sections 6.4 and 6.5 the A-C and R-G methods are introduced using this example. For a general introduction to compositional methods, and the definition of a compositional proof method, we refer to Section 1.6.

In Chapter 7 we investigate the assumption-commitment proof method for synchronous distributed message passing, which we present in three stages.

First, we investigate the semantic foundations of a compositional proof method for top-level synchronous transition diagrams. Technically, we combine so-called *compositionally*-inductive assertion networks for reasoning about the sequential parts of concurrent systems with compositional proof rules for deducing properties of the whole system, giving rigorous soundness and completeness proofs for the resulting theory. The basic idea of a compositionally-inductive assertion network is here the definition of the verification conditions in terms of a *logical* history variable which records the sequence of communications generated by the component (logical variables only occur in assertions, never in programs). The parallel combination of these compositionally-inductive assertion networks is defined in terms of a simple semantic characterisation of the variables and channels *involved in* a predicate. (The semantic notion "involved in" of a variable approximates to the corresponding syntactic notion of occurrence.) More specifically, the notion of the channels involved in a predicate is defined in terms of a natural generalisation of a *projection* operation on communication histories to predicates.

Secondly, we extend this compositional proof method to nested synchronous transition diagrams, which can be composed sequentially or in parallel. The complicating proof-theoretic consequence of introducing a parallel combination of compositionally-inductive assertion networks in this nested setting is that it requires the introduction of the so-called *prefix-invariance* axiom (initially formulated in [Zwi89]). This axiom basically expresses that the history of communications of a system grows monotonically, because this property is not expressible using the parallel composition rule. One of the main conceptual advantages of our semantic approach, as opposed to an approach in which assertions are expressed in a given logical assertion language, is that it provides a simple semantic explanation of this prefix-invariance axiom.

Thirdly, we present the semantic foundations of the assumption-commitment proof method for nested synchronous transition diagrams. This method incorporates as a new element that a property of a process is expressed by a pair (A, C) consisting of a commitment C that the component will satisfy provided

358 6 Introduction to Compositional Reasoning

the environment of the component satisfies the assumption property A. As we shall see, this method enables the formulation of a parallel composition rule which relates to parallel composition in the same way as Hoare's while rule, formulated in Sections 9.1.3 and 9.5, relates to while loops, in that they both incorporate an induction argument which is proved once and for all in the soundness proofs of these rules. That is, when applying these rules this inductive argument needs not be proved over and over again. This method is by far the best-studied and most-applied compositional proof method.

In Chapter 8 we investigate the rely-guarantee proof method for shared-variable concurrency, and present it in two stages.

First, we examine the semantic foundations of a compositional proof method for top-level shared-variable transition diagrams. In fact, we have encountered this method before implicitly, namely in the disguise of the inductive asser-tion networks defined in the completeness proof for the (noncompositional) Owicki & Gries method! The completeness proof for this method shows that for certain local assertion networks the requirement of interference freedom is trivially satisfied, essentially because the predicates of the local assertion networks specify the meaning of a component process in terms of its interac-tions with an *arbitrary* concurrent environment. In Section 8.3 we show how one can obtain a compositional proof method by incorporating in the local ver-ification conditions *all possible interleavings* with an arbitrary environment. The local transitions themselves will be described in terms of a logical history variable, assuming this history variable to be part of the state.

Secondly, we investigate the semantic foundations of the rely-guarantee proof method, in particular which compositional semantic model is appropri-ate for defining its validity. For there are two basically different compositional semantic models for shared-variable concurrency: *reactive-sequence* seman-tics [dBKPR91], and *Aczel-trace* semantics [Acz83]. A reactive sequence of a process P is a sequence of computation steps $\langle \sigma, \sigma' \rangle$ which represent the execution of atomic actions of P in state σ with resulting state σ', where σ' does not necessarily coincide with the initial state of the subsequent computa-tion step in the sequence. These 'gaps' represent the state-changes induced by the (parallel) environment. Note that in this way a reactive sequence abstracts from the *number and granularity* of the environmental actions. In contrast, an Aczel trace of a process records *all* the state-changes (both of the process and its environment) at the level of the atomic actions.

We shall prove that the Aczel semantics provides the correct notion of valid-ity for the R-G proof method. Technically, we introduce the concept of R-G-inductive assertion networks for reasoning about the sequential components, i.e., the transition diagrams, of a concurrent system. By combining these with compositional proof rules such assertion networks can be used for deducing properties of the whole system. The main technical contribution of Chapter 8 is a new semantic completeness proof of the R-G method, which considerably simplifies previous approaches; this completeness proof requires the introduction of one fresh auxiliary variable h. A soundness proof is also provided.

An early formalisation of the R-G paradigm, which reduces its soundness and completeness to that of the Owicki & Gries method, was given by Stirling [Sti88]. Our results in Section 8.4.6 imply that this reduction is justified, since Stirling's rely and guarantee predicates, when transposed to our setting, are reflexive and transitive.

6.3 Assume-Guarantee-based Reasoning

The main emphasis in Chapters 6, 7 and 8 on compositional reasoning will be on the above mentioned assume-guarantee (A-G) proof method for concurrent systems since that is the best-studied approach to the compositional verification of concurrency [MC81, Jon83, Oss83, Sou84, Pnu85, ZdBdR84, BK85, Sta85, ZdRvEB85, GdR86, Lar87, Sti88, Zwi89, Jos90, Hoo91b, PJ91, XH91, AL93, AP93, Col93, Jos93, KR93, Col94b, CMP94, DH94, XCC94, AL95, DJS95, XdRH97, McM97, McM98, HQRT98, McM99].

As mentioned before, Francez and Pnueli developed in [Fra76, FP78] the first method for reasoning compositionally about concurrency.

The basic intuition underlying the assume-guarantee paradigm can be explained by considering the very simple example of an adder component P shown in Figure 6.1 that adds two input numbers x and y and places the output in z. We owe this example to Natarajan Shankar [Sha98b].

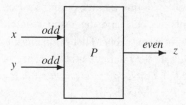

Fig. 6.1. Even number generator P.

Here x, y and z can be program variables, signals, or latches, depending on the chosen model of computation. The system containing P as the component might require its output z to be an even number, but obviously P cannot unconditionally guarantee this property of the output z. It might be reasonable to assume that the environment always provides odd number inputs at x and y, so that with this assumption it is easy to show that the output numbers at z are always even. Only local reasoning in terms of P is needed to establish that z is always even when given odd number inputs at x and y.

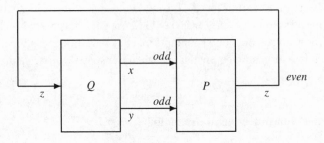

Fig. 6.2. Odd and even number generators.

If, as shown in Figure 6.2, P is now composed with another component Q that generates the inputs at x and y, then to preserve the property that only even numbers are output at z, Q must be shown to output only odd numbers at x and y. However, the demonstration that Q provides only odd numbers as outputs at x and y might require assumptions on the inputs taken by Q, where z itself might be such an input. If in showing that Q produces odd outputs at x and y, one has to assume that the z input is always even, then we have an obvious circularity and nothing can be concluded about the oddness or evenness of x, y and z. If this circularity can somehow be broken, then we have a form of well-founded mutual recursion between P and Q which admits a proof by simultaneous induction that x and y are always odd and z is always even. The circularity can be broken by noting that a z output for P is even as long as the *preceding* x and y inputs are odd, and the x and y outputs for Q are odd as long as the *preceding* z input is even. That is, using the terminology of the assume-guarantee paradigm, the guarantee that output z is even is satisfied by *P as long as the assumption that its previous inputs x and y are odd has always been satisfied before by P's environment.*

In the assume-guarantee approach for reasoning about concurrency, a property of a component process is expressed by a pair (A, G) consisting of a commitment G that the component will satisfy provided the environment of the component satisfies the assumption property A. The interpretation of (A, G) has to be carefully defined to be non-circular. Informally, a component P satisfies (A, G) if the environment of P must violate A before the component P can fail to satisfy G. That is, P satisfies (A, G) if at any stage of an on-going computation P's actions satisfy G as long as A is satisfied by all actions from P's environment. When two components, P_1 satisfying (A_1, G_1) and P_2 satisfying (A_2, G_2), are composed into a larger component $P_1 \| P_2$, the assumption A of $P_1 \| P_2$ together with property G_1 of component P_1 must be used to show that assumption A_2 is not violated, and, correspondingly, A and G_2 must be used to show that assumption A_1 is not violated.

6.4 Assumption-Commitment-based Reasoning

The main variant of the A-G paradigm for message passing systems is called assumption-commitment-based reasoning. It was discovered by Jayadev Misra and Mani Chandy in 1981 [MC81].

Formally, an assumption-commitment correctness formula (or A-C formula for short) has the form:

$$\langle A, C \rangle : \{\varphi\} \, P \, \{\psi\},$$

where P denotes a program and A, φ, ψ, C denote predicates. For an A-C formula we require that A and C are predicates whose values do not depend on the values of any program variables.

Informally, a valid A-C formula has the following meaning:

If φ holds in the initial state, including the communication history, in which P starts its execution, then

(i) *C holds initially, and C holds after every communication provided A holds after all preceding communications, and*

(ii) *if P terminates and A holds after all previous communications (including the last one) then ψ holds in the final state including the final communication history.*

Here A expresses an *assumption* describing the expected behaviour of the environment of P, C expresses a *commitment* which is guaranteed by process P itself as long as the environment does not violate assumption A, and φ and ψ express pre- and postconditions upon the state of P. In general, assumption and commitment reflect the communication interface between parallel components and do *not* refer to the local program variables of a process, whereas pre- and postconditions facilitate reasoning about sequential composition and iteration as in Hoare logic, and *do* refer to these variables. All predicates can refer to logical variables.

As an illustration of A-C-based reasoning a formal specification of module P from Figure 6.1 is given below.

Example 6.1 We continue the example from Figure 6.1 and propose an implementation of *P* using distributed communication in Figure 6.3.

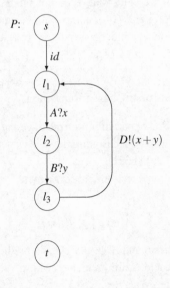

Fig. 6.3. Structure of adder *P*.

We have the following A-C correctness formula for *P* in an arbitrary environment

$$\langle true, \#D = \#A = \#B \geq 1 \rightarrow last(D) = last(A) + last(B) \rangle :$$
$$\{\#D = \#A = \#B = 0\} \, P \, \{false\}.$$

(Here, for *chan* ∈ CHAN, *#chan* denotes the number of communications via channel *chan*, and *last*(*chan*) refers to the latest value sent via channel *chan*.)

Note that the antecedent $\#D = \#A = \#B \geq 1$ of the implication in the commitment expresses that control of *P* is at l_1 (see Fig. 6.3). Now, in order for *x* and *y* to be properly initialised, and the value of $x + y$ to have been sent along channel *D*, the loop (l_1, l_2, l_3, l_1) should have been executed at least once, under the assumption that, initially, the number of recorded communications is zero, as expressed by the precondition $\#D = \#A = \#B = 0$. Since *P* does not terminate, its postcondition is *false*.

We want to use program *P* as the even number generator, but obviously we cannot unconditionally guarantee that all values sent via channel *D* are even. By introducing as a restriction on the environment that it always provides odd numbers along channels *A* and *B*, we obtain for *P* the following A-C correctness formula:

$$\langle Ass_1, (\#A \geq 1) \wedge (\#B \geq 1) \wedge (\#D \geq 1) \to even(last(D)) \rangle :$$
$$\{\#D = \#A = \#B = 0\} \, P \, \{false\},$$

where

$$Ass_1 \stackrel{\text{def}}{=} (\#A > 0 \to odd(last(A))) \wedge (\#B > 0 \to odd(last(B)))$$

($odd(v)$ or even (v) states that v denotes an odd or even value), respectively. $\square$

The full theory of assumption-commitment-based reasoning is worked out in Section 7.5.

The assumption-commitment paradigm can be regarded as a compositional reformulation of the method of Apt, Francez & de Roever [AFdR80] for the simple reason that their associated notions of validity can be based on the same underlying semantic models, as we show in Chapter 7.

The difference between the method of Apt, Francez & de Roever and the A-C paradigm can be best understood by analysing the different ways in which these two methods require the environment of a process to be characterised. The AFR-method operates in two stages by:

- providing a sound local sequential assertion network for every process in a network, and
- proving that all communications occurring in these proof outlines satisfy a *cooperation test*, reflecting the global effect of a communication.

Consequently, the former method characterises the environment only in terms of *concretely known* processes, and is therefore only appropriate for characterising *closed* systems. That is, the AFR-method provides no abstract characterisation of an environmental action.

In contrast, the A-C paradigm expresses the property which should be satisfied by an environmental step by means of an assumption. This is a predicate which only relates to the the communication *interface*. Consequently, the A-C paradigm provides an abstraction from the actual implementation of the environment, since it does not refer to any known process in that environment. This explains why it also characterises open systems, and can be used for the formal derivation of open synchronously-communicating networks of processes.

6.5 Rely-Guarantee-based Reasoning

As stated above, the main variant of the A-G paradigm for shared-variable concurrency is called rely-guarantee-based reasoning and was discovered by

Cliff Jones in [Jon81, Jon83]. An R-G specification describes conditions under which the program is used, and the expected behaviour of the program when it is used under these conditions.

Satisfaction of an R-G specification by a process P amounts to proving validity of some R-G correctness formula

$$\langle rely, guar \rangle : \{\varphi\}\, P\, \{\psi\}.$$

Traditionally, φ and ψ impose conditions upon the initial and final, respectively, state of a computation of P, whereas *rely* and *guar* impose conditions upon environmental transitions and transitions of P itself, respectively. This is captured by the following intuitive characterisation of validity of an R-G correctness formula:

If

- *P is invoked in an initial state which satisfies φ, and*
- *whenever at some moment during the computation of P all past environmental transitions satisfy rely,*

then

- *all transitions by P up to that moment satisfy guar, and*
- *if this computation terminates, its final state satisfies ψ.*

As an illustration of R-G-based reasoning a formal specification of module P from Figure 6.1 is given below.

Example 6.2 We continue the example from Figure 6.1 and in Figure 6.4 we suggest an implementation of P using shared-variable concurrency .

$$z := x + y$$

Fig. 6.4. Structure of adder P.

The value of the R-G method for shared variables is based on the fact that in an arbitrary environment without any restrictions it is impossible to derive any appropriate state description of a shared-variable process. For the process above of Figure 6.4 we know that it sets the value of z to the sum of the values of x and y – yet immediately afterwards some environmental process can assign some other value to either z, x or y, thereby invalidating the assertion $z = x + y$. Thus in the case of an arbitrary environment, validity of the R-G specification

$$\langle true, z' = x + y \rangle : \{true\} \, P \, \{false\}$$

gives as the only information that immediately after P's transition the value of z is the sum of the values of x and y.

Since *rely* and *guar* describe the behaviour of an atomic action by pairs (σ, σ') consisting of a state σ and the state σ' produced by that action in σ, we use the convention that in these predicates unprimed variables such as $x, y, \ldots$ refer to their value in σ and primed variables $x', y', \ldots$ refer to their value in σ'.

If we use P as the even number generator, i.e., if we want to guarantee that the value of z is generated by P and is always even, the following restriction on the environment suffices: it should not change the value of z, i.e., we need that $\models rely \rightarrow z = z'$.

The value of z (as the sum of x and y) is even if x and y have odd values whenever P takes its only transition. Since P might take this transition without any guard, i.e., at any moment, the environment has to ensure that after every environmental step x and y have odd values, as formally expressed by $\models rely \rightarrow odd(x') \wedge odd(y')$.

Since P may sum up x and y before any environmental process acts, we have to ensure also that x and y have initially odd values. These considerations lead to the following R-G specification of P as an even number generator:

$$\langle z = z' \wedge odd(x') \wedge odd(y'), even(z') \rangle : \{odd(x) \wedge odd(y)\} \, P \, \{false\}.$$

However, this is not yet the full specification of P needed to guarantee that P, in the context of Q depicted in Figure 6.2, is an even number generator. To see this, consider Q from Figure 6.2. Similar considerations to those above lead to the following R-G interface specification for Q as the generator of pairs of odd numbers:

$$\langle x = x' \wedge y = y' \wedge even(z'), odd(x') \wedge odd(y') \rangle : \{even(z)\} \, Q \, \{false\}.$$

The extra element required for the network depicted in Figure 6.2 to function, is that the *guarantee*-part of Q's specification should imply the *rely*-part of P's specification, and that the *guarantee*-part of P's specification should imply the *rely*-part of Q's specification. This leads to the following specifications for P and Q:

$$\langle z = z' \wedge odd(x') \wedge odd(y'), even(z') \wedge x = x' \wedge y = y' \rangle :$$
$$\{odd(x) \wedge odd(y)\}\ P\ \{false\},$$

and

$$\langle x = x' \wedge y = y' \wedge even(z'), odd(z') \wedge odd(y') \wedge z = z' \rangle : \{even(z')\}\ Q\ \{false\}.$$

□

The full theory of rely-guarantee-based reasoning is worked out in Section 8.4.

Again, the difference between the method of Owicki & Gries and the R-G paradigm is that the former method characterises the environment only in terms of concretely known processes and is therefore only appropriate for characterising closed systems, whereas the latter also applies to (the development of) open systems (as explained in Sections 1.5.6 and 1.6).

Exercises

6.1   Suggest an implementation of Q as a generator of pairs of odd numbers, provided input z is even, within the synchronous communication model. Then determine an A-G specification of Q. Finally, check that the *guarantee*-part of P's specification implies the *assumption*-part of Q's specification, and, vice-versa, that the *guarantee*-part of Q's specification implies the *assumption*-part of P's specification. These two properties guarantee that when Q and P are put together, as in Figure 6.2, the resulting network Q operates as a generator of pairs of odd numbers along channels A and B, and P operates as a generator of even numbers along channel D.

7

Compositional Proof Methods: Synchronous Message Passing

7.1 Objective and Introduction

In this chapter we investigate the semantic foundations of compositional proof methods for concurrent transition diagrams which communicate by synchronous message passing. Technically, we combine so-called *compositionally-*inductive and *A-C-inductive* assertion networks, used for reasoning about the sequential parts of concurrent systems, with compositional proof rules for deducing properties of their parallel composition, giving rigorous soundness and completeness proofs for the resulting theory. The basic idea of such inductive assertion networks for synchronous transition diagrams is the definition of verification conditions in terms of a single *logical* history variable h which records the sequence of communications generated by the component. Logical variables only occur in assertions (or predicates), but never in transition diagrams. This is in contrast to *auxiliary* variables, which do occur in transition diagrams, but which do not influence their control flow.

What happens in the definition of compositionally-inductive and A-C-inductive assertion networks is that the usual assignments to auxiliary variables are simulated at the logical level by appropriately defined verification conditions for the inductive assertion networks for the sequential components of a program. As a result of using this one logical variable, one can simulate the local (communication) histories of those sequential components. Consequently, the main challenge in defining a compositional proof method for this form of concurrent programs is *the formulation of a sound and complete proof rule for parallel composition!* For this to succeed it is mandatory that the specification for a component only *involves* the variables and channels which are associated with that component, since, otherwise, this local specification could be invalidated by the other parallel components. This requirement is a consequence of the fact that such a rule should transfer the only locally verified information about the components into global information about the whole program. And that is accomplished by *projecting* the communication histories encoded in this logical variable on the actions of that component. This also explains why compositional proof methods always involve some form of projection mechanism.

After recalling the basic concepts of a compositional semantics for synchronous transition diagrams from Chapter 4, we give in Section 7.3.2 a compositional proof method for top-level parallelism, i.e., for the same kind of diagrams as treated in the Apt, Francez & de Roever method and the method of Levin & Gries. This proof method requires finding *compositionally-inductive assertion networks* for each process P_i, and then the application of a parallel composition rule, provided the specifications of the constituent processes P_i satisfy the above mentioned restrictions.

In Section 7.4 this approach is extended to nested parallelism, requiring some special attention to the use made of the logical history variable h in the context of parallel composition, which is provided by the *prefix-invariance* axiom. Apart from a larger example illustrating the verify-while-develop paradigm, soundness and completeness proofs of the resulting proof method are given.

The extension of this proof method to the assumption-commitment specification style, which allows also for the specification of infinite computations and open systems and, hence, enables the specification of reactive systems, is investigated in Section 7.5. The semantics for synchronous transition diagrams as defined in Section 7.3.1 is extended to suit this further range of application, and culminates in the proof method developed in Section 7.5.3. Its soundness and completeness proofs are given in Section 7.5.4 and Section 7.5.5, respectively. Related work is discussed in Section 7.6.

7.2 Structure of the Chapter

After describing the main technical features of this chapter in Section 7.1, Section 7.3.1 contains a description of a compositional proof method for top-level synchronous message passing, a simple application of this method in Section 7.3.3, and a description of its soundness and completeness proofs.

Section 7.4 is devoted to extending this method to nested parallelism, that is, systems which are constructed from sequential synchronous transition diagrams by means of the operations of sequential and parallel composition. Compared with the compositional method of top-level parallelism given in the previous section, the main difference in the case of nested parallelism is the need for the so-called *prefix-invariance axiom*, which is extensively discussed. Section 7.4.3 features as an application of this compositional method the top-down derivation of a distributed priority queue, illustrating the verify-while-develop paradigm. Sections 7.4.4 and 7.4.5 contain soundness and completeness proofs of this method.

In Section 7.5 we investigate the semantic foundations of the compositional assumption-commitment proof method for nested synchronous message passing, giving detailed proofs of the example from Chapter 6 and some related examples, and soundness and completeness proofs for this method in Sections 7.5.4 and 7.5.5. In Section 7.6 we describe the history of compositional proof methods for message passing, and discuss related work. Then follows a list of exercises.

7.3 A Compositional Proof Method for Top-level Synchronous Message Passing

7.3.1 *Semantics*

In this section we consider parallel systems (or programs) $P_1 \| \dots \| P_n$ in which the components $P_1, \dots, P_n$ are sequential synchronous transition diagrams as defined in Section 4.3. Such networks are called *top-level* synchronous networks (in order to distinguish them from the networks considered in Section 7.4, which can also be sequentially composed).

Labels on edges in P_i can have the following form:

(i) A boolean condition b followed by a state transformation f:

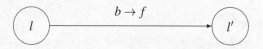

Transitions of the above form are called *internal* transitions.

(ii) A guarded io-statement followed by a state transformation, for which there are two possibilities:

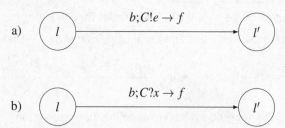

These transitions are called *communication* or *input-output* transitions.

For all communication channels C, program variables x and semantic expressions e, we use the following abbreviations:

- (i) when $b \equiv true$ or $f = id_\Sigma$, $b;C?x \to f$ is abbreviated to, respectively, $C?x \to f$ or $b;C?x$,
- (ii) these conventions can be combined, and
- (iii) they also apply to $b;C!e \to f$.

These sequential transition diagrams (or processes) are disjoint, i.e., they do not share variables and communicate by means of synchronous message passing along unidirectional channels which connect at most two different processes. The semantics of these diagrams is given by the labelled transition relation of Definition 4.13 which we repeat below.

Definition 7.1 Let $P \equiv (L, T, s, t)$ be a sequential synchronous transition diagram.

- In the case of an internal transition $l \xrightarrow{a} l' \in T$, $a \equiv b \to f$, we have

$$\langle l; \sigma \rangle \xrightarrow{()} \langle l'; \sigma' \rangle,$$

  if $\sigma \models b$ and $\sigma' = f(\sigma)$.
- In the case of an output transition $l \xrightarrow{a} l' \in T$, $a \equiv b;C!e \to f$, we have, for $v = e(\sigma)$,

$$\langle l; \sigma \rangle \xrightarrow{(C,v)} \langle l'; \sigma' \rangle,$$

  if $\sigma \models b$ and $\sigma' = f(\sigma)$.
- In the case of an input transition $l \xrightarrow{a} l' \in T$, with $a \equiv b;C?x \to f$, we define, for an *arbitrary* value $v \in VAL$,

$$\langle l; \sigma \rangle \xrightarrow{(C,v)} \langle l'; \sigma' \rangle,$$

  if $\sigma \models b$ and $\sigma' = f(\sigma : x \mapsto v)$.
- Furthermore, we have the following rules for computing the reflexive, transitive closure of the transition relation generated by $\xrightarrow{()}$ and $\xrightarrow{(C,v)}$:

$$\langle l; \sigma \rangle \xrightarrow{()} \langle l; \sigma \rangle \quad \text{and} \quad \frac{\langle l; \sigma \rangle \xrightarrow{\theta} \langle l'; \sigma' \rangle \quad \langle l'; \sigma' \rangle \xrightarrow{\theta'} \langle l''; \sigma'' \rangle}{\langle l; \sigma \rangle \xrightarrow{\theta \cdot \theta'} \langle l''; \sigma'' \rangle}. \qquad \square$$

Using this transition relation we define the compositional semantics of a sequential synchronous transition diagram, in which the value received by an input transition is selected by local guessing.

Definition 7.2 Let $P \equiv (L,T,s,t)$ be a sequential synchronous transition diagram and $l \in L$. We define

$$O_l(P) \stackrel{\text{def}}{=} \{(\sigma,\sigma',\theta) \mid \langle s;\sigma \rangle \stackrel{\theta}{\longrightarrow} \langle l;\sigma' \rangle \}.$$

Observe that we can now define the initial-final state semantics of P by $O_t(P)$. Observe also that σ and σ' assign values to the logical variable h. These values should be identical, since h, being a logical variable, does not occur in P, and, hence, its value is not changed by execution of P. ☐

In the following definition we extend the above semantics in a compositional manner to parallel systems, using the fact that the variables of P_1 and P_2 are disjoint.

Definition 7.3 For P a parallel system $P_1 \parallel P_2$, we define

$$O(P) \stackrel{\text{def}}{=} \{(\sigma,\sigma',\theta) \mid (\sigma,\sigma'_i,\theta_i) \in O(P_i), \ i=1,2, \text{ where}$$
$$\sigma'(x) \stackrel{\text{def}}{=} \begin{cases} \sigma'_1(x), & \text{if } x \in var(P_1), \\ \sigma'_2(x), & \text{if } x \in var(P_2), \\ \sigma(x), & \text{otherwise} \}. \end{cases}$$

The history θ_i denotes the projection $\theta \downarrow Chan(P_i)$ of θ along the channels of P_i, for which we also use the notation $\theta \downarrow P_i$. ☐

Remark 7.4 Note that for $(\sigma,\sigma',\theta) \in O(P)$ we have that $\sigma(x) = \sigma'(x)$ for all $x \notin var(P)$ for both sequential synchronous transition diagrams and parallel systems.

Lemma 7.5 (Associativity of the semantics of parallel systems) Given the disjoint synchronous transition systems P_1, P_2, and P_3 we have that

$$(P_1 \parallel P_2) \parallel P_3 = P_1 \parallel (P_2 \parallel P_3).$$

Proof The proof of this lemma is left as Exercise 7.1 [Han00]. ☐

By the above lemma we can suppress the parentheses in a parallel composition and simply write $P_1 \parallel \ldots \parallel P_n$.

Remark 7.6 For a closed program $P_1 \parallel \ldots \parallel P_n$ the O semantics coincides with the $\mathcal{M}$ semantics of Section 4.3. In Theorem 4.19 this has been proved already.

7.3.2 *Proof Method*

Next we introduce compositionally-inductive assertion networks for reasoning about the sequential components P_i of a parallel system $P \equiv P_1 \| \ldots \| P_n$. Then we introduce compositional proof rules for deducing properties of the whole system. The basic idea of a compositionally-inductive assertion network is the definition of the verification conditions of P_i in terms of a single *logical* history variable h which records the sequence of communications generated by that component.

Here one distinguished *history variable* h is assumed to exist, $h \in VAR$. A state $\sigma \in \Sigma$ thus assigns as the meaning to h a sequence of communications, i.e., $\sigma(h) \in (CHAN \times VAL)^*$ denotes a sequence of communication records, which are pairs consisting of a channel name and a value. The idea behind this is that history variable h represents the sequence of communications of the given concurrent system. For every basic synchronous transition diagram P we require for every state transformation f and boolean condition b of P that $VAR(f) \subseteq (VAR \setminus \{h\})$ and $VAR(b) \subseteq (VAR \setminus \{h\})$. This requirement formalises the condition that the history variable h does not occur in any program.

The parallel combination of these compositionally-inductive assertion networks is defined in terms of a simple semantic characterisation of the variables and channels involved in a predicate. The notion of channels involved in a predicate is defined in terms of a natural generalisation of the projection operation on histories to predicates.

In order to model an input statement $C?x$ which involves the assignment of an *arbitrary* value to x, we need the introduction of quantifiers.

For a predicate φ we define $\sigma \models \forall x.\varphi$ iff for every semantic expression $e : \Sigma \to VAL$, we have $(\sigma : x \mapsto e(\sigma)) \models \varphi$, and similarly $\sigma \models \exists x.\varphi$ by $\sigma \models \neg\forall x.\neg\varphi$.

Definition 7.7 (Compositionally-inductive assertion network) The local assertion network Q for a *sequential* synchronous transition diagram $P \equiv (L, T, s, t)$ is called *compositionally inductive* if:

- For $l \xrightarrow{a} l'$ a local transition of P, i.e., $a \equiv b \to f$ for some boolean b and state transformation f, one has

$$\models Q_l \wedge b \to Q_{l'} \circ f.$$

- For $l \xrightarrow{a} l'$ an output transition of P, i.e., $a \equiv b; C!e \to f$, for some boolean b, channel C and state transformation f, one has

$$\models Q_l \wedge b \to Q_{l'} \circ (f \circ g),$$

where $g(\sigma) \stackrel{\text{def}}{=} (\sigma : h \mapsto \sigma(h) \cdot (C, e(\sigma)))$.

- For $l \xrightarrow{a} l'$ an input transition of P, i.e., $a \equiv b; C?x \to f$, for some boolean b, channel C and state transformation f, one has

$$\models Q_l \wedge b \to \forall x. Q_{l'} \circ (f \circ g),$$

where $g(\sigma) \overset{\text{def}}{=} (\sigma : h \mapsto \sigma(h) \cdot (C, \sigma(x)))$.

We denote by $P \vdash Q$ that Q is a compositionally-inductive assertion network for P. □

Definition 7.8 A *partial correctness statement* is of the form $\{\varphi\}\ P\ \{\psi\}$, where φ and ψ are predicates, also called the precondition and postcondition, which involve, amongst others, logical variable h, and P denotes either a synchronous transition diagram or a parallel system. □

Formally, validity of a partial correctness statement $\{\varphi\}\ P\ \{\psi\}$, notation: $\models \{\varphi\}\ P\ \{\psi\}$, is defined with respect to the semantics O.

Definition 7.9 (Validity of partial correctness formulae) We define $\models \{\varphi\}$ $P\ \{\psi\}$, with $P = (L, T, s, t)$ a sequential synchronous transition diagram, by: for every $(\sigma, \sigma', \theta) \in O_t(P)$ such that $(\sigma : h \mapsto \langle\rangle) \models \varphi$, we have

$$(\sigma' : h \mapsto \theta) \models \psi.$$

Similarly, we define $\models \{\varphi\}\ P\ \{\psi\}$, for P a parallel system, in terms of $O(P)$ by:

for every $(\sigma, \sigma', \theta) \in O(P)$ such that $(\sigma : h \mapsto \langle\rangle) \models \varphi$, we have

$$(\sigma' : h \mapsto \theta) \models \psi.$$ □

In this way the validity of a partial correctness statement $\{\varphi\}\ P\ \{\psi\}$ is defined with respect to computations of P which start in a state in which the history variable h is initialised to the empty sequence, reflecting the fact that we only consider top-level synchronous networks. We can impose this restriction because we do not consider the sequential composition of parallel systems (that is, we consider only top-level parallelism). For a discussion on the consequences of such an operation we refer to Section 7.4 on nested parallelism.

Rule 7.1 (Basic diagram rule) For $P \equiv (L, T, s, t)$ a sequential synchronous transition diagram, we have the following basic diagram rule:

$$\frac{P \vdash Q}{\{Q_s\}\ P\ \{Q_t\}}$$

Moreover, for synchronous transition diagrams we have the following initialisation rule.

Rule 7.2 (Initialisation rule)

$$\frac{\{\varphi \wedge (h = \langle \rangle)\}P\{\psi\}}{\{\varphi\}P\{\psi\}}$$

where $\sigma \models h = \langle \rangle \Leftrightarrow \sigma(h) = \langle \rangle$.

The choice of a single history variable h enforces restrictions on the parallel composition rule which serve the same purpose as the condition on disjointness of the (program) variables. In order to define a rule for parallel composition we introduce the following operation on predicates, known as *chaotic closure* [Zwi89].

We formulate these conditions in terms of a predicate also *involving*, apart from program variables, *channel names*. We introduce the chaotic closure $\varphi \uparrow \bar{C}$ of φ w.r.t. $\bar{C}$, where $\bar{C}$ expresses a set of channel names, to indicate that the value of φ, as far as h is concerned, only depends on the *projection* of the global history h on the channels $\bar{C}$. Formally, we have the following definition.

Definition 7.10 (Semantic characterisation of channel dependency) Let φ be a predicate and $\bar{C}$ a set of channels. We denote by the *chaotic closure* $\varphi \uparrow \bar{C}$ the predicate

$$\sigma \models \varphi \uparrow \bar{C} \Leftrightarrow \quad \text{there exists } \sigma' \models \varphi \text{ s.t. } \sigma(x) = \sigma'(x), \text{for } x \in \text{VAR} \setminus \{h\},$$
$$\text{and } \sigma(h){\downarrow}\bar{C} = \sigma'(h){\downarrow}\bar{C}.$$

That is, if $\sigma \models \varphi$ then $\sigma' \models \varphi \uparrow \bar{C}$ holds for all σ' which are obtained from σ by interleaving $\sigma(h)$ with *arbitrary* communication records (D, v) with $D \notin \bar{C}$, thus justifying the name *chaotic* closure.

Note that $\varphi \uparrow \bar{C} = \varphi$ indicates that, as far as the dependency of the value of φ upon the value of h is concerned, the value of φ only depends on the *projection* of the global history h on the channels $\bar{C}$. More formally, $\varphi \uparrow \bar{C} = \varphi$ indicates that for every σ and σ', such that σ and σ' are the same, except that $\sigma(h){\downarrow}\bar{C} = \sigma'(h){\downarrow}\bar{C}$ holds for the values which they assign to the history variable h, we have

$$\sigma \models \varphi \text{ if and only if } \sigma' \models \varphi.$$

If $\varphi \uparrow \bar{C} = \varphi$ then we also say that 'φ *only involves the channels of* $\bar{C}$'. $Chan(\varphi)$ is defined as the minimal set of channels $\bar{C}$ such that $\varphi \uparrow \bar{C} = \varphi$. □

Example 7.11 In this example we explain the definition of the chaotic closure operator, and the notion that 'φ *only involves the channels of* $\bar{C}$'.

(i) Which channels are involved in $(h{\downarrow}\{C\}) = \langle C, 0 \rangle$? In $((h \downarrow \{C\}) = \langle C, 0 \rangle) \uparrow \{C\}$ we interleave the value of h with arbitrary communication records over channels different from C. However, the projection operator ${\downarrow}\{C\}$ applied to the resulting communication sequence projects all communications not involving channel C. That is, the values of $(h{\downarrow}\{C\} = \langle C, 0 \rangle) \uparrow \{C\}$ and $(h{\downarrow}\{C\} = \langle C, 0 \rangle)$ are the same. This implies that $((h{\downarrow}\{C\}) = \langle C, 0 \rangle)$ only involves channel C.

(ii) Which channels are involved in $(h = \langle C, 0 \rangle)$? In $(h = \langle C, 0 \rangle) \uparrow \{C\}$ we interleave the value of h, as above, with arbitrary communication records over channels different from C. This influences the value of $(h = \langle C, 0 \rangle)$, because these arbitrary interleavings are visible through the occurrence of h in $(h = \langle C, 0 \rangle)$. Hence, $(h = \langle C, 0 \rangle) \uparrow \{C\}$ and $(h = \langle C, 0 \rangle)$ are different. Therefore, $(h = \langle C, 0 \rangle)$ does not involve $\{C\}$.

(iii) Considering $h = \langle C, 0 \rangle$, again, we ask ourselves which channels are involved in $h = \langle C, 0 \rangle$. In $(h = \langle C, 0 \rangle) \uparrow (\text{CHAN} \setminus \{C\})$ we interleave h with arbitrary communication records involving C, only. This leads to values, which are different from those of $h = \langle C, 0 \rangle$ without those interleavings. That is, only by considering the chaotic closure of $h = \langle C, 0 \rangle$ with respect to the full set of available channels CHAN, i.e., only by *not interleaving h with any communication records at all*, do we obtain $(h = \langle C, 0 \rangle) \uparrow \text{CHAN} = (h = \langle C, 0 \rangle)$. This implies that $h = \langle C, 0 \rangle$ involves (the whole of) CHAN, which is a consequence of the unprojected occurrence of h in $h = \langle C, 0 \rangle$. □

Similarly, as in Section 2.4.1, we restrict ourselves in the applications of the proof methods discussed in the remainder of this chapter to predicates φ for which there exist finite sets of channels which they involve. For such predicates φ one can prove that $Chan(\varphi)$ exists and is finite.

We can now formulate the following rule for parallel composition.

Rule 7.3 Let $P \equiv P_1 \parallel P_2$ in the rule

$$\frac{\{\varphi_1\}\, P_1\, \{\psi_1\},\ \{\varphi_2\}\, P_2\, \{\psi_2\}}{\{\varphi_1 \wedge \varphi_2\}\, P\, \{\psi_1 \wedge \psi_2\}},$$

provided ψ_i does not involve the variables of P_j and $\psi_i \uparrow Chan(P_i) = \psi_i$, $i \neq j$. (Recall that $Chan(P_i)$ indicates the channels of P_i.)

The following example shows that the restriction on channels is necessary.

Example 7.12 Consider a network $C!0 \parallel D!0$ (abstracting from the locations of the components). Locally, we can prove

$$\{h = \langle\rangle\}\ C!0\ \{h = \langle(C,0)\rangle\}\ \text{and}\ \{h = \langle\rangle\}\ D!0\ \{h = \langle(D,0)\rangle\}.$$

Applying the above rule (without checking whether its restrictions hold) leads to

$$\{h = \langle\rangle\}\ C!0 \parallel D!0\ \{false\},$$

which gives rise to incorrect results when we further compose the open system $C!0 \parallel D!0$. However, we observe that this specification of $C!0 \parallel D!0$ does hold (and can be derived by the AFR-method) when we view $C!0 \parallel D!0$ as a *closed* system (i.e., under the semantics $\mathcal{M}$). In the example above we derive that, e.g., postcondition $h = \langle(C,0)\rangle$ involves *all* channels, and, hence, the conditions upon the postconditions ψ_i in the above rule for parallel composition are violated. □

We conclude the exposition of the proof method with the following consequence and initialisation rules.

Rule 7.4 For P a sequential synchronous transition diagram or a parallel system we have the usual consequence rule:

$$\frac{\varphi \rightarrow \varphi',\ \{\varphi'\}\ P\ \{\psi'\},\ \psi' \rightarrow \psi}{\{\varphi\}\ P\ \{\psi\}}.$$

Rule 7.5 For P a parallel system we have the initialisation rule:

$$\frac{\{\varphi\}\ P\ \{\psi\}}{\{\varphi \circ f\}\ P\ \{\psi\}},$$

where f is a state function such that its write variables are not involved in P or ψ.

We denote derivability of a partial correctness statement $\{\varphi\}\ P\ \{\psi\}$, using the rules above, we denote by $\vdash \{\varphi\}\ P\ \{\psi\}$.

7.3.3 Application

Example 7.13 We consider the parallel system $P \equiv P_1 \| P_2 \| P_3$ and prove that

$$\vdash \{true\}\ P\ \{x = 1 \wedge y = 2 \wedge z = 0\}.$$

P_1:

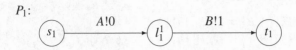

P_2:

P_3:

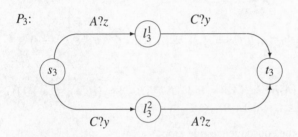

As the assertion network we use for P_1 the following set of predicates which is compositionally inductive:

$$Q_{s_1} \stackrel{\text{def}}{=} h{\downarrow}\{A,B\} = \langle\rangle$$
$$Q_{l_1^1} \stackrel{\text{def}}{=} h{\downarrow}\{A,B\} = \langle(A,0)\rangle$$
$$Q_{t_1} \stackrel{\text{def}}{=} h{\downarrow}\{A,B\} = \langle(A,0),(B,1)\rangle.$$

Similarly we have for P_2:

$$Q_{s_2} \stackrel{\text{def}}{=} h{\downarrow}\{B,C\} = \langle\rangle$$
$$Q_{l_2^1} \stackrel{\text{def}}{=} h{\downarrow}\{B,C\} = \langle(B,x)\rangle$$
$$Q_{t_2} \stackrel{\text{def}}{=} h{\downarrow}\{B,C\} = \langle(B,x),(C,x+1)\rangle.$$

And for P_3:

$$Q_{s_3} \stackrel{\text{def}}{=} h{\downarrow}\{A,C\} = \langle\rangle$$
$$Q_{l_3^1} \stackrel{\text{def}}{=} h{\downarrow}\{A,C\} = \langle(A,z)\rangle$$
$$Q_{l_3^2} \stackrel{\text{def}}{=} h{\downarrow}\{A,C\} = \langle(C,y)\rangle$$
$$Q_{t_3} \stackrel{\text{def}}{=} (h{\downarrow}\{A,C\} = \langle(A,z),(C,y)\rangle \vee h{\downarrow}\{A,C\} = \langle(C,y),(A,z)\rangle).$$

Applying Rule 7.1 we derive

$$\vdash \{h{\downarrow}\{A,B\} = \langle\rangle\}\ P_1\ \{h{\downarrow}\{A,B\} = \langle(A,0),(B,1)\rangle\}$$
$$\vdash \{h{\downarrow}\{B,C\} = \langle\rangle\}\ P_2\ \{h{\downarrow}\{B,C\} = \langle(B,x),(C,x+1)\rangle\}$$
$$\vdash \{h{\downarrow}\{A,C\} = \langle\rangle\}\ P_3\ \{(h{\downarrow}\{A,C\} = \langle(A,z),(C,y)\rangle$$
$$\vee\, h{\downarrow}\{A,C\} = \langle(C,y),(A,z)\rangle)\}.$$

Observe that the restrictions on the parallel composition rule 7.3 are satisfied, and we derive

$$\vdash\ \{h{\downarrow}\{A,B\} = \langle\rangle \wedge h{\downarrow}\{B,C\} = \langle\rangle\}$$
$$P_1\|P_2$$
$$\{h{\downarrow}\{A,B\} = \langle(A,0),(B,1)\rangle \wedge h{\downarrow}\{B,C\} = \langle(B,x),(C,x+1)\rangle\}.$$

Since

$$\models h{\downarrow}\{A,B,C\} = \langle\rangle \to h{\downarrow}\{A,B\} = \langle\rangle \wedge h{\downarrow}\{B,C\} = \langle\rangle$$

and

$$\models\ (h{\downarrow}\{A,B\} = \langle(A,0),(B,1)\rangle \wedge h{\downarrow}\{B,C\} = \langle(B,x),(C,x+1)\rangle) \to$$
$$h{\downarrow}\{A,C\} = \langle(A,0),(C,2)\rangle \wedge x = 1,$$

we obtain by the consequence rule

$$\vdash \{h{\downarrow}\{A,B,C\} = \langle\rangle\}\ P_1\|P_2\ \{h{\downarrow}\{A,C\} = \langle(A,0),(C,2)\rangle \wedge x = 1\}.$$

Again we apply the parallel composition rule to $(P_1\|P_2)$ and P_3 and derive

$$\vdash \{h{\downarrow}\{A,B,C\} = \langle\rangle \wedge h{\downarrow}\{A,C\} = \langle\rangle\}$$
$$(P_1\|P_2)\|P_3$$
$$\{\ h{\downarrow}\{A,C\} = \langle(A,0),(C,2)\rangle \wedge x = 1 \wedge$$
$$(h{\downarrow}\{A,C\} = \langle(A,z),(C,y)\rangle \vee h{\downarrow}\{A,C\} = \langle(C,y),(A,z)\rangle)\}.$$

Now

$$\models (h{\downarrow}\{A,B,C\} = \langle\rangle) \to (h{\downarrow}\{A,B,C\} = \langle\rangle \wedge h{\downarrow}\{A,C\} = \langle\rangle),$$

and the postcondition above implies

$$x = 1 \wedge y = 2 \wedge z = 0.$$

By the consequence rule we derive, therefore,

$$\vdash \{h{\downarrow}\{A,B,C\} = \langle\rangle\}\ P_1\|P_2\|P_3\ \{x = 1 \wedge y = 2 \wedge z = 0\},$$

and the initialisation rule leads to

$$\vdash \{true\}\ P_1\|P_2\|P_3\ \{x = 1 \wedge y = 2 \wedge z = 0\}. \qquad \square$$

7.3.4 Soundness and Completeness

A closer examination of the presented proof method reveals that it is a compositional reformulation of the ideas worked out in Section 4.6. The formulation of compositionally-inductive assertion networks is a variant of Definition 4.41, and Rule 4.1 in fact unites the main rules of this section, namely the basic transition diagram rule 7.1 and the parallel composition rule 7.3. In particular the restrictions formulated in Rule 7.3 are consistent with the restrictions formulated in Section 4.6.3. Since one can interpret the proof method presented in Section 7.3.2 as a special case of the Levin & Gries method, soundness follows immediately from soundness of the latter.

An examination of the completeness proof for the method of Levin & Gries in Section 4.5.3 shows that the strongest postcondition predicates as defined in Definition 4.33 indeed satisfy the restrictions imposed in Section 7.3.2 and hence we can analogously prove completeness. An independent completeness proof for the proof method discussed in this section can be obtained as a special case of the completeness proof given in Section 7.4.5 for the extension of this method to nested parallelism.

7.4 A Compositional Proof Method for Nested Parallelism

In this section we extend the compositional proof method of Section 7.3 and show how one can reason compositionally about systems which are constructed from sequential synchronous transition diagrams by means of sequential and parallel composition. Such *composite* systems give rise to *nested parallelism* and play a dominant rôle in more advanced chapters such as Chapter 12 on layered design. Formally, we have the following definition of composite systems.

Definition 7.14 We assume as given a set $\mathcal{B}$, with typical element B, of *basic systems*, that is, sequential synchronous transition diagrams. We define the set of *composite systems*, with typical element P, inductively as follows:

$$P ::= B \mid P_1 ; P_2 \mid P_1 \parallel P_2.$$ $\qquad\qquad\square$

7.4.1 Compositional Semantics

The semantics of basic synchronous transition systems is given in Definitions 7.1 and 7.2. These definitions form the basis of our definition of a compositional semantics for composite systems which is defined inductively w.r.t. their structure.

Definition 7.15 The semantics $O(B)$ of a basic synchronous transition diagram $B \equiv (L, T, s, t)$ is simply defined as $O_t(B)$.

For $P \equiv P_1; P_2$ we define

$$O(P) \stackrel{\text{def}}{=} \{(\sigma, \sigma', \theta) \mid \text{There exist } \sigma_1, \theta_1, \theta_2 \text{ such that } (\sigma, \sigma_1, \theta_1) \in O(P_1),$$
$$(\sigma_1, \sigma', \theta_2) \in O(P_2) \text{ and } \theta = \theta_1 \cdot \theta_2\}.$$

For $P \equiv P_1 \parallel P_2$ we define

$$O(P) \stackrel{\text{def}}{=} \{(\sigma, \sigma', \theta) \mid i = 1, 2, (\sigma, \sigma_i', \theta \downarrow P_i) \in O(P_i) \wedge \theta = \theta \downarrow Chan(P_1 \parallel P_2),$$
$$\text{where } \sigma'(x) \stackrel{\text{def}}{=} \begin{cases} \sigma_1'(x), & \text{if } x \in var(P_1), \\ \sigma_2'(x), & \text{if } x \in var(P_2), \\ \sigma(x), & \text{otherwise}\}. \end{cases} \qquad \square$$

Remark 7.16 For a composite system we have that $\sigma(x) = \sigma'(x)$ for all $x \notin var(P)$ and $(\sigma, \sigma', \theta) \in O(P)$.

Observe that, due to the condition $\theta = \theta \downarrow Chan(P_1 \parallel P_2)$ in the definition of $O(P_1 \parallel P_2)$, O does not contain information about communications along channels not occurring in $P_1 \parallel P_2$. We paraphrase this property by saying that O defines a *precise* semantics, or that "θ contains no dirt."

It is easy to see that the semantic operation of parallel composition defined above is commutative and associative [Han00].

We observe that in the above definition the requirement that a local history of a basic transition diagram can be obtained as the projection of a global history θ guarantees that an input on a channel is indeed synchronised with a corresponding output.

7.4.2 A Compositional Proof Method

We generalise our compositional proof method of Section 7.3 to nested parallelism by repeating the definition of compositionally-inductive assertion networks, Definition 7.7, for reasoning about the basic sequential components of a composite system, and giving proof rules for composite systems together with the *prefix-invariance axiom* which is discussed in detail below.

Definition 7.17 (Compositional local verification conditions) Let $B \equiv (L, T, s, t)$ be a basic sequential synchronous transition diagram and $l \stackrel{a}{\rightarrow} l'$ be a transition of B. A local assertion network Q for B is called *compositionally inductive* if:

- $l \overset{a}{\to} l'$ is a local transition, i.e., $a \equiv b \to f$ for some boolean b and state-transformation f and

$$\models Q_l \wedge b \to Q_{l'} \circ f,$$

- $l \overset{a}{\to} l'$ is an output transition, i.e., $a \equiv b; C!e \to f$, for some boolean b, channel C and state-transformation f and

$$\models Q_l \wedge b \to Q_{l'} \circ (f \circ g),$$

where $g(\sigma) \overset{\text{def}}{=} (\sigma : h \mapsto \sigma(h) \cdot (C, e(\sigma)))$,

- $l \overset{a}{\to} l'$ is an input transition, i.e., $a \equiv b; C?x \to f$, for some boolean b, channel C and state-transformation f and

$$\models Q_l \wedge b \to \forall x. Q_{l'} \circ (f \circ g),$$

where $g(\sigma) \overset{\text{def}}{=} (\sigma : h \mapsto \sigma(h) \cdot (C, \sigma(x)))$.

We denote by $B \vdash Q$ that Q is a compositionally inductive assertion network for B. □

Based on these verification conditions we can derive partial correctness $\models \{\varphi\} B \{\psi\}$ of a sequential transition diagram B if there exists a compositionally-inductive assertion network Q for B in the sense of Definition 7.17 such that φ implies Q_s and Q_t implies ψ, where s and t are the entry and exit locations of B. This definition is extended to composite systems.

Defining validity of a specification means linking the meaning of a program with the meaning of a specification. Here we relate the information about the communication behaviour of a composite system P as recorded in the semantics by θ to the history variable h used in the verification conditions.

Formally, validity of a partial correctness statement $\{\varphi\} P \{\psi\}$ is defined with respect to the semantics O.

Definition 7.18 We define $\models \{\varphi\} P \{\psi\}$ as follows:

for every $(\sigma, \sigma', \theta) \in O(P)$ such that $\sigma \models \varphi$, we have $(\sigma' : h \mapsto \sigma(h) \cdot \theta) \models \psi$. □

The only difference with the notion of validity given in Definition 7.9 is that we do not require the initial history to be empty. This is clearly necessary when we want to reason about sequential composition.

Rule 7.6 For $B \equiv (L, T, s, t)$ a basic synchronous transition diagram, we have the following basic diagram rule:

$$\frac{B \vdash Q}{\{Q_s\} \, B \, \{Q_t\}}.$$

Rule 7.7 For sequentially composed $P \equiv P_1; P_2$ we have the following rule:

$$\frac{\{\varphi\} \, P_1 \, \{\xi\}, \, \{\xi\} \, P_2 \, \{\psi\}}{\{\varphi\} \, P \, \{\psi\}}.$$

Next, we formulate a correct rule for the parallel composition of nested synchronous transition systems.

Rule 7.8 For $P \equiv P_1 \parallel P_2$ one has

$$\frac{\{\varphi_1\} \, P_1 \, \{\psi_1\}, \, \{\varphi_2\} \, P_2 \, \{\psi_2\}}{\{\varphi_1 \wedge \varphi_2\} \, P \, \{\psi_1 \wedge \psi_2\}},$$

provided ψ_i does not involve the variables of P_j and

$$Chan(\psi_i) \cap Chan(P_j) \subseteq Chan(P_i), \, i \neq j.$$

In the formulation of the parallel composition rule above, one might have expected $Chan(\psi_i) \subseteq Chan(P_i)$ to be a condition upon the channels of ψ_i. However, that would have introduced a source of incompleteness, because one would not have been able to prove that a network does not influence communication histories over channels which do not occur in it. For in the present context of nested parallelism this can be expressed by a valid correctness formula, in contrast to the context of the previous section in which only preconditions implying $h = \langle \rangle$ are allowed.

However Rule 7.8 is still incomplete!

Example 7.19 We cannot derive the valid partial correctness formula

$$\{\langle (D, 0), (C, 1) \rangle = h {\downarrow} \{C, D\}\} D!2 \parallel C!3 \{\langle (D, 0), (C, 1) \rangle \preceq h {\downarrow} \{C, D\}\},$$

which tells us that, if initially the projection of h on the channels C and D equals $\langle (D, 0), (C, 1) \rangle$, i.e., first a communication along D occurred and then one along C, then after the communications $D!2$ and $C!3$ one has that $\langle (D, 0), (C, 1) \rangle$ is a *prefix* of the projection of h on the channels C and D.   □

It is not difficult to see that we cannot derive this correctness statement because of the restrictions on the postconditions in the rule for parallel composition, namely that they should not involve the channels of the other components in the network.

In order to derive this correctness statement we have to introduce the following prefix-invariance axiom which allows us to reason about a possibly nonempty initial history:

Axiom 7.9 (Prefix invariance)

$$\{t = h\} \, P \, \{t \preceq h\}, \text{ for logical variable } t.$$

In Exercise 7.13 we sketch how one can prove formally that the prefix-invariance axiom is independent from the other rules and axioms of our proof method [HZ].

Additionally we have the usual consequence rule (as given by Rule 7.4), a conjunction rule and a suitable initialisation rule. Sometimes we need the following invariance rule, which is actually deducible within our method.

Rule 7.10 (Invariance)

$$\{\varphi\} \, P \, \{\varphi\},$$

for φ not involving the variables and neither the channels of P.

Using the rules above, we denote derivability of a partial correctness statement $\{\varphi\} \, P \, \{\psi\}$ for composite system P by $\vdash \{\varphi\} \, P \, \{\psi\}$.

7.4.3 An Extended Example – Specification and Correctness of a Distributed Priority Queue

In this section we illustrate the compositional proof techniques for nested systems, presented above, by giving a correctness proof for a distributed priority queue, formerly presented in [Zwi89]. This example illustrates in particular the verify-while-develop paradigm since we start with a top-level specification and derive sequential synchronous transition diagrams used for "implementing" the specified system. Every design step is directly linked to a verification step, i.e., an application of a rule of our proof method, resulting in a correctness proof when reaching the level of basic transition diagrams.

Example 7.20 We derive a program implementing a distributed priority queue from its specifications, together with its correctness proof. In particular, we present for any $n \in \mathbb{N}, n \geq 1$, a program P_n which can receive n values along channel A_n, and which sends a descending sequence of these n values along output channel B_n (note that the set of input values equals the set of output values). Here we use the following abbreviations:

- $h_{cset} \equiv h{\downarrow}cset, h_C \equiv h{\downarrow}\{C\}, h_{CD} \equiv h{\downarrow}\{C,D\}, h_{ABC} \equiv h{\downarrow}\{A,B,C\}$, etc.
- $A_n[i] \stackrel{\text{def}}{=} h_{A_n}[i], B_n[i] \stackrel{\text{def}}{=} h_{B_n}[i]$, where $seq[i]$ denotes the i-th element of communication sequence seq, and
- $\#(seq)$ denotes the length of seq.

Formally P_n is specified by $\{h_{A_n B_n} = \langle\rangle\}\, P_n\, \{q_n\}$, with q_n defined as

$$q_n \stackrel{\text{def}}{=} \#h_{A_n} = \#h_{B_n} = n \wedge \{B_n[1],\dots,B_n[n]\} = \{A_n[1],\dots,A_n[n]\} \wedge$$
$$B_n[1] \geq \dots \geq B_n[n],$$

where $\{A_n, B_n\} \subseteq Chan(P_n)$. The syntactic interface of P_n with the environment is presented in Figure 7.1.

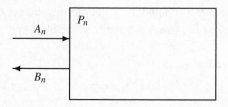

Fig. 7.1. External interface of program P_n.

The main idea is to design P_n, for any $n > 1$, using P_{n-1}, and to implement P_1 directly.

So, the first step is to implement P_n as the parallel composition of P_{n-1} and a process M_n, which computes the maximum of the inputs received on A_n and sends this value as the first output along B_n. All other inputs are forwarded to P_{n-1} via channel A_{n-1}, and the resulting output along B_{n-1} is copied to B_n after the maximum input value has been sent along B_n (see Figure 7.2). This results in $P_n \stackrel{\text{def}}{=} M_n \| P_{n-1}$ as depicted in Figure 7.2.

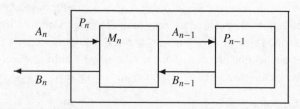

Fig. 7.2. Structure of P_n for $n > 1$.

For this inductive definition we need program P_1, and for any $n \in \mathbb{N}, n > 1$, we have to construct program M_n. Considering that P_1 just has one input value to select, the specification reduces to the requirement that the output value equals the input value, which is fulfilled by the transition system P_1 depicted in Figure 7.3.

$$P_1:$$

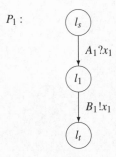

Fig. 7.3. Structure of P_1.

It is obvious that for P_1 the partial correctness formula

$$\{h_{A_1B_1} = \langle\rangle\}\ P_1\ \{\ \#h_{A_1} = \#h_{B_1} = 1 \wedge \{B_1[1]\} = \{A_1[1]\}\ \}$$

holds.

As described above, the process M_n uses all the input values to compute their maximum, and outputs this value; all other values are forwarded to process P_{n-1}, and the resulting output of P_{n-1} along B_{n-1} is forwarded to B_n. Therefore, we can decompose M_n sequentially into an input part and an output part. We give the transition systems for IN_n in Figure 7.4, and for OUT_n in Figure 7.5, where $M_n \stackrel{\text{def}}{=} IN_n; OUT_n$.

Proof To prove partial correctness of $P_n \stackrel{\text{def}}{=} M_n \| P_{n-1}$, we need M_n to be partially correct w.r.t. precondition $h_{A_nB_nA_{n-1}B_{n-1}} = \langle\rangle$ and postcondition q_{M_n}, where

$$q_{M_n} \stackrel{\text{def}}{=} \#h_{A_n} = \#h_{B_n} = n \wedge \#h_{A_{n-1}} = \#h_{B_{n-1}} = n-1 \wedge$$
$$\{A_{n-1}[1], \dots, A_{n-1}[n-1]\} = \{A_n[1], \dots, A_n[n]\} \setminus \{max_n\} \wedge$$
$$B_n[1] = max_n \wedge \forall i: 2 \leq i \leq n.B_n[i] = B_{n-1}[i-1],$$

and

$$max_n \stackrel{\text{def}}{=} max\{A_n[1], \dots, A_n[n]\}.$$

The proof proceeds by induction on n. For $n > 1$ we prove first that the above specification of M_n suffices for proving the given specification of P_n correct assuming that the corresponding specification for P_{n-1} is correct. Then we prove correctness of M_n.

For $n = 1$ we observe that P_1, as given above, already satisfies its specification. Taken together, this proves that P_n is a correct distributed implementation of a priority queue of length n.

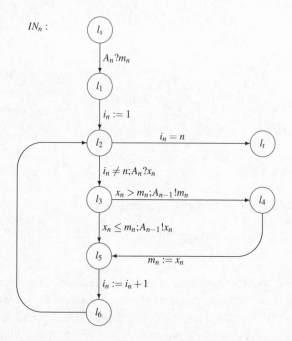

Fig. 7.4. Structure of IN_n for $n > 1$.

Correctness of the parallel composition. Assuming that the specification of P_{n-1} given above holds, it can be proved that $M_n \| P_{n-1}$ satisfies the specification of P_n. To apply the parallel composition rule, observe that

$$Chan(q_{M_n}) \subseteq \{A_n, B_n, A_{n-1}, B_{n-1}\} \subseteq Chan(M_n)$$
$$\text{implies} \quad Chan(q_{M_n}) \cap Chan(P_{n-1}) \subseteq Chan(M_n),$$

and

$$Chan(q_{n-1}) \subseteq \{A_{n-1}, B_{n-1}\} \subseteq Chan(P_{n-1})$$
$$\text{implies} \quad Chan(q_{n-1}) \cap Chan(M_n) \subseteq Chan(P_{n-1}).$$

Further note that the assertions q_{M_n} and q_{n-1} do not refer to program variables. Hence the restrictions of the parallel composition rule are fulfilled and we obtain

$$\vdash \{h_{A_n B_n A_{n-1} B_{n-1}} = \langle\rangle \wedge h_{A_{n-1} B_{n-1}} = \langle\rangle\} \; M_n \| P_{n-1} \; \{q_{M_n} \wedge q_{n-1}\}.$$

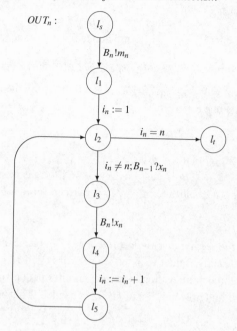

OUT_n:

Fig. 7.5. Structure of OUT_n for $n > 1$.

We show that $\models q_{M_n} \wedge q_{n-1} \to q_n$:

- $\#h_{A_n} = \#h_{B_n} = n$ follows from q_{M_n}.
- Next, we conclude:

$$
\begin{aligned}
\{B_n[1],\dots,B_n[n]\} &= \{max_n, B_{n-1}[1],\dots,B_{n-1}[n-1]\} && \text{(by } q_{M_n}) \\
&= \{max_n\} \cup \{A_{n-1}[1],\dots,A_{n-1}[n-1]\} && \text{(by } q_{n-1}) \\
&= \{max_n\} \cup (\{A_n[1],\dots,A_n[n]\} \setminus \{max_n\}) && \text{(by } q_{M_n}) \\
&= \{A_n[1],\dots,A_n[n]\}.
\end{aligned}
$$

- Furthermore, we have

$$
\begin{aligned}
B_n[1] = max_n &\geq max(\{A_n[1],\dots,A_n[n]\} \setminus \{max_n\}) \\
&= max\{A_{n-1}[1],\dots,A_{n-1}[n-1]\} && \text{(by } q_{M_n}) \\
&= max\{B_{n-1}[1],\dots,B_{n-1}[n-1]\} = B_{n-1}[1] && \text{(by } q_{n-1}).
\end{aligned}
$$

Thus $B_n[1] \geq B_{n-1}[1] = B_n[2]$. For $i \in \{2,\dots,n-1\}$ we have

$$
B_n[i] = B_{n-1}[i-1] \geq B_{n-1}[i] = B_n[i+1].
$$

Hence, we obtain $B_n[1] \geq \dots \geq B_n[n]$.

Thus $\models q_{M_n} \wedge q_{n-1} \rightarrow q_n$. Further note that $h_{A_nB_n} = \langle\rangle \wedge h_{A_{n-1}B_{n-1}} = \langle\rangle$ implies $h_{A_nB_nA_{n-1}B_{n-1}} = \langle\rangle \wedge h_{A_{n-1}B_{n-1}} = \langle\rangle$, and hence the consequence rule leads to

$$\vdash \{h_{A_nB_n} = \langle\rangle \wedge h_{A_{n-1}B_{n-1}} = \langle\rangle\}\, M_n\|P_{n-1}\,\{q_n\}.$$

Since $Chan(h_{A_nB_n} = \langle\rangle, q_n) \cap \{A_{n-1}, B_{n-1}\} = \emptyset$, by using the initialisation and consequence rule one establishes

$$\vdash \{h_{A_nB_n} = \langle\rangle\}\, M_n\|P_{n-1}\,\{q_n\},$$

using the convention that $Chan(\varphi_1, \ldots, \varphi_n) \stackrel{\text{def}}{=} \bigcup_{i=1}^n Chan(\varphi_i)$. Together with $Chan(M_n\|P_{n-1}) \supseteq \{A_n, B_n\}$, this proves that $M_n\|P_{n-1}$ is a correct implementation of P_n. Now it remains to prove M_n is correct, for $n > 1$, according to its specification.

Correctness of the sequential composition of M_n. To prove that $IN_n; OUT_n$ implements M_n correctly, inductive assertion networks will be given for both. To prove the sequential composition is correct an intermediate predicate as postcondition of IN_n and precondition of OUT_n is needed. This predicate r_n is

$$r_n \stackrel{\text{def}}{=} h_{B_nB_{n-1}} = \langle\rangle \wedge \#h_{A_n} = n \wedge \#h_{A_{n-1}} = n - 1 \wedge m_n = max_n \wedge$$
$$\{A_{n-1}[1], \ldots, A_{n-1}[n-1]\} = \{A_n[1], \ldots, A_n[n]\} \setminus \{max_n\}.$$

Note that by

$$Chan(IN_n; OUT_n) = Chan(IN_n) \cup Chan(OUT_n) \supseteq \{A_n, B_n, A_{n-1}, B_{n-1}\}$$

and the sequential composition rule, we have that $IN_n; OUT_n$ satisfies the specification of M_n, provided $\{h_{A_nB_nA_{n-1}B_{n-1}} = \langle\rangle\}\, IN_n\,\{r_n\}$ and $\{r_n\}\, OUT_n\,\{q_{M_n}\}$ are valid, for $n > 1$.

Correctness of IN_n. The transition system for IN_n uses an iteration to receive n values along A_n. The invariant for this iteration can be derived from assertion r_n by replacing each occurrence of variable n in r_n by a variable i_n.

Define I_n as

$$I_n \stackrel{\text{def}}{=} h_{B_nB_{n-1}} = \langle\rangle \wedge \#h_{A_n} = i_n \wedge \#h_{A_{n-1}} = i_n - 1 \wedge$$
$$m_n = max\{A_n[1], \ldots, A_n[i_n]\} \wedge$$
$$\{A_{n-1}[1], \ldots, A_{n-1}[i_n - 1]\} = \{A_n[1], \ldots, A_n[i_n]\} \setminus \{m_n\}.$$

Now, we give the assertion network for IN_n. We have to establish that this assertion network is compositionally inductive.

Assertion network for IN_n

$Q_{I_s} \stackrel{\text{def}}{=} h_{A_nB_nA_{n-1}B_{n-1}} = \langle\rangle$

$Q_{I_1} \stackrel{\text{def}}{=} h_{B_nA_{n-1}B_{n-1}} = \langle\rangle \wedge m_n = A_n[1] \wedge \#h_{A_n} = 1$

$Q_{l_2} \overset{\text{def}}{=} I_n$

$Q_{l_3} \overset{\text{def}}{=} h_{B_n B_{n-1}} = \langle\rangle \wedge i_n \neq n \wedge x_n = A_n[i_n + 1] \wedge \#h_{A_n} = i_n + 1 \wedge$
$\qquad \#h_{A_{n-1}} = i_n - 1 \wedge m_n = max\{A_n[1], \ldots, A_n[i_n]\} \wedge$
$\qquad \{A_{n-1}[1], \ldots, A_{n-1}[i_n - 1]\} = \{A_n[1], \ldots, A_n[i_n]\} \setminus \{m_n\}$

$Q_{l_4} \overset{\text{def}}{=} h_{B_n B_{n-1}} = \langle\rangle \wedge i_n \neq n \wedge x_n = A_n[i_n + 1] \wedge \#h_{A_n} = i_n + 1 \wedge$
$\qquad \#h_{A_{n-1}} = i_n \wedge m_n = max\{A_n[1], \ldots, A_n[i_n]\} \wedge$
$\qquad \{A_{n-1}[1], \ldots, A_{n-1}[i_n]\} = \{A_n[1], \ldots, A_n[i_n]\} \wedge x_n > m_n$

$Q_{l_5} \overset{\text{def}}{=} h_{B_n B_{n-1}} = \langle\rangle \wedge i_n \neq n \wedge x_n = A_n[i_n + 1] \wedge \#h_{A_n} = i_n + 1 \wedge$
$\qquad \#h_{A_{n-1}} = i_n \wedge m_n = max\{A_n[1], \ldots, A_n[i_n + 1]\} \wedge$
$\qquad \{A_{n-1}[1], \ldots, A_{n-1}[i_n]\} = \{A_n[1], \ldots, A_n[i_n + 1]\} \setminus \{m_n\}$

$Q_{l_6} \overset{\text{def}}{=} I_n$

$Q_{l_t} \overset{\text{def}}{=} I_n \wedge i_n = n.$

To illustrate the proof of compositional inductiveness we prove that the transitions l_s to l_1 (an input statement) and l_3 to l_5 (an output statement) are compositionally inductive. For an input transition l to l' labelled with $b;C?x$

$$\models Q_l \wedge b \to \forall x. Q_{l'} \circ g,$$

with $g(\sigma) \overset{\text{def}}{=} (\sigma : h \mapsto \sigma(h) \cdot (C, x))$, has to hold, where Q_l and $Q_{l'}$ are, respectively, the assertions associated with the corresponding locations. For the transition from l_s to l_1 this reduces to checking:

$$\models h_{A_n B_n A_{n-1} B_{n-1}} = \langle\rangle \to$$
$$\forall m_n.(h_{B_n A_{n-1} B_{n-1}} = \langle\rangle \wedge m_n = A_n[1] \wedge \#h_{A_n} = 1) \circ g,$$

with $g(\sigma) \overset{\text{def}}{=} (\sigma : h \mapsto \sigma(h) \cdot (A_n, m_n))$, which obviously holds. For an output transition from l to l' labelled with $b;C!e$ one has to prove that

$$\models (Q_l \wedge b) \to Q_{l'} \circ g$$

holds, with $g(\sigma) = (\sigma : h \mapsto \sigma(h) \cdot (C, e(\sigma)))$. For the transition from l_3 to l_5 this reduces to checking

$$\models (h_{B_n B_{n-1}} = \langle\rangle \wedge i_n \neq n \wedge x_n = A_n[i_n + 1] \wedge \#h_{A_n} = i_n + 1 \wedge$$
$$\#h_{A_{n-1}} = i_n - 1 \wedge m_n = max\{A_n[1], \ldots, A_n[i_n]\} \wedge$$
$$\{A_{n-1}[1], \ldots, A_{n-1}[i_n - 1]\} = \{A_n[1], \ldots, A_n[i_n]\} \setminus \{m_n\})$$
$$\wedge x_n \leq m_n \to$$
$$(h_{B_n B_{n-1}} = \langle\rangle \wedge i_n \neq n \wedge x_n = A_n[i_n + 1] \wedge \#h_{A_n} = i_n + 1 \wedge$$
$$\#h_{A_{n-1}} = i_n \wedge m_n = max\{A_n[1], \ldots, A_n[i_n + 1]\} \wedge$$
$$\{A_{n-1}[1], \ldots, A_{n-1}[i_n]\} = \{A_n[1], \ldots, A_n[i_n + 1]\} \setminus \{m_n\}) \circ g,$$

with $g(\sigma) = (\sigma : h \mapsto \sigma(h) \cdot (A_{n-1}, x_n))$, as can be easily established. The same applies to the other transitions. Furthermore, note that $\models I_n \wedge i_n = n \to r_n$, and therefore IN_n satisfies the given specification.

Correctness of OUT_n. We must prove $\{r_n\}OUT_n\{q_{m_n}\}$, for $n > 1$. For OUT_n one has that $Chan(OUT_n) \cap \{A_n, A_{n-1}\} = \emptyset$ holds. So, we can deduce with the (derivable) invariance rule

$$\vdash \{\#h_{A_n} = n \wedge \#h_{A_{n-1}} = n - 1 \wedge$$
$$\{A_{n-1}[1], \ldots, A_{n-1}[n-1]\} = \{A_n[1], \ldots, A_n[n]\} \setminus \{max_n\}\}$$
$$OUT_n$$
$$\{\#h_{A_n} = n \wedge \#h_{A_{n-1}} = n - 1 \wedge$$
$$\{A_{n-1}[1], \ldots, A_{n-1}[n-1]\} = \{A_n[1], \ldots, A_n[n]\} \setminus \{max_n\}\}.$$

It remains to prove that

$$\vdash \{h_{B_n B_{n-1}} = \langle\rangle \wedge m_n = max_n\}$$
$$OUT_n$$
$$\{\#h_{B_n} = n \wedge \#h_{B_{n-1}} = n - 1 \wedge$$
$$B_n[1] = max_n \wedge \forall i : 2 \leq i \leq n.B_n[i] = B_{n-1}[i-1]\},$$

using the conjunction rule to obtain $\vdash \{r_n\}OUT_n\{q_{m_n}\}$. To prove the former we use as loop invariant

$$L_n \stackrel{\text{def}}{=} \#h_{B_n} = i_n \wedge \#h_{B_{n-1}} = i_n - 1 \wedge B_n[1] = max_n \wedge$$
$$\forall i : 2 \leq i \leq i_n.B_n[i] = B_{n-1}[i-1].$$

Therefore, the assertion network for OUT_n looks as follows.

Assertion network for OUT_n

$Q_{J_s} \stackrel{\text{def}}{=} h_{B_n B_{n-1}} = \langle\rangle \wedge m_n = max_n$

$Q_{J_1} \stackrel{\text{def}}{=} h_{B_{n-1}} = \langle\rangle \wedge \#h_{B_n} = 1 \wedge B_n[1] = max_n$

$Q_{J_2} \stackrel{\text{def}}{=} L_n$

$Q_{J_3} \stackrel{\text{def}}{=} i_n \neq n \wedge x_n = B_{n-1}[i_n] \wedge \#h_{B_n} = i_n \wedge \#h_{B_{n-1}} = i_n \wedge B_n[1] = max_n \wedge$
$\qquad \forall i : 2 \leq i \leq i_n.B_n[i] = B_{n-1}[i-1]$

$Q_{J_4} \stackrel{\text{def}}{=} i_n \neq n \wedge \#h_{B_n} = i_n + 1 \wedge \#h_{B_{n-1}} = i_n \wedge B_n[1] = max_n \wedge$
$\qquad \forall i : 2 \leq i \leq i_n + 1.B_n[i] = B_{n-1}[i-1]$

$Q_{J_5} \stackrel{\text{def}}{=} L_n$

$Q_{J_t} \stackrel{\text{def}}{=} L_n \wedge i_n = n$

Proving compositional inductiveness is similar to the proof for IN_n. Thus, we obtain correctness of OUT_n. $\qquad\qquad\qquad\qquad\qquad\qquad\qquad\qquad \Box$

7.4.4 Soundness

A proof of the soundness of the method presented in Section 7.4 proceeds by induction on the structure of P. Here we treat only the basic case and the parallel composition rule. See also Exercise 7.6.

Theorem 7.21

Let $B \equiv (L,T,s,t)$ be a basic synchronous transition diagram and Q be a compositionally-inductive assertion network for B. We have that $B \vdash Q$ implies $\models \{Q_s\} B \{Q_t\}$.

Proof It suffices to prove that for every computation

$$\langle s;\sigma \rangle \xrightarrow{\theta} \langle l;\sigma' \rangle$$

of $B \equiv (L,T,s,t)$, we have that $\sigma \models Q_s$ implies $(\sigma' : h \mapsto \sigma(h) \cdot \theta) \models Q_l$, where Q is a compositionally-inductive assertion network for B. We proceed by induction on the length of the computation.

For a computation of length 0 we have trivially that $\sigma \models Q_s$ implies

$$(\sigma : h \mapsto \sigma(h) \cdot \langle \rangle) \models Q_s.$$

We only discuss the case that the last transition involves the execution of a guarded input $b; C?x \to f$.

Let

$$\langle s;\sigma \rangle \xrightarrow{\theta} \langle l';\sigma' \rangle \quad \text{and} \quad \langle l';\sigma' \rangle \xrightarrow{(C,v)} \langle l;\sigma'' \rangle,$$

with $\sigma \models Q_s$, $\sigma' \models b$ and $\sigma'' = f(\sigma' : x \mapsto v)$ for an arbitrary value v. Since $\langle s;\sigma \rangle \xrightarrow{\theta} \langle l';\sigma' \rangle$ and $\langle l';\sigma' \rangle \xrightarrow{(C,v)} \langle l;\sigma'' \rangle$ together imply $\langle s;\sigma \rangle \xrightarrow{\theta \cdot (C,v)} \langle l;\sigma'' \rangle$ by Definition 7.1, we have to prove

$$(\sigma'' : h \mapsto \sigma(h) \cdot \theta \cdot (C,v)) \models Q_l.$$

By the induction hypothesis we have

$$(\sigma' : h \mapsto \sigma(h) \cdot \theta) \models Q_{l'}.$$

Now from $\sigma' \models b$ and $h \notin var(b)$ we have

$$(\sigma' : h \mapsto \sigma(h) \cdot \theta) \models b,$$

and hence

$$(\sigma' : h \mapsto \sigma(h) \cdot \theta) \models Q_{l'} \wedge b.$$

We are given that Q is compositionally inductive, so we have

$$\models Q_{l'} \wedge b \to \forall x. Q_l \circ (f \circ g),$$

where, in general, $g(\sigma) \stackrel{\text{def}}{=} (\sigma : h \mapsto \sigma(h) \cdot (C,\sigma(x)))$.

Consequently,

$$(\sigma' : h \mapsto \sigma(h) \cdot \theta) \models \forall x. Q_J \circ (f \circ g)$$
$$\Leftrightarrow ((\sigma' : h \mapsto \sigma(h) \cdot \theta) : x \mapsto v) \models Q_J \circ (f \circ g), \text{ with } v \text{ an arbitrary value,}$$
$$\Leftrightarrow (f \circ g)((\sigma' : h \mapsto \sigma(h) \cdot \theta) : x \mapsto v) \models Q_J, \text{ by definition of } g,$$
$$\Leftrightarrow f((\sigma' : h \mapsto \sigma(h) \cdot \theta \cdot (C, v)) : x \mapsto v) \models Q_J,$$
$$\Leftrightarrow (f(\sigma' : x \mapsto v) : h \mapsto \sigma(h) \cdot \theta \cdot (C, v)) \models Q_J, \text{ as } f \text{ does not involve } h,$$
$$\Leftrightarrow (\sigma'' : h \mapsto \sigma(h) \cdot \theta \cdot (C, v)) \models Q_J. \qquad \square$$

Next we prove soundness of the parallel composition rule.

Theorem 7.22

Let $P \equiv P_1 \parallel P_2$. We have that $\models \{\varphi_1\} P_1 \{\psi_1\}$ and $\models \{\varphi_2\} P_2 \{\psi_2\}$ imply $\models \{\varphi_1 \wedge \varphi_2\} P \{\psi_1 \wedge \psi_2\}$, provided ψ_i does not involve the variables of P_j and $Chan(\psi_i) \cap Chan(P_j) \subset Chan(P_i)$, $i \neq j$.

Proof Let $(\sigma, \sigma', \theta) \in O(P)$ such that $\sigma \models \varphi_1 \wedge \varphi_2$. By the definition of $O(P)$ we have that

$$(\sigma, \sigma'_i, \theta \downarrow P_i) \in O(P_i), \ i = 1, 2, \text{ and } \theta = \theta \downarrow Chan(P_1 \parallel P_2),$$

where

$$\sigma'(x) \overset{\text{def}}{=} \begin{cases} \sigma'_1(x), & \text{if } x \in var(P_1), \\ \sigma'_2(x), & \text{if } x \in var(P_2), \\ \sigma(x), & \text{otherwise.} \end{cases}$$

We must prove that $(\sigma' : h \mapsto \sigma(h) \cdot \theta) \models \psi_1 \wedge \psi_2$. By the hypothesis $\models \{\varphi_i\} P_i \{\psi_i\}$ we have that

$$(\sigma'_i : h \mapsto \sigma(h) \cdot \theta \downarrow P_i) \models \psi_i \text{ for } i = 1, 2.$$

Since ψ_i does not involve the variables of P_j for $i \neq j$, this implies

$$(\sigma' : h \mapsto \sigma(h) \cdot \theta \downarrow P_i) \models \psi_i \text{ for } i = 1, 2.$$

Also we have that $Chan(\psi_i) \cap Chan(P_j) \subset Chan(P_i)$, $i \neq j$. Let

$$C_i \overset{\text{def}}{=} \overline{Chan(P_j)} \cup Chan(P_i) \text{ for } i \neq j,$$

where $\overline{Chan(P_j)}$ abbreviates $\text{CHAN} \setminus Chan(P_j)$. Observe that $Chan(\psi_i) \cap Chan(P_j) \subset Chan(P_i)$ is equivalent to $Chan(\psi_i) \subseteq C_i$. Then $(\theta \downarrow (P_1 \parallel P_2)) \downarrow C_i = \theta \downarrow (Chan(P_1 \parallel P_2) \cap C_i) = \theta \downarrow (Chan(P_i) \cap C_i) = (\theta \downarrow P_i) \downarrow C_i$, and we infer, using $Chan(\psi_i) \subseteq C_i$, that $(\sigma' : h \mapsto \sigma(h) \cdot \theta \downarrow (P_1 \parallel P_2)) \models \psi_i$, $i = 1, 2$. Since $\theta = \theta \downarrow (P_1 \parallel P_2)$ we conclude that $(\sigma' : h \mapsto \sigma(h) \cdot \theta) \models \psi_i$, $i = 1, 2$, as was to be proved. $\qquad \square$

7.4.5 *Semantic Completeness*

We want to prove completeness, that is, we want to prove that every valid partial correctness statement of a composite system P is derivable, i.e.,

Theorem 7.23

$$\models \{\varphi\}\, P\, \{\psi\} \;\Rightarrow\; \vdash \{\varphi\}\, P\, \{\psi\}.$$

We prove this by induction on the structure of P, restricting ourselves to the cases of basic transition diagrams and parallel composition. To this end we introduce the following characterisation of *strongest postconditions*.

Definition 7.24 Given a basic synchronous transition diagram $B \equiv (L, T, s, t)$, $l \in L$, and a precondition φ we define

$$SP_l(\varphi B) \overset{\text{def}}{=} \{\sigma \,|\, \text{there exists } \sigma', \sigma'', \theta \text{ s.t. } \sigma' \models \varphi,$$
$$(\sigma', \sigma'', \theta) \in O_l(B), \text{ and } \sigma = (\sigma'' : h \mapsto \sigma'(h) \cdot \theta)\}.$$

By $SP(\varphi, B)$, for $B \equiv (L, T, s, t)$, we denote $SP_t(\varphi, B)$. Similarly we define $SP(\varphi, P)$, for P a composite system, in terms of $O(P)$. $\qquad\square$

For the strongest postcondition we have the following properties.

Lemma 7.25 For P a sequential synchronous transition diagram or a composite system, one has that

$$\models \{\varphi\}\, P\, \{SP(\varphi, P)\},$$

and

$$\models \{\varphi\}\, P\, \{\psi\} \;\Rightarrow\; \models SP(\varphi, P) \to \psi.$$

Proof See Exercise 7.7. $\qquad\square$

We now prove our completeness result by induction on the complexity of composite systems, starting with basic synchronous transition diagrams.

Lemma 7.26 For B a basic synchronous transition diagram, we have

$$\models \{\varphi\}\, B\, \{\psi\} \;\Rightarrow\; \vdash \{\varphi\}\, B\, \{\psi\}.$$

Proof Let $B \equiv (L, T, s, t)$ and let Q be the assertion network which associates with each location l of B the predicate $SP_l(\varphi, B)$.

We first prove that this assertion network is compositionally inductive. We only treat the case of an input transition $l \xrightarrow{a} l' \in T$, with $a \equiv b; C?x \to f$. We have to prove that

$$\models SP_l(\varphi, B) \land b \to \forall x.SP_{l'}(\varphi, B) \circ (f \circ g),$$

where $g(\sigma) \stackrel{\text{def}}{=} (\sigma : h \mapsto \sigma(h) \cdot (C, \sigma(x)))$.

Let $\sigma \models SP_l(\varphi, B) \land b$. By Definition 7.24, $\sigma \models SP_l(\varphi, B)$ means that there exist $\sigma', \sigma'', \theta$ such that $\sigma' \models \varphi$, $(\sigma', \sigma'', \theta) \in O_l(B)$ and $\sigma = (\sigma'' : h \mapsto \sigma'(h) \cdot \theta)$.

Now $\sigma \models b$ implies $\sigma'' \models b$, because h is a logical variable not involved in b. That is,

$$\langle l; \sigma'' \rangle \xrightarrow{(C,v)} \langle l'; f(\sigma'' : x \mapsto v) \rangle, \text{ by Definition 7.1,}$$

and

$$\langle s; \sigma' \rangle \xrightarrow{\theta \cdot (C,v)} \langle l'; f(\sigma'' : x \mapsto v) \rangle$$

with $\sigma' \models \varphi$ and $v \in VAL$ an arbitrary value, from above and Definition 7.1. Therefore,

$$(f(\sigma'' : x \mapsto v) : h \mapsto \sigma'(h) \cdot \theta \cdot (C,v)) \models SP_{l'}(\varphi, B). \tag{$*$}$$

However, we have to prove that

$$\sigma \models \forall x.SP_{l'}(\varphi, B) \circ (f \circ g)$$
$$\Leftrightarrow \quad (\sigma : x \mapsto v) \models SP_{l'}(\varphi, B) \circ (f \circ g), \qquad \text{for arbitrary } v$$
$$\Leftrightarrow \quad f \circ g(\sigma : x \mapsto v) \models SP_{l'}(\varphi, B), \qquad \text{for arbitrary } v$$
$$\Leftrightarrow \quad f((\sigma : x \mapsto v) : h \mapsto \sigma(h) \cdot (C, v)) \models SP_{l'}(\varphi, B),$$

by applying the definition of g, for arbitrary v.

Now,

$f((\sigma : x \mapsto v) : h \mapsto \sigma(h) \cdot (C, v)) = $ (by definition of σ)
$f(((\sigma'' : h \mapsto \sigma'(h) \cdot \theta) : x \mapsto v) : h \mapsto \sigma'(h) \cdot \theta \cdot (C, v)) = $
(by a property of the $(\sigma : x \mapsto exp)$ operator)
$f((\sigma'' : x \mapsto v) : h \mapsto \sigma'(h) \cdot \theta \cdot (C, v)) = $
(f does not depend on h, and neither do the write variables of f contain h)
$(f(\sigma'' : x \mapsto v)) : h \mapsto \sigma'(h) \cdot \theta \cdot (C, v)$.

Hence we obtain from $(*)$ that

$$f((\sigma : x \mapsto v) : h \mapsto \sigma(h) \cdot (C, v)) \models SP_{l'}(\varphi, B),$$

which we had to prove.

Coming back to our main argument, we derive by Rule 7.6 that

$$\vdash \{SP_s(\varphi, B)\} \ P \ \{SP_t(\varphi, B)\}.$$

Next we observe that $\models \varphi \to SP_s(\varphi, B)$, and by Lemma 7.25 $\models SP_t(\varphi, B) \to \psi$, so an application of the consequence rule gives us

$$\vdash \{\varphi\} \, B \, \{\psi\}. \qquad \qquad \Box$$

Now we continue our induction on the structure of P and prove

Lemma 7.27 For $P \equiv P_1 \parallel P_2$ we have

$$\models \{\varphi\} \, P \, \{\psi\} \Rightarrow \vdash \{\varphi\} \, P \, \{\psi\}.$$

Proof We first introduce the following sets of variables and channels.

- $\bar{x} = var(\varphi) \cup var(P)$,
- $\bar{x}_i = var(P_i)$, $i = 1, 2$,
- $C_i = \overline{Chan(P_j)} \cup Chan(P_i)$, $i \neq j$.

By the induction hypothesis we have that

$$\models \{\varphi'\} P_i \{\psi_i\} \Rightarrow \vdash \{\varphi'\} P_i \{\psi_i\}, i = 1, 2,$$

holds; since $\models \{\varphi'\} P_i \{SP(\varphi', P_i)\}$ holds by Lemma 7.25, we obtain $\vdash \{\varphi'\} \, P_i$ $\{SP(\varphi', P_i)\}$, $i = 1, 2$, where $\varphi' \equiv (\varphi \wedge \bar{z} = \bar{x} \wedge t = h)$, with t a "fresh" logical history variable and $\bar{z}$ a sequence of "fresh" logical variables corresponding to $\bar{x}$ (here $\bar{z} = \bar{x}$ denotes the set of states σ such that $\sigma(z_i) = \sigma(x_i)$, for every $z_i \in \bar{z}$ and corresponding x_i). The variables t and $\bar{z}$ are used to *freeze* the initial values of $\bar{x}$ and h; the predicate $\bar{z} = \bar{x}$ initialises the variables of $\bar{z}$ to the values of the corresponding $\bar{x}$. Similarly, $t = h$ sets the value of t to the initial value of h.

Applying the consequence rule we obtain

$$\vdash \{\varphi'\} \, P_i \, \{\exists \bar{x}_j.(SP(\varphi', P_i) \uparrow C_i)\}, \ i, j \in \{1, 2\}, i \neq j,$$

using that $\models SP(\varphi', P_i) \to \exists \bar{x}_j.(SP(\varphi', P_i) \uparrow C_i)$ follows from the definition of SP.

Below we write $\exists \bar{x}_j.SP(\varphi', P_i) \uparrow C_i$ (dropping the parentheses); this is justified because $\exists \bar{x}_j.(SP(\varphi', P_i) \uparrow C_i) = (\exists \bar{x}_j.SP(\varphi', P_i)) \uparrow C_i$. Clearly the conditions of the parallel composition rule are satisfied. So we obtain

$$\vdash \{\varphi'\} \, P \, \{\exists \bar{x}_2.SP(\varphi', P_1) \uparrow C_1 \wedge \exists \bar{x}_1.SP(\varphi', P_2) \uparrow C_2\}.$$

Next we apply the conjunction rule to the above and the prefix invariance axiom, obtaining

$$\vdash \{\varphi' \wedge t = h\} \, P \, \{\exists \bar{x}_2.SP(\varphi', P_1) \uparrow C_1 \wedge \exists \bar{x}_1.SP(\varphi', P_2) \uparrow C_2 \wedge t \preceq h\}.$$

(Note that actually $t = h$ is already implied by φ'.) To proceed we need the following main lemma, which is proved later, claiming that this postcondition indeed implies the strongest postcondition.

Lemma 7.28

$$\models (\exists \bar{x}_2.SP(\varphi',P_1) \uparrow C_1 \wedge \exists \bar{x}_1.SP(\varphi',P_2) \uparrow C_2 \wedge t \preceq h) \rightarrow SP(\varphi',P).$$

Applying the consequence rule we thus obtain $\vdash \{\varphi'\} \, P \, \{SP(\varphi',P)\}$.

Since $\models SP(\varphi',P) \rightarrow SP(\varphi,P)$ (because $\models \varphi' \rightarrow \varphi$ and SP is monotone in its first argument), we derive by another application of the consequence rule

$$\vdash \{\varphi'\} \, P \, \{SP(\varphi,P)\}.$$

An application of the initialisation rule yields

$$\vdash \{\varphi\} \, P \, \{SP(\varphi,P)\}. \qquad \qquad \square$$

It remains to prove Lemma 7.28.

Proof Let $\sigma \models \exists \bar{x}_2.SP(\varphi',P_1) \uparrow C_1 \wedge \exists \bar{x}_1.SP(\varphi',P_2) \uparrow C_2 \wedge t \preceq h$. Hence, there exist states σ_1 and σ_2 such that $\sigma_i \models SP(\varphi',P_i)$ and σ differs from σ_i only with respect to the variables $\bar{x}_j$ ($i \neq j$) and h, with $\sigma(h){\downarrow}C_i = \sigma_i(h){\downarrow}C_i$, $i,j \in \{1,2\}$.

By definition of $SP(\varphi',P_i)$ there exist states σ'_i and σ''_i and histories θ_i, $i = 1,2$, such that $\sigma'_i \models \varphi'$ and

$$(\sigma'_i,\sigma''_i,\theta_i) \in O(P_i),$$

with $\sigma_i = (\sigma''_i : h \mapsto \sigma'_i(h) \cdot \theta_i)$, $i = 1,2$.

Since $\sigma'_i(\bar{z}) = \sigma''_i(\bar{z}) = \sigma'_i(\bar{x})$ (and $\sigma'_i(t) = \sigma'_i(h)$) and $\sigma(\bar{z}) = \sigma_i(\bar{z}) = \sigma'_i(\bar{z})$ (and $\sigma(t) = \sigma_i(t) = \sigma'_i(t) = \sigma''_i(t)$), it follows that σ'_1 and σ'_2 agree with respect to the (program) variables $\bar{x}$ and the history variable h. Moreover, for any other variable y we have that $\sigma(y) = \sigma_i(y) = \sigma'_i(y) = \sigma''_i(y)$. Summarising, we have established that $\sigma'_1 = \sigma'_2$. Let us denote this state by σ_0.

We are given that $\sigma(t) \preceq \sigma(h)$, so let θ be such that $\sigma(h) = \sigma(t) \cdot \theta$.

Since $\sigma(t) = \sigma'_i(t) = \sigma'_i(h)$ and $\sigma(h){\downarrow}C_i = \sigma_i(h){\downarrow}C_i = \sigma'_i(h){\downarrow}C_i \cdot \theta_i{\downarrow}C_i$, it follows, by $\sigma(t) = \sigma'_i(h)$ and $\sigma(h){\downarrow}C_i = (\sigma(t).\theta){\downarrow}C_i = (\sigma(t){\downarrow}C_i).(\theta{\downarrow}C_i)$, that $\theta_i{\downarrow}C_i = \theta{\downarrow}C_i$. Since $Chan(P_i) \subseteq C_i$, it follows from the definition of O that $\theta_i = \theta_i{\downarrow}C_i$, because O is a precise semantics, and, hence, θ_i contains no dirt. Thus we arrive at $\theta_i = \theta{\downarrow}C_i$.

Since

$$(\sigma'_i,\sigma''_i,\theta_i) \in O(P_i)$$

and $\sigma_0 = \sigma_i'$, we have

$$(\sigma_0, \sigma_i'', \theta_i) \in O(P_i).$$

We obtain $\tilde{\sigma}_i$ from σ by assigning to the variables not belonging to process P_i their corresponding values in σ_0, observing that, for $i = 1, 2$,

- $\tilde{\sigma}_i(\bar{x}_j) = \sigma_0(\bar{x}_j) = \sigma_i'(\bar{x}_j) = \sigma_i''(\bar{x}_j) = \sigma_i(\bar{x}_j), j \neq i,$
- $\tilde{\sigma}_i(\bar{x}_i) = \sigma(\bar{x}_i) = \sigma_i(\bar{x}_i),$ and
- $\tilde{\sigma}_i(h) = \sigma_0(h) = \sigma_i'(h).$

Clearly we have that

$$(\sigma_0, \tilde{\sigma}_i, \theta_i) \in O(P_i).$$

Now $\theta = \theta \!\downarrow\! Chan(P_1 \| P_2)$ follows from $\theta \!\downarrow\! Chan(P_i) = \theta \!\downarrow\! C_i = \theta_i$, because θ contains no dirt and $Chan(P_i) \subseteq C_i$.

We have established

$$(\sigma_0, \tilde{\sigma}_i, \theta \!\downarrow\! P_i) \in O(P_i) \wedge \theta = \theta \!\downarrow\! (P_1 \| P_2), i = 1, 2,$$

and by Definition 7.15 this implies $(\sigma_0, \tilde{\sigma}, \theta) \in O(P)$ with

$$\tilde{\sigma}(x) \overset{\text{def}}{=} \begin{cases} \tilde{\sigma}_i(x), & \text{if } x \in \bar{x}_i, \\ \sigma_0(x), & \text{otherwise.} \end{cases}$$

Now $\sigma \models SP(\varphi', P)$ follows immediately, since $\sigma_0 \models \varphi'$ and

$$\sigma = (\tilde{\sigma} : h \mapsto \sigma_0(h) \cdot \theta). \qquad \square$$

Another strategy for proving completeness is sketched in Exercise 7.14, and is based on the use of weakest precondition instead of strongest postcondition operators.

7.5 Assumption-Commitment-based Reasoning

In this section we present the assumption-commitment (A-C) method by providing its semantic foundations, stating its proof rules, and proving the soundness and semantic completeness of these rules.

The intuition behind reasoning by means of assumptions and commitments about a process is quite simple. When reasoning in isolation about a given process (which communicates by synchronous message passing with its environment), one should ask the question: *About which quantities do I need information?*

First of all, one needs information about the initial state of a process. That information is supplied by a precondition φ limiting the range of the initial states of a process.

Secondly, one needs information about its inputs. That information is supplied by providing an assumption A, which expresses at any moment during an ongoing (or terminated) computation the properties that are assumed for its previous inputs.

Of course, when one considers properties concerning the possible blocking of a process and the like, one also needs information on whether the outputs of a process are, indeed, synchronised with inputs in its environment. But since we consider in Part III only partial-correctness properties, we will not take such information into account, and refer to [Pan88, PJ91] for the proof theory of other properties.

So, once the necessary properties of the initial state of a process are expressed by requiring φ to hold, and the necessary properties of its inputs are supplied by requiring A to hold *after every input* during an ongoing computation, it should be possible to state which properties hold for the outputs of a process, and in case it also terminates, for its final state. These properties are expressed, respectively, by the commitment C of a process, and its postcondition ψ.

Next, we discuss our formal setting for this paradigm.

Networks will be built from basic transition diagrams, and can be composed using sequential and parallel composition, as before. The transition diagrams of such concurrent systems communicate by means of synchronous message passing along unidirectional channels which connect at most two different processes.

The new element in the A-C method is that it allows for the specification (and verification) of the ongoing interaction between a process and its environment, and therefore also applies to infinite computations and open systems. Consequently, one can also specify *reactive systems* [HP85] using this method. The A-C method captures the behaviour of these systems on the level of correctness formulae because assumption and commitment are required to hold for both finished (i.e., terminated) and unfinished (nonterminated) computations. That is, we shall introduce a prefix-closed semantics and require the assumption-commitment relationship to hold for all prefixes of a computation as described in the semantics. More precisely, this requirement not only involves the initial-final state semantics of processes, but also checking correctness of the assumption-commitment relationship after exchange of every intermediate message. In order to capture all intermediate stages of a computation, we define the semantics of a process in terms of a set of four-tuples consisting of the initial state, the current state, a termination flag, and a communication history. This representation of the semantics of a process by such four-tuples satisfies the property that for all prefixes of a communication history, whose termination flag indicates that the computation is finished, there exist four-tuples in the semantics with the same initial state and a termination flag indicating that the computation in question is unfinished.

Technically, we introduce the new concept of *A-C-inductive assertion networks* for reasoning about the sequential parts, i.e., the transition diagrams, of a concurrent system. By means of compositional proof rules such assertion networks can be used for deducing properties of the whole system. Our main technical instrument for obtaining a compositional method is again the introduction of a single *logical history* variable which records the sequence of communications generated by each component.

We slightly modify the definition of our basic program components, the sequential synchronous transition diagrams.

Definition 7.29 A sequential synchronous transition diagram is a quadruple (L, T, s, t), where L is a finite set of locations l, T is a finite set of transitions (l, a, l') with a an instruction as discussed above, and s and t are the entry and exit locations, respectively, with exit location t having no outgoing edge, and entry location s *having no incoming edge*. □

Note that requiring s to have no incoming edge is no substantial restriction since we can always introduce a new entry location s' and a new transition (s', id, s). This condition simplifies the formulation of our proof method. As in Section 7.4, *composite systems* are either basic sequential synchronous transition diagrams B, sequentially composed composite systems $P_1; P_2$, or the parallel composition $P_1 \| P_2$ of two composite systems. We call a composite transition diagram also a *program* or (if it is a component of a parallel composition) a *process*.

7.5.1 Semantics

The definition of a compositional semantics for composite transition diagrams reflects the fact that we consider both finished and unfinished computations in the A-C formalism in contrast to, e.g., the previous section. Yet the semantics $O[\![P]\!]$ for basic transition diagrams is based on the same labelled transition relation as in Definition 7.1 which is used to define the semantics $O_l(P)$ as in Definition 7.2. For basic transition diagrams B we extend these definitions by adding a *termination flag* $\tau \in \{\top, \bot\}$, where termination for a basic transition diagram – this is indicated by setting τ to $\top$ – is characterised by the fact that its exit location t is reached.

A *computation* of a process is characterised by its initial state σ, its end state σ', its communication sequence θ and a termination flag τ where $\tau = \top$ indicates a terminated computation and $\tau = \bot$ indicates a nonterminated (or "unfinished") one. We compose two computations sequentially if the first computation is a terminated one. Parallel composition of computations is defined by requiring that the projection of the resulting communication sequences on the channels which belong to their associated processes are local communication sequences of these processes.

Definition 7.30 The compositional semantics $O[\![P]\!]$ of a program P is defined as follows. For $B \equiv (L,T,s,t)$,

- $O[\![B]\!] \overset{\text{def}}{=} \bigcup_{l \in L}\{(\sigma,\sigma',\theta,\bot)|(\sigma,\sigma',\theta) \in O_l(B)\}$
  $\qquad \cup \{(\sigma,\sigma',\theta,\top)|(\sigma,\sigma',\theta) \in O_t(B)\}$,

- $O[\![P_1;P_2]\!] \overset{\text{def}}{=} \{(\sigma,\sigma_1,\theta,\bot)|(\sigma,\sigma_1,\theta,\bot) \in O[\![P_1]\!]\}$
  $\qquad \cup \{(\sigma,\sigma_2,\theta,\tau)|\exists\sigma_1,\theta_1,\theta_2.(\sigma,\sigma_1,\theta_1,\top) \in O[\![P_1]\!]$
  $\qquad\qquad \wedge (\sigma_1,\sigma_2,\theta_2,\tau) \in O[\![P_2]\!] \wedge \theta = \theta_1 \cdot \theta_2\}$,

- $O[\![P_1\|P_2]\!] \overset{\text{def}}{=} \{(\sigma,\sigma',\theta,\tau)|\text{for } i = 1,2,\ (\sigma,\sigma_i',\theta{\downarrow}P_i,\tau_i) \in O[\![P_i]\!]$
  $\qquad \wedge \theta = \theta{\downarrow}Chan(P_1\|P_2)$
  $\qquad \wedge (\tau = \top \leftrightarrow (\tau_1 = \top \wedge \tau_2 = \top)),$
  $\qquad \text{where}$

$$\sigma'(x) = \begin{cases} \sigma_1'(x), & \text{if } x \in var(P_1), \\ \sigma_2'(x), & \text{if } x \in var(P_2), \\ \sigma(x), & \text{otherwise}\}. \end{cases} \qquad \square$$

Note that, due to the condition $\theta = \theta{\downarrow}Chan(P_1\|P_2)$ in the definition of $O[\![P_1\|P_2]\!]$, θ does not contain communications along channels not occurring in $P_1\|P_2$.

It is easy to see that the semantic operation of parallel composition defined above is commutative and associative.

Observe that in the above definition the requirement that a local history of a basic transition diagram can be obtained as the projection of one global history θ guarantees that an input on a channel is indeed synchronised with the corresponding output. Observe also that for basic transition diagrams only terminated computations are marked with $\top$. Finally observe that only when *both* P_1 and P_2 have reached their exit locations, is the resulting computation of $P_1\|P_2$ marked as terminated.

Note that the $O[\![P]\!]$ semantics also contains nonterminated computations.

These are needed because the validity (or truth) of an A-C correctness formula for a transition diagram P requires $O[\![P]\!]$ to contain all prefixes of communication sequences of P. Recall from Section 6.4 that a process P satisfies (A,C) provided that P's environment must violate A *before* P can violate C, i.e., *at any stage of an on-going computation P's actions should satisfy C as long as A has been satisfied before by P's environment*. This is mathematically expressed by requiring (A,C) to be satisfied by all prefixes of a computation (precisely, by the prefixes of communication sequences) of P. This we obtain for a basic transition diagram P by defining $O[\![P]\!]$ as the union of all unfinished and terminated computations, and for a composed transition diagram P by observing that the definitions of ";" and "$\|$" given above preserve prefix closure. Note that we consider $(\sigma, \sigma', \theta, \bot)$ as the prefix of $(\sigma, \sigma', \theta, \top)$.

7.5.2 *Validity*

Recall that an A-C correctness formula has the form

$$\langle A, C \rangle : \{\varphi\} \, P \, \{\psi\},$$

where A and C are trace predicates (defined below) and φ and ψ ordinary predicates.

Definition 7.31 A trace predicate A is a predicate which involves no program variables $\bar{x} \subseteq Pvar$; its satisfaction depends only on the communication sequence which is recorded in the value of h and on its logical variables. For a trace predicate A we have that for all σ and σ',

$$\sigma \models A \; \Leftrightarrow \; \sigma' \models A \text{ iff } \sigma(x) = \sigma'(x), \text{ for } x \in Lvar \cup \{h\}. \qquad \square$$

Now validity of an A-C correctness formula $\langle A, C \rangle : \{\varphi\}P\{\psi\}$ has the following intuitive meaning:

If φ holds in the initial state, including the communication history, in which P starts its execution, then

(i) *C holds initially, and C holds after every communication provided A holds after all preceding communications, and*

(ii) *if P terminates and A holds after all previous communications (including the last one) then ψ holds in the final state, including the final communication history.*

Formally, validity of A-C formulae is defined as below.

Definition 7.32 (Validity)

$$\models \langle A, C \rangle : \{\varphi\}\, P\, \{\psi\} \quad \text{if}$$

$$\forall (\sigma, \sigma', \theta, \tau) \in O[\![P]\!].$$
$$\sigma \models \varphi \Rightarrow$$
$$((\forall \theta' \prec \theta.(\sigma : h \mapsto \sigma(h) \cdot \theta') \models A) \Rightarrow (\sigma : h \mapsto \sigma(h) \cdot \theta) \models C) \wedge$$
$$((\tau = \top \wedge (\forall \theta' \preceq \theta.(\sigma : h \mapsto \sigma(h) \cdot \theta') \models A)) \Rightarrow (\sigma' : h \mapsto \sigma(h) \cdot \theta) \models \psi).$$

$\square$

We need to explain why this formal definition covers the informal one given above.

The sub-formula

$$((\forall \theta' \prec \theta.(\sigma : h \mapsto \sigma(h) \cdot \theta') \models A) \Rightarrow (\sigma : h \mapsto \sigma(h) \cdot \theta) \models C)$$

for $\theta = \langle \rangle$ implies that $\sigma \models C$. This means that $\models \langle A, C \rangle : \{\varphi\}\, P\, \{\psi\}$ implies that if the precondition φ holds also the commitment C must hold initially.

Secondly, Definition 7.32 expresses that if φ holds in the initial state σ (with communication history $\sigma(h)$) in which P starts its execution then C must hold after every communication, say, resulting in local communication history θ, provided A holds in $\sigma(h) \cdot \theta'$ for all prefixes θ' of θ. This differs from clause (i) of the intuitive meaning of validity of an A-C formula in that A should also hold for $\sigma(h)$ (obtained by taking the empty sequence $\langle \rangle$ as prefix of θ).

In case $\sigma(h) = \langle \rangle$ one can without loss of generality require that $\sigma \models A$ holds, since this choice is left open in clause (i).

The case $\sigma(h) \neq \langle \rangle$ corresponds to sequential composition with a previous composite transition diagram P_1. Since, by soundness and completeness of our proof method, Rule 7.16 suffices to reason about sequential composition, one can safely assume that $\sigma \models A$ holds, too, because, otherwise, one could not be sure that $\sigma \models \varphi$ would hold (i.e., $\sigma \models \xi$ in Rule 7.16).

Clause (ii) of the intuitive meaning of $\models \langle A, C \rangle : \{\varphi\}\, P\, \{\psi\}$ is covered by Definition 7.32 on similar grounds.

7.5.3 *Proof Method and Application*

A-C-inductive assertion networks

We adapt Floyd's method to the additional requirements of A-C formulae and define for $B \equiv (L, T, s, t)$ an A-C-inductive assertion network $Q(A, C) : L \to \mathcal{P}(\Sigma)$, i.e., we associate with each location l of B a predicate Q_l as follows:

Definition 7.33 (A-C-inductive assertion networks) Q is an A-C-inductive assertion network w.r.t. A and C for $B \equiv (L, T, s, t)$ if:

- $\models Q_s \to C$.
- In case of an internal transition $l \xrightarrow{a} l' \in T$, $a \equiv b \to f$, we require

$$\models Q_l \wedge b \wedge A \to Q_{l'} \circ f.$$

- In case of an output transition $l \xrightarrow{a} l' \in T$, $a \equiv b; D!e \to f$, we require, for $v = e(\sigma)$,

$$\models Q_l \wedge A \wedge b \to ((A \to Q_{l'}) \wedge C) \circ (f \circ g),$$

where $g(\sigma) \stackrel{\text{def}}{=} (\sigma : h \mapsto \sigma(h) \cdot (D, v))$.

- In case of an input transition $l \xrightarrow{a} l' \in T$, with $a \equiv b; D?x \to f$, we require, for an *arbitrary* value $v \in VAL$,

$$\models Q_l \wedge A \wedge b \to ((A \to Q_{l'}) \wedge C) \circ (f \circ g),$$

where $g(\sigma) \stackrel{\text{def}}{=} (\sigma : x, h \mapsto v, \sigma(h) \cdot (D, v))$. □

Remark 7.34 In the last two clauses of this definition we require only $(A \to Q_{l'})$ to hold after the transition, since the idea behind A-C reasoning is to use the assumption A whenever possible.

We abbreviate the existence of an A-C-inductive assertion network Q w.r.t. A and C for B by $Q(A, C) \vdash B$. We have the following rule for deriving A-C specifications of basic transition diagrams.

Rule 7.11 (Basic diagram rule) For $B \equiv \langle L, T, s, t \rangle$:

$$\frac{Q(A, C) \vdash B}{\langle A, C \rangle : \{Q_s\} B \{Q_t\}}.$$

Example 7.35 (Even number generator) We demonstrate the application of the method by verifying the first specification of Example 6.1, i.e., for the program P of Figure 6.3 one has

$$\models \langle true, \#D = \#A = \#B \geq 1 \to last(D) = last(A) + last(B) \rangle :$$
$$\{\#D = \#A = \#B = 0\} P \{false\}.$$

We have the following assertion network for P:

$$Q_s \stackrel{\text{def}}{=} \#D = \#A = \#B = 0,$$
$$Q_{l_1} \stackrel{\text{def}}{=} \#D = \#A = \#B,$$
$$Q_{l_2} \stackrel{\text{def}}{=} \#B = \#D = (\#A - 1) \wedge last(A) = x,$$
$$Q_{l_3} \stackrel{\text{def}}{=} \#A = \#B = (\#D + 1) \wedge last(A) = x \wedge last(B) = y, \text{ and}$$
$$Q_l \stackrel{\text{def}}{=} false.$$

We have to check five implications to prove that the assertion network above is an A-C-inductive assertion network w.r.t. assumption $Ass \equiv true$ and commitment $C \equiv (\#D = \#A = \#B \geq 1 \rightarrow last(D) = last(A) + last(B))$.

- $\models Q_s \rightarrow C$ and $\models Q_s \rightarrow Q_{l_1}$ follow from the definition above.

- $\models Q_{l_1} \rightarrow (Q_{l_2} \wedge C) \circ g$, where $g(\sigma) \stackrel{\text{def}}{=} (\sigma : x, h \mapsto v, \sigma(h) \cdot (A, v))$ for arbitrary v, holds since only a communication via A took place and, consequently, the value received is the last value received via A. Since $\#A \neq \#B = \#D$ holds, we have also satisfied C. (Note that, since the assumption is identically true, it suffices to check that $Q_{l_2} \circ g$ holds.)

- $\models Q_{l_2} \rightarrow (Q_{l_3} \wedge C) \circ g$, where $g(\sigma) \stackrel{\text{def}}{=} (\sigma : x, h \mapsto v, \sigma(h) \cdot (B, v))$ for arbitrary v, holds analogously.

- The most interesting verification condition is related to the output transition of P:

$$\models Q_{l_3} \rightarrow (Q_{l_1} \wedge C) \circ g,$$

where $g(\sigma) \stackrel{\text{def}}{=} (\sigma : h \mapsto \sigma(h) \cdot (D, \sigma(x) + \sigma(y)))$.

We have one communication via channel D and, hence, Q_{l_1} is satisfied. Furthermore, $last(D) = x + y = last(A) + last(B)$, and, hence, C holds after the transition.

The application of the basic diagram rule establishes the correctness formula above. $\square$

Example 7.36 (Continuation of the previous example) The assumption that the environment always provides odd numbers via channels A and B is formalised by

$$Ass_1 \stackrel{\text{def}}{=} (\#A > 0 \rightarrow odd(last(A))) \wedge (\#B > 0 \rightarrow odd(last(B))).$$

Using this assumption and the following assertion network:

$$Q_s \overset{\text{def}}{=} \quad \#D = \#A = \#B = 0,$$
$$Q_{l_1} \overset{\text{def}}{=} \quad \#D = \#A = \#B,$$
$$Q_{l_2} \overset{\text{def}}{=} \quad \#B = \#D = (\#A - 1) \wedge last(A) = x \wedge odd(last(A)),$$
$$Q_{l_3} \overset{\text{def}}{=} \quad \#A = \#B = (\#D + 1) \wedge last(A) = x \wedge last(B) = y \wedge$$
$$\qquad \quad odd(last(A)) \wedge odd(last(B)), \text{ and}$$
$$Q_t \overset{\text{def}}{=} \quad false,$$

one can prove similarly, as above,

$$\models \langle Ass_1, C_1 \rangle : \{\#D = \#A = \#B = 0\} P \{false\},$$

where $C_1 \overset{\text{def}}{=} (\#D = \#A = \#B \geq 1 \to even(last(D)))$. Here we observe the use of assumption Ass_1 for proving the verification conditions. Consider, e.g., the transition $(l_2, B?y, l_3)$. The associated verification condition is

$$\models Q_{l_2} \wedge Ass_1 \to ((Ass_1 \to Q_{l_3}) \wedge C_1) \circ g,$$

where $g(\sigma) \overset{\text{def}}{=} (\sigma : h \mapsto \sigma(h) \cdot (B, \sigma(y)))$.

While we can conclude that $y = last(B)$ holds as before, the claim of Q_{l_3} that $odd(last(B))$ holds, i.e., that y is an odd number, is not provable without the information of assumption Ass_1 that also for this last communication via channel B one can assume that $odd(last(B))$ holds. $\qquad \square$

Some general rules

For a valid formula $\langle A, C \rangle : \{\varphi\} P \{\psi\}$ we can always weaken the commitment or the postcondition without invalidating the formula. Symmetrically we can assure the same commitment/postcondition whenever we impose stricter restrictions on P's environment, i.e., the assumption and the precondition. This justifies the consequence rule below.

Rule 7.12 (Consequence rule)

$$\frac{\langle A, C \rangle : \{\varphi\} P \{\psi\}}{\begin{array}{c} A' \to A, \ \varphi' \to \varphi, \\ C \to C', \ \psi \to \psi' \end{array}}{\langle A', C' \rangle : \{\varphi'\} P \{\psi'\}}$$

Another observation on valid assumption-commitment formulae is that we cannot change the communication history that was generated *before* the process at hand was invoked.

Rule 7.13 (Prefix invariance) Let $cset \subseteq CHAN$ be a set of channels, and $t \in Lvar$.

$$\frac{\langle A, C \rangle : \{\varphi\}\, P\, \{\psi\}}{\langle A, C \wedge t \preceq h{\downarrow}cset \rangle : \{\varphi \wedge t = h{\downarrow}cset\}\, P\, \{\psi \wedge t \preceq h{\downarrow}cset\}}.$$

An immediate consequence of the definition of the validity of A-C formulae is the fact that for any valid formulae not only the commitment holds after any communication action but also the assumption holds for all proper prefixes up to that point, i.e., the latter is an additional commitment.

Rule 7.14 (Assumption closure) Let $cset$ satisfy $Chan(A) \subseteq cset \subseteq CHAN$ and $t \in Lvar$.

$$\frac{\langle A, C \rangle : \{\varphi\}\, P\, \{\psi\}}{\substack{\langle A, C \wedge \forall t.(t_0 \preceq t \prec h{\downarrow}cset \to A\{t/h\}) \rangle : \\ \{\varphi \wedge t_0 = h{\downarrow}cset\}\, P\, \{\psi \wedge \forall t.(t_0 \preceq t \preceq h{\downarrow}cset \to A\{t/h\})\}}}$$

Here $A\{t/h\}$ denotes substitution, i.e., $A\{t/h\} \stackrel{\text{def}}{=} A \circ f$, with $f : \Sigma \mapsto \Sigma$, $f(\sigma)(x) \stackrel{\text{def}}{=} \sigma(x)$ for $x \neq h$, and $f(\sigma)(h) \stackrel{\text{def}}{=} \sigma(t)$. Observe that this rule is consistent with Definition 7.32 in that also $A\{t_0/h\}$ is required to hold in the C and ψ parts of its conclusion.

Additionally we have a conjunction rule and an initialisation rule.

Rule 7.15 (Initialisation)

$$\frac{\langle A, C \rangle : \{\varphi\}\, P\, \{\psi\}}{\langle A, C \rangle : \{\varphi \circ f\}\, P\, \{\psi\}}$$

where f is a function such that its write variables constitute a set of (logical) variables that do not occur in $P, A, C,$ or ψ.

Composition rules

The rule for sequential composition of processes is standard.

Rule 7.16 (Sequential composition)

$$\frac{\langle A, C \rangle : \{\varphi\}\, P_1\, \{\xi\}, \ \langle A, C \rangle : \{\xi\}\, P_2\, \{\psi\}}{\langle A, C \rangle : \{\varphi\}\, P_1; P_2\, \{\psi\}}.$$

Next we discuss the proof obligations for assumptions and commitments in the parallel composition rule.

Rule 7.17 (Parallel Composition)

$$\langle A_1, C_1 \rangle : \{\varphi_1\} \, P_1 \, \{\psi_1\},$$
$$\langle A_2, C_2 \rangle : \{\varphi_2\} \, P_2 \, \{\psi_2\},$$
$$A \wedge C_1 \to A_2, A \wedge C_2 \to A_1$$

$$\langle A, C_1 \wedge C_2 \rangle : \{\varphi_1 \wedge \varphi_2\} \, P_1 \| P_2 \, \{\psi_1 \wedge \psi_2\}$$

provided

(i) $var(A_1, C_1, \psi_1) \cap var(P_2) = \emptyset$, $var(A_2, C_2, \psi_2) \cap var(P_1) = \emptyset$, and
(ii) $Chan(A_1, C_1, \psi_1) \cap Chan(P_2) \subseteq Chan(P_1)$,
$Chan(A_2, C_2, \psi_2) \cap Chan(P_1) \subseteq Chan(P_2)$.

Consider the parallel composition $P_1 \| P_2$, and assume we have assumption-commitment pairs (A_1, C_1) satisfied by P_1 and (A_2, C_2) satisfied by P_2. Which conditions have to be verified to obtain a pair (A, C) satisfied by $P_1 \| P_2$? Consider first assumption A_2 of P_2:

- If A_2 contains assumptions about joint channels of P_1 and P_2 which connect these two processes, these assumptions should be justified by the commitment C_1 of P_1.
- If A_2 contains assumptions about external channels of P_2, i.e., channels that are not connected with P_1, these assumptions should be justified by the new network assumption A for $P_1 \| P_2$.

Imposing both these conditions leads to requiring validity of the following verification condition:

$$A \wedge C_1 \to A_2.$$

Validity of $A \wedge C_2 \to A_1$ is argued similarly.

The soundness of a parallel composition rule with these implications depends heavily on the definition of validity of the formula $\langle A_i, C_i \rangle : \{\varphi_i\} \, P_i \, \{\psi_i\}$, for $i = 1, 2$. Observe that if in this definition one had chosen a simple implication between A_i and C_i to hold instead of $\langle A_i, C_i \rangle : \{\varphi_i\} P_i \{\psi_i\}$, then the above rule would have led to circular reasoning, since then $A_1 \to C_1 \to A_2 \to C_2 \to A_1$ might have been implied. Because of this reason the rule would have become unsound. To see this, choose $A \equiv true$ and $A_1 \equiv A_2 \equiv C_1 \equiv C_2 \equiv false$. Then in this changed interpretation, the above rule would have implied $\langle true, false \rangle \{\varphi\} \, P \, \{false\}$, which contradicts the intuitive meaning of A-C formulae given earlier.

To avoid such problems, in defining the validity of $\langle A_i, C_i \rangle : \{\varphi_i\} \, P_i \, \{\psi_i\}$, we have required that if φ_i holds in the initial state then:

(i) C_i holds initially, and

(ii) C_i holds after every communication provided A_i holds after all **preceding** communications.

Hence, *false* cannot be used as the commitment in a valid A-C formula with assumption *true*, i.e., the definition of the validity of A-C correctness formulae incorporates an induction step. The associated inductive argument is part of the soundness proof of the parallel composition rule, and no longer needs to be given, when applying this rule.

Consequently, the above rule plays the same rôle for the parallel composition of synchronously communicating processes as Hoare's **loop** rule (Rule 9.9 in Chapter 9) plays for iterative constructs.

Derivability of an A-C formula $\langle A, C \rangle : \{\varphi\} \, P \, \{\psi\}$ in this A-C proof method is expressed by

$$\vdash \langle A, C \rangle : \{\varphi\} \, P \, \{\psi\}.$$

Application of the above proof method

We illustrate the assumption-commitment paradigm by continuing Examples 6.1 and 7.35, and construct the environment for process P as in Figure 6.3.

Example 7.37 Since we want to use P as an even number generator, we have to provide a program Q_1 that sends odd values via channels A and B as required in the assumption Ass_1 in Example 7.36. This program sends odd numbers via

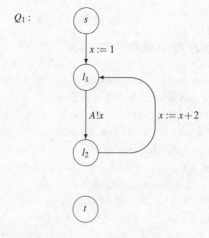

Fig. 7.6. Odd numbers generator.

channel A and can serve as part of the environment of P. We can give a local proof of

$$\vdash \langle true, \#A \geq 1 \to odd(last(A)) \rangle : \{\#A = 0\} \ Q_1 \ \{false\}.$$

If we modify the program Q_1 of Figure 7.6 such that the output statement $A!x$ is replaced by $B!y$, and call the resulting process Q_2, then $Q_1 \| Q_2$ constitutes an environment in which P will generate only even numbers.

Because

$$\vdash \langle true, \#B \geq 1 \to odd(last(B)) \rangle : \{\#B = 0\} \ Q_2 \ \{false\},$$

by an application of the parallel composition rule we deduce that

$$\vdash \langle true, ((\#A \geq 1 \to odd(last(A))) \land (\#B \geq 1 \to odd(last(B)))) \rangle :$$
$$\{\#A = \#B = 0\} \ Q_1 \| Q_2 \ \{false\},$$

since $\models true \land (\#A \geq 1 \to odd(last(A))) \to true$ and $\models true \land (\#B \geq 1 \to odd(last(B))) \to true$.

We see that the commitment of $Q_1 \| Q_2$ is exactly the assumption Ass_1 of Example 7.36, and since

$$\models true \land ((\#A \geq 1 \to odd(last(A))) \land (\#B \geq 1 \to odd(last(B)))) \to Ass_1$$

and

$$\models true \land \#D = \#A = \#B \geq 1 \to even(last(D)) \to true$$

hold, we can apply the parallel composition rule again to obtain (after some simplifications using the consequence rule):

$$\vdash \langle true, \#D = \#A = \#B \geq 1 \to even(last(D)) \rangle :$$
$$\{\#A = \#B = \#D = 0\} \ Q_1 \| Q_2 \| P \ \{false\}.$$

That is, with Q_1 and Q_2 as the input generating environment, P acts as an even number generator, as desired. $\qquad\qquad\square$

Next we illustrate the case of mutually dependent processes when the output of P is an input for Q and vice versa.

Example 7.38 We have a process Env as the environment for P, getting input via D and sending values via A and B. The output of process Env depends on its inputs via channel D, except for the first values sent via A and B. We now assume that all inputs via D are even values by defining assumption $Ass_2 \overset{\text{def}}{=} \#D \geq 1 \to even(last(D))$.

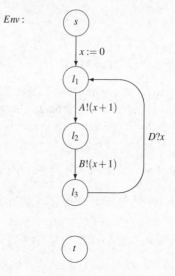

Fig. 7.7. Another odd numbers generator.

Under this assumption all outputs via A and B are odd numbers, as expressed by commitment

$$C_2 \stackrel{\text{def}}{=} (\#A \geq 1 \to (odd(last(A)) \land (A,1) \preceq h{\downarrow}\{A\})) \land$$
$$(\#B \geq 1 \to (odd(last(B)) \land (B,1) \preceq h{\downarrow}\{B\})).$$

For process Env we prove

$$\vdash \langle Ass_2, C_2 \rangle : \{\#A = \#B = \#D = 0\} \; Env \; \{false\}.$$

We are still interested in the property that all values transmitted via channel D are even values. The program $Env\|P$ satisfies this property as can be seen as follows:

P has to wait for input via A and B. First, Env sends 1 via both A and B. Then P adds these values and sends back 2 via D. Now Env receives an even value and sends odd values back, P receives these odd values and sends their (even) sum back, etc.

This intuitive explanation why the program $Env\|P$ behaves correctly contains explicitly an induction argument. Our formal proof of the property mentioned does not require such an inductive argument explicitly. Our only proof obligations are

$$\models true \land C_2 \to Ass_1$$

and

$$\models true \land (\#D = \#A = \#B \geq 1 \to even(last(D))) \to Ass_2.$$

Applying the parallel composition rule (and some simplifications) then leads to

$$\vdash \langle true, (\#D = \#A = \#B \geq 1 \to even(last(D)))\rangle :$$
$$\{\#A = \#B = \#D = 0\} \, Env\|P \, \{false\}. \qquad \square$$

The assumption-commitment paradigm allows for compositional reasoning. In particular, while verifying one component of a parallel program, some other components may not have been implemented yet – we only use their specifications. Note that the parallel composition rule only refers to the specification of P and Env and not to their implementation, and is therefore compositional.

Example 7.39 Consider the process R in Figure 7.8, which is just a slight modification of process Env above. Process R can replace process Env as

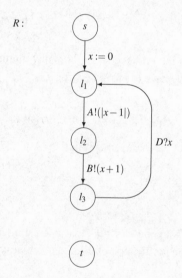

Fig. 7.8. And yet another odd numbers generator.

environment for P since one can also prove that

$$\langle Ass_2, C_2 \rangle : \{\#A = \#B = \#D = 0\} \, R \, \{false\}$$

is a valid correctness formula, and hence $P\|R$ will also satisfy

$$\models \langle true, (\#D = \#A = \#B \geq 1 \to even(last(D)))\rangle :$$
$$\{\#A = \#B = \#C = 0\} \, P\|R \, \{false\}. \qquad \square$$

Example 7.40 Whereas all previous formulae refer only to the last value sent via a channel, process R allows another use of program P: in environment R, P will send 2^i as the i-th value over D (here we abbreviate the i-th value sent along channel D by $D[i]$).

We get as the specification for the adder P

$$\langle Ass_3, C_3 \rangle : \{\#A = \#B = \#D = 0\} \ P \ \{false\}$$

with $C_3 \overset{\text{def}}{=} \#D \geq 1 \to D[i] = 2^i$, and

$$Ass_3 \overset{\text{def}}{=} (\#A \geq 1 \to A[i] = 2^{(i-1)} - 1) \wedge (\#B \geq 1 \to B[i] = 2^{(i-1)} + 1).$$

Since P is still the same program as in Figure 6.3, what are the restrictions on the environment to guarantee that output behaviour?

P just adds the values previously received via A and B. If we assume that we receive as $A[i]$ the value $2^{(i-1)} - 1$ and as $B[i]$ the value $2^{(i-1)} + 1$ then we have that

$$D[i] = A[i] + B[i] = (2^{(i-1)} - 1) + (2^{(i-1)} + 1) = 2 * 2^{(i-1)} = 2^i$$

as desired.

Now similarly as in the odd-even case, P and R mutually depend on each other's output. What we have to prove now for R is:

$$\vdash \langle C_3, Ass_3 \rangle : \{\#A = \#B = \#D = 0\} \ R \ \{false\},$$

which is done again by verifying an appropriate A-C-inductive assertion network.   □

7.5.4 Soundness

In this part we prove soundness of the most interesting rules. First we prove that our approach to the verification of basic sequential synchronous transition diagrams is sound.

Soundness of the basic diagram rule

Theorem 7.41

The basic diagram rule is sound.

Let $B \equiv (L, T, s, t)$ and Q be an A-C-inductive assertion network for B w.r.t. A and C, i.e., $Q(A, C) \vdash B$. We must prove $\models \langle A, C \rangle : \{Q_s\} B \{Q_t\}$.

Let $(\sigma, \sigma', \theta, \tau) \in O[\![B]\!]$ and let $\sigma \models Q_s$. Since Q is A-C-inductive, we have immediately $\sigma \models C$.

From Definition 7.30 of the semantics we know that $(\sigma, \sigma', \theta, \tau) \in O[\![B]\!]$ implies that there is a location $l_n \in L$ such that $(\sigma, \sigma', \theta) \in O_{l_n}(B)$ and a sequence of computation steps

$$\langle l_0; \sigma_0 \rangle \xrightarrow{\pi_1} \langle l_1; \sigma_1 \rangle \xrightarrow{\pi_2} \cdots \xrightarrow{\pi_n} \langle l_n; \sigma_n \rangle,$$

where $l_0 = s$, $\sigma = \sigma_0$, $\sigma' = \sigma_n$ and $\theta \stackrel{\text{def}}{=} \pi_1 \cdot \ldots \cdot \pi_n$. Let $\theta_i \stackrel{\text{def}}{=} \pi_1 \cdot \ldots \cdot \pi_i$, for $i = 1, \ldots, n$, and $\theta_0 \stackrel{\text{def}}{=} \langle \rangle$. Note that computation steps may be local and thus some of the labels π_i may represent the empty sequence $\langle \rangle$.

Lemma 7.42 Given the above, we have for $i = 0, \ldots, n$ that:

   (i) $(\forall \theta' \preceq \theta_i.(\sigma : h \mapsto \sigma(h) \cdot \theta') \models A) \Rightarrow (\sigma_i : h \mapsto \sigma(h) \cdot \theta_i) \models Q_{l_i}$.

   (ii) $(\forall \theta' \prec \theta_i.(\sigma : h \mapsto \sigma(h) \cdot \theta') \models A) \Rightarrow (\sigma_i : h \mapsto \sigma(h) \cdot \theta_i) \models C$, where $Q_{l_0} = Q_s$, and $Q_{l_n} = Q_t$.

Proof By induction on the length i of the above sequence of computation steps.

(i) First, we have for $i = 0$ that $\sigma = \sigma_0$ and $\sigma_0 \models Q_s$.

Now assume that $(\forall \theta' \preceq \theta_{i+1}.(\sigma : h \mapsto \sigma(h) \cdot \theta') \models A)$. This immediately implies that $(\forall \theta' \preceq \theta_i.(\sigma : h \mapsto \sigma(h) \cdot \theta') \models A)$ and, in particular, $(\sigma : h \mapsto \sigma(h) \cdot \theta_i) \models A$.

Now consider the three options to get from $\langle l_i; \sigma_i \rangle$ to $\langle l_{i+1}; \sigma_{i+1} \rangle$:

- By a local transition $b \to f$:
  By the induction hypothesis we have $(\sigma_i : h \mapsto \sigma(h) \cdot \theta_i) \models Q_{l_i}$, by our assumption we have $(\sigma : h \mapsto \sigma(h) \cdot \theta_i) \models A$, and since A is a trace predicate, we also have $(\sigma_i : h \mapsto \sigma(h) \cdot \theta_i) \models A$. Furthermore we have that $\sigma_i \models b$ (the transition is taken) and since h is not involved in b we also have $(\sigma_i : h \mapsto \sigma(h) \cdot \theta_i) \models b$.
  Since Q is an A-C-inductive assertion network we have that

  $$f(\sigma_i : h \mapsto \sigma(h) \cdot \theta_i) \models Q_{l_{i+1}},$$

  and since f does not involve h,

  $$(f(\sigma_i) : h \mapsto \sigma(h) \cdot \theta_i) \models Q_{l_{i+1}}.$$

  Note that $f(\sigma_i) = \sigma_{i+1}$ and that $\theta_{i+1} = \theta_i$. Thus we have that

  $$(\sigma_{i+1} : h \mapsto \sigma(h) \cdot \theta_{i+1}) \models Q_{l_{i+1}}.$$

- By an output transition $b; D!e \to f$:
  We have $(\sigma_i : h \mapsto \sigma(h) \cdot \theta_i) \models Q_{l_i}$ by the induction hypothesis, $(\sigma_i : h \mapsto \sigma(h) \cdot \theta_i) \models A$ by assumption (and A is a trace predicate), and

$(\sigma_i : h \mapsto \sigma(h) \cdot \theta_i) \models b$ (the transition is taken, and b does not involve h). As the result of this transition we have $\sigma_{i+1} = f(\sigma_i)$ and $\theta_{i+1} = \theta_i \cdot (D, e(\sigma_i))$.

From the fact that Q is A-C-inductive we obtain that

$$(f \circ g)(\sigma_i : h \mapsto \sigma(h) \cdot \theta_i) \models (A \to Q_{l_{i+1}}) \wedge C.$$

Applying g and dropping the commitment C this implies

$$f(\sigma_i : h \mapsto \sigma(h) \cdot \theta_i \cdot (D, e(\sigma_i))) \models (A \to Q_{l_{i+1}}),$$

and since f does not involve h, $f(\sigma_i) = \sigma_{i+1}$, and therefore

$$(\sigma_{i+1} : h \mapsto \sigma(h) \cdot \theta_i \cdot (D, e(\sigma_i))) \models (A \to Q_{l_{i+1}}).$$

Since we additionally assume that $(\sigma : h \mapsto \sigma(h) \cdot \theta_{i+1}) \models A$ (and hence also $(\sigma_{i+1} : h \mapsto \sigma(h) \cdot \theta_{i+1}) \models A$) we conclude that

$$(\sigma_{i+1} : h \mapsto \sigma(h) \cdot \theta_{i+1}) \models Q_{l_{i+1}}.$$

- By an input transition $b; D?x \to f$: similar to the above.

(ii) For the second claim we proceed analogously.

For $i = 0$ we have immediately that $\sigma \models C$.

Now assume that $(\forall \theta' \prec \theta_{i+1}.(\sigma : h \mapsto \sigma(h) \cdot \theta') \models A)$. Again there are three ways to get from $\langle l_i; \sigma_i \rangle$ to $\langle l_{i+1}; \sigma_{i+1} \rangle$:

- By a local transition:
  Since $\theta_{i+1} = \theta_i$ and $(\sigma_i : h \mapsto \sigma(h) \cdot \theta_i) \models C$ by the induction hypothesis we immediately have that $(\sigma_{i+1} : h \mapsto \sigma(h) \cdot \theta_{i+1}) \models C$, since C is a trace predicate.

- By an output transition:
  Then $\sigma_{i+1} = f(\sigma_i)$ and $\theta_{i+1} = \theta_i \cdot (D, e(\sigma_i))$.
  Note that $(\sigma_i : h \mapsto \sigma(h) \cdot \theta_i) \models Q_{l_i}$ from (i), $(\sigma : h \mapsto \sigma(h) \cdot \theta_i) \models A$ (and hence $(\sigma_i : h \mapsto \sigma(h) \cdot \theta_i) \models A$), and $(\sigma_i : h \mapsto \sigma(h) \cdot \theta_i) \models b$, as above.
  Since Q is A-C-inductive and f does not involve h we conclude that

  $$(f(\sigma_i) : h \mapsto \sigma(h) \cdot \theta_{i+1}) \models C.$$

- By an input transition: similar to the above.   □

If $\tau = \top$ we know by definition of the semantics that $l_n = t$ and, hence Lemma 7.42 (i) implies

$$\models \tau = \top \wedge (\forall \theta' \preceq \theta_n.(\sigma_n : h \mapsto \sigma(h) \cdot \theta') \models A) \Rightarrow (\sigma_n : h \mapsto \sigma(h) \cdot \theta_n) \models Q_t.$$

This finishes our proof of Theorem 7.41.   □

Soundness of the sequential composition rule

Theorem 7.43

The sequential composition rule 7.16 is sound.

Soundness of the parallel composition rule

Theorem 7.44

The parallel composition rule 7.17 is sound.

Proof Assume

$$\models \langle A_1, C_1 \rangle : \{\varphi_1\} \, P_1 \, \{\psi_1\}, \quad \models \langle A_2, C_2 \rangle : \{\varphi_2\} \, P_2 \, \{\psi_2\}, \tag{1}$$

$$\models A \wedge C_1 \to A_2, \quad \models A \wedge C_2 \to A_1, \tag{2}$$

$$var(A_1, C_1, \psi_1) \cap var(P_2) = \emptyset, \quad var(A_2, C_2, \psi_2) \cap var(P_1) = \emptyset, \text{ and} \tag{3}$$

$$\begin{aligned} Chan(A_1, C_1, \psi_1) \cap Chan(P_2) &\subseteq Chan(P_1), \\ Chan(A_2, C_2, \psi_2) \cap Chan(P_1) &\subseteq Chan(P_2). \end{aligned} \tag{4}$$

We have to prove $\models \langle A, C_1 \wedge C_2 \rangle : \{\varphi_1 \wedge \varphi_2\} \, P_1 \| P_2 \, \{\psi_1 \wedge \psi_2\}$.

Let $(\sigma_0, \sigma, \theta, \tau) \in O[\![P_1 \| P_2]\!]$ and $\sigma_0 \models \varphi_1 \wedge \varphi_2$. Then there exist σ_1, σ_2 such that, for $i = 1, 2$, $(\sigma_0, \sigma_i, \theta{\downarrow}P_i, \tau_i) \in O[\![P_i]\!]$, $\theta = \theta{\downarrow}(P_1 \| P_2)$ and $\tau = \top \leftrightarrow (\tau_1 = \top \wedge \tau_2 = \top)$, where

$$\sigma_i(x) \stackrel{\text{def}}{=} \begin{cases} \sigma(x), & \text{if } x \in var(P_i), \\ \sigma_0(x), & \text{if } x \notin var(P_i). \end{cases}$$

We have to prove:

(i) $(\forall \theta' \prec \theta.(\sigma_0 : h \mapsto \sigma_0(h) \cdot \theta') \models A) \Rightarrow (\sigma_0 : h \mapsto \sigma_0(h) \cdot \theta) \models C_1 \wedge C_2$.

(ii) $\tau = \top \wedge \forall \theta' \preceq \theta.((\sigma_0 : h \mapsto \sigma_0(h) \cdot \theta' \models A) \Rightarrow$
$(\sigma : h \mapsto \sigma_0(h) \cdot \theta) \models \psi_1 \wedge \psi_2$.

Proof

(i) We prove point (i) by induction on the length of θ. Assume that

$$(\forall \theta' \prec \theta.(\sigma_0 : h \mapsto \sigma_0(h) \cdot \theta') \models A).$$

Now we prove a stronger claim, namely that

$$\forall \theta' \preceq \theta.(\sigma_0 : h \mapsto \sigma_0(h) \cdot \theta') \models C_1 \wedge C_2.$$

This immediately implies $(\sigma_0 : h \mapsto \sigma_0(h) \cdot \theta) \models C_1 \wedge C_2$ as desired.

Base Step:

Let $\theta = \langle \rangle$. Then $\theta{\downarrow}P_i = \langle \rangle$, and hence

$$\forall \theta' \prec \theta{\downarrow}P_i.(\sigma_0 : h \mapsto \sigma_0(h) \cdot \theta') \models A_i, i = 1, 2,$$

is vacuously fulfilled, as a result of which (1) yields

$$\forall \theta' \preceq \langle \rangle.(\sigma_0 : h \mapsto \sigma_0(h) \cdot \theta') \models C_1 \wedge C_2.$$

Induction Step:

Let $\theta = \theta_1 \cdot (C, \mu)$. By the induction hypothesis we have

$$\forall \theta' \preceq \theta_1.(\sigma_0 : h \mapsto \sigma_0(h) \cdot \theta') \models C_1 \wedge C_2. \tag{5}$$

Now assume $\forall \theta' \prec \theta_1 \cdot (C, \mu).(\sigma_0 : h \mapsto \sigma_0(h) \cdot \theta') \models A$.

By (2), for all $\theta' \preceq \theta_1$, we have that $(\sigma_0 : h \mapsto \sigma_0(h) \cdot \theta') \models A$ and $(\sigma_0 : h \mapsto \sigma_0(h) \cdot \theta') \models C_1 \wedge C_2$ imply $(\sigma_0 : h \mapsto \sigma_0(h) \cdot \theta') \models A_i$, for $i = 1, 2$.

We want to apply (1), but in order to do so we first need to derive $(\sigma_0 : h \mapsto \sigma_0(h) \cdot \theta') \models A_i$ for all $\theta' \preceq \theta_1{\downarrow}P_i$, $i = 1, 2$.

Clearly $A_i \uparrow Chan(A_i) = A_i$, and from (4) one obtains that A_i does not depend on those channels of P_j which are not connected to P_i, $i \neq j$.

Also for $(\sigma_0, \sigma', \theta', \tau) \in O[\![P_1\|P_2]\!]$, one has that $\theta' = \theta'{\downarrow}(P_1\|P_2)$ by Definition 7.30 and therefore

$$\begin{aligned}
&\theta'{\downarrow}Chan(A_i) = \theta'{\downarrow}(P_1\|P_2){\downarrow}Chan(A_i) = \\
&\theta'{\downarrow}(Chan(P_1\|P_2) \cap Chan(A_i)) = \quad \text{by (4)} \\
&\theta'{\downarrow}(Chan(P_i) \cap Chan(A_i)) = (\theta'{\downarrow}P_i){\downarrow}Chan(A_i).
\end{aligned}$$

From $\forall \theta' \preceq \theta_1.(\sigma_0 : h \mapsto \sigma_0(h) \cdot \theta') \models A_i$ one thus also obtains that

$$\forall \theta'{\downarrow}P_i \preceq \theta_1{\downarrow}P_i.(\sigma_0 : h \mapsto \sigma_0(h) \cdot \theta'{\downarrow}P_i) \models A_i,$$

i.e.,

$$\forall \theta' \preceq \theta_1{\downarrow}P_i.(\sigma_0 : h \mapsto \sigma_0(h) \cdot \theta') \models A_i.$$

Thus we have

$$(\forall \theta' \prec (\theta_1 \cdot (C, \mu)){\downarrow}P_i.(\sigma_0 : h \mapsto \sigma_0(h) \cdot \theta') \models A_i),$$

and since (1) yields

$$\begin{aligned}
&(\forall \theta' \prec (\theta_1 \cdot (C, \mu)){\downarrow}P_i.(\sigma_0 : h \mapsto \sigma_0(h) \cdot \theta') \models A_i) \Rightarrow \\
&(\sigma_0 : h \mapsto \sigma_0(h) \cdot (\theta_1 \cdot (C, \mu)){\downarrow}P_i) \models C_i,
\end{aligned}$$

we have that

$$(\sigma_0 : h \mapsto \sigma_0(h) \cdot (\theta_1 \cdot (C, \mu)){\downarrow}P_i) \models C_i.$$

Similarly as above one deduces $\theta' {\downarrow} Chan(C_i) = (\theta' {\downarrow} P_i) {\downarrow} Chan(C_i)$ for $(\sigma_0, \sigma', \theta', \tau) \in O[\![P_1 \| P_2]\!]$ and, hence,

$$(\sigma_0 : h \mapsto \sigma_0(h) \cdot \theta_1 \cdot (C, \mu)) \models C_i, i = 1, 2.$$

Together with formula (5) of the previous page, we obtain

$$\forall \theta' \preceq \theta.(\sigma_0 : h \mapsto \sigma_0(h) \cdot \theta') \models C_1 \wedge C_2.$$

(ii) If $\tau = \top$ then $\tau_1 = \tau_2 = \top$ and

for all $x \in VAR$: $\sigma(x) \stackrel{\text{def}}{=} \begin{cases} \sigma_i(x), & \text{if } x \in var(P_i), i = 1, 2, \\ \sigma_0(x), & \text{if } x \notin var(P_1 \| P_2). \end{cases}$

Furthermore, assume $(\sigma_0 : h \mapsto \sigma_0(h) \cdot \theta') \models A$, for all $\theta' \preceq \theta$.
As above this leads to $(\sigma_0 : h \mapsto \sigma_0(h) \cdot \theta') \models A_i$, for all $\theta' \preceq \theta {\downarrow} P_i$.
Thus by (1) we obtain $(\sigma_i : h \mapsto \sigma_0(h) \cdot \theta {\downarrow} P_i) \models \psi_i$.
By (3, 4) this again leads to $(\sigma : h \mapsto \sigma_0(h) \cdot \theta) \models \psi_i, i = 1, 2.$ ☐

7.5.5 Completeness

This section presents the semantic completeness proof of the proof method presented in Section 7.5.3, i.e., we prove that every valid A-C-formula is derivable with this proof method, as expressed by:

Theorem 7.45

$$\models \langle A, C \rangle : \{\varphi\}\, P\, \{\psi\} \Rightarrow \vdash \langle A, C \rangle : \{\varphi\}\, P\, \{\psi\}.$$

The proof of this theorem proceeds by induction on the structure of program P. First we discuss the structure of this proof.

Given program P and restrictions on the environment consisting of an assumption A and a precondition φ, we will construct the *strongest postcondition* w.r.t. φ, A and P, and the *strongest commitment* w.r.t. φ, A and P, in order to characterise precisely all reachable states of P which are consistent with the environment specified by A and φ, and all possible traces of P which are consistent with that environment.

These two kinds of predicates will be used for constructing A-C-inductive assertion networks for basic transition diagrams. For given precondition φ, assumption A and basic synchronous transition diagram B, they allow us to generate the A-C-inductive assertion network $Q(A, SC(\varphi, A, B))$ w.r.t. assumption A and strongest commitment $SC(\varphi, A, B)$, by associating with each node l of B the strongest postcondition $SP_l(\varphi, A, B)$. That this yields an A-C-inductive assertion network will be established in Lemma 7.49 below, and allows one to apply the basic diagram rule 7.11, after which some applications of the consequence rule yield the desired result.

To establish completeness for composite systems P one proceeds inductively. In this part we shall apply the usual notion of strongest postcondition $SP(\varphi,A,P)$ generalised to our setting.

The simple case is that of sequential composition: $P \equiv P_1;P_2$.

Here the induction hypothesis will be used to prove:

  (i) completeness w.r.t. φ and A for P_1, and
  (ii) completeness w.r.t. $SP(\varphi,A,P_1)$ and A for P_2,

after which the sequential composition rule will be applied to establish

$$\vdash \langle A,C \rangle : \{\varphi\}\ P_1;P_2\ \{SP(SP(\varphi,A,P_1),A,P_2)\}.$$

Using that $SP(SP(\varphi,A,P_1),A,P_2) = SP(\varphi,A,P_1;P_2)$ holds as usual, the result then follows from Lemma 7.53 (ii).

The most interesting case is $P \equiv P_1\|P_2$.

The problem here is that when

$$\models \langle A,C \rangle : \{\varphi\}\ P_1\|P_2\ \{\psi\}$$

holds, in general C cannot be equivalently expressed as $C_1 \wedge C_2$, and, similarly, ψ cannot be written as $\psi_1 \wedge \psi_2$, where $C_i,\psi_i, i = 1,2$, satisfy the restrictions imposed in the parallel composition rule.

As a result, the A-C formulae which can be proved directly using this rule are too weak. In fact, a second rule, the prefix-invariance rule, is needed to overcome some of these limitations. This can be seen as follows.

One restriction mentioned in the parallel composition rule is that

$$Chan(A_i,C_i,\psi_i) \cap Chan(P_j) \subseteq Chan(P_i), i \neq j, i,j = 1,2,$$

i.e., A_i, C_i and ψ_i do not involve channels of P_j which are not connected to P_i. In general, this rule only allows us to deduce commitments of the form $C_1 \wedge C_2$ and postconditions of the form $\psi_1 \wedge \psi_2$. However, when C_1 and ψ_1 refer to a channel D of P_1 which is not connected to P_2, and C_2 and ψ_2 to a channel E of P_2 which is not connected to P_1, the relative order to the communications over D and E prior to execution of $P_1\|P_2$ cannot be expressed this way (this order may have been referred to in φ). It is here that the application of the prefix-invariance axiom is crucial to establish completeness.

Another problem arises from the fact that, as remarked previously, validity of A-C formulae embodies an induction argument (this has been worked out in [ZdBdR84]). This, together with the fact that $\models A \wedge C_i \rightarrow A_j, i \neq j$, $i,j = 1,2$, occurs in the premise of the parallel composition rule, suggests a mutually recursive relationship between C_i and A_j, whose explicit expression would considerably complicate proofs. To get around this problem a purely combinatorial trick is used, which is based on the assumption-closure rule, and on Lemma 7.55, which captures this recursive dependency between C_i and A_j as a property of the underlying data domain, which on the level of our completeness proof can be incorporated using the consequence rule.

As a consequence, the case $P \equiv P_1 \| P_2$ of our completeness proof has a rather combinatorial flavour.

An alternative strategy for proving completeness appears in Exercises 7.15 and 7.16. This strategy is based on the use of weakest l-condition, precondition and weakest assumption operators w.r.t. commitment C and postcondition ψ.

Completeness for basic transition diagrams

The *strongest postcondition* for a basic transition diagram B characterises essentially those states that are reached by some communication history at a location l of B when starting in a state satisfying φ such that A holds for all prefixes of that communication history.

Definition 7.46 For $l \neq s$,

$$
\begin{aligned}
SP_l(\varphi, A, B) \overset{\text{def}}{=} \{ \sigma \mid \; &\exists \sigma_0, \sigma', \theta.(\sigma_0, \sigma', \theta) \in O_l(B) \\
&\wedge \sigma = (\sigma' : h \mapsto \sigma_0(h) \cdot \theta) \\
&\wedge \sigma_0 \models \varphi \wedge \forall \theta' \preceq \theta.(\sigma_0 : h \mapsto \sigma_0(h) \cdot \theta') \models A \} \\
SP_s(\varphi, A, B) \overset{\text{def}}{=} \{ \sigma \mid \; &\sigma \models \varphi \}.
\end{aligned}
$$

Observe that $SP_s(\varphi, A, B)$ is defined separately. This is because we want to simplify the formulation of the basic diagram rule and, in particular, to obtain that the assertion network $\mathcal{SP} : l \mapsto SP_l(\varphi, A, B)$ results in an A-C-inductive assertion network for basic transition diagrams. The latter requires, amongst others, that $\models SP_s(\varphi, A, B) \to SC(\varphi, A, B)$, and this is exactly what our definitions of $SP_s(\varphi, A, B)$ and $SC(\varphi, A, B)$ ensure (this condition is essential for starting the inductive argument in the soundness proof of the parallel composition rule).

Similarly we define the *strongest commitment* for a basic transition diagram B as the predicate characterising essentially those communication histories of B which start in a state satisfying φ such that A holds for all *proper* prefixes of those communication histories.

Definition 7.47

$$
\begin{aligned}
SC(\varphi, A, B) \overset{\text{def}}{=} \{ \sigma \mid \; &\exists l, \sigma_0, \sigma', \theta.(\sigma_0, \sigma', \theta) \in O_l(B) \wedge \sigma(h) = \sigma_0(h) \cdot \theta \\
&\wedge \sigma_0 \models \varphi \wedge \forall \theta' \prec \theta.(\sigma_0 : h \mapsto \sigma_0(h) \cdot \theta') \models A \}.
\end{aligned}
$$

Note that $SC(\varphi, A, B)$ is indeed a trace predicate.

We have the following properties of the strongest postcondition and commitment predicates for a basic transition diagram B.

Lemma 7.48

(i) $\models \langle A, SC(\varphi, A, B) \rangle : \{\varphi\} \, B \, \{SP_t(\varphi, A, B)\}$.

(ii) $\models \langle A, C \rangle : \{\varphi\} \, B \, \{\psi\} \Rightarrow$

    (a) $\models SP_t(\varphi, A, B) \rightarrow \psi$.

    (b) $\models SC(\varphi, A, B) \rightarrow C$.

Proof

(i) Let $(\sigma_0, \sigma, \theta, \tau) \in O[\![B]\!]$, and let $\sigma_0 \models \varphi$. We split the proof into two parts, one for establishing $SC(\varphi, A, B)$ and a second for establishing $SP_t(\varphi, A, B)$.

    (a) By Definition 7.32 of the validity of A-C formulae, one has to prove that $\forall \theta' \prec \theta.(\sigma_0 : h \mapsto \sigma_0(h) \cdot \theta') \models A$ implies

$$(\sigma_0 : h \mapsto \sigma_0(h) \cdot \theta) \models SC(\varphi, A, B).$$

    So assume $\forall \theta' \prec \theta.(\sigma_0 : h \mapsto \sigma_0(h) \cdot \theta') \models A$.

    Now $(\sigma_0, \sigma, \theta, \tau) \in O[\![B]\!]$ implies that some location l of B exists such that $(\sigma_0, \sigma, \theta) \in O_l(B)$. By Definition 7.47 one has that $\sigma \models SC(\varphi, A, B)$ if $\sigma(h) = \sigma_0(h) \cdot \theta$.

    Clearly the state $(\sigma_0 : h \mapsto \sigma_0(h) \cdot \theta)$ satisfies this property. Hence $(\sigma_0 : h \mapsto \sigma_0(h) \cdot \theta) \models SC(\varphi, A, B)$.

    (b) By Definition 7.32 of the validity of A-C formulae, one has to prove that $\tau = \top \wedge \forall \theta' \preceq \theta.(\sigma_0 : h \mapsto \sigma_0(h) \cdot \theta') \models A$ implies

$$(\sigma : h \mapsto \sigma_0(h) \cdot \theta) \models SP_t(\varphi, A, B).$$

    So assume the former property and notice that $\tau = \top$ implies that $(\sigma_0, \sigma, \theta) \in O_t(B)$. By Definition 7.46 one has that $\sigma' \models SP_t(\varphi, A, B)$ if $\sigma' = (\sigma : h \mapsto \sigma_0(h) \cdot \theta)$, provided $\sigma_0 \models \varphi$ and $\forall \theta' \preceq \theta.(\sigma_0 : h \mapsto \sigma_0(h) \cdot \theta') \models A$. Since the latter holds by assumption, $(\sigma : h \mapsto \sigma_0(h) \cdot \theta) \models SP_t(\varphi, A, B)$ follows.

(ii) Let $\models \langle A, C \rangle : \{\varphi\} \, B \, \{\psi\}$.

    (a) Assume that $\sigma \models SP_t(\varphi, A, B)$. Expanding Definition 7.46 this means that

$$\exists \sigma_0, \sigma', \theta.(\sigma_0, \sigma', \theta) \in O_t(B) \wedge \sigma = (\sigma' : h \mapsto \sigma_0(h) \cdot \theta)$$
$$\wedge \sigma_0 \models \varphi \wedge \forall \theta' \preceq \theta.(\sigma_0 : h \mapsto \sigma_0(h) \cdot \theta') \models A.$$

Now, $(\sigma_0, \sigma', \theta) \in O_l(B)$ implies that $(\sigma_0, \sigma', \theta, \top) \in O[\![B]\!]$.
Since $\sigma_0 \models \varphi$ we deduce from $\models \langle A, C \rangle : \{\varphi\}\, B\, \{\psi\}$ that

$$\forall \theta' \preceq \theta.(\sigma_0 : h \mapsto \sigma_0(h) \cdot \theta') \models A \Rightarrow (\sigma' : h \mapsto \sigma_0(h) \cdot \theta) \models \psi.$$

Thus we have that $(\sigma' : h \mapsto \sigma_0(h) \cdot \theta) \models \psi$, as was to be proved.
  (b) The proof of $\models SC(\varphi, A, B) \to C$ is similar. $\qquad\qquad\square$

We associate predicates $SP_l(\varphi, A, B)$ with each location l of B, and prove that
they constitute an A-C-inductive assertion network w.r.t. A and $SC(\varphi, A, B)$.

Lemma 7.49 $S\!P : l \mapsto SP_l(\varphi, A, B)$ is an A-C-inductive assertion network
w.r.t. A and $SC(\varphi, A, B)$ w.r.t. B.

Proof

- Let $l \xrightarrow{b \to f} l'$ be a local transition. Let $\sigma \models SP_l(\varphi, A, B) \wedge A \wedge b$.
  We have to prove that $f(\sigma) \models SP_{l'}(\varphi, A, B)$.
  $\sigma \models SP_l(\varphi, A, B) \wedge A \wedge b$ means by Definition 7.46 that
  $\exists \sigma_0, \sigma', \theta.\ \sigma_0 \models \varphi \wedge (\sigma_0, \sigma', \theta) \in O_l(B) \wedge \sigma = (\sigma' : h \mapsto \sigma_0(h) \cdot \theta)$
  $\wedge \forall \theta' \preceq \theta.(\sigma_0 : h \mapsto \sigma_0(h) \cdot \theta') \models A \wedge \sigma \models A \wedge \sigma \models b$.
  As a result of the above transition we have $(\sigma_0, \sigma'', \theta'') \in O_{l'}(B)$ where
  $\sigma'' = f(\sigma')$ and $\theta'' = \theta$. From $\theta'' = \theta$ we conclude that
  $\forall \theta' \preceq \theta''.(\sigma_0 : h \mapsto \sigma_0(h) \cdot \theta') \models A$.
  Hence we have that $(\sigma'' : h \mapsto \sigma_0(h) \cdot \theta) \models SP_{l'}(\varphi, A, B)$.
  But since f does not involve h we have $(\sigma'' : h \mapsto \sigma_0(h) \cdot \theta) = (f(\sigma') : h \mapsto \sigma_0(h) \cdot \theta) = f(\sigma' : h \mapsto \sigma_0(h) \cdot \theta) = f(\sigma)$, and hence we
  have $f(\sigma) \models SP_{l'}(\varphi, A, B)$, as was to be proved.
- Let $l \xrightarrow{b;D!e \to f} l'$ be an output transition. Let $\sigma \models SP_l(\varphi, A, B) \wedge A \wedge b$.
  This means that
  $\exists \sigma_0, \sigma', \theta.\sigma_0 \models \varphi \wedge (\sigma_0, \sigma', \theta) \in O_l(B) \wedge \sigma = (\sigma' : h \mapsto \sigma_0(h) \cdot \theta)$
  $\wedge \forall \theta' \preceq \theta.(\sigma_0 : h \mapsto \sigma_0(h) \cdot \theta') \models A \wedge \sigma \models b \wedge \sigma \models A$.
  We have to prove that for $\mu = e(\sigma)$

  $$(f(\sigma) : h \mapsto \sigma(h) \cdot (D, \mu)) \models ((A \to SP_{l'}(\varphi, A, B)) \wedge SC(\varphi, A, B)).$$

  Taking the transition above results in $\sigma'' = f(\sigma')$, $\theta'' = \theta \cdot (D, \mu)$. Thus
  $(\sigma_0, \sigma'', \theta'') \in O_{l'}(B)$. We have that $\sigma_0 \models \varphi$ and
  $\forall \theta' \prec \theta \cdot (D, \mu).(\sigma_0 : h \mapsto \sigma_0(h) \cdot \theta') \models A$. This implies by Definition 7.47 that

  $$(\sigma'' : h \mapsto \sigma_0(h) \cdot \theta \cdot (D, \mu)) \models SC(\varphi, A, B),$$

and, since f does not involve h,

$$(f(\sigma) : h \mapsto \sigma_0(h) \cdot \theta \cdot (D,\mu)) \models SC(\varphi,A,B).$$

If we assume additionally $(f(\sigma) : h \mapsto \sigma(h) \cdot (D,\mu)) \models A$, we also have $(\sigma_0 : h \mapsto \sigma(h) \cdot (D,\mu)) \models A$, since A is a trace predicate. Consequently, $\forall \theta' \preceq \theta \cdot (D,\mu).(\sigma_0 : h :\mapsto \sigma_0(h) \cdot \theta') \models A$, and we conclude from Definition 7.46

$$(f(\sigma) : h \mapsto \sigma_0(h) \cdot \theta \cdot (D,\mu)) \models SP_{l'}(\varphi,A,B).$$

- The case of an input transition $l \xrightarrow{b;D?x \to f} l'$ is similarly proved.

Although $SP_s(\varphi,A,B)$ is defined separately, the verification conditions for transitions (s,a,l) are satisfied as above, since we always have A in the premise. $\qquad \square$

After these preliminaries we start with our induction proof of Theorem 7.45 and consider the case that program B is a basic synchronous transition diagram (L,T,s,t) such that

$$\models \langle A,C \rangle : \{\varphi\}\, B\, \{\psi\}.$$

For predicates A and φ we construct SP_l predicates which form by Lemma 7.49 an A-C-inductive assertion network for B w.r.t. A and $SC(\varphi,A,B)$. Thus we can apply the basic diagram rule 7.11 and derive

$$\vdash \langle A,SC(\varphi,A,B) \rangle : \{SP_s(\varphi,A,B)\}\, B\, \{SP_t(\varphi,A,B)\}.$$

Since by Lemma 7.48 $\models SP_t(\varphi,A,B) \to \psi$ and $\models SC(\varphi,A,B) \to C$ hold, and $\models \varphi \to SP_s(\varphi,A,B)$ by definition of SP_s, we derive by an application of the consequence rule the desired result

$$\vdash \langle A,C \rangle : \{\varphi\}\, B\, \{\psi\}.$$

This establishes completeness in the sense of Theorem 7.45 for basic synchronous transition diagrams.

Strongest postcondition and strongest commitment for composed programs

We adapt Definitions 7.46 and 7.47 to the semantics of Definition 7.30.

Definition 7.50

$$SP(\varphi,A,P) \stackrel{\text{def}}{=} \{\sigma \mid \exists \sigma_0, \sigma', \theta.(\sigma_0,\sigma',\theta,\top) \in O[\![P]\!]$$
$$\wedge \sigma = (\sigma' : h \mapsto \sigma_0(h) \cdot \theta)$$
$$\wedge \sigma_0 \models \varphi \wedge \forall \theta' \preceq \theta.(\sigma_0 : h \mapsto \sigma_0(h) \cdot \theta') \models A \}. \qquad \square$$

Remark 7.51 For a basic diagram B we have $\models SP_t(\varphi, A, B) \Leftrightarrow SP(\varphi, A, B)$.

Definition 7.52

$$SC(\varphi, A, P) \overset{\text{def}}{=} \{\sigma \mid \exists \sigma_0, \sigma', \theta, \tau.(\sigma_0, \sigma', \theta, \tau) \in O[\![P]\!]$$
$$\wedge \sigma(h) = \sigma_0(h) \cdot \theta$$
$$\wedge \sigma_0 \models \varphi \wedge \forall \theta' \prec \theta.(\sigma_0 : h \mapsto \sigma_0(h) \cdot \theta') \models A \}. \qquad \square$$

The strongest precondition SP and strongest commitment SC satisfy the following properties:

Lemma 7.53

(i) $\models \langle A, SC(\varphi, A, P) \rangle : \{\varphi\} \ P \ \{SP(\varphi, A, P)\}$.

(ii) $\models \langle A, C \rangle : \{\varphi\} \ P \ \{\psi\} \Rightarrow$

(a) $\models SP(\varphi, A, P) \to \psi$.

(b) $\models SC(\varphi, A, P) \to C$.

Proof Similar to that of Lemma 7.48. $\square$

Completeness for sequentially composed programs

Given a program $P_1; P_2$ such that

$$\models \langle A, C \rangle : \{\varphi\} \ P_1; P_2 \ \{\psi\}.$$

we show that this is derivable with our proof method. By Lemma 7.53 we have

$$\models \langle A, SC(\varphi, A, P_1) \rangle : \{\varphi\} \ P_1 \ \{SP(\varphi, A, P_1)\}$$

and

$$\models \langle A, SC(SP(\varphi, A, P_1), A, P_2) \rangle : \{SP(\varphi, A, P_1)\} \ P_2 \ \{SP(SP(\varphi, A, P_1), A, P_2)\}.$$

By our induction hypothesis, these correctness statements are provable, i.e., we have

$$\vdash \langle A, SC(\varphi, A, P_1) \rangle : \{\varphi\} \ P_1 \ \{SP(\varphi, A, P_1)\}$$

and

$$\vdash \langle A, SC(SP(\varphi, A, P_1), A, P_2) \rangle : \{SP(\varphi, A, P_1)\} \ P_2 \ \{SP(SP(\varphi, A, P_1), A, P_2)\}.$$

Next we prove the following implications.

Lemma 7.54

- $\models SP(SP(\varphi, A, P_1), A, P_2) \to SP(\varphi, A, (P_1; P_2))$,
- $\models SC(\varphi, A, P_1) \to SC(\varphi, A, (P_1; P_2))$,

- $\models SC(SP(\varphi, A, P_1), A, P_2) \to SC(\varphi, A, (P_1; P_2))$.

Proof

- Let $\sigma \models SP(SP(\varphi, A, P_1), A, P_2)$.
  This means by Definition 7.50 that

  $$\exists \sigma_0, \sigma', \theta_2. (\sigma_0, \sigma', \theta_2, \top) \in O[\![P_2]\!] \wedge \sigma = (\sigma' : h \mapsto \sigma_0(h) \cdot \theta_2)$$
  $$\wedge \sigma_0 \models SP(\varphi, A, P_1) \wedge \forall \theta' \preceq \theta_2. (\sigma_0 : h \mapsto \sigma_0(h) \cdot \theta') \models A.$$

  By expanding $SP(\varphi, A, P_1)$ this means that

  $$\exists \sigma_0, \sigma', \theta_2. (\sigma_0, \sigma', \theta_2, \top) \in O[\![P_2]\!] \wedge \sigma = (\sigma' : h \mapsto \sigma_0(h) \cdot \theta_2)$$
  $$\wedge \forall \theta' \preceq \theta_2. (\sigma_0 : h \mapsto \sigma_0(h) \cdot \theta') \models A$$
  $$\wedge \exists \sigma_{00}, \sigma'', \theta_1. (\sigma_{00}, \sigma'', \theta_1, \top) \in O[\![P_1]\!]$$
  $$\wedge \sigma_0 = (\sigma'' : h \mapsto \sigma_{00}(h) \cdot \theta_1)$$
  $$\wedge \sigma_{00} \models \varphi \wedge \forall \theta'' \preceq \theta_1. (\sigma_{00} : h \mapsto \sigma_{00}(h) \cdot \theta'') \models A.$$

  Since A is a trace predicate, $(\sigma_0 : h \mapsto \sigma_0(h) \cdot \theta') \models A$ implies that also $(\sigma_{00} : h \mapsto \sigma_0(h) \cdot \theta') \models A$. We have $h \notin var(P_1)$, hence $\sigma''(h) = \sigma_{00}(h)$, and we conclude that $\sigma'' = (\sigma_0 : h \mapsto \sigma_{00}(h)$. Furthermore $h \notin var(P_2)$, and we also have that

  $$((\sigma_0 : h \mapsto \sigma_{00}(h)), (\sigma : h \mapsto \sigma_{00}(h)), \theta_2, \top) \in O[\![P_2]\!].$$

  By definition of $O[\![P_1; P_2]\!]$ one obtains from this

  $$\exists \sigma_{00}, \sigma', \theta_1, \theta_2. (\sigma_{00}, (\sigma' : h \mapsto \sigma_{00}(h)), (\theta_1 \cdot \theta_2), \top) \in O[\![P_1; P_2]\!]$$
  $$\wedge \sigma = (\sigma' : h \mapsto \sigma_{00} \cdot (\theta_1 \cdot \theta_2))$$
  $$\wedge \forall \theta' \preceq \theta_2. (\sigma_{00} : h \mapsto (\sigma_{00}(h) \cdot \theta_1) \cdot \theta') \models A$$
  $$\wedge \sigma_{00} \models \varphi \wedge \forall \theta'' \preceq \theta_1. (\sigma_{00} : h \mapsto \sigma_{00}(h) \cdot \theta'') \models A.$$

  Furthermore $\forall \theta' \preceq \theta_2. (\sigma_{00} : h \mapsto (\sigma_{00}(h) \cdot \theta_1) \cdot \theta') \models A$ and $\forall \theta'' \preceq \theta_1. (\sigma_{00} : h \mapsto \sigma_{00}(h) \cdot \theta'') \models A$ together imply

  $$\forall \theta' \preceq (\theta_1 \cdot \theta_2). (\sigma_{00} : h \mapsto \sigma_{00}(h) \cdot \theta') \models A.$$

  Now this leads to

  $$\exists \sigma_{00}, \sigma', \theta_1, \theta_2. (\sigma_{00}, \sigma', (\theta_1 \cdot \theta_2), \top) \in O[\![P_1; P_2]\!]$$
  $$\wedge \sigma = (\sigma' : h \mapsto \sigma_{00} \cdot (\theta_1 \cdot \theta_2))$$
  $$\wedge \sigma_{00} \models \varphi \wedge \forall \theta' \preceq (\theta_1 \cdot \theta_2). (\sigma_{00} : h \mapsto \sigma_{00}(h) \cdot \theta') \models A.$$

  By Definition 7.50 this means that $\sigma \models SP(\varphi, A, (P_1; P_2))$.
- The second claim follows immediately from Definition 7.52 and the definition of sequential composition.
- The third claim is proven analogously to the first implication. $\square$

Using these implications we derive the following formulae by applying the consequence rule:

$$\vdash \langle A, SC(\varphi, A, (P_1; P_2)) \rangle : \{\varphi\} \; P_1 \; \{SP(\varphi, A, P_1)\}$$

and

$$\vdash \langle A, SC(\varphi, A, (P_1; P_2)) \rangle : \{SP(\varphi, A, P_1)\} \; P_2 \; \{SP(\varphi, A, (P_1; P_2))\}.$$

Now we can apply the sequential composition rule and derive

$$\vdash \langle A, SC(\varphi, A, (P_1; P_2)) \rangle : \{\varphi\} \; P_1; P_2 \; \{SP(\varphi, A, (P_1; P_2))\}.$$

Again Lemma 7.53 (ii) and the consequence rule lead to

$$\vdash \langle A, C \rangle : \{\varphi\} \; P_1; P_2 \; \{\psi\}.$$

Completeness for parallel processes

Now given a program $P \equiv P_1 \| P_2$ such that

$$\models \langle A, C \rangle : \{\varphi\} \; P_1 \| P_2 \; \{\psi\},$$

we proceed as follows with our semantic completeness proof.
We define the following sets of variables and channels:

$$\bar{x} \stackrel{\text{def}}{=} var(\varphi, P),$$
$$\bar{x}_i \stackrel{\text{def}}{=} var(P_i), i = 1, 2,$$
$$C_i \stackrel{\text{def}}{=} CHAN \setminus (Chan(P_j) \setminus Chan(P_i)), i, j = 1, 2, i \neq j.$$

We freeze the initial values of $\bar{x}$ and h in the precondition using fresh logical variables $\bar{z}$ and t_0:

$$\varphi' \stackrel{\text{def}}{=} \varphi \wedge \bar{x} = \bar{z} \wedge t_0 = h.$$

In order to avoid circularity – in fact to avoid an inductive construction of *SP/SC* – when constructing the strongest commitment/postcondition for each process P_i, we employ *true* as the assumption, i.e., at first we do not restrict the communication behaviour of the environment. The adaptation to the actual assumption A concerned is done afterwards using the assumption rule; this strategy was suggested by Paritosh Pandya.

For precondition φ' and assumption *true* we have by Lemma 7.53

$$\models \langle true, SC(\varphi', true, P_i) \rangle : \{\varphi'\} \; P_i \; \{SP(\varphi', true, P_i)\},$$

for $i = 1, 2$, and by the induction hypothesis

$$\vdash \langle true, SC(\varphi', true, P_i) \rangle : \{\varphi'\} \; P_i \; \{SP(\varphi', true, P_i)\}.$$

Since

$$\models SP(\varphi', true, P_i) \to \exists \bar{x}_j (SP(\varphi', true, P_i) \uparrow C_i),$$

and similarly

$$\models SC(\varphi', true, P_i) \to SC(\varphi', true, P_i) \uparrow C_i,$$

we derive by the consequence rule

$$\vdash \langle true, SC(\varphi', true, P_i) \uparrow C_i \rangle : \{\varphi'\} \ P_i \ \{\exists \bar{x}_j (SP(\varphi', true, P_i) \uparrow C_i)\}.$$

Trivially $\models true \wedge SC(\varphi', true, P_i) \uparrow C_i \to true$ holds for $i = 1, 2$, and the side conditions of the parallel composition rule are satisfied, hence we obtain

$$\vdash \langle true, SC(\varphi', true, P_1) \uparrow C_1 \wedge SC(\varphi', true, P_2) \uparrow C_2 \rangle :$$
$$\{\varphi'\}$$
$$P_1 \| P_2$$
$$\{\exists \bar{x}_2 (SP(\varphi', true, P_1) \uparrow C_1) \wedge \exists \bar{x}_1 (SP(\varphi', true, P_2) \uparrow C_2)\}.$$

Using the prefix-invariance axiom (and the conjunction rule), taking CHAN for *cset*, we derive

$$\vdash \langle true, SC(\varphi', true, P_1) \uparrow C_1 \wedge SC(\varphi', true, P_2) \uparrow C_2 \wedge t_0 \preceq h \rangle :$$
$$\{\varphi' \wedge t_0 = h\}$$
$$P_1 \| P_2$$
$$\{\exists \bar{x}_2 (SP(\varphi', true, P_1) \uparrow C_1) \wedge \exists \bar{x}_1 (SP(\varphi', true, P_2) \uparrow C_2) \wedge t_0 \preceq h\}.$$

We introduce the assumption A by means of the consequence rule and apply the assumption rule to reflect this restriction in the commitment and in the postcondition:

$$\vdash \langle A, SC(\varphi', true, P_1) \uparrow C_1 \wedge SC(\varphi', true, P_2) \uparrow C_2 \wedge t_0 \preceq h$$
$$\wedge \forall t. (t_0 \preceq t \prec h \to A\{t/h\}) \rangle :$$
$$\{\varphi' \wedge t_0 = h\}$$
$$P_1 \| P_2$$
$$\{ \exists \bar{x}_2 (SP(\varphi', true, P_1) \uparrow C_1) \wedge \exists \bar{x}_1 (SP(\varphi', true, P_2) \uparrow C_2) \wedge t_0 \preceq h$$
$$\wedge \forall t. (t_0 \preceq t \preceq h \to A\{t/h\}) \}.$$

The crucial step now is the proof that the commitment constructed here is in fact the strongest commitment $SC(\varphi', A, P_1 \| P_2)$ and that the postcondition developed above is in fact the strongest postcondition $SP(\varphi', A, P_1 \| P_2)$. This is proved in Lemma 7.55 below and is the very reason why another application of the consequence rule leads to the derivation of

$$\vdash \langle A, SC(\varphi', A, P_1 \| P_2) \rangle : \{\varphi'\} \ P_1 \| P_2 \ \{SP(\varphi', A, P_1 \| P_2)\},$$

and by Lemma 7.53 (ii), the initialisation rule, and the consequence rule we conclude that

$$\vdash \langle A, C \rangle : \{\varphi\}\ P_1 \| P_2\ \{\psi\},$$

as desired.

This ends our completeness proof for composed transition diagrams $P_1 \| P_2$.

The crucial detail in the completeness proof for the parallel composition of composite transition diagrams is formulated in the following lemma.

Lemma 7.55

- $\models (\exists \bar{x}_2 (SP(\varphi', true, P_1) \uparrow C_1) \wedge \exists \bar{x}_1 (SP(\varphi', true, P_2) \uparrow C_2) \wedge t_0 \preceq h$
  $\wedge \forall t.(t_0 \preceq t \preceq h \to A\{t/h\})) \Rightarrow SP(\varphi', A, P_1 \| P_2).$
- $\models SC(\varphi', true, P_1) \uparrow C_1 \wedge SC(\varphi', true, P_2) \uparrow C_2 \wedge t_0 \preceq h$
  $\wedge \forall t.(t_0 \preceq t \prec h \to A\{t/h\}) \Rightarrow SC(\varphi', A, P_1 \| P_2).$

Proof

We prove the first claim only; the proof of the second claim proceeds analogously.

Let

$$\sigma \models (\exists \bar{x}_2 (SP(\varphi', true, P_1) \uparrow C_1) \wedge \exists \bar{x}_1 (SP(\varphi', true, P_2) \uparrow C_2)$$
$$\wedge t_0 \preceq h \wedge \forall t.(t_0 \preceq t \preceq h \to A\{t/h\})).$$

There exist states σ_1 and σ_2 such that

$$\sigma_i \models SP(\varphi', true, P_i),$$

and σ differs from σ_i only w.r.t. the variables $\bar{x}_j$ ($i \neq j$), and $\sigma(h){\downarrow}C_i = \sigma_i(h){\downarrow}C_i$.

By definition of $SP(\varphi', true, P_i)$ there exist σ_i^0, σ_i' and θ_1^i such that $\sigma_i^0 \models \varphi'$ and

$$(\sigma_i^0, \sigma_i', \theta_1^i, \tau_i) \in O[\![P_i]\!]$$

and $\sigma_i = (\sigma_i' : h \mapsto \sigma_i^0(h) \cdot \theta_1^i)$.

Since $\sigma_i^0 \models \varphi'$ we know that $\sigma_i^0(\bar{x}) = \sigma_i^0(\bar{z})$, $i = 1, 2$, and since $\sigma_i^0(\bar{z}) = \sigma_i'(\bar{z}) = \sigma_i(\bar{z}) = \sigma(\bar{z})$ we conclude that σ_1^0 and σ_2^0 agree on all variables in $\bar{x}$. For all other variables y we have that $\sigma(y) = \sigma_i(y) = \sigma_i'(y) = \sigma_i^0(y)$, hence σ_1^0 and σ_2^0 agree also on all variables not in $\bar{x}$. We denote this state by σ_0.

We have that $\sigma(t_0) \preceq \sigma(h)$, so define $\hat{\theta}$ such that $\sigma(h) = \sigma(t_0) \cdot \hat{\theta}$. We additionally know that $\sigma_i^0(h) = \sigma(t_0)$. Furthermore we have $\sigma(h){\downarrow}C_i = \sigma_i(h){\downarrow}C_i$.

Since $\sigma_i(h) = \sigma_i^0(h) \cdot \theta_1^i$, we also have that

$$\sigma(h){\downarrow}C_i = \sigma_i(h){\downarrow}C_i = \sigma_i^0(h){\downarrow}C_i \cdot \theta_1^i{\downarrow}C_i.$$

It follows from $\sigma(h) = \sigma(t_0) \cdot \hat{\theta}$ and $\sigma_i^0(h) = \sigma(t_0)$ that $\hat{\theta} \downarrow C_i = \theta_1^i \downarrow C_i$.

Moreover, the computation sequences in the O semantics are precise, thus we have that $\theta_1^i = \theta_1^i \downarrow P_i$, and since $Chan(P_i) \subseteq C_i$ we also have $\theta_1^i = \theta_1^i \downarrow C_i$.

We conclude that

$$\theta_1^i = \theta_1^i \downarrow C_i = \hat{\theta} \downarrow C_i.$$

Now $(\sigma_i^0, \sigma_i', \theta_1^i, \tau_i) \in O[\![P_i]\!]$; since σ_0 agrees with σ_i^0 on all variables we also have $(\sigma_0, \sigma_i', \theta_1^i, \tau_i) \in O[\![P_i]\!]$.

Recall that $\theta_1^i = \theta_1^i \downarrow P_i$, i.e., $Chan(\theta_1^i) = Chan(P_i)$. Additionally we have that $\hat{\theta} \downarrow C_i = \theta_1^i \downarrow C_i = \theta_1^i = \theta_1^i \downarrow P_i$. Since $Chan(P_i) \subseteq C_i$ we conclude that $\theta_1^i \downarrow P_i = \hat{\theta} \downarrow P_i$. Thus we have

$$(\sigma_0, \sigma_i', \hat{\theta} \downarrow P_i, \tau_i) \in O[\![P_i]\!].$$

Since $C_1 \cup C_2 = CHAN$ we have $\hat{\theta} = \hat{\theta} \downarrow CHAN = \hat{\theta} \downarrow (C_1 \cup C_2)$. Now

$$Chan(\hat{\theta}) = Chan(\hat{\theta} \downarrow (C_1 \cup C_2)) = Chan(\hat{\theta} \downarrow C_1) \cup Chan(\hat{\theta} \downarrow C_2) =$$
$$Chan(\hat{\theta} \downarrow P_1) \cup Chan(\hat{\theta} \downarrow P_2) \subseteq Chan(P_1) \cup Chan(P_2) = Chan(P_1 \| P_2)$$

and consequently $\hat{\theta} = \hat{\theta} \downarrow (P_1 \| P_2)$.

Now we construct σ' as follows: σ' agrees with σ_0 for all variables except for $\bar{x}_1$ and $\bar{x}_2$, and with σ_i' on $\bar{x}_i$.

- $\sigma'(\bar{x}_i) \stackrel{\text{def}}{=} \sigma_i'(\bar{x}_i) = \sigma_i(\bar{x}_i)$, $i = 1, 2$,
- $\sigma'(h) \stackrel{\text{def}}{=} \sigma_0(h)$,
- $\sigma'(y) \stackrel{\text{def}}{=} \sigma_0(y)$, for all $y \notin \bar{x}_1, y \notin \bar{x}_2, y \neq h$.

Thus, by definition of the semantics we have that

$$(\sigma_0, \sigma', \hat{\theta}, \tau) \in O[\![P_1 \| P_2]\!],$$

where $\tau = \top \leftrightarrow (\tau_1 = \top \wedge \tau_2 = \top)$.

Since $\sigma(\bar{x}_i) = \sigma'(\bar{x}_i)$, $i = 1, 2$, and $\sigma(h) = \sigma_0(h) \cdot \hat{\theta}$ we have

$$\sigma = (\sigma' : h \mapsto \sigma_0(h) \cdot \hat{\theta}).$$

Now recall that

$$\sigma(t_0) = \sigma_0(h) \preceq \sigma(h) = \sigma_0(h) \cdot \hat{\theta}.$$

We have that $\sigma \models \forall t.(t_0 \preceq t \preceq h \to A\{t/h\})$. Let $\sigma(t)$ be such that $\sigma(t_0) \preceq \sigma(t) \preceq \sigma(h)$. Then obviously $\sigma(t) = \sigma_0(h) \cdot \theta'$ for some θ' such that $\theta' \preceq \hat{\theta}$, and $(\sigma : t \mapsto \sigma_0(h) \cdot \theta') \models A\{t/h\}$. This is equivalent to $(\sigma : h \mapsto \sigma_0(h) \cdot \theta') \models A$ and since θ' is an arbitrary prefix of $\hat{\theta}$ we have proven that

$$\forall \theta' \preceq \hat{\theta}.(\sigma : h \mapsto \sigma_0(h) \cdot \theta') \models A.$$

Since A is a trace predicate we also have that

$$\forall \theta' \preceq \hat{\theta}.(\sigma_0 : h \mapsto \sigma_0(h) \cdot \theta') \models A.$$

Recalling that $\sigma_0 \models \varphi'$ we collect the requirements of Definition 7.50, and we have that

$$\sigma \models SP(\varphi', A, P_1 \| P_2). \qquad \Box$$

7.6 Historical Notes

The compositional proof methods discussed below are all based on *traces*, i.e., sequences of communication records. These appear for the first time in the dissertation of Yonezawa [Yon77].

One of the founding papers in the area of compositional program proving is [MC81] by Jayadev Misra and K. Mani Chandy, in which they show how to reason compositionally about synchronous networks. In [Oss83] some applications of their theory – compositional correctness proofs for the alternating bit and parts of an HDLC protocol – are presented. However, [Zwi89] states that both the programming language, assertion language and proof system used in [MC81] remained to be precisely defined. The latter is undertaken in [ZdBdR84]; as a consequence, incompleteness of their proof system became immediately apparent, as was observed, independently, by Nguyen [Ngu85]. In [ZdRvEB84] a sound and complete proof system for these networks is presented, identifying as previous sources of incompleteness the properties of *prefix invariance* – a network prolongs its initial communication history – and *assumption closure* – a valid A-C formula not only assures that its commitment holds after every communication but also that its assumption holds for all proper prefixes of the communication history. [ZdRvEB85] presents a sound and complete proof system for partial correctness properties of synchronously communicating networks of processes, which is based on trace invariants, pre- and postconditions. In [Pan88, PJ91] a proof system for the A-C paradigm is presented which also enables compositional proofs for total correctness and, e.g., absence of deadlock, together with its soundness and completeness proofs. The extension to more general liveness properties is discussed in [Pnu85, Pan90].

Job Zwiers' monograph on compositional logics for synchronous communication appears in 1989 [Zwi89]. He introduces a "telescope" of increasingly sophistical logics – each of which can be embedded in the previous one – for reasoning compositionally about synchronously communicating processes, and gives their soundness and completeness proofs. In particular, he proves that these logics can be embedded in his most fundamental compositional formalism, the so-called *SAT*-formalism [Pnu77, Hoa85a].

Neelam Soundararajan, partly in collaboration with Ole-Johan Dahl, formulates compositional logics for proving partial and total correctness of synchronous networks in [SD82, Sou84, Sou86], using an input axiom which holds independently from any environment. This axiom is incorporated in the definition of compositionally-inductive assertion networks in this chapter, by requiring, for all nodes l', assertion $\forall x. Q_{l'}$ to hold after input transitions leading to l', which expresses that $Q_{l'}$ holds for all input values of x.

Serious attempts at simplification of proof rules for concurrency and communication are undertaken in Rick Hehner's monographs [Heh84, Heh93], with [HH83] as predecessor.

An interesting result is stated in [Sou97], in which Soundararajan looks back upon an old problem, and draws the conclusion that some attempts at its solution failed. The problem concerns the comparison of the expressive power of trace invariants for channels and for processes; it draws its interest from the observation that channel invariants are simpler than process invariants. Here channel invariants characterise the communication behaviour along separate channels of a process, whereas process invariants characterise the interface of a process by interleaving communication records of different channels whenever necessary. The problem originates from incompleteness of early trace-based proof systems [ZH81, Hoa81a, MC81, ZdBdR84, Hoa85a], as observed in, e.g., [BA81, Ngu85], and leads to the complete logics of [ZdRvEB84, NDOG86]. As observed in [WGS87] "the modifications [required to obtain complete trace-based proof systems] tend to be extensive and cumbersome; the simplicity of the underlying logic is lost". Subsequently, in [Wid87, WGS87, WGS92] simpler trace-based proof systems are suggested, together with associated completeness proofs. Now Soundararajan explains in [Sou97, Sou00] giving a precise analysis, why these proof systems are not complete. In doing so, he establishes the incompleteness of any proof system based only on channel invariants. In particular, he establishes that, if the invariant for each process is allowed to talk only about traces along channels that connect it to external processes, then the Widom–Gries proof system [WGS87, WGS92] is incomplete. This result is closely related to that of Bengt Jonsson and Joost Kok [JK89] concerning a fully abstract characterisation of processes in Kahn networks [Kah74]. The need for such a characterisation was already apparent from the so-called "Brock-Ackermann paradox" [BA81], showing that some form of interleaving of communication along different channels is indispensable when characterising processes which communicate with their environment.

An interesting area of investigation is the compositional characterisation of concurrency by means of predicate transformers. In the case of synchronous message passing, the predicates involved denote sets of pairs of states and traces, whereas the semantics of a process is given by a set of triples consisting of an initial and a final state, together with the trace of communications occurring in the computation between these two states. To characterise the predicate transformers induced by the latter, one generalises predicate transformers to relation transformers, i.e., pre- and postspecifications in the sense of [HHS87]. The resulting theory enables a unified compositional theory of concurrency, which is sketched, e.g., in [ZdR89, Din99a] and its relationship with compositional refinement [Zwi90, Bro97]. This theory is further discussed in Section 8.5.

Returning to the assumption-commitment paradigm, a clear explanation of its rules, its application to UNITY [CM88], and its correspondence with the rely-guarantee paradigm, are discussed in, e.g., [Col93, Col94a, CS95a, CS96, XCC94, CC96], and extended in the context of UNITY to reasoning about component-based designs in [CC99].

Continuing the discussion of the work of Ernst-Rüdiger Olderog from Section 4.10, in his monograph [Old91a] Olderog presents three views of concurrent processes: *Petri nets* describe processes as concurrent and interacting machines, *algebraic process terms* stress their composition and *logical trace formulae* specify the intended communication behaviour. For the top-down design of concurrent processes two sets of transformation rules are given. The first one can be used to transform logical formulae stepwise into process terms, whilst process terms can be transformed into Petri nets by the second set. In later work, Olderog extends these results in a series of publications to the compositional derivation of real-time systems within the context of the ProCoS project; this is discussed below.

The ProCoS project (for "Provably Correct Systems") [HHF+94] is a comprehensive wide-spectrum verification project that studies embedded, concurrent and communicating systems at various levels of abstraction. These encompass requirements' capture, specification language and machine language. The principal goal of the project is to formally connect all these different levels of abstraction through stepwise transformation and thus allow the development of concurrent systems that are correct by construction. A specification language is used that combines trace-based with state-based assertional reasoning. Using a set of transformation rules, a specification is first successively transformed into a distributed, concurrent OCCAM-like program [INM84, ORSS92, OR93, OD98]. The resulting program is then mapped to a machine language. The theoretical foundation of ProCoS is strongly influenced by [Old91a].

The FOCUS project also aims, similarly to ProCoS, at supporting the systematic formal specification and development of distributed interactive systems [BDD+92]. The notion of a trace (here the term *stream* is used) forms the foundation of the framework of Manfred Broy's [Bro86]. The behaviour of system components is described in FOCUS by means of stream-processing functions which specify how tuples of input traces are mapped to output traces. Methods for the compositional development and verification of concurrent systems, which are specified in this way, are given in [BDD+92, Bro98].

An interesting application of trace-based reasoning is the area of VLSI design. This concerns, especially, the design of so-called *delay-insensitive* circuits, i.e., circuits whose functioning does not depend on any timing regime. Initiated in Martin Rem's [Rem81], this area is investigated in [Udd84, vdS85, Ebe89, Zwa89, Sch92, vB93, JU93, Ver94, Ver98, Mal00].

Compositional theories of asynchronous communication are presented in works of Bengt Jonsson, Nancy Lynch and Mark Tuttle [Jon85, Jon87a, LT87, Lyn96, Jon94].

A major application area of the theory developed in this chapter is the compositional verification of real-time properties of synchronously communicating processes. Based on the semantics of synchrony and real-time presented in [KSdR+85], Jozef Hooman started his research in this area with [Hoo87, Hoo90, Hoo91b, Hoo93, Hoo96, HdR91, HRdR92, HvR97, SH94], focussing in later work on machine-checked compositional correctness proofs of real-time algorithms [Hoo95, Hoo98, HvR97], using PVS as supporting tool [ORS92]. In [ZH95] an atomic broadcast protocol due to Flaviu Cristian is proved correct, using a compositional proof system for local clocks.

In [CMP94] a temporal-logic-based formalism is presented for the compositional specification and verification of real-time systems, in the school of Zohar Manna and Amir Pnueli. In [Mos98] Ben Moszkowski presents a compositional methodology for specification and proof using fixpoints in Interval Temporal Logic (ITL). Ben developed an interpreter for ITL's executable subset Tempura, which incorporates compositional reasoning [Mos83, Mos86, Mos94].

For the work of many other equally important researchers in the area of compositional formalisms for real-time systems, such as Michael Hansen, Hans Hansson, F. Jahanian, Mathai Joseph, Leslie Lamport, Simon S. Lam, Insup Lee, Ziming Liu, Aloysius Mok, Jonathan Ostroff, Jan Peleska, Anders Ravn, A. Udaya Shankar, and Chao-Chen Zhou, we refer to our companion volume [HdRP+00] and to surveys of literature in this field [Jos88, dBHdRR92,

Vyt91, vTK91, Vyt93, dBdRR94, LdRV94, JP96, Jos96, RR98, Jos00]. For further work of the Oxford Timed-CSP group, consisting of Steve Brookes, Jim Davies, Tony Hoare, Dave Jackson, Joy Reed, Mike Reed, Bill Roscoe, and Steve Schneider, we also refer to Section 4.10, as well as to [Ros98, Sch99b].

Presently an influential approach from an industrial view point is the *Synchronous Languages* approach, pioneered by Gérard Berry, Albert Benveniste, Paul Caspi, Paul le Guernic, Nicolas Halbwachs, David Harel, and Florence Maraninchi, of which we list only a few pointers to the recent literature [Har87, HCP91, Hal93, BCGH94, BGA98, MR98, Ber99, Ber00, BBF$^+$00]. A result of foundational importance is Berry's [Ber99], based upon [SBT96, SSB$^+$96], in which three kinds of approaches to defining the semantics of synchronous languages (applied to ESTEREL) are proved to be equivalent:

- The *constructive behavioural* semantics, the simplest of the three, which is based on what a program *must* and *cannot* do.
- The *constructive operational* semantics, which is based on an interpretation scheme defining microstep sequences.
- The *electrical* semantics, which is based on the translation of synchronous programs into synchronous circuits.

This result shows that from the point of view of both physics, logic and computer science a stable concept of semantics has been obtained.

Exercises

7.1   Prove associativity of the parallel composition (Lemma 7.5) as defined in Definition 7.3, i.e., given the disjoint synchronous transition systems P_1, P_2, and P_3 we have that

$$O((P_1 \parallel P_2) \parallel P_3) = O(P_1 \parallel (P_2 \parallel P_3))$$

7.2   Deduce the invariance rule 7.10 using the proof rules of Section 7.4.2. Hence the soundness of the compositional method for nested parallelism implies soundness of this rule.

7.3   Derive the correctness of

$$\{h_{A_1B_1} = \langle\rangle\} P_1 \{ \#h_{A_1} = \#h_{B_1} = 1 \wedge \{B_1[1]\} = \{A_1[1]\} \}$$

for P_1 as given in Figure 7.3 in detail.

7.4   Prove that the given assertion network for IN_n in Example 7.20 is compositionally-inductive.

7.5   Prove that the given assertion network for OUT_n in Example 7.20 is compositionally-inductive.

7.6   Prove soundness of the sequential composition rule 7.7 and the prefix-invariance axiom 7.9.

7.7   Let f_1 and f_2 be two total functions over *VAL*. The purpose of this exercise is to develop a compositional design of a composite system P that first receives a value v on a channel A, then computes $f_1(f_1(v) + f_2(v))$ and $f_2(f_1(v) + f_2(v))$, and finally transmits these values along channel B.

Formally, P should satisfy

$$\{h_{AB} = \langle\rangle\}$$
$$P$$
$$\{\exists v(h_{AB} = \langle(A,v),(B,f_1(f_1(v) + f_2(v))),(B,f_2(f_1(v) + f_2(v))))\rangle)\}.$$

Here $h_{AB} = h\!\downarrow\!\{A,B\}$.

To give an implementation for P, assume we are given two basic components C_1 and C_2 that satisfy, for any arithmetical expression *exp*,

- $\{x_1 = exp\} C_1 \{y_1 = f_1(exp)\}$, $var(C_1) = \{x_1, y_1\}$, $Chan(C_1) = \emptyset$
- $\{x_2 = exp\} C_2 \{y_2 = f_2(exp)\}$, $var(C_2) = \{x_2, y_2\}$, $Chan(C_2) = \emptyset$

Derive an implementation for P using the compositional proof method for nested parallelism developed in Section 7.4.

Hint: The first design step is to write P as a sequential composition of P_0, that receives a value on channel A and stores it in x_1 and x_2, using a system $\hat{P}$. Then $\hat{P}$ is refined to $P_1 ; P_2$, where P_1 computes the desired values and stores them in y_1 and y_2, and P_2 sends these along channel B, as desired. Subsequently, P_1 is refined into $P_{11} \| P_{12}$. P_{11} and P_{12} first compute, respectively, $f_1(v)$ and $f_2(v)$. Then they exchange these results using auxiliary channels. Finally P_{11} and P_{12} compute, respectively, $f_1(f_1(v) + f_2(v))$ and $f_2(f_1(v) + f_2(v))$, storing these values in y_1 and y_2.

Observe that the resulting refinements satisfy their desired specifications because compositional proof rules do not use the program text of the components, but operate on their specifications. This is used, e.g., in establishing that correctness of P follows from the specifications of P_0 and $\hat{P}$, although the implementation of P_0 and $\hat{P}$ is not yet known. Check this.

Now all these processes can be implemented independently according to their specifications.

7.8   Prove Lemma 7.25.

7.9   Give detailed proofs for Example 7.39.

7.10   Give detailed proofs for Example 7.40.

7.11   Apply the assumption-commitment formalism to Example 7.12, i.e., the aim is to prove that

$$\langle h\downarrow\{A,B,C\} = \langle\rangle, h\downarrow\{A,B,C\} \preceq \langle(A,0),(B,1),(C,2)\rangle\rangle : \atop \{true\} \ P_1\|P_2\|P_3 \ \{x=1 \wedge y=2 \wedge z=0\}. \tag{E7.1}$$

For this task we want to use the correctness formulae

$$\langle A_1, C_1\rangle : \{h\downarrow\{A,B\} = \langle\rangle\} \ P_1 \ \{true\}$$
$$\langle A_2, C_2\rangle : \{h\downarrow\{B,C\} = \langle\rangle\} \ P_2 \ \{x=1\}$$
$$\langle A_3, C_3\rangle : \{h\downarrow\{A,C\} = \langle\rangle\} \ P_3 \ \{y=2 \wedge z=0\}$$

(a) Give A_1, C_1, A_2, C_2, A_3 and C_3 such that

1. the three above formulae are valid, and

2. formula E7.1 can be derived from these formulae.

(b) Give this last derivation.

7.12   Prove Theorem 7.43, i.e., soundness of the sequential composition rule for the A-C proof method.

7.13   **(Independence of the prefix-invariance axiom)** The purpose of this exercise is to prove that the prefix-invariance axiom is independent of the other axioms and proof rules of the proof method given in Section 7.4. To this end we define an alternative semantics O_{alt} in which all these other axioms and rules are valid, but not the prefix-invariance axiom.

Since in Section 7.4.4 we have proved soundness of our proof method , and this proof method includes the prefix-invariance axiom, we have two semantics in one of which this axiom holds, whereas in the other one it does not hold. Had it been possible to derive the prefix-invariance axiom from the other axioms and rules of our proof method, then this would not have been the case by the soundness of our method. Consequently, this proves that the prefix-invariance axiom is independent from those other axioms and rules.

The fact that in O_{alt} the prefix-invariance axiom does not hold implies that there exists a composite system whose executions according to O_{alt} changes its initial communication history. We define this to be the case for $D!o\|E!o$, where $D, E \in CHAN$ are specially selected.

O_{alt} is defined as follows:

- $O_{alt}(C!e) \stackrel{\text{def}}{=} \{(\sigma, \sigma, (C, e(\sigma))) \mid C \in CHAN\}.$

- $O_{alt}(D!o\|E!o) \overset{\text{def}}{=} \{(\sigma,(\sigma:h \mapsto shuffle(\sigma(h))),\theta)\,|\,\text{s.t.}$
$$(\sigma,(\sigma:h \mapsto \langle\rangle),\theta{\downarrow}D) \in O_{alt}(D!o) \,\wedge$$
$$(\sigma,(\sigma:h \mapsto \langle\rangle),\theta{\downarrow}E) \in O_{alt}(E!o) \,\wedge$$
$$\theta = \theta{\downarrow}\{D,E\}\},$$

  with $shuffle(\theta)$ defined by:

  – $shuffle(\theta) \overset{\text{def}}{=} \theta$, for $length(\theta) \leq 1$, and
  – $shuffle(\langle(C_1,v_1),(C_2,v_2)\rangle \cdot \theta) \overset{\text{def}}{=}$
$$\begin{cases} \langle(C_2,v_2),(C_1,v_1)\rangle \cdot shuffle(\theta), \text{ if } (C_1 = E \wedge C_2 = D \,\vee \\ \qquad\qquad\qquad\qquad\qquad\qquad C_1 = D \wedge C_2 = E), \text{ and} \\ \langle(C_1,v_1),(C_2,v_2)\rangle \cdot shuffle(\theta), \text{ otherwise.} \end{cases}$$

- $O_{alt}(P) \overset{\text{def}}{=} \emptyset$, for all remaining composite systems.

Validity $\models \{\varphi\}P\{\psi\}$ under semantics O_{alt} is defined similarly as $\models \{\varphi\}P\{\psi\}$ under O, using O_{alt} instead of O.

  (a) Check that the prefix-invariance axiom does not hold in semantics O_{alt}.
  (b) Prove that all remaining axioms and rules are valid under semantics O_{alt}, in particular, the parallel composition rule 7.8.
  (c) Extend these results to the assumption-commitment method.

7.14 This exercise extends Exercises 2.16 and 2.17 concerning the *weakest l-condition operator* $wp_l(P,\psi)(\sigma)$ of transition diagram P w.r.t. postcondition ψ, to synchronously-communicating composite systems.

  (a) Extend the definition of $wp_l(P,\psi)$ to the semantics O_l and O from Definition 7.15.
  (b) Prove that $\{wp_l(P,\psi)\,|\,l \in L\}$ is a compositionally-inductive assertion network for $P = (L,T,s,t)$ a basic transition diagram.
  (c) Prove $\models \{wp_s(P,\psi)\}P\{\psi\}$, that $\{\varphi\}P\{\psi\}$ implies $\models \varphi \to wp_s(P,\psi)$ and $\models wp_t(P,\psi) \to \psi$, for P a basic transition diagram, and that similar results hold for an arbitrary composite system P. Consequently one could also have based the completeness proof in Section 7.4 on such weakest l-condition operators.

7.15 **(Open problem)** Extend Exercise 7.14 to the assumption-commitment method [Hol99].

  (a) In particular, define the weakest l-condition and precondition operators $wp_l(B,C,\psi)$ and $wp(B,C,\psi)$ of basic transition diagram B w.r.t. commitment C and postcondition ψ, and the weakest assumption operator $WA(B,C,\psi)$ of B w.r.t. commitment C and postcondition ψ.

(b) Prove $\models \langle WA(B,C,\psi),C \rangle : \{wp_s(B,C,\psi)\}B\{\psi\}$.

(c) Prove $\models \langle A,C \rangle : \{\varphi\}B\{\psi\} \Rightarrow$

　　1. $\models \varphi \Rightarrow wp_s(B,C,\psi)$

　　2. $\models A \Rightarrow WA(B,C,\psi)$

　　3. $\models wp_t(B,C,\psi) \rightarrow \psi$

(d) Prove that $\{wp_l(B,C,\psi) \,|\, l \in L_B\}$ is an A-C-inductive assertion network w.r.t. assumption $WA(B,C,\psi)$ and commitment C.

(e) Let $\models \langle A,C \rangle : \{\varphi\}B\{\psi\}$, for B a basic synchronous transition diagram.

Prove

$$\vdash \langle WA(B,C,\psi),C \rangle : \{wp_s(B,C,\psi)\}B\{wp_t(B,C,\psi)\}$$

and derive from this $\vdash \langle A,C \rangle : \{\varphi\}B\{\psi\}$.

7.16　**(Open problem)** Give a proof of completeness of the assumption-commitment method which is based on the notions of weakest l-condition, precondition and weakest assumption operators w.r.t. commitment C and postcondition ψ [Hol99], and extends Exercise 7.15.

8

Compositional Proof Methods: Shared-Variable Concurrency

8.1 Introduction and Overview

In this chapter we investigate the semantic foundations of compositional proof methods for concurrent transition diagrams which communicate by shared variables.

After in Section 8.2 briefly recalling the basic definitions of the compositional semantics of shared-variable concurrency from Chapter 3, we focus in Section 8.3 on a simple compositional proof method for top-level concurrency, and explore how to characterise closed systems.

The main point of this chapter is the presentation in Section 8.4 of the rely-guarantee method, of which we prove soundness and semantic completeness.

The R-G method is presented on the basis of auxiliary variables rather than logical variables, because auxiliary variables allow greater flexibility in proofs. For, although a presentation based on logical variables is equally well possible, these record the full communication history, whereas auxiliary variables in general only record an abstraction of this history.

Both proof methods are based on the notion of *compositionally-inductive assertion networks* for reasoning about the sequential parts of transition diagrams, using compositional proof rules for deducing properties of the whole system. Whereas in the proof method for top-level shared-variable concurrency we incorporate in the local verification conditions all possible interleavings by an arbitrary environment, in the R-G-based proof method only those environmental state changes are considered which satisfy the *rely* condition. The latter set-up immediately leads to the question whether the *rely* condition is transitive. And indeed, of the two compositional semantics for shared-variable concurrency which are investigated, reactive sequence and Aczel-trace semantics [Acz83], we prove that reactive sequences only provide a sound model for the R-G method when the *rely* condition is transitive.

438

In order to illustrate the R-G method we prove correctness of a small mutual-exclusion algorithm due to Dijkstra in Section 8.4.3, and of a concurrent program for finding the first positive number in an integer array.

Related work is discussed in Section 8.5, after which a list of exercises is provided.

8.2 Concurrent Transition Diagrams

We use the following definition of a basic transition diagram.[1]

Definition 8.1 A basic transition diagram is a quadruple (L, T, s, t), where L is a finite set of locations l, T is a finite set of transitions $(l, b \to f, l')$, and s and t are the entry and exit locations, respectively, which are different ($s \neq t$). There are no outgoing transitions starting in t. □

For the formal definition of reactive sequence semantics as introduced in, e.g., [dBKPR91], we recall the definition of the transition relation from Definition 3.31.

Definition 8.2 For a given basic transition diagram $P \equiv (L, T, s, t)$,

$$l \xrightarrow{\langle \sigma, \sigma' \rangle} l'$$

denotes a transition of P when for some $(l, b \to f, l') \in T$ one has that $\sigma \models b$ and $\sigma' = f(\sigma)$.

The following axiom and rule allow us to compute the reflexive transitive closure of this transition relation:

$$l \xrightarrow{\varepsilon} l \quad \text{and} \quad \frac{l \xrightarrow{w} l', l' \xrightarrow{w'} l''}{l \xrightarrow{w \cdot w'} l''},$$

where ε denotes the empty sequence, and "$\cdot$" the operation of concatenation of sequences. □

Given a basic transition diagram P, $l \xrightarrow{w} l'$ thus indicates that, starting at l, execution of P can generate the sequence of computation steps w arriving at l'. Such a sequence w is called a *reactive sequence*. A reactive sequence $w = \langle \sigma_1, \sigma_1' \rangle \langle \sigma_2, \sigma_2' \rangle \cdots \langle \sigma_n, \sigma_n' \rangle$ is called a *connected* sequence if for all $i = 1, \ldots, n - 1$ we have that $\sigma_i' = \sigma_{i+1}$. A 'gap' $\langle \sigma_i', \sigma_{i+1} \rangle$ between two consecutive computation steps $\langle \sigma_i, \sigma_i' \rangle$ and $\langle \sigma_{i+1}, \sigma_{i+1}' \rangle$ in a reactive sequence

---

[1] In order to simplify this chapter's presentation, we have slightly changed Definition 2.2 of a transition diagram by stipulating s and t to be different; this implies that one-point transition diagrams are not considered in this chapter.

represents the state-transformation induced by the (concurrent) environment. As a consequence, reactive sequences describe *open* systems. Note that such a gap abstracts from the *granularity* of the environment, i.e., the actual number of atomic computation steps performed by the environment which transform σ'_i into σ_{i+1}.

The function $head(w)$ extracts the first state pair in a nonempty reactive sequence, i.e., $head(\langle \sigma, \sigma' \rangle \cdot w') \stackrel{\text{def}}{=} \langle \sigma, \sigma' \rangle$. Analogously, we define $tail(w)$ to retrieve the last state pair of a nonempty reactive sequence w. For a nonempty reactive sequence w, the function $first(w)$ extracts the first state of $head(w)$, i.e., $first(\langle \sigma, \sigma' \rangle \cdot w') \stackrel{\text{def}}{=} \sigma$ and $last(w)$ is used to access the last state of the sequence, i.e., $last(w' \cdot \langle \sigma, \sigma' \rangle) \stackrel{\text{def}}{=} \sigma'$.

Formally, the reactive-sequence semantics of open (basic) transition diagrams is defined recursively below.

Definition 8.3 For a basic transition diagram $P \equiv (L, T, s, t)$, $l \in L$ we define

$$\mathcal{R}_l[\![P]\!] \stackrel{\text{def}}{=} \{ w \mid s \xrightarrow{w} l \}.$$

Let $l \equiv \langle l_1, \ldots, l_n \rangle$ be a location of $P \equiv P_1 \| \ldots \| P_n$, then

$$\mathcal{R}_l[\![P]\!] \stackrel{\text{def}}{=} \mathcal{R}_{l_1}[\![P_1]\!] \, \tilde{\|} \ldots \tilde{\|} \mathcal{R}_{l_n}[\![P_n]\!],$$

where $\tilde{\|}$ denotes the operation of interleaving. $\qquad\qquad\Box$

8.3 A Compositional Proof Method: Top-level Shared-Variable Concurrency

As the stepping stone for our presentation of the compositional rely-guarantee method for developing open shared-variable systems in the next section, we, as we shall see, reformulate the compositional approach from Section 3.5.4. This approach was used to prove (semantic) completeness of the method of Owicki & Gries for closed systems consisting of the parallel composition of basic transition diagrams – so-called top-level shared-variable concurrency. As a result we become acquainted with a compositional reformulation of the notion of inductive assertion networks for open systems, and a much needed characterisation of closed systems used for converting properties of open systems to closed ones without which only a little can be expressed about shared-variable concurrency. An example will illustrate this point.

That the method of Owicki & Gries only works for closed systems is simple to see. It operates in two stages:

- providing a sound local sequential proof outline for every process in a network,
- proving that each predicate occurring in that proof outline is invariant under the actions of the other processes in that network.

Consequently, this method characterises such an environment only in terms of *concretely known processes* , and is therefore only appropriate for characterising closed systems. That is, the method of Owicki & Gries provides no abstract characterisation of an environmental action.

Next, recall that in the completeness proof of this method we use two kinds of semantics:

- reactive sequences, for characterising the semantics of shared-variable processes compositionally, and
- process-indexed state sequences, which are called histories.

The latter are needed to define strongest postcondition operators, in terms of which the local assertion networks are formulated (which turn out to be compositionally-inductive, as we shall see). The completeness proof of the proof method of Owicki & Gries in Section 3.5.4 shows that for these local assertion networks the requirement of interference freedom is trivially satisfied, essentially because the predicates of these networks specify the meaning of the component in terms of its interactions with an *arbitrary* concurrent environment. We will show how one can obtain a compositional proof method from this observation by incorporating in the local verification conditions *all possible interleavings* by an arbitrary environment. The local transitions themselves will be described in this section in terms of a distinguished logical history variable h which records a sequence of process-indexed states representing the individual contributions of the processes to the overall computation. That is, we use the logical variable h for the same task for which we introduced h as an auxiliary variable in the completeness proof of Section 3.5.4. Observe that h is not a program variable; it is used in assertions to allow reasoning about the global computation.

We formally define *histories*, i.e., sequences of process-indexed states of the form (i, σ), as follows.

Definition 8.4 Given a set of process indices I, a history θ is a sequence of indexed states (i, σ), $i \in I$, indicating that the i-th component is active in state σ, and responsible for the change of state from σ. □

Next we recall the definition of the projection operator which, given some set of (indices of) sequential components and a final state, transforms a history into a reactive sequence consisting of all the computation steps involving the given components.

Definition 8.5 We introduce $\theta[I](\sigma)$ to denote the reactive sequence which records the transitions of processes with indices from the set I:

$$\varepsilon[I](\sigma) \stackrel{\text{def}}{=} \varepsilon,$$

$$(\theta \cdot (i, \sigma'))[I](\sigma) \stackrel{\text{def}}{=} \begin{cases} \theta[I](\sigma') \cdot \langle \sigma', \sigma \rangle, & \text{if } i \in I, \\ \theta[I](\sigma'), & \text{otherwise}, \end{cases}$$

where ε expresses the *empty* reactive sequence. $\square$

When the index set I contains all indices occurring in θ, then $\theta[I](\sigma)$ is connected. The pair $\langle \sigma, \theta \rangle$ itself represents a connected sequence with additional information about the identity of the active components: Let $\theta = (i_0, \sigma_0) \cdot \ldots \cdot (i_k, \sigma_k) \cdot \ldots \cdot (i_n, \sigma_n)$; then process i_m, $1 \leq m \leq n$, transforms state σ_m into σ_{m+1}, where $\sigma_{n+1} = \sigma$.

Note that the projection operation above is different from the usual operation of projection $\theta \downarrow I$ which filters (indexed states (j, σ) for $j \notin I$ from) sequence θ. Operation $\theta \downarrow I$ is here applied to histories:

$$\varepsilon \downarrow I \stackrel{\text{def}}{=} \varepsilon,$$

$$((i, \sigma) \cdot \theta) \downarrow I \stackrel{\text{def}}{=} \begin{cases} (i, \sigma) \cdot (\theta \downarrow I), & \text{if } i \in I, \\ \theta \downarrow I, & \text{otherwise}. \end{cases}$$

Given a parallel program $P \equiv P_1 \parallel \cdots \parallel P_n$ with $P_1, \ldots, P_n$ basic transition diagrams, we identify the set of indices $\{1, \ldots, n\}$ with the program P itself and the index i with the component P_i; correspondingly one has notation $\theta[P](\sigma)$ for $\theta[\{1, \ldots, n\}](\sigma)$ and $\theta[P_i](\sigma)$ for $\theta[\{i\}](\sigma)$.

Definition 8.6 (Compositional local verification conditions) Let $P \equiv P_1 \parallel \cdots \parallel P_n$. A local assertion network Q_i for P_i is called *compositionally-inductive* if:

- Every transition $l_i \xrightarrow{a} l_i'$ of P_i with $a \equiv b \rightarrow f$ satisfies the following verification condition:

$$\models Q_{l_i} \wedge b \rightarrow Q_{l_i'} \circ g,$$

where $g(\sigma) \stackrel{\text{def}}{=} (f(\sigma) : h \mapsto \sigma(h) \cdot (i, \sigma))$.
- For every location l_i of P_i, we have:

$$\models Q_{l_i} \rightarrow Q_{l_i} \circ f,$$

where $f(\sigma) \stackrel{\text{def}}{=} \{\sigma' \mid \sigma'(h)[P_i](\sigma') = \sigma(h)[P_i](\sigma)\}$.

Note that this introduces a nondeterministic state transformation. For $f : \Sigma \rightarrow 2^{\Sigma}$ we define $\sigma \models \varphi \circ f$, if for all $\sigma' \in f(\sigma)$ we have that $\sigma' \models \varphi$. Observe that f describes the possible interference by the environment at node l_i.

If Q_i is a compositionally-inductive assertion network for P_i, we denote this by $P_i \vdash Q_i$. $\qquad\qquad\qquad\qquad\qquad\qquad\qquad\qquad\qquad\qquad\qquad\qquad\quad\square$

The new local verification conditions guarantee that the local predicates not only specify the initial/final state behaviour of the component but also take into account *all possible interleavings*, because the second condition ensures interference freedom with respect to *any* possible parallel environment. The first verification condition corresponds to the usual local verification condition apart from the additional update to the history.

Note that according to our definition of compositionally-inductive assertion networks, it is not necessary to augment the program with assignments to auxiliary variables – instead we use the history component θ for the purpose of recording the computation steps of a program, and let by convention the logical variable h refer to this component within assertions.

We now define validity of a correctness formula $\{\varphi\} P \{\psi\}$:

Definition 8.7 A partial correctness formula is valid, denoted by

$$\models \{\varphi\} P \{\psi\},$$

if for all $w \in \mathcal{R}_I [\![P]\!]$, where $w = \langle \sigma_0, \sigma'_0 \rangle \ldots \langle \sigma_n, \sigma'_n \rangle$, we have that, if $(\sigma_0 : h \mapsto \varepsilon) \models \varphi$, then $(\sigma'_n : h \mapsto \theta) \models \psi$ for all θ such that $\theta[P]\sigma'_n = w$. $\quad\square$

These concepts lead to the following proof rules.

Rule 8.1 (Basic diagram) For $P \equiv (L, T, s, t)$ a basic synchronous transition diagram, we have the following main rule:

$$\frac{P \vdash Q}{\{Q_s\} P \{Q_t\}}.$$

Now we can formulate the following compositional proof rule for parallel programs.

Rule 8.2 (Parallel composition)

$$\frac{\{\varphi_i\} P_i \{\psi_i\}, \ i = 1, \ldots, n}{\{\bigwedge_{i=1}^{n} \varphi_i\} P_1 \| \ldots \| P_n \{\bigwedge_{i=1}^{n} \psi_i\}}.$$

Additionally, we have the following initialisation rule.

Rule 8.3 (Initialisation)

$$\frac{\{\varphi \wedge h = \varepsilon\} \, P \, \{\psi\}}{\{\varphi\} \, P \, \{\psi\}}.$$

As usual, derivability of a correctness formula $\{\varphi\} \, P \, \{\psi\}$, using the above proof method, is denoted by

$$\vdash \{\varphi\} \, P \, \{\psi\}.$$

The above approach raises problems due to its generality. Implicitly we assume that for every process there is some environment that possibly alters all variables randomly. And this is true also for the parallel composition of such processes! Consequently, very few valid partial correctness formulae exist which state global claims about the values of shared variables in such networks, because these values can be changed arbitrarily by the environment. The following example illustrates the consequences of this approach. But first we need the following definition:

Definition 8.8 (First state upon which P operates) Define $Init(\theta, P)(\sigma)$ as follows, for θ a history:

$$Init(\theta, P)(\sigma) \stackrel{\text{def}}{=} \begin{cases} \sigma, & \text{if } \theta[P]\sigma = \varepsilon, \\ first(\theta[P]\sigma), & \text{otherwise.} \end{cases} \qquad \square$$

Example 8.9 Consider the following *closed* program $P \equiv P_1 \| P_2$.

We would like to prove

$$\{x = z\} \, P_1 \| \, P_2 \, \{x = z + 2\},$$

using only (projections of) the history variable h. The crucial point in this proof is the assumption that $P_1 \| P_2$ is a *closed* system. We have the following compositionally inductive assertion network for P_i, $i \in \{1, 2\}$:

$$Q_{s_i} \stackrel{\text{def}}{=} \{(\sigma : h \mapsto \theta) \mid \theta[P_i]\sigma = \varepsilon,$$
$$Q_{t_i} \stackrel{\text{def}}{=} \{(\sigma : h \mapsto \theta) \mid \theta[P_i]\sigma = \langle \sigma_i, (\sigma_i : x \mapsto \sigma_i(x) + 1) \rangle$$
$$\wedge \, \sigma_i = Init(\theta, P_i)(\sigma)\}.$$

By the basic rule we derive $\vdash \{Q_{s_i}\} \, P_i \, \{Q_{t_i}\}$ and by the parallel composition rule we derive for $P_1 \| P_2$

$$\vdash \{Q_{s_1} \wedge Q_{s_2}\} \, P_1 \| P_2 \, \{Q_{t_1} \wedge Q_{t_2}\}.$$

The postcondition $Q_{J_1} \wedge Q_{J_2}$ now implies

$$\{(\sigma : h \mapsto \theta) \mid \theta[P]\sigma = \langle \sigma_1, (\sigma_1 : x \mapsto \sigma_1(x) + 1)\rangle \cdot \langle \sigma_2, (\sigma_2 : x \mapsto \sigma_2(x) + 1)\rangle$$
$$\vee \theta[P]\sigma = \langle \sigma_2, (\sigma_2 : x \mapsto \sigma_2(x) + 1)\rangle \cdot \langle \sigma_1, (\sigma_1 : x \mapsto \sigma_1(x) + 1)\rangle\},$$

where σ_i is the first state of the state pair given by $\theta[P_i]\sigma$, $i = 1, 2$. That is, the postcondition $Q_{J_1} \wedge Q_{J_2}$ implies that the program P has increased the value of x twice by one – that is all. This does not establish $x = z + 2$ since an external agent might also have set x to 666. That is, the specification of $P_1 \| P_2$ does not yet reflect that $P_1 \| P_2$ is a closed system. $\square$

The limiting factor in this compositional approach is the possibility of interference by other processes which may alter the value of x arbitrarily. Although we developed the above rule from the completeness proof for the Owicki & Gries method, the interpretation of $P_1 \| \dots \| P_n$ has changed. Whereas in Chapter 3 this parallel system was assumed to be closed, this assumption has been dropped in the compositional approach above.

The additional step required is *to restrict $P_1 \| \dots \| P_n$ to be closed*, i.e., to ensure that no other process is interfering during its execution. In this case we know that the value of $\theta[P]\sigma$ after termination is a connected sequence, starting in the initial state and ending in the final state. This is made explicit by defining $\langle P_1 \| \dots \| P_n \rangle$ as the closed version of the $P_1 \| \dots \| P_n$ program, by stipulating that the reactive sequences in the meaning of $\langle P_1 \| \dots \| P_n \rangle$ are connected, and by formulating a separate closure rule.

Definition 8.10

$$\mathcal{R}[\![\langle P \rangle]\!] \stackrel{\text{def}}{=} \{w \in \mathcal{R}[\![P]\!] \mid w \text{ is a connected reactive sequence}\}. \qquad \square$$

Rule 8.4 (Closure rule) Let $var(P) \subseteq \bar{x}$, and $\bar{z}$ be a list of fresh logical variables of the same length as $\bar{x}$.

$$\frac{\{\varphi\}\, P\, \{\psi\}}{\{\varphi \wedge \bar{x} = \bar{z}\}\, \langle P \rangle\, \{\psi \wedge h \downarrow P = h \wedge Init(h, P)(\bar{x}) = \bar{z}\}}.$$

The assertion $h \downarrow P = h$ expresses that only the processes belonging to P have contributed to the computation, i.e., that the reactive sequence which is extracted out of h is connected. Note that for σ such that $\sigma \models h \downarrow P = h$ we do not only have that $\sigma(h)[P]\sigma$ is connected, but also that for a nonempty h we have that $last(\sigma(h)[P]\sigma) = \sigma$.

Example 8.11 (Example 8.9 continued) We continue our example by applying this rule, and deduce from the postcondition that

$$(\sigma : h \mapsto \theta) \models Q_{t_1} \wedge Q_{t_2} \wedge h \downarrow P = h \wedge \mathit{Init}(h, P)(x) = z$$

$$\Leftrightarrow$$

$$(\ \theta[P]\sigma = \langle \sigma_1, \sigma_2 \rangle \cdot \langle \sigma_2, \sigma \rangle$$
$$\wedge \sigma_2 = (\sigma_1 : x \mapsto \sigma_1(x) + 1) \wedge \sigma_1(x) = \sigma(z) \wedge \sigma = (\sigma_2 : x \mapsto \sigma_2(x) + 1))$$
$$\vee (\theta[P]\sigma = \langle \sigma_2, \sigma_1 \rangle \cdot \langle \sigma_1, \sigma \rangle$$
$$\wedge \sigma_1 = (\sigma_2 : x \mapsto \sigma_2(x) + 1) \wedge \sigma_2(x) = \sigma(z) \wedge \sigma = (\sigma_1 : x \mapsto \sigma_1(x) + 1)).$$

From this we obtain that

$$(\sigma : h \mapsto \theta) \models Q_{t_1} \wedge Q_{t_2} \wedge h \downarrow P = h \wedge \mathit{Init}(h, P)(x) = z$$

implies that $\sigma(x) = \sigma(z) + 2$, i.e., we have established

$$\vdash \{x = z\} \ \langle P_1 \| P_2 \rangle \ \{x = z + 2\}. \qquad \qquad \square$$

Together with this closure rule 8.4, our proof method consisting of the basic rule 8.1, the parallel composition rule 8.2, the initialisation rule 8.3, and the usual consequence, initialisation and conjunction rules is capable of generating all valid correctness formulae for closed systems, i.e., all correctness formulae we can derive using the method of Owicki & Gries. Note that this completeness result follows in a straightforward manner since the local networks defined in the completeness proof of the Owicki & Gries proof method are easily seen to satisfy the new local verification conditions.

Now we have two different approaches to the compositional verification of shared-variable concurrency. Using the above closure rule we have obtained a compositional method to prove correctness of programs which are composed in parallel in top-level fashion, allowing for more independence of local proofs, but which applies only to the parallel composition of processes to closed systems. I.e., in the end one imposes that the environment does not change the program variables.

Within these limits we can extend the above proof method to nested concurrency, where a program P is defined inductively to be either a basic transition diagram, the sequential composition $P_1; P_2$ of programs P_1 and P_2, or the parallel composition $P_1 \| P_2$ of programs P_1 and P_2. Again in order to allow for substantial claims in correctness formulae, the final program has to be *closed* in that approach; this is the subject of an exercise.

Faced with these two extremes of allowing the environment to do anything whatsoever or nothing, we prefer instead an approach which allows us to use explicitly formulated assumptions about the environment at any stage of the verification process, resulting in greater clarity and flexibility. Such an approach is provided by the rely-guarantee formalism in the next section.

8.4 The Rely-Guarantee Method

The approach which is followed in this section is based again on the inductive-assertion method. We introduce the concept of R-G-inductive assertion networks for reasoning about transition diagrams which constitute a concurrent system, and present compositional proof rules for deducing properties of such systems. Since validity of a rely-guarantee formula depends not only on the initial-final state relation of a process, we develop a so-called *Aczel semantics* for characterising the meaning of such a formula by prefix-closed sets of computations of a process in Section 8.4.1. Section 8.4.2 presents the proof method with respect to this Aczel semantics. Applications of this proof method are given in Section 8.4.3, and soundness and completeness proofs for the rely-guarantee-based method are given in Sections 8.4.4 and 8.4.5. Section 8.4 ends with a discussion on the relationship between reactive-sequence semantics and Aczel semantics.

Note that in the previous section we employed a logical history variable h as our only means of recording communication between processes. The example given there showed that this requires coding all relevant observable behaviour into this variable. For ease of proofs we use in the remainder of this chapter an auxiliary variable h rather than a logical history. This auxiliary variable is introduced only for reasoning about parallel composition and for proving completeness of the parallel composition rule.

8.4.1 Semantics

In the rely-guarantee formalism we have to characterise not only the initial-final state behaviour but also the effect of single transitions of the process or the environment. This is accomplished by the use of *action predicates*, called *rely* and *guar*, which denote sets of state pairs reflecting the effect of a state transformation (or action) on a state, i.e., *rely* and *guar* denote subsets of $\Sigma \times \Sigma$. When we interpret action predicates we use as the convention that unprimed variables x refer to the program state before a transition, whereas primed variables x' refer to the state after the transition, i.e., given a pair of states $\langle \sigma, \sigma' \rangle$, the variable x in an action predicate denotes $\sigma(x)$ and the variable x' denotes $\sigma'(x)$.

Definition 8.12 For a reactive sequence $w = \langle \sigma_1, \sigma'_1 \rangle \cdots \langle \sigma_n, \sigma'_n \rangle$, and action predicate *act*, $w \models act$ indicates that $\langle \sigma_i, \sigma_i' \rangle \models act$, $i = 1, \ldots, n$, i.e., that $\langle \sigma_i, \sigma_i' \rangle$ belongs to the denotation of *act*.   □

We analyse the R-G formalism for nested concurrent programs built up from basic transition diagrams.

Definition 8.13 A *program* P is either a basic transition diagram or defined inductively as a sequential composition $P_1; P_2$ or parallel composition $P_1 \parallel P_2$ of two programs P_1 and P_2.   □

We assume a set *Id* of *process identifiers* with typical elements $i_1, i_2, \ldots$. The complement of a set of identifiers $V \subseteq Id$ is denoted by $\overline{V} \stackrel{\text{def}}{=} Id \setminus V$. With each program P we associate a set of identifiers denoted by $Lab(P)$. These sets of identifiers are necessary in the case of parallel composition, because we need to trace which contributions are made by P_1 and which by P_2. In order to differentiate between these contributions we label them by identifiers from $Lab(P_1)$ and $Lab(P_2)$, according to which process made the contribution. This explains why we introduce label sets. The idea behind this extension is that each basic transition diagram has a unique identifier. Thus computation steps of a composed system are indexed by the process identifiers of the components of this system.

Definition 8.14 The set of identifiers $Lab(P)$ of a program P is defined as follows.

For a basic transition diagram P

$$Lab(P) \stackrel{\text{def}}{=} \{i\}, \text{ for some } i \in Id.$$

For a composed program P we have

$Lab(P_1; P_2) \stackrel{\text{def}}{=} Lab(P_1) \cup Lab(P_2)$, where $Lab(P_1) \cap Lab(P_2) = \emptyset$, and
$Lab(P_1 \parallel P_2) \stackrel{\text{def}}{=} Lab(P_1) \cup Lab(P_2)$, where $Lab(P_1) \cap Lab(P_2) = \emptyset$.   □

An Aczel-trace is a connected sequence of process-indexed state pairs. It can thus be seen as the extension of connected reactive sequences in which every atomic action contains as additional information the identifier of the process which executed that action.

Definition 8.15 A process-indexed state pair is a triple $\langle \sigma, i, \sigma' \rangle \in \Sigma \times Id \times \Sigma$. An Aczel-trace π is a *nonempty* connected sequence of process-indexed state pairs.

For an Aczel-trace π we define $first(\pi)$ and $last(\pi)$ by the first and last state of the sequence, respectively: $first(\langle \sigma, i, \sigma' \rangle) \stackrel{\text{def}}{=} \sigma$ and $last(\langle \sigma, i, \sigma' \rangle) \stackrel{\text{def}}{=} \sigma'$, and

$first(\langle\sigma,i,\sigma'\rangle\cdot\pi')\stackrel{\text{def}}{=}\sigma$ and $last(\pi'\cdot\langle\sigma,i,\sigma'\rangle)\stackrel{\text{def}}{=}\sigma'$. The reason for the requirement that an Aczel-trace is always nonempty, is that it simplifies our central definition, that of validity of an R-G correctness formula (Definition 8.23). $\square$

For the formal definition of process-indexed state-pair-sequence semantics we introduce the following representation of a transition step.

Definition 8.16 (Transition step) For a given basic transition diagram $P \equiv (L,T,s,t)$, we denote by $\langle l;\sigma\rangle \to \langle l';\sigma'\rangle$ a transition step of P, when for $l,l' \in L$ and $(l,b \to f,l') \in T$ one has that $\sigma \models b$ and $\sigma' = f(\sigma)$. $\square$

Definition 8.17 (Aczel-traces) For a given basic transition diagram $P \equiv (L, T,s,t)$, each process transition is recorded by its start state, end state *and process index*:

$$l \stackrel{\langle\sigma,i,\sigma'\rangle}{\longrightarrow} l' \text{ if } \langle l;\sigma\rangle \to \langle l';\sigma'\rangle, \text{ and } Lab(P) = \{i\}.$$

At any point the environment (consisting of other processes) is allowed to perform environmental transitions:

$$l \stackrel{\langle\sigma,j,\sigma'\rangle}{\longrightarrow} l, \text{ if } j \notin Lab(P).$$

The following rule allows us to compute the transitive closure:

$$\frac{l \stackrel{\pi}{\to} l', l' \stackrel{\pi'}{\to} l''}{l \stackrel{\pi\cdot\pi'}{\to} l''} \text{ if } last(\pi) = first(\pi'),$$

where π and π' denote nonempty sequences of process-indexed state pairs, called *Aczel-traces*. The requirement $last(\pi) = first(\pi')$ ensures that we have connected sequences, since the environmental transitions are also included. $\square$

Definition 8.18 For a basic transition diagram $P \equiv (L,T,s,t)$, and $l \in L$ we define

$$\mathcal{Acz}_l [\![P]\!] \stackrel{\text{def}}{=} \{\pi \,|\, s \stackrel{\pi}{\to} l\}. \qquad \square$$

The rely-guarantee paradigm aims at specifying both terminating *and nonterminating* computations in a compositional style.

We distinguish sequences which are *terminated* w.r.t. the executing process by ending them with the $\sqrt{}$ symbol. *Computations* are either Aczel-traces or Aczel-traces followed by a $\sqrt{}$ symbol. Therefore, if a computation π contains a $\sqrt{}$, it is of the form $\pi'\sqrt{}$ with π' an Aczel-trace containing no $\sqrt{}$ symbol. We extend the definition of $last(\pi)$ by the clause $last(\pi\sqrt{}) \stackrel{\text{def}}{=} last(\pi)$.

We concatenate two computations sequentially if the first computation is a terminated one; this condition is our motivation for introducing the $\sqrt{}$ symbol. Parallel composition of computations is defined by a modified intersection operator, to capture the characterisation of termination correctly; this operator is associative and commutative.

Definition 8.19 Let X and Y denote sets of computations.

$$X;Y \stackrel{\text{def}}{=} \{\pi \mid \pi \in X \wedge \pi \neq \pi'\sqrt{}\} \cup \{\pi \cdot \pi' \mid \pi\sqrt{} \in X \wedge \pi' \in Y\}$$

$$X \bar{\cap} Y \stackrel{\text{def}}{=} \{\pi \mid \pi \in X \wedge \pi \in Y\} \cup \{\pi \mid \pi\sqrt{} \in X \wedge \pi \in Y\}$$
$$\cup \{\pi \mid \pi \in X \wedge \pi\sqrt{} \in Y\} \cup \{\pi\sqrt{} \mid \pi\sqrt{} \in X \wedge \pi\sqrt{} \in Y\},$$

where π does not contain $\sqrt{}$. $\square$

Definition 8.20 (Aczel semantics) The semantics $\mathcal{A}cz[\![P]\!]$ of labelled nested transition systems $P \equiv (L,T,s,t)$ is defined by

$$\mathcal{A}cz[\![P]\!] \stackrel{\text{def}}{=} \bigcup_{l \in L} \mathcal{A}cz_l[\![P]\!] \cup \{\pi\sqrt{} \mid \pi \in \mathcal{A}cz_t[\![P]\!]\}.$$

For composed programs we have

$$\mathcal{A}cz[\![P_1;P_2]\!] \stackrel{\text{def}}{=} \mathcal{A}cz[\![P_1]\!];\mathcal{A}cz[\![P_2]\!],$$

and

$$\mathcal{A}cz[\![P_1\|P_2]\!] \stackrel{\text{def}}{=} \mathcal{A}cz[\![P_1]\!] \bar{\cap} \mathcal{A}cz[\![P_2]\!]. \qquad \square$$

Observe that only sequences corresponding to terminated computations are marked with $\sqrt{}$, i.e., for basic transition diagrams P we only mark sequences $\pi \in \mathcal{A}cz_t[\![P]\!]$. Also observe that in the definition of $\mathcal{A}cz[\![P_1;P_2]\!]$ only terminated sequences from P_1 are concatenated with sequences from P_2. Finally observe that only when *both* P_1 and P_2 have reached their exit locations, are the resulting sequences of $P_1\|P_2$ marked with $\sqrt{}$.

The semantics $\mathcal{A}cz[\![P]\!]$ contains all the finite nonempty prefixes of all the computations of P, including those of *nonterminating* computations. We call this property *prefix closure* of $\mathcal{A}cz[\![P]\!]$, where it is understood that there is no such thing as an empty Aczel-trace. These prefixes are needed for defining validity of R-G correctness formulae in the next section. This can be understood by recalling from Section 6.3 that a process P satisfies (R,G) provided P's environment must violate R *before* P can violate G, i.e., *at any stage of an on-going computation P*'s actions should satisfy *G as long as R remains satisfied by P's environment*. This is mathematically expressed by requiring (R, G) to be satisfied by all nonempty prefixes of a computation of P.

We define the following projection operation of Aczel-traces to reactive sequences.

Definition 8.21 Let $V \subseteq Id$ be a set of process identifiers.

$$\langle \sigma, i, \sigma' \rangle [V] \quad \stackrel{\text{def}}{=} \begin{cases} \varepsilon, & \text{if } i \notin V, \\ \langle \sigma, \sigma' \rangle, & \text{if } i \in V. \end{cases}$$

$$(\langle \sigma, i, \sigma' \rangle \cdot \pi)[V] \quad \stackrel{\text{def}}{=} \begin{cases} \pi[V], & \text{if } i \notin V, \\ \langle \sigma, \sigma' \rangle \cdot \pi[V], & \text{if } i \in V. \end{cases}$$

$$\pi \sqrt{}[V] \quad \stackrel{\text{def}}{=} \pi[V]\sqrt{}. \qquad \qquad \square$$

This projection function is applied to extract the steps of components P, with $Lab(P) = V$, from an Aczel-trace π (which is always nonempty). Note that the result of this projection is a reactive sequence which might end with the $\sqrt{}$ symbol. We extend Definition 8.12 of the satisfaction of an action predicate *act* by a reactive sequence w to $w\sqrt{} \models act$ by defining that $w\sqrt{} \models act$ holds if $w \models act$ holds.

8.4.2 A Complete R-G Proof Method for Aczel Semantics

In this section we first give a definition of rely-guarantee correctness formulae and their validity, and then present a proof method for this type of correctness formula that is fairly standard as far as the composition rules are concerned [XdRH97]. For correctness formulae that reason about basic transition diagrams we adapt Floyd's inductive assertion network method to the additional requirements of the R-G method.

Definition 8.22 Let φ and ψ be predicates denoting sets of states, *rely* and *guar* be action predicates, and P be a program, then $\langle rely, guar \rangle : \{\varphi\} P \{\psi\}$ is called an R-G correctness formula. $\qquad \qquad \square$

Traditionally, φ and ψ impose conditions, respectively, upon the initial and final states of a computation, whereas *rely* and *guar* impose conditions, respectively, upon environmental transitions and transitions of the process itself. This is captured by the following intuitive characterisation of validity of an R-G formula:

Whenever

1) *P is invoked in an initial state which satisfies* φ, *and*
2) *at some moment during the computation of P all* past *environment transitions satisfy rely,*

then

3) *all transitions by P up to that moment satisfy guar, and*
4) *if this computation terminates, its final state satisfies* ψ.

We define validity of R-G correctness formulae as follows.

Definition 8.23 (Aczel-validity of R-G correctness formulae) We define

$$\models_A \langle rely, guar \rangle : \{\varphi\}\ P\ \{\psi\}$$

by:

> For all $\pi \in \mathcal{A}cz[\![P]\!]$, if $first(\pi) \models \varphi$ and $\pi[\overline{Lab(P)}] \models rely$
> then $\pi[Lab(P)] \models guar$, and if $\pi = \pi'\sqrt{}$, this implies that $last(\pi) \models \psi$.   □

Observe that Aczel-validity of an R-G formula $\langle rely, guar \rangle : \{\varphi\}\ P\ \{\psi\}$ implies that ψ is invariant under *rely*.

We generalise Floyd's method to the additional requirements of R-G formulae and define an R-G-inductive assertion network $Q(rely, guar)$ for $P \equiv (L, T, s, t)$, i.e., we associate with each location l of P a predicate Q_l as follows.

Definition 8.24 (R-G-inductive assertion networks) An assertion network Q is R-G-inductive for $P \equiv (L, T, s, t)$ w.r.t. *rely* and *guar* if:

- For every $(l, b \rightarrow f, l') \in T$ and state σ:
  if $\sigma \models Q_l \wedge b$ then $\langle \sigma, f(\sigma) \rangle \models guar$ and $f(\sigma) \models Q_{l'}$.
- For every $l \in L$ and states σ and σ′:
  if $\sigma \models Q_l$ and $\langle \sigma, \sigma' \rangle \models rely$ then $\sigma' \models Q_l$.

We abbreviate that Q is an R-G-inductive assertion network for P w.r.t. *rely* and *guar* by $Q(rely, guar) \vdash P$.   □

We have the following rule for deriving R-G specifications about basic transition diagrams.

Rule 8.5 (Basic diagram rule)   For $P \equiv (L, T, s, t)$:

$$\frac{Q(rely, guar) \vdash P}{\langle rely, guar \rangle : \{Q_s\}\ P\ \{Q_t\}}.$$

The rule for sequential composition is standard.

Rule 8.6 (Sequential composition rule)

$$\frac{\langle rely, guar \rangle : \{\varphi\}\, P_1\, \{\chi\}, \, \langle rely, guar \rangle : \{\chi\}\, P_2\, \{\psi\}}{\langle rely, guar \rangle : \{\varphi\}\, P_1; P_2\, \{\psi\}}.$$

Rule 8.7 (Parallel composition rule)

$$\frac{\begin{array}{c} \models (rely \vee guar_1) \rightarrow rely_2 \\ \models (rely \vee guar_2) \rightarrow rely_1 \\ \models (guar_1 \vee guar_2) \rightarrow guar \\ \langle rely_i, guar_i \rangle : \{\varphi\}\, P_i\, \{\psi_i\}, i = 1, 2 \end{array}}{\langle rely, guar \rangle : \{\varphi\}\, P_1 \| P_2\, \{\psi_1 \wedge \psi_2\}}.$$

This rule for parallel composition expresses that:

- every transition of P_i (which is characterised by $guar_i$) and every transition of the common environment of P_1 and P_2 (characterised by $rely$) is seen by $P_j, i \neq j$ as an environmental transition which has to satisfy $rely_j$,
- every transition by P_1 or P_2 is a transition of $P_1 \| P_2$, and therefore has to satisfy $guar$, and
- since validity of $\langle rely_i, guar_i \rangle : \{\varphi\}\, P_i\, \{\psi_i\}$ implies that ψ_i is invariant under $rely_i$, $\psi_1 \wedge \psi_2$ holds upon termination of $P_1 \| P_2$; since $rely$ implies $rely_i$, $i = 1, 2$, this implies that $\psi_1 \wedge \psi_2$ is invariant under $rely$ after $P_1 \| P_2$ has terminated, too.

Rule 8.8 (Consequence rule)

$$\frac{\begin{array}{c} \langle rely, guar \rangle : \{\varphi\}\, P\, \{\psi\} \\ \models \varphi_1 \rightarrow \varphi, \models \psi \rightarrow \psi_1, \\ \models rely_1 \rightarrow rely, \models guar \rightarrow guar_1 \end{array}}{\langle rely_1, guar_1 \rangle : \{\varphi_1\}\, P\, \{\psi_1\}}.$$

Completeness of the method presented here depends on the use of auxiliary variables when applying the parallel composition rule. We therefore need the following rule for deleting such variables:

Rule 8.9 (Auxiliary variables rule) Let $\bar{z}$ be a set of auxiliary variables of P'.

$$\frac{\langle rely, guar \rangle : \{\varphi\}\, P'\, \{\psi\}}{\langle rely, guar \rangle : \{\varphi\}\, P\, \{\psi\}},$$

provided *guar* and ψ do not involve $\bar{z}$, and P is obtained from P' by restricting the state transformations of P' to all variables of P excluding the auxiliary variable set $\bar{z}$. More precisely, let f be a state transformation of P' such that $f = g \circ h$, where g does not involve $\bar{z}$ and the write variables of h are among $\bar{z}$, then g is the corresponding state transformation of P.

Rule 8.10 (Initialisation rule)

$$\frac{\langle rely, guar \rangle : \{\varphi\}\, P\, \{\psi\}}{\langle rely \circ g, guar \rangle : \{\varphi \circ f\}\, P\, \{\psi\}},$$

where f is a state function such that its write variables constitute a set of auxiliary variables for P which neither occur in *guar* nor in ψ, and g is a function over state pairs $\langle \sigma, \sigma' \rangle$, defined below:

$$g(\langle \sigma, \sigma' \rangle) \stackrel{\text{def}}{=} \langle g_1(\langle \sigma, \sigma' \rangle), g_2(\langle \sigma, \sigma' \rangle) \rangle,$$

with g_1 and g_2 functions from state pairs to states such that their write variables constitute a set of auxiliary variables for P which do neither occur in *guar* nor in ψ.

Derivability of an R-G formula $\langle rely, guar \rangle : \{\varphi\}\, P\, \{\psi\}$ within this proof method is expressed by

$$\vdash \langle rely, guar \rangle : \{\varphi\}\, P\, \{\psi\}.$$

Finally, how does one reason about closed programs? This is done by requiring *rely* to be the diagonal relation, i.e., the graph of the identity function on states, and thus requiring the projection of the computation at hand onto the labels of such programs to be a connected reactive sequence. For this allows the environment only to perform stuttering steps [dBKPR91, XH91, Bro93a, Lam94a, Bro96] which do not affect the state. We bring in these stuttering steps here to allow a later discussion on the abstractness of semantics, with the idea that for any system there is always some acting, but not influencing, environment (see Definition 8.48).

8.4.3 Application

As an application of the R-G method we give a compositional proof of the mutual exclusion property of the program discussed in Example 3.19 (which is due to Edsger W. Dijkstra [Dij65b]).

Example 8.25 We want to establish that $P_1 \| P_2$, with P_i as in Figure 8.1, satisfies the mutual exclusion property.

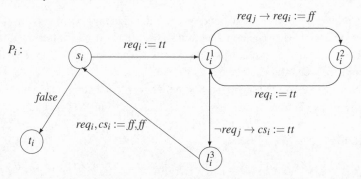

Fig. 8.1. Dijkstra's mutual exclusion algorithm.

An analysis of the Owicki-Gries-style proof of Section 3.5.2 reveals the following observations.

In the assertions Q_i of P_i the clause $cs_j \rightarrow req_j$ is used as an invariant that is not influenced by any transition of P_i, while $cs_i \rightarrow req_i$ can be seen as an invariant guaranteed by P_i.

Our next observation is that in the rely-guarantee method the interface is expressed in terms of action predicates rather than by state predicates as used in the method of Owicki & Gries.

In order to represent the transitions of each process adequately, we choose

$$G_i \stackrel{\text{def}}{=} \quad \neg(cs_1 \land cs_2) \land \neg(cs'_1 \land cs'_2)$$
$$\land\, (cs_i \rightarrow req_i) \land (cs'_i \rightarrow req'_i)$$
$$\land\, cs_j = cs'_j \land req_j = req'_j$$

as guarantee predicate for P_i, under the assumption that we can rely on the fact that

$$R_i \stackrel{\text{def}}{=} ((cs_j \rightarrow req_j) \land (cs'_j \rightarrow req'_j) \land cs_i = cs'_i \land req_i = req'_i) \lor id$$

is satisfied by all steps of the environment.

First we define an assertion network Q_i for each process P_i:

$$Q_i(s_i) \stackrel{\text{def}}{=} \quad \neg cs_i \land \neg req_i \land (cs_j \rightarrow req_j)$$
$$Q_i(l^1_i) \stackrel{\text{def}}{=} \quad \neg cs_i \land req_i \land (cs_j \rightarrow req_j)$$
$$Q_i(l^2_i) \stackrel{\text{def}}{=} \quad \neg cs_i \land \neg req_i \land (cs_j \rightarrow req_j)$$
$$Q_i(l^3_i) \stackrel{\text{def}}{=} \quad cs_i \land req_i \land (cs_j \rightarrow req_j)$$
$$Q_i(t_i) \stackrel{\text{def}}{=} \quad false\,.$$

Here we make an interesting observation: We still have to add the state information $(cs_j \rightarrow req_j)$ to each assertion to successfully prove R-G-inductiveness.

Even though the R-G method incorporates some inductive argument, this is *not* observable for basic transition diagrams! This is clear from the formulation of the R-G-inductive assertion networks where establishing *guar* is independent from the *rely* condition.

We have to prove that this assertion network is locally correct. In this case, for the rely-guarantee method, we prove that Q_i is an R-G-inductive assertion network for P_i w.r.t. R_i and G_i by establishing the following verification conditions:

- Let $\sigma \models Q_i(s_i)$, and $f_1(\sigma) \stackrel{\text{def}}{=} (\sigma : req_i \mapsto tt)$. Then $f_1(\sigma) \models Q_i(l_i^1)$ and $(\sigma, f_1(\sigma)) \models G_i$.
- Let $\sigma \models Q_i(l_i^1) \wedge req_j$, and $f_2(\sigma) \stackrel{\text{def}}{=} (\sigma : req_i \mapsto ff)$. Then $f_2(\sigma) \models Q_i(l_i^2)$ and $(\sigma, f_2(\sigma)) \models G_i$.
- Let $\sigma \models Q_i(l_i^2)$, and $f_3(\sigma) \stackrel{\text{def}}{=} (\sigma : req_i \mapsto tt)$. Then $f_3(\sigma) \models Q_i(l_i^1)$ and $(\sigma, f_3(\sigma)) \models G_i$.
- The only interesting transition is again the one leading from l_i^1 to l_i^3, entering the critical section.

  Let $\sigma \models Q_i(l_i^1) \wedge \neg req_j$, and $f_4(\sigma) \stackrel{\text{def}}{=} (\sigma : cs_i \mapsto tt)$.

  We have that $\sigma \models \neg cs_i \wedge req_i \wedge (cs_j \rightarrow req_j) \wedge \neg req_j$ which implies that $\sigma \models \neg cs_i \wedge req_i \wedge \neg cs_j \wedge \neg req_j$. Thus, $f_4(\sigma) \models cs_i \wedge req_i \wedge \neg cs_j \wedge \neg req_j$ and $f_4(\sigma) \models Q_i(l_i^3)$. From these characterisations of σ and $f_4(\sigma)$ we immediately conclude that $(\sigma, f_4(\sigma)) \models G_i$.
- Let $\sigma \models Q_i(l_i^3)$, and $f_5(\sigma) \stackrel{\text{def}}{=} (\sigma : req_i, cs_i \mapsto ff, ff)$. Obviously

$$f_5(\sigma) \models Q_i(s_i), \text{ and } (\sigma, f_5(\sigma)) \models G_i.$$

- $\models Q_i(s_i) \wedge false \rightarrow false \wedge G_i(\sigma, \sigma)$ is satisfied trivially.

Invariance of the assertion network under R_i is satisfied immediately.

By the basic diagram and consequence rules we derive for each process P_i:

$$\vdash \langle R_i, G_i \rangle : \{\neg cs_i \wedge \neg req_i \wedge \neg cs_j \wedge \neg req_j\} \, P_i \, \{false\}.$$

For these local proofs

$$\vdash \langle R_1, G_1 \rangle : \{\neg cs_1 \wedge \neg req_1 \wedge \neg cs_2 \wedge \neg req_2\} \, P_1 \, \{false\}$$

and

$$\vdash \langle R_2, G_2 \rangle : \{\neg cs_1 \wedge \neg req_1 \wedge \neg cs_2 \wedge \neg req_2\} \, P_2 \, \{false\}$$

we choose appropriate action predicates to apply the parallel composition rule. As assumption for the composed program we choose $Rely \stackrel{\text{def}}{=} id$, and for the desired guarantee the mutual exclusion property

$$Guar \stackrel{\text{def}}{=} \neg(cs_1 \wedge cs_2) \wedge \neg(cs_1' \wedge cs_2').$$

Next, we prove the remaining conditions of the parallel composition rule:

- $\models (Rely \vee G_1) \rightarrow R_2$: If $(\sigma, \sigma') \models Rely$, we have $\sigma = \sigma'$ and

$$(\sigma, \sigma) \models ((cs_1 \rightarrow req_1) \wedge (cs_1' \rightarrow req_1') \wedge cs_2 = cs_2' \wedge req_2 = req_2') \vee id.$$

Let $(\sigma, \sigma') \models G_1$. Then

$$(\sigma, \sigma') \models (cs_1 \rightarrow req_1) \wedge (cs_1' \rightarrow req_1') \wedge cs_2 = cs_2' \wedge req_2 = req_2'$$

and, hence, $(\sigma, \sigma') \models R_2$.
- $\models (Rely \vee G_2) \rightarrow R_1$ follows by symmetry considerations.
- $\models (G_1 \vee G_2) \rightarrow Guar$: This follows from the definition of G_i, $i = 1, 2$.

Now we can apply the parallel composition rule and derive

$$\vdash \langle id, \neg(cs_1 \wedge cs_2)\rangle : \{\neg cs_1 \wedge \neg req_1 \wedge \neg cs_2 \wedge \neg req_2\} \; P_1 \| P_2 \; \{false\}.$$

Using the R-G method, we have to prove two verification conditions for each transition in order to show that Q_i is R-G-inductive, i.e., 24 verification conditions, and three conditions for the application of the parallel rule. This is reduced further due to symmetry of the processes. $\qquad \square$

Example 8.26 The second example concerns the problem of finding the index of the first positive number in an integer array $A[1 \ldots n]$. The suggested solution [OG76a, Jon83, XCC94] consists of two parallel processes, one searching the odd positions, and the other one searching the even ones. A global integer variable k is used to store the index found, initially set to $n + 1$, and which is not changed if there are no positive numbers in the array. Process P_1 which searches the odd positions is given in Figure 8.3. For this process we define the following assertion network.

$$
\begin{aligned}
Q_s &\stackrel{\text{def}}{=} k \leq n + 1 \wedge (k \leq n \rightarrow A[k] > 0) \\
Q_l &\stackrel{\text{def}}{=} k \leq n + 1 \wedge (k \leq n \rightarrow A[k] > 0) \\
&\quad \wedge \forall u.((odd(u) \wedge u < i) \rightarrow A[u] \leq 0) \\
Q_t &\stackrel{\text{def}}{=} (A[k] > 0 \vee k = n + 1) \wedge \\
&\quad \forall u.((odd(u) \wedge A[u] > 0) \rightarrow k \leq u).
\end{aligned}
$$

The assumption we rely on when using process P_1 is

$$Rel_1 \stackrel{\text{def}}{=} (k' = k \vee (k' < k \wedge A[k'] > 0)) \wedge A' = A \wedge i' = i,$$

i.e., the environment (which P_2 belongs to) neither changes the values in the array A nor the counter i of P_1. The guarantee, satisfied by all transitions of P_1, is similar, since P_1 guarantees that neither the array A nor the counter j of

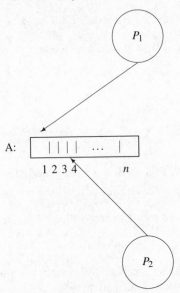

Fig. 8.2. Distributed search in array A.

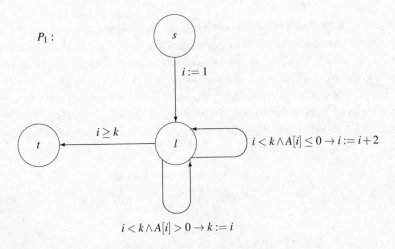

Fig. 8.3. P_1 searches the odd positions of A.

P_2 is subject to change, and that k is only decreased when it corresponds to a positive value in A.

$$Guar_1 \stackrel{\text{def}}{=} (k' = k \vee (k' < k \wedge A[k'] > 0)) \wedge A' = A \wedge j' = j.$$

We have to prove that this assertion network is R-G-inductive w.r.t. Rel_1 and $Guar_1$, i.e., we establish:

- $\sigma \models Q_s$ implies $(\sigma : i \mapsto 1) \models Q_J$ vacuously, and $\langle \sigma, (\sigma : i \mapsto 1) \rangle \models Guar_1$,
- if $\sigma \models Q_J \wedge i < k \wedge A[i] \leq 0$ we increment i by 2; consequently, $\langle \sigma, (\sigma : i \mapsto \sigma(i) + 2) \rangle \models Guar_1$. Since $A[i] \leq 0$, also $(\sigma : i \mapsto \sigma(i) + 2) \models Q_J$,
- if $\sigma \models Q_J \wedge i < k \wedge A[i] > 0$, a positive number is found and k is set to i, i.e., $k' = i$ and from $i < k$ we infer that $(k' < k \wedge A[k'] > 0)$; hence $\langle \sigma, (\sigma : k \mapsto \sigma(i)) \rangle \models Guar_1$ and $(\sigma : k \mapsto \sigma(i)) \models Q_J$, and
- we also have $\models Q_J \wedge i \geq k \rightarrow Q_t$; notice that the state transformation is the identity function and that for all σ, $\langle \sigma, \sigma \rangle \models Guar_1$.

The second condition for this assertion network to be R-G-inductive, invariance under *rely* transitions, is also satisfied.

By the basic diagram rule we thus have

$$\vdash \langle Rel_1, Guar_1 \rangle : \{Q_s\} \, P_1 \, \{Q_t\}.$$

Similarly, we prove for process P_2 which searches through the even numbers

$$\vdash \langle Guar_1, Rel_1 \rangle : \{Q_{s'}\} \, P_2 \, \{Q_{t'}\},$$

where

$$
\begin{aligned}
Q_{s'} &\overset{\text{def}}{=} k \leq n+1 \wedge (k \leq n \rightarrow A[k] > 0), \\
Q_{t'} &\overset{\text{def}}{=} (A[k] > 0 \vee k = n+1) \wedge \\
&\quad \forall u.(even(u) \wedge A[u] > 0) \rightarrow k \leq u.
\end{aligned}
$$

To these correctness formulae we apply the parallel composition rule, choosing $Rel \overset{\text{def}}{=} k' = k \wedge A' = A \wedge i' = i \wedge j' = j$ and $Guar \overset{\text{def}}{=} true$, and the consequence rule to obtain

$$\vdash \langle k' = k \wedge A' = A \wedge i' = i \wedge j' = j, true \rangle : \{k = n+1\} \, P_1 \| P_2 \, \{\psi\},$$

with $\psi \overset{\text{def}}{=} (A[k] > 0 \vee k = n+1) \wedge (\forall u.A[u] > 0 \rightarrow k \leq u)$.

We require an appropriate environment to preserve the values of k, i, j and the array A. On termination either k still equals $n+1$, indicating that no positive value was found, or k is the index of the first positive number in A. □

8.4.4 Soundness

We only give soundness proofs for the basic diagram rule and the parallel composition rule; soundness of the remaining rules is proved in a fairly standard way.

Lemma 8.27 The basic diagram rule 8.5 is sound.

Proof Let Q be an R-G-inductive assertion network for $P \equiv (L,T,s,t)$ w.r.t. *rely* and *guar*. We prove for all computations

$$\pi = \langle \sigma_1, i_1, \sigma_2 \rangle \cdots \langle \sigma_n, i_n, \sigma_{n+1} \rangle \in \mathcal{A}cz[\![P]\!],$$

if $\sigma_1 \models Q_s$ and for all environmental steps of π of the form $\langle \sigma_j, i_j, \sigma_{j+1} \rangle$ with $i_j \notin Lab(P)$ $\langle \sigma_j, \sigma_{j+1} \rangle \models rely$ holds, then

- for all program steps of π of the form $\langle \sigma_j, i_j, \sigma_{j+1} \rangle$ with $i_j \in Lab(P)$ we have that $\langle \sigma_j, \sigma_{j+1} \rangle \models guar$, and
- for all nonempty prefixes π' of π, if

$$\pi' = \langle \sigma_1, i_1, \sigma_2 \rangle \cdots \langle \sigma_j, i_j, \sigma_{j+1} \rangle \in \mathcal{A}cz_l[\![P]\!], 1 \le j \le n,$$

we have that $\sigma_{j+1} \models Q_l$.

We proceed by induction on the length of π.
$|\pi| = 1$. So we have $\pi = \langle \sigma_1, i_1, \sigma_2 \rangle$.

- Let $i_1 \in Lab(P)$. In this case $\langle \sigma_1, \sigma_2 \rangle$ is the first computation step of P, and is the result of a transition $(s, b \to f, l) \in T$ with $\sigma_1 \models b$ that reaches $l \in L$. Since $\sigma_1 \models Q_s$ and Q is an R-G-inductive assertion network, we conclude that $\langle \sigma_1, \sigma_2 \rangle \models guar$, $\pi \in \mathcal{A}cz_l[\![P]\!]$ and $\sigma_2 \models Q_l$.
- Let $i_1 \notin lab(P)$. In this case $\langle \sigma_1, \sigma_2 \rangle$ is an environment step which satisfies *rely*, and $\pi \in \mathcal{A}cz_s[\![P]\!]$. Since $\sigma_1 \models Q_s$, and since Q is an R-G-inductive assertion network, we conclude that $\sigma_2 \models Q_s$.

Now let $\pi = \pi' \cdot \langle \sigma_j, i_j, \sigma_{j+1} \rangle$. Since $\pi \in \mathcal{A}cz[\![P]\!]$ and $\mathcal{A}cz[\![P]\!]$ is prefix-closed, also $\pi' \in \mathcal{A}cz[\![P]\!]$, i.e., there is a location l such that $\pi' \in \mathcal{A}cz_l[\![P]\!]$. By the induction hypothesis we have that $\sigma_j \models Q_l$, and prove our claim by the same case distinction on i_j as above.

Consequently, all process steps satisfy *guar*. Now if π is a terminated computation (of the form $\pi'\sqrt{}$ with $last(\pi') = \sigma_{n+1}$) we know from the definition of the Aczel semantics, that $\pi' \in \mathcal{A}cz_t[\![P]\!]$. By our second claim proved above, $\sigma_{n+1} \models Q_t$. □

Theorem 8.28
The parallel composition rule 8.7 is sound.

Proof Let

$$\models (rely \lor guar_1) \to rely_2,$$
$$\models (rely \lor guar_2) \to rely_1,$$
$$\models (guar_1 \lor guar_2) \to guar,$$
$$\text{and } \models \langle rely_i, guar_i \rangle : \{\varphi\} \, P_i \, \{\psi_i\}, i = 1, 2.$$

Furthermore, let $\pi \in \mathcal{A}cz[\![P_1\|P_2]\!]$ such that we have $first(\pi) \models \varphi$ and $\pi[\overline{Lab(P_1\|P_2)}] \models rely$. By definition of $\mathcal{A}cz[\![P_1\|P_2]\!]$ we also have that $\pi \in \mathcal{A}cz[\![P_i]\!], i = 1, 2$. We prove that $\pi[Lab(P_1\|P_2)] \models guar$ by induction on the length of π. Moreover, we also need to prove that $\pi[\overline{Lab(P_i)}] \models rely_i, i = 1, 2$, in order to deduce later that $last(\pi) \models \psi_1 \land \psi_2$.

Let $\pi = \langle \sigma_1, i_1, \sigma_1' \rangle$.

- If $i_1 \in Lab(P_i)$, we have that $\pi[\overline{Lab(P_i)}] = \varepsilon \models rely_i$.

  Since $\pi \in \mathcal{A}cz[\![P_i]\!]$, we have by validity of $\langle rely_i, guar_i \rangle : \{\varphi\} \, P_i \, \{\psi_i\}$ that $\pi[Lab(P_i)] \models guar_i$. From $\models guar_1 \lor guar_2 \to guar$ we deduce that $\pi[Lab(P_i)] \models guar$ and since in this case $\pi[Lab(P_i)] = \pi[Lab(P_1\|P_2)]$, we conclude that $\pi[Lab(P_1\|P_2)] \models guar$.

  Since $\pi[Lab(P_i)] \models guar_i$ we have $\pi[Lab(P_i)] \models rely_j$ from the first two assumptions above. Now $\pi[Lab(P_i)] = \langle \sigma_1, \sigma_1' \rangle = \pi[\overline{Lab(P_j)}]$ for this particular choice of π, $\pi[\overline{Lab(P_j)}] \models rely_j$ holds, too.

- If $i_1 \in Lab(P_j)$, $i \neq j$, we have, by the same arguments as above, that $\pi[Lab(P_1\|P_2)] \models guar$, $\pi[\overline{Lab(P_i)}] \models rely_i$ and $\pi[\overline{Lab(P_j)}] \models rely_j$.

- If $i_1 \notin Lab(P_i) \cup Lab(P_j)$, we have that $\pi[Lab(P_1\|P_2)] = \varepsilon \models guar$. Since $i_1 \in \overline{Lab(P_1\|P_2)}$ and $\pi[\overline{Lab(P_1\|P_2)}] \models rely$ we also have that $\langle \sigma_1, \sigma_1' \rangle \models rely$. But as $i_1 \in \overline{Lab(P_i)}$ and $\models rely \lor guar_j \to rely_i$, we conclude that $\pi[\overline{Lab(P_i)}] \models rely_i$. By the same argument we establish $\pi[\overline{Lab(P_j)}] \models rely_j$.

Now let $\pi = \pi' \cdot \langle \sigma_n, i_n, \sigma_n' \rangle$. Since the semantics is prefix-closed, we have that $\pi' \in \mathcal{A}cz[\![P_1\|P_2]\!]$, since $\pi \in \mathcal{A}cz[\![P_1\|P_2]\!]$ is assumed. This implies $\pi' \in \mathcal{A}cz[\![P_i]\!]$ for $i = 1, 2$. Thus, we get from the induction hypothesis that $\pi'[Lab(P_1 \|P_2)] \models guar$ and $\pi'[\overline{Lab(P_i)}] \models rely_i$ for $i = 1, 2$.

- If $i_n \in Lab(P_i)$, $i \neq j$, then $\pi[\overline{Lab(P_i)}] = \pi'[\overline{Lab(P_i)}]$. Since $\pi'[\overline{Lab(P_i)}] \models rely_i$ we have by the above that also $\pi[\overline{Lab(P_i)}] \models rely_i$. Since $first(\pi) \models \varphi$, $\pi \in \mathcal{A}cz[\![P_i]\!]$, and as shown above, $\pi[\overline{Lab(P_i)}] \models rely_i$ and $\langle rely_i, guar_i \rangle : \{\varphi\} \, P_i \, \{\psi_i\}$, we have that $\pi[Lab(P_i)] \models guar_i$. Since $\models (guar_1 \lor guar_2) \to guar$, which implies that $\models guar_i \to guar$, we also have that $\pi[Lab(P_i)] \models guar$. Now $\pi'[Lab(P_1\|P_2)] \models guar$ and $\pi[Lab(P_i)] \models guar$ together imply $\pi[Lab(P_1\|P_2)] \models guar$. Since we showed above that $\pi[Lab(P_i)] \models guar_i$, we also have that $\langle \sigma_n, i_n, \sigma_n' \rangle$

$[Lab(P_i)] \models guar_i$. Because $\models (rely \lor guar_i) \to rely_j$, this implies that $\langle \sigma_n, i_n, \sigma'_n \rangle [Lab(P_i)] \models rely_j$. Since $\langle \sigma_n, i_n, \sigma'_n \rangle [Lab(P_i)] = \langle \sigma_n, \sigma'_n \rangle = \langle \sigma_n, i_n, \sigma'_n \rangle [Lab(P_j)]$, we have that $\langle \sigma_n, i_n, \sigma'_n \rangle [Lab(P_j)] \models rely_j$. As we also have $\pi'[Lab(P_j)] \models rely_j$, we can conclude that $\pi[Lab(P_j)] \models rely_j$.

- If $i_n \in Lab(P_j)$, $i \neq j$, the same proof applies with i and j interchanged.
- If $i_n \notin Lab(P_i) \cup Lab(P_j)$, $i \neq j$, then $\pi[Lab(P_1 \| P_2)] = \pi'[Lab(P_1 \| P_2)]$. Thus we can conclude from $\pi'[Lab(P_1 \| P_2)] \models guar$ that $\pi[Lab(P_1 \| P_2)] \models guar$. Since $i_n \in \overline{Lab(P_1 \| P_2)}$ and $\pi[Lab(P_1 \| P_2)] \models rely$, we also have that $\langle \sigma_n, \sigma'_n \rangle \models rely$. Since $\models (rely \lor guar_j) \to rely_i$, we can conclude that $\langle \sigma_n, \sigma'_n \rangle \models rely_i$. But as $i_n \in \overline{Lab(P_i)}$, we can conclude that $\langle \sigma_n, i_n, \sigma'_n \rangle [\overline{Lab(P_i)}] \models rely_i$. Since we have $\pi'[\overline{Lab(P_i)}] \models rely_i$, we can conclude from the above that $\pi[\overline{Lab(P_i)}] \models rely_i$. Furthermore, since $\models (rely \lor guar_i) \to rely_j$, we can also conclude from $\langle \sigma_n, \sigma'_n \rangle \models rely$ that $\langle \sigma_n, \sigma'_n \rangle \models rely_j$. But as $i_n \in \overline{Lab(P_j)}$, we can conclude that $\langle \sigma_n, i_n, \sigma'_n \rangle [\overline{Lab(P_j)}] \models rely_j$. As we have $\pi'[\overline{Lab(P_j)}] \models rely_j$, we can conclude from the above that $\pi[\overline{Lab(P_j)}] \models rely_j$.
- If additionally $\pi = \pi' \sqrt{}$, we have by the fact that the semantics is being prefix-closed that $\pi' \in \mathcal{A}cz[\![P_i]\!]$ for $i = 1, 2$. Thus, we get from the induction hypothesis that $\pi'[Lab(P_i)] \models rely_i$ for $i = 1, 2$. From Definition 8.21 we can conclude that $\pi[Lab(P_i)] \models rely_i$ for $i = 1, 2$.

Since $first(\pi) \models \varphi$, $\pi[\overline{Lab(P_i)}] \models rely_i$ for $i = 1, 2$, and $\langle rely_i, guar_i \rangle : \{\varphi\} P_i \{\psi_i\}$ is valid for $i = 1, 2$, we can conclude that $last(\pi) \models \psi_i$, $i = 1, 2$, and thus $last(\pi) \models \psi_1 \land \psi_2$. □

8.4.5 Completeness

This section presents the completeness proof for our proof method in a similar fashion as that in the previous chapter for assumption-commitment-based reasoning.

Theorem 8.29

The proof method presented in Section 8.4.2 is (semantically) complete w.r.t. the Aczel-trace semantics, i.e.,

$$\models_A \langle rely, guar \rangle : \{\varphi\} P \{\psi\} \text{ implies } \vdash \langle rely, guar \rangle : \{\varphi\} P \{\psi\}. \quad \square$$

We prove the derivability of an Aczel-valid R-G specification by induction on the structure of the program P.

Basic case

Given a valid R-G specification $\models_A \langle rely, guar \rangle : \{\varphi\} \ P \ \{\psi\}$, with $P \equiv (L, T, s, t)$ a basic transition diagram, we associate with every location l of P the *strongest postcondition* $SP_l(\varphi, rely, P)$. The resulting network we denote by $S\mathcal{P}$. Intuitively, a state σ belongs to $SP_l(\varphi, rely, P)$ if there is a computation of P *together with its environment* that reaches location l of P, starting in a state satisfying φ, such that all environment steps satisfy *rely*.

Definition 8.30 For $P \equiv (L, T, s, t)$, $l \in L$, and $\sigma \in \Sigma$ we define

$$\sigma \models SP_l(\varphi, rely, P)$$

by

$(l = s \wedge \sigma \models \varphi)$ or there exists some $\pi \in \mathcal{A}cz_l[\![P]\!]$, with $last(\pi) = \sigma$, $first(\pi) \models \varphi$ and $\pi[\overline{Lab(P)}] \models rely$. □

Note that if σ satisfies $SP_l(\varphi, rely, P)$ all states σ' which can be reached by a sequence of environmental steps, which satisfy *rely*, also satisfy $SP_l(\varphi, rely, P)$. Hence $SP_l(\varphi, rely, P)$ is invariant under *rely*.

We also need a characterisation of the computation steps of a program P. This is given by the *strongest guarantee* $SG(\varphi, rely, P)$, an action predicate describing those transitions of P which are actually executed by P in some computation, provided φ is satisfied initially, and every environmental transition satisfies *rely*.

Definition 8.31 Let P be an arbitrary program. We define

$$\langle \sigma, \sigma' \rangle \models SG(\varphi, rely, P),$$

if there exists some $\pi \in \mathcal{A}cz[\![P]\!]$ with $first(\pi) \models \varphi$ and $\pi[\overline{Lab(P)}] \models rely$, such that $\langle \sigma, \sigma' \rangle = tail(\pi[Lab(P)])$, i.e., $\langle \sigma, \sigma' \rangle$ is the last action of P in such π. □

The following basic properties of SP_l and SG follow immediately from their definitions.

Lemma 8.32 For P a basic transition diagram we have

(i) $\models_A \langle rely, SG(\varphi, rely, P) \rangle : \{\varphi\} \ P \ \{SP_t(\varphi, rely, P)\}$.

(ii) $\models_A \langle rely, guar \rangle : \{\varphi\} \ P \ \{\psi\}$ implies

    (a) $\models SP_t(\varphi, rely, P) \rightarrow \psi$.

    (b) $\models SG(\varphi, rely, P) \rightarrow guar$.

(iii) $\models \varphi \rightarrow SP_s(\varphi, rely, P)$. □

We have the following lemma.

Lemma 8.33 Given a basic transition diagram $P \equiv (L, T, s, t)$, $\mathcal{SP}$ is an R-G-inductive assertion network for P w.r.t. *rely* and $SG(\varphi, rely, P)$.

Proof Let $l \in L$ and $\sigma \models SP_l(\varphi, rely, P)$. This means that either there exists π such that $\pi \in \mathcal{A}cz_l \llbracket P \rrbracket$, $first(\pi) \models \varphi$, $\pi[\overline{Lab(P)}] \models rely$ and $last(\pi) = \sigma$, or $l = s$ and $\sigma \models \varphi$. The proof proceeds by induction on the length of π.

- Let $\sigma \models b$ and $(l, b \rightarrow f, l') \in T$. By executing $(l, b \rightarrow f, l')$ we reach l' with $\sigma' = f(\sigma)$. We have to prove that $\sigma' \models SP_{l'}(\varphi, rely, P)$ and $\langle \sigma, \sigma' \rangle \models SG(\varphi, rely, P)$.

  – Since $\pi \in \mathcal{A}cz_l \llbracket P \rrbracket$ we get that $\pi' = \pi \cdot \langle \sigma, i, \sigma' \rangle \in \mathcal{A}cz_{l'} \llbracket P \rrbracket$ and $i \in Lab(P)$ (the case $\pi' = \langle \sigma, i, \sigma' \rangle$ is discussed below). We have that $first(\pi) = first(\pi') \models \varphi$. Also, $\pi[\overline{Lab(P)}] \models rely$ and $\pi[\overline{Lab(P)}] = \pi'[\overline{Lab(P)}]$. Thus, $\pi'[\overline{Lab(P)}] \models rely$. Obviously we have $last(\pi') = \sigma'$ and therefore $\sigma' \models SP_{l'}(\varphi, rely, P)$. Additionally, we observe that $\langle \sigma, \sigma' \rangle = tail(\pi'[Lab(P)])$, and derive that $\langle \sigma, \sigma' \rangle \models SG(\varphi, rely, P)$.

  – If $l = s$ and $\sigma \models \varphi$, we have an Aczel-trace $\langle \sigma, i, \sigma' \rangle \in \mathcal{A}cz_{l'} \llbracket P \rrbracket$ with $i \in Lab(P)$, i.e., this process-indexed state pair is the first and only transition so far of P. Then $first(\langle \sigma, i, \sigma' \rangle) = \sigma \models \varphi$, and $\langle \sigma, i, \sigma' \rangle[\overline{Lab(P)}] = \varepsilon \models rely$. Since $last(\langle \sigma, i, \sigma' \rangle) = \sigma'$ we have that $\sigma' \models SP_{l'}(\varphi, rely, P)$, and, as above, $\langle \sigma, \sigma' \rangle \models SG(\varphi, rely, P)$.

- Next let $\langle \sigma, \sigma' \rangle \models rely$, and $\langle \sigma, \sigma' \rangle$ originate from an environmental transition.

  – We have for $i \notin Lab(P)$ that $\pi' = \pi \cdot \langle \sigma, i, \sigma' \rangle \in \mathcal{A}cz_l \llbracket P \rrbracket$. The case $\pi' = \langle \sigma, i, \sigma' \rangle$ is considered below. Again we have that $first(\pi) = first(\pi') \models \varphi$. Since $\pi[\overline{Lab(P)}] \models rely$, $\langle \sigma, \sigma' \rangle \models rely$ and $\pi'[\overline{Lab(P)}] = \pi[\overline{Lab(P)}] \cdot \langle \sigma, \sigma' \rangle$ we conclude that $\pi'[\overline{Lab(P)}] \models rely$. Finally, $last(\pi') = \sigma'$. Thus, $\sigma' \models SP_l(\varphi, rely, P)$.

  – If $l = s$ and $\sigma \models \varphi$ we have for $i \notin Lab(P)$ that $\pi' = \langle \sigma, i, \sigma' \rangle$, again with $first(\pi') \models \varphi$ and $\pi'[\overline{Lab(P)}] = \langle \sigma, \sigma' \rangle \models rely$.
    As above $last(\pi') = \sigma'$ and $\sigma' \models SP_l(\varphi, rely, P)$.   □

By our basic rule 8.5 we thus derive that

$$\vdash \langle rely, SG(\varphi, rely, P) \rangle : \{SP_s(\varphi, rely, P)\} \, P \, \{SP_t(\varphi, rely, P)\}.$$

Since by Lemma 8.32

- $\models \varphi \rightarrow SP_s(\varphi, rely, P)$,

- $\models SP_t(\varphi, rely, P) \rightarrow \psi$, and
- $\models SG(\varphi, rely, P) \rightarrow guar$

hold, we derive by the consequence rule

$$\vdash \langle rely, guar \rangle : \{\varphi\} \, P \, \{\psi\}.$$

Composed programs

Next we consider the remaining cases $P \equiv P_1; P_2$ and $P \equiv P_1 \parallel P_2$. First we generalise Definition 8.30.

Definition 8.34 For every program P we define

$$\sigma \models SP(\varphi, rely, P)$$

if there exists some $\pi\sqrt{} \in \mathcal{A}cz[\![P]\!]$, with $first(\pi) \models \varphi$, $\pi[\overline{Lab(P)}] \models rely$, and $last(\pi) = \sigma$. □

Note that for $P \equiv (L, T, s, t)$ a basic transition diagram

$$SP(\varphi, rely, P) = SP_t(\varphi, rely, P).$$

The basic properties of Lemma 8.32 carry over to the general case.

Lemma 8.35 For every system P we have

(i) $\models_A \langle rely, SG(\varphi, rely, P) \rangle : \{\varphi\} \, P \, \{SP(\varphi, rely, P)\}$.
(ii) $\models_A \langle rely, guar \rangle : \{\varphi\} \, P \, \{\psi\}$ implies

    (a) $\models SP(\varphi, rely, P) \rightarrow \psi$.
    (b) $\models SG(\varphi, rely, P) \rightarrow guar$.

Sequential composition

Now we consider the case of sequential composition. Let

$$\models_A \langle rely, guar \rangle : \{\varphi\} \, P_1; P_2 \, \{\psi\}.$$

This implies

$$\models_A \langle rely, guar \rangle : \{\varphi\} \, P_1 \, \{SP(\varphi, rely, P_1)\}$$

and

$$\models_A \langle rely, guar \rangle : \{SP(\varphi, rely, P_1)\} \, P_2 \, \{\psi\},$$

and by the induction hypothesis we have

$$\vdash \langle rely, guar \rangle : \{\varphi\} \, P_1 \, \{SP(\varphi, rely, P_1)\}$$

and

$$\vdash \langle rely, guar \rangle : \{SP(\varphi, rely, P_1)\} \; P_2 \; \{\psi\}.$$

An application of the rule for sequential composition concludes the proof.

Parallel composition

We now investigate the most interesting case: $P \equiv P_1 \| P_2$. Therefore, assume

$$\models_A \langle rely, guar \rangle : \{\varphi\} \; P_1 \| P_2 \; \{\psi\}.$$

Proving $\models_A \langle rely', guar \rangle : \{\varphi'\} \; P_1' \| P_2' \; \{\psi\}$ requires some technical prepara-
tions. Similarly to Section 3.5.4 we assume given a fresh auxiliary variable h
as history variable (i.e., h does not occur in P nor in the given predicates *rely*,
guar, φ, and ψ). For h a history variable, $\sigma(h)$ denotes a computation history.

Our first step is to augment every transition of $P_1 \| P_2$ with the correspond-
ing update to the fresh history variable h. This variable records the history
of P, i.e., the sequence of state changes of process P *together with its environment*, plus the active components responsible for these changes. Without
loss of generality we may assume that P_1 and P_2 are two distinct process identifiers *representing* $Lab(P_1)$ and, respectively, $Lab(P_2)$. We then transform
each transition $(l, b \rightarrow f, l')$ of a constituent of P_i to $(l, b \rightarrow f \circ g, l')$, where
$g \stackrel{\text{def}}{=} (\sigma : h \mapsto h \cdot (\mathsf{P}_i, \sigma))$, i.e., $g(\sigma)$ is like σ, except for the value of h which is
extended by (P_i, σ). This augmented version of P_i will be denoted by P_i'.

Our task is to construct predicates that fit the hypotheses of the parallel composition rule 8.7. In particular we have to define predicates $rely_i$, $guar_i$, φ, ψ_i,
$i = 1, 2$, such that for the augmented P_i' the R-G specifications

$$\models_A \langle rely_i, guar_i \rangle : \{\varphi\} \; P_i' \; \{\psi_i\}, i = 1, 2,$$

and the corresponding side conditions hold.

Note that in the augmented process $P' \equiv P_1' \| P_2'$ boolean conditions do not
involve the history variable h, and that h does not occur in assignments to non-
history variables. That is, the history variable h is indeed an *auxiliary variable*
which does not influence the flow-of-control of a process. Also, h does not
occur in *rely*, *guar*, φ or ψ.

We have to ensure, *in order to have the complete computation history recorded in* h, that every possible environmental action should update the history
variable correctly. That is, we prevent some environmental process setting,
e.g., $h := \varepsilon$, by formulating additional requirements upon *rely*; we also change

the given precondition φ to ensure that initially h denotes the empty sequence ε.[2]

Definition 8.36 We define

- $\langle \sigma, \sigma' \rangle \models rely'$ if and only if $\langle \sigma, \sigma' \rangle \models rely$ and $\sigma'(h) = \sigma(h) \cdot (E, \sigma)$,
- $\sigma \models \varphi'$ if and only if $\sigma \models \varphi$ and $\sigma(h) = \varepsilon$,

where $E \in Id$ is a process identifier representing "the environment", and *rely* and φ do not involve h. E is distinct from P_1 and P_2, and does not occur in $Lab(P_1) \cup Lab(P_2)$.[3]
□

We have

Lemma 8.37

$$\models_A \langle rely, guar \rangle : \{\varphi\} \, P_1 \| P_2 \, \{\psi\}$$

implies

$$\models_A \langle rely', guar \rangle : \{\varphi'\} \, P_1' \| P_2' \, \{\psi\}.$$

Proof Let

$$\langle \sigma_1', i_1, \sigma_2' \rangle \cdots \langle \sigma_n', i_n, \sigma_{n+1}' \rangle (\sqrt{}) \in \mathcal{A}cz[\![P_1' \| P_2']\!],$$

such that $\sigma_1' \models \varphi'$ and $\langle \sigma_k', \sigma_{k+1}' \rangle \models rely'$, for $i_k \notin Lab(P_1 \| P_2)$ and $1 \le k \le n$. Let $\sigma_k = (\sigma_k' : h \mapsto \sigma_1'(h))$, for $1 \le k \le n$. From the construction of $P_1' \| P_2'$ it follows that

$$\langle \sigma_1, i_1, \sigma_2 \rangle \cdots \langle \sigma_n, i_n, \sigma_{n+1} \rangle (\sqrt{}) \in \mathcal{A}cz[\![P_1 \| P_2]\!].$$

From $\sigma_1' \models \varphi'$ and Definition 8.36 we conclude that $\sigma_1 \models \varphi$, and from $\langle \sigma_k', \sigma_{k+1}' \rangle \models rely'$ and Definition 8.36 we conclude that $\langle \sigma_k, \sigma_{k+1} \rangle \models rely$, for $i_k \notin Lab(P_1 \| P_2)$ and $1 \le k \le n$.

From $\sigma_1 \models \varphi$, $\langle \sigma_k, \sigma_{k+1} \rangle \models rely$, for $i_k \notin Lab(P_1 \| P_2)$ and $1 \le k \le n$, the validity of $\langle rely, guar \rangle : \{\varphi\} \, P_1 \| P_2 \, \{\psi\}$, and

$$\langle \sigma_1, i_1, \sigma_2 \rangle \cdots \langle \sigma_n, i_n, \sigma_{n+1} \rangle (\sqrt{}) \in \mathcal{A}cz[\![P_1 \| P_2]\!],$$

we conclude that $\langle \sigma_k, \sigma_{k+1} \rangle \models guar$, for $i_k \in Lab(P_1 \| P_2)$ and $1 \le k \le n$, and $\sigma_{n+1} \models \psi$ (in the case of a terminated computation).

---

[2] Note that we use the same symbol for expressing the empty computation history and the empty reactive sequence.

[3] Alternatively, one could have changed every environmental transition $(l, b \to f, l')$ into $(l, b \to f \circ g, l')$, where $g(\sigma) \stackrel{def}{=} (\sigma : h \mapsto h \cdot (E, \sigma))$.

Since h is supposed not to occur in *guar* or ψ, we also conclude that $\langle \sigma'_k,$
$\sigma'_{k+1} \rangle \models guar$, for $i_k \in Lab(P'_1 \| P'_2)$ and $1 \leq k \leq n$ and $\sigma'_{n+1} \models \psi$ (in the case
of a terminated computation). $\square$

Moreover, we introduce the following rely-condition env_i which ensures a
correct update of the history variable h by the environment of P'_i when exe-
cuted in the context $P'_1 \| P'_2$. Note that the environment of P'_i in the context of
$P'_1 \| P'_2$ consists of both the common environment of P'_1 and P'_2 and the other
component P'_j, $i \neq j$.

Definition 8.38 Let for $i = 1, 2$,

$$\langle \sigma, \sigma' \rangle \models env_i$$

be defined by

$$\sigma'(h) = \sigma(h) \cdot (\mathrm{E}, \sigma) \text{ or } \sigma'(h) = \sigma(h) \cdot (\mathrm{P}_j, \sigma),$$

where $i \neq j (\in \{1, 2\})$. $\square$

We now define the predicates that satisfy, as we shall prove, the requirements
of the parallel composition rule.

Definition 8.39 We define for $i = 1, 2$ the following predicates:

- $rely_i \stackrel{\text{def}}{=} rely' \vee SG(\phi', env_j, P'_j)$, for $i \neq j$,
- $\psi_i \stackrel{\text{def}}{=} SP(\phi', rely_i, P'_i)$, and
- $guar_i \stackrel{\text{def}}{=} SG(\phi', rely_i, P'_i)$. $\square$

The predicate $rely_i$ is intended to specify the steps of the environment of P'_i
in the context of $P'_1 \| P'_2$ and of the environment of $P'_1 \| P'_2$. The computation
steps of the common environment of P'_1 and P'_2 are specified by the action predicate $rely'$, whereas the computation steps of the other component are specified
by the action predicate $SG(\phi', env_j, P'_j)$ which states the existence of a corresponding computation of P'_j in which the environment correctly updates the
history variable h.

Now we are sufficiently prepared to prove

Theorem 8.40

$$\models_A \langle rely, guar \rangle : \{\phi\} \ P_1 \| P_2 \ \{\psi\}$$

implies

$$\vdash \langle rely, guar \rangle : \{\phi\} \ P_1 \| P_2 \ \{\psi\}.$$

Proof Let

$$\models_A \langle rely, guar \rangle : \{\varphi\}\ P_1\|P_2\ \{\psi\}.$$

By augmenting P_i as described above we obtain P_i', $i = 1, 2$. Defining $rely'$ and φ' as in Definition 8.36, we apply Lemma 8.37 to deduce

$$\models_A \langle rely', guar \rangle : \{\varphi'\}\ P_1'\|P_2'\ \{\psi\}.$$

For the predicates of Definition 8.39 we have by Lemma 8.35 for $i = 1, 2$,

$$\models_A \langle rely_i, guar_i \rangle : \{\varphi'\}\ P_i'\ \{\psi_i\}.$$

Recall from the beginning of Section 8.4.5 that the completeness proof is given by induction on the structure of program P, using as induction hypotheses

$$\models_A \langle rely, guar \rangle : \{\varphi\}\ P\ \{\psi\} \Rightarrow\ \vdash \langle rely, guar \rangle : \{\varphi\}\ P\ \{\psi\}.$$

Hence we obtain from this induction hypothesis that

$$\vdash \langle rely_i, guar_i \rangle : \{\varphi'\}\ P_i'\ \{\psi_i\}.$$

In order to apply the parallel composition rule we have to prove its corresponding requirements:

$$\models (rely' \vee guar_i) \rightarrow rely_j,$$

for $i, j = 1, 2$ and $i \neq j$ is proved in Lemma 8.41 below, and

$$\models (guar_1 \vee guar_2) \rightarrow guar$$

in Lemma 8.42. By an application of the parallel composition rule we thus obtain

$$\vdash \langle rely', guar \rangle : \{\varphi'\}\ P_1'\ \|\ P_2'\ \{\psi_1 \wedge \psi_2\}.$$

We prove

$$\models (\psi_1 \wedge \psi_2) \rightarrow \psi$$

in Lemma 8.43.

Having proved these lemmas, we obtain, by an application of the consequence rule,

$$\vdash \langle rely', guar \rangle : \{\varphi'\}\ P_1'\ \|\ P_2'\ \{\psi\}.$$

Next we apply the auxiliary variables rule and obtain

$$\vdash \langle rely', guar \rangle : \{\varphi'\}\ P_1\ \|\ P_2\ \{\psi\}.$$

After that we apply the initialisation rule with $f(\sigma) \stackrel{\text{def}}{=} (\sigma : h \mapsto \varepsilon)$,

$g_1(\langle\sigma,\sigma'\rangle) \stackrel{\text{def}}{=} (\sigma : h \mapsto \varepsilon)$, and $g_2(\langle\sigma,\sigma'\rangle) \stackrel{\text{def}}{=} (\sigma' : h \mapsto (\text{E},\sigma))$. Finally, we conclude after an application of the consequence rule (using $\models rely \to rely' \circ g$ and $\models \varphi \to \varphi' \circ f$),

$$\vdash \langle rely, guar\rangle : \{\varphi\}\, P_1 \parallel P_2 \,\{\psi\}. \qquad \square$$

We now prove the remaining lemmas.

Lemma 8.41 We have for $i, j = 1, 2$ and $i \neq j$,

$$\models rely' \vee guar_i \to rely_j.$$

Proof The validity of the implication

$$rely' \vee guar_i \to rely_j$$

follows, after substituting the definitions of $guar_i$ and $rely_j$, from the validity of the implication

$$SG(\varphi', rely_i, P_i') \to SG(\varphi', env_i, P_i').$$

Validity of the latter follows from the validity of the implication $rely_i \to env_i$. Let $\langle\sigma,\sigma'\rangle \models rely_i$. In case $\langle\sigma,\sigma'\rangle \models rely'$, by definition of $rely'$, we have that $\sigma'(h) = \sigma(h) \cdot (\text{E},\sigma)$; otherwise, $\langle\sigma,\sigma'\rangle \models SG(\varphi', env_j, P_j')$ and so we have by definition of SG and the construction of P_j', that $\sigma'(h) = \sigma(h) \cdot (\text{P}_j,\sigma)$. $\qquad \square$

The following proof is rather combinatorial. Starting with a computation π of P_i' with last computation step $\langle\sigma, i, \sigma'\rangle$ satisfying $guar_i$, $i \in Lab(P_i')$, we construct an Aczel-trace $\tilde{\pi}$ of $P_1' \parallel P_2'$ such that $\tilde{\pi}[\overline{Lab(P_1' \parallel P_2')}] \models rely'$, $first(\tilde{\pi}) \models \varphi'$ and $\langle\sigma, i, \sigma'\rangle$ is a computation step of $\tilde{\pi}$. Then we infer from the validity of

$$\models_A \langle rely', guar\rangle : \{\varphi'\}\, P_1' \parallel P_2' \,\{\psi\}$$

that $\langle\sigma,\sigma'\rangle \models guar$. This construction is possible because we have stored sufficient information in the history h, and ensured that the history is always updated correctly.

Lemma 8.42 We have

$$\models guar_1 \vee guar_2 \to guar.$$

Proof Let $\langle\sigma,\sigma'\rangle \models guar_i$. By definition of $guar_i$ there exists

$$\pi = \langle\sigma_1, i_1, \sigma_2\rangle \cdots \langle\sigma_n, i_n, \sigma_{n+1}\rangle \in \mathcal{A}cz[\![P_i']\!],$$

such that $\sigma_1 \models \varphi'$, $\sigma_n = \sigma$, $\sigma_{n+1} = \sigma'$, $i_n \in Lab(P_i')$, and $\langle\sigma_k, \sigma_{k+1}\rangle \models rely_i$, whenever $i_k \notin Lab(P_i')$.

Either there is a last P'_j step in Aczel-trace π or there is not.

• If there is no P'_j step in π we have for all $\langle \sigma_k, i_k, \sigma_{k+1} \rangle$ with $i_k \notin Lab(P'_i)$ that $i_k \notin Lab(P'_i) \cup Lab(P'_j)$. From above we have that $\langle \sigma_k, \sigma_{k+1} \rangle \models rely_i$, i.e., by Definition 8.39, $\langle \sigma_k, \sigma_{k+1} \rangle \models rely' \vee SG(\varphi', env_j, P'_j)$. Now assume $\langle \sigma_k, \sigma_{k+1} \rangle \models SG(\varphi', env_j, P'_j)$. By the definition of $SG(\varphi', env_j, P'_j)$ this would mean that $\langle \sigma_k, \sigma_{k+1} \rangle$ is the last P'_j step of a computation π', i.e., $i_k \in Lab(P'_j)$. This contradicts the fact that there is no P'_j step in π, hence $\langle \sigma_k, \sigma_{k+1} \rangle \models rely'$ for all $i_k \notin Lab(P'_i) \cup Lab(P'_j)$. Moreover, $\pi \in \mathcal{Acz}[\![P'_j]\!]$ because there are no P'_j steps in π. Hence $\pi \in \mathcal{Acz}[\![P'_1 \| P'_2]\!]$ and by validity of

$$\models_A \langle rely', guar \rangle : \{\varphi'\} \, P'_1 \| P'_2 \, \{\psi\}$$

we derive that $\langle \sigma_j, \sigma_{j+1} \rangle \models guar$ when $i_j \in Lab(P'_1 \| P'_2)$: since $i_n \in Lab(P'_i)$ we indeed have that $\langle \sigma, \sigma' \rangle \models guar$.

• Now let $\langle \sigma_l, i_l, \sigma_{l+1} \rangle$ be the last P'_j step in Aczel-trace π, with $i_l \in Lab(P'_j)$, for $i \neq j$. By definition of $rely_i$ and construction of P'_j, $i_k \notin Lab(P'_i)$ implies either $\sigma_{k+1}(h) = \sigma_k(h) \cdot (E, \sigma_k)$ or $\sigma_{k+1}(h) = \sigma_k(h) \cdot (P_j, \sigma_k)$. Moreover, for $i_k \in Lab(P'_i)$ we have by construction of P'_i that $\sigma_{k+1}(h) = \sigma_k(h) \cdot (P_i, \sigma_k)$.

Thus we may assume that $\sigma_{k+1}(h) = \sigma_k(h) \cdot (id_k, \sigma_k), k = 1, \ldots, n$, with $id_k \in \{E, P_1, P_2\}$. From $\sigma_1 \models \varphi'$ and Definition 8.36 we conclude that $\sigma_1(h) = \varepsilon$. And from this, we derive by induction that

$$\sigma_{k+1}(h) = (id_1, \sigma_1) \cdots (id_k, \sigma_k), \; k = 1, \ldots, n.$$

We can retrieve an abstraction of the Aczel-trace π from the value of h in the last state σ_{n+1} which is accurate w.r.t. the states occurring in the sequences, but which abstracts from the process identifiers, in that we abstract from the exact identifiers of environmental processes, replacing them by E, and from the exact identifiers of processes occurring in P'_i replacing them by P_i. Defining

$$abst(\varepsilon, \sigma) \stackrel{\text{def}}{=} \varepsilon,$$
$$abst(\theta \cdot (id, \sigma'), \sigma) \stackrel{\text{def}}{=} abst(\theta, \sigma') \cdot \langle \sigma', id, \sigma \rangle,$$

we conclude that

$$abst(\sigma_{n+1}(h), \sigma_{n+1}) = \langle \sigma_1, id_1, \sigma_2 \rangle \cdots \langle \sigma_n, id_n, \sigma_{n+1} \rangle,$$

where $id_i \in \{E, P_1, P_2\}$. Furthermore we know from the construction of P'_i that $i_k \in Lab(P'_i)$ for π implies that $id_k = P_i$ in $abst(\sigma_{n+1}(h), \sigma_{n+1})$.

Now $\langle \sigma_l, i_l, \sigma_{l+1} \rangle$ is the last P'_j step in π. By construction of P'_j we have that $\sigma_{l+1}(h) = \sigma_l(h) \cdot (P_j, \sigma_l)$, and hence $\langle \sigma_l, \sigma_{l+1} \rangle \not\models rely'$.

But since $\langle \sigma_l, \sigma_{l+1} \rangle \models rely_i$ we conclude that $\langle \sigma_l, \sigma_{l+1} \rangle \models SG(\varphi', env_j, P'_j)$.

By definition of $SG(\varphi', env_j, P'_j)$ there exists

$$\pi' = \langle \sigma'_1, i'_1, \sigma'_2 \rangle \cdots \langle \sigma'_m, i'_m, \sigma'_{m+1} \rangle \in Acz[\![P'_j]\!],$$

such that $\sigma'_1 \models \varphi'$, $\sigma'_m = \sigma_l$, $\sigma'_{m+1} = \sigma_{l+1}$, $i'_m \in Lab(P'_j)$, and $\langle \sigma'_k, \sigma'_{k+1} \rangle \models env_j$, whenever $i'_k \notin Lab(P'_j)$.

By definition of env_j and the construction of P'_j, in a similar manner as argued above, we have that $\sigma'_{k+1}(h) = \sigma'_k(h) \cdot (id'_k, \sigma'_k)$, $k = 1, \ldots, m$, and $id'_k \in \{E, P_1, P_2\}$. Since $\sigma'_1(h) = \varepsilon$, we thus derive by straightforward induction that $\sigma'_{k+1}(h) = (id'_1, \sigma'_1) \cdots (id'_k, \sigma'_k)$, $k = 1, \ldots, m$.

As above we can retrieve an abstracted Aczel-trace from $\sigma'_{m+1}(h)$:

$$abst(\sigma'_{m+1}(h), \sigma'_{m+1}) = \langle \sigma'_1, id'_1, \sigma'_2 \rangle \cdots \langle \sigma'_m, id'_m, \sigma'_{m+1} \rangle,$$

where $id'_i \in \{E, P_1, P_2\}$. Moreover we know that if $i'_j \in Lab(P'_j)$ in π' we have that $id'_j = P_j$ in $abst(\sigma'_{m+1}(h), \sigma'_{m+1})$.

Since $\sigma'_{m+1} = \sigma_{l+1}$ we also have $\sigma'_{m+1}(h) = \sigma_{l+1}(h)$. Since h also stores the past states together with the identifiers of the processes which have acted on those states, we conclude that $\sigma'_i = \sigma_i$ and $id'_i = id_i$, for $i = 1, \ldots, l$. Consequently, from the definition of the semantics we deduce that it is not necessary to know the precise process identifier of environmental transitions, i.e, for an Aczel-trace $\pi \in Acz[\![P]\!]$ we can rename the identifiers in $\overline{Lab(P)}$ by other identifiers in $\overline{Lab(P)}$ and the resulting Aczel-trace π' also belongs to $Acz[\![P]\!]$.

Now $\pi' \in Acz[\![P'_j]\!]$. Since $Lab(P'_i) \cap Lab(P'_j) = \emptyset$ we can replace each process identifier i'_k in π' by i_k whenever $id'_k = P_i$. For the resulting Aczel-trace π_1 we also have that $\pi_1 \in Acz[\![P'_j]\!]$.

Similarly we replace each process identifier i'_k in π' by i_k whenever $id'_k = E$ and again for the resulting Aczel-trace π_2 we have that $\pi_2 \in Acz[\![P'_j]\!]$. Notice that π_2 contains the same P'_i steps as π up to the l-th computation step. Since the Aczel semantics is prefix-closed, we deduce from $\pi \in Acz[\![P'_i]\!]$ that also $\pi_2 \in Acz[\![P'_i]\!]$ and hence $\pi_2 \in Acz[\![P'_i \| P'_2]\!]$. If we extend π_2 by those process-indexed state pairs following $\langle \sigma_l, i_l, \sigma_{l+1} \rangle$ in π, we obtain the Aczel-trace $\tilde{\pi}$, i.e.,

$$\tilde{\pi} \stackrel{\text{def}}{=} \langle \sigma_1, \tilde{i}_1, \sigma_2 \rangle \cdots \langle \sigma_l, \tilde{i}_l, \sigma_{l+1} \rangle \cdots \langle \sigma_n, i_n, \sigma_{n+1} \rangle,$$

where $\tilde{i}_k \stackrel{\text{def}}{=} i_k$ if $id_k \neq P_j$ and $\tilde{i}_k \stackrel{\text{def}}{=} i'_k$ if $id_k = P_j$ for $i = 1, \ldots, l$. Since $\tilde{\pi}$ is an extension of π_2 consisting of non-P'_j steps only, by definition of $Acz[\![P'_j]\!]$ we also derive that $\tilde{\pi} \in Acz[\![P'_j]\!]$.

π_2 contains the same sequence of P'_i steps as π up to the l-th computation step; in fact only those process identifiers i_k were renamed with $i_k \in Lab(P'_j)$. Thus $\tilde{\pi}$ is identical to π except for the process identifiers $i_k \in Lab(P'_j)$, and since

$Lab(P_i') \cap Lab(P_j') = \emptyset$ we conclude by the observation above on renaming process identifiers that $\tilde{\pi} \in \mathcal{A}cz[\![P_i']\!]$. Consequently $\tilde{\pi} \in \mathcal{A}cz[\![P_1' \| P_2']\!]$.

The state transformations in $\tilde{\pi}$ are the same as in π. Thus we have that $\tilde{\pi}[\overline{Lab(P_1') \cup Lab(P_2')}]$ satisfies $rely_i$. We now prove that $\tilde{\pi}[\overline{Lab(P_1') \cup Lab(P_2')}]$ $\models rely'$. By Definition 8.39, $rely_i = rely' \vee SG(\varphi', env_j, P_j')$. Assume $\langle \sigma, \sigma' \rangle \in \tilde{\pi}[\overline{Lab(P_1') \cup Lab(P_2')}]$ satisfies $rely'$. This case is fulfilled trivially. Now assume that $\langle \sigma, \sigma' \rangle \in \tilde{\pi}[\overline{Lab(P_1') \cup Lab(P_2')}]$ satisfies $SG(\varphi', env_j, P_j')$, for $i \neq j$. By Definition 8.31 this implies that $\langle \sigma, \sigma' \rangle$ is the last action of P_j' in the found π. This contradicts the assumption $\langle \sigma, \sigma' \rangle \in \tilde{\pi}[\overline{Lab(P_1') \cup Lab(P_2')}]$. Hence, since $\tilde{\pi}[\overline{Lab(P_1') \cup Lab(P_2')}] \models rely'$ and $\sigma_1 \models \varphi'$, we infer from the validity of

$$\models_A \langle rely', guar \rangle : \{\varphi'\} P_1' \| P_2' \{\psi\}$$

that $\langle \sigma, \sigma' \rangle \models guar$.

Summarising, from $\langle \sigma, \sigma' \rangle \models guar_i$ we obtain an Aczel-trace $\pi \in \mathcal{A}cz[\![P_i']\!]$, whose first state σ_1 satisfies φ', and whose state pairs $\langle \sigma_k, \sigma_{k+1} \rangle \models rely_i$ whenever $\langle \sigma_k, i_k, \sigma_{k+1} \rangle$ satisfies $i_k \notin Lab(P_i')$.

This trace π we split into two parts $\pi = \pi^* \cdot \pi^{**}$ with π^* ending with the last P_j' step, $\langle \sigma_l, i_l, \sigma_{l+1} \rangle$, in π with $i_l \in Lab(P_j')$. Observing that $\langle \sigma_l, \sigma_{l+1} \rangle \models SG(\varphi, env_j, P_j')$, and using the value of the history variable $\sigma_{l+1}(h)$ in σ_{l+1}, we deduce the existence of an Aczel trace $\pi' \in \mathcal{A}cz[\![P_j']\!]$, which is, up to identifiers, identical to π^*. In this trace π' we change the non-P_j' identifiers to the corresponding ones in π^*, resulting in trace π_2, $\pi_2 \in \mathcal{A}cz[\![P_j']\!]$. Trace π_2 we concatenate with π^{**} to $\tilde{\pi} = \pi_2 \cdot \pi^{**}$. Since $\pi_2 \in \mathcal{A}cz[\![P_j']\!]$ and π^{**} does not contain any P_j' steps, also $\tilde{\pi} \in \mathcal{A}cz[\![P_j']\!]$. On the other hand, $\tilde{\pi}$ is identical to π up to the identifiers in $Lab(P_j')$, and hence $\tilde{\pi} \in \mathcal{A}cz[\![P_i']\!]$. That is, $\tilde{\pi} \in \mathcal{A}cz[\![P_1' \| P_2']\!]$.

Since $\tilde{\pi}$'s first state satisfies φ' and its non-$P_1' \| P_2'$ moves satisfy $rely'$ we obtain from

$$\models_A \langle rely', guar \rangle : \{\varphi'\} P_1' \| P_2' \{\psi\}$$

that its last pair of states, $\langle \sigma, \sigma' \rangle$, satisfies $guar$, i.e.,

$$\models guar_1 \vee guar_2 \to guar. \qquad \square$$

Finally, we prove

Lemma 8.43 $\models \psi_1 \wedge \psi_2 \to \psi$.

Proof Let $\sigma \models \psi_1 \wedge \psi_2$. By definition of ψ_1 and ψ_2 there exist computations

$$\pi = \langle \sigma_1, i_1, \sigma_2 \rangle \cdots \langle \sigma_n, i_n, \sigma_{n+1} \rangle \sqrt{} \in \mathcal{A}cz[\![P_i']\!]$$

and

$$\pi' = \langle \sigma_1', i_1', \sigma_2' \rangle \cdots \langle \sigma_m', i_m', \sigma_{m+1}' \rangle \sqrt{} \in \mathcal{A}cz[\![P_j']\!]$$

such that $\sigma = \sigma_{n+1} = \sigma_{m+1}'$, $\sigma_1 \models \varphi'$, $\sigma_1' \models \varphi'$, and $\langle \sigma_k, \sigma_{k+1} \rangle \models rely_1$, whenever $i_k \notin Lab(P_1')$, and $\langle \sigma_k', \sigma_{k+1}' \rangle \models rely_2$, whenever $i_k' \notin Lab(P_2')$.

By definition of $rely_i$ and construction of P_i' $(i = 1, 2)$ we may assume that

$$\sigma_{k+1}(h) = \sigma_k(h) \cdot (id_k, \sigma_k), \; k = 1, \ldots, n,$$

and

$$\sigma_{k+1}'(h) = \sigma_k'(h) \cdot (id_k', \sigma_k'), \; k = 1, \ldots, m$$

($id_k, id_k' \in \{P_1, P_2, E\}$ as above). Since $\sigma_1(h) = \sigma_1'(h) = \varepsilon$, we derive by induction that $\sigma_{n+1}(h) = (id_1, \sigma_1) \cdots (id_n, \sigma_n)$ and $\sigma_{m+1}'(h) = (id_1', \sigma_1') \cdots (id_m', \sigma_m')$. Thus we derive from $\sigma_{n+1}(h) = \sigma_{m+1}'(h)$ that $m + 1 = n + 1$ and, consequently, $abst(\sigma_{n+1}(h), \sigma_{n+1}) = abst(\sigma_{m+1}(h), \sigma_{m+1})$. By the same argument as above we get that $\pi' \in \mathcal{A}cz[\![P_i']\!]$ and thus $\pi' \in \mathcal{A}cz[\![P_1'\|P_2']\!]$. By the given validity of the R-G-specification

$$\models_A \langle rely, guar \rangle : \{\varphi\} P_1\|P_2 \{\psi\}$$

we obtain from Lemma 8.37 that

$$\models_A \langle rely', guar \rangle : \{\varphi'\} P_1'\|P_2' \{\psi\}.$$

Let us collect our information: $\sigma_1' \models \varphi'$; $\langle \sigma_k', \sigma_{k+1}' \rangle \models rely_2$, whenever $i_k' \notin Lab(P_2')$; and, finally, $\pi' \in \mathcal{A}cz[\![P_1'\|P_2']\!]$.

We need to show that $\langle \sigma_k', \sigma_{k+1}' \rangle \models rely'$, whenever $i_k' \notin Lab(P_1') \cup Lab(P_2')$. By Definition 8.39, $rely_2 = rely' \vee SG(\varphi', env_1, P_1')$. Pick $\langle \sigma_k', \sigma_{k+1}' \rangle$ such that $i_k' \notin Lab(P_1') \cup Lab(P_2')$, and thus also $i_k' \notin Lab(P_2')$. Since $\langle \sigma_k', \sigma_{k+1}' \rangle \models rely_2$, we have $\langle \sigma_k', \sigma_{k+1}' \rangle \models rely'$ or $\langle \sigma_k', \sigma_{k+1}' \rangle \models SG(\varphi', env_1, P_1')$. As in the proof of Lemma 8.42, the latter case leads to a contradiction.

Consequently, we derive from $\models_A \langle rely', guar \rangle : \{\varphi'\} P_1'\|P_2' \{\psi\}$, $\sigma_1' \models \varphi'$, $\langle \sigma_k', \sigma_{k+1}' \rangle \models rely'$, with $i_k' \notin Lab(P_1') \cup Lab(P_2')$, and $\pi' \in \mathcal{A}cz[\![P_1'\|P_2']\!]$, and the fact that π' represents a terminated computation, that $\sigma \models \psi$, since $\sigma = \sigma_{m+1}'$, which is the final state of π'.   □

8.4.6 The R-G Method and Reactive Sequences

Since the approach to rely-guarantee reasoning using Aczel semantics is rather straightforward, the reader might wonder why we did not directly use the reactive-sequence semantics. In this section we investigate the relation between reactive-sequence semantics and rely-guarantee reasoning and discover that additional requirements have to be imposed for the parallel composition rule to be sound, in case reactive sequences are used as models. First we extend the reactive-sequence semantics of Section 8.3 to the R-G formalism by defining both finite and infinite computations (characterising the latter by their finite prefixes). The semantics used in this section is based on the reactive-sequence semantics for basic transition diagrams as given by Definition 8.3.

Definition 8.44 The reactive-sequence semantics $\mathcal{R}[\![P]\!]$ of a basic program P is defined as follows:

For $P \equiv (L, T, s, t)$ we define

$$\mathcal{R}[\![P]\!] \overset{\text{def}}{=} \bigcup_{l \in L} \mathcal{R}_l[\![P]\!] \cup \{w\sqrt{} \mid w \in \mathcal{R}_l[\![P]\!]\}.$$

For $P \equiv P_1; P_2$ we define

$$\mathcal{R}[\![P]\!] \overset{\text{def}}{=} \{w \mid w \in \mathcal{R}'[\![P_1]\!]\} \cup \{w \cdot w' \mid w\sqrt{} \in \mathcal{R}[\![P_1]\!] \wedge w' \in \mathcal{R}[\![P_2]\!]\},$$

where $\mathcal{R}'[\![P_1]\!]$ denotes the set of nonterminated sequences of P_1, that is, those sequences not ending with $\sqrt{}$. Finally, for $P \equiv P_1 \parallel P_2$ we define

$$\mathcal{R}[\![P]\!] \overset{\text{def}}{=} \{w \mid w \in w_1 \tilde{\parallel} w_2, w_1 \in \mathcal{R}[\![P_1]\!], w_2 \in \mathcal{R}[\![P_2]\!]\},$$

where $w_1 \tilde{\parallel} w_2$ denotes the set of all interleavings of w_1 and w_2, ending in $\sqrt{}$ if and only if both w_1 and w_2 end in $\sqrt{}$. □

Note that the semantics $\mathcal{R}[\![P]\!]$ contains all the finite prefixes of all the computations of P, including those of *nonterminating* computations.

In order to define the validity of an R-G specification $\langle rely, guar \rangle : \{\varphi\} P \{\psi\}$ w.r.t. the reactive-sequence semantics we have first to determine the exact meaning of the precondition φ and the postcondition ψ within a formula which specifies an open system.

For closed systems, the definition of $\models \{\varphi\} P \{\psi\}$ is that for any *initial* state σ of P, if $\sigma \models \varphi$ holds and P starting in σ terminates in *final* state τ, then $\tau \models \psi$ holds.

However, what are the initial and final states of an open system, of which P is merely a component? Observe that the meaning of $\langle rely, guar \rangle : \{\varphi\} P \{\psi\}$ should be defined using these notions. We shall introduce the following convention:

Any state σ of this open system, which occurs before P is, or starts to be, executed, is an initial state of the open system; and any state τ of this open system, occurring when P terminates, or after P has terminated, is a finite state of this system.

Observe that this convention is consistent w.r.t. defining the sequential composition of two systems P_1 and P_2 in Section 8.4.1 in Definition 8.20. In that definition, a final state of P_1 is the last state of an Aczel-trace π such that $\pi \in \mathcal{A}cz_t \llbracket P_1 \rrbracket$, and this implies that π may end in an arbitrary finite number of environmental transitions by Definitions 8.17 and 8.18.

Similarly, an initial state is, according to Definition 8.23, any state σ such that $\sigma = first(\pi)$ and $\pi \in \mathcal{A}cz \llbracket P \rrbracket$ (observe that by Definition 8.15, Aczel-traces are always nonempty). This implies that π may start with an environmental action, as stated in our convention. Now that the notions of initial and final states of an open system, of which P is a component, are clarified, we proceed with the definition of validity of R-G specifications, using reactive sequences as semantic basis, instead.

We define for a reactive sequence w and states σ, σ' the *complement* of w with respect to initial state σ and final state σ', denoted by $\overline{\langle \sigma, w, \sigma' \rangle}$, as follows:

Definition 8.45 We define

$$\overline{\langle \sigma, \varepsilon, \sigma' \rangle} \overset{\text{def}}{=} \langle \sigma, \sigma' \rangle,$$
$$\overline{\langle \sigma, \sqrt{}, \sigma' \rangle} \overset{\text{def}}{=} \langle \sigma, \sigma' \rangle, \text{ and}$$
$$\overline{\langle \sigma, \langle \sigma_1, \sigma_2 \rangle \cdot w, \sigma' \rangle} \overset{\text{def}}{=} \langle \sigma, \sigma_1 \rangle \cdot \overline{\langle \sigma_2, w, \sigma' \rangle}. \qquad \Box$$

The complement of a reactive sequence w with respect to a given initial state σ and final state σ' thus specifies the behaviour of the environment.

Note that our definition of the complement suggests we should choose a *reflexive rely*-predicate: Observing a computation of a process without interference from the environment may result in a connected sequence

$$w = \langle \sigma, \sigma_1 \rangle \langle \sigma_1, \sigma_2 \rangle \langle \sigma_2, \sigma_3 \rangle \dots$$

Clearly the complement of this computation $\overline{\langle \sigma, w, \sigma' \rangle}$ then starts with stuttering steps $\langle \sigma, \sigma \rangle \langle \sigma_1, \sigma_1 \rangle \langle \sigma_2, \sigma_2 \rangle \dots$. These stuttering steps which model the fact that the environment may not act at all between two consecutive computation steps thus enforce the choice of a reflexive *rely*-predicate.

Now we are sufficiently equipped to introduce the following notion of the validity of R-G specifications w.r.t. reactive sequence semantics.

Definition 8.46 (R-validity of R-G correctness formulae) We define

$$\models_R \langle rely, guar \rangle : \{\varphi\} \ P \ \{\psi\}$$

by:

for all $w \in \mathcal{R} \llbracket P \rrbracket$, states σ and σ', if $\sigma \models \varphi$ and $\overline{\langle \sigma, w, \sigma' \rangle} \models rely$, then

$w \models guar$, and if additionally $w = w'\sqrt{}$, for some w', this implies $\sigma' \models \psi$.

□

Intuitively, an R-G specification $\langle rely, guar \rangle : \{\varphi\}\ P\ \{\psi\}$ is R-valid if for every reactive sequence w of P, initial state σ and final state σ' (of the parallel composition of P with its environment) the following holds:

- if the initial state σ satisfies φ and all the steps of the environment as specified by $\overline{\langle \sigma, w, \sigma' \rangle}$ satisfy *rely* then all the steps of w satisfy *guar*, and
- upon termination the final state σ' satisfies ψ.

We have the following *counterexample* to the soundness of the parallel composition rule with respect to the notion of R-validity above.

Example 8.47 Let $x := x+1$ abbreviate the transition diagram $(\{s,t\}, \{(s, true \rightarrow f, t)\}, s, t)$, where f increments x by 1. It is not difficult to check that

$$\models_R \langle x' = x+1, x' = x+1 \rangle : \{x = 0\}\ x := x+1\ \{x = 3\},$$

since all terminating $w \in \mathcal{R}\llbracket x := x+1 \rrbracket$ are of the form $w = \langle \sigma_1, \sigma_1' \rangle \sqrt{}$ where $\sigma_1'(x) = \sigma_1(x) + 1$, and for all $\sigma, \sigma' \in \Sigma$ we have $\overline{\langle \sigma, w, \sigma' \rangle} = \langle \sigma, \sigma_1 \rangle \cdot \langle \sigma_1', \sigma' \rangle$. By an application of the parallel composition rule to $x := x+1 \| x := x+1$, where both assignments $x := x+1$ are specified as above, we would then derive

$$\langle x' = x+1, x' = x+1 \rangle : \{x = 0\}\ x := x+1 \| x := x+1\ \{x = 3\},$$

which is clearly not R-valid, because environmental actions can increase x by one at least three times:

(i) Before execution of $x := x+1 \| x := x+1$.
(ii) Between the execution of $x := x+1$ and the next execution of $x := x+1$.
(iii) After the execution of the two processes.

Therefore, $x = 5$ is also possible as postcondition. □

Soundness of the parallel composition rule 8.7 with respect to this notion of validity requires all *rely*-predicates to be *transitive*, i.e., that $\langle \sigma, \sigma' \rangle \models rely$ and $\langle \sigma', \sigma'' \rangle \models rely$ imply $\langle \sigma, \sigma'' \rangle \models rely$ (see Exercise 8.10).

This observation motivates why we gave a different interpretation of R-G specifications in terms of Aczel-traces which provide more detailed information about environmental steps. As observed above, the reactive sequences semantics $\mathcal{R}$ does not provide a correct interpretation of R-G specifications. More precisely, it requires the predicates $rely_1$ and $rely_2$ in the parallel composition rule to be transitive. However, we can obtain such a correct interpretation of R-G specifications by the introduction of arbitrary *stutter steps* of the form $\langle \sigma, \sigma \rangle$.

Definition 8.48 Let $\mathcal{R}_\tau [\![P]\!]$ be the smallest set containing $\mathcal{R} [\![P]\!]$ which satisfies the following:

$$w_1 \cdot w_2 \in \mathcal{R}_\tau [\![P]\!] \text{ implies } w_1 \cdot \langle \sigma, \sigma \rangle \cdot w_2 \in \mathcal{R}_\tau [\![P]\!] . \qquad \Box$$

This abstraction operation is required in order to obtain a *fully abstract* semantics (see [dBKPR91, Bro93a, Lam94a, Bro96]). We observe that the corresponding notion of validity, which we denote by $\models_{R_\tau}$, requires the *guar* predicate to be *reflexive*, i.e., $\langle \sigma, \sigma \rangle \models guar$, for every state σ. Given this restriction we have that the two different notions of validity $\models_A$ and $\models_{R_\tau}$ coincide.

Theorem 8.49

Let $\langle rely, guar \rangle : \{\varphi\} \, P \, \{\psi\}$ be such that *guar* is reflexive. Then

$$\models_A \langle rely, guar \rangle : \{\varphi\} \, P \, \{\psi\} \text{ if and only if } \models_{R_\tau} \langle rely, guar \rangle : \{\varphi\} \, P \, \{\psi\}.$$

Proof Let $\models_A \langle rely, guar \rangle : \{\varphi\} \, P \, \{\psi\}$ and $w \in \mathcal{R}_\tau [\![P]\!]$. Furthermore let σ and σ' be such that $\sigma \models \varphi$, $\overline{\langle \sigma, w, \sigma' \rangle} \models rely$. Then the requirements of $\models_{R_\tau}$ are satisfied because of the existence of a corresponding $\pi \in \mathcal{A}cz [\![P]\!]$. Formally, we obtain such a corresponding π by defining the Aczel-trace $A(\sigma, w, \sigma')$ by induction on the length of w. Let $E \notin Lab(P)$ and $i \in Lab(P)$. Then

$$
\begin{aligned}
A(\sigma, \varepsilon, \sigma') &\stackrel{\text{def}}{=} \langle \sigma, E, \sigma' \rangle, \\
A(\sigma, \langle \sigma_1, \sigma_2 \rangle \cdot w, \sigma') &\stackrel{\text{def}}{=} \langle \sigma, E, \sigma_1 \rangle \cdot \langle \sigma_1, i, \sigma_2 \rangle \cdot A(\sigma_2, w, \sigma').
\end{aligned}
$$

Conversely, let $\models_{R_\tau} \langle rely, guar \rangle : \{\varphi\} P \{\psi\}$ and

$$\pi = \langle \sigma_1, i_1, \sigma_2 \rangle \cdots \langle \sigma_n, i_n, \sigma_{n+1} \rangle \in \mathcal{A}cz [\![P]\!]$$

such that $\sigma_1 \models \varphi$ and $\langle \sigma_k, \sigma_{k+1} \rangle \models rely$, for $i_k \notin Lab(P)$. Then the requirements of $\models_A$ are satisfied because of the existence of a corresponding $w \in \mathcal{R}_\tau [\![P]\!]$. Formally, we define $R_P(\pi)$ by induction on the length of π:

$$
\begin{aligned}
R_P(\varepsilon) &\stackrel{\text{def}}{=} \varepsilon, \\
R_P(\langle \sigma_1, i_1, \sigma_2 \rangle \cdot \pi) &\stackrel{\text{def}}{=} \begin{cases} \langle \sigma_1, \sigma_2 \rangle \cdot R_P(\pi) & i_1 \in Lab(P) \\ \langle \sigma_2, \sigma_2 \rangle \cdot R_P(\pi) & i_1 \notin Lab(P), \end{cases}
\end{aligned}
$$

and use $R_P(\pi) \in \mathcal{R}_\tau [\![P]\!]$ as a reactive sequence corresponding to π to prove that *guar* and ψ hold in their respective (pairs of) states. Note that the insertion of stutter steps is used to obtain the 'gaps' corresponding to the environmental steps in π, in order to provide extra observation points. $\qquad \Box$

These results imply that Colin Stirling's reduction of the rely-guarantee formalism [Sti88] to that of Owicki & Gries is justified, since, by transposing his system into our setting, one obtains rely and guarantee predicates which are reflexive and transitive by definition. This is explained in the next section.

8.5 Historical Notes

Some researchers, e.g., Leslie Lamport and Natarajan Shankar, consider Ed Ashcroft's method of global invariants [Ash75] as the main practical noncompositional proof method for shared-variable concurrency. For example, Lamport writes in [Lam94b] that

The concept of invariance was introduced by Ashcroft; it is hidden inside the machinery of the Owicki-Gries method. A proof is essentially the same when carried out in either method.

Others consider the method of Owicki and Gries as a step forward w.r.t. Ashcroft's method. For example, Zohar Manna and Amir Pnueli write in [MP95, page 165]:

It is possible to view Owicki and Gries' method as the association of an assertion φ_l with each location l in the program, i.e., going back to Floyd's original method. This can be viewed as an improvement on Ashcroft's method which associates an assertion with each tuple of locations.

And we wrote earlier on page 143:

As such the present method [i.e., of Owicki and Gries] intrinsically involves a so-called *compositional* way of reasoning since it allows one to obtain a proof of correctness of an entire system from local correctness proofs of its components.

All these points of view are correct in their own way. Granted, *technically speaking,* the method of Owicki and Gries can be seen as a mere reformulation of Ashcroft's method. However, *conceptually speaking,* Owicki and Gries introduce an important separation of concerns, paving the way for compositional reasoning. Namely, that between *local* correctness proofs, valid when considering a process *in isolation,* and the interference *caused by its environment.* From here it is but a small step to Cliff Jones' summary of the basic philosophy of the rely-guarantee paradigm on page 43: "to *specify* the interference allowed by the environment of a component during its execution *without endangering its purpose*".

Rely-Guarantee-based reasoning was first proposed by Francez and Pnueli [FP78] and Jones [Jon81]. Given a parallel composition $P_1 \| P_2$, program P_1 is shown to behave correctly, assuming that P_2 behaves in a certain way, and similarly for P_2. Sometimes the correctness of P_1 and the correctness of P_2 are mutually dependent: the guarantees of P_1 influence the assumptions of P_2 which influence the guarantees of P_2, influencing the assumptions of P_1, and so on. Care must be taken to ensure that the reasoning does not become circular and unsound. Consider, for instance, the following two programs.

$$P_1 \equiv y := 0 \,; \mathbf{wait}\ y = 1 \,; x := 1$$
$$P_2 \equiv x := 0 \,; \mathbf{wait}\ x = 1 \,; y := 1$$

Let $P(x,y)$ stand for:

$P(x,y) \equiv$ If the environment eventually sets x to 1,
then the program will eventually set y to 1.

Although P_1 and P_2 satisfy $P(y,x)$ and $P(x,y)$, respectively, it is not the case that $P_1 \| P_2$ will eventually set x and y to 1, since x being set to 1 by P_1 depends on y being set to 1 by P_2 which depends on $\dots$. The reasoning is circular and unsound. While all proof systems using rely-guarantee reasoning in the literature are based on the idea of explicitly specifying the rely and guarantee conditions of a program, there is a lot of variation in the way they break this symmetry.

In [FP78], Francez and Pnueli consider shared-variable parallel programs in which each variable is either a local variable, an input variable or an output variable. The behaviour is modelled by sequences of states

$$\sigma_0 \to \sigma_1 \to \sigma_2 \dots$$

where some of the steps may have been performed by the environment. A compositional treatment of parallel composition is obtained because program and environmental transitions are identifiable by the variable that they change. Specifications are of the form (φ, ψ) where φ and ψ are formulae involving an explicit time variable. A behaviour meets the specification (φ, ψ) iff it satisfies ψ whenever it satisfies φ. The rule for parallel composition uses explicit induction over some wellfounded set. The induction not only avoids circularity, but also allows arbitrary formulae (including liveness properties) to be used as assumptions and commitments. Pnueli later extended the approach to linear temporal logic [Pnu85].

In [Sta84, Sta85], Stark extends the partial-correctness-oriented formalism of [Jon81, Jon83] to specifying liveness properties within the Rely-Guarantee framework, and breaks the above-mentioned symmetry within his proof rule for parallel composition by introducing an explicit argument. In [Sta88], he extends his formalism to proving refinement and proves soundness and completeness of the resulting framework.

Complete compositional proof systems for Jones' rely-guarantee paradigm are presented in [Stø90a, Xu92].

Colin Stirling presents a generalisation of Owicki and Gries' proof system. Again, compositionality is achieved using rely-guarantee reasoning [Sti88]. Specifications of the form

$$[P, \Gamma] \, C \, [Q, \Delta]$$

are used to express that, if executed in an initial state satisfying P and in a parallel environment preserving all predicates in Γ, C promises to terminate in a state satisfying Q and to preserve all predicates in Δ. In Stirling's setting, Γ typically does not imply Q, because C is *not* subject to interference after termination – this is in contrast to the set-up in the present chapter. As in Jones' work, proofs are modular due to the use of rely-guarantee reasoning and thus program development is supported.

A difference between Jones' (and our) formulation of the rely-guarantee paradigm and that of Stirling is that in Jones' setting a rely (respectively, guarantee) predicate is a single predicate over primed *and* unprimed variables. However, in Stirling's setting a rely (respectively, guarantee) predicate is given by a set Γ (respectively, Δ) of predicates over unprimed variables, only. The idea is that every single environment (respectively, component) step has to preserve *all* predicates in Γ (respectively, Δ).

So, if, for instance, $P \in \Gamma$ and the environment makes a step from state σ to σ', and also $\models P(\sigma)$, then $\models P(\sigma')$ has to hold, too. Intuitively, this means that one cannot force the environment to change the state in a certain way, as in, e.g., $x > x'$. One can only *prevent* the environment from making certain state changes, namely, the ones that would change the value of some predicate $P \in \Gamma$ from true to false. The same holds for guarantee predicates.

So one can think of the Stirling-style rely Γ predicate as the following Jones-style rely predicate:

$$\forall P \in \Gamma.(P \rightarrow P'),$$

and of the Stirling-style guarantee Δ predicate as the Jones-style guarantee predicate

$$\forall P \in \Delta.(P \rightarrow P'),$$

both of which are reflexive and transitive. In other words, using sets of predicates as rely and guarantee predicates, as proposed by Colin Stirling, gives one in Jones' setting rely and guarantee predicates which are reflexive and transitive *by definition*.[4]

---

[4] We owe this observation to Jürgen Dingel.

The primary concern in the UNITY framework of Jayadev Misra and Mani Chandy is the logical design of concurrent programs [CM88], which is also discussed in Chapter 12. Thus, UNITY separates *what* problem is to be solved from *when, where,* and *how* this can be achieved. The what is specified in a program, whereas the when, where and how are specified in a *mapping* which describes how the constructs and variables are to be mapped to a particular architecture. This separation allows for a simple programming notation that is appropriate for a wide variety of architectures. Together with a strong emphasis on non-operational reasoning, it is this strategy that makes the UNITY approach very appealing.

However, due to the absence of control flow in UNITY, existing theories for program development and verification are not applicable. Considerable insight is required to introduce such a fundamental operator as ";" into UNITY, as done in [SdR94], and worked out in Chapter 12.

Also, UNITY, as presented in [CM88], has the drawback that it is based on a noncompositional computational model. The behaviour of a composite program is not described solely in terms of its components, making it hard to reason compositionally. This deficiency has been addressed in [Col93, CK95] which view a UNITY program as an *open* system which is subject to interrupts and intermediate state changes by the environment. In his thesis [Col94a] Pierre Collette defines a compositional trace semantics for UNITY based on Aczel traces. He augments the UNITY logic with rely-guarantee specifications and uses a composition principle similar to that proposed by Abadi and Lamport [AL93] to equip UNITY with a compositional parallel proof rule for rely-guarantee specifications.

In [GN90, GNL90], Grønning, Nielsen and Løvengreen introduce a formalism for refinement and composition of transition-based Rely-Guarantee specifications with auxiliary variables, which aims at proving safety properties, and includes a proof rule for hiding.

Martín Abadi and Leslie Lamport free themselves of any particular program syntax or paradigm and study parallel programming from a very abstract point of view that strives to replace operational by logical reasoning. In [AL93], they isolate in very general terms the conditions under which assumption-guarantee specifications for the components of a system imply an assumption-guarantee specification of the overall system. These conditions are captured in a proof rule called the composition principle.

We mention, next, some results of Simon S. Lam and A. Udaya Shankar [LS84a, SL87, SL90, SL90]. Their work concerns, e.g., the verification of network protocols using refinement methods, and compositional verification methods [LS92a, LS94], which influence recent work on the compositional verification of component-based design using UNITY [MS96, CC99]. An interesting format in between distributed message passing and shared-variable concurrency is the restriction of the latter to an access discipline in which every shared variable can be modified ("is owned") by only one process and read by all others. Verification theories for this format have been presented in [KKPR99, CC99].

Another question concerns the comparison of verification theories for synchronous message passing and shared-variable concurrency. For synchronous message passing [Zwi89, ZdRvEB84] introduce a "telescope" of four formalisms:

- the *SAT*-formalism,
- a variant of Hoare Logic – utilising Vaughan Pratt's suggestion in [Pra82] that pre- and postconditions are assertions over a combination of communication traces and states,
- trace-invariant-based reasoning, and
- assume-guarantee-based reasoning.

This suggests looking for a similar telescope of proof formats for shared-variable concurrency. These have been developed partly in [dBTdRvH96, dBHdR97a, dBHdR97b] based on the idea of characterising computations through so-called *timing diagrams*. These are mappings from a discrete, total, and wellfounded ordering to states, which, when combined with certain action predicates, result in a compositional formalism.

A promising direction of research is initiated in Jürgen Dingel's PhD thesis [Din99a, Din99b], in which compositional reasoning is combined with the refinement calculus of Caroll Morgan and Paul Gardiner [Mor90, GM93], resulting in a formal compositional framework for the development of parallel programs, for both shared-variable concurrency and distributed message passing. The usage and applicability of Dingel's framework is demonstrated through a wide variety of examples that involve shared-variable parallel programs, distributed programs and mutual exclusion algorithms. More specifically, Dingel employs a mixed-term formalism in which executable programs and specifications can be combined by both program and specification operators. The specification language is given a compositional *trace semantics* based on Brooke's work [Bro96], from which it inherits many properties. A *context-sensitive* notion of *approximation* is defined that allows the comparison of two programs with respect to a particular context. This notion of approximation is combined with assumption-guarantee-based reasoning to form the *refinement relation,* supporting stepwise, top-down program development and compositional reasoning, the introduction of local variables and channels, and the seamless treatment of message-passing and shared-variable concurrency. The *refinement calculus* identifies a number of rules that govern the refinement relation. Most of these rules are compositional. Summarising, Dingel's work constitutes one of the most recent developments of compositional reasoning about, and compositional derivation of, concurrent programs.[5]

Exercises

8.1   **(Hard)** Formulate a compositional proof theory for shared variable concurrency using the following simplification of the associated models:

> A shared variable can be updated by only one process, and read by the other ones, i.e., for every shared variable only one process has write access.

8.2   Generalise the proof method for closed top-level shared-variable concurrency to nested concurrency.
Hints:

- Adapt the definition of $\models \{\varphi\} \, P \, \{\psi\}$ such that it takes into account the sequential composition of programs.
- Give a new definition of $\models \{\varphi\} \, \langle P \rangle \, \{\psi\}$ with $\langle P \rangle$ a closed program.
- Introduce a separate rule for $\{\varphi\} \, \langle P \rangle \, \{\psi\}$ which takes into account that one may start with an arbitrary initial history (introduce a freeze variable to denote the initial trace).

8.3   Let $\pi \in \mathcal{A}cz \llbracket P \rrbracket$. Let f be a *renaming function* which replaces process identifiers $i \in \overline{Lab(P)}$ occurring in π by process identifiers $j \in \overline{Lab(P)}$. Formalise the concept of renaming functions and prove that $f(\pi) \in \mathcal{A}cz \llbracket P \rrbracket$.

8.4   Let $P \equiv P_1 \parallel P_2 \parallel P_3$ as given in Figure 8.4. Prove $\models \langle y = y', true \rangle : \{y = 0\} \, P \, \{y = 3\}$.

8.5   Formulate the rely-guarantee proof method using a logical history variable similar to that of Section 8.3.

8.6   Give a detailed proof that process P_2 indeed satisfies its specification in Example 8.26.

8.7   Prove soundness of the sequential composition rule 8.6 and the initialisation rule 8.10.

8.8   Prove Lemma 8.32 and Lemma 8.35.

---

[5] Some parts of this section originate from his thesis.

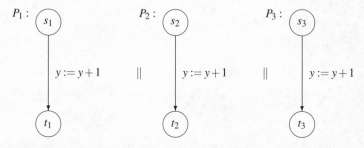

Fig. 8.4. Program $P \equiv P_1 \parallel P_2 \parallel P_3$ for Exercise 8.4.

8.9 Prove that

$$\pi \in \mathcal{A}cz[\![P]\!] \Leftrightarrow \pi[Lab(P)] \in \mathcal{R}[\![P]\!].$$

8.10 Prove soundness of the parallel composition rule 8.7 w.r.t. R-validity under the assumption that the action predicates $rely_1$ and $rely_2$ are transitive.

8.11 **(Open problem)** In Section 1.6.4 the notion of a complete adaptation rule is explained. In [ZHLdR95] such a rule has been formulated for synchronous message passing in the context of the assumption-commitment formalism. In the formulation of this rule the notions of strongest postcondition and strongest commitment operators play a central rôle. The present chapter develops similar notions for shared-variable concurrency in the context of the rely-guarantee formalism. However, the problem how to formulate a complete adaptation rule for shared-variable concurrency in the context of the latter formalism is not yet solved. Formulate such a rule, using the techniques developed in this chapter and in [ZHLdR95]. (The research involved is roughly that required for a Master's Thesis at the University of Kiel.)

Part IV
Hoare Logic

9

A Proof System for Sequential Programs Using Hoare Triples

9.1 Introduction and Overview of Hoare Logics

9.1.1 Overview of Part IV

In Part II of this volume we have presented sound and (semantically) complete methods for proving correctness of concurrent programs, which communicate by means of shared variables, and of distributed programs, which communicate by synchronous message passing. The method used is that of inductive assertions in which a finite number of verification conditions are generated whose validity is both sufficient to guarantee correctness of a program, and necessary in that, once a program is correct, the validity of an appropriate set of verification conditions is guaranteed. Also we have proved that these verification conditions can be expressed as assertions from first-order predicate logic over the natural numbers, using Gödel encoding.

Next, we have developed in Part III compositional proof methods for these kinds of concurrent programs which are also based on the inductive assertion method. As argued in Section 1.6, these enable us to *verify a program during the process of its development from its specification,* a strategy called the *verify-while-develop* paradigm. This contrasts with *a posteriori* program verification which applies to program correctness *after* a program has been designed. Since programs are almost always incorrect, the attempt to prove their correctness usually results in the detection of errors in their code, after which the cycle of program redesign and correctness proof starts all over again. This is not the case for the verify-while-develop paradigm, which should therefore be applied, whenever possible.

However, the above programme is not yet complete.

First of all, the compositional proof methods from Part III apply to nested concurrency only, i.e., to systems which are built from basic (synchronous) transition diagrams using sequential and parallel composition. Therefore they reduce the verification of such systems to the verification of these basic transition diagrams. Using the terminology of the verify-while-develop paradigm, the methods developed until now for the systematic derivation of such systems from their specifications provide no help once specifications of basic transition diagrams are obtained. This is unacceptable, for such basic diagrams correspond to sequential programs or processes, and the systematic derivation of such programs from their specifications constitutes one of computer science's major tasks. Solutions to this problem have been developed under the heading of "structured programming", especially by Edsger W. Dijkstra and his group of colleagues since the end of the sixties, see, e.g., [Dij69b, Wir71, DDH72, Dij76, Jon80, Gri81, Rey81, Dij82, Heh84, Jon86, Bac86, Bor87, Spi88, DF88, Mor90, Kal90, Dah92, Heh93, vdS93, BEKV94] – and this list is by no means complete.

Consequently, in these chapters we extend the methods developed in the previous chapters to sequential program operators (the incorporation of data structures is beyond the scope of this work).

Secondly, what was missing in the previous chapters was *a direct link between program verification and the textual representation of programs.*

The need for such a link became clear when proving Szymanski's mutual exclusion algorithm correct in Example 3.19. There, textual representations of transition diagrams and their associated assertion networks were needed to obtain readable correctness arguments. Also, a readable correctness proof for a correct concurrent garbage collector, see Section 1.4.3, requires program text. This is immediately obvious from the proof of such an algorithm given in Section 10.5; that proof would have been unreadable had it been based directly on transition diagrams. In fact, all extended examples presented in the previous chapters suffered to a certain degree from the fact that there was no such link.

A solution to both these problems is provided by (sequential) *Hoare logic* [Hoa69]. First, this logic is compositional w.r.t. its sequential programming operators and, therefore, extends the compositional methods developed for concurrency in the previous chapters to sequential programming. Second, Hoare logic provides an immediate link between program verification and program text. These points are explained below.

A programming language has an algebraic structure which is defined by its operations and which is reflected in its programs. Now *Hoare logic reflects this algebraic structure at the level of its logic,* i.e., by its axioms and rules.

In Part II, such a structure was absent within our basic formalism, that of (sequential) transitions diagrams, with (various forms of) parallel composition as the only operation. Consequently, we first introduced the algebraically-unstructured inductive assertion method for sequential transition diagrams, and later various rules for parallel composition.

In Part III, our atomic building blocks for programs were again (sequential) transition diagrams, with sequential and parallel composition as operations; application of these operations did result in programs but did not result in sequential transition diagrams (defining these operations at the level of transition diagrams would have defied our purpose). This algebraic structure of programs was reflected at the level of proof methods by compositionally-inductive assertion methods for sequential transition diagrams, and corresponding proof rules for these two operations.

Hoare logic extends this development even further towards adding more operations plus corresponding proof rules in that it *only features the application of rules* (axioms being regarded as rules with empty premises).

In these chapters we shall give a broader interpretation to Hoare logic than that suggested above, namely by *regarding this logic as a structured proof method for the inductive construction of inductive assertion networks for programs.* This includes program proving by the systematic "decoration" of program text by means of assertions from first-order predicate logic. In case these assertions are inductive, this results in so-called *proof-outlines.* Thus, by integrating the algebraic structure of programs within our proof system, we obtain a representation of transition diagrams which allows one to construct assertion networks inductively (and concisely) using annotated programs as their representation.

In the context of sequential programming, Hoare logic is compositional when considered in its original form, which excludes the decoration of program text by assertions [Hoa69]. For Dijkstra's guarded-command language such a Hoare logic will be developed in this chapter, and illustrated by various examples. We shall prove two equivalences between this Hoare logic and the inductive assertion method. Also the corresponding proof-outline logic will be worked out, and proved to be equivalent in expressive power to the inductive assertion method. Consequently, the soundness and semantic completeness of the inductive assertion method will be shown to carry over to the soundness and relative completeness of these logics.

We will present Hoare logics for shared-variable concurrency and synchronous message passing in Chapters 10 and 11. These logics are based on a syntactic formulation, within the context of Hoare logic, of the interference freedom and cooperation tests from Chapters 3 and 4 by means of proof outlines. Also for these logics we prove equivalence with their corresponding inductive assertion methods. And, similarly as above, the soundness and semantic completeness of these inductive assertion methods immediately implies soundness and relative completeness of these logics. They are noncompositional, because the syntactic formulation of the interference freedom and cooperation tests requires reference to the program text, and this is not allowed according to the compositionality principle. To obtain compositional Hoare logics for these forms of concurrency, the compositionally-inductive assertion networks plus proof rules developed in Chapters 7 and 8 have to be reformulated as proof rules for each operation concerned (for compositionally-inductive assertion networks this especially introduces a considerable amount of complexity). This is worked out in the companion volume. How to obtain such a reformulation in the case of the parallel composition of synchronous diagrams is the subject of Section 11.6.

Also the program development method presented in Chapter 12, *layered composition*, is presented using program text, because it is based on program transformations, and these require a textual representation of programs.

Finally, complicated and long correctness arguments, such as required for, e.g., networks of real-time processes, should be machine verified in order to be really convincing. For this purpose the textual representation of programs is the only option presently available. This provides additional motivation for using Hoare logic as the basic formalism in the companion volume.

9.1.2 Hoare Triples

Our framework for the specification and verification of programs in these chapters is based on *Hoare triples*, that is, formulae of the form $\{p\} \ S \ \{q\}$, where

- p is an assertion, called the *precondition*,
- S is a *statement*, written in some programming language,
- q is an assertion, called the *postcondition*.

Informally, (validity of) such a triple expresses that if p holds in the initial state of S, i.e., for the variables at the start of the execution of S, then q holds for any final state of S, that is, if a computation of S terminates then q holds for the values of the variables at termination. For instance, the Hoare triple $\{x = 5\} \ x := x + 1 \ \{x = 6\}$ is valid. Hoare triples are also called *correctness formulae*, because they express the notion of program correctness dealt with in our theory.

Similarly to Chapter 5, assertions p and q are expressed in a first-order assertion language (over N). As well as program variables, as used in the example above and collected in the set *Pvar*, we also use *logical variables* , which are collected in the set *Lvar*. For example, in order to express that the program $x := x + 1$ increments x by 1, logical variable $x_0 \in Lvar$ is used as follows:

$\{x = x_0\}\ x := x + 1\ \{x = x_0 + 1\}$. The need for such variables has already been argued in Section 2.4.1, where they are called logical or freeze variables. Obviously, the sets of program variables and logical variables are assumed to be disjoint.

Our aim is to develop proof systems in which valid Hoare triples can be formally derived. As a first step towards this goal we consider in this chapter the correctness of sequential programs written in a variant of Dijkstra's guarded command language GCL [Dij76]; this variant we call GCL^+. GCL^+ is the textual equivalent of the language of sequential transition diagrams from Chapter 2. (This follows from a result by Böhm & Jacopini [BJ66] which states essentially that transition diagrams can be converted into nested loops using boolean variables for recording the values of tests in those diagrams.) With each program S in this language we associate a transition diagram $T\,[\![S]\!]$ in order to define the semantics $O[\![S]\!]$ of S by $O[\![T\,[\![S]\!]]\!]$, the semantics of its associated transition diagram. Thus we reduce S semantically to a transition diagram. This strategy allows us to regard programs as a notation for transition diagrams *with a syntactic structure*, and, consequently, to take this syntactic structure into account when reasoning about them. For example, one can define $T\,[\![S_1;S_2]\!]$ as the sequential composition of $T\,[\![S_1]\!]$ and $T\,[\![S_2]\!]$, and derive such structural properties as $O[\![S_1;S_2]\!] = \{(\sigma,\tau) \mid$ there exists ρ s.t. $(\sigma,\rho) \in O[\![S_1]\!]$ and $(\rho,\tau) \in O[\![S_2]\!]\} = O[\![S_1]\!]\,;O[\![S_2]\!]$.

More interestingly, *this point of view allows us to regard Hoare logic as a syntactically-structured mechanism for proving correctness statements about transition diagrams inductively*. To be precise, Hoare logic has as an additional advantage over inductive assertion based methods that it uses the algebraic structure of programs to impose a corresponding structure on proofs about programs. Notice that such a structure is absent in the proof methods from Chapters 2, 3, and 4, since we did not define Floyd's inductive assertion method by induction on the associated transition diagrams, and neither did we define the methods due to Owicki & Gries and Apt, Francez & de Roever that way.

Abbreviating the existence of a proof of $\{p\}S\{q\}$ in Hoare logic by $\vdash \{p\}S\{q\}$, and the existence of a proof that $\models \{p\}T\,[\![S]\!]\,\{q\}$ holds using the method of inductive assertions by $\vdash \{p\}T\,[\![S]\!]\,\{q\}$, we prove as the key result in Theorem 9.17 that

$$\vdash \{p\}S\{q\} \text{ iff } \vdash \{p\}T\,[\![S]\!]\,\{q\}. \tag{a}$$

Since the fact that the semantics of S is defined by $T\,[\![S]\!]$ immediately implies

$$\models \{p\}S\{q\} \text{ iff } \models \{p\}T\,[\![S]\!]\,\{q\}, \tag{b}$$

soundness and (relative) completeness of the inductive assertion method,

$$\models \{p\}T[\![S]\!]\{q\} \text{ iff } \vdash \{p\}T[\![S]\!]\{q\}, \tag{c}$$

implies the soundness and (relative) completeness of Hoare logic (Theorem 9.18) as formulated below:

$$\models \{p\}S\{q\} \overset{\text{(b)}}{\Longleftrightarrow} \models \{p\}T[\![S]\!]\{q\} \overset{\text{(c)}}{\Longleftrightarrow} \vdash \{p\}T[\![S]\!]\{q\} \overset{\text{(a)}}{\Longleftrightarrow} \vdash \{p\}S\{q\}.$$

In the next two chapters, GCL^+ is extended to a simple programming language for shared-variable concurrency with synchronisation, SVL^+, and an OCCAM-like language for synchronous message passing.

Similarly to the proof methods of Owicki & Gries and Apt, Francez & de Roever in the previous chapters, the associated Hoare logics for shared-variable concurrency and synchronous message passing in Chapters 10 and 11 yield their proofs in a two-stage process.

First, local proofs are generated for each of the parallel processes in isolation using the sequential part of Hoare logic which enables proving properties of purely sequential statements. Secondly, interference and cooperation tests are used to deduce properties of concurrent programs. The problem is now: *"To which (syntactically structured) objects should these tests in Hoare logic be applied?"*.

We know already by our above key result that any proof of $\vdash \{p\}S\{q\}$ for a sequential statement corresponds to an inductive assertion network correct w.r.t. p and q, and vice versa, and for such inductive assertion networks the appropriate notions for IFT and COOP have been defined already. So all that remains is to reformulate our question as: *To which syntactically structured notation do inductive assertion networks correspond?*. The solution to this problem has been given by Owicki & Gries [OG76a] by introducing the notion of *proof outline*.

We adopt this solution for shared-variable concurrency in Chapter 10. For synchronous message passing in Chapter 11 we adopt Apt's notion of proofs from assumptions [Apt84], which separates proofs for sequential statements from any assumptions regarding communication.

A proof outline is a sequential statement which is systematically annotated with assertions and which is inductively defined (according to the structure of that statement's syntax) in such a way that the generated assertions are related by verification conditions to the annotated text. For example, $\{p\}x := e\{q\}$ is a proof outline for $x := e$ if $\models p \to q[e/x]$ holds, and $\{p\}A(S_1); \{r\}A(S_2)\{q\}$ is a proof outline for $S_1; S_2$ provided $\{p\}A(S_1)\{r\}$ and $\{r\}A(S_2)\{q\}$ are proof outlines for, respectively, S_1 and S_2.

We will view proof outlines as structured syntactic representations of inductive assertion networks, in the same vein as the program S is viewed as a structured notation for the transition system $T[\![S]\!]$. Hence, the contents of these chapters on Hoare logic can be summarised by:

- The translation of a program S into a transition system $T[\![S]\!]$ allows us to define the semantics of a program in terms of the semantics of its corresponding transition system, and therefore to regard programs as a structured notation for transition systems.

- Consequently, a correctness proof of a program S in Hoare logic corresponds to an inductive assertion network for $T[\![S]\!]$, and vice-versa, with the added difference that a proof in Hoare logic now reflects the algebraic structure of the program in question.

- A proof outline of a program S denotes an inductive assertion network for $T[\![S]\!]$, but displays the algebraic structure of S.

- As a result, Hoare-style proof outlines allow one to construct assertion networks inductively using their representation as annotated programs.

9.1.3 Hoare Triples, Compositionality and the Verify-While-Develop Paradigm

A compositional proof system first of all requires a compositional (assertional) specification language, in which the specification of a compound (non-atomic) construct is implied by suitable sub-specifications for its direct components, without any additional information concerning their implementation. For a compositional proof system one additionally needs that the proof rules specific to each type of compound construct are compositional, i.e., satisfy the following format: their hypotheses consist of properties of their direct components and a number of implications, while their conclusion lists a property of the combined construct in question, again without additional information about, or reference to, any possible implementation of those components.

An example of such a compositional proof rule is Hoare's rule for the while statement:

Hoare's while-statement rule

$$\frac{\{I \wedge b\}S\{I\}}{\{I\} \text{ while } b \text{ do } S \text{ od } \{I \wedge \neg b\}} \, .$$

This rule states the conclusion, that the compound statement **while** b **do** S **od** satisfies the partial correctness formula $\{I\}$ **while** b **do** S **od** $\{I \wedge \neg b\}$, once its premise above the line, $\{I \wedge b\} \ S \ \{I\}$, which is a partial correctness formula for the component S (its body) of **while** b **do** S **od** , has been proved.

In order to understand why a compositional proof system allows the verify-while-develop strategy and why a specification format based on Hoare triples does not in general result in a compositional proof system for shared-variable concurrency or synchronous message passing, we explain how to obtain Hoare logics technically.

Consider again the above while rule. Of course we already know how partial correctness of S is established. For Floyd's inductive assertion method from Chapter 2 already provides the answer, be it that in that case S is a sequential transition diagram instead of a GCL^+ statement. So, as mentioned already, first we define the semantics of a GCL^+ statement S as being that of the corresponding transition diagram $T \ [\![S]\!]$. (Ultimately program execution consists of the execution of assignment statements and control flow. Since these are provided by the semantics of transition diagrams, why bother about formulating a new format for defining semantics if no essentially new element is introduced?) This step implies that partial correctness of S, $\models \{p\} \ S \ \{q\}$ is equivalent to partial correctness of $T \ [\![S]\!]$, $\models \{p\} \ T \ [\![S]\!] \ \{q\}$, which is defined in Chapter 2.

Moreover one can also take into account the rule of consequence:

Rule of consequence

$$\frac{p \rightarrow p_0, \{p_0\} \ S \ \{q_0\}, q_0 \rightarrow q}{\{p\} \ S \ \{q\}} .$$

The *new* element provided by the while rule and the rule of consequence is that a *structural transformation* is given between the sets of verification conditions required for establishing $\models \{I \wedge b\}S\{I\}$ and establishing $\models \{p\}$ **while** b **do** S **od** $\{q\}$; namely, only the implications $\models p \rightarrow I$ and $\models I \wedge \neg b \rightarrow q$ should additionally hold!

For the argument below, it is important to observe the following fact about the formulation of this compositional rule – that in this rule S occurs in the context **while** b **do** S **od** is not reflected in any way in its hypothesis, apart from requiring S to satisfy $\{I \wedge b\}S\{I\}$, and requiring $(p \rightarrow I)$ and $(I \wedge \neg b \rightarrow q)$ to be valid. The mere fact of establishing $\{I \wedge b\}S\{I\}$, *regardless of how S is eventually implemented*, together with $\models p \rightarrow I$ and $\models I \wedge \neg b \rightarrow q$ already guarantees $\{p\}$ **while** b **do** S **od** $\{q\}$ will hold. No further connections between the implementation of S and this occurrence of S in the context **while** b **do** S **od** w.r.t. precondition p and postcondition q have to be taken into account to establish the rule's conclusion.

That is, if one's aim is to develop a statement S which satisfies the Hoare triple $\{p\}$ **while** b **do** S **od** $\{q\}$, then the development step: "Find an assertion I s.t. $(p \rightarrow I)$ and $(I \wedge \neg b \rightarrow q)$ are valid", brings us one step nearer to that goal, provided the next goal is to develop S such that $\{I \wedge b\}S\{I\}$ holds. This illustrates why compositional proof rules support the "verify-while-develop" paradigm in this particular case. Moreover, it is important to observe that once the implications $(p \rightarrow I)$ and $(I \wedge \neg b \rightarrow q)$ are proved, *any later development step of S does not in any way influence the validity of the "present" step*, consisting of establishing validity of $p \rightarrow I$ and $I \wedge \neg b \rightarrow q$. How the Hoare logic given in this chapter can be used to combine program development with program verification is further illustrated in Section 9.9.

Why the verify-while-develop strategy works in this case can be understood by observing that $\models p \rightarrow I$, $\models I \wedge \neg b \rightarrow q$ and $\models \{I \wedge b\}S\{I\}$ all express conditions upon the *interface* between S and its environment **while** b **do** ... **od**, in order for their combination to satisfy $\models \{p\}$ **while** b **do** S **od** $\{q\}$. This interface consists in this sequential context of sets of pairs of initial plus corresponding final states of S, the *observable behaviour* of S. In this sequential context there is no way S can interact with its environment *except through this observable behaviour*. Hence its interface with its environment is expressed in terms of this behaviour: requiring a certain precondition $(I \wedge b)$ and a certain postcondition (I) to hold for its observable behaviour, and guaranteeing consistency w.r.t. the pre- and postconditions p and q imposed upon its environment by requiring validity of $p \rightarrow I$ and $I \wedge \neg b \rightarrow q$.

Observe that this argument does not apply when there are *more ways to interact* with an environment than only through initial and final states, as is the case with parallel composition. Then the interface can no longer be expressed in terms of the initial and final states of a process, as a result of which it can no longer be expressed through corresponding Hoare triples with assertions imposing restrictions only upon this initial-final-state behaviour. The resulting parallel composition rules then require additional noncompositional modes of expression for their formulation, in order to express conditions upon these additional ways of interaction between a process and its parallel environment during its execution, in this case the noncompositional notion of *proof outline* mentioned previously. For considering $\{pre\}P_1\|P_2\{post\}$ we already know that the development of P_1 in isolation of P_2 only on the basis of satisfying some Hoare triple $\{pre_1\}P_1\{post_1\}$ is not adequate (assuming again that the semantics of the textual statement $P_1\|P_2$ has been defined by that of its associated transition diagram). For, e.g., in the case of shared-variable concurrency one has to establish that the assertions generated during the development of P_1 (including pre_1 and $post_1$) *should be invariant* under the execution of assignments in the eventual program text of P_2, as required by the interference freedom test (IFT). The same holds, mutatis mutandis, for distributed message passing on account of the need to satisfy the cooperation test (COOP). Recall that for GCL (and GCL$^+$) *no such relation exists* between the correctness of the "present" development step made on the basis of the while rule above, and any future development steps of S, i.e., the "present" step in the development of **while** b **do** S **od** cannot be invalidated by any "future" development step of S. This separation of concerns forms the main attraction of compositional proof systems, and explains why so much effort is put into developing compositional proof systems for parallelism.

Thus compositional proof systems for shared-variable communication and synchronous message passing cannot be formulated within a simplistic set-up where only initial and final states are observable, because for compositionality additional information concerning intermediate steps during program execution is required, as worked out in Part III. In Chapters 10 and 11 this type of information is provided in a noncompositional set-up by *inserting* the assertions whose invariance must be checked or established, as required by IFT and COOP, *within the program text itself*, resulting in the already mentioned notions of proof outline and proofs from assumptions. Consequently any claim regarding compositionality is given up, precisely because that final program text must be there in order to formulate proof outlines (and proofs from assumptions).

That compositionality can be obtained in a different setting in which the intermediate events through which a process interacts with its environment are also observable, and in which the specification of these events is incorporated within the Hoare-triple format, is worked out in the companion volume.

As an aside, observe that, had the *labels* of the intermediate program text been regarded as observable, then the assertions attached to those labels, whose invariance has to be checked, could have been specified, too, in an appropriate format for these observables, and a compositional proof method would have resulted. This is the approach followed by Gerth and de Roever in [GdR86], in which compositional proof systems for monitor-based languages, such as concurrent ADA, are developed.

9.2 Structure of this Chapter

Section 9.3 contains the syntax and the informal semantics of the Language of Guarded Commands GCL of Dijkstra [Dij76], and of a variant called GCL$^+$ introduced for the sake of mathematical elegance. GCL programs can be seen as abbreviations of GCL$^+$ programs. Both are the textual counterpart of the language of transition diagrams from Chapter 2. The semantics of the language GCL$^+$, and thus of GCL, is defined in Section 9.4 by associating with every GCL$^+$ program S a transition diagram $T[\![S]\!]$ for which the semantics has already been defined in Chapter 2. Partial correctness is specified by Hoare triples, using pre- and postconditions expressed in the assertion language defined in Chapter 5. A proof system called PS_{seq} in which such Hoare triples can be derived is formulated in Section 9.5. Section 9.9 describes some examples of how GCL$^+$ programs can be specified, developed and verified. Soundness and relative completeness of this proof system are proved in Section 9.6, whereas proof outlines, a representation of inductive assertion networks for $T[\![S]\!]$ in terms of a version of S which is annotated with assertions, are introduced in Section 9.7. Some alternative definitions of proof outlines are given in Section 9.8. Section 9.10 gives the historical background of this chapter, and the end of this chapter consists of a list of exercises.

9.3 Syntax and Informal Meaning of GCL$^+$ Programs

The programming languages in these chapters are based on classes of expressions e, and boolean expressions b. These two types of expression are used also within the assertions of Hoare formulae. Their syntax is given in Table 9.1.

Table 9.1. *Syntax of expressions and boolean expressions.*

Expression	$e ::=\quad c \mid x \mid (e_1 + e_2) \mid (e_1 - e_2) \mid (e_1 * e_2)$
Boolean Expression	$b ::=\quad e_1 = e_2 \mid e_1 < e_2 \mid (\neg b) \mid (b_1 \wedge b_2)$

The programming language called GCL is based on Dijkstra's guarded-command language. Due to its elegant mathematical flavour, this language is well suited for the construction and verification of sequential algorithms. A typical aspect of GCL is that nondeterminism is an essential aspect of the language constructs for conditionals and for loops. These nondeterministic counterparts of the **if** $-$ **then** $-$ **else** and **while** constructs are especially useful when developing algorithms.

Let *Pvar* be a nonempty set of program variables, and *VAL* be a domain of values. Let $x \in Pvar$, and $c \in VAL$.

We have chosen fairly small classes of expressions; other arithmetical and boolean operations that can be seen as abbreviations will be used freely in examples. For instance, we use $b_1 \vee b_2 \stackrel{\text{def}}{=} \neg((\neg b_1) \wedge (\neg b_2))$. In examples we also often omit parentheses, relying on the usual precedence rules for arithmetical and boolean operators.

The syntax of GCL is given in Table 9.2.

Table 9.2. *Syntax of the Programming Language GCL.*

Statement	$S ::=$	$\bar{x} := \bar{e}$	$\mid$	$S_1 ; S_2$	$\mid$	**if** $[]_{i=1}^{n} b_i \rightarrow S_i$ **fi**	$\mid$	**do** $[]_{i=1}^{n} b_i \rightarrow S_i$ **od**

Guarded commands were invented to express *sequential* programs, and atomicity of operations was therefore not an important issue. By the principle of separation of concerns, assignments and boolean tests are strictly separated, and not combined in one action of the form of a guarded assignment $\langle b \rightarrow \bar{x} := \bar{e} \rangle$, as is the case for transition systems. In the following chapters, where we study concurrency, we take in essence GCL as the point of departure, and add language constructs like parallel composition and communication commands. Here, atomicity is of foremost importance, and we need a language construct like the guarded assignment. Such guarded assignments form the basis of our transition systems, and also of many other formal methods for concurrency, such as the development styles due to Ralph Back, see, e.g., [Bac80] and [Bac90], and to Jay Misra & Mani Chandy [CM88]. Therefore, we introduce an extension, called GCL$^+$, that incorporates guarded assignments and, for instance, allows such guarded assignments at places where in GCL only boolean guards are allowed. GCL$^+$ as such will be used mainly in theoretical investigations concerning soundness and completeness results, and is therefore chosen such that it has a simple syntax and, more importantly, provides for a straightforward translation of GCL$^+$ programs to equivalent transition systems. The language constructs of GCL$^+$ correspond to natural composition operations for transition systems. All GCL$^+$ operations amount, on the level of transition systems, to taking the disjoint union of the component graphs, followed by identification of the appropriate entry and/or exit labels. For instance, the choice construct **if** $[]_{i=1}^{n} S_i$ **fi** at the level of transition systems amounts to taking the disjoint union of the graphs denoted by the components S_i, whereafter the entries for all components are merged into one entry for the whole, and similarly, all exit locations are merged into one exit (see Figure 9.3 on page 503). Observe that, on the level of transition systems, this expresses the nondeterministic union of $S_1, \ldots, S_n$, which is, indeed, the informal meaning of **if** $[]_{i=1}^{n} S_i$ **fi**. The loop construct in GCL$^+$ is somewhat less elegant than that of GCL, due to the fact that in transition systems the transition that terminates a loop must be given explicitly. Therefore, the loop construct in GCL$^+$ has the form **do** S_B $[]$ S_E ; **exit od**, including an explicit exit branch. Informally, when such a loop is executed, the guards of the initial transitions of the "body" S_B

Table 9.3. *Syntax of the Programming Language* GCL^+.

Statement $S ::=$ $\langle b \to \bar{x} := \bar{e} \rangle$ | $S_1 ; S_2$ | **if** $[\![_{i=1}^n S_i$ **fi** |
do S_B $[\![$ S_E ; **exit od**

and the "exit branch" S_E are evaluated, and one of the transitions with a guard that evaluates to "*true*" is nondeterministically chosen. If some S_B transition is chosen, then the rest of S_B is executed and, upon reaching the exit location of S_B, the whole process is repeated; if some S_E transition is chosen, then after executing the rest of S_E and upon reaching the exit location of S_E the iteration terminates. Below we show how the loop construct from GCL^+ can be used to simulate the GCL loop and the more conventional **while** − **do** construct. One can also simulate a construct S^* which executes S zero or more times, where the actual number of iterations is chosen nondeterministically. (This is analogous to the Kleene star operator for regular languages). The intended meaning for S^* is captured by the GCL^+ statement **do** $S [\![\textbf{skip} ; \textbf{exit od}$, where **skip** denotes the guarded assignment with guard "*true*" and an assignment to an empty list of variables.

The following restrictions are imposed. Let $\equiv$ denote syntactic equality.

- For an assignment $\bar{x} := \bar{e}$, with $\bar{x} \equiv (x_1, \ldots, x_k)$ and $\bar{e} \equiv (e_1, \ldots, e_k)$, for $i = 1, \ldots, k$, the variables $x_i \in Pvar$ must all be distinct. This also applies to the assignment part of a *guarded assignment* $\langle b \to \bar{x} := \bar{e} \rangle$.
- The statements S_i, S_B and S_E in **if** $[\![_{i=1}^n S_i$ **fi** and **do** S_B $[\![$ S_E ; **exit od** must be *guarded*, where we say that S is guarded if

  – S is an action, that is, of the form $\langle b \to \bar{x} := \bar{e} \rangle$, or
  – S is of the form $S_1 ; S_2$, and S_1 is guarded, or
  – S is of the form **if** $[\![_{i=1}^n S_i$ **fi**, and S_i is guarded, for $i = 1, \ldots, n$.

The meaning of the GCL^+ constructs is obtained by translating GCL^+ statements into transition systems, which is done in Section 9.4. The guardedness of S_i in **if** $[\![_{i=1}^n S_i$ **fi** and of S_B, S_E in **do** S_B $[\![$ S_E ; **exit od** is needed in order to define the semantics of these constructs in terms of transition systems as described below. We will come back to the issue of guardedness in the next section.

GCL statements are formally introduced as abbreviations of GCL^+ statements; their translation is straightforward:

- An assignment $\bar{x} := \bar{e}$ abbreviates $\langle true \to \bar{x} := \bar{e} \rangle$.

- We also need **skip** , which abbreviates a multiple assignment with an *empty* list of variables.
- The *guarded command* notation **if** $[]_{i=1}^n b_i \to S_i$ **fi** abbreviates

$$\textbf{if } []_{i=1}^n \langle b_i \to \textbf{skip} \rangle ; S_i \textbf{ fi} .$$

- The guarded loop, **do** $[]_{i=1}^n b_i \to S_i$ **od** abbreviates **do if** $[]_{i=1}^n b_i \to S_i$ **fi** $[]$ $\langle \neg b_G \to \textbf{skip} \rangle$; **exit od**, where $b_G \equiv b_1 \lor \cdots \lor b_n$.

Note that, according to our translation, a GCL guard is executed as a transition of its own, i.e., not combined with any assignment to program variables. For sequential programs this difference hardly matters; for concurrent programs this difference is crucial because of the possibility of interference between the guard and the assignment. We return to this question in Chapter 10.

Observe that not only GCL programs, but also many other conventional programming constructs can be defined as an abbreviation:

- Sometimes, a boolean guard of the form b is used as a statement itself, which is then called a *filter*, and abbreviates $\langle b \to \textbf{skip} \rangle$.
- As an alternative to the guarded command notation one also uses constructs in the style of ALGOL, PASCAL, ADA, etc. E.g., **if** b **then** S_1 **else** S_2 **fi** abbreviates **if** $b \to S_1 [] \neg b \to S_2$ **fi** and **while** b **do** S **od** abbreviates **do** $[]_{i=1}^1 b \to S$ **od**, which is called a while statement.

In examples we will sometimes use boolean variables, ranging over $\{tt, ff\}$. Conventional abbreviations are used, such as $tt \stackrel{\text{def}}{=} 0 = 0$, $ff \stackrel{\text{def}}{=} \neg tt$, $b_1 \land b_2 \stackrel{\text{def}}{=} \neg(\neg b_1 \lor \neg b_2)$, etc.

9.4 Semantics of GCL$^+$

9.4.1 A Compositional Translation of GCL$^+$ to Transition Systems

The semantics of GCL$^+$ statements is defined by associating a transition system $T[\![S]\!]$ with program S. Recall that the difference between a transition system and a transition diagram is that a transition system is an equivalence class of transition diagrams, obtained by abstracting from the particular names of nodes of such diagrams, cf. Section 2.3. We use transition systems, but almost always define operations on such systems in terms of their representative transition diagrams. The main advantage of transition systems over transition diagrams is that operations such as sequential composition become associative by definition, since the semantics of a transition diagram does not depend on the particular names chosen for its nodes.

The translation from GCL$^+$ statements to transition systems is in a compositional style. The first step is to define composition operations for transition systems. All definitions below are given relative to a fixed state space Σ.

Definition 9.1 (Operations on transition systems)

- For a guarded assignment, we define **step**($\langle b \rightarrow \bar{x} := \bar{e} \rangle$) as the transition system represented by $(\{s,t\}, \{(s, b \rightarrow \bar{x} := \bar{e}, t)\}, s, t)$.
- Let P_1 and P_2 be transition systems represented by (L_1, T_1, s, r) and (L_2, T_2, r, t), and assume that $L_1 \cap L_2 = \{r\}$. We define $P_1 \, ; P_2$ as the transition system represented by $(L_1 \cup L_2, T_1 \cup T_2, s, t)$.
- Let P_i be transition systems represented by (L_i, T_i, s, t), for $i = 1, \ldots, n$, where we assume that $L_i \cap L_j = \{s, t\}$, for $1 \leq i < j \leq n$.
  We define **if** $[\,]_{i=1}^{n} P_i$ **fi** as the transition system represented by

$$(\bigcup_{i=1}^{n} L_i, \bigcup_{i=1}^{n} T_i, s, t).$$

- Let P_B be a transition system represented by (L_B, T_B, s, r) and let P_E be a transition system represented by (L_E, T_E, s, t), such that $L_E \cap L_B = \{s\}$. We define **do** $P_B \, [\,] \, P_E \, ; \textbf{exit} \, \textbf{od}$ as the transition system represented by $((L_B \setminus \{r\}) \cup L_E, T_B' \cup T_E, s, t)$, where T_B' is like T_B except that transitions of the form $(l, b \rightarrow \bar{x} := \bar{e}, r)$ have been replaced by $(l, b \rightarrow \bar{x} := \bar{e}, s)$. $\qquad\square$

From the above definitions one can see why transition systems rather than diagrams are useful, because one can choose in every one of the above clauses representatives such that the constraints on the label sets L_i are satisfied. Now that we have operations on transition systems that match the language operations of GCL$^+$, it is easy to define the T function, which translates GCL$^+$ programs to transition systems:

Definition 9.2 (Semantics of GCL$^+$ statements)

- $T [\![\langle b \rightarrow \bar{x} := \bar{e} \rangle]\!] \stackrel{\text{def}}{=} \textbf{step}(\langle b \rightarrow \bar{x} := \bar{e} \rangle)$, cf. Figure 9.1.

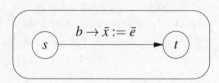

Fig. 9.1. The transition system $T [\![\langle b \rightarrow \bar{x} := \bar{e} \rangle]\!]$.

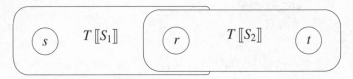

Fig. 9.2. The transition system $T[\![S_1 ; S_2]\!]$.

- $T[\![S_1 ; S_2]\!] \overset{\text{def}}{=} T[\![S_1]\!] ; T[\![S_2]\!]$, cf. Figure 9.2.
- $T[\![\textbf{if } []_{i=1}^{n} S_i \textbf{ fi}]\!] \overset{\text{def}}{=} \textbf{if } []_{i=1}^{n} T[\![S_i]\!] \textbf{ fi}$, cf. Figure 9.3.

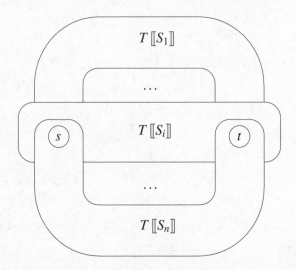

Fig. 9.3. The transition system $T[\![\textbf{if } []_{i=1}^{n} S_i \textbf{ fi}]\!]$.

- $T[\![\textbf{do } S_B [] S_E ; \textbf{exit od}]\!] \overset{\text{def}}{=} \textbf{do } T[\![S_B]\!] [] T[\![S_E]\!] ; \textbf{exit od}$, cf. Figure 9.4. $\square$

Let us explain why the assumption of guardedness in the choice construct $\textbf{if } []_{i=1}^{n} S_i \textbf{ fi}$ and loop construct $\textbf{do } S_B [] S_E ; \textbf{exit od}$ is essential. Consider for instance program $S_1 \overset{\text{def}}{=}$

$$\textbf{if do } \langle x > 2 \rightarrow x := x - 2 \rangle [] \langle x \leq 2 \rightarrow \textbf{skip} \rangle ; \textbf{exit od } [] \langle \textit{true} \rightarrow y := 2 \rangle \textbf{ fi}$$

with transition system $T[\![S_1]\!]$ given in Figure 9.5. Note that S_1 is not guarded because $\textbf{do } \langle x > 2 \rightarrow x := x + 2 \rangle [] \langle x \leq 2 \rightarrow \textbf{skip} \rangle ; \textbf{exit od}$ is not guarded.

Now one can easily show that there exist computations of S_1 which execute part of the loop

$$\textbf{do } \langle x > 2 \rightarrow x := x + 2 \rangle; [] \langle x \leq 2 \rightarrow \textbf{skip} \rangle ; \textbf{exit od},$$

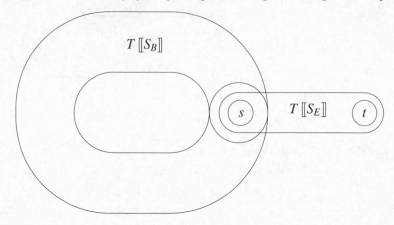

Fig. 9.4. The transition system $T[\![\,\mathbf{do}\ S_B\ [\!]\ S_E\,;\mathbf{exit}\ \mathbf{od}\,]\!]$.

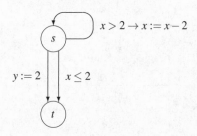

Fig. 9.5. $T[\![S_1]\!]$.

and then $\langle true \to y := 2 \rangle$, without ever passing the guard $x \leq 2$. This is not consistent with the intuitive meaning of computations generated by the loop construct. For another example, consider the program

$$S_2 \overset{\text{def}}{=}$$

 if

   do $\langle x > 2 \to x := x - 2 \rangle\ [\!]\ \langle x \leq 2 \to \mathbf{skip}\,\rangle\,;\mathbf{exit}\ \mathbf{od}$

  $[\!]$

   do $\langle y > 3 \to y := y - 1 \rangle\ [\!]\ \langle y \leq 3 \to \mathbf{skip}\,\rangle\,;\mathbf{exit}\ \mathbf{od}$

 fi.

The transition system $T[\![S_2]\!]$ is shown in Figure 9.6. As can be seen, this transition system allows for computations where execution of the body of one of the two loops alternates with execution of the body of the other loop, as long as both conditions $x > 2$ and $y > 3$ are satisfied. Of course this is not the

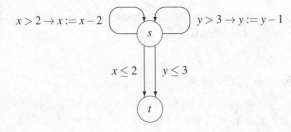

Fig. 9.6. $T[\![S_2]\!]$.

intended meaning of the choice construct, where the choice which of the two loops will be executed is made immediately when the choice construct starts executing. This kind of anomaly can be excluded by imposing the guardedness condition. One can prove, see Exercise 9.12, that if S is guarded then for every transition diagram (L, T, s, t) representing $T[\![S]\!]$ one has $(l, a, s) \notin T$ for all labels l of L and for all actions a. That is, the start location s has no incoming transitions, and hence such anomalies, as illustrated above, cannot arise.

We can define an operational semantics $O[\![P]\!]$ for arbitrary transition systems P as in Definition 3.26 of Chapter 3.

Definition 9.3 The initial-final state behaviour of transition system P represented by (L, T, s, t) is defined by:

$$O[\![P]\!] \stackrel{\text{def}}{=} \{(\sigma, \sigma') \mid \langle s; \sigma \rangle \rightarrow^* \langle t; \sigma' \rangle\},$$

where $\rightarrow^*$ denotes the reflexive transitive closure of the computation step relation $\rightarrow$ between configurations defined in Section 2.3. $\qquad\square$

Indirectly, this also associates an operational semantics with GCL$^+$ programs:

Definition 9.4 (Operational semantics of GCL$^+$) For GCL$^+$ programs S we define: $O[\![S]\!] \stackrel{\text{def}}{=} O[\![T[\![S]\!]]\!]$. $\qquad\square$

(We have overloaded the O symbol here; from the context it is clear which function is meant). Notice this definition implies that we abstract from the internal states of a program. For instance $x := x + 2$ and $x := x + 1; x := x + 1$ obtain the same semantics. Since we consider partial correctness in this chapter, only the initial and final state of a terminating computation are observable. Observe also that this semantics only records the effect of terminating computations. For example, $O[\![\textbf{do } true \rightarrow \textbf{skip} \quad \textbf{od}]\!] = \emptyset$.

This definition of $O[\![S]\!]$ is not a compositional one, as the definition of $O[\![P]\!]$ is not in a compositional style.

9.4.2 An Alternative Approach

For GCL$^+$ programs one can improve upon this situation, due to the regular structure of the transition systems that are denoted by GCL$^+$ programs. We illustrate this in a lemma below, after introducing a few relational operations:

Definition 9.5 For $R, R_1, R_2 \subseteq \Sigma \times \Sigma$,

- $R_1; R_2 \overset{\text{def}}{=} \{(\sigma, \tau) \mid \text{ there exists a } \rho \in \Sigma \text{ s.t. } (\sigma, \rho) \in R_1 \text{ and } (\rho, \tau) \in R_2 \}$
- for $i \in N$, R^i is defined by $R^0 \overset{\text{def}}{=} id_\Sigma$, $R^{i+1} \overset{\text{def}}{=} R^i; R$
- R^* is defined by $R^* \overset{\text{def}}{=} \bigcup_{i \in N} R^i$
- if $[]_{i=1}^n R_i$ fi $\overset{\text{def}}{=} \bigcup_{i=1}^n R_i$
- do R_1 $[]$ R_2 ; exit od $\overset{\text{def}}{=} R_1^*; R_2$. $\qquad\qquad$ □

Lemma 9.6

(i) $O[\![\bar{x} := \bar{e}]\!] = \{(\sigma, \tau) \mid \tau = (\sigma : x_1 \mapsto \mathcal{E}[\![e_1]\!]\sigma, \ldots, x_k \mapsto \mathcal{E}[\![e_k]\!]\sigma)\}$, where $\mathcal{E}$ denotes the semantic function from Chapter 5 mapping expressions to value expressions.

(ii) $O[\![b]\!] = \{(\sigma, \tau) \mid \mathcal{B}[\![b]\!]\sigma = tt \wedge \tau = \sigma\}$, where $\mathcal{B}$ denotes the semantic function from Chapter 5 mapping boolean expressions to truth values.

(iii) $O[\![\langle b \to \bar{x} := \bar{e}\rangle]\!] = O[\![b]\!]$; $O[\![\bar{x} := \bar{e}]\!]$.

(iv) $O[\![S_1; S_2]\!] = O[\![S_1]\!]; O[\![S_2]\!]$.

(v) $O[\![\text{if } []_{i=1}^n S_i \text{ fi }]\!] = \bigcup_{i=1}^n O[\![S_i]\!]$.

(vi) $O[\![\text{do } S_B [] S_E ; \text{exit od}]\!] = \text{do } O[\![S_B]\!] [] O[\![S_E]\!]$; exit od.

Proof See Exercise 9.4. $\qquad\qquad$ □

In Chapter 10 this alternative compositional definition of $O[\![S]\!]$ would not be correct due to interference of other programs with S, which can alter the final state of S. For instance, clause (iii) does not hold anymore when introducing concurrency.

9.5 A Proof System for GCL$^+$ Programs

To describe partial correctness of a program S, we use correctness formulae of the form $\{p\}S\{q\}$, where p, q are assertions, p is called a *precondition* and q a *postcondition*. We often refer to a formula $\{p\}S\{q\}$ as a *Hoare triple* or *correctness formula*. Informally, such a triple expresses that if p holds in the initial state of S, i.e., for the values of the variables at the start of the execution of S, then q holds for any final state of S, that is, if a computation of S terminates then q holds for the values of the variables at termination; for instance, $\{x = 5\} x := x + 1 \{x = 6\}$ is valid according to the definition below. As observed previously, e.g., in Section 2.4.1, apart from program variables, one in general needs logical variables, collected in the set *Lvar*, in order to characterise programs by means of pre- and postconditions. Therefore, let $VAR \stackrel{\text{def}}{=} Lvar \cup Pvar$ and let $\Sigma \stackrel{\text{def}}{=} VAR \to VAL$ in the definition of $T \llbracket S \rrbracket$.

Definition 9.7 (Validity of a correctness formula) For a program S and assertions p and q, a correctness formula $\{p\}S\{q\}$ is *valid*, if $\models \{p\}T \llbracket S \rrbracket \{q\}$. This is expressed by $\models \{p\}S\{q\}$. $\qquad\qquad\square$

Observe that such a formula expresses partial correctness, since validity of $\{p\}T \llbracket S \rrbracket \{q\}$ expresses partial correctness for the underlying transition system $T \llbracket S \rrbracket$ of S.

In the previous section we defined the semantics $O \llbracket S \rrbracket$. One can also characterise correctness of Hoare formulae in terms of this simple relational semantics:

Lemma 9.8 $\models \{p\}S\{q\}$ iff for all σ, if $\sigma \models p$ and $(\sigma, \tau) \in O \llbracket S \rrbracket$, then $\tau \models q$.

Proof For arbitrary transition systems P, the definition of $\{p\}P\{q\}$, from Chapter 2, amounts to the following, when choosing $T \llbracket S \rrbracket$ for P:

$\models \{p\}T \llbracket S \rrbracket \{q\}$ iff for all σ, if $\sigma \models p$ and $(\sigma, \tau) \in O \llbracket T \llbracket S \rrbracket \rrbracket$, then $\tau \models q$. Together with Definition 9.4, stating that $O \llbracket S \rrbracket = O \llbracket T \llbracket S \rrbracket \rrbracket$, the lemma follows immediately. $\qquad\qquad\square$

Next we formulate a proof system PS_{seq} in which all valid Hoare triples can be formally derived. In such a proof system we can derive formulae of the form $\{p\} S \{q\}$ by means of *axioms*, which allow the derivation of Hoare triples without any assumption, and *rules* of the form

$$\frac{\ldots, \{p_i\} S_i \{q_i\}, \ldots, p_j \to q_k, \ldots}{\{p\} S \{q\}},$$

by which the formula below the line, called the *conclusion* of the rule, can be derived if we have derived all the formulae above the line, which constitute the *premises* of the rule.

The basic axioms are as follows.

Axiom 9.1 (Skip) $\{p\}$ **skip** $\{p\}$.

Axiom 9.2 (Assignment) $\{q[\bar{e}/\bar{x}]\}\ \bar{x} := \bar{e}\ \{q\}$.

Example 9.9 Since $(x = 5 \wedge y = 3)[x + y/x] \equiv x + y = 5 \wedge y = 3$, the assignment axiom yields $\{x + y = 5 \wedge y = 3\}\ x := x + y\ \{x = 5 \wedge y = 3\}$. $\square$

Axiom 9.3 (Guard) $\{b \to q\}\ b\ \{q\}$.

Axiom 9.4 (Guarded assignment) $\{b \to q[\bar{e}/\bar{x}]\}\ \langle b \to \bar{x} := \bar{e} \rangle\ \{q\}$.

Observe that the above set of axioms is not minimal: Axioms 9.1, 9.2, and 9.3 can all be derived from Axiom 9.4.

First we give a general rule which can be applied to any statement. With this rule the precondition of an already derived Hoare triple can be strengthened and the postcondition can be weakened.

Rule 9.5 (Consequence)

$$\frac{p \to p_0,\ \{p_0\}\ S\ \{q_0\}, q_0 \to q}{\{p\}\ S\ \{q\}}.$$

Example 9.10 From Example 9.9 above we have $\{x + y = 5 \wedge y = 3\}\ x := x + y\ \{x = 5 \wedge y = 3\}$. Assuming that we can derive the valid implication $(x = 2 \wedge y = 3) \to (x + y = 5 \wedge y = 3)$, the consequence rule leads to

$$\{x = 2 \wedge y = 3\}\ x := x + y\ \{x = 5 \wedge y = 3\}.$$ $\square$

Rule 9.6 (Sequential composition)

$$\frac{\{p\}\ S_1\ \{r\},\ \{r\}\ S_2\ \{q\}}{\{p\}\ S_1; S_2\ \{q\}}.$$

Example 9.11 By the assignment axiom and the consequence rule one can derive $\{x = 2\}\ y := 3\ \{x = 2 \wedge y = 3\}$, and $\{x = 2 \wedge y = 3\}\ x := x + y\ \{x = 5 \wedge y = 3\}$. Hence, the sequential composition rule leads to

$$\{x = 2\}\ y := 3; x := x + y\ \{x = 5 \wedge y = 3\}.$$ $\square$

Rule 9.7 (Choice)

$$\frac{\{p\}\ S_i\ \{q\},\ \text{for all } i \in \{1, \ldots, n\}}{\{p\}\textbf{if}\ [\!]_{i=1}^{n} S_i\ \textbf{fi}\ \{q\}}.$$

Rule 9.8 (Guarded command)

$$\frac{\{p \land b_i\}\, S_i\, \{q\}, \text{for all } i \in \{1, \dots, n\}}{\{p\}\, \textbf{if}\ \; []_{i=1}^{n}\, b_i \to S_i\ \, \textbf{fi}\ \; \{q\}}.$$

Example 9.12 Since we can derive $\{y = 0 \land x = 0\}\, y := 1\, \{x = 0 \land y = 1\}$, the rule for guarded command leads to

$$\{y = 0\}\ \textbf{if}\ \; x = 0 \to y := 1\ \, \textbf{fi}\ \; \{x = 0 \land y = 1\}. \qquad \square$$

For the iteration construct we have the following rules:

Rule 9.9 (Exit-loop)

$$\frac{\{p\}S_B\{p\},\ \{p\}S_E\{q\}}{\{p\}\textbf{do}\ S_B\ []\ S_E\,;\textbf{exit}\ \ \textbf{od}\{q\}}.$$

Rule 9.10 (Do-loop)

$$\frac{\{p \land b_i\}\, S_i\, \{p\}}{\{p\}\ \textbf{do}\ \; []_{i=1}^{n}\, b_i \to S_i\ \, \textbf{od}\ \{p \land \neg b_G\}}.$$

Example 9.13 (Greatest common divisor) Consider

$$\textbf{do}\ x < y \to y := y - x\,[]\,x > y \to x := x - y\ \textbf{od}.$$

We would like to derive

$$\{x = n \land y = m\}$$
$$\textbf{do}\ x < y \to y := y - x\,[]\,x > y \to x := x - y\ \textbf{od}$$
$$\{x = y = gcd(n, m)\}.$$

How this is done, using the above axiom system, is shown below.

By Axiom 9.2 one derives

$$\{gcd(x, y - x) = gcd(n, m)\}\, y := y - x\, \{gcd(x, y) = gcd(n, m)\},$$

and by the consequence rule

$$\{x < y \land gcd(x, y - x) = gcd(n, m)\}\, y := y - x\, \{gcd(x, y) = gcd(n, m)\}.$$

Since

$$\models (x < y \land gcd(x, y - x) = gcd(n, m)) \leftrightarrow (x < y \land gcd(x, y) = gcd(n, m)),$$

this yields, again by the consequence rule,

$$\{x < y \land gcd(x, y) = gcd(n, m)\}\, y := y - x\, \{gcd(x, y) = gcd(n, m)\}.$$

Similarly one derives

$$\{x > y \land gcd(x,y) = gcd(n,m)\} \, x := x - y \, \{gcd(x,y) = gcd(n,m)\}.$$

Then Rule 9.10 leads to

$$\{gcd(x,y) = gcd(n,m)\}$$
$$\textbf{do } x < y \to y := y - x [\![x > y \to x := x - y \textbf{ od}$$
$$\{gcd(x,y) = gcd(n,m) \land x = y\}.$$

By the consequence rule we derive

$$\{x = n \land y = m\}$$
$$\textbf{do } x < y \to y := y - x [\![x > y \to x := x - y \textbf{ od}$$
$$\{x = y = gcd(n,m)\}. \qquad\qquad \Box$$

Example 9.14 (Integer division: proof system approach) One of the simplest algorithms for division of a non-negative integer x by a positive integer y is based on repeated subtraction, and is represented in GCL as follows:

$Div_1 \equiv$

$q,r := 0,x;$

do

$\quad y \leq r \to q,r := q + 1, r - y$

od.

The desired postcondition of this program is given by $x = q * y + r \land 0 \leq r < y$. We show how one can prove the above algorithm correct, using the proof system of this section. By Axiom 9.2 we derive

$$\{x = (q+1) * y + r - y \land y \leq r\}q,r := q + 1, r - y\{x = q * y + r \land 0 \leq r\}.$$

By the consequence rule and some properties of N we derive

$$\{(x = q * y + r \land 0 \leq r) \land y \leq r\}q,r := q + 1, r - y\{x = q * y + r \land 0 \leq r\}$$

and hence by the do-loop rule

$$\{x = q * y + r \land 0 \leq r\}$$
$$\textbf{do } y \leq r \to q,r := q + 1, r - y \textbf{ od}$$
$$\{(x = q * y + r \land 0 \leq r) \land r < y\}.$$

Again we apply the assignment Axiom 9.2 to derive

$$\{x = 0 * y + x \land 0 \leq x\} \, q,r := 0,x\{x = q * y + r \land 0 \leq r\}.$$

We see that the above precondition is equivalent to $0 \leq x$, so after another application of the consequence rule 9.5 we finally derive by the sequential composition rule 9.6

$\{0 \leq x\}$
$q, r := 0, x;$
do
$\quad y \leq r \rightarrow q, r := q + 1, r - y$
od
$\{(x = q * y + r \wedge 0 \leq r) \wedge r < y\}.$

Observe that the derived postcondition is equivalent to the desired postcondition. Hence we obtain

$$\{0 \leq x\} \; Div_1 \; \{x = q * y + r \wedge 0 \leq r < y\}. \qquad \square$$

Note that the rules in PS_{seq} only use the pre- and postconditions of the Hoare triples above the line. The structure of the programs in these triples is not relevant and hence in the rule for a compound construct the components can be considered as black boxes. With such a proof system we can verify the design steps during the process of top-down program development, as will be illustrated in Section 9.9. As has been discussed in Sections 1.6 and 9.1.3, in general, verification during program design requires a compositional proof system.

Observe that PS_{seq} is compositional, according to the definition of this concept in Section 1.6.2.

9.6 Soundness and Relative Completeness

We write $\vdash \{p\} \; S \; \{q\}$ if formula $\{p\} \; S \; \{q\}$ can be derived in proof system PS_{seq}. For such a proof system there are two basic questions that have to be considered:

- Is the proof system *sound*, that is, is every formula that can be derived valid? Formally, the soundness of the proof system is expressed as follows: if $\vdash \{p\} \; S \; \{q\}$ then $\models \{p\} \; S \; \{q\}$.
- Is the proof system *complete*, that is, is it possible to derive every valid formula? Formally, this can be expressed as: if $\models \{p\} \; S \; \{q\}$ then $\vdash \{p\} \; S \; \{q\}$.

Usually, soundness of a proof system is demonstrated by proving that its axioms are valid and that its rules preserve validity, i.e., if the hypotheses of a rule are valid then so is its conclusion. An induction argument on the length of the derivation of a correctness formula then suffices to prove validity of any formula derived in that system.

In our set-up a slightly different strategy is followed because validity of a Hoare-style correctness formula for S is by definition equivalent to validity of the corresponding correctness formula for $T\,[\![S]\!]$, and for the latter a sound and complete characterisation has been already given. Hence, soundness and relative completeness of our Hoare logic will be proved as a corollary of the following key result of this chapter, which states that correctness of a program in Hoare logic corresponds with the existence of an inductive assertion network for its associated transition diagram, and vice versa.

In order to prove this result, we need to establish the structural properties of assertion networks for transition diagrams corresponding to GCL^+ statements, e.g., that an assertion network Q for $T\,[\![S_1;S_2]\!]$ can be obtained as a composition $Q_1;Q_2$ (defined below) of assertion networks for $T\,[\![S_i]\!]$, $i = 1,2$. When examining the composition operations for transition systems one sees that essentially the component networks are "glued" together by unifying the appropriate entry and exit locations. The composition operations for assertion networks assume that the assertions for these unified locations are the same for all the component assertion networks. As a consequence, the composition operations for assertion networks are *partial* functions.

Notice that in the present syntactic set-up, an assertion network for $T\,[\![S]\!] \stackrel{\text{def}}{=} (L,T,s,t)$ is a function Q associating an *assertion* $Q(l)$ with every location $l \in L$. This is justified in Chapter 5 where it is shown that every predicate needed in (the semantic completeness proofs of) Chapters 2, 3 and 4 can be expressed as an assertion from first-order logic over N.

Definition 9.15 (Operations on assertion networks)

- Let P_1 and P_2 be transition systems represented by (L_1,T_1,s,r) and (L_2,T_2,r,t), where $L_1 \cap L_2 = \{r\}$, and assume that Q_1 and Q_2 are assertion networks for P_1 and P_2. The assertion network $Q_1;Q_2$ for $P_1;P_2$ is defined as follows, provided that $Q_1(r) \equiv Q_2(r)$, i.e., $Q_1(r)$ and $Q_2(r)$ are syntactically equal:

$$(Q_1;Q_2)(l) \stackrel{\text{def}}{=} Q_1(l), \qquad \text{for } l \in L_1,$$
$$\stackrel{\text{def}}{=} Q_2(l), \qquad \text{for } l \in L_2.$$

- Let P_i be a transition system represented by (L_i,T_i,s,t), for $i = 1,\dots,n$, where $L_i \cap L_j = \{s,t\}$, for $1 \leq i < j \leq n$, and assume that Q_i is an assertion network for P_i, for $i = 1,\dots,n$. The assertion network $\textbf{if } [\!]_{i=1}^{n} Q_i \textbf{ fi}$ is defined for $\textbf{if } [\!]_{i=1}^{n} P_i \textbf{ fi}$ provided that $Q_i(s) \equiv Q_j(s)$ and $Q_i(t) \equiv Q_j(t)$ for

$1 \leq i < j \leq n$:

$$\textbf{if } [\,]_{i=1}^{n} Q_i \textbf{ fi } (l) \stackrel{\text{def}}{=} Q_i(l), \qquad \text{for } l \in L_i.$$

- Let P_B and P_E be transition systems represented by (L_B, T_B, s, r) and (L_E, T_E, s, t), where $L_B \cap L_E = \{s\}$. Assume that Q_B and Q_E are assertion networks for P_B and P_E. The assertion network $\textbf{do } Q_B [\,] Q_E \textbf{; exit od}$ for $\textbf{do } P_B [\,] P_E \textbf{; exit od}$ is defined provided that $Q_B(s) \equiv Q_B(r)$, and $Q_B(s) \equiv Q_E(s)$:

$$
\begin{aligned}
\textbf{do } Q_B [\,] Q_E \textbf{; exit od}(l) \;&\stackrel{\text{def}}{=}\; Q_B(l), && \text{for } l \in L_B \setminus \{r\}, \\
&\stackrel{\text{def}}{=}\; Q_E(l), && \text{for } l \in L_E. \qquad \square
\end{aligned}
$$

The operations introduced above are *partial* operations. If for some operation and assertion networks Q_i the operation is defined, then we say that the Q_i networks are *compatible*.

Lemma 9.16 (Structural properties of (inductive) assertion networks)

  (i) Q is an assertion network for $P_1 ; P_2$ iff there exist compatible assertion networks Q_1 and Q_2 for P_1 and P_2 s.t. $Q = Q_1 ; Q_2$. Moreover, Q is inductive iff Q_1 and Q_2 are inductive.

  (ii) Q is an assertion network for $\textbf{if } [\,]_{i=1}^{n} P_i \textbf{ fi}$ iff there exist compatible assertion networks $Q_1, \ldots, Q_n$ for $P_1, \ldots, P_n$, with $Q = \textbf{if } [\,]_{i=1}^{n} Q_i \textbf{ fi}$. Moreover, Q is inductive iff $Q_1, \ldots, Q_n$ are inductive.

  (iii) Q is an assertion network for $\textbf{do } P_B [\,] P_E \textbf{; exit od}$ iff there exist compatible assertion networks Q_B and Q_E for P_B and P_E, such that $Q = \textbf{do } Q_B [\,] Q_E \textbf{; exit od}$. Moreover, Q is inductive iff Q_B and Q_E are inductive.

Proof First we recall the definition from Section 2.5.1 of the set $V(P, Q)$ of verification conditions for an assertion network Q of transition system P represented by (L, T, s, t):

$$V(P, Q) \stackrel{\text{def}}{=} \{ Q(l) \wedge b \rightarrow Q(l')[e/x] \mid (l, b \rightarrow x := e, l') \in T \}.$$

The assertion network is called inductive if all the verification conditions in $V(P, Q)$ are valid.

  (i) $\Leftarrow$: By the definition of $Q_1 ; Q_2$.
  $\Rightarrow$: Let $P_1 \equiv (L_1, T_1, s, r)$ and $P_2 \equiv (L_2, T_2, r, t)$. Let Q_i be Q restricted to L_i. It is clear that $Q_1(r) \equiv Q(r) \equiv Q_2(r)$, so the assertion networks Q_1 and Q_2 are compatible. Since $V(P, Q) = V(P_1, Q_1) \cup V(P_2, Q_2)$, it is clear that Q is inductive iff Q_1 and Q_2 are inductive.

  (ii) Left as Exercise 9.5.

(iii) $\Leftarrow$: by the definition of **do** $Q_B \,[\!] \, Q_E$; **exit od**.

$\Rightarrow$: Let $P_B \equiv (L_B, T_B, s, r)$ and $P_E \equiv (L_E, T_E, s, t)$. The assertion network Q_E for P_E can be chosen as the restriction of Q to L_E. The assertion network Q_B for P_B is as follows:

$$Q_B(l) \;\stackrel{\text{def}}{=}\; Q(l), \qquad \text{for } l \in L_B \setminus \{r\},$$
$$\stackrel{\text{def}}{=}\; Q(s), \qquad \text{for } l \equiv t.$$

Since $V(P, Q) = V(P_B, Q_B) \cup V(P_E, Q_E)$, it is clear that Q is inductive iff Q_B and Q_E are inductive (notice that , since $Q_B(s) = Q_B(r)$, the verification conditions for P_B and the program resulting from the redirection of transitions are indeed the same). $\qquad\qquad\square$

Before we state the relation between a Hoare-logic proof and the existence of inductive assertion networks we first introduce some notation. Let S be a GCL$^+$ program: let $\vdash \{p\}Q(S)\{q\}$ abbreviate the claim that there exists an inductive assertion network $Q(S)$ for $T\,[\![S]\!]$ such that for the entry location s one has $Q(S)(s) = p$, and for the exit location t one has $Q(S)(t) = q$. Let $\vdash \{p\}T\,[\![S]\!]\{q\}$ abbreviate the claim that there exists an inductive assertion network for $T\,[\![S]\!]$ which is correct w.r.t. p and q. One should notice the difference between $\vdash \{p\}Q(S)\{q\}$ and $\vdash \{p\}T\,[\![S]\!]\{q\}$. The latter formula states that there exists an inductive assertion network Q for $T\,[\![S]\!]$ such that for the entry location s one has that $\models p \to Q(s)$ holds, and for the exit location t that $\models Q(t) \to q$ holds.

Theorem 9.17 (Equivalence between Hoare logic and Floyd's inductive assertion method)

Let S be a GCL$^+$ program.

- If S is guarded then

$$\vdash \{p\}S\{q\} \text{ iff } \vdash \{p\}Q(S)\{q\}.$$

- If S is not guarded then

$$\vdash \{p\}S\{q\} \text{ iff there exists an } I \text{ such that } \models p \to I \text{ and } \vdash \{I\}Q(S)\{q\}.$$

- $\vdash \{p\}S\{q\}$ iff $\vdash \{p\}T\,[\![S]\!]\{q\}$.

Proof Observe that the last claim of the theorem follows directly from the first two. Next we simultaneously prove, by induction on the syntactic structure of S, the implication ($\Rightarrow$) for the first two claims.

Basic case: Guarded assignment.

Let $S \equiv \langle b \to \bar{x} := \bar{e} \rangle$ and assume $\vdash \{p\}S\{q\}$. This formula can only be derived from Axiom 9.4 by applying the rule of consequence several times. Hence there exist p' and q' with

$$\vdash \{p'\}S\{q'\} \text{ with } p' \equiv b \to q'[\bar{e}/\bar{x}], \models p \to p', \text{ and } \models q' \to q.$$

From this we deduce $\models p \to (b \to q'[e/x])$, hence $\models p \to (b \to q[\bar{e}/\bar{x}])$, which is equivalent to $\models p \wedge b \to q[\bar{e}/\bar{x}]$. This is, by definition of inductive, exactly the verification condition for a syntactic assertion network for $T \llbracket \langle b \to \bar{x} := \bar{e} \rangle \rrbracket$ with assertion p for the entry location, and assertion q for the exit location. Hence

$$\vdash \{p\} Q(\langle b \to \bar{x} := \bar{e} \rangle)\{q\}.$$

Induction step:

- Sequential composition.

  Let $S \equiv S_1 ; S_2$ and assume $\vdash \{p\}S\{q\}$. This formula can only be derived from the sequential composition rule, and by applying the rule of consequence several times afterwards. Hence there exist p', q', and r such that

  $$\vdash \{p'\}S_1\{r\}, \vdash \{r\}S_2\{q'\} \text{ and } \models p \to p', \models q' \to q.$$

  Hence by the rule of consequence $\vdash \{r\}S_2\{q\}$. Thus by the induction hypothesis, there exists an r' with $\models r \to r'$ and $\vdash \{r'\}Q(S_2)\{q\}$, choosing $r' \stackrel{\text{def}}{=} r$ in case S_2 is guarded. Moreover, again by the rule of consequence applied to $\models p \to p'$, $\models r \to r'$ and $\vdash \{p'\}S_1\{r\}$ we deduce $\vdash \{p\}S_1\{r'\}$. By the induction hypothesis, there exists an I with $\models p \to I$, $\vdash \{I\}Q(S_1)\{r'\}$, and $p \equiv I$ if S_1 is guarded. Notice that the premises for the sequential composition of $Q(S_1)$ and $Q(S_2)$ are met, cf. Definition 9.15, and by Lemma 9.16 this sequential composition is inductive. Hence $\vdash \{I\}Q(S_1 ; S_2)\{q\}$. Moreover $p \equiv I$ if S_1 and thus S is guarded.

- Guarded choice.

  Let $S \equiv \mathbf{if} \; \llbracket_{i=1}^{n} S_i \; \mathbf{fi}$ with all S_i guarded, and assume $\vdash \{p\}S\{q\}$. Then by the same arguments as above there exist p' and q' such that $\models p \to p'$, $\models q' \to q$ and $\vdash \{p'\}\mathbf{if} \; \llbracket_{i=1}^{n} S_i \; \mathbf{fi} \{q'\}$ is deduced from the choice rule 9.7. Hence $\vdash \{p'\}S_i\{q'\}$ for all i. Now by the rule of consequence $\vdash \{p\}S_i\{q\}$ for all i. Moreover all S_i are guarded, hence by the induction hypothesis $\vdash \{p\}Q(S_i)\{q\}$. Also the premises for the choice construct between assertion networks are met, and by Lemma 9.16 this choice is inductive. Hence $\vdash \{p\}Q(\mathbf{if} \; \llbracket_{i=1}^{n} S_i \; \mathbf{fi})\{q\}$.

- Iteration.

  Let $S \equiv \textbf{do } S_B \,[\!]\, S_E \,; \textbf{exit od}$ with S_B and S_E guarded, and assume $\vdash \{p\}\, S\, \{q\}$. By the same arguments as above we deduce the existence of I and q' such that $\models p \to I$, $\models q' \to q$, $\vdash \{I\}S_B\{I\}$ and $\vdash \{I\}S_E\{q'\}$, and therefore $\vdash \{I\}S_E\{q\}$. By the induction hypothesis we deduce $\vdash \{I\}Q(S_B)\{I\}$ and $\vdash \{I\}Q(S_E)\{q\}$ since S_B and S_E are guarded. This yields, using Lemma 9.16,

$$\vdash \{I\}Q(\textbf{do } S_B \,[\!]\, S_E \,; \textbf{exit od})\{q\}.$$

  Since $\models p \to I$ the result follows.

This finishes the proof of the implication $\Rightarrow$ for the first two claims. For the converse implication we only have to prove that $\vdash \{p\}Q(S)\{q\}$ implies $\vdash \{p\}S\{q\}$, since in case $\models p \to I$ and $\vdash \{I\}\,Q(S)\,\{q\}$ this implies $\vdash \{I\}S\{q\}$, and therefore $\vdash \{p\}S\{q\}$. This is quite straightforward, so that we only prove the basic case and one induction step.

Basic case: Guarded assignment.

Assume $\vdash \{p\}Q(\langle b \to \bar{x} := \bar{e}\rangle)\{q\}$, then by definition of inductiveness $\models p \wedge b \to q[\bar{e}/\bar{x}]$, which is equivalent to $\models p \to (b \to q[\bar{e}/\bar{x}])$. Hence by the consequence rule and the guarded assignment axiom: $\vdash \{p\}\langle b \to \bar{x} := \bar{e}\rangle\{q\}$.

Induction step:

- Sequential composition.

  Let $S \equiv S_1 \,; S_2$ and assume $\vdash \{p\}Q(S_1 \,; S_2)\{q\}$. By the structural properties of inductive assertion networks, cf. Lemma 9.16, there exist inductive assertion networks Q_1 for S_1, and Q_2 for S_2, such that $Q(S_1 \,; S_2) = Q_1 \,; Q_2$. By Definition 9.15 we have that $Q_1(r) = Q_2(r)$, where r is the exit location of S_1 and the entry location of S_2. Put $r' \stackrel{\text{def}}{=} Q_1(r)$, then $\vdash \{p\}Q(S_1)\{r'\}$ and $\vdash \{r'\}Q(S_2)\{q\}$. Hence by induction hypothesis $\vdash \{p\}S_1\{r'\}$ and $\vdash \{r'\}S_2\{q\}$. Applying the sequential composition rule yields $\vdash \{p\}S_1 \,; S_2\{q\}$, the desired result.

- The other cases are left as Exercise 9.11. $\qquad\qquad \square$

In the above theorem, the existence of an I which satisfies $\models p \to I$ and also $\vdash \{I\}Q(S)\{q\}$ is essential in case S is a loop construct, as can be seen from Example 9.13, see also the exercises.

Now soundness and relative completeness of our Hoare logic for GCL^+ can be established as a corollary of Theorem 9.17 (as demonstrated in Section 9.1.2).

Theorem 9.18 (Soundness and relative completeness)
Proof system PS_{seq} for GCL^+ is sound and relatively complete. $\qquad\qquad \square$

9.7 Proof Outlines

Theorem 9.17 expresses that an inductive assertion network can be viewed as a (graphical) representation of a proof in our Hoare style proof system PS_{seq}. In the literature it is customary to use a *linear* representation of such a proof by means of a so-called *proof outline* [Apt83, Apt81a, Apt81b, Owi75].

Proof outlines are a special instance of the more general notion of *annotated programs*. We will view such annotated programs as structured syntactic representations of assertion networks, in the same vein as S is viewed as a structured notation for the transition system $T[\![S]\!]$.

Definition 9.19 (Annotated program) An annotated program, or *annotation* for short, $\{p\}A(S)\{q\}$, is a statement $S \in \mathrm{GCL}^+$ augmented with pre- and postassertions p and q, and with assertions at its internal locations. The syntax of $A(S)$ is given in Table 9.4, in which r denotes an assertion.

Table 9.4. *Syntax of $A(S)$*.

$$
\begin{aligned}
A(S) \quad ::= \quad & \langle b \to \bar{x} := \bar{e} \rangle \mid A(S_1); \{r\}A(S_2) \mid \textbf{if } [\!]_{i=1}^{n} A(S_i) \textbf{ fi} \\
& \mid \textbf{ do } A(S_B) [\!] A(S_E); \textbf{exit od}
\end{aligned}
$$

The same restrictions as for the syntax of GCL^+ apply. In particular, the program components of the choice and iteration constructs are required to be guarded. $\qquad \square$

For guarded commands of GCL we use the following convention: In case of the GCL do-loop $\textbf{do } [\!]_{i=1}^{n} b_i \to S_i \textbf{ od}$, its annotation is defined by

$$\{p\} \textbf{ do } [\!]_{i=1}^{n} b_i \to \{p_i\} A(S_i) \textbf{ od}\{q\}.$$

Notice that this is a consequence of the abbreviations introduced in Section 9.3. The GCL loop $\textbf{do } [\!]_{i=1}^{n} b_i \to S_i \textbf{ od}$ abbreviates

$$\textbf{do if } [\!]_{i=1}^{n} \langle b_i \to \textbf{skip} \rangle; S_i \textbf{ fi } [\!] \langle \neg b_G \to \textbf{skip} \rangle; \textbf{exit od},$$

and by the definition above an annotation for the latter generates the need for an assertion $\{p_i\}$ in between $\langle b_i \to \textbf{skip} \rangle$ and $A(S_i)$. This we express by conventions as $b_i \to \{p_i\} A(S_i)$.

A similar remark applies to the GCL choice construct.

Annotations according to our definition are rather sparse in that assertions are attached to only a minimal set of positions in the program text. For instance, there are no assertions at the positions before and after the branches of **if** $--$ **fi** and **do** $--$ **od** programs. The informal reason for this is that those textual positions do not represent independent locations in the underlying transition system; rather they coincide with the positions before and after the **if** $--$ **fi** and **do** $--$ **od** programs as a whole. In practice one therefore often duplicates the assertions before and/or after the branches of conditionals and loops by putting them before and after the branches of those constructs, just to improve readability of annotated programs and proof outlines.

Next we define partial operations for composing annotated programs. For example, there is a defining clause for a sequential composition of annotated programs but only for the case that the postcondition of the first component matches the precondition of the second component. Analogously to assertion networks we call annotated programs compatible for a certain composition operator if that composition operation is defined for the annotated programs.

Definition 9.20 (Operations on annotations)

- $\{p\}A(S_1)\{r\} \; ; \; \{r\}A(S_2)\{q\} \overset{\text{def}}{=} \{p\}A(S_1);\{r\}A(S_2)\{q\}$
- **if** $[]_{i=1}^n\{p\}A(S_i)\{q\}$ **fi** $\overset{\text{def}}{=} \{p\}$**if** $[]_{i=1}^n A(S_i)$ **fi** $\{q\}$
- **do** $\{p\}A(S_B)\{p\}$ $[]$ $\{p\}A(S_E)\{q\}$; **exit od** $\overset{\text{def}}{=}$
  $\{p\}$**do** $A(S_B)$ $[]$ $A(S_E)$; **exit od** $\{q\}$. $\qquad\qquad\square$

Annotated programs and assertion networks are close analogues. We make the relation between the two explicit by defining a translation function $\mathcal{A}$ that maps an annotated program of the form $\{p\}A(S)\{q\}$ to an assertion network $\mathcal{A}(\{p\}A(S)\{q\})$ for the transition system $T[\![S]\!]$.

Definition 9.21 Let $\{p\}A(S)\{q\}$ be an annotated program where $T[\![S]\!]$ is represented by (L,T,s,t). We define the assertion network $\mathcal{A}(\{p\}A(S)\{q\})$, by induction on the structure of S:

- $S \equiv \langle b \to \bar{x} := \bar{e} \rangle$:
  $\mathcal{A}(\{p\}A(S)\{q\})(s) \overset{\text{def}}{=} p$ and $\mathcal{A}(\{p\}A(S)\{q\})(t) \overset{\text{def}}{=} q$.
- $S \equiv S_1; S_2$:
  $\mathcal{A}(\{p\}A(S_1);\{r\}A(S_2)\{q\}) \overset{\text{def}}{=} \mathcal{A}(\{p\}A(S_1)\{r\});\mathcal{A}(\{r\}A(S_2)\{q\})$.
- $S \equiv$ **if** $[]_{i=1}^n S_i$ **fi** :
  $\mathcal{A}(\{p\}$**if** $[]_{i=1}^n A(S_i)$ **fi** $\{q\}) \overset{\text{def}}{=}$ **if** $[]_{i=1}^n \mathcal{A}(\{p\}A(S_i)\{q\})$ **fi** .
- $S \equiv$ **do** S_B $[]$ S_E ; **exit od**:
  $\mathcal{A}(\{p\}$**do** $A(S_B)$ $[]$ $A(S_E)$; **exit od** $\{q\}) \overset{\text{def}}{=}$
  do $\mathcal{A}(\{p\}A(S_B)\{p\})$ $[]$ $\mathcal{A}(\{p\}A(S_E)\{q\})$; **exit od**. $\qquad\square$

A simple induction on S shows that if $\{p\}A(S)\{q\}$ is an annotation then $\mathcal{A}(\{p\}A(S)\{q\})$ is an assertion network. We also define a function which transforms an assertion network of a transition system $T\ [\![S]\!]$ into a corresponding annotated program.

Definition 9.22 We define a function $\mathcal{P}$ which transforms an assertion network Q for $T\ [\![S]\!]$ into a corresponding annotated program. The definition of $\mathcal{P}$ proceeds by induction on S:

- $S \equiv \langle b \to \bar{x} := \bar{e} \rangle$:
  $\mathcal{P}(Q) \stackrel{\text{def}}{=} \{Q(s)\}S\{Q(t)\}$, where s and t are the entry and exit locations of $T\ [\![\langle b \to \bar{x} := \bar{e} \rangle]\!]$.
- $S \equiv S_1; S_2$:
  Let $Q = Q_1; Q_2$. $\mathcal{P}(Q) \stackrel{\text{def}}{=} \mathcal{P}(Q_1); \mathcal{P}(Q_2)$.
- $S \equiv \textbf{if}\ []_{i=1}^{n} S_i\ \textbf{fi}$:
  Let $Q = \textbf{if}\ []_{i=1}^{n} Q_i\ \textbf{fi}$. $\mathcal{P}(Q) \stackrel{\text{def}}{=} \textbf{if}\ []_{i=1}^{n} \mathcal{P}(Q_i)\ \textbf{fi}$.
- $S \equiv \textbf{do}\ S_B\ []\ S_E$; **exit od**:
  Let $Q = \textbf{do}\ Q_B\ []\ Q_E$; **exit od**. $\mathcal{P}(Q) \stackrel{\text{def}}{=} \textbf{do}\ \mathcal{P}(Q_B)\ []\ \mathcal{P}(Q_E)$; **exit od**. $\square$

An interesting observation is that $\mathcal{P}$ and $\mathcal{A}$ are isomorphisms. (A proof of this isomorphism is given below.) Consequently, annotations and assertion networks are isomorphic notions. Therefore one can define various notions for annotated programs via corresponding notions for assertion networks.

Definition 9.23 (Proof outlines)

- The verification conditions of an annotated program are defined as follows:

$$V(\{p\}A(S)\{q\}) \stackrel{\text{def}}{=} V(T\ [\![S]\!], \mathcal{A}(\{p\}A(S)\{q\})).$$

- An annotated program $\{p\}A(S)\{q\}$ is a proof outline if all its verification conditions are valid.
- A proof outline $\{p\}A(S)\{q\}$ is defined to be *correct* w.r.t. the assertions *pre* and *post*, if additionally $\models pre \to p$ and $\models q \to post$ hold, notation: $\vdash \{pre\}A(S)\{post\}$. $\square$

An immediate consequence of the definitions is:

Theorem 9.24 (Equivalence of proof outlines and inductive assertion networks)

- An annotated program $\{p\}A(S)\{q\}$ is a proof outline iff $\mathcal{A}(\{p\}A(S)\{q\})$ is inductive.

- An assertion network Q for $T[\![S]\!]$ is inductive iff $\mathcal{P}(Q)$ is a proof outline.
- $\vdash \{p\}T[\![S]\!]\{q\}$ iff $\vdash \{p\}A(S)\{q\}$. □

Theorem 9.25 (Isomorphism between assertion networks and annotated programs)

(i) $\mathcal{P} \circ \mathcal{A}(\{p\}A(S)\{q\}) = \{p\}A(S)\{q\}$, with $\{p\}A(S)\{q\}$ an annotation for S.

(ii) $\mathcal{A} \circ \mathcal{P}(Q) = Q$, with Q an assertion network for $T[\![S]\!]$.

Proof By induction on the structure of S.

First we prove (i), for $S \equiv S_1; S_2$:

Let $\{p\}A(S_1; S_2)\{q\}$ be an annotation for S.

$$
\begin{aligned}
&\mathcal{P} \circ \mathcal{A}(\{p\}A(S_1; S_2)\{q\}) &&= \text{(by Definition 9.19)} \\
&\mathcal{P} \circ \mathcal{A}(\{p\}A(S_1); \{r\}A(S_2)\{q\}) &&= \text{(by Definition 9.21)} \\
&\mathcal{P}(\mathcal{A}(\{p\}A(S_1)\{r\}); \mathcal{A}(\{r\}A(S_2)\{q\})) &&= \text{(by Definition 9.22)} \\
&(\mathcal{P} \circ \mathcal{A}(\{p\}A(S_1)\{r\})); (\mathcal{P} \circ \mathcal{A}(\{r\}A(S_2)\{q\})) &&= \text{(induction step)} \\
&\{p\}A(S_1)\{r\}; \{r\}A(S_2)\{q\} &&= \text{(by Definition 9.19)} \\
&\{p\}A(S_1; S_2)\{q\}.
\end{aligned}
$$

Next we prove (ii), also for $S \equiv S_1; S_2$:

Let Q denote an assertion network for $T(S_1; S_2)$. Hence, by Lemma 9.16 (ii), $Q = Q_1; Q_2$. Therefore,

$$
\begin{aligned}
&\mathcal{A} \circ \mathcal{P}(Q) &&= \\
&\mathcal{A} \circ \mathcal{P}(Q_1; Q_2) &&= \text{(by Definition 9.22)} \\
&\mathcal{A}(\mathcal{P}(Q_1); \mathcal{P}(Q_2)) &&= \text{(by Definitions 9.21 and 9.19)} \\
&(\mathcal{A} \circ \mathcal{P}(Q_1)); (\mathcal{A} \circ \mathcal{P}(Q_2)) &&= \text{(induction hypothesis)} \\
&Q_1; Q_2. &&\qquad\qquad\square
\end{aligned}
$$

A proof outline constitutes a linear representation of a proof in Hoare logic. It should be stressed, however, that the other way around – to every Hoare logic proof there corresponds an isomorphic proof outline – is not generally the case, due to the rule of consequence.

Example 9.26 (The greatest common divisor: proof outline approach)
Consider the gcd program from Example 9.13 and its correctness proof, establishing

$$
\vdash \qquad \{x = n \wedge y = m\}
$$
$$
\mathbf{do}\ x < y \to y := y - x [\!] x > y \to x := x - y\ \mathbf{od}
$$
$$
\{y = gcd(n, m) \wedge x = y\}.
$$

From this proof one can extract the following proof outline:

$\{gcd(x,y) = gcd(n,m)\}$
do
$\quad x < y \rightarrow \{gcd(x,y) = gcd(n,m) \wedge x < y\}\ y := y - x\{gcd(x,y) = gcd(n,m)\}$
$\quad [\!]\ x > y \rightarrow \{gcd(x,y) = gcd(n,m) \wedge x > y\}\ x := x - y\{gcd(x,y) = gcd(n,m)\}$
od
$\{y = gcd(n,m) \wedge x = y\}.$

Observe that, since $x = n \wedge y = m$ is no invariant of this program, replacing precondition $gcd(x,y) = gcd(n,m)$ of this proof outline by $x = n \wedge y = m$ does not lead to a proof outline in the sense of Definition 9.20 above. $\qquad\square$

The above example illustrates the need for the notion of correctness of a proof outline *with respect to some given pre- and postconditions p and q*. But we do have the analogue of Theorem 9.17:

Theorem 9.27 (Transformation of Hoare logic proofs to proof outlines)
- If $\vdash \{p\}S\{q\}$, then there exists a proof outline of the form $\{I\}A(S)\{q\}$ for some assertion I such that $\models p \rightarrow I$.
- If $\vdash \{p\}S\{q\}$ and S is guarded, there exists a proof outline of the form $\{p\}A(S)\{q\}$. $\qquad\square$

The theorem follows directly from the equivalence between Hoare logic and inductive assertion networks, see Theorem 9.17, on the one hand, and the equivalence between proof outlines and inductive assertion networks, stated by Theorem 9.24, on the other.

9.8 Alternative Definitions of Proof Outlines

In the literature, different definitions of proof outlines are given, see for instance [Apt83, Apt81a, Apt81b, Owi75]. In our set up, Definition 9.20 of proof outline is induced by Definition 9.15 and Lemma 9.16. For instance, an alternative definition of the notion of a proof outline would characterise a loop by $\{p\}$**do** $\{I\}A(S_B)\{I\}\ [\!]\ \{I\}A(S_E)\{q\}$; **exit od**$\{q\}$, with $\models p \rightarrow I$, where p should hold when arriving at the loop, and p *only implies* the loop invariant. (Our definition requires p to be *identical* to the loop invariant.) The alternative definition is in fact more in line with Hoare logic, since it allows one to represent applications of the rule of consequence within a proof outline. For instance, the situation sketched above represents such an application, where the formula $\{I\}$**do** $S_B [\!] S_E$; **exit od**$\{q\}$ is adapted to $\{p\}$**do** $S_B [\!] S_E$; **exit od**$\{q\}$.

The problem with these alternative proof outlines is that they attach more than one assertion to certain locations, which is not possible in assertion networks. All that one can do at the level of assertion networks is to create some auxiliary program locations by means of adding **skip** actions to the program. We therefore introduce the following convention.

In annotations we allow consecutive assertions of the form "$\{p\}\{p'\}$". We interpret this formally as "$\{p\}$**skip** $\{p'\}$". Consequently, the implication $p \to p'$ is one of the verification conditions of the annotation.

So, an annotation $A(S)$ with occurrences of consecutive assertions is formally an annotation $A(S^\dagger)$ for a program $S^\dagger$ which is different from S. In fact, S can be obtained from $S^\dagger$ by omitting certain **skip** actions from the program text, or equivalently $S^\dagger$ is obtained from S by adding **skip** actions.

Theorem 9.28 (Omitting auxiliary skip actions)
Let S and $S^\dagger$ be GCL$^+$ programs, such that S can be obtained from $S^\dagger$ by removing one or more **skip** actions. Then $\models \{p\}S^\dagger\{q\}$ iff $\models \{p\}S\{q\}$. $\Box$

The proof is based on a lemma that states that for each S computation h there is an $S^\dagger$ computation h' which is like h except for the addition of "skip" steps at certain locations. The proof of the lemma is by induction on the length of computation sequences in $Comp(S)$ and $Comp(S^\dagger)$. It depends crucially on the assumption that both S and $S^\dagger$ are legal GCL$^+$ programs. This implies that these programs, in particular S, satisfy the side conditions with respect to *guardedness*. The details are left as an exercise.

The phenomenon that, in order to prove the correctness of program S, one first verifies a variant $S^\dagger$ of S will reoccur in Chapter 10, when we consider parallel programs.

9.9 Examples of Verification during Program Development

We continue the discussion in Section 9.1.3 and show by means of a few simple examples how GCL programs can be specified, developed and verified at the same time.

Example 9.29 (Integer division: proof outline approach) We now show how to derive the algorithm from Example 9.14 for division of non-negative integer x by a positive integer y, yielding a quotient q and a remainder r. So, we seek a GCL program Div, satisfying the specification

$$\{x \geq 0 \wedge y > 0\} \; Div \; \{post\_div\},$$

where $post\_div \equiv x = q*y + r \wedge 0 \leq r < y$. Moreover, Div should not modify x and y. As observed in Example 9.14, one of the simplest algorithms for division is based on repeated subtraction, and is represented in GCL as follows:

$Div_1 \equiv$

$q,r := 0,x;$

do

    $y \leq r \rightarrow q,r := q+1, r-y$

od.

A loop invariant I can often be constructed from the postcondition of the loop by weakening the postcondition (e.g., see [Gri81, Chapter 6] for an early reference to such techniques). In this case, for instance, we know that

$$(I \wedge \neg(y \leq r)) \rightarrow post\_div$$

should hold, and so a possible candidate for I is:

$$I \equiv x = q * y + r \wedge 0 \leq r.$$

With this choice for I we create an annotation for Div_1:

$\{x \geq 0 \wedge y > 0\}$

$q,r := 0,x;$

$\{I\}$

do $\{I\}$

    $y \leq r \rightarrow \{I \wedge y \leq r\}\, q,r := q+1, r-y\, \{I\}$

od $\{I \wedge \neg(y \leq r)\}$

$\{post\_div\}$.

The next step is to check that this annotation is actually a *proof outline*, that is, we must check that the following verification conditions hold:

(i) The need for the annotated action $\{x \geq 0 \wedge y > 0\}\, q,r := 0,x\, \{I\}$ is logically a consequence of Definition 9.21 and generates the verification condition:

$$(x \geq 0 \wedge y > 0) \rightarrow (x = 0 * y + x \wedge 0 \leq x).$$

This condition is clearly valid, i.e., the formula holds for all x and y.

(ii) Similarly, the annotated action $\{I \wedge y \leq r\}\, q,r := q+1, r-y\, \{I\}$ generates the verification condition:

$$(x = q * y + r \wedge 0 \leq r \wedge y \leq r)$$
$$\rightarrow (x = (q+1) * y + (r-y) \wedge 0 \leq (r-y)).$$

We have obtained the right hand side of this implication as the substitution $I[q+1/q, r-y/r]$. Note that we must here (re-)introduce parentheses around $q+1$ and $r-y$ to obtain the correct parsing of the resulting formula. Checking the validity of the verification condition is left to the reader.

(iii) We must check the validity of:

$$(I \wedge \neg(y \leq r)) \rightarrow post\_div.$$

This is obvious; in fact we have chosen I such that this implication holds.   □

Example 9.30 (Integer division once more) The division algorithm from the previous Example 9.29 is quite inefficient, as in each iteration of the loop r is decreased by an amount no more than y. A more efficient algorithm for division improves upon this by subtracting *multiples* of y. We take this idea into account by changing the invariant from the previous example into the following one:

$$I_2 \equiv x = q * w + r \wedge w = 2^p * y \wedge 0 \leq r,$$

and by developing a loop which maintains this invariant. The idea is to subtract w from r, as long as $w \leq r$. The reader should check that the following Hoare formula is valid:

$$\{I_2 \wedge w \leq r\}\, q, r := q+1, r-w\, \{I_2\}.$$

Apart from decreasing r, we need an action for decreasing w, such that upon termination we have reached a state where $w = y$. Again the reader should check the validity of:

$$\{I_2 \wedge w > y\}\, q, w, p := q * 2, w \div 2, p-1\, \{I_2\},$$

and also the validity of the following implication:

$$(I_2 \wedge \neg(w > y) \wedge \neg(w \leq r)) \rightarrow post\_div.$$

Note that we have used the operation "$\div 2$"; we assume that such a "binary shift" operation can be used in our division algorithm. From the validity of the previous two Hoare formulae and the implication above, it follows that the following is a proof outline:

$$\{I_2\}$$
do $\{I_2\}$
$\quad w \leq r \rightarrow \{I_2 \wedge w \leq r\}\, q, r := q+1, r-w\, \{I_2\}$

$[]\ w > y \rightarrow \{I_2 \wedge w > y\}\ q, w, p := q * 2, w \div 2, p - 1 \{I_2\}$
od $\{I_2 \wedge \neg (w \leq r \vee w > y)\}$
$\{post\_div\}$.

Consequently we have succeeded in our task to develop a loop maintaining invariant I_2. As the next step, we must find some way of initialising variables such that I_2 holds. A trivial way is embodied in the following Hoare formula:

$$\{x \geq 0 \wedge y > 0\}\ q, r, w, p := 0, x, y, 0 \{I_2\}.$$

Not for correctness, but rather for efficiency reasons, we would like to set w to a larger value than y, before starting the loop that we verified above. This is done by doubling w as long as it is smaller than r. Check the validity of:

$$\{I_2 \wedge q = 0 \wedge w < r\}\ w, p := w * 2, p + 1 \{I_2\}.$$

This justifies the following proof outline:

$\{I_2\}$
do $\{I_2\}$
$\quad w \leq r \rightarrow \{I_2 \wedge w \leq r\}\ w, p := w * 2, p + 1 \{I_2\}$
od $\{I_2 \wedge \neg (w \leq r)\}$
$\{I_2\}$.

Now we can compose the three components that we verified thus far. Formally this is done by means of the sequential composition rule. We present this part of our proof by the following annotation, where we have retained only the pre-postconditions of the components:

$\{x \geq 0 \wedge y > 0\}$
$q, r, w, p := 0, x, y, 0;$
$\{I_2\}$
do $\{I_2\}$
$\quad w \leq r \rightarrow \{I_2 \wedge w \leq r\}\ w, p := w * 2, p + 1 \{I_2\}$
od; $\{I_2 \wedge \neg (w \leq r)\}$
$\{I_2\}$
do $\{I_2\}$
$\quad w \leq r \rightarrow \{I_2 \wedge w \leq r\}\ q, r := q + 1, r - w \{I_2\}$
$\quad [] \ w > y \rightarrow \{I_2 \wedge w > y\}\ q, w, p := q * 2, w \div 2, p - 1 \{I_2\}$
od $\{I_2 \wedge \neg (w \leq r \vee w > y)\}$

Thus, we have reached a correct solution which by starting out with a new loop invariant and developing the corresponding loop is considerably more efficient than the previous algorithm. We can make a few modifications to the final solution. First of all, note that we can omit the variable p without affecting the correctness of the whole. The reason for this is that p does not occur in the postcondition of the program, is not used in a boolean test, and is never used within assignments to variables other than p itself. Such a variable is called an *auxiliary variable*. In the following chapters auxiliary variables are indispensable tools for showing the correctness of concurrent programs. For sequential programs, auxiliary variables are sometimes useful for simplifying correctness proofs, as we have done here, but one can always avoid them. We could have avoided the p variable here by using $\exists p.I_2$, rather than I_2, as loop invariant.

Finally we remark that we can strengthen the guard "$w > y$" in the second loop of the program to $w > y \wedge w > r$, without affecting the correctness of the proof outline. Note that after this modification the program has become deterministic, since in any state at most one of the two guards "$w > y \wedge w > r$" and "$w \leq r$" can be true. Such a transformation into a deterministic program is necessary if we want to implement the algorithm in a more conventional language such as PASCAL. We leave it to the reader to work this out in detail.

$\square$

9.10 Historical Notes

Hoare logic is a formal system for reasoning about Hoare triples. It originates from C.A.R. Hoare's 1969 paper *An axiomatic basis for computer programming* [Hoa69], which introduces an axiom system for proving partial correctness of programs which are constructed using assignment statements, sequential composition, conditional and while statements. Soundness and, especially, relative completeness proofs for this logic were given for the first time in S.A. Cook's *Soundness and completeness of an axiom system for program verification* [Coo78].

In this chapter, and in Part IV, Hoare logic is viewed as the structural analysis of R.W. Floyd's semantically based inductive assertion method [Flo67] which is discussed in Chapter 2 (and in Chapters 3 and 4). For our sequential constructs this viewpoint is formally expressed by Theorem 9.17 (and for our concurrent and synchronous constructs by Lemmas 10.28 and 11.18). This theorem enables one to "lift" the corresponding soundness and semantic completeness results which are established in Chapter 2 for the inductive assertion method (w.r.t. partial correctness) to soundness and relative completeness of the Hoare logic given in Section 9.6 (using the expressibility results of Chapter 5 to express the predicates occurring in the proofs of these results syntactically). This strategy of lifting soundness and completeness proofs for the inductive assertion method to Hoare logics is original.

Hoare's approach has received a great deal of attention ever since its introduction, and has had a significant impact on methods both for designing and verifying programs. It is seen by us as owing its success to three factors:

1. It is *state based*, i.e., characterises programming constructs as state transformers, and therefore applies in principle to every such construct.
2. It is *syntax directed* and can, therefore, also be regarded as a design calculus.
3. The extraordinarily simple way in which it characterises sequential composition and iteration.

Hoare logics have been formulated for almost every language construct in sequential and concurrent programming alike, with applications ranging from pattern matching to graphical languages, and to fault tolerance as well as real time (see [HdRP+00]). We do not aim to give an exhaustive bibliography of this subject, since this has already been given elsewhere, see for instance [dB80, Apt81b, And91, Dah92] and the section on historical notes in Chapter 4 of [Sch97]. For the reader interested in user-oriented texts on Hoare logic a number of excellent books are already available, see for instance [Gri81, DF88, Kal90, Coh90, And91, Dah92]. As to mathematical rigour and depth, J.W. de Bakker's scholarly handbook [dB80] and K.R. Apt's 50 page survey [Apt81b] remain the standard sources for the foundations of Hoare logic for sequential programming (especially regarding the procedure concept).

Ernst-Rüdiger Olderog publishes in 1983 one of the lesser-known jewels of Hoare logic, his *On the notion of expressiveness and the rule of adaptation* [Old83b], straightening out the relationship between verification theories for top-down and bottom-up reasoning about program construction, and exposing a number of unsound and incomplete proof rules. Olderog shows how to integrate bottom-up reasoning within top-down reasoning about program verification, by introducing semantically complete adaptation rules, a topic briefly discussed in Sections 1.6.4 and 3.5.5. Together with [MC81] Olderog's paper had a decisive influence upon the writing of the first monograph on compositional theories for concurrent program verification [Zwi89], in which adaptation rules play a major rôle.

Closely related to Hoare logics are calculi for *predicate transformers*. In the latter approach one characterises the semantics of programming language

concepts by functions mapping predicates to predicates, called predicate transformers after E.W. Dijkstra's [Dij75a], rather than by means of functions mapping states to (sets of) states as in the present approach. The first guarded
command language has been introduced and characterised by means of predicate transformers in [Dij75a]. For an overview of predicate transformer-based
calculi, as well as their historical background, the reader is referred to Chapter 10 of [dRE98].

Proof outlines originate from S. Owicki's dissertation [Owi75], and have
been formalised by K.R. Apt [Apt81a, Apt83] and by L. Lamport [Lam80].
Later, F. Schneider developed a logic, called Proof Outline Logic, in which
proof outlines are properties [SA86]; see also Chapter 4 of [Sch97] and our
Chapter 10.

Exercises

9.1   Prove that

    (a) $\models \{x = m \wedge m \geq 0 \wedge y = 1 \wedge z \neq 0\}$
        while $x > 0$ **do** $y := y * z; x := x - 1$ **od**
        $\{x = 0 \wedge m \geq 0 \wedge y = z^m \wedge z \neq 0\}$

    (b) $\models \{x = m \wedge m \geq 0 \wedge y = 1\}$
        while $x > 0$ **do** $y := x * y; x := x - 1$ **od**
        $\{x = 0 \wedge m \geq 0 \wedge y = m!\}$.

9.2   Which of the following inferences are sound?

    (a) $\dfrac{\{p \wedge b\}S\{p\}, \quad p \wedge \neg b \to q}{\{p\} \textbf{ while } b \textbf{ do } S \textbf{ od } \{q\}}$

    (b) $\dfrac{\{p\}S\{q\}, \quad q \to ((b \to p) \wedge (\neg b \to r))}{\{q\} \textbf{ while } b \textbf{ do } S \textbf{ od } \{r\}}$

    (c) $\dfrac{\{q\}S\{p\}, \quad p \to ((b \to q) \wedge (\neg b \to r))}{\{q\} \textbf{ while } b \textbf{ do } S \textbf{ od } \{r\}}$.

9.3   An assertion p is called the weakest precondition of assertion q and
    statement S iff:

    • $\models \{p\}S\{q\}$ holds and
    • for all assertions r, if $\models \{r\}S\{q\}$ then $\models r \to p$.

    Give a characterisation of the weakest precondition for assignment
    statements, sequential composition, conditional statements, and guar-
    ded commands.

9.4   Prove Lemma 9.6.

9.5 Prove Lemma 9.16, part (ii), i.e., the structural properties of assertion networks for guarded commands.

9.6 Recall that **if** b **then** S_1 **else** S_2 **fi** $\equiv$ **if** $b \to S_1 [] \neg b \to S_2$ **fi**. Prove soundness of the following rule.

Rule 9.11 (if-then-else) $\dfrac{\{p \wedge b\}\, S_1\, \{q\}, \quad \{p \wedge \neg b\}\, S_2\, \{q\}}{\{p\}\ \textbf{if}\ b\ \textbf{then}\ S_1\ \textbf{else}\ S_2\ \textbf{fi}\ \{q\}}$

9.7 Let **repeat** S **until** $b \equiv S; \textbf{do}\ \neg b \to S\ \textbf{od}$. Prove soundness of the following rule.

Rule 9.12 (Repeat) $\dfrac{\{p\}\, S\, \{q\}, \quad q \wedge \neg b \to p}{\{p\}\ \textbf{repeat}\ S\ \textbf{until}\ b\ \{q \wedge b\}}$

9.8 An assertion q is a *strongest postcondition* of a precondition p and a statement S if

   (a) $\models \{p\}S\{q\}$

   (b) for all r, if $\models \{p\}S\{r\}$ then $\models q \to r$.

Give a strongest postcondition characterisation of **skip**, assignment, sequential composition, and guarded command.

9.9 Let $x := ?$ denote a *random assignment* which assigns a random value to x.

   (a) Extend the operational semantics to random assignments.

   (b) Extend the proof system with an axiom for random assignments.

   (c) Prove soundness and relative completeness of the extended proof system.

9.10 Define, for an assertion p, $[\![p]\!] = \{\sigma \in \Sigma \mid \sigma \models p\}$. Prove

   (a) $[\![\neg p]\!] = \Sigma \setminus [\![p]\!]$

   (b) $[\![p_1 \vee p_2]\!] = [\![p_1]\!] \cup [\![p_2]\!]$

   (c) $[\![p_1 \wedge p_2]\!] = [\![p_1]\!] \cap [\![p_2]\!]$

   (d) $\models p_1 \to p_2$ iff $[\![p_1]\!] \subseteq [\![p_2]\!]$

   (e) $\models p_1 \leftrightarrow p_2$ iff $[\![p_1]\!] = [\![p_2]\!]$.

Define, for a set of states $\Upsilon \subseteq \Sigma$,
$O^{\dagger}[\![S]\!]\Upsilon = \{\sigma \mid$ there exists a $\sigma_0 \in \Upsilon$ such that $(\sigma_0, \sigma) \in O[\![S]\!]\ \}$.
Prove

   (f) $\models \{p\}\, S\, \{q\}$ iff $O^{\dagger}[\![S]\!]\, [\![p]\!] \subseteq [\![q]\!]$.

9.11   Prove from Theorem 9.17 the "$\Leftarrow$" part, in case $S \equiv$ **if** $[]_{i=1}^{n} S_i$ **fi** and $S \equiv$ **do** $S_B [] S_E$; **exit od**.

9.12   Show that if S is guarded, then, for every transition diagram given as (L, T, s, t) representing $T[\![S]\!]$, one has for all labels l of L, and for actions a, $(l, a, s) \notin T$.

9.13   Show that the implication

$$\vdash \{p\} S \{q\} \Rightarrow \vdash \{p\} Q(S) \{q\}$$

is in general not valid.

9.14   Prove by induction on the structure of S that if $\{p\} A(S) \{q\}$ is a proof outline and $\models q \rightarrow r$, then $\{p\} A(S) \{r\}$ is a proof outline.

9.15   (**Hard**) Define

$$\{p\} \textbf{do} \{I\} A(S_B) \{I\} [] \{I\} A(S_E) \{q\} ; \textbf{exit od} \{q\}$$

as the proof outline for the guarded loop **do** $S_B [] S_E$; **exit od** by requiring $\models p \rightarrow I$, cf. Section 9.8. Which changes should be made to Definition 9.20 and Lemma 9.16 to prove that $\vdash \{pre\} T(S) \{post\}$ iff there exists a proof outline $\{pre\} A(S) \{post\}$, using this new definition?

9.16   Prove Theorem 9.28.

10

A Hoare Logic for Shared-Variable Concurrency

10.1 Introduction and Overview

In this chapter we discuss a Hoare logic for the classical proof method of Owicki & Gries [OG76a] for concurrent programs that communicate by shared variables.

In Section 10.2 we introduce the shared-variable language SVL, which is an extension of the guarded-command language GCL. SVL incorporates a parallel composition operator, and a synchronisation construct that allows a statement to *wait* until a certain condition becomes true. Parallel composition in SVL is treated on an equal footing with other language constructs such as, for instance, sequential composition; it is therefore possible to have programs with nested parallelism. We also introduce a small extension of SVL, called SVL$^+$, which is technically more convenient than SVL itself from the point of view of giving soundness and completeness proofs for Hoare logic. The operational semantics of SVL$^+$ (and therefore of SVL) is defined in Section 10.3, and is based on the semantics of its associated transition diagrams.

Section 10.4 starts by recalling that, within the current framework, specifying processes by pre- and postassertions forms too narrow a basis for reasoning about parallel composition. Proof outlines, which in the previous chapter could be seen as mere abbreviations of Hoare-style proofs, now become much more important. In fact we will use proof outlines as the formal objects that appear in both the premises and the conclusion of our proof rules. The resulting logic is called a proof-outline logic [Sch97], to distinguish it from Hoare logic. The reason for this change is the rule for parallel composition. As explained before, to verify the correctness of an assertion network for the parallel composition of transition systems, one needs to require interference freedom of their associated inductive assertion networks. Since in this chapter we aim at providing a structured notation for such inductive-assertion-style proof methods, this requirement translates into imposing a corresponding notion of interference freedom upon the objects used to express inductive assertion networks within our formalism, i.e., their corresponding proof outlines. Observe that pre-post specifications can no longer be used for sequential constructs. For example, consider a program $S \equiv [(S_1 ; S_2) \parallel S_3]$. The Owicki & Gries-style rule can be applied here, provided that we have proof outlines for the components $(S_1 ; S_2)$ and S_3. So, the rule for sequential composition that we would like to apply to $S_1 ; S_2$ must have a *proof outline* as its conclusion, rather than a Hoare formula.

We mention that the original Owicki & Gries rule for parallel composition from [OG76a] has a Hoare formula, rather than a proof outline, as its conclusion. The reason for this is that in [OG76a] the parallel composition of programs is no longer used as a component of a larger system. So in [OG76a] a restricted class of SVL programs is considered, where parallel composition is allowed only as a "top-level" operation, excluding for instance a program of the form $[((S_1 \parallel S_2) ; [S_3 \parallel S_4]) \parallel S_5]$. For this reason we use a modified version of the Owicki & Gries rule that does have a proof outline as its conclusion, since we shall need nested parallelism in its full generality in Chapter 12 (see, for instance, Section 12.10).

Section 10.5 illustrates a more complicated application of the method of Owicki & Gries, namely that of proving concurrent garbage collectors correct. This section presents a general strategy for generating correctness proofs for such complex algorithms, using concurrent garbage collection as an example. First an abstract version of a concurrent garbage collector is proved correct, and then a correctness proof is given for a concrete version, in which the proof for its abstract version is used.

Finally, Section 10.6 contains a proof of (relative) completeness of this Owicki & Gries proof-outline logic for closed programs, which is inspired by earlier work of Leslie Lamport [Lam80, Lam88]. A list of exercises appears at the end of this chapter.

10.2 Syntax and Informal Meaning of SVL Programs

This section contains a description of the syntax and the informal meaning of the shared-variable language SVL. SVL is an extension of the guarded-command language GCL, introduced in Chapter 9. The new aspects are a parallel composition operator, and the concept of program components *waiting* for a certain boolean condition to become true. SVL is in essence the GCL language from Chapter 9 to which parallel composition has been added. Apart from this syntactical extension, the meaning of GCL constructs is affected by the presence of concurrency. For instance, now a guarded assignment of the form $\langle b \to \bar{x} := \bar{e} \rangle$ will cause the control flow to *wait,* if necessary, until the guard b becomes true, whereafter the assignment can be executed. Note that such waiting makes sense only in a language with concurrency; in a purely sequential language like GCL, the program would wait forever in case $\models b \leftrightarrow false$. It is important that passing the boolean guard and executing the assignment comprises one *atomic* action. "Atomic" here means: without being interfered with by the execution of statements from other concurrent processes. SVL incorporates the guarded-command constructs from GCL, such as for instance **if** $[]_{i=1}^{n} b_i \to S_i$ **fi** . For the **if** $[]_{i=1}^{n} b_i \to S_i$ **fi** statement we have again the possibility of *waiting* if no guard can be passed upon arrival at the **if** $\cdots$ **fi** statement. It is important here that evaluation of a guard b_i is a *separate* atomic action in the latter construct, i.e., interference between the evaluation of b_i and the execution of S_i is possible here; to express this we shall also use the terminology that there exists an *interleaving point* in between b_i and S_i.

The fact that SVL programs can be executed concurrently with other programs has a profound impact on the way such programs are specified. As already explained above, we use *proof outlines* as specifications for SVL programs. We introduce a separate syntactic class of *closed programs*, which are just SVL programs, except that one cannot incorporate them as components in a larger system. Consequently, closed programs have a simpler semantics, and can be specified by means of simple Hoare triples, rather than by proof outlines.

Just as we created an extension GCL$^+$ of GCL in Chapter 9, we introduce here an extension of SVL, called SVL$^+$. We have argued before, in Chapter 3, that in order to verify concurrent programs one must sometimes introduce so-called *auxiliary variables*, and augment actions and boolean guards with assignments to these auxiliary variables. For instance, in Example 10.19, describing Dekker's mutual exclusion algorithm, this facility is applied to the loop exit. Such augmentations lead in general to SVL$^+$ programs, even when the original program without auxiliary variables is an SVL program. Formally, the switch from SVL to SVL$^+$ programs is dealt with by regarding SVL programs simply as abbreviations of SVL$^+$ programs. Although our theoretical investigations concerning the soundness and completeness of proof systems are centred around SVL$^+$, we mainly use SVL to present concurrent algorithms in our examples.

Synchronisation constructs, in the form of so-called P and V operations on *semaphores*, have been introduced for the first time in the "THE" multiprogramming system developed by Edsger W. Dijkstra and his five colleagues at the Eindhoven University of Technology [Dij68c] ("THE" is the former Dutch acronym for this institution). Dijkstra called these constructs $P(s)$ and $V(s)$ operations, for the Dutch words "passeren" – to pass – and "verhogen" – to increase. Later on, atomic execution of a statement S in a programming language was expressed by $\langle S \rangle$, following a convention introduced by Leslie Lamport. This notation is used to express the guarded assignments of transition systems both syntactically and in SVL$^+$. In SVL, the P and V operations are represented, using guarded assignments, as $P(s) \equiv \langle s > 0 \to s := s - 1 \rangle$ and $V(s) \equiv \langle true \to s := s + 1 \rangle$.

Next the syntax of SVL is defined. The syntax of variables x, expressions e and boolean expressions b is taken from Table 9.1 in Section 9.3. The syntax of SVL is given below in Table 10.1. For guarded commands of the form:

$$\textbf{if }\ b_1 \to S_1\ [] \cdots [] \ b_n \to S_n\ \textbf{fi}\ \text{ and}$$

$$\textbf{do }\ b_1 \to S_1\ [] \cdots [] \ b_n \to S_n\ \textbf{od},$$

we use the following abbreviations: $\textbf{if }\ []_{i=1}^n b_i \to S_i\ \textbf{fi}$ and $\textbf{do }\ []_{i=1}^n b_i \to S_i\ \textbf{od}$.

Table 10.1. *Syntax of the Programming Language SVL.*

Statement	$S ::=$	$\langle b \to \bar{x} := \bar{e} \rangle\ \mid\ S_1 ; S_2\ \mid\ \textbf{if }\ []_{i=1}^n b_i \to S_i\ \textbf{fi}\ \mid$
		$\textbf{do }\ []_{i=1}^n b_i \to S_i\ \textbf{od}\ \mid\ [S_1 \parallel S_2]$
Closed Program	$Sys ::=$	$\langle S \rangle$

Next we introduce the SVL-extension SVL$^+$. The syntax of SVL$^+$ is derived in a straightforward manner from the GCL$^+$ language by adding parallel composition.

Table 10.2. *Syntax of the Programming Language SVL$^+$.*

Statement	$S ::=$	$\langle b \to \bar{x} := \bar{e} \rangle\ \mid\ S_1 ; S_2\ \mid\ \textbf{if }\ []_{i=1}^n S_i\ \textbf{fi}\ \mid$
		$\textbf{do }\ S_B\ []\ S_E ; \textbf{exit}\ \textbf{od}\ \mid\ [S_1 \parallel S_2]$
Closed Program	$Sys ::=$	$\langle S \rangle$

Since '; ' will be interpreted by relational composition, and this operation is associative, there is no need for brackets around $S_1 ; S_2$.

The definition of guardedness given in Section 9.3 is extended to parallel composition by considering a parallel statement of the form $[S_1 \parallel S_2]$ as unguarded. Given this new definition we restrict SVL$^+$ programs to those in which the statements S_i, S_B, and S_E in **if** $[]_{i=1}^{n} S_i$ **fi** and **do** S_B $[]$ S_E ; **exit od** are guarded. In essence this amounts to the requirement that branches S_i, S_B, and S_E as above cannot start with a loop or a parallel composition operation.

SVL programs are seen as abbreviations of SVL^+ programs. The translation is similar to the translation from GCL to GCL^+, as described in Chapter 9:

- The *guarded command* notation **if** $[]_{i=1}^{n} b_i \rightarrow S_i$ **fi** from SVL is regarded as an abbreviation of **if** $[]_{i=1}^{n} \langle b_i \rightarrow \textbf{skip} \rangle$; S_i **fi** (which is an SVL^+ program when S_i is one).

- Similarly, **do** $[]_{i=1}^{n} b_i \rightarrow S_i$ **od** abbreviates **do if** $[]_{i=1}^{n} b_i$; S_i **fi** $[]$ $\neg b_G$; **exit od**, where b_i and $\neg b_G$ are regarded as filters, abbreviating $\langle b_i \rightarrow \textbf{skip} \rangle$ and $\langle b_G \rightarrow \textbf{skip} \rangle$ as in Chapter 9, and $b_G \equiv b_1 \vee \cdots \vee b_n$.

Similarly to the conventions introduced in Chapter 9, we also use abbreviations like **skip** , **if** $\cdots$ **then** $\cdots$ **else** $\cdots$ **fi** , etc.

Throughout this chapter (and in Chapter 12) we shall often abbreviate $\langle true \rightarrow x := e \rangle$ by $x := e$, whenever this does not lead to confusion. Note that, according to our translation, an SVL guard is executed as an atomic transition. It is not combined with any assignment to variables. For instance, compare the SVL program S with the SVL^+ program T, defined by:

$$S \equiv \textbf{if } x > 0 \rightarrow x := x - 1 ; y := 0 \; [] \; x = 0 \rightarrow \textbf{skip } \textbf{fi}$$

$$T \equiv \textbf{if } \langle x > 0 \rightarrow x := x - 1 \rangle ; y := 0 \; [] \; \langle x = 0 \rightarrow \textbf{skip} \rangle \textbf{ fi} .$$

Program S abbreviates the SVL^+ program S':

$$S' \equiv \textbf{if } \langle x > 0 \rightarrow \textbf{skip} \rangle ; x := x - 1 ; y := 0 \; [] \; \langle x = 0 \rightarrow \textbf{skip} \rangle \textbf{ fi} .$$

Notice that S' differs from T in that the guard $x > 0$ and the assignment $x := x - 1$ are executed in two steps in S' with an interleaving point in between, whereas T executes them in one step (i.e., as an atomic transition).

For future use we introduce the notation **wait** b for $\langle b \rightarrow \textbf{skip} \rangle$.

Example 10.1 Consider the program $[S_1 \parallel S_2]$ due to Dijkstra [Dij68a], with S_1 and S_2 given in Figure 10.1.

The claim is that $[S_1 \parallel S_2]$ guarantees the mutual exclusion of the statements *critical section1* and *critical section 2*, when *in*1 and *in*2 do not occur amongst the variables of the critical sections *critical section*1 and *critical section*2. Consequently $[S_1 \parallel S_2]$ is called a *mutual exclusion* algorithm (see Section 1.3 for basic terminology).

$S_1 \equiv$ $S_2 \equiv$

$in1 := true$; $in2 := true$;

do   **do**

   $in2 \rightarrow in1 := false$; $in1 := true$ $in1 \rightarrow in2 := false$; $in2 := true$

od;   **od**;

*critical section*1;   *critical section*2;

$in1 := false$; $in2 := false$;

*noncritical section*1   *noncritical section*2

Fig. 10.1. A mutual exclusion algorithm.

Program $[S_1 \parallel S_2]$ does not necessarily terminate. There exists an interleaving of the atomic actions of S_1 and S_2, called *"after-you-no-after-you blocking"*, which leads to an infinite computation sequence, namely:

$$in1 := true; in2 := true;$$
$$(in1 := false; in1 := true; in2 := false; in2 := true;)^{\infty}.$$

The solution $[S_1 \parallel S_2]$ of the mutual exclusion problem is not acceptable when we reject solutions which feature after-you-no-after-you blocking. This danger is eliminated in Dekker's solution. This solution is presented in Section 10.4.2, where we also describe Dijkstra's correctness proof of mutual exclusion for $[S_1 \parallel S_2]$ and his own correctness arguments for Dekker's algorithm. The mutual exclusion inside $[S_1 \parallel S_2]$ is caused by the nontermination of its corresponding $[R_1 \parallel R_2]$-part, given by:

$R_1 \equiv$ $R_2 \equiv$

$in1 := true$; $in2 := true$;

do   **do**

   $in2 \rightarrow in1 := false$; $in1 := true$ $in1 \rightarrow in2 := false$; $in2 := true$

od   **od**

This guarantees that, when, e.g., R_1 terminates, R_2 does not terminate and, therefore, execution of *critical section*1 inside S_1 cannot overlap with that of *critical section*2 inside S_2, because no assignment to $in1$ occurs inside *critical section*1. Only when *critical section*1, $in1 := false$ has been executed, is R_2 allowed to terminate. Then *critical section*2 is executed, thus guaranteeing the required property of mutual exclusion. Nontermination of $[R_1 \parallel R_2]$ can be easily expressed in our partial correctness framework and will be proved in Section 10.4.1, cf. Examples 10.16, 10.17, 10.18 and 10.19.   □

10.3 Semantics of SVL$^+$

First we recall our motivation for the choice of (operational) semantics chosen to model the execution of a concurrent shared-variable SVL$^+$ program.

The informal description of the meaning of concurrent programs is not satisfactory. Consider, for instance,

$$[(x := 0 ; x := x + 2) \parallel (x := 1 ; x := x + 3)].$$

What is the precise meaning of executing the statements $x := 0$ and $x := 1$ in parallel? Is there any assumption that these actions are executed atomically, in any order, resulting in $x = 0$ or $x = 1$? For instance, in Section 3.2 we give two different interpretations for executing such assignments in parallel, whose resulting states are different. Similarly, consider the execution of $x := x + 2 \parallel$ $x := x + 3$ in a state in which x has the value 0. What will be the final value of x? If both statements first read x, next $x := x + 2$ assigns 2 to x, and then $x := x + 3$ assigns 3 to x, we obtain a final state in which x has the value 3. But if these assignments are executed atomically, without interruption, then the resulting value of x will be 5. Clearly, a decision must be made about which actions are considered to be atomic. Here we make the following assumptions:

- $\langle b \rightarrow \bar{x} := \bar{e} \rangle$ and $\langle b \rightarrow \bar{x} := \bar{e} \rangle$; **exit** constructs are executed *atomically* in a state in which b holds. That is, during its execution other concurrent processes may not change x nor the variables occurring in e and b. As a consequence $\bar{x} := \bar{e}$ is also executed atomically.
- Concurrent processes proceed asynchronously. No assumptions are made about the relative speeds at which processes execute their actions, as long as these speeds are positive.

By this last assumption, in $[(x := 0 ; x := x + 2) \parallel (x := 1 ; x := x + 3)]$ first $x := 0 ; x := x + 2$ might be executed, followed by $x := 1 ; x := x + 3$, yielding $x = 4$. Or $x := 0$ might be executed first, followed by $x := 1 ; x := x + 3$, and finally $x := x + 2$, resulting in $x = 6$. With the assumptions mentioned above, this leads to a final state in which the value of x is either $2, 4, 5$ *or* 6.

Observe that $[x := x + 1 \parallel y := y + 3]$ can be implemented by executing the statements $x := x + 1$ and $y := y + 3$ concurrently on different processors, but that *this has the same net effect on the values of the variables as executing them in any order*. Thus $[x := x + 1 \parallel y := y + 3]$ should have the same semantics as $x := x + 1 ; y := y + 3$ and $y := y + 3 ; x := x + 1$. Note that we have this equivalence because *we only observe the values of variables and not, for instance, the termination time of programs.* This justifies the transition system semantics given below, where we model the execution of a concurrent program

$[S_1 \parallel \dots \parallel S_n]$ as the parallel composition of the corresponding transition systems $T[\![S_i]\!]$, for $i = 0, \dots, n$.

Continuing now our formal development, as in Chapter 9 we similarly associate a transition system $T[\![S]\!]$ with an SVL$^+$ program S. For every $S \in$ SVL$^+$ we define its corresponding transition system by induction on the syntactic structure of S. For program constructs like $S_1 ; S_2$, introduced already in GCL$^+$ in Section 9.3, we use the corresponding construction on transition systems, in this case $T[\![S_1]\!] ; T[\![S_2]\!]$, as given in Definition 9.2. Thus, in order to obtain a compositional semantics for $T[\![S]\!]$ we only have to define $T[\![S_1 \parallel S_2]\!]$ in terms of $T[\![S_1]\!]$ and $T[\![S_2]\!]$. In essence this has already been done in Definition 3.9, but we recall this definition below.

Definition 10.2 (Transitions for $T[\![S]\!], S \in$ SVL$^+$) For SVL$^+$ statements S, the transition system $T[\![S]\!]$ is defined using the following definition that extends Definition 9.2:

- $T[\![\langle b \to \bar{x} := \bar{e}\rangle]\!] = \mathbf{step}(\langle b \to \bar{x} := \bar{e}\rangle)$
- $T[\![S_1 ; S_2]\!] = T[\![S_1]\!] ; T[\![S_2]\!]$
- $T[\![\mathbf{if}\ []_{i=1}^n S_i\ \mathbf{fi}\ ]\!] = \mathbf{if}\ []_{i=1}^n T[\![S_i]\!]\ \mathbf{fi}$
- $T[\![\mathbf{do}\ S_B\ []\ S_E ; \mathbf{exit\ od}]\!] = \mathbf{do}\ T[\![S_B]\!]\ []\ T[\![S_E]\!] ; \mathbf{exit\ od}$
- For parallel composition $[S_1 \parallel S_2]$, the transition system $T[\![[S_1 \parallel S_2]]\!]$ is defined by $T[\![S_1]\!] \parallel T[\![S_2]\!]$, where the parallel composition of transition systems is given by Definition 3.9, which is recalled below. This reflects our choice to use interleaving of actions to model the execution of concurrent programs. □

In Section 3.5 the parallel composition of two transition systems represented by transition diagrams $P_i \stackrel{\text{def}}{=} (L_i, T_i, s_i, t_i)$, $i = 1, 2$ has been defined as the transition system represented by (L, T, s, t) where

- $L = L_1 \times L_2$
- $T = \{(l, a, l') \mid l = \langle l_1, l_2\rangle, l' = \langle l'_1, l'_2\rangle, \text{s.t. } (l_i, a, l'_i) \in T_i, l_j = l'_j, j \neq i\}$
- $s = \langle s_1, s_2\rangle$
- $t = \langle t_1, t_2\rangle$.

As a result, for every S in SVL$^+$ a *syntactic* transition diagram in the sense of Chapter 5 is obtained.

We recall Lemma 3.10 from Chapter 3:

Parallel composition of transition systems is associative and commutative. That is, for transition systems P_1, P_2, and P_3, $[[P_1 \parallel P_2] \parallel P_3]$ is equivalent to $[P_1 \parallel [P_2 \parallel P_3]]$, and $[P_1 \parallel P_2]$ is equivalent to $[P_2 \parallel P_1]$. □

It follows directly from these definitions that parallel composition of SVL$^+$ statements inherits associativity and commutativity from transition systems. For instance, if S_1, S_2 and S_3 are SVL$^+$ programs, then $[[S_1 \parallel S_2] \parallel S_3]$ and $[S_1 \parallel [S_2 \parallel S_3]]$ denote the same class of transition systems. As a consequence, we are free to use notations like $[S_1 \parallel S_2 \parallel \cdots \parallel S_n]$ without (semantic) ambiguity.

The semantics of *closed* programs differs considerably from the semantics of (non-closed) programs. Closed programs *Sys* of the form $\langle S \rangle$ have a state transformer semantics, defined by the O function.

Definition 10.3 (Operational semantics of closed programs) The operational semantics $O[\![\langle S \rangle]\!]$ of a closed SVL$^+$ program $\langle S \rangle$ is defined by

$$O[\![\langle S \rangle]\!] \stackrel{\text{def}}{=} O[\![T [\![S]\!]]\!],$$

where O on the right hand side of this definition is given by Definition 9.3. $\square$

We do not define the state-transformer semantics of general SVL$^+$ programs S. Technically speaking, there is no reason why we could not define such a semantics. With slight abuse of notation, we might define $O[\![S]\!] \stackrel{\text{def}}{=} O[\![T [\![S]\!]]\!]$. Yet, it makes no sense to do so. Consider, for instance, the following two programs:

$$S_1 \equiv x := x + 2 \text{ and } S_2 \equiv x := x + 1 \,; x := x + 1.$$

Although the transition systems $T [\![S_1]\!]$ and $T [\![S_2]\!]$ are different, the overall state transformation calculated by the two programs is the same. (They both increase x by 2.) Therefore, $O[\![S_1]\!] = O[\![S_2]\!]$. The problem is that when we place S_1 or S_2 in a parallel context, their behaviour is different, and, moreover, the difference shows up even when we are interested only in the O semantics of the parallel system. For instance, consider $S_1' \equiv [S_1 \parallel y := x]$ versus $S_2' \equiv [S_2 \parallel y := x]$. For the final states reached by S_1' we have either $y = x$ or $y = x - 2$. But for S_2', we have that $y = x$, $y = x - 1$, or $y = x - 2$, and so, $O[\![S_1']\!] \neq O[\![S_2']\!]$. We conclude that the O semantics is *too abstract*, in the sense that it hides too much of the relevant behaviour of statements. Technically, this means that the definition of $O[\![S]\!]$ is *not compositional* with respect to parallel composition. In particular, the result of Lemma 9.6 cannot be extended to concurrency. For this reason, we stick to the $T [\![S]\!]$ semantics for SVL$^+$, and reserve O for *closed* programs only.

10.4 A Proof System for SVL Programs

In this section proof systems for our languages for shared-variable concurrency SVL and SVL$^+$ are defined, based on the notion of *interference-free proof outlines* due to Owicki & Gries [OG76a].

We use Hoare-style correctness formulae of the form $\{p\}\langle S\rangle\{q\}$ to describe partial correctness of closed programs S.

Definition 10.4 (Validity of Hoare formulae) For a closed program of the form $\langle S\rangle$ and assertions p and q, a correctness formula $\{p\}\langle S\rangle\{q\}$ is *valid*, expressed by $\models \{p\}\langle S\rangle\{q\}$, if $\models \{p\}T[\![S]\!]\{q\}$.   □

For non-closed SVL$^+$ programs, the situation is different. For essentially the same reasons that we did not define a state-transformer semantics for such programs, we also cannot define a satisfactory Hoare logic for SVL$^+$. For instance, consider again the two programs

$$S_1 \equiv x := x + 2 \text{ and } S_2 \equiv x := x + 1 \, ; x := x + 1.$$

With the validity of Hoare formulae defined in the style of the above Definition 10.4 we would have obtained, for all p and q, that

$$\models \{p\}S_1\{q\} \text{ iff } \models \{p\}S_2\{q\}.$$

Hence we cannot distinguish S_1 and S_2 by pre- and postconditions, although in a parallel context they behave differently. For instance, we would expect the following to be true:

$$\models \{x = 0\}[S_1 \parallel y := x]\{y = 0 \vee y = 2\}$$

but *not*

$$\models \{x = 0\}[S_2 \parallel y := x]\{y = 0 \vee y = 2\}.$$

Thus a sound and (relatively) complete compositional proof system purely based on Hoare logic is not possible in the current framework. In accordance with the $T[\![S]\!]$ semantics for SVL$^+$, we develop a proof system based on *annotated programs*. Such annotations are seen as generalisations of Hoare formulae, in that assertions are attached to *all* control locations rather than only to the entry and exit points of programs. The resulting logic based upon annotated programs is called *proof-outline logic* [SA86]. A program annotation, and therefore proof-outline logic, does not abstract at all from any internal syntactic detail of its program text. This is a drawback when one wants to construct larger systems, where system components should be specified in such a way that internal syntactic details are not observable. If we had based our framework on the compositional semantics from Chapter 8, a compositional proof method would have been the result, based on introducing a special variable h to record the computation history of process-indexed states. Within the inductive assertion framework this can be done in Part III, whereas for Hoare logic it is one of the subjects of our companion volume.

So why develop a proof-outline logic for shared-variable concurrency at all? The answer is simple. It is currently the only logic capable of scaling up to examples of the complexity of those discussed in Chapter 12! Consequently, we develop such a logic in the present chapter, and refer to [Sch97] for alternative approaches to proof-outline logics.

First we extend the notion of proof outline and its properties as developed in Section 9.7 to SVL$^+$, adopting the conventions introduced in that section. As before, proof outlines are closely related to assertion networks. It is relatively simple to define parallel composition for the latter, so we first extend Definition 9.15.

Definition 10.5 (Operations on assertion networks)
- For sequential composition, choice, and iteration, the defining clauses are those of Definition 9.15.
- Let P_1 be a transition system represented by (L_1, T_1, s_1, t_1) and P_2 be a transition system represented by (L_2, T_2, s_2, t_2), and assume that Q_1 and Q_2 are assertion networks for P_1 and P_2, respectively. The assertion network $Q_1 \parallel Q_2$ for $P_1 \parallel P_2$ is defined as follows:

$$(Q_1 \parallel Q_2)(\langle l, m \rangle) \stackrel{\text{def}}{=} Q_1(l) \wedge Q_2(m) \qquad \text{for } \langle l, m \rangle \in L_1 \times L_2. \qquad \square$$

The next step is to extend the definition of annotations to concurrent programs.

Definition 10.6 (Annotated SVL$^+$ statement) An annotated statement, or *annotation* for short, $\{p\}A(S)\{q\}$, is a statement $S \in \text{SVL}^+$ augmented with pre- and postcondition p and q, and with assertions at its internal locations. The syntax of $A(S)$ is given in Table 10.3 below, in which r, p_1, p_2, q_1 and q_2 denote assertions.

Table 10.3. *Syntax of $A(S)$.*

$A(S) ::=$	$\langle b \rightarrow \bar{x} := \bar{e} \rangle \mid A(S_1); \{r\} A(S_2) \mid \textbf{if } []_{i=1}^{n} A(S_i) \textbf{ fi} \mid$
	$\textbf{do } A(S_B) [] A(S_E); \textbf{exit od} \mid [\{p_1\}A(S_1)\{q_1\} \parallel \{p_2\}A(S_2)\{q_2\}]$

The same restrictions as for the syntax of SVL^+ apply. That is, the program components of the choice and iteration constructs are required to be guarded. Moreover, for a parallel composition within a context of the form $\{p\}[\{p_1\}A(S_1)\{q_1\} \parallel \{p_2\}A(S_2)\{q_2\}]\{q\}$ we require that $p \equiv p_1 \wedge p_2$ and $q \equiv q_1 \wedge q_2$. □

The restriction for annotations of concurrent programs is needed to enable a simple translation into assertion networks. In practice, one can relax the requirements $p \equiv p_1 \wedge p_2$ to $\models p \rightarrow p_1 \wedge p_2$ and $q \equiv q_1 \wedge q_2$ to $\models q_1 \wedge q_2 \rightarrow q$. Formally, this can be justified by inserting extra **skip** actions as follows :

$$\{p\}\textbf{skip} \; ; \{p_1 \wedge p_2\}[\{p_1\}A(S_1)\{q_1\} \parallel \{p_2\}A(S_2)\{q_2\}]\{q_1 \wedge q_2\} \, ; \textbf{skip} \; \{q\}.$$

The introduction of such **skip** actions is sometimes unavoidable in order to satisfy the constraints for annotations. For instance, a program of the form $[S_1 \parallel S_2] ; [T_1 \parallel T_2 \parallel T_3]$ cannot be analysed in our setting without adding (at least one) **skip** step between the two parallel constructs $[S_1 \parallel S_2]$ and $[T_1 \parallel T_2 \parallel T_3]$. Similar remarks can be made when a concurrent program is incorporated as the body of an iteration construct.

Annotations for SVL^+ statements can be translated into assertion networks for transition systems:

Definition 10.7 Let $\{p\} A(S)\{q\}$ be an annotated SVL^+ statement. We define the assertion network $\mathcal{A}(\{p\}A(S)\{q\})$ for $T [\![S]\!]$ by induction on the structure of S. The clauses are the same as in Definition 9.21, except for the addition of the following clause for parallel composition:

$$\mathcal{A}(\{p\}[\{p_1\}A(S_1)\{q_1\} \parallel \{p_2\}A(S_2)\{q_2\}]\{q\}) \stackrel{\text{def}}{=}$$
$$(\mathcal{A}(\{p_1\}A(S_1)\{q_1\}) \parallel \mathcal{A}(\{p_2\}A(S_2)\{q_2\})).$$

□

Observe that, with this new clause added, there no longer exists an *isomorphism* between annotated programs and assertion networks. Indeed, different annotations for concurrent programs are mapped onto the same assertion network. This is due to the choice of an interleaving model for concurrency, where concurrent programs translate (in our case) to nondeterministic transition systems. To give a concrete example, consider the two annotations $\{p_1 \wedge p_2\} A(S_1) \{q_1 \wedge q_2\}$ and $\{p_1 \wedge p_2\} A(S_2) \{q_1 \wedge q_2\}$, where $A(S_1)$ and $A(S_2)$ are given by:

$$A(S_1) \stackrel{\text{def}}{=} [\{p_1\}x := 0\{q_1\} \parallel \{p_2\}x := 2\{q_2\}]$$

and

$$A(S_2) \stackrel{\text{def}}{=} \textbf{if} \; (x := 0; \{q_1 \wedge p_2\}x := 2) \; [\!] \; (x := 2; \{p_1 \wedge q_2\}x := 0) \; \textbf{fi} \; .$$

Then $\mathcal{A}(\{p_1 \wedge p_2\} A(S_1) \{q_1 \wedge q_2\})$ and $\mathcal{A}(\{p_1 \wedge p_2\} A(S_2) \{q_1 \wedge q_2\})$ define the same assertion network. (Observe that for this to work, S_1 and S_2 should be regarded as transition systems, rather than as transition diagrams.) Hence it is impossible to reconstruct a unique program text from the resulting transition system.

Annotated SVL^+ programs can be seen as elaborate abbreviations of assertion networks. We exploit this view by defining various useful notions for annotated SVL^+ programs via their translation to assertion networks.

Definition 10.8 (Proof outlines)

- The verification conditions of an annotated program are defined as follows:

$$V(\{p\}A(S)\{q\}) \stackrel{\text{def}}{=} V(T \, [\![S]\!] , \mathcal{A}(\{p\}A(S)\{q\})).$$

- An annotated program $\{p\}A(S)\{q\}$ is called a *proof outline* if all its verification conditions are valid, that is, if $\mathcal{A}(\{p\}A(S)\{q\})$ is inductive.
- To express that $\{p\}A(S)\{q\}$ is a proof outline we use the following notation, $\vdash \{p\}A(S)\{q\}$. $\qquad\qquad\square$

These definitions are not very helpful when it comes to actually verifying that a given annotation is a proof outline. It is not clear how to determine the set of verification conditions directly from the annotated program texts, for one should first translate the annotated program to an assertion network. The latter is prohibitively expensive, since transition systems for concurrent programs can be very large. Let us focus on the form of the verification conditions as they occur in $V(\{p_1 \wedge p_2\}[\{p_1\}A(S_1)\{q_1\} \parallel \{p_2\}A(S_2)\{q_2\}]\{q_1 \wedge q_2\})$. Consider some location $\langle l, m \rangle$ in the transition system $T \, [\![S_1 \parallel S_2]\!]$, and some outgoing transition towards a location $\langle l', m \rangle$, labelled by an action of the form $\langle b \rightarrow \bar{x} := \bar{e} \rangle$. Assume that the annotation for S_1 attaches assertions r_1 and r_1' to the locations l and l', and similarly, the annotation for S_2 attaches r_2 to location m. The verification condition for this transition is:

$$(r_1 \wedge r_2 \wedge b) \rightarrow ((r_1' \wedge r_2)[\bar{e}/\bar{x}]). \qquad\qquad (*)$$

We can split this condition into a *local verification condition* and an *interference freedom test:*

- $(r_1 \wedge b) \rightarrow (r_1'[\bar{e}/\bar{x}]),$ (local verification condition)
- $(r_1 \wedge r_2 \wedge b) \rightarrow (r_2[\bar{e}/\bar{x}]).$ (interference freedom test)

These two conditions can also be derived directly from the annotated program texts for $\{p_1\}A(S_1)\{q_1\}$ and $\{p_2\}A(S_2)\{q_2\}$, that is, without first constructing an inductive assertion network for the product transition system $T \, [\![S_1 \parallel S_2]\!]$.

The local verification conditions are just the verification conditions for S_1 and S_2 when these are regarded as stand-alone statements; i.e., if $\{p_1\}A(S_1)\{q_1\}$ and $\{p_2\}A(S_2)\{q_2\}$ are their annotations. The interference freedom tests take into account (annotated) actions from one component, and assertions from the annotation for the other component. The method that we thus arrive at is the well-known Owicki & Gries method, from Chapter 3! Note that the two conditions together *imply* (∗), but in fact, they are *stronger* than (∗), since the local verification condition does not take the precondition r_2 into account. Omitting r_2 from the local verification condition has the following consequences:

- This "local verification condition" refers to the annotated program text $\{p_1\}$ $A(S_1)\{q_1\}$, but not to the annotation for S_2. In particular, it is independent of the assertion attached to the S_2 location m. Consequently, the local verification conditions have to be checked only once, rather than anew for each possible S_2 location.
- Choosing the appropriate local assertions in order for them to pass the interference freedom test requires in general the introduction of *auxiliary variables*. In essence these auxiliary variables allow one to strengthen assertions like r_1 such that the local verification conditions and the interference-freedom tests together are equivalent to global verification conditions of the form (∗).

Since annotations can be translated into assertion networks, it is clear that a notion of interference-free proof outlines can be defined analogously to interference-free assertion networks in Chapter 3. Thus, annotations $\{p_1\}A(S_1)\{q_1\}$ and $\{p_2\}A(S_2)\{q_2\}$ are interference free when the corresponding assertion networks $\mathcal{A}(\{p_1\}A(S_1)\{q_1\})$ and $\mathcal{A}(\{p_2\}A(S_2)\{q_2\})$ are. Of course one can also formulate interference freedom for annotations directly in terms of the assertions and annotated guarded assignments within these annotations themselves.

Definition 10.9 (Assertions and annotated actions of annotated programs)
For an annotated program of the form $\{p\}A(S)\{q\}$, we define the set of annotated actions $Act(\{p\}A(S)\{q\})$ and the set of assertions $Assn(\{p\}A(S)\{q\})$ by induction on the structure of S:

- Let $A(S)$ be $\langle b \rightarrow \bar{x} := \bar{e}\rangle$, then
  - $Act(\{p\}A(S)\{q\}) \stackrel{\text{def}}{=} \{\{p\}\langle b \rightarrow \bar{x} := \bar{e}\rangle\{q\}\}$
  - $Assn(\{p\}A(S)\{q\}) \stackrel{\text{def}}{=} \{p, q\}$.
- Let $A(S)$ be $A(S_1)\,;\,\{r\}A(S_2)$, then
  - $Act(\{p\}A(S)\{q\}) \stackrel{\text{def}}{=} Act(\{p\}A(S_1)\{r\}) \cup Act(\{r\}A(S_2)\{q\})$
  - $Assn(\{p\}A(S)\{q\}) \stackrel{\text{def}}{=} Assn(\{p\}A(S_1)\{r\}) \cup Assn(\{r\}A(S_2)\{q\})$.

- Let $A(S)$ be **if** $[]_{i=1}^{n} A(S_i)$ **fi**, then
    - $Act(\{p\}A(S)\{q\}) \stackrel{\text{def}}{=} \bigcup_{i=1}^{n} Act(\{p\}A(S_i)\{q\})$
    - $Assn(\{p\}A(S)\{q\}) \stackrel{\text{def}}{=} \bigcup_{i=1}^{n} Assn(\{p\}A(S_i)\{q\})$.
- Let $A(S)$ be **do** $A(S_B)$ $[]$ $A(S_E)$; **exit od**, then
    - $Act(\{p\}A(S)\{q\}) \stackrel{\text{def}}{=} Act(\{p\}A(S_B)\{p\}) \cup Act(\{p\}A(S_E)\{q\})$
    - $Assn(\{p\}A(S)\{q\}) \stackrel{\text{def}}{=} Assn(\{p\}A(S_B)\{p\}) \cup Assn(\{p\}A(S_E)\{q\})$.
- Let $A(S)$ be $[\{p_1\}A(S_1)\{q_1\} \parallel \{p_2\}A(S_2)\{q_2\}]$, then
    - $Act(\{p\}A(S)\{q\}) \stackrel{\text{def}}{=} Act(\{p_1\}A(S_1)\{q_1\}) \cup Act(\{p_2\}A(S_2)\{q_2\})$
    - $Assn(\{p\}A(S)\{q\}) \stackrel{\text{def}}{=} Assn(\{p_1\}A(S_1)\{q_1\}) \cup Assn(\{p_2\}A(S_2)\{q_2\})$. $\square$

Definition 10.10 (Interference free annotations) We call the annotations $\{p_1\}A(S_1)\{q_1\}$ and $\{p_2\}A(S_2)\{q_2\}$ *interference free*, if for $i,k \in \{1,2\}, i \neq k$, for every assertion r in $Assn(\{p_k\}A(S_k)\{q_k\})$ and for every guarded assignment $\{p\}\langle b \to \bar{x} := \bar{e}\rangle\{q\}$ in $Act(\{p_i\}A(S_i)\{q_i\})$ the verification condition $(p \wedge r \wedge b) \to (r[\bar{e}/\bar{x}])$ is valid. In other words: every assertion occurring in one of the annotations has to be proved invariant under guarded assignments which belong to the process associated with the other annotation. $\square$

Note that the components S_i in this definition are not restricted to sequential programs. Each of the S_i could be a parallel composition itself, or it could be a sequential program containing nested parallelism. The essence of the Owicki & Gries rule for parallel composition is the observation that proof outlines that are interference free w.r.t. each other constitute a proof outline for the parallel composition of the two statements considered.

Lemma 10.11 (Soundness of the Owicki & Gries rule)
Let $\{p_1\}A(S_1)\{q_1\}$ and $\{p_2\}A(S_2)\{q_2\}$ be proof outlines that are interference free according to Definition 10.10. Then

$$\{p_1 \wedge p_2\}[\{p_1\}A(S_1)\{q_1\} \parallel \{p_2\}A(S_2)\{q_2\}]\{q_1 \wedge q_2\}$$

is a proof outline.

Proof The essence of the proof is given in the above analysis of the verification conditions for the annotation of a concurrent program. It was shown that the validity of these "global" verification conditions follows from the validity of the local verification conditions and the validity of the interference freedom tests. The assumption that $\{p_1\}A(S_1)\{q_1\}$ and $\{p_2\}A(S_2)\{q_2\}$ are proof outlines implies the validity of the local verification conditions. Obviously, the assumption that the two proof outlines are interference free implies the validity of the interference freedom tests. $\square$

We now present the rules of the proof-outline logic. Apart from the Owicki & Gries rule, of which the soundness has been shown above, we have rules for the sequential constructs of SVL^+. The soundness of these latter rules follows from the results on assertion networks and proof outlines in Chapter 9. As an example, consider the rule for sequential composition. Consider annotations $\{p\} A(S_1) \{r\}$ and $\{r\} A(S_2) \{q\}$. Let $P_1 = T[[S_1]], P_2 = T[[S_2]], Q_1 = \mathcal{A}(\{p\} A(S_1) \{r\})$, and let $Q_2 = \mathcal{A}(\{r\} A(S_2) \{q\})$. The premise of the sequential composition rule asserts that the two annotations are proof outlines, that is, Q_1 and Q_2 are inductive assertion networks for diagrams P_1 and P_2. From Lemma 9.16 it follows that $Q \stackrel{\text{def}}{=} Q_1 ; Q_2$ is an inductive assertion network for $P_1 ; P_2$. According to Definition 9.21, Q is the assertion network corresponding to annotation $\{p\} A(S_1) ; \{r\} A(S_2) \{q\}$, and so we conclude that the latter is actually a proof outline. This is exactly the conclusion of the sequential composition rule.

Rule 10.1 (Guarded assignment)

$$\frac{(p \wedge b) \rightarrow q[\bar{e}/\bar{x}]}{\{p\} \langle b \rightarrow \bar{x} := \bar{e} \rangle \{q\}} .$$

Rule 10.2 (Sequential composition)

$$\frac{\{p\} A(S_1) \{r\}, \ \{r\} A(S_2) \{q\}}{\{p\} A(S_1) ; \{r\} A(S_2) \{q\}} .$$

Rule 10.3 (Choice)

$$\frac{\{p\} A(S_i) \{q\}, \text{for all } i \in \{1, \dots, n\}}{\{p\} \text{ if } []_{i=1}^{n} A(S_i) \text{ fi } \{q\}} .$$

Rule 10.4 (Exit-loops)

$$\frac{\{I\} A(S_B)\{I\}, \ \{I\} A(S_E)\{q\}}{\{I\} \text{ do } A(S_B) \ [] \ A(S_E) ; \textbf{exit } \textbf{od}\{q\}} .$$

Rule 10.5 (Parallel composition)

$$\frac{\{p_1\} A(S_1) \{q_1\} \text{ and } \{p_2\} A(S_2) \{q_2\} \text{ are interference free proof outlines}}{\{p_1 \wedge p_2\} [\{p_1\}A(S_1)\{q_1\} \ || \ \{p_2\}A(S_2)\{q_2\}]\{q_1 \wedge q_2\}} .$$

Thus, one has the following theorem.

Theorem 10.12

The proof rules 10.1, 10.2, 10.3, 10.4 and 10.5 are sound.   □

10.4.1 A Hoare Logic for Closed Shared-Variable Programs

Proof outlines are not completely satisfactory as specification for closed programs, as they display the full program text. A more abstract specification, that determines only the initial-final-state behaviour, can be given in terms of Hoare-style pre-postconditions. First of all, Hoare formulae allow one to abstract from internal control points. Second, one often introduces auxiliary variables during a correctness proof. For Hoare logic, there are proof rules that allow one to remove such variables. For proof outlines no such rules exist. We now discuss the rule for transforming a proof outline for an SVL^+ program S to a Hoare formula for S, where S is considered as a *closed* program, i.e., as $\langle S \rangle$. In the simplest case, the rule states that if $\{p\}A(S_0)\{q\}$ is a proof outline, then $\{p\}\langle S_0 \rangle\{q\}$ is a valid Hoare formula. That is, we simply forget in $A(S_0)$ the internal control points and their associated assertions. However, in many cases S_0 will have been created from a simpler program S, by adding assignments to auxiliary variables. We recall that auxiliary variables are introduced for the sake of verification. These variables are not allowed in boolean guards and should not occur in the original assignments of the program. Thus the values of program variables and, a fortiori, control flow are not affected by the addition to a program of assignments to auxiliary variables. In the end we want to remove these variables, both from the program text, as well as from the assertions. An appropriate place to do so is when we make the transition from proof outlines to Hoare formulae for closed programs. First of all, we must define (formally) the instances when a set of variables can be regarded as "auxiliary".

Definition 10.13 (Auxiliary variables)
Consider a program S_0. Let $A \subseteq var(S_0)$, where $var(S_0)$ denotes the set of variables that occur (within assignments and boolean tests) in S_0. We call A a *set of auxiliary variables of* S_0 if the following conditions are satisfied:

- Each variable from A occurs in S_0 only within assignments, that is, it may *not* occur within the boolean tests b of guarded assignments and guarded commands.
- When it occurs in an assignment $x_1,\ldots,x_n := e_1,\ldots,e_n$ it does so only within its components (x_i,e_i) when $x_i \in A$. In words: a variable from A cannot be used in assignments to variables outside A. □

Note that this definition is consistent with Definition 3.13 of an auxiliary variable set A for $T[\![S]\!]$ (see for instance Section 5.6). S obtains its meaning from $T[\![S]\!]$ whose transitions are in general of the form $(\mathcal{B}[\![b]\!] \to \lambda\sigma.\sigma : \bar{x} \mapsto$

$\mathcal{E}[\![\bar{e}]\!]\sigma$), which we abbreviate to $b \to f$. Now by the above definition $A \cap var(b) = \emptyset$ and $f = g \circ h$ s.t. $A \cap var(g) = \emptyset$ and the write variables of h are among A, i.e., Definition 3.13 applies.

Next we present a version of the auxiliary-variables rule. Note that the premise of the rule has the form of a proof outline, whereas its conclusion is a Hoare formula.

Rule 10.6 (Auxiliary variables)

$$\frac{\{p\}\,A(S_0)\,\{q\}}{\{p\}\,\langle S \rangle\,\{q\}},$$

where, for some set of auxiliary variables A of S_0 with $A \cap var(q) = \emptyset$, program S results from S_0 by deleting all assignments to the variables in A, and, in case this results in **skip** statements, dropping the latter.

In the literature, the auxiliary-variable rule is usually formulated slightly differently. For instance, in [OG76a] the step from proof outlines to Hoare logic is incorporated in the rule for parallel composition. The auxiliary-variables rule is then formulated as a Hoare-style rule, i.e., with a premise in the form of a Hoare formula, rather than a proof outline. As we have seen, this approach has the disadvantage that a concurrent program cannot be a component of a larger system, but is automatically treated as a closed program.

We remark that, although the rule does not *forbid* auxiliary variables within the precondition p of the conclusion $\{p\}\langle S\rangle\{q\}$, one usually aims at a Hoare formula without them. A common situation is the one in which one does have a proof outline $\{p'\}A(S_0)\{q'\}$ with pre- and postconditions still including free occurrences of auxiliary variables so that the auxiliary variables rule is not immediately applicable. Assume that $\bar{z}$ is a list of auxiliary variables, and that $\bar{z} := \bar{e}_0$ is an assignment in which the expressions in $\bar{e}_0$ do not contain auxiliary variables. Let $p \stackrel{\text{def}}{=} p'[\bar{e}_0/\bar{z}]$. Moreover, assume that q is an assertion without auxiliary variables such that $q' \to q$ is valid; how to obtain such an assertion q will be discussed later. Then we can construct the following proof outline, with a precondition p and postcondition q neither of which contains auxiliary variables:

$$\{p\}\,\bar{z} := \bar{e}_0\,;\,\{p'\}\,A(S_0)\,\{q'\}\,\{q\}.$$

We have used the convention, introduced in Chapter 6, that two consecutive assertions such as $\{q'\}\{q\}$ abbreviate a proof outline of the form $\{q'\}\mathbf{skip}\{q\}$. Now the auxiliary variables rule allows one to deduce $\{p\}\langle S\rangle\{q\}$, with S obtained from S_0 as above.

As already observed above, the standard formulation of the Owicki & Gries method differs slightly from the set of rules presented thus far, in particular with respect to the treatment of auxiliary variables. We briefly discuss the rules associated with this standard formulation below.

Rule 10.7 (Parallel composition for the Owicki & Gries system)

$$\frac{\{p_1\}\, A(S_1)\, \{q_1\} \text{ and } \{p_2\}\, A(S_2)\, \{q_2\} \text{ are interference free proof outlines}}{\{p_1 \wedge p_2\}\, \langle [S_1 \parallel S_2] \rangle \{q_1 \wedge q_2\}}$$

The auxiliary variables rule for Hoare logic is similar to the above auxiliary variables rule for proof outlines. The only difference being that the premise of the rule is formulated in terms of closed programs:

Rule 10.8 (Auxiliary variables for the Owicki & Gries system)

$$\frac{\{p\}\, \langle S_0 \rangle\, \{q\}}{\{p\}\, \langle S \rangle\, \{q\}} \; ,$$

where, for some set of auxiliary variables A of S_0 with $A \cap var(q) = \emptyset$, S results from S_0 by deleting all assignments to the variables in A, and, when this results in **skip** statements, dropping the latter.

Although this rule *looks* very similar to rule 10.6, it is less powerful, since it does not allow for the elimination of auxiliary variables in the pre- and postcondition of a Hoare-style specification by means of the technique sketched above. The Owicki & Gries system contains some extra rules, well-known from Hoare logic for sequential programs with recursive procedures [Apt81b, Gor75]: the well-known consequence and so-called substitution rules. The latter occurs in the literature in various forms; the one most resembling our elimination technique above is as follows.

Rule 10.9 (Substitution for the Owicki & Gries system)

$$\frac{\{p\}\, \langle S \rangle\, \{q\}}{\{\exists \bar{z}.p\}\, \langle S \rangle\, \{q\}} \; ,$$

where $\{\bar{z}\} \cap var(q) = \emptyset$, for some set of auxiliary variables $\bar{z}$ for S.

Elimination of auxiliary variables from the pre- and postcondition of a Hoare specification by means of assignment statements judiciously-placed before and after a parallel program is not possible in the original Owicki & Gries system. The rules above would be used as follows, to obtain the same result. First the standard Owicki & Gries rule for parallel composition is used, resulting in a conclusion in the form of a Hoare formula of the form $\{p'\}S_0\{q'\}$, where both p' and q' might contain auxiliary variables $\bar{z}$.

Rule 10.10 (Consequence) $$\frac{p \to p_0, \ \{p_0\} \ S \ \{q_0\}, \ q_0 \to q}{\{p\} \ S \ \{q\}} \quad.$$

The consequence rule is applied to weaken the postcondition, yielding the formula $\{p'\}S_0\{q\}$, where q does not contain auxiliary variables. For example, one could choose $q \equiv \exists \bar{z}.q'$, if $\bar{z}$ is the list of auxiliary variables, since $q' \to (\exists \bar{z}.q')$ is a valid formula. Note that the consequence rule cannot be used to do the same with the precondition, for $\exists \bar{z}.p'$ does not imply p'. However, since q does not contain free occurrences of $\bar{z}$ variables, the substitution rule applies, and yields the formula $\{\exists \bar{z}.p'\}\langle S\rangle\{\exists \bar{z}.q'\}$. In this last formula, both the pre- and postcondition no longer contain free occurrences of auxiliary variables. (Often it is desirable to apply the consequence rule once more, so as to rewrite the pre- and postcondition into equivalent forms without existential quantifiers.)

In the literature [Gor75, dB80] one also encounters the following variation of the substitution rule, originally used within a proof system for sequential programs with recursive procedures:

Rule 10.11 (Substitution for the Gorelick system)

$$\frac{\{p\} \ \langle S\rangle \ \{q\}}{\{p[\bar{e}/\bar{z}]\} \ \langle S\rangle \ \{q\}} \ ,$$

where $\{\bar{z}\} \cap var(q) = \emptyset$, for some set of auxiliary variables $\bar{z}$ for S.

This rule resembles quite closely the elimination technique for auxiliary variables by means of the addition of extra assignments as discussed above. The rule follows from the substitution rule for the Owicki & Gries system and the rule of consequence, since $p[\bar{e}/\bar{z}] \to \exists \bar{z}.p$ is a valid formula.

In all the examples below we use the convention, introduced previously, that $\langle true \to x := e\rangle$ is abbreviated to $x := e$ whenever this does not lead to confusion.

As before, desirability of a correctness formula using these rules is expressed by prefixing "⊢" to this formula.

Example 10.14 We prove $\{x = 0\} \ \langle \ [x := x + 1 \ \| \ x := x + 2] \ \rangle \ \{x = 3\}$.

Observe that, by applying the rules for assignment,

$$\{x = 0 \lor x = 2\} x := x + 1 \{x = 1 \lor x = 3\}$$

and

$$\{x = 0 \lor x = 1\} x := x + 2 \{x = 2 \lor x = 3\}$$

are proof outlines. To prove interference freedom of these, we have to prove the verification conditions generated by the following four assignments:

- $\{(x = 0 \lor x = 2) \land (x = 0 \lor x = 1)\ x := x + 1\ \{x = 0 \lor x = 1\}$,
- $\{(x = 0 \lor x = 2) \land (x = 2 \lor x = 3)\ x := x + 1\ \{x = 2 \lor x = 3\}$,
- $\{(x = 0 \lor x = 1) \land (x = 0 \lor x = 2)\ x := x + 2\ \{x = 0 \lor x = 2\}$, and
- $\{(x = 0 \lor x = 1) \land (x = 1 \lor x = 3)\ x := x + 2\ \{x = 1 \lor x = 3\}$.

These formulae follow from the guarded-assignment rule. By applying the parallel composition rule we obtain the following proof outline:

$$\{(x = 0 \lor x = 2) \land (x = 0 \lor x = 1)\}$$
$$[\quad \{x = 0 \lor x = 2\}\, x := x + 1\, \{x = 1 \lor x = 3\}$$
$$\|\quad \{x = 0 \lor x = 1\}\, x := x + 2\, \{x = 2 \lor x = 3\}$$
$$]\,\{(x = 1 \lor x = 3) \land (x = 2 \lor x = 3)\}.$$

Since

$$\models x = 0 \to (x = 0 \lor x = 2) \land (x = 0 \lor x = 1)$$

and

$$\models (x = 1 \lor x = 3) \land (x = 2 \lor x = 3) \to x = 3,$$

we can extend this to a proof outline of the form:

$$\{x = 0\}$$
$$\{(x = 0 \lor x = 2) \land (x = 0 \lor x = 1)\}$$
$$[\cdots \| \cdots]$$
$$\{(x = 1 \lor x = 3) \land (x = 2 \lor x = 3)\}$$
$$\{x = 3\}.$$

By applying the consequence rule, we can transform this into the desired Hoare formula: $\vdash \{x = 0\}\ \langle\, [x := x + 1\ \|\ x := x + 2]\, \rangle\ \{x = 3\}$. $\qquad\square$

Example 10.15 As the next example consider $\langle\, [x := x + 1\ \|\ x := x + 1]\, \rangle$. The aim is to prove $\{x = 0\}\langle\, [x := x + 1\ \|\ x := x + 1]\, \rangle\{x = 2\}$. Analogous to the previous example, we first have to try using the proof outlines

$$\{x = 0 \lor x = 1\} x := x + 1 \{x = 1 \lor x = 2\}$$

and

$$\{x = 0 \lor x = 1\}x := x + 1\{x = 1 \lor x = 2\}.$$

These proof outlines, however, are not interference free. For instance, $\{(x = 0 \lor x = 1) \land (x = 0 \lor x = 1)\}\, x := x + 1\, \{x = 0 \lor x = 1\}$ is not valid. A second problem is that the conjunction of the postassertions $(x = 1 \lor x = 2) \land (x = 1 \lor x = 2)$ does not imply the desired postassertion $x = 2$. As proved in Example 3.12 within the context of the inductive assertion method, it is even impossible to prove $\{x = 0\}x := x + 1 \parallel x := x + 1\{x = 2\}$ by making use of assertions whose only free variable is x. This proof carries over to the present framework.

As we saw before, a solution to this problem is the use of *auxiliary variables*. In our example we can use, for instance, two auxiliary variables *done*1 and *done*2, which record whether the assignment has been performed in, respectively, the first or second process.

Now consider the following proof outlines:

$$\{\neg done1 \land (\neg done2 \to x = 0) \land (done2 \to x = 1)\}$$
$$x, done1 := x + 1, true$$
$$\{done1 \land (\neg done2 \to x = 1) \land (done2 \to x = 2)\}$$

and

$$\{\neg done2 \land (\neg done1 \to x = 0) \land (done1 \to x = 1)\}$$
$$x, done2 := x + 1, true$$
$$\{done2 \land (\neg done1 \to x = 1) \land (done1 \to x = 2)\}.$$

These proof outlines are interference free. For instance,

$$\{\neg done1 \land (\neg done2 \to x = 0) \land (done2 \to x = 1) \land$$
$$\neg done2 \land (\neg done1 \to x = 0) \land (done1 \to x = 1)\}$$
$$x, done1 := x + 1, true$$
$$\{\neg done2 \land (\neg done1 \to x = 0) \land (done1 \to x = 1)\}$$

is valid, since its precondition is equivalent to $\neg done1 \land \neg done2 \land x = 0$. Consequently, we can apply the parallel composition rule. We also introduce an initialisation of the auxiliary variables, and obtain the proof outline below, where we have used the following abbreviations:

$$p_1 \stackrel{def}{=} \neg done1 \land (\neg done2 \to x = 0) \land (done2 \to x = 1)$$
$$p_2 \stackrel{def}{=} \neg done2 \land (\neg done1 \to x = 0) \land (done1 \to x = 1)$$
$$q_1 \stackrel{def}{=} done1 \land (\neg done2 \to x = 1) \land (done2 \to x = 2)$$
$$q_2 \stackrel{def}{=} done2 \land (\neg done1 \to x = 1) \land (done1 \to x = 2).$$

The proof outline is given by

$\{x = 0\}$
$done1, done2 := false, false;$
$\{p_1 \wedge p_2\}$
$[\quad \{p_1\}\, x, done1 := x+1, true\, \{q_1\}$
$\|\quad \{p_2\}\, x, done2 := x+1, true\, \{q_2\}$
$]\, \{q_1 \wedge q_2\}$
$\{x = 2\}.$

By the auxiliary variables rule we obtain

$$\vdash \{x = 0\}\langle [x := x+1 \,\|\, x := x+1]\rangle \{x = 2\}. \qquad \Box$$

In the next example we sketch how Example 10.1 can be proved correct by both augmenting assignment statements and loop exits with auxiliary variables.

Example 10.16 In this example we continue the study of the mutual exclusion algorithm $[R_1 \,\|\, R_2]$ from Example 10.1.

$R_1 \equiv$ $R_2 \equiv$
$in1 := true;$ $in2 := true;$
do   **do**
      $in2 \to in1 := false; in1 := true$ $in1 \to in2 := false; in2 := true$
od   **od**

As mentioned in Example 10.1, our aim is to prove that this program does not terminate (since that implies mutual exclusion for the original program $[S_1 \,\|\, S_2]$). Formally, this is expressed by $\vdash \{true\}\, \langle\, [R_1 \,\|\, R_2]\,\rangle\, \{false\}$. Here we present a proof of this formula inspired by the proof given in [Dij82] (consult Section 10.4.2 for Dijkstra's proof of the original algorithm). Two auxiliary variables *luck1* and *luck2* are added to the program, and the guarded commands are extended with an explicit exit branch. Below we give an annotated program for the resulting processes R_1' and R_2':

$R_1' \equiv$ $R_2' \equiv$
$\{p_0\} in1 := true;$ $\{q_0\} in2 := true;$
$\{p_1\}$**do** $in2 \to \{p_2\} in1 := false;$ $\{q_1\}$**do** $in1 \to \{q_2\} in2 := false;$
               $\{p_3\} in1 := true$ $\{q_3\} in2 := true$
    $[]\langle \neg in2 \to luck1 := true\rangle;$ **exit** $[]\langle \neg in1 \to luck2 := true\rangle;$ **exit**
    od   **od**
$\{p_4\}$ $\{q_4\}$

with the following set of abbreviations:

$p_0 : \neg luck1 \wedge (luck2 \to in2)$ $q_0 : \neg luck2 \wedge (luck1 \to in1)$

$p_1 : \neg luck1 \wedge in1 \wedge (luck2 \to in2)$ $q_1 : \neg luck2 \wedge in2 \wedge (luck1 \to in1)$

$p_2 : \neg luck1 \wedge in1 \wedge (luck2 \to in2)$ $q_2 : \neg luck2 \wedge in2 \wedge (luck1 \to in1)$

$p_3 : \neg luck1 \wedge \neg in1 \wedge (luck2 \to in2)$ $q_3 : \neg luck2 \wedge \neg in2 \wedge (luck1 \to in1)$

$p_4 : luck1 \wedge \neg luck2$ $q_4 : luck2 \wedge \neg luck1.$

It is easy to see that these annotations form a proof outline. For the step from p_1 to p_4 observe that $luck2 \to in2$ and $\neg in2$ together imply $\neg luck2$. Also the proof of interference freedom is rather straightforward. For instance, observe that $luck2 \to in2$ in the assertions of R_1' can be falsified by $in2 := false$ and $luck2 := true$ in R_2'. However, precondition q_2 of $in2 := false$ contains $\neg luck2$ and precondition q_1 of $luck2 := true$ contains $in2$, which implies that $luck2 \to in2$ remains valid. Hence, by the parallel composition rule for proof outlines we obtain a proof outline of the form:

$$\{p_0 \wedge q_0\} \, A([R_1' \parallel R_2']) \, \{p_4 \wedge q_4\}.$$

By adding an initialisation for the auxiliary variables, and since $p_4 \wedge q_4$ implies *false*, the following proof outline results:

$$\{true\} \; luck1, luck2 := false, false \,; \{p_0 \wedge q_0\} \, A([R_1' \parallel R_2']) \, \{p_4 \wedge q_4\} \, \{false\}.$$

By applying the auxiliary variables rule 10.6, we obtain the desired Hoare formula:

$$\vdash \{true\} \, \langle \, [R_1 \parallel R_2] \, \rangle \, \{false\}. \qquad\qquad \square$$

In the next example we sketch how the example above can be proved correct by only augmenting assignment statements with auxiliary variables. That is, in this case one does not use synchronisation of auxiliary variables with loop exits; in fact the whole verification can be done within the limited syntax of SVL, rather than that of SVL$^+$.

Example 10.17 Consider again the program $[R_1 \parallel R_2]$ as given in Example 10.1. The aim is to prove $\{true\} \, \langle [R_1 \parallel R_2] \rangle \, \{false\}$ by only adding auxiliary variables to already-present assignments. In the next annotated program we have added a single auxiliary variable *last*:

$R_1' \equiv$ $R_2' \equiv$

$\{p_0\}in1, last := true, 1\,;$ $\{q_0\}in2, last := true, 2\,;$

$\{p_1\}$ $\{q_1\}$

do   **do**

     $in2 \to \{p_2\}in1 := false\,;$ $in1 \to \{q_2\}in2 := false\,;$

         $\{p_3\}in1, last := true, 1$ $\{q_3\}in2, last := true, 2$

od   **od**

$\{p_4\}$ $\{q_4\}$

with the following abbreviations:

$p_0 : true$	$q_0 : true$
$p_1 : in1$	$q_1 : in2$
$p_2 : true$	$q_2 : true$
$p_3 : true$	$q_3 : true$
$p_4 : in1 \wedge (\neg in2 \vee last = 2)$	$q_4 : in2 \wedge (\neg in1 \vee last = 1).$

It is easy to see that this annotated program is a proof outline. Observe also that $in1 \wedge \neg in2$ instead of p_4 would lead to a proof outline for R_1, but we have weakened this assertion to achieve interference freedom. Note that $\neg in2 \vee last = 2$ can only be falsified by R_2' if it sets $in2$ to *true*, but in the same atomic action *last* is assigned the value 2. Hence one can show that we have interference-free proof outlines; the parallel composition rule then leads to a proof outline of the form $\{p_0 \wedge q_0\} [R_1' \parallel R_2'] \{p_4 \wedge q_4\}$. Observe that $p_4 \wedge q_4$ implies *false*. Thus, analogous to the above derivation, we can construct a proof outline of the form $\{true\} \{p_0 \wedge q_0\} [R_1' \parallel R_2'] \{p_4 \wedge q_4\} \{false\}$. By the auxiliary variables rule, we finally obtain $\vdash \{true\} \langle [R_1 \parallel R_2] \rangle \{false\}$. $\square$

10.4.2 A Historical Note / EWD 554

The mutual exclusion algorithm from Example 10.1 has been taken from *A personal summary of the Gries–Owicki theory*, EWD 554, by Edsger W. Dijkstra, dated 14 March 1976, and reprinted in [Dij82]. This EWD (see footnote 1.4.3 of Chapter 1 on page 21 for an explanation) is one of de Roever's favourites, reflecting the spirit of the golden era of programming when program construction was regarded as an art worthy of gods, and programming concepts were described by mythical terms such as "daemon" and "exorcising". In accordance with this EWD, we first give Dijkstra's proof of the simple mutual exclusion algorithm and then present Dekker's algorithm, which avoids after-you-no-after-you blocking, with Dijkstra's correctness arguments.

Example 10.18 Let S_1 and S_2 be the same as in Example 10.1. Below we give proof outlines for these processes.

$S_1 \equiv$ $S_2 \equiv$

$\{p_0\} in1 := true;$ $\{q_0\} in2 := true;$

$\{p_1\}$**do** $in2 \rightarrow \{p_1\} in1 := false;$ $\{q_1\}$**do** $in1 \rightarrow \{q_1\} in2 := false;$

          $\{p_2\} in1 := true$ $\{q_2\} in2 := true$

$[] \langle \neg in2 \to luck1 := true \rangle$; **exit**
od ;
$\{p_3\} critical\ section1$;
$\{p_3\} luck1, in1 := false, false$;
$\{p_4\} noncritical\ section1$
$\{p_4\}$

$[] \langle \neg in1 \to luck2 := true \rangle$; **exit**
od ;
$\{q_3\} critical\ section2$;
$\{q_3\} luck2, in2 := false, false$;
$\{q_4\} noncritical\ section2$
$\{q_4\}$

With $p_0 : \neg luck1$, one can prove:

$$p_1 : \neg luck1 \land in1$$
$$p_2 : \neg luck1 \land \neg in1$$
$$p_3 : luck1 \land in1$$
$$p_4 : \neg luck1 \land \neg in1,$$

and similarly for the q_i assertions in process S_2. Furthermore observe that all assertions p_i imply p defined by $p \stackrel{\text{def}}{=} luck1 \to in1$, and similarly, that all the q_i's imply q defined by $q \stackrel{\text{def}}{=} luck2 \to in2$.

We can now replace all the original assertions p_i in process S_1 by $p_i \land q_j$ for any j; the proofs remain valid, because process S_1 does not change the variables mentioned in q_j. Similarly one can replace all the original forms for q_i in process S_2 by $q_i \land p_j$ for any j; again the proofs remain valid, i.e., these proof outlines are interference free! Having thus proved that the assertions of each of the processes are invariant with respect to the other process, we conclude the invariance of $p \land q$.

Finally consider assertion $r : \neg(luck1 \land luck2)$. This assertion can also be added to all assertions; it is also invariant. The critical assignment in process S_1 that could destroy its validity is, of course, $luck1 := true$, but it is safe, because

$$\vdash \{\neg luck2\} luck1 := true \{r\},$$

and $\neg luck2$ is implied by $q \land \neg in2$.

(*Notice that this way of reasoning is sound solely because* $\langle \neg in2 \to luck1 := true \rangle$ *is considered as an atomic action. Notice also that mutual exclusion is specified here in the form of an invariant of a proof outline for* $[S_1 \parallel S_2]$. *It is not possible to specify this property in the form of a Hoare formula for the closed program* $\langle [S_1 \parallel S_2] \rangle$ [note added by the authors].)

This solution for the mutual exclusion problem essentially uses two shared variables: $in1$ and $in2$. They are really the only two variables that matter: the variables $luck1$ and $luck2$ are auxiliary variables which have only been introduced for the sake of being able to formulate what we mean by "mutual exclusion" and of being able to formulate the proofs. In the actual programs to be executed they – and all the operations carried out on them – can be eliminated.

□

Example 10.19 (Dekker's algorithm [Dij65b]) The possibility of after-you-no-after-you blocking, present in the above algorithm, is eliminated in the mutual exclusion algorithm of T.J. Dekker's below.

Let the initial value of the shared integer variable *turn* be either 1 or 2. We only give process S_1; process S_2 can be obtained from it by interchanging 1's and 2's. We recall that **wait** b is an abbreviation for $\langle b \rightarrow \textbf{skip} \rangle$.

$S_1:$ $in1 := true$;

     if $in2 \rightarrow$ **if** $turn = 1 \rightarrow$ **skip**

         $[] turn = 2 \rightarrow in1 := false$; **wait** $turn = 1$; $in1 := true$

         fi ; **wait** $\neg in2$; $luck1 := true$

     $[] \langle \neg in2 \rightarrow luck1 := true \rangle$

     fi ;

     *critical section*1 ;

     $turn := 2$;

     $luck1, in1 := false, false$;

     *noncritical section*1

Again one can derive that, provided $\neg(luck1 \wedge luck2)$ is initially satisfied by $S_1 \parallel S_2$, this expression is an invariant for $S_1 \parallel S_2$, and, therefore, that this program is a mutual exclusion algorithm. Its difference is that it does not feature any after-you-no-after-you blocking. One needs a weaker assumption about the "daemon" that chooses how to interleave actions from S_1 and S_2 to be sure of termination. With the program from Example 10.1, this daemon could select an unbounded number of units of actions from S_1 and an unbounded number of units of actions from S_2, without even one of the critical sections being selected. With our new program this is no longer true [Dij82].

(*This weaker assumption is called fairness, as, e.g., expressed by* **Requirement 3** *in Section 3.2* [Note added by the authors].)

Below we give a proof outline for process S_1; a proof outline for process S_2 can be obtained from it by interchanging 1's by 2's and p's by q's.

$\{p_0\}$ $in1 := true$;

$\{p_1\}$ **if** $in2 \rightarrow$

     $\{p_2\}$ **if** $turn = 1 \rightarrow \{p_3\}$ **skip**

         $[] turn = 2 \rightarrow \{p_4\}$ $in1 := false$; $\{p_5\}$ **wait** $turn = 1$;

                 $\{p_6\}$ $in1 := true$

       fi ; $\{p_3\}$ **wait** $\neg in2$; $\{p_3\}$ $luck1 := true$

     $[] \langle \neg in2 \rightarrow luck1 := true \rangle$

     fi ;

$\{p_7\}$ *critical section*1 ;

$\{p_7\}$ $turn := 2$;

$\{p_7\}$ $luck1, in1 := false, false$;
$\{p_8\}$ $noncritical$ $section$
$\{p_8\}$

Studying this process in relative isolation we derive, under the assumption that $p_0 : \neg luck1$, the following assertions:

$$p_1 : \neg luck1 \wedge in1$$
$$p_2 : p_1$$
$$p_3 : \neg luck1 \wedge in1 \wedge turn = 1$$
$$p_4 : \neg luck1$$
$$p_5 : \neg luck1 \wedge \neg in1$$
$$p_6 : \neg luck1 \wedge \neg in1 \wedge turn = 1$$
$$p_7 : luck1 \wedge in1$$
$$p_8 : \neg luck1 \wedge \neg in1.$$

Again the assertion $luck1 \to in1$ is implied by all of them, and together with process S_2 and its proof outline we can derive the invariance of $\neg(luck1 \wedge luck2)$ as before. The difference between the programs from Example 10.18 and $S_1 \parallel S_2$ is, as mentioned before, that $S_1 \parallel S_2$ does not display after-you-no-after-you blocking. This is proved next. Nontermination of S_1 implies, because it contains only two **wait** statements, invariance of $(p_5 \wedge turn \neq 1) \vee (p_3 \wedge in2)$, i.e., of

$$(\neg in1 \wedge turn \neq 1) \vee (in1 \wedge in2 \wedge turn = 1). \tag{10.1}$$

(Note that $turn = 1$ in the p_i's is invariant w.r.t. process S_2.) For process S_2 we have the corresponding assertion

$$(\neg in2 \wedge turn \neq 2) \vee (in1 \wedge in2 \wedge turn = 2). \tag{10.2}$$

The conjunction of (10.1) and (10.2) reduces to $(\neg in1 \wedge \neg in2 \wedge turn \neq 1 \wedge turn \neq 2)$. And, indeed, when we start the two processes with, say, $turn = 3$, nontermination, i.e. blocking, of both processes is quite easily realised. If, however, we start them – and so we assume – with

$$turn = 1 \vee turn = 2, \tag{10.3}$$

then it is easily seen that (10.3) is invariant w.r.t. both processes, thus implying the negation of the conjunction of (10.1) and (10.2). This is usually taken as the proof that there is no danger of the after-you-no-after-you blocking (and, a fortiori, the absence of the danger of deadlock).

The conclusion that the machine executing the process's units of action in interleaved fashion will eventually terminate formally rests on the assumption that the daemon that chooses how to interleave actions will not be so grossly unfair as to always select the next unit of action from the same program. $\square$

10.4.3 Labelling

Auxiliary variables play an important rôle in the Owicki & Gries method. *Labels* attached to certain program locations can be made visible and recorded using a special kind of auxiliary variable. Such labels will be used in Chapter 12, for instance, to indicate that certain actions are ready to execute. Labels are also used in our completeness proof for the Owicki & Gries method for SVL$^+$. We shall show that a set of auxiliary variables in the form of a canonical labelling suffices for any Owicki & Gries-style proof. Labels l can occur in assertions, where, informally, **at**(l) is "true" in those states in which execution of a program has reached the control point labelled by l. Note that a *concurrent* program can reside at two or more local locations at the same time, so one can have a state in which both **at**(l_1) and **at**(l_2) are true.

Program labels can be introduced formally in various ways. Probably the simplest solution is to assume that program locations are part of the program state, as is done for instance in [Lam88]. Thus, program locations are values of special variables that are updated implicitly during a transition. When program locations are seen as separate entities, as is the case for the Owicki & Gries method in [OG76a], then auxiliary variables that keep track of the value of program locations can be introduced. This is the approach which will be followed below.

A labelled statement is in essence just an ordinary statement to which auxiliary variables, called "counters", have been added to keep track of the locations. These counters reflect the parallel structure of the program. For instance, if S is a parallel statement of the form $[S_1 \parallel S_2]$, then the counter m for S will have the form of a pair $\langle m_1, m_2 \rangle$, where m_1 and m_2 are counters for S_1 and S_2. In general, we consider SVL$^+$ statements S where parallel composition and sequential constructs can be *nested*, and so the number of parallel components that is active at some point during execution may vary. Informally, this leads to a program counter for S in the form of a nested tuple of variables for which the degree of nesting varies throughout the execution; the general form of this tuple is determined by the syntax of S. We indicate a simple way of encoding such complicated counters by means of a fixed set of auxiliary variables.

Definition 10.20 (Parallel components and concurrent actions) Call statement S_i a *parallel component* of S if it occurs in S within a (sub)statement of the form $[S_i \parallel S_j]$ or $[S_j \parallel S_i]$ for some S_j (S_j is of course a parallel component, too). We call two guarded assignments $a_1 \stackrel{\text{def}}{=} \langle b_1 \rightarrow \bar{x}_1 := \bar{e}_1 \rangle$ and $a_2 \stackrel{\text{def}}{=} \langle b_2 \rightarrow \bar{x}_2 := \bar{e}_2 \rangle$ occurring in S *concurrent* actions if there is within S a sub-statement of the form $S_i \parallel S_j$ such that a_1 occurs in S_i and a_2 occurs in S_j.

$\square$

Note that this definition includes not only the direct syntactic components of S, but also its *nested* components. For example, in a program S of the form $S_1 ; [S_2 \parallel (S_3 ; [S_4 \parallel S_5]; S_6)]$, we have the following parallel components: S_2, S_4, S_5, and $(S_3 ; [S_4 \parallel S_5]; S_6)$. Informally, at any moment some subset of a statement's parallel components will be active, i.e., is being executed. For instance, for the example above one of the possible situations is one in which the execution of S_1 has been finished, the S_2 and $(S_3 ; [S_4 \parallel S_5]; S_6)$ components are active, and the latter has activated the S_4 and S_5 components, and, hence, S_3 and S_6 are currently inactive. In order to keep track of which parallel component is active at which location inside those components, we introduce a collection of *label counters* which are variables $m_1, \ldots, m_n$, ranging over natural numbers. We introduce one counter m_0 for the program as a whole and one counter m_i for each parallel component S_i of S. Strictly positive values for m_i are used to denote the locations *inside* the S_i component. A value $m_i = 0$ denotes a location of S in which S_i is not active. We construct a labelled statement $S^\dagger$ from S by adding assignments to such counter variables. Therefore, we consider three types of program actions and that $T[\![S_i]\!]$ is represented by a transition diagram P_i of the form (L, T, l_1, l_{n_i}) where the set L of locations is $\{l_1, l_2, \ldots, l_{n_i}\}$. The initial value of m_0 is 1 while every other component is inactive. We distinguish the following cases:

- **Sequential step**: An action in a sequential context is executed. Within the corresponding transition diagram this means a step from a location l_j to a location l_k. The counter variable for the enclosing component has to be set to k. Using guarded assignments this is an atomic action (e.g., $\langle b \rightarrow x, m_i := \bar{e}, k \rangle$).

- **Entering a parallel statement**: The next action in component S_i is a parallel statement. The enclosed parallel components have to become active while S_i has to be deactivated. This means that m_i has to be set to 0 and the counter variables for the enclosed parallel components have to be set to 1.

- **Return from a parallel statement**: The parallel components within a parallel statement of S_i reach their exit locations. Then their counter variables have to be set to 0 while m_i is set to k which corresponds to the next location

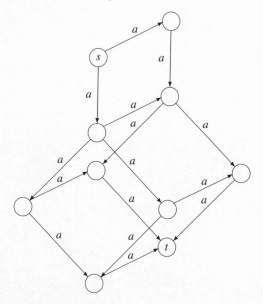

Fig. 10.2. The transition system for $[(y := y+1; [y := y+1 \parallel y := y+1]) \parallel y := y+1]$ with a denoting the assignment $y := y+1$.

l_k in S_i. The enclosed parallel components are deactivated and the enclosing component is reactivated.

Example 10.21 (Labelling) Consider the programs $S_1 \stackrel{\text{def}}{=} y := y+1; [y := y+1 \parallel y := y+1]$ and $S_2 \stackrel{\text{def}}{=} y := y+1$. A representative for the transition system $T[\![[S_1 \parallel S_2]]\!]$ is sketched in Figure 10.2.

The canonical labelling for S is given by $S^\dagger$, where $S^\dagger \stackrel{\text{def}}{=} [S_1^\dagger \parallel S_2^\dagger]$ is given by

$$S_1^\dagger \stackrel{\text{def}}{=} \langle y, m_1 := y+1, 2 \rangle ; \langle m_1, m_2, m_3 := 0, 1, 1 \rangle ;$$
$$[\langle y, m_2 := y+1, 2 \rangle \parallel \langle y, m_3 := y+1, 2 \rangle]$$

and

$$S_2^\dagger \stackrel{\text{def}}{=} \langle y, m_4 := y+1, 2 \rangle.$$

A transition network representing $T[\![S^\dagger]\!]$ is given in Figure 10.3. $\qquad\square$

Basing them on labelled statements we now introduce assertion networks denoted by "**at**". Let S be some labelled statement, and let P be a transition diagram representing $T[\![S]\!]$. Intuitively, if l is some location of P then **at**(l) is an assertion that is "true" during some execution if and only if control resides

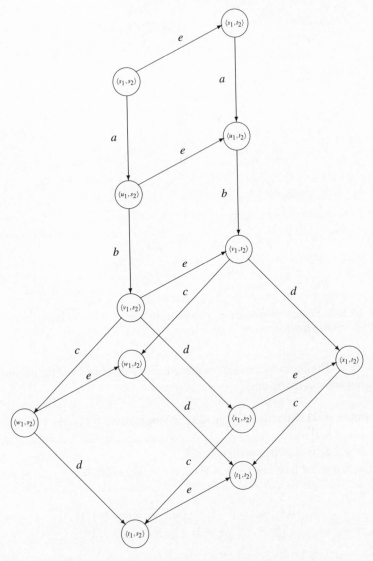

Fig. 10.3. This transition diagram for $T[\![S^\dagger]\!]$ uses the following abbreviations: $a \equiv y, m_1 := y+1, 2$; $b \equiv m_1, m_2, m_3 := 0, 1, 1$; $c \equiv y, m_2 := y+1, 2$; $d \equiv y, m_3 := y+1, 2$; and $e \equiv y, m_4 := y+1, 2$.

at location l. We call a location l of $T[\![S]\!]$ a *global* location for S. When S can be decomposed into parallel components, say $S \stackrel{\text{def}}{=} [S_1 \parallel \cdots \parallel S_n]$, we also call locations l_i of $T[\![S_i]\!]$ *local* locations of $T[\![S_i]\!]$. Therefore, a location l could be a *simple location* l_j in front of a sequential statement but l could also be a location in front of a parallel statement. In the latter case, l is a *tuple* of the form $\langle l_1, \ldots, l_n \rangle$, where each of the components l_i is (recursively) a location. For each simple location l, one can identify the parallel component S_i and the transition diagram $T[\![S_i]\!]$ in which l occurs. Now let l correspond to node $l_j \in L_i$. Then we define $\textbf{at}(l)$ as the predicate $m_i = j$. If l is a tuple of the form $\langle l_1, \ldots, l_n \rangle$, then we define, recursively, $\textbf{at}(l) \stackrel{\text{def}}{=} \textbf{at}(l_1) \wedge \cdots \wedge \textbf{at}(l_n)$. Notice that when S_i is one of the parallel components of S, then $\textbf{at}$ restricted to the locations of S_i is an inductive assertion network for $T[\![S_i]\!]$ (see Exercise 10.20). We also denote such restricted assertion networks by "$\textbf{at}$".

Example 10.22 (at network) Consider the labelled program $S^\dagger \stackrel{\text{def}}{=} [S_1^\dagger \parallel S_2^\dagger]$ of the previous example. The corresponding $\textbf{at}$ network is given by

$$\textbf{at}(\langle s_1, s_2 \rangle) \stackrel{\text{def}}{=} m_1 = 1 \wedge m_2 = 0 \wedge m_3 = 0 \wedge m_4 = 1$$
$$\textbf{at}(\langle s_1, t_2 \rangle) \stackrel{\text{def}}{=} m_1 = 1 \wedge m_2 = 0 \wedge m_3 = 0 \wedge m_4 = 2$$
$$\textbf{at}(\langle u_1, s_2 \rangle) \stackrel{\text{def}}{=} m_1 = 2 \wedge m_2 = 0 \wedge m_3 = 0 \wedge m_4 = 1$$
$$\textbf{at}(\langle u_1, t_2 \rangle) \stackrel{\text{def}}{=} m_1 = 2 \wedge m_2 = 0 \wedge m_3 = 0 \wedge m_4 = 2$$
$$\textbf{at}(\langle v_1, s_2 \rangle) \stackrel{\text{def}}{=} m_1 = 0 \wedge m_2 = 1 \wedge m_3 = 1 \wedge m_4 = 1$$
$$\textbf{at}(\langle v_1, t_2 \rangle) \stackrel{\text{def}}{=} m_1 = 0 \wedge m_2 = 1 \wedge m_3 = 1 \wedge m_4 = 2$$
$$\textbf{at}(\langle w_1, s_2 \rangle) \stackrel{\text{def}}{=} m_1 = 0 \wedge m_2 = 2 \wedge m_3 = 1 \wedge m_4 = 1$$
$$\textbf{at}(\langle w_1, t_2 \rangle) \stackrel{\text{def}}{=} m_1 = 0 \wedge m_2 = 2 \wedge m_3 = 1 \wedge m_4 = 2$$
$$\textbf{at}(\langle x_1, s_2 \rangle) \stackrel{\text{def}}{=} m_1 = 0 \wedge m_2 = 1 \wedge m_3 = 2 \wedge m_4 = 1$$
$$\textbf{at}(\langle x_1, t_2 \rangle) \stackrel{\text{def}}{=} m_1 = 0 \wedge m_2 = 1 \wedge m_3 = 2 \wedge m_4 = 2$$
$$\textbf{at}(\langle t_1, s_2 \rangle) \stackrel{\text{def}}{=} m_1 = 0 \wedge m_2 = 2 \wedge m_3 = 2 \wedge m_4 = 1$$
$$\textbf{at}(\langle t_1, t_2 \rangle) \stackrel{\text{def}}{=} m_1 = 0 \wedge m_2 = 2 \wedge m_3 = 2 \wedge m_4 = 2 \,.$$

$\square$

We have defined labelled versions $S^\dagger$ of SVL$^+$ statements S, based on the one-to-one correspondence between the guarded assignments in S and transitions in $T[\![S]\!]$. This is *not* the case for SVL programs because boolean guards inside SVL programs do not have an assignment part. Therefore, if one labels an SVL program S', then we must treat S' as an abbreviation of an SVL$^+$ program S'', and the result of labelling will be some SVL$^+$ program $S''^\dagger$ rather than an SVL program, because boolean guards have been augmented by means of assignments to counters.

10.5 An Extended Example: Concurrent Garbage Collection

As a more ambitious application, we consider concurrent garbage collectors, such as the program discussed already in Section 1.4.3. A formal correctness proof by means of Hoare logic of the garbage collector from [DLM+78] has first been given in [Gri77]. Here we develop this garbage collector in two steps. First, we present a more abstract version of garbage-collector algorithms based on the abstract data types sets and relations for representing graphs, inspired by [Rey81]. Second, we replace the abstract set-typed variables by concrete variables in the form of arrays and integer-typed variables. This approach simplifies the correctness proof, and allows many variations, all derived from the same abstract algorithm, but with different choices made during the second development step [DLM+78, BA82, And91].

10.5.1 The Mutator and the Collector

We consider graphs with a set of nodes called *Nodes* and a set of directed edges called *Edges*. A convenient way to describe such graphs is by means of a successor function $Succ : Nodes \rightarrow \mathcal{P}(Nodes)$. The intuition is that for a node x the set $Succ(x)$ denotes the set $\{y_1, \ldots, y_n\}$ of graph nodes y_i such that there is an edge from x to y_i. It is customary to extend the *Succ* function to sets of nodes. If X is a set of nodes $\{x_1, \ldots, x_n\}$, then we define $Succ(X) \stackrel{\text{def}}{=} Succ(x_1) \cup \cdots \cup Succ(x_n)$. We can define the set of nodes *reachable* from X, denoted by $Succ^*(X)$, as follows:

(i) $X \subseteq Succ^*(X)$,

(ii) $Succ(Succ^*(X)) \subseteq Succ^*(X)$, and

(iii) a node x is a member of $Succ^*(X)$ if and only if this follows from clauses (i) and (ii) above. In other words, $Succ^*(X)$ is the *smallest* set satisfying these two clauses.

We assume that there is a given set of *root nodes* that we denote by *Roots*. We define the set of reachable nodes as $Reachable \stackrel{\text{def}}{=} Succ^*(Roots)$. All unreachable nodes, i.e., the nodes from the set $Garbage \stackrel{\text{def}}{=} Nodes \setminus Reachable$, are called *garbage nodes*.

The concurrent garbage-collector algorithm consists of two main components called the *mutator* and the *collector*, running in parallel, thus:

$$GCsystem \stackrel{\text{def}}{=} [Mutator \parallel Collector].$$

The mutator symbolises a user program that has access to the graph nodes via the root nodes. From the point of view of the garbage-collector algorithm, all the mutator does is to continuously add or delete edges between nodes. In concrete garbage-collection algorithms, as in [DLM+78], the mutator can also allocate nodes from some list of "free" nodes. We introduce the equivalent of this free list by partitioning the set *Roots* into two sets: *DataRoots* and *FreeRoots*. The set of nodes *FreeNodes* $\stackrel{\text{def}}{=}$ *Succ**(*FreeRoots*) is considered as the set of free nodes. At the abstract level, allocating a free node simply consists of adding and deleting a few edges, to the effect that some node x that was formerly reachable via *FreeRoots* has now instead become reachable via *DataRoots*. The important observation here is that all mutator actions boil down to adding and deleting edges between nodes that are reachable from nodes in *Roots*. We therefore specify two abstract mutator actions called *AddEdge* and *DeleteEdge*. It is assumed that only these two actions can modify the graph, so that all other mutator actions cannot possibly interfere with the correct functioning of the collector. We specify these two actions by means of Hoare formulae that are in a suitable form for applying the interference freedom test when we verify our collector program. This means that we give assignments describing the effect of these actions, together with preconditions that we may assume will hold when these actions are executed. Since the postcondition is of no importance as far as the interference freedom test is concerned, we choose here the assertion "*true*". The specification uses the well-known *functional overriding* notation $f \oplus \{x \mapsto v\}$, which is defined by the following two clauses:

(1) $(f \oplus \{x \mapsto v\})(x) \stackrel{\text{def}}{=} v$,
(2) $(f \oplus \{x \mapsto v\})(y) \stackrel{\text{def}}{=} f(y)$, for $y \not\equiv x$.

The mutator actions are specified thus:

> *AddEdge*:
> $\{x, y \in Reachable\}$ *Succ* := *Succ* $\oplus \{x \mapsto Succ(x) \cup \{y\}\}$ $\{true\}$
> $\{x \notin Reachable \vee y \notin Reachable\}$ *AddEdge* $\{false\}$[1]

> *DeleteEdge*:
> $\{x, y \in Reachable\}$ *Succ* := *Succ* $\oplus \{x \mapsto Succ(x) \setminus \{y\}\}$ $\{true\}$
> $\{x \notin Reachable \vee y \notin Reachable\}$ *DeleteEdge* $\{false\}$[1]

When the mutator deletes some edge, then some nodes might become unreachable from *Roots*, i.e., turn into garbage nodes. It is the task of the collector to detect such garbage nodes, and to add these to the set of free nodes, by making them reachable again via the nodes in *FreeRoots*. An important aspect of *concurrent* garbage collection is that while garbage is being collected new garbage can be created at the same time. In fact, some node that has just been added to the free nodes can be allocated by the mutator and then a few moments later

---

[1] These correctness formulae express that these actions do not terminate when the precondition $x, y \in Reachable$ is not fulfilled. This holds for all definitions of mutator actions discussed in Section 10.5, and will no longer be mentioned explicitly.

become garbage again. Consequently, we cannot specify the garbage collector as a terminating program with a postcondition that requires (in the form of some predicate formula) that upon termination all garbage has been collected. Rather we will construct a collector in the form of a *cyclic* program, i.e., a nonterminating program of the form

$$Collector \stackrel{\text{def}}{=} \textbf{do } Marking\,;\,Collecting \textbf{ od}.$$

We aim to specify that (at least) all nodes that are garbage at the start of a cycle will be detected during the *Marking* phase, and recollected during the subsequent *Collecting* phase of that cycle. Specifying the latter property is not completely straightforward since nodes that are added to the *FreeNodes* set by the *Collecting* phase could be allocated by the mutator, and turned into garbage again a few moments later, even during the same *Collecting* phase. So, we cannot claim that a garbage node that has been discovered during the *Marking* phase is a free node upon termination of the *Collecting* phase. The best we can claim is that such nodes have been added to the *FreeNodes* set at some moment during the *Collecting* phase. Hoare logic is not the ideal logic for specifying this sort of property, because pre- and postconditions specify only properties of the initial and final state of a computation, and cannot specify any property of intermediate states. We can specify the desired property by means of a *proof outline* for the garbage-collection cycle of the following form:

$$\{true\}$$
$$Reachable_0 := Reachable\,;\, Marking\,\{Garbage_0 \subseteq Garb\}\,;\, Collecting$$
$$\{Garb = \emptyset\}$$

Here, $Reachable_0$ is an auxiliary variable, used to "freeze" the set of reachable nodes at the start of the collector cycle. We use $Garbage_0$ as an abbreviation of $Nodes \setminus Reachable_0$. The intermediate condition $Garbage_0 \subseteq Garb$ specifies that a program variable $Garb$ contains at least all nodes in $Garbage_0$. It might contain more, since nodes that turn into garbage during the *Marking* phase might still be detected during that phase. If they are not detected, then (validity of) the specification implies that they will be taken care of during the *next* cycle. The postcondition specifies that upon termination of the *Collecting* phase all nodes in $Garb$ have been removed from that set. In itself that would not be a very useful property, and therefore we also require the following property of the program text for the *Collecting* phase: the only actions inside *Collecting* that modify $Garb$ are of the form

$$FreeNodes, Garb := FreeNodes \cup \{x\}, Garb \setminus \{x\}.$$

Together with the given assertions this enforces that any node x in $Garbage_0$ is added to *FreeNodes* somewhere during the *Collecting* phase.

10.5.2 The Abstract Collector Algorithm

The abstract algorithm for the *Collector* program is based on set-typed variables P, U, and *Garb*. For a variable like U we use an action "*picksome(U)*". This is a nondeterministic operation that chooses some arbitrary element from U, provided the set is nonempty. This abstract operation will later be replaced by simple SVL^+ operations; here it is sufficient to treat *picksome(U)* as an abstract operation that satisfies a certain specification. If I is a state formula that does not have x as a free variable, then (validity of) the following Hoare formula specifies the *picksome* action:

$$\{I \wedge U \neq \emptyset\} \, x := picksome(U) \, \{I \wedge x \in U\}.$$

The program for the abstract collector is as follows:

$Collector_A \overset{\text{def}}{=}$

do

    $P, U, Reachable_0 := \emptyset, Roots, Reachable$;

    do

        $U \neq \emptyset \rightarrow x := picksome(U)$;

                $P, U := P \cup \{x\}, (U \setminus \{x\}) \cup (Succ(x) \setminus (P \cup \{x\}))$

    od;

    $Garb := Nodes \setminus P$;

    do

        $Garb \neq \emptyset \rightarrow y := picksome(Garb)$;

                $FreeNodes, Garb := FreeNodes \cup \{y\}, Garb \setminus \{y\}$

    od

od

The informal explanation of the algorithm is that both P and U contain nodes that are "marked" as being reachable. Nodes x in P are called "processed" nodes, meaning that it is ensured that all successor nodes $Succ(x)$ are included in either P or U. For the "unprocessed" nodes x in U, this property is not yet guaranteed. The first loop makes progress by picking some arbitrary unprocessed node x. If x has any successor nodes that are not yet in P or U, then these successors are added to U. The node x itself has now become a "processed" node, and is moved from U to P. If U becomes empty, then P satisfies the conditions (i) and (ii) of the definition of $Succ^*(Roots)$, and therefore contains all reachable nodes.

The invariants and proof outline for the abstract collector

We give a list of definitions $D_1, \ldots, D_4$, for the notions that were introduced above, which will be used in the proofs below.

(D_1)　$Reachable \stackrel{\text{def}}{=} Succ^*(Roots)$,

(D_2)　$Garbage \stackrel{\text{def}}{=} Nodes \setminus Reachable$,

(D_3)　$Garbage_0 \stackrel{\text{def}}{=} Nodes \setminus Reachable_0$,

(D_4)　$FreeNodes \stackrel{\text{def}}{=} Succ^*(FreeRoots)$.

The correctness proof is based upon a number of predicate formulae $I_1, \ldots, I_6$, that formalise the intuitive descriptions of the sets P and U, and that are used as loop invariants. Invariants I_1 and I_2 together imply that P includes all reachable nodes when U has become empty. Invariant I_5 holds during the marking phase, and states that reachable nodes can become unreachable, but not vice versa. Invariant I_6 also holds during the marking phase, and states, together with I_1, I_2 and I_4, that the reachable nodes are always a subset of $Reachable_0$.

(I_1)　$Roots \subseteq P \cup U$,

(I_2)　$Succ(P) \subseteq P \cup U$,

(I_3)　$P \cap U = \emptyset$,

(I_4)　$P \cup U \subseteq Reachable_0$,

(I_5)　$Reachable \subseteq Reachable_0$,

(I_6)　$Succ(Reachable_0) \subseteq Reachable_0$.

Based upon these invariants, we formulate the following proof outline. As mentioned above, it is the proof outline as a whole, and not only its pre- and postconditions, that expresses correctness of the collector. Note that in the second half of the program, a node y is removed from *Garb* within the same atomic action that adds it to the *FreeNodes* set. Thus, upon termination, i.e., when $Garb = \emptyset$, we know that all *Garb* nodes have been inserted into *FreeNodes*. (As explained above, this does not imply that all *Garb* nodes are *still* within *FreeNodes* when the collector terminates, due to the presence of the mutator.)

do $\{true\}$

　　$P, U, Reachable_0 := \emptyset, Roots, Reachable$;

　　$\{I_1 \wedge I_2 \wedge I_3 \wedge I_4 \wedge I_5 \wedge I_6\}$

　　do

　　　　$U \neq \emptyset \to x := picksome(U)$; $\{I_1 \wedge I_2 \wedge I_3 \wedge I_4 \wedge I_5 \wedge I_6 \wedge x \in U\}$

　　　　　　$P, U := P \cup \{x\}, (U \setminus \{x\}) \cup (Succ(x) \setminus (P \cup \{x\}))$

　　od ;

　　$\{I_1 \wedge I_2 \wedge I_3 \wedge I_4 \wedge I_5 \wedge I_6 \wedge U = \emptyset\}$

　　$\{Reachable \subseteq P \subseteq Reachable_0\}$

$Garb := Nodes \setminus P$;
$\{Garb \cap Reachable = \emptyset \wedge Garbage_0 \subseteq Garb\}$
$\{true\}$
do

    $Garb \neq \emptyset \rightarrow y := picksome(Garb)$;
                         $FreeNodes, Garb := FreeNodes \cup \{y\}, Garb \setminus \{y\}$
od

    $\{Garb = \emptyset\}$
od

The assignment to $FreeNodes := FreeNodes \cup \{y\}$ is an operation, which adds and removes edges in such a way that afterwards y is a free node. It should be remarked, that $Succ(y)$ should also be changed, e.g., to the empty set (or at least such that $Succ(y) \subseteq FreeNodes$). Otherwise, there could exist an old edge going from y to a non-garbage node z. In such a case, z would then afterwards be reachable from *DataRoots* and from *FreeRoots*.

The local correctness of the abstract collector

The local verification conditions of this proof outline are readily verified. The main part of the proof is to show that the assignment in the first loop satisfies the following Hoare formula:

$$\{I_1 \wedge I_2 \wedge I_3 \wedge I_4 \wedge I_5 \wedge I_6 \wedge x \in U\} \, P, U := \widetilde{P}, \widetilde{U} \, \{I_1 \wedge I_2 \wedge I_3 \wedge I_4 \wedge I_5 \wedge I_6\}, \quad (**)$$

where $\widetilde{P} \stackrel{\text{def}}{=} P \cup \{x\}$, and $\widetilde{U} \stackrel{\text{def}}{=} (U \setminus \{x\}) \cup (Succ(x) \setminus (P \cup \{x\}))$. It turns out that we can show the correctness of a number of simpler specifications, which together imply the correctness of $(**)$.

(1) $\{I_1\} \, P, U := \widetilde{P}, \widetilde{U} \, \{I_1\}$. To show this, we must show validity of the verification condition $I_1 \rightarrow I_1[\widetilde{P}/P, \widetilde{U}/U]$. That is:
$\models Roots \subseteq P \cup U \rightarrow Roots \subseteq (P \cup \{x\}) \cup ((U \setminus \{x\}) \cup (Succ(x) \setminus (P \cup \{x\})))$. This implication is obvious.

(2) $\{I_2\} \, P, U := \widetilde{P}, \widetilde{U} \, \{I_2\}$. This boils down to showing the validity of the following implication:
$Succ(P) \subseteq P \cup U \rightarrow Succ(P \cup \{x\}) \subseteq (P \cup \{x\}) \cup ((U \setminus \{x\}) \cup (Succ(x) \setminus (P \cup \{x\})))$.
Using the property $\models Succ(P \cup \{x\}) = Succ(P) \cup Succ(x)$, this verification condition also follows easily.

(3) $\{I_3\} \, P, U := \widetilde{P}, \widetilde{U} \, \{I_3\}$. What must be shown is the following implication:
$P \cap U = \emptyset \rightarrow (P \cup \{x\}) \cap ((U \setminus \{x\}) \cup (Succ(x) \setminus (P \cup \{x\}))) = \emptyset$.
Assuming $P \cap U = \emptyset$, it suffices to show that:

(i) $\models (P \cup \{x\}) \cap (U \setminus \{x\}) = \emptyset$, and

(ii) $\models (P \cup \{x\}) \cap (Succ(x) \setminus (P \cup \{x\})) = \emptyset$,

both of which are easily seen to hold.

(4) $\{I_4 \wedge I_6 \wedge x \in U\}\ P, U := \widetilde{P}, \widetilde{U}\ \{I_4\}$. We must show the validity of the implication:

$(P \cup U \subseteq Reachable_0 \wedge Succ(Reachable_0) \subseteq Reachable_0 \wedge x \in U) \to$
$(P \cup \{x\}) \cup ((U \setminus \{x\}) \cup (Succ(x) \setminus (P \cup \{x\}))) \subseteq Reachable_0.$

Assuming $(P \cup U \subseteq Reachable_0 \wedge Succ(Reachable_0) \subseteq Reachable_0 \wedge x \in U)$, it follows immediately that $(P \cup \{x\}) \cup (U \setminus \{x\}) \subseteq Reachable_0$ and $x \in Reachable_0$, which in turn implies $Succ(x) \subseteq Reachable_0$ using I_6 and that the $Succ$ function is not modified.

(5) $\{I_5\}\ P, U := \widetilde{P}, \widetilde{U}\ \{I_5\}$. Since the assignment does not modify the $Succ$ function, it follows that $Reachable$ and $Reachable_0$ are not modified, from which preservation of I_5 follows immediately.

(6) $\{I_6\}\ P, U := \widetilde{P}, \widetilde{U}\ \{I_6\}$. Again, since the assignment does not modify $Succ$ or $Reachable_0$, preservation of I_6 follows immediately.

We leave the remainder of the local verification conditions for the collector as an exercise.

The interference freedom tests for the abstract collector

The next step in our correctness proof is to prove interference freedom under mutator actions of the assertions in the above proof outline. Again we concentrate on interference that concerns the invariants $I_1, \dots, I_6$. (The remaining interference freedom tests are straightforward.) First, we focus on invariant I_2, which should be preserved by the *AddEdge* and *DeleteEdge* actions, executed by the mutator. Here a problem arises with the *AddEdge* action. If this action adds an edge from node x to node y, and $x \in P$, but $y \notin P \cup U$, then I_2 will be violated. Note, since y must be a *reachable* node, that there must exist some other edge, say, from some node z to y. If the latter edge is deleted before the successors of z are marked, then node y will never be marked, and so our design thus far is *incorrect*. The well-known solution here is that the mutator must *itself* mark nodes like y. In our abstract algorithm, this means that y, unless it happens to be in the set P already, must be inserted in the set U. (It cannot be inserted in P, since we do not have any guarantee that the successors of y are in $P \cup U$. Technically speaking, inserting y in P might cause another violation of I_2.) So, we define the *AddEdge* and *DeleteEdge* actions as follows:

modified *AddEdge*:

$\{x,y \in Reachable\} \; U, Succ := U \cup (\{y\} \setminus P), Succ \oplus \{x \mapsto Succ(x) \cup \{y\}\}$
$\{true\}$

DeleteEdge:

$\{x,y \in Reachable\} \; Succ := Succ \oplus \{x \mapsto Succ(x) \setminus \{y\}\} \; \{true\}$

Note that the expression $(\{y\} \setminus P)$, used in the modified *AddEdge* action, denotes either $\emptyset$ or $\{y\}$, depending on whether y is in P or not. For these two (modified) actions we must check the interference freedom conditions. For the *DeleteEdge* action this is simple; the effect of deleting an edge is that $Succ(P)$, and therefore *Reachable*, either remain unchanged or else become *smaller* sets. Since P and U remain unchanged too, it follows that $I_1, \ldots, I_6$ are preserved.

We focus on preservation of I_2 by the modified *AddEdge* action. The interference freedom test requires us to show the validity of:

$\{Succ(P) \subseteq P \cup U \wedge x,y \in Reachable\}$
$U, Succ := U \cup (\{y\} \setminus P), Succ \oplus \{x \mapsto Succ(x) \cup \{y\}\}$
$\{Succ(P) \subseteq P \cup U\}.$

What must be shown is, assuming the precondition $Succ(P) \subseteq P \cup U$ and $x,y \in Reachable$, that $Succ \oplus \{x \mapsto Succ(x) \cup \{y\}\}(P) \subseteq P \cup (U \cup (\{y\} \setminus P))$. This follows from:

(1) $Succ \oplus \{x \mapsto Succ(x) \cup \{y\}\}(P) \subseteq Succ(P) \cup \{y\}$, and
(2) $P \cup (U \cup (\{y\} \setminus P)) = P \cup U \cup \{y\}$.

A second assertion that occurs in the proof outline is $I_1 \wedge I_2 \wedge I_3 \wedge I_4 \wedge I_5 \wedge I_6 \wedge U = \emptyset$. We consider here preservation of the $U = \emptyset$ part by the modified *AddEdge* action. At first sight, this assertion looks suspect; the mutator might add a new edge at any time, and, therefore, could insert a node in U, which would not preserve the assertion at hand. The interference freedom test requires us to show the validity of:

$\{I_1 \wedge I_2 \wedge I_3 \wedge I_4 \wedge I_5 \wedge I_6 \wedge U = \emptyset \wedge x,y \in Reachable\}$
$U, Succ := U \cup (\{y\} \setminus P), Succ \oplus \{x \mapsto Succ(x) \cup \{y\}\}$
$\{U = \emptyset\}.$

The precondition of this Hoare formula implies $y \in Reachable \subseteq P$. Therefore, the initial state for the *AddEdge* action satisfies the assertion $\{y\} \setminus P = \emptyset$. Apparently, when the collector has arrived at this point every node that the mutator adds a link to is already in P. Therefore, we can construct the following valid annotated fragment, which shows the invariance of the above assertion:

$\{I_1 \wedge I_2 \wedge I_3 \wedge I_4 \wedge I_5 \wedge I_6 \wedge U = \emptyset \wedge x, y \in \textit{Reachable}\}$
$\{\{y\} \setminus P = \emptyset \wedge U = \emptyset\}$
$U, \textit{Succ} := U \cup (\{y\} \setminus P), \textit{Succ} \oplus \{x \mapsto \textit{Succ}(x) \cup \{y\}\}$
$\{\dots \wedge U = \emptyset\}.$

The details of the remaining interference freedom tests are left as an exercise. We only mention here that one should not only verify that assertions from the proof outline for the collector are preserved by the mutator actions, but also vice versa, that the assertion $x, y \in \textit{Reachable}$ is preserved by collector actions.

Refining the grain of granularity

The modified *AddEdge* action used thus far has one defect: it is hard to implement since it requires that both a graph link is added and an element is inserted in U within the same *atomic* action. Of course, there are more of these simultaneous assignments in the *Collector* algorithm, but most of these can be split into simple assignments satisfying Reynolds' criterion, explained in Section 3.2. For instance, consider the action A, defined by:

$$A \overset{\text{def}}{=} P, U := P \cup \{x\}, (U \setminus \{x\}) \cup (\textit{Succ}(x) \setminus (P \cup \{x\})).$$

As a first step, one could split A into two actions A_1 ; A_2 as follows:

$$A_1 ; A_2 \overset{\text{def}}{=} U := U \cup (\textit{Succ}(x) \setminus P) ; P, U := P \cup \{x\}, U \setminus \{x\}.$$

One could go one step further and, for instance, implement A_1 as a loop that enumerates the elements of $\textit{Succ}(x)$ and inserts the elements not already in P into U, one by one. On the other hand, the next section shows that the A_2 action is easily implemented as an atomic action, so splitting it into two separate assignments to P and U is unnecessary. Splitting atomic actions introduces extra control points, and for each of these an appropriate assertion has to be attached. Usually, checking the local verification conditions is fairly straightforward. For instance, the precondition for A, i.e., the assertion $I_1 \wedge I_2 \wedge I_3 \wedge I_4 \wedge I_5 \wedge I_6 \wedge x \in U$, can also be used for the control point between A_1 and A_2. What is easily overlooked, however, is that an extra control point also means that there is an extra *interference freedom test* to be performed. In this particular case, there is, obviously, no problem, since we could use the precondition for A for the new control point, and this precondition has been checked for interference freedom already. But now let us consider the (modified) *AddEdge* action, specified by:

$\models \{x, y \in \textit{Reachable}\} \; U, \textit{Succ} := U \cup (\{y\} \setminus P), \textit{Succ} \oplus \{x \mapsto \textit{Succ}(x) \cup \{y\}\}$
$\quad \{\textit{true}\}.$

We would like to split *AddEdge* such that the following fragment remains valid:

$$\{x, y \in Reachable\} \; U := U \cup (\{y\} \setminus P) \; ; \{x, y \in Reachable \wedge y \in P \cup U\}$$
$$Succ := Succ \oplus \{x \mapsto Succ(x) \cup \{y\}\} \; \{true\}.$$

Checking local correctness presents no problems. The interference freedom tests, in which we check that the above two actions do not interfere with the assertions for the collector proof outline, are also not difficult, and are left as an exercise. Note that the extra conjunct $y \in P \cup U$ is essential to show that the assignment to *Succ* preserves invariant I_2. The last check that we should make is that the collector actions preserve the new assertion, in particular, that they preserve the $y \in P \cup U$ assertion.

Exercise: *Show that this last test fails; $y \in P \cup U$ is not preserved!*

Amazingly, we can reverse the order of these two actions, and implement the *AddEdge* action *correctly* as follows:

$$\{x, y \in Reachable\}$$
$$Succ := Succ \oplus \{x \mapsto Succ(x) \cup \{y\}\} \; ;$$
$$U := U \cup (\{y\} \setminus P) \; \{true\}$$

At a first look, one is convinced this must be wrong; before we added the assignment $U := U \cup (\{y\} \setminus P)$ the problem was that the collector could exit its first loop, because $U = \emptyset$ held, without having inserted y in P, so that y would, incorrectly, be considered as garbage. Here we have introduced a new control location that has the same problem as before, or so it seems. There is a subtle difference, however. The mutator's next action will insert y into U, and, in particular, *it cannot delete any edge before it has done this insertion*. Because of this, and because y must be reachable before the *AddEdge* action starts, we know that there must be an alternative way to reach y, that is, different from using the newly added edge. This alternative guarantees that the collector cannot exit its first loop without having y inserted into P. (Note that this implies the assumption that the mutator itself is a *sequential* program, not a parallel program that could add and delete several edges concurrently.) Of course this sort of informal reasoning is hardly trustworthy. To show the correctness of this argument formally, we introduce an auxiliary variable $\widetilde{Succ}$. This auxiliary variable is meant to "shadow" *Succ*, except at the new control point of the *AddEdge* action. The $\widetilde{Succ}$ variable is used to make the split mutator action (the assignments to U and *Succ*) *atomic* again with respect to the proof. The modifications done to *Succ* in the *AddEdge* action are also done to $\widetilde{Succ}$, but delayed for one mutator step and, hence, simultaneously with the assignment to U. This is needed, because with respect to I_2, the changes must be simultaneous. Otherwise, we would have interference. So, we introduce

$$\tilde{I}_2 \stackrel{\text{def}}{=} \widetilde{Succ}(P) \subseteq P \cup U$$

and replace I_2 by $\tilde{I}_2$ in the proof outline. Then, the interference test for $\tilde{I}_2$ is in principle the same as in the previous proof for I_2. But we have to redo the local correctness proofs where I_2 was involved. Establishing local correctness for I_1, I_3, I_4, I_5, and I_6 remains the same as before. Note that I_2 is not used in most of these local correctness proofs. For $\tilde{I}_2$, we need some more information and introduce two new assertions. First, we add the formula

$$I_7 \stackrel{\text{def}}{=} Reachable = \widetilde{Reachable}$$

to all control points of the collector. Since the marking part of the collector program does not modify $Succ$ or $\widetilde{Succ}$, checking the local correctness conditions for I_7 there is obvious. And for the collecting part, local correctness will be simple, because we assume simultaneous assignments to $Succ$ and $\widetilde{Succ}$. Second, we must restrict the relationship between $Succ$ and $\widetilde{Succ}$, and introduce the formula

$$I_8 \stackrel{\text{def}}{=} Succ = \widetilde{Succ} \vee \exists x,y \in Reachable : Succ = \widetilde{Succ} \oplus \{x \mapsto Succ(x) \cup \{y\}\}$$

which is added to every control location of the collector program.

We introduce a formula $M_1 \stackrel{\text{def}}{=} \widetilde{Succ} = Succ$, which we use as an invariant for the mutator. The *AddEdge* action now becomes annotated as follows:

$\{x,y \in Reachable \wedge M_1\}$
$Succ, \widetilde{Succ} := Succ \oplus \{x \mapsto Succ(x) \cup \{y\}\}, Succ;$
$\{x,y \in Reachable \wedge \widetilde{Succ} \oplus \{x \mapsto Succ(x) \cup \{y\}\} = Succ\}$
$U, \widetilde{Succ} := U \cup (\{y\} \setminus P), Succ$
$\{M_1\}.$

The *DeleteEdge* action should of course be modified too, such that it preserves M_1. The modified proof outline thus becomes as follows:

do $\{I_7 \wedge I_8\}$
　　$P, U, Reachable_0 := \emptyset, Roots, Reachable;$
　　$\{I_1 \wedge \tilde{I}_2 \wedge I_3 \wedge I_4 \wedge I_5 \wedge I_6 \wedge I_7 \wedge I_8\}$
　　do
　　　　$U \neq \emptyset \rightarrow x := picksome(U);\ \{I_1 \wedge \tilde{I}_2 \wedge I_3 \wedge I_4 \wedge I_5 \wedge I_6 \wedge I_7 \wedge I_8 \wedge x \in U\}$
　　　　　　$P, U := P \cup \{x\}, (U \setminus \{x\}) \cup (Succ(x) \setminus (P \cup \{x\}))$
　　od;
　　$\{I_1 \wedge \tilde{I}_2 \wedge I_3 \wedge I_4 \wedge I_5 \wedge I_6 \wedge I_7 \wedge I_8 \wedge U = \emptyset\}$
　　$\{\widetilde{Reachable} \subseteq P \subseteq Reachable_0 \wedge I_7 \wedge I_8\}$

$\{Reachable \subseteq P \subseteq Reachable_0 \wedge I_7 \wedge I_8\}$
$Garb := Nodes \setminus P;$
$\{Garb \cap Reachable = \emptyset \wedge Garbage_0 \subseteq Garb \wedge I_7 \wedge I_8\}$
$\{I_7 \wedge I_8\}$
do
$\quad Garb \neq \emptyset \rightarrow y := picksome(Garb)\,; \;\{I_7 \wedge I_8\}$
$\quad\quad\quad\quad FreeNodes, Garb := FreeNodes \cup \{y\}, Garb \setminus \{y\}$
od
$\quad\{Garb = \emptyset \wedge I_7 \wedge I_8\}$
od

As mentioned above, we must redo the local correctness proof for $\tilde{I}_2$. We concentrate on the critical transitions which are the assignment to P and U in the first loop, and its exit. For the assignment we have to show that

$$I_1 \wedge \tilde{I}_2 \wedge I_3 \wedge I_4 \wedge I_5 \wedge I_6 \wedge I_7 \wedge I_8 \wedge x \in U$$
$$\rightarrow \quad \widetilde{Succ}(P \cup \{x\}) \subseteq \tilde{P} \cup \tilde{U}$$

with $\tilde{P} = P \cup \{x\}$ and $\tilde{U} = ((U \setminus \{x\}) \cup (Succ(x) \setminus (P \cup \{x\})))$. Then, $\tilde{U} \supseteq U \setminus \{x\}$. Consequently, $P \cup U \subseteq P \cup \{x\} \cup (U \setminus \{x\}) \subseteq \tilde{P} \cup \tilde{U}$. Since $\widetilde{Succ}$ is not changed, we gain, using $\tilde{I}_2$, that $\widetilde{Succ}(P) \subseteq P \cup U \subseteq \tilde{P} \cup \tilde{U}$. What is left to show is $\widetilde{Succ}(x) \subseteq \tilde{P} \cup \tilde{U}$. From I_8 and the choice of $\tilde{P}$ and $\tilde{U}$ we infer that $\widetilde{Succ}(x) \subseteq Succ(x) \subseteq \tilde{P} \cup \tilde{U}$. When the first loop exits, we cannot be sure that $\widetilde{Succ} = Succ$, so at first we only infer, from $I_1 \wedge \tilde{I}_2 \wedge U = \emptyset$, that $\widetilde{Reachable} \subseteq P$. However, from I_7 we *do* know that $\widetilde{Succ}^*(Roots) = Succ^*(Roots)$, and thus we infer that $Reachable \subseteq P$, as desired.

Furthermore, the local correctness proof for I_7 and I_8 has to be done. For I_7, this is already explained above, and for I_8 it is obvious, because we require the collector to always assign simultaneously the same to $Succ$ and $\widetilde{Succ}$.

An interesting part of the correctness proof is of course to check whether the interference freedom tests are satisfied. The test that mutator actions preserve the collector assertions is almost the same as before, where we assumed that *AddEdge* was executed as a single atomic action. For I_1, I_3, and I_4 this is obvious, since they do not depend on $Succ$, so there is no difference between a simultaneous and a split assignment (the assignment to $Succ$ has no influence on these formulae). For I_5 and I_6 the same argument applies, but this time the assignment to U is not observable with respect to the formulae. The only critical formula, which depends both on U and on $Succ$, is I_2, but this one is changed to $\tilde{I}_2$. Invariant $\tilde{I}_2$ is not affected by the assignment to $Succ$, and the assignment to $\widetilde{Succ}$ is combined with the assignment to U into an atomic action. Hence, the proof for I_2 can be taken.

Now we prove interference freedom for invariant I_7. Consider the *AddEdge* operation. The first assignment adds an edge from x to y to *Succ*. But since $\widetilde{Succ}$ is not changed, y is also in $\widetilde{Reachable}$ after the first assignment. Then, one can conclude that I_7 also holds there. The second assignment is simple, because afterwards $\widetilde{Succ} = Succ$.

The interference freedom test for I_8 is obvious by definition of the *AddEdge* operation. The *DeleteEdge* operation should preserve M_1, hence there can be no interference with I_7 or I_8.

The other tests are either trivial or depend only on one of U and *Succ*. Therefore, they are not complicated and left to the reader.

The test whether collector actions preserve the mutator assertions, in particular M_1 and the assertion for the new control location, is not difficult. The first loop from the collector does not assign to *Succ* or $\widetilde{Succ}$, so all mutator assertions are preserved trivially. For the second loop of the collector, this is not completely obvious, since we have not specified in any detail how the action *FreeNodes* := *FreeNodes* $\cup \{y\}$ is implemented, other than that it can be done by adding and deleting a number of edges. Note that adding edges by the collector is different from adding edges by the mutator: since the collector is clearly not in its marking phase, there is no need to include an assignment to U. Therefore, we may assume that these collector actions have the following form:

$$Succ(x), \widetilde{Succ}(x) := Succ(x) \cup \{y\}, \widetilde{Succ}(x) \cup \{y\}, \text{ and}$$
$$Succ(x), \widetilde{Succ}(x) := Succ(x) \setminus \{y\}, \widetilde{Succ}(x) \setminus \{y\}.$$

It is obvious that these actions preserve the assertions for the mutator proof outline, and so we conclude the same for the second loop of the collector. Remember that simultaneously with these assignments, $Succ(y)$ and $\widetilde{Succ}(y)$ should be changed (see also page 569).

10.5.3 A Concrete Implementation of the Garbage Collector

We discuss a more concrete implementation of the garbage collector, that is, a program where we use simple integer variables and arrays, rather than abstract sets. The work done for the abstract algorithm is not lost, however; we will see that the abstract set variables can be used to explain and verify the more concrete algorithm. We consider the algorithm originally proposed by Dijkstra et al. [DLM$^+$78]. The algorithm can be seen as an implementation of the abstract algorithm, where suitable representations have been chosen for the graph and for variables like the sets P and U. For the [DLM$^+$78] algorithm, the graph nodes and the successor function are represented by means of arrays with index set $[1..n]$, where n is some constant, denoting the number of nodes. The successor set $Succ(x)$ of some node x is limited to at most two successors, called $Left(x)$ and $Right(x)$. $Left(x)$ or $Right(x)$ can be $n+1$, which is used to indicate that there is no left or right successor. We use Nil to denote $n+1$. So, we have arrays $Left : [1..n] \to [1..n] \cup \{Nil\}$ and $Right : [1..n] \to [1..n] \cup \{Nil\}$. The set $Roots$ is restricted here to the set $\{Root, Free\}$, where $Root$ and $Free$ are node indices, i.e., two (different) constants in the range $[1..n]$. A characteristic of the [DLM$^+$78] algorithm is that the sets P and U are encoded in such a way that very little storage is needed. This is an important aspect, since these sets have to be stored in the same memory as is used for the graph nodes. Consider the situation where almost all nodes are in the set *FreeNodes*. The collector would mark these free nodes, resulting in a set P that contains almost all graph nodes. A naive implementation could result in a set P that occupies *more* memory than is available for storing nodes. What is used in [DLM$^+$78] is an array $Color : [1..n] \cup \{Nil\} \to \{White, Grey, Black\}$, and an integer valued variable k. Since $Color(x)$ can take on only three values, one actually needs only two bits per node to store $Color$, which is considered to be acceptable. The idea here is that the collector marks nodes by colouring them black. The distinction between processed and unprocessed nodes is made by means of the index k. Nodes in the range $[1..k-1]$ that are black belong to the set P, whereas other black nodes belong to U. The grey colour is reserved for the *mutator* action *AddEdge*. This action can insert some node y into the set U by colouring it grey. However, when this y node has been coloured black already by the collector, then it is a member of P or U, and it should therefore remain black. When the collector finds a grey node it will colour it black and, in the next step, ensure that the successors of the node become black if necessary. This indicates the division of labour between the mutator and the collector; the former must ensure only that the target of an *AddEdge* action is in U or P by means of colouring it grey, whereas further processing of these nodes is the task of the latter. The test whether the set U is empty becomes for the concrete algorithm a test that $k > n$ holds and that, moreover, no grey nodes are left. The latter test is of course more substantial than the simple "$U = \emptyset$" test from the abstract algorithm, and in fact leads to an extra loop construct. The resulting concrete version of *Collector* is as follows:

$Collector_C \stackrel{\text{def}}{=}$
do
    $Color(Nodes) := White$;
    $Color(Nil), Color(Root), Color(Free) := Black, Black, Black$;
    $k, PossibleGrey := 1, true$;

do
$$[]\ \ k \leq n \wedge Color(k) = White \rightarrow k := k+1$$
$$[]\ \ k \leq n \wedge Color(k) = Grey \rightarrow Color(k) := Black$$
$$[]\ \ k \leq n \wedge Color(k) = Black \wedge Color(Left(k)) = Black \wedge$$
$$\wedge Color(Right(k)) = Black$$
$$\rightarrow k := k+1$$
$$[]\ \ k \leq n \wedge Color(k) = Black \wedge$$
$$\wedge (Color(Left(k)) \neq Black \vee Color(Right(k)) \neq Black)$$
$$\rightarrow Color(Left(k)), Color(Right(k)), k :=$$
$$Black, Black, \min(k+1, Left(k), Right(k))$$
$$[]\ \ k > n \wedge PossibleGrey \rightarrow\ \ j := 1;$$
$$\mathbf{do}\ j \leq n \wedge Color(j) \neq Grey \rightarrow\ \ j := j+1\ \mathbf{od};$$

if
$$[]\ \ j > n \rightarrow PossibleGrey := false$$
$$[]\ \ j \leq n \rightarrow k := j$$
fi

od;
$$k := n;$$
do
$$[]\ \ k > 0 \wedge Color(k) = Black \rightarrow\ \ Color(k), k := White, k-1$$
$$[]\ \ k > 0 \wedge Color(k) = White \rightarrow\ \ FreeNodes, k := FreeNodes \cup \{k\}, k-1$$
od
od

Relating the concrete algorithm to the abstract algorithm

The variables P, U, *Succ*, and *Garb* of the abstract algorithm do not occur explicitly in this algorithm. Yet, we can introduce these abstract variables as *abbreviations* in terms of the concrete variables *Color*, *Left*, *Right*, and k, as follows:

(RI_1) $P \stackrel{\text{def}}{=} \{ i \mid 1 \leq i < k \wedge Color(i) = Black \}$,

(RI_2) $U \stackrel{\text{def}}{=} \{ i \mid k \leq i \leq n \wedge Color(i) = Black \} \cup \{ i \mid 1 \leq i \leq n \wedge Color(i) = Grey \}$,

(RI_3) $Succ(x) \stackrel{\text{def}}{=} \{ Left(x), Right(x) \} \setminus \{ Nil \}$,

(RI_4) $Garb \stackrel{\text{def}}{=} \{ i \mid 1 \leq i \leq k \wedge Color(i) = White \}$,

(RI_5) $Roots \stackrel{\text{def}}{=} \{ Root, Free \}$.

Using these abbreviations, we can give a proof outline for the concrete collector inspired by the proof outline for the abstract collector. We introduce invariants J_1, J_2, J_3 and definitions I_{1-6} and D_6 :

(I_{1-6}) $I_1 \wedge I_2 \wedge I_3 \wedge I_4 \wedge I_5 \wedge I_6$,

(J_1) $Color(Nil) = Black \wedge k > 0$,

(J_2) $\neg PossibleGrey \rightarrow k > n \wedge \forall x. 1 \leq x \leq n \rightarrow Color(x) \neq Grey$,

(J_3) $k > n \wedge ((\forall x. 1 \leq x < j \rightarrow Color(x) \neq Grey) \vee$
$\qquad\qquad (\exists y. j \leq y \leq n \wedge Color(y) = Grey))$,

(D_6) $SuccessorsBlack(k) \stackrel{\text{def}}{=} Color(Left(k)) = Black \wedge Color(Right(k)) = Black$.

We again use the invariants $I_1, \ldots, I_6$ and definitions $D_1, \ldots, D_4$ given on page 568. The concrete proof outline is as follows:

$\{true\}$
do
$\quad Reachable_0 := Reachable$;
$\quad Color(Nodes) := White$;
$\quad Color(Nil), Color(Root), Color(Free) := Black, Black, Black$;
$\quad k, PossibleGrey := 1, true$;
$\quad \{I_{1-6} \wedge J_1 \wedge J_2\}$
$\quad$**do**
$\quad [] \quad k \leq n \wedge Color(k) = White \rightarrow k := k + 1$
$\quad [] \quad k \leq n \wedge Color(k) = Grey \rightarrow Color(k) := Black$
$\quad [] \quad k \leq n \wedge Color(k) = Black \wedge SuccessorsBlack(k) \rightarrow k := k + 1$
$\quad [] \quad k \leq n \wedge Color(k) = Black \wedge \neg SuccessorsBlack(k) \rightarrow$
$\quad\quad Color(Left(k)), Color(Right(k)), k :=$
$\quad\quad Black, Black, \min(k + 1, Left(k), Right(k))$
$\quad [] \quad k > n \wedge PossibleGrey \rightarrow j := 1$;
$\quad\quad\quad \{I_{1-6} \wedge J_1 \wedge J_2 \wedge J_3 \wedge PossibleGrey \wedge j > 0\}$
$\quad\quad\quad$**do** $j \leq n \wedge Color(j) \neq Grey \rightarrow j := j + 1$ **od**;
$\quad\quad\quad \{I_{1-6} \wedge J_1 \wedge J_2 \wedge J_3 \wedge PossibleGrey \wedge j > 0\}$
$\quad\quad\quad$**if**
$\quad\quad\quad [] \quad j > n \rightarrow PossibleGrey := false$
$\quad\quad\quad [] \quad j \leq n \rightarrow k := j$
$\quad\quad\quad$**fi**
$\quad\quad\quad \{I_{1-6} \wedge J_1 \wedge J_2\}$
$\quad$**od**;
$\quad \{I_{1-6} \wedge J_1 \wedge J_2 \wedge k > n \wedge \neg PossibleGrey\}$
$\quad \{I_{1-6} \wedge U = \emptyset \wedge J_2 \wedge \neg PossibleGrey\}$
$\quad \{Reachable \subseteq P \subseteq Reachable_0 \wedge I_{1-6} \wedge J_2 \wedge \neg PossibleGrey\}\}$
$\quad k := n$;
$\quad \{Garb \cap Reachable = \emptyset \wedge Garbage_0 \subseteq Garb \wedge k \geq 0 \wedge$

$$\wedge \, Reachable \subseteq \{x | Color(x) = Black\}\}$$
$$\{k \geq 0\}$$
do
$$[] \quad k > 0 \wedge Color(k) = Black \; \rightarrow \; Color(k), k := White, k - 1$$
$$[] \quad k > 0 \wedge Color(k) = White \; \rightarrow \; FreeNodes, k := FreeNodes \cup \{k\}, k - 1$$
od
$$\{Garb = \emptyset\}$$
od

The assignment to *FreeNodes* should also modify $Succ(y)$; there should be no node in $Succ(y)$ which is also reachable from *Root* (see also page 569).

Checking the verification conditions for the concrete algorithm

The next step is to check the validity of the local verification conditions, as well as the interference freedom tests. For the latter, we must adapt the model of the mutator, since this component, too, must operate in terms of the concrete variables *Left*, *Right*, and *Color*. We replace the abstract *AddEdge* and *DeleteEdge* actions by the following six concrete ones. We list here only the three actions that assign to *Left*; the other three, that assign to *Right* rather than *Left*, are treated analogously.

- $\{x, y \in Reachable\} \; Color(y) = White \; \rightarrow \; Left(x), Color(y) := y, Grey \; \{true\}$
- $\{x, y \in Reachable\} \; Color(y) \neq White \; \rightarrow \; Left(x) := y \; \{true\}$
- $\{x, y \in Reachable\} \; Left(x) := Nil \; \{true\}$

It will by now be clear that the actual verification in terms of the concrete variables will be quite laborious. This is caused by the fact that there are more actions on the concrete level than on the abstract level, and also because the definitions of abstract variables by means of invariants like $I_1, \ldots, I_6$ must be first expanded before we can actually verify that such invariants are preserved by concrete actions. Invariants J_1, J_2, and J_3 are not based on abbreviations, which makes the proof of them simpler. The verification of the *local* correctness for these invariants is not difficult, and is left as an exercise.

The *interference freedom test* for J_1 is obvious, since the mutator actions do not modify $Color(Nil)$ or k. The interference freedom test for J_2 can, similarly to the abstract assertion $U = \emptyset$, show under the assumption that I_{1-6} are valid. Hence, we have to show that $I_{1-6} \wedge J_2$ is preserved under the mutator operations. The only critical operation is the first *AddEdge*, the other operations do not modify *Color*, k, or *PossibleGrey*. Formally, we have to show:

$$\models (I_{1-6} \land J_2 \land x, y \in Reachable \land Color(y) = White)$$
$$\rightarrow J_2[Color \oplus \{y \mapsto Grey\}/Color].$$

(Note that *Left* does not occur freely in J_2, so there is no need to substitute y for *Left*(x) in the latter assertion.) Assume that the premise holds. In case *PossibleGrey* is true, J_2 is obviously preserved by the transition. Otherwise, we have $k > n \land \forall x. 1 \leq x \leq n \rightarrow Color(x) \neq Grey$. That implies $U = \emptyset$. Thus, with I_1 and I_2 it follows that *Reachable* $\subseteq P$ and $x, y \in P$. This leads to a contradiction since then $Color(y) = Black$. Therefore, the transition is never enabled in case of $I_{1-6} \land J_2$, and the formula is valid.

The interference freedom test for J_3 is rather subtle. We focus again on the "most dangerous" mutator action specified by:

$$\models \{x, y \in Reachable \land Color(y) = White\} \, Left(x), Color(y) := y, Grey \, \{true\}.$$

Unlike the other mutator actions, this one actually turns a white node y into a grey one, and so, if $y < j$, J_3 would *not* be preserved, *unless* we can show that in the initial state of that action, some grey node g already exists, in the range $j \leq g \leq n$. What *formally* must be shown is the following:

$$\models (I_{1-6} \land J_1 \land J_2 \land J_3 \land x, y \in Reachable \land Color(y) = White) \rightarrow J_3[Color \oplus \{y \mapsto Grey\}/Color].$$

(Again, *Left* does not occur freely in J_3.) To prove this verification condition, assume that the premise of the implication holds. Since this implies J_3, we have either that $\forall z. 1 \leq z < j \rightarrow Color(z) \neq Grey$, or else that $\exists g. j \leq g \leq n \land Color(g) = Grey$ holds. In the second case, it follows immediately that $J_3[Color \oplus \{y \mapsto Grey\}/Color]$ holds. So assume the first case. It follows from I_1, I_2, $y \in Reachable$ and $Color(y) = White$ that in this case $U \neq \emptyset$ holds, for, otherwise, we would have had that $y \in P$, and consequently that $Color(y) \neq White$. So we infer that there exists some node $g \in U$. Since J_3 implies $k > n$, we infer that $Color(g) = Grey$. Since we assume that $\forall z. 1 \leq z < j \rightarrow Color(z) \neq Grey$ holds, we conclude that $j \leq g \leq n$, and so that $\exists g. j \leq g \leq n \land Color(g) = Grey$ holds. This implies $J_3[Color \oplus \{y \mapsto Grey\}/Color]$, as was to be shown.

Checking the local correctness and interference freedom for the remaining assertions in the proof outline is left to the reader. The more difficult part of this is to check for the various branches of the main loop that $I_1, \ldots, I_6$ are preserved.

Local correctness of the concrete algorithm

Whenever possible, we split the assertions into a number of simpler specifications similarly to the proofs for the abstract algorithm. Then, we simultaneously prove $\{I_j\}\tau\{I_j\}$ for a couple of transitions τ.

It is obvious that invariant I_3 is trivially valid by definition of P and U. Moreover, we have only to consider the marking phase of the algorithm, since the I_j assertions only appear in this part.

The exact proof that $I_{1-6} \wedge J_1 \wedge J_2$ is valid after the first four transitions is left to the reader. For this proof, certain assertions must be inserted in between the transitions. For example, after the assignment to $Reachable_0$, $I_3 \wedge I_5 \wedge I_6$ is valid. Here, I_4 is not required to hold since the mutator can first colour some nodes grey and delete edges to make them unreachable. After the assignment, these nodes are members of U, but not of $Reachable_0$. After the second assignment, I_4 is also valid and $\forall x.Color(x) \neq Black$.

Now, we have to show that once initialised, every assertion is preserved by each transition of the first loop.

For I_1, local correctness is easily established, because the root nodes are coloured black in the beginning, and black nodes are not changed to white or grey in the marking phase.

Also I_5 and I_6 are trivially fulfilled after initialisation, because they only depend on *Left* and *Right*, but these functions are not modified during this phase of the collector.

Thus, only I_2 and I_4 remain. Since *Succ* is not modified, only the changes to P and U affect the validity of I_2 and I_4. By definition of P and U this means that we have to check for modifications of *Color* and k.

- $k \leq n \wedge Color(k) = White \rightarrow k := k+1$
  Here, $I_2 \wedge I_4$ is preserved since potentially only node k could be added to P and removed from U, but this node is white and thus not in $P \cup U$. Consequently, P and U are unchanged.

- $k \leq n \wedge Color(k) = Grey \rightarrow Color(k) := Black$
  Since node k was already in U before the transition was taken, P and U are also unchanged by this transition.

- $k \leq n \wedge Color(k) = Black \wedge SuccessorsBlack(k) \rightarrow k := k+1$
  The effect of this transition is that node k is removed from U and added to P. Hence I_4 is preserved. For I_2 we have to ensure that $Succ(k) \subseteq P \cup U$ after the transition is taken. This is obviously ensured by the transition guard.

- $k \leq n \wedge Color(k) = Black \wedge \neg SuccessorsBlack(k) \rightarrow$
  $Color(Left(k)), Color(Right(k)), k :=$
  $Black, Black, \min(k+1, Left(k), Right(k))$

The modification of *Color* has the effect that the successor nodes of k are added to U (because k is set to a value less than or equal to $Left(k)$ and $Right(k)$, these nodes will not be added to P). The assignment to k can have several effects, either some nodes from P are moved to U, or node k is moved from U to P. By definition of P and U it is easily seen that a modification of k does not influence the set $P \cup U$, because this is just the set of all nodes coloured black or grey.

From the guard we can derive that node k was coloured black, thus node k was in $P \cup U$. With $I_4 \wedge I_6$ it then follows that initially $Succ(k) \subseteq Reachable_0$. Consequently, I_4 is preserved by the transition.

Let $m = \min(Left(k), Right(k))$.

- $k + 1 \leq m$. In this case, k is increased by 1. Thus, node k is added to P. For I_2 we have to ensure that $Succ(k) \subseteq P \cup U$ which is valid since the successors of k are coloured black by this transition.
- $m < k + 1$. Then, the value m is assigned to k. Let P' be the value of P before the transition, and P'' the value after taking it. Since k is not increased, we get $P'' \subseteq P'$. Moreover, $P \cup U$ does not change. Consequently, we derive $Succ(P'') \subseteq Succ(P') \subseteq P \cup U$ and I_2 is valid.

- $k > n \wedge PossibleGrey \rightarrow j := 1; \ldots$ and the inner loop. There is only one critical modification to k in the whole part, namely the transition $j \leq n \rightarrow k := j$.

Since modifications of k do not change $P \cup U$, invariant I_4 is trivially preserved.

From J_3 we know that $k > n$. Moreover, the guard ensures $j \leq n$. Hence, this transition reduces P. Then, since I_2 was valid before the transition was taken, it must also be valid afterwards.

Most of the local correctness conditions for the collecting phase are easily proven, they are left as an exercise.

10.5.4 Conclusion of the Extended Example

What have we actually accomplished in Section 10.5?

With some goodwill, i.e., some extra work done by the reader (see the list of exercises), one can argue that we proved the abstract version of the collector correct, i.e., both locally correct and that its assertions are invariant under the actions of the abstract version of the mutator.

However, the arguments given for arguing correctness of the version of the concrete concurrent garbage collection algorithm presented above are less complete, more complex, and require a lot more detail before they are fully convincing. Of course, we, its authors, have the added luxury of hindsight, since a correct argument has already been presented in [Gri77] for this concrete garbage collector.

We just gave a different presentation of Gries' argument, making use of the facts that:

(i) it can also be interpreted as establishing correctness of the abstract collector presented in this section, and

(ii) the correctness of the abstract collector can be used in the correctness proof for the concrete collector.

However, would a complete formal proof have been more convincing? In our opinion, such a proof would not have convinced everybody, because of its enormous amount of detail. It would have been more convincing, but not *totally convincing*.

Going one step further, one might produce a machine-verified proof. That would be really a lot more convincing! And, indeed, such a proof has been given by Klaus Havelund [Hav99].

But, does Havelund's proof result in a 100%-secure proof? No, because it is known that machine verifiers contain errors, and there exists the probability (which is actually not as low as one would like) that, due to such an error, a flaw in an alleged correctness proof would have been undetected.

So, even then, one cannot be 100% confident! By human standards, all one can do is increase one's confidence in the correctness of such very complex algorithms by investing ever more work in their correctness proofs. This can be done by testing, by formal proofs, by checking the correctness of such proofs electronically, even by checking the correctness of the used proof checkers, and the used machines, and so on.

But one will never establish absolute confidence. This is one of the reasons why testing such complex programs still remains necessary.

10.6 Completeness of the Owicki & Gries Method

Correctness proofs for concurrent programs are inherently more complex than proofs for sequential programs, because the interference between processes has to be expressed by interference-free proof outlines. In general, it is necessary to introduce auxiliary variables to obtain a proof using the Owicki & Gries method. This aspect has a profound influence on the completeness proof for this method. For the correctness proof of a given program, one might be able to make a "clever" choice as to which auxiliaries have to be used. A completeness proof, however, should apply to every program and must, therefore, rely on a *canonical* way of introducing auxiliary variables. One possibility is the use of a so-called *history* variable h. Informally speaking, history variables record the complete observable behaviour of the system. A second possibility, that we will use here, relies on *labels* that indicate the control points that a program passes through. Labelled statements to enable correctness proofs are frequently used in temporal-logic-related formalisms, such as described in, e.g., [MP82, Lam88, Ger89]. Informally, one attaches labels to (local) locations in a program, acting as names for these program locations.

The main technical result proved in this section is a decomposition property (formulated as Lemma 10.26) of inductive assertion networks Q for concurrent transition diagrams of the form $T [[S_1 \| S_2]]$ whose components S_i have been labelled in the sense above. This property states that, when each location in $[S_1 \| S_2]$ has been labelled, Q can be decomposed into inductive assertion networks for $T [[S_1]]$ and $T [[S_2]]$ which are interference free, provided $\models Q(l) \to \mathbf{at}(l)$, where $\mathbf{at}$ is the inductive assertion network for $T [[S_1 \| S_2]]$ corresponding to the labels of $[S_1 \| S_2]$ as defined above. In other words, we extend Lemma 9.16 to parallel composition. The completeness proof itself is then rather straightforward.

10.6.1 The Decomposition Lemmas

As in Chapter 9, this completeness proof is based upon decomposition lemmas that show how a given assertion network Q for a composed transition system P can be decomposed into assertion networks for the constituents of P. For most constructs the results from Chapter 9 carry over. But for parallel composition this decomposition lemma is quite subtle, and depends on the use of auxiliary variables. We first give a preview for this result by means of an example of such a decomposition.

Example 10.23 (Decomposition of assertion networks) As an illustration of the labelling technique, consider the two programs $S_1 \overset{\text{def}}{=} y := y + 1$ and $S_2 \overset{\text{def}}{=} y := y + 1$ from Section 3.5. The transition diagram for $T [[S_1 \| S_2]]$ is sketched in Figures 3.9 and 3.10. In order to prove the specification $\langle y = 0, y = 2 \rangle$ one can construct a global inductive assertion network Q for $T [[S_1 \| S_2]]$ as follows:

$$Q(\langle s_1, s_2 \rangle) \overset{\text{def}}{=} y = 0$$
$$Q(\langle s_1, t_2 \rangle) \equiv Q(\langle t_1, s_2 \rangle) \overset{\text{def}}{=} y = 1$$
$$Q(\langle t_1, t_2 \rangle) \overset{\text{def}}{=} y = 2.$$

But as explained in Example 3.12 it is impossible to decompose this Q into inductive assertion networks for $T[[S_i]]$, $i = 1, 2$, which are interference free. Next reconsider Figure 3.13, where another transition diagram is given for $[S_1 \parallel S_2]$, augmented with the auxiliary variables z_1 and z_2 which act as program counters. The assertion network Q, defined above, is still inductive w.r.t. this augmented transition system and constitutes a proof for the specification $\langle y = 0, y = 2 \rangle$. We show how to obtain from Q inductive assertion networks Q_i for $T[[S_i]]$, $i = 1, 2$, which are interference free, and moreover have the property that $(Q_1 \parallel Q_2)(\langle l_1, l_2 \rangle) \to Q(\langle l_1, l_2 \rangle)$. Abbreviating $z_1 = 0$ by $\mathbf{at}(s_1)$, $z_1 = 1$ by $\mathbf{at}(t_1)$, $z_2 = 0$ by $\mathbf{at}(s_2)$ and $z_2 = 1$ by $\mathbf{at}(t_2)$, we define a so-called *global invariant* GI for $T[[[S_1 \parallel S_2]]]$ by:

$$GI \overset{\text{def}}{=} ((\mathbf{at}(s_1) \wedge \mathbf{at}(s_2)) \to Q(\langle s_1, s_2 \rangle)) \wedge$$
$$((\mathbf{at}(t_1) \wedge \mathbf{at}(s_2)) \to Q(\langle t_1, s_2 \rangle)) \wedge$$
$$((\mathbf{at}(s_1) \wedge \mathbf{at}(t_2)) \to Q(\langle s_1, t_2 \rangle)) \wedge$$
$$((\mathbf{at}(t_1) \wedge \mathbf{at}(t_2)) \to Q(\langle t_1, t_2 \rangle)).$$

The name "global invariant" stems from the fact that we can define an inductive assertion network GQ for $T[[[S_1 \parallel S_2]]]$ as follows:

$$GQ(\langle s_1, s_2 \rangle) \equiv GQ(\langle s_1, t_1 \rangle) \equiv GQ(\langle t_1, s_1 \rangle) \equiv GQ(\langle t_1, t_2 \rangle) \overset{\text{def}}{=} GI,$$

i.e., we attach the *same* assertion to every location! Global invariants were introduced by Ed Ashcroft in [Ash75], and constitute, in the opinion of Leslie Lamport, the first practical method for reasoning about concurrent algorithms. Now define Q_i by

$$Q_i(s_i) \overset{\text{def}}{=} \mathbf{at}(s_i) \wedge GI \text{ and } Q_i(t_i) \overset{\text{def}}{=} \mathbf{at}(t_i) \wedge GI.$$

So in particular

$$Q_1(s_1) = (z_1 = 0) \wedge (z_2 = 0 \to y = 0) \wedge (z_2 = 1 \to y = 1)$$
$$Q_1(t_1) = (z_1 = 1) \wedge (z_2 = 0 \to y = 1) \wedge (z_2 = 1 \to y = 2),$$

and similarly for Q_2. Then, as explained after Figure 3.13, the Q_i are inductive and interference free. Therefore, by the soundness of the Owicki & Gries method $Q_1 \parallel Q_2$ is also inductive. Moreover, observe that

$$(Q_1 \parallel Q_2)(\langle l_1, l_2 \rangle) = \mathbf{at}(l_1) \wedge \mathbf{at}(l_2) \wedge Q(\langle l_1, l_2 \rangle).$$

From this it follows that $\models (Q_1 \parallel Q_2)(\langle l_1, l_2 \rangle) \to Q(\langle l_1, l_2 \rangle)$.

Notice that we have not yet reached the goal of proving the specification $\langle y = 0, y = 2 \rangle$. Rather, we have shown correctness of the specification $\langle y = 0 \wedge \mathbf{at}(s_1) \wedge \mathbf{at}(s_2), y = 2 \wedge \mathbf{at}(t_1) \wedge \mathbf{at}(t_2) \rangle$. By similar techniques as applied in

Example 10.15, one can transform this proof into one for the desired specification $\langle y = 0, y = 2 \rangle$. □

First, we recapitulate the structural properties of inductive assertion networks for the sequential language constructs. The proof is identical to that of Lemma 9.16.

Lemma 10.24 (Structural properties of assertion networks (1))

a) Q is an assertion network for $P_1 ; P_2$ iff there exist compatible assertion networks Q_1 and Q_2 for P_1 and P_2 s.t. $Q = Q_1 ; Q_2$. Moreover, Q is inductive iff Q_1 and Q_2 are inductive.

b) Q is an assertion network for **if** $\big[\big]_{i=1}^{n} P_i$ **fi** iff there exist compatible assertion networks Q_i for P_i, $i = 1, \dots, n$, such that $Q = $ **if** $\big[\big]_{i=1}^{n} Q_i$ **fi**. Moreover, Q is inductive iff $Q_1, \dots, Q_n$ are inductive.

c) Q is an assertion network for **do** $P_B \, [] \, P_E$; **exit od** iff there exist compatible assertion networks Q_B for P_B and Q_E for P_E, such that

$$Q = \textbf{do } Q_B \, [] \, Q_E ; \textbf{exit od}.$$

Moreover, Q is inductive iff Q_B and Q_E are inductive. □

As shown in the introduction to this section – in fact, already after Figure 3.10 – it is not possible to extend the above structural properties in this general form to parallel composition. But for *labelled* transition systems, the situation is different.

Example 10.25 (Labelling) Consider again the programs $S_1 \stackrel{\text{def}}{=} y := y + 1$; $[y := y + 1 \, \| \, y := y + 1]$ and $S_2 \stackrel{\text{def}}{=} y := y + 1$. A representative of the transition system $T \, [\![[S_1 \, \| \, S_2]]\!]$ is given in Figure 10.2. One can easily construct a *global* inductive assertion network to prove the specification $\langle y = 0, y = 4 \rangle$. One would like to turn this into a proof according to the Owicki & Gries method. To this end, one must introduce auxiliary variables, for instance in the form of *labels*, as introduced in Sections 3.5 and 10.4.3. Again one could construct a *global* inductive assertion network Q to prove the specification $\langle y = 0 \wedge m_1 = 1 \wedge m_2 = 0 \wedge m_3 = 0 \wedge m_4 = 1, \ y = 4 \rangle$. But this time we construct interference free inductive assertion networks Q_1 and Q_2 for $T \, [\![S_1^\dagger]\!]$ and $T \, [\![S_2^\dagger]\!]$, respectively, such that $\models Q_1(l_1) \wedge Q_2(l_2) \to Q(l_1, l_2)$. In the sequel we show that these networks Q_1 and Q_2 can be derived in a canonical way from the global network Q. This construction is a vital step in the completeness proof below. □

Lemma 10.26 (Structural properties of assertion networks (2)) Let P be a transition diagram representing $T[\![S]\!]$ for some labelled SVL^+ statement S. Moreover, assume that $S = [S_1 \parallel S_2]$, and assume that $P = P_1 \parallel P_2$, where P_1 and P_2 represent $T[\![S_1]\!]$ and $T[\![S_2]\!]$. Let "**at**" be the corresponding assertion network for P derived from the labelling, as defined in Section 10.4.3. Assume that Q_{par} is some inductive assertion network for P. Then there exist inductive assertion networks Q_1 and Q_2 for P_1 and P_2 such that $\models Q_1 \parallel Q_2 \leftrightarrow Q_{par} \wedge$ **at**. Moreover, Q_1 and Q_2 are interference free with respect to P_2 and P_1, respectively.

Proof Recall that the set of locations L for $P_1 \parallel P_2$ is given by a Cartesian product of the form $L_1 \times L_2$, where L_1 and L_2 represent the sets of locations of P_1 and P_2. From the definition of **at** it follows that for locations $\langle l_1, l_2 \rangle \in L$, we have that

$$\mathbf{at}(\langle l_1, l_2 \rangle) = \mathbf{at}(l_1) \wedge \mathbf{at}(l_2).$$

We use the **at** assertion network to define a global invariant $\mathcal{G}I$ for $P_1 \parallel P_2$, as follows:

$$\mathcal{G}I \stackrel{\mathrm{def}}{=} \bigwedge_{\langle l_1, l_2 \rangle \in L} (\mathbf{at}(\langle l_1, l_2 \rangle) \to Q_{par}(\langle l_1, l_2 \rangle)).$$

Intuitively, $\mathcal{G}I$ is an invariant which holds irrespective of any particular location in P. This invariant allows us to decompose the assertion network Q_{par} for P into networks Q_1 for P_1 and Q_2 for P_2:

$$Q_1(l_1) \stackrel{\mathrm{def}}{=} \mathbf{at}(l_1) \wedge \mathcal{G}I, \text{ for } l_1 \in L_1, \quad \text{and} \quad Q_2(l_2) \stackrel{\mathrm{def}}{=} \mathbf{at}(l_2) \wedge \mathcal{G}I, \text{ for } l_2 \in L_2.$$

Since $\mathbf{at}(\langle l_1, l_2 \rangle) = \mathbf{at}(l_1) \wedge \mathbf{at}(l_2)$ one can simplify Q_1 (and analogously Q_2) to:

$$Q_1(l_1) = \mathbf{at}(l_1) \wedge \bigwedge_{l_2 \in L_2} (\mathbf{at}(l_2) \to Q_{par}(\langle l_1, l_2 \rangle)).$$

By definition of the parallel composition of assertion networks,

$$(Q_1 \parallel Q_2)(\langle l_1, l_2 \rangle) = Q_1(l_1) \wedge Q_2(l_2).$$

When $P_1 \parallel P_2$ is being executed, at every moment control resides at precisely one location in P_1 and one location in P_2. That is, at every moment $\mathbf{at}(l_1)$ is true for only one label $l_1 \in L_1$, and similarly for $\mathbf{at}(l_2)$ with $l_2 \in L_2$. Therefore,

$$\models Q_1(l_1) \wedge Q_2(l_2) \leftrightarrow \mathbf{at}(l_1) \wedge \mathbf{at}(l_2) \wedge Q_{par}(\langle l_1, l_2 \rangle) \leftrightarrow \mathbf{at}(\langle l_1, l_2 \rangle) \wedge$$
$$\wedge Q_{par}(\langle l_1, l_2 \rangle).$$

We claim that Q_1 and Q_2 are inductive and interference free. We first check that Q_1 is inductive for P_1. (By symmetry, it then follows that Q_2 is inductive for P_2.) Consider some transition $b \to \bar{x} := \bar{e}$ in P_1 from some L_1- location l_1 to l_1'. We must check validity of the following verification condition:

$$(Q_1(l_1) \wedge b) \to Q_1(l_1')[\bar{e}/\bar{x}].$$

By expanding the definitions of Q_1 and Q_2 this is equivalent to showing:

$$\models (\mathbf{at}(l_1) \wedge \bigwedge_{l_2 \in L_2} (\mathbf{at}(l_2) \to Q_{par}(\langle l_1, l_2 \rangle)) \wedge b) \to$$
$$(\mathbf{at}(l_1') \wedge \bigwedge_{l_2 \in L_2} (\mathbf{at}(l_2) \to Q_{par}(\langle l_1', l_2 \rangle))))[\bar{e}/\bar{x}]. \tag{+}$$

As we have seen above, the assertions $\mathbf{at}(l_1)$ and $\mathbf{at}(l_1')$ have in general the form of conjuncts involving the values of one or more counters. The transition $b \to \bar{x} := \bar{e}$ includes assignments to some of these counters, with the effect that $\mathbf{at}(l_1) \to (\mathbf{at}(l_1')[\bar{e}/\bar{x}])$ is a valid formula. (This amounts to the fact that the $\mathbf{at}$ assertion network itself is *inductive*.) This takes care of the $\mathbf{at}(l_1')[\bar{e}/\bar{x}]$ part on the right hand side of $(+)$. The same analysis also shows that the substitution $[\bar{e}/\bar{x}]$ has no effect on $\mathbf{at}(l_2)$, for l_2 is a location for P_2, and P_2 has counters that are distinct from all P_1 counters. It follows that the proof of $(+)$ reduces to proving:

$$\models (\bigwedge_{l_2 \in L_2} (\mathbf{at}(l_2) \to Q_{par}(\langle l_1, l_2 \rangle)) \wedge b) \to$$
$$\bigwedge_{l_2 \in L_2} (\mathbf{at}(l_2) \to (Q_{par}(\langle l_1', l_2 \rangle)))[\bar{e}/\bar{x}]. \tag{++}$$

Now, from the assumption that Q_{par} is an *inductive* assertion network for P, we know that for all locations $l_2 \in L_2$,

$$\models (Q_{par}(\langle l_1, l_2 \rangle) \wedge b) \to Q_{par}(\langle l_1', l_2 \rangle)[\bar{e}/\bar{x}].$$

From this, the truth of $(++)$ follows immediately.

Next we have to prove the validity of the interference freedom tests. Consider an assertion $Q_1(l_1)$ for some P_1 location l_1, and a transition $b \to \bar{x} := \bar{e}$ made by P_2 from some location l_2 to l_2'. We must show that $Q_1(l_1)$ is preserved under this transition, i.e., validity of the following interference freedom test:

$$(Q_1(l_1) \wedge Q_2(l_2) \wedge b) \to Q_1(l_1)[\bar{e}/\bar{x}]. \tag{+++}$$

Again we use the assumption that Q_{par} is inductive, so we know that the following holds:

$$\models (Q_{par}(\langle l_1, l_2 \rangle) \wedge b) \to Q_{par}(\langle l_1, l_2' \rangle)[\bar{e}/\bar{x}].$$

By an analysis similar to that above, one can show that, in this case, $\mathbf{at}(l_1)$ is not affected by the substitution $[\bar{e}/\bar{x}]$, and that $\mathbf{at}(l_2) \rightarrow (\mathbf{at}(l_2')[\bar{e}/\bar{x}])$ is valid. Combining this with the above, we see that the following is valid:

$$\mathbf{at}(l_1) \wedge \mathbf{at}(l_2) \wedge Q_{par}(\langle l_1, l_2 \rangle) \wedge b \rightarrow (\mathbf{at}(l_1) \wedge \mathbf{at}(l_2') \wedge Q_{par}(\langle l_1, l_2' \rangle))[\bar{e}/\bar{x}].$$

It follows from the definitions of Q_1 and Q_2 listed above that this implies:

$$\models (Q_1(l_1) \wedge Q_2(l_2) \wedge b) \rightarrow (Q_1(l_1) \wedge Q_2(l_2'))[\bar{e}/\bar{x}].$$

It is clear that this implies validity of formula $(+++)$, as had to be shown.

$\square$

Example 10.27 (Examples 10.21 and 10.22 continued) Consider the labelled program $S^\dagger \stackrel{\text{def}}{=} [S_1^\dagger \parallel S_2^\dagger]$ of Example 10.21. The transition system $T[\![S^\dagger]\!]$ is represented by the transition diagram in Figure 10.3. Define the inductive assertion network for $T[\![S^\dagger]\!]$ by

$$\begin{aligned}
Q(s) &= Q(\langle s_1, s_2 \rangle) \stackrel{\text{def}}{=} y = 0 \\
Q(\langle s_1, t_2 \rangle) &= Q(\langle u_1, s_2 \rangle) = Q(\langle v_1, s_2 \rangle) \stackrel{\text{def}}{=} y = 1 \\
Q(\langle u_1, t_2 \rangle) &= Q(\langle v_1, t_2 \rangle) = Q(\langle w_1, s_2 \rangle) = Q(\langle x_1, s_2 \rangle) \stackrel{\text{def}}{=} y = 2 \\
Q(\langle t_1, s_2 \rangle) &= Q(\langle x_1, t_2 \rangle) = Q(\langle w_1, t_2 \rangle) \stackrel{\text{def}}{=} y = 3 \\
Q(t) &= Q(\langle t_1, t_2 \rangle) \stackrel{\text{def}}{=} y = 4,
\end{aligned}$$

then indeed Q is inductive. In analogy with the observation in Section 3.5.1, there do not exist inductive assertion networks Q_1 and Q_2 for $T[\![S_1^\dagger]\!]$ and $T[\![S_2^\dagger]\!]$ which are interference free such that $Q = Q_1 \wedge Q_2$. Therefore one again takes recourse to introducing counters (auxiliary variables) in a canonical way. Applying the techniques described above, a global invariant GI for the transition system $T[\![S^\dagger]\!]$ is given by the following assertion:

$$\begin{aligned}
GI \stackrel{\text{def}}{=} &((m_1 = 1 \wedge m_2 = 0 \wedge m_3 = 0 \wedge m_4 = 1) \rightarrow y = 0) \wedge \\
&((m_1 = 2 \wedge m_2 = 0 \wedge m_3 = 0 \wedge m_4 = 1) \rightarrow y = 1) \wedge \\
&((m_1 = 1 \wedge m_2 = 0 \wedge m_3 = 0 \wedge m_4 = 2) \rightarrow y = 1) \wedge \\
&((m_1 = 0 \wedge m_2 = 1 \wedge m_3 = 1 \wedge m_4 = 1) \rightarrow y = 1) \wedge \\
&((m_1 = 2 \wedge m_2 = 0 \wedge m_3 = 0 \wedge m_4 = 2) \rightarrow y = 2) \wedge \\
&((m_1 = 0 \wedge m_2 = 1 \wedge m_3 = 1 \wedge m_4 = 2) \rightarrow y = 2) \wedge \\
&((m_1 = 0 \wedge m_2 = 2 \wedge m_3 = 1 \wedge m_4 = 1) \rightarrow y = 2) \wedge \\
&((m_1 = 0 \wedge m_2 = 1 \wedge m_3 = 2 \wedge m_4 = 1) \rightarrow y = 2) \wedge \\
&((m_1 = 0 \wedge m_2 = 2 \wedge m_3 = 1 \wedge m_4 = 2) \rightarrow y = 3) \wedge \\
&((m_1 = 0 \wedge m_2 = 1 \wedge m_3 = 2 \wedge m_4 = 2) \rightarrow y = 3) \wedge
\end{aligned}$$

$$((m_1 = 0 \land m_2 = 2 \land m_3 = 2 \land m_4 = 1) \to y = 3) \land$$
$$((m_1 = 0 \land m_2 = 2 \land m_3 = 2 \land m_4 = 2) \to y = 4) \, .$$

From $\mathcal{G}I$ we construct the corresponding inductive and interference free assertion network Q_1 for $T[\![S_1^\dagger]\!]$:

$$Q_1(s_1) \overset{\text{def}}{=} (m_1 = 1 \land m_2 = 0 \land m_3 = 0 \land \mathcal{G}I)$$
$$= m_1 = 1 \land m_2 = 0 \land m_3 = 0 \land (m_4 = 1 \to y = 0) \land (m_4 = 2 \to y = 1)$$
$$Q_1(u_1) \overset{\text{def}}{=} (m_1 = 2 \land m_2 = 0 \land m_3 = 0 \land \mathcal{G}I)$$
$$= m_1 = 2 \land m_2 = 0 \land m_3 = 0 \land (m_4 = 1 \to y = 1) \land (m_4 = 2 \to y = 2)$$
$$Q_1(v_1) \overset{\text{def}}{=} (m_1 = 0 \land m_2 = 1 \land m_3 = 1 \land \mathcal{G}I)$$
$$= m_1 = 0 \land m_2 = 1 \land m_3 = 1 \land (m_4 = 1 \to y = 1) \land (m_4 = 2 \to y = 2)$$
$$Q_1(w_1) \overset{\text{def}}{=} (m_1 = 0 \land m_2 = 2 \land m_3 = 1 \land \mathcal{G}I)$$
$$= m_1 = 0 \land m_2 = 2 \land m_3 = 1 \land (m_4 = 1 \to y = 2) \land (m_4 = 2 \to y = 3)$$
$$Q_1(x_1) \overset{\text{def}}{=} (m_1 = 0 \land m_2 = 1 \land m_3 = 2 \land \mathcal{G}I)$$
$$= m_1 = 0 \land m_2 = 1 \land m_3 = 2 \land (m_4 = 1 \to y = 2) \land (m_4 = 2 \to y = 3)$$
$$Q_1(t_1) \overset{\text{def}}{=} (m_1 = 0 \land m_2 = 2 \land m_3 = 2 \land \mathcal{G}I)$$
$$= m_1 = 0 \land m_2 = 2 \land m_3 = 2 \land (m_4 = 1 \to y = 3) \land (m_4 = 2 \to y = 4).$$

The assertion network Q_2 can be derived in a similar way. Then Q_1 and Q_2 indeed are interference free inductive assertion networks for $T[\![S_1^\dagger]\!]$ and $T[\![S_2^\dagger]\!]$, respectively, and moreover $\models Q_1(l_1) \land Q_2(l_2) \leftrightarrow Q(l_1, l_2) \land \mathbf{at}(l_1) \land \mathbf{at}(l_2)$. $\square$

10.6.2 The Completeness Proof

Assertion networks Q for SVL^+ statements S that are enriched by auxiliary variables in the form of labels, as above, have the nice property that they can be decomposed according to the syntactical structure of S. This follows from the decomposition lemmas from the previous section. As a result, we can transform the (global) assertion network Q into a *proof outline* for S. This is the content of the following lemma:

Lemma 10.28 (Translation from assertion networks to proof outlines) Let S be a labelled SVL^+ program and let $T[\![S]\!]$ be represented by $P \equiv (L, T, s, t)$. Let Q be an inductive assertion network for P with the property that, for $l \in L$, $Q(l) \leftrightarrow (Q(l) \land \mathbf{at}(l))$. Then there exists a proof outline for S of the form $\{Q(s)\} A(S) \{Q(t)\}$.

Proof The proof is by induction on the structure of S. $\square$

Case: sequential language constructs

In essence, this case follows from the results of Chapter 9. We consider sequential composition as an example. So assume that S is of the form $S_1 \, ; S_2$. Let $P = P_1 \, ; P_2$, where P_1 and P_2 represent $T \, [\![S_1]\!]$ and $T \, [\![S_2]\!]$, r is the common location for P_1 and P_2, and L_1 and L_2 are the label sets of, respectively, P_1 and P_2. By Lemma 9.16 from Chapter 9, there are inductive assertion networks Q_1 and Q_2 for P_1 and P_2 such that $Q = Q_1 \, ; Q_2$. Now assumption $\models Q(l) \leftrightarrow (Q(l) \wedge \mathbf{at}(l))$, $l \in L$, implies that for Q_1 and Q_2 one has the similar assumption $\models Q_i(l) \leftrightarrow (Q_i(l) \wedge \mathbf{at}(l))$, $l \in L_i$ and $i = 1, 2$. Consequently, by induction we may assume that there are proof outlines of the form $\{Q_1(s)\}A(S_1)\{Q_1(r)\}$ and $\{Q_2(r)\}A(S_2)\{Q_2(t)\}$. Moreover, from $Q = Q_1 \, ; Q_2$ it follows that $Q_1(s) = Q(s), Q_1(r) = Q_2(r)$, and $Q_2(t) = Q(t)$. So, these two proof outlines are compatible, and by composing them we obtain a proof outline of the form $\{Q(s)\}A(S)\{Q(t)\}$, as desired.

Case: parallel composition

Assume that S is a labelled SVL$^+$ program of the form $[S_1 \parallel S_2]$, and that P_1 and P_2 are transition systems representing $T \, [\![S_1]\!]$ and $T \, [\![S_2]\!]$. Assume also that $s = \langle s_1, s_2 \rangle$ and $t = \langle t_1, t_2 \rangle$, where s_1, s_2, t_1, and t_2 are the entry and exit locations for P_1 and P_2. Further assume that Q is an inductive assertion network for $[P_1 \parallel P_2]$ satisfying $\models Q(l) \leftrightarrow (Q(l) \wedge \mathbf{at}(l))$, for $l \in L_1 \times L_2$, with L_i the set of labels of P_i. By Lemma 10.26 there are interference free assertion networks Q_1 and Q_2 for P_1 and P_2 such that $\models Q_1 \parallel Q_2 \leftrightarrow Q \wedge \mathbf{at}$.

Again, this implies that using assumption $\models Q(l) \leftrightarrow (Q(l) \wedge \mathbf{at}(l))$, for $l \in L_1 \times L_2$, one obtains after some manipulation that the following holds for Q_1 and Q_2:

$$\models Q_i(l_i) \leftrightarrow (Q(l_i) \wedge \mathbf{at}(l_i)), \text{ for } l_i \in L_i \text{ and } i = 1, 2.$$

Consequently, by induction one may assume that these assertion networks can be translated into corresponding proof outlines for S_1 and S_2. From the interference freedom of Q_1 and Q_2 it follows that these proof outlines are interference free too. The two proof outlines can be combined into the following one for S:

$$\{Q(s)\}[\{Q_1(s_1)\}A(S_1)\{Q_1(t_1)\} \parallel \{Q_2(s_2)\}A(S_2)\{Q_2(t_2)\}]\{Q(t)\},$$

as had to be shown. $\square$

Finally, we arrive at the main theorem of this section: the soundness and completeness of the Owicki & Gries method. The soundness part has been shown already in Section 10.4. What remains to prove is its *relative* completeness.

Theorem 10.29 (Completeness of the Owicki & Gries method)
Let $\langle S \rangle$ be a closed SVL$^+$ program. If $\models \{p\}\langle S \rangle\{q\}$ then $\vdash \{p\}\langle S \rangle\{q\}$.

Proof Assume that

$$\models \{p\}\langle S \rangle\{q\}. \tag{10.4}$$

Let $S^\dagger$ be a labelled version of S and let $P = (L, T, s, t)$ represent $T[\![S^\dagger]\!]$. Let $p^\dagger$ denote $p \wedge \textbf{at}(s)$, and similarly, let $q^\dagger$ denote $q \wedge \textbf{at}(t)$. From (10.4) and the definition of **at**, it follows that

$$\models \{p^\dagger\}\langle S^\dagger \rangle\{q^\dagger\},$$

and therefore:

$$\models \{p^\dagger\}\, P\, \{q^\dagger\}. \tag{10.5}$$

From completeness Theorem 2.15 (or rather Theorem 5.19) for the inductive assertion method one can infer that

$$\vdash \{p^\dagger\}\, P\, \{q^\dagger\}, \tag{10.6}$$

that is, there exists some inductive assertion network Q for P, such that $\models p^\dagger \to Q(s)$ and $\models Q(t) \to q^\dagger$. It is clear that (10.6) also holds for assertion network Q', where Q' is defined by $Q'(l) \equiv Q(l) \wedge \textbf{at}(l)$, for $l \in L$. From the above Lemma 10.28, it follows that there is a proof outline for $S^\dagger$ of the form:

$$\{Q'(s)\}A(S^\dagger)\{Q'(t)\}.$$

Since $S^\dagger$ is labelled, we have some counter m for $S^\dagger$ itself, and $\textbf{at}(s)$ and $\textbf{at}(t)$ are assertions of the form "$m = 1$" and "$m = r$", for some natural number r. We can therefore extend the proof outline above into the following one, where we use the fact that $\models Q'(t) \to q$, and $\models p \to (p \wedge \textbf{at}(s))[1/m]$ hold:

$$\{p\}m := 1\,;\{Q'(s)\}\, A(S^\dagger)\,;\{Q'(t)\}\textbf{skip}\ \{q\}.$$

Next, we apply the auxiliary variables rule, and obtain the desired result:

$$\vdash \{p\}\,\langle S \rangle\,\{q\}.$$

In this last step, we have dropped the assignments to the counters, and also all **skip** statements that were added to construct a proof outline for $S^\dagger$. $\qquad\square$

Exercises

10.1   Let S_1 and S_2 be the following statements $S_1 \equiv x := x + 1$ and $S_2 \equiv z := x; z := z + 1; x := z$.

Give a parallel context S for S_1 and S_2 such that

$$O[\![S \parallel S_1]\!] \neq O[\![S \parallel S_2]\!].$$

10.2   Prove that

$$\vdash \{true\} \langle x := 0 \parallel x := x + 2 \rangle \{x = 0 \vee x = 2\}$$

cannot be proved without auxiliary variables.

10.3   Let S and T be nonempty, finite sets of integers. We describe a "set-partitioning" algorithm which uses shared variables. Using $|S|$ and $|T|$ to denote the number of elements in S and T, respectively, we want a program P such that

$$\vdash \{S = S_0 \neq \emptyset \wedge T = T_0 \neq \emptyset \wedge S \cap T = \emptyset\}$$
$$\langle P \rangle$$
$$\{|S| = |S_0| \wedge |T| = |T_0| \wedge$$
$$S \cup T = S_0 \cup T_0 \wedge max(S) < min(T)\}.$$

Consider the following program $P_1 \parallel P_2$, where:

$P_1 \stackrel{\text{def}}{=}$ $mx, count_1 := max(S), count_1 + 1$;
         do $count_1 \neq count_2 \to$ **skip** **od** ;
         do $mn < mx \to$
            $S := (S - \{mx\}) \cup \{mn\}$;
            $mx, count_1 := max(S), count_1 + 1$;
            do ; $count_1 \neq count_2 \to$ **skip** **od** ;
         od

$P_2 \stackrel{\text{def}}{=}$ $mn, count_2 := min(T), count_2 + 1$;
         do $count_1 \neq count_2 \to$ **skip** **od** ;
         do $mn < mx \to$
            $T := (T - \{mn\}) \cup \{mx\}$;
            $mn, count_2 := min(T), count_2 + 1$;
            do $count_1 \neq count_2 \to$ **skip** **od** ;
         od .

Note that $count_1$ and $count_2$ are used to synchronise the programs.

(a) Show that this program does not satisfy the above specification of P, i.e., give sets S and T and describe an execution yielding a final state that does not satisfy the postcondition.

To obtain a correct program we add a synchronisation point:

$P_1 \stackrel{\text{def}}{=} \quad mx, count_1 := max(S), count_1 + 1 ;$
$\qquad \textbf{do } count_1 > count_2 \rightarrow \textbf{skip od} ;$
$\qquad \textbf{do } mn < mx \rightarrow$
$\qquad\qquad S, count_1 := (S - \{mx\}) \cup \{mn\}, count_1 + 1 ;$
$\qquad\qquad \textbf{do } count_1 > count_2 \rightarrow \textbf{skip od} ;$
$\qquad\qquad mx, count_1 := max(S), count_1 + 1 ;$
$\qquad\qquad \textbf{do } count_1 > count_2 \rightarrow \textbf{skip od} ;$
$\qquad \textbf{od}$

$P_2 \stackrel{\text{def}}{=} \quad mn, count_2 := min(T), count_2 + 1 ;$
$\qquad \textbf{do } count_1 > count_2 \rightarrow \textbf{skip od} ;$
$\qquad \textbf{do } mn < mx \rightarrow$
$\qquad\qquad T, count_2 := (T - \{mn\}) \cup \{mx\}, count_2 + 1 ;$
$\qquad\qquad \textbf{do } count_1 < count_2 \rightarrow \textbf{skip od} ;$
$\qquad\qquad mn, count_2 := max(T), count_2 + 1 ;$
$\qquad\qquad \textbf{do } count_1 < count_2 \rightarrow \textbf{skip od} ;$
$\qquad \textbf{od} .$

(b) Prove

$$\vdash \{count_1 = count_2 = 0 \wedge S = S_0 \neq \emptyset$$
$$\wedge T = T_0 \neq \emptyset \wedge S \cap T = \emptyset\}$$
$$\langle P_1 \parallel P_2 \rangle$$
$$\{|S| = |S_0| \wedge |T| = |T_0| \wedge$$
$$S \cup T = S_0 \cup T_0 \wedge max(S) < min(T)\}$$

by means of the Owicki & Gries method of this chapter.

10.4   Consider a closed program $\langle [S_1 \parallel S_2] \rangle$, with
$S_1 \stackrel{\text{def}}{=} \quad \textbf{do}$
$\qquad x > 0 \rightarrow y := 0 ; \textbf{if } \langle y = 0 \rightarrow x := x - 1 \rangle \,[\!]$
$\qquad\qquad\qquad\qquad\qquad\qquad \langle y \neq 0 \rightarrow y := 0 \rangle \textbf{ fi}$
$\quad \textbf{od},$
and
$S_2 \stackrel{\text{def}}{=} \quad \textbf{do}$
$\qquad x > 0 \rightarrow y := 1 ; \textbf{if } \langle y = 1 \rightarrow x := x - 1 \rangle \,[\!]$
$\qquad\qquad\qquad\qquad\qquad\qquad \langle y \neq 1 \rightarrow y := 1 \rangle \textbf{ fi}$
$\quad \textbf{od}.$

Describe the semantics of $[S_1 \parallel S_2]$, i.e., give a formal characterisation of $O[\![[S_1 \parallel S_2]]\!]$. Does $[S_1 \parallel S_2]$ always terminate?

10.5   Give an alternative proof of $\{x = 0\}\langle x := x + 1 \parallel x := x + 1\rangle\{x = 2\}$ by transforming the program into

$$\langle (x, z_1 := x + 1, z_1 + 1) \parallel (x, z_2 := x + 1, z_2 + 1)\rangle$$

and using as invariant $x = z_1 + z_2$.

10.6   Show by means of an example that the following rule is not sound:

$$\frac{\{p_1\}S_1\{q_1\}, \dots, \{p_n\}S_n\{q_n\}}{\{p_1 \wedge \dots \wedge p_n\}\langle S_1 \parallel \dots \parallel S_n\rangle\{q_1 \wedge \dots \wedge q_n\}} \; ,$$

where $\{p_i\}S_i\{q_i\}$ denote proof outlines.

10.7   A semaphore s is an integer variable which is only changed by the operations $P(s)$ and $V(s)$, defined by

$$P(s) \stackrel{\text{def}}{=} \langle s > 0 \rightarrow s := s - 1\rangle \text{ and } V(s) \stackrel{\text{def}}{=} \langle s := s + 1\rangle.$$

They are axiomatised by the axiom

$$\vdash \{q[s + 1/s]\}V(s)\{q\}$$

and the rule

$$\frac{p \wedge s > 0 \rightarrow q[s - 1/s]}{\{p\}P(s)\{q\}} \; .$$

Prove soundness of the rule for $P(s)$ in two ways:

(a) By computing $O[\![P(s)]\!]$ and showing that

$$\models p \wedge s > 0 \rightarrow q[s - 1/s] \text{ implies } \models \{p\}P(s)\{q\}.$$

(b) By showing that it is a derived rule in our proof system.

As a very simple example of these operations, prove

(c) $\models \{x = 0 \wedge s = 1\}\langle S_1 \parallel S_2\rangle\{x = 2\}$,
     where

$$S_1 \stackrel{\text{def}}{=} P(s) \, ; t_1 := x \, ; x := t_1 + 1 \, ; V(s) \text{ and}$$
$$S_2 \stackrel{\text{def}}{=} P(s) \, ; t_2 := x \, ; x := t_2 + 1 \, ; V(s).$$

10.8   Use the method of Owicki and Gries to prove the following formulae:

(a) $\{x = 0\}\langle t_1 := x \, ; x := t_1 + 1 \parallel t_2 := x \, ; x := t_2 + 1\rangle\{x = 1 \vee x = 2\}$

(b) $\{true\}\langle\langle x = 0 \rightarrow x := x + 1\rangle\rangle \parallel \langle x = 0 \rightarrow x := x + 1\rangle\{false\}$.

10.9   Prove that the auxiliary variables rule, Rule 10.6, is sound.

10.10 Investigate the restrictions on the auxiliary variables rule (Rule 10.6). Show by examples that this rule is not sound if A is not a set of auxiliary variables, i.e., if

    (a) A contains variables that occur in an assignment $x := e$ where $x \notin A$, or

    (b) A contains variables that occur in a boolean expression.

Furthermore, show that the rule is not sound if

    (c) A is a set of auxiliary variables, but $A \cap var(q) \neq \emptyset$.

10.11 Prove Lemma 10.11.

10.12 To find a point where a function f from integers to integers is zero, we consider the closed program $\langle S_1 \parallel S_2 \rangle$ with:

$$S_1 \equiv \quad x := 0;$$
$$\textbf{do}$$
$$\quad \neg \text{FOUND} \rightarrow x := x+1; \textbf{if } f(x) = 0 \rightarrow \text{FOUND} := \textit{true } \textbf{fi}$$
$$\textbf{od}$$

and

$$S_2 \equiv \quad y := 1;$$
$$\textbf{do}$$
$$\quad \neg \text{FOUND} \rightarrow y := y-1; \textbf{if } f(y) = 0 \rightarrow \text{FOUND} := \textit{true } \textbf{fi}$$
$$\textbf{od}$$

Prove $\vdash \{\text{FOUND} = \textit{false}\}\langle S_1 \parallel S_2 \rangle \{f(x) = 0 \lor f(y) = 0\}$.

10.13   (a) Prove that the proof outlines given in Example 10.16 are interference free.

    (b) Prove that the proof outlines given in Example 10.17 are interference free.

10.14 An *alternative* definition of $Succ^*$ is the following one:

    (a) $Succ^0(X) \stackrel{\text{def}}{=} X$,

    (b) $Succ^{i+1}(X) \stackrel{\text{def}}{=} Succ(Succ^i(X))$, for $i \geq 0$,

    (c) $Succ^*(X) \stackrel{\text{def}}{=} \bigcup_{i \geq 0} Succ^i(X)$.

Show that this is the same as the definition given by clauses (i), (ii), and (iii) on page 564. Hint: First, show that a function $Succ$ satisfying (a), (b), (c) also satisfies clauses (i), (ii), and (iii). Second, show the reverse: clauses (a), (b), and (c) follow from (i), (ii), (iii).

10.15   The initialisation of the abstract *Collector* algorithm on page 568 is annotated as follows:

$$\{true\}$$
$$P, U, Reachable_0 := \emptyset, Roots, Reachable$$
$$\{I_1 \wedge I_2 \wedge I_3 \wedge I_4 \wedge I_5 \wedge I_6\}$$

Show the local verification condition for this part of the proof outline.

10.16   The second half of the abstract collector algorithm on page 568 has been annotated thus:

$$\{I_1 \wedge I_2 \wedge I_3 \wedge I_4 \wedge I_5 \wedge I_6 \wedge U = \emptyset\}$$
$$\{Reachable \subseteq P \subseteq Reachable_0\}$$
$$Garb := Nodes \setminus P;$$
$$\{Garb \cap Reachable = \emptyset \wedge Garbage_0 \subseteq Garb\}$$
do
$$\{true\}$$
$$\quad Garb \neq \emptyset \rightarrow y := picksome(Garb);$$
$$\qquad\qquad FreeNodes, Garb := FreeNodes \cup \{y\}, Garb \setminus \{y\}$$
od
$$\{Garb = \emptyset\}.$$

Show the local correctness of this part of the proof outline.

10.17   The interference freedom test for the abstract collector in the main text has been done rather sketchily. In essence, only the preservation of I_2 and the assertion $U = \emptyset$ after the first loop have been checked. Correct this by checking the remaining verification conditions.

10.18   The interference freedom test on page 571 that shows preservation of the $U = \emptyset$ assertion, used the fact that $\models (I_1 \wedge I_2 \wedge I_3 \wedge I_4 \wedge I_5 \wedge I_6 \wedge U = \emptyset \wedge x, y \in Reachable) \rightarrow y \in Reachable \subseteq P$ holds. Show this.

10.19   Consider Example 10.27.

   (a) Derive the assertion network Q_2.
   (b) Prove that both Q_1 and Q_2 are indeed inductive.
   (c) Prove that both Q_1 and Q_2 are indeed interference free.
   (d) Construct the proof outlines for $S_1^\dagger$ and $S_2^\dagger$ corresponding to Q_1 and Q_2 respectively.
   (e) Prove, using the proof system of Section 10.4, that

   $$\models \{y = 0\}\langle[S_1 \parallel S_2]\rangle\{y = 4\}.$$

10.20   Prove that **at** is an inductive assertion network.

10.21　Indicate how to construct a proof outline for a labelled statement S, such that the corresponding assertion network coincides with the **at** assertion network for S.

10.22　Assume that we take the proof system consisting of the standard rules for proof outlines, but where the auxiliary variables rule (Rule 10.6) has been replaced by the following one:

Rule 10.12 (Closed programs)

$$\frac{\{p\}\, A(S)\, \{q\}}{\{p\}\, \langle S \rangle\, \{q\}}\,.$$

Explain why this system is *incomplete*. Next, determine which Hoare-style rules from the Owicki & Gries-proof system should be added to obtain a complete system. Show, on the basis of the completeness proof in Section 10.6, why the augmented system is complete. (Hint: only a small part of the completeness proof is concerned with auxiliary variables; you can change this part so that it uses the new rules only.)

11

A Hoare Logic for Synchronous Message Passing

11.1 Structure of this Chapter

In this chapter we formulate a Hoare logic for a simple programming language for *synchronous* message passing, called DML for *D*istributed *M*essage passing *L*anguage. Historically, DML is inspired by Occam [INM88] and its predecessor *C*ommunicating *S*equential *P*rocesses (CSP) [Hoa85a, Hoa78]. We give an informal overview of the language constructs in Section 11.2 and provide a formal semantics in Section 11.3, relying on transition systems as defined in Chapter 4. In Section 11.4 a Hoare logic for synchronous message passing is formulated. Soundness and relative completeness of this Hoare logic are proved in Section 11.5 as a consequence of this chapter's key result that Hoare-style proofs for synchronous message-passing programs are equivalent to the existence of assertion networks for their component diagrams which cooperate w.r.t. a global invariant I and for which all verification conditions for local transitions are satisfied. Crucial elements in the proof of this result are the following facts:

(i) Cooperation can immediately be integrated into proofs by introducing so-called (proofs from) *assumptions*.

(ii) Proofs from cooperating assumptions imply cooperation of their corresponding locally-inductive assertion networks, where "locally" refers to the fact that all verification conditions for local transitions are satisfied, and vice-versa, if locally-inductive assertion networks are cooperating then so are the assumptions associated with their corresponding proofs.

In Section 11.6 a compositional rule for synchronous message passing is formulated, after introducing the proof system of Levin & Gries; at the end of this chapter, one finds a list of exercises.

11.2 Syntax and Informal Meaning of DML Programs

This section contains a description of the syntax and informal meaning of the programming language DML for distributed communication using synchronous message passing along unidirectional channels. The main constructs for expressing distributed communication in this language are its message-passing primitives. They function both as communication and synchronisation statements and are either an *input statement C?x* or an *output statement C!e*. Output statement $C!e$ is used to send the value of expression e along channel C and input statement $C?x$ to receive a value via C and to assign this value to variable x, assuming synchronous communication. Here C typically denotes a channel from a set of (unidirectional) channels *CHAN*, e an arithmetic expression over the local program variables of the process in which $C!e$ occurs and x is a local program variable of the process in which $C?x$ occurs. This convention on local variables is not accidental, because, since communication and synchronisation are already taken care of by these message-passing constructs, the only remaining use of variables is that of performing local computations *inside* a (sequential) process. Consequently, program variables in DML are always local.

Synchronisation in DML is primarily expressed within guarded commands by so-called *input guards*, i.e., input statements which additionally function as a mechanism for testing whether communication along a certain channel is possible. If such is the case, then the input guard may be selected for execution and subsequently be "passed". When such a guard is nondeterministically selected for execution, this selection is made from all those guards in a guarded command which can be passed (by convention a purely boolean guard can be passed if it evaluates to *true*). Consequently, when compared with GCL the *programming nucleus of DML* contains as a new element guarded commands whose guards may also contain input statements. In addition to the possibility (already present in GCL) of a purely boolean guard in a guarded statement of the form $b \to S$, we introduce in DML the further possibility of combining a boolean guard with an input guard, where in both cases such guards are called *open* if their boolean components evaluate to *true*. If none of the guards is open, the execution of the guarded command stops, resulting in termination or abortion. Otherwise, execution waits until one of the open guards can be passed and then continues with the corresponding statement. By convention guards of the form $true; C?x$ are abbreviated to $C?x$. The resulting programming nucleus is basically an extension of the GCL language of Chapter 9 with communication statements $C?x$ and $C!e$; it is described in Table 11.1.

Thus DML contains two kinds of guarded commands: *guarded selections*

Table 11.1. *Programming nucleus.*

< Statement >	$S ::=$	$b \to \bar{x} := \bar{e} \mid C!e \mid C?x \mid S_1; S_2 \mid$
		if $\big[\!\big]_{i=1}^{l} G_i$ **fi** $\mid$ **do** $\big[\!\big]_{i=1}^{l} G_i$ **od**
< Guarded Statement >	$G ::=$	$b \to S \mid b; C?x \to S$
< Program >	$P ::=$	$S_1 \| \ldots \| S_n$

of the form **if** $\big[\!\big]_{i=1}^{l} G_i$ **fi** , and *guarded loops* of the form **do** $\big[\!\big]_{i=1}^{l} G_i$ **od**. Their difference is that, whereas execution of a guarded selection aborts when none of the (constituent) guards of its guarded statements are open, execution of a guarded loop terminates if such is the case, and otherwise continues to execute from its body a guarded statement whose guard is open. Notice that output statements do not function as guards in guarded commands. The reason for this stipulation is to restrict the concept of nondeterminism in DML to *local nondeterminism* only, since this requires only local schedulers for its implementation. This can be understood as follows.

Example 11.1 Consider the following distributed CSP-like program $P_1 \| P_2$:

$$S_1 : \quad \textbf{if} \ \ C?x \to S_3 \ \big[\big] \ D?y \to S_4 \ \textbf{fi}$$

$$S_2 : \quad \textbf{if} \ \ C!2 \to S_5 \ \big[\big] \ D!6 \to S_6 \ \textbf{fi} \ .$$

If the nondeterminism expressed by **if** $-$ **fi** is implemented by only local schedulers, i.e., one for S_1 and a second one for S_2, and these local schedulers function only on the basis of purely local information ("they just toss a coin"), then these local selections (between the guarded statements inside S_1 and S_2) result in four global possibilities being offered for execution, out of which only the two associated with the pairs $\langle C?x, C!2 \rangle$ and $\langle D?y, D!6 \rangle$ lead to successful communication, and the remaining two to deadlock. In order to prevent selection of these deadlocked combinations, the local choices have to be *coordinated*, i.e, the mechanism behind this choice should somehow "know" *both* S_1 and S_2. This is called *global nondeterminism* [FHLdR79]: nondeterministic choices are resolved at the global level by a global scheduler which in principle affects all processes of the network by its requests for information and decisions. In contrast, local nondeterminism requires only local schedulers for making nondeterministic choices, i.e., one scheduler per process. We illustrate the latter by modifying S_2 in accordance with our syntactical restrictions:

$$S_2' : \quad \textbf{if} \ \ true \to C!2; S_5 \ \big[\big] \ true \to D!6; S_6 \ \textbf{fi} \ .$$

In this case there is no global choice mechanism but only a local one needed in S_2' for determining which path to follow and, consequently, which of the pairs $\langle C?x, C!2 \rangle$, $\langle D?y, D!6 \rangle$ will in fact be executed in the overall computation. This decision is driven only by the control flow inside process S_2', thus eliminating to also involve the need for a scheduler S_1. □

As pointed out in Chapter 4 we need to introduce additional constructs in DML to *reason about* its programming nucleus. In the case of DML, and as in Chapter 10 for the passing of boolean guards, we now need to express that input guards are passed, leading to additional guards of the form of communication statement $\langle b; C?x \rightarrow \bar{z} := \bar{e} \rangle$, where assignment $\bar{z} := \bar{e}$ to the auxiliary variables $\bar{z}$ is added in order to obtain completeness of our proof method. As in Chapter 4 we also need communication statements of the form $\langle C?x \rightarrow \bar{z} := \bar{e} \rangle$ and $\langle C!e \rightarrow \bar{z} := \bar{e} \rangle$. Since we have to express that the "$\rightarrow$" addition by $\bar{z} := \bar{e}$ should be part of the same atomic step as that in which the communication is performed, we use atomic brackets '$\langle$' and '$\rangle$' for expressing that $\langle \ldots \rangle$ should be viewed as one atomic action: the resulting $\langle \ldots \rangle$ constructs are called *bracketed sections*.

The purpose of these assignments to auxiliary variables is to encode information about the communication actions that have been executed. Such communication actions will be characterised first assigning of the transmitted values to the variable named in the receiving processes and then by updating the auxiliary variables, considering especially these transmitted values.

Recall that $var(P)$ consists of the set of variables occurring in the statement or program P, and $var(q)$ of the set of free variables occurring in assertion q.

Next the syntax of DML is defined. As in Chapter 10 we need the concept of an *auxiliary variables* set of a program P, with typical element z, repeating its definition below.

Definition 11.2 (Auxiliary variables) For a program P we call a set $AVar(P)$ of program variables of P, with typical element $z \in Pvar$, a *set of auxiliary variables of P* if

- for any boolean expression b in P, $AVar(P) \cap var(b) = \emptyset$,
- each variable $z \in AVar(P)$ occurs only within assignments, and when it occurs within an assignment $x_1, \ldots, x_k := e_1, \ldots, e_k$ it does so only within components (z_i, e_i) with $z_i \in AVar(P)$. □

In this chapter we use $\bar{x}$ for a set of program variables $x_1, \ldots, x_k$ and $\bar{z}$ for a set of auxiliary (program) variables $z_1, \ldots, z_k$. Also we stipulate that in DML auxiliary variables only occur within bracketed sections, in particular:

(i) When an auxiliary variable $z_i \in \bar{z}$ occurs in some program P, it does so only within its bracketed sections, and

(ii) $\bar{z}$ is contained in the auxiliary variable set of P.

These restrictions will be reflected in our syntax of DML, given in Table 11.2 below, where $x_1, \ldots, x_k$ (and similarly $z_1, \ldots, z_k$) are all different program variables, $k, l, n \in N$, $n > 0$, $\mu \in VAL$ and $C \in CHAN$. Observe that DML does not feature nested parallelism.

Table 11.2. *Syntax of DML.*

$<$ *Expression* $>$	$e ::=$	$\mu \mid x \mid e_1 + e_2 \mid e_1 - e_2 \mid e_1 * e_2$
$<$ *Boolean Expression* $>$	$b ::=$	$e_1 = e_2 \mid e_1 < e_2 \mid \neg b \mid b_1 \vee b_2$
$<$ *Statement* $>$	$S ::=$	$b \to \bar{x} := \bar{e} \mid \langle C!e \to \bar{z} := \bar{e} \rangle \mid$
		$\langle b; C?x \to \bar{z} := \bar{e} \rangle \mid S_1 ; S_2 \mid \mathbf{if} \ []_{i=1}^{l} S_i \ \mathbf{fi} \mid$
		$\mathbf{do} \ S_B [] S_E ; \mathbf{exit} \ \mathbf{od}$
$<$ *Assignment* $>$	$\bar{x} := \bar{e} ::=$	$x_1, \ldots, x_k := e_1, \ldots, e_k$
$<$ *Program* $>$	$P ::=$	$S_1 \| \ldots \| S_n$

Syntactic restrictions

The statements S_i, S_B and S_E in $\mathbf{if} \ []_{i=1}^{l} S_i \ \mathbf{fi}$ and $\mathbf{do} \ S_B [] S_E ; \mathbf{exit} \ \mathbf{od}$ must be *guarded*, where we say that S is guarded, provided

- S is a local assignment, i.e., of the form $b \to \bar{x} := \bar{e}$,
- S is a guarded input statement, i.e., of the form $\langle b; C?x \to \bar{z} := \bar{e} \rangle$,
- S is of the form $S_1 ; S_2$ and S_1 is guarded, and
- S is of the form $\mathbf{if} \ []_{i=1}^{l} S_i \ \mathbf{fi}$, and S_i is guarded, for $i = 1, \ldots, l$.

To guarantee that channels are unidirectional and connect at most two processes, we introduce the following syntactic constraints.

- For $S_1 ; S_2$ we require that if S_1 contains $C!e$ then S_2 does not contain $C?x$, and if S_1 contains $C?x$ then S_2 does not contain $C!e$.
- For $\mathbf{if} \ []_{i=1}^{l} S_i \ \mathbf{fi}$ (and similarly for $\mathbf{do} \ S_B [] S_E ; \mathbf{exit} \ \mathbf{od}$) we require that, for all $i, j \in \{1, \ldots, l\}$ $(i, j \in \{B, E\})$, $i \neq j$, if S_i contains $C!e$ then S_j does not contain $C?x$.
- For $S_1 \| \ldots \| S_n$ we require that for all $i, j \in \{1, \ldots, n\}, i \neq j$, if S_i contains $C!e_1$ then S_j does not contain $C!e_2$, and if S_i contains $C?x_1$ then S_j does not contain $C?x_2$.

The fact that in DML parallel processes do not share program variables is formalised as follows:

- For $S_1 \| \ldots \| S_n$ we require, for all $i, j \in \{1, \ldots, n\}, i \neq j$, that

$$var(S_i) \cap var(S_j) = \emptyset.$$

Conventions

- $true \to \bar{x} := \bar{e}$ is abbreviated to $\bar{x} := \bar{e}$,
- **skip** is an abbreviation for an assignment to the empty list of variables,
- $b \to S$ is an abbreviation for $b \to$ **skip** $; S$, and, similarly, $b; C?x \to S$ is an abbreviation for $\langle b; C?x \to$ **skip** $\rangle; S$,
- $\langle true; C?x \to$ **skip** $\rangle$ and $\langle C!e \to$ **skip** $\rangle$ are abbreviated to $C?x$ and, respectively, $C!e$,
- **do** $[]_{i=1}^{l} G_i$ **od** abbreviates **do if** $[]_{i=1}^{l} G_i$ **fi** $[] \langle \neg b_G \to$ **skip** $\rangle;$ **exit od**, where $\neg b_G \stackrel{\text{def}}{=} (\neg b_1 \wedge \ldots \wedge \neg b_l)$ (here b_i is the boolean condition of the guard with which the guarded statement G_i starts),
- In case $n = 1, S_1 \| \ldots \| S_n$ reduces to a sequential statement not involving any communication,
- In case $n \geq 2, S_1 \| \ldots \| S_n$ is called a distributed program; the components S_i are also called *processes*.

With these conventions GCL and the programming nucleus of DML described in Table 11.1 become proper sub-languages of DML. We illustrate this programming nucleus by a variation upon the set-partitioning algorithm of Chapter 4.

Example 11.3 (Partitioning a set) The distributed program below partitions the union of two disjoint (nonempty) finite sets of integers S and T into two subsets S' and T' of the same size as S and T such that every element of S' is smaller than every element of T'. Its intuitive explanation is as follows: P_0 chooses the maximum *max* of S, P_1 chooses the minimum *min* of T and these values are exchanged and then essentially compared for *max* of $S > min$ of T; if this test is false the processes terminate. However, since that test would require sharing of variables between P_0 and P_1, which is disallowed in DML, localised versions of this global test are introduced. We express this algorithm, similarly to the one discussed in Example 4.2, within our language by:

$P_0:$ $max := max(S);$
       $C?mn; D!max;$
       do
         $max > mn \to S := (S \setminus \{max\}) \cup \{mn\}; max := max(S); C?mn; D!max$
       od

$P_1:$ $min := min(T);$

$C!min; D?mx;$
do
$\quad mx > min \rightarrow T := (T \setminus \{min\}) \cup \{mx\}; min := min(T); C!min; D?mx$
od

without assignments to auxiliary variables which will become inevitable in the correctness proof of this algorithm. We prove in Section 11.4.2 that this program satisfies the Hoare formula

$$\{S = S_0 \neq \emptyset \wedge T = T_0 \neq \emptyset \wedge S \cap T = \emptyset\}$$
$$P_0 \| P_1$$
$$\{max(S) < min(T) \wedge |S| = |S_0| \wedge |T| = |T_0| \wedge S \cup T = S_0 \cup T_0\},$$

where S_0 and T_0 are, as usual, logical variables.   □

11.3 Semantics of DML

Continuing our formal development, we extend the definitions of Section 9.4 with the following operations on synchronous transition systems, associate a synchronous transition system $T[\![S]\!]$ with a DML program S, and define the operational semantics $O[\![S]\!]$ by $\mathcal{M}[\![T[\![S]\!]]\!]$, with $\mathcal{M}$ expressing the semantics of synchronous transition systems, defined in Section 4.3.

Definition 11.4 (Operations on synchronous transition systems)

- For a guarded assignment statement or a communication statement S we define **step**(S) as the synchronous transition system represented by

$$(\{s,t\},\{(s,b \rightarrow \bar{x} := \bar{e},t)\},s,t),$$
$$(\{s,t\},\{(s,C!e \rightarrow \bar{z} := \bar{e},t)\},s,t), \text{ or}$$
$$(\{s,t\},\{(s,b;C?x \rightarrow \bar{z} := \bar{e},t)\},s,t).$$

- Let P_1 and P_2 be synchronous transition systems represented by (L_1,T_1,s,r) and (L_2,T_2,r,t), and assume that $L_1 \cap L_2 = \{r\}$. We define $P_1 ; P_2$ as the synchronous transition system represented by $(L_1 \cup L_2, T_1 \cup T_2, s, t)$.
- Let P_i be a synchronous transition system represented by (L_i,T_i,s,t), for $i = 1,\dots,l$, where we assume that $L_i \cap L_j = \{s,t\}$, for $1 \leq i < j \leq l$. We define **if** $[\!]_{i=1}^{l} P_i$ **fi** as the synchronous transition system represented by

$$(\bigcup_{i=1}^{l} L_i, \bigcup_{i=1}^{l} T_i, s, t).$$

- Let P_B be a transition system represented by (L_B, T_B, s, r) and let P_E be a transition system represented by (L_E, T_E, s, t). We define **do** P_B $[]$ P_E ; **exit od** as the transition system represented by $(L_B \setminus \{r\} \cup L_E, T_B' \cup T_E, s, t)$, where T_B' is like T_B except that transitions of the form $(l, b \to \bar{x} := \bar{e}, r)$ have been replaced by $(l, b \to \bar{x} := \bar{e}, s)$.

- For synchronous transition systems $P_i = (L_i, T_i, s_i, t_i)$, $i = 1, \ldots, n$ we define their synchronous product $P_1 \| \ldots \| P_n \stackrel{\text{def}}{=} (L, T, s, t)$ by

  – $L = L_1 \times \ldots \times L_n$
  – $s = \langle s_1, \ldots, s_n \rangle$
  – $t = \langle t_1, \ldots, t_n \rangle$
  – $T = \{(l, a, l') \mid l = \langle l_1, \ldots, l_i, \ldots, l_n \rangle, l' = \langle l_1', \ldots, l_i', \ldots, l_n' \rangle,$
  $\qquad s.t. \; l_j = l_j', j \neq i, (l_i, a, l_i') \in T_i, \text{ and } a \equiv b \to \bar{x} := \bar{e} \}$
  $\cup \{(l, a, l') \mid l = \langle l_1, \ldots, l_i, \ldots, l_n \rangle, l' = \langle l_1', \ldots, l_i', \ldots, l_n' \rangle,$
  $\qquad a \equiv b_j \to x, \bar{z}_i, \bar{z}_j := exp, \bar{e}_i, (\bar{e}_j[exp/x]), \text{ if } (l_i, a_i, l_i') \in T_i,$
  $\qquad (l_j, a_j, l_j') \in T_j, j \neq i, a_i \equiv C!exp \to \bar{z}_i := \bar{e}_i,$
  $\qquad a_j \equiv b_j; C?x \to \bar{z}_j := \bar{e}_j, l_k = l_k', k \neq j, k \neq i \}. \qquad \Box$

Remark: For constructs from the programming nucleus we have labels $(C!e \to id), (C?x \to id)$ and $(b; C?x \to id)$ for transitions, where id denotes the identity state transformation $\lambda\sigma.\sigma$.

Definition 11.5 (Transition systems $T[\![S]\!]$, $S \in$ DML)

- $T[\![b \to \bar{x} := \bar{e}]\!] \stackrel{\text{def}}{=} \textbf{step}(\langle b \to \bar{x} := \bar{e} \rangle)$
- $T[\![\langle C!exp \to \bar{z} := \bar{e} \rangle]\!] \stackrel{\text{def}}{=} \textbf{step}(\langle C!exp \to \bar{z} := \bar{e} \rangle)$
- $T[\![\langle b; C?x \to \bar{z} := \bar{e} \rangle]\!] \stackrel{\text{def}}{=} \textbf{step}(\langle b; C?x \to \bar{z} := \bar{e} \rangle)$
- $T[\![S_1; S_2]\!] \stackrel{\text{def}}{=} T[\![S_1]\!]; T[\![S_2]\!]$
- $T[\![\textbf{if} \; []_{i=1}^{l} S_i \; \textbf{fi}]\!] \stackrel{\text{def}}{=} \textbf{if} \; []_{i=1}^{l} T[\![S_i]\!] \; \textbf{fi}$
- $T[\![\textbf{do} \; S_B \; [] \, S_E; \textbf{exit od}]\!] \stackrel{\text{def}}{=} \textbf{do} \; T[\![S_B]\!] \; [] \, T[\![S_E]\!]; \textbf{exit od}$
- $T[\![S_1 \| \ldots \| S_n]\!] \stackrel{\text{def}}{=} T[\![S_1]\!] \| \ldots \| T[\![S_n]\!]. \qquad \Box$

As a result, for $P \equiv S_1 \| \ldots \| S_n$ a *semantic* synchronous transition diagram in the sense of Chapter 4 is obtained, to which the semantics function $\mathcal{M}$ is applied, interpreting such a diagram as a state transformer.

As in Chapter 9, the meaning $O[\![P]\!]$ of a DML program P is then defined as a binary relation, obtained by restricting the graph of $\mathcal{M}[\![T[\![P]\!]]\!]$ to $\Sigma \times \Sigma$. Consequently $O[\![P]\!]$ does not contain any information regarding possible deadlocks or nonterminating computations. But since our aim in Part IV is to characterise only partial correctness, the meaning of P needed to define partial correctness should be given. That is, given an initial state σ one is only interested in possible final states of $T[\![P]\!]$ resulting in termination in exit node t. This explains why we restrict the graph of $\mathcal{M}[\![T[\![P]\!]]\!]$ to $\Sigma \times \Sigma$.

Definition 11.6 (Operational semantics of DML) The operational semantics $O[\![P]\!]$ of a DML program $P \equiv S_1 \|\ldots\| S_n$ is defined by

$$O[\![P]\!] \stackrel{\text{def}}{=} \{(\sigma,\sigma') \mid \sigma,\sigma' \in \Sigma \quad \text{and} \quad \sigma' \in \mathcal{M}[\![T[\![P]\!]]\!]\sigma\}.$$

Note that this definition includes the semantics of sequential GCL statements for $n = 1$ where $T[\![P]\!]$ is not a parallel composition, i.e., does not involve any communication operations.   □

11.4 A Hoare Logic for Synchronous Message Passing

To specify programs P we use Hoare triples with the assertion language from Chapter 5. Their validity is as previously defined, be it that now the operational semantics O from Definition 11.6 is used:

$$\models \{pre\}\, P\, \{post\} \text{ iff for all } (\sigma_0,\sigma) \in O[\![P]\!] : \text{ if } \sigma_0 \models pre \text{ then } \sigma \models post.$$

Note that since O is based on $\mathcal{M}$, and $\mathcal{M}$ is noncompositional w.r.t. parallelism, this is also the case for O.

Our aim in this chapter is to characterise the set of all valid Hoare triples for DML by a corresponding logic. The general approach in providing rules for the sequential statements and constructing a rule for parallelism is based on the inductive assertion method. We point out, in particular, that the presence of logical variables within assertions allows one to characterise communication of values syntactically (see Example 11.7).

11.4.1 Proofs from Assumptions and the Cooperation Test

The proof system for synchronous message passing developed in this section is in many aspects quite different from that for shared-variable concurrency in Chapter 10. This difference is primarily caused by the fact that only *pairs* of *actually communicating* input and output statements display any observable behaviour. One cannot give any *observable* operational semantics to a single communication statement considered in isolation. This contrasts with the way proofs are carried out in Hoare logic. There, for *every* atomic statement pre- and postconditions are introduced, and such assertions are generated for their combinations according to fixed rules. As a consequence, in Hoare logic one is forced to introduce pre- and postconditions for single communication statements, whereas, as argued above, only suitable combinations of them display any observable behaviour. This contrast finds its reflection in the following proof strategy.

For single communication statements β, occurring inside a given statement S, we record pre- and postconditions $pre(\beta)$ and $post(\beta)$ in a *set of assumptions* A for S, which consists of Hoare triples of the form $\{pre(\beta)\}\ \beta\ \{post(\beta)\}$ for all communication statements β in S. Since these triples are used to generate a Hoare-style proof for S, A contains at least one such triple for every communication statement β contained in S. Because the same β may occur at various places inside S, correspondingly different pre- and postconditions for β may be needed to generate such a proof. Consequently A may contain syntactically different triples $\{pre(\beta)\}\ \beta\ \{post(\beta)\}$, $\{pre'(\beta)\}\ \beta\ \{post'(\beta)\}$ for the same statement β occurring in S. Since proofs for S are now generated *relative to A*, using these triples as pre-post characterisations for the communication statements contained in S, one simply selects the most suitable triple $\{\widetilde{pre}(\beta)\}\ \beta\ \{\widetilde{post}(\beta)\}$ in A for each occurrence of β in S in order to generate a proof of $\{pre\}\ S\ \{post\}$. The notation for such proofs is $A \vdash \{pre\}\ S\ \{post\}$, denoting a proof of $\{pre\}\ S\ \{post\}$ using the axioms and rules for sequential Hoare logic plus the triples of A as additional axioms.

This does not as yet imply that such triples provide a consistent characterisation of communication statements. Consistency can only be established by *comparing* the various assumption sets A_i required for generating proofs for the processes S_i in $S_1 \| \ldots \| S_n$ with themselves, because only when comparing triples with the communication they intend to characterise can one establish whether these triples make any sense. This is illustrated next.

When considering communications between, say, $C?x$ and $C!7$ one expects the postcondition of $C?x$ to somehow imply that $x = 7$ holds, since a postcondition characterises the state *after* execution of a statement. On the other hand, at the receiving end of a channel there is no knowledge available of which inputs will be received, for if such knowledge had been available before receiving them, there would have been no need to receive these values. Consequently, this information can only be provided by the postcondition of $C!7$. Let assumption set A_1 for $C?x$ contain $\{pre_1\}\ C?x\ \{post_1\}$ and assumption set A_2 for $C!7$ contain $\{pre_2\}\ C!7\ \{post_2\}$. Since only the combination of $C?x$ and $C!7$ displays any observable behaviour, namely $x := 7$, we require a proof of

$$\{pre_1 \wedge pre_2\}\ C?x\|C!7\ \{post_1 \wedge post_2\},$$

where, in general, $(C?x\|C!e) \stackrel{\text{def}}{=} x := e$, for $C \in CHAN$. Such a consistency proof is called a *cooperation test*. Call pairs of triples of the form

$$\langle \{pre_1\}\ C?x\ \{post_1\}, \{pre_2\}\ C!7\ \{post_2\}\rangle$$

for a pair of input and output statements which refer to the same channel *syntactically-matching* triples. Then assumption sets A_1 and A_2 *cooperate* if all pairs of syntactically-matching triples $\langle t_1, t_2 \rangle$ with $t_1 \in A_1, t_2 \in A_2$ satisfy their cooperation test. Consistency of the sets of assumptions $A_1, \ldots, A_n$ required for generating proofs for the sequential processes $S_1 \| \ldots \| S_n$ is defined by requiring that *all* pairs $\langle A_i, A_j \rangle$, $i \neq j$, cooperate; if such is the case we also say that $A_1, \ldots, A_n$ cooperate.

To give an idea of what these notions are good for, we sketch below for a simple network how its Hoare-style proof would look, postponing a more formal development, based on the formulation of a rule for parallel composition, to a later stage.

Example 11.7 Consider process network $S_1 \| S_2 \| S_3$ where $S_1 \equiv C!x, S_2 \equiv C?y;$ $D!y$ and $S_3 \equiv D?u$. We would like to prove

$$\{true\} \; S_1 \| S_2 \| S_3 \; \{x = u\}. \tag{11.1}$$

First we generate the following proofs from assumptions. Let

$$
\begin{aligned}
A_1 &\stackrel{\text{def}}{=} \langle \{x = z_0\} \; C!x \; \{x = z_0\} \rangle, \\
A_2 &\stackrel{\text{def}}{=} \langle \{true\} \; C?y \; \{y = z_0\}, \; \{y = z_0\} \; D!y \; \{y = z_0\} \rangle, \\
A_3 &\stackrel{\text{def}}{=} \langle \{true\} \; D?u \; \{u = z_0\} \rangle,
\end{aligned}
$$

then obviously

$$
\begin{aligned}
A_1 &\vdash \{x = z_0\} \; C!x \; \{x = z_0\}, \\
A_2 &\vdash \{true\} \; C?y; D!y \; \{y = z_0\}, \\
A_3 &\vdash \{true\} \; D?u \; \{u = z_0\}.
\end{aligned}
$$

It is required that the assertions used in the proofs of $A_i \vdash \{pre_i\} \; S_i \; \{post_i\}$ do not contain free variables subject to change in S_j, for $i \neq j$, because, otherwise, one would get interference problems and have to postulate interference freedom. Since z_0 is a logical variable, which by definition is not free in any program construct, this requirement is automatically satisfied. Next we check for cooperation of A_1, A_2 and A_3. This follows from

$$\{x = z_0 \wedge true\} \; y := x \; \{x = z_0 \wedge y = z_0\} \text{ and}$$

$$\{y = z_0 \wedge true\} \; u := y \; \{y = z_0 \wedge u = z_0\},$$

which are proved using the assignment axiom.

Because the proofs $A_i \vdash \{pre_i\} \; S_i \; \{post_i\}$ do not interfere and A_1, A_2 and A_3 cooperate, we conclude

$$\vdash \{x = z_0 \wedge true \wedge true\} \; S_1 \| S_2 \| S_3 \; \{x = z_0 \wedge y = z_0 \wedge u = z_0\}, \tag{11.2}$$

since A_1, A_2 and A_3 are no longer needed, because no unchecked triple is left in $A_1 \cup A_2 \cup A_3$ and, therefore, these assumptions have played their rôle. Using the consequence and substitution rules as usual, one obtains (11.1) from (11.2). □

In the above example the identification of syntactically-matching triples raises no problems – clearly only $\langle \{x = z_0\} \, C!x \, \{x = z_0\}, \{true\} \, C?y \, \{y = z_0\} \rangle$ and $\langle \{y = z_0\} \, D!y \, \{y = z_0\}, \{true\} \, D?u \, \{u = z_0\} \rangle$ qualify – and these triples concern pairs of communication statements which actually communicate inside $(S_1 \| S_2 \| S_3)$ above.

The latter is no longer the case in the following example.

Example 11.8

$$Q \equiv Q_1 \| Q_2, \text{ where } Q_1 \equiv C!1; C!2 \text{ and } Q_2 \equiv C?x; C?x.$$

Let $(C?x)_i$ identify the i-th occurrence of $C?x$ in Q_2, $i = 1, 2$, then $Q_2 = (C?x)_1; (C?x)_2$. □

Notice that now the pairs of occurrences of syntactically-matching triples inside Q are

$$\{\langle C!1, (C?x)_1\rangle, \langle C!1, (C?x)_2\rangle, \langle C!2, (C?x)_1\rangle, \langle C!2, (C?x)_2\rangle\},$$

and that *not all of these* correspond with actual communications inside Q. Only the pairs $\langle C!1, (C?x)_1\rangle$ and $\langle C!2, (C?x)_2\rangle$ actually communicate; such pairs are called *semantically-matching* triples. The remaining pairs,

$$\langle C!1, (C?x)_2\rangle \text{ and } \langle C!2, (C?x)_1\rangle,$$

do not correspond with any communication, although they are syntactically matching according to our definition. This situation is an immediate consequence of the contrast signalled at the beginning of this section, namely between the operational semantics for communication statements which can only be given to actually communicating pairs, and Hoare-style proofs which require a triple for every isolated occurrence of a single communication statement.

An immediate implication of the existence of syntactically- but not semantically-matching pairs for Q is that our formulation of the cooperation test becomes unsatisfactory, because we can no longer find cooperating assumption sets A_1 and A_2 for Q_1 and Q_2; this is proved in the example below.

Example 11.9 (Continued) Clearly

$$\models \{true\} \, Q_1 \| Q_2 \, \{x = 2\} \tag{11.3}$$

holds, with Q_1 and Q_2 as defined above.

In order to try to prove this formula we have to find sets of assumptions A_i for Q_i:

$$A_1 \stackrel{\text{def}}{=} \langle \{pre_{11}\} \, C!1 \, \{post_{11}\}, \{pre_{12}\} \, C!2 \, \{post_{12}\} \rangle$$
$$A_2 \stackrel{\text{def}}{=} \langle \{pre_{21}\} \, C?x \, \{post_{21}\}, \{pre_{22}\} \, C?x \, \{post_{22}\} \rangle.$$

Observe that we give one assumption for each occurrence of a communication statement.

The proof of (11.3) requires first that $\models true \to pre_{11} \wedge pre_{21}$ and $\models post_{12} \wedge post_{22} \to x = 2$. Furthermore, the program variable x of Q_2 does not occur in $pre_{11}, post_{11}, pre_{12}$ or $post_{12}$. Since a sound derivation of a correctness formula for the sequential composition requires that $\models post_{i1} \to pre_{i2}$, we might assume for simplicity that $post_{i1} = pre_{i2}$.

There are four syntactically-matching pairs and we assume that the cooperation test as sketched above holds for each of them, i.e.,

$$\vdash \{pre_{11} \wedge pre_{21}\} \, x := 1 \, \{post_{11} \wedge post_{21}\} \tag{1}$$
$$\vdash \{pre_{11} \wedge pre_{22}\} \, x := 1 \, \{post_{11} \wedge post_{22}\} \tag{2}$$
$$\vdash \{pre_{12} \wedge pre_{21}\} \, x := 2 \, \{post_{12} \wedge post_{21}\} \tag{3}$$
$$\vdash \{pre_{12} \wedge pre_{22}\} \, x := 2 \, \{post_{12} \wedge post_{22}\}. \tag{4}$$

Now there exists a state σ such that $\sigma \models true \to pre_{11} \wedge pre_{21}$. From (1) we obtain that $(\sigma : x \mapsto 1) \models post_{11} \wedge post_{21}$ and since, as argued above, $\models post_{11} \wedge post_{21} \to pre_{12} \wedge pre_{22}$ by (4) we get $(\sigma : x \mapsto 2) \models post_{12} \wedge post_{22}$. Since x does not occur in $post_{12}$, $(\sigma : x \mapsto 2) \models post_{12}$ implies also that $(\sigma : x \mapsto 1) \models post_{12}$. Analogously, $\sigma \models pre_{11}$ implies that $(\sigma : x \mapsto 1) \models pre_{11}$.

Thus $(\sigma : x \mapsto 1) \models pre_{11} \wedge post_{12}$ and, therefore, $(\sigma : x \mapsto 1) \models pre_{11} \wedge pre_{22}$. By (2) this leads to $(\sigma : x \mapsto 1) \models post_{11} \wedge post_{22}$, in particular $(\sigma : x \mapsto 1) \models post_{22}$. Since our assumptions were chosen such that $\models post_{12} \wedge post_{22} \to x = 2$ this leads to $(\sigma : x \mapsto 1) \models x = 2$. Contradiction.

Hence no such cooperating assumption sets exist for $Q_1 \| Q_2$. $\square$

To get more insight into this problem we generalise Q to two communicating loops:

$$Q_1 \equiv S_1; \, \textbf{do} \ldots C?x \ldots \textbf{od} \ldots,$$
$$Q_2 \equiv S_2; \, \textbf{do} \ldots C!y \ldots \textbf{od} \ldots,$$

and regard $Q_1 \| Q_2$ in which every passage through the loop bodies results in one communication, and S_1 and S_2 do not contain communications along channel C. Certainly the third occurrence of $C?x$ does not communicate with the fifth occurrence of $C!y$! Yet these two occurrences match syntactically (as can be seen by expanding the loops) and should therefore satisfy the cooperation test according to our definition.

These two examples suggest that we need a new formulation of the co-operation test which enables the identification of such syntactically- but not semantically-matching pairs. In order to express this distinction in Hoare-style proofs, we annotate each communication statement with an assignment to *auxiliary variables* in such a way that their combination becomes an atomic action, called *bracketed section* in Section 11.2. Next we introduce a *global (communication) invariant I* and reformulate our notion of the cooperation test and, consequently, that of cooperating assumptions, so as to be able to generate cooperating assumptions for programs such as Q above. In order to obtain a sound proof method, the free variables of I should be logical variables or auxiliary variables which only occur within bracketed sections. The cooperation test is now reformulated *relative to I*: two syntactically-matching triples $\langle \{pre(\alpha)\} \ \alpha \ \{post(\alpha)\}, \{pre(\bar{\alpha})\} \ \bar{\alpha} \ \{post(\bar{\alpha})\} \rangle$ for pairs of bracketed sections $\langle \alpha, \bar{\alpha} \rangle$ should satisfy

$$\vdash \{pre(\alpha) \wedge pre(\bar{\alpha}) \wedge I\} \ \alpha \| \bar{\alpha} \ \{post(\alpha) \wedge post(\bar{\alpha}) \wedge I\},$$

where $\alpha \| \bar{\alpha}$, for $\alpha \equiv \langle b; C?x \to \overline{aux}_1 := \bar{e}_1 \rangle$ and $\bar{\alpha} \equiv \langle C!exp \to \overline{aux}_2 := \bar{e}_2 \rangle$, is defined by $(\alpha \| \bar{\alpha}) \stackrel{\text{def}}{=} b \to (x, \overline{aux}_1, \overline{aux}_2 := exp, \bar{e}_1[exp/x], \bar{e}_2)$. (Here syntactical/semantical matching is generalised from communication statements to bracketed sections α and $\bar{\alpha}$, and to Hoare triples for α and $\bar{\alpha}$ by stipulating that the communication statements inside α and $\bar{\alpha}$ match syntactically/semantically.) It is the intention that $pre(\alpha)$, $pre(\bar{\alpha})$ and I are chosen in such a way that for syntactically-matching pairs $\langle \alpha, \bar{\alpha} \rangle$ which do not match semantically $pre(\alpha) \wedge pre(\bar{\alpha}) \wedge I$ evaluates to *false*, in which case the cooperation test trivially follows using the assignment axiom.

For instance, in the case of the communicating loops example suggested above, we use the following annotations for Q_1 and Q_2, resulting in the program $Q_1' \| Q_2'$ with

$$Q_1' \equiv S_1; \ \textbf{do} \ \dots \langle C?x \to i := i+1 \rangle \dots \ \textbf{od} \dots,$$
$$Q_2' \equiv S_2; \ \textbf{do} \ \dots \langle C!y \to j := j+1 \rangle \dots \ \textbf{od} \dots,$$

and choose $I \stackrel{\text{def}}{=} i = j$ as invariant, assuming that auxiliary variables i and j do not occur in the original loops, and $C?x$ and $C!y$ to be the only occurrences of communicating statements inside them. The definition of cooperation between assumption sets $A_1, \dots, A_n$ is now called cooperation *w.r.t. I*. In this formulation the sequential flow of control within every single process is expressed by the pre- and postconditions $pre(\alpha)$ and $post(\alpha)$ (and $pre(\bar{\alpha})$ and $post(\bar{\alpha})$), and the matching between communicating pairs by the global invariant I. The effect of this reformulation is to check whether the matching between bracketed sections α and $\bar{\alpha}$, as expressed by I, is *consistent* with the sequential control flow inside every process participating in the communication, as encoded in the $pre(\alpha)$, $pre(\bar{\alpha})$, $post(\alpha)$ and $post(\bar{\alpha})$ assertions. This leads to the formulation of the following proof strategy for the parallel composition of DML processes.

Given proofs $A_i \vdash \{pre_i\}\, S_i\, \{post_i\}$, $i = 1, \dots, n$, where

- $A_1, \dots, A_n$ cooperate w.r.t. I,
- the variables occurring freely in $A_i \vdash \{pre_i\}\, S_i\, \{post_i\}$ are not subject to change in S_j, $j \neq i$, and
- the only free variables contained in I are logical variables and auxiliary variables.

One can conclude:

$$\vdash \{\bigwedge_{i=1}^{n} pre_i \wedge I\}\, S_1 \| \dots \| S_n\, \{\bigwedge_{i=1}^{n} post_i \wedge I\}.$$

These concepts are illustrated in the examples below.

Example 11.10 (Illustrating the cooperation test) Consider program Q above, defined by:

$$Q \equiv Q_1 \| Q_2, \text{ with } Q_1 \equiv C!1; C!2 \text{ and } Q_2 \equiv C?x; C?x.$$

Our intention is to prove $\vdash \{true\}\, Q\, \{x = 2\}$.

First we annotate the communication statements of Q with assignments to auxiliary variables k_1 and k_2, resulting in Q_1' and Q_2':

$$Q_1' \equiv \langle C!1 \rightarrow k_1 := 1 \rangle; \langle C!2 \rightarrow k_1 := 2 \rangle, \text{ and}$$
$$Q_2' \equiv \langle C?x \rightarrow k_2 := 1 \rangle; \langle C?x \rightarrow k_2 := 2 \rangle,$$

choosing $k_1 = k_2$ as invariant I.

As assumption sets we choose

$$A_1 \stackrel{\text{def}}{=} \langle\quad \{k_1 = 0\} \langle C!1 \rightarrow k_1 := 1 \rangle\, \{k_1 = 1\},$$
$$\{k_1 = 1\} \langle C!2 \rightarrow k_1 := 2 \rangle\, \{k_1 = 2\} \rangle \text{ for } Q_1', \text{and}$$
$$A_2 \stackrel{\text{def}}{=} \langle\quad \{k_2 = 0\} \langle C?x \rightarrow k_2 := 1 \rangle\, \{x = 1 \wedge k_2 = 1\},$$
$$\{k_2 = 1\} \langle C?x \rightarrow k_2 := 2 \rangle\, \{x = 2 \wedge k_2 = 2\} \rangle \text{ for } Q_2',$$

and prove $A_1 \vdash \{k_1 = 0\}\, Q_1'\, \{k_1 = 2\}$ and $A_2 \vdash \{k_2 = 0\}\, Q_2'\, \{x = 2 \wedge k_2 = 2\}$. To prove cooperation of A_1 and A_2 w.r.t. I we have to check the following four combinations:

$$\vdash \{k_1 = 0 \wedge k_2 = 0 \wedge k_1 = k_2\}$$
$$x, k_1, k_2 := 1, 1, 1$$
$$\{k_1 = k_2 \wedge k_1 = 1 \wedge x = 1 \wedge k_2 = 1\},$$

$$\vdash \{k_1 = 0 \wedge k_2 = 1 \wedge k_1 = k_2\}$$
$$x, k_1, k_2 := 1, 1, 2$$
$$\{k_1 = k_2 \wedge k_1 = 1 \wedge x = 1 \wedge k_2 = 2\},$$

$$\vdash \{k_1 = 1 \wedge k_2 = 0 \wedge k_1 = k_2\}$$
$$x, k_1, k_2 := 2, 2, 1$$
$$\{k_1 = k_2 \wedge k_1 = 2 \wedge x = 2 \wedge k_2 = 1\}, \text{ and}$$

$$\vdash \{k_1 = 1 \wedge k_2 = 1 \wedge k_1 = k_2\}$$
$$x, k_1, k_2 := 2, 2, 2$$
$$\{k_1 = k_2 \wedge k_1 = 2 \wedge x = 2 \wedge k_2 = 2\}.$$

Clearly both the second formula and the third formula evaluate their precondition to *false* which we interpret as indicating that a communication consisting of the two involved statements will never happen – a fact which can actually be proved [Apt83]. The first and fourth formulae are established as easily. Consequently we conclude

$$\vdash \{k_1 = 0 \wedge k_2 = 0 \wedge k_1 = k_2\} \ Q_1' \| Q_2' \ \{k_1 = k_2 \wedge k_1 = 2 \wedge x = 2 \wedge k_2 = 2\},$$

from which $\vdash \{k_1 = 0 \wedge k_2 = 0 \wedge k_1 = k_2\} \ Q_1' \| Q_2' \ \{x = 2\}$ follows by the consequence rule, which implies $\vdash \{k_1 = 0 \wedge k_2 = 0 \wedge k_1 = k_2\} \ Q_1 \| Q_2 \ \{x = 2\}$ by a suitable version of the auxiliary variables rule, and $\vdash \{true\} \ Q \ \{x = 2\}$ by the substitution rule. $\qquad \square$

Notice that, since we use a semantics in which the parallel composition of, e.g., $\langle C?y \rightarrow k_1 := 1 \rangle$ and $\langle C!1 \rightarrow k_2 := 1 \rangle$ is expressed by the single atomic assignment $\langle y, k_1, k_2 := 1, 1, 1 \rangle$, the global invariant $k_1 = k_2$ is maintained. Were we to use a semantics in which this parallel composition had been described by, e.g., interleaving the assignments $y := 1$, $k_1 := 1$ and $k_2 := 1$, then this global invariant would have been violated (for precondition $k_1 = k_2 = 0$) after executing $k_1 := 1$ and before executing $k_2 := 1$.

Next we ask ourselves why this strategy is sound, and why it leads to a (relatively) complete proof system. The formal proofs of these claims follow in Section 11.5. However, their basic intuition can be given already now.

The central question to be asked first is: *Does global invariant I always single out which syntactically-matching pairs are also semantically matching?*

The answer is : not in general! The only consequence of the introduction of

I is that for certain syntactically-matching pairs the proof of the cooperation test becomes particularly simple because

$$\models pre(\alpha) \wedge pre(\bar{\alpha}) \wedge I \leftrightarrow false.$$

Of course, in our completeness proof we do give a characterisation of global invariant I which identifies the semantically-matching pairs.

Sometimes it is not even necessary to distinguish between syntactic and semantic matching! This is for instance the case for such programs as

$$Q' : \quad (C?x; C?x) \, \| (C!1; C!1),$$

in which the values actually communicated are the same as those assigned in the cooperation test for the semantically-non-matching pairs. As a result, on the level of proof these two kinds of pairs need not be distinguished inside Q'. The global invariant can even single out only semantically-non-matching pairs, as in the example below!

Example 11.11 (Choosing a "wrong" invariant) This example is similar to the one above, except that we use the "wrong" invariant $J \stackrel{\text{def}}{=} k_1 \neq k_2$, in that J does not express semantic matching, and replace A_2 by A_2' defined by

$$A_2' \stackrel{\text{def}}{=} \langle \quad \{k_2 = 0\}\langle C?x \rightarrow k_2 := 1\rangle \, \{x = 2 \wedge k_2 = 1\},$$
$$\{k_2 = 1\}\langle C?x \rightarrow k_2 := 2\rangle \, \{x = 1 \wedge k_2 = 2\}\rangle.$$

It is easy to check that A_1 and A_2' cooperate w.r.t. J.
We have $A_1 \vdash \{k_1 = 0\} \, Q_1' \, \{k_1 = 2\}$ and $A_2' \vdash \{k_2 = 0\} \, Q_2' \, \{x = 1 \wedge k_2 = 2\}$!
Consequently we conclude

$$\vdash \{k_1 = 0 \wedge k_2 = 0 \wedge k_1 \neq k_2\} \, Q_1' \| Q_2' \, \{k_1 = 2 \wedge x = 1 \wedge k_2 = 2\},$$

from which $\vdash \{false\} \, Q \, \{x = 1\}$ follows. We interpret this result as follows: since J is not established initially it is also not preserved and, consequently, nothing can be proved relative to J. $\qquad \square$

We conclude that a global invariant does *not* always single out the semantically-matching communication statements of a program. This slightly baffling result makes a soundness proof of our proof strategy the more urgent.

Therefore we give the intuition behind such a soundness proof below, and present a more formal version, which is based on the soundness proof for the corresponding inductive assertion method, in Section 11.5. Intuitively, soundness of this strategy for parallel DML processes $S_1 \| \dots \| S_n$ is due to three factors:

- Initially, $\bigwedge_{i=1}^{n} pre_i \wedge I$ is required to hold as precondition for $S_1\|\ldots\|S_n$.
- The values of the free variables of I are only changed within bracketed sections.
- The purely sequential parts in the proofs from assumptions $A_i \vdash \{pre_i\}S_i$ $\{post_i\}$, i.e., those parts not involving A_i, correspond to inductive assertion networks.

Due to the first factor, one only needs to consider computation sequences of $P_1\|\ldots\|P_n$ starting in an initial state σ_o which satisfies I, as well as $\bigwedge_i pre_i$. The third factor guarantees that $\sigma_0 \models \bigwedge_i pre_i$ implies that the (first) communication takes place in a state σ satisfying the two preconditions, pre'_k and pre'_l, of the communicating pair $\langle \alpha, \bar{\alpha} \rangle$ concerned, i.e., $\sigma \models pre'_k \wedge pre'_l$. Since $\sigma_0 \models I$ holds and the free variables of I do not change their values in the meantime on account of the second factor, also $\sigma \models I$ holds. By soundness of the assignment axiom, one obtains that by the cooperation test

$$\vdash \{pre'_k \wedge pre'_l \wedge I\} \ \alpha\|\bar{\alpha} \ \{post'_k \wedge post'_l \wedge I\}$$

(where $\alpha\|\bar{\alpha}$ also abbreviates the assignment to the auxiliary variables as above) $\sigma \models pre'_k \wedge pre'_l \wedge I$ implies $\tau \models post'_k \wedge post'_l \wedge I$, with τ denoting the state after executing $\alpha\|\bar{\alpha}$. Iterating this argument leads for terminating computation sequences to $\sigma_n \models \bigwedge_i post_i \wedge I$ for final state σ_n.

Completeness of our strategy follows from the corresponding result in Section 4.5 for (locally-)inductive assertion networks which satisfy the cooperation test and the fact that the predicates used can be expressed as assertions over the standard model of the natural numbers as proved in Section 5.7.

These considerations lead to the proof system for DML presented in the next section.

11.4.2 A Proof System for DML

A formal proof system for DML contains first of all axioms and rules for the sequential statements inside S_i in $P \equiv S_1\|\ldots\|S_n$. Each of the proofs for S_i is obtained relative to a set of assumptions. In a second step the parallel composition of these processes is proven correct using a global cooperation test for the assumption sets w.r.t. an invariant I. One usually introduces *logical variables* (i.e., variables which do not occur within program statements and which are not changed during the execution of a program) in order to express assumption sets satisfying the cooperation test. Recall that the set of such logical variables is referred to as *Lvar*.

Definition 11.12 (Assumptions) Let α denote a bracketed section, i.e., α is of the form $\langle C!e \to \bar{z} := \bar{e} \rangle$ or $\langle b; C?x \to \bar{z} := \bar{e} \rangle$, occurring in process S_i. The set of assumptions A_i of process S_i is a set of correctness formulae $\{p'\} \, \alpha \, \{q'\}$ covering all communication actions of S_i in the sense that for each bracketed section α in S_i an assumption $\{p'\} \, \alpha \, \{q'\}$ exists with $\{p'\} \, \alpha \, \{q'\} \in A_i$.

We write $A_i \vdash \{p_i\} \, S_i \, \{q_i\}$ to denote the fact that $\{p_i\} \, S_i \, \{q_i\}$ is provable from the set of assumptions A_i, using the axioms and rules as listed below. $\square$

Note that this definition allows us to introduce more than one assumption for one particular communication statement, and also that one assumption may cover two (or more) different occurrences of a bracketed section. This is a syntactical construction, the effect of this characterisation by assumptions being only visible in the cooperation test.

Assumption sets cooperate w.r.t. an invariant I only under certain syntactical restrictions on the variables occurring in the pre- and postconditions and in the invariant. Recall that in DML auxiliary variables occur only inside bracketed sections and that no variable of S_i occurs in S_j, $i \neq j$. The definition of $var(P)$ and $var(q)$ is extended to correctness formulae as follows:

$$var(\{pre\} \, P \, \{post\}) \stackrel{\text{def}}{=} var(pre) \cup var(P) \cup var(post).$$

Definition 11.13 (Cooperating Assumptions) Let $P \equiv S_1 \| \ldots \| S_n$. We say that the syntactically-matching pair of assumptions $\{p_i\} \, \langle C!e \to \bar{z}_i := \bar{e}_i \rangle \, \{q_i\}$ and $\{p_j\} \, \langle b; C?x \to \bar{z}_j := \bar{e}_j \rangle \, \{q_j\}$ occurring in S_i and, respectively, S_j, $i \neq j$, cooperate w.r.t. I iff

  (i) $var(I) \subseteq AVar(P) \cup Lvar$,
  (ii) $var(\{p_i\} \, \langle C!e \to \bar{z}_i := \bar{e}_i \rangle \, \{q_i\}) \cap var(\{p_j\} \, \langle b; C?x \to \bar{z}_j := \bar{e}_j \rangle \, \{q_j\}) \subseteq$ $Lvar$, and
  (iii) $\vdash \{p_i \wedge p_j \wedge b \wedge I\} \, x, \bar{z}_i, \bar{z}_j := e, \bar{e}_i, \bar{e}_j[e/x] \, \{q_i \wedge q_j \wedge I\}$ hold.

Given two sets of assumptions A_i and A_j, we say that these sets *cooperate w.r.t. some invariant* I if all syntactically matching pairs inside $A_i \times A_j$ cooperate w.r.t. I. This notation is extended to sets of assumptions $A_1, \ldots, A_n$ which have to cooperate pairwise w.r.t. I. $\square$

Notice that the syntax of DML programs already requires that sets of auxiliary variables which belong to different processes are disjoint.

The proof system for DML reflects a two-stage approach to the verification of distributed programs using proofs from assumptions. First the processes are verified in isolation, each process relative to its own set of assumptions, and then a check is made that these sets pass the cooperation test, which represents a global verification effort. Although the sequential constructs of DML are merely extensions of GCL statements, the proof rules for the sequential constructs have to be adapted to this different style of proof system.

Axiom 11.1 (Skip)

$$\emptyset \vdash \{p\} \textbf{ skip } \{p\}.$$

Axiom 11.2 (Local guarded assignment)

$$\emptyset \vdash \{b \to q[e/x]\} \, b \to x := e \, \{q\}.$$

In our proof system, all correctness formulae for communication statements are introduced by the assumption sets.

Axiom 11.3 (Output)

$$A \vdash \{p\} \, \langle C!e \to \bar{z} := \bar{e} \rangle \, \{q\},$$

provided $\{p\} \, \langle C!e \to \bar{z} := \bar{e} \rangle \, \{q\} \in A$.

Axiom 11.4 (Input)

$$A \vdash \{p\} \, \langle b; C?x \to \bar{z} := \bar{e} \rangle \, \{q\},$$

provided $\{p\} \, \langle b; C?x \to \bar{z} := \bar{e} \rangle \, \{q\} \in A$.

Rule 11.5 (Sequential composition)

$$\frac{A_1 \vdash \{p\} \, S_1 \, \{r\}, \ A_2 \vdash \{r\} \, S_2 \, \{q\}}{A \vdash \{p\} \, S_1; S_2 \, \{q\}}, \text{ where } A \stackrel{\text{def}}{=} A_1 \cup A_2.$$

Rule 11.6 (Guarded DML selection)

$$\frac{A_i \vdash \{p\} \, S_i \, \{q\}, \text{ for } i = 1, \ldots, l}{A \vdash \{p\} \textbf{ if } []_{i=1}^{l} S_i \textbf{ fi } \{q\}}, \text{ where } A \stackrel{\text{def}}{=} \bigcup_{i=1}^{l} A_i.$$

Rule 11.7 (Guarded DML loop)

$$\frac{A_B \vdash \{I\} \, S_B \, \{I\}, A_E \vdash \{I\} \, S_E \, \{q\}}{A \vdash \{I\} \textbf{ do } S_B [] S_E; \textbf{exit od } \{q\}}, \text{ where } A \stackrel{\text{def}}{=} A_B \cup A_E.$$

We need additionally a rule of consequence for this sequential part.

Rule 11.8 (Consequence)

$$\frac{p \to p_1, A \vdash \{p_1\} \, S \, \{q_1\}, q_1 \to q}{A \vdash \{p\} \, S \, \{q\}} \ .$$

Observe that these are merely extensions of the corresponding rules for GCL.

The step towards the verification of distributed processes is made explicit by the following rule for parallel composition. Note that this rule requires knowledge about the local proofs generated for all constituent processes – or, to be more precise, knowledge about all sets of assumptions that belong to these local proofs. Since we consider only top-level parallelism we do not have to verify any additional communications and can omit these sets of assumptions in the conclusion of the rule below.

Rule 11.9 (Distributed communication (Proofs from assumptions))

$$\frac{\text{There exist proofs } A_i \vdash \{p_i\} \, S_i\{q_i\}, i = 1, \ldots n,}{\{I \wedge \bigwedge_{i=1}^{n} p_i\} \, S_1 \| \ldots \| S_n \, \{I \wedge \bigwedge_{i=1}^{n} q_i\}} \ .$$

Observe that this rule still makes sense when $n = 1$, with $I = true$ and $A_i = \emptyset$. In that case, its task is formal removal of the empty assumption set.

The consequence rule is also needed for distributed programs P.

Rule 11.10 (Consequence)

$$\frac{p \to p_1, \{p_1\} \, P \, \{q_1\}, q_1 \to q}{\{p\} \, P \, \{q\}} \ .$$

Notice that up until now all axioms and rules cover the full DML programming language, including bracketed sections and auxiliary variables. While the latter are inevitable for verification since they express the flow of control of the distributed program at the level of assertions, they should not occur within the eventual program text. Thus we have to remove them from the program and the precondition to obtain correctness formulae for the programming nucleus.

Rule 11.11 (Auxiliary variables)

$$\frac{\{p\} \, P_0 \, \{q\}}{\{p\} \, P \, \{q\}} \ ,$$

where, for some set of auxiliary variables *Aux* of P_0 with $Aux \cap var(q) = \emptyset$, program P results from P_0 by deleting all assignments to the variables in *Aux* and using our conventions for suppressing **skip** statements inside bracketed sections.

Finally we should be able to remove the auxiliary variables from the precondition. This can be done by the substitution rule.

Rule 11.12 (Substitution)

$$\frac{\{p\} \, P \, \{q\}}{\{p[\overline{exp}/\overline{z}]\} \, P \, \{q\}} \, ,$$

provided $\overline{z} \cap (var(P) \cup var(q)) = \emptyset$ and $\overline{exp}$ is arbitrary.

By $\vdash \{p\} \, P \, \{q\}$ we denote that the distributed program is provable w.r.t. precondition p and postcondition q using the above rules and appropriate assumption sets for the processes constituting P.

Example 11.14 We demonstrate the use of assumptions in the verification of the set-partitioning algorithm sketched in Example 11.3. We immediately start with the version of the program with auxiliary variables,

$$P'_0: \quad max := max(S);$$
$$\langle C?mn \to mnS := mnS \cup \{mn\}\rangle; \langle D!max \to mxS := mxS \cup \{max\}\rangle;$$
$$\mathbf{do}$$
$$max > mn \to \quad S := (S \setminus \{max\}) \cup \{mn\};$$
$$max := max(S);$$
$$\langle C?mn \to mnS := mnS \cup \{mn\}\rangle;$$
$$\langle D!max \to mxS := mxS \cup \{max\}\rangle$$
$$\mathbf{od}$$

$$P'_1: \quad min := min(T);$$
$$\langle C!min \to mnT := mnT \cup \{min\}\rangle; \langle D?mx \to mxT := mxT \cup \{mx\}\rangle;$$
$$\mathbf{do}$$
$$mx > min \to \quad T := (T \setminus \{min\}) \cup \{mx\};$$
$$min := min(T);$$
$$\langle C!min \to mnT := mnT \cup \{min\}\rangle;$$
$$\langle D?mx \to mxT := mxT \cup \{mx\}\rangle$$
$$\mathbf{od}$$

and prove

$$\{S = S_0 \neq \emptyset \wedge T = T_0 \neq \emptyset \wedge S \cap T = \emptyset \wedge mnS = mnT = mxS = mxT = \emptyset\}$$
$$P_0' \| P_1'$$
$$\{max(S) < min(T) \wedge |S| = |S_0| \wedge |T| = |T_0| \wedge S \cup T = S_0 \cup T_0\},$$

using the global invariant I defined below:

$$I \stackrel{\text{def}}{=} mnT = mnS \wedge mxT = mxS \wedge |mxT| \leq |mnT| \leq |mxT| + 1 \wedge S_0 \cap T_0 = \emptyset.$$

At the input side of channel C the values received in P_0' are unknown prior to reception and are collected in the auxiliary set variable mnS. At the output side of channel C in P_1' the values sent are known, collected in the auxiliary set variable mnT and known to be minimal values of T (whence the name mnT). The global invariant I characterises the values sent along channel C therefore by $mnS = mnT$. Similarly, the values sent along channel D are characterised in the global invariant by $mxS = mxT$, where mxS collects the maximal values of S. We need the assertion $|mxT| \leq |mnT| \leq |mxT| + 1$ in I to separate between syntactically- and semantically-matching pairs (as in Example 11.10). The assertion $S_0 \cap T_0 = \emptyset$ has been added to I for reasons of convenience (in order to delete it in the local proofs).

Next we list the local proofs for P_0' and P_1' and their assumption sets A_0 and A_1. We do this in the form of a proof outline, which, as this concept has not been formally defined for DML, can be regarded as an abbreviation of the corresponding sequential proofs (note that proofs for bracketed sections are provided by the cooperation test).

$$\{\, S = S_0 \wedge S \neq \emptyset \wedge S_0 \cap T_0 = \emptyset \wedge mnS = \emptyset \wedge mxS = \emptyset \,\} \qquad \{p_0\}$$

$$max := max(S);$$

$$\{\, S = S_0 \wedge mnS = \emptyset \wedge mxS = \emptyset \wedge max \in S \wedge max = max(S) \,\} \qquad \{p_1\}$$

$$\langle C?mn \rightarrow mnS := mnS \cup \{mn\}\rangle;$$

$$\left\{ \begin{array}{l} S = S_0 \cup (mnS \setminus \{mn\}) \wedge mxS = \emptyset \wedge S \subseteq S_0 \cup T_0 \\ \wedge\, max \in S \wedge max = max(S) \wedge |S| = |S_0| \wedge |mnS| = |mxS| + 1 \\ \wedge\, mn = max(mnS) \wedge mn \notin S \wedge mn \in S_0 \cup T_0 \wedge mn \in mnS \end{array} \right\} \qquad \{p_2\}$$

$$\langle D!max \rightarrow mxS := mxS \cup \{max\}\rangle;$$

$$\left\{ \begin{array}{l} S = (S_0 \setminus (mxS \setminus \{max\})) \cup (mnS \setminus \{mn\}) \wedge max \in S \\ \wedge\, mn \in S_0 \cup T_0 \wedge mn \notin S \wedge max = max(S) \wedge max \in mxS \\ \wedge\, mn \in mnS \wedge |S| = |S_0| \wedge |mnS| = |mxS| > 0 \\ \wedge\, S \subseteq S_0 \cup T_0 \wedge mn = max(mnS) \wedge max = min(mxS) \end{array} \right\} \quad \{p_3\}$$

$$\textbf{do} \quad max > mn \rightarrow$$

$$\left\{ \begin{array}{l} S = (S_0 \setminus (mxS \setminus \{max\})) \cup (mnS \setminus \{mn\}) \wedge mn < max \\ \wedge\, max \in S \wedge mn \in S_0 \cup T_0 \wedge mn \notin S \wedge max = max(S) \\ \wedge\, max \in mxS \wedge mn \in mnS \wedge |S| = |S_0| \wedge |mnS| = |mxS| > 0 \\ \wedge\, S \subseteq S_0 \cup T_0 \wedge mn = max(mnS) \wedge max = min(mxS) \end{array} \right\} \quad \{p_4\}$$

$$S := (S \setminus \{max\}) \cup \{mn\};$$

$$\left\{ \begin{array}{l} S = (S_0 \setminus mxS) \cup mnS \wedge max \notin S \wedge mn < max \wedge |S| = |S_0| \\ \wedge\, |mnS| = |mxS| > 0 \wedge S \subseteq S_0 \cup T_0 \wedge max > max(S) \\ \wedge\, mn = max(mnS) \wedge max = min(mxS) \wedge max \in mxS \end{array} \right\} \quad \{p_5\}$$

$$max := max(S);$$

$$\left\{ \begin{array}{l} S = (S_0 \setminus mxS) \cup mnS \wedge max \in S \wedge |S| = |S_0| \\ \wedge\, max < min(mxS) \wedge mn < min(mxS) \wedge max = max(S) \\ \wedge\, |mnS| = |mxS| > 0 \wedge S \subseteq S_0 \cup T_0 \wedge mn = max(mnS) \end{array} \right\} \quad \{p_6\}$$

$$\langle C?mn \rightarrow mnS := mnS \cup \{mn\} \rangle;$$

$$\left\{ \begin{array}{l} S = (S_0 \setminus mxS) \cup (mnS \setminus \{mn\}) \wedge max \in S \wedge mn \notin S \\ \wedge\, mn \in S_0 \cup T_0 \wedge max < min(mxS) \wedge |S| = |S_0| \\ \wedge\, max = max(S) \wedge 0 < |mnS| = (|mxS| + 1) \\ \wedge\, mn = max(mnS) \wedge mn \in mnS \wedge S \subseteq S_0 \cup T_0 \end{array} \right\} \quad \{p_7\}$$

$$\langle D!max \rightarrow mxS := mxS \cup \{max\} \rangle$$

$$\left\{ \begin{array}{l} S = (S_0 \setminus (mxS \setminus \{max\})) \cup (mnS \setminus \{mn\}) \wedge mn \notin S \\ \wedge\, max \in S \wedge mn \in S_0 \cup T_0 \wedge max = max(S) \wedge max \in mxS \\ \wedge\, mn \in mnS \wedge |S| = |S_0| \wedge |mnS| = |mxS| > 0 \wedge S \subseteq S_0 \cup T_0 \\ \wedge\, max = min(mxS) \wedge mn = max(mnS) \end{array} \right\} \quad \{p_8\}$$

od

$$\left\{ \begin{array}{l} S = (S_0 \setminus (mxS \setminus \{max\})) \cup (mnS \setminus \{mn\}) \wedge max \leq mn \\ \wedge\, max \in S \wedge mn \in S_0 \cup T_0 \wedge mn \notin S \wedge max = max(S) \\ \wedge\, max \in mxS \wedge mn \in mnS \wedge |S| = |S_0| \wedge |mnS| = |mxS| > 0 \\ \wedge\, S \subseteq S_0 \cup T_0 \wedge mn = max(mnS) \wedge max = min(mxS) \end{array} \right\} \quad \{p_9\}$$

Similarly we have for P_1':

$$\{\, T = T_0 \wedge T \neq \emptyset \wedge T_0 \cap S_0 = \emptyset \wedge mnT = \emptyset \wedge mxT = \emptyset \,\} \qquad \{q_0\}$$

$$min := min(T);$$

$$\{\, T = T_0 \wedge mnT = \emptyset \wedge mxT = \emptyset \wedge min = min(T) \wedge min \in T \,\} \qquad \{q_1\}$$

$$\langle C!min \rightarrow mnT := mnT \cup \{min\}\rangle;$$

$$\left\{ \begin{array}{l} T = (T_0 \setminus (mnT \setminus \{min\}) \wedge mxT = \emptyset \wedge min = min(T) \\ \wedge\, |T| = |T_0| \wedge T \subseteq S_0 \cup T_0 \wedge min \in mnT \wedge min \in T \\ \wedge\, |mnT| = |mxT| + 1 \wedge min = max(mnT) \end{array} \right\} \quad \{q_2\}$$

$$\langle D?mx \rightarrow mxT := mxT \cup \{mx\}\rangle;$$

$$\left\{ \begin{array}{l} T = (T_0 \setminus (mnT \setminus \{min\})) \cup (mxT \setminus \{mx\}) \wedge mx \notin T \\ \wedge\, min \in T \wedge |T| = |T_0| \wedge T \subseteq S_0 \cup T_0 \wedge mx = min(mxT) \\ \wedge\, min = min(T) \wedge mx \in S_0 \cup T_0 \wedge min \in mnT \\ \wedge\, |mnT| = |mxT| > 0 \wedge min = max(mnT) \wedge mx \in mxT \end{array} \right\} \quad \{q_3\}$$

do $mx > min \rightarrow$

$$\left.\begin{array}{l} mx > min \wedge T = (T_0 \setminus (mnT \setminus \{min\})) \cup (mxT \setminus \{mx\}) \\ \wedge\, min \in T \wedge |T| = |T_0| \wedge T \subseteq S_0 \cup T_0 \wedge mx = min(mxT) \\ \wedge\, mx \notin T \wedge mx \in S_0 \cup T_0 \wedge min \in mnT \wedge mx \in mxT \\ \wedge\, |mnT| = |mxT| > 0 \wedge min = min(T) \wedge min = max(mnT) \end{array}\right\} \quad \{q_4\}$$

$$T := (T \setminus \{min\}) \cup \{mx\};$$

$$\left.\begin{array}{l} mx > min \wedge min < min(T) \wedge T = (T_0 \setminus mnT) \cup mxT \\ \wedge\, min \notin T \wedge |T| = |T_0| \wedge T \subseteq S_0 \cup T_0 \wedge mx = min(mxT) \\ \wedge\, |mnT| = |mxT| > 0 \wedge min = max(mnT) \end{array}\right\} \quad \{q_5\}$$

$$min := min(T);$$

$$\left.\begin{array}{l} mx > max(mnT) \wedge min = min(T) \wedge T = (T_0 \setminus mnT) \cup mxT \\ \wedge\, min \in T \wedge |T| = |T_0| \wedge T \subseteq S_0 \cup T_0 \wedge mx = min(mxT) \\ \wedge\, |mnT| = |mxT| > 0 \wedge min > max(mnT) \end{array}\right\} \quad \{q_6\}$$

$$\langle C!min \to mnT := mnT \cup \{min\}\rangle;$$

$$\left.\begin{array}{l} min = min(T) \wedge T = (T_0 \setminus (mnT \setminus \{min\})) \cup mxT \\ \wedge\, min \in T \wedge |T| = |T_0| \wedge T \subseteq S_0 \cup T_0 \wedge mx = min(mxT) \\ \wedge\, |mnT| = |mxT| + 1 > 0 \wedge min = max(mnT) \wedge min \in mnT \end{array}\right\} \quad \{q_7\}$$

$$\langle D?mx \to mxT := mxT \cup \{mx\}\rangle$$

$$\left.\begin{array}{l} T = (T_0 \setminus (mnT \setminus \{min\})) \cup (mxT \setminus \{mx\}) \wedge mx \notin T \\ \wedge\, min \in T \wedge |T| = |T_0| \wedge T \subseteq S_0 \cup T_0 \wedge mx = min(mxT) \\ \wedge\, min = min(T) \wedge mx \in S_0 \cup T_0 \wedge min \in mnT \\ \wedge\, |mnT| = |mxT| > 0 \wedge min = max(mnT) \wedge mx \in mxT \end{array}\right\} \quad \{q_8\}$$

od

$$\left.\begin{array}{l} T = (T_0 \setminus (mnT \setminus \{min\})) \cup (mxT \setminus \{mx\}) \wedge mx \leq min \\ \wedge\, min \in T \wedge |T| = |T_0| \wedge T \subseteq S_0 \cup T_0 \wedge mx = min(mxT) \\ \wedge\, min = min(T) \wedge mx \in S_0 \cup T_0 \wedge min \in mnT \wedge mx \notin T \\ \wedge\, |mnT| = |mxT| > 0 \wedge min = max(mnT) \wedge mx \in mxT \end{array}\right\} \quad \{q_9\}$$

Formally, we have to introduce the assumption sets of these two processes first. Using the abbreviations on the right hand side of this "proof outline" we define for P'_0 the assumption set

$$A_0 \stackrel{\text{def}}{=} \left\{ \begin{array}{l} \{p_1\}\ \langle C?mn \rightarrow mnS := mnS \cup \{mn\}\rangle\ \{p_2\}, \\ \{p_2\}\ \langle D!max \rightarrow mxS := mxS \cup \{max\}\rangle\ \{p_3\}, \\ \{p_6\}\ \langle C?mn \rightarrow mnS := mnS \cup \{mn\}\rangle\ \{p_7\}, \\ \{p_7\}\ \langle D!max \rightarrow mxS := mxS \cup \{max\}\rangle\ \{p_8\} \end{array} \right\}$$

and, similarly, for P'_1 the assumption set

$$A_1 \stackrel{\text{def}}{=} \left\{ \begin{array}{l} \{q_1\}\ \langle C!min \rightarrow mnT := mnT \cup \{min\}\rangle\ \{q_2\}, \\ \{q_2\}\ \langle D?mx \rightarrow mxT := mxT \cup \{mx\}\rangle\ \{q_3\}, \\ \{q_6\}\ \langle C!min \rightarrow mnT := mnT \cup \{min\}\rangle\ \{q_7\}, \\ \{q_7\}\ \langle D?mx \rightarrow mxT := mxT \cup \{mx\}\rangle\ \{q_8\} \end{array} \right\}.$$

We omit the following proofs of the various assignments (they are combinations of the assignment axiom and the consequence rule):

$$A_0 \vdash \{p_0\}\ max := max(S)\ \{p_1\},$$
$$A_0 \vdash \{p_4\}\ S := (S \setminus \{max\}) \cup \{mn\}\ \{p_5\},$$
$$A_0 \vdash \{p_5\}\ max := max(S)\ \{p_6\},$$
$$A_1 \vdash \{q_0\}\ min := min(T)\ \{q_1\},$$
$$A_1 \vdash \{q_4\}\ T := (T \setminus \{min\}) \cup \{mx\}\ \{q_5\},\ \text{and}$$
$$A_1 \vdash \{q_5\}\ min := min(T)\ \{q_6\}.$$

as well as those parts of the proof that establish, e.g.,

$$A_0 \vdash \{p_4\} \quad S := (S \setminus \{max\}) \cup \{mn\}; max := max(S);$$
$$\langle C?mn \rightarrow mnS := mnS \cup \{mn\}\rangle;$$
$$\langle D!max \rightarrow mxS := mxS \cup \{max\}\rangle\ \{p_8\}$$

by applying the sequential composition rule and the consequence rule several times. Note that the assertion p_3 constitutes the loop invariant and $p_9 \equiv p_3 \wedge max \leq mn$ is the postcondition of the loop.

Cooperation test

The global verification step consists of the cooperation test w.r.t. I; the above assumption sets A_0 and A_1 satisfy this test, as can be checked easily. We have a closer look at the semantically-matching pair of communication statements along channel C within the loop construct:

$$
\left\{
\begin{aligned}
&\left.
\begin{aligned}
&S = (S_0 \setminus mxS) \cup mnS \wedge max \in S \wedge |S| = |S_0| \\
&\wedge\, max < min(mxS) \wedge mn < min(mxS) \wedge max = max(S) \\
&\wedge\, |mnS| = |mxS| > 0 \wedge S \subseteq S_0 \cup T_0 \wedge mn = max(mnS)
\end{aligned}
\right\} \equiv p_6 \\[8pt]
&\left.
\begin{aligned}
&\wedge\, mx > max(mnT) \wedge min = min(T) \wedge T = (T_0 \setminus mnT) \cup mxT \\
&\wedge\, min \in T \wedge |T| = |T_0| \wedge T \subseteq S_0 \cup T_0 \wedge mx = min(mxT) \\
&\wedge\, |mnT| = |mxT| > 0 \wedge min > max(mnT)
\end{aligned}
\right\} \equiv q_6 \\[8pt]
&\left.
\begin{aligned}
&\wedge\, mnT = mnS \wedge mxT = mxS \wedge S_0 \cap T_0 = \emptyset \\
&\wedge\, |mxT| \le |mnT| \le |mxT| + 1
\end{aligned}
\right\} \equiv I
\end{aligned}
\right\}
$$

$$
mn := min;\, mnS, mnT := mnS \cup \{min\}, mnT \cup \{min\}
$$

$$
\left\{
\begin{aligned}
&\left.
\begin{aligned}
&S = (S_0 \setminus mxS) \cup (mnS \setminus \{mn\}) \wedge max \in S \wedge mn \notin S \\
&\wedge\, mn \in S_0 \cup T_0 \wedge max < min(mxS) \wedge |S| = |S_0| \\
&\wedge\, max = max(S) \wedge 0 < |mnS| = (|mxS| + 1) \\
&\wedge\, mn = max(mnS) \wedge mn \in mnS \wedge S \in S_0 \cup T_0
\end{aligned}
\right\} \equiv p_7 \\[8pt]
&\left.
\begin{aligned}
&\wedge\, min = min(T) \wedge T = (T_0 \setminus (mnT \setminus \{min\})) \cup mxT \\
&\wedge\, min \in T \wedge |T| = |T_0| \wedge T \subseteq S_0 \cup T_0 \wedge mx = min(mxT) \\
&\wedge\, |mnT| = |mxT| + 1 > 0 \wedge min = max(mnT) \wedge min \in mnT
\end{aligned}
\right\} \equiv q_7 \\[8pt]
&\left.
\begin{aligned}
&\wedge\, mnT = mnS \wedge mxT = mxS \wedge S_0 \cap T_0 = \emptyset \\
&\wedge\, |mxT| \le |mnT| \le |mxT| + 1
\end{aligned}
\right\} \equiv I
\end{aligned}
\right\}
$$

The only interesting point in this proof is proving postcondition $mn \notin S$, which is needed in the local proof for P_0' to guarantee that $|S|$ remains invariant under $S := (S \setminus \{max\}) \cup \{mn\}$. This postcondition $mn \notin S$ can be obtained as follows: Since $mnT = mnS$ and $mxT = mxS$, we also have that $min = max(mnT) = max(mnS) = mn$ and, analogously, $max = mx$. Furthermore the following holds:

$$
\begin{aligned}
S_0 \cup T_0 \subseteq\ &((S_0 \setminus mxS) \cup mxS) \cup (T_0 \setminus (mnS \setminus \{min\})) \cup (mnS \setminus \{min\}) \\
=\ &(S_0 \setminus mxS) \cup (mnS \setminus \{mn\}) \cup (T_0 \setminus (mnT \setminus \{min\})) \cup mxS = S \cup T.
\end{aligned}
$$

Together with $S \cup T \subseteq S_0 \cup T_0$ this implies that $S \cup T = S_0 \cup T_0$, and since $S_0 \cap T_0 = \emptyset$ and $|S| = |S_0| \wedge |T| = |T_0|$ we conclude that $S \cap T = \emptyset$. Thus $min \in T$ implies $mn \notin S$.

The cooperation test for the other semantically-matching pairs is similar and left as an exercise. The cooperation test for the only syntactically-matching pairs follows from the observation that within the loops $|mnS| > 0$ and $|mxS| >$

0 hold, whereas in the initialisation phase we have the explicit precondition that $mnS = \emptyset$ and $mxS = \emptyset$.

Hence we have

$$A_0 \vdash \quad \{\, S = S_0 \wedge S \neq \emptyset \wedge S_0 \cap T_0 = \emptyset \wedge mnS = \emptyset \wedge mxS = \emptyset \,\}$$

$$P_0'$$

$$\left\{ \begin{array}{c} max \leq mn \wedge S = (S_0 \setminus (mxS \setminus \{max\})) \cup (mnS \setminus \{mn\}) \\ \wedge\, max \in S \wedge max = max(S) \wedge |S| = |S_0| \wedge S \subseteq S_0 \cup T_0 \\ \wedge max = min(mxS) \wedge mn = max(mnS) \end{array} \right\}$$

and

$$A_1 \vdash \quad \{\, T = T_0 \wedge T \neq \emptyset \wedge T_0 \cap S_0 = \emptyset \wedge mnT = \emptyset \wedge mxT = \emptyset \,\}$$

$$P_1'$$

$$\left\{ \begin{array}{c} mx \leq min \wedge T = (T_0 \setminus (mnT \setminus \{min\})) \cup (mxT \setminus \{mx\}) \\ \wedge\, min \in T \wedge min = min(T) \wedge |T| = |T_0| \wedge T \subseteq S_0 \cup T_0 \\ \wedge\, mx = min(mxT) \wedge min = max(mnT) \end{array} \right\}$$

with sets of assumptions cooperating w.r.t. I. Thus Rule 11.9 for distributed communication applies and leads (after some simplification) to the formula

$$\left\{ \begin{array}{c} T = T_0 \neq \emptyset \wedge S = S_0 \neq \emptyset \wedge S \cap T = \emptyset \wedge mnT = mnS = \emptyset \\ \wedge |mxT| \leq |mnT| \leq (|mxT| + 1) \wedge mxT = mxS = \emptyset\} \end{array} \right\}$$

$$P_0' \| P_1'$$

$$\left\{ \begin{array}{l} max \leq mn \wedge S = (S_0 \setminus (mxS \setminus \{max\})) \cup (mnS \setminus \{mn\}) \\ \wedge\, max \in S \wedge max = max(S) \wedge max = min(mxS) \wedge mn = max(mnS) \\[4pt] \wedge\, |S| = |S_0| \wedge S \subseteq S_0 \cup T_0 \wedge |T| = |T_0| \wedge T \subseteq S_0 \cup T_0 \\[4pt] \wedge\, mx \leq min \wedge T = (T_0 \setminus (mnT \setminus \{min\})) \cup (mxT \setminus \{mx\}) \\ \wedge\, min \in T \wedge min = min(T) \wedge mx = min(mxT) \wedge min = max(mnT) \\[4pt] \wedge\, mnT = mnS \wedge mxT = mxS \wedge S_0 \cap T_0 = \emptyset \\ \wedge |mxT| \leq |mnT| \leq (|mxT| + 1) \end{array} \right\} .$$

From its postcondition we derive the following consequence:

$$max(S) = max = min(mxS) = mx \leq min = max(mnT) = mn = min(T)$$
$$\wedge\, S \cup T \subseteq S_0 \cup T_0 \wedge S_0 \cap T_0 = \emptyset \wedge |S| = |S_0| \wedge |T| = |T_0|$$
$$\wedge\, S \cup T = (S_0 \setminus (mxS \setminus \{max\})) \cup (mnS \setminus \{mn\}) \cup$$
$$(T_0 \setminus (mnT \setminus \{min\})) \cup (mxT \setminus \{mx\}).$$

The last equation together with $mn = min$, $mnS = mnT$, $mxS = mxT$ and $mx = max$ implies $S \cup T \supseteq S_0 \cup T_0$. Consequently, the above formula implies the new postcondition

$$max(S) \leq min(T) \wedge |S| = |S_0| \wedge |T| = |T_0| \wedge S \cup T = S_0 \cup T_0 \wedge S_0 \cap T_0 = \emptyset.$$

But this implies also that $S \cap T = \emptyset$, since, otherwise, $|S_0 \cup T_0| = |S \cup T| < |S| + |T| = |S_0| + |T_0|$, contradicting $S \cup T = S_0 \cup T_0$. And since $max(S) \in S$ and $min(T) \in T$, we conclude that $max(S) \neq min(T)$, implying the desired postcondition

$$max(S) < min(T) \wedge |S| = |S_0| \wedge |T| = |T_0| \wedge S \cup T = S_0 \cup T_0.$$

Now that we have given a proof for

$$\left\{ \begin{array}{c} T = T_0 \neq \emptyset \wedge S = S_0 \neq \emptyset \wedge S \cap T = \emptyset \wedge mnT = mnS = \emptyset \\ \wedge |mxT| \leq |mnT| \leq (|mxT| + 1) \wedge mxT = mxS = \emptyset \end{array} \right\}$$

$$P_0' \| P_1'$$

$$\{max(S) < min(T) \wedge |S| = |S_0| \wedge |T| = |T_0| \wedge S \cup T = S_0 \cup T_0\},$$

the last step to perform is an application of the auxiliary variables rule 11.11 and the substitution rule 11.12 to obtain the desired Hoare formula

$$\{S = S_0 \neq \emptyset \wedge T = T_0 \neq \emptyset \wedge S \cap T = \emptyset\}$$

$$P_0 \| P_1$$

$$\{max(S) < min(T) \wedge |S| = |S_0| \wedge |T| = |T_0| \wedge S \cup T = S_0 \cup T_0\}. \qquad \square$$

A clearer structured proof of this set-partitioning algorithm is given in Section 12.10.

Technical Note

Our proof system adapts the original Hoare-style AFR proof method [AFdR80] to the inductive assertion method for transition systems as described in Chapter 4. In the original paper it is possible to extend bracketed sections with local assignments and consider these as "atomic" from a global point of view in that these local assignments do not affect other processes. Our bracketed sections are smaller than those in [AFdR80]. This is a consequence of our strategy to reduce the proofs of soundness and completeness of our Hoare logic to those of the corresponding inductive assertion method.

11.5 Soundness and Relative Completeness of this Hoare Logic

In this section we prove soundness and relative completeness of our Hoare logic for synchronous message passing. Our technique to do so is to relate the method of Apt, Francez & de Roever developed in Chapter 4 to DML programs, thereby obtaining the result that *derivability in this Hoare logic is equivalent to provability using the inductive assertion method.*

Similarly to the soundness and completeness proof for the sequential statements of GCL in Chapter 9 we first have to show how to construct assertion networks for the synchronous transition diagrams corresponding to DML.

Definition 11.15 (Operations on assertion networks for synchronous transition diagrams)

- Let P_1 and P_2 be synchronous transition systems represented by (L_1, T_1, s, r) and (L_2, T_2, r, t), where $L_1 \cap L_2 = \{r\}$, and assume that Q_1 and Q_2 are assertion networks for P_1 and P_2. Then assertion network $Q_1; Q_2$ for $P_1; P_2$ is defined as follows, provided that $Q_1(r) \equiv Q_2(r)$:

$$
\begin{aligned}
(Q_1; Q_2)(l) &\stackrel{\text{def}}{=} Q_1(l), &&\text{for } l \in L_1, \\
&\stackrel{\text{def}}{=} Q_2(l), &&\text{for } l \in L_2.
\end{aligned}
$$

- Let P_i be synchronous transition systems represented by (L_i, T_i, s, t), for $i = 1, \ldots, l$, where $L_j \cap L_k = \{s, t\}$, for $1 \leq j < k \leq l$, and assume that Q_i is an assertion network for P_i, for $i = 1, \ldots, l$. Then assertion network **if** $[]_{i=1}^{l} Q_i$ **fi** is defined for **if** $[]_{i=1}^{l} P_i$ **fi** provided that $Q_j(s) \equiv Q_k(s)$ and $Q_j(t) \equiv Q_k(t)$ for $1 \leq j < k \leq l$:

$$
\textbf{if } []_{i=1}^{l} Q_i \textbf{ fi } (l) \stackrel{\text{def}}{=} Q_i(l), \qquad \text{for } l \in L_i.
$$

- Let P_B and P_E be synchronous transition systems represented by (L_B, T_B, s, r) and (L_E, T_E, s, t), where $L_B \cap L_E = \{s\}$. Assume that Q_B and Q_E are assertion networks for P_B and P_E. Assertion network **do** Q_B $[]$ Q_E ; **exit od** is defined for **do** P_B $[]$ P_E ; **exit od** provided $Q_B(s) \equiv Q_B(r)$ and $Q_B(s) \equiv Q_E(s)$ hold:

$$
\begin{aligned}
\textbf{do } Q_B \text{ } [] \text{ } Q_E \textbf{ ; exit od}(l) &\stackrel{\text{def}}{=} Q_B(l), &&\text{for } l \in L_B \backslash \{r\}, \\
&\stackrel{\text{def}}{=} Q_E(l), &&\text{for } l \in L_E.
\end{aligned}
$$
     $\square$

Definition 11.16 (Locally-inductive assertion networks) An assertion network Q for $T[\![S]\!]$ is called *locally inductive* if all verification conditions for local transitions in $T[\![S]\!]$ hold. $\square$

As with the operations defined in Lemma 9.16 assertion networks Q_i are called *compatible* for some operation if this operation is defined for these assertion networks.

Lemma 11.17 (Structural properties of locally-inductive assertion networks) Let P_i, for $i = 1, \ldots, l$, $l \geq 2$, P_B and P_E be synchronous transition systems.

   (i) Q is an assertion network for $P_1; P_2$ iff there exist compatible assertion networks Q_1 and Q_2 for P_1 and P_2 s.t. $Q = Q_1; Q_2$. Moreover, Q is locally inductive iff Q_1 and Q_2 are locally inductive.

   (ii) Q is an assertion network for **if** $[]_{i=1}^{l} P_i$ **fi** iff one can find compatible assertion networks $Q_1, \ldots, Q_l$ for $P_1, \ldots, P_l$ which satisfy $Q =$ **if** $[]_{i=1}^{l} Q_i$ **fi**. Moreover, Q is locally inductive iff $Q_1, \ldots, Q_l$ are locally inductive.

   (iii) Q is an assertion network for **do** P_B $[]$ P_E ; **exit od** iff there exist compatible assertion networks Q_B and Q_E for P_B and P_E, such that $Q =$ **do** Q_B $[]$ Q_E ; **exit od**. Moreover, Q is locally inductive iff Q_B and Q_E are locally inductive.

Proof The proof of this lemma is similar to that of Lemma 9.16 (see Exercise 11.9). $\square$

A few remarks on the relation between the programming nucleus of DML and full DML are necessary. The addition of assignments to auxiliary variables and bracketed sections around communication statements is caused by the requirement to obtain a (complete) proof method and as such is not part of the program text, whose sole purpose is to describe how its execution affects the value of its variables. The following key result refers to DML programs which belong to the programming nucleus of DML.

Lemma 11.18 (Key result: equivalence between our Hoare logic applied to DML programs and the inductive assertion method) Let $S_1 \| \ldots \| S_n$ be a program in the programming nucleus of DML, $T[\![S_i]\!]$ the transition system corresponding to S_i, and $\vdash \{p\}\ T[\![S_1]\!] \| \ldots \| T[\![S_n]\!]\ \{q\}$ abbreviate the claim that $T[\![S_1]\!] \| \ldots \| T[\![S_n]\!]$ can be proved correct w.r.t. $< T[\![p]\!], T[\![q]\!] >$ using the inductive assertion method of Apt, Francez & de Roever. Then:

$$\vdash \{p\}\ S_1 \| \ldots \| S_n\ \{q\} \text{ iff } \vdash \{p\} T[\![S_1]\!] \| \ldots \| T[\![S_n]\!] \{q\}.$$

Proof

$$\vdash \{p\}\, S_1 \|\ldots\| S_n\, \{q\}$$

$\overset{(1)}{\Longleftrightarrow}$ There exist proofs from assumptions $A_i \vdash \{p_i\}\, S_i'\, \{q_i\}, i = 1,\ldots,n$ such that $A_1,\ldots,A_n$ cooperate w.r.t. an invariant I, $\models I \wedge \bigwedge_i q_i \to q$ and $\models p \to (I \wedge \bigwedge_i p_i)[\overline{exp}/\bar{z}]$, where S_i' is obtained from S_i by adding assignments to auxiliary variables $\bar{z}$ and enclosing these assignments and input-output statements in bracketed sections as described before.

$\overset{(2)}{\Longleftrightarrow}$ There exist locally-inductive assertion networks $Q_1,\ldots,Q_n$ for $T[\![S_1']\!]$, $\ldots, T[\![S_n']\!]$ ($T[\![S_i]\!]$ is represented by (L_i, T_i, s_i, t_i)) that cooperate w.r.t. $T[\![I]\!]$, s.t. $Q_i(s_i) = T[\![p_i]\!]$ and $Q_i(t_i) = T[\![q_i]\!], \models I \wedge \bigwedge_i Q_i(t_i) \to T[\![q]\!]$, and $\models T[\![p]\!] \to (I \wedge \bigwedge_i Q_i(s_i)) \circ f$ for some state transformation f whose write variables belong to the set of auxiliary variables $\bar{z}$.

$\overset{(3)}{\Longleftrightarrow}$ The method of Apt, Francez & de Roever as described in Definition 4.8 applies to proving $\{T[\![p]\!]\}\, T[\![S_1]\!] \|\ldots\| T[\![S_n]\!]\, \{T[\![q]\!]\}$.

$\Longleftrightarrow \vdash \{p\}\, T[\![S_1]\!] \|\ldots\| T[\![S_n]\!]\, \{q\}$. ☐

We have to prove equivalences $\overset{1}{\Longleftrightarrow}$, $\overset{2}{\Longleftrightarrow}$ and $\overset{3}{\Longleftrightarrow}$; this is done below.

Subproof $\overset{1}{\Longleftrightarrow}$:

$\Leftarrow$: Immediate from the distributed communication rule 11.9, the consequence rule, and the substitution and auxiliary variables rules (see Example 11.10).

$\Rightarrow$: Follows from the fact that the distributed communication rule had to be used exactly once in the derivation of $\vdash \{p\}\, S_1 \|\ldots\| S_n\{q\}$ and hence such assumption sets, annotations and an appropriate global invariant exist. Additionally only rules that do not refer to the composition of program constructs may have been applied (consequence, substitution, …), and this is expressed in the side conditions. ☐

Subproof $\overset{2}{\Longleftrightarrow}$ (Isomorphism between proofs from assumptions and locally-inductive assertion networks) :

Subproof $\overset{2}{\Leftarrow}$:

Assume we have found locally-inductive assertion networks $Q_1,\ldots,Q_n$ for $T[\![S_1']\!],\ldots,T[\![S_n']\!]$ which cooperate w.r.t. I as described above. As indicated in Section 5.7 there exist syntactic assertion networks $\mathcal{AN}_1,\ldots,\mathcal{AN}_n$ corresponding to these semantic assertion networks. We prove that there exist proofs from assumptions for $S_1',\ldots,S_n'$, that these assumptions are cooperating w.r.t. an assertion $\tilde{I}$ such that $T[\![\tilde{I}]\!] = I$, and that the side conditions are satisfied.

There exist proofs from assumptions for $S_1',\ldots,S_n'$.
We prove this by structural induction on the complexity of the augmented pro-

cesses S_i'. For the sake of readability we will denote these in the proof by $S, S_1, \ldots$ without primes.

Given a transition diagram $T[\![S]\!] = (L, T, s, t)$ with a locally-inductive syntactic assertion network $\mathcal{AN}$ we construct a set of assumptions A and a pair of pre- and postconditions $\langle p, q \rangle$ for S such that $A \vdash \{p\} \, S\{q\}$ is a proof, $p = \mathcal{AN}(s)$ and $q = \mathcal{AN}(t)$.

- $S \equiv b \to \bar{x} := \bar{e}$
  $A \stackrel{\text{def}}{=} \emptyset$, $p \stackrel{\text{def}}{=} \mathcal{AN}(s)$, $q \stackrel{\text{def}}{=} \mathcal{AN}(t)$. Since $\mathcal{AN}$ is inductive, one has $\models p \wedge b \to q[\bar{e}/\bar{x}]$, i.e., by Axiom 11.2 that $A \vdash \{p\} \, S \, \{q\}$ is a proof.

- $S \equiv \langle C!e \to \bar{z} := \bar{e} \rangle$
  $A \stackrel{\text{def}}{=} \langle \, \{\mathcal{AN}(s)\} \, S \, \{\mathcal{AN}(t)\} \, \rangle$, $p \stackrel{\text{def}}{=} \mathcal{AN}(s)$, $q \stackrel{\text{def}}{=} \mathcal{AN}(t)$. By Axiom 11.3 this is a proof.

- $S \equiv \langle b; C?x \to \bar{z} := \bar{e} \rangle$
  $A \stackrel{\text{def}}{=} \langle \, \{\mathcal{AN}(s)\} \, S \, \{\mathcal{AN}(t)\} \, \rangle$, $p \stackrel{\text{def}}{=} \mathcal{AN}(s)$, $q \stackrel{\text{def}}{=} \mathcal{AN}(t)$. By Axiom 11.4 $A \vdash \{p\} \, S\{q\}$ is a proof.

- $S \equiv S_1; S_2$
  The locally-inductive syntactic assertion network $\mathcal{AN}$ for S corresponds to an inductive assertion network Q for $T[\![S_1; S_2]\!]$, and by Lemma 11.17 $Q = Q_1; Q_2$ where Q_i is a locally-inductive assertion network for $T[\![S_i]\!]$, $i = 1, 2$. Let $T[\![S_1]\!]$ be represented by (L_1, T_1, s, r) and let $T[\![S_2]\!]$ be represented by (L_2, T_2, r, t). By definition of $Q_1; Q_2$, Q_1 is defined by Q restricted to the nodes of L_1, Q_2 by restriction of Q to the nodes of L_2 and $Q_1(r) \equiv Q_2(r)$. Again there exist syntactical assertion networks $\mathcal{AN}_i$ corresponding to Q_i, $i = 1, 2$. By the induction hypothesis one can construct sets of assumptions A_i such that $A_i \vdash \{p_i\} \, S_i \, \{q_i\}$ is a proof, $i = 1, 2$, with $p_1 \equiv \mathcal{AN}(s)$, $q_1 \equiv \mathcal{AN}(r) \equiv p_2$, $q_2 \equiv \mathcal{AN}(t)$. Since $q_1 \equiv p_2$, by Rule 11.5 for sequential composition we conclude that $A_1 \cup A_2 \vdash \{p_1\} \, S_1; S_2\{q_2\}$ is a proof, and $p_1 \equiv \mathcal{AN}(s)$ and $q_2 \equiv \mathcal{AN}(t)$.

- $S \equiv \text{if } [\!]_{i=1}^l S_i \text{ fi}$ and $S \equiv \text{do } Q_B [\!] Q_E; \text{exit od}$
  The structure of the proof for these cases is similar to the case above.

The assumptions so obtained are cooperating

The assertion networks $Q_1, \ldots, Q_n$ for $T[\![S_1']\!], \ldots, T[\![S_n']\!]$ cooperate w.r.t. the invariant I. This means that for transitions $l_i \xrightarrow{a} l_i'$ and $l_j \xrightarrow{a'} l_j'$ with labels $a \equiv C!e \to \bar{z} := \bar{e}$ and $a' \equiv b; C?x \to \bar{z}' := \bar{e}'$ the associated assertions $Q_i(l_i), Q_i(l_i')$, $Q_j(l_j), Q_j(l_j')$ as in Definition 4.8 satisfy:

$$\models (I \wedge Q_i(l_i) \wedge Q_j(l_j) \wedge b) \to (I \wedge Q_i(l_i') \wedge Q_j(l_j')) \circ f,$$

where f is the state transformation corresponding to the communication and the assignments to auxiliary variables, i.e., $f(\sigma) = (((\sigma : x \mapsto e) : \bar{z} \mapsto \bar{e}) : \bar{z}' \mapsto \bar{e}')$. Since the variables in $\bar{z}'$ and $\bar{e}'$ are disjoint from those in $\bar{z}$ and $\bar{e}$, these assignments may be executed simultaneously. For the same reason the variable x does not occur in $\bar{e}$. As x may occur in $\bar{e}'$, we have to consider the new value of x in the assignment to $\bar{z}'$, namely that of expression e. The state transformation above is thus represented by the assignment $x, \bar{z}, \bar{z}' := e, \bar{e}, \bar{e}'[e/x]$. The transition with label a corresponds to some statement $S \equiv \langle C!e \to \bar{z} := \bar{e} \rangle$; the one with label a' to $S' \equiv \langle b; C?x \to \bar{z}' := \bar{e}' \rangle$. By the construction above assumptions $\{\mathcal{AN}_i(l_i)\} \, S \, \{\mathcal{AN}_i(l_i')\}$ and $\{\mathcal{AN}_j(l_j)\} \, S' \, \{\mathcal{AN}_j(l_j')\}$ are generated and added to the corresponding assumption sets. From the above we obtain the cooperation test:

$$\models \{I \wedge \mathcal{AN}_i(l_i) \wedge \mathcal{AN}_j(l_j) \wedge b\}$$
$$x, \bar{z}, \bar{z}' := e, \bar{e}, (\bar{e}'[e/x])$$
$$\{I \wedge \mathcal{AN}_i(l_i') \wedge \mathcal{AN}_j(l_j')\}.$$

Side conditions
Immediate from the construction of pre- and postconditions and the interpretation functions $\mathcal{B}$ and $\mathcal{E}$ of Chapter 5. □

Subproof $\overset{2}{\Rightarrow}$:
Given are processes $S_1, \ldots, S_n$, s.t. there exist augmented processes $S_1', \ldots, S_n'$ (where S_i' is obtained from S_i by adding assignments to auxiliary variables $\bar{z}$ and enclosing these assignments together with input-output statements in bracketed sections) and proofs from assumptions $A_i \vdash \{p_i'\} \, S_i' \, \{q_i'\}$ that cooperate w.r.t. I. We have to show how to transform these proofs and their associated annotated programs S_i' into locally-inductive syntactic assertion networks $\mathcal{AN}_i$ which correspond by Definition 11.16 and, analogous to Lemma 5.12, to locally-inductive semantic assertion networks Q_i for $T[\![S_i']\!]$; then we prove that these assertion networks cooperate w.r.t. I, and finally that the side conditions are satisfied.

How to transform these proofs and their associated annotated programs S_i' to locally-inductive assertion networks Q_i for $T[\![S_i']\!] = (L_i, T_i, s, t)$.
Additionally we have if $A \vdash \{p\} \, S' \, \{q\}$ is a proof then $Q(s) \leftrightarrow T[\![p]\!]$ and $Q(t) \leftrightarrow T[\![q]\!]$, as follows from the construction below. We prove this part by induction on the complexity of S_i'.

- $S' \equiv b \to \bar{x} := \bar{e}$
  Then $A \vdash \{p\} \, b \to \bar{x} := \bar{e} \, \{q\}$ is a proof and we define $\mathcal{AN}(s) \overset{\text{def}}{=} p$ and $\mathcal{AN}(t) \overset{\text{def}}{=} q$, hence

$$Q(s) \leftrightarrow T[\![p]\!] \text{ and } Q(t) \leftrightarrow T[\![q]\!].$$

Notice that Q is (locally) inductive: the only way to derive $A \vdash \{p\} \, b \rightarrow \bar{x} := \bar{e} \, \{q\}$ is to weaken the precondition of the axiom $A \vdash \{b \rightarrow q[e/x]\} \, b \rightarrow \bar{x} := \bar{e} \, \{q\}$, using the consequence rule in case $\models p \rightarrow (b \rightarrow q[e/x])$ or, equivalently $\models p \wedge b \rightarrow q[e/x]$, which is exactly the syntactic formulation of the verification condition for $T[\![(b \rightarrow \bar{x} := \bar{e})]\!]$.

- $S' \equiv \langle C!e \rightarrow \bar{z} := \bar{e} \rangle$

  We have $\{p\} \, \langle C!e \rightarrow \bar{z} := \bar{e} \rangle \{q\} \in A$, defining $\mathcal{AN}(s) \stackrel{\text{def}}{=} p$ and $\mathcal{AN}(t) \stackrel{\text{def}}{=} q$. Then

  $$Q(s) \leftrightarrow T[\![p]\!], \text{ and } Q(t) \leftrightarrow T[\![q]\!].$$

  Observe that Q is by definition locally inductive since no local verification conditions need to be satisfied.

- $S' \equiv \langle b; C?x \rightarrow \bar{z} := \bar{e} \rangle$

  We have $\{p\} \, \langle b; C?x \rightarrow \bar{z} := \bar{e} \rangle \{q\} \in A$, we define $\mathcal{AN}(s) \stackrel{\text{def}}{=} p$ and $\mathcal{AN}(t) \stackrel{\text{def}}{=} q$. Then

  $$Q(s) \leftrightarrow T[\![p]\!], \text{ and } Q(t) \leftrightarrow T[\![q]\!].$$

  Observe that Q is by definition locally inductive since no local verification conditions need to be satisfied.

- $S' \equiv S_1; S_2$

  Let $T[\![S_1]\!] = (L_1, T_1, s, r)$ and $T[\![S_2]\!] = (L_2, T_2, r, t)$. We have a proof for $A \vdash \{p\} \, S_1; S_2 \{q\}$ and since Rule 11.5 must have been applied, we conclude that p', r' and q', A_1 and A_2 exist such that $A_1 \vdash \{p'\} \, S_1 \, \{r'\}$ and $A_2 \vdash \{r'\} \, S_2 \, \{q'\}$ are proofs, $\models p \rightarrow p'$, $\models q' \rightarrow q$ and $A_1 \cup A_2 = A$. Hence by the consequence rule, also $A_1 \vdash \{p\} \, S_1 \, \{r'\}$ and $A_2 \vdash \{r'\} \, S_2 \, \{q\}$ are proofs. By induction there exist locally-inductive assertion networks Q_1 for $T[\![S_1]\!]$ and Q_2 for $T[\![S_2]\!]$, where $Q_1(r) \leftrightarrow T[\![r']\!] \leftrightarrow Q_2(r)$. According to Lemma 11.17 $Q \equiv Q_1; Q_2$ is locally inductive, $Q(s) = Q_1(s) \leftrightarrow T[\![p]\!]$ and $Q(t) = Q_2(t) \leftrightarrow T[\![q]\!]$.

- $S' \equiv \textbf{if } []_{i=1}^{l} S_i \textbf{ fi}$

  Let $T[\![S_i]\!] = (L_i, T_i, s, t)$. Since we have a proof $A \vdash \{p\} \textbf{ if } []_{i=1}^{l} S_i \textbf{ fi} \{q\}$, this has been derived by an application of the guarded selection rule in combination with (zero or more applications of) the consequence rule, and we obtain that there exist p_i, q_i, p', q' and A_i such that $A_i \vdash \{p_i\} \, S_i \, \{q_i\}$, for $i = 1, \ldots, l$ are proofs, $\models q_i \rightarrow q'$, $\models p' \rightarrow p_i$, $\models p \rightarrow p'$, $\models q' \rightarrow q$ and $\bigcup_{i=1}^{l} A_i = A$. Thus, also $A_i \vdash \{p'\} \, S_i \, \{q'\}$ are proofs. By the induction hypothesis, there exist locally-inductive assertion networks $Q_1, \ldots, Q_l$ for $T[\![S_i]\!]$, $i = 1, \ldots, l$ with $Q_1(s) = \ldots = Q_l(s) \leftrightarrow T[\![p']\!]$ and $Q_1(t) = \ldots = Q_l(t) \leftrightarrow T[\![q']\!]$. According to Lemma 11.17, $Q = \textbf{if } []_{i=1}^{l} Q_l \textbf{ fi}$ is inductive, and $Q(s) = Q_i(s) \leftrightarrow T[\![p']\!]$, $Q(t) = Q_i(t) \leftrightarrow T[\![q']\!]$. Since $\models p \rightarrow p'$

and $\models q' \to q$ and S' is guarded, the assertion network Q' defined by

$$Q'(l) \overset{\text{def}}{=} \mathcal{T}[\![p]\!] \quad \text{if } l = s,$$
$$Q'(l) \overset{\text{def}}{=} \mathcal{T}[\![q]\!] \quad \text{if } l = t,$$
$$Q'(l) \overset{\text{def}}{=} Q(l) \quad \text{if } l \neq s, l \neq t,$$

is also locally inductive.

- $S \equiv \mathbf{do}\ S_B\ []\ S_E;\mathbf{exit}\ \ \mathbf{od}$
  Similar to the case above.

These assertion networks cooperate w.r.t. I:
Directly from the definitions of cooperation and the construction above.

The **side conditions** are satisfied by construction, substitution Lemma 5.8 and interpretation functions $\mathcal{B}$ and $\mathcal{E}$. $\square$

Subproof $\overset{3}{\Longleftrightarrow}$:

$\Rightarrow$: Let S_i' be the program obtained from S_i by adding assignments to auxiliary variables $\bar{z}$ and enclosing these in bracketed sections as described before. Let $T[\![S_i]\!] = (L_i, T_i, s_i, t_i)$ and $T[\![S_i']\!] = (L_i, T_i', s_i, t_i)$. We show that the proof method of Apt, Francez & de Roever can be applied to the transition diagrams $T[\![S_1]\!], \ldots, T[\![S_n]\!]$ corresponding to the processes $S_1, \ldots, S_n$, if locally-inductive assertion networks $Q_1, \ldots, Q_n$ for $T[\![S_1']\!], \ldots, T[\![S_n']\!]$ are given which cooperate w.r.t. the invariant I such that $Q_i(s_i) = \mathcal{T}[\![p_i]\!]$ and $Q_i(t_i) = \mathcal{T}[\![q_i]\!]$, $\models I \wedge \bigwedge_i Q_i(t_i) \to \mathcal{T}[\![q]\!]$, and $\models \mathcal{T}[\![p]\!] \to (I \wedge \bigwedge_i Q_i(s_i')) \circ f$ with $f \overset{\text{def}}{=} (\lambda\sigma.\sigma : \bar{z} \mapsto \mathcal{E}[\![\bar{e}\bar{x}p]\!]\sigma)$ overwriting only the values of the auxiliary variables $\bar{z}$. We deal separately with every condition of Definition 4.8.

- First we augment $T[\![S_i]\!]$ as follows, obtaining $T[\![S_i]\!]'$, and prove that $T[\![S_i]\!]' = T[\![S_i']\!]$.

  A transition π with label $(C!e \to \mathbf{skip}\ )$ in $T[\![S_i]\!]$ is transformed into $(C!e \to \bar{z} := \bar{e})$ in $T[\![S_i]\!]'$, whenever:
  (1) There exists a corresponding occurrence π' of $C!e$ in S_i which has been transformed to $\langle C!e \to \bar{z} := \bar{e} \rangle$ in S_i', and
  (2) π' has been transformed into a transition with label π by application of Definition 11.5.

  Similarly, a transition π with label $(b;C?x \to \mathbf{skip}\ )$ in $T[\![S_i]\!]$ is transformed into $(b;C?x \to \bar{z} := \bar{e})$ in $T[\![S_i]\!]'$, whenever:
  (1) There exists a corresponding occurrence π' of $\langle b;C?x \to \mathbf{skip}\ \rangle$ in S_i which has been transformed to $\langle b;C?x \to \bar{z} := \bar{e} \rangle$ in S_i', and
  (2) π' has been transformed into a transition with label π by application of Definition 11.5.

Then $T[\![S_i]\!]' = T[\![S_i']\!]$ follows.

- With each transition diagram $T[\![S_i]\!]'$ with annotations we associate our *given* assertion network Q_i which satisfies the requirements (ii) and (iii) of the AFR proof method, since the Q_i are locally inductive.

- Requirement (iv) of the AFR-method is satisfied because the assertion networks $Q_1, \ldots, Q_n$ cooperate w.r.t I, and the given assertion networks Q_i are associated with each annotated transition diagram $T[\![S_i]\!]'$.

- We are given above that $\models I \wedge \bigwedge_i Q_i(t_i) \rightarrow \mathcal{T}[\![q]\!]$ and
$\models \mathcal{T}[\![p]\!] \rightarrow (I \wedge \bigwedge_i Q_i(s_i)) \circ f$. Therefore Point (v) follows immediately. $\square$

$\Leftarrow$: Given are (synchronous) transition diagrams $T[\![S_i]\!]$ and locally-inductive assertion networks $Q_1, \ldots, Q_n$ for annotated transition diagrams $T[\![S_i]\!]'$, which are obtained by the method of Apt, Francez & de Roever, which cooperate w.r.t. I. We have to construct locally-inductive assertion networks for the transition diagrams $T[\![S_i']\!]$. Therefore we show how to construct annotated programs S_i' from S_i provided the diagrams $T[\![S_i]\!]'$ are given:
(1) Let $C!e$ occur in S_i, i.e., we have a transition $\pi = (C!e \rightarrow \textbf{skip})$ in $T[\![S_i]\!]$. This statement is transformed into $\langle C!e \rightarrow \bar{z} := \bar{e} \rangle$ in S_i' whenever $(C!e \rightarrow \bar{z} := \bar{e})$ is the label of a transition in $T[\![S_i]\!]'$ that is obtained by augmenting π.
(2) Let $\langle b; C?x \rightarrow \textbf{skip} \rangle$ occur in S_i, i.e., we have a transition $\pi = (b; C?x \rightarrow \textbf{skip})$ in $T[\![S_i]\!]$. This statement is transformed into $\langle b; C?x \rightarrow \bar{z} := \bar{e} \rangle$ in S_i' whenever $(b; C?x \rightarrow \bar{z} := \bar{e})$ is the label of a transition in $T[\![S_i]\!]'$ that is obtained by augmenting π.

Thus we obtain that $T[\![S_i']\!] = T[\![S_i]\!]'$ holds for $i = 1, \ldots, n$ and that the assertion networks $Q_1, \ldots, Q_n$ for $T[\![S_1]\!]', \ldots, T[\![S_n]\!]'$ are also locally-inductive assertion networks for $T[\![S_1']\!], \ldots, T[\![S_n']\!]$ which cooperate w.r.t. I. From Point 5 of the AFR-method we derive the desired side conditions concerning the pre- and postcondition. $\square$

Theorem 11.19 (Soundness and relative completeness of our Hoare logic for DML)

The Hoare logic presented in Section 11.4.2 is sound and relatively complete.

Proof Our basic technique for inferring soundness and relative completeness of Hoare logics from soundness and semantic completeness for the corresponding inductive assertion method, using key result Lemma 11.18 above, has already been formulated in Section 9.1.2. In more detail, the proof goes as follows (note that we identify p and q with, respectively, $\mathcal{T}[\![p]\!]$ and $\mathcal{T}[\![q]\!]$ here since the interpretation of assertions is clear from Section 5.3.3):

$$\vdash \{p\} \, S_1 \| \ldots \| S_n \, \{q\}$$

$\Longleftrightarrow \vdash \{p\}\, T[\![S_1]\!]\,\|\ldots\|\, T[\![S_n]\!]\, \{q\}$, by Lemma 11.18.

$\Longleftrightarrow \models \{p\}\, T[\![S_1]\!]\|\ldots\|\, T[\![S_n]\!]\, \{q\}$, by:

$\Longrightarrow$: Soundness of the proof method of Apt, Francez & de Roever.

$\Longleftarrow$: Semantic completeness of the proof method of Apt, Francez & de Roever.

$\Longleftrightarrow \models \{p\}\, T[\![S_1\|\ldots\|S_n]\!]\, \{q\}$, by Definition 11.5.

$\Longleftrightarrow \models \{p\}\, S_1\|\ldots\|S_n\, \{q\}$, by Definition 11.6. $\square$

11.6 Technical Note: Modifications Towards Compositionality

Now that we have developed a sound and relatively complete proof system
for DML we observe that we can give a proof for a program only if the entire program text is available in order to determine the corresponding sets of
assumptions for each single process and check then for cooperation w.r.t. an invariant suited only for this particular combination of processes. Our very aim
is a *compositional* proof system where we can give proofs for each process
in isolation and combine them into a proof for a distributed program without
precise knowledge about the internal details of each process, i.e., on the basis
of the Hoare triples of the constituent processes only, as indicated in Section
9.1.3. As a first step we introduce proof outlines for DML programs, similar
to the approach in Section 9.7, as an alternative representation of a proof from
assumptions. This concept of proof outlines is essential for the presentation of
a proof system based on *shared* auxiliary variables as developed by Levin &
Gries. On the basis of this proof system and the foundations of its completeness proof we can restrict ourselves in the use of auxiliary variables to a *single
global history variable* only and simplify proofs by removing the interference
freedom test and the cooperation test due to restrictions on the assertions allowed in the proofs for the components of a distributed program.

11.6.1 Proof Outlines

Historically, in [AFdR80] a different set-up has been followed for obtaining
a parallel composition rule for synchronous communication. In the original
approach, a proof outline logic is used to prove correctness of distributed systems. The definition of a proof outline for DML is similar to the definition
given in Section 9.7 for GCL$^+$ since only sequential processes are annotated
in order to generate proof outlines: The problem of parallel composition is
delegated again to a cooperation test. We start with the definition of annotated
DML statements.

Definition 11.20 (Annotated DML statement) An *annotation* $\{p\} \, A(S) \, \{q\}$ is a DML statement S augmented with pre- and postconditions p and q and with assertions at internal locations. The syntax of $A(S)$ is given in Table 11.3 below, in which r denotes an assertion.   □

Table 11.3. *Syntax of $A(S)$ for DML.*

$$
\begin{aligned}
A(S) \quad ::= \quad & \bar{x} := \bar{e} \mid \langle C!e \to \bar{z} := \bar{e} \rangle \mid \langle b; C?x \to \bar{z} := \bar{e} \rangle \mid A(S_1); \{r\} A(S_2) \\
& \textbf{if } []_{i=1}^{l} A(S_i) \textbf{ fi} \mid \textbf{do } A(S_B) [] A(S_E); \textbf{exit od}
\end{aligned}
$$

Definition 11.21 (Proof outline) A proof outline is an annotated statement with some restrictions that express the verification conditions in the Hoare-style proof system as far as the sequential statements are concerned.

- $\{p\} \, b \to \bar{x} := \bar{e} \, \{q\}$ is a proof outline if $\models b \land p \to q[\bar{e}/\bar{x}]$.
- $\{p\} \, \langle C!e \to \bar{z} := \bar{e} \rangle \, \{q\}$ is a proof outline.
- $\{p\} \, \langle b; C?x \to \bar{z} := \bar{e} \rangle \, \{q\}$ is a proof outline.
- $\{p\} \, A(S_1); \{r\} A(S_2) \, \{q\}$ is a proof outline if both $\{p\} \, A(S_1) \, \{r\}$ and $\{r\} \, A(S_2) \, \{q\}$ are proof outlines.
- $\{p\} \, \textbf{if } []_{i=1}^{l} A(S_i) \textbf{ fi } \, \{q\}$ is a proof outline if for $i = 1, \ldots, l$, $\{p\} \, A(S_i) \, \{q\}$ is a proof outline.
- $\{p\} \, \textbf{do } A(S_B) [] A(S_E); \textbf{exit od } \{q\}$ is a proof outline if both $\{p\} \, A(S_B) \, \{p\}$ and $\{p\} \, A(S_E) \, \{q\}$ are proof outlines.   □

According to this definition one obtains proof outlines for processes in a similar way as proofs from assumptions, the difference between these two styles of local proof being that when using proof outlines one does not introduce the assumptions explicitly but uses the following "axioms" for communication statements.

Axiom 11.13 (Input)

$$\{p\} \, \langle b; C?x \to \bar{z} := \bar{e} \rangle \, \{q\}.$$

Axiom 11.14 (Output)

$$\{p\} \, \langle C!e \to \bar{z} := \bar{e} \rangle \, \{q\}.$$

"Axioms" like $\{true\} \, C?x \, \{false\}$ and $\{true\} \, C!e \, \{false\}$ allow the generation of proof outlines for the processes constituting a program. Because from

$\{true\}\ S\ \{false\}$ one can deduce $\{p\}\ S\ \{q\}$ for arbitrary assertions p and q, these "axioms" allow for adaptation of the Hoare triples for communication statements to the usual sequential correctness conditions imposed by the definition of proof outlines. The following axioms and rules repeat Definition 11.21 and show how to generate proof outlines for sequential processes.

Axiom 11.15 (Skip)

$$\{p\}\ \mathbf{skip}\ \{p\}.$$

Note that this is merely an instance of Axiom 11.16.

Axiom 11.16 (Local guarded assignment)

$$\{b \to q[e/x]\}\ b \to x := e\ \{q\}.$$

Rule 11.17 (Sequential composition)

$$\frac{\{p\}\ A(S_1)\ \{r\},\ \{r\}\ A(S_2)\ \{q\}}{\{p\}\ A(S_1);\{r\}A(S_2)\ \{q\}}.$$

Rule 11.18 (Guarded DML selection)

$$\frac{\{p\}\ A(S_i)\ \{q\},\ \text{for } i = 1,\dots,l}{\{p\}\ \mathbf{if}\ []_{i=1}^{l}A(S_i)\ \mathbf{fi}\ \{q\}}.$$

Rule 11.19 (Guarded DML loop)

$$\frac{\{I\}\ A(S_B)\ \{I\},\ \{I\}\ A(S_E)\ \{q\}}{\{I\}\ \mathbf{do}\ A(S_B)[]A(S_E);\mathbf{exit\ od}\ \{q\}}.$$

These proof outlines are then subject to a cooperation test. We adapt Definition 11.13 to the proof outline concept.

Definition 11.22 (Cooperation test for proof outlines (AFR)) Given $P \equiv S_1\|\dots\|S_n$, two proof outlines $\{p_i\}\ A(S_i)\ \{q_i\}$ and $\{p_j\}\ A(S_j)\ \{q_j\}$, $i \neq j$, $i,j \in \{1,\dots,n\}$, cooperate w.r.t. an invariant I if:

(i) $var(I) \subseteq AVar(P) \cup Lvar$,

and for all pairs of syntactically-matching bracketed sections $\{p\}\ \langle C!e \to \bar{z} := \bar{e}\rangle\ \{q\}$ in $\{p_i\}\ A(S_i)\ \{q_i\}$ and $\{p'\}\ \langle b;C?x \to \bar{z}' := \bar{e}'\rangle\ \{q'\}$ in $\{p_j\}\ A(S_j)\ \{q_j\}$ the following holds:

(ii) $var(p,q) \cap var(p',q') \subseteq Lvar$, and

(iii) $\vdash \{p \wedge p' \wedge b \wedge I\} \, x, \bar{z}, \bar{z}' := e, \bar{e}, \bar{e}'[e/x] \, \{q \wedge q' \wedge I\}$.

The set of proof outlines $\{p_1\} \, A(S_1) \, \{q_1\}, \ldots, \{p_n\} \, A(S_n) \, \{q_n\}$ cooperates w.r.t. I if each pair of these proof outlines cooperates w.r.t. I. □

These definitions lead to the following proof rule for parallel composition for proof outlines, in line with the AFR framework:

Rule 11.20 (Distributed communication (AFR proof outlines))

There exist proof outlines $\{pre_i\} \, A(S_i) \, \{post_i\}, i = 1, \ldots, n$
which cooperate w.r.t I

$$\overline{\{\bigwedge_{i=1}^{n} pre_i \wedge I\} \, S_1 \| \ldots \| S_n \, \{\bigwedge_{i=1}^{n} post_i \wedge I\}} \quad .$$

Together with Rules 11.10, 11.11 and 11.12 we obtain a proof system that is equivalent to the system using proofs from assumption.

Lemma 11.23 Let $P \equiv S_1 \| \ldots \| S_n$ be a program in the programming nucleus of DML.

$\{p\} \, P \, \{q\}$ is provable in the proof system of Section 11.4.2 iff $\{p\} \, P \, \{q\}$ is provable in the above proof system.

Proof

- For a sequential DML process S: There exists a set of assumptions A such that $A \vdash \{p\} \, S \, \{q\}$ iff $\{p\} \, A(S) \, \{q\}$ is a proof outline.
- For a program $P \equiv S_1 \| \ldots \| S_n$: Given proofs from assumptions $A_1 \vdash \{p_i\} \, S_i \, \{q_i\}, i = 1, \ldots, n$, the assumption sets A_i cooperate w.r.t. an invariant I iff the corresponding proof outlines $\{p_i\} \, A(S_i) \, \{q_i\}$ cooperate w.r.t. I. □

Although we provide a sound and (relative) complete proof system on this basis, in our opinion inserting pieces of "proofs" of the form $\{true\} \, S \, \{false\}$ does not express one's operational insight during verification (and development) of a program. For it cannot be our intention to derive arbitrary postconditions and to guess the appropriate ones. This led us to adopt the approach in Section 11.4 of using assumption sets which has been suggested by K.R. Apt [Apt84]. This approach allows in our opinion a more natural introduction of Hoare triples for communication statements into the verification process. For one should know *a priori* which communications should occur and use assumptions about these which express this intuition. These assumptions form the *logical* basis for reasoning about the actual behaviour of communication actions. We note that this is also the more pragmatic solution from the developer's point of view.

11.6.2 The Proof System of Levin & Gries

As mentioned in Section 4.4.3, Levin & Gries [LG81] developed a proof system for synchronous communication on the basis of the interference freedom test of Owicki & Gries. As with the method of Apt, Francez & de Roever assignments to auxiliary variables have to be added to the program text within bracketed sections, in order to obtain a complete proof system. In contrast to the AFR-method, auxiliary variables can be *shared* by several processes. The addition of shared auxiliary variables to processes and their proof outlines allows assertions in distinct processes to refer to non-disjoint state spaces. This is important in order to relate the program variables of one process with the program variables of another. As a consequence, a global invariant is no longer needed to connect the information about the individual processes as recorded in the auxiliary variables. Dropping the requirement that auxiliary variables sets are disjoint for different processes, the method of Levin & Gries is also based on proof outlines as defined above in Definition 11.21.

Although these auxiliary variables may appear only

- in any assertion of any process, and
- in expressions being assigned to auxiliary variables,

we are not allowed to arbitrarily augment the program with assignments to these auxiliary variables. Since they are introduced to record the effect of communications, it is sufficient to augment communication statements only with assignments to auxiliary variables in one atomic step, resulting in the same notion of bracketed sections as in the AFR-method. Furthermore we have to ensure that communication statements are augmented in such a way that no auxiliary variable is changed both in the input statement and in the output statement of a syntactically-matching pair. The cooperation test for this method is simplified due to the shared auxiliary variables.

Definition 11.24 (Cooperation test for proof outlines (Levin & Gries)) Let $P \equiv S_1 \| \ldots \| S_n$. Two proof outlines $\{p_i\} A(S_i) \{q_i\}$ and $\{p_j\} A(S_j) \{q_j\}$ cooperate iff for all syntactically matching occurrences pairs of bracketed sections $\{p\} \langle C!e \to \bar{z}_i := \bar{e}_i \rangle \{q\}$ and $\{p'\} \langle b; C?x \to \bar{z}_j := \bar{e}_j \rangle \{q'\}$ occurring in $\{p_i\} A(S_i) \{q_i\}$ and, respectively, $\{p_j\} A(S_j) \{q_j\}$ the following holds:

(i) $var(\{p\}\ \langle C!e \to \bar{z}_i := \bar{e}_i\rangle\ \{q\}) \cap var(\{p'\}\ \langle b;C?x \to \bar{z}_j := \bar{e}_j\rangle\ \{q'\}) \subseteq (AVar(P) \cup Lvar)$,

(ii) $\bar{z}_i \cap \bar{z}_j = \emptyset$, and

(iii) $\vdash \{p \wedge p' \wedge b\}\ x,\bar{z}_i,\bar{z}_j := e,\bar{e}_i,\bar{e}_j[e/x]\ \{q \wedge q'\}$. $\qquad\qquad\square$

While this cooperation test is needed for the same reason (checking consistency) as before, the introduction of shared auxiliary variables leads to an additional requirement. Since auxiliary variables might be changed in all processes and are also allowed in the assertions of all processes, we have to guarantee that these assertions remain valid under all actions of other processes. Thus an interference freedom test is necessary in this set-up, which is similar to that of Definition 10.10. This test is based on proof outlines, in order to take all intermediate steps of the processes (including communication) into account.

Definition 11.25 (Interference free proof outlines) The proof outlines $\{p_i\}$ $A(S_i)$ $\{q_i\}$, $i = 1,\dots,n$ are *interference free* iff for any assertion r_k in $\{p_k\}$ $A(S_k)$ $\{q_k\}$, if bracketed section $\{r_i\}\ \langle C!e \to \bar{z}_i := \bar{e}_i\rangle\ \{r'_i\}$ occurs in $\{p_i\} A(S_i)$ $\{q_i\}$ and bracketed section $\{r_j\}\ \langle b;C?x \to \bar{z}_j := \bar{e}_j\rangle\ \{r'_j\}$ occurs in $\{p_j\} A(S_j)$ $\{q_j\}$, $i \neq k$, $j \neq k$ (and $i \neq j$) then

$$\vdash \{r_i \wedge r_j \wedge r_k \wedge b\}\ x,\bar{z}_i,\bar{z}_j := e,\bar{e}_i,\bar{e}_j[e/x]\ \{r_k\}. \qquad\square$$

The Levin & Gries rule for parallel composition now refers to proof outlines that are interference free and cooperate.

Rule 11.21 (Distributed communication (Levin & Gries))

$$\frac{\begin{array}{c}\text{There exist proof outlines}\\ \{p_i\}\ A(S_i)\ \{q_i\},i = 1,\dots n\\ \text{which are interference free and cooperate}\end{array}}{\{\bigwedge_{i=1}^{n} p_i\}\ S_1\|\cdots\|S_n\ \{\bigwedge_{i=1}^{n} q_i\}}$$

The restriction placed on auxiliary variables that they must not be changed both in an augmented input statement and in a syntactically-matching augmented output statement can be satisfied trivially if we augment only output statements with assignments to shared auxiliary variables. As we can see from the completeness proof in Chapter 4 this strategy is sufficient to obtain a complete proof system. In order to illustrate the proof method of Levin & Gries we look again at Example 11.8.

Example 11.26 Again we want to prove that

$$\{true\}\ C!1;C!2\ \|\ C?x;C?x\ \{x = 2\}$$

holds. We annotate only the output statements with assignments to a single auxiliary variable k. The new task is thus to prove that

$$\{k = 0\}\ \langle C!1 \rightarrow k := k + 1\rangle; \langle C!2 \rightarrow k := k + 1\rangle \,\|\, C?x; C?x\ \{x = 2\}$$

holds. We give the following proof outlines

$$\{k = 0\}\ \langle C!1 \rightarrow k := k + 1\rangle; \{k = 1\}\ \langle C!2 \rightarrow k := k + 1\rangle\ \{k = 2\}$$
$$\{k = 0\}\ C?x;\ \{k = 1\}\ C?x\ \{x = 2 \wedge k = 2\}.$$

Now the cooperation test for the Levin & Gries method is satisfied for all four syntactically matching pairs:

- For $\{k = 0\}\ \langle C!1 \rightarrow k := k + 1\rangle\ \{k = 1\}$ and $\{k = 0\}\ C?x\ \{k = 1\}$ one can prove that $\{k = 0\}\ x, k := 1, k + 1\ \{k = 1\}$.
- For $\{k = 1\}\ \langle C!2 \rightarrow k := k + 1\rangle\ \{k = 2\}$ and $\{k = 1\}\ C?x\ \{k = 2 \wedge x = 2\}$ one can prove that $\{k = 1\}\ x, k := 2, k + 1\ \{k = 2 \wedge x = 2\}$.
- For $\{k = 0\}\ \langle C!1 \rightarrow k := k + 1\rangle\ \{k = 1\}$ and $\{k = 1\}\ C?x\ \{k = 2 \wedge x = 2\}$ the cooperation test holds trivially since $k = 0 \wedge k = 1$ yields *false* as precondition.
- For $\{k = 1\}\ \langle C!2 \rightarrow k := k + 1\rangle\ \{k = 2\}$ and $\{k = 0\}\ C?x\ \{k = 1\}$ one has again that the precondition of the cooperation test yields *false*.

The proof outlines above cooperate and since there is no process that can interfere with $C!1; C!2$ and $C?x; C?x$, hence we can derive the desired result by the parallel composition rule.

Now suppose that a third process is executed concurrently with these two processes, e.g.,

$$Q' \equiv C!1; C!2 \,\|\, C?x; C?x \,\|\, \mathbf{skip}.$$

The proof outline $\{k = 0\}\ \mathbf{skip}\ \{k = 0\}$ clearly cooperates with the above two proof outlines, yet the distributed communication rule (Levin & Gries) without the interference freedom test would lead to

$$\{k = 0\}$$
$$\langle C!1 \rightarrow k := k + 1\rangle; \langle C!2 \rightarrow k := k + 1\rangle \,\|\, C?x; C?x \,\|\, \mathbf{skip}$$
$$\{k = 2 \wedge x = 2 \wedge k = 0\},$$

i.e., we would derive $\vdash \{k = 0\}\ P\ \{false\}$, although this is not valid.

This conclusion is excluded by the interference freedom test since for $r_k \equiv k = 0$ none of the possible communications can establish this assertion as postcondition. A different proof outline for the **skip** process has to be found, e.g., $\{true\}\ \mathbf{skip}\ \{true\}$. $\qquad\qquad\qquad\qquad\qquad \Box$

Note that we can transform every proof in the AFR proof system of Section 11.4.2 to a proof using the method of Levin & Gries. Using the assumptions from our assumption sets as instances for the input axiom 11.13 and the output axiom 11.14 for communication statements occurring in the program, we can obtain proof outlines for a program from our proof system. In order to obtain annotations that pass the cooperation test of Levin & Gries, each annotation p is modified to $p' \overset{\text{def}}{=} p \wedge I$ where I is the global invariant of the AFR-method. Since I refers only to auxiliary and logical variables the syntactic restrictions on the annotations (only auxiliary and logical variables are shared) are satisfied, and a cooperation test in the Levin & Gries method

$$\vdash \{p_i' \wedge p_j' \wedge b\} \, x, \bar{z}_i, \bar{z}_j := e, \bar{e}_i, \bar{e}_j[e/x] \, \{q_i' \wedge q_j'\}$$

holds iff the cooperation test for the AFR-method

$$\vdash \{I \wedge p_i \wedge p_j \wedge b\} \, x, \bar{z}_i, \bar{z}_j := e, \bar{e}_i, \bar{e}_j[e/x] \, \{I \wedge q_i \wedge q_j\}$$

holds in the proof system for proofs from assumptions (where we assume w.l.o.g. that process j contains the input statement and process i contains the output statement). For local steps I is invariant as it refers to auxiliary variables that are only changed inside bracketed sections.

We still have to prove interference freedom of our proof outlines, i.e., that $p_k \wedge I$ occurring in the proof outline for P_k is invariant under execution of the assignment $x, \bar{z}_i, \bar{z}_j := e, \bar{e}_i[e/x], \bar{e}_j[e/x])$ with precondition $I \wedge p_i \wedge p_j$ which models communication between P_i and P_j, $i \neq j$, $k \neq i$, $k \neq j$. Since no variable occurring in p_k is changed by this assignment (all variable sets are disjoint), it remains invariant under this assignment, and as a consequence of the AFR cooperation test I still holds as postcondition.

11.6.3 Removing the Interference Freedom Test

Observe that the proof system given in the previous section is not compositional, since the rule for parallel composition contains a cooperation test and an interference freedom test which require the complete program text – annotated with assertions – of the processes involved.

In this section we discuss how this noncompositional method can be adapted to obtain a compositional proof system. In general, proofs in the methods described in [AFdR80, LG81] will use different auxiliary variables for different programs. The first idea is to use the same auxiliary variable for the proofs of all programs. By always using the same, standard, auxiliary variable there is no need to augment programs explicitly with assignments to this auxiliary variable. This auxiliary variable can be updated implicitly in the semantics of programs. Then bracketed sections are no longer needed and, hence, also no auxiliary variables rule is needed to remove these sections.

The use of standard auxiliary variables in all proofs is justified by the completeness proof given in Section 4.4.3, which discusses soundness and semantic completeness of the method of Levin & Gries. This completeness result shows that any valid Hoare triple for a parallel program can be proved by adding a single, global, history variable h to the program. This variable records the global communication history of the whole program during its execution. We first show that we can remove the interference freedom test and the cooperation test from the method of Levin & Gries, once this single auxiliary variable is used.

The main idea for removing the interference freedom test is to use projections on the history variable. A communication history, also called a *trace*, is a finite sequence $\langle (C_1,\mu_1),\ldots,(C_m,\mu_m)\rangle$, with $m \in N$, $C_i \in CHAN$ and $\mu_i \in VAL$, for $i = 1,\ldots,m$. Again $\langle\rangle$ is used to denote the empty sequence. The *concatenation* of two traces $\theta_1 \equiv \langle (C_{11},\mu_{11}),\ldots,(C_{1k},\mu_{1k})\rangle$ and $\theta_2 \equiv \langle (C_{21},\mu_{21}),\ldots,(C_{2m},\mu_{2m})\rangle$, is denoted by $\theta_1 \cdot \theta_2$ (and also by $\theta_1\theta_2$), and defined as the trace $\langle (C_{11},\mu_{11}),\ldots,(C_{1k},\mu_{1k}),(C_{21},\mu_{21}),\ldots,(C_{2m},\mu_{2m})\rangle$. We often use $\theta \cdot (C,\mu)$ as an abbreviation of $\theta \cdot \langle (C,\mu)\rangle$. For two traces θ_1 and θ_2 we use $\theta_1 \preceq \theta_2$ to denote that θ_1 is a prefix of θ_2, that is, there exists a trace θ_3 such that $\theta_1 \cdot \theta_3 = \theta_2$.

Let *TRACE* be the set of traces, that is, the smallest set such that

- $\langle\rangle \in TRACE$,
- if $\theta \in TRACE$, $C \in CHAN$, and $\mu \in D$ then $\theta \cdot (C,\mu) \in TRACE$.

Definition 11.27 (Channels occurring in a trace) The set of channels occurring in a trace θ, notation $Chan(\theta)$, is defined by

- $Chan(\langle\rangle) \stackrel{\text{def}}{=} \emptyset$,
- $Chan(\theta \cdot (C,\mu)) \stackrel{\text{def}}{=} Chan(\theta) \cup \{C\}$. $\square$

We also define projection on traces.

Definition 11.28 (Projection) For a trace $\theta \in TRACE$ and a set of channels $cset \subseteq CHAN$, we define the *projection* of θ onto $cset$, denoted by $\theta{\downarrow}cset$, as the sequence obtained from θ by deleting all records with channels not in $cset$. Formally,

$$\theta{\downarrow}cset \stackrel{\text{def}}{=} \begin{cases} \langle\rangle & \text{if } \theta \equiv \langle\rangle \\ \theta_0{\downarrow}cset & \text{if } \theta \equiv \theta_0 \cdot (C,\mu) \text{ and } C \notin cset \\ \theta_0{\downarrow}cset \cdot (C,\mu) & \text{if } \theta \equiv \theta_0 \cdot (C,\mu) \text{ and } C \in cset. \end{cases}$$ $\square$

Note that $\theta \downarrow Chan(\theta) = \theta$. The assertion language is also extended with projections on variables: for a variable h that ranges over *TRACE* we define $\mathcal{E}(h \downarrow cset)\sigma \stackrel{\text{def}}{=} (\sigma(h)) \downarrow cset$.

Recall that we need interference freedom test because variable h denotes the communication history of the complete program and h might occur in the assertions of each process. Hence these assertions can refer to the global trace of the complete program. For instance, a process that only communicates on channels A and B is allowed to use h in its assertions, and thus can state properties about a channel C connecting other processes. This can be avoided by the following requirement:

> In a proof for a program $S_1 \| \cdots \| S_n$ the assertions in the proof outline for process S_i only refer to h by means of projections onto channels of S_i, that is, h occurs only in the form $h \downarrow cset$ with $cset \subseteq Chan(S_i)$, for $i = 1, \ldots, n$.

By this restriction each process only uses its own view of the global history. What it asserts about the global trace is directly under its control and cannot be changed by other processes without participation of the process itself.

To avoid interference for program variables we have the following requirement.

> In a proof for a program $S_1 \| \cdots \| S_n$ all program variables occurring in the proof outline for process S_i are program variables of S_i, for $i = 1, \ldots, n$. Thus if $x \in var(S_1 \| \ldots \| S_n)$ and x occurs in the proof outline for process S_i then $x \in var(S_i)$, for $i = 1, \ldots, n$, i.e., $x \notin var(S_j)$ for $j \neq i$.

Since processes do not share variables, this requirement implies that a proof outline for one process does not refer to program variables of other processes. Next we argue that with these two requirements the interference freedom test is trivially satisfied and hence not needed. By the restriction above, the only variable in the proof outline of a process that might change by executing statements in other processes is history variable h. To prove interference freedom, consider assertion r_k in a proof outline for process S_k, suppose $\{r_1^i\} \langle C!e \rightarrow h := h \cdot (C, e) \rangle \{r_2^i\}$ occurs in a proof outline for S_i, and $\{r_1^j\} \, C?x \, \{r_2^j\}$ occurs in a proof outline for S_j, $i \neq k, j \neq k$. Then each h in r_k occurs in the form $h \downarrow cset$ with $cset \subseteq Chan(S_k)$. Since channel C connects S_i and S_j and a channel connects at most two processes, we have $C \notin Chan(S_k)$, and thus $C \notin cset$. But then the value of $h \downarrow cset$ is not affected by the assignment $h := h \cdot (C, e)$, and hence r_k remains valid under the C-communication.

11.6.4 Removing the Cooperation Test

Recall that the cooperation test has been introduced to verify the postconditions of io-statements in the local proof outline of a process. These assertions represent assumptions about the communication behaviour of the environment of this process. Hence, to remove the cooperation test, we should disallow such assumptions about the environment and restrict the proof outlines such that they are valid in any environment. This is achieved by changing the definition of a proof outline for io-statements.

Definition 11.29 (Proof outline revised)   Replace in the definition of a proof outline the clauses for io-statements by:

- $\{p\}\ \langle C!e \to h := h \cdot (C,e)\rangle\ \{q\}$ is a proof outline iff $p \to q[h \cdot (C,e)/h]$.
- $\{p\}\ C?x\ \{q\}$ is a proof outline iff $p \to \forall v : q[h \cdot (C,v)/h, v/x]$.   □

In general, we can prove that with these restricted proof outlines the cooperation test is always fulfilled. Suppose $\{r_1^i\}\ \langle C!e \to h := h \cdot (C,e)\rangle\ \{r_2^i\}$ occurs in a proof outline for S_i and $\{r_1^j\}\ C?x\ \{r_2^j\}$ occurs in a proof outline for S_j.
Then $r_1^i \to r_2^i[h \cdot (C,e)/h]$ and $r_1^j \to \forall v : r_2^j[h \cdot (C,v)/h, v/x]$.
Hence, using e for v, $r_1^j \to r_2^j[h \cdot (C,e)/h, e/x]$.
Since $x \in var(S_j)$, x does not occur in assertions of S_i , and thus
$r_1^i \wedge r_1^j \to (r_2^i \wedge r_2^j)[h \cdot (C,e)/h, e/x]$.
Since x does not occur in e (which follows from $var(S_i) \cap var(S_j) = \emptyset$), we have that
$(r_2^i \wedge r_2^j)[h \cdot (C,e)/h, e/x] \to (r_2^i \wedge r_2^j)[h \cdot (C,e)/h][e/x]$, and thus
$r_1^i \wedge r_1^j \to (r_2^i \wedge r_2^j)[h \cdot (C,e)/h][e/x]$.
Hence $\{r_1^i \wedge r_1^j\}\ x := e; h := h \cdot (C,e)\ \{r_2^i \wedge r_2^j\}$.
Summarising, we have removed the interference freedom test and the cooperation test as follows:

(i)   Always use a single auxiliary variable h which records the global communication history of the program. Therefore each output statement $C!e$ in the program is transformed into $\langle C!e \to h := h \cdot (C,e)\rangle$.

(ii)   Require that assertions in a proof outline of a process refer only to program variables of the process itself and to h by means of projections onto the channels of the process.

(iii)   Restrict the proof outlines of io-statements such that they are valid in any environment.

Using Definition 11.29 we obtain

Rule 11.22
$$\frac{\text{There exist proof outlines } \{p_i\}\, A(S_i)\, \{q_i\},\ i = 1,\ldots,n}{\{p_1 \wedge \ldots \wedge p_n\}\, S_1 \|\cdots\| S_n\, \{q_1 \wedge \ldots \wedge q_n\}}\ ,$$

provided

- each output statement $C!e$ is included in a bracketed section $\langle C!e \to h := h \cdot (C,e)\rangle$,
- all program variables occurring in an assertion in $\{p_i\}\, A(S_i)\, \{q_i\}$ are program variables of S_i, for $i = 1,\ldots,n$, and
- history variable h occurs in assertions in $\{p_i\}\, A(S_i)\, \{q_i\}$ only in the form $h{\downarrow}cset$ with $cset \subseteq Chan(S_i)$, for $i = 1,\ldots,n$.

Finally, observe that we can remove the auxiliary variables rule by updating variable h as a *logical* variable only. Section 7.3 gives an idea how to use h as a logical variable, i.e., without explicitly updating statements of the processes involved.

Observe that in Rule 11.22 only the pre- and postconditions of the proof outlines are used. Therefore, with suitable restrictions, we have the following compositional rule for parallel composition.

Rule 11.23 (Parallel composition)

$$\frac{\{p_i\}\, S_i\, \{q_i\},\ i = 1,\ldots,n}{\{p_1 \wedge \cdots \wedge p_n\}\, S_1 \|\cdots\| S_n\, \{q_1 \wedge \cdots \wedge q_n\}}\ .$$

Exercises

11.1   Does

$$\textbf{if}\ \ \langle C!e \to \textbf{skip }\rangle; S_1\, [\!]\, \langle D?x \to \textbf{skip }\rangle; S_2\ \textbf{fi}$$

belong to DML for appropriate S_1 and S_2?

11.2   The correctness proof of the distributed program in Example 11.14 is easier to handle if one uses the following "axiom":

Axiom 11.24 (Invariance)

$$A \vdash \{p\}\, S\, \{p\},$$
$$provided\ var(p) \cap var(S) = \emptyset.$$

Prove that $\models \{p\}\, S\, \{p\}$ holds under this condition.

11.3   Consider the processes

$$S_1 \equiv A!0; B!1; A!2 \quad \text{and}$$
$$S_2 \equiv A?x; \textbf{if } A?y \rightarrow B?z [\!] \ B?y \rightarrow A?z \textbf{ fi } .$$

Prove $\{true\} \ S_1 \| S_2 \ \{x = 0 \wedge y = 1 \wedge z = 2\}$.

11.4   Consider the following processes. First we have two producers S_1 and S_2.

$$S_1 \equiv \quad A!0; \textbf{if } \ true \rightarrow A!3 [\!] true \rightarrow \textbf{skip fi}$$
$$S_2 \equiv \quad B!1; \textbf{if } \ true \rightarrow B!2 [\!] true \rightarrow \textbf{skip fi}$$

Process M merges the output of S_1 and S_2 and sends it along channel C.

$$M \equiv A?x; B?y; \textbf{if } \ x < y \rightarrow C!x; A?x [\!] \ x \geq y \rightarrow C!y; B?y \textbf{ fi}$$

Finally we have a consumer C.

$$C \equiv C?z.$$

Give a proof from assumptions for

$$\vdash \{true\} \ S_1 \| S_2 \| M \| C \ \{x = 3 \wedge y = 1 \wedge z = 0\}.$$

11.5   Let $N \geq 0$ be a constant and consider two array variables A and B with domain $\{0, \dots, N\}$. We use $A[i]$ to denote the i th element of array A. Define the processes

$$S_1 \equiv \quad j := 0; \textbf{do } j \leq N \rightarrow C!A[j]; j := j + 1 \textbf{ od}$$
$$S_2 \equiv \quad k := 0; \textbf{do } k \leq N \rightarrow C?B[k]; k := k + 1 \textbf{ od}.$$

Give a proof from assumptions for

$$\vdash \{true\} \ S_1 \| S_2 \ \{\forall i.0 \leq i \leq N \rightarrow A[i] = B[i]\}.$$

11.6   Give the detailed proof of the cooperation test of Example 11.14 for the communication along channel D for all syntactically-matching pairs.

11.7   Prove that proof outlines as defined in Definition 11.21 and locally-inductive assertion networks are isomorphic.

11.8   With processes S_1, S_2, M and C as in Exercise 11.4, use the method of Levin & Gries to prove that

$$\vdash \{true\} \ S_1 \| S_2 \| M \| C \ \{x = 3 \wedge y = 1 \wedge z = 0\},$$

where only output statements are annotated with assignments to auxiliary variables.

11.9   With processes S_1 and S_2 as in Exercise 11.5, use the method of Levin & Gries to prove that

$$\vdash \{true\}\; S_1 \| S_2\; \{\forall i.0 \leq i \leq N \rightarrow A[i] = B[i]\},$$

where only output statements are annotated with assignments to auxiliary variables.

11.10   Prove Lemma 11.17.

11.11   (Proof of Lemma 11.18)

Prove that for an $S' \equiv \mathbf{do}\; S_B \,[\!]\, S_E; \mathbf{exit}\;\mathbf{od}$ and a proof $A \vdash \{p\}\; S'\; \{q\}$ there exists a locally-inductive assertion network Q for $T\,[\![S']\!]$ with $\models Q(s) \leftrightarrow T\,[\![p]\!]$ and $\models Q(t) \leftrightarrow T\,[\![q]\!]$.

11.12   Prove that the assertion networks as obtained by the construction in the proof of part $\overset{2}{\Rightarrow}$ of Lemma 11.18 indeed cooperate w.r.t. the invariant I.

Part V
Layered Design

12

Transformational Design and Hoare Logic

12.1 Introduction and Overview

Program development can be guided by the syntactic structure of a program, as explained and advocated in Chapters 9, 10 and 11. Using this approach, the structure of program components that have been developed already, be it in a top-down or bottom-up fashion, usually remains fixed throughout the rest of the design process. An alternative is to start off with a relatively simple program, prove it correct, and then *transform* it into the final program. The motivation for this transformational approach is that protocols for distributed programs are often not only very complicated to develop but are even more complicated to understand by persons other than the designers. Such protocols are often the result of a process of transforming, refining and optimising a basically simple algorithm; however, in the final result these transformations cannot be traced anymore within the syntactic structure of a program. The result is a program that can be very hard to verify by means of the structured techniques of Chapters 9, 10 and 11. A notorious example is the algorithm for determining minimum-weight spanning trees by Gallager, Humblet and Spira [GHS83]. There are several published correctness proofs of this algorithm [SdR87, WLL88, CG88, SdR89, FFG90, JZ92a, Hes96], some of which rely on a protocol structure for the verification process that differs from the structure of the final algorithm.

In this chapter we take the point of view that, in order to explain and clarify the final resulting protocol, as opposed to its mere verification, *the structure of a correctness proof should reflect the structure of the original design process*, rather than the structure of the final resulting program. To this end we introduce program-transformation techniques that should be used in combination with the Owicki & Gries-style of program verification of Chapter 10.

A transformational method is particularly attractive for the design of con-

654

current and distributed programs. Unlike in the sequential case, algorithms for concurrent and distributed programs usually take the system architecture into account. By "system architecture" we refer to such aspects as the number of parallel processing units available, and the structure and the performance of the network connecting those processing units. This leads to a wide variety of algorithms, each one tailored to some particular architecture, for solving one and the same task. Informally we often make a distinction between the "physical structure" and the "logical structure" of programs. The physical structure refers to a program S_D that has a syntactic structure that is reasonably close to the actual physical architecture that will be used to execute the program. For instance, one expects a simple and straightforward mapping from the parallel processes of S_D to the actual processing units available in a given system architecture. We assume here that the physical structure can be described as a collection of distributed and communicating network nodes P_j, each of which executes a number of "phases" $P_{0,j}, \cdots, P_{n,j}$ sequentially (the term "phase" is borrowed from the literature on protocols). Schematically, this can be described as a program of the following form:

$$S_D \stackrel{\text{def}}{=} [(P_{0,0}; P_{1,0}; \cdots; P_{n,0}) \parallel \cdots \parallel (P_{0,m}; P_{1,m}; \cdots; P_{n,m})].$$

As an example, consider the following variation of the set-partitioning example 11.3:

$$SetPart_D \stackrel{\text{def}}{=} \left[\begin{array}{l|l} max := \max(S) & min := \min(T) \\ ; & ; \\ \mathbf{send}(C, max) & \mathbf{receive}(C, mx) \\ ; & ; \\ \mathbf{receive}(D, mn) & \mathbf{send}(D, min) \\ ; & ; \\ \mathbf{while}\ max > mn\ \mathbf{do} & \mathbf{while}\ mx > min\ \mathbf{do} \\ \quad S := (S \setminus \{max\}) \cup \{mn\} & \quad T := (T \setminus \{min\}) \cup \{mx\} \\ ; & ; \\ \quad max := \max(S) & \quad min := \min(T) \\ ; & ; \\ \quad \mathbf{send}(C, max) & \quad \mathbf{receive}(C, mx) \\ ; & ; \\ \quad \mathbf{receive}(D, mn) & \quad \mathbf{send}(D, min) \\ \mathbf{od} & \mathbf{od} \end{array} \right].$$

The **send** and **receive** actions in this program are asynchronous communication actions that can be seen as abbreviations of shared-variable actions, as explained in Section 12.3. (In all other respects, the algorithm is the same as in Example 11.3.) Consequently, the Owicki & Gries method can be used to specify and verify the correctness of this algorithm. However, in this chapter we propose an alternative route for this correctness proof.

The first step is to recognise that there is a sequential version of the algorithm, which is easier to prove correct. For the set-partitioning problem, the following program could serve this rôle:

$$
SetPart_S \stackrel{\text{def}}{=} \left\{
\begin{array}{l}
max, min := \max(S), \min(T) \,; \\
\textbf{while } max > min \textbf{ do} \\
S, T := (S \setminus \{max\}) \cup \{min\}, (T \setminus \{min\}) \cup \{max\}; \\
max, min := \max(S), \min(T) \\
\quad \textbf{od}
\end{array}
\right.
$$

The correctness of the latter sequential program is easily shown, using the Hoare-style proof system of Chapter 9. The main idea of design by means of sequentially-layered programs is that many distributed algorithms are derived from such simple sequential algorithms.

The second step is to construct a concurrent program consisting of a number of sequential phases, where each phase itself is a concurrent program. For the set-partitioning example the following program is a good choice:

$$
SetPart_L \stackrel{\text{def}}{=} \left\{
\begin{array}{lcl}
[max := \max(S) & \| & min := \min(T)] \\
& ; & \\
[\textbf{send}(C, max) & \| & \textbf{receive}(C, mx)] \\
& ; & \\
[\textbf{receive}(D, mn) & \| & \textbf{send}(D, min)] \\
& ; & \\
\textbf{while } max > min \textbf{ do} & & \\
[S := (S \setminus \{max\}) \cup \{mn\} & \| & T := (T \setminus \{min\}) \cup \{mx\}] \\
& ; & \\
[max := \max(S) & \| & min := \min(T)] \\
& ; & \\
[\textbf{send}(C, max) & \| & \textbf{receive}(C, mx)] \\
& ; & \\
[\textbf{receive}(D, mn) & \| & \textbf{send}(D, min)] \\
\textbf{od} & &
\end{array}
\right.
$$

Informally speaking, such sequentially-phased programs can often be obtained from a sequential program by applying various simple program transformations. One might rely here on correctness-preserving transformations, in which case the correctness of the sequentially-phased program follows from the correctness of the sequential version. Alternatively, one can show the correctness of the sequentially-phased program directly, using for instance the Owicki & Gries method. Because each of the sequential phases is a much simpler program than the program as a whole, this verification task will turn out to be rather simple, and often can be derived from the proof for the sequential version in a straightforward manner. As observed in, for instance, [EF82, SdR87, JZ92a], the logical structure, i.e., the structure that one uses to explain concurrent algorithms and protocols often appears to be sequentially phased, and corresponds to a program of the form:

$$S_L \overset{\text{def}}{=} [P_{0,0} \parallel \cdots \parallel P_{0,m}] ; \cdots ; [P_{n,0} \parallel \cdots \parallel P_{n,m}].$$

The aim of this chapter is to explain under which circumstances such sequentially-phased programs S_L are actually *equivalent* to their corresponding distributed version S_D, where "equivalent" is to be understood as "computing the same initial-final state relation". For instance, it can be shown that the layered version of the set-partitioning algorithm is equivalent to the distributed version mentioned above. Therefore, the correctness of the distributed version follows from the correctness of the layered version.

The idea of program transformation applied to the design of concurrent and distributed programs can also be found in, e.g., [Bac88, CM88, BS89, Bac90, BS90, BS91, BS92], and is based on the major idea that one should start off with a so-called *action system*. Within the programming language of this chapter (or Chapter 10), such an action system can be seen as a program of the form

$$\bar{x} := \bar{e}_{init} ; \mathbf{do} \ []_{i=1}^{n} b_i \rightarrow \bar{x}_i := \bar{e}_i \ \mathbf{od}.$$

The idea is that programs in this particularly simple form are also rather simple to verify. Obviously, after this has been done, the action system must be transformed into a concurrent or distributed program. The approach followed in this chapter differs from the action-system approach in that the initial design is not an action system but rather a sequentially-phased program as described above. Here the idea is that the sequential phases are relatively small concurrent programs, and therefore simple to verify. These phases are combined by means of sequential composition, which allows for relatively simple (Hoare-logic-style) techniques. Moreover, similarly to the action-system approach, afterwards we also need to transform, since usually a sequentially-phased program does not match the imposed physical system structure.

Here we have transformations in mind which are based on the seemingly simple notion of *commuting actions*. Two guarded assignments a_1 and a_2 are said to be commuting if the following holds:

- executing a_1 in a state in which a_2 is enabled, i.e., in which the boolean guard of a_2 is "*true*", will not disable a_2,
- vice versa, executing a_2 will not disable a_1,
- the net effect on the state of executing a_1 ; a_2 is the same as that of executing a_2 ; a_1.

Let us compare the following two programs:

$$S_L \overset{\text{def}}{=} [P_{0,0} \parallel \cdots \parallel P_{0,m}] ; \cdots ; [P_{n,0} \parallel \cdots \parallel P_{n,m}]$$

and

$$S_D \overset{\text{def}}{=} [(P_{0,0} ; P_{1,0} ; \cdots ; P_{n,0}) \parallel \cdots \parallel (P_{0,m} ; P_{1,m} ; \cdots ; P_{n,m})].$$

If one can show that *the ordering of non-commuting actions in the distributed program S_D is the same as in the sequentially-phased program S_L* then the two versions S_D and S_L are equivalent. For the above distributed program S_D this boils down to the restriction that for every pair of non-commuting actions a_1 and a_2 with a_1 an action of $P_{i,j}$ and a_2 an action of $P_{i',j'}$, $i < i'$ and $j \neq j'$, one must show that in every computation of S_D occurrences of a_1 are not preceded by occurrences of a_2. Actually, we use only a simple so-called *syntactic approximation* of commutativity, based on the idea that when some action a_1 reads and writes variables which all belong to some set V_1, a_2 reads and writes variables that belong to V_2, and V_1 and V_2 are disjoint sets, then certainly a_1 and a_2 are commuting actions.

In this chapter we consider both shared-variable concurrency and programs with explicit communication actions. The latter class is regarded here as a subclass of all shared-variable programs, where shared variables are used only in the form of communication buffers and synchronisation flags. The techniques based on commuting actions remain valid for communication-based programs, i.e., programs with explicit communication actions. But, due to the restrictions involved, a more attractive formulation of the transformation laws is possible than for *general* shared-variable programs. This formulation is the principle of *communication-closed-layers* (CCL), and has been originally proposed in [EF82]. Informally, for a program S_L as above, a sequential phase of the form $L_i \overset{\text{def}}{=} [P_{i,0} \parallel \cdots \parallel P_{i,m}]$, is called communication-closed if for every communication channel C the number of **send** actions executed inside L_i equals the number of **receive** actions for C executed inside L_i. The communication-closed-layers law claims that when all sequential phases L_i, for $0 \leq i \leq n$, are communication-closed, then S_L is equivalent to the distributed version S_D. Technically speaking this law can be justified on the basis of the laws for commuting actions. In practice however, "counting" **send** and **receive** actions is often simpler than reasoning directly in terms of commuting actions. Moreover, communication-closedness is a property that can be checked for each sequential phase *in isolation*, that is, without consideration of other phases. On the other hand, for (general) shared-variable programs, one has to reason about ordering of non-commuting actions *across sequential phases*.

The techniques introduced in this chapter are based on *precedence relations* among program actions. Basically, such properties have the form "a_1 *precedes* a_2", with the meaning that in every possible computation of the program the points in the execution where a_1 is executed all precede the points in the execution where a_2 is executed. The question is how to deal with this class of properties within proofs in the style of the Owicki & Gries method. In principle, the Owicki & Gries method uses assertions on *states*, whereas precedence properties are assertions that are interpreted over *computations*.

For instance, an assertion that expresses that "all occurrences of action a_1 precede all occurrences of action a_2" cannot be interpreted as being "*true*" or "*false*" in an arbitrary program state σ. A possible solution is to introduce a boolean-typed auxiliary variable for action a_2, called "$a_2.occ$", which is set to "*true*" as soon as an instance of action a_2 occurs. (This is done by incorporating an assignment of the form $a_2.occ := true$ within the a_2 action.) In this way, the above precedence relation can be verified by means of an Owicki & Gries-style proof outline where a_1 has a precondition that implies "$\neg a_2.occ$".

Instead, we prefer to give a more systematic approach, based on so-called *temporal logic* [Krö87, Lam83c, MP91b], and then use the proof strategy sketched above to prove formulae from the subset of temporal logic we actually need. Temporal logic is a logic with formulae ϕ interpreted over computations, rather than over states, which is perfect for formulating precedence properties. Readers already familiar with temporal logic will recognise that we use only a small fragment of temporal logic, TL^-, with operators that refer to the past history of a given state. Moreover, we only touch upon the subject of proving temporal formulae valid for a given program. The interested reader is referred to [MP91b, MP95] for a full account on this topic. The temporal logic used here is called *linear time* temporal logic. Its characteristic is that its underlying model is based on computations in the form of "linear" sequences. Other models, based on partial orders, as in [Pra86, Maz89, JPZ91, PZ93, JPXZ94], are slightly more natural for dealing with precedence relations among actions. (In essence, a computation in the partial-order model, can be seen as a collection of actions together with a set of precedence relations on these actions.) Closely related are logics such as Interleaving Set Temporal Logic (ISTL) [KP87, KP89, KP92]. These techniques are outside the scope of this book, in which only linear computation sequences are used. A clear advantage of linear time temporal logic is that its models are relatively simple, compared to most other mathematical models.

12.2 Structure of this Chapter

Section 12.3 introduces the syntax of SVL^{++}, a language which is actually an extension of the shared-variable language SVL from Chapter 10 that includes a form of asynchronous communication. The semantics of SVL^{++} is given in Section 12.4. The small fragment of temporal logic which is needed for formulating the communication-closed-layers principle (CCL) is discussed in Section 12.5. In Sections 12.6 and 12.8 several versions of the CCL laws are formulated and proved correct. A generalisation of the CCL laws, based on loop unfolding, is given in Section 12.9. Two main examples of program transformation are given. In Section 12.7 correctness of the two-phase commit protocol are discussed and in Section 12.10 correctness of the set-partitioning algorithm. Both are proven correct using the above proof principles, associated with communication-closed-layers. Finally, Section 12.11 discusses related work; the chapter ends with a list of exercises.

12.3 Syntax and Informal Meaning of SVL^{++} Programs

This section provides the syntax and informal meaning of an extension, called SVL^{++}, of the shared-variable languages SVL and SVL^{+} from Chapter 10. SVL^{++} augments SVL^{+} by introducing *asynchronous communication* constructs in the form of **send** and **receive** actions. These extensions can be defined as abbreviations of certain guarded assignments. Moreover, we introduce *action naming*, which is a device for assigning unique names to individual guarded assignments within a program text.

As usual, we use variables x, expressions e and boolean expressions b. For channel names we use c, and for action names we use a. The syntax of SVL^{++} is given in Table 12.1 below.

Table 12.1. *Syntax of the Programming Language SVL^{++}.*

Actions	$act ::=$	$\langle b \rightarrow \bar{x} := \bar{e} \rangle \mid$ **send**$(c,e) \mid$ **receive**(c,x)
Programs	$S ::=$	$a : act \mid S_1 ; S_2 \mid$ **if** $[\!]_{i=1}^{n} S_i$ **fi** $\mid$
		do S_B $[\!]$ S_E ; **exit** **od** $\mid$ $[S_1 \parallel S_2]$
Closed programs	$Sys ::=$	$\langle S \rangle$

The definitions and restrictions concerning guardedness carry over from Chapters 9 and 10. Also, we assume that communication channels in SVL^{++} programs are unidirectional point-to-point channels. Finally we require that all action names a within a program S are *unique*. In practice we suppress most of these labels and put only labels in front of those actions that are referred to in formulae that are used to specify and verify a particular program. Formally speaking we assume in such cases that, implicitly, some labelling scheme is used that assigns unique names to all unlabelled actions.

We use also the same abbreviations as in Chapters 9 and 10. These are the following (where we have suppressed action labels):

- An assignment $\bar{x} := \bar{e}$ abbreviates $\langle true \to \bar{x} := \bar{e}\rangle$.
- **if** $[\,]_{i=1}^{n} b_i \to S_i$ **fi** is an abbreviation of **if** $[\,]_{i=1}^{n} \langle b_i \to \mathbf{skip}\rangle$; S_i **fi** .
- **do** $[\,]_{i=1}^{n} b_i \to S_i$ **od** abbreviates
  do if $[\,]_{i=1}^{n} b_i \to S_i$ **fi** $[\,]$ $\langle \neg b_G \to \mathbf{skip}\rangle$; **exit od**, where $b_G \equiv b_1 \vee \cdots \vee b_n$.
- **if** b **then** S_1 **else** S_2 **fi** abbreviates **if** $b \to S_1 [\,] \neg b \to S_2$ **fi** and
  while b **do** S **od** abbreviates **do** $b \to S$ **od**, as usual.

SVL^{++} as Special Case of SVL^{+}

SVL^{++} programs can be seen as SVL^{+} programs provided we treat the communication actions "**send**" and "**receive**" as abbreviations. The **send** and **receive** actions of SVL^{++} model *asynchronous send* and *receive* actions for a channel with a one-place buffer. Informally, **send**(c,e) evaluates expression e and sends the result along channel c, where it is temporarily stored in a one-place buffer $c.buf$. In case the buffer is filled up already, the send action waits until the buffer is emptied. The receive action **receive**(c,x) waits until a message is put in the buffer associated with the channel, retrieves it, and stores the message in a variable x. Consequently, **send** and **receive** actions can be defined using guarded assignments:

$$\mathbf{send}(c,e) \stackrel{\text{def}}{=} \langle \neg c.full \to c.full, c.buf := true, e\rangle,$$
$$\mathbf{receive}(c,x) \stackrel{\text{def}}{=} \langle c.full \to c.full, x := false, c.buf\rangle.$$

For closed programs we assume that initially all *semaphores* (cf. Section 10.2) of the form $c.full$ associated with communication channels c are set to "*false*", guaranteeing that all channels $c.buf$ are empty initially. Formally speaking, we take care of this by assuming that the preconditions of Hoare formulae for closed programs implicitly contain a conjunct of the form $\neg c.full$ for all relevant channels c.

12.4 The Semantics of SVL^{++} Programs

Based on the compositional reactive-sequence semantics from Chapter 3, Section 3.5.4, we develop a similar semantics for SVL^{++} programs. A slight extension is the addition of *action names* to computation steps. This results in a semantics with computation steps of the form $\langle \sigma \overset{a}{\to} \sigma' \rangle$, where action label a is the name of the program action that caused the state transformation $\langle \sigma, \sigma' \rangle$. Such a computation step $\langle \sigma \overset{a}{\to} \sigma' \rangle$ with action label a is called an a-event. Note that although action names are unique it is possible that several a-events occur within a single reactive sequence, due to the presence of loops. As explained in Section 3.5.4, a reactive sequence models a computation of a program which takes into account possible interactions by parallel components. This is modelled using "gaps" whenever two subsequent computation steps have non-identical final and initial states. So we use action-labelled reactive sequences θ of the form:

$$\langle \sigma_0 \overset{a_0}{\to} \sigma_0' \rangle \langle \sigma_1 \overset{a_1}{\to} \sigma_1' \rangle \ldots \langle \sigma_{i-1} \overset{a_{i-1}}{\to} \sigma_{i-1}' \rangle \langle \sigma_i \overset{a_i}{\to} \sigma_i' \rangle \langle \sigma_{i+1} \overset{a_{i+1}}{\to} \sigma_{i+1}' \rangle \ldots$$

We provide here a semantics $\mathcal{RA}[\![S]\!]$ for SVL^{++} programs S which defines the reactive sequences corresponding to properly terminating computations of S. (It is possible to define deadlock behaviour and divergent computations in a similar style, but since we are aiming here at partial correctness only, we will not need those here.)

Definition 12.1 (Reactive-event-sequence semantics) For SVL^{++} programs S we define the reactive-event-sequence semantics $\mathcal{RA}[\![S]\!]$ in the following compositional way. For the semantics of **send** and **receive** actions we refer to the definitions above.

- $\mathcal{RA}[\![a : \langle b \to \bar{x} := \bar{e} \rangle]\!] \overset{\text{def}}{=} \{ \langle \sigma \overset{a}{\to} \sigma' \rangle \mid \sigma \models b \wedge \sigma' = \mathcal{A}_I[\![\bar{x} := \bar{e}]\!] \sigma \}$, where the meaning of an assignment $\mathcal{A}_I$ has been defined in Section 5.3.2.
- $\mathcal{RA}[\![S_1 ; S_2]\!] \overset{\text{def}}{=} \mathcal{RA}[\![S_1]\!] \,^\frown \mathcal{RA}[\![S_2]\!]$, where $^\frown$ is the operation of concatenation of sequences, pointwise extended to sets of reactive sequences.
- $\mathcal{RA}[\![\textbf{if } []_{i=1}^{n} S_i \textbf{ fi }]\!] \overset{\text{def}}{=} \bigcup_{i=1}^{n} \mathcal{RA}[\![S_i]\!]$.
- Let $R^{(0)} \overset{\text{def}}{=} \mathcal{RA}[\![S_E]\!]$, and let $R^{(i+1)} \overset{\text{def}}{=} \mathcal{RA}[\![S_B]\!] \,^\frown R^{(i)}$, for $i \geq 0$. Then:

$$\mathcal{RA}[\![\textbf{do } S_B \,[]\, S_E ; \textbf{exit od}]\!] \overset{\text{def}}{=} \bigcup \{ R^{(i)} \mid i \geq 0 \}.$$

- $\mathcal{RA}[\![S_1 \parallel S_2]\!] \overset{\text{def}}{=} \mathcal{RA}[\![S_1]\!] \,\tilde{\parallel}\, \mathcal{RA}[\![S_2]\!]$, where $\tilde{\parallel}$ denotes the operation of interleaving, cf. Theorem 3.34.

Finally, we define the semantics of *closed* programs. We say that a reactive sequence θ of the form

$$\langle \sigma_0 \xrightarrow{a_0} \sigma_0' \rangle \langle \sigma_1 \xrightarrow{a_1} \sigma_1' \rangle \ldots \langle \sigma_i \xrightarrow{a_i} \sigma_i' \rangle \langle \sigma_{i+1} \xrightarrow{a_{i+1}} \sigma_{i+1}' \rangle \ldots \langle \sigma_n \xrightarrow{a_n} \sigma_n' \rangle$$

is *connected* iff $\sigma_i' = \sigma_{i+1}$ for all indices i such that σ_i' and σ_{i+1} belong both to θ. For a closed program $\langle S \rangle$ no interaction with parallel components from outside of S is assumed, hence we require that for such closed programs the reactive sequences do not contain "gaps", i.e., are connected.

- Define the reactive-sequence semantics $\mathcal{RA}[\![\langle S \rangle]\!]$ of a closed program $\langle S \rangle$ by

$$\mathcal{RA}[\![\langle S \rangle]\!] \stackrel{\text{def}}{=} \{\theta \in \mathcal{RA}[\![S]\!] \mid \theta \text{ is connected}\}. \qquad \square$$

Definition 12.2 For the sake of readability we introduce

$$O_{cl}[\![S]\!] \stackrel{\text{def}}{=} O[\![\langle S \rangle]\!],$$

with $O[\![\langle S \rangle]\!]$ as defined in Definition 10.3. $\qquad \square$

The $O_{cl}[\![S]\!]$ semantics can be derived from $\mathcal{RA}[\![\langle S \rangle]\!]$. First we define an auxiliary function $IO(\eta)$ for reactive sequences η, that constructs the initial-final state pair from a (finite) reactive sequence:

$$IO(\langle \sigma_0 \xrightarrow{a_0} \sigma_0' \rangle \ldots \langle \sigma_n \xrightarrow{a_n} \sigma_n' \rangle) = (\sigma_0, \sigma_n').$$

The $O_{cl}[\![S]\!]$ semantics of programs is easily determined from the reactive sequence semantics of the *closed* program $\langle S \rangle$:

Theorem 12.3

$$O_{cl}[\![S]\!] = \{IO(\eta) \mid \eta \in \mathcal{RA}[\![\langle S \rangle]\!]\}.$$

Proof Exercise. $\qquad \square$

12.5 Partial Orders and Temporal Logic

Program specification by means of pre- and postconditions is adequate for sequential programs, but does not suffice for proving parallel programs correct. This has already become clear in Chapter 10, where no pre-postcondition formulae but rather proof outlines were used in the Owicki & Gries proof system. Pre-postcondition formulae specify only the initial and final states of computations. A proof outline, on the other hand, can be seen as an *invariant* of the computation, expressing informally that upon arrival at program location l the corresponding assertion from the proof outline is satisfied. Note that this invariant is satisfied *throughout the whole computation*, and not just at the point of termination. Specification of such invariants is just an example of a much wider class of specifications that all have in common and that they apply to *computations as a whole,* rather than to single program states. Prime examples of specification formalisms in this style are various forms of trace logics [Hoa81a, MC81, ZH81, OH83, Sou84, ZdRvEB85, HdR86, OH86, Old86, ZdR89, Zwi89, Zwi90, Hoo91b, Old91a, PJ91], which are discussed in the companion volume, as well as various forms of *temporal logic* [Pnu77, Lam83c, Pnu86, Krö87, MP91b, MP95]. In this chapter we focus on a variant of temporal logic, called pasttime temporal logic.

To understand the operators of temporal logic intuitively, one should consider reactive sequences θ, of the form $\theta_0 \theta_1 \ldots \theta_n$, where each of the sequence elements θ_i is a computation step of the form $\langle \sigma_i \xrightarrow{a_i} \sigma_i' \rangle$. A temporal logic formula is a logic formula that has a truth value that depends on the whole sequence, unlike Hoare formulae, which have a truth value that depends only on the start state of the first computation step and the final state of the last computation step in the sequence. A temporal formula ϕ is interpreted as being "true" or "false" for combinations of the form (θ, i), where i is some natural number such that $i \leq n$. We call i the "reference point" for the formula. Intuitively, reference point i indicates one particular transition θ_i which is assumed to happen "now", at the moment of time defined by that reference point. All other transitions are classified as being in the future or in the past, all relative to the reference point. When we specify a program S by means of a temporal formula ϕ, we use a correctness formula of the form S **psat** ϕ. This correctness formula expresses that *all* (finite) computation sequences of S satisfy ϕ at reference point $j = 0$.

The temporal logic that we actually use here is a variant of Lamport's *temporal logic of actions*, inspired by the logic TLA [Lam94a]. Since we aim at specifying and verifying so-called *open programs*, with a semantics based on reactive sequences, this form of temporal logic fits in naturally. We remark that the temporal logic used in, for instance, [MP95] (with the exception of Sections 0.4 and 4.3) is based on *closed* programs. Consequently, the temporal logic in [MP95] is based on sequences of states, rather than reactive sequences. Such state sequences can be identified with the *connected* reactive sequences of closed programs, as defined in Section 12.4, if we omit the action labels.

The simplest cases of temporal formulae are formulae called *assertions*. Assertions specify the single computation step that is indicated by the reference point. A computation step of type $\langle \sigma_j \overset{a_j}{\to} \sigma'_j \rangle$ is defined by its label a_j and its state transformation, i.e., the step from state σ_j to state σ'_j. We therefore introduce two basic forms of assertions:

(i) Assertions in the form of *action labels*. We say that the assertion of the form "a" is satisfied at reference point j if the j-th computation step in θ has a as its label.

(ii) Basic assertions for specifying the *state transformation* of a computation step. These are much like the assertions used as pre-postconditions in Hoare formulae. A new aspect is that program variables x can occur in two variations: *unprimed*, in the form x, and *primed*, in the form x'. The two variations refer to the values of x before and after the execution of the computation step, that is, the value of x in σ_j and the value of x in σ'_j. An example of such an assertion is the formula $p \overset{\text{def}}{=} I \to I'$, where I is an assertion without primed variables, and where I' is like I except that all its variables have been changed into their primed counterparts. When this assertion p is true for some computation step, then one says that I is *preserved* by this step. By "preserved" we mean that if I holds at the beginning of the step, then it still holds after executing the step. For example, if the state formula I is chosen to be $x > 0$, then $I \to I'$ expresses that if the computation step at the reference point starts in a state where $x > 0$, then this step leaves x unchanged or it increases the value of x, but it cannot decrease its value. However, should the step start in a state where $x \leq 0$ then anything could happen with the value of x but I is still preserved.

An important special class of assertions is that of so-called *state formulae*, which consists of all assertions without action labels and without free occurrences of primed variables, for instance, the assertion I in the example above. These are the assertions of temporal logic for closed programs, and are the same as those in [MP95].

On top of assertions, temporal logic defines a number of temporal operators. The first of these operators is the "always" operator "$\Box$". A temporal formula of the form "$\Box \phi$" ("always ϕ") holds at some position j if ϕ holds at *all* positions k after j, including position j itself. As an example, consider a formula ϕ of the form $\Box(x > 0 \to x' > 0)$. This formula is true for a sequence θ when the computation step at the reference point and all steps thereafter *preserve* the state formula $x > 0$. For instance, if S is some SVL^{++} program where all assignments to variable x are of the form $x := x + 1$, then all computation sequences of S satisfy ϕ, from reference point $j = 0$ onwards. This fact can be denoted by the correctness formula S **psat** ϕ.

We contrast this with temporal formula ψ of the form $x > 0 \rightarrow \Box(x > 0)$, again interpreted at reference point $j = 0$. This formula states, for any reactive-event sequence, that if x is greater than zero in the start state of the first transition, then it will always be greater than zero in the start states of all remaining transitions. The computation sequences of program S will not satisfy this ψ formula in general, since the start states of transitions are, in general, not determined by the actions of S, since the latter may be executed by some (unknown) parallel environment. Consequently, the start-state condition for the unprimed x on the right hand side of the implication may become false although $x > 0$ was true at the reference point. This situation changes if, rather than considering some open program S, we consider the *closed* program $\langle S \rangle$. Since we know that S preserves the assertion $x > 0$, and since there are no possible interfering actions from the outside of S, we conclude that ψ is actually valid for all computation sequences of $\langle S \rangle$, and we denote this by (validity of) the correctness formula $\langle S \rangle$ **psat** $x > 0 \rightarrow \Box(x > 0)$.

The second temporal operator that we discuss is the "eventually" operator "$\Diamond$". A formula of the form $\Diamond\phi$ expresses that ϕ holds at the reference position j or at *some* position $k > j$. For example, a formula of the form $\Diamond a$, interpreted in $(\theta, 0)$, expresses that somewhere in θ a step occurs that has as its action label "a". When we use a correctness formula of the form S **psat** $\Diamond\phi$, then by definition *all* computation sequences of S satisfy $\Diamond a$ at the reference point $j = 0$. That is, some a labelled action is bound to occur in every S computation. Informally we say in this case that "a is *unavoidable*". We will use this sort of formula when we have chains of actions $a_0, a_1, \ldots, a_n$, where we know that a_i precedes a_{i+1}, for $i = 0, \ldots, n - 1$. We would like to infer that a_0 precedes a_n, by transitivity of the ordering relation. This reasoning breaks down, however, if some of the intermediate actions $a_1, \ldots, a_{n-1}$ are not *necessarily* executed in all possible computations of the program S under consideration. To exclude this possibility, one must show that all intermediate actions are *unavoidable*, that is, that S **psat** $\Diamond a_i$ is also satisfied for all a_i, $0 \le i \le n - 1$.

There are so-called pasttime variants of $\Box\phi$ and $\Diamond\phi$, denoted by $\blacksquare\phi$ and $\blacklozenge\phi$. For instance, $\blacklozenge\phi$ expresses that ϕ holds for some position j or some *earlier* position, i.e., for some $k < j$, s.t. $k \ge 0$.

The syntax of the fragment of temporal logic that we use is given in Table 12.2. In this table, a denotes an action name. We assume a given class of assertions p which is the same class as in earlier chapters, except that for program variables x we allow both x as well as its primed version x' to occur in expressions. We use standard abbreviations, such as $\phi_1 \vee \phi_2$ for $\neg(\neg\phi_1 \wedge \neg\phi_2)$.

We define a type of correctness formula of the form S **psat** ϕ, where S de-

Table 12.2. *Syntax of the Temporal Logic fragment* TL^-.

| TL^- *formulae* | $\phi ::=$ | $a \mid p \mid \phi_1 \wedge \phi_2 \mid \phi_1 \rightarrow \phi_2 \mid \neg\phi$ |
| | | $\mid \Box\phi \mid \Diamond\phi \mid \blacksquare\phi \mid \blacklozenge\phi$ |

notes an SVL^{++} program, possibly a closed program. Validity of the formula S **psat** ϕ expresses that all reactive sequences of S satisfy temporal logic formula ϕ. Similarly, (validity of) $\langle S \rangle$ **psat** ϕ expresses that all reactive sequences of $\langle S \rangle$, that is, all *connected* reactive sequences of S, satisfy the temporal formula ϕ. We remark that in the literature on temporal logic of reactive systems one uses a different type of correctness formula of the form "S **sat** ϕ". Often one simply specifies the temporal formula ϕ, and leaves the system S implicit. Such formulae require a temporal logic formula ϕ to hold for all finite and infinite computations of program $\langle S \rangle$. Our " **psat** " relation requires ϕ to hold for *terminating* computations only, and therefore is suited only for stating partial correctness properties, i.e., properties that should hold *for terminating computations*. The generalisation towards liveness properties, based on infinite computations, is outside the scope of this volume.

Let $\theta = \langle \sigma_0 \overset{a_0}{\rightarrow} \sigma_0' \rangle \ldots \langle \sigma_n \overset{a_n}{\rightarrow} \sigma_n' \rangle \in \mathcal{RA}[\![S]\!]$ be a reactive sequence of a program S, and (θ, j) abbreviate $\langle \sigma_j \overset{a_j}{\rightarrow} \sigma_j' \rangle$. We define the relation $(\theta, j) \models \phi$, i.e., " ϕ holds at position j in sequence θ", for all j, $0 \leq j \leq n$, as follows:

- For action names a, we define:

$$(\theta, j) \models a \text{ if } a_j = a.$$

- For assertion p we define:

$$(\theta, j) \models p \text{ if } \langle \sigma_j, \sigma_j' \rangle \models p.$$

Here the relation $\langle \sigma, \sigma' \rangle \models p$ is defined similarly to the relation $\sigma \models p$ in Chapter 5, except that it is understood that the value of *unprimed* variables x is interpreted as the value $\sigma(x)$, whereas the value of *primed* variables x' is interpreted as the value $\sigma'(x)$.

- For boolean connectives we define:

$$(\theta, j) \models \phi_1 \wedge \phi_2 \text{ if } (\theta, j) \models \phi_1 \text{ and } (\theta, j) \models \phi_2,$$
$$(\theta, j) \models \phi_1 \rightarrow \phi_2 \text{ if } (\theta, j) \models \phi_1 \text{ implies } (\theta, j) \models \phi_2,$$
$$(\theta, j) \models \neg\phi \text{ if not } (\theta, j) \models \phi.$$

- For temporal operators we define:

$$(\theta, j) \models \Box \phi \text{ if } (\theta, k) \models \phi \text{ for all } k, \ j \le k \le n,$$
$$(\theta, j) \models \Diamond \phi \text{ if } (\theta, k) \models \phi \text{ for some } k, \ j \le k \le n,$$
$$(\theta, j) \models \blacksquare \phi \text{ if } (\theta, k) \models \phi \text{ for all } k, \ 0 \le k \le j,$$
$$(\theta, j) \models \blacklozenge \phi \text{ if } (\theta, k) \models \phi \text{ for some } k, \ 0 \le k \le j.$$

Definition 12.4 (Meaning of a correctness formula) We define the meaning of a correctness formula as follows:

$$S \ \mathbf{psat} \ \phi \text{ is valid (or holds) if for all } \theta \in \mathcal{R}\mathcal{A}[\![S]\!], (\theta, 0) \models \phi$$

notation $\models S \ \mathbf{psat} \ \phi$. □

This style of defining the meaning of temporal logic formulae is called the "anchored version", and has been introduced in [MP89] (for connected sequences). "Anchored" here refers to the fixed reference point $j = 0$.

We introduce a number of general proof rules for temporal logic, aimed at verifying safety properties; they are not intended to provide a complete axiomatisation of these properties. Safety properties of a program express that the program maintains some invariant, which excludes 'bad' things from happening [Lam77], such as violation of the assertions of a proof outline. First we consider a collection of rules for open programs that are intended to show that certain state formulae are *preserved* while executing a given program S. Additional rules for closed programs are considered to show that certain state formulae are *invariants*. These rules can be seen as the temporal logic counterparts of the Owicki & Gries-style proof rules from Chapter 10. In fact, after introducing labels for all program locations, as explained in Section 10.4.3, an annotation for a parallel program S can be seen as a (rather formidable) state formula $\mathcal{G}I$ of the form:

$$\mathcal{G}I \overset{\text{def}}{=} \bigwedge_{l_i \in L} (\mathbf{at} \ l_i \to \phi_i),$$

where L is the collection of all labels for S, ϕ_i is the assertion that, within the proof outline at hand, is associated with the location labelled 'l_i', and **at** l_i is an auxiliary boolean variable which should be true iff control resides at location l_i. A claim that such an annotation is a proof outline can be compared to a proof of the temporal logic formula $S \ \mathbf{psat} \ \Box(\mathcal{G}I \to \mathcal{G}I')$. For an example we refer to the "global invariants", used in Example 10.23. The temporal logic counterpart of a proof outline for an open program S is a proof that a formula of the form $\mathcal{G}I$ is preserved by S. We now introduce the temporal proof rules that allow one to give such proofs. In the rules to follow, general temporal formulae are denoted by ϕ, ψ, whereas I denotes a state formula.

Rule 12.1 (Conjunction)

$$\frac{S \textbf{ psat } \phi_1, \ S \textbf{ psat } \phi_2}{S \textbf{ psat } \phi_1 \wedge \phi_2} .$$

Rule 12.2 (Consequence)

$$\frac{S \textbf{ psat } \phi, \ \phi \rightarrow \psi}{S \textbf{ psat } \psi} .$$

Rule 12.3 (Guarded assignment)

$$\frac{(I \wedge b) \rightarrow I[\bar{e}/\bar{x}]}{\langle b \rightarrow \bar{x} := \bar{e} \rangle \ \textbf{ psat } \Box(I \rightarrow I')} .$$

Rule 12.4 (Sequential composition)

$$\frac{S_1 \textbf{ psat } \Box(I \rightarrow I'), \ S_2 \textbf{ psat } \Box(I \rightarrow I')}{S_1 ; S_2 \textbf{ psat } \Box(I \rightarrow I')} .$$

Rule 12.5 (Choice)

$$\frac{S_i \textbf{ psat } \Box(I \rightarrow I'), \text{ for all } i \in \{1, \ldots, n\}}{\textbf{if } []_{i=1}^{n} S_i \ \textbf{fi} \ \textbf{ psat } \Box(I \rightarrow I')} .$$

Rule 12.6 (Do-loops)

$$\frac{S_B \textbf{ psat } \Box(I \rightarrow I'), \ S_E \textbf{ psat } \Box(I \rightarrow I')}{\textbf{do } S_B [] S_E ; \textbf{exit od psat } \Box(I \rightarrow I')} .$$

Rule 12.7 (Parallel composition)

$$\frac{S_1 \textbf{ psat } \Box(I \rightarrow I'), \ S_2 \textbf{ psat } \Box(I \rightarrow I')}{[S_1 \ || \ S_2] \textbf{ psat } \Box(I \rightarrow I')} .$$

Finally we have two rules that are of interest for *closed* programs. According to the semantics of SVL^{++}, every (necessarily connected) reactive sequence of $\langle S \rangle$ is also a possible reactive sequence of S. This fact, combined with the definition of the **psat** relation, then implies the following result:

Rule 12.8 (From open to closed programs)

$$\frac{S \text{ psat } \phi}{\langle S \rangle \text{ psat } \phi}.$$

If some state formula I holds initially, and is preserved by program S, than I will *always* hold for the closed program $\langle S \rangle$, since there are no other programs that could cause I to be violated. This is formulated as a proof rule:

Rule 12.9 (Invariants for closed programs)

$$\frac{S \text{ psat } \Box(I \to I')}{\langle S \rangle \text{ psat } I \to \Box I}.$$

These rules merely serve as an example illustrating how temporal logic can be used for proving safety properties of certain open and closed programs.

12.5.1 Action Ordering

Apart from verifying invariants, temporal logic can be used to specify and verify the ordering of actions occurring in some parallel program. Action ordering plays a major rôle in the transformation laws for parallel programs, which we discuss in the next section.

Definition 12.5 (Action ordering) For actions a_1 and a_2, we define the *weak precedence relation* $a_1 \twoheadrightarrow a_2$:

$$a_1 \twoheadrightarrow a_2 \overset{\text{def}}{=} \Box(a_1 \to \neg \blacklozenge a_2). \qquad \Box$$

Informally, $a_1 \twoheadrightarrow a_2$ requires that when both a_1 and a_2 occur in some execution sequence, then all a_1-events precede all a_2-events within that execution sequence. Note that this relation does not require a_1 or a_2 to be executed at all; for instance, an execution sequence with some a_2-event but no a_1-event does satisfy "$a_1 \twoheadrightarrow a_2$". This explains why the ordering is called "weak".

So, weak precedence is expressed by a temporal logic formula. The question is: how does one *verify* such formulae , and in particular, how does one verify $\Box(a_1 \to \neg \blacklozenge a_2)$ within the Owicki & Gries-style proof method? Let us assume that we have a closed program $\langle S \rangle$ with actions a_1 and a_2, and we would like to verify the property $a_1 \twoheadrightarrow a_2$. One would like to construct a proof outline for S, in the sense of Chapter 10, where the precondition for action a_1, say $pre(a_1)$, would imply the formula $\neg \blacklozenge a_2$. Formally speaking this would not be possible since $pre(a_1)$ is a state formula, whereas a temporal formula such as $\neg \blacklozenge a_2$

cannot be interpreted in a single state. Fortunately, the formula that we are interested in is expressed by means of pasttime operators only, and therefore one can transform it into a state formula by introducing auxiliary variables. In this case one introduces a fresh boolean auxiliary variable "$a_2.occ$" that records whether a_2 did occur at least once thus far, or not. Let action a_2 be of the form $\langle b_2 \to \bar{x}_2 := \bar{e}_2 \rangle$. Then one modifies the program S and constructs a proof outline for S, as follows:

- The action a_2 in S is replaced by $\langle b_2 \to \bar{x}_2, a_2.occ := \bar{e}_2, true \rangle$. No other assignments to $a_2.occ$ are added within S.
- Construct a proof outline $\{\neg a_2.occ\} A(S) \{q\}$, cf. Chapter 10, for S such that the verification condition $pre(a_1) \to \neg a_2.occ$ is valid.

Then S satisfies the condition $a_1 \twoheadrightarrow a_2$.

Theorem 12.6 (Verifying action ordering)
Let $\{\neg a_2.occ\} A(S) \{q\}$ be a proof outline for program S, augmented with an auxiliary variable $a_2.occ$ as described above. Let the precondition for action a_1 in this proof outline be denoted by $pre(a_1)$ and assume that $\models pre(a_1) \to \neg a_2.occ$. Then $\langle S \rangle$ **psat** $a_1 \twoheadrightarrow a_2$ holds.

Proof Let η be some reactive sequence of $\langle S \rangle$, and assume, to the contrary, that η does not satisfy the formula $a_1 \twoheadrightarrow a_2$. That is, $\eta \not\models a_1 \to \neg \blacklozenge a_2$. From the interpretation of temporal logic, it follows that η must be of the form below, where actions a_1 and a_2 occur at least once, and moreover, at least one a_2-event precedes at least one a_1-event, as indicated:

$$\eta = \langle \sigma_0 \xrightarrow{\bar{a}} \sigma_0' \rangle \dots \langle \sigma_i \xrightarrow{a_2} \sigma_i' \rangle \dots \langle \sigma_j \xrightarrow{a_1} \sigma_j' \rangle \dots$$

Note that $a_2.occ$ is an auxiliary variable. It is not used in boolean guards, nor does its value affect the values assigned to other program variables of $\langle S \rangle$. If σ_0 does not satisfy the condition $\neg a_2.occ$, then we construct a variant η' of η that is like η except for the values assigned to $a_2.occ$. Because of the auxiliary-variable nature of $a_2.occ$ we can choose these values such that the initial state of η' does satisfy $\neg a_2.occ$, and, moreover, η' is a $\langle S \rangle$ computation and $\eta' \not\models a_1 \to \neg \blacklozenge a_2$. Because of this reason we assume from now on, without loss of generality, that σ_0 satisfies the condition $\neg a_2.occ$. From the assumption that action a_2 incorporates the assignment "$a_2.occ := true$" we infer that $\sigma_i'(a_2.occ) = true$. Because $\langle S \rangle$ is a closed program, η is a *connected* sequence. From this, and the assumption that no other assignments to $a_2.occ$ falsify $a_2.occ$ inside S, we infer that for all $k > i$, we have that $\sigma_k(a_2.occ) =$

$\sigma'_k(a_2.occ) = true$. This in particular implies that $\sigma_j(a_2.occ) = true$. However, from the assumption that $\{\neg a_2.occ\}A(S)\{q\}$ is a proof outline for S and the fact that we assume that η has an initial state satisfying $\neg a_2.occ$, it follows that in state σ_j the condition $pre(a_1)$ holds, which in turn implies that $\sigma_j(a_2.occ) = false$. From this contradiction we infer that $\langle S \rangle$ has no computations like η, and therefore all $\langle S \rangle$ computations satisfy the formula $a_1 \twoheadrightarrow a_2$.

$\square$

A slightly more powerful version of this theorem is presented in Exercise 12.6. Observe that although the premise of Theorem 12.6 requires that one constructs a proof outline for a program S, the *conclusion* of the theorem is about the *closed* program $\langle S \rangle$. The reason for this is that the mere existence of a proof outline $\{p\}A(S)\{q\}$ for S in isolation does not imply invariance of its associated inductive assertion network when S were executed in parallel with another program S'. In that case the verification conditions of the combined network would not necessarily be fulfilled because there is no guarantee that the assertions contained in $\{p\}A(S)\{q\}$ are invariant under the actions of S'. Note that S *itself* could be a parallel program too. In that case, Definition 10.8 of proof outline $\{p\}A(S)\{q\}$ requires the usual interference freedom tests for the parallel components of S.

Theorem 12.6 begs the question why do we use weak precedence relations to verify programs. After all, the theorem suggests that you must *already* have a proof outline in order to show that certain precedence relations hold. However, the strategy that we propose *for verifying the distributed program S_D* is as follows:

- First, set up a proof outline that is used *only* to verify weak precedence properties of S_D. That is, this proof outline does not show the correctness of S_D with respect to its specification by means of the pre- and postconditions p and q. Therefore, this proof outline can usually be fairly simple.

- Second, after having verified the necessary weak precedence properties of S_D, forget the first proof outline, and use these precedence properties in combination with one of the communication-closed-layers laws, that are discussed later on in this chapter, to transform the original distributed program S_D into a *simplified* layered version S_L.

- Finally, use new proof outlines to show the correctness of the layered version S_L with respect to the original specification of the program.

In practice the proof outlines needed to verify precedence properties follow a few predefined patterns. We explore some of these patterns below. For some of these, we must consider program fragment S *within a certain larger program context.* When a program S is part of a larger context, we denote the program as a whole by "$C[S]$", where "$C[\cdot]$" denotes the rest of the program, surrounding S. One calls a construct of the form "$C[\cdot]$" a *context*, where the "dot" suggests that an arbitrary program S can be substituted for "$\cdot$" inside C.

Theorem 12.7 (Ordering caused by sequential composition)
Assume that S_1 is a program containing action label a_1 and S_2 is a program containing action label a_2. Let $C[S]$ denote program S in a certain context such that the S component does not occur inside the body of any loop construct, and S occurs only once inside $C[S]$. Then $\langle C[S_1 ; S_2]\rangle$ **psat** $a_1 \twoheadrightarrow a_2$ holds.

Proof **(Sketch)**
We construct a proof outline for $C[S_1 ; S_2]$ that can be used in Theorem 12.6 to verify $\langle C[S_1 ; S_2]\rangle$ **psat** $a_1 \twoheadrightarrow a_2$. For $C[S_1 ; S_2]$ as a whole, we use a proof outline of the form $\{\neg a_2.occ\}A(C[S_1 ; S_2])\{true\}$. For the locations inside C, we construct a proof outline by means of induction on the structure of C. In the cases discussed below we split C into parts. For instance, C might be of the form $C_1 ; C_2$, where C_1 or C_2 (but not both, since S occurs only once inside $C[S]$) contains the $S_1 ; S_2$ part. The proof outline for the latter part is then constructed inductively. The other part, i.e., the one *not* containing $S_1 ; S_2$ always has a postcondition that is either *true* or else it equals its precondition; we choose for all locations *inside* this part the same assertion as the postcondition. Since the $S_1 ; S_2$ part is assumed not to occur inside the body of a loop, we distinguish the following cases:

- $C[S_1 ; S_2]$ has the form $C_1[S_1 ; S_2] ; C_2$. Choose as annotation:

$$\{\neg a_2.occ\}A(C_1[S_1 ; S_2]) ; \{true\}A(C_2)\{true\}.$$

- $C[S_1 ; S_2]$ has the form $C_1 ; C_2[S_1 ; S_2]$. Choose as annotation:

$$\{\neg a_2.occ\}A(C_1) ; \{\neg a_2.occ\}A(C_2[S_1 ; S_2])\{true\}.$$

- $C[S_1 ; S_2]$ has the form **if** $C_1 [] \cdots [] C_i[S_1 ; S_2] [] \cdots [] C_n$ **fi**. Choose as annotation:

$$\{\neg a_2.occ\}\textbf{if } A(C_1) [] \cdots [] A(C_i[S_1 ; S_2]) [] \cdots [] A(C_n) \textbf{ fi} \{true\}.$$

- $C[S_1 ; S_2]$ has the form $[C_1[S_1 ; S_2] \| C_2]$. Choose as annotation:

$$\{\neg a_2.occ\}[\{\neg a_2.occ\}A(C_1[S_1;S_2])\{true\} \| \{true\}A(C_2)\{true\}]\{true\}.$$

Finally we must choose assertions for locations inside $S_1 ; S_2$. The construction above associates the following pre- and postcondition with the $S_1 ; S_2$ part: $\{\neg a_2.occ\}A(S_1 ; S_2)\{true\}$. We extend this to an annotation for the whole of

S_1; S_2. All locations inside S_1 are assigned the assertion $\{\neg a_2.occ\}$, whereas the entry location of S_2 as well as all locations inside S_2 are assigned the assertion $\{true\}$.

Note that in particular the action labelled by a_1 receives the precondition $\{\neg a_2.occ\}$.

The last task is then to check that the annotation constructed above is a valid proof outline. This is straightforward. For instance, in the above second case this follows because:

- Action a_2 does not occur inside C_1, and, hence, the value of $a_2.occ$ is preserved by the guarded actions of C_1; therefore, the annotated program $\{\neg a_2.occ\}A(C_1)\{\neg a_2.occ\}$ associating $\neg a_2.occ$ with all the internal locations of C_1 is a proof outline.
- $\{\neg a_2.occ\}A(C_2[S_1 ; S_2])\{true\}$ is a proof outline according to the induction hypothesis.
- Once $\{\neg a_2.occ\}A(C_1)\{\neg a_2.occ\}$ and $\{\neg a_2.occ\}A(C_2[S_1 ; S_2])\{true\}$ are proof outlines, $\{\neg a_2.occ\}A(C_1)$; $\{\neg a_2.occ\}A(C_2[S_1 ; S_2])\{true\}$ is a proof outline . This follows from Definitions 9.20 case (i), 9.21 case (ii), 9.23 cases (i) and (ii), and Lemma 9.16 case (i).

In the fourth case above, the interference freedom tests are satisfied because C_2 does not contain any actions changing the value of $a_2.occ$.   □

An alternative method for imposing and deducing an ordering is based upon *binary semaphores*. Recall that a binary semaphore is a boolean shared variable s that is initialised to "*true*", and that is read and modified exclusively by $P(s)$ and $V(s)$ operations, where we define:

- $P(s) \stackrel{\text{def}}{=} \langle s \to s := false \rangle$
- $V(s) \stackrel{\text{def}}{=} \langle \neg s \to s := true \rangle$.

Theorem 12.8 (Ordering caused by semaphores)
Let S_1 and S_2 be programs containing a single $P(s)$ operation within S_1, and a single $V(s)$ operation within S_2. Then

$$\models \langle S_1 \parallel S_2 \rangle \ \mathbf{psat} \ \ s \to (P(s) \twoheadrightarrow V(s)).$$

Proof Exercise 12.2.   □

Weak precedence is *not* a transitive relation, that is, from $a_1 \twoheadrightarrow a_2$ and $a_2 \twoheadrightarrow a_3$ it does *not* follow that $a_1 \twoheadrightarrow a_3$ holds, for some computation η. To see this, consider some reactive sequence η with no a_2-events at all. Then $a_1 \twoheadrightarrow a_2$ and $a_2 \twoheadrightarrow a_3$ both hold for η, trivially. But of course $a_1 \twoheadrightarrow a_3$ need not hold for η.

This "counterexample" suggests a useful theorem. Assume that the program S satisfies the formula $\Diamond a_2$, so we know that in every computation of S at least one a_2-event occurs. Informally, we say that a_2 is *unavoidable*. Now, if in this situation the formulae $a_1 \twoheadrightarrow a_2$ and $a_2 \twoheadrightarrow a_3$ are valid for S, then one may conclude that $a_1 \twoheadrightarrow a_3$ is also a valid formula for S. To prove this, assume to the contrary that there exists an execution sequence where some a_1-event occurs that is preceded by some a_3-event. We know that some a_2-event is also bound to occur. By the $a_1 \twoheadrightarrow a_2$ and $a_2 \twoheadrightarrow a_3$ relations, it follows that this a_2-event has to follow the a_1-event and precede the a_3-event. This contradicts the assumption that the a_3-event precedes the a_1-event, and so, by reductio ad absurdum, we conclude that $a_1 \twoheadrightarrow a_3$ must be valid for S. We formulate a theorem below that is a simple extension of what we have just shown.

Theorem 12.9 (Conditional transitivity of action ordering)
Let a_1 and a_2 be action names and let $\tilde{a}_i$, where $i \in I$ for some nonempty finite index set I, be an action name. If S **psat** $a_1 \twoheadrightarrow \tilde{a}_i$ and S **psat** $\tilde{a}_i \twoheadrightarrow a_2$ hold, for all $i \in I$, and S **psat** $((\Diamond a_1 \wedge \Diamond a_2) \to \bigvee_{i \in I} \Diamond \tilde{a}_i)$ also holds, then S **psat** $a_1 \twoheadrightarrow a_2$ holds.

Proof Exercise 12.3. □

We do not aim to formulate a complete proof system for temporal logic here (the interested reader is referred to [MP91b], or to [Lam94a]). Rather, we provide a few basic rules, and thereafter concentrate on simple rules that we need in order to prove order constraints. We emphasise that some of these rules are formulated for *open* programs. Recall that S **psat** $\Diamond a$ means that in every reactive sequence of S, action a is executed. This is a much stronger requirement than the claim that $\Diamond a$ holds for a *closed* program $\langle S \rangle$. For the latter, only connected sequences are considered. Informally, the formula S **psat** $\Diamond a$, for an open program S, implies that a will be executed by S, *regardless of what a possible parallel environment might do*. For example, consider the program

$$S_1 \equiv x := 1 \,;\, \textbf{if } x = 1 \textbf{ then } a : y := 1 \textbf{ fi} \,.$$

If one interprets S_1 as a closed program, as is usually done in the literature on temporal logic, then S_1 clearly satisfies the formula $\Diamond a$. But if S_1 is considered to be an open program, then S_1 **psat** $\Diamond a$ is not a valid formula. To see this, consider a parallel environment of the form $S_2 \equiv x := 2$. It will be clear that the a action is not executed for every terminating computation of $S_1 \parallel S_2$, so that $\Diamond a$ is not valid for S_1. Because the distinction between open programs and closed programs is rather important, we make it clearly visible, by using S for open, and $\langle S \rangle$ for closed programs. Using this notation, we can now say that

$\langle S_1 \rangle$ **psat** $\Diamond a$ is valid, whereas S_1 **psat** $\Diamond a$ is *not*. We also stress that the theorem below is formulated in terms of the "S **psat** ϕ" relation, which requires formula ϕ to hold for *terminating* computations only. A nonterminating program S satisfies *every* partial correctness formula of the form $\{p\} S \{q\}$, and also satisfies *every* formula of the form S **psat** ϕ. So, a formula of the form S **psat** $\Diamond a$ should be read as: "If S terminates, then at some moment during the execution of S an a action must have occurred". This is the reason why a formula of the form $a : \langle b \to \bar{x} := \bar{e} \rangle$ **psat** $\Diamond a$ is valid, because, *if* the program terminates, it must have executed the a action.

Theorem 12.10 (Properties of $\Diamond$ for open programs)

- $a : A$ **psat** $\Diamond a$ holds, for every action $A \in act$.

- If S_1 **psat** $\Diamond a$ holds then, for any S_2, $S_1 ; S_2$ **psat** $\Diamond a$ and $S_2 ; S_1$ **psat** $\Diamond a$ hold.

- If S_1 **psat** $\Diamond a$ holds then, for any S_2, $[S_1 \parallel S_2]$ **psat** $\Diamond a$ and $[S_2 \parallel S_1]$ **psat** $\Diamond a$ hold.

- If S_i **psat** $\Diamond a_i$ holds for $i = 1, \ldots, n$, then **if** $[]_{i=1}^{n} b_i \to S_i$ **fi** **psat** $\bigvee_{i=1,\ldots,n} \Diamond a_i$ holds.

Proof We give a proof of the claim that the validity of S_1 **psat** $\Diamond a$ implies that $[S_1 \parallel S_2]$ **psat** $\Diamond a$ holds. The proof of the other claims is in the same style and is left as an exercise. So, assume that S_1 **psat** $\Diamond a$ is valid. Let η be a reactive sequence of $[S_1 \parallel S_2]$. From Definition 12.1 it follows that η is the interleaving of two reactive sequences η_1 and η_2, where η_i is a reactive sequence of S_i, for $i = 1, 2$. Because S_1 **psat** $\Diamond a$ is valid, every reactive sequence of S_1 satisfies the formula $\Diamond a$, and in particular, η_1 satisfies $\Diamond a$, that is, one of the computation steps in η_1 has a as its label. But then η, which includes all η_1 steps, also has at least one a-labelled step, and so satisfies $\Diamond a$. Since η was an arbitrary reactive sequence of $[S_1 \parallel S_2]$, we have shown that $[S_1 \parallel S_2]$ **psat** $\Diamond a$ is valid. □

12.6 The Communication-Closed-Layers Laws

We discuss a group of related program transformations, collectively referred to as "Communication-Closed-Layers laws" (CCL laws). The phrase "communication closed" stems from a paper by Tzilla Elrad and Nissim Francez [EF82], where communication closedness of CSP programs was introduced. We refer here to a more general setting where we ask under which conditions an arbitrary program S_L of the form $[S_{0,0} \parallel S_{0,1}] ; [S_{1,0} \parallel S_{1,1}]$ can be considered equivalent to a program S_D of the form $[(S_{0,0}\,;S_{1,0})\;\|\;(S_{0,1}\,;S_{1,1})]$. The interest here lies in program development where one starts off with *(sequentially-) layered* programs S_L, which are considered simpler to design and verify than *distributed programs* S_D. After S_L has been verified, it is then *transformed* into the form S_D.

There are a number of related transformation laws, where the variation originates from the following factors:

- A variation in communication mechanisms is possible. For example, CSP-style communication or shared-variable-based communication.

- The side conditions under which the equivalence holds. There is a choice between simple syntactic conditions and more complex verification conditions, where the latter are applicable in more general situations than the simple ones.

- The notion of program equivalence that we are interested in. As a minimum we will require that "equivalent" programs define the same initial-final state relation when we consider them as state transformers. This implies that equivalent programs satisfy the same Hoare formulae for partial correctness. A stronger condition is to insist that "equivalent" programs have the same deadlock behaviour. By this we mean that when two programs S_1 and S_2 are "equivalent" and one of them, say S_1, cannot get into a deadlocked configuration when started in some initial state σ, then S_2 will not deadlock either when started in σ. Next, one might define "equivalence" as *semantic equality*, based on the *Comp* semantics defined in Chapter 2. Programs S_1 and S_2 are considered equivalent iff they have the same sets of computations, i.e., when $Comp\,[\![S_1]\!] = Comp\,[\![S_2]\!]$. The latter is clearly a rather strong requirement, implying that S_1 and S_2 have the same initial-final state behaviour, the same deadlock behaviour as well as the same divergence behaviour. On top of that we know that any temporal logic formula satisfied by S_1 would also be satisfied by S_2 and vice versa. Moreover, we know that semantic equality yields not only an equivalence but even what is called a *congruence*. To understand congruences, consider the case where (say) S_1 is a syntactic component of a larger SVL^{++} program, say of the form $C[S_1]$. Program congruence (w.r.t. the observability criterion of initial-final state behaviour) states that when S_1 is congruent to S_2, then $C[S_1]$ and $C[S_2]$ should display the same initial-final state behaviour, for any possible context $C[\cdot]$ within the given programming language SVL^{++}. We recall the discussion in Chapter 3, where it was shown that program equivalence based on initial-final state behaviour is *not* a congruence. For instance, consider $S_1 \equiv x := x+1\,;x := x+1$ versus $S_2 \equiv x := x+2$. Obviously, S_1 and S_2 have the same initial-final state behaviour. Yet, when placed in a context $C[\cdot]$ of the form $z := x \parallel \cdot$, one then sees that $C[S_1] \equiv z := x \parallel (x := x+1; x := x+1)$ and $C[S_2] \equiv z := x \parallel x := x+2$ do *not* have the same initial-final state behaviour.

Despite the obvious advantages of program congruence there is also a serious disadvantage: if "equivalent" programs are required to have identical computations, then not much room for interesting transformations remains. In this chapter we therefore focus on equivalence in the sense of identical initial-final state behaviour.

Definition 12.11 (io-equivalence) We define io-equivalence for SVL^{++} programs, denoted by $S_1 \stackrel{IO}{=} S_2$ iff $O_{cl}[\![S_1]\!] = O_{cl}[\![S_2]\!]$, where O_{cl} is the semantics given by Definition 12.2, see also Theorem 12.3. □

Note that io-equivalence, because it is based on the O_{cl} semantics, considers programs as *closed* programs, in accordance with our explanation above that io-equivalence is not a congruence. In the sections below we show soundness of various transformation laws by considering the action-labelled reactive-sequence semantics $\mathcal{RA}[\![S]\!]$ of programs. From the definition of io-equivalence and the definitions of the semantic functions it follows that io-equivalence between S_1 and S_2 holds iff the following is true: For any computation $\eta \in \mathcal{RA}[\![\langle S_1 \rangle]\!]$ (respectively, $\mathcal{RA}[\![\langle S_2 \rangle]\!]$) of the form

$$\langle \sigma_0 \stackrel{a_0}{\to} \sigma_1 \rangle \langle \sigma_1 \stackrel{a_1}{\to} \sigma_2 \rangle \ldots \langle \sigma_{n-1} \stackrel{a_{n-1}}{\to} \sigma \rangle$$

there is a computation $\eta' \in \mathcal{RA}[\![\langle S_2 \rangle]\!]$ (respectively, $\mathcal{RA}[\![\langle S_1 \rangle]\!]$) of the form

$$\langle \sigma_0 \stackrel{a'_0}{\to} \sigma'_1 \rangle \langle \sigma'_1 \stackrel{a'_1}{\to} \sigma'_2 \rangle \ldots \langle \sigma'_{m-1} \stackrel{a'_{m-1}}{\to} \sigma \rangle.$$

That is, for any possible computation η which starts with an initial state σ_0 and terminates in a state σ of one of the two programs, there is an io-equivalent computation η', i.e., with the same initial and final state, for the other program. Note that io-equivalent computations need not go through the same intermediate states, and that they need not be of the same length.

Theorem 12.12

Let S and S' be io-equivalent programs and let $C[\cdot]$ be a context such that S is not a statement within a parallel component of $C[S]$, i.e., S is not within the scope of a parallel composition operator inside $C[S]$, cf. Definition 10.20. Then

$$C[S] \stackrel{IO}{=} C[S'].$$

Proof See Exercise 12.4. □

This theorem implies that io-equivalence is a congruence for the language GCL of Chapter 9.

12.6.1 CCL Laws for Shared Variables

The CCL laws for shared variables are based on the fairly simple idea of *syntactically-commuting actions*. First, let a be the name of some $\langle b \to \bar{x} := \bar{e} \rangle$ action. We define the set of read variables $R(a) \stackrel{\text{def}}{=} var(b) \cup var(\bar{e})$, and the set of write variables $W(a) \stackrel{\text{def}}{=} \{x_1, \ldots, x_n\}$, where $\bar{x} = \langle x_1, \ldots, x_n \rangle$. We say that two actions $a_1 \equiv \langle b_1 \to \bar{x}_1 := \bar{e}_1 \rangle$ and $a_2 \equiv \langle b_2 \to \bar{x}_2 := \bar{e}_2 \rangle$ are *syntactically commuting* if the following three conditions are satisfied:

(i) $W(a_1) \cap R(a_2) = \emptyset$,
(ii) $W(a_2) \cap R(a_1) = \emptyset$,
(iii) $W(a_1) \cap W(a_2) = \emptyset$.

Actions which do not syntactically commute are said to be *in conflict* and, depending on which condition above is violated, we speak of read-write or write-write conflicts. When a_1 and a_2 are in conflict we denote this by $a_1 - a_2$ and otherwise, i.e., when they commute syntactically, by $a_1 \not\!\!\!- a_2$.

Definition 12.13 (Concurrent actions) Two actions a and a' occurring in S are called *concurrent* actions if there are two different parallel components S_1 and S_2 of S, cf. Definition 10.20, such that a occurs in S_1 and a' occurs in S_2. □

The soundness of the CCL laws that we discuss below depends on the following principal property of commuting concurrent actions:

Lemma 12.14 (Commuting actions) Let a and a' be concurrent actions of a closed program $\langle S \rangle$ and suppose that a and a' are syntactically-commuting actions, i.e., $a \not\!\!\!- a'$. Let $\eta \in \mathcal{RA}[\![\langle S \rangle]\!]$ be a computation of $\langle S \rangle$, of the form:

$$\langle \sigma_0 \stackrel{a_0}{\to} \sigma_1 \rangle \ldots \langle \sigma_{i-1} \stackrel{a_{i-1}}{\to} \sigma_i \rangle \langle \sigma_i \stackrel{a_i}{\to} \sigma_{i+1} \rangle \langle \sigma_{i+1} \stackrel{a_{i+1}}{\to} \sigma_{i+2} \rangle \langle \sigma_{i+2} \stackrel{a_{i+2}}{\to} \sigma_{i+3} \rangle \ldots .$$

Assume that for some index i, event a_i is an occurrence of action a, and a_{i+1} is an occurrence of a'. Let η' be defined as η with a_i and a_{i+1} exchanged, i.e., of the form:

$$\langle \sigma_0 \stackrel{a_0}{\to} \sigma_1 \rangle \ldots \langle \sigma_{i-1} \stackrel{a_{i-1}}{\to} \sigma_i \rangle \langle \sigma_i \stackrel{a_{i+1}}{\to} \sigma'_{i+1} \rangle \langle \sigma'_{i+1} \stackrel{a_i}{\to} \sigma_{i+2} \rangle \langle \sigma_{i+2} \stackrel{a_{i+2}}{\to} \sigma_{i+3} \rangle \ldots ,$$

where σ'_{i+1} results from applying action a_{i+1} to σ_i. We claim that η', also, is a computation of $\langle S \rangle$. That is: $\eta' \in \mathcal{R}\mathcal{A}[\![\langle S \rangle]\!]$.

Proof Note that η' determines the same sequence of states except for state σ'_{i+1}, which in general differs from σ_{i+1}. We take a closer look at these two states. Let a and a' be of the form $\langle b_1 \to \bar{x}_1 := \bar{e}_1 \rangle$ and $\langle b_2 \to \bar{x}_2 := \bar{e}_2 \rangle$, respectively. The semantics from Chapter 5 for expressions and boolean guards associates conditions c_1 and c_2 with b_1 and b_2, and state transformations f_1 and f_2 with the assignments $\bar{x}_1 := \bar{e}_1$ and $\bar{x}_2 := \bar{e}_2$. From the semantic definitions we derive the following facts:

- $c_1(\sigma_i) = tt$,
- $\sigma_{i+1} = f_1(\sigma_i)$,
- $c_2(\sigma_{i+1}) = tt$,
- $\sigma_{i+2} = f_2(\sigma_{i+1})$.

From the assumption that $a \not\to a'$ one can infer the following:

- $c_1 \circ f_2 = c_1$,
- $f_2 \circ f_1 = f_1 \circ f_2$,
- $c_2 \circ f_1 = c_2$.

Moreover, the assumption that a and a' occur in distinct parallel components of S implies that when execution has reached state σ_i then the locations reached within these parallel components are those in front of a and a'. Executing a in this situation will not affect the control location of the component in which a' resides, and vice versa, executing a' does not affect the control location for a. If we define $\sigma'_{i+1} = f_2(\sigma_i)$ then from the facts above we infer the following:

- $c_2(\sigma_i) = tt$,
- $c_1(\sigma'_{i+1}) = tt$,
- $\sigma_{i+2} = f_1(\sigma'_{i+1})$.

Consequently, executing action a will neither enable nor disable a', and vice versa, executing a' does not affect enabledness of a. Therefore, we may conclude that η' as introduced in the lemma is indeed a computation of $\langle S \rangle$. $\square$

The next theorem is the first example of a CCL law. It is based on the independence of program fragments, where we define $S_1 \not\to S_2$ by requiring that for all actions a_1 occurring in S_1 and all actions a_2 occurring in S_2 we have that $a_1 \not\to a_2$.

Theorem 12.15 (Communication-Closed-Layers 1)
Let S_L and S_D be programs defined as follows:

$$S_L \stackrel{\text{def}}{=} \begin{matrix} [S_{0,0} \quad || \quad \cdots \quad || \quad S_{0,m}] \\ ; \\ \vdots \qquad \vdots \qquad \vdots \\ ; \\ [S_{n,0} \quad || \quad \cdots \quad || \quad S_{n,m}] \end{matrix}$$

and

$$S_D \stackrel{\text{def}}{=} \begin{bmatrix} S_{0,0} & || & \cdots & || & S_{0,m} \\ ; & & \cdots & & ; \\ \vdots & || & \vdots & || & \vdots \\ ; & & \cdots & & ; \\ S_{n,0} & || & \cdots & || & S_{n,m} \end{bmatrix}.$$

Assume that $S_{i,j} \not\vdash S_{i',j'}$ for $i \neq i'$ and $j \neq j'$, then $S_L \stackrel{IO}{=} S_D$. $\qquad\square$

The intuitive justification of this law is simple. Consider the simple case where $S_L \stackrel{\text{def}}{=} [S_{0,0} \ || \ S_{0,1}] ; [S_{1,0} \ || \ S_{1,1}]$ and $S_D \stackrel{\text{def}}{=} [S_{0,0} ; S_{1,0} \ || \ S_{0,1} ; S_{1,1}]$. It will be clear that any computation for $\langle S_L \rangle$ is also a possible computation for $\langle S_D \rangle$. The reverse does not in general hold, since, for instance, $S_{1,0}$ actions can occur in S_D as soon as the $S_{0,0}$ part has terminated, so possibly *before* the $S_{0,1}$ part has terminated. However, since it is assumed in the above theorem that $S_{0,1}$ actions and $S_{1,0}$ actions commute syntactically, such computations are equivalent to computations where $S_{1,0}$ actions occur only *after* all $S_{0,1}$ actions, that is, such $\langle S_D \rangle$ computations are equivalent to some $\langle S_L \rangle$ computation. Although a proof, using Lemma 12.14, is simple, we do not provide a formal proof here, since Theorem 12.15 follows as a simple corollary from our second CCL law. The idea of this second CCL law is as follows. Assume that we have programs S_L and S_D as above, but this time assume, for instance, that condition $S_{1,0} \not\vdash S_{0,1}$ does *not* hold. That is, there are actions a_1 in $S_{0,1}$ and a_2 in $S_{1,0}$ such that $a_1 - a_2$. In general, an S_D computation where an instance of a_2 precedes an instance of a_1 will not be equivalent to any S_L computation. Let us assume, however, that (for all such pairs of conflicting actions) we can show that S_D satisfies the formula $a_1 \twoheadrightarrow a_2$. That is, a_2-events simply do not precede a_1-events. Then reasoning as above S_D computations can be shown to be equivalent to S_L computations via the technique of permuting occurrences of commuting actions.

We introduce some extra notation in order to formulate our second version of the CCL law. For actions a_1 and a_2 let $a_1 \stackrel{C}{\twoheadrightarrow} a_2$ abbreviate the formula $a_1 \twoheadrightarrow$

a_2 if $a_1 - a_2$, and let it denote *"true"* otherwise. We call $a_1 \overset{C}{\twoheadrightarrow} a_2$ "conflict-based ordering". We extend the notation to programs: $S_1 \overset{C}{\twoheadrightarrow} S_2$ abbreviates the following formula:

$$\bigwedge \{a_1 \overset{C}{\twoheadrightarrow} a_2 \mid a_1 \text{ occurs in } S_1, a_2 \text{ occurs in } S_2\}.$$

Informally, $S_1 \overset{C}{\twoheadrightarrow} S_2$ expresses that a_1-events of S_1 precede those a_2-events of S_2 that are in conflict with them.

Theorem 12.16 (Communication-Closed-Layers 2)

Let S_L and S_D be programs defined as follows:

$$S_L \overset{\text{def}}{=} \begin{array}{ccc} [S_{0,0} & \| \quad \cdots \quad \| & S_{0,m}] \\ & ; & \\ \vdots & \vdots & \vdots \\ & ; & \\ [S_{n,0} & \| \quad \cdots \quad \| & S_{n,m}] \end{array}$$

and

$$S_D \overset{\text{def}}{=} \begin{bmatrix} S_{0,0} & \| & \cdots & \| & S_{0,m} \\ ; & & \cdots & & ; \\ \vdots & \| & \vdots & \| & \vdots \\ ; & & \cdots & & ; \\ S_{n,0} & \| & \cdots & \| & S_{n,m} \end{bmatrix}.$$

Assume that $\models \langle S_D \rangle$ **psat** $(S_{i,j} \overset{C}{\twoheadrightarrow} S_{i',j'})$ holds for all $i < i'$ and $j \neq j'$. Then $S_L \overset{IO}{=} S_D$.

Proof We must show that for every computation in $\mathcal{RA}[\![\langle S_L \rangle]\!]$ there is an equivalent computation in $\mathcal{RA}[\![\langle S_D \rangle]\!]$, and vice versa.

It follows from the semantic definitions that when $\eta \in \mathcal{RA}[\![\langle S_L \rangle]\!]$, then also $\eta \in \mathcal{RA}[\![\langle S_D \rangle]\!]$, which constitutes the easy half of the proof.

For the reverse case, we only consider the case $n = 1$. The general case $n > 1$ can be shown analogously. So assume $\eta \in \mathcal{RA}[\![\langle S_D \rangle]\!]$. It follows from the semantic definitions that η is an interleaving of events $S_{0,0}; S_{1,0}, S_{0,1}; S_{1,1}, \ldots$, and $S_{0,m}; S_{1,m}$. In general, η will contain $S_{1,j}$-events a_1 that precede $S_{0,j'}$-events a_0, for some $j \neq j'$. Let k denote the number of such event pairs (a_1, a_0). We show by induction on k that η is equivalent to some $\langle S_L \rangle$ computation.

First, assume that $k = 0$. Then, apparently, η can be split in two parts, the first half consisting only of events stemming from $S_{0,j}$, the second half containing only events stemming from $S_{1,j'}$. It is easily seen that in this special case η is *itself* a possible computation of $\langle S_L \rangle$.

Second, assume that the claim has been shown for a certain value k. Assume that η has $k+1$ pairs of actions (a_1, a_0) as indicated. We claim that we can identify at least one pair (a_1, a_0) such that a_0 *immediately follows* a_1 within η.

To prove this claim one reasons as follows. Let a_0 be the *first* $S_{0,j}$-event that is preceded by some $S_{1,j'}$ action. Then, for this choice of a_0, let a_1 be the *last* $S_{1,j'}$ action that precedes a_0. The action (immediately) following a_1 cannot be some $S_{1,j'}$ action, since it would precede a_0 and still be later than a_1. Therefore, a_1 is immediately followed by some $S_{0,j}$ action. It cannot be anything else but a_0, because otherwise we would have found some $S_{0,j}$ action *earlier* than a_0 that is preceded by some $S_{1,j'}$ action.

Now, returning to the main proof, assume that we have some pair (a_1, a_0) such that a_0 immediately follows a_1 within η, and assume, without loss of generality, that a_0 stems from some $S_{0,0}$ action a_0 and a_1 from some $S_{1,1}$ action a_1. From the assumption that $\models \langle S_D \rangle$ **psat** $S_{0,0} \overset{C}{\twoheadrightarrow} S_{1,1}$ it follows that a_0 and a_1 must be commuting actions, i.e., $a_0 \nparallel a_1$. Therefore, Lemma 12.14 applies, showing that one can exchange the a_1- and a_0-events within η, resulting in a computation η' of $\langle S_D \rangle$ that is equivalent to η. Moreover, η' is, by induction, equivalent to some $\langle S_L \rangle$ computation η''. It follows that also η is equivalent to η'', which had to be shown. □

Example 12.17 (Communication-Closed-Layers) Consider the program S given by

$$
S \overset{\text{def}}{=}
\begin{bmatrix}
a_1 : z := 2 & \Big\| & a_1' : x := 2 \\
; & & ; \\
P_1 : P(s) & & V_1 : V(s) \\
; & & ; \\
a_2 : w := 1 & & a_2' : v := 1 \\
; & & ; \\
P_2 : P(s) & & V_2 : V(s) \\
; & & ; \\
a_3 : z := x + 1 & & a_3' : v := w + 1
\end{bmatrix}.
$$

One can show that, under the implicit assumption that initially s holds, cf. Exercise 12.8, S satisfies the following:

$$
\models \langle S \rangle \ \textbf{psat} \ (P_1 \twoheadrightarrow V_1) \wedge (V_1 \twoheadrightarrow P_2) \wedge (P_2 \twoheadrightarrow V_2).
$$

Moreover using Theorem 12.10 above one can deduce

$$\models \langle S \rangle \ \textbf{psat} \ \Diamond P_1 \wedge \Diamond V_1 \wedge \Diamond P_2 \wedge \Diamond V_2.$$

Therefore, using Theorem 12.9, we also infer that $\models \langle S \rangle \ \textbf{psat} \ (P_1 \twoheadrightarrow V_2)$. Note that for a layered version of S, as shown below, the conflicting actions for $S_{0,0}$ and $S_{1,1}$ are $P_1 - V_2$ and $a_2 - a_3'$. Also, for $S_{1,0}$ and $S_{0,1}$ the conflicts are $P_2 - V_1$ and $a_3 - a_1'$. Using Theorems 12.7, 12.10, and 12.9 one can also show that $\models \langle S \rangle \ \textbf{psat} \ a_2 \twoheadrightarrow a_3'$ and $\models \langle S \rangle \ \textbf{psat} \ a_1' \twoheadrightarrow a_3$ hold. Altogether we have shown for $S \stackrel{\text{def}}{=} [(S_{0,0} ; S_{1,0}) \ \| \ (S_{0,1} ; S_{1,1})]$ that formulae $\langle S \rangle \ \textbf{psat} \ S_{0,0} \stackrel{C}{\twoheadrightarrow} S_{1,1}$ and $\langle S \rangle \ \textbf{psat} \ S_{0,1} \stackrel{C}{\twoheadrightarrow} S_{1,0}$ hold. Therefore, Theorem 12.16 applies, and one can deduce that $\langle S \rangle$ is io-equivalent with the layered program $\langle S_1 ; S_2 \rangle$ where

$$S_1 \stackrel{\text{def}}{=} [S_{0,0} \ \| \ S_{0,1}] \stackrel{\text{def}}{=} \begin{bmatrix} a_1 : z := 2 & \| & a_1' : x := 2 \\ ; & & ; \\ P_1 : P(s) & \| & V_1 : V(s) \\ ; & & ; \\ a_2 : w := 1 & \| & a_2' : v := 1 \end{bmatrix}$$

and

$$S_2 \stackrel{\text{def}}{=} [S_{1,0} \ \| \ S_{1,1}] \stackrel{\text{def}}{=} \begin{bmatrix} P_2 : P(s) & \| & V_2 : V(s) \\ ; & & ; \\ a_3 : z := x+1 & \| & a_3' : v := w+1 \end{bmatrix}.$$

This io-equivalent layered version readily implies $\models \{s\}\langle S \rangle \{z = 3 \wedge v = 2\}$ holds. $\qquad\qquad\qquad\qquad\qquad\qquad\qquad\qquad\qquad\qquad\qquad\qquad\qquad\qquad\quad \Box$

12.6.2 CCL Law for Communication-Based Programs

In this section we consider distributed programs in which the components only communicate with each other through send and receive actions. Recall that, since these are SVL^{++} programs, their channels are unidirectional point-to-point channels. The CCL law for such communication-based programs is derived from Theorem 12.16. So, we assume that we have programs $S_L \stackrel{\text{def}}{=} [S_{0,0} \ \| \ S_{0,1}] ; [S_{1,0} \ \| \ S_{1,1}]$, and $S_D \stackrel{\text{def}}{=} [S_{0,0} ; S_{1,0} \ \| \ S_{0,1} ; S_{1,1}]$. The CCL law from Theorem 12.16 states that $S_L \stackrel{IO}{=} S_D$, provided that for the distributed program S_D the formula $\langle S_D \rangle \ \textbf{psat} \ (S_{0,0} \stackrel{C}{\twoheadrightarrow} S_{1,1}) \wedge (S_{0,1} \stackrel{C}{\twoheadrightarrow} S_{1,0})$ is valid. In general, the conditions on S_D for this property to hold are not always so easy to verify. However, assume that communication between $(S_{0,0} ; S_{1,0})$ and $(S_{0,1} ; S_{1,1})$ is by means of explicit **send** and **receive** actions only, i.e. there are no shared variables except for those associated with communication channels. We call a single layer, such as $L_0 \equiv [S_{0,0} \parallel S_{0,1}]$, *communication closed* if it has the following property:

- For each **send** event inside L_0 for some channel c, there is a "matching" **receive** event within L_0.

By "matching" we refer to a simple counting argument: the number of **send** events for channel c is the same as the number of **receive** events for c. We claim that when both $L_0 \stackrel{\text{def}}{=} [S_{0,0} \parallel S_{0,1}]$ and $L_1 \stackrel{\text{def}}{=} [S_{1,0} \parallel S_{1,1}]$ are communication-closed-layers, then the side conditions of the form $(S_{0,0} \stackrel{c}{\twoheadrightarrow} S_{1,1})$ and $(S_{0,1} \stackrel{c}{\twoheadrightarrow} S_{1,0})$ are satisfied.

First we formalise this counting argument. Here we do not aim at the most general situation, since that would lead to verifying conditions that are as complicated as program verification in general. Rather, we identify a few simple cases, for which the idea is that the number of **send** events along a channel c in a program S should be in one-to-one correspondence with the syntactic occurrences of **send** and **receive** actions, and, moreover, that this number can be deterministically determined, even if S itself is nondeterministic. Section 12.8 contains a semantic characterisation of the number of **send** and **receive** events in a program.

Definition 12.18 (Syntactic send and receive counters) For a channel c we define the partial functions $ns_c(S)$, the number of **send** events in S along channel c, and $nr_c(S)$, the number of **receive** events is S along channel c. The definition is given by induction on the syntactic structure of S.

- $ns_c(\mathbf{send}(c,e)) \stackrel{\text{def}}{=} 1$, and $ns_c(a) \stackrel{\text{def}}{=} 0$ for all other atomic actions a.
- $nr_c(\mathbf{receive}(c,x)) \stackrel{\text{def}}{=} 1$, and $nr_c(a) \stackrel{\text{def}}{=} 0$ for all other atomic actions a.
- $ns_c(S_1 ; S_2) \stackrel{\text{def}}{=} ns_c(S_1) + ns_c(S_2)$, $nr_c(S_1 ; S_2) \stackrel{\text{def}}{=} nr_c(S_1) + nr_c(S_2)$. (Both numbers are defined only when the corresponding numbers for S_1 and S_2 are defined.)
- $ns_c(\mathbf{if} \; []_{i=1}^n b_i \rightarrow S_i \; \mathbf{fi}) \stackrel{\text{def}}{=} ns_c(S_1)$, if $ns_c(S_i) = ns_c(S_j)$ for all i and j, and is not defined otherwise.
  $nr_c(\mathbf{if} \; []_{i=1}^n b_i \rightarrow S_i \; \mathbf{fi}) \stackrel{\text{def}}{=} nr_c(S_1)$, if $nr_c(S_i) = nr_c(S_j)$ for all i and j, and is not defined otherwise.
  This implies that $ns_c(\mathbf{if} \; []_{i=1}^n b_i \rightarrow S_i \; \mathbf{fi})$ (respectively, $nr_c(\mathbf{if} \; []_{i=1}^n b_i \rightarrow S_i \; \mathbf{fi})$) is defined iff the number of **send** or **receive** events can be determined deterministically.

- $ns_c(S_1 \parallel S_2) \stackrel{\text{def}}{=} ns_c(S_1) + ns_c(S_2)$, $nr_c(S_1 \parallel S_2) \stackrel{\text{def}}{=} nr_c(S_1) + nr_c(S_2)$. (Both numbers are defined only when the corresponding numbers for S_1 and S_2 are defined.)

- $ns_c(\textbf{do} \ []_{i=1}^{n} b_i \to S_i \ \textbf{od}) \stackrel{\text{def}}{=} 0$, if $ns_c(S_i) = 0$ for all i, and is not defined, otherwise.

  $nr_c(\textbf{do} \ []_{i=1}^{n} b_i \to S_i \ \textbf{od}) \stackrel{\text{def}}{=} 0$, if $nr_c(S_i) = 0$ for all i, and is not defined, otherwise. $\qquad\qquad\qquad\qquad\qquad\qquad\qquad\qquad\qquad\qquad\qquad\qquad\quad \square$

The clause for loops in the last definition is rather crude, caused by the fact that one does not know beforehand the number of iterations of a loop that will be executed. Therefore, the only sensible definition in this syntactic approximation is to state that $ns_c(\textbf{do} \ []_{i=1}^{n} b_i \to S_i \ \textbf{od})$ and $nr_c(\textbf{do} \ []_{i=1}^{n} b_i \to S_i \ \textbf{od})$ are defined only if there are *no* **send** and **receive** actions at all along channel c within the loop body. The effect of this is that the communication-closed-layers law discussed next does not apply when some of the components of a distributed program contain communications inside loops. We reconsider this situation in later sections, where we discuss a generalisation of the communication-closed-layers law, called loop distribution.

Finally, we can give a *formal* definition of communication closedness.

Definition 12.19 (Channel-based communication closedness) Let $L \stackrel{\text{def}}{=} [S_0 \parallel S_1 \parallel \cdots \parallel S_m]$ be a program that uses some channel c. Assume that process S_i contains all the send actions for c and some other process S_j contains all the receive actions for c. L is called *communication closed for channel c* if $ns_c(S_i)$ and $nr_c(S_j)$ are defined and $ns_c(S_i) = nr_c(S_j)$.

L is called *communication closed* if it is communication closed for all channels occurring in it. $\qquad\qquad\qquad\qquad\qquad\qquad\qquad\qquad\qquad\qquad\qquad\qquad\quad \square$

Note that the above definition assumes that for each channel there is one process doing all the send actions and one process doing all the receive actions. This unidirectional point to point pattern of communication is syntactically required for SVL^{++} programs. Moreover, the condition $ns_c(S_i) = nr_c(S_j)$ implies that both $ns_c(S_i)$ and $nr_c(S_j)$ must be *defined* quantities in the sense of Definition 12.18, implying for instance that no communication actions occur inside loops.

Theorem 12.20 (Communication-Closed-Layers 3)

Let S_L and S_D be communication-based programs defined as follows:

$$S_L \overset{\text{def}}{=} \begin{array}{ccc} [S_{0,0} & \| \cdots \| & S_{0,m}] \\ & ; & \\ \vdots & \vdots & \vdots \\ & ; & \\ [S_{n,0} & \| \cdots \| & S_{n,m}] \end{array}$$

and

$$S_D \overset{\text{def}}{=} \begin{bmatrix} S_{0,0} & \cdots & S_{0,m} \\ ; & \cdots & ; \\ \vdots & \vdots & \vdots \\ ; & \cdots & ; \\ S_{n,0} & \cdots & S_{n,m} \end{bmatrix} .$$

Assume that each layer $L_i \overset{\text{def}}{=} [S_{i,0} \| \cdots \| S_{i,m}]$, where $1 \leq i \leq n$, is communication closed. Then $S_L \overset{IO}{=} S_D$.

Proof Using Theorem 12.16 we only need to prove $\models \langle S_D \rangle$ **psat** $(S_{i,j} \overset{c}{\twoheadrightarrow} S_{i',j'})$ for all $i < i'$ and $j \neq j'$. Again the general case $n > 1$ follows from the case $n = 1$ and Theorem 12.12. By symmetry it is sufficient to show that $\models \langle S_D \rangle$ **psat** $S_{0,1} \overset{c}{\twoheadrightarrow} S_{1,0}$ holds. Assume, to the contrary, that $S_{0,1} \overset{c}{\twoheadrightarrow} S_{1,0}$ does *not* hold, i.e., assume that there is a *terminating* computation η of $\langle S_D \rangle$ and an event in η stemming from $S_{1,0}$ that precedes an event in η that stems from $S_{0,1}$ and that is in conflict with this latter event. Let $a_{1,0}$ be the *first* event of $S_{1,0}$ in the computation η preceding some conflicting event $a_{0,1}$ of $S_{0,1}$. Since conflicts can only arise due to communication, both events must be communication events along some common channel, say c. We distinguish two cases:

Case 1: $S_{0,0}$ contains **send** events along channel c and $S_{0,1}$ contains **receive** events along channel c, i.e., $a_{0,1}$ is of the form **receive**(c,x).

Due to the syntactic constraint $a_{1,0}$ must be a **send** event along channel c. All **send** events along channel c preceding $a_{1,0}$ must stem from $S_{0,0}$, since $a_{1,0}$ is assumed to be the *first* $S_{1,0}$-event preceding some conflicting $S_{0,1}$-event. Hence within the computation η, $a_{1,0}$ is preceded by precisely $ns_c(S_{0,0})$ **send** events along channel c. It follows that $a_{1,0}$ is preceded by exactly $ns_c(S_{0,0})$ **receive** events along channel c, cf. Exercise 12.1. All these **receive** events must be events from $S_{0,1}$; they cannot stem from $S_{1,1}$ since $a_{1,0}$ precedes (by assumption) some $S_{0,1}$-event, viz. $a_{0,1}$, and all $S_{1,1}$-events succeed $a_{0,1}$. Hence $S_{0,1}$ has at least $ns_c(S_{0,0}) + 1$ **receive** events along channel c, contradicting the assumption $ns_c(S_{0,0}) = nr_c(S_{0,1})$.

Case 2: $S_{0,0}$ contains all the **receive** events along channel c and $S_{0,1}$ contains all the **send** events along channel c, i.e. $a_{0,1}$ is of the form **send**(c, e) and $a_{1,0}$ is of the form **receive**(c, x).

First note that by similar arguments as in case 1, $a_{1,0}$ is preceded by $nr_c(S_{0,0})$ **receive** events from $S_{0,0}$, and is not preceded by any **send** event from $S_{1,1}$. So again using Exercise 12.1 we conclude that $a_{1,0}$ is preceded by exactly $nr_c(S_{0,0})$ **send** events for c. All these **send** events are events of $S_{0,1}$, hence $ns_c(S_{0,1}) \geq nr_c(S_{0,0}) + 1$, contradicting the assumption $nr_c(S_{0,0}) = ns_c(S_{0,1})$. This finishes the proof of the theorem. □

12.7 The Two-Phase Commit Protocol

The Two-Phase Commit protocol belongs to the family of *atomic commit protocols* that are used in distributed databases to guarantee *consistency* of the database [BHG87]. A distributed database consists of a number of *sites* connected by some network, where every site has a local database. Data are therefore distributed over a number of sites. In such a distributed database system *transactions* are executed which consist of a series of read and write actions. Reading and writing database items is done by forwarding the action to the site where the item is stored. Terminating the transaction, however, involves *all* sites accessed in the transaction, as all sites must agree on the decision to be taken – which is either to *commit* or to *abort* – in order to guarantee consistency. In the case of an abort all changes made by the transaction are undone, in the case of a commit they are made permanent. A protocol that guarantees such consistency is called an atomic commit protocol.

A possible implementation of an atomic commit protocol is an algorithm consisting of two phases. In the first phase all sites are requested to vote whether they can commit or not, then these votes are collected and a decision is taken. And in the second phase all sites are informed of the decision. This protocol is known as the *Two-Phase Commit protocol*. In this section we derive an implementation of the Two-Phase Commit protocol from its specification. The basic structure of the initial design is the composition of a number of layers. Using the communication-closed-layers law we transform this program with a *layered structure* to a program with a *distributed structure* corresponding to the network architecture.

We start with an informal description of the requirements of an atomic commit protocol and of the rôle of such protocols in distributed databases (see, for example, [BHG87, Ray88, LMWF94]). Then the general idea of the Two-Phase Commit protocol (TPC) for a fully connected network is described, after which we give a formal correctness proof of a layered implementation of TPC that is then transformed to a (distributed) process-oriented implementation. Since all the transformation steps preserve initial-final state behaviour, a new correctness proof for the second implementation is not required.

More precisely, an algorithm that guarantees consistent termination of distributed database transactions is called an *Atomic Commit Protocol* (ACP). Let us precisely state the requirements of an ACP. We assume that the transaction involves a coordinator process *C*, and a set of participating processes *P* for all sites that were accessed. Every participating process has one vote: YES or NO, and every process can reach one of two decisions: COMMIT or ABORT. An ACP must obey the following requirements [BHG87]:

ACP1 *All processes that reach a decision reach the same one.*

ACP2 *A process cannot reverse its decision after it has reached one.*

ACP3 *The* COMMIT *decision can only be reached if all processes voted* YES.

ACP4 *If there are no failures and all processes voted* YES, *then the decision will be* COMMIT.

ACP5 *If there are no failures for sufficiently a long period, then all processes will reach a decision.*

We do not take into account the possibility of communication failures or site failures, that is, we assume that every message sent is eventually delivered and that all sites are working correctly. This does not remove the necessity of an ACP; we still have to take into account system failures and media failures which can lead to the abortion of a transaction. The addition of communication failures and site failures is very well possible, but leads – amongst other things – to the introduction of recovery algorithms in the protocol. Here we treat the simpler case only.

The *Two-Phase Commit protocol* (TPC) is the simplest and most popular algorithm for this kind of problem. In the absence of communication failures it informally behaves as follows:

(i) The protocol starts when the coordinator receives a VOTE_REQ message from the system.

(ii) The coordinator starts by sending VOTE_REQ to all participants.

(iii) When a participant receives a VOTE_REQ it decides what to vote and sends its vote (YES or NO) to the coordinator, according to whether it can commit or not.

(iv) The coordinator collects all votes, and decides to COMMIT if all votes including its own vote were YES, and to ABORT, otherwise. It sends the decision to every participant, after which it acts accordingly, that is, it commits or aborts.

(v) When the participants receive the decision they act accordingly.

Observe that in the informal description above, the coordinator has to collect *all* votes before it takes a decision. This is not necessary when it receives a NO vote from some participant, because in that case the coordinator can immediately decide to abort without waiting for the not-yet-received votes. It does not even have to finish sending all the vote requests. Thus for a more efficient behaviour the fourth clause above should be changed into:

(iv) When, during the collection of votes, the coordinator receives a NO vote then it can immediately take the decision to abort, without waiting for the votes not yet received, and can start sending this decision to all the participants. If all votes are collected and all voted YES (including its own vote), the coordinator decides to commit and sends this decision to all the participants. Afterwards it acts accordingly.

As observed before, the protocol consists conceptually of two phases: a first phase in which the votes are collected and a decision is made, and a second phase in which all processes are informed of the decision and act accordingly.

12.7.1 Derivation of a Layered Implementation

The usual way to present this distributed algorithm is as a number of communicating processes running in parallel. Compared to sequential algorithms, however, this complicates the correctness proof due to the fact that one has to take into account the possibility of interference between processes running in parallel. Here we take the approach that algorithms will be modelled in the initial design stages as *compositions of layers.* These layers can be viewed as if they were executed sequentially one after the other. This leads to a simple correctness proof, in which we can use the proof methods presented in the previous sections, without resorting to interference freedom tests.

After having constructed our initial design of the TPC protocol in the form of a layered program, we transform it so as to meet the *distributed* structure of the network. This is done by means of correctness-preserving (algebraic) transformation steps (which hold when certain syntactic side conditions are fulfilled). Thus the actual correctness proof of the distributed program is relatively simple, because we need not consider interference freedom of different parallel components.

Specification of the protocol

We start off with the specification of the protocol. The set of sites involved in a transaction T is $\{S_i \mid i \in I\}$, where $I = \{0, 1, \ldots, n\}$ and S_0 is the site where the coordinator process is located.

Let dec_i be the variable containing the decision made by site S_i for $i \in I$, and let $vote_i$ be the variable containing the vote of process i. Let dec be the decision taken by the coordinator process. We do not model the initial vote request message sent to the coordinator. We recall the convention, introduced in Section 12.3, according to which the precondition for the *ACP* program implicitly includes the assertion $\neg c.full$, for all channels c that occur in *ACP*. This expresses that channels are initially empty.

We use the following specification of an ACP:

$$\{\forall i \in I. (dec_i = \text{NONE} \wedge vote_i = \text{NONE})\}$$
$$\langle ACP \rangle$$
$$\{(dec = \text{COMMIT} \vee dec = \text{ABORT}) \wedge$$
$$(dec = \text{COMMIT} \leftrightarrow \forall i \in I. (vote_i = \text{YES})) \wedge \forall i \in I. (dec_i = dec)\}.$$

We now derive an implementation of the Two-Phase Commit protocol that satisfies the ACP specification.

Decomposing the protocol

Our layered initial design consists of two phases which can be split up into a number of distinct actions. The specifications of these phases are:

$$\{\forall i \in I. (dec_i = \text{NONE} \wedge vote_i = \text{NONE})\}$$
$$\langle Phase_1 \rangle$$
$$\{(dec = \text{COMMIT} \vee dec = \text{ABORT}) \wedge$$
$$(dec = \text{COMMIT} \leftrightarrow \forall i \in I. (vote_i = \text{YES}))\}$$

and

$$\{(dec = \text{COMMIT} \vee dec = \text{ABORT}) \wedge$$
$$(dec = \text{COMMIT} \leftrightarrow \forall i \in I. (vote_i = \text{YES}))\}$$
$$\langle Phase_2 \rangle$$
$$\{(dec = \text{COMMIT} \vee dec = \text{ABORT}) \wedge$$
$$(dec = \text{COMMIT} \leftrightarrow \forall i \in I. (vote_i = \text{YES})) \wedge \forall i \in I. (dec_i = dec)\}.$$

These specifications immediately imply that the sequential composition of the two phases $Phase_1$; $Phase_2$ satisfies the ACP specification, by the rule for sequential composition.

Communication between the coordinator and the participants takes place via a set of channels cp_i from the coordinator to participant i, and a set of channels pc_i from participant i to the coordinator.

The first phase consists of the parallel composition of the coordinator and the participants. The coordinator sends a vote request to all the participants, collects the votes, and makes a decision. The participants receive a vote request and send their vote to the coordinator afterwards. Each participant uses a local boolean variable $stable_i$ to determine the vote.

$$Phase_1 \stackrel{\text{def}}{=} [C_1 \parallel P_1^1 \parallel P_1^2 \parallel \dots \parallel P_1^n]$$

with the coordinator part defined by

$$C_1 \stackrel{\text{def}}{=} [Q_1 \parallel R_1 \parallel Decide],$$

where

$$Q_1 \stackrel{\text{def}}{=} [\textbf{send}(cp_1, \text{VOTE\_REQ}) \parallel \textbf{send}(cp_2, \text{VOTE\_REQ}) \parallel \dots \parallel$$
$$\textbf{send}(cp_n, \text{VOTE\_REQ})],$$
$$R_1 \stackrel{\text{def}}{=} [\textbf{receive}(pc_1, vote_1) \parallel \textbf{receive}(pc_2, vote_2) \parallel \dots \parallel \textbf{receive}(pc_n, vote_n)],$$

and

$$
\begin{aligned}
Decide \stackrel{\text{def}}{=}\ &\textbf{if}\ \ stable_0\ \textbf{then}\ vote_0 := \text{YES}\ \textbf{else}\ \ vote_0 := \text{NO}\ \textbf{fi}\ ; \\
&\textbf{if}\ \ []_{i=0}^n vote_i = \text{NO} \rightarrow dec := \text{ABORT} \\
&[]\ \bigwedge_{i=0}^n vote_i = \text{YES} \rightarrow dec := \text{COMMIT} \\
&\textbf{fi}\ .
\end{aligned}
$$

The decision process *Decide* is composed in parallel with the send process Q_1 and the receive program R_1. Note that a decision can be taken immediately after a NO vote has been received.

Each participant executes the following program

$$
\begin{aligned}
P_1^i \stackrel{\text{def}}{=}\ &\textbf{receive}(cp_i, msg)\ ; \\
&\textbf{if}\ \ stable_i\ \textbf{then}\ v_i := \text{YES}\ \textbf{else}\ v_i := \text{NO}\ \textbf{fi}\ ; \\
&\textbf{send}(pc_i, v_i).
\end{aligned}
$$

Observe that the receive action is only used for synchronisation, i.e., it initiates the sending of the vote. In the second phase the decision made by the coordinator is broadcasted via the cp_i channel to each participating site P_i. The second phase of the protocol is defined by:

$$Phase_2 \stackrel{\text{def}}{=} [C_2 \parallel P_2^1 \parallel P_2^2 \parallel \dots \parallel P_2^n],$$

with the coordinator part C_2 defined by

$$C_2 \stackrel{\text{def}}{=} [Q_2 \parallel dec_0 := dec]$$

and where Q_2 is given by

$$Q_2 \stackrel{\text{def}}{=} [\mathbf{send}(cp_1, dec) \parallel \mathbf{send}(cp_2, dec) \parallel \ldots \parallel \mathbf{send}(cp_n, dec)].$$

In the second phase the part P_2^i of each participant is defined by

$$P_2^i \stackrel{\text{def}}{=} \mathbf{receive}(cp_i, dec_i).$$

That these implementations of *Phase₁* and *Phase₂* satisfy the above specifications can be proven, using the proof system of Chapter 10.

The implementation of the TPC protocol we have obtained until now is the sequential composition *Phase₁* ; *Phase₂* of the two phases and is given by the following program:

$$TPClayered \stackrel{\text{def}}{=} \begin{array}{c} [C_1 \parallel P_1^1 \parallel P_1^2 \parallel \ldots \parallel P_1^n] \\ ; \\ [C_2 \parallel P_2^1 \parallel P_2^2 \parallel \ldots \parallel P_2^n]. \end{array}$$

The next step is to transform this layered protocol *TPClayered*, using the CCL 3 law from Theorem 12.20. The communication closedness of the two layers is established by calculating the numbers $ns_{cp_i}, nr_{cp_i}, ns_{pc_i}$, and nr_{pc_i} for each layer. As is easily verified, we have the required equalities $ns_{cp_i}(Phase_1) = nr_{cp_i}(Phase_1), ns_{pc_i}(Phase_1) = nr_{pc_i}(Phase_1), ns_{cp_i}(Phase_2) = nr_{cp_i}(Phase_2)$, and $ns_{pc_i}(Phase_2) = nr_{pc_i}(Phase_2)$. The CCL law now states that *TPClayered* is io-equivalent to the following distributed protocol:

$$TPCdistr \stackrel{\text{def}}{=} \begin{bmatrix} C_1 & \big\| & P_1^1 & \big\| & P_1^2 & \big\| & \ldots & \big\| & P_1^n \\ ; & & ; & & ; & & & & ; \\ C_2 & \big\| & P_2^1 & \big\| & P_2^2 & \big\| & \ldots & \big\| & P_2^n \end{bmatrix}.$$

The CCL law preserves correctness of Hoare formulae; hence, this distributed version satisfies the initial specification of the TPC protocol.

In this distributed version each participant executes the following program:

$$P_{impl}^i \stackrel{\text{def}}{=} \begin{array}{l} \mathbf{receive}(cp_i, msg) \, ; \\ \mathbf{if} \;\; stable_i \; \mathbf{then} \; v_i := \text{YES} \; \mathbf{else} \;\; v_i := \text{NO} \; \mathbf{fi} \, ; \\ \mathbf{send}(pc_i, v_i) \, ; \\ \mathbf{receive}(cp_i, dec_i) \end{array}$$

The implementation of the coordinator is given by:

$$C_{impl} \stackrel{\text{def}}{=} \begin{array}{c} [Q_1 \parallel R_1 \parallel Decide] \\ ; \\ [Q_2 \parallel dec_0 := dec]. \end{array}$$

The result is a correct implementation of the Two-Phase Commit protocol.

12.8 Assertion-Based Program Transformations

A characteristic of the transformation laws discussed thus far is that they are of the general form "S_1 is equivalent to S_2 provided certain *syntactic* side conditions are fulfilled". Because of the syntactic nature of the side conditions one calls these transformation laws *algebraic*. In this section we introduce a generalisation of the communication-closed-layers laws that depends on side conditions in the form of *assertions*. To be precise, we introduce a law that is of the form "S_1 is equivalent to S_2, provided that these programs start in an initial state satisfying precondition *pre*". Let us assume that we have a program of the form $C[S_1]$, where $C[\cdot]$ is the program context of S_1. If one wants to transform this program into $C[S_2]$ by applying this transformation law, then one has to show that, within the given context $C[S_1]$, the required precondition *pre* holds whenever S_1 starts executing.

We first introduce a generalised version of the operational semantics O_{cl}, which in essence captures the semantics of a closed program provided that it starts in a state satisfying a given precondition. Formally speaking, we define a semantic function $O_{cl}[\![(pre, S)]\!]$ that maps pairs consisting of a precondition and a program to sets of state pairs, in the same style as the operational semantics $O_{cl}[\![S]\!]$. We use the notation $O_{cl}[\![\{pre\}S]\!]$, rather than $O_{cl}[\![(pre, S)]\!]$.

Definition 12.21 (Precondition-based semantics)

$$O_{cl}[\![\{pre\}S]\!] \stackrel{\text{def}}{=} \{(\sigma, \sigma') \mid \exists \eta.\sigma \models pre \wedge (\sigma, \sigma') = IO(\eta) \ \wedge \ \eta \in \mathcal{RA}[\![\langle S \rangle]\!] \}.$$
□

The next step is the generalisation of io-equivalence.

Definition 12.22 (Precondition-based io-equivalence) Define precondition-based io-equivalence between two SVL^{++} programs S_1 and S_2, expressed by

$$\{p_1\}S_1 \stackrel{IO}{=} \{p_2\}S_2,$$

if $O_{cl}[\![\{p_1\}S_1]\!] = O_{cl}[\![\{p_2\}S_2]\!]$.   □

For the next series of definitions we assume that extra auxiliary variables "*c.sent*" and "*c.received*" have been introduced for all relevant channels c, acting as counters for the number of times that **send** and **receive** actions have been executed. Since the **send** and **receive** actions incorporate updates to these auxiliary variables, they are redefined by:

$$\mathbf{send}(c, e) \stackrel{\text{def}}{=} \langle \neg c.full \rightarrow c.full, c.buf, c.sent := true, e, c.sent + 1 \rangle,$$
$$\mathbf{receive}(c, x) \stackrel{\text{def}}{=} \langle c.full \rightarrow c.full, x, c.received := false, c.buf, c.received + 1 \rangle.$$

Assume that the preconditions of Hoare formulae for closed programs implicitly contain conjuncts of the form $\neg c.full$ and $c.sent = c.received = 0$, expressing that initially all channels are empty, and no messages have been sent. Obviously the $c.sent$ and $c.received$ variables for a program S are closely related to the $ns_c(S)$ and $nr_c(S)$ functions defined in Definition 12.18. It is not difficult to check (Exercise 12.1) that *when* $ns_c(S)$ *and* $nr_c(S)$ *are defined*, the following Hoare formula is valid:

$$\{c.sent = c.received = 0\}\langle S\rangle\{c.sent = ns_c(S) \wedge c.received = nr_c(S)\}.$$

This formula suggests how to generalise the notion of communication closedness. Call a program communication closed if the Hoare formula

$$\{c.sent = c.received\}\langle S\rangle\{c.sent = c.received\}$$

is valid for all relevant channels c. The latter formula applies also in situations where $ns_c(S)$ and $nr_c(S)$ are *not* defined, for instance because of the presence of communication actions inside loops. In fact, we need to take one more aspect into account, namely, that the number of executed **send** actions equals the number of executed **receive** actions *provided that the program starts in a state satisfying a certain precondition pre*. (For instance, one might be able to predict the number of iterations for a loop containing communication actions only when the initial state satisfies a certain precondition.) We therefore generalise the notion of communication closedness, introduced in Definition 12.19, as follows:

Definition 12.23 (Channel-based Communication-Closed-Layers 2) A program S with precondition *pre* is called *communication closed for channel c* if the following Hoare formula is valid:

$$\{pre \wedge c.sent = c.received\}\langle S\rangle\{c.sent = c.received\},$$

and **send**(c,e) and **receive**(c,x) are defined as above. A program or layer with precondition *pre* is called *communication closed* if it is communication closed for all of its channels. □

According to the remarks above, programs that were called communication closed according to Definition 12.19 are still communication closed under the new definition if we take as precondition "*true*". Moreover, we claim that Theorem 12.20 remains valid for the new definition of communication closedness.

Theorem 12.24 (Communication-Closed-Layers 4)
Let S_L and S_D be communication-based programs, and let S_L be annotated as

follows:

$$S_L \stackrel{\text{def}}{=} \begin{array}{c} \{p_0\} \\ [S_{0,0} \quad \| \quad \cdots \quad \| \quad S_{0,m}] \\ ; \\ \{p_1\} \\ \vdots \qquad \vdots \qquad \vdots \\ ; \\ \{p_n\} \\ [S_{n,0} \quad \| \quad \cdots \quad \| \quad S_{n,m}] \end{array}$$

and

$$S_D \stackrel{\text{def}}{=} \begin{bmatrix} S_{0,0} & \| & \cdots & \| & S_{0,m} \\ ; & & \cdots & & ; \\ \vdots & \vdots & \vdots & & \vdots \\ ; & & \cdots & & ; \\ S_{n,0} & \| & \cdots & \| & S_{n,m} \end{bmatrix} .$$

Assume that each layer with precondition

$$L_i \stackrel{\text{def}}{=} \{p_i\}[S_{i,0} \| \cdots \| S_{i,m}]$$

is communication closed, and that $\{p_i\}[S_{i,0} \| \cdots \| S_{i,m}]\{p_{i+1}\}$ is valid for $i = 0, \ldots, n-1$. Then $\{p_0\}S_L \stackrel{IO}{=} \{p_0\}S_D$.

Proof Exercise 12.10　　　　　　　　　　　　　　　　　　　　　　□

12.9 Loop Distribution

In this section we derive certain laws for distributing loops over parallel composition. Conditions will be given under which a loop of the form

while b **do** $[S_1 \| S_2]$ **od**

can be considered equivalent to a distributed loop of the form:

$[$**while** b_1 **do** S_1 **od** $\|$ **while** b_2 **do** S_2 **od**$]$.

The notion of equivalence that we rely on here is weaker than simple io-equivalence; it can be paraphrased as "io-equivalence provided the initial states satisfy a certain precondition", as defined previously. Before we consider loop distribution we first discuss loop unfolding.

Lemma 12.25 (Loop unfolding) For all contexts $C[\cdot]$ we have

$$O_{cl}\, [\![C[\textbf{while } b \textbf{ do } S \textbf{ od}]]\!] = \bigcup_{j\in N} O_{cl}\, [\![C[(b;S)^j;\neg b]]\!].$$

Proof The proof follows directly from the compositional setup of the $\mathcal{RA}[\![\cdot]\!]$ semantics, cf. Definition 12.1, the relation of the $\mathcal{RA}[\![\cdot]\!]$ semantics with the $O_{cl}[\![\cdot]\!]$ semantics, cf. Theorem 12.3, and the fact that $\bigcup_{j\in N}$ distributes over the (semantic) operators of SVL^{++}. $\qquad\square$

A direct consequence of this lemma is that preconditions can be incorporated as follows:

$$O_{cl}\, [\![\{pre\}\, C[\textbf{while } b \textbf{ do } S \textbf{ od}]]\!] = \bigcup_{j\in N} O_{cl}\, [\![\{pre\}\, C[(b;S)^j;\neg b]]\!].$$

In terms of program correctness the above equality can, therefore, be stated as:

$$\models \{p\}\langle C[\textbf{while } b \textbf{ do } S \textbf{ od}]\rangle\{q\}$$

$$\Longleftrightarrow$$

$$\forall j \geq 0.\ \models \{p\}\langle C[(b;S)^j;\neg b]\rangle\{q\}.$$

We now turn again to the problem of distributing a loop over parallel composition. What are sufficient conditions under which a loop of the form

$$\textbf{while } b \textbf{ do }\ [S_1 \parallel S_2]\ \textbf{od}$$

can be transformed into a loop of the form

$$[\textbf{while } b_1 \textbf{ do } S_1 \textbf{ od} \parallel \textbf{while } b_2 \textbf{ do } S_2 \textbf{ od}]\ ?$$

Such a transformation is not valid in general, but depends on the relation between the guard b and the guards b_1 and b_2, and an appropriate loop invariant. The loop bodies S_1 and S_2 should satisfy Definition 12.23 of channel-based communication-closed-layers, shown above. And, also variables of the guard b_i should be local variables of the loop body S_i.

Theorem 12.26 (Loop distribution)
Consider a program $\textbf{while } b \textbf{ do }\ [S_1 \parallel S_2]\ \textbf{od}$, guards b_1, b_2, and assertions p and I with the following properties:

(i) I is a loop invariant, i.e.,

$$\models \{I \wedge b\}\langle[S_1 \parallel S_2]\rangle\{I\}.$$

(ii) $\models p \rightarrow I$.

(iii) The variables of b_i are local to S_i, $i = 1, 2$, and moreover the following is valid:

$$\models I \rightarrow ((b \leftrightarrow b_1) \wedge (b \leftrightarrow b_2)).$$

(iv) $\{I\}[S_1 \parallel S_2]$ is communication closed. (In particular we assume that no shared variables are used except for those associated with the channels.)

Then

$$\{p\} \text{ while } b \text{ do } [S_1 \parallel S_2] \text{ od}$$

$$\stackrel{IO}{=}$$

$$\{p\} [\text{while } b_1 \text{ do } S_1 \text{ od} \parallel \text{while } b_2 \text{ do } S_2 \text{ od}]$$

and $\{p\} [\text{while } b_1 \text{ do } S_1 \text{ od} \parallel \text{while } b_2 \text{ do } S_2 \text{ od}]$ is communication closed.

Proof From Lemma 12.25, it follows that

$$O_{cl} \llbracket \{p\} \text{while } b \text{ do } [S_1 \parallel S_2] \text{ od} \rrbracket = \bigcup_{j \in N} O_{cl} \llbracket \{p\}(b;[S_1 \parallel S_2])^j; \neg b \rrbracket.$$

Take some arbitrary but fixed j and consider a connected computation sequence η of $\{p\}(b;[S_1 \parallel S_2])^j; \neg b$, so we assume that for initial state σ_0 of η we have $\sigma_0 \models p$. We deduce from properties (i) and (ii) that for every intermediate state σ where the guard b or the the guard $\neg b$ are evaluated at the positions indicated above, we have $\sigma \models I$. Property (iii) now implies that $\sigma \models b$ iff $\sigma \models b_1 \wedge b_2$ and that $\sigma \models \neg b$ iff $\sigma \models \neg b_1 \wedge \neg b_2$. So we conclude

$$\{p\}(b;[S_1 \parallel S_2])^j; \neg b \stackrel{IO}{=} \{p\}((b_1 \wedge b_2);[S_1 \parallel S_2])^j; (\neg b_1 \wedge \neg b_2).$$

(Here we regard a boolean expression as *filter*, which concept is introduced in Section 9.3.) By Exercise 12.11,

$$(b_1 \wedge b_2) \stackrel{IO}{=} [b_1 \parallel b_2] \text{ and } (\neg b_1 \wedge \neg b_2) \stackrel{IO}{=} [\neg b_1 \parallel \neg b_2].$$

By Theorem 12.12 we can replace $b_1 \wedge b_2$ by $[b_1 \parallel b_2]$ and $\neg b_1 \wedge \neg b_2$ by $[\neg b_1 \parallel \neg b_2]$ in the above program, yielding an io-equivalent program. Hence we deduce:

$$\{p\}((b_1 \wedge b_2);[S_1 \parallel S_2])^j; (\neg b_1 \wedge \neg b_2)$$
$$\stackrel{IO}{=} \{p\}([b_1 \parallel b_2];[S_1 \parallel S_2])^j; [\neg b_1 \parallel \neg b_2].$$

Next consider the sub-term of the form

$$[b_1 \parallel b_2];[S_1 \parallel S_2].$$

By property (iv) this term satisfies the premises of the CCL 1 law, Theorem 12.15, yielding

$$[b_1 \parallel b_2]; [S_1 \parallel S_2] \stackrel{IO}{=} [b_1; S_1 \parallel b_2; S_2].$$

Hence

$$\{p\}(b; [S_1 \parallel S_2])^j; \neg b \stackrel{IO}{=} \{p\}([b_1; S_1 \parallel b_2; S_2])^j; [\neg b_1 \parallel \neg b_2].$$

Next we transform the term $([b_1; S_1 \parallel b_2; S_2])^j$. If $j > 1$, it can be written as

$$[b_1; S_1 \parallel b_2; S_2]; [b_1; S_1 \parallel b_2; S_2]; ([b_1; S_1 \parallel b_2; S_2])^{j-2}.$$

By property (iv) we can apply the CCL 3 law, Theorem 12.20, to the first part, obtaining

$$[b_1; S_1 \parallel b_2; S_2]; [b_1; S_1 \parallel b_2; S_2] \stackrel{IO}{=} [(b_1; S_1)^2 \parallel (b_2; S_2)^2].$$

By repeated application of the CCL 3 law, we arrive at the following equivalences:

$$([b_1; S_1 \parallel b_2; S_2])^j \stackrel{IO}{=}$$

$$[(b_1; S_1)^2 \parallel (b_2; S_2)^2]; ([b_1; S_1 \parallel b_2; S_2])^{j-2} \stackrel{IO}{=} \cdots \stackrel{IO}{=}$$

$$[(b_1; S_1)^j \parallel (b_2; S_2)^j].$$

Applying the CCL 3 law once more, we finally obtain:

$$([b_1; S_1 \parallel b_2; S_2])^j; [\neg b_1 \parallel \neg b_2] \stackrel{IO}{=} [(b_1; S_1)^j; \neg b_1 \parallel (b_2; S_2)^j; \neg b_2].$$

Combining the above io-equivalences we obtain

$$\{p\}(b; [S_1 \parallel S_2])^j; \neg b \stackrel{IO}{=} \{p\}[(b_1; S_1)^j; \neg b_1 \parallel (b_2; S_2)^j; \neg b_2].$$

Summarising:

$$\begin{aligned} &O_{cl}\,[\![\{p\}\mathbf{while}\ b\ \mathbf{do}\ [S_1 \parallel S_2]\ \mathbf{od}]\!] \\ =\ &\bigcup_{j \in N} O_{cl}\,[\![\{p\}(b; [S_1 \parallel S_2])^j; \neg b]\!] \\ =\ &\bigcup_{j \in N} O_{cl}\,[\![\{p\}[(b_1; S_1)^j; \neg b_1 \parallel (b_2; S_2)^j; \neg b_2]]\!]. \end{aligned}$$

Next we claim that, for all j,

$$\begin{aligned} &O_{cl}\,[\![\{p\}[(b_1; S_1)^j; \neg b_1 \parallel (b_2; S_2)^j; \neg b_2]]\!] \\ =\ &\bigcup_{k \in N} O_{cl}\,[\![\{p\}[(b_1; S_1)^j; \neg b_1 \parallel (b_2; S_2)^k; \neg b_2]]\!]. \end{aligned}$$

The validity of this claim can be seen as follows. Assume that $j \neq k$, and, without loss of generality, that $j < k$. By applying a series of CCL transformations analogously to the transformations shown above, we deduce

$$[(b_1;S_1)^j; \neg b_1 \parallel (b_2;S_2)^k; \neg b_2] \overset{IO}{=}$$
$$([b_1 \parallel b_2]; [S_1 \parallel S_2])^j; [\neg b_1 \parallel b_2]; (S_2;b_2)^{k-j-1}; S_2; \neg b_2.$$

For computations of this last program, with initial state satisfying p, the loop invariant I holds at the state where the guard $[\neg b_1 \parallel b_2]$ is evaluated. But then by property (iii) this guard evaluates to "false", and cannot be passed. So we can conclude that for $j \neq k$

$$O_{cl} \llbracket \{p\}[(b_1;S_1)^j; \neg b_1 \parallel (b_2;S_2)^k; \neg b_2] \rrbracket = \emptyset.$$

This shows the validity of the claim.

Proceeding with the main proof, we now deduce by the above equivalences, Lemma 12.25, the compositionality of the reactive-event-sequence semantics $\mathcal{RA}$, and the fact that $\bigcup_{j \in N}$ distributes over $\bar{\parallel}$:

$$O_{cl} \llbracket \{p\} \textbf{while } b \textbf{ do } [S_1 \parallel S_2] \textbf{ od} \rrbracket$$
$$= \bigcup_{j \in N} O_{cl} \llbracket \{p\}(b;[S_1 \parallel S_2])^j; \neg b \rrbracket$$
$$= \bigcup_{j \in N} O_{cl} \llbracket \{p\}[(b_1;S_1)^j; \neg b_1 \parallel (b_2;S_2)^j; \neg b_2] \rrbracket$$
$$= \bigcup_{j \in N} \bigcup_{k \in N} O_{cl} \llbracket \{p\}[(b_1;S_1)^j; \neg b_1 \parallel (b_2;S_2)^k; \neg b_2] \rrbracket$$
$$= \bigcup_{j \in N} O_{cl} \llbracket \{p\}[(b_1;S_1)^j; \neg b_1 \parallel \textbf{while } b_2 \textbf{ do } S_2 \textbf{ od}] \rrbracket$$
$$= O_{cl} \llbracket \{p\}[\textbf{while } b_1 \textbf{ do } S_1 \textbf{ od} \parallel \textbf{while } b_2 \textbf{ do } S_2 \textbf{ od}] \rrbracket .$$

The communication closedness of $\{p\}[\textbf{while } b_1 \textbf{ do } S_1 \textbf{ od} \parallel \textbf{while } b_2 \textbf{ do } S_2$ $\textbf{od}]$ follows according to Definition 12.23 directly from the communication closedness of $\{p\}\textbf{while } b \textbf{ do } [S_1 \parallel S_2] \textbf{ od}$, since both programs are io-equivalent and hence satisfy the same pre-postconditions. This finishes the proof of the theorem. $\square$

12.10 Set-partitioning Revisited

In this section a variation of the set-partitioning algorithm is developed. The main difference between the algorithms of, e.g., Examples 4.2 and 11.3 and the version discussed here is that we base our formalism on asynchronous communication, instead of synchronous communication as used in, e.g., the previous chapter. Again we start with a provably-correct top-level layered program, and afterwards transform this layered program, *while preserving correctness* to a distributed version.

As already seen before, the pre-post specification of the set-partitioning algorithm is given by

$$\{S = S_0 \neq \emptyset \wedge T = T_0 \neq \emptyset \wedge S \cap T = \emptyset\}$$
$$\langle P \rangle$$
$$\{\mid S \mid = \mid S_0 \mid \wedge \mid T \mid = \mid T_0 \mid \wedge S \cup T = S_0 \cup T_0 \wedge max(S) < min(T)\}.$$

The initial version of this algorithm is based on a shared-variable approach, and is given by:

$$P_{sv} \stackrel{\text{def}}{=} \left\{ \begin{array}{l} [max := max(S) \qquad\qquad \| \qquad\qquad min := min(T)] \\ \quad; \\ \textbf{while } max > min \textbf{ do} \\ [S := (S \setminus \{max\}) \cup \{min\} \quad \| \quad T := (T \setminus \{min\}) \cup \{max\}] \\ \quad; \\ [max := max(S) \qquad\qquad \| \qquad\qquad min := min(T)] \\ \textbf{od} \end{array} \right.$$

One can easily show that the above program P_{sv} is correct with respect to the desired pre- and postconditions. P_{sv} requires sharing of variables between the two parallel components. As the communication between processes will be modelled by send and receive actions, we will introduce these actions and some local auxiliary variables *mn* (a copy of *min*) and *mx* (a copy of *max*) for storing the communicated values. This leads to the following program P_{init}, which will be the starting point of the design and transformation strategy. Observe that in P_{init} shared variables no longer occur.

$$P_{init} \stackrel{\text{def}}{=} \left\{ \begin{array}{l} [max := max(S) \qquad\qquad \| \qquad\qquad min := min(T)] \\ \quad; \\ [[\textbf{send}(C,max) \| \textbf{receive}(D,mn)] \quad \| \quad [\textbf{receive}(C,mx) \| \textbf{send}(D,min)]] \\ \quad; \\ \textbf{while } max > min \textbf{ do} \\ \quad [S := (S \setminus \{max\}) \cup \{mn\} \quad \| \quad T := (T \setminus \{min\}) \cup \{mx\}] \\ \quad; \\ [max := max(S) \qquad\qquad \| \qquad\qquad min := min(T)] \\ \quad; \\ [[\textbf{send}(C,max) \| \textbf{receive}(D,mn)] \| [\textbf{receive}(C,mx) \| \textbf{send}(D,min)]] \\ \textbf{od} \end{array} \right.$$

The partial correctness of the above program can be shown using the loop invariant

$$I \stackrel{\text{def}}{=} \ \mid S \mid = \mid S_0 \mid \ \wedge \ \mid T \mid = \mid T_0 \mid \ \wedge S \cup T = S_0 \cup T_0 \wedge S \cap T = \emptyset \ \wedge$$
$$S \neq \emptyset \wedge T \neq \emptyset \wedge mn = min = \min(T) \ \wedge \ mx = max = \max(S).$$

First we transform the initialisation phase

$$[max := \max(S) \qquad\qquad \| \qquad\qquad min := \min(T)]$$
$$;$$
$$[[\mathbf{send}(C,max) \ \| \ \mathbf{receive}(D,mn)] \quad \| \quad [\mathbf{receive}(C,mx) \ \| \ \mathbf{send}(D,min)]] \,.$$

One easily checks that the premises of the communication-based CCL 3 law, Theorem 12.20, are satisfied. Hence this initialisation phase can be transformed into the following io-equivalent program:

$$\left[\begin{array}{c} max := \max(S) \\ ; \\ [\mathbf{send}(C,max) \ \| \ \mathbf{receive}(D,mn)] \end{array} \right\| \left. \begin{array}{c} min := \min(T) \\ ; \\ [\mathbf{receive}(C,mx) \ \| \ \mathbf{send}(D,min)] \end{array} \right] .$$

Next we transform the loop body

$$[S := (S \setminus \{max\}) \cup \{mn\} \qquad \| \qquad T := (T \setminus \{min\}) \cup \{mx\}]$$
$$;$$
$$[max := \max(S) \qquad\qquad \| \qquad\qquad min := \min(T)]$$
$$;$$
$$[[\mathbf{send}(C,max) \ \| \ \mathbf{receive}(D,mn)] \quad \| \quad [\mathbf{receive}(C,mx) \ \| \ \mathbf{send}(D,min)]]$$

to a distributed version. This loop body also satisfies the premises of the communication-based CCL 3 law, Theorem 12.20. Hence this loop body can be transformed into the following io-equivalent program:

$$[B_1 \ \| \ B_2]$$

with

$$B_1 \stackrel{\text{def}}{=} \left\{ \begin{array}{c} S := (S \setminus \{max\}) \cup \{mn\} \\ ; \\ max := \max(S) \\ ; \\ [\mathbf{send}(C,max) \ \| \ \mathbf{receive}(D,mn)] \end{array} \right.$$

and

$$B_2 \stackrel{\text{def}}{=} \left\{ \begin{array}{c} T := (T \setminus \{min\}) \cup \{mx\} \\ ; \\ min := \min(T) \\ ; \\ [\mathbf{receive}(C,mx) \ \| \ \mathbf{send}(D,min)] \,. \end{array} \right.$$

Finally we distribute the guard **while** $max > min$ **do** $[B_1 \parallel B_2]$ **od** over the parallel composition. As explained before in Section 12.9 on loop distribution, once the premises of Theorem 12.26 are satisfied, this can be done if we are able to express for each parallel component the global guard in terms of local variables, and if the layer $B_1 \parallel B_2$ is communication closed. In this particular case we use the auxiliary variables mn, a copy of min, and mx, a copy of max, cf. the loop invariant I. Hence we have at the start of the loop that

$$\models I \rightarrow (max > min \leftrightarrow mx > min) \wedge (max > min \leftrightarrow max > mn)$$

holds. The second and fourth inequality are expressed using the local variables of B_2 and B_1, respectively. Moreover one can easily check the communication closedness of the layer $B_1 \parallel B_2$. Consequently the premises of Theorem 12.26 are satisfied, and the guard can be distributed over the parallel composition. This yields the following io-equivalent, distributed and correct version of the loop **while** $max > min$ **do** $[B_1 \parallel B_2]$ **od**:

$$\left[\begin{array}{c} \textbf{while } max > mn \textbf{ do} \\ B_1 \\ \textbf{od} \end{array} \middle\| \begin{array}{c} \textbf{while } mx > min \textbf{ do} \\ B_2 \\ \textbf{od} \end{array} \right].$$

As an intermediate result we have obtained the following program:

$$P_{inter_1} \stackrel{\text{def}}{=} \left\{ \begin{array}{c} [Init_1 \quad \parallel \quad Init_2] \\ ; \\ \left[\begin{array}{c} \textbf{while } max > mn \textbf{ do} \\ B_1 \\ \textbf{od} \end{array} \middle\| \begin{array}{c} \textbf{while } mx > min \textbf{ do} \\ B_2 \\ \textbf{od} \end{array} \right] \end{array} \right.$$

with

$$Init_1 \stackrel{\text{def}}{=} \left\{ \begin{array}{c} max := \max(S) \\ ; \\ [\textbf{send}(C, max) \parallel \textbf{receive}(D, mn)] \end{array} \right.$$

and

$$Init_2 \stackrel{\text{def}}{=} \left\{ \begin{array}{c} min := \min(T) \\ ; \\ [\textbf{receive}(C, mx) \parallel \textbf{send}(D, min)]. \end{array} \right.$$

By Theorem 12.26 the distributed loop (layer)

$$\{I\}[\textbf{while } max > mn \textbf{ do } B_1 \textbf{ od} \parallel \textbf{while } mx > min \textbf{ do } B_2 \textbf{ od}]$$

is communication closed. So one can apply the precondition-based communication-closed-layers law CCL 4, Theorem 12.24, to the distributed initialisation phases and the distributed loops, yielding the following distributed program

$$
P_{impl} \overset{\text{def}}{=}
\left[
\begin{array}{c|c}
Init_1 & Init_2 \\
; & ; \\
\textbf{while } max > mn \textbf{ do} & \textbf{while } mx > min \textbf{ do} \\
B_1 & B_2 \\
\textbf{od} & \textbf{od}
\end{array}
\right] .
$$

Expanding the definition of $Init_1$, $Init_2$, B_1 and B_2 results in:

$$
P_{impl} \equiv
\left[
\begin{array}{c|c}
max := \max(S) & min := \min(T) \\
; & ; \\
[\textbf{send}(C,max) \parallel \textbf{receive}(D,mn)] & [\textbf{send}(D,min) \parallel \textbf{receive}(C,mx)] \\
; & ; \\
\textbf{while } max > mn \textbf{ do} & \textbf{while } mx > min \textbf{ do} \\
S := (S \setminus \{max\}) \cup \{mn\} & T := (T \setminus \{min\}) \cup \{mx\} \\
; & ; \\
max := \max(S) & min := \min(T) \\
; & ; \\
[\textbf{send}(C,max) \parallel \textbf{receive}(D,mn)] & [\textbf{send}(D,min) \parallel \textbf{receive}(C,mx)] \\
\textbf{od} & \textbf{od}
\end{array}
\right] .
$$

And we can conclude that the above program P_{impl} is a partially-correct implementation of the set-partitioning algorithm P_{sv}.

12.11 Historical Notes

Stomp and de Roever [SdR87, SdR94] introduce what is called a *principle for sequentially-phased reasoning* which allows the formulation of *semantically-defined* layers that are used to capture the intuition of protocol designers. In [Sto89, Sto90b] this principle is applied to the derivation of a broadcast protocol. Chou and Gafni [CG88] group classes of actions and define a sequential structure on such classes. This strategy is called *stratification*. Both approaches are closely related to the idea of *communication-closed-layers* for synchronous-communication-based programs, which are introduced by Elrad and Francez in [EF82] and studied in [GS86]. In [JZ92a, JZ93, ZJ94] an explanation of [GHS83] is given, inspired by ideas from [SdR87, SdR89], based on *layered composition,* sometimes called "conflict (-based) composition" or "weak sequential composition" [JPZ91, FPZ93, RW94, Jan94]. This layer-composition operator "•" is a program composition operator similar to parallel or sequential composition, used for composing "sequential phases" or "communication-closed-layers". The idea is that when a program of the form $S_1 \bullet S_2 \bullet \cdots \bullet S_n$ runs as a "closed program", that is, without interference by other parallel programs, its initial-final state behaviour is the same as that of the sequential program $S_1 ; S_2 ; \cdots ; S_n$. Therefore, it can be analysed and shown correct by means of classical Hoare logic for sequential programs, at least on this level of detail. On a *more* detailed level of design the components $S_1, S_2, \ldots, S_n$ themselves can be *parallel programs*. The layer composition operator turns out to be different from ordinary sequential composition: actions a_1 and a_2 from different layers are sequentially ordered only if a_1 and a_2 are non-commuting. Using the layer composition operator one can describe the distributed version S_D and the sequentially-phased or layered version S_L of concurrent programs, that we discussed in the introduction, as follows:

$$S_D \stackrel{\text{def}}{=} [(P_{0,0} \bullet P_{1,0} \bullet \cdots \bullet P_{n,0}) \parallel \cdots \parallel (P_{0,m} \bullet P_{1,m} \bullet \cdots \bullet P_{n,m})],$$
$$S_L \stackrel{\text{def}}{=} [P_{0,0} \parallel \cdots \parallel P_{0,m}] \bullet \cdots \bullet [P_{n,0} \parallel \cdots \parallel P_{n,m}].$$

A generalised version of the communication-closed-layers (CCL) law was proposed in [JPZ91] for shared variables rather than synchronous communication, and based on layered composition rather than sequential composition. In [JZ92b] layered composition is used to derive the two-phase commit protocol, which is a typical example of layering. The side conditions (in [JPZ91]) for the CCL law are that actions from $P_{i,j}$ must commute with actions from $P_{k,l}$ unless $i = k$ or $j = l$. Under these conditions the programs S_L and S_D are semantically identical, that is, they have identical sets of computations. This certainly *implies* that S_L and S_D have the same initial-final state relation, but it is also a stronger property. For it implies that S_L can replace S_D, or vice versa, *in arbitrary contexts,* including contexts where processes run concurrently with S_L or S_D. Technically, one says that the equivalence between S_L and S_D is a *congruence.* On the other hand, when one replaces layered composition in S_L and S_D by sequential composition, then, under the same side conditions, initial-final state equivalence is still guaranteed, but this equivalence is *not* preserved when processes run concurrently. That is, S_L can be replaced by S_D within sequential contexts only. This limitation is not significant when S_D can be seen as a complete, self-contained algorithm, such as, for instance, the set-partitioning example introduced in earlier chapters, and studied again in this chapter. After all, one does not expect the correctness of such algorithms to be preserved when run in an arbitrary concurrent context that could read and modify the shared variables used by the algorithm. When an algorithm like "set partitioning" might be incorporated into a larger concurrent program, then one should take care that no interference is possible between the algorithm and the rest of the program, for instance by declaring the shared variables of the algorithm to be "private" variables [MP91b] of the algorithm. For programs like the two-phase commit protocol, which we also use as an example, the situation is more complex. Such a protocol is usually only a small part of more elaborate protocols, for instance a protocol dealing with reliable atomic transactions in distributed databases [BHG87]. In such cases the final (distributed) algorithm has to be combined with other protocols that interact in a non-trivial way. In such situations one needs either a congruence between layered and distributed version of the protocol, or else one must be careful when combining protocols. Mechanisms for combining protocols that do not depend on compositional program operators, and therefore do not depend on congruence properties, are discussed in [CM88, BS92, Kat93].

Exercises

12.1   Consider a program S which communicates via a channel c. Introduce auxiliary variables ns and nr and augment every communication action along channel c with assignments to ns and nr as follows:

$$\mathbf{send}'(c,e) \overset{\text{def}}{=} \langle \neg c.full \rightarrow c.full, c.buf, ns := true, e, ns + 1 \rangle$$
$$\mathbf{receive}'(c,x) \overset{\text{def}}{=} \langle c.full \rightarrow c.full, x, nr := false, c.buf, nr + 1 \rangle.$$

Prove that under the precondition $\neg c.full \wedge (ns = nr)$,

$$GI \overset{\text{def}}{=} (\neg c.full \leftrightarrow ns = nr) \wedge (c.full \leftrightarrow ns = nr + 1)$$

is a global invariant of S. In other words, at every moment in a computation of S the number of **send** actions minus the number of **receive** actions along channel c equals 1 or 0. Conclude:

(a) In a computation of S every $\mathbf{send}(c,e)$ event is preceded by an equal number of **send** and **receive** events along channel c.

(b) In a computation of S every $\mathbf{receive}(c,x)$ event is preceded by one more **send** event than **receive** events along channel c.

12.2   Prove Theorem 12.8.

12.3   Prove Theorem 12.9.

12.4   Let S and S' be io-equivalent programs. Prove that for all programs S_1:

- $S_1 ; S \overset{IO}{=} S_1 ; S'$,
- $S ; S_1 \overset{IO}{=} S' ; S_1$,
- **if** $S [] S_1$ **fi** $\overset{IO}{=}$ **if** $S' [] S_1$ **fi** ,
- **do** $S \; [] \; S_1$; **exit od** $\overset{IO}{=}$ **do** $S' \; [] \; S_1$; **exit od**,

- **do** S_1 [] S; **exit od** $\overset{IO}{=}$ **do** S_1 [] S'; **exit od**.

Prove Theorem 12.12, using the above io-equivalences.

12.5   Let S be a program and $C[.]$ be a context such that $C[S]$ is well-defined. Prove that

$$C[S] \overset{IO}{=} C[\textbf{skip} ; S] \overset{IO}{=} C[S ; \textbf{skip}].$$

12.6   Theorem 12.6 requires that a proof outline is given with a precondition of the form $\neg a_2.occ$. Assume that $\langle v_1, \ldots, v_n \rangle$ is a list of auxiliary variables for S, and that p is a predicate formula with $var(p) \subseteq \{v_1, \ldots, v_n\}$. Moreover, assume that $\exists v_1, \ldots, v_n . p$ is a valid predicate formula. Show that in Theorem 12.6 the existence of a proof outline of the form $\{p\}A(S)\{q\}$ suffices to establish that $\langle S \rangle$ **psat** $a_1 \twoheadrightarrow a_2$ is valid. (Remark: in practice $a_2.occ$ will always be one of these auxiliary variables v_i, and $p \to \neg a_2.occ$ will be a valid assertion. But for the soundness of the theorem this is not required.)

12.7   Consider the program

$$S \overset{\text{def}}{=} [x := 1 ; P(s) \parallel V(s) ; x := 2].$$

Intuitively it is clear that S satisfies the specification

$$\models \{s\} \langle S \rangle \{x = 2\}$$

but how is this proved?

First use the above Exercise 12.5 to show that

$$S \overset{IO}{=} [x := 1 ; P(s) ; \textbf{skip} \parallel \textbf{skip} ; V(s) ; x := 2]$$

holds. Under the precondition s, the $P(s)$ action precedes the $V(s)$ action, i.e., $\langle \{s\}S \rangle$ **psat** $P(s) \twoheadrightarrow V(s)$ holds, where $\langle \{s\}S \rangle$ **psat** ϕ is defined in Exercise 12.8. Use Theorem 12.9 and Theorem 12.16 to show that

$$S \overset{IO}{=} [x := 1 ; P(s) \parallel \textbf{skip}] ; [\textbf{skip} \parallel V(s) ; x := 2]$$

holds. Finally deduce

$$\models \{s\} \langle S \rangle \{x = 2\}.$$

12.8   Consider the program S of Example 12.17, given by

$$S \stackrel{\text{def}}{=} \begin{bmatrix} z := 2 & \Bigg\| & x := 2 \\ ; & & ; \\ P_1 : P(s) & & V_1 : V(s) \\ ; & & ; \\ w := 1 & & v := 1 \\ ; & & ; \\ P_2 : P(s) & & V_2 : V(s) \\ ; & & ; \\ z := x + 1 & & v := w + 1 \end{bmatrix}.$$

(a) Define

$$\langle \{pre\}S \rangle \ \textbf{psat} \ \phi \stackrel{\text{def}}{=} \langle S \rangle \ \textbf{psat} \ pre \to \phi.$$

Prove for the above program the validity of the following precedence relation:

$$\langle \{s\}S \rangle \ \textbf{psat} \ P_1 \twoheadrightarrow V_1 \wedge V_1 \twoheadrightarrow P_2 \wedge P_2 \twoheadrightarrow V_2.$$

(b) Show also that

$$\models \langle \{s\}S \rangle \ \textbf{psat} \ \Diamond P_1 \wedge \Diamond V_1 \wedge \Diamond P_2 \wedge \Diamond V_2$$

holds.

(c) Prove that $\{s\}S$ is io-equivalent to $\{s\}S_1 ; S_2$ with

$$S_1 \stackrel{\text{def}}{=} \begin{bmatrix} z := 2 & \Bigg\| & x := 2 \\ ; & & ; \\ P_1 : P(s) & & V_1 : V(s) \\ ; & & ; \\ w := 1 & & v := 1 \end{bmatrix}$$

and

$$S_2 \stackrel{\text{def}}{=} \begin{bmatrix} P_2 : P(s) & \Bigg\| & V_2 : V(s) \\ ; & & ; \\ z := x + 1 & & v := w + 1 \end{bmatrix}.$$

(d) Prove that S satisfies

$$\models \{s\}\langle S \rangle \{z = 3 \wedge v = 2\}.$$

12.9   Why is the following conclusion false?

Consider

$$L_0 \stackrel{\text{def}}{=} [\mathbf{send}(a,0) \parallel \mathbf{if}\ false \to \mathbf{receive}(a,x)\ \mathbf{fi}\,],$$
$$L_1 \stackrel{\text{def}}{=} [\mathbf{send}(a,1) \parallel \mathbf{receive}(a,y)],\ \text{and}$$
$$S_D \stackrel{\text{def}}{=} [\mathbf{send}(a,0);\mathbf{send}(a,1) \parallel$$
$$\stackrel{\text{def}}{=} \mathbf{if}\ false \to \mathbf{receive}(a,x)\ \mathbf{fi}\,;\mathbf{receive}(a,y)].$$

L_0 and L_1 are communication closed according to Definition 12.19.
By the proof of Theorem 12.20 this implies that

$$\models \langle S_D \rangle\ \mathbf{psat}\ (\mathbf{send}(a,0) \stackrel{C}{\twoheadrightarrow} \mathbf{receive}(a,y)),$$

which is clearly false, since $\mathbf{send}(a,0)$ and $\mathbf{receive}(a,y)$ match semantically. Consequently the proof of Theorem 12.20 is false.

12.10   Prove Theorem 12.24, by adapting the proof of Theorem 12.20.

12.11   Show that

$$b_1 \wedge b_2 \stackrel{IO}{=} [b_1 \parallel b_2].$$

Use the above io-equivalence to prove:

$$(b_1 \wedge b_2)\,;S \stackrel{IO}{=} [b_1 \parallel b_2]\,;S.$$

12.12   Give a formal derivation of the distributed version $SetPart_D$ of the set-partitioning algorithm given in Section 12.1, from its sequential version $SetPart_L$. Use the communication-closed-layers laws developed in this chapter.

Bibliography

[Abr87] S. Abramsky. Domain theory in logical form. In *Annual Symposium on Logic in Computer Science*, pages 47–53. IEEE CS, 1987. Extended version in *Annals of Pure and Applied Logic* 51:1–77, 1991.

[Acz83] Peter Aczel. On an inference rule for parallel composition. Unpublished letter to Cliff Jones, March 1983. Univ. of Manchester, cited in [dR85b, page 202].

[Ada83] United States Department of Defense and American National Standards Institute. *The Programming Language Ada reference manual*, 1983. Published as volume 155 of Lecture Notes in Computer Science, Springer-Verlag.

[AdAHM99] R. Alur, L. de Alfaro, T. Henzinger, and F. Mang. Automating modular verification. In *10th International Conference on Concurrency Theory (CONCUR 1999)*, volume 1664 of *LNCS*, pages 82–97. Springer-Verlag, 1999.

[AdB94] P.H.M. America and F.S. de Boer. Reasoning about dynamically evolving process structures. *Formal Aspects of Computing*, 6(3):269–317, 1994.

[AdBKR86] P.H.M America, J.W. de Bakker, J.N. Kok, and J.J.M.M. Rutten. Operational semantics of a parallel object-oriented language. In *Conference Record of the 13th Symposium on Principles of Programming Languages, St. Petersburg Beach, Florida, January 1986*, pages 194–208, 1986.

[ADH+99] H. Akhiani, D. Doligez, P. Harter, L. Lamport, J. Scheid, M. Tuttle, and Y. Yu. Cache coherence verification with TLA+. In J.M. Wing, J. Woodcock, and J. Davies, editors, *FM '99: World Congress on Formal Methods in the Development of Computing Systems, Toulouse, France, September 1999*, volume 1709 of *LNCS*, page 1871 (vol. II). Springer-Verlag, 1999.

[AdLFS93] T. Anderson, R. de Lemos, J.S. Fitzgerald, and A. Saeed. On formal support for industrial-scale requirements analysis. In *Workshop on Theory of Hybrid Systems*, volume 736 of *LNCS*, pages 426–451, 1993.

[AFdR80] K.R. Apt, N. Francez, and W. P. de Roever. A proof system for communicating sequential processes. *ACM Transactions on Programming Languages and Systems*, 2:359–385, 1980.

[AFV01] L. Aceto, W. Fokkink, and C. Verhoef. Structural operational semantics. In Bergstra et al. [BPS01].

[AG00] R. Alur and R. Grosu. Modular refinement of hierarchic state machines. In *Proc. 27th ACM Symposium on Principles of Programming Languages (POPL '00), New York (N.Y.)*. ACM, 2000.

[AH96] Rajeev Alur and Thomas A. Henzinger, editors. *Proceedings of CAV '96: Computer aided verification: 8th international conference, New Brunswick, NJ, USA, July 31–August 3, 1996*, volume 1102 of *LNCS*. Springer-Verlag, 1996.

[AH99] R. Alur and T.A. Henzinger. Reactive modules. *Formal Methods in System Design*, 15(1):7–48, 1999. Invited submission to FloC '96 special issue. A preliminary version appears in *Proc. 11th LICS, 1996, pp. 207–218*.

[AHK98] R. Alur, T.A. Henzinger, and O. Kupferman. Alternating-time temporal logic. In de Roever et al. [dRLP98], pages 23–60.

[AHM+98] R. Alur, T. Henzinger, F. Mang, S. Qadeer, S. Rajamani, and S. Tasiran. MOCHA: Modularity in model checking. In *Proc. of the 10th International Conference on Computer Aided Verification*, volume 1427 of *LNCS*, pages 516–520. Springer-Verlag, 1998.

[AL91] Martin Abadi and Leslie Lamport. The existence of refinement mappings. *Theoretical Computer Science*, 82(2):253–284, 1991.

[AL93] Martin Abadi and Leslie Lamport. Composing specifications. *ACM TOPLAS*, 15(1):73–132, 1993.

[AL95] Martin Abadi and Leslie Lamport. Conjoining specifications. *ACM TOPLAS*, 17(3):507–534, May 1995.

[ÁMdB00] E. Ábrahám-Mumm and F. de Boer. Proof-outlines for threads in JAVA. In *Proceedings of CONCUR 2000*, LNCS. Springer-Verlag, 2000.

[Ame87] P.H.M. America. A proof theory for sequential POOL. Technical report, Philips Research, 1987. ESPRIT project 415 A.

[Ame89] P.H.M. America. Issues in the design of a parallel object-oriented language. *Formal Aspects of Computing*, 1(4):366–411, 1989.

[And91] Gregory R. Andrews. *Concurrent Programming, Principles and Practice*. The Benjamin/Cummings Publishing Company, Redwood City, CA, 1991.

[Ang67] Ignacio Angelelli, editor. *Gottlob Frege. Kleine Schriften*. Georg Olms, Hildesheim, 1967.

[AO91] K.R. Apt and E.-R. Olderog. *Verification of Sequential and Concurrent Programs*. Springer-Verlag, 1991.

[AP93] Martin Abadi and Gordon D. Plotkin. A logical view of composition. *Theoretical Computer Science*, 114(1):3–30, 1993.

[Apt81a] K.R. Apt. Recursive assertions and parallel programs. *Acta Informatica*, 1981.

[Apt81b] K.R. Apt. Ten years of Hoare logic: a survey – part I. *ACM Transactions on Programming Languages and Systems*, 3(4):431–483, October 1981.

[Apt83] K.R. Apt. Formal justification of a proof system for Communicating Sequential Processes. *Journal of the ACM*, 30(1):197–216, January 1983.

[Apt84] K.R. Apt. Proving correctness of CSP programs – a tutorial. Technical Report 84–24, L.I.P.T., Université Paris 7, 1984.

[Apt85] K.R. Apt, editor. *Logics and Models of Concurrent Systems*, volume 13 of *NATO Advanced Science Institutes Series F: Computer and System Sciences*. Springer-Verlag, 1985.

[Arn94] André Arnold. *Finite Transition Systems: Semantics of Communicating Systems*. Prentice Hall International Series in Computer Science. Prentice Hall, Hemel Hampstead, 1994.

[AS85] B. Alpern and F.B. Schneider. Defining liveness. *Information Processing Letters*, 21(4):181–185, October 1985.

[Ash75] Ed. A. Ashcroft. Proving assertions about parallel programs. *JCSS*, 10:110–135, February 1975.

[BA81] J.D. Brock and W.B. Ackermann. Scenarios: A model of nondeterminate computation. In J. Diaz and I. Ramos, editors, *Formalization of Programming Concepts*, volume 107 of *LNCS*, pages 252–259. Springer-Verlag, 1981.

[BA82] M. Ben-Ari. On-the-fly garbage collection: New algorithms inspired by program proofs. In *ICALP 82*, volume 140 of *LNCS*, pages 14–23. Springer-Verlag, 1982.

[BA84] Mordechai Ben-Ari. Algorithms for on-the-fly garbage collection. *ACM Transaction on Programming Languages and Systems (TOPLAS)*, 6(3):333–344, July 1984.

[Bac78] R.J.R. Back. *On the Correctness of Refinement Steps in Program Development*. PhD thesis, Department of Computer Science, University of Helsinki, 1978. Report A-1978-4.

[Bac80] R.J.R. Back. Correctness preserving program refinements: Proof theory and applications. Mathematical Centre Tracts 131, Mathematisch Centrum, Amsterdam, 1980. Revised version of [Bac78].

[Bac86] Roland C. Backhouse. *Program Construction and Verification*. Prentice Hall, 1986.

[Bac88] R.J.R. Back. A calculus of refinements for program derivations. *Acta Informatica*, 25, 1988.

[Bac90] R. Back. Refinement calculus, part II: Parallel and reactive programs. In de Bakker et al. [dBdRR90], pages 67–93.

[BB91] A. Benveniste and G. Berry. The synchronous approach to reactive and real-time systems. In *Proceedings of the IEEE*, volume 79 (9), pages 1270–1282, 1991.

[BBC+95] N. S. Bjørner, A. Browne, E.S. Chang, M. Colón, A. Kapur, Z. Manna, H.B. Sipma, and T.E. Uribe. STeP : The Stanford Temporal Prover, User's Manual. Technical Report STAN-CS-TR-95-1562, Stanford University, Stanford, CA, November 1995.

[BBF+00] G. Berry, A. Bouali, X. Fornari, E. Ledinot, E. Nassor, and R. de Simone. Esterel: a formal method applied to avionic software development. *Science of Computer Programming*, 36:5–25, 2000.

[BC95] R.E. Bryant and Y.-A. Chen. Verification of arithmetic circuits with binary moment diagrams. In *Proceedings of the 32nd Design Automation Conference*, pages 535–541, June 1995.

[BCC98] S. Berezin, S. Campos, and E.M. Clarke. Compositional reasoning in model checking. In de Roever et al. [dRLP98], pages 81–102.

[BCGH94] A. Benveniste, P. Caspi, P. Le Guernic, and N. Halbwachs. Data-flow synchronous languages. In de Bakker et al. [dBdRR94], pages 1–45.

[BCJ94] Guy E. Blelloch, K. Mani Chandy, and Suresh Jagannathan, editors. *Specification of Parallel Algorithms*, volume 18 of *DIMACS Series in Discrete Mathematics and Theoretical Computer Science*. American Mathematical Society, 1994.

[BDD+92] Manfred Broy, Frank Dederich, Claus Dendorfer, Max Fuchs, Thomas Gritzner, and Rainer Weber. The design of distributed systems – an introduction to FOCUS. Technical Report TUM-I9202, Technische Universität München, 1992.

[Bek71] Hans Bekić. Towards a mathematical theory of processes. Technical Report TR 25.125, IBM Laboratory Vienna, 1971. Also published in: [Jon84, pages 168–206].

[BEKV94] Krysia Broda, Susan Eisenbach, Hessam Khoshnevisan, and Steve Vickers. *Reasoned Programming*. Prentice Hall, 1994.

[Ber99] Gérard Berry. The constructive semantics of Esterel. Draft book, current version 3.0, July 2, 1999. http://www-sop.inria.fr/meije/personnel/ Gerard.Berry.html, 1999.

[Ber00] Gérard Berry. The foundations of Esterel. In G. Plotkin, C. Stirling, and M. Tofte, editors, *Proof, Language and Interaction: Essays in Honour of Robin Milner*, Foundations of Computing Series. MIT Press, 2000.

[BG88] G. Berry and G. Gonthier. The ESTEREL synchronous programming language: Design, semantics, implementation. Technical Report 842, Ecole Nationale Supérieure des Mines de Paris, 1988.

[BGA98] A. Benveniste, P. Le Guernic, and P. Aubry. Compositionality in dataflow synchronous languages: Specification and code generation. In de Roever et al. [dRLP98].

[BGJ91] Albert Benveniste, Paul Le Guernic, and Christian Jacquemot. Synchronous programming with events and relations: the SIGNAL language and its semantics. *Science of Computer Programming*, 16(2):103–149, September 1991.

[BH95a] Jonathan P. Bowen and Michael G. Hinchey. Seven more myths of formal methods. *IEEE Software*, 12(4):34–41, July 1995.

[BH95b] Jonathan P. Bowen and Michael G. Hinchey. Ten commandments of formal methods. *IEEE Computer*, 28(4):56–63, April 1995.

[BHG87] P. Bernstein, V. Hadzilacos, and N. Goodman. *Concurrency Control and Recovery in Database Systems*. Addison-Wesley, 1987.

[BHR84] S.D. Brookes, C.A.R. Hoare, and A.W. Roscoe. A theory of communicating sequential processes. *JACM*, 31(3):560–599, 1984.

[BJ66] C. Böhm and G. Jacopini. Flow diagrams, Turing machines, and Languages with only two formation rules. *CACM*, 9:366–372, 1966.

[BK84] J.A. Bergstra and J.W. Klop. Process algebra for synchronous communication. *Information and Control*, 60(1/3):109–137, 1984.

[BK85] H. Barringer and R. Kuiper. Hierarchical development of concurrent systems in a temporal logic framework. In *Proc. of a Seminar on Concurrency*, volume 197 of *LNCS*. Springer-Verlag, 1985.

[BK95] Manuel Blum and Sampath Kannan. Designing programs that check their work. *JACM*, 42(1):269–291, January 1995.

[BKP84] Howard Barringer, Ruurd Kuiper, and Amir Pnueli. Now you may compose temporal logic specifications. In *Proceedings of the 16th ACM Symposium on the Theory of Computing, Washington, 1984*, pages 51–63, New York, 1984. ACM.

[BLA⁺99] G. Behrmann, K. Larsen, H. Andersen, H. Hulgaard, and J. Lind-Nielsen. Verification of hierarchical state/event systems using reusability and compositionality. In *TACAS '99: Fifth International Conference on Tools and Algorithms for the Construction and Analysis of Software*, 1999.

[BLO98a] S. Bensalem, Y. Lakhnech, and S. Owre. Computing abstractions of infinite state systems compositionally and automatically. In *CAV '98*, volume 1427 of *LNCS*. Springer-Verlag, 1998.

[BLO98b] S. Bensalem, Y. Lakhnech, and S. Owre. InVeSt: A tool for the verification of invariants. In Alan J. Hu and Moshe Y. Vardi, editors, *CAV '98*, volume 1427 of *LNCS*, pages 505–510. Springer-Verlag, 1998.

[BLR89] M. Blum, M. Luby, and R. Rubinfeld. Program result checking against adaptive programs and in cryptographic settings. In *Proc. of DIMACS Workshop on Distributed Computing and Cryptography*, 1989.

[BM97] R.S. Boyer and J. S. Moore. *A Computational Logic Handbook*. Academic Press, second edition, 1997.

[Bor87] R. Bornat. *Programming from First Principles*. Prentice Hall, 1987.

[Bou88] L. Bougé. On the existence of symmetric algorithms to find leaders in networks of communicating sequential processes. *Acta Informatica*, 25:179–201, 1988.

[BPS01] J.A. Bergstra, A. Ponse, and S.A. Smolka, editors. *Handbook of Process Algebra*. Elsevier, 2001.

[Bro83] S.D. Brookes. *A model for communicating sequential processes*. PhD thesis, Oxford University, 1983.

[Bro86] M. Broy. A theory for nondeterminism, parallelism, communication, and concurrency. *Theoretical Computer Science*, 45(1):1–61, 1986.

[Bro93a] S. Brookes. Full abstraction for a shared variable parallel language. In *Proceedings 8th Annual IEEE Symposium on Logic in Computer Science, Montreal, Canada, June 19–23, 1993*, pages 98–109. IEEE, IEEE Computer Society Press, 1993.

[Bro93b] Manfred Broy. Interaction refinement – the easy way. In M. Broy, editor, *Program Design Calculi*, volume 118 of *NATO Advanced Science Institutes Series F: Computer and System Sciences*. Springer-Verlag, 1993.

[Bro96] S.D. Brookes. Full abstraction for a shared-variable parallel language. *Information and Computation*, 127(2):145–163, June 1996.

[Bro97] Manfred Broy. Compositional refinement of interactive systems. *Journal of the ACM*, 44(6):850–891, November 1997.

[Bro98] M. Broy. Compositional refinement of interactive systems modelled by relations. In de Roever et al. [dRLP98].

[Bry95] R.E. Bryant. Bit-level analysis of an SRT divider circuit. Technical Report CMU-CS-95-140, School of Computer Science, Carnegie Mellon University, Pittsburgh, PA, April 1995.

[BS89] R. Back and K. Sere. Stepwise refinement of action systems. In Jan L. A. Van de Snepscheut, editor, *Mathematics of program construction: 375th anniversary of the Groningen University: international conference, Groningen, The Netherlands, June 26–30, 1989*, volume 375 of *LNCS*, pages 115–138. Springer-Verlag, 1989.

[BS90] R. Back and K. Sere. Stepwise refinement of parallel algorithms. *Science of Computer Programming*, 1:133–180, 1990.

[BS91] R. Back and K. Sere. Stepwise refinement of action systems. *Structured Programming*, 12:17–30, 1991.

[BS92] R. Back and K. Sere. Superposition refinement of parallel algorithms. In K.R. Parker and G.A. Rose, editors, *Formal Description Techniques IV*. IFIP Transaction C-2, North-Holland, 1992.

[BS01] Manfred Broy and Ketil Stølen. *Specification and Development of Interactive Systems: FOCUS on Streams, Interfaces, and Refinement*. Springer-Verlag, 2001. To appear.

[BST98] S. Bornot, J. Sifakis, and S. Tripakis. Modeling urgency in timed systems. In de Roever et al. [dRLP98], pages 103–129.

[BvW90] Ralph J.R. Back and Joakim von Wright. Refinement calculus, part I: Sequential nondeterministic programs. In de Bakker et al. [dBdRR90], pages 43–66.

[C⁺86] R.L. Constable et al. *Implementing Mathematics with the Nuprl Proof Development System*. Prentice Hall, 1986.

[Cau96] Antonio Cau. Compositional verification and specification of refinement for reactive systems in a dense time temporal logic. Technical Report Bericht Nr. 9601, Institut für Informatik und Praktische Mathematik, University of Kiel, 1996.

[Cau00] Antonio Cau. Composing and refining dense temporal logic specifications. *Formal Aspects of Computing*, 12(1):52–70, 2000.

[CC96] Pierre Collette and Antonio Cau.   Parallel composition of assumption-commitment specifications: a unifying approach for shared variable and distributed message passing concurrency. *Acta Informatica*, 33(2):153–176, 1996.

[CC99] M. Charpentier and K. Mani Chandy. Towards a compositional approach to the design and verification of distributed systems. In J.M. Wing, J. Woodcock, and J. Davies, editors, *FM '99: World Congress on Formal Methods in the Development of Computing Systems, Toulouse, France, September 1999*, volume 1708 of *LNCS*, pages 570–589 (vol. I). Springer-Verlag, 1999.

[CdR93] A. Cau and W.-P. de Roever. Specifying fault tolerance within Stark's formalism. In *Proc. 23rd Symposium on Fault-Tolerant Computing*, pages 392–401. IEEE Computer Society Press, 1993.

[CE82] E.M. Clarke and E.A. Emerson.   Design and synthesis of synchronization skeletons for branching time temporal logic. In Dexter Kozen, editor, *Logics of Programs Workshop, IBM Watson Research Center, Yorktown Heights, New York, May 1981*, volume 131 of *LNCS*, pages 52–71. Springer-Verlag, 1982.

[CG88] C. Chou and E. Gafni. Understanding and verifying distributed algorithms using stratified decomposition. In *Proceedings 7th ACM Symposium on Principles of Distributed Computing*, 1988.

[CGP99] Edmund M. Clarke, Orna Grumberg, and Doron A. Peled. *Model Checking*. MIT Press, December 1999.

[CGZ96] E.M. Clarke, S.M. German, and X. Zhao. Verifying the SRT division algorithm using theorem proving techniques. In Alur and Henzinger [AH96], pages 111–122.

[CH88] T. Coquand and G. Huet. The Calculus of Constructions. *Information and Computation*, 76(2/3):95–120, 1988.

[CH93] J. Coenen and J. Hooman. Parameterized semantics for fault tolerant real-time systems. In J. Vytopil, editor, *Formal Techniques in Real-Time and Fault Tolerant Systems*, pages 51–78. Kluwer Academic Publishers, 1993.

[Cha94] K. Mani Chandy. Properties of concurrent programs. *Formal Aspects of Computing*, 6(6):607–619, 1994.

[CK95] P. Collette and E. Knapp. Logical foundations for compositional verification and development of concurrent programs in UNITY. In *Proceedings of the 4th International Conference on Algebraic Methodology and Software Technology (AMAST '95)*, volume 936 of *LNCS*, pages 353–367. Springer-Verlag, 1995.

[CK97] Pierre Collette and Edgar Knapp. A foundation for modular reasoning about safety and progress properties of state-based concurrent programs. *Theoretical Computer Science*, 183(2):253–279, 1997.

[CKdR92] A. Cau, R. Kuiper, and W.-P. de Roever. Formalising Dijkstra's development strategy within Stark's formalism. In Jones, Shaw, and Denvir, editors, *Proc. 5th Refinement Workshop*. Workshops in Computing Series, Springer-Verlag, 1992.

[CL85] K. Mani Chandy and Leslie Lamport. Distributed snapshots: Determining global states of distributed systems. *ACM Transactions on Computing Systems*, 3(1):63–75, February 1985.

[Cla85] E.M. Clarke. The characterization problem for Hoare logics. *Mathematical Logic and Programming Languages*, 1985. Prentice Hall.

[Cli73] M. Clint. Program proving: Coroutines. *Acta Informatica*, 2(1):50–63, 1973.

[CLM89] Ed M. Clarke, D.E. Long, and K.L. McMillan. Compositional model checking. In *Proc. LICS '89*, pages 353–362. IEEE Computer Society Press, 1989.

[CM84] K.M. Chandy and J. Misra. The drinking-philosophers problem. *TOPLAS*, 6(4):632–646, 1984.

[CM88] K.M. Chandy and J. Misra. *Parallel Program Design: A Foundation*. Addison-Wesley, 1988.

[CMP94] Edward Chang, Zohar Manna, and Amir Pnueli. Compositional verification of real-time systems. In *Proc. LICS '94*. IEEE Computer Society Press, 1994.

[Coe93] J. Coenen. Top-down development of layered fault tolerant systems and its problems – a deontic perspective. *Annals of Mathematics and Artificial Intelligence*, 9:133–150, 1993.

[Coh90] E. Cohen. *Programming in the 1990s*. Springer-Verlag, 1990.

[Col93] Pierre Collette. Application of the composition principle to UNITY-like specifications. In Gaudel and Jouannaud [GJ93].

[Col94a] P. Collette. *Design of Compositional Proof Systems based on Assumption-Commitment Specifications – Application to UNITY*. PhD thesis, Université Catholique de Louvain, Belgium, 1994.

[Col94b] Pierre Collette. An explanatory presentation of composition rules for assumption-commitment specifications. *Information Processing Letters*, 50(1):31–35, 1994.

[Coo78] S.A. Cook. Soundness and completeness of an axiom system for program verification. *SIAM Journal on Computing*, 7(1):70–90, 1978.

[Cri85] F. Cristian. A rigorous approach to fault-tolerant programming. *IEEE Transactions on Software Engineering*, SE-11(1):23–31, 1985.

[Cri89] F. Cristian. Probabilistic clock synchronization. *Distributed Computing*, 3:146–156, 1989.

[CS95a] K. Mani Chandy and Beverly A. Sanders. Predicate transformers for reasoning about concurrent programs. *Science of Computer Programming*, 24:129–148, 1995.

[CS95b] K.M. Chandy and B.A. Sanders. Predicate transformers for reasoning about concurrent computation. *Science of Computer Programming*, 24(2):129–148, 1995.

[CS96] K. Mani Chandy and Beverly A. Sanders. Reasoning about program composition. Technical Report 96-035, University of Florida, Department of Computer and Information Science and Engineering, 1996.

[CT91] K. Mani Chandy and Stephen Taylor. *Introduction to Parallel Programming*. Jones & Bartlett, 1991.

[CZ95] E.M. Clarke and X. Zhao. Word level symbolic model checking: A new approach for verifying arithmetic circuits. Technical Report CMU-CS-95-161, School of Computer Science, Carnegie Mellon University, Pittsburgh, PA, April 1995.

[Dah92] Ole-Johan Dahl. *Verifiable Programming*. Prentice Hall, 1992.

[Dam98] Mads Dam. Proving properties of dynamic process networks. *Information and Computation*, 140:95–114, 1998. A preliminary version appeared as "Compositional Proof Systems for Model Checking Infinite State Processes", CONCUR '95, LNCS 962, 12–26, Springer-Verlag, 1995.

[Dav93] J.W.M. Davies. *Specification and proof in real-time CSP*. Cambridge University Press, 1993.

[dB67] N.G. de Bruijn. Letter to the editor: Additional comments on a problem in concurrent programming control. *Communications of the ACM*, 10(3):137–138, March 1967.

[dB69] J.W. de Bakker. Semantics of programming languages. *Advances in Information Systems Science*, 2, 1969. Plenum Press.

[dB80] J.W. de Bakker. *Mathematical Theory of Program Correctness*. Prentice Hall, London, 1980.

[dB86] F.S. de Boer. A proof rule for process creation. In M. Wirsing, editor, *Formal Description of Programming Concepts*, 3rd IFIP WG 2.2 working conference, GI. Avernæs, Ebberup, Denmark, 1986.

[dB90] F.S. de Boer. A proof system for the parallel object-oriented language POOL. In M.S. Patterson, editor, *Proc. of ICALP '90*, volume 443 of *LNCS*. Springer-Verlag, 1990.

[dB91a] F.S. de Boer. A compositional proof system for dynamic process creation. In *Proceedings of the sixth annual IEEE symposium on Logics in Computer Science LICS*. IEEE Computer Society Press, Amsterdam, The Netherlands, 1991.

[dB91b] F.S. de Boer. *Reasoning about Dynamically Evolving Process Structures: A proof theory for the parallel object-oriented language POOL*. PhD thesis, Free University, Amsterdam, 1991.

[dB94] F.S. de Boer. Compositionality in the inductive assertion method for concurrent systems. In Olderog [Old94], pages 282–302.

[dB98] F.S. de Boer. Reasoning about asynchronous communication in dynamically evolving object structures. In *CONCUR '98*, volume 1466 of *LNCS*. Springer-Verlag, 1998.

[dB99] F.S. de Boer. A WP-calculus for OO. In *Proceedings of Foundations of Software Science and Computation Structures, FOSSACS '99*, volume 1578 of *LNCS*. Springer-Verlag, 1999.

[dB02] F.S. de Boer. Reasoning about asynchronous communication in dynamically evolving object structures. *Theoretical Computer Science*, 272(1–2), 2002. To appear.

[dBdR72] J.W. de Bakker and W.-P. de Roever. A calculus for recursive program schemes. In Maurice Nivat, editor, *Automata, Languages, and Programming, Proc. of a Symposium organized by IRIA*, pages 167–196. North-Holland/American Elsevier, July 1972.

[dBdRR89] J.W. de Bakker, W.-P. de Roever, and G. Rozenberg, editors. *Linear Time, Branching Time and Partial Order in Logics and Models for Concurrency*, volume 354 of *LNCS*. Springer-Verlag, 1989.

[dBdRR90] J.W. de Bakker, W.P. de Roever, and G. Rozenberg, editors. *Proceedings of the REX Workshop on Stepwise Refinement of Distributed Systems: models, formalisms, correctness, Mook, The Netherlands, May 29–June 2, 1989*, volume 430 of *LNCS*. Springer-Verlag, 1990.

[dBdRR94] J.W. de Bakker, W.-P. de Roever, and G. Rozenberg, editors. *Proceedings of the REX School/Symposium "A Decade of Concurrency: Reflections and Perspectives", Noordwijkerhout, June 1–4, 1993*, volume 803 of *LNCS*. Springer-Verlag, 1994.

[dBFvHS98] Frank S. de Boer, Nissim Francez, Marten van Hulst, and Frank Stomp. A proof theory of asynchronously communicating sequential processes. In David Gries and Willem-Paul de Roever, editors, *Programming Concepts and Methods PROCOMET'98*, pages 49–67. Chapman & Hall, 1998.

[dBH92] F.S. de Boer and J. Hooman. The real time behaviour of asynchronously communicating processes. In *2nd Symposium Formal Techniques in Real-Time and Fault-Tolerant Systems, Nijmegen*, volume 571 of *LNCS*, pages 451–472. Springer-Verlag, 1992.

[dBHdR97a] F.S. de Boer, U. Hannemann, and W.-P. de Roever. A compositional proof system for shared-variable concurrency. In John Fitzgerald, Cliff B. Jones, and Peter Lucas, editors, *FME '97: Industrial Applications and Strengthened Foundations of Formal Methods*, volume 1313 of *LNCS*, pages 515–532, Berlin, Heidelberg, New York, 1997. Springer-Verlag.

[dBHdR97b] F.S. de Boer, U. Hannemann, and W.-P. de Roever. Hoare-style compositional proof systems for reactive shared variable concurrency. In *FSTTCS '97: Foundations of Software Technology and Theoretical Computer Science*, volume 1346 of *LNCS*, Berlin, Heidelberg, New York, 1997. Springer-Verlag.

[dBHdR99a] Frank de Boer, Ulrich Hannemann, and Willem-Paul de Roever. Formal justification of the rely-guarantee paradigm for shared-variable concurrency: A semantic approach. In Jeannette Wing, Jim Woodcock, and Jim Davies, editors, *FM '99 – Formal Methods*, volume 1709 of *LNCS*, pages 1245–1265, Berlin, Heidelberg, New York, 1999. Springer-Verlag.

[dBHdR99b] Frank de Boer, Ulrich Hannemann, and Willem-Paul de Roever. The semantic foundations of a compositional proof method for synchronously communicating processes. In Mirosław Kutyłowski, Lescek Pacholski, and Tomasz Wierzbicki, editors, *Mathematical Foundations of Computer Science 1999*, number 1672 in LNCS, pages 343–353, Berlin, Heidelberg, New York, 1999. Springer-Verlag.

[dBHdRR92] J.W. de Bakker, C. Huizing, W.-P. de Roever, and G. Rozenberg, editors. *Proc. of the REX Workshop Real-Time: Theory in Practice, Mook, June 1991*, volume 600 of *LNCS*. Springer-Verlag, June 1992.

[dBKPR91] F.S. de Boer, J.N. Kok, C. Palamidessi, and J.J.M.M. Rutten. The failure of failures: towards a paradigm for asynchronous communication. In Baeten and Groote, editors, *CONCUR '91*, volume 527 of *LNCS*. Springer-Verlag, 1991.

[dBM75] J.W. de Bakker and L.G.L.T. Meertens. On the completeness of the inductive assertion method. *Computer and System Sciences*, 11:323–357, 1975.

[dBP94] F.S. de Boer and C. Palamidessi. Embedding as a tool for language comparison. *Information and Computation*, 108(1), 1994.

[dBS69] J.W. de Bakker and Dana S. Scott. A theory of programs. Unpublished manuscript. Reprinted in [KMR89, pages 1–30], 1969.

[dBTdRvH96] F.S. de Boer, H. Tej, W.-P. de Roever, and M. van Hulst. Compositionality in real-time shared-variable concurrency. In *Proc. of the 17th Conference on Foundations of Software Technology and Theoretical Computer Science (FSTTCS 96)*, volume 1180 of *LNCS*. Springer-Verlag, 1996.

[DD99] Bernard Dion and Sylvan Dissoubray. Modeling and implementing critical real-time systems with SyncCharts/Esterel. *Real-Time Magazine*, 1:58–63, 1999.

[DDH72] Ole-Johan Dahl, Edsger W. Dijkstra, and C.A.R Hoare. *Structured Programming*, volume 8 of *APIC Studies in Data Processing*. Academic Press, 1972.

[DF88] Edsger W. Dijkstra and Wim H.J. Feijen. *A Method of Programming*. Addison Wesley, 1988.

[DF95] J. Dingel and T. Filkorn. Model checking for infinite state systems using data abstraction, assumption-commitment style reasoning and theorem proving. In *Proceedings of the Seventh International Conference on Computer Aided Verification (CAV '95)*, number 939 in LNCS, pages 54–69, Liege, Belgium, July 1995. Springer-Verlag.

[DH94] Werner Damm and Johannes Helbig. Linking visual formalisms: A compositional proof system for statecharts based on symbolic timing diagrams. In *IFIP Working Conference on Programming Concepts, Methods and Calculi (PRO-COMET '94). North-Holland*, pages 337–356, 1994.

[Dij59] E.W. Dijkstra. *Communication with an automatic computer*. Proefschrift (dissertation), University of Amsterdam, 1959. Published by Excelsior, Rijswijk, Netherlands.

[Dij62] E.W. Dijkstra. Some meditations on advanced programming. In *Proceedings of the IFIP Congress 1962*, pages 535–538, 1962.

[Dij65a] E.W. Dijkstra. Programming considered as a human activity. In *Proceedings of the IFIP Congress 1965*, pages 213–217, 1965.

[Dij65b] E.W. Dijkstra. Solution of a problem in concurrent programming control. *CACM*, 8(9), 1965.

[Dij68a] E.W. Dijkstra. Cooperating sequential processes. In F. Genuys, editor, *Programming Languages*, pages 43–112. Academic Press, New York, 1968.

[Dij68b] E.W. Dijkstra. Go to statement considered harmful. *CACM*, 11:147–148, 1968.

[Dij68c] E.W. Dijkstra. The structure of the "THE" multiprogramming system. *CACM*, 11(5):341–346, 1968.

[Dij69a] E.W. Dijkstra. EWD 264. Published in an extended version as [Dij69b], August 1969.

[Dij69b] E.W. Dijkstra. Structured programming. In J.N. Buxton and B. Randell, editors, *Software Engineering Techniques, Report on a conference sponsored by the NATO Science Committee*, pages 84–88. NATO Science Committee, 1969.

[Dij71] E.W. Dijkstra. A short introduction to the art of computer programming. Technical report, Technische Hogeschool, Eindhoven, 1971.

[Dij72a] E.W. Dijkstra. Hierarchical ordering of sequential processes. In C.A.R. Hoare and R.H. Perrot, editors, *Operating Systems Techniques*, pages 72–98, London and New York, 1972. Academic Press. Proceedings of a seminar held at Queen's University, Belfast, 1971.

[Dij72b] E.W. Dijkstra. The humble programmer. *Communications of the ACM*, 15(10):859–866, October 1972. 1972 ACM Turing Award Lecture.

[Dij72c] E.W. Dijkstra. Notes on structured programming. In *Structured Programming* [DDH72].

[Dij74] E.W. Dijkstra. Self-stabilizing systems in spite of distributed control. *Communications of the ACM*, 17(11):643–644, November 1974.

[Dij75a] Edsger W. Dijkstra. Guarded commands, nondeterminacy and formal derivation of programs. *Communications of the ACM*, 18(8):453–457, 1975.

[Dij75b] E.W. Dijkstra. EWD 500: After many a sobering experience. Technical report, Burroughs, Nuenen, The Netherlands, 1975. Obtainable from Ir. Wim Feijen, Eindhoven University of Technology.

[Dij76] E.W. Dijkstra. *A discipline of programming*. Prentice Hall, 1976.

[Dij77] E.W. Dijkstra. A correctness proof for communicating processes-a small exercise. Technical Report EWD-607, Burroughs, Nuenen, The Netherlands, 1977.

[Dij82] E.W. Dijkstra. *Selected Writings on Computing: A Personal Perspective.* Springer-Verlag, 1982.

[Din96] J. Dingel. Modular verification for shared-variable concurrent programs. In *Proceedings of the Seventh International Conference on Concurrency Theory (CONCUR '96)*, volume 1119 of *LNCS*, pages 703–718, Pisa, Italy, August 1996. Springer-Verlag.

[Din99a] J. Dingel. *Systematic Parallel Programming*. PhD thesis, Computer Science Department, Carnegie Mellon University, Pittsburgh, USA, November 1999. Technical report CMU-CS-99-172.

[Din99b] J. Dingel. A trace-based refinement calculus for shared-variable parallel programs. In *Proceedings of the Seventh International Conference on Algebraic Methodology and Software Technology (AMAST '98)*, number 1548 in LNCS, pages 231–247, Amazonia, Brazil, January 1999. Springer-Verlag.

[DJHP98] Werner Damm, Bernhard Josko, Hardi Hungar, and Amir Pnueli. A compositional real-time semantics of STATEMATE designs. In de Roever et al. [dRLP98], pages 186–238.

[DJS95] W. Damm, B. Josko, and R. Schlör. Specification and verification of VHDL-based system-level hardware designs. In E. Börger, editor, *Specification and Validation Methods*, pages 331–410. Oxford University Press, 1995.

[DLM$^+$78] E.W. Dijkstra, L. Lamport, A.J. Martin, C.S. Scholten, and E.F.M. Steffens. On-the-fly garbage collection: An exercise in cooperation. *CACM*, 21(11):966–974, 1978.

[dR76] W.-P. de Roever. Recursive program schemes: Semantics and proof theory. Mathematical Centre Tracts 70, Mathematisch Centrum, Amsterdam, 1976. Appeared first as PhD. thesis, Vrije Universiteit Amsterdam, January 1975.

[dR85a] W.-P. de Roever. The cooperation test: a syntax-oriented verification method. In Apt [Apt85].

[dR85b] W.-P. de Roever. The quest for compositionality – a survey of assertion-based proof systems for concurrent programs, part 1: Concurrency based on shared variables. In *Proc. of IFIP Working Conf., The Role of Abstract Models in Computer Science, North-Holland*, 1985.

[dR98] Willem-Paul de Roever. The need for compositional proof systems: A survey. In de Roever et al. [dRLP98], pages 1–22.

[dRE98] W.-P. de Roever and K. Engelhardt. *Data Refinement.* Cambridge University Press, 1998.

[dRLP98] Willem-Paul de Roever, Hans Langmaack, and Amir Pnueli, editors. *Compositionality: The Significant Difference, Proceedings of the International Symposium COMPOS '97, Malente, Germany, September 7–12, 1997,* volume 1536 of *LNCS.* Springer-Verlag, 1998.

[DS92] J.W.M. Davies and S.A. Schneider. A brief history of Timed CSP. Computing Laboratory Monograph PRG-96, Oxford University, 1992.

[Ebe89] Jo C. Ebergen. Translating Programs into Delay-Insensitve Circuits. CWI Tracts Vol. 56, CWI (Centre for Mathematics and Computer Science), Amsterdam, 1989.

[EF82] T. Elrad and N. Francez. Decomposition of distributed programs into communication closed layers. *Science of Computer Programming,* 2:155–173, 1982.

[EGL93] Urban Engberg, Peter Grønning, and Leslie Lamport. Mechanical verification of concurrent systems with TLA. In von Bochmann and Probst [vBP93], pages 44–55.

[Eme81] E.A. Emerson. *Branching Time Temporal Logic and the Design of Correct Concurrent Programs.* PhD thesis, Harvard University, August 1981.

[FF96] Nissim Francez and Ira Forman. *Interacting processes: a multiparty approach to coordinated distributed programming.* Addison-Wesley, 1996.

[FFG90] L. Fix, N. Francez, and O. Grumberg. Semantics-driven decompositions for the verification of distributed programs. In M. Broy and C. Jones, editors, *Programming Concepts and Methods,* pages 101–123. Elsevier Science Publishers, 1990.

[FHLdR79] N. Francez, C.A.R. Hoare, D. Lehmann, and W.P. de Roever. Semantics of nondeterminism, concurrency and communication. *JCSS,* 19:290–308, 1979.

[Flo67] R.W. Floyd. Assigning meanings to programs. In *Proceedings AMS Symposium Applied Mathematics,* volume 19, pages 19–31, Providence, R.I., 1967. American Mathematical Society.

[Flo79] Robert W. Floyd. The paradigms of programming. *CACM,* 22(8):455–460, 1979.

[FLP80] N. Francez, D. Lehmann, and A. Pnueli. A linear history semantics for distributed languages (extended abstract). In *21st Annual Symposium on Foundations of Computer Science,* pages 143–151, Syracuse, New York, October 1980. IEEE. See [FLP84] for the journal version.

[FLP84] N. Francez, D. Lehmann, and A. Pnueli. A linear-history semantics for languages for distributed programming. *Theoretical Computer Science,* 32:25–46, 1984.

[FM98] Marcela F. Frias and Roger D. Maddux. Completeness of a relational calculus for program schemes. In *Proc. 13th Annual IEEE Symposium on Logic in Computer Science (LICS '98), Indianapolis, Indiana, June 21–24, 1998,* pages 127–134. IEEE Computer Society, 1998.

[FMS98] B. Finkbeiner, Z. Manna, and H. Sipma. Deductive verification of modular systems. In de Roever et al. [dRLP98], pages 239–275.

[FP78] N. Francez and A. Pnueli. A proof method for cyclic programs. *Acta Informatica,* 9:133–157, 1978.

[FPZ93] M. Fokkinga, M. Poel, and J. Zwiers. Modular completeness for communication closed layers. In Eike Best, editor, *Proceedings CONCUR '93*, volume 715 of *LNCS*, pages 50–65. Springer-Verlag, 1993.

[FR80] Nissim Francez and Michael Rodeh. Achieving distributed termination without freezing. Technical Report TR 72, IBM Israel Scientific Center, 1980.

[FR82] Nissim Francez and Michael Rodeh. Achieving distributed termination without freezing. *IEEE Transactions on Software Engineering*, 8(2):287–292, 1982.

[Fra76] N. Francez. *The Analysis of Cyclic Programs*. PhD thesis, Weizmann Institute of Science, Rehovot, Israel, 1976.

[Fra79] Nissim Francez. On achieving distributed termination. In Kahn [Kah79], pages 300–315.

[Fra80] Nissim Francez. Distributed termination. *ACM TOPLAS*, 2(1):42–55, January 1980.

[Fra86] N. Francez. *Fairness*. Springer-Verlag, New York, 1986.

[Fra92] Nissim Francez. *Program Verification*. Addison-Wesley, Wokingham, 1992.

[Fre79] Gottlob Frege. *Begriffsschrift, eine der arithmetischen nachgebildete Formelsprache des reinen Denkens*. Louis Nebert, Halle, 1879. Reprinted in [Ang67, pp. 89–93].

[Fre84] Gottlob Frege. *Die Grundlagen der Arithmetik. Eine logisch-mathematische Untersuchung über den Begriff der Zahl*. W. Koebner, Breslau, 1884. Reprint published by Georg Olms, Hildesheim, 1961. Translated as [Fre53].

[Fre23] Gottlob Frege. Logische Untersuchungen. Dritter Teil: Gedankengefüge. *Beiträge zur Philosophie des Deutschen Idealismus*, 3(1):36–51, 1923. Reprinted in [Ang67, pp. 378–394]. English translation in [Fre77].

[Fre53] Gottlob Frege. *The foundations of arithmetic. A logico-mathematical enquiry into the concept of number*. Basil Blackwell, Oxford, second revised edition, 1953. Translation (with original text) by J.L. Austin.

[Fre77] Gottlob Frege. Compound thoughts. In P. Geach and N. Black, editors, *Logical Investigations*. Blackwells, Oxford, 1977.

[FRS81] Nissim Francez, Michael Rodeh, and Michel Sintzoff. Distributed termination with interval assertions. In J. Diaz and I. Ramos, editors, *Proc. International Colloquium on Formalization of programming concepts, Peniscola, Spain, April 19–25, 1981*, volume 107, 1981.

[Fut88] The Institute of Electrical and Electronics Engineers, Inc. *IEEE Standard Backplane Bus Specification for Multiprocessor Architectures: Futurebus*, 1988.

[FvG99] W.H.J. Feijen and A.J.M. van Gasteren. *On a Method of Multiprogramming*. Monographs in Computer Science. Springer-Verlag, 1999.

[GB87] R. Gerth and A. Boucher. A timed failures model for extended communicating processes. In Th. Ottmann, editor, *Proceedings of the 14th ICALP Colloquium*, volume 267 of *LNCS*, pages 95–114. Springer-Verlag, 1987.

[GdR84] R.T. Gerth and W.-P. de Roever. A proof system for concurrent ADA programs. *Science of Computer Programming*, 4:159–204, 1984.

[GdR86] R.T. Gerth and W.-P. de Roever. Proving monitors revisited: A first step towards verifying object-oriented systems. *Fundamenta Informatica, North-Holland*, IX:371–400, 1986. A list of errata, required to make the proof system complete, appears in a later issue; this list can also be obtained directly from W.-P. de Roever.

[GdRR82] R. Gerth, W.-P. de Roever, and M. Roncken. Procedures and concurrency: a proof theoretical study. In M. Dezani-Ciancaglini and U. Montanari, editors, *Pro-*

ceedings of the International Symposium on Programming: 5th colloquium, Turin, April 6–8, 1982, volume 137 of *LNCS*. Springer-Verlag, 1982.

[Ger84] R. Gerth. Transition logic: How to reason about temporal properties in a compositional way. In *Proceedings of the 16th Annual ACM Symposium on the Theory of Computing (STOC)*, pages 39–50, New York, NY, 1984. ACM, ACM Press.

[Ger89] R.T. Gerth. *Syntax-directed verification of distributed systems*. PhD thesis, University of Utrecht, 1989.

[Ger90] Rob Gerth. Foundations of compositional program refinement. In de Bakker et al. [dBdRR90], pages 777–808.

[GFMdR81] O. Grumberg, N. Francez, J.A. Makowski, and W.-P. de Roever. A proof rule for fair termination of guarded commands. In J.W. de Bakker and H. van Vliet, editors, *Proc. of Symposium on Algorithmic Languages*. North-Holland, 1981. In revised form in: *Information and Control* 66, no 1/2, pp. 83–102, 1985.

[GG91] S.J. Garland and J.V. Guttag. A guide to LP, the LARCH prover. Technical Report SRC Report 82, Digital Systems Research Center, 1991.

[GHS83] R. Gallager, P. Humblet, and P. Spira. A distributed algorithm for minimum-weight spanning trees. *ACM TOPLAS*, 5(1):66–77, January 1983.

[GJ93] M.-C. Gaudel and J.-P. Jouannaud, editors. *TAPSOFT '93: theory and practice of software development: 4th International Joint Conference CAAP/FASE, Orsay, France, April 13–17, 1993*, volume 668 of *LNCS*. Springer-Verlag, 1993.

[GJS81a] J.A.G. Groenendijk, T.M.V. Janssen, and M.B.J. Stokhof, editors. *Formal methods in the study of language. Proceedings of the third Amsterdam colloquium. Part 1*, number 135 in CWI Tracts, Amsterdam, 1981. Centre for Mathematics and Computer Science.

[GJS81b] J.A.G. Groenendijk, T.M.V. Janssen, and M.B.J. Stokhof, editors. *Formal methods in the study of language. Proceedings of the third Amsterdam colloquium. Part 2*, number 136 in CWI Tracts, Amsterdam, 1981. Centre for Mathematics and Computer Science.

[GJS96] J. Gosling, B. Joy, and G. Steele. *The Java Language Specification*. Addison-Wesley, 1996.

[GL94] Orna Grumberg and David Long. Model checking and modular verification. *ACM TOPLAS*, 16(3):843–871, 1994.

[GM93] Paul H.B. Gardiner and Carroll C. Morgan. A single complete rule for data refinement. *Formal Aspects of Computing*, 5(4):367–382, 1993.

[GN90] P. Grønning and T. Qvist Nielsen. Compositional specification and verification of concurrent systems. Master's thesis, Dept. of Computer Science, Technical University of Denmark, Lyngby, 1990.

[GNL90] Peter Grønning, Thomas Qvist Nielsen, and Hans Henrik Løvengreen. Refinement and composition of transition-based rely-guarantee specifications with auxiliary variables. In K.V. Nori and C.E. Veni Madhavan, editors, *Proc. of FST/TCS, Bangalore, India, 17-19 Dec.*, volume 472 of *LNCS*. Springer-Verlag, 1990.

[GNRR93] R. Grossman, A. Nerode, A. Ravn, and H. Rischel, editors. *Hybrid Systems*, volume 736 of *LNCS*. Springer-Verlag, 1993.

[Göd31] K. Gödel. Über formal unentscheidbare Sätze der Principia Mathematica und verwandter Systeme. *Monatshefte für Mathematik und Physik*, 38:173–198, 1931.

[Gor75] G.A. Gorelick. A complete axiomatic system for proving assertions about recursive and non-recursive programs. Technical report, University of Toronto, 1975.

[GR84] A. Goldberg and D. Robson. *Smalltalk-80, The Language and its Implementation.* Addison-Wesley, 1984.

[GR90] Rob Gerth and Marly Roncken. A denotational semantics for synchronous and asynchronous behavior with multiform time. In *Proceedings of the BCS-FACS Workshop on Semantics of Concurrency, Leicester*, Workshops in Computing, London, July 1990. Springer-Verlag.

[Gri77] D. Gries. An exercise in proving parallel programs correct. *CACM*, 20(12):921–930, 1977.

[Gri81] D. Gries. *The Science of Programming.* Texts and Monographs in Computer Science. Springer-Verlag, 1981.

[Gri96] E.P. Gribomont. Atomicity refinement and trace reduction theorems. In Alur and Henzinger [AH96], pages xii + 472.

[Grø90] Peter Grønning. Compositional specification and verification using protocols. Technical report, Technical University of Denmark, Lyngby, 1990.

[GS86] R. Gerth and L. Shira. On proving communication closedness of distributed layers. In *Proceedings 6th Conference on Foundations of Software Technology and Theoretical Computer Science*, 1986.

[Gun92] Carl A. Gunter. *Semantics of Programming Languages: Structures and Techniques.* Foundations of Computing Series. The MIT Press, Cambridge, Massachusetts, 1992.

[Gur91] Y. Gurevich. Evolving algebras: A tutorial introduction. *Bulletin of the EATCS*, 43:264–284, 1991.

[GvN47] H.H. Goldstine and J. von Neumann. Planning and coding problems for an electronic computer. In Traub [Tra63], pages 80–235.

[Hal93] Nicolas Halbwachs. *Synchronous programming of reactive systems.* Kluwer Academic Publishers, 1993.

[Han00] Ulrich Hannemann. *Semantic Analysis of Compositional Proof Methods for Concurrency.* PhD thesis, Department of Computer Science, University of Utrecht, October 2000.

[Har78] David Harel. *Logics of Programs: Axiomatics and Descriptive Power.* PhD thesis, Massachusetts Institute of Technology, May 1978. Technical report MIT/LCS/TR-200, appeared also as [Har79].

[Har79] David Harel. *First-Order Dynamic Logic*, volume 68 of *LNCS*. Springer-Verlag, 1979. A revision of [Har78].

[Har87] David Harel. Statecharts: A visual formalism for complex systems. *Science of Computer Programming*, 8(3):231–274, 1987.

[Hav99] K. Havelund. Mechanical verification of a garbage collector. In J. Rolim et al., editor, *Parallel and Distributed Processing*, volume 1586 of *LNCS*, pages 1258–1283. Springer-Verlag, 1999.

[HC70] A. Holt and F. Commoner. Events and conditions. In *Record of the Project MAC Conference on Concurrent Systems and Parallel Computation, June 1970*, pages 3–52, 1970.

[HCP91] N. Halbwachs, P. Caspi, and D. Pilaud. The synchronous dataflow programming language LUSTRE. *Proceedings of the IEEE, Another Look at Real-time Programming*, 79(9):1305–1319, September 1991. Special issue.

[HdR86] J. Hooman and W.-P. de Roever. The quest goes on: A survey of proof systems for partial correctness of CSP. In J.W. de Bakker, W.-P. de Roever, and G. Rozenberg, editors, *Current Trends in Concurrency*, volume 224 of *LNCS*, pages 343–395. Springer-Verlag, 1986.

[HdR91] J.J.M. Hooman and W.-P. de Roever. Verification and specification of concurrent programs. Technical report 9111, Institut für Informatik und Praktische Mathematik, Kiel University, 1991.

[HdR94] U. Hannemann and W.-P. de Roever. Modular completeness of state-trace-based proof systems for partial correctness of concurrent programs. Technical report, Institut für Informatik und Praktische Mathematik, Kiel University, 1994.

[HdRP$^+$00] J. Hooman, W.-P. de Roever, P. Pandya, H. Schepers, Q. Xu, and P. Zhou. *Compositional Theory of Concurrency*. Cambridge University Press, 2000. To appear.

[Heh84] Eric C.R. Hehner. *The Logic of Programming*. Prentice Hall, 1984.

[Heh93] Eric C.R. Hehner. *A Practical Theory of Programming*. Texts and Monographs in Computer Science. Springer-Verlag, 1993.

[Hen88] Matthew Hennessy. *Algebraic Theory of Processes*. The MIT Press, Cambridge, Massachusetts, 1988.

[Hes96] Wim H. Hesselink. The verified incremental design of a distributed spanning tree algorithm. Computing Science Report CSR 9602, Rijksuniversiteit Groningen, 1996. Extended abstract in *Formal Aspects of Computing* 11(1): 45–55, 1999.

[HGdR87] C. Huizing, R. Gerth, and W.-P. de Roever. Full abstraction of a real-time denotational semantics for an OCCAM-like language. In *Proc. of the 1987 ACM Symposium on Principles of Programming Languages POPL*, pages 223–237, New York, 1987. ACM.

[HGdR88] C. Huizing, R. Gerth, and W.-P. de Roever. Modeling statecharts' behaviour in a fully abstract way. In *Proc. CAAP'88*, volume 299 of *LNCS*. springer, 1988.

[HH83] E.C.R. Hehner and C.A.R. Hoare. A more complete model of communicating processes. *Theoretical Computer Science*, 26:105–120, September 1983.

[HH98] C.A.R. Hoare and J. He. *Unifying Theories of Programming*. Prentice Hall Series in Computer Science. Prentice Hall, 1998.

[HHF$^+$94] Jifeng He, C.A.R. Hoare, Martin Fränzle, Markus Müller-Olm, Ernst-Rüdiger Olderog, Michael Schenke, Michael R. Hansen, Anders P. Ravn, and Hans Rischel. Provably correct systems. In Langmaack et al. [LdRV94], pages 288–335.

[HHS87] C.A.R. Hoare, Jifeng He, and Jeff W. Sanders. Prespecification in data refinement. *Information Processing Letters*, 25(2):71–76, May 1987.

[HJ00] M. Huisman and B. Jacobs. Java program verification via a Hoare logic with abrupt termination. In T. Maibaum, editor, *Fundamental Approaches to Software Engineering (FASE '00)*, number 1783 in LNCS, pages 284–303. Springer-Verlag, 2000.

[HLN$^+$90] David Harel, Hagi Lachover, Amnon Naamad, Amir Pnueli, Michal Politi, Rivi Sherman, Aharon Shtull-Trauring, and Mark B. Trakhtenbrot. STATEMATE: a working environment for the development of complex reactive systems. *IEEE Transactions on Software Engineering*, 16(4):403–414, April 1990.

[HO81] Brent T. Hailpern and Susan Owicki. Modular verification of computer communication protocols. Research Report RC8726, IBM, 1981.

[HO83] Brent T. Hailpern and Susan Owicki. Modular verification of computer communication protocols,. *IEEE Transactions on Communications*, COM-31(1):56–68, January 1983.

[Hoa69] C.A.R. Hoare. An axiomatic basis for computer programming. *CACM*, 12(10):576–580,583, 1969.

[Hoa78] C.A.R. Hoare. Communicating sequential processes. *CACM*, 21(8):666–677, 1978.

[Hoa80] C.A.R. Hoare. A model for communicating sequential processes. In R.M. McKeag and A.M. MacNaughten, editors, *On the Construction of Programs*, pages 229–254. Cambridge University Press, 1980.

[Hoa81a] C.A.R. Hoare. A calculus of total correctness for communicating processes. *Science of Computer Programming*, 1(1-2):49–72, October 1981.

[Hoa81b] C.A.R. Hoare. A model for communicating sequential processes. Technical Monograph PRG-22, Programming Research Group, Oxford University, 1981.

[Hoa85a] C.A.R. Hoare. *Communicating Sequential Processes*. Prentice-Hall International, Hemel Hempstead, 1985.

[Hoa85b] C.A.R. Hoare. Programs are predicates. In C.A.R. Hoare and J.C. Shepherdson, editors, *Mathematical Logic and Programming Languages*, Prentice-Hall International Series in Computer Science, pages 141–155. Prentice Hall, 1985.

[Hol99] Leszek Holenderski. Incremental verification of synchronous networks. Submitted to FTRTFT 2000, 1999.

[Hoo87] J. Hooman. A compositional proof theory for real-time distributed message passing. In *Proceedings of Parallel Architectures and Languages Europe PARLE '87*, volume 259 of *LNCS*, pages 315–332. Springer-Verlag, 1987.

[Hoo90] J. Hooman. Compositional verification of distributed real-time systems. In *Proceedings Workshop on Real-Time Systems-Theory and Applications*, pages 1–20. North-Holland, 1990.

[Hoo91a] J. Hooman. A denotational real-time semantics for shared processors. In *Proceedings of Parallel Architectures and Languages Europe PARLE '91, vol. II*, volume 506 of *LNCS*, pages 184–201. Springer-Verlag, 1991.

[Hoo91b] J. Hooman. *Specification and compositional verification of real-time systems*, volume 558 of *LNCS*. Springer-Verlag, 1991.

[Hoo92a] J. Hooman. Compositional verification of real-time systems using Extended Hoare Triples. In de Bakker et al. [dBHdRR92].

[Hoo92b] J. Hooman. Program verification. Course Notes, 1992. Technical University of Eindhoven.

[Hoo93] J. Hooman. A compositional approach to the design of hybrid systems. In *Workshop on Theory of Hybrid Systems*, volume 736, pages 121–148. LNCS, 1993.

[Hoo95] Jozef Hooman. Verifying part of the ACCESS.bus protocol using PVS. In *Proc. of 15th FSTTCS*, volume 1026 of *LNCS*. Springer-Verlag, 1995.

[Hoo96] J. Hooman. Assertional specification and verification. In M. Joseph, editor, *Real-time Systems: Specification, Verification and Analysis*, chapter 5, pages 97–146. Prentice Hall, 1996.

[Hoo98] Jozef Hooman. Compositional verification of real-time applications. In de Roever et al. [dRLP98], pages 276–300.

[HP72] P. Hitchcock and David M.R. Park. Induction rules and termination proofs. In Maurice Nivat, editor, *Automata, Languages, and Programming, Proceedings of a*

Symposium Organized by IRIA, pages 225–251. North-Holland/American Elsevier, 1972.

[HP85] D. Harel and A. Pnueli. On the development of reactive systems. In Apt [Apt85], pages 477–498.

[HP98] David Harel and Michal Politi. *Modeling Reactive Systems with Statecharts: The Statemate Approach.* McGraw-Hill, 1998.

[HP99] N. Halbwachs and D. Peled, editors. *Computer Aided Verification, 11th International Conference, CAV '99*, number 1633 in LNCS. Springer-Verlag, July 1999.

[HPS77] D. Harel, A. Pnueli, and J. Stavi. A complete axiomatic system for proving deductions about recursive programs. In *Proc. of the 9th ACM Symposium on Theory of Computing, Boulder, May 1977*, pages 249–260, 1977.

[HQR98] T.A. Henzinger, S. Qadeer, and S. Rajamani. You assume, we guarantee: Methodology and case studies. In *CAV '98: Computer-aided Verification*, volume 1427 of *LNCS*, pages 521–525, 1998.

[HQRT98] T.A. Henzinger, S. Qadeer, S.K. Rajamani, and S. Tasiran. An assume-guarantee rule for checking simulation. In *Proceedings of FMCAD '98*, volume 1522 of *LNCS*. Springer-Verlag, 1998.

[HRdR92] J. Hooman, S. Ramesh, and W.-P. de Roever. A compositional axiomatization of statecharts. *Theoretical Computer Science*, 101:289–335, 1992.

[HvR97] J. Hooman and O. van Roosmalen. Platform-independent verification of real-time programs. In *Proc. of the Joint Workshop on Parallel and Distributed Real-Time Systems*, pages 183–192. IEEE Computer Society Press, 1997.

[Hym66] H. Hyman. Comments on a problem in concurrent programming control. *Communications of the ACM*, 9(1):45, January 1966.

[HZ] J. Hooman and J. Zwiers. Combining sequential and parallel composition: Unexpected implications for compositional proofsystems. Unpublished note.

[INM84] INMOS Limited. *occam Programming Manual*, 1984. Prentice-Hall International.

[INM88] INMOS Limited. *occam 2 Reference Manual*, 1988. Prentice-Hall International.

[Jac91] D.M. Jackson. A temporal logic proof system for timed CSP. Technical Report TR-2-91, Oxford University, Programming Research Group, 1991.

[Jan84] T.M.V. Janssen. Individual concepts are useful. In F. Landman and F. Veltman, editors, *Varieties of formal semantics*, number 3 in GRASS, pages 171–192. Foris, Dordrecht, 1984.

[Jan86a] T.M.V. Janssen. *Foundations and Applications of Montague Grammar: part 1, Philosophy, Framework, Computer Science*. Number 19 in CWI Tracts. Centre for Mathematics and Computer Science, Amsterdam, 1986.

[Jan86b] T.M.V. Janssen. *Foundations and Applications of Montague Grammar: part 2, Applications to Natural Language*. Number 28 in CWI Tracts. Centre for Mathematics and Computer Science, Amsterdam, 1986.

[Jan94] W. Janssen. *Layered Design of Parallel Systems*. PhD thesis, University of Twente, 1994.

[Jan97] T.M.V. Janssen. Compositionality (with an appendix by B. Partee). In van Benthem and ter Meulen [vBtM97], chapter 7, pages 417–473.

[Jan98] T.M.V. Janssen. Algebraic translations, correctness and algebraic compiler construction. *Theoretical Computer Science*, 199:25–26, 1998.

[Jan01] T.M.V. Janssen. Frege, compositionality and contextuality. *Journal of Logic Language and Information*, 2001.

[JG89] M. Joseph and A. Goswami. Relating computation and time. Research Report RR138, Department of Computer Science, University of Warwick, 1989.

[JH87] H. Jifeng and C.A.R. Hoare. Algebraic specification and proof of a distributed recovery algorithm. *Distributed Computing*, 2:1–12, 1987.

[JK89] Bengt Jonsson and Joost N. Kok. Comparing two fully abstract dataflow models. In E. Odijk, M. Rem, and J.-C. Syre, editors, *Proceedings of PARLE '89: Parallel Architectures and Languages Europe, Eindhoven, The Netherlands, June 12–16, 1989*, volume 366 of *LNCS*, pages 217–234. Springer-Verlag, 1989.

[JL96] R. Jones and R. Lins. *Garbage Collection*. Wiley & Sons, Chichester etc., 1996.

[JMS87] M. Joseph, A. Moitra, and N. Soundararajan. Proof rules for fault tolerant distributed programs. *Science of Computer Programming*, 8:43–67, 1987.

[Jon80] Cliff B. Jones. *Software Development: a Rigorous Approach*. Prentice Hall, 1980.

[Jon81] C.B. Jones. *Development methods for computer programs including a notion of interference*. PhD thesis, Oxford University Computing Laboratory, 1981.

[Jon83] C.B. Jones. Tentative steps towards a development method for interfering programs. *ACM Transactions on Programming Languages and Systems*, 5(4):596–619, 1983.

[Jon84] Cliff B. Jones, editor. *Programming Languages and their Definition, Selected Papers of H. Bekić*, volume 177 of *LNCS*. Springer-Verlag, 1984.

[Jon85] B. Jonsson. A model and proof system for asynchronous networks. In *Proceedings of the 4TH ACM SIGACT-SIGOPS Symposium on Principles of Distributed Computing*, pages 49–58, 1985.

[Jon86] Cliff B. Jones. *Systematic Software Development using VDM*. Prentice Hall, 1986.

[Jon87a] B. Jonsson. Modular verification of asynchronous networks. In *6th ACM Symposium on Principles of Distributed Computing, Vancouver, Canada*, pages 152–166, 1987.

[Jon87b] Bengt Jonsson. *Compositional Verification of Distributed Systems*. PhD thesis, Uppsala University, Department of Computer Systems, Uppsala, Sweden, 1987. Available as report DoCS 87/09.

[Jon90a] Cliff B. Jones. *Systematic Software Development using VDM*. Prentice Hall, 2nd edition, 1990.

[Jon90b] B. Jonsson. On decomposing and refining specifications of distributed systems. In de Bakker et al. [dBdRR90], pages 361–385.

[Jon94] Bengt Jonsson. Compositional specification and verification of distributed systems. *ACM TOPLAS*, 16(2):259–303, March 1994.

[Jon96] Cliff B. Jones. Accommodating interference in the formal design of concurrent object-based programs. *Formal Methods in System Design*, 8(2):105–121, October 1996.

[Jos88] M. Joseph, editor. *Proceedings of the Symposium on Formal Techniques in Real-Time and Fault-Tolerant Systems, Warwick, UK, September 22–23, 1988*, volume 331 of *LNCS*. Springer-Verlag, 1988.

[Jos90] B. Josko. Verifying the correctness of AADL-modules using model checking. In de Bakker et al. [dBdRR90].

[Jos93] Bernhard Josko. *Modular Specification and Verification of Reactive Systems.* Habilitationsschrift, Universität Oldenburg, 1993.

[Jos96] Mathai Joseph, editor. *Real-time Systems: Specification, Verification and Analysis.* Prentice-Hall International Series in Computer Science. Prentice-Hall International, 1996.

[Jos00] Mathai Joseph, editor. *6th International Symposium on Formal Techniques in Real-Time and Fault-Tolerant Systems (FTRTFT 2000), September 20–22, 2000, Pune, India,* LNCS. Springer-Verlag, 2000.

[JP87] M. Joseph and P. Pandya. Specification and verification of total correctness of distributed programs. Technical Report RR96, University of Warwick, 1987. Research Report.

[JP96] Bengt Jonsson and Joachim Parrow, editors. *Proceedings of the 4th International Symposium on Formal Techniques in Real-Time and Fault-Tolerant Systems (FTRTFT), Uppsala, Sweden, September 9–13, 1996,* volume 1135 of *LNCS.* Springer-Verlag, 1996.

[JPXZ94] W. Janssen, M. Poel, Q. Xu, and J. Zwiers. Layering of real-time distributed processes. In Langmaack et al. [LdRV94], pages 393–417.

[JPZ91] W. Janssen, M. Poel, and J. Zwiers. Action systems and action refinement in the development of parallel systems. In *Proceedings of CONCUR '91,* volume 527 of *LNCS,* pages 298–316. Springer-Verlag, 1991.

[JT95] B. Jonsson and Y.-K. Tsay. Assumption/guarantee specifications in linear-time temporal logic. In Mosses et al. [MNS95], pages 262–276. See [JT96] for the journal version.

[JT96] B. Jonsson and Y.-K. Tsay. Assumption/guarantee specifications in linear-time temporal logic. *Theoretical Computer Science,* 167(1–2):47–72, October 1996.

[JU93] Mark B. Josephs and Jan Tijmen Udding. An overview of DI algebra. In *Proc. Hawaii International Conference on System Sciences, vol. I.* IEEE Computer Society Press, 1993.

[JvEB77a] T.M.V. Janssen and P. van Emde Boas. The expressive power of intensional logic in the semantics of programming languages. In J. Gruska, editor, *Mathematical foundations of computer science, 1977: proceedings, 6th Symposium, Tatranska Lomnica, September 5–9, 1977,* volume 53 of *LNCS,* pages 303–311. Springer-Verlag, 1977. Preprint: Report ZW 98, Mathematical Centre, Amsterdam, 1977.

[JvEB77b] T.M.V. Janssen and P. van Emde Boas. On the proper treatment of referencing, dereferencing and assignment. In A. Salomaa and M. Steinby, editors, *Automata, languages and programming: fourth colloquium, University of Turku, Finland, July 18–22, 1977,* volume 52 of *LNCS,* pages 282–300. Springer-Verlag, 1977.

[JvEB80] T.M.V. Janssen and P. van Emde-Boas. The impact of Frege's compositionality principle for the semantics of programming and natural languages. In D. Alexander, editor, *Proc. of the First Frege Memorial Conference, May '79, Jena,* pages 110–129. Friedrich-Schiller Universität Jena, May 1980. Previously as preprint, Report MI-UVA-79-07, Mathematisch Centrum, Amsterdam, 1979.

[JZ92a] W. Janssen and J. Zwiers. From sequential layers to distributed processes, deriving a distributed minimum weight spanning tree algorithm, (extended abstract). In

Proceedings 11th ACM Symposium on Principles of Distributed Computing, pages 215–227. ACM, 1992.

[JZ92b] W. Janssen and J. Zwiers. Protocol design by layered decomposition, a compositional approach. In J. Vytopil, editor, *Proceedings Formal Techniques in Real-Time and Fault-Tolerant Systems*, volume 571 of *LNCS*, pages 307–326. Springer-Verlag, 1992.

[JZ93] W. Janssen and J. Zwiers. Specifying and proving communication closedness in protocols. In A. Dantine, G. Leduc, and P. Wolper, editors, *Proceedings 13th IFIP Symp. on Protocol Specification, Testing and Verification*, pages 323–339. Elsevier Science Publishers, 1993.

[Kah74] Gilles Kahn. The semantics of simple language for parallel programming. In Jack L. Rosenfeld, editor, *Proceedings of the 6th IFIP Congress, Stockholm, Sweden, August 5–10, 1974*, volume 74 of *Information Processing*, pages 471–475. North-Holland, 1974.

[Kah79] Gilles Kahn, editor. *Proceedings of the International Symposium on Semantics of Concurrent Computation, Evian, France, July 2–4, 1979*, volume 70 of *LNCS*. Springer-Verlag, 1979.

[Kal90] Anne Kaldewaij. *Programming: The Derivation of Algorithms*. Prentice Hall, 1990.

[Kat93] S. Katz. A superimposition control construct for distributed systems. *ACM Transactions on Programming Languages and Systems*, 15(2), 1993.

[Kay93] A. Kay. A theory of rely and guarantee for timed CSP. Technical Report PRG-TR-12-93, Oxford University Programming Research Group, 1993.

[KdR82] R. Kuiper and W.-P. de Roever. Fairness assumption for CSP in a Temporal Logic Framework. In D. Bjørner, editor, *Proc. of the IFIP Working Conference on Formal Description of Programming Concepts II, Garmisch-Partenkirchen, June 1–4, 1982*. North-Holland Publ. Co., 1982.

[Kel76] R.M. Keller. Formal verification of parallel programs. *Communications of the ACM*, 19(7):371–384, July 1976.

[KKPR99] Y. Kesten, A. Klein, A. Pnueli, and G. Raanan. A perfecto verification: Combining model checking with deductive analysis to verify real-life software. In J.M. Wing, J. Woodcock, and J. Davies, editors, *Proc. FM '99 – Formal Methods*, volume 1708 of *LNCS*. Springer-Verlag, 1999.

[KKZ89] R. Koymans, R. Kuiper, and E. Zijlstra. Specification specified. In *R. Kuiper, Ph.D. Thesis*. University of Eindhoven, 1989.

[KL93] Rob P. Kurshan and Leslie Lamport. Verification of a multiplier: 64 bits and beyond. In *Computer-Aided Verification, Proc. of the 5th Int. Conf. CAV '94*, volume 697 of *LNCS*, pages 166–174. Springer-Verlag, 1993.

[Kle93] S. Kleuker. Case study: Stepwise development of a communication processor using trace logic. In Andrews, Groote, and Middelburg, editors, *Proc. of the International Workshop on Semantics of Specification Languages SoSL*, Utrecht, 1993.

[KM94] M. Kaufmann and J.S. Moore. Design goals of ACL2. Technical Report 101, Computational Logic, Inc., August 1994.

[KMR89] J.W. Klop, J.-J.Ch. Meijer, and J.J.M.M. Rutten, editors. *J.W. de Bakker: 25 jaar semantiek, Liber Amoricum*. CWI, Amsterdam, 1989.

[Knu66] D.E. Knuth. Additional comments on a problem in concurrent programming control. *Communications of the ACM*, 9(5):321–322, May 1966.

[Knu99] Donald Ervin Knuth. *Digital Typography*. Number 78 in CSLI Lecture Notes. CSLI Publications, Stanford, California, 1999.

[Kön32] D. König. Theorie der endlichen und unendlichen Graphen. Technical report, Leipzig, 1932.

[Koy90] R. Koymans. Specifying real-time properties with metric temporal logic. *Real-Time Systems*, 2(4):255–299, 1990.

[KP87] S. Katz and D. Peled. Interleaving set temporal logic. In *Proceedings of the 6th ACM Symposium on Principles of Distributed Computing, Vancouver*, pages 178–190, 1987.

[KP89] S. Katz and D. Peled. An efficient verification method for parallel and distributed programs. In *Proceedings of the REX workshop on Linear Time, Branching Time and Partial order in Logics and Models for Concurrency*, volume 354 of *LNCS*, pages 489–507. Springer-Verlag, 1989.

[KP90] S. Katz and D. Peled. Interleaving set temporal logic. *Theoretical Computer Science*, 75(2), 1990.

[KP92] S. Katz and D. Peled. Verification of distributed programs using representative interleaving sequences. *Distributed Computing*, 6(2), 1992.

[KR90] A. Kay and J.N. Reed. A specification of a telephone exchange in timed CSP. Technical Report PRG-TR-19-90, Oxford University Programming Research Group, 1990.

[KR91] A. Kay and J.N. Reed. Using rely and guarantee in timed CSP. Technical Report PRG-TR-11-91, Oxford University Programming Research Group, 1991.

[KR93] A. Kay and J.N. Reed. A rely and guarantee method for timed CSP. *IEEE Transactions on Software Engineering*, 19(6), 1993.

[Kri99] K.J. Kristoffersen. *Compositional Verification of Concurrent Systems: A possible cure for the state explosion problem*. Report no. r 98-5009, Aalborg University, January 1999.

[Krö87] F. Kröger. *Temporal Logic of Programs*. EATCS Monographs on Theoretical Computer Science. Springer-Verlag, 1987.

[KSdR+85] R. Koymans, R.K. Shyamasundar, W.-P. de Roever, R. Gerth, and S. Arun-Kumar. Compositional semantics for real-time distributed computing. In *Proc. of the Workshop on Logics of Programs '85*, volume 193 of *LNCS*, pages 167–189. Springer-Verlag, 1985. An extended version appeared in [KSdR+88].

[KSdR+88] R. Koymans, R.K. Shyamasundar, W.-P. de Roever, R. Gerth, and S. Arun-Kumar. Compositional semantics for real-time distributed computing. *Information and Computation*, 79(3):210–256, December 1988. Academic Press.

[KV96] Orna Kupferman and Moshe Y. Vardi. Module checking. In Alur and Henzinger [AH96], pages xii + 472.

[KV98] O. Kupferman and M.Y. Vardi. Modular model checking. In de Roever et al. [dRLP98], pages 381–401.

[KVdR83] R. Koymans, J. Vytopil, and W.-P. de Roever. Real time programming and asynchronous message passing. In *2nd ACM Symposium on Distributed Computing, Montreal*, pages 187–197, 1983.

[LA90] P.A. Lee and T. Anderson. *Fault tolerance: Principles and practice*. Springer-Verlag, 1990.

[Lam76] L. Lamport. Formal correctness proofs for multiprocess algorithms. In *Proc. of the 2ème Colloque International sur la programmation, Paris*, April 1976.

[Lam77] L. Lamport. Proving the correctness of multiprocess programs. *IEEE Transactions on Software Engineering*, SE-3(2):125–143, 1977.

[Lam78] L. Lamport. Time, clocks, and the ordering of events in a distributed system. *Communications of the ACM*, 21(7):558–565, 1978.

[Lam80] L. Lamport. The "Hoare Logic" of concurrent programs. *Acta Informatica*, 14:21–37, 1980.

[Lam83a] L. Lamport. Solved problems, unsolved problems and non-problems in concurrency. In *PODC84: Proceedings of the Third Annual ACM Symposium on Principles of Distributed Computing*, pages 63–67, 1983.

[Lam83b] L. Lamport. Specifying concurrent program modules. *ACM TOPLAS*, 5(2), 1983.

[Lam83c] L. Lamport. What good is temporal logic. In R.E.A. Mason, editor, *Information Processing 83: Proceedings of the IFIP 9th World Congress*, pages 657–668, Paris, September 1983. IFIP, North-Holland.

[Lam88] L. Lamport. Control predicates are better than dummy variables for reasoning about program control. *ACM TOPLAS*, 10(2):267–281, 1988.

[Lam90] L. Lamport. win and sin: Predicate transformers for concurrency. *ACM Transactions on Programming Languages and Systems (ToPLaS)*, 12(3):396–428, July 1990. Also appeared as SRC Research Report 17.

[Lam94a] L. Lamport. The temporal logic of actions. *ACM Transactions on Programming Languages and Systems*, 16(3):872–923, May 1994.

[Lam94b] Leslie Lamport. Verification and specification of concurrent programs. In de Bakker et al. [dBdRR94], pages 347–374.

[Lam98] Leslie Lamport. Composition: A way to make proofs harder. In de Roever et al. [dRLP98], pages 402–423.

[Lam99] L. Lamport. On the Dijkstra on-the-fly garbage collector. Private communication, 1999.

[Lar87] Kim G. Larsen. A context-dependent bisimulation between processes. *Theoretical Computer Science*, 49, 1987.

[LdRV94] H. Langmaack, W.-P. de Roever, and J. Vytopil, editors. *Formal techniques in real-time and fault-tolerant systems (FTRTFT '94): third international symposium organized jointly with the Working Group Provably Correct Systems (ProCoS), Lübeck, Germany, September 19–23, 1994*, volume 863 of *LNCS*. Springer-Verlag, 1994.

[Lev80] Gary M. Levin. *Proof Rules for Communicating Sequential Processes*. PhD thesis, Cornell University, August 1980.

[LF79] Nancy A. Lynch and M. J. Fisher. On describing the behavior and implementation of distributed systems. In Kahn [Kah79], pages 147–171.

[LG81] G.M. Levin and D. Gries. A proof technique for Communicating Sequential Processes. *Acta Informatica*, 15:281–302, 1981.

[Lip75] Richard J. Lipton. Reduction: A method for proving properties of parallel programs. *CACM*, 18(12):717–721, 1975.

[LJ93] Z. Liu and M. Joseph. Specification and verification of recovery in asynchronous communicating systems. In J. Vytopil, editor, *Formal Techniques in Real-Time and Fault Tolerant Systems*, pages 137–165. Kluwer Academic Publishers, 1993.

[LJ94] Z. Liu and M. Joseph. Stepwise development of fault-tolerant reactive systems. In Langmaack et al. [LdRV94], pages 529–546.

[LMR+98] Phillipe Lacan, Jean Nöel Monfort, Le Vinh Quy Ribal, Alain Deutsch, and Georges Gonthier. ARIANE 5 the software reliability verification process: the ARIANE 5 example. In *DASIA '98 Data Systems in Aerospace*. ESA Publications, May 1998.

[LMWF94] N. Lynch, M. Merritt, W. Weihl, and A. Fekete. *Atomic Transactions*. Morgan Kaufman Publishers, 1994.

[LO80] H. Langmaack and E.-R. Olderog. Present-day Hoare-like systems for programming languages with procedures: power, limits and most likely extensions. In J.W. de Bakker and J. van Leeuwen, editors, *Automata, Languages and Programming (Proc. 7th ICALP)*, volume 85 of *LNCS*, pages 363–373. Springer-Verlag, 1980.

[Loy92] L. Loyens. *A design method for parallel programs*. PhD thesis, Eindhoven University of Technology, 1992.

[LPZ85] O. Lichtenstein, A. Pnueli, and L. Zuck. The glory of the past. In R. Parikh, editor, *12th ACM Symposium on Logics of Programs*, volume 193 of *LNCS*, pages 196–218. Springer-Verlag, 1985.

[LS84a] S.S. Lam and A.U. Shankar. Protocol verification via projections. *IEEE Transactions on Software Engineering*, SE-10(4):325–342, July 1984.

[LS84b] L. Lamport and F.B. Schneider. The "Hoare Logic" of CSP and all that. *ACM TOPLAS*, 6(2):281–296, April 1984.

[LS84c] J. Loeckx and K. Sieber. *The Foundation of Program Verification*. Wiley, 1984.

[LS90] Simon S. Lam and A. Udaya Shankar. Refinement and projection of relational specifications. In de Bakker et al. [dBdRR90], pages 454–486.

[LS92a] S. Lam and A. Shankar. Specifying modules to satisfy interfaces – a static transition approach. *Distributed Computing*, 6(1):39–63, July 1992.

[LS92b] Kim G. Larsen and Arne Skou. Compositional verification of probabilistic processes. In W.R. Cleaveland, editor, *Proc. of CONCUR '92*, volume 630 of *LNCS*. Springer-Verlag, 1992.

[LS94] S. Lam and A. Shankar. A theory of interfaces and modules i: Composition theorem. *IEEE Transactions on Software Engineering*, 20(1):55–71, January 1994.

[LS97a] Y. Lakhnech and M. Siegel. Deductive verification of stabilizing systems. In *Proceedings of the Third Workshop on Self-Stabilizing Systems, Santa Barbara, 1997*. Carleton University Press, 1997.

[LS97b] Y. Lakhnech and M. Siegel. Temporal logic for stabilizing systems. In *Proc. of the Second International Conference on Temporal Logic, ICTL '97, Manchester, England, 14–18 July, 1997*. Kluwer, 1997.

[LSZ94] Y. Lakhnech, F.A. Stomp, and J. Zwiers. Modular completeness revisited. Technical report, Kiel University, 1994.

[LT87] Nancy A. Lynch and Mark R. Tuttle. Hierarchical correctness proofs for distributed algorithms. In *Proc. PoDC '87*, ACM, New York, 1987.

[LT91] Kim G. Larsen and Bent Thomsen. Partial specifications and compositional specification. *Theoretical Computer Science*, 88:15–32, 1991.

[Luc68] Peter Lucas. Two constructive realizations of the block concept and their equivalence. Technical Report TR 25.085, IBM Laboratory Vienna, January 1968.

[Lyn96] Nancy A. Lynch. *Distributed Algorithms*. Morgan Kaufmann Publishers, San Francisco, 1996.

[Mal00] Willem C. Mallon. *Theories and Tools for the Design of Delay-Insensitive Communicating Processes*. PhD thesis, Dept. of Math. and C.S., University of Groningen, 2000.

[Man69] Z. Manna. The correctness of programs. *Computer and System Sciences*, 3:119–127, 1969.

[Man74] Z. Manna. *Mathematical Theory of Computation*. McGraw-Hill, New York, 1974.

[Maz77] A. Mazurkiewicz. Concurrent program schemes and their interpretations. DAIMI Report PB-78, Aarhus University, Aarhus, Denmark, 1977.

[Maz89] A. Mazurkiewicz. Basic notions of trace theory. In J.W. de Bakker, W.-P. de Roever, and G. Rozenberg, editors, *Linear Time, Branching Time and Partial Order in Logics and Models for Concurrency*, volume 354 of *LNCS*. Springer-Verlag, 1989.

[MC81] J. Misra and K.M. Chandy. Proofs of networks of processes. *IEEE Transactions on Software Engineering*, 7(7):417–426, 1981.

[McC89] E.R. McCurly. Auxiliary variables in partial correctness programming logics. *Information Processing Letters*, 33:131–133, 1989.

[McM97] K.L. McMillan. A compositional rule for hardware design refinement. In *Computer-Aided Verification CAV '97*, volume 1254 of *LNCS*, pages 24–35. Springer-Verlag, 1997.

[McM98] K.L. McMillan. Verification of an implementation of Tomasulo's algorithm by compositional model checking. In *Proceedings of CAV '98*, volume 1427 of *LNCS*. Springer-Verlag, 1998.

[McM99] K.L. McMillan. Circular compositional reasoning about liveness. In *Proceedings of CHARME '99*, volume 1703 of *LNCS*. Springer-Verlag, 1999.

[MCS82] J. Misra, K.M. Chandy, and T. Smith. Proving safety and liveness of communicating processes with examples. In *Proc. PoDC '82*, ACM, New York, 1982.

[Mel86] S. Meldal. Axiomatic semantics of access type tasks in ADA. Technical Report 100, Institute of Informatics, University of Oslo, Norway, May 1986. To appear in Distributed Computing.

[Mey88] B. Meyer. *Object-Oriented Software Construction*. Prentice Hall, 1988.

[Mil73] R. Milner. Processes: A mathematical model of computing agents. In *Proc.: Logic Colloquium*, Amsterdam, 1973. North-Holland.

[Mil80] Robin Milner. *A Calculus of Communicating Systems*, volume 92 of *LNCS*. Springer-Verlag, 1980.

[Mil89] Robin Milner. *Communication and Concurrency*. Prentice Hall International, 1989.

[Mis01] J. Misra. *A Discipline of Multiprogramming*. Texts and Monographs in Computer Science. Springer-Verlag, 2001. To appear. Parts of the manuscript are available at http://www.cs.utexas.edu/users/psp/discipline.ps.gz.

[ML96] Paul S. Miner and James F. Leathrum, Jr. Verification of IEEE compliant subtractive division algorithms. In Srivas and Camilleri [SC96], pages 64–78.

[MLK98] J Strother Moore, Tom Lynch, and Matt Kaufmann. A mechanically checked proof of the correctness of the kernel of the AMD5K6 floating-point division algorithm. *IEEE Transactions on Computers*, 47(9):913–926, September 1998.

[MMP92] O. Maler, Z. Manna, and A. Pnueli. From timed to hybrid systems. In de Bakker et al. [dBHdRR92], pages 447–484.

[MNS95] Peter Mosses, M. Nielsen, and Michael I. Schwartzbach, editors. *Proceedings of TAPSOFT '95: theory and practice of software development: 6th International Joint Conference CAAP/FASE, Aarhus, Denmark, May 22–26, 1995*, volume 915 of *LNCS*. Springer-Verlag, 1995.

[MO97] Markus Müller-Olm. *Modular Verification: A Refinement-Algebraic Approach Advocating Stepwise Abstraction*, volume 1283 of *LNCS*. Springer-Verlag, 1997.

[Moo96] J S. Moore. *Piton: A Mechanically-Verified Assembly-Level Language*. Kluwer Academic Press, Dordrecht, The Netherlands, 1996.

[Moo01] J Strother Moore. On the verification of the AMD K5 floating point operations. Private communication, February 2001.

[Mor82] J.M. Morris. Assignment and linked data structures. In Broy and Schmidt, editors, *Theoretical Foundations of Programming Methodology*, pages 35–41. Reidel, 1982.

[Mor90] C. Morgan. *Programming from Specifications*. Prentice Hall, 1990.

[Mos83] Ben Moszkowski. *Reasoning about Digital Circuits*. PhD thesis, Stanford University, Stanford, California, 1983.

[Mos86] Ben Moszkowski. *Executing Temporal Logic Programs*. Cambridge University Press, Cambridge, England, 1986.

[Mos94] Ben Moszkowski. Some very compositional temporal properties. In Olderog [Old94], pages 307–326.

[Mos95] Ben Moszkowski. Compositional reasoning about projected and infinite time. In *Proc. of the First IEEE Int. Conf. on Engineering of Complex Computer Systems (ICECCS '95)*, pages 238–245. IEEE Computer Society Press, 1995.

[Mos98] B.U. Moszkowski. Compositional reasoning using interval temporal logic and Tempura. In de Roever et al. [dRLP98], pages 439–464.

[MP82] Z. Manna and A. Pnueli. Verification of concurrent programs: a temporal proof system. In *Foundations of Computer Science IV, Distributed Systems: Part 2*, volume 159 of *Mathematical Centre Tracts*, pages 163–255, 1982.

[MP84] Z. Manna and A. Pnueli. Adequate proof principles for invariance and liveness properties of concurrent programs. *Science of Computer Programming*, 4(3):257–289, 1984.

[MP89] Z. Manna and A. Pnueli. The anchored version of the temporal framework. In J.W. de Bakker, W.-P. de Roever, and G. Rozenberg, editors, *School/Workshop, Noordwijkerhout, May/June 1988*, number 354 in LNCS, pages 201–284. Springer-Verlag, 1989.

[MP90] Z. Manna and A. Pnueli. An exercise in the verification of multi-process programs. In W.H.J. Feijen, A.J.M. van Gasteren, D. Gries, and J. Misra, editors, *Beauty is Our Business*, pages 289–301. Springer-Verlag, 1990.

[MP91a] Z. Manna and A. Pnueli. Completing the temporal picture. *Theoretical Computer Science*, 83(1):97–130, 1991.

[MP91b] Z. Manna and A. Pnueli. *The Temporal Logic of Reactive and Concurrent Systems: Specification*. Springer-Verlag, 1991.

[MP91c] Z. Manna and A. Pnueli. Tools and rules for the practicing verifier. In

R. Rashid, editor, *Carnegie Mellon Computer Science: A 25-year Commemorative*, pages 125–159. ACM Press and Addison-Wesley, 1991.

[MP95] Z. Manna and A. Pnueli. *Temporal verification of Reactive Systems: Safety*. Springer-Verlag, 1995.

[MP99] Z. Manna and A. Pnueli. Temporal verification of reactive systems: Progress. Technical report, The Weizmann Institute of Science, 1999.

[MR98] F. Maraninchi and Y. Rémond. Compositionality criteria for defining mixed-styles synchronous languages. In de Roever et al. [dRLP98], pages 424–438.

[MS96] R. Manohar and P. Snilotti. Composing processes using modified rely-guarantee specifications. Technical Report CS-TR-96-22, California Institute of Technology, 1996.

[MW85] Z. Manna and R. Waldinger. *The Logical Basis for Computer Programming, Volume 1: Deductive Reasoning*. Addison-Wesley, 1985.

[MW90] Z. Manna and R. Waldinger. *The Logical Basis for Computer Programming, Volume 2: Deductive Systems*. Addison-Wesley, 1990.

[NAS99] Mars climate orbiter team finds likely cause of loss. NASA Press Release 99-113, September 1999. http://mars.jpl.nasa.gov/msp98/news/mco990930.html.

[Nau66] P. Naur. Proof of algorithms by general snapshots. *BIT*, 6:310–316, 1966.

[NDOG86] V. Nguyen, A. Demers, S. Owicki, and D. Gries. A modal and temporal proof system for networks of processes. *Distributed Computing*, 1(1):7–25, 1986.

[Ngu85] V. Nguyen. The incompleteness of Misra and Chandy's proof system. *Information Processing Letters*, 21:93–96, August 1985.

[Nor93] J. Nordahl. Design for dependability. In *Proc. 3rd IFIP Int. Working Conference on Dependable Computing for Critical Applications,*, volume 8 of *Dependable Computing and Fault Tolerant Systems*, pages 65–89. Springer-Verlag, 1993.

[NT00] Kedar S. Namjoshi and Richard J. Trefler. On the completeness of compositional reasoning. In *Proceedings of CAV 2000*, LNCS, pages 139–153. Springer-Verlag, 2000.

[OD98] E.-R. Olderog and H. Dierks. Decomposing real-time specifications. In de Roever et al. [dRLP98], pages 465–489.

[OG76a] S. Owicki and D. Gries. An axiomatic proof technique for parallel programs. *Acta Informatica*, 6:319–340, 1976.

[OG76b] S. Owicki and D. Gries. Verifying properties of parallel programs: An axiomatic approach. *Communications of the ACM*, 19(5):279–286, May 1976.

[OH83] E.-R. Olderog and C.A.R. Hoare. Specification oriented semantics for communicating processes. In *Proceedings of the 10th ICALP conference*, volume 154 of *LNCS*. Springer-Verlag, 1983.

[OH86] E.-R. Olderog and C.A.R. Hoare. Specification-oriented semantics for communicating processes. *Acta Informatica*, 23:9–66, 1986.

[OL82] Susan Owicki and Leslie Lamport. Proving liveness properties of concurrent programs. *ACM TOPLAS*, 4(3):455–495, July 1982.

[Old81] E.-R. Olderog. Sound and complete Hoare-like calculi based on copy rules. *Acta Informatica*, 16:161–197, 1981.

[Old83a] E.-R. Olderog. A characterization of Hoare's logic for programs with Pascal-like procedures. In *Proc. 15th ACM Symp. on Theory of Computing*, pages 320–329. ACM Press, April 1983. Boston, Mass.

[Old83b] E.-R. Olderog. On the notion of expressiveness and the rule of adaptation. *Theoretical Computer Science*, 24:337–347, 1983.

[Old84a] E.-R. Olderog. Correctness of programs with Pascal-like procedures without global variables. *Theoretical Computer Science*, 30:49–90, 1984.

[Old84b] E.-R. Olderog. Hoare's logic for programs with procedures – what has been achieved? In E.M. Clarke and D. Kozen, editors, *Proc. Logics of Programs*, volume 164 of *LNCS*, pages 383–395. Springer-Verlag, 1984.

[Old86] E.-R. Olderog. Process theory: Semantics, specification and verification. In *ESPRIT/LPC Advanced School on Current Trends in Concurrency*, volume 224 of *LNCS*. Springer-Verlag, 1986.

[Old91a] E.-R. Olderog. *Nets, Terms and Formulas*. Number 23 in Cambridge Tracts in Theoretical Computer Science. Cambridge University Press, 1991.

[Old91b] E.-R. Olderog. Towards a design calculus for communicating programs. In J.C.M. Baeten and J.F. Groote, editors, *Proc. CONCUR '91*, volume 527 of *LNCS*, pages 61–72. Springer-Verlag, 1991.

[Old94] E.-R. Olderog, editor. *Proceedings of the IFIP TC2 Working Conference on Programming Concepts, Methods and Calculi (PROCOMET 1994)*, volume A-56 of *IFIP Transactions A: Computer Science and Technology*. North-Holland, 1994.

[OR93] E.-R. Olderog and S. Rössig. A case study in transformational design of concurrent systems. In Gaudel and Jouannaud [GJ93], pages 90–104.

[ORS92] S. Owre, J. Rushby, and N. Shankar. PVS: A prototype verification system. In *11th Conference on Automated Deduction*, volume 607 of *Lecture Notes in Artificial Intelligence*, pages 748–752. Springer-Verlag, 1992.

[ORSS92] E.-R. Olderog, S. Rössig, J. Sander, and M. Schenke. ProCoS at Oldenburg: The interface between specification language and occam-like programming language. Technical Report 3/92, University of Oldenburg, Department of Computer Science, 1992.

[ORSvH93] S. Owre, J. Rushby, N. Shankar, and F. von Henke. Formal verification for fault-tolerant architectures: some lessons learned. In J.C.P. Woodcock and P.G. Larsen, editors, *FME '93: Industrial-Strength Formal Methods*, volume 670 of *LNCS*, pages 482–500. Springer-Verlag, 1993.

[ORSvH95] S. Owre, J. Rushby, N. Shankar, and F. von Henke. Formal verification for fault-tolerant architectures: Prolegomena to the design of PVS. *IEEE Transactions on Software*, 21(2):107–125, 1995.

[Oss83] M. Ossefort. Correctness proofs of communicating processes: Three illustrative examples from the literature. *ACM Transactions on Programming Languages and Systems*, 5(4):620–640, 1983.

[Owi75] S. Owicki. *Axiomatic proof techniques for parallel programs*. Report tr 75-251, Cornell University, Ithaca N.Y., Department of Computer Science, 1975.

[Owi76] S. Owicki. A consistent and complete deductive system for the verification of parallel programs. In *Proc. of the 8th ACM Symposium on the Theory of Computing (STOC '76), Hershey, Pennsylvania, May 3–5, 1976*, pages 73–86. ACM, 1976.

[Pan88] Paritosh K. Pandya. *Compositional Verification of Distributed Systems*. PhD thesis, University of Bombay/TIFR, 1988.

[Pan90] P.K. Pandya. Some comments on the assumption-commitment framework for compositional verification of distributed programs. In de Bakker et al. [dBdRR90], pages 622–640.

[Par80] David M.R. Park. On the semantics of fair parallelism. In *Abstract Software Specification*, volume 86 of *LNCS*, pages 504–526. Springer-Verlag, 1980.

[Par81a] David M.R. Park. Concurrency and automata on infinite sequences. In Peter Deussen, editor, *Theoretical Computer Science: 5th GI-Conference, Karlsruhe*, volume 104 of *LNCS*, pages 167–183. Springer-Verlag, March 1981.

[Par81b] David M.R. Park. A predicate transformer for weak fair iteration. In *6th IBM Symposium on Mathematical Foundations of Computer Science, Hakone, Japan*, 1981.

[Pel91] J. Peleska. Design and verification of fault tolerant systems with CSP. *Distributed Computing*, 5:95–106, 1991.

[Pet62] C.A. Petri. Kommunikation mit Automaten. Technical Report Schriften des IIM No. 2, Institut für Instrumentelle Mathematik, Bonn, 1962. English translation: [Pet66].

[Pet63] C.A. Petri. Fundamentals of a theory of asynchronous information flow. In *Proc. of IFIP Congress 62*, pages 386–390, Amsterdam, 1963. North-Holland Publishing Company.

[Pet66] C.A. Petri. Communication with automata. Technical Report RADC-TR-65-377, Vol. 1, Suppl. 1, Applied Data Research, Princeton, NJ, 1966.

[Pet81] J.L. Peterson. *Petri Net Theory and Modeling of Systems*. Prentice Hall, Englewood Cliffs, N.J., 1981.

[Pet83] G.L. Peterson. A new solution to Lamport's concurrent programming problem using small shared variables. *ACM TOPLAS*, 5(1):56–65, 1983.

[PH98] A. Poigné and L. Holenderski. On the combination of synchronous languages. In de Roever et al. [dRLP98], pages 490–514.

[PJ91] P. Pandya and M. Joseph. P-A logic – a compositional proof system for distributed programs. *Distributed Computing*, 4(4), 1991.

[PJ93] D. Peled and M. Joseph. A compositional approach for fault tolerance using specification transformation. In *Proc. Parallel Architectures and Languages Europe (PARLE) '93*, volume 694 of *LNCS*, pages 173–184. Springer-Verlag, 1993.

[Plo76] Gordon D. Plotkin. A powerdomain construction. *SIAM Journal on Computation*, 5(3):452–487, 1976.

[Plo79] Gordon D. Plotkin. Dijkstra's predicate transformer and Smyth's powerdomain. In Dines Bjørner, editor, *Proceedings of the Winter School on Abstract Software Specification*, volume 86 of *LNCS*, pages 527–553. Springer-Verlag, 1979.

[Plo81] G.D. Plotkin. Structural operational semantics. DAIMI report FN-19, Aarhus University, Denmark, 1981.

[Plo82] G.D. Plotkin. An operational semantics for CSP. In D. Bjørner, editor, *Proc. of a TC-2 Working Conference*. North-Holland, 1982.

[Plo83] Gordon D. Plotkin. Domains. Lecture notes, 1983. Available, e.g, at URL ftp://ftp.funet.fi/pub/sci/math/misc/papers/plotkin/.

[Pnu67] A. Pnueli. *Tides in Simple Basins*. PhD thesis, Dept. of Applied Mathematics, Weizmann Institute of Science, Rehovot, 1967.

[Pnu77] Amir Pnueli. The temporal logic of programs. In *Proceedings of the 18th Symposium on Foundations of Programming Semantics*, pages 46–57, 1977.

[Pnu85] Amir Pnueli. In transition from global to modular reasoning about programs. In Apt [Apt85], pages 123–144.

[Pnu86] A. Pnueli. Applications of temporal logic to the specification and verification of reactive systems: A survey of current trends. In J.W. de Bakker, W.-P. de Roever, and G. Rozenberg, editors, *Current Trends in Concurrency*, volume 224 of *LNCS*, pages 510–584. Springer-Verlag, 1986.

[PP68a] A. Pnueli and C.L. Pekeris. Free tidal oscillations in rotating flat basins of the form of rectangles and of sectors of circles. *Philosophical Transactions: Mathematical, Physical and Engineering Sciences*, A 263:149–171, 1968.

[PP68b] A. Pnueli and C.L. Pekeris. Tides in oceans in the form of a cross. *Philosophical Transactions: Mathematical, Physical and Engineering Sciences*, A 305:219–233, 1968.

[Pra76] Vaughan R. Pratt. Semantical considerations on Floyd-Hoare logic. Technical Report MIT/LCS/TR-168, Massachusetts Institute of Technology, August 1976.

[Pra82] Vaughan R. Pratt. On the composition of processes. In *Proceedings of the 9th ACM Symposium on Principles of Programming Languages*, pages 213–223, 1982.

[Pra86] V. Pratt. Modelling concurrency with partial orders. *International Journal of Parallel Programming*, 1(15):33–71, 1986.

[Pra95] Vaughan Pratt. Anatomy of the Pentium bug. In Mosses et al. [MNS95], pages 97–107.

[PSS98] A. Pnueli, M. Siegel, and O. Shtrichman. Translation validation for synchronous languages. In K.G. Larsen, S. Skyum, and G. Winskel, editors, *Proceedings of ICALP '98: Automata, languages, and programming: 25th international colloquium, Aalborg, Denmark, July 13–17, 1998*, volume 1443 of *LNCS*, pages 235–246. Springer-Verlag, 1998.

[PvdBJ00] E. Poll, J. van den Berg, and B. Jacobs. Specification of the JavaCard API in JML. In *Fourth SmartCard Research and Advanced Application Conference (IFIP CARDIS2000)*. Kluwer Academic Press, 2000. Also as Technical Report CSI-R0005, University of Nijmegen.

[PZ93] M. Poel and J. Zwiers. Layering techniques for development of parallel systems. In von Bochmann and Probst [vBP93], pages 16–29.

[QS81] J.P. Queille and J. Sifakis. Specification and verification of concurrent systems in CESAR. Technical Report RR no 254, Lab. IMAG, Grenoble, France, June 1981. Published as [QS82].

[QS82] J.P. Queille and J. Sifakis. Specification and verification of concurrent systems in CESAR. In M. Dezani-Ciancaglini and U. Montanari, editors, *Proceedings of the 5th International Symposium on Programming, Turin, April 6–8, 1982*, pages 337–350. Springer-Verlag, 1982.

[Que81] J.P. Queille. The CESAR system: An aided design and certification system for distributed applications. In *Proc. 2nd Int. Conf. on Distributed Computing Systems*, pages 149–161, April 1981.

[Que82] J.P. Queille. *Le système CESAR: Description, spécification et analyse des applications réparties*. PhD thesis, I.N.P., Grenoble, France, June 1982.

[Ram90] S. Ramesh. On the completeness of modular proof systems. *Information Processing Letters*, pages 195–201, 1990.

[Ray86] M. Raynal. *Algorithms for Mutual Exclusion*. Scientific Computation Series. The MIT Press, Cambridge, Massachusetts, 1986.

[Ray88] M. Raynal. *Distributed Algorithms and Protocols*. John Wiley & Sons, 1988.

[Rei85] W. Reisig. *Petri Nets*. Springer-Verlag, 1985.

[Rei98] Wolfgang Reisig. *Elements of Distributed Algorithms: Modeling and Analysis with Petri Nets*. Springer-Verlag, 1998.

[Rem81] M. Rem. The VLSI challenge: complexity bridling. In J.B. Gray, editor, *VLSI '81 (Very Large Scale Integration)*. Academic Press, 1981.

[Rey81] John C. Reynolds. *The Craft of Programming*. Prentice Hall, 1981.

[RF00] W. Reisig and A. Foremniak. The temporal logic of distributed actions. Technical report, Humboldt-Universität zu Berlin, Berlin, August 2000.

[Ros82] A.W. Roscoe. *A mathematical theory of communicating processes*. PhD thesis, Oxford University, 1982.

[Ros94a] A.W. Roscoe. Model-checking CSP. In A.W. Roscoe, editor, *A Classical Mind: Essays in Honour of C.A.R. Hoare*, pages 353–378. Prentice Hall International, 1994.

[Ros94b] M.T. Rosetta. *Compositional Translation*. The Kluwer International Series in Engineering and Computer Science 230. Kluwer Academic Publishers, Dordrecht, 1994. M.T. Rosetta is penname of L. Appelo, T. Janssen, F. de Jong, J. Landsbergen (eds.).

[Ros98] A.W. Roscoe. *The Theory and Practice of Concurrency*. Prentice-Hall International, 1998.

[RR86] G.M. Reed and A.W. Roscoe. A timed model for communicating sequential processes. In *Proc. 13th International Colloquium on Automata, Languages and Programming (ICALP '86), Rennes, France, July 15–19, 1986*, volume 226 of *LNCS*, pages 314–323. Springer-Verlag, 1986.

[RR88] G. Reed and A. Roscoe. A timed model for communicating sequential processes. *Theoretical Computer Science*, 58:249–261, 1988.

[RR98] Anders P. Ravn and Hans Rischel, editors. *Proceedings of the 5th International Symposium on Formal Techniques in Real-Time and Fault-Tolerant Systems FTRTFT '98, Lyngby, Denmark, September 14–18, 1998*, volume 1486 of *LNCS*. Springer-Verlag, 1998.

[RSS96] H. Rueß, N. Shankar, and M.K. Srivas. Modular verification of SRT division. In Alur and Henzinger [AH96], pages 123–134.

[RSS99] H. Rueß, N. Shankar, and M.K. Srivas. Modular verification of SRT division. *Formal Methods in Systems Design*, 14(1):45–73, January 1999.

[Rud90] M. Rudalics. Correctness of distributed garbage collection algorithms. Technical report RISC-Linz series no. 90-40.0, University of Linz, 1990.

[Rus99] David M. Russinoff. A mechanically checked proof of IEEE compliance of the AMD K5 floating-point square root microcode. *Formal Methods in System Design*, 14(1):75–125, January 1999. Special Issue on Verification of Arithmetic Hardware.

[RW94] A. Rensink and H. Wehrheim. Weak sequential composition in process algebras. In *Proceedings CONCUR '94*, volume 836 of *LNCS*, pages 226–241. Springer-Verlag, 1994.

[SA86] F.B. Schneider and G.R. Andrews. Concepts for concurrent programming. In de Bakker, de Roever, and Rozenberg, editors, *Current Trends in Concurrency*, volume 224 of *LNCS*, pages 669–716. Springer-Verlag, 1986.

[SBT96] Thomas R. Shiple, Gérard Berry, and Hervé Touati. Constructive analysis of cyclic circuits. In *Proc. International Design and Testing Conference (IDTC '96), Paris, France, 1996*, 1996.

[SC96] Mandayam Srivas and Albert Camilleri, editors. *Proceedings of FMCAD '96: Formal methods in computer-aided design: first international conference, Palo Alto, CA, USA, November 6–8, 1996*, volume 1166 of *LNCS*. Springer-Verlag, 1996.

[Sca97] Verilog S.A. *A Solution Second to None for the Production of Safety Critical Real-Time Embedded Systems*, 1997.

[Sch77] J. Schwarz. Generic commands – a tool for partial correctness formalisms. *The Computer Journal*, 20:151–155, 1977.

[Sch86] David A. Schmidt. *Denotational Semantics: A Methodology for Language Development*. Allyn and Bacon Inc., Newton, Massachusetts, 1986.

[Sch87] Fred B. Schneider. Decomposing properties into safety and liveness using predicate logic. Technical Report 87–874, Dept. of Computer Science, Cornell University, Ithaca, NY, 1987.

[Sch89] S.A. Schneider. *Correctness and communication in real-time systems*. PhD thesis, Oxford University, 1989.

[Sch90] F.B. Schneider. Implementing fault tolerant services using the state machine approach: A tutorial. *ACM Computing Surveys*, 22(4):299–319, 1990.

[Sch92] Huub Schols. *Delay-insensitive Communication*. PhD thesis, Dept. of Math. and C.S., Eindhoven University of Technology, 1992.

[Sch93] H. Schepers. Terminology and paradigms for fault tolerance. In J. Vytopil, editor, *Formal Techniques in Real-Time and Fault Tolerant Systems*, pages 3–31. Kluwer Academic Publishers, 1993.

[Sch94] H. Schepers. *Fault tolerance and timing of distributed systems: Compositional specification and verification*. PhD thesis, Eindhoven University of Technology, 1994.

[Sch97] F.B. Schneider. *On Concurrent Programming*. Graduate Texts in Computer Science. Springer-Verlag, 1997.

[Sch99a] Michael Schenke. Transformational design of real-time systems – part 2: from program specifications to programs. *Acta Informatica*, 36:67–99, 1999.

[Sch99b] Steve Schneider. *Concurrent and Real Time Systems*. John Wiley & Sons Publishers, 1999.

[Sco79] D.S. Scott. Identity and existence in intuitionistic logic. In M.P. Fourman, C.J. Mulvey, and D.S. Scott, editors, *Applications of Sheaves. Proceedings, Durham 1977*, volume 753 of *Lecture Notes in Mathematics*, pages 660–696. Springer-Verlag, 1979.

[SD82] N. Soundararajan and O.J. Dahl. Partial correctness semantics for communicating sequential processes. Research Report 66, Institute for Informatics, University of Oslo, 1982.

[SDJ⁺92] S.A. Schneider, J. Davies, D.M. Jackson, G.M. Reed, J.N. Reed, and A.W. Roscoe. Timed CSP: Theory and Practice. In de Bakker et al. [dBHdRR92].

[SdR87] F. Stomp and W.-P. de Roever. A correctness proof of a distributed minimum-weight spanning tree algorithm (extended abstract). In *Proceedings of the 7th ICDCS*, 1987.

[SdR89] F. Stomp and W.-P. de Roever. Designing distributed algorithms by means of formal sequentially phased reasoning. In J.-C. Bermond and M. Raynal, editors, *Proceedings of the 3rd International Workshop on Distributed Algorithms, Nice*, volume 392 of *LNCS*, pages 242–253. Springer-Verlag, 1989.

[SdR94] F. Stomp and W.-P. de Roever. A principle for sequential reasoning about distributed systems. *Formal Aspects of Computing*, 6(6):716–737, 1994.

[SdRG89] F.A. Stomp, W.-P. de Roever, and R.T. Gerth. The μ-calculus as an assertion-language for fairness arguments. *Information and Computation*, 82 (3):278–322, September 1989.

[SH94] H. Schepers and J. Hooman. A trace-based compositional proof theory for fault tolerant distributed systems. *Theoretical Computer Science*, 128(1&2):127–157, June 1994.

[Sha89] E.Y. Shapiro. The family of concurrent logic programming languages. *ACM Computing Surveys*, 21(3):412–510, 1989.

[Sha94] Natarajan Shankar. *Metamathematics, Machines, and Gödel's Proof*, volume 38 of *Cambridge Tracts in Theoretical Computer Science*. Cambridge University Press, 1994.

[Sha98a] N. Shankar. Machine-assisted verification using theorem proving and model checking. *Mathematical Methods in Program Development*, 1998.

[Sha98b] Natarajan Shankar. Lazy compositional verification. In de Roever et al. [dRLP98], pages 541–564.

[Sha01] Natarajan Shankar. On the Pentium floating point division bug. Private communication, February 2001.

[Sie95] M. Siegel. A refinement theory that supports both "decrease of nondeterminism" and "increase of parallelism". In S. Smolka, editor, *CONCUR '95*, volume 962 of *LNCS*. Springer-Verlag, 1995.

[Sie96] M. Siegel. *Phased Design and Verification of Stabilizing Systems*. PhD thesis, Institut für Informatik und Praktische Mathematik, Univ. of Kiel, July 1996. Technical Report no. 9705.

[Sit74] R.L. Sites. *Proving that computer programs terminate cleanly*. PhD thesis, Stanford University, 1974.

[SL87] A. Udaya Shankar and Simon S. Lam. Time-dependent distributed systems: Proving safety, liveness and real-time properties. *Distributed Computing*, 2(2):61–79, 1987.

[SL90] A. Udaya Shankar and Simon S. Lam. Construction of network protocols by stepwise refinement. In de Bakker et al. [dBdRR90], pages 669–695.

[Smy78] Michael B. Smyth. Powerdomains. *Journal of Computer and System Sciences*, pages 23–36, 1978.

[SO99] Michael Schenke and E.-R. Olderog. Transformational design of real-time systems – part 1: from requirements to program specifications. *Acta Informatica*, 36:1–65, 1999.

[Sou84] N. Soundararajan. Axiomatic semantics of communicating sequential processes. *ACM TOPLAS*, 6:647–662, 1984.

[Sou86] N. Soundararajan. Total Correctness of CSP Programs. *Acta Informatica*, 23:193–215, 1986.

[Sou97] N. Soundarajan. Communication traces in the verification of distributed programs. In D.J. Duke and A.S. Evans, editors, *Proc. of the 2nd BCS-FACS Northern Formal Methods Workshop*, Electronic Workshops in Computing. Springer-Verlag, 1997.

[Sou00] N. Soundarajan. Channel-trace versus process-trace-based reasoning. E-mail to de Roever, July 2000.

[Spi88] J. Michael Spivey. *Understanding Z – A Specification Language and its Formal Semantics*. Cambridge Tracts in Computer Science. Cambridge University Press, 1988.

[SS71] Dana S. Scott and Christopher Strachey. Toward a mathematical semantics for computer languages. In J. Fox, editor, *Proceedings Symposium on Computers and Automata*, pages 19–46. Polytechnic Institute of Brooklyn Press, 1971.

[SS83] R.D. Schlichting and F.B. Schneider. Fail-stop processors: An approach to designing fault tolerant computing systems. *ACM Transactions on Computer Systems*, 1(3):222–238, 1983.

[SS84] R.D. Schlichting and F.B. Schneider. Using message passing for distributed programming: Proof rules and disciplines. *ACM TOPLAS*, 3(6):402–431, July 1984.

[SS94] M. Siegel and F. Stomp. Extending the limits of sequentially phased reasoning. In P.S. Thiagarajan, editor, *Proc. FST&TCS 14*, volume 880 of *LNCS*. Springer-Verlag, 1994.

[SSB⁺96] Thomas R. Shiple, Vigyan Singhal, Gérard Berry, Robert K. Brayton, and Alberto L. Sangiovanni-Vincentelli. Analysis of combinational cycles. Technical Report UCB/ERL M96, Electronics Research Laboratory, College of Engineering, University of California, Berkeley, 1996.

[Sta84] Eugene W. Stark. *Foundations of a Theory of Specification for Distributed Systems*. PhD thesis, Massachusetts Institute of Technology, Laboratory for Computer Science, Cambridge, MA, 1984. Published as Technical Report MIT/LCS/TR-342.

[Sta85] Eugene W. Stark. A proof technique for rely/guarantee properties. In *Proceedings of 5th Conference on Foundations of Software Technology and Theoretical Computer Science*, volume 206 of *LNCS*, pages 369–391. Springer-Verlag, 1985.

[Sta88] Eugene W. Stark. Proving entailment between conceptual state specifications. *Theoretical Computer Science*, 56(1):135–154, January 1988.

[Sti88] Colin Stirling. A generalization of Owicki & Gries's Hoare logic for a concurrent while language. *Theoretical Computer Science*, 58:347–359, 1988.

[Sto77] Joseph E. Stoy. *Denotational Semantics: The Scott-Strachey Approach to Programming Language Theory*. The MIT Series in Computer Science. The MIT Press, Cambridge, Massachusetts, and London, England, 1977.

[Sto89] F. Stomp. *Design and Verification of Distributed Network Algorithms: Foundations and Applications*. PhD thesis, Eindhoven University of Technology, 1989.

[Stø90a] K. Stølen. *Development of Parallel Programs on Shared Data-structures*. PhD thesis, Computer Science Department, Manchester University, 1990.

[Sto90b] F. Stomp. A derivation of a broadcasting protocol using sequentially phased reasoning. In de Bakker et al. [dBdRR90], pages 696–730.

[Stø91] K. Stølen. A method for the development of totally correct shared-state parallel programs. In Baeten and Groote, editors, *Proc. of CONCUR '91*, volume 527 of *LNCS*. Springer-Verlag, 1991.

[Str66] Christopher Strachey. Towards a formal semantics. *Formal Language Description Languages for Computer Programming*, pages 198–220, 1966. T.B. Steel Jr., editor.

[SY96] Joseph Sifakis and Serge Yovine. Compositional specification of timed systems. In *Proc. of STACS '96*, volume 1046 of *LNCS*. Springer-Verlag, 1996.

[Szy88] B.K. Szymanski. A simple solution to Lamport's concurrent programming problem with linear wait. In *Proceedings of International Conference on Super-computing Systems 1988*, pages 621–626, St. Malo, France, July 1988.

[Szy90] B.K. Szymanski. Mutual exclusion revisited. In *Proc. Fifth Jerusalem Conference on Information Technology*, pages 110–117, Los Alamitos, CA, 1990. IEEE Computer Society Press.

[Tra] B.A. Trakhtenbrot. On the power of compositional proofs for nets: relationships between completeness and modularity. Dedicated to the memory of Helena Rasiowa. Undated draft.

[Tra63] A.H. Traub, editor. *Collected Works of John von Neumann*, volume 5. Pergamon Press, Oxford, 1963.

[Tur49] A. Turing. On checking a large routine. Report of a conference on high-speed automatic calculating machines, University Mathematical Laboratory, Cambridge, 1949.

[TZ88] J.V. Tucker and J.I. Zucker. Program correctness over abstract data types, with error-state semantics. CWI Monograph Series 6, Centre for Mathematics and Computer Science, 1988. North-Holland.

[Udd84] Jan Tijmen Udding. *Classification and Composition of Delay-Insensitive Circuits*. PhD thesis, Dept. of Math. and C.S., Eindhoven University of Technology, 1984.

[vB93] Kees van Berkel. *Handshake Circuits: An Asynchronous Architecture for VLSI Programming*. Cambridge University Press, 1993.

[vBP93] Gregor von Bochmann and D.K. Probst, editors. *Proceedings of the 4th International Workshop on Computer Aided Verification (CAV '92), Montreal, Canada, June 29–July 1, 1992*, volume 663 of *LNCS*. Springer-Verlag, 1993.

[vBtM97] J. van Benthem and A. ter Meulen, editors. *Handbook of Logic and Language*. Elsevier, Amsterdam and The MIT Press, Cambridge, Mass., 1997.

[vdS85] Jan L.A. van de Snepscheut. *Trace Theory and VLSI Design*, volume 200 of *LNCS*. Springer-Verlag, 1985.

[vdS93] Jan L.A. van de Snepscheut. *What Computing is all about*. Text and Monographs in Computer Science. Springer-Verlag, 1993.

[Ver94] Tom Verhoeff. *A theory of delay-insensitive systems*. PhD thesis, Dept. of Math. and C.S., Eindhoven University of Technology, 1994.

[Ver98] Tom Verhoeff. Analyzing specifications for delay-insensitive circuits. In *Proc. 4th International Symposium on Advanced Research in Asynchronous Circuits and Systems, April 1998, San Diego*. IEEE Computer Society Press, 1998.

[vTK91] André M. van Tilborg and Gary M. Koob, editors. *Foundations of Real-Time Computing: Formal Specifications and Methods*. Kluwer Academic Publishers, 1991.

[Vyt91] J. Vytopil, editor. *Proceedings of the 2nd International Symposium on Formal Techniques in Real-Time and Fault-Tolerant Systems, Nijmegen, The Netherlands, January 8–10, 1992*, volume 571 of *LNCS*. Springer-Verlag, 1991.

[Vyt93] Jan Vytopil, editor. *Formal Techniques in Real-Time and Fault-Tolerant Systems*. Kluwer International Series in Engineering and Computer Science. Kluwer Academic Publishers, 1993.

[WB97] Hal Wasserman and Manuel Blum. Software reliability via run-time result-checking. *JACM*, 44(1):826–849, November 1997.

[WD88] J.C.P. Woodcock and B. Dickinson. Using VDM with rely and guarantee-conditions, experiences from a real project. In *2nd VDM-Europe Symposium*, volume 328 of *LNCS*. Springer-Verlag, 1988.

[Web89] D.G. Weber. Formal specification of fault-tolerance and its relation to computer security. *ACM Software Engineering Notes*, 14(3):273–277, 1989.

[WGS87] J. Widom, D. Gries, and F.B. Schneider. Completeness and incompleteness of trace-based network proof systems. In *Proceedings of the 14th Annual ACM SIGACT-SIGPLAN Symposium on Principles of Programming Languages (POPL), Munich, Germany, January 1987*, pages 27–38, New York, 1987. ACM.

[WGS92] J. Widom, D. Gries, and F. Schneider. Trace-based network proof systems: Expressiveness and completeness. *ACM Transactions on Programming Languages and Systems*, 14(3):396–416, July 1992.

[Wid87] J. Widom. *Trace-based network proof systems: Expressiveness and Completeness*. PhD. thesis 87-833, Cornell University, Ithaca, New York, 1987.

[Win93] Glynn Winskel. *The Formal Semantics of Programming Languages*. The MIT Press, Cambridge, Massachusetts, 1993.

[Wir71] Niklaus Wirth. Program development by stepwise refinement. *Communications of the ACM*, 14:221–227, 1971.

[WLL88] J. Welch, L. Lamport, and N. Lynch. A lattice-structured proof technique applied to a minimum weight spanning tree algorithm. In *Proceedings of the 7th Annual Symposium on Principles of Distributed Computing*. ACM, 1988.

[XCC94] Q. Xu, A. Cau, and P. Collette. On unifying assumption-commitment style proof rules for concurrency. In Jonsson and Parrow, editors, *Proc. of CONCUR '94*, volume 836 of *LNCS*. Springer-Verlag, 1994.

[XdRH95] Q. Xu, W.-P. de Roever, and J. He. Rely-guarantee method for verifying shared-variable concurrent programs. Institutsbericht 9502, Christian-Albrechts-Universität zu Kiel, March 1995.

[XdRH97] Q. Xu, W.-P. de Roever, and J. He. The rely-guarantee method for verifying shared-variable concurrent programs. *Formal Aspects of Computing*, 9(2):149–174, 1997.

[XH91] Q. Xu and J. He. A theory of state-based parallel programming: Part 1. In Morris, editor, *Proceedings of BCS FACS 4th Refinement Workshop*. Springer-Verlag, January 1991.

[Xu92] Q. Xu. *A theory of state-based parallel programming*. PhD thesis, Oxford University Computing Laboratory, 1992.

[Yon77] A. Yonezawa. *Specification and verification techniques for parallel programs based on message passing semantics*. PhD thesis, Massachusetts Institute of Technology, 1977. MIT/LCS/TR-191.

[ZCdR92] J. Zwiers, J. Coenen, and W.-P. de Roever. A note on compositional refinement. In C.B. Jones, R.G. Shaw, and T. Denvir, editors, *Proc. 5th Refinement Workshop*, Workshops in Computing, pages 342–366. Springer-Verlag, 1992.

[ZdBdR84] J. Zwiers, A. de Bruin, and W.-P. de Roever. A proof system for partial correctness of dynamic networks of processes. In *Proceedings of the Conference on Logics of Programs 1983*, volume 164 of *LNCS*, 1984.

[ZdR89] J. Zwiers and W.-P. de Roever. Predicates are predicate transformers: a unified theory for concurrency. In *Proceedings of the ACM conference on Principles of Distributed Computing, August 14–16, 1989*, Edmonton, Canada, 1989. ACM.

[ZdRvEB84] J. Zwiers, W.-P. de Roever, and P. van Emde Boas. Compositionality and concurrent networks: soundness and completeness of a proof system. Technical report 57, University of Nijmegen, The Netherlands, 1984.

[ZdRvEB85] J. Zwiers, W.-P. de Roever, and P. van Emde Boas. Compositionality and concurrent networks: soundness and completeness of a proof system. In *Proceedings of 12th ICALP, July 15–19, 1985*, volume 194 of *LNCS*, pages 509–519, Nafplion, Greece, July 1985. Springer-Verlag.

[ZH81] Chao-Chen Zhou and C.A.R. Hoare. Partial correctness of communicating sequential processes. In *Proceedings of 2nd IEEE International Conference on Distributed Computing Systems*, pages 1–12. IEEE Computer Society Press, 1981.

[ZH95] P. Zhou and J. Hooman. Formal specification and compositional verification of an atomic broadcast protocol. *Real-Time Systems*, 9(2):119–145, 1995.

[ZHLdR95] J. Zwiers, U. Hannemann, Y. Lakhnech, and W.-P. de Roever. Synthesizing different development paradigms: Combining top-down with bottom-up reasoning about distributed systems. In *Proceedings of FST & TCS Bangalore*, volume 1026 of *LNCS*. Springer-Verlag, 1995.

[ZHR91] Chao-Chen Zhou, C.A.R. Hoare, and A.P. Ravn. A calculus of durations. *Information Processing Letters*, 40(5), 1991.

[ZJ94] J. Zwiers and W. Janssen. Partial order based design of concurrent systems. In de Bakker et al. [dBdRR94].

[Zwa89] Gerard Zwaan. *Parallel Computations*. PhD thesis, Dept. of Math. and C.S., Eindhoven University of Technology, January 1989.

[Zwi89] J. Zwiers. *Compositionality and Partial Correctness*, volume 321 of *LNCS*. Springer-Verlag, 1989.

[Zwi90] J. Zwiers. Predicates, predicate transformers and refinement. In de Bakker et al. [dBdRR90], pages 759–776.

[Zwi92] J. Zwiers. Layering and action refinement for timed systems. In de Bakker et al. [dBHdRR92], pages 687–723.

Glossary of Symbols

Chapter 3

Chapter 4

Chapter 5

Chapter 8

Chapter 11

Index